Advance Praise for
A Journey Through the Landscape of Philosophy: A Reader

"This is a text that will reach out to students by acknowledging the topics that they are concerned with. It illustrates how philosophical reflection and self-expression go hand in hand, and will provide students with confidence in their own critical reasoning skills as well as a means to interpret a variety of philosophers' works, while still finding their own reflective voice."

— Christine James,
Valdosta State University

"I appreciate the accessibly written explanations and introductions to each reading, and the multicultural and gender-mixed nature of the range of selections. Bowen shows the drama and excitement of philosophy."

— Roben Torosyan,
Fairfield University

"My students love *The Dream Weaver*, but they struggle with the readings I assign. Bowen's approach in this reader helps mightily—he has done a masterful job."

— Blanche Premo-Hopkins,
University of South Carolina

"The discussion questions were good, thought-provoking, and constructive, and I could use the reading questions as the basis of weekly reading quizzes."

— Sharon Crasnow,
Riverside Community College

A Journey Through
The Landscape
of Philosophy

A Reader

Jack Bowen
DeAnza College
Menlo School

PENGUIN ACADEMICS

PEARSON
Longman

New York Boston San Francisco
London Toronto Sydney Tokyo Singapore Madrid
Mexico City Munich Paris Cape Town Hong Kong Montreal

Editor-in-Chief: Eric Stano
Executive Marketing Manager: Ann Stypuloski
Supplements Editor: Brian Belardi
Production Manager: Stacey Kulig
Project Coordination, Text Design, and Electronic Page Makeup: Electronic
    Publishing Services Inc., New York City
Senior Cover Designer/Manager: Nancy Danahy
Cover Designer: Kay Petronio
Cover Image: © Jack Bowen
Manufacturing Buyer: Lucy Hebard
Printer and Binder: R.R. Donnelley and Sons/Harrisonburg
Cover Printer: Phoenix Color Corporation/Hagerstown

Library of Congress Cataloging-in-Publication Data
Bowen, Jack.
A journey through the landscape of philosophy : a reader / Jack Bowen.—1st ed.
    p. cm.
  ISBN-13: 978-0-321-32824-3
  ISBN-10: 0-321-32824-8
  1. Philosophy.   I. Title.
BD31.B69 2008
100—dc22

                                                                2007031439

Copyright © 2008 by Pearson Education, Inc.

All rights reserved. No part of this publication may be reproduced, stored in a
retrieval system, or transmitted, in any form or by any means, electronic, mechanical,
photocopying, recording, or otherwise, without the prior written permission of the
publisher. Printed in the United States.

Please visit us at www.ablongman.com

ISBN 13: 978-0-321-32824-3
ISBN 10: 0-321-32824-8

2 3 4 5 6 7 8 9 10—DOH—10 09 08 07

Dedicated to all those who inspired, challenged, and encouraged me in the classroom.

It is the supreme art of the teacher to awaken joy in creative expression and knowledge.
> —ALBERT EINSTEIN

Especially my philosophy professors at Stanford and California State University, Long Beach—that a dedication to this volume may provide at least a glimpse of my profound experience with you.

Give me a fish and I eat for a day. Teach me to fish and I eat for a lifetime.
> —CHINESE PROVERB

And to my students and athletes over the past seven years—that you see your fingerprints throughout this volume and realize you have shared with me as much as I have with you.

To teach is to learn twice.
> —JOSEPH JOUBERT

Contents

CHAPTER 3   Science   172

CHAPTER 4   God and Creation   257

CHAPTER 5   The Religious Problem of Evil   337

CHAPTER 10   Aesthetics   543

CHAPTER 11   Morality   558

Preface

You will learn from me not philosophy, but how to philosophize.

—IMMANUEL KANT

Introduction

As an author and philosopher I expect that readers approach this book for any number of reasons. It could derive from a genuine interest as to what philosophy is all about. Or maybe from some sort of school-related requirement. And it might be a follow-up to previous endeavors—either as revisiting prior philosophically related discussions, or an already heightened interest in philosophical issues, or maybe even as a result from reading this book's corresponding novel, *The Dream Weaver*. Regardless, this is a book for everyone— everyone interested in coming to know the world around him or her, in exploring new ideas, in challenging one's currently held point of view, and in exploring one's own place in the world.

The true nature of philosophy is difficult to pinpoint. One could decipher the roots of the Greek word *philosophia*—*love of wisdom*—though that paints a very broad picture. Philosophy initially earned the designation Queen of Sciences, as it illuminated underlying issues of all other disciplines as well as giving rise to new branches of science. My real hope here is, instead of my defining it, that you take an active role in this yourself. The ideal result for the readers is that they learn to *philosophize*, as well as learn *about* philosophy.

In my research over the years, I have encountered hundreds of academic experiments which capture elements of human and animal nature and also relate directly to important themes within philosophy. Three in particular stand out.

In the first of these, experimenters place five monkeys in a cage containing a ladder leading to a banana. When a monkey ascends the ladder, the other four are hosed down with cold water. To avoid further water-dousing, the monkeys attack any monkey who attempts to climb the ladder in the future. The experimenters then replace one of the monkeys. When that replacement inevitably goes for the banana, the other four attack him. Again, one of the four remaining original monkeys is replaced and again the four attack him when he ascends the ladder. This occurs until all five monkeys in the cage are new—*none* of them have any knowledge of the cold-water punishment because none of the original monkeys are in the group. Yet anytime a monkey gets to the ladder, the other four attack him—just because.

In the second experiment, an infamous 1964 study done at Yale University by Stanley Milgram, volunteer subjects (referred to as "readers") are instructed to read word pairs to a "learner" (who the reader believes is also a volunteer) who is supposed to memorize them. The reader first watches as the learner is strapped down to a chair in an adjacent room and connected to an "electroshock device." Subjects are told that the purpose of the experiment is to test the effects of punishment on learning. Anytime the learner gives an incorrect answer, the reader is instructed to administer an electric shock to the learner. The shocks begin very mildly (15 volts) and increase by 15 volts every time the learner responds incorrectly. Along the way, the learner begins to yell out in pain, pleading that they cease the experiment, complaining of a heart condition and eventually (if the reader continues long enough) the feedback stops all together. Of the 40 volunteers who participated, 65 percent administered the strongest shock possible (450 volts) *despite* the learner's pleading and eventual lack of response.

(See footnote below before continuing.)* In the third of the studies, a subject views a 25-second film depicting two teams of three people (one team in black, the other in white). Each team has a basketball. Subjects are asked to determine how many passes the white team makes to themselves. After about 10 seconds, a person dressed in a gorilla outfit slowly walks into the room, stands in the middle of the room beating his chest, and then slowly walks off. Despite being on the screen for 9 seconds and in clear view, *half* of the 10,000 subjects *failed* to see the gorilla. When shown the video again and told to look for the gorilla, it appeared so obvious that subjects often accused the experimenter of showing two different videos.

What can we discern from these studies? The monkeys illustrate that we may often act without even realizing *why* we do so. Yet it seems like we should at least question the reasons behind why we do something instead of doing it *just because "that's how it's done"*—especially in a case where others incur

---

* If you would like to experience the study before reading about it (and thus before being biased) visit http://viscog.beckman.uiuc.edu/grafs/demos/15.html. There you can watch a 25-second video in which you need only count the number of times the team in white shirts passes the basketball to each other.

harm. This is not to say that we ought to spend our time questioning *all* commonly held beliefs *all* the time. But doing so some of the time can result in two things. In certain cases, it can help illuminate an important truth upon which we can act. As Kofi Annan opined in his 1997 commencement address at MIT, "To live is to choose. But to choose well, you must know who you are, what you stand for, where you want to go, and why you want to go there." The second shortcoming that results from failure to question the *status quo* can be seen through more of a personal lens: In failing to investigate the truths that we take for granted, we may miss out on a deeper understanding of that particular phenomenon. As T. S. Elliot wrote in *Four Quartets*:

We shall not cease from exploration
And the end of all our exploring
Will be to arrive where we started
And know the place for the first time.

The "invisible gorilla" illuminates just how biased and limited we can be in our ability to perceive the world. Given our unique respective upbringings and environments, we become blind to things outside our scope of attention. We literally do not see things that are there—whether they be physical objects or ideas that may run counter to our own. Once we realize what most often directs our attention—television, education, politicians, advertisers, religion—we can then make changes accordingly or, at the least, gain awareness of these forces. These biases abound in many areas of life. For example:

- It has been shown that parents are more likely to buckle their children in the car if the child is considered more attractive.
- When told that a person on the other end of the phone is of a minority race, the speaker laughs half as much at the same jokes told when they perceive the speaker as non-minority.
- When scientific grant proposals are reviewed anonymously, they are meted out evenly amongst males and females. When the same grants display gender-specific names, males are three times more likely to win the award.
- In a survey inquiring as to who would earn entry into heaven, while only 65 percent predicted Michael Jordan, 79 percent believed Mother Teresa. But the person that 87 percent of survey takers believed would be *most* likely to make it to heaven was themselves. (This bias is also illustrated by the College Entrance Examination Board's survey of 829,000 high school seniors of which *zero* percent rated themselves as below average in "ability to get along with others.")

Clearly, our biases reach out to others and the way we treat them, inward to the way we view our own ideas, and deeply inward to the way we view ourselves.

The Milgram experiment clearly demonstrates the importance of thinking for oneself. While nearly everyone values another's right to be free from harm more than a scientist's desire to conduct an experiment, a majority acted totally counter to this. Without first establishing a sound foundation for our beliefs, we may act from either a position of ignorance or from other factors out of our control. Stanley Milgram referenced Nazi henchmen as just another group who did what they were told without thinking through it. As Hitler himself noted, "What good fortune for those in power that people don't know how to think."

In short, these three findings encourage us to learn how to think for ourselves and to examine what we know and how we know it.

In a brief introductory précis to the compendium that follows, I will try to summarize just what philosophy "does." Philosophy not only enlightens us by logically framing often difficult issues, but it also provides an opportunity to "do for the sake of doing." Imagine avoiding questions such as "Do we have a soul?" and "What is beauty?" and "In what way do we have free will?"—all because you fear not getting an answer. At the least, this quest for answers will illuminate your own limits to knowledge. At the most it will provide you with great insight about yourself and the world. Certainly, though, it will encourage you to think for yourself—and the ability to think for oneself is essential to becoming a self-sustaining person. After all, most of us forget the Krebs Cycle and how to solve differential equations—or, at the least, we can locate the information quickly on the Internet. But once you learn to think, it becomes a part of you and is something that one could not otherwise quickly access in a book or on a computer.

And so your answer to the age-old question "What is the meaning of life?" may well differ from mine. In some sense, it is like asking, "What is the most valuable thing?" If I offer you the choice between one million dollars and a truckload of water, I imagine the money would have considerably greater value to you. Yet the same offer made to a castaway on a deserted isle yields the opposite answer. Coming to opposing yet "correct" answers does not render the meaning-of-life question useless. The quest itself provides meaning.

Everyone uses philosophy, thinks philosophically, and benefits from the fruits of philosophical discourse. In delving deeper, you will hopefully become aware of this in yourself and will realize new and different ways to expand your own horizons. The practical use of philosophy, its application to real-world issues, and its ability to enlighten just happen to be very compelling by-products—the icing on the cake, as they say. Or maybe it's the other way around. You can decide for yourself.

Song Lyrics and Movie Titles

Song Lyrics

Included at the end of each chapter you will find a list of song titles. These songs were selected because of their philosophical relevance and relation to the topics of each respective chapter. My hope for the reader is that you explore these lyrics on your own and with friends and classmates and decipher your own meaning:

- What particular philosophical relevance does the song have?
- How does it relate to any of the readings, issues, or theories discussed in the chapter?
- Are there any especially poignant stanzas or phrases?
- What does it mean to you, in your own life?

You are also encouraged to find philosophically relevant lyrics in your own music collection (and email them to the author if you're feeling especially motivated!). You will likely realize that, once again, philosophical inquiry is not limited to academia but, instead, is prevalent in our daily culture.

The lyrics to most songs are easily accessible on the Internet through various search engines by entering the song title (typically in quotations), performer's name, and the word "lyrics."

For examples of five songs (accompanied with questions), visit the book's website—www.dreamweaverphilosophy.com—and go to the "Music Picks" section under "Ian in Your World."

Movie Titles

Also included following each chapter is a list of movie titles with a brief synopsis or philosophically relevant question. Again, see how you can apply the ideas from each chapter to the themes and issues in each movie.

Lyrics to the Book's Theme Song*

Beautiful Colors

The world is quite peaceful,
With my head down in the sand.
It's cool and it's quiet here,
no need to understand
Life's great mysteries,
seeing only shadows of reality.
So I lift my head to the world,
and I'm blinded by the light.

If you see the world in black and white,
you're missing out on all the beautiful colors.

Dark and light, wrong and right,
May or might, and all the rest.
If you keep on traveling to the east,
You'll end up west.
Your paradigms are affected,
When you see it's all connected.
You embrace both heart and mind
in seeking what you find.

You have no idea my son.
Your journey's just begun.
If you look with eyes wide open,
you realize the world wonders,
and you are not alone.

The world is quite full of wonder,
with my head out of the sand.

Discussion Questions

1. People often say, "Ignorance is bliss." In what ways might this be true? What are the negative consequences of this ideal? How do you evaluate

*The song can be heard at the book's website home page: www.dreamweaverphilosophy.com.

the opening and closing stanzas of the song that seem to be totally opposing views?

2. What virtue might there be in seeing the world in "black and white"? What would this mean? If right-and-wrong (morality) is not a black-and-white issue, then how could we come to any answers regarding morality? If morality is a matter of black and white, why can't we all agree on moral issues?

3. What produces greater insights for you—your heart (intuition, faith, passion) or mind (logic, math, reason)? Is one "better" than the other?

4. What kind of things affect your paradigm (world-view)— Science? Advertising? Religion? "Society"? With all of these influences, how can you make truly authentic choices?

5. Do you find greater beauty/wonder in something the more or less you know about it? How does your answer affect the way you approach knowing your self, others, and the world around you?

Guide to Critical Thinking and Logic

Many people would sooner die than think. In fact they do.

—Bertrand Russell

He that will not reason is a bigot; he that cannot reason is a fool; and he that dares not reason is a slave.

—William Drummond

I was initially a bit apprehensive about including such a guide in what could already be an intimidating book. But given the power of critical thinking in so many ventures, I figured that this might end up being the most important part of the book for the introductory-level reader. Furthermore, a background in logic may actually make your study of philosophy more enjoyable, as logic is often considered the "nuts and bolts" of philosophy.

A basic understanding of logic provides many additional benefits. A sharp critical eye helps to dispel many of the logical tricks often used by others who attempt to manipulate us or convince us of something that is not true—politicians, for example, and advertisers, the media, certain religious persons, cults, Internet scams, etc. As Adolf Hitler frighteningly illustrated, "Thank goodness for those in power that people don't know how to think."

Just as importantly, having an understanding of logic and its pitfalls can help one avoid drawing incorrect conclusions themselves as well as to help us avoid speaking illogically when we attempt to do otherwise.

And critical thinking can actually be fun, as you will soon see. It often helps to illuminate exactly what conclusion is drawn and *how* it is defended—and then one can discover deeper truths in a more lucid manner.

Lastly, critical thinking helps to determine not just what you think but *why* you think it, and why others think what they think as well. In deciphering exactly what conclusion another defends and *how* they defend it, you will not only learn a lot about that person, but you will have a chance to learn a lot about your own position on a given topic. Learning about what you think teaches you something about who you are, for in many ways we are what we think. Thinking critically will take you beyond the banter often heard when people are merely sharing their opinions. While people are certainly free to have opinions (though I wouldn't go so far as to say they have a *right* to them as is often said, for I'm not sure who would grant this right), these opinions are not worth much if they are not backed up by anything more than a mere feeling. In any case, having the right to an opinion doesn't make that opinion right.

Instead of merely asserting a belief or repeatedly contradicting someone, one can formulate an argument. The reader should note that the term "argument" here may differ from the usual use and is not to be confused with the oft-referenced *argument* or impassioned verbal dispute in which friends, lovers, and political assailants often participate. Instead, it refers to the logical use of the word—the defense of a conclusion through the use of any number of premises.[1]

In what follows, I provide the basic structure of an argument along with a method for assessment including a basic overview of some of the more important laws of logic. Once we determine a *good* argument, I illustrate some of the more prevalent pitfalls ("fallacies") incurred in developing an argument.

Detecting and devising an argument is simple—look for a conclusion and then look for supporting evidence (**premises**) used to defend that conclusion.

Once you have done this, line the premises up to see how they defend the conclusion. Here is a simple example of this: "We know that all humans are mammals and realize that Ian is a human. Thus, we can conclude that Ian is a mammal." This is a very basic argument with two premises and a conclusion. It can be **standardized** as follows:

1. All humans are mammals. (premise 1)
2. Ian is a human. (premise 2)
3. Therefore, Ian is a mammal. (conclusion)

In this case, the premises of the argument are "All humans are mammals" and "Ian is a human."[2] The conclusion is "Ian is a mammal." This is an example of a **deductively valid** argument—if all the premises are true, then the conclusion *must* be true. In this case, determining the truth of the premises is quite easy, as it is mostly couched in definition. But look at the following argument:

1. The death penalty is a cheaper punishment than a life sentence in prison.
2. We should employ the cheaper of two punishments.

3. Therefore, we should employ the death penalty.

In this case, the argument is **valid**—if the premises are true, then the conclusion is true. But two problems arise with this argument. First, the second premise is questionable: Do we really want to base our penal system only on cost? If so, then we should not have death row and instead should immediately kill the condemned prisoner, though this will likely result in more deaths of those wrongly accused. So this premise needs to be explored in greater depth.[3] Secondly, the first premise is not true: Because of the appeals process and many other factors, the death penalty costs the state considerably more than a life term in prison. So, while this argument is valid, it is not *sound*. A **sound** argument is one in which the premises of a valid argument are true.

An important note (and oft-made mistake): Just because an argument is invalid or unsound, this does not necessitate that the conclusion is unacceptable. For example, while the previous argument is not sound, the conclusion *could* still be true, but for other reasons. Be aware of someone claiming a conclusion is wrong *just because* it was defended poorly.

Another thing to be aware of in arguments is a **missing premise.** Very often, a premise will either be assumed or intentionally left out of an argument. Look at the following argument:

1. The death penalty most closely matches the crime.
2. Therefore, we should employ the death penalty.

In this case, the unstated (missing) premise is, "We should employ punishments that most closely match the crime." While you may agree with the first premise,[4] you would also need to agree with the missing premise in order for the argument to be *sound*—deductively valid with true premises. The argument can be rewritten to include the missing premise:

1. The death penalty matches the crime.
2. (We should employ punishments that match the crime.)
3. Therefore, we should employ the death penalty.

Once we have done this, we can assess the missing premise along with the stated premise in order to determine the soundness of the argument. (Question: How do you assess this premise?)

For the sake of follow-up on the role of opinion in an argument, we can standardize an argument that is actually based on opinion. Here is how it would look:

1. I feel the death penalty is wrong.
2. Therefore, the death penalty is wrong.

As you can now see, there is a missing premise in this argument: "What I feel to be wrong *is* wrong." While it may be true that I think the death penalty is wrong, the missing premise certainly does not hold true—there is no reason to believe that I can somehow set the standard of morality for everyone, that "thinking makes it so." Considerably more work needs to be done in defense of this conclusion.

Obviously, one key to deeming an argument *sound* is determining whether it is *valid*. All sound arguments are valid. Some argument forms are always valid in that they follow a logical law. There are many logical laws, some considerably complex. Here are just a few (Question: How do you assess the premises and overall arguments in the following arguments?):

Logical Law: *Disjunctive Syllogism*

1. Either A or B
2. Not A
3. Therefore, B

Here is an example of a valid argument in the form of a *disjunctive syllogism*:

1. The universe is either a result of mere chance or an intelligent designer.
2. The universe is not a result of mere chance.
3. Therefore, the universe is a result of an intelligent designer.

Because this argument is in the form of a disjunctive syllogism, we know that it is valid. All we need to do is assess the two premises as true and we have a sound argument.

Logical Law: *Modus Ponens*

1. If A, then B
2. A
3. Therefore, B

Here is an example of a valid argument in the form of *modus ponens*:

1. If the universe looks designed, then it must have been designed by an intelligent designer.
2. The universe looks designed.
3. Therefore, the universe was designed by an intelligent designer.

Logical Law: *Modus Tollens*

1. If A, then B
2. Not B
3. Therefore, not A

Here is an example of a valid argument in the form of *modus tollens*:

1. If God created the universe, then it would be free of all evil.
2. The universe is not free of all evil.
3. Therefore, God did not create the universe.

These arguments are all deductively *valid* arguments. Even the arguments with just the A's and B's are valid based on their structure: If the premises were true, then the argument would be sound.

We should also examine arguments that are **inductive** (as opposed to *deductive*). A *cogent inductive* argument is one based on probability and one in which, while the premises are true, the conclusion could still be false.[5] Inductive arguments rely on the assumption that trends observed from past experiences or data will continue in the future. Whereas deductive arguments aim to provide conclusive support for a conclusion, inductive arguments provide probable support for a conclusion. For example:

1. Every day the sun has risen.
2. Therefore, tomorrow the sun will rise.

This is a very *strong* inductive argument because we have a lot of data and experience (i.e., all the days throughout history) and assume that tomorrow should resemble previous days in all relevant respects. But look at this inductive argument:

1. All ten crows I have seen are black.
2. Therefore, all crows are black.

This is a very *weak* inductive argument: A sample size of ten crows is not a good representation of all crows that exist.[6] A better formulation of this would be:

1. All ten crows I have seen are black.
2. Therefore, most crows are probably black.

Though you can see here that the conclusion is not very strong, as it now includes "most" and "probably." Last, look at this argument:

1. I have seen 10,000 crows throughout the world and they were all black.
2. Therefore, all crows are black.

This is certainly a much stronger inductive argument. While we can imagine that the premise could be true yet the conclusion be false it is just very unlikely.[7] One of the difficulties in assessing inductive arguments is to determine when the inductive claim can be generalized. And remember, we still need to determine the acceptability and relevance of the premises of inductive arguments.

Now that we have a basic overview of logic and methods of devising valid, sound arguments, it is important to take a brief look at common errors or, in some cases, common sleights of hand—known as **red herrings**[8]—that occur when developing an argument. The following is a list of logical fallacies.

Ad Hominem—Latin for "at the man" (often referred to as an **ad hom attack**), this error occurs when one's argument is attacked based on the character of the one making the argument. For example, if a death row inmate provides a seemingly sound argument against the death penalty, one might respond (wrongly), "That's a bad argument because you're a terrible person and committed a horrendous crime." While that may be true, the character of the arguer is irrelevant to the argument presented.

This also occurs when the motive of the arguer is in question or when the person arguing does not abide by his or her own logic. For example, if someone is late to class and another truant classmate says:

1. Walking into class late disrupts the class for all the other students.
2. You shouldn't disrupt the class for all the other students.
3. Therefore, you shouldn't be late to class.

The response may be, "You're late all the time. Why should I listen to you?"— but this would be committing the *ad hom* fallacy. The truancy of the arguer is not what is in question.

This fallacy occurs more often than you may realize, as it is a very powerful way of diverting an argument (as a *red herring*). It does not strike at the logic of the argument but at the character of the arguer. As the philosopher G. F. Hegel wrote, "It is a matter of perfect indifference where a thing originated. The only question is: 'is it true in and for itself?'"

The only time that one's character is relevant to an argument is when a premise relies on such facts. For example, when considering for whom we should vote as President, the premise "He's a convicted felon" is relevant in support of the conclusion "You should not vote for him for President."

Begging the Question—This error occurs when the truth of the conclusion is assumed in a premise. It is also referred to as **circular reasoning.** For example, one cannot logically claim that the death penalty is wrong based on the premise "It is unethical for the government to kill criminals." Both of those statements say basically the same thing:

1. It is unethical to have the government kill criminals.
2. Therefore, it is wrong to implement the death penalty.

In this case, the same thing is being said in the premise as in the conclusion but with different words: The word "wrong" is substituted with "unethical" and the phrase "death penalty" with "government kill criminals." Here's another common example:

1. God is all-powerful.
2. In order for a being to be all-powerful, that being must exist.
3. Therefore, God exists.

This example is slightly trickier, as it does not simply redefine words. Instead, premise one *assumes* the truth of the conclusion. The argument tries to prove that God exists, yet this is the point of contention. So the evidence for God's existence (the premises) cannot rely on the assumption that God exists (as in premise one). In this case, premise one begs the question by assuming God's existence by stating, "God *is* . . ."—that is the very question that the argument attempts to answer (i.e., *Is* God?).[9]

Equivocation—This error occurs when an arguer uses the *same* word in two premises to mean different things. For example,

1. All *men* are created equal.
2. No women are *men*.
3. Therefore, women are not equal to men.

Here the term "men" is used differently. In the first premise, it is used as a referent for "human beings" (i.e., both men and women), while in the second premise it is used as the plural of "man." It becomes more apparent when rewritten:

1. All human beings are created equal.
2. No women are males.
3. Therefore . . .

What is important is the *meaning* of the word and not the word itself.

Mary Anne Warren argues that the typical argument against abortion fails for this same reason (see her article in this anthology). Here is how it looks (and you can decide for yourself):

1. It is wrong to kill an innocent *human being*.
2. The fetus is an innocent *human being*.
3. Therefore, it is wrong to kill a fetus.

Warren argues that "human being" is used to mean two different (i.e., unequivocal) things. In premise one it means "person with moral rights" and in premise two it means, "organism with human DNA." (And, according to Warren, if you change the second premise to avoid this fallacy, then it commits the fallacy of begging the question. Can you see why? Do you agree?)

Appeal to Popularity—This error occurs when an argument relies on "what a majority of people think." It is often hidden as an unstated premise, which I show here:

1. A majority of people think that slavery is a good thing.
2. (What the majority of people think is a good thing must be a good thing.)
3. Therefore, slavery is a good thing.

You can see from the argument above that we must defend a conclusion based on something more than what a majority of people think. As Giordano Bruno writes, "Truth does not change because it is, or is not, believed by a majority of the people."

False Dilemma—This error occurs when an either/or premise is given, yet there are more than just two options. For example,

1. Either the medicine cured her cancer or the magic words cured her.
2. The medicine did not cure her.
3. Therefore, the magic words cured her.

While this argument is valid in form (Can you see why? Which logical law does it follow?), it commits the fallacy of false dilemma. Premise one presents an either/or situation in which there are other options for a cure—radiotherapy, for example, or in some cases this occurs naturally.

Ignorance—This error occurs when the arguer claims either (a) Because X cannot be proven false that it must be true or (b) Because X cannot be proven true that it must be false. For example:

1. No one has proven that alien life does not exist.
2. Therefore, alien life exists.

    OR

1. There is no proof that alien life exists.
2. Therefore, alien life does not exist.

Something other than a lack of ability to prove something one way or another must be given in proper support of a conclusion. As Carl Sagan noted, "Absence of evidence is not evidence of absence."

Post Hoc—Short for *post hoc ergo propter hoc* ("after this, therefore, because of this"), this error occurs when one argues that X caused Y *just because* X came before Y. While that may be relevant, it is certainly not sufficient. For example:

1. I ate tree bark last night and woke up today and my cold was gone.
2. Therefore, eating tree bark cures colds.

In this case, *just because* you ate tree bark and *then* your cold went away is not evidence enough to say that eating tree bark cures colds. This is an example of **anecdotal evidence**—something that occurs once and is thus assumed to work universally. An event simply preceding another event is not enough to say that the first event *caused* the later event.

Slippery Slope—This error occurs when one argues that allowing A would result in B and therefore we should not allow A. For example:

1. If we allow legalized abortion in the first trimester, this will lead to legalized abortion in the second trimester, which will lead to legalized abortion in the third trimester, which will lead to the legalized killing of infants.
2. We should not allow for something that will lead to the legalized killing of infants.
3. Therefore, we should not allow legalized abortion in the first trimester.

While abortion in the first trimester may be considered immoral (remember, just because an argument is fallacious, this does not necessarily mean that the conclusion is wrong), it should not be considered so for what *may* happen in the future.

Naturalistic Fallacy—This error occurs when one argues that because something *is* one way that it *ought* to be that way. It wrongly mixes a value judgment with a factual claim. For example:

1. Males of a species are biologically disposed to act promiscuously.
2. Therefore, adultery in human males should be permitted.

Here, a biological (i.e., *natural*) claim is being transformed into a moral claim. *Just because* something is natural does not necessitate it being moral. As the Russian playwright Anton Chekhov wrote, "Man will become better when you show him what he is like." Simply being naturally predisposed to stealing (kleptomania) does not in itself make it morally acceptable to steal.

Denying the Antecedent—This error occurs when an argument is in the following logical form:

1. If A, then B
2. Not A
3. Therefore, not B

While this may look similar to the deductively valid *modus tollens*, there is an important difference. Given the truth of "If A, then B," then just because A (the antecedent—*ante* meaning "before") is not the case, it does not necessitate that *B* is not the case. For example:

1. If you drink the poison, then you will die.
2. You did not drink the poison.
3. Therefore, you will not die.

This fallacy should be obvious once this example is understood.

Affirming the Consequent—This error occurs when an argument is in the following logical form:

1. If A, then B
2. B
3. Therefore, A

While this may look similar to the deductively valid *modus ponens*, there is an important difference. Given the truth of "If A, then B," then just because B (the consequent) is the case, it does not necessitate that A is the case. For example:

1. If you drink the poison, then you will die.
2. You will die.
3. Therefore, you will drink the poison.

This fallacy should be obvious once this example is understood.

Hundreds of books have been written on this topic and this brief guide explores only introductory issues in logic and critical thinking, though with this background you should have enough tools to decipher what is being said (and what *you* are saying) in an argument. When engaged in philosophical discourse, one key skill is often overlooked—*listening*. Make sure you clearly understand another's position so that instead of talking past each other, you can tackle the issue directly. It is here that real intellectual growth occurs. As John Stuart Mill wrote in his famous essay, *On Liberty* (in defense of free speech, though the theme certainly applies here):

> The peculiar evil of silencing the expression of an opinion is, that it is robbing the human race . . . If the opinion is right, they are deprived of the opportunity of exchanging error for truth: if wrong, they lose, what is almost as great a benefit, the clearer perception and livelier impression of truth, produced by its collision with error.

Notes

1. For a more comical view of an argument, read this dialogue from the Monty Python skit, the "Argument Clinic":

   MAN: An argument isn't just contradiction.
   MR. V.: Well, it can be.

MAN: No it can't. An argument is a connected series of statements intended to establish a definite proposition.

MR V.: No it isn't.

MAN: Yes it is. It isn't just contradiction.

MR V.: Look, if I argue with you, I must take up a contrary position.

MAN: But it isn't just saying "No it isn't."

MR V.: Yes it is.

MAN: No it isn't. An argument is an intellectual process. Contradiction is just the automatic gainsaying of anything the other person says.

MR V.: No it isn't.

MAN: Yes it is.

2. The arguments in this brief guide all have one or two premises. This is done for the sake of simplicity. An argument can have any number of premises and many have more than one or two.

3. When a premise requires more discussion, a *sub-argument* is required. A **sub-argument** is a set of premises used to defend the premise of another argument— typically a premise that is not widely received. In this example, because the second premise is not clearly acceptable, it will need to be defended by a sub-argument.

4. Some do not agree, arguing that the death penalty results in considerably more suffering than the crime itself. French existentialist writer Albert Camus wrote that for a proper match, "the death penalty would have to punish a criminal who had warned his victim of the date at which he would inflict a horrible death on him and who, from the moment onward, had confined him at his mercy for months."

5. Many use the term "**cogent**" instead of "sound" to refer to a *valid* inductive argument.

6. This error in logic is referred to as committing the fallacy of **hasty generalization**. It occurs when the arguer makes a generalization (i.e., *all* X's exhibit property Y) based on a very small sample size. This can also occur when the generalization is based on a biased or poorly sampled group—for example, if you interview 10,000 people and they all believe in God but the people you interviewed were all at a particular church, you would be wrong to claim, "Therefore, *all people* believe in God."

7. An example of this occurring is this: Before the discovery of Australia, the inductive conclusion "All swans are white" was highly confirmed and considered very strong, as many swans had been sighted and all were white. But upon discovering Australia, black swans were also discovered.

8. When a logical fallacy is intentionally used to divert the discussion, it is referred to as a **red herring**. The term is believed to derive from a ploy criminals have used to avoid capture. A herring is a type of fish that becomes red when cooked and then emits a pungent odor. When being tracked by dogs, a criminal would use the red herring to divert the bloodhounds in order to avoid detection. It is also purported that activists opposed to fox hunting would use red herrings to divert dogs involved in fox hunting.

9. You could prove the existence of anything if this move were permissible:
   1. Martians are crazy.
   2. For a thing to be crazy, it must exist.
   3. Therefore, Martians exist.

Acknowledgments

In a project as immense as this there are many people to thank and acknowledge. I once again found great comfort in the advice and suggestions provided by my then-professors (now colleagues) Al Spangler, Paul Tang, and Sara Goering. I will always consider you "my professors."

I must also thank those who offered their time and expertise in sharing in my quest to provide both breadth and depth in a book like this: Jeff Broome, Arapahoe Community College; Sharon Crasnow, Riverside Community College; John Elia, University of Georgia; Richard Field, Northwest Missouri State University; Christine James, Valdosta State University; Nicholas Jones, Ohio State University; Hey-Kyung Kim, University of Wisconsin-Green Bay; Blanche Premo-Hopkins, University of South Carolina-Aiken; Yvonne Raley, Felician College; Rob Reich, Stanford University; Mary Schatz, Palomar College; Edward Schoen, Western Kentucky University; Roben Torosyan, Fairfield Univeristy; Kathryn Valdivia, Cuyamaca College.

I would also like to thank De Anza College and Menlo School, not just for their support of me as a writer and educator, but also for their commitment to education.

And to the team at Longman Publishers who helped with the multitude of behind-the-scenes details: Donna Garnier, Deborah Bergeson, Eric Stano, and Liz Hoens. And to Katy Leclerq and Rebecca Coleman at EPS. And of course, my editor (times two) Priscilla McGeehon—it's been an amazing adventure and I have you to thank for it. Thank you to Michael Shermer at *Skeptic* magazine for sharing your advice and to Richard Dawkins for his aid in securing copyrights.

Prologue

Philosophy

As the introduction to this book states, the best way to answer the question "What is Philosophy?" is to read and study philosophy. This section, though, provides a good overview and introduction by painting a broad picture of philosophy. The articles in this chapter will also serve as a great intellectual quest to revisit after working your way through the entire book. You will likely have some different reactions to the issues posed in the articles in this section, or at least will have shed new light on your initial views.

This book examines all of the major branches of philosophy as briefly categorized here:

Epistemology—Study of knowledge

Metaphysics—Study of reality and issues that are "beyond physics" (i.e., time, the soul and mind, numbers, free will, etc.)

Philosophy of Religion—Study of God and religion

Ethics—Study of how we should live and what we *ought* to do morally (also includes "Applied Ethics," in which we apply ethical and moral principles to specific actions and situations)

Political and Social Philosophy—Study of society and government and the issues that relate to them, such as economics, distribution of goods, justification of punishment, rights

Logic—Study of reasoning and application of rules in determining the validity and soundness of arguments, both inductive and deductive

Aesthetics—Study of art and beauty

This selection of readings not only helps to highlight philosophical issues, but it also provides a motivation for examining them. These articles frame one of the greatest virtues of studying philosophy: learning for its own sake. And as a very valuable side product of this venture, one can better grapple with the major issues both outwardly in society and inwardly on a personal level.

The Allegory of the Cave
Plato

Mathematician and philosopher Alfred North Whitehead once characterized the tradition of European philosophy as consisting of "a series of footnotes to Plato." While considered by most to be a slight exaggeration, it illuminates the importance of Plato's influence on all of philosophy and, certainly, on its inception.

After Plato's service with the army of Athens throughout the Peloponnesian War (431–404 B.C.) and Corinthian War (395–386), he went on to pursue a life of politics. His interest in politics was tainted, though, by numerous instances: one being an overtly corrupt and unjust coup that took over rule in Athens, and another, when Plato was 28, in which the government condemned to death his friend and teacher Socrates for supposed "corruption of the youth" and denigration of the gods (see other selection in this section). This prompted Plato and other students of Socrates to leave Athens and go to Megara, Greece.

It was at this time that Plato supposedly wrote most of his works, a majority of them in the form of dialogue. While he never referenced himself nor explicitly stated his position in these dialogues, he often used Socrates as a character. Many believe that Socrates represents Plato's views.

Plato returned to Athens and, at age 42, founded the Academy—the first Western university. It was at this university that many philosophical issues were studied for the first time. Plato taught many students at the Academy (including Aristotle, who arrived at the Academy at age 17) and remained until his death at age 80. The Academy remained until A.D. 529 when Christian rulers closed it due to its teachings that ran counter to the church's doctrine.

In this reading, Plato presents what has come to be one of the most well-known allegories throughout history. While he wrote it to put forth his metaphysical foundation for the existence of objects, this allegory also provides great motivation for our study of philosophy. For those without philosophical inclination, it is as though they are stuck in a cave of false reality, watching mere shadows on the wall. It is not until one pursues the "blindingly" difficult process of education that one can come to know reality, as illuminated by the sun.

In the conversation leading up to this discussion of the allegory, Plato defends himself as an "essentialist"—objects have essences or, in his terms, "Forms." These *Forms* allow us to know that one thing is a chair while another is not. We realize that no two chairs are exactly the same: They can have four legs, three legs, a back, no back, no legs (a bean-bag chair), are colored, wooden, plastic, etc. But, Plato argued, because each of these items shares in the Form of *chairness*, we call them all by the same name and know them as chairs. This Form of the chair exists objectively as the perfect chair—an ideal model of a chair—that maintains a greater sense of reality than the worldly examples (instantiations) of chairs that we see around us. (The term "Platonic Form" often refers to the perfect instantiation of something in our lives.)

When one emerged from the cave and became acclimated to the light, they could come to know these Forms. The Latin roots of the word "educate" are "to lead out." Plato held that the ideal leaders for the republic would be Philosopher Kings—those who had emerged from the cave and achieved this sort of knowledge.

Source: From Plato, *Republic*, 2nd Edition, translated by G.M.A. Grube, revised by C.D.C. Reeve, copyright © 1992 by Hackett Publishing Company, Inc. Reprinted by permission of Hackett Publishing Company, Inc. All rights reserved.

Reading Questions

1. How does Socrates imagine the prisoner would feel once his eyes became accustomed to the sunlight? What point is he making here?
2. What would happen if the prisoner returned from the outside back into the cave?
3. What does Socrates say about the soul and how this knowledge should relate to education?

Compare the effect of education and of the lack of it on our nature to an experience like this: Imagine human beings living in an underground, cavelike *514* dwelling with an entrance a long way up, which is both open to the light and as wide as the cave itself. They've been there since childhood, fixed in the same place, with their necks and legs fettered, able to see only in front of them, because their bonds prevent them from turning their heads around. Light is provided by a fire burning far above and behind them. Also behind them, but on higher ground, there is a path stretching between them and the fire. Imagine that *b* along this path a low wall has been built, like the screen in front of puppeteers above which they show their puppets.

I'm imagining it.

Then also imagine that there are people along the wall, carrying all kinds of artifacts that project above it—statues of people and other animals, made out of stone, wood, and every material. And, as you'd expect, some of the carriers are *c* talking, and some are silent. *515*

It's a strange image you're describing, and strange prisoners.

They're like us. Do you suppose, first of all, that these prisoners see anything of themselves and one another besides the shadows that the fire casts on the wall in front of them?

How could they, if they have to keep their heads motionless throughout life? *b*

What about the things being carried along the wall? Isn't the same true of them?

Of course.

And if they could talk to one another, don't you think they'd suppose that the names they used applied to the things they see passing before them?[1]

They'd have to.

And what if their prison also had an echo from the wall facing them? Don't you think they'd believe that the shadows passing in front of them were talking whenever one of the carriers passing along the wall was doing so?

I certainly do.

Then the prisoners would in every way believe that the truth is nothing other *c* than the shadows of those artifacts.

They must surely believe that.

Consider, then, what being released from their bonds and cured of their ignorance would naturally be like if something like this came to pass. When one of them was freed and suddenly compelled to stand up, turn his head, walk, and look up toward the light, he'd be pained and dazzled and unable to see the things

d   whose shadows he'd seen before. What do you think he'd say, if we told him that what he'd seen before was inconsequential, but that now—because he is a bit closer to the things that are and is turned towards things that are more—he sees more correctly? Or, to put it another way, if we pointed to each of the things passing by, asked him what each of them is, and compelled him to answer, don't you think he'd be at a loss and that he'd believe that the things he saw earlier were truer than the ones he was now being shown?

Much truer.

And if someone compelled him to look at the light itself, wouldn't his eyes

e   hurt, and wouldn't he turn around and flee towards the things he's able to see, believing that they're really clearer than the ones he's being shown?

He would.

And if someone dragged him away from there by force, up the rough, steep path, and didn't let him go until he had dragged him into the sunlight, wouldn't

516   he be pained and irritated at being treated that way? And when he came into the light, with the sun filling his eyes, wouldn't he be unable to see a single one of the things now said to be true?

He would be unable to see them, at least at first.

I suppose, then, that he'd need time to get adjusted before he could see things in the world above. At first, he'd see shadows most easily, then images of men and other things in water, then the things themselves. Of these, he'd be able to study the things in the sky and the sky itself more easily at night, looking at the light of the

b   stars and the moon, than during the day, looking at the sun and the light of the sun.

Of course.

Finally, I suppose, he'd be able to see the sun, not images of it in water or some alien place, but the sun itself, in its own place, and be able to study it.

Necessarily so.

And at this point he would infer and conclude that the sun provides the seasons and the years, governs everything in the visible world, and is in some way the

c   cause of all the things that he used to see.

It's clear that would be his next step.

What about when he reminds himself of his first dwelling place, his fellow prisoners, and what passed for wisdom there? Don't you think that he'd count himself happy for the change and pity the others?

Certainly.

And if there had been any honors, praises, or prizes among them for the one who was sharpest at identifying the shadows as they passed by and who best

d   remembered which usually came earlier, which later, and which simultaneously, and who could thus best divine the future, do you think that our man would desire these rewards or envy those among the prisoners who were honored and held power? Instead, wouldn't he feel, with Homer, that he'd much prefer to "work the earth as a serf to another, one without possessions,"[2] and go through any sufferings, rather than share their opinions and live as they do?

I suppose he would rather suffer anything than live like that.   *e*

Consider this too. If this man went down into the cave again and sat down in his same seat, wouldn't his eyes—coming suddenly out of the sun like that—be filled with darkness?

They certainly would.

And before his eyes had recovered—and the adjustment would not be quick—while his vision was still dim, if he had to compete again with the perpetual prisoners in recognizing the shadows, wouldn't he invite ridicule? Wouldn't it   *517* be said of him that he'd returned from his upward journey with his eyesight ruined and that it isn't worthwhile even to try to travel upward? And, as for anyone who tried to free them and lead them upward, if they could somehow get their hands on him, wouldn't they kill him?

They certainly would.

This whole image, Glaucon, must be fitted together with what we said before.   *b* The visible realm should be likened to the prison dwelling, and the light of the fire inside it to the power of the sun. And if you interpret the upward journey and the study of things above as the upward journey of the soul to the intelligible realm, you'll grasp what I hope to convey, since that is what you wanted to hear about. Whether it's true or not, only the god knows. But this is how I see it: In the knowable realm, the form of the good is the last thing to be seen, and it is reached only with difficulty. Once one has seen it, however, one must conclude that it is the cause of all that is correct and beautiful in anything, that it produces both light   *c* and its source in the visible realm, and that in the intelligible realm it controls and provides truth and understanding, so that anyone who is to act sensibly in private or public must see it.

I have the same thought, at least as far as I'm able.

Come, then, share with me this thought also: It isn't surprising that the ones who get to this point are unwilling to occupy themselves with human affairs and that their souls are always pressing upwards, eager to spend their time above, for, after all, this is surely what we'd expect, if indeed things fit the image I described before.   *d*

It is.

What about what happens when someone turns from divine study to the evils of human life? Do you think it's surprising, since his sight is still dim, and he hasn't yet become accustomed to the darkness around him, that he behaves awkwardly and appears completely ridiculous if he's compelled, either in the courts or elsewhere, to contend about the shadows of justice or the statues of which they are the shadows and to dispute about the way these things are understood by people who have never seen justice itself?   *e*

That's not surprising at all.

No, it isn't. But anyone with any understanding would remember that the   *518* eyes may be confused in two ways and from two causes, namely, when they've come from the light into the darkness *and* when they've come from the darkness into the light. Realizing that the same applies to the soul, when someone sees a soul disturbed and unable to see something, he won't laugh mindlessly, but he'll take into consideration whether it has come from a brighter life and is dimmed

through not having yet become accustomed to the dark or whether it has come from greater ignorance into greater light and is dazzled by the increased brilliance. Then he'll declare the first soul happy in its experience and life, and he'll
b pity the latter—but even if he chose to make fun of it, at least he'd be less ridiculous than if he laughed at a soul that has come from the light above.

What you say is very reasonable.

If that's true, then here's what we must think about these matters: Education isn't what some people declare it to be, namely, putting knowledge into souls that
c lack it, like putting sight into blind eyes.

They do say that.

But our present discussion, on the other hand, shows that the power to learn is present in everyone's soul and that the instrument with which each learns is like an eye that cannot be turned around from darkness to light without turning the whole body. This instrument cannot be turned around from that which is coming into being without turning the whole soul until it is able to study that which is
d and the brightest thing that is, namely, the one we call the good. Isn't that right?

Yes.

Then education is the craft concerned with doing this very thing, this turning around, and with how the soul can most easily and effectively be made to do it. It isn't the craft of putting sight into the soul. Education takes for granted that sight is there but that it isn't turned the right way or looking where it ought to look, and it tries to redirect it appropriately.

So it seems.

Discussion Questions

1. How could you know if you were living in a "false reality"? Imagine a tiger born in a zoo—a cave-like reality. Would he know that he is missing out on the jungle, or would he likely think that the zoo habitat just *is* the one true reality? Is it possible that humans live in such a false reality? What would that mean?

2. In the movie *The Truman Show*, the main character is born into a false reality— a huge television set that serves as the ultimate "reality show." Everyone on the set is an actor (including his wife, friends, and boss), and viewers at home watch Truman grow up. Even though everything is taken care of for Truman—the weather, his job, relationships, etc.—do you somehow feel that he has missed out on something important? Explain.

3. Where do you put yourself on the spectrum of ignorant-and-blissful on one end and knowledgeable-and-miserable on the other? Do you think that ignorance is bliss? In what ways is being knowledgeable *unblissful*? Do you agree with these dichotomies?

4. How much truth is there to the phrase "What you don't know can't hurt you"?

5. In what ways is it selfish and even harmful to adhere to the phrase "Ignorance is bliss"?

6. In what ways does your education involve putting information "into your soul," as Socrates suggests? In what ways does it involve drawing it out of you? Is one better than the other? Which do you value more?

The Value of Philosophy

Bertrand Russell

Bertrand Russell began his education in mathematics at Trinity College in Cambridge and there, three years after he arrived, he began his study of philosophy. He went on to teach at Cambridge and refine his theories of mathematics (he later published a highly renowned book in 1910 with Alfred North Whitehead called *Principia Mathematica*). Russell was outspoken and this caused much strife in his life: His public atheism prevented him from holding positions in Parliament; his outward opposition to World War I (though a pacifist) caused his teaching position at Cambridge to be terminated and eventually led to his six-month imprisonment in 1918 (and again in 1961 for one week for civil disobedience); and his liberal views on sex prevented him from acquiring a teaching assignment at New York City College.

In 1936 he went to the United States to teach and in 1950 won the Nobel Prize for literature for his book, *A History of Western Philosophy*. He returned to Cambridge and focused on the dangers and pitfalls of the war.

The following selection is the final chapter of his book, *The Problems of Philosophy*. In it he provides a brief overview of what philosophy is—and is not. More importantly, he lays out the virtues of philosophical pursuit and how in can help prevent us from being stuck in a "Plato's Cave" situation—ignorant and cut off from the world.

Reading Questions

1. To whom does Russell refer as the " 'practical' man"? How are they "wrongly" called this? What does it have to do with the value of philosophy?
2. According to Russell, what are the two reasons that philosophy has no "body of truths"?
3. What value does Russell suggest can be found in locating our *un*certainty?
4. How does philosophic contemplation help escape the potential narrow-mindedness of our own surroundings? How does it aid in the "enlargement of the Self"?

It will be well to consider . . . what is the value of philosophy and why it ought to be studied. It is the more necessary to consider this question, in view of the fact that many men, under the influence of science or of practical affairs, are inclined to doubt whether philosophy is anything better than innocent but useless trifling, hair-splitting distinctions, and controversies on matters concerning which knowledge is impossible.

This view of philosophy appears to result, partly from a wrong conception of the ends of life, partly from a wrong conception of the kind of goods which philosophy strives to achieve. Physical science, through the medium of inventions, is useful to innumerable people who are wholly ignorant of it; thus the study of

Source: Excerpt from *The Problems of Philosophy* by Bertrand Russell, 1959, pp. 153–161. By permission of Oxford University Press.

physical science is to be recommended, not only, or primarily, because of the effect on the student, but rather because of the effect on mankind in general. Thus utility does not belong to philosophy. If the study of philosophy has any value at all for others than students of philosophy, it must be only indirectly, through its effects upon the lives of those who study it. It is in these effects, therefore, if anywhere, that the value of philosophy must be primarily sought.

But further, if we are not to fail in our endeavour to determine the value of philosophy, we must first free our minds from the prejudices of what are wrongly called 'practical' men. The 'practical' man, as this word is often used, is one who recognizes only material needs, who realizes that men must have food for the body, but is oblivious of the necessity of providing food for the mind. If all men were well off, if poverty and disease had been reduced to their lowest possible point, there would still remain much to be done to produce a valuable society; and even in the existing world the goods of the mind are at least as important as the goods of the body. It is exclusively among the goods of the mind that the value of philosophy is to be found; and only those who are not indifferent to these goods can be persuaded that the study of philosophy is not a waste of time.

Philosophy, like all other studies, aims primarily at knowledge. The knowledge it aims at is the kind of knowledge which gives unity and system to the body of the sciences, and the kind which results from a critical examination of the grounds of our convictions, prejudices, and beliefs. But it cannot be maintained that philosophy has had any very great measure of success in its attempts to provide definite answers to its questions. If you ask a mathematician, a mineralogist, a historian, or any other man of learning, what definite body of truths has been ascertained by his science, his answer will last as long as you are willing to listen. But if you put the same question to a philosopher, he will, if he is candid, have to confess that his study has not achieved positive results such as have been achieved by other sciences. It is true that this is partly accounted for by the fact that, as soon as definite knowledge concerning any subject becomes possible, this subject ceases to be called philosophy, and becomes a separate science. The whole study of the heavens, which now belongs to astronomy, was once included in philosophy; Newton's great work was called 'the mathematical principles of natural philosophy.' Similarly, the study of the human mind, which was a part of philosophy, has now been separated from philosophy and has become the science of psychology. Thus, to a great extent, the uncertainty of philosophy is more apparent than real: Those questions which are already capable of definite answers are placed in the sciences, while those only to which, at present, no definite answer can be given, remain to form the residue which is called philosophy.

This is, however, only a part of the truth concerning the uncertainty of philosophy. There are many questions—and among them those that are of the profoundest interest to our spiritual life—which, so far as we can see, must remain insoluble to the human intellect unless its powers become of quite a different order from what they are now. Has the universe any unity of plan or purpose, or is it a fortuitous concourse of atoms? Is consciousness a permanent part of the universe, giving hope of indefinite growth in wisdom, or is it a transitory accident on a small planet on which life must ultimately become impossible? Are good and evil of importance to the universe or only to man? Such questions are asked by philosophy, and variously answered by various philosophers. But it would seem that, whether answers be otherwise discoverable or not, the answers suggested by philosophy are none of them demonstrably true. Yet, however slight may be the hope of discovering an answer, it is part of the business of philosophy to continue the consideration of such questions, to make us aware of their importance, to examine all the approaches to them, and to keep alive that speculative interest in the universe which is apt to be killed by confining ourselves to definitely ascertainable knowledge.

Many philosophers, it is true, have held that philosophy could establish the truth of certain answers to such fundamental questions. They have supposed that what is of most importance in religious beliefs could be proved by strict demonstration to be true. In order to judge of such attempts, it is necessary to take a survey of human knowledge, and to form an opinion as to its methods and its limitations. On such a subject it would be unwise to pronounce dogmatically; but if the investigations of our previous chapters have not led us astray, we shall be compelled to renounce the hope of finding philosophical proofs of religious beliefs. We cannot, therefore, include as part of the value of philosophy any definite set of answers to such questions. Hence, once more, the value of philosophy must not depend upon any supposed body of definitely ascertainable knowledge to be acquired by those who study it.

The value of philosophy is, in fact, to be sought largely in its very uncertainty. The man who has no tincture of philosophy goes through life imprisoned in the prejudices derived from common sense, from the habitual beliefs of his age or his nation, and from convictions which have grown up in his mind without the co-operation or consent of his deliberate reason. To such a man the world tends to become definite, finite, obvious; common objects rouse no questions, and unfamiliar possibilities are contemptuously rejected. As soon as we begin to philosophize, on the contrary, we find . . . that even the most everyday things lead to problems to which only very incomplete answers can be given. Philosophy, though unable to tell us with certainty what is the true answer to the doubts which it raises, is able to suggest many possibilities which enlarge our thoughts and free them from the tyranny of custom. Thus, while diminishing our feeling of certainty as to what things are, it greatly increases our knowledge as to what they may be; it removes the somewhat arrogant dogmatism of those who have never traveled into the region of liberating doubt, and it keeps alive our sense of wonder by showing familiar things in an unfamiliar aspect.

Apart from its utility in showing unsuspected possibilities, philosophy has a value—perhaps its chief value—through the greatness of the objects which it contemplates, and the freedom from narrow and personal aims resulting from this contemplation. The life of the instinctive man is shut up within the circle of his private interests: Family and friends may be included, but the outer world is not regarded except as it may help or hinder what comes within the circle of instinctive wishes. In such a life there is something feverish and confined, in comparison with which the philosophic life is calm and free. The private world of instinctive interests is a small one, set in the midst of a great and powerful world which must, sooner or later, lay our private world in ruins. Unless we can so enlarge our interests as to include the whole outer world, we remain like a garrison in a beleaguered fortress, knowing that the enemy prevents escape and that ultimate surrender is inevitable. In such a life there is no peace, but a constant strife between the insistence of desire and the powerlessness of will. In one way or another, if our life is to be great and free, we must escape this prison and this strife.

One way of escape is by philosophic contemplation. Philosophic contemplation does not, in its widest survey, divide the universe into two hostile camps—friends and foes, helpful and hostile, good and bad—it views the whole impartially. Philosophic contemplation, when it is unalloyed, does not aim at proving that the rest of the universe is akin to man. All acquisition of knowledge is an enlargement of the Self, but this enlargement is best attained when it is not directly sought. It is obtained when the desire for knowledge is alone operative, by a study which does not wish in advance that its objects should have this or that character, but adapts the Self to the characters which it finds in its objects. This enlargement of Self is not obtained when, taking the Self as it is, we try to show that the world is so similar to this Self that knowledge of it is possible without any admission of what seems alien. The desire to prove this is a form of self-assertion and, like all self-assertion, it is an obstacle to the growth of Self which it desires, and of which the Self knows that it is capable. Self-assertion, in philosophic speculation as elsewhere, views the world as a means to its own ends; thus it makes the world of less account than Self, and the Self sets bounds to the greatness of its goods. In contemplation, on the contrary, we start from the not-Self, and through its greatness the boundaries of Self are enlarged; through the infinity of the universe the mind which contemplates it achieves some share in infinity.

For this reason greatness of soul is not fostered by those philosophies which assimilate the universe to Man. Knowledge is a form of union of Self and not-Self; like all union, it is impaired by dominion, and therefore by any attempt to force the universe into conformity with what we find in ourselves. There is a widespread philosophical tendency towards the view which tells us that Man is the measure of all things, that truth is man-made, that space and time and the world of universals are properties of the mind, and that, if there be anything not created by the mind, it is unknowable and of no account for us. This view, if our previous discussions were correct, is untrue; but in addition to being untrue, it has the effect of robbing philosophic contemplation of all that gives it value, since it fetters contemplation of Self. What it calls knowledge is not a union with the not-Self, but a set of prejudices, habits, and desires, making an impenetrable veil between us and the world beyond. The man who finds pleasure in such a theory of knowledge is like the man who never leaves the domestic circle for fear his word might not be law.

The true philosophic contemplation, on the contrary, finds its satisfaction in every enlargement of the not-Self, in everything that magnifies the objects contemplated, and thereby the subject contemplating. Everything, in contemplation, that is personal or private, everything that depends upon habit, self-interest, or desire, distorts the object, and hence impairs the union which the intellect seeks. By thus making a barrier between subject and object, such personal and private things become a prison to the intellect. The free intellect will see as God might see, without a *here* and *now*, without hopes and fears, without the trammels of customary beliefs and traditional prejudices, calmly, dispassionately, in the sole and exclusive desire of knowledge—knowledge as impersonal, as purely contemplative, as it is possible for man to attain. Hence also the free intellect will value more the abstract and universal knowledge into which the accidents of private history do not enter, than the knowledge brought by the senses, and dependent, as such knowledge must be, upon an exclusive and personal point of view and a body whose sense-organs distort as much as they reveal.

The mind which has become accustomed to the freedom and impartiality of philosophic contemplation will preserve something of the same freedom and impartiality in the world of action and emotion. It will view its purposes and desires as parts of the whole, with the absence of insistence that results from seeing them as infinitesimal fragments in a world of which all the rest is unaffected by any one man's deeds. The impartiality which, in contemplation, is the unalloyed desire for truth, is the very same quality of mind which, in action, is justice, and in emotion is that universal love which can be given to all, and not only to those who are judged useful or admirable. Thus contemplation enlarges not only the objects of our thoughts, but also the objects of our actions and our affections: it makes us citizens of the universe, not only of one walled city at war with all the rest. In this citizenship of the universe consists man's true freedom, and his liberation from the thraldom of narrow hopes and fears.

Thus, to sum up our discussion of the value of philosophy; Philosophy is to be studied, not for the sake of any definite answers to its questions, since no definite answers can, as a rule, be known to be true, but rather for the sake of the questions themselves; because these questions enlarge our conception of what is possible, enrich our intellectual imagination and diminish the dogmatic assurance which closes the mind against speculation; but above all because, through the greatness of the universe which philosophy contemplates, the mind also is rendered great, and becomes capable of that union with the universe which constitutes its highest good.

Discussion Questions

1. Which of Russell's motivations persuade you most about the study of philosophy?
2. What prejudices, habits, and desires might prevent you from finding truth?
3. What danger is there in a person being "shut up within the circle of his private interests," as Russell writes?
4. Russell refers to the "ends" of life—i.e., the goals or the purpose of life. Is there one answer to this or does it vary according to each person? How do you answer this question?
5. Do you find any value in realizing what it is that you do *not* (or *cannot*) know?

The Function of Education

Jiddu Krishnamurti

Jiddu Krishnamurti—the eighth child in his family, named after Krishna, who is the eighth reincarnation of Vishnu, the Hindu god—was born in India in 1895. He became a very well known and respected philosopher, yet refused to take on disciples (though he could have), as he felt that relationship to be exploitive; instead he preferred to explore issues *with* people and to "walk as two friends." His conversations were published in over fifty books and over fifty languages as well. He was awarded the United Nations Peace Medal in 1984, two years before his death.

A principle aim in his lectures and writings was to free others from the influence of any sort of ideology, religion, or dogma and, like him, to learn about the world and (more importantly) about oneself in a freer, more authentic sense. This comes through in the following selection.

Reading Questions

1. According to Krishnamurti, what is wrong with a view of education aimed solely at preparing one to earn a living?
2. How does he define "intelligence"?
3. According to Krishnamurti, what causes anxiety? And what alleviates it?
4. Why does Krishnamurti suggest that we revolt against everything?
5. What does he say about "living safely"? What does that mean? Why is it difficult?
6. Why is conforming seen in a negative light by Krishnamurti?
7. How does he answer the question as to whether an all-out revolt would result in chaos?
8. Why does he argue that it is so important to find out what you love to do?

I wonder if we have ever asked ourselves what education means. Why do we go to school, why do we learn various subjects, why do we pass examinations and compete with each other for better grades? What does this so-called education mean, and what is it all about? This is really a very important question, not only for the students, but also for the parents, for the teachers, and for everyone who loves this earth. Why do we go through the struggle to be educated? Is it merely in order to pass some examinations and get a job? Or is it the function of education to prepare us while we are young to understand the whole process of life? Having a job and earning one's livelihood is necessary—but is that all? Are we being educated only for that? Surely, life is not merely a job, an occupation; life is something extraordinarily wide and profound, it is a great mystery, a vast realm in which we

Source: The Function of Education. Chapter 1, pp. 9–16, from *Think on These Things* by J. Krishnamurti. Copyright © 1964 by the Krishnamurti Foundation of America. Reprinted by permission of HarperCollins Publishers.

function as human beings. If we merely prepare ourselves to earn a livelihood, we shall miss the whole point of life; and to understand life is much more important than merely to prepare for examinations and become very proficient in mathematics, physics, or what you will.

So, whether we are teachers or students, is it not important to ask ourselves why we are educating or being educated? And what does life mean? Is not life an extraordinary thing? The birds, the flowers, the flourishing trees, the heavens, the stars, the rivers and the fish therein—all this is life. Life is the poor and the rich; life is the constant battle between groups, races and nations; life is meditation; life is what we call religion, and it is also the subtle, hidden things of the mind—the envies, the ambitions, the passions, the fears, fulfilments and anxieties. All this and much more is life. But we generally prepare ourselves to understand only one small corner of it. We pass certain examinations, find a job, get married, have children, and then become more and more like machines. We remain fearful, anxious, frightened of life. So, is it the function of education to help us understand the whole process of life, or is it merely to prepare us for a vocation, for the best job we can get?

What is going to happen to all of us when we grow to be men and women? Have you ever asked yourselves what you are going to do when you grow up? In all likelihood you will get married, and before you know where you are you will be mothers and fathers; and you will then be tied to a job, or to the kitchen, in which you will gradually wither away. Is that all that *your* life is going to be? Have you ever asked yourselves this question? Should you not ask it? If your family is wealthy you may have a fairly good position already assured, your father may give you a comfortable job, or you may get richly married; but there also you will decay, deteriorate. Do you see?

Surely, education has no meaning unless it helps you to understand the vast expanse of life with all its subtleties, with its extraordinary beauty, its sorrows and joys. You may earn degrees, you may have a series of letters after your name and land a very good job; but then what? What is the point of it all if in the process your mind becomes dull, weary, stupid? So, while you are young, must you not seek to find out what life is all about? And is it not the true function of education to cultivate in you the intelligence which will try to find the answer to all these problems? Do you know what intelligence is? It is the capacity, surely, to think freely, without fear, without a formula, so that you begin to discover for yourself what is real, what is true; but if you are frightened you will never be intelligent. Any form of ambition, spiritual or mundane, breeds anxiety, fear; therefore ambition does not help to bring about a mind that is clear, simple, direct, and hence intelligent.

You know, it is really very important while you are young to live in an environment in which there is no fear. Most of us, as we grow older, become frightened; we are afraid of living, afraid of losing a job, afraid of tradition, afraid of what the neighbours, or what the wife or husband would say, afraid of death. Most of us have fear in one form or another; and where there is fear there is no intelligence. And is it not possible for all of us, while we are young, to be in an environment where there is no fear but rather an atmosphere of freedom—freedom, not just to do what we like, but to understand the whole process of living? Life is really very beautiful, it is not this ugly thing that we have made of it; and you can appreciate its richness, its depth, its extraordinary loveliness only when you revolt against everything—against organized religion, against tradition, against the present rotten society—so that you as a human being find out for yourself what is true. Not to imitate but to discover—*that* is education, is it not? It is very easy to conform to what your society or your parents and teachers tell you. That is a safe and easy way of existing; but that is not living, because in it there is fear, decay, death. To live is to find out for yourself what is true, and you can do this only when there is freedom, when there is continuous revolution inwardly, within yourself.

But you are not encouraged to do this; no one tells you to question, to find out for yourself what God is, because if you were to rebel you would become a danger to all that is false. Your parents and society want you to live safely, and you also want to live safely. Living safely generally means living in imitation and therefore in fear. Surely, the function of education is to help each one of us to live freely and without fear, is it not? And to create an atmosphere in which there is no fear requires a great deal of thinking on your part as well as on the part of the teacher, the educator.

Do you know what this means—what an extraordinary thing it would be to create an atmosphere in which there is no fear? And we *must* create it, because we see that the world is caught up in endless wars; it is guided by politicians who are always seeking power; it is a world of lawyers, policemen and soldiers, of ambitious men and women all wanting position and all fighting each other to get it. Then there are the so-called saints, the religious *gurus* with their followers; they also want power, position, here or in the next life. It is a mad world, completely confused, in which the communist is fighting the capitalist, the socialist is resisting both, and everybody is against somebody, struggling to arrive at a safe place, a position of power or comfort. The world is torn by conflicting beliefs, by caste and class distinctions, by separative nationalities, by every form of stupidity and cruelty—and this is the world you are being educated to fit into. You are encouraged to fit into the framework of this disastrous society; your parents want you to do that, and you also want to fit in.

Now, is it the function of education merely to help you to conform to the pattern of this rotten social order, or is it to give you freedom—complete freedom to grow and create a different society, a new world? We want to have this freedom, not in the future, but now, otherwise we may all be destroyed. We must create immediately an atmosphere of freedom so that you can live and find out for yourselves what is true, so that you become intelligent, so that you are able to face the world and understand it, not just conform to it, so that inwardly, deeply, psychologically you are in constant revolt; because it is only those who are in constant revolt that discover what is true, not the man who conforms, who follows some tradition. It is only when you are constantly inquiring, constantly observing, constantly learning, that you find truth, God, or love; and you cannot inquire, observe, learn, you cannot be deeply aware, if you are afraid. So the function of education, surely, is to eradicate, inwardly as well as outwardly, this fear that destroys human thought, human relationship and love.

Questioner: If all individuals were in revolt, don't you think there would be chaos in the world?

KRISHNAMURTI: Listen to the question first, because it is very important to understand the question and not just wait for an answer. The question is: If all individuals were in revolt, would not the world be in chaos? But is the present society in such perfect order that chaos would result if everyone revolted against it? Is there not chaos *now*? Is everything beautiful, uncorrupted? Is everyone living happily, fully, richly? Is man not against man? Is there not ambition, ruthless competition? So the world is already in chaos, that is the first thing to realize. Don't take it for granted that this is an orderly society; don't mesmerize yourself with words. Whether, here in Europe, in America or Russia, the world is in a process of decay. If you see the decay, you have a challenge: You are challenged to find a way of solving this urgent problem. And how you respond to the challenge is important, is it not? If you respond as a Hindu or a Buddhist, a Christian or a communist, then your response is very limited—which is no response at all. You can respond fully, adequately only if there is no fear in you, only if you don't think as a Hindu, a communist or a capitalist, but as a total human being who is trying to solve this problem; and you cannot solve it unless you yourself are in revolt against the whole thing, against the ambitious acquisitiveness on which society is based. When you yourself are not ambitious, not acquisitive, not clinging to your own security—only then can you respond to the challenge and create a new world.

Questioner: To revolt, to learn, to love—are these three separate processes, or are they simultaneous?

KRISHNAMURTI: Of course they are not three separate processes; it is a unitary process. You see, it is very important to find out what the question means. This question is based on theory, not on experience; it is merely verbal, intellectual, therefore it has no validity. A man who is fearless, who is really in revolt, struggling to find out what it means to learn, to love—such a man does not ask if it is one process or three. We are so clever with words, and we think that by offering explanations we have solved the problem.

Do you know what it means to learn? When you are really learning you are learning throughout your life and there is no one special teacher to learn from. Then everything teaches you—a dead leaf, a bird in flight, a smell, a tear, the rich and the poor, those who are crying, the smile of a woman, the haughtiness of a man. You learn from everything, therefore there is no guide, no philosopher, no guru. Life itself is your teacher, and you are in a state of constant learning.

Questioner: Is it true that society is based on acquisitiveness and ambition; but if we had no ambition would we not decay?

KRISHNAMURTI: This is really a very important question, and it needs great attention.

Do you know what attention is? Let us find out. In a classroom, when you stare out of the window or pull somebody's hair, the teacher tells you to pay attention. Which means what? That you are not interested in what you are studying and so the teacher compels you to pay attention—which is not attention at all. Attention comes when you are deeply interested in something, for then you love to find out all about it; then your whole mind, your whole being is there. Similarly, the moment you see that this question—if we had no ambition, would we not decay?—is really very important, you are interested and want to find out the truth of the matter.

Now, is not the ambitious man destroying himself? That is the first thing to find out, not to ask whether ambition is right or wrong. Look around you, observe all the people who are ambitious. What happens when you are ambitious? You are thinking about yourself, are you not? You are cruel, you push other people aside because you are trying to fulfil your ambition, trying to become a big man, thereby creating in society the conflict between those who are succeeding and those who are falling behind. There is a constant battle between you and the others who are also after what you want; and is this conflict productive of creative living? Do you understand, or is this too difficult?

Are you ambitious when you love to do something for its own sake? When you are doing something with your whole being, not because you want to get somewhere, or have more profit, or greater results, but simply because you love to do it—in that there is no ambition, is there? In that there is no competition; you are not struggling with anyone for first place. And should not education help you to find out what you really love to do so that from the beginning to the end of your life you are working at something which you feel is worthwhile and which for you has deep significance? Otherwise, for the rest of your days, you will be miserable. Not knowing what you really want to do, your mind falls into a routine in which there is only boredom, decay and death. That is why it is very important to find out while you are young what it is you really *love* to do; and this is the only way to create a new society.

Discussion Questions

1. For what reason(s) do you spend so much time and effort becoming educated?
2. How would you approach your education if you did not need it in order to make a living (imagine that you had a job lined up for yourself when you were ready for it, after finishing college, for example)?
3. Do you agree that intelligence alleviates fear? Why/why not?
4. Does (did) your education alleviate fear for you? In what ways does it provide you with more freedom? In what ways does it take away from your freedom?
5. In what ways do you feel that you're being asked to fit in or conform to society? By your parents? Religion? Politics? Advertisers? Educators? Is conforming a bad thing? Why/why not?
6. What do you think of his answer as to whether an all-out revolt would result in chaos?
7. What does he mean when he writes, "We are so clever with words, and we think that by offering explanations we have solved the problem"?
8. Think of the most exciting moments in your education—when you really felt like you learned. What was unique to that time? How was it different from times when you were being taught but not truly learning?

The Official Theory

Steven Pinker

Steven Pinker has been a professor in the department of psychology at Harvard University since 2003, prior to which he served as the director of the Center for Cognitive Neuroscience at MIT. He has written six books, two of which were finalists for the Pulitzer Prize, including the book from which this selection is extracted—*The Blank Slate: The Modern Denial of Human Nature*. He was also declared as one of the "World's Top 100 Public Intellectuals" in 2005 by *Prospect* and *Foreign Policy* and as one of the "Top 100 Most Influential People in the World Today" (2004) by *Time*.

This selection serves two purposes. First, it introduces three of the major philosophical theories that have shaped modern education, religion, and social policy. In Pinker's brief overview, he not only summarizes these theories but also examines their respective competing theories. (In doing so, he reviews four of the readings from this anthology—Locke, Descartes, Ryle, and Hobbes.) Secondly, Pinker shows how relevant philosophical theories can be and that these theories are more than mere ideas—they are the foundation for much of what motivates our beliefs in both our private and political lives.

Reading Questions

1. What is the theory of the "Blank Slate"? In what ways did Locke's theory about knowledge and the Blank Slate affect his socio-political theories?
2. What other effects has the idea of a Blank Slate had?
3. What are the ramifications of the Noble Savage (and its counterpart in Hobbes) in both political and private life?
4. How does Descartes's view of the soul (Ghost in the Machine) contrast with Hobbes' mechanical view in terms of our ability to freely choose?
5. Pinker refers to Dennett: The brain transplant is "the one transplant operation in which it is better to be the donor than the recipient." What does his reference signify?
6. How does Pinker suggest that all three doctrines—empiricism, romanticism, and dualism—are connected?
7. How does the Ghost in the Machine affect the moral status of stem-cell research and abortion?

"Blank Slate" is a loose translation of the medieval Latin term *tabula rasa*—literally, "scraped tablet." It is commonly attributed to the philosopher John Locke (1632–1704), though in fact he used a different metaphor. Here is the famous passage from *An Essay Concerning Human Understanding*:

> Let us then suppose the mind to be, as we say, white paper void of all characters, without any ideas. How comes it to be furnished? Whence comes it by

Source: "The Official Theory," from *The Blank Slate* by Steven Pinker, copyright © 2002 by Steven Pinker. Used by permission of Viking Penguin, a division of Penguin Group (USA) Inc.

that vast store which the busy and boundless fancy of man has painted on it with an almost endless variety? Whence has it all the materials of reason and knowledge? To this I answer, in one word, from EXPERIENCE.

Locke was taking aim at theories of innate ideas in which people were thought to be born with mathematical ideals, eternal truths, and a notion of God. His alternative theory, empiricism, was intended both as a theory of psychology—how the mind works—and as a theory of epistemology—how we come to know the truth. Both goals helped motivate his political philosophy, often honored as the foundation of liberal democracy. Locke opposed dogmatic justifications for the political status quo, such as the authority of the church and the divine right of kings, which had been touted as self-evident truths. He argued that social arrangements should be reasoned out from scratch and agreed upon by mutual consent, based on knowledge that any person could acquire. Since ideas are grounded in experience, which varies from person to person, differences of opinion arise not because one mind is equipped to grasp the truth and another is defective, but because the two minds have had different histories. Those differences therefore ought to be tolerated rather than suppressed. Locke's notion of a blank slate also undermined a hereditary royalty and aristocracy, whose members could claim no innate wisdom or merit if their minds had started out as blank as everyone else's. It also spoke against the institution of slavery, because slaves could no longer be thought of as innately inferior or subservient.

During the past century the doctrine of the Blank Slate has set the agenda for much of the social sciences and humanities. As we shall see, psychology has sought to explain all thought, feeling, and behavior with a few simple mechanisms of learning. The social sciences have sought to explain all customs and social arrangements as a product of the socialization of children by the surrounding culture: a system of words, images, stereotypes, role models, and contingencies of reward and punishment. A long and growing list of concepts that would seem natural to the human way of thinking (emotions, kinship, the sexes, illness, nature, the world) are now said to have been "invented" or "socially constructed."

The Blank Slate has also served as a sacred scripture for political and ethical beliefs. According to the doctrine, any differences we see among races, ethnic groups, sexes, and individuals come not from differences in their innate constitution but from differences in their experiences. Change the experiences—by reforming parenting, education, the media, and social rewards—and you can change the person. Underachievement, poverty, and antisocial behavior can be ameliorated; indeed, it is irresponsible not to do so. And discrimination on the basis of purportedly inborn traits of a sex or ethnic group is simply irrational.

The Blank Slate is often accompanied by two other doctrines, which have also attained a sacred status in modern intellectual life. My label for the first of the two is commonly attributed to the philosopher Jean-Jacques Rousseau

(1712–1778), though it really comes from John Dryden's *The Conquest of Granada*, published in 1670:

I am as free as Nature first made man,
Ere the base laws of servitude began,
When wild in woods the noble savage ran.

The concept of the noble savage was inspired by European colonists' discovery of indigenous peoples in the Americas, Africa, and (later) Oceania. It captures the belief that humans in their natural state are selfless, peaceable, and untroubled, and that blights such as greed, anxiety, and violence are the products of civilization. In 1755 Rousseau wrote:

> So many authors have hastily concluded that man is naturally cruel, and requires a regular system of police to be reclaimed; whereas nothing can be more gentle than him in his primitive state, when placed by nature at an equal distance from the stupidity of brutes and the pernicious good sense of civilized man. . . .
>
> The more we reflect on this state, the more convinced we shall be that it was the least subject of any to revolutions, the best for man, and that nothing could have drawn him out of it but some fatal accident, which, for the public good, should never have happened. The example of the savages, most of whom have been found in this condition, seems to confirm that mankind was formed ever to remain in it, that this condition is the real youth of the world, and that all ulterior improvements have been so many steps, in appearance towards the perfection of individuals, but in fact towards the decrepitness of the species.

First among the authors that Rousseau had in mind was Thomas Hobbes (1588–1679), who had presented a very different picture:

> Hereby it is manifest, that during the time men live without a common power to keep them all in awe, they are in that condition which is called war; and such a war as is of every man against every man. . . .
>
> In such condition there is no place for industry, because the fruit thereof is uncertain: and consequently no culture of the earth; no navigation, nor use of the commodities that may be imported by sea; no commodious building; no instruments of moving and removing such things as require much force; no knowledge of the face of the earth; no account of time; no arts; no letters; no society; and which is worst of all, continual fear, and danger of violent death; and the life of man, solitary, poor, nasty, brutish, and short.

Hobbes believed that people could escape this hellish existence only by surrendering their autonomy to a sovereign person or assembly. He called it a leviathan, the Hebrew word for a monstrous sea creature subdued by Yahweh at the dawn of creation.

Much depends on which of these armchair anthropologists is correct. If people are noble savages, then a domineering leviathan is unnecessary. Indeed, by forcing people to delineate private property for the state to recognize—property they might otherwise have shared—the leviathan creates the very greed and belligerence it is designed to control. A happy society would be our birthright; all we would need to do is eliminate the institutional barriers that keep it from us. If, in contrast, people are naturally nasty, the best we can hope for is an uneasy truce enforced by police and the army. The two theories have implications for private life as well. Every child is born a savage (that is, uncivilized), so if savages are naturally gentle, childrearing is a matter of providing children with opportunities to develop their potential, and evil people are products of a society that has corrupted them. If savages are naturally nasty, then childrearing is an arena of discipline and conflict, and evil people are showing a dark side that was insufficiently tamed.

The actual writings of philosophers are always more complex than the theories they come to symbolize in the textbooks. In reality, the views of Hobbes and Rousseau are not that far apart. Rousseau, like Hobbes, believed (incorrectly) that savages were solitary, without ties of love or loyalty, and without any industry or art (and he may have out-Hobbes'd Hobbes in claiming they did not even have language). Hobbes envisioned—indeed, literally drew—his leviathan as an embodiment of the collective will, which was vested in it by a kind of social contract; Rousseau's most famous work is called *The Social Contract*, and in it he calls on people to subordinate their interests to a "general will."

Nonetheless, Hobbes and Rousseau limned contrasting pictures of the state of nature that have inspired thinkers in the centuries since. No one can fail to recognize the influence of the doctrine of the Noble Savage in contemporary consciousness. We see it in the current respect for all things natural (natural foods, natural medicines, natural childbirth) and the distrust of the man-made, the unfashionability of authoritarian styles of childrearing and education, and the understanding of social problems as repairable defects in our institutions rather than as tragedies inherent to the human condition.

The other sacred doctrine that often accompanies the Blank Slate is usually attributed to the scientist, mathematician, and philosopher René Descartes (1596–1650):

> There is a great difference between mind and body, inasmuch as body is by nature always divisible, and the mind is entirely indivisible. . . . When I consider the mind, that is to say, myself inasmuch as I am only a thinking being, I cannot distinguish in myself any parts, but apprehend myself to be clearly one and entire; and though the whole mind seems to be united to the whole body, yet if a foot, or an arm, or some other part, is separated from the body, I am aware that nothing has been taken from my mind. And the faculties of willing, feeling, conceiving, etc. cannot be properly speaking said to be its parts, for it is one and the same mind which employs itself in willing and in feeling and understanding. But it is quite otherwise with corporeal or extended objects, for there is not one of them imaginable by me which my mind cannot

easily divide into parts. . . . This would be sufficient to teach me that the mind or soul of man is entirely different from the body, if I had not already been apprised of it on other grounds.

A memorable name for this doctrine was given three centuries later by a detractor, the philosopher Gilbert Ryle (1900–1976):

> There is a doctrine about the nature and place of minds which is so prevalent among theorists and even among laymen that it deserves to be described as the official theory. . . . The official doctrine, which hails chiefly from Descartes, is something like this. With the doubtful exception of idiots and infants in arms every human being has both a body and a mind. Some would prefer to say that every human being is both a body and a mind. His body and his mind are ordinarily harnessed together, but after the death of the body his mind may continue to exist and function. Human bodies are in space and are subject to mechanical laws which govern all other bodies in space. . . . But minds are not in space, nor are their operations subject to mechanical laws. . . .
> . . . Such in outline is the official theory. I shall often speak of it, with deliberate abusiveness, as "the dogma of the Ghost in the Machine."

The Ghost in the Machine, like the Noble Savage, arose in part as a reaction to Hobbes. Hobbes had argued that life and mind could be explained in mechanical terms. Light sets our nerves and brain in motion, and that is what it means to see. The motions may persist like the wake of a ship or the vibration of a plucked string, and that is what it means to imagine. "Quantities" get added or subtracted in the brain, and that is what it means to think.

Descartes rejected the idea that the mind could operate by physical principles. He thought that behavior, especially speech, was not *caused* by anything, but freely *chosen*. He observed that our consciousness, unlike our bodies and other physical objects, does not feel as if it is divisible into parts or laid out in space. He noted that we cannot doubt the existence of our minds—indeed, we cannot doubt that we *are* our minds—because the very act of thinking presupposes that our minds exist. But we *can* doubt the existence of our bodies, because we can imagine ourselves to be immaterial spirits who merely dream or hallucinate that we are incarnate.

Descartes also found a moral bonus in his dualism (the belief that the mind is a different kind of thing from the body): "There is none which is more effectual in leading feeble spirits from the straight path of virtue, than to imagine that the soul of the brute is of the same nature as our own, and that in consequence, after this life we have nothing to fear or to hope for, any more than the flies and the ants." Ryle explains Descartes's dilemma:

> When Galileo showed that his methods of scientific discovery were competent to provide a mechanical theory which should cover every occupant of space, Descartes found in himself two conflicting motives. As a man of scientific

genius he could not but endorse the claims of mechanics, yet as a religious and moral man he could not accept, as Hobbes accepted, the discouraging rider to those claims, namely that human nature differs only in degree of complexity from clockwork.

It can indeed be upsetting to think of ourselves as glorified gears and springs. Machines are insensate, built to be used, and disposable; humans are sentient, possessing of dignity and rights, and infinitely precious. A machine has some workaday purpose, such as grinding grain or sharpening pencils; a human being has higher purposes, such as love, worship, good works, and the creation of knowledge and beauty. The behavior of machines is determined by the ineluctable laws of physics and chemistry; the behavior of people is freely chosen. With choice comes freedom, and therefore optimism about our possibilities for the future. With choice also comes responsibility, which allows us to hold people accountable for their actions. And of course if the mind is separate from the body, it can continue to exist when the body breaks down, and our thoughts and pleasures will not someday be snuffed out forever.

As I mentioned, most Americans continue to believe in an immortal soul, made of some nonphysical substance, which can part company with the body. But even those who do not avow that belief in so many words still imagine that somehow there must be more to us than electrical and chemical activity in the brain. Choice, dignity, and responsibility are gifts that set off human beings from everything else in the universe, and seem incompatible with the idea that we are mere collections of molecules. Attempts to explain behavior in mechanistic terms are commonly denounced as "reductionist" or "determinist." The denouncers rarely know exactly what they mean by those words, but everyone knows they refer to something bad. The dichotomy between mind and body also pervades everyday speech, as when we say "Use your head," when we refer to "out-of-body experiences," and when we speak of "John's body," or for that matter "John's brain," which presupposes an owner, John, that is somehow separate from the brain it owns. Journalists sometimes speculate about "brain transplants" when they really should be calling them "body transplants," because, as the philosopher Dan Dennett has noted, this is the one transplant operation in which it is better to be the donor than the recipient.

The doctrines of the Blank Slate, the Noble Savage, and the Ghost in the Machine—or, as philosophers call them, empiricism, romanticism, and dualism—are logically independent, but in practice they are often found together. If the slate is blank, then strictly speaking it has neither injunctions to do good nor injunctions to do evil. But good and evil are asymmetrical: there are more ways to harm people than to help them, and harmful acts can hurt them to a greater degree than virtuous acts can make them better off. So a blank slate, compared with one filled with motives, is bound to impress us more by its inability to do harm than by its inability to do good. Rousseau did not literally believe in a blank slate, but he did believe that bad behavior is a product of learning and socialization. "Men are wicked," he wrote; "a sad and constant experience makes proof unnecessary." But this wickedness comes from society: "There is no original perversity in the human heart. There is not a single vice to be found in it of which it cannot be said how and whence it entered." If the metaphors in everyday speech are a clue, then all of us, like Rousseau, associate blankness with virtue rather than with nothingness. Think of the moral connotations of the adjectives *clean, fair, immaculate, lily-white, pure, spotless, unmarred,* and *unsullied,* and of the nouns *blemish, blot, mark, stain,* and *taint.*

The Blank Slate naturally coexists with the Ghost in the Machine, too, since a slate that is blank is a hospitable place for a ghost to haunt. If a ghost is to be at the controls, the factory can ship the device with a minimum of parts. The ghost can read the body's display panels and pull its levers, with no need for a high-tech executive program, guidance system, or CPU. The more not-clockwork there is controlling behavior, the less clockwork we need to posit. For similar reasons, the Ghost in the Machine happily accompanies the Noble Savage. If the machine behaves ignobly, we can blame the ghost, which freely chose to carry out the iniquitous acts; we need not probe for a defect in the machine's design.

Philosophy today gets no respect. Many scientists use the term as a synonym for effete speculation. When my colleague Ned Block told his father that he would major in the subject, his father's reply was "Luft!"—Yiddish for "air." And then there's the joke in which a young man told his mother he would become a Doctor of Philosophy and she said, "Wonderful! But what kind of disease is philosophy?"

But far from being idle or airy, the ideas of philosophers can have repercussions for centuries. The Blank Slate and its companion doctrines have infiltrated the conventional wisdom of our civilization and have repeatedly surfaced in unexpected places. William Godwin (1756–1835), one of the founders of liberal political philosophy, wrote that "children are a sort of raw material put into our hands," their minds "like a sheet of white paper." More sinisterly, we find Mao Zedong justifying his radical social engineering by saying, "It is on a blank page that the most beautiful poems are written." Even Walt Disney was inspired by the metaphor. "I think of a child's mind as a blank book," he wrote. "During the first years of his life, much will be written on the pages. The quality of that writing will affect his life profoundly."

Locke could not have imagined that his words would someday lead to Bambi (intended by Disney to teach self-reliance); nor could Rousseau have anticipated Pocahontas, the ultimate noble savage. Indeed, the soul of Rousseau seems to have been channeled by the writer of a recent Thanksgiving op-ed piece in the *Boston Globe:*

> I would submit that the world native Americans knew was more stable, happier, and less barbaric than our society today. . . . there were no employment problems, community harmony was strong, substance abuse unknown, crime nearly nonexistent. What warfare there was between tribes

was largely ritualistic and seldom resulted in indiscriminate or wholesale slaughter. While there were hard times, life was, for the most part, stable and predictable. . . . Because the native people respected what was around them, there was no loss of water or food resources because of pollution or extinction, no lack of materials for the daily essentials, such as baskets, canoes, shelter, or firewood. . . .

The third doctrine, too, continues to make its presence felt in modern times. In 2001 George W. Bush announced that the American government will not fund research on human embryonic stem cells if scientists have to destroy new embryos to extract them (the policy permits research on stem-cell lines that were previously extracted from embryos). He derived the policy after consulting not just with scientists but with philosophers and religious thinkers. Many of them framed the moral problem in terms of "ensoulment," the moment at which the cluster of cells that will grow into a child is endowed with a soul. Some argued that ensoulment occurs at conception, which implies that the blastocyst (the five-day-old ball of cells from which stem cells are taken) is morally equivalent to a person and that destroying it is a form of murder. That argument proved decisive, which means that the American policy on perhaps the most promising medical technology of the twenty-first century was decided by pondering the moral issue as it might have been framed centuries before: When does the ghost first enter the machine?

These are just a few of the fingerprints of the Blank Slate, the Noble Savage, and the Ghost in the Machine on modern intellectual life. In the following chapters we will see how the seemingly airy ideas of Enlightenment philosophers entrenched themselves in modern consciousness, and how recent discoveries are casting those ideas in doubt.

Discussion Questions

1. Imagine the difference in your philosophy of life if you changed your opinion about the doctrines explained by Pinker. What would change if you believed differently regarding:
   a. The Blank Slate (versus having innate human nature)
   b. The Noble Savage (versus humans as naturally cruel)
   c. The Ghost in the Machine (versus the materialist notion of no immaterial mind or soul)

   Would it somehow be *better* if people believed one or the other in each (a–c) above? Does the practical advantage of one position outweigh the truth of the matter—i.e., is it better to hold a certain position simply because its results are better?

2. In the preface to Pinker's book, he quotes Chekhov: "Man will become better when you show him what he is like." Do you agree? What significance does this have?

The Apology
Plato
(For a brief biography of Plato, see the earlier selection by Plato.)

In this reading, we see Plato's account of Socrates' "apology" before his sentence of death. It is not to be read as an apology in the true sense of being sorry and regretful for his actions. Instead, Socrates here defends his actions, displaying the inconsistencies inherent in the government of his time. One of the benefits of philosophy, according to Socrates, is to allow one to remain balanced—participating equally in the concepts of truth, beauty, and goodness. With this, along with Socrates' strong belief in the afterlife, he was able to remain calm up until the state forced him to drink the poisonous hemlock.

Reading Questions
1. What does the Oracle say about Socrates? How does he attempt to disprove the Oracle?
2. How does Socrates *prove* his belief in the gods? Do you agree with his proof?
3. How does Socrates use the analogy of himself as a gadfly (horsefly) and the government as a horse?
4. How does Socrates attempt to argue that death should not be feared?

How you, O Athenians, have been affected by my accusers, I cannot tell; but I know that they almost made me forget who I was—so persuasively did they speak; and yet they have hardly uttered a word of truth. But of the many falsehoods told by them, there was one which quite amazed me;—I mean when they said that you should be upon your guard and not allow yourselves to be deceived by the force of my eloquence. To say this, when they were certain to be detected as soon as I opened my lips and proved myself to be anything but a great speaker, did indeed appear to me most shameless—unless by the force of eloquence they mean the force of truth; for if such is their meaning, I admit that I am eloquent. But in how different a way from theirs! Well, as I was saying, they have scarcely spoken the truth at all; but from me you shall hear the whole truth: not, however, delivered after their manner in a set oration duly ornamented with words and phrases. No, by heaven! but I shall use the words and arguments which occur to me at the moment; for I am confident in the justice of my cause (Or, I am certain that I am right in taking this course.): at my time of life I ought not to be appearing before you, O men of Athens, in the character of a juvenile orator—let no one expect it of me. . . . Never mind the manner, which may or may not be good; but think only of the truth of my words, and give heed to that: Let the speaker speak truly and the judge decide justly. . . .

Translated by Benjamin Jowett

I will begin at the beginning, and ask what is the accusation which has given rise to the slander of me, and in fact has encouraged Meletus to proof this charge against me. Well, what do the slanderers say? They shall be my prosecutors, and I will sum up their words in an affidavit: 'Socrates is an evil-doer, and a curious person, who searches into things under the earth and in heaven, and he makes the worse appear the better cause; and he teaches the aforesaid doctrines to others.' Such is the nature of the accusation: It is just what you have yourselves seen in the comedy of Aristophanes (Aristoph., Clouds.), who has introduced a man whom he calls Socrates, going about and saying that he walks in air, and talking a deal of nonsense concerning matters of which I do not pretend to know either much or little—not that I mean to speak disparagingly of any one who is a student of natural philosophy. I should be very sorry if Meletus could bring so grave a charge against me. But the simple truth is, O Athenians, that I have nothing to do with physical speculations. Very many of those here present are witnesses to the truth of this, and to them I appeal. Speak then, you who have heard me, and tell your neighbours whether any of you have ever known me hold forth in few words or in many upon such matters . . . You hear their answer. And from what they say of this part of the charge you will be able to judge of the truth of the rest.

As little foundation is there for the report that I am a teacher, and take money; this accusation has no more truth in it than the other. Although, if a man were really able to instruct mankind, to receive money for giving instruction would, in my opinion, be an honour to him. . . .

I dare say, Athenians, that some one among you will reply, 'Yes, Socrates, but what is the origin of these accusations which are brought against you; there must have been something strange which you have been doing? All these rumours and this talk about you would never have arisen if you had been like other men: tell us, then, what is the cause of them, for we should be sorry to judge hastily of you.' Now I regard this as a fair challenge, and I will endeavour to explain to you the reason why I am called wise and have such an evil fame. Please to attend then. And although some of you may think that I am joking, I declare that I will tell you the entire truth. Men of Athens, this reputation of mine has come of a certain sort of wisdom which I possess. If you ask me what kind of wisdom, I reply, wisdom such as may perhaps be attained by man, for to that extent I am inclined to believe that I am wise; . . . And here, O men of Athens, I must beg you not to interrupt me, even if I seem to say something extravagant. For the word which I will speak is not mine. I will refer you to a witness who is worthy of credit; that witness shall be the God of Delphi—he will tell you about my wisdom, if I have any, and of what sort it is. You must have known Chaerephon; he was early a friend of mine, and also a friend of yours, for he shared in the recent exile of the people, and returned with you. Well, Chaerephon, as you know, was very impetuous in all his doings, and he went to Delphi and boldly asked the oracle to tell him whether—as I was saying, I must beg you not to interrupt—he asked the oracle to tell him whether anyone was wiser than I was, and the Pythian prophetess answered, that there was no man wiser. Chaerephon is dead himself; but his brother, who is in court, will confirm the truth of what I am saying.

Why do I mention this? Because I am going to explain to you why I have such an evil name. When I heard the answer, I said to myself, What can the god mean? and what is the interpretation of his riddle? for I know that I have no wisdom, small or great. What then can he mean when he says that I am the wisest of men? And yet he is a god, and cannot lie; that would be against his nature. After long consideration, I thought of a method of trying the question. I reflected that if I could only find a man wiser than myself, then I might go to the god with a refutation in my hand. I should say to him, 'Here is a man who is wiser than I am; but you said that I was the wisest.' Accordingly I went to one who had the reputation of wisdom, and observed him—his name I need not mention; he was a politician whom I selected for examination—and the result was as follows: When I began to talk with him, I could not help thinking that he was not really wise, although he was thought wise by many, and still wiser by himself; and thereupon I tried to explain to him that he thought himself wise, but was not really wise; and the consequence was that he hated me, and his enmity was shared by several who were present and heard me. So I left him, saying to myself, as I went away: Well, although I do not suppose that either of us knows anything really beautiful and good, I am better off than he is,—for he knows nothing, and thinks that he knows; I neither know nor think that I know. In this latter particular, then, I seem to have slightly the advantage of him. Then I went to another who had still higher pretensions to wisdom, and my conclusion was exactly the same. Whereupon I made another enemy of him, and of many others besides him.

Then I went to one man after another, being not unconscious of the enmity which I provoked, and I lamented and feared this: but necessity was laid upon me,—the word of God, I thought, ought to be considered first. And I said to myself, Go I must to all who appear to know, and find out the meaning of the oracle. And I swear to you, Athenians, by the dog I swear!—for I must tell you the truth—the result of my mission was just this: I found that the men most in repute were all but the most foolish; and that others less esteemed were really wiser and better. I will tell you the tale of my wanderings and of the 'Herculean' labours, as I may call them, which I endured only to find at last the oracle irrefutable. After the politicians, I went to the poets; tragic, dithyrambic, and all sorts. And there, I said to myself, you will be instantly detected; now you will find out that you are more ignorant than they are. Accordingly, I took them some of the most elaborate passages in their own writings, and asked what was the meaning of them—thinking that they would teach me something. Will you believe me? I am almost ashamed to confess the truth, but I must say that there is hardly a person present who would not have talked better about their poetry than they did themselves. Then I knew that not by wisdom do poets write poetry, but by a sort of genius and inspiration; they are like diviners or soothsayers who also say many fine things, but do not understand the meaning of them. The poets appeared to me to be much in the same case; and I further observed that upon the strength of their poetry they believed themselves to be the wisest of men in other things in which they were not wise. So I departed, conceiving myself to be superior to them for the same reason that I was superior to the politicians.

At last I went to the artisans. I was conscious that I knew nothing at all, as I may say, and I was sure that they knew many fine things; and here I was not mistaken, for they did know many things of which I was ignorant, and in this they certainly were wiser than I was. But I observed that even the good artisans fell into the same error as the poets;—because they were good workmen they thought that they also knew all sorts of high matters, and this defect in them overshadowed their wisdom; and therefore I asked myself on behalf of the oracle, whether I would like to be as I was, neither having their knowledge nor their ignorance, or like them in both; and I made answer to myself and to the oracle that I was better off as I was.

This inquisition has led to my having many enemies of the worst and most dangerous kind, and has given occasion also to many calumnies. And I am called wise, for my hearers always imagine that I myself possess the wisdom which I find wanting in others: but the truth is, O men of Athens, that God only is wise; and by his answer he intends to show that the wisdom of men is worth little or nothing; he is not speaking of Socrates, he is only using my name by way of illustration, as if he said, He, O men, is the wisest, who, like Socrates, knows that his wisdom is in truth worth nothing. And so I go about the world, obedient to the god, and search and make enquiry into the wisdom of any one, whether citizen or stranger, who appears to be wise; and if he is not wise, then in vindication of the oracle I show him that he is not wise; and my occupation quite absorbs me, and I have no time to give either to any public matter of interest or to any concern of my own, but I am in utter poverty by reason of my devotion to the god.

There is another thing:—young men of the richer classes, who have not much to do, come about me of their own accord; they like to hear the pretenders examined, and they often imitate me, and proceed to examine others; there are plenty of persons, as they quickly discover, who think that they know something, but really know little or nothing; and then those who are examined by them instead of being angry with themselves are angry with me: This confounded Socrates, they say; this villainous misleader of youth!—and then if somebody asks them, Why, what evil does he practise or teach? they do not know, and cannot tell; but in order that they may not appear to be at a loss, they repeat the ready-made charges which are used against all philosophers about teaching things up in the clouds and under the earth, and having no gods, and making the worse appear the better cause; for they do not like to confess that their pretence of knowledge has been detected—which is the truth; and as they are numerous and ambitious and energetic, and are drawn up in battle array and have persuasive tongues, they have filled your ears with their loud and inveterate calumnies. . . .

I have said enough in my defence against the first class of my accusers; I turn to the second class. They are headed by Meletus, that good man and true lover of his country, as he calls himself. Against these, too, I must try to make a defence:— Let their affidavit be read: It contains something of this kind: It says that Socrates is a doer of evil, who corrupts the youth; and who does not believe in the gods of the state, but has other new divinities of his own. Such is the charge; and now let us examine the particular counts. He says that I am a doer of evil, and corrupt the youth; but I say, O men of Athens, that Meletus is a doer of evil, in that he pretends to be in earnest when he is only in jest, and is so eager to bring men to trial from a pretended zeal and interest about matters in which he really never had the smallest interest. And the truth of this I will endeavour to prove to you.

Come hither, Meletus, and let me ask a question of you. You think a great deal about the improvement of youth?

Yes, I do.

Tell the judges, then, who is their improver; for you must know, as you have taken the pains to discover their corrupter, and are citing and accusing me before them. Speak, then, and tell the judges who their improver is. . . .

The laws.

But that, my good sir, is not my meaning. I want to know who the person is, who, in the first place, knows the laws.

The judges, Socrates, who are present in court.

What, do you mean to say, Meletus, that they are able to instruct and improve youth?

Certainly they are.

What, all of them, or some only and not others?

All of them.

By the goddess Here, that is good news! There are plenty of improvers, then. And what do you say of the audience,—do they improve them?

Yes, they do.

And the senators?

Yes, the senators improve them.

But perhaps the members of the assembly corrupt them?—or do they too improve them?

They improve them.

Then every Athenian improves and elevates them; all with the exception of myself; and I alone am their corrupter? Is that what you affirm?

That is what I stoutly affirm.

I am very unfortunate if you are right. But suppose I ask you a question: How about horses? Does one man do them harm and all the world good? Is not the exact opposite the truth? One man is able to do them good, or at least not many;—the trainer of horses, that is to say, does them good, and others who have to do with them rather injure them? Is not that true, Meletus, of horses, or of any other animals? Most assuredly it is; whether you and Anytus say yes or no. Happy indeed would be the condition of youth if they had one corrupter only, and all the rest of the world were their improvers. But you, Meletus, have sufficiently shown that you never had a thought about the young: Your carelessness is seen in your not caring about the very things which you bring against me.

And now, Meletus, I will ask you another question—by Zeus I will: Which is better, to live among bad citizens, or among good ones? Answer, friend, I say; the question is one which may be easily answered. Do not the good do their neighbours good, and the bad do them evil?

Certainly.

And is there anyone who would rather be injured than benefited by those who live with him? Answer, my good friend, the law requires you to answer—does any one like to be injured?

Certainly not.

And when you accuse me of corrupting and deteriorating the youth, do you allege that I corrupt them intentionally or unintentionally?

Intentionally, I say.

But you have just admitted that the good do their neighbours good, and the evil do them evil. Now, is that a truth which your superior wisdom has recognized thus early in life, and am I, at my age, in such darkness and ignorance as not to know that if a man with whom I have to live is corrupted by me, I am very likely to be harmed by him; and yet I corrupt him, and intentionally, too—so you say, although neither I nor any other human being is ever likely to be convinced by you. But either I do not corrupt them, or I corrupt them unintentionally; and on either view of the case you lie. If my offence is unintentional, the law has no cognizance of unintentional offences: you ought to have taken me privately, and warned and admonished me; for if I had been better advised, I should have left off doing what I only did unintentionally—no doubt I should; but you would have nothing to say to me and refused to teach me. And now you bring me up in this court, which is a place not of instruction, but of punishment.

It will be very clear to you, Athenians, as I was saying, that Meletus has no care at all, great or small, about the matter. But still I should like to know, Meletus, in what I am affirmed to corrupt the young. I suppose you mean, as I infer from your indictment, that I teach them not to acknowledge the gods which the state acknowledges, but some other new divinities or spiritual agencies in their stead. These are the lessons by which I corrupt the youth, as you say.

Yes, that I say emphatically.

Then, by the gods, Meletus, of whom we are speaking, tell me and the court, in somewhat plainer terms, what you mean! for I do not as yet understand whether you affirm that I teach other men to acknowledge some gods, and therefore that I do believe in gods, and am not an entire atheist—this you do not lay to my charge,—but only you say that they are not the same gods which the city recognizes—the charge is that they are different gods. Or, do you mean that I am an atheist simply, and a teacher of atheism?

I mean the latter—that you are a complete atheist.

What an extraordinary statement! Why do you think so, Meletus? Do you mean that I do not believe in the godhead of the sun or moon, like other men?

I assure you, judges, that he does not: for he says that the sun is stone, and the moon earth. . . .

And so, Meletus, you really think that I do not believe in any god?

I swear by Zeus that you believe absolutely in none at all.

Nobody will believe you, Meletus, and I am pretty sure that you do not believe yourself. I cannot help thinking, men of Athens, that Meletus is reckless and impudent, and that he has written this indictment in a spirit of mere wantonness and youthful bravado. Has he not compounded a riddle, thinking to try mo? He said to himself:—I shall see whether the wise Socrates will discover my facetious contradiction, or whether I shall be able to deceive him and the rest of them. For he certainly does appear to me to contradict himself in the indictment as much as if he said that Socrates is guilty of not believing in the gods, and yet of believing in them—but this is not like a person who is in earnest.

I should like you, O men of Athens, to join me in examining what I conceive to be his inconsistency; and do you, Meletus, answer. And I must remind the audience of my request that they would not make a disturbance if I speak in my accustomed manner:

Did ever man, Meletus, believe in the existence of human things, and not of human beings? . . . I wish, men of Athens, that he would answer, and not be always trying to get up an interruption. Did ever any man believe in horseman-ship, and not in horses? or in flute-playing, and not in flute-players? No, my friend; I will answer to you and to the court, as you refuse to answer for yourself. There is no man who ever did. But now please to answer the next question: Can a man believe in spiritual and divine agencies, and not in spirits or demigods?

He cannot.

How lucky I am to have extracted that answer, by the assistance of the court! But then you swear in the indictment that I teach and believe in divine or spiritual agen-cies (new or old, no matter for that); at any rate, I believe in spiritual agencies,—so you say and swear in the affidavit; and yet if I believe in divine beings, how can I help believing in spirits or demigods;—must I not? To be sure I must; and therefore I may assume that your silence gives consent. Now what are spirits or demigods? Are they not either gods or the sons of gods?

Certainly they are.

But this is what I call the facetious riddle invented by you: the demigods or spir-its are gods, and you say first that I do not believe in gods, and then again that I do believe in gods; that is, if I believe in demigods. For if the demigods are the illegiti-mate sons of gods, whether by the nymphs or by any other mothers, of whom they are said to be the sons—what human being will ever believe that there are no gods if they are the sons of gods? You might as well affirm the existence of mules, and deny that of horses and asses. Such nonsense, Meletus, could only have been intended by you to make trial of me. You have put this into the indictment because you had nothing real of which to accuse me. But no one who has a particle of understanding will ever be convinced by you that the same men can believe in divine and superhuman things, and yet not believe that there are gods and demigods and heroes.

I have said enough in answer to the charge of Meletus: any elaborate defence is unnecessary, but I know only too well how many are the enmities which I have incurred, and this is what will be my destruction if I am destroyed;—not Meletus, nor yet Anytus, but the envy and detraction of the world, which has been the death of many good men, and will probably be the death of many more; there is no danger of my being the last of them.

Some one will say: And are you not ashamed, Socrates, of a course of life which is likely to bring you to an untimely end? To him I may fairly answer: There you are mistaken: A man who is good for anything ought not to calculate the chance of living or dying; he ought only to consider whether in doing anything he is doing right or wrong—acting the part of a good man or of a bad. . . . For wherever a man's place is, whether the place which he has chosen or that in which he has been placed by a commander, there he ought to remain in the hour of danger; he should not think of death or of anything but of disgrace. And this, O men of Athens, is a true saying.

Strange, indeed, would be my conduct, O men of Athens, if I who, when I was ordered by the generals whom you chose to command me at Potidaea and Amphipolis and Delium, remained where they placed me, like any other man, facing death—if now, when, as I conceive and imagine, God orders me to fulfil the philosopher's mission of searching into myself and other men, I were to desert my post through fear of death, or any other fear; that would indeed be strange, and I might justly be arraigned in court for denying the existence of the gods, if I disobeyed the oracle because I was afraid of death, fancying that I was wise when I was not wise. For the fear of death is indeed the pretence of wisdom, and not real wisdom, being a pretence of knowing the unknown; and no one knows whether death, which men in their fear apprehend to be the greatest evil, may not be the greatest good. Is not this ignorance of a disgraceful sort, the ignorance which is the conceit that a man knows what he does not know? And in this respect only I believe myself to differ from men in general, and may perhaps claim to be wiser than they are:—that whereas I know but little of the world below, I do not suppose that I know: but I do know that injustice and disobedience to a better, whether God or man, is evil and dishonourable, and I will never fear or avoid a possible good rather than a certain evil. And therefore if you let me go now, and are not convinced by Anytus, who said that since I had been prosecuted I must be put to death; (or if not that I ought never to have been prosecuted at all); and that if I escape now, your sons will all be utterly ruined by listening to my words—if you say to me, Socrates, this time we will not mind Anytus, and you shall be let off, but upon one condition, that you are not to enquire and speculate in this way any more, and that if you are caught doing so again you shall die;—if this was the condition on which you let me go, I should reply: Men of Athens, I honour and love you; but I shall obey God rather than you, and while I have life and strength I shall never cease from the practice and teaching of philosophy, exhorting any one whom I meet and saying to him after my manner: You, my friend,—a citizen of the great and mighty and wise city of Athens,—are you not ashamed of heaping up the greatest amount of money and honour and reputation, and caring so little about wisdom and truth and the greatest improvement of the soul, which you never regard or heed at all? And if the person with whom I am arguing, says: Yes, but I do care; then I do not leave him or let him go at once; but I proceed to interrogate and examine and cross-examine him, and if I think that he has no virtue in him, but only says that he has, I reproach him with undervaluing the greater, and overvaluing the less. And I shall repeat the same words to every one whom I meet, young and old, citizen and alien, but especially to the citizens, inasmuch as they are my brethren. For know that this is the command of God; and I believe that no greater good has ever happened in the state than my service to the

God. For I do nothing but go about persuading you all, old and young alike, not to take thought for your persons or your properties, but first and chiefly to care about the greatest improvement of the soul. I tell you that virtue is not given by money, but that from virtue comes money and every other good of man, public as well as private. This is my teaching, and if this is the doctrine which corrupts the youth, I am a mischievous person. But if any one says that this is not my teaching, he is speaking an untruth. Wherefore, O men of Athens, I say to you, do as Anytus bids or not as Anytus bids, and either acquit me or not; but whichever you do, understand that I shall never alter my ways, not even if I have to die many times.

Men of Athens, do not interrupt, but hear me; there was an understanding between us that you should hear me to the end: I have something more to say, at which you may be inclined to cry out; but I believe that to hear me will be good for you, and therefore I beg that you will not cry out. I would have you know, that if you kill such an one as I am, you will injure yourselves more than you will injure me. Nothing will injure me, not Meletus nor yet Anytus—they cannot, for a bad man is not permitted to injure a better than himself. I do not deny that Anytus may, perhaps, kill him, or drive him into exile, or deprive him of civil rights; and he may imagine, and others may imagine, that he is inflicting a great injury upon him: but there I do not agree. For the evil of doing as he is doing—the evil of unjustly taking away the life of another—is greater far.

And now, Athenians, I am not going to argue for my own sake, as you may think, but for yours, that you may not sin against the God by condemning me, who am his gift to you. For if you kill me you will not easily find a successor to me, who, if I may use such a ludicrous figure of speech, am a sort of gadfly, given to the state by God; and the state is a great and noble steed who is tardy in his motions owing to his very size, and requires to be stirred into life. I am that gadfly which God has attached to the state, and all day long and in all places am always fastening upon you, arousing and persuading and reproaching you. You will not easily find another like me, and therefore I would advise you to spare me. I dare say that you may feel out of temper (like a person who is suddenly awakened from sleep), and you think that you might easily strike me dead as Anytus advises, and then you would sleep on for the remainder of your lives, unless God in his care of you sent you another gadfly. When I say that I am given to you by God, the proof of my mission is this:—if I had been like other men, I should not have neglected all my own concerns or patiently seen the neglect of them during all these years, and have been doing yours, coming to you individually like a father or elder brother, exhorting you to regard virtue; such conduct, I say, would be unlike human nature. If I had gained anything, or if my exhortations had been paid, there would have been some sense in my doing so; but now, as you will perceive, not even the impudence of my accusers dares to say that I have ever exacted or sought pay of any one; of that they have no witness. And I have a sufficient witness to the truth of what I say—my poverty. . . .

But I shall be asked, Why do people delight in continually conversing with you? I have told you already, Athenians, the whole truth about this matter: they like to hear the cross-examination of the pretenders to wisdom; there is amusement in it. Now this duty of cross-examining other men has been imposed upon me by God;

and has been signified to me by oracles, visions, and in every way in which the will of divine power was ever intimated to any one. This is true, O Athenians, or, if not true, would be soon refuted. If I am or have been corrupting the youth, those of them who are now grown up and have become sensible that I gave them bad advice in the days of their youth should come forward as accusers, and take their revenge; or if they do not like to come themselves, some of their relatives, fathers, brothers, or other kinsmen, should say what evil their families have suffered at my hands. Now is their time. Many of them I see in the court. . . . I might mention a great many others, some of whom Meletus should have produced as witnesses in the course of his speech; and let him still produce them, if he has forgotten—I will make way for him. And let him say, if he has any testimony of the sort which he can produce. Nay, Athenians, the very opposite is the truth. For all these are ready to witness on behalf of the corrupter, of the injurer of their kindred, as Meletus and Anytus call me; not the corrupted youth only—there might have been a motive for that—but their uncorrupted elder relatives. Why should they too support me with their testimony? Why, indeed, except for the sake of truth and justice, and because they know that I am speaking the truth, and that Meletus is a liar. . . .

But, setting aside the question of public opinion, there seems to be something wrong in asking a favour of a judge, and thus procuring an acquittal, instead of informing and convincing him. For his duty is, not to make a present of justice, but to give judgment; and he has sworn that he will judge according to the laws, and not according to his own good pleasure; and we ought not to encourage you, nor should you allow yourselves to be encouraged, in this habit of perjury—there can be no piety in that. Do not then require me to do what I consider dishonourable and impious and wrong, especially now, when I am being tried for impiety on the indictment of Meletus. For if, O men of Athens, by force of persuasion and entreaty I could overpower your oaths, then I should be teaching you to believe that there are no gods, and in defending should simply convict myself of the charge of not believing in them. But that is not so—far otherwise. For I do believe that there are gods, and in a sense higher than that in which any of my accusers believe in them. And to you and to God I commit my cause, to be determined by you as is best for you and me.

. . . [He is found guilty by 281 votes to 220.]

There are many reasons why I am not grieved, O men of Athens, at the vote of condemnation. I expected it, and am only surprised that the votes are so nearly equal; for I had thought that the majority against me would have been far larger. . . .

And so he proposes death as the penalty. And what shall I propose on my part, O men of Athens? Clearly that which is my due. And what is my due? What return shall be made to the man who has never had the wit to be idle during his whole life; but has been careless of what the many care for—wealth, and family interests, and military offices, and speaking in the assembly, and magistracies, and plots, and parties. Reflecting that I was really too honest a man to be a politician and live, I did not go where I could do no good to you or to myself; but where I could do the greatest good privately to every one of you, thither I went, and sought to persuade every man among you that he must look to himself, and seek virtue and wisdom before he looks to his private interests, and look to the state before he looks to the interests of the state; and that this should be the order which he observes in all his actions. What shall be done to such an one? . . .

Perhaps you think that I am braving you in what I am saying now, as in what I said before about the tears and prayers. But this is not so. I speak rather because I am convinced that I never intentionally wronged anyone, although I cannot convince you—the time has been too short; if there were a law at Athens, as there is in other cities, that a capital cause should not be decided in one day, then I believe that I should have convinced you. But I cannot in a moment refute great slanders; and, as I am convinced that I never wronged another, I will assuredly not wrong myself. I will not say of myself that I deserve any evil, or propose any penalty. Why should I? because I am afraid of the penalty of death which Meletus proposes? When I do not know whether death is a good or an evil, why should I propose a penalty which would certainly be an evil? Shall I say imprisonment? And why should I live in prison, and be the slave of the magistrates of the year—of the Eleven? Or shall the penalty be a fine, and imprisonment until the fine is paid? There is the same objection. I should have to lie in prison, for money I have none, and cannot pay. And if I say exile (and this may possibly be the penalty which you will affix), I must indeed be blinded by the love of life, if I am so irrational as to expect that when you, who are my own citizens, cannot endure my discourses and words, and have found them so grievous and odious that you will have no more of them, others are likely to endure me. No indeed, men of Athens, that is not very likely. And what a life should I lead, at my age, wandering from city to city, ever changing my place of exile, and always being driven out! For I am quite sure that wherever I go, there, as here, the young men will flock to me; and if I drive them away, their elders will drive me out at their request; and if I let them come, their fathers and friends will drive me out for their sakes.

Some one will say: Yes, Socrates, but cannot you hold your tongue, and then you may go into a foreign city, and no one will interfere with you? Now I have great difficulty in making you understand my answer to this. For if I tell you that to do as you say would be a disobedience to the God, and therefore that I cannot hold my tongue, you will not believe that I am serious; and if I say again that daily to discourse about virtue, and of those other things about which you hear me examining myself and others, is the greatest good of man, and that the unexamined life is not worth living, you are still less likely to believe me. Yet I say what is true, although a thing of which it is hard for me to persuade you. Also, I have never been accustomed to think that I deserve to suffer any harm. Had I money I might have estimated the offence at what I was able to pay, and not have been much the worse. But I have none, and therefore I must ask you to proportion the fine to my means. Well, perhaps I could afford a mina, and therefore I propose that penalty: Plato, Crito, Critobulus, and Apollodorus, my friends here, bid me say thirty minae, and they will be the sureties. Let thirty minae be the penalty; for which sum they will be ample security to you.

[He is condemned to death.]

Not much time will be gained, O Athenians, in return for the evil name which you will get from the detractors of the city, who will say that you killed Socrates, a wise man; for they will call me wise, even although I am not wise, when they want to reproach you. If you had waited a little while, your desire would have been fulfilled in the course of nature. For I am far advanced in years, as you may perceive, and not far from death. I am speaking now not to all of you, but only to those who have condemned me to death. And I have another thing to say to them: you think that I was convicted because I had no words of the sort which would have procured my acquittal—I mean, if I had thought fit to leave nothing undone or unsaid. Not so; the deficiency which led to my conviction was not of words—certainly not. But I had not the boldness or impudence or inclination to address you as you would have liked me to do, weeping and wailing and lamenting, and saying and doing many things which you have been accustomed to hear from others, and which, as I maintain, are unworthy of me. I thought at the time that I ought not to do anything common or mean when in danger: nor do I now repent of the style of my defence; I would rather die having spoken after my manner, than speak in your manner and live. For neither in war nor yet at law ought I or any man to use every way of escaping death. Often in battle there can be no doubt that if a man will throw away his arms, and fall on his knees before his pursuers, he may escape death; and in other dangers there are other ways of escaping death, if a man is willing to say and do anything. The difficulty, my friends, is not to avoid death, but to avoid unrighteousness; for that runs faster than death. I am old and move slowly, and the slower runner has overtaken me, and my accusers are keen and quick, and the faster runner, who is unrighteousness, has overtaken them. And now I depart hence condemned by you to suffer the penalty of death,—they too go their ways condemned by the truth to suffer the penalty of villainy and wrong; and I must abide by my award—let them abide by theirs. I suppose that these things may be regarded as fated,—and I think that they are well.

And now, O men who have condemned me, I would fain prophesy to you; for I am about to die, and in the hour of death men are gifted with prophetic power. And I prophesy to you who are my murderers, that immediately after my departure punishment far heavier than you have inflicted on me will surely await you. Me you have killed because you wanted to escape the accuser, and not to give an account of your lives. But that will not be as you suppose: far otherwise. For I say that there will be more accusers of you than there are now; accusers whom hitherto I have restrained: and as they are younger they will be more inconsiderate with you, and you will be more offended at them. If you think that by killing men you can prevent some one from censuring your evil lives, you are mistaken; that is not a way of escape which is either possible or honourable; the easiest and the noblest way is not to be disabling others, but to be improving yourselves. This is the prophecy which I utter before my departure to the judges who have condemned me. . . .

It is an intimation that what has happened to me is a good, and that those of us who think that death is an evil are in error. For the customary sign would surely have opposed me had I been going to evil and not to good.

Let us reflect in another way, and we shall see that there is great reason to hope that death is a good; for one of two things—either death is a state of nothingness and utter unconsciousness, or, as men say, there is a change and migration of the soul from this world to another. Now if you suppose that there is no consciousness, but a sleep like the sleep of him who is undisturbed even by dreams, death will be an unspeakable gain. For if a person were to select the night in which his sleep was undisturbed even by dreams, and were to compare with this the other days and nights of his life, and then were to tell us how many days and nights he had passed in the course of his life better and more pleasantly than this one, I think that any man, I will not say a private man, but even the great king will not find many such days or nights, when compared with the others. Now if death be of such a nature, I say that to die is gain; for eternity is then only a single night. But if death is the journey to another place, and there, as men say, all the dead abide, what good, O my friends and judges, can be greater than this? If indeed when the pilgrim arrives in the world below, he is delivered from the professors of justice in this world, and finds the true judges who are said to give judgment there, Minos and Rhadamanthus and Aeacus and Triptolemus, and other sons of God who were righteous in their own life, that pilgrimage will be worth making. What would not a man give if he might converse with Orpheus and Musaeus and Hesiod and Homer? Nay, if this be true, let me die again and again. I myself, too, shall have a wonderful interest in there meeting and conversing with Palamedes, and Ajax the son of Telamon, and any other ancient hero who has suffered death through an unjust judgment; and there will be no small pleasure, as I think, in comparing my own sufferings with theirs. Above all, I shall then be able to continue my search into true and false knowledge; as in this world, so also in the next; and I shall find out who is wise, and who pretends to be wise, and is not. What would not a man give, O judges, to be able to examine the leader of the great Trojan expedition; or Odysseus or Sisyphus, or numberless others, men and women too! What infinite delight would there be in conversing with them and asking them questions! In another world they do not put a man to death for asking questions: assuredly not. For besides being happier than we are, they will be immortal, if what is said is true.

Wherefore, O judges, be of good cheer about death, and know of a certainty, that no evil can happen to a good man, either in life or after death. He and his are not neglected by the gods; nor has my own approaching end happened by mere chance. But I see clearly that the time had arrived when it was better for me to die and be released from trouble; wherefore the oracle gave no sign. For which reason, also, I am not angry with my condemners, or with my accusers; they have done me no harm, although they did not mean to do me any good; and for this I may gently blame them.

Still I have a favour to ask of them. When my sons are grown up, I would ask you, O my friends, to punish them; and I would have you trouble them, as I have troubled you, if they seem to care about riches, or anything, more than about virtue; or if they pretend to be something when they are really nothing,—then reprove them, as I have reproved you, for not caring about that for which they ought to care, and thinking that they are something when they are really nothing. And if you do this, both I and my sons will have received justice at your hands.

The hour of departure has arrived, and we go our ways—I to die, and you to live. Which is better God only knows.

Discussion Questions

1. Is there any principle or set of principles that you would be willing to die for? If so, what? If not, do you think Socrates "gave up" too easily?
2. How would you apply the Oracle's notion of wisdom—that the wise person is the person who knows that he knows nothing—to your own life?
3. Do you think Socrates deserves to be punished?
4. How effective is Socrates' method—asking questions—compared to other methods of argument, such as asserting truths? Why?
5. Socrates was punished because he espoused ideas deemed dangerous by the government. Can you think of any ideas that you find dangerous? That the government finds dangerous? That past cultures have considered dangerous?
6. Socrates is often quoted as saying "an unexamined life is not worth living." Do you agree? In what way do you "examine" life? In what way would you disagree with Socrates here?

Movie Titles

1. *The Truman Show* —Provides a close analogue to Plato's Cave. Should Truman be happy living in a manmade utopia? Do you somehow feel that he's missing out on something?
2. *Waking Life* (R)—Animated. The plot centers around the main character trying to determine his waking from his dreaming life. Along his journey, he has numerous conversations that directly relate to philosophical issues.

Song Lyrics

Monty Python—"Meaning of Life"
Less Than Jake—"Growing Up On A Couch"
Joni Mitchell—"Both Sides Now"
Amboy Kelso—"What If I Were?"
Pink Floyd—"Another Brick In The Wall"
Edie Brickell & The New Bohemians—"What I Am"
Hoobastank—"Same Direction"
Nine Inch Nails—"Right Where It Belongs"
Cloud Cult—"I Guess This Dream Is For Me"
Thrice—"Stare at the Sun"

Chapter 1

||

Knowledge

A proper starting place for any investigation—especially one of a philosophical nature—is to determine just *how* we can assert knowledge in the first place.

Think of things that you currently claim to know:

- You know where your car is parked.
- God exists (or doesn't exist).
- 2 + 2 = 4.
- The sky is blue.
- You are not dreaming right now.
- Water is made of two hydrogen atoms and one oxygen atom.
- Murder is immoral.
- You have a soul (or don't have a soul).

To what degree are you *certain* of these claims? Would you bet money (all of your money?) on any of these? How did you come to know them? Have you ever changed your mind regarding things that you know or been wrong regarding a knowledge claim?

Philosophers throughout history have struggled with issues in *epistemology*—the study of knowledge. This branch of philosophy involves defining knowledge, determining how we can justify this knowledge, and also exploring areas where knowledge may not be possible.

On the one hand, some take a *skeptical* approach: Because our senses are faulty (the moon appears very small and sticks seem bent in the water) and reason imperfect (logical paradoxes abound and there is no universal agreement on moral issues), knowledge is thus impossible, or at least very difficult, to acquire. Others assert that we can rightly claim to know things. Some through our senses (*empiricists*), others through reason (*rationalists*), and still others (*idealists*) hold that the physical world as we know it does not exist but is instead a result of our mental experiences.

These are all represented in the readings that follow. Plato questions what it means to know and then suggests criteria to determine which claims can be considered knowledge. Descartes first presents what appears to be a very skeptical position but then uses this to defend the rationalist view of knowledge. Berkeley puts forth the idealist (immaterialist) position and Locke the empiricist position. Russell illustrates problems with all "epistemological frameworks," and Code accounts for the subjective nature of knowledge and applies that to a feminist framework.

Theaetetus

Plato

(For a brief biography of Plato, see the first selection featuring him in the prologue.)

In the following selection, Socrates and Theaetetus discuss the criteria necessary for claiming knowledge. What Socrates aims to do here is to discover exactly what is needed in order to attain knowledge. He is especially careful to avoid relying only on notions of *truth* and *belief*, as many people believe true things for the wrong reason.

Reading Questions

1. Briefly explain the three criteria required for knowledge according to Socrates.
2. Why does Socrates add the term "account" to "true belief" for his criteria for knowledge?
3. What are the three meanings for "account" that Socrates suggests?
4. What is the purpose of the discussion about the wagon?

SOCR: . . . What is one to say that knowledge is? For surely we are not going to give up yet.

THEAET: Not unless you do so.

SOCR: Then tell me: what definition can we give with the least risk of contradicting ourselves?

THEAET: The one we tried before, Socrates. I have nothing else to suggest.

SOCR: What was that?

THEAET: That true belief is knowledge. Surely there can at least be no mistake in believing what is true and the consequences are always satisfactory.

SOCR: Try, and you will see, Theaetetus, as the man said when he was asked if the river was too deep to ford. So here, if we go forward on our search, we may stumble upon something that will reveal the thing we are looking for. We shall make nothing but, if we stay where we are.

THEAET: True; let us go forward and see.

SOCR: Well, we need not go far to see this much: You will find a whole profession to prove that true belief is not knowledge.

THEAET: How so? What profession?

SOCR: The profession of those paragons of intellect known as orators and lawyers. There you have men who use their skill to produce conviction, not by instruction, but by making people believe whatever they want them to believe. You can hardly imagine teachers so clever as to be able, in the short time allowed by the clock, to instruct their hearers thoroughly in the

Source: *Plato's Theory of Knowledge: The Theaetetus and the Sophist of Plato*, translated by F. M. Cornford, New York: Harcourt, Brace and Co., 1935. (Gould, p. 240).

true facts of a case of robbery or other violence which those hearers had not witnessed.

THEAET: No, I cannot imagine that; but they can convince them.

SOCR: And by convincing you mean making them believe something.

THEAET: Of course.

SOCR: And when a jury is rightly convinced of facts which can be known only by an eye-witness, then, judging by hearsay and accepting a true belief, they are judging without knowledge, although, if they find the right verdict, their conviction is correct?

THEAET: Certainly.

SOCR: But if true belief and knowledge were the same thing, the best of jurymen should never have a correct belief without knowledge. It now appears that they must be different things.

THEAET: Yes, Socrates, I have heard someone make the distinction. I had forgotten, now it comes back to me. He said that true belief with the addition of an account (*logos*) was knowledge, while belief without an account was outside its range. Where no account could be given of a thing, it was not "knowable"—that was the word he used—where it could, it was knowable.

SOCR: Well then, what is this term "account" intended to convey to us? I think it must mean one of three things.

THEAET: What are they?

SOCR: The first will be giving overt expression to one's thought by means of vocal sound with names and verbs, casting an image of one's notion on the stream that flows through the lips, like a reflection in a mirror or in water. Do you agree that expression of that sort is an "account"?

THEAET: I do. We certainly call that expressing ourselves in speech.

SOCR: On the other hand, that is a thing that anyone can do more or less readily. If a man is not born deaf or dumb, he can signify what he thinks on any subject. So in this sense anyone whatever who has a correct notion evidently will have it "with an account," and there will be no place left anywhere for a correct notion apart from knowledge.

THEAET: True.

SOCR: Then we must not be too ready to charge the author of the definition of knowledge now before us with talking nonsense. Perhaps that is not what he meant. He may have meant: being able to reply to the question, what any given thing is, by enumerating its elements.

THEAET: For example, Socrates?

SOCR: For example, Hesiod says about a wagon, "In a wagon are a hundred pieces of wood." I could not name them all; no more, I imagine, could you. If we were asked what a wagon is, we should be content if we could mention wheels, axle, body, rails, yoke.

THEAET: Certainly.

SOCR: But I dare say he would think us just as ridiculous as if we replied to the question about your own name by telling the syllables. We might think and express ourselves correctly, but we should be absurd if we fancied ourselves to be grammarians and able to give such an account of the name Theaetetus as a grammarian would offer. He would say it is impossible to give a scientific account of anything, short of adding to your true notion a complete catalogue of the elements, as, I think, was said earlier.

THEAET: Yes, it was.

SOCR: In the same way, he would say, we may have a correct notion of the wagon, but the man who can give a complete statement of its nature by going through those hundred parts has thereby added an account to his correct notion and, in place of mere belief, has arrived at a technical knowledge of the wagon's nature, by going through all the elements in the whole.

THEAET: Don't you approve, Socrates?

SOCR: Tell me if you approve, my friend, and whether you accept the view that the complete enumeration of elements is an account of any given thing, whereas description in terms of syllables or of any larger unit still leaves it unaccounted for. Then we can look into the matter further.

THEAET: Well, I do accept that.

SOCR: Do you think, then, that anyone has knowledge of whatever it may be, when he thinks that one and the same thing is a part sometimes of one thing, sometimes of a different thing; or again when he believes now one and now another thing to be part of one and the same thing?

THEAET: Certainly not.

SOCR: Have you forgotten, then, that when you first began learning to read and write, that was what you and your schoolfellows did?

THEAET: Do you mean, when we thought that now one letter and now another was part of the same syllable, and when we put the same letter sometimes into the proper syllable, sometimes into another?

SOCR: That is what I mean.

THEAET: Then I have certainly not forgotten; and I do not think that one has reached knowledge so long as one is in that condition.

SOCR: Well then, if at that stage you are writing "Theaetetus" and you think you taught to write T and H and E and do so, and again when you are trying to write "Theodorus", you think you ought to write T and E and do so, can we say that you now the first syllable of your two names?

THEAET: No; we have just agreed that one has not knowledge so long as one is in that condition.

SOCR: And there is no reason why a person should not be in the same condition with respect to the second, third, and fourth syllables as well?

THEAET: None whatever.

SOCR: Can we, then, say that whenever in writing "Theaetetus" he puts down all the letters in order, then he is in possession of the complete catalogue of elements together with correct belief?

THEAET: Obviously.

SOCR: Being still, as we agree, without knowledge, though his beliefs are correct?

THEAET: Yes.

SOCR: Although he possesses the "account" in addition to right belief. For when he wrote he was in possession of the catalogue of the elements, which we agreed was the "account."

THEAET: True.

SOCR: So, my friend, there is such a thing as right belief together with an account, which is not yet entitled to be called knowledge.

THEAET: I am afraid so.

SOCR: Then, apparently, our idea that we had found the perfectly true definition of knowledge was no better than a golden dream. Or shall we not condemn the theory yet? Perhaps the meaning to be given to "account" is not this, but the remaining one of the three, one of which we said must be intended by anyone who defines knowledge as correct belief together with an account.

THEAET: A good remainder; there is still one meaning left. The first was what might called the image of thought in spoken sound; and the one we have just discussed going all through the elements to arrive at the whole. What is the third?

SOCR: The meaning most people would give: being able to name some mark by which the thing one is asked about differs from everything else.

THEAET: Could you give me an example of such an account of a thing?

SOCR: Take the sun as an example. I dare say you will be satisfied with the account of it as the brightest of the heavenly bodies that go round the earth.

THEAET: Certainly.

SOCR: Let me explain the point of this example. It is to illustrate what we were just saying: That if you get hold of the difference distinguishing any given thing from all others, then, so some people say, you will have an "account" of it; whereas, so long as you fix upon something common to other things, your account will embrace all the things that share it.

THEAET: I understand. I agree that what you describe may fairly be called an "account".

SOCR: And if, besides a right notion about a thing, whatever it may be, you also grasp its difference from all other things, you will have arrived at knowledge of what, till then, you had only a notion of.

THEAET: We do say that, certainly.

SOCR: Really, Theaetetus, now I come to look at this statement at close quarters, it is like a scene-painting: I cannot make it out at all, though, so long as I kept at a distance, there seemed to be some sense in it.

THEAET: What do you mean? Why so?

SOCR: I will explain, if I can. Suppose I have a correct notion about you; if I add to that the account of you, then, we are to understand, I know you. Otherwise I have only a notion.

THEAET: Yes.

SOCR: And "account" means putting your differentness into words.

THEAET: Yes.

SOCR: So, at the time when I had only a notion, my mind did not grasp any of the points in which you differ from others?

THEAET: Apparently not.

SOCR: Then I must have had before my mind one of those common things which belong to another person as much as to you.

THEAET: That follows.

SOCR: But look here! If that was so, how could I possibly be having a notion of you rather than of anyone else? Suppose I was thinking: Theaetetus is one who is a man and has a nose and eyes and a mouth and so forth, enumerating every part of the body. Will thinking in that way result in my thinking of Theaetetus rather than of Theodorus or, as they say, of the man in the street?

THEAET: How should it?

SOCR: Well, now suppose I think not merely of a man with a nose and eyes, but of one with a snub nose and prominent eyes, once more shall I be having a notion of you any more than of myself or anyone else of that description?

THEAET: No.

SOCR: In fact, there will be no notion of Theaetetus in my mind, I suppose, until this particular snubness has stamped and registered within me a record distinct from all the other cases of snubness that I have seen; and so with every other part of you. Then, if I meet you tomorrow, that trait will revive my memory and give me a correct notion about you.

THEAET: Quite true.

SOCR: If that is so, the correct notion of anything must itself include the differentness of that thing.

THEAET: Evidently.

SOCR: Then what meaning is left for getting hold of an "account" in addition to the correct notion? If, on the one hand, it means adding the notion of how a thing differs from other things, such an injunction is simply absurd.

THEAET: How so?

SOCR: When we have a correct notion of the way in which certain things differ from other things, it tells us to add a correct notion of the way in which they differ from other things. On this showing, the most vicious of circles would be nothing to this injunction. It might better deserve to be called the sort of direction a blind man might give: To tell us to get hold of something we already have, in order to get to know something we are already thinking of, suggests a state of the most absolute darkness.

THEAET: Whereas, if ———? The supposition you made just now implied that you would state some alternative: what was it?

SOCR: If the direction to add an "account" means that we are to get to *know* the differentness, as opposed to merely having a notion of it, this most admirable of all definitions of knowledge will be a pretty business; because "getting to know" means acquiring knowledge, doesn't it?

THEAET: Yes.

SOCR: So, apparently, to the question, What is knowledge? our definition will reply "Correct belief together with knowledge of a differentness"; for, according to it, "adding an account" will come to that.

THEAET: So it seems.

SOCR: Yes; and when we are inquiring after the nature of knowledge, nothing could be sillier than to say that it is correct belief together with a *knowledge* of differentness or of anything whatever.

So, Theaetetus, neither true belief, nor the addition of an "account" to true belief can be knowledge.

THEAET: Apparently not.

SOCR: Are we in labour, then, with any further child, my friend, or have we brought to birth all we have to say about knowledge?

THEAET: Indeed we have; and for my part I have already, thanks to you, given utterance to more than I had in me.

SOCR: All of which our midwife's skill pronounces to be mere wind-eggs and not worth the rearing?

THEAET: Undoubtedly.

SOCR: Then supposing you should ever henceforth try to conceive afresh. Theaetetus, if you succeed, your embryo thoughts will be the better as a consequence of today's scrutiny; and if you remain barren, you will be gentler and more agreeable to your companions, having the good sense not to fancy you know what you do not know. For that, and no more, is all that my art can effect; nor have I any of that knowledge possessed by all the great and admirable men of our own day or of the past. But this midwife's art is a gift from heaven; my mother had it for women, and I for young men of a generous spirit and for all in whom beauty dwells.

Discussion Questions

1. Think of statements that you claim to know. How are you justified in knowing them? What about:
   a. I know where my bike/car is parked.
   b. I know the Earth is spherical.
   c. I know God exists (or, I know God does not exist).
   d. I know all ravens are black.
   e. I know aliens exist (or, I know aliens do not exist).
2. In the movie *Thank You for Smoking*, the main character seems more interested in creating a certain belief versus a "true" belief. He is very skilled in *rhetoric*: the ability to persuade. Socrates seems to denounce this when he mentions orators and lawyers. How can you go about distinguishing mere rhetoric from a more justified account of the truth? Should advertisers and lawyers have the responsibility of promoting the truth or should it be the listener's responsibility to be able to sift through the rhetoric?
3. Would you rather be more skilled in rhetoric—convincing others to believe your stance—or more skilled in knowledge-gathering and coming to know the truth, despite what others believe? Why?
4. If you find the truth and believe it but do so in an unjustified way, does that matter? If one believes that Zeus throws lightning bolts when he's angry and this helps them to predict when and how lightning occurs and it provides a sense of comfort, what value would you place on this?
5. What would it take to justify your knowing whether aliens do not exist?

Meditations I and II

René Descartes

Like many philosophers of his time, Descartes explored the sciences as well as philosophy. He published *The Meditations* in 1641 in French for a mass audience: They were meant to be read by everyone, not just philosophers and theologians, and were literally meant as a sort of meditation that non-philosophers could do. Considered one of the most influential philosophers throughout history, Descartes helped to add credence to the *dualist* position—that there exist two separate types of "substances" in the world: the material (such as our bodies and things that occupy space) and the mental (such as our minds and souls).

Descartes hopes to overcome the skeptic challenge that absolute knowledge is impossible, though throughout the first meditation he appears quite skeptical. Eventually, by the end of the sixth and final meditation, Descartes not only demonstrates that knowledge is possible, but helps to define just what we can know, including (not in this section) knowledge of an immaterial soul and the existence of an all-good God.

Reading Questions

1. Descartes explains many ways in which it seems that knowledge may not be possible—what are they?
2. How does he eventually overturn the skeptical position and prove that absolute knowledge is possible?

Meditation I

Of the Things Which May Be Brought Within the Sphere of the Doubtful

It is now some years since I detected how many were the false beliefs that I had from my earliest youth admitted as true, and how doubtful was everything I had since constructed on this basis; and from that time I was convinced that I must once for all seriously undertake to rid myself of all the opinions which I had formerly accepted, and commence to build anew from the foundation, if I wanted to establish any firm and permanent structure in the sciences. But as this enterprise appeared to be a very great one, I waited until I had attained an age so mature that I could not hope that at any later date I should be better fitted to execute my design. This reason caused me to delay so long that I should feel that I was doing wrong were I to occupy in deliberation the time that yet remains to me for action. Today, then, since very opportunely for the plan I have in view I have delivered my mind from every care [and am happily agitated by no passions] and since I have procured for myself an assured leisure in a peaceable retirement. I shall at last seriously and freely address myself to the general upheaval of all my former opinions.

Source: "Meditation I" and "Meditation II" from *The Philosophical Works of Descartes,* translated by Elizabeth S. Haldone and G.R.T. Ross. Copyright © 1931, 1967 by Cambridge University Press. Reprinted with the permission of Cambridge University Press.

Now for this object it is not necessary that I should show that all of these are false—I shall perhaps never arrive at this end. But in as much as reason already persuades me that I ought no less carefully to withhold my assent from matters which are not entirely certain and indubitable than from those which appear to me manifestly to be false, if I am able to find in each one some reason to doubt, this will suffice to justify my rejecting the whole. And for that end it will not be requisite that I should examine each in particular, which would be an endless undertaking; for owing to the fact that the destruction of the foundations of necessity brings with it the downfall of the rest of the edifice, I shall only in the first place attack those principles upon which all my former opinions rested.

All that up to the present time I have accepted as most true and certain I have learned either from the senses or through the senses; but it is sometimes proved to me that these senses are deceptive, and it is wiser not to trust entirely to any thing by which we have once been deceived.

But it may be that although the senses sometimes deceive us concerning things which are hardly perceptible, or very far away, there are yet many others to be met with as to which we cannot reasonably have any doubt, although we recognise them by their means. For example, there is the fact that I am here, seated by the fire, attired in a dressing gown, having this paper in my hands and other similar matters. And how could I deny that these hands and this body are mine, were it not perhaps that I compare myself to certain persons, devoid of sense, whose cerebella are so troubled and clouded by the violent vapours of black bile, that they constantly assure us that they think they are kings when they are really quite poor, or that they are clothed in purple when they are really without covering, or who imagine that they have an earthenware head or are nothing but pumpkins or are made of glass. But they are mad, and I should not be any the less insane were I to follow examples so extravagant.

At the same time I must remember that I am a man, and that consequently I am in the habit of sleeping, and in my dreams representing to myself the same things or sometimes even less probable things, than do those who are insane in their waking moments. How often has it happened to me that in the night I dreamt that I found myself in this particular place, that I was dressed and seated near the fire, whilst in reality I was lying undressed in bed! At this moment it does indeed seem to me that it is with eyes awake that I am looking at this paper, that this head which I move is not asleep, that it is deliberately and of set purpose that I extend my hand and perceive it; what happens on sleep does not appear so clear nor so distinct as does all this. But in thinking over this I remind myself that on many occasions I have in sleep been deceived by similar illusions, and in dwelling carefully on this reflection I see so manifestly that there are no certain indications by which we may clearly distinguish wakefulness from sleep that I am lost in astonishment. And my astonishment is such that it is almost capable of persuading me that I now dream.

Now let us assume that we are asleep and that all these particulars, for example, that we open our eyes, shake our head, extend our hands, and so on, are but false delusions; and let us reflect that possibly neither our hands nor our whole body are such as they appear to us to be. At the same time we must at least confess that the things which are represented to us in sleep are like painted representations which can only have been formed as the counterparts of something real and true, and that in this way those general things at least, that is, eyes, a head, hands, and a whole body, are not imaginary things, but things really existent. For, as a matter of fact, painters, even when they study with the greatest skill to represent sirens and satyrs by forms the most strange and extraordinary, cannot give them natures which are entirely new, but merely make a certain medley of the members of different animals; or if their imagination is extravagant enough to invent something so novel that nothing similar has ever before been seen, and that their work represents a thing purely fictitious and absolutely false, it is certain all the same that the colours of which this is composed are necessarily real. And for the same reason, although these general things, to wit, [a body], eyes, a head, hands, and such like, may be imaginary, we are bound at the same time to confess that there are at least some other objects yet more simple and more universal, which are real and true; and of these just in the same way as with certain real colours, all these images of things which dwell in our thoughts, whether true and real or false and fantastic, are formed.

To such a class of things pertains corporeal nature in general, and its extension, the figure of extended things, their quantity or magnitude and number, as also the place in which they are, the time which measures their duration, and so on.

That is possibly why our reasoning is not unjust when we conclude from this that Physics, Astronomy, Medicine, and all other sciences which have as their end the consideration of composite things are very dubious and uncertain; but that Arithmetic, Geometry and other sciences of that kind which only treat of things that are very general, without taking great trouble to ascertain whether they are actually existent or not, contain some measure of certainty and an element of the indubitable. For whether I am awake or asleep, two and three together always form five, and the square can never have more than four sides, and it does not seem possible that truths so clear and apparent can be suspected of any falsity [or uncertainty].

Nevertheless I have long had fixed in my mind the belief that an all-powerful God existed by whom I have been created such as I am. But how do I know that He has not brought it to pass that there is no earth, no heaven, no extended body, no magnitude, no place, and that nevertheless [I possess the perceptions of all these things and that] they seem to me to exist just exactly as I now see them? And, besides, as I sometimes imagine that others deceive themselves in the things which they think they know best, how do I know that I am not deceived every time that I add two and three, or count the sides of a square, or judge of things yet simpler, if anything simpler can be imagined? But possibly God has not desired that I should be thus deceived, for He is said to be supremely good. If, however, it is contrary to His goodness to have made me such that I constantly deceive myself, it would also appear to be contrary to His goodness to permit me to be sometimes deceived, and nevertheless I cannot doubt that He does permit this.

There may indeed be those who would prefer to deny the existence of a God so powerful, rather than believe that all other things are uncertain. But let us not oppose them for the present, and grant that all that is here said of a God is a fable; nevertheless in whatever way they suppose that I have arrived at the state of being that I have reached—whether they attribute it to fate or to accident, or make out that it is by a continual succession of antecedents, or by some other method—since to err and deceive oneself is a defect, it is clear that the greater will be the probability of my being so imperfect as to deceive myself ever, as is the Author to whom they assign my origin the less powerful. To these reasons I have certainly nothing to reply, but at the end I feel constrained to confess that there is nothing in all that I formerly believed to be true, of which I cannot in some measure doubt, and that not merely through want of thought or through levity, but for reasons which are very powerful and maturely considered; so that henceforth I ought not the less carefully to refrain from giving credence to these opinions than to that which is manifestly false, if I desire to arrive at any certainty [in the sciences].

But it is not sufficient to have made these remarks, we must also be careful to keep them in mind. For these ancient and commonly held opinions still revert frequently to my mind, long and familiar custom having given them the right to occupy my mind against my inclination and rendered them almost masters of my belief; nor will I ever lose the habit of deferring to them or of placing my confidence in them, so long as I consider them as they really are, i.e., opinions in some measure doubtful, as I have just shown, and at the same time highly probable, so that there is much more reason to believe in than to deny them. That is why I consider that I shall not be acting amiss, if, taking of set purpose a contrary belief, I allow myself to be deceived, and for a certain time pretend that all these opinions are entirely false and imaginary, until at least, having thus balanced my former prejudices with my latter [so that they cannot divert my opinions more to one side than to the other], my judgment will no longer be dominated by bad usage or turned away from the right knowledge of the truth. For I am assured that there can be neither peril nor error in this course, and that I cannot at present yield too much to distrust, since I am not considering the question of action, but only of knowledge.

I shall then suppose, not that God who is supremely good and the fountain of truth, but some evil genius not less powerful than deceitful, has employed his whole energies deceiving me; I shall consider that the heavens, the earth, colours, figures, sound, and all other external things are nought but the illusions and dreams of which this genius has availed himself in order to lay traps for my credulity; I shall consider myself as having no hands, no eyes, no flesh, no blood, nor any senses, yet falsely believing myself to possess all these things; I shall remain obstinately attached to this idea, and if by this means it is not in my power to arrive at the knowledge of any truth I may at least do what is in my power [i.e., suspend my judgment] and with firm purpose avoid giving credence to any false thing, or being imposed upon by this arch deceiver, however powerful and deceptive he may be. But this task is a laborious one, and insensibly a certain lassitude leads me into the course of my ordinary life. And just as a captive who in sleep enjoys an imaginary liberty, when he begins to suspect that his liberty is but a dream, fears to awaken, and conspires with these agreeable illusions that the deception may be prolonged, so insensibly of my own accord I fall back into my former opinions, and I dread awakening from this slumber, lest the laborious wakefulness which would follow the tranquility of this repose should have to be spent not in daylight, but in the excessive darkness of the difficulties which have just been discussed.

Meditation II

Of the Nature of the Human Mind, and That It Is More Easily Known Than the Body

The Meditation of yesterday filled my mind with so many doubts that it is no longer in my power to forget them. And yet I do not see in what manner I can resolve them; and, just as if I had all of a sudden fallen into very deep water, I am so disconcerted that I can neither make certain of setting my feet on the bottom, nor can I swim and so support myself on the surface. I shall nevertheless make an effort and follow anew the same path as that on which I yesterday entered, that is, I shall proceed by setting aside all that in which the least doubt could be supposed to exist, just as if I had discovered that it was absolutely false; and I shall ever follow in this road until I have met with something which is certain, or at least, if I can do nothing else, until I have learned for certain that there is nothing in the world that is certain. Archimedes, in order that he might draw the terrestrial globe out of its place, and transport it elsewhere, demanded only that one point should be fixed and immoveable; in the same way I shall have the right to conceive high hopes if I am happy enough to discover one thing only which is certain and indubitable.

I suppose, then, that all the things that I see are false; I persuade myself that nothing has ever existed of all that my fallacious memory represents to me. I consider that I possess no senses; I imagine that body, figure, extension, movement, and place are but the fiction of my mind. What, then, can be esteemed as true? Perhaps nothing at all, unless that there is nothing in the world that is certain.

But how can I know there is not something different from those things that I have just considered, of which one cannot have the slightest doubt? Is there not some God, or some other being by whatever name we call it, who puts these reflections into my mind? That is not necessary, for is it not possible that I am capable of producing them myself? I myself, am I not at least something? But I have already denied that I had senses and body. Yet I hesitate, for what follows from that? Am I so dependent on body and senses that I cannot exist without these? But I was persuaded that there were no minds, nor any bodies: Was I not then likewise persuaded that I did not exist? Not at all; of a surety I myself did exist since I persuaded myself of something [or merely because I thought of something]. But there is some deceiver or other, very powerful and very cunning, who ever employs his ingenuity in deceiving me. Then without doubt I exist also if he deceives me, and let him deceive me as much as he will, he can never cause me to be nothing so long as I think that I am something. So that after having reflected well and carefully examined all things, we must come to the definite conclusion that this proposition: I am, I exist, is necessarily true each time that I pronounce it, or that I mentally conceive it.

Discussion Questions

1. Do you agree that when one conceives of the phrase "I am, I exist" this statement must be "necessarily true"? Is there any way that it could be false?
2. Given the doubts cast in *Meditation I*, how does that change how you know things and what your own limits might be with regard to knowledge?
3. In the movie *The Matrix*, a false world is portrayed—for example, what appears to us as a nicely cooked steak is *actually* a pile of grey mush. If this were the case, would you rather live in the "false-steak reality" or in the true reality of grey mush? Why?
4. Have you had dreams that seem real at the time? Descartes argues that we have all had this experience, and thus it is at least possible that you are dreaming right now. How could you know that you are not?
5. Certainty here requires indubitability. If something *can* be doubted, then we can't be certain about it. Certainty is more a philosophical term, while indubitability is psychological. Thus, in the opening of this piece he hopes to show that everything can be doubted and that nothing is certain. Can you think of anything that you know *without a doubt*? Do you agree that to be certain about something you must not be *able* to doubt it?

Three Dialogues Between Hylas and Philonous

George Berkeley

George Berkeley was a bishop in the protestant Church of Ireland. He is most well known for his theory of *idealism*—that there are no material objects, only mental. He is most often quoted as writing, "To be is to be perceived"—in order to *be* (exist), a thing must be perceived (or, consequently, must be a *perceiver*).

In this dialogue, Philonous—translated as "Friend of the Mind"—represents Berkeley's view. In contrast, Hylas (*hyle* is Greek for "matter") represents the materialist/mechanistic position. This later position was supported by the work of well-known scientists such as Robert Boyle and Isaac Newton, as well as philosopher John Locke. Berkeley believed that their views eventually led to ultimate skepticism and that his *idealism* avoided this.

Source: George Berkeley, *Three Dialogues.* First published in 1713, reissued in 1725, and then revised for a third ed. in 1734. The text here is from the third ed.

Reading Questions

1. How does Hylas define what it means to be a skeptic?
2. How does Philonous defend his position (idealism) with regard to the following?
   a. Heat and its relation to sensation and pain
   b. The example of having two hands in hot and cold buckets of water
   c. The subjective nature of taste
   d. Color and the clouds
3. What is the "material substratum" that Hylas refers to?
4. In the end, how has Philonous defended the notion of idealism?

Three dialogues between Hylas and Philonous, the design of which is plainly to demonstrate the reality and perfection of human knowledge, the incorporeal nature of the soul, and the immediate providence of a deity: in opposition to sceptics and atheists; also to open a method for rendering the sciences more easy, useful, and compendious.

The First Dialogue

HYLAS: You were represented, in last night's conversation, as one who maintained the most extravagant opinion that ever entered into the mind of man, to wit, that there is no such thing as *material substance* in the world.

PHILONOUS: That there is no such thing as what *philosophers call material substance*, I am seriously persuaded: But if I were made to see anything absurd or sceptical in this, I should then have the same reason to renounce this that I imagine I have now to reject the contrary opinion.

HYLAS: What! Can anything be more fantastical, more repugnant to common sense, or a more manifest piece of scepticism, than to believe there is no such thing as *matter*?

PHILONOUS: Softly, good Hylas. What if it should prove that you, who hold there is, are by virtue of that opinion a greater sceptic, and maintain more paradoxes and repugnances to common sense, than I who believe no such thing?

HYLAS: You may as soon persuade me the part is greater than the whole, as that, in order to avoid absurdity and scepticism, I should ever be obliged to give up my opinion in this point.

PHILONOUS: Well then, are you content to admit that opinion for true, which upon examination shall appear most agreeable to common sense, and remote from scepticism?

HYLAS: With all my heart. Since you are for raising disputes about the plainest things in nature, I am content for once to hear what you have to say.

PHILONOUS: Pray, Hylas, what do you mean by a *sceptic*?

HYLAS: I mean what all men mean—one that doubts of everything.

PHILONOUS: He then who entertains no doubts concerning some particular point, with regard to that point cannot be thought a sceptic.

HYLAS: I agree with you.

PHILONOUS: Whether doth doubting consist in embracing the affirmative or negative side of a question?

HYLAS: In neither; for whoever understands English cannot but know that *doubting* signifies a suspense between both.

PHILONOUS: He then that denies any point, can no more be said to doubt of it, than he who affirmeth it with the same degree of assurance.

HYLAS: True.

PHILONOUS: And, consequently, for such his denial is no more to be esteemed a sceptic than the other.

HYLAS: I acknowledge it.

PHILONOUS: How cometh it to pass then, Hylas, that you pronounce me *a sceptic*, because I deny what you affirm, to wit, the existence of matter? Since, for aught you can tell, I am as peremptory in my denial, as you in your affirmation.

HYLAS: Hold, Philonous, I have been a little out in my definition; but every false step a man makes in discourse is not to be insisted on. I said indeed that a *sceptic* was one who doubted of everything; but I should have added, or who denies the reality and truth of things.

PHILONOUS: What things? Do you mean the principles and theorems of sciences? But these you know are universal intellectual notions, and consequently independent of matter. The denial therefore of this doth not imply the denying them.

HYLAS: I grant it. But are there no other things? What think you of distrusting the senses, of denying the real existence of sensible things, or pretending to know nothing of them. Is not this sufficient to denominate a man a *sceptic*?

PHILONOUS: Shall we therefore examine which of us it is that denies the reality of sensible things, or professes the greatest ignorance of them; since, if I take you rightly, he is to be esteemed the greatest *sceptic*?

HYLAS: That is what I desire.

PHILONOUS: What mean you by sensible things?

HYLAS: Those things which are perceived by the senses. Can you imagine that I mean anything else?

PHILONOUS: Pardon me, Hylas, if I am desirous clearly to apprehend your notions, since this may much shorten our inquiry. Suffer me then to ask you this farther question. Are those things only perceived by the senses which are perceived immediately? Or, may those things properly be said to be *sensible* which are perceived mediately, or not without the intervention of others?

HYLAS: I do not sufficiently understand you.

PHILONOUS: In reading a book, what I immediately perceive are the letters; but mediately, or by means of these, are suggested to my mind the notions of God, virtue, truth, &c. Now, that the letters are truly sensible things, or perceived by sense, there is no doubt: but I would know whether you take the things suggested by them to be so too.

HYLAS: No, certainly: it were absurd to think *God* or *virtue* sensible things; though they may be signified and suggested to the mind by sensible marks, with which they have an arbitrary connexion.

PHILONOUS: It seems then, that by *sensible things* you mean those only which can be perceived *immediately* by sense?

HYLAS: Right. [. . .] I tell you once for all, that by *sensible things* I mean those only which are perceived by sense; and that in truth the senses perceive nothing which they do not perceive *immediately*: for they make no inferences. The deducing therefore of causes or occasions from effects and appearances, which alone are perceived by sense, entirely relates to reason.

PHILONOUS: This point then is agreed between us—That *sensible things are those only which are immediately perceived by sense.* You will farther inform me, whether we immediately perceive by sight anything beside light, and colours, and figures; or by hearing, anything but sounds; by the palate, anything beside tastes; by the smell, beside odours; or by the touch, more than tangible qualities.

HYLAS: We do not.

PHILONOUS: It seems, therefore, that if you take away all sensible qualities, there remains nothing sensible?

HYLAS: I grant it.

PHILONOUS: Sensible things therefore are nothing else but so many sensible qualities, or combinations of sensible qualities?

HYLAS: Nothing else.

PHILONOUS: Heat then is a sensible thing?

HYLAS: Certainly.

PHILONOUS: Doth the *reality* of sensible things consist in being perceived? or, is it something distinct from their being perceived, and that bears no relation to the mind?

HYLAS: To *exist* is one thing, and to be *perceived* is another.

PHILONOUS: I speak with regard to sensible things only. And of these I ask, whether by their real existence you mean a subsistence exterior to the mind, and distinct from their being perceived?

HYLAS: I mean a real absolute being, distinct from, and without any relation to, their being perceived.

PHILONOUS: Heat therefore, if it be allowed a real being, must exist without the mind?

HYLAS: It must.

PHILONOUS: Tell me, Hylas, is this real existence equally compatible to all degrees of heat, which we perceive; or is there any reason why we should attribute it to some, and deny it to others? And if there be, pray let me know that reason.

HYLAS: Whatever degree of heat we perceive by sense, we may be sure the same exists in the object that occasions it.

PHILONOUS: What! the greatest as well as the least?

HYLAS: I tell you, the reason is plainly the same in respect of both. They are both perceived by sense; nay, the greater degree of heat is more sensibly perceived; and consequently, if there is any difference, we are more certain of its real existence than we can be of the reality of a lesser degree.

PHILONOUS: But is not the most vehement and intense degree of heat a very great pain?

HYLAS: No one can deny it.

PHILONOUS: And is any unperceiving thing capable of pain or pleasure?

HYLAS: No, certainly.

PHILONOUS: Is your material substance a senseless being, or a being endowed with sense and perception?

HYLAS: It is senseless without doubt.

PHILONOUS: It cannot therefore be the subject of pain?

HYLAS: By no means.

PHILONOUS: Nor consequently of the greatest heat perceived by sense, since you acknowledge this to be no small pain?

HYLAS: I grant it.

PHILONOUS: What shall we say then of your external object; is it a material substance, or no?

HYLAS: It is a material substance with the sensible qualities inhering in it.

PHILONOUS: How then can a great heat exist in it, since you own it cannot in a material substance? I desire you would clear this point.

HYLAS: Hold, Philonous, I fear I was out in yielding intense heat to be a pain. It should seem rather, that pain is something distinct from heat, and the consequence or effect of it.

PHILONOUS: Upon putting your hand near the fire, do you perceive one simple uniform sensation, or two distinct sensations?

HYLAS: But one simple sensation.

PHILONOUS: Is not the heat immediately perceived?

HYLAS: It is.

PHILONOUS: And the pain?

HYLAS: True.

PHILONOUS: Seeing therefore they are both immediately perceived at the same time, and the fire affects you only with one simple or uncompounded idea, it follows that this same simple idea is both the intense heat immediately perceived, and the pain; and, consequently, that the intense heat immediately perceived is nothing distinct from a particular sort of pain.

HYLAS: It seems so.

PHILONOUS: Again, try in your thoughts, Hylas, if you can conceive a vehement sensation to be without pain or pleasure.

HYLAS: I cannot.

PHILONOUS: Or can you frame to yourself an idea of sensible pain or pleasure in general, abstracted from every particular idea of heat, cold, tastes, smells? &c.

HYLAS: I do not find that I can.

PHILONOUS: Doth it not therefore follow, that sensible pain is nothing distinct from those sensations or ideas, in an intense degree?

HYLAS: It is undeniable; and, to speak the truth, I begin to suspect a very great heat cannot exist but in a mind perceiving it.

PHILONOUS: What! are you then in that sceptical state of suspense, between affirming and denying?

HYLAS: I think I may be positive in the point. A very violent and painful heat cannot exist without the mind.

PHILONOUS: It hath not therefore according to you, any *real* being?

HYLAS: I own it.

PHILONOUS: Is it therefore certain, that there is no body in nature really hot?

HYLAS: I have not denied there is any real heat in bodies. I only say, there is no such thing as an intense real heat.

PHILONOUS: But, did you not say before that all degrees of heat were equally real; or, if there was any difference, that the greater were more undoubtedly real than the lesser?

HYLAS: True: but it was because I did not then consider the ground there is for distinguishing between them, which I now plainly see. And it is this: Because intense heat is nothing else but a particular kind of painful sensation; and pain cannot exist but in a perceiving being; it follows that no intense heat can really exist in an unperceiving corporeal substance. But this is no reason why we should deny heat in an inferior degree to exist in such a substance.

PHILONOUS: But how shall we be able to discern those degrees of heat which exist only in the mind from those which exist without it?

HYLAS: That is no difficult matter. You know the least pain cannot exist unperceived; whatever, therefore, degree of heat is a pain exists only in the mind. But, as for all other degrees of heat, nothing obliges us to think the same of them.

PHILONOUS: I think you granted before that no unperceiving being was capable of pleasure, any more than of pain.

HYLAS: I did.

PHILONOUS: And is not warmth, or a more gentle degree of heat than what causes uneasiness, a pleasure?

HYLAS: What then?

PHILONOUS: Consequently, it cannot exist without the mind in an unperceiving substance, or body.

HYLAS: So it seems.

PHILONOUS: Since, therefore, as well those degrees of heat that are not painful, as those that are, can exist only in a thinking substance; may we not conclude that external bodies are absolutely incapable of any degree of heat whatsoever? . . . Can any doctrine be true that necessarily leads a man into an absurdity?

HYLAS: Without doubt it cannot.

PHILONOUS: Is it not an absurdity to think that the same thing should be at the same time both cold and warm?

HYLAS: It is.

PHILONOUS: Suppose now one of your hands hot, and the other cold, and that they are both at once put into the same vessel of water, in an intermediate state; will not the water seem cold to one hand, and warm to the other?

HYLAS: It will.

PHILONOUS: Ought we not therefore, by your principles, to conclude it is really both cold and warm at the same time, that is, according to your own concession, to believe an absurdity?

HYLAS: I confess it seems so.

PHILONOUS: Consequently, the principles themselves are false, since you have granted that no true principle leads to an absurdity.

HYLAS: But, after all, can anything be more absurd than to say, *there is no heat in the fire?*

PHILONOUS: To make the point still clearer; tell me whether, in two cases exactly alike, we ought not to make the same judgment?

HYLAS: We ought.

PHILONOUS: When a pin pricks your finger, doth it not rend and divide the fibres of your flesh?

HYLAS: It doth.

PHILONOUS: And when a coal burns your finger, doth it any more?

HYLAS: It doth not.

PHILONOUS: Since, therefore, you neither judge the sensation itself occasioned by the pin, nor anything like it to be in the pin; you should not, conformably to what you have now granted, judge the sensation occasioned by the fire, or anything like it, to be in the fire.

HYLAS: Well, since it must be so, I am content to yield this point, and acknowledge that heat and cold are only sensations existing in our minds. But there still remain qualities enough to secure the reality of external things.

PHILONOUS: But what will you say, Hylas, if it shall appear that the case is the same with regard to all other sensible qualities, and that they can no more be supposed to exist without the mind, than heat and cold?

HYLAS: Then indeed you will have done something to the purpose; but that is what I despair of seeing proved.

PHILONOUS: Let us examine them in order. What think you of *tastes*, do they exist without the mind, or no?

HYLAS: Can any man in his senses doubt whether sugar is sweet, or wormwood bitter?

PHILONOUS: Inform me, Hylas. Is a sweet taste a particular kind of pleasure or pleasant sensation, or is it not?

HYLAS: It is.

PHILONOUS: And is not bitterness some kind of uneasiness or pain?

HYLAS: I grant it.

PHILONOUS: If therefore sugar and wormwood are unthinking corporeal substances existing without the mind, how can sweetness and bitterness, that is, pleasure and pain, agree to them?

HYLAS: Hold, Philonous, I now see what it was deluded me all this time. You asked whether heat and cold, sweetness and bitterness, were not particular sorts of pleasure and pain; to which I answered simply, that they were. Whereas I should have thus distinguished: Those qualities, as perceived by us, are pleasures or pains, but not as existing in the external objects. We must not therefore conclude absolutely, that there is no heat in the fire, or sweetness in the sugar, but only that heat or sweetness, as perceived by us, are not in the fire or sugar. What say you to this?

PHILONOUS: I say it is nothing to the purpose. Our discourse proceeded altogether concerning sensible things, which you defined to be, *the things we immediately perceive by our senses*. Whatever other qualities, therefore, you speak of as distinct from these, I know nothing of them, neither do they at all belong to the point in dispute. You may, indeed, pretend to have discovered certain qualities which you do not perceive, and assert those insensible qualities exist in fire and sugar. But what use can be made of this to your present purpose, I am at a loss to conceive. Tell me then once more, do you acknowledge that heat and cold, sweetness and bitterness (meaning those qualities which are perceived by the senses), do not exist without the mind?

HYLAS: I see it is to no purpose to hold out, so I give up the cause as to those mentioned qualities. Though I profess it sounds oddly, to say that sugar is not sweet.

PHILONOUS: But, for your farther satisfaction, take this along with you: that which at other times seems sweet, shall, to a distempered palate, appear bitter. And, nothing can be plainer than that divers persons perceive different tastes in the same food; since that which one man delights in, another abhors. And how could this be, if the taste was something really inherent in the food?

HYLAS: I acknowledge I know not how. . . .

PHILONOUS: Then as to *sounds*, what must we think of them: are they accidents really inherent in external bodies, or not?

HYLAS: That they inhere not in the sonorous bodies is plain from hence: because a bell struck in the exhausted receiver of an air-pump sends forth no sound. The air, therefore, must be thought the subject of sound.

PHILONOUS: What reason is there for that, Hylas?

HYLAS: Because, when any motion is raised in the air, we perceive a sound greater or lesser, according to the air's motion; but without some motion in the air, we never hear any sound at all.

PHILONOUS: And granting that we never hear a sound but when some motion is produced in the air, yet I do not see how you can infer from thence, that the sound itself is in the air.

HYLAS: It is this very motion in the external air that produces in the mind the sensation of *sound*. For, striking on the drum of the ear, it causeth a vibration, which by the auditory nerves being communicated to the brain, the soul is thereupon affected with the sensation called *sound*.

PHILONOUS: What! is sound then a sensation?

HYLAS: I tell you, as perceived by us, it is a particular sensation in the mind.

PHILONOUS: And can any sensation exist without the mind?

HYLAS: No, certainly.

PHILONOUS: How then can sound, being a sensation, exist in the air, if by the *air* you mean a senseless substance existing without the mind?

HYLAS: You must distinguish, Philonous, between sound as it is perceived by us, and as it is in itself; or (which is the same thing) between the sound we immediately perceive, and that which exists without us. The former, indeed, is a particular kind of sensation, but the latter is merely a vibrative or undulatory motion the air.

PHILONOUS: I thought I had already obviated that distinction, by the answer I gave when you were applying it in a like case before. But, to say no more of that, are you sure then that sound is really nothing but motion?

HYLAS: I am.

PHILONOUS: Whatever therefore agrees to real sound, may with truth be attributed to motion?

HYLAS: It may.

PHILONOUS: It is then good sense to speak of *motion* as of a thing that is *loud, sweet, acute,* or *grave.*

HYLAS: I see you are resolved not to understand me. Is it not evident those accidents or modes belong only to sensible sound, or sound in the common acceptation of the word, but not to *sound* in the real and philosophic sense; which, as I just now told you, is nothing but a certain motion of the air?

PHILONOUS: It seems then there are two sorts of sound—the one vulgar, or that which is heard, the other philosophical and real?

HYLAS: Even so.

PHILONOUS: And the latter consists in motion?

HYLAS: I told you so before.

PHILONOUS: Tell me, Hylas, to which of the senses, think you, the idea of motion belongs? to the hearing?

HYLAS: No, certainly; but to the sight and touch.

PHILONOUS: It should follow then, that, according to you, real sounds may possibly be *seen* or *felt,* but never *heard.*

HYLAS: Look you, Philonous, you may, if you please, make a jest of my opinion, but that will not alter the truth of things. I own, indeed, the inferences you draw me into sound something oddly; but common language, you know, is framed by, and for the use of the vulgar: We must not therefore wonder if expressions adapted to exact philosophic notions seem uncouth and out of the way.

PHILONOUS: Is it come to that? I assure you, I imagine myself to have gained no small point, since you make so light of departing from common phrases and opinions; it being a main part of our inquiry, to examine whose notions are widest of the common road, and most repugnant to the general sense of the world. But, can you think it no more than a philosophical paradox, to say that *real sounds are never heard,* and that the idea of them is obtained by some other sense? And is there nothing in this contrary to nature and the truth of things?

HYLAS: To deal ingenuously, I do not like it. And, after the concessions already made, I had as well grant that sounds too have no real being without the mind.

PHILONOUS: And I hope you will make no difficulty to acknowledge the same of *colours.*

HYLAS: Pardon me: the case of colours is very different. Can anything be plainer than that we see them on the objects?

PHILONOUS: The objects you speak of are, I suppose, corporeal substances existing without the mind?

HYLAS: They are.

PHILONOUS: And have true and real colours inhering in them?

HYLAS: Each visible object hath that colour which we see in it.

PHILONOUS: How! is there anything visible but what we perceive by sight?

HYLAS: There is not.

PHILONOUS: And, do we perceive anything by sense which we do not perceive immediately?

HYLAS: How often must I be obliged to repeat the same thing? I tell you, we do not.

PHILONOUS: Have patience, good Hylas; and tell me once more, whether there is anything immediately perceived by the senses, except sensible qualities. I know you asserted there was not; but I would now be informed, whether you still persist in the same opinion.

HYLAS: I do.

PHILONOUS: Pray, is your corporeal substance either a sensible quality, or made up of sensible qualities?

HYLAS: What a question that is! who ever thought it was?

PHILONOUS: My reason for asking was, because in saying, *each visible object hath that colour which we see in it,* you make visible objects to be corporeal substances; which implies either that corporeal substances are sensible qualities, or else that there is something besides sensible qualities perceived by sight; but, as this point was formerly agreed between us, and is still maintained by you, it is a clear consequence, that your *corporeal substance* is nothing distinct from *sensible qualities.*

HYLAS: You may draw as many absurd consequences as you please, and endeavour to perplex the plainest things; but you shall never persuade me out of my senses. I clearly understand my own meaning.

PHILONOUS: I wish you would make me understand it too. But, since you are unwilling to have your notion of corporeal substance examined, I shall urge that point no farther. Only be pleased to let me know, whether the same colours which we see exist in external bodies, or some other.

HYLAS: The very same.

PHILONOUS: What! are then the beautiful red and purple we see on yonder clouds really in them? Or do you imagine they have in themselves any other form than that of a dark mist or vapour?

HYLAS: I must own, Philonous, those colours are not really in the clouds as they seem to be at this distance. They are only apparent colours.

PHILONOUS: *Apparent* call you them? How shall we distinguish these apparent colours from real?

HYLAS: Very easily. Those are to be thought apparent which, appearing only at a distance, vanish upon a nearer approach.

PHILONOUS: And those, I suppose, are to be thought real which are discovered by the most near and exact survey.

HYLAS: Right.

PHILONOUS: Is the nearest and exactest survey made by the help of a microscope, or by the naked eye?

HYLAS: By a microscope, doubtless.

PHILONOUS: But a microscope often discovers colours in an object different from those perceived by the unassisted sight. And, in case we had microscopes magnifying to any assigned degree, it is certain that no object whatsoever, viewed through them, would appear in the same colour which it exhibits to the naked eye.

HYLAS: And what will you conclude from all this? You cannot argue that there are really and naturally no colours on objects: because by artificial managements they may be altered, or made to vanish.

PHILONOUS: I think it may evidently be concluded from your own concessions, that all the colours we see with our naked eyes are only apparent as those on the clouds, since they vanish upon a more close and accurate inspection which is afforded us by a microscope. . . .

HYLAS: Colours, sounds, tastes, in a word all those termed *secondary qualities,* have certainly no existence without the mind. But by this acknowledgment I must not be supposed to derogate the reality of matter, or external objects; seeing it is no more than several philosophers maintain, who nevertheless are the farthest imaginable from denying matter. For the clearer understanding of this, you must know sensible qualities are by philosophers divided into *primary* and *secondary.* The former are extension, figure, solidity, gravity, motion, and rest; and these they hold exist really in bodies. The latter are those above enumerated; or, briefly, *all sensible qualities beside the primary,* which they assert are only so many sensations or ideas existing nowhere but in the mind. But all this, I doubt not, you are apprised of. For my part, I have been a long time sensible there was such an opinion current among philosophers, but was never thoroughly convinced of its truth until now.

PHILONOUS: You are still then of opinion that *extension* and *figures* are inherent in external unthinking substances?

HYLAS: I am.

PHILONOUS: But what if the same arguments which are brought against secondary qualities will hold good against these also?

HYLAS: Why then I shall be obliged to think, they too exist only in the mind.

PHILONOUS: Is it your opinion the very figure and extension which you perceive by sense exist in the outward object or material substance?

HYLAS: It is.

PHILONOUS: Have all other animals as good grounds to think the same of the figure and extension which they see and feel?

HYLAS: Without doubt, if they have any thought at all.

PHILONOUS: Answer me, Hylas. Think you the senses were bestowed upon all animals for their preservation and well-being in life? or were they given to men alone for this end?

HYLAS: I make no question but they have the same use in all other animals.

PHILONOUS: If so, is it not necessary they should be enabled by them to perceive their own limbs, and those bodies which are capable of harming them?

HYLAS: Certainly.

PHILONOUS: A mite therefore must be supposed to see his own foot, and things equal or even less than it, as bodies of some considerable dimension; though at the same time they appear to you scarce discernible, or at best as so many visible points?

HYLAS: I cannot deny it.

PHILONOUS: And to creatures less than the mite they will seem yet larger?

HYLAS: They will.

PHILONOUS: Insomuch that what you can hardly discern will to another extremely minute animal appear as some huge mountain?

HYLAS: All this I grant.

PHILONOUS: Can one and the same thing be at the same time in itself of different dimensions?

HYLAS: That were absurd to imagine.

PHILONOUS: But, from what you have laid down it follows that both the extension by you perceived, and that perceived by the mite itself, as likewise all those perceived by lesser animals, are each of them the true extension of the mite's foot; that is to say, by your own principles you are led into an absurdity.

HYLAS: There seems to be some difficulty in the point.

PHILONOUS: Again, have you not acknowledged that no real inherent property of any object can be changed without some change in the thing itself?

HYLAS: I have.

PHILONOUS: But, as we approach to or recede from an object, the visible extension varies, being at one distance ten or a hundred times greater than another. Doth it not therefore follow from hence likewise that it is not really inherent in the object?

HYLAS: I own I am at a loss what to think.

PHILONOUS: Your judgement will soon be determined, if you will venture to think as freely concerning this quality as you have done concerning the rest. Was it not admitted as a good argument, that neither heat nor cold was in the water, because it seemed warm to one hand and cold to the other?

HYLAS: It was.

PHILONOUS: Is it not the very same reasoning to conclude, there is no extension or figure in an object, because to one eye it shall seem little, smooth, and round, when at the same time it appears to the other, great, uneven, and regular?

HYLAS: The very same. But does this latter fact ever happen?

PHILONOUS: You may at any time make the experiment, by looking with one eye bare, and with the other through a microscope.

HYLAS: I know not how to maintain it; and yet I am loath to give up *extension*, I see so many odd consequences following upon such a concession.

PHILONOUS: Odd, say you? After the concessions already made, I hope you will stick at nothing for its oddness. But, on the other hand, should it not seem very odd, if the general reasoning which includes all other sensible qualities did not also include extension? If it be allowed that no idea, nor anything like an idea, can exist in an unperceiving substance, then surely it follows that no figure, or mode of extension, which we can either perceive, or imagine, or have any idea of, can be really inherent in matter; not to mention the peculiar difficulty there must be in conceiving a material substance, prior to and distinct from extension, to be the *substratum* of extension. Be the sensible quality what it will—figure, or sound, or colour, it seems alike impossible it should subsist in that which doth not perceive it.

HYLAS: I give up the point for the present, reserving still a right to retract my opinion, in case I shall hereafter discover any false step in my progress to it. . . .

PHILONOUS: Do but consider that if *extension* be once acknowledged to have no existence without the mind, the same must necessarily be granted of motion, solidity, and gravity; since they all evidently suppose extension. It is therefore superfluous to inquire particularly concerning each of them. In denying extension, you have denied them all to have any real existence. . . . Can you even separate the ideas of extension and motion from the ideas of all those qualities which they who make the distinction term *secondary*?

HYLAS: What! is it not an easy matter to consider extension and motion by themselves, abstracted from all other sensible qualities? Pray how do the mathematicians treat of them?

PHILONOUS: I acknowledge, Hylas, it is not difficult to form general propositions and reasonings about those qualities, without mentioning any other; and, in this sense, to consider or treat of them abstractedly. But, how doth it follow that, because I can pronounce the word *motion* by itself, I can form the idea of it in my mind exclusive of body? or, because theorems may be made of extension and figures, without any mention of *great* or *small*, or any other sensible mode or quality, that therefore it is possible such an abstract idea of extension, without any particular size or figure, or sensible quality, should be distinctly formed, and apprehended by the mind? Mathematicians treat of quantity, without regarding what other sensible qualities it is attended with, as being altogether indifferent to their demonstrations. But, when laying aside the words, they contemplate the bare ideas, I believe you will find, they are not the pure abstracted ideas of extension.

HYLAS: But what say you to *pure intellect*? May not abstracted ideas be framed by that faculty?

PHILONOUS: Since I cannot frame abstract ideas at all, it is plain I cannot frame them by the help of pure *intellect*, whatsoever faculty you understand by those words. Besides, not to inquire into the nature of pure intellect and its spiritual objects, as *virtue, reason, God*, or the like, thus much seems manifest—that sensible things are only to be perceived by sense, or represented by the imagination. Figures, therefore, and extension, being originally perceived by sense, do not belong to pure intellect: but, for your farther satisfaction, try if you can frame the idea of any figure, abstracted from all particularities of size, or even from other sensible qualities.

HYLAS: Let me think a little—I do not find that I can.

PHILONOUS: And can you think it possible that should really exist in nature which implies a repugnancy in its conception?

HYLAS: By no means.

PHILONOUS: Since therefore it is impossible even for the mind to disunite the ideas of extension and motion from all other sensible qualities, doth it not follow, that where the one exist there necessarily the other exist likewise?

HYLAS: It should seem so.

PHILONOUS: Consequently, the very same arguments which you admitted as conclusive against the secondary qualities are, without any farther application of force, against the primary too. Besides, if you will trust your senses, is it not plain all sensible qualities coexist, or to them, appear as being in the same place? Do they ever represent a motion, or figure, as being divested of all other visible and tangible qualities?

HYLAS: You need say no more on this head. I am free to own, if there be no secret error or oversight in our proceedings hitherto, that all sensible qualities are alike to be denied existence without the mind. But, my fear is that I have been too liberal in my former concessions, or overlooked some fallacy or other. In short, I did not take time to think. . . . I acknowledge, Philonous, that, upon a fair observation of what passes in my mind, I can discover nothing else but that I am a thinking being, affected with variety of sensations; neither is it possible to conceive how a sensation should exist in an unperceiving substance. But then, on the other hand, when I look on sensible things in a different view, considering them as so many modes and qualities, I find it necessary to suppose a *material substratum,* without which they cannot be conceived to exist.

PHILONOUS: Material substratum call you it? Pray, by which of your senses came you acquainted with that being?

HYLAS: It is not itself sensible; its modes and qualities only being perceived by the senses.

PHILONOUS: I presume then it was by reflexion and reason you obtained the idea of it?

HYLAS: I do not pretend to any proper positive *idea* of it. However, I conclude it exists, because qualities cannot be conceived to exist without a support.

PHILONOUS: It seems then you have only a relative *notion* of it, or that you conceive it not otherwise than by conceiving the relation it bears to sensible qualities?

HYLAS: Right.

PHILONOUS: Be pleased therefore to let me know wherein that relation consists.

HYLAS: Is it not sufficiently expressed in the term *substratum,* or *substance*?

PHILONOUS: If so, the word *substratum* should import that it is spread under the sensible qualities or accidents?

HYLAS: True.

PHILONOUS: And consequently under extension?

HYLAS: I own it.

PHILONOUS: It is therefore somewhat in its own nature entirely distinct from extension?

HYLAS: I tell you, extension is only a mode, and matter is something that supports modes. And is it not evident the thing supported is different from the thing supporting?

PHILONOUS: So that something distinct from, and exclusive of, extension is supposed to be the *substratum* of extension?

HYLAS: Just so.

PHILONOUS: Answer me, Hylas. Can a thing be spread without extension? or is not the idea of extension necessarily included in *spreading*?

HYLAS: It is.

PHILONOUS: Whatsoever therefore you suppose spread under anything must have in itself an extension distinct from the extension of that thing under which it is spread?

HYLAS: It must.

PHILONOUS: Consequently, every corporeal substance, being the *substratum* of extension, must have in itself another extension, by which it is qualified to be a *substratum:* and so on to infinity. And I ask whether this be not absurd in itself, and repugnant to what you granted just now, to wit, that the *substratum* was something distinct from and exclusive of extension?

HYLAS: Aye but, Philonous, you take me wrong. I do not mean that matter is *spread* in a gross literal sense under extension. The word *substratum* is used only to express in general the same thing with *substance*.

PHILONOUS: Well then, let us examine the relation implied in the term *substance*. Is it not that it stands under accidents?

HYLAS: The very same.

PHILONOUS: But, that one thing may stand under or support another, must it not be extended?

HYLAS: It must.

PHILONOUS: Is not therefore this supposition liable to the same absurdity with the former?

HYLAS: You still take things in a strict literal sense. That is not fair, Philonous.

PHILONOUS: I am not for imposing any sense on your words: you are at liberty to explain them as you please. Only, I beseech you, make me understand something by them. You tell me matter supports or stands under accidents. How! is it as your legs support your body?

HYLAS: No; that is the literal sense.

PHILONOUS: Pray let me know any sense, literal or not literal, that you understand it in.—How long must I want for an answer, Hylas?

HYLAS: I declare I know not what to say. I once thought I understood well enough what was meant by matter's supporting accidents. But now, the more I think on it the less can I comprehend it: In short I find that I know nothing of it.

PHILONOUS: It seems then you have no idea at all, neither relative nor positive, of matter; you know neither what it is in itself, nor what relation it bears to accidents?

HYLAS: I acknowledge it.

PHILONOUS: And yet you asserted that you could not conceive how qualities or accidents should really exist, without conceiving at the same time a material support of them?

HYLAS: I did.

PHILONOUS: That is to say, when you conceive the real existence of qualities, you do withal conceive something which you cannot conceive?

HYLAS: It was wrong, I own. . . .

PHILONOUS: Can you see a thing which is at the same time unseen?

HYLAS: No, that were a contradiction.

PHILONOUS: Is it not as great a contradiction to talk of *conceiving* a thing which is *unconceived*?

HYLAS: It is.

PHILONOUS: The, tree or house therefore which you think of is conceived by you?

HYLAS: How should it be otherwise?

PHILONOUS: And what is conceived is surely in the mind?

HYLAS: Without question, that which is conceived is in the mind.

PHILONOUS: How then came you to say, you conceived a house or tree existing independent and out of all minds whatsoever?

HYLAS: That was I own an oversight; but stay, let me consider what led me into it.—It is a pleasant mistake enough. As I was thinking of a tree in a solitary place, where no one was present to see it, methought that was to conceive a tree as existing unperceived or unthought of; not considering that I myself conceived it all the while. But now I plainly see that all I can do is to frame ideas in my own mind. I may indeed conceive in my own thoughts the idea of a tree, or a house, or a mountain, but that is all. And this is far from proving that I can conceive them *existing out of the minds of all spirits.*

PHILONOUS: You acknowledge then that you cannot possibly conceive how any one corporeal sensible thing should exist otherwise than in the mind?

HYLAS: I do.

PHILONOUS: And yet you will earnestly contend for the truth of that which you cannot so much as conceive?

HYLAS: I profess I know not what to think; but still there are some scruples remain with me. Is it not certain I see things at a distance? Do we not perceive the stars and moon, for example, to be a great way off? Is not this, I say, manifest to the senses?

PHILONOUS: Do you not in a dream too perceive those or the like objects?

HYLAS: I do.

PHILONOUS: And have they not then the same appearance of being distant?

HYLAS: They have.

PHILONOUS: But you do not thence conclude the apparitions in a dream to be without the mind?

HYLAS: By no means.

PHILONOUS: You ought not therefore to conclude that sensible objects are without the mind, from their appearance, or manner wherein they are perceived.

HYLAS: I acknowledge it. But doth not my sense deceive me in those cases? . . .

PHILONOUS: Allowing that distance was truly and immediately perceived by the mind, yet it would not thence follow it existed out of the mind. For, whatever is immediately perceived is an idea: And can any idea exist out of the mind?

HYLAS: To suppose that were absurd: But, inform me, Philonous, can we perceive or know nothing beside our ideas?

PHILONOUS: As for the rational deducing of causes from effects, that is beside our inquiry. And, by the senses you can best tell whether you perceive anything which is not immediately perceived. And I ask you, whether the things immediately perceived are other than your own sensations or ideas? You have indeed more than once, in the course of this conversation, declared yourself on those points; but you seem, by this last question, to have departed from what you then thought.

HYLAS: To speak the truth, Philonous, I think there are two kinds of objects:—the one perceived immediately, which are likewise called *ideas*, the other are real things or external objects, perceived by the mediation of ideas, which are their images and representations. Now, I own ideas do not exist without the mind; but the latter sort of objects do. I am sorry I did not think of this distinction sooner; it would probably have cut short your discourse.

PHILONOUS: Are those external objects perceived by sense or by some other faculty?

HYLAS: They are perceived by sense.

PHILONOUS: How! is there any thing perceived by sense which is not immediately perceived?

HYLAS: Yes, Philonous, in some sort there is. For example, when I look on a picture or statue of Julius Caesar, I may be said after a manner to perceive him (though not immediately) by my senses.

PHILONOUS: It seems then you will have our ideas, which alone are immediately perceived, to be pictures of external things: and that these also are perceived by sense, inasmuch as they have a conformity or resemblance to our ideas?

HYLAS: That is my meaning.

PHILONOUS: And, in the same way that Julius Caesar, in himself invisible, is nevertheless perceived by sight; real things, in themselves imperceptible, are perceived by sense.

HYLAS: In the very same.

PHILONOUS: Tell me, Hylas, when you behold the picture of Julius Caesar, do you see with your eyes any more than some colours and figures, with a certain symmetry and composition of the whole?

HYLAS: Nothing else.

PHILONOUS: And would not a man who had never known anything of Julius Caesar see as much?

HYLAS: He would.

PHILONOUS: Consequently he hath his sight, and the use of it, in as perfect a degree as you?

HYLAS: I agree with you.

PHILONOUS: Whence comes it then that your thoughts are directed to the Roman emperor, and his are not? This cannot proceed from the sensations or ideas of sense by you then perceived; since you acknowledge you have no advantage over him in that respect. It should seem therefore to proceed from reason and memory: should it not?

HYLAS: It should.

PHILONOUS: Consequently, it will not follow from that instance that anything is perceived by sense which is not immediately perceived. Though I grant we may, in one acceptation, be said to perceive sensible things mediately by sense: that is, when, from a frequently perceived connexion, the immediate perception of ideas by one sense *suggests* to the mind others, perhaps belonging to another sense, which are wont to be connected with them. For instance, when I hear a coach drive along the streets, immediately I perceive only the sound; but, from the experience I have had that such a sound is connected with a coach, I am said to hear the coach. It is nevertheless evident that, in truth and strictness, nothing can be *heard* but *sound;* and the coach is not then properly perceived by sense, but suggested from experience. So likewise when we are said to see a red-hot bar of iron; the solidity and heat of the iron are not the objects of sight, but suggested to the imagination by the colour and figure which are properly perceived by that sense. In short, those things alone are actually and strictly perceived by any sense, which would have been perceived in case that same sense had then been first conferred on us. As for other things, it is plain they are only suggested to the mind by experience, grounded on former perceptions. But, to return to your comparison of Caesar's picture, it is plain, if you keep to that, you must hold the real things, or archetypes of our ideas, are not perceived by sense, but by some internal faculty of the soul, as reason or memory. I would therefore fain know what arguments you can draw from reason for the existence of what you call *real things* or *material objects*. Or, whether you remember to have seen them formerly as they are in themselves; or, if you have heard or read of any one that did.

HYLAS: I see, Philonous, you are disposed to raillery; but that will never convince me.

PHILONOUS: My aim is only to learn from you the way to come at the knowledge of *material beings*. Whatever we perceive is perceived immediately or mediately: by sense, or by reason and reflexion. But, as you have excluded sense, pray shew me what reason you have to believe their existence; or what *medium* you can possibly make use of to prove it, either to mine or your own understanding.

HYLAS: To deal ingenuously, Philonous, now I consider the point, I do not find I can give you any good reason for it. But, thus much seems pretty plain, that it is at least possible such things may really exist. And, as long as there is no absurdity in supposing them, I am resolved to believe as I did, till you bring good reasons to the contrary.

PHILONOUS: What! Is it come to this, that you only *believe* the existence of material objects, and that your belief is founded barely on the possibility of its being true? Then you will have me bring reasons against it: though another would think it reasonable the proof should lie on him who holds the affirmative.

And, after all, this very point which you are now resolved to maintain, without any reason, is in effect what you have more than once during this discourse seen good reason to give up. But, to pass over all this; if I understand you rightly, you say our ideas do not exist without the mind, but that they are copies, images, or representations, of certain originals that do?

HYLAS: You take me right.

PHILONOUS: They are then like external things?

HYLAS: They are.

PHILONOUS: Have those things a stable and permanent nature, independent of our senses; or are they in a perpetual change, upon our producing any motions in our bodies—suspending, exerting, or altering, our faculties or organs of sense?

HYLAS: Real things, it is plain, have a fixed and real nature, which remains the same notwithstanding any change in our senses or in the posture and motion of our bodies; which indeed may affect the ideas in our minds, but it were absurd to think they had the same effect on things existing without the mind.

PHILONOUS: How then is it possible that things perpetually fleeting and variable as our ideas should be copies or images of anything fixed and constant? Or, in other words, since all sensible qualities, as size, figure, colour, &c., that is, our ideas, are continually changing, upon every alteration in the distance, medium, or instruments of sensation; how can any determinate material objects be properly represented or painted forth by several distinct things, each of which is so different from and unlike the rest? Or, if you say it resembles some one only of our ideas, how shall we be able to distinguish the true copy from all the false ones?

HYLAS: I profess, Philonous, I am at a loss. I know not what to say to this.

PHILONOUS: But neither is this all. Which are material objects in themselves—perceptible or imperceptible?

HYLAS: Properly and immediately nothing can be perceived but ideas. All material things, therefore, are in themselves insensible, and to be perceived only by our ideas.

PHILONOUS: Ideas then are sensible, and their archetypes or originals insensible?

HYLAS: Right.

PHILONOUS: But how can that which is sensible be like that which is insensible? Can a real thing, in itself *invisible*, be like a *colour*, or a real thing, which is not *audible*, be like a *sound*? In a word, can anything be like a sensation or idea, but another sensation or idea?

HYLAS: I must own, I think not.

PHILONOUS: Is it possible there should be any doubt on the point? Do you not perfectly know your own ideas?

HYLAS: I know them perfectly; since what I do not perceive or know can be no part of my idea.

PHILONOUS: Consider, therefore, and examine them, and then tell me if there be anything in them which can exist without the mind: Or if you can conceive anything like them existing without the mind.

HYLAS: Upon inquiry, I find it is impossible for me to conceive or understand how anything but an idea can be like an idea. And it is most evident that *no idea can exist without the mind.*

PHILONOUS: You are therefore, by your principles, forced to deny the *reality* of sensible things; since you made it to consist in an absolute existence exterior to the mind. That is to say, you are a downright sceptic. So I have gained my point, which was to shew your principles led to scepticism.

HYLAS: For the present I am, if not entirely convinced, at least silenced.

Discussion Questions

1. A favorite question of philosophers is: If a tree falls in the forest and no one is there to hear it, does it make a sound? How would Berkeley answer this question? An answer of *no* seems counterintuitive—what would it mean to answer "no" to this? Would it be different for other sensible qualities?
   a. If a ripe lemon is in the forest and no one sees it, is it yellow?
   b. If honey is in the forest and no one tastes it, is it sweet?
2. When you do the experiment that Berkeley suggests of putting your hands in cold and hot water and then placing them in the same tepid bucket of water, what does that tell you about your experience of sensible qualities?
3. In what way does the definition of things (sound, for example) affect our view of reality?

An Essay Concerning Human Understanding

John Locke

John Locke wrote not only on epistemology (theory of knowledge) and theories of reality, but also on government (see the later selection in this book), economics, education, religion, and gardening. As one of the preeminent British empiricists (from the Greek word, *empeiria*: "experience"), Locke held that knowledge is gathered through sense experience onto a sort of blank slate—*tabula rasa*. It is from this that our ideas and knowledge base become formed. (See Pinker's article for an overview.)

Locke's approach directly conflicts with that of such *rationalists* as Plato and Descartes, who held that our ideas are innate and can be accessed by inward reflection.

In this reading, Locke defends the notion of the *tabula rasa* and then goes on to describe the qualities of objects (both primary and secondary) and how we formulate ideas (what we know) about them.

Source: John Locke, "An Essay Concerning Human Understanding." First published in 1690, reprinted from Locke's ten-volume *Collected Works* (first published in 1714 and reprinted with corrections in 1823).

Reading Questions

1. How does Locke use the painter/dyer example to support his position?
2. What are primary and secondary qualities? How does our perception of them differ?
3. How does Locke distinguish between a simple and a complex idea?

Book II

Of Ideas

Chapter I

Of Ideas in general, and their Original

(1) *Idea is the object of thinking.* Every man being conscious to himself that he thinks; and that which his mind is applied about whilst thinking being the ideas that are there, it is past doubt that men have in their minds several ideas,— such as are those expressed by the words whiteness, hardness, sweetness, thinking, motion, man, elephant, army, drunkenness, and others: It is in the first place then to be inquired, How he comes by them?

I know it is a received doctrine, that men have native ideas, and original characters, stamped upon their minds in their very first being. This opinion I have at large examined already; and, I suppose what I have said in the foregoing Book will be much more easily admitted, when I have shown whence the understanding may get all the ideas it has; and by what ways and degrees they may come into the mind;—for which I shall appeal to every one's own observation and experience.

(2) *All ideas come from sensation or reflection.* Let us then suppose the mind to be, as we say, white paper, void of all characters, without any ideas:—How comes it to be furnished? Whence comes it by that vast store which the busy and boundless fancy of man has painted on it with an almost endless variety? Whence has it all the materials of reason and knowledge? To this I answer, in one word, from EXPERIENCE. In that all our knowledge is founded; and from that it ultimately derives itself. Our observation employed either, about external sensible objects, or about the internal operations of our minds perceived and reflected on by ourselves, is that which supplies our understandings with all the materials of thinking. These two are the fountains of knowledge, from whence all the ideas we have, or can naturally have, do spring.

(3) *The objects of sensation one source of ideas.* First, our Senses, conversant about particular sensible objects, do convey into the mind several distinct perceptions of things, according to those various ways wherein those objects do affect them. And thus we come by those ideas we have of yellow, white, heat, cold, soft, hard, bitter, sweet, and all those which we call sensible qualities; which when I say the senses convey into the mind, I mean, they from external objects convey into the mind what produces there those perceptions. This great source of most of the

ideas we have depending wholly upon our senses, and derived by them to the understanding, I call SENSATION.

(4) *The operations of our minds, the other source of them.* Secondly, the other fountain from which experience furnisheth the understanding with ideas is,—the perception of the operations of our own mind within us, as it is employed about the ideas it has got;—which operations, when the soul comes to reflect on and consider, do furnish the understanding with another set of ideas, which could not be had from things without. And such are perception, thinking, doubting, believing, reasoning, knowing, willing, and all the different actings of our own minds—which we being conscious of, and observing in ourselves, do from these receive into our understandings as distinct ideas as we do from bodies affecting our senses. This source of ideas every man has wholly in himself; and though it be not sense, as having nothing to do with external objects, yet it is very like it, and might properly enough be called internal sense. But as I call the other SENSATION, so I Call this REFLECTION, the ideas it affords being such only as the mind gets by reflecting on its own operations within itself. By reflection then, in the following part of this discourse, I would be understood to mean, that notice which the mind takes of its own operations, and the manner of them, by reason whereof there come to be ideas of these operations in the understanding. These two, I say, viz. external material things, as the objects of SENSATION, and the operations of our own minds within, as the objects of REFLECTION, are to me the only originals from whence all our ideas take their beginnings. The term operations here I use in a large sense, as comprehending not barely the actions of the mind about its ideas, but some sort of passions arising sometimes from them, such as is the satisfaction or uneasiness arising from any thought.

(5) *All our ideas are of the one or the other of these.* The understanding seems to me not to have the least glimmering of any ideas which it doth not receive from one of these two. External objects furnish the mind with the ideas of sensible qualities, which are all those different perceptions they produce in us; and the mind furnishes the understanding with ideas of its own operations.

These, when we have taken a full survey of them, and their several modes, combinations, and relations, we shall find to contain all our whole stock of ideas: And that we have nothing in our minds which did not come in one of these two ways. Let any one examine his own thoughts, and thoroughly search into his understanding; and then let him tell me, whether all the original ideas he has there, are any other than of the objects of his senses, or of the operations of his mind, considered as objects of his reflection. And how great a mass of knowledge soever he imagines to be lodged there, he will, upon taking a strict view, see that he has not any idea in his mind but what one of these two have imprinted;— though perhaps, with infinite variety compounded and enlarged by the under-standing, as we shall see hereafter. . . .

(25) *In the reception of simple ideas, the understanding is for the most part passive.* In this part the understanding is merely passive; and whether or no it will have these beginnings, and as it were materials of knowledge, is not in its own power. For the objects of our senses do, many of them, obtrude their particular

ideas upon our minds whether we will or not; and the operations of our minds will not let us be without, at least, some obscure notions of them. No man can be wholly ignorant of what he does when he thinks. These simple ideas, when offered to the mind, the understanding can no more refuse to have, nor alter when they are imprinted, nor blot them out and make new ones itself, than a mirror can refuse, alter, or obliterate the images or ideas which the objects set before it do therein produce. As the bodies that surround us do diversely affect our organs, the mind is forced to receive the impressions; and cannot avoid the perception of those ideas that are annexed to them.

Chapter II

Of Simple Ideas

(1) *Uncompounded appearances.* The better to understand the nature, manner, and extent of our knowledge, one thing is carefully to be observed concerning the ideas we have; and that is, that some of them are simple and some complex.

Though the qualities that affect our senses are, in the things themselves, so united and blended, that there is no separation, no distance between them; yet it is plain, the ideas they produce in the mind enter by the senses simple and unmixed. For, though the sight and touch often take in from the same object, at the same time, different ideas;—as a man sees at once motion and colour; the hand feels softness and warmth in the same piece of wax: Yet the simple ideas thus united in the same subject, are as perfectly distinct as those that come in by different senses. The coldness and hardness which a man feels in a piece of ice being as distinct ideas in the mind as the smell and whiteness of a lily; or as the taste of sugar, and smell of a rose. And there is nothing can be plainer to a man than the clear and distinct perception he has of those simple ideas; which, being each in itself uncompounded, contains in it nothing but one uniform appearance, or conception in the mind, and is not distinguishable into different ideas.

(2) *The mind can neither make nor destroy them.* These simple ideas, the materials of all our knowledge, are suggested and furnished to the mind only by those two ways above mentioned, viz. sensation and reflection. When the understanding is once stored with these simple ideas, it has the power to repeat, compare, and unite them, even to an almost infinite variety, and so can make at pleasure new complex ideas. But it is not in the power of the most exalted wit, or enlarged understanding, by any quickness or variety of thought, to invent or frame one new simple idea in the mind, not taken in by the ways before mentioned: Nor can any force of the understanding destroy those that are there. The dominion of man, in this little world of his own understanding being muchwhat the same as it is in the great world of visible things; wherein his power, however managed by art and skill, reaches no farther than to compound and divide the materials that are made to his hand; but can do nothing towards the making the least particle of new matter, or destroying one atom of what is already in being. The same inability will every one find in himself, who shall go about to fashion in his understanding one simple idea, not received in by his senses from external objects, or by reflection from the

operations of his own mind about them. I would have any one try to fancy any taste which had never affected his palate; or frame the idea of a scent he had never smelt: and when he can do this, I will also conclude that a blind man hath ideas of colours, and a deaf man true distinct notions of sounds. . . .

Chapter VIII

Some further considerations concerning our Simple Ideas of Sensation

(1) *Positive ideas from privative causes.* Concerning the simple ideas of Sensation, it is to be considered,—that whatsoever is so constituted in nature as to be able, by affecting our senses, to cause any perception in the mind, doth thereby produce in the understanding a simple idea; which, whatever be the external cause of it, when it comes to be taken notice of by our discerning faculty, it is by the mind looked on and considered there to be a real positive idea in the understanding, as much as any other whatsoever; though, perhaps, the cause of it be but a privation of the subject.

(2) *Ideas in the mind distinguished from that in things which gives rise to them.* Thus the ideas of heat and cold, light and darkness, white and black, motion and rest, are equally clear and positive ideas in the mind; though, perhaps, some of the causes which produce them are barely privations, in those subjects from whence our senses derive those ideas. These the understanding, in its view of them, considers all as distinct positive ideas, without taking notice of the causes that produce them: which is an inquiry not belonging to the idea, as it is in the understanding, but to the nature of the things existing without us. These are two very different things, and carefully to be distinguished; it being one thing to perceive and know the idea of white or black, and quite another to examine what kind of particles they must be, and how ranged in the superficies, to make any object appear white or black.

(3) *We may have the ideas when we are ignorant of their physical causes.* A painter or dyer who never inquired into their causes hath the ideas of white and black, and other colours, as clearly, perfectly, and distinctly in his understanding, and perhaps more distinctly, than the philosopher who hath busied himself in considering their natures, and thinks he knows how far either of them is, in its cause, positive or privative; and the idea of black is no less positive in his mind than that of white, however the cause of that colour in the external object may be only a privation.

(4) *Why a privative cause in nature may occasion a positive idea.* If it were the design of my present undertaking to inquire into the natural causes and manner of perception, I should offer this as a reason why a privative cause might, in some cases at least, produce a positive idea; viz. that all sensation being produced in us only by different degrees and modes of motion in our animal spirits, variously agitated by external objects, the abatement of any former motion must as necessarily produce a new sensation as the variation or increase of it; and so introduce a new idea, which depends only on a different motion of the animal spirits in that organ. . . .

(7) *Ideas in the mind, qualities in bodies.* To discover the nature of our ideas the better, and to discourse of them intelligibly, it will be convenient to distinguish

them as they are ideas or perceptions in our minds; and as they are modifications of matter in the bodies that cause such perceptions in us: that so we may not think (as perhaps usually is done) that they are exactly the images and resemblances of something inherent in the subject; most of those of sensation being in the mind no more the likeness of something existing without us, than the names that stand for them are the likeness of our ideas, which yet upon hearing they are apt to excite in us.

(8) *Our ideas and the qualities of bodies.* Whatsoever the mind perceives in itself, or is the immediate object of perception, thought, or understanding, that I call idea; and the power to produce any idea in our mind, I call quality of the subject wherein that power is. Thus a snowball having the power to produce in us the ideas of white, cold, and round,—the power to produce those ideas in us, as they are in the snowball, I call qualities; and as they are sensations or perceptions in our understandings, I call them ideas; which ideas, if I speak of sometimes as in the things themselves, I would be understood to mean those qualities in the objects which produce them in us.

(9) *Primary qualities of bodies.* Qualities thus considered in bodies are, *First,* such as are utterly inseparable from the body, in what state soever it be; and such as in all the alterations and changes it suffers, all the force can be used upon it, it constantly keeps; and such as sense constantly finds in every particle of matter which has bulk enough to be perceived; and the mind finds inseparable from every particle of matter, though less than to make itself singly be perceived by our senses: v.g. Take a grain of wheat, divide it into two parts; each part has still solidity, extension, figure, and mobility: Divide it again, and it retains still the same qualities; and so divide it on, till the parts become insensible; they must retain still each of them all those qualities. For division (which is all that a mill, or pestle, or any other body, does upon another, in reducing it to insensible parts) can never take away either solidity, extension, figure, or mobility from any body, but only makes two or more distinct separate masses of matter, of that which was but one before; all which distinct masses, reckoned as so many distinct bodies, after division, make a certain number. These I call original or primary qualities of body, which I think we may observe to produce simple ideas in us, viz. solidity, extension, figure, motion or rest, and number.

(10) *Secondary qualities of bodies. Secondly,* such qualities which in truth are nothing in the objects themselves but power to produce various sensations in us by their primary qualities, i.e., by the bulk, figure, texture, and motion of their insensible parts, as colours, sounds, tastes, etc. These I call secondary qualities. To these might be added a third sort, which are allowed to be barely powers; though they are as much real qualities in the subject as those which I, to comply with the common way of speaking, call qualities, but for distinction, secondary qualities. For the power in fire to produce a new colour, or consistency, in wax or clay,—by its primary qualities, is as much a quality in fire, as the power it has to produce in me a new idea or sensation of warmth or burning, which I felt not before,—by the same primary qualities, viz. the bulk, texture, and motion of its insensible parts.

(11) *How bodies produce ideas in us.* The next thing to be considered is, how bodies produce ideas in us; and that is manifestly by impulse, the only way which we can conceive bodies to operate in.

(12) *By motions, external, and in our organism.* If then external objects be not united to our minds when they produce ideas therein; and yet we perceive these original qualities in such of them as singly fall under our senses, it is evident that some motion must be thence continued by our nerves, or animal spirits, by some parts of our bodies, to the brains or the seat of sensation, there to produce in our minds the particular ideas we have of them. And since the extension, figure, number, the motion of bodies of an observable bigness, may be perceived at a distance by the sight, it is evident some singly imperceptible bodies must come from them to the eyes, and thereby convey to the brain some motion; which produces these ideas which we have of them in us.

(13) *How secondary qualities produce their ideas.* After the same manner, that the ideas of these original qualities are produced in us, we may conceive that the ideas of secondary qualities are also produced, viz. by the operation of insensible particles on our senses. For, it being manifest that there are bodies and good store of bodies, each whereof are so small, that we cannot by any of our senses discover either their bulk, figure, or motion,—as is evident in the particles of the air and water, and others extremely smaller than those; perhaps as much smaller than particles of air and water, as the particles of air and water are smaller than peas or hail-stones;—let us suppose at present that the different motions and figures, bulk and number, of such particles, affecting the several organs of our senses, produce in us those different sensations which we have from the colours and smells of bodies; v.g. that a violet, by the impulse of such insensible particles of matter, of peculiar figures and bulks, and in different degrees and modifications of their motions, causes the ideas of the blue colour, and sweet scent of that flower to be produced in our minds. It being no more impossible to conceive that God should annex such ideas to such motions, with which they have no similitude, than that he should annex the idea of pain to the motion of a piece of steel dividing our flesh, with which that idea hath no resemblance.

(14) *They depend on the primary qualities.* What I have said concerning colours and smells may be understood also of tastes and sounds, and other the like sensible qualities; which, whatever reality we by mistake attribute to them, are in truth nothing in the objects themselves, but powers to produce various sensations in us; and depend on those primary qualities, viz. bulk, figure, texture, and motion of parts as I have said.

(15) *Ideas of primary qualities are resemblances; of secondary, not.* From whence I think it easy to draw this observation,—that the ideas of primary qualities of bodies are resemblances of them, and their patterns do really exist in the bodies themselves, but the ideas produced in us by these secondary qualities have no resemblance of them at all. There is nothing like our ideas, existing in the bodies themselves. They are, in the bodies we denominate from them, only a power to produce those sensations in us: and what is sweet, blue, or warm in idea, is but the certain bulk, figure, and motion of the insensible parts, in the bodies themselves, which we call so.

(16) *Examples.* Flame is denominated hot and light; snow, white and cold; and manna, white and sweet, from the ideas they produce in us. Which qualities are commonly thought to be the same in those bodies that those ideas are in us, the one the perfect resemblance of the other, as they are in a mirror, and it would by most men be judged very extravagant if one should say otherwise. And yet he that will consider that the same fire that, at one distance produces in us the sensation of warmth, does, at a nearer approach, produce in us the far different sensation of pain, ought to bethink himself what reason he has to say—that this idea of warmth, which was produced in him by the fire, is actually in the fire; and his idea of pain, which the same fire produced in him the same way, is not in the fire. Why are whiteness and coldness in snow, and pain not, when it produces the one and the other idea in us; and can do neither, but by the bulk, figure, number, and motion of its solid parts?

(17) *The ideas of the primary alone really exist.* The particular bulk, number, figure, and motion of the parts of fire or snow are really in them,—whether any one's senses perceive them or no: And therefore they may be called real qualities, because they really exist in those bodies. But light, heat, whiteness, or coldness, are no more really in them than sickness or pain is in manna. Take away the sensation of them; let not the eyes see light or colours, nor the ears hear sounds; let the palate not taste, nor the nose smell, and all colours, tastes, odours, and sounds, as they are such particular ideas, vanish and cease, and are reduced to their causes, i.e., bulk, figure, and motion of parts. . . .

(21) *Explains how water felt as cold by one hand may be warm to the other.* Ideas being thus distinguished and understood, we may be able to give an account how the same water, at the same time, may produce the idea of cold by one hand and of heat by the other: Whereas it is impossible that the same water, if those ideas were really in it, should at the same time be both hot and cold. For, if we imagine warmth, as it is in our hands, to be nothing but a certain sort and degree of motion in the minute particles of our nerves or animal spirits, we may understand how it is possible that the same water may, at the same time, produce the sensations of heat in one hand and cold in the other; which yet figure never does, that never producing—the idea of a square by one hand which has produced the idea of a globe by another. But if the sensation of heat and cold be nothing but the increase or diminution of the motion of the minute parts of our bodies, caused by the corpuscles of any other body, it is easy to be understood, that if that motion be greater in one hand than in the other; if a body be applied to the two hands, which has in its minute particles a greater motion than in those of one of the hands, and a less than in those of the other, it will increase the motion of the one hand and lessen it in the other; and so cause the different sensations of heat and cold that depend thereon.

(22) *An excursion into natural philosophy.* I have in what just goes before been engaged in physical inquiries a little further than perhaps I intended. But, it being necessary to make the nature of sensation a little understood; and to make the difference between the qualities in bodies, and the ideas produced by them in the mind, to be distinctly conceived, without which it were impossible to discourse intelligibly of them;—I hope I shall be pardoned this little excursion into natural

philosophy; it being necessary in our present inquiry to distinguish the primary and real qualities of bodies, which are always in them (viz. solidity, extension, figure, number, and motion, or rest, and are sometimes perceived by us. viz. when the bodies they are in are big enough singly to be discerned), from those secondary and imputed qualities, which are but the powers of several combinations of those primary ones, when they operate without being distinctly discerned;— whereby we may also come to know what ideas are, and what are not, resemblances of something really existing in the bodies we denominate from them.

(23) *Three sorts of qualities in bodies.* The qualities, then, that are in bodies, rightly considered, are of three sorts:—

> First, the bulk, figure, number, situation, and motion or rest of their solid parts. Those are in them, whether we perceive them or not; and when they are of that size that we can discover them, we have by these an idea of the thing as it is in itself; as is plain in artificial things. These I call primary qualities.
>
> Secondly, the power that is in any body, by reason of its insensible primary qualities, to operate after a peculiar manner on any of our senses, and thereby produce in us the different ideas of several colours, sounds, smells, tastes, etc. These are usually called sensible qualities.
>
> Thirdly, the power that is in any body, by reason of the particular constitution of its primary qualities, to make such a change in the bulk, figure, texture, and motion of another body, as to make it operate on our senses differently from what it did before. Thus the sun has a power to make wax white, and fire to make lead fluid. These are usually called powers.

The first of these, as has been said, I think may be properly called real, original, or primary qualities; because they are in the things themselves, whether they are perceived or not: and upon their different modifications it is that the secondary qualities depend.

The other two are only powers to act differently upon other things: which powers result from the different modifications of those primary qualities.

(24) *The first are resemblances; the second thought to be resemblances, but are not; the third neither are nor are thought so.* But, though the two latter sorts of qualities are powers barely, and nothing but powers, relating to several other bodies, and resulting from the different modifications of the original qualities, yet they are generally otherwise thought of. For the second sort, viz., the powers to produce several ideas in us, by our senses, are looked upon as real qualities in the things thus affecting us: But the third sort are called and esteemed barely powers. v.g. The idea of heat or light, which we receive by our eyes, or touch, from the sun, are commonly thought real qualities existing in the sun, and something more than mere powers in it. But when we consider the sun in reference to wax, which it melts or blanches, we look on the whiteness and softness produced in the wax, not as qualities in the sun, but effects produced by powers in it. Whereas, if rightly considered, these qualities of light and warmth, which are perceptions in me when I am warmed or enlightened by

the sun, are no otherwise in the sun, than the changes made in the wax, when it is blanched or melted, are in the sun. They are all of them equally powers in the sun, depending on its primary qualities; whereby it is able, in the one case, so to alter the bulk, figure, texture, or motion of some of the insensible parts of my eyes or hands, as thereby to produce in me the idea of light or heat; and in the other, it is able so to alter the bulk, figure, texture, or motion of the insensible parts of the wax, as to make them fit to produce in me the distinct ideas of white and fluid.

(25) *Why the secondary are ordinarily taken for real qualities, and not for bare powers.* The reason why the one are ordinarily taken for real qualities, and the other only for bare powers, seems to be, because the ideas we have of distinct colours, sounds, etc., containing nothing at all in them of bulk, figure, or motion, we are not apt to think them the effects of these primary qualities; which appear not, to our senses, to operate in their production, and with which they have not any apparent congruity or conceivable connexion. Hence it is that we are so forward to imagine, that those ideas are the resemblances of something really existing in the objects themselves: Since sensation discovers nothing of bulk, figure, or motion of parts in their production; nor can reason show how bodies, by their bulk, figure, and motion, should produce in the mind the ideas of blue or yellow, etc. But, in the other case, in the operations of bodies changing the qualities one of another, we plainly discover that the quality produced hath commonly no resemblance with anything in the thing producing it; wherefore we look on it as a bare effect of power. For, through receiving the idea of heat or light from the sun, we are apt to think it is a perception and resemblance of such a quality in the sun; yet when we see wax, or a fair face, receive change of colour from the sun, we cannot imagine that to be the reception or resemblance of anything in the sun, because we find not those different colours in the sun itself. For, our senses being able to observe a likeness or unlikeness of sensible qualities in two different external objects, we forwardly enough conclude the production of any sensible quality in any subject to be an effect of bare power, and not the communication of any quality which was really in the efficient, when we find no such sensible quality in the thing that produced it. But our senses, not being able to discover any unlikeness between the idea produced in us, and the quality of the object producing it, we are apt to imagine that our ideas are resemblances of something in the objects, and not the effects of certain powers placed in the modification of their primary qualities, with which primary qualities the ideas produced in us have no resemblance.

(26) *Secondary qualities twofold; first, immediately perceivable; secondly, mediately perceivable.* To conclude. Besides those before-mentioned primary qualities in bodies, viz. bulk, figure, extension, number, and motion of their solid parts; all the rest, whereby we take notice of bodies, and distinguish them one from another, are nothing else but several powers in them, depending on those primary qualities; whereby they are fitted, either by immediately operating on our bodies to produce several different ideas in us; or else, by operating on other bodies, so to change their primary qualities as to render them capable of producing ideas in us different from what before they did. The former of these, I think, may be called secondary qualities immediately perceivable: the latter, secondary qualities, mediately perceivable.

Discussion Questions

1. Close your eyes. Turn your head in either direction and then open your eyes. Pay attention to your first thought when your eyes open. What control did you have over it? What *caused* this thought? (Does this support or take away from Locke's point in Book II, Chapter 1, #25?)
2. If knowledge is not innate, how do we gain our knowledge of moral principles, math, and logic? Locke references the numerous different and conflicting religions as evidence that there cannot be any universal innate idea of God. How would you address this?
3. What significance would it have on your life if it really were the case that color, for example, was not *in* objects but instead in the observer?

Appearance and Reality

Bertrand Russell

(For a brief biography, see the selection from Russell in the prologue.)

This selection, from the first chapter of his book *The Problems of Philosophy,* attempts to discover knowledge that is *certain* and unable to be doubted. Russell takes a skeptical approach in hopes of determining this (which he does determine in subsequent chapters). In doing so, he mentions Berkeley's view (see his selection in this section) as well as others, including subtle references to Locke's view (see his selection in this section) and that of science.

Reading Questions

1. What does Russell say in his comparison of the painter's and philosopher's view of the table? How do they view the table differently?
2. How does Russell defend his claim that there is no inherent color in the table?
3. What role does the microscope play in viewing the "real" texture of the table?
4. What is "sense-data" and how does it differ from "sensation"? How does Russell frame Berkeley's position in terms of sense-data and sensations? Mind and matter?
5. What is an "idealist"? What does Russell say about this idea?
6. What answers does Russell provide about what the real table is in terms of answers given by Leibniz, Berkeley, and by science?
7. According to Russell, what value is there in merely framing these questions, even without answers?

Source: Appearance and Reality. Chapter 1 (with slight edit) from *The Problems of Philosophy,* by Bertrand Russell, 1959, pp. 7–16. By permission of Oxford University Press.

Is there any knowledge in the world which is so certain that no reasonable man could doubt it? This question, which at first sight might not seem difficult, is really one of the most difficult that can be asked. When we have realized the obstacles in the way of a straightforward and confident answer, we shall be well launched on the study of philosophy—for philosophy is merely the attempt to answer such ultimate questions, not carelessly and dogmatically, as we do in ordinary life and even in the sciences, but critically, after exploring all that makes such questions puzzling, and after realizing all the vagueness and confusion that underlie our ordinary ideas.

In daily life, we assume as certain many things which, on a closer scrutiny, are found to be so full of apparent contradictions that only a great amount of thought enables us to know what it is that we really may believe. In the search for certainty, it is natural to begin with our present experiences, and in some sense, no doubt, knowledge is to be derived from them. But any statement as to what it is that our immediate experiences make us know is very likely to be wrong. It seems to me that I am now sitting in a chair, at a table of a certain shape, on which I see sheets of paper with writing or print. By turning my head I see out of the window buildings and clouds and the sun. I believe that the sun is about ninety-three million miles from the earth; that it is a hot globe many times bigger than the earth; that, owing to the earth's rotation, it rises every morning, and will continue to do so for an indefinite time in the future. I believe that, if any other normal person comes into my room, he will see the same chairs and tables and books and papers as I see, and that the table which I see is the same as the table which I feel pressing against my arm. All this seems to be so evident as to be hardly worth stating, except in answer to a man who doubts whether I know anything. Yet all this may be reasonably doubted, and all of it requires much careful discussion before we can be sure that we have stated it in a form that is wholly true.

To make our difficulties plain, let us concentrate attention on the table. To the eye it is oblong, brown, and shiny, to the touch it is smooth and cool and hard; when I tap it, it gives out a wooden sound. Any one else who sees and feels and hears the table will agree with this description, so that it might seem as if no difficulty would arise; but as soon as we try to be more precise our troubles begin. Although I believe that the table is 'really' of the same colour all over, the parts that reflect the light look much brighter than the other parts, and some parts look white because of reflected light. I know that, if I move, the parts that reflect the light will be different, so that the apparent distribution of colours on the table will change. It follows that if several people are looking at the table at the same moment, no two of them will see exactly the same distribution of colours, because no two can see it from exactly the same point of view, and any change in the point of view makes some change in the way the light is reflected.

For most practical purposes these differences are unimportant, but to the painter they are all-important: The painter has to unlearn the habit of thinking that things seem to have the colour which common sense says they 'really' have, and to learn the habit of seeing things as they appear. Here we have already the beginning of one of the distinctions that cause most trouble in philosophy—the distinction between appearance' and 'reality,' between what things seem to be and what they are. The painter wants to know what things seem to be, the practical man and the philosopher want to know what they are; but the philosopher's wish to know this is stronger than the practical man's, and is more troubled by knowledge as to the difficulties of answering the question.

To return to the table. It is evident from what we have found, that there is no colour which preeminently appears to be *the* colour of the table, or even of any one particular part of the table—it appears to be of different colours from different points of view, and there is no reason for regarding some of these as more really its colour than others. And we know that even from a given point of view the colour will seem different by artificial light, or to a colour-blind man, or to a man wearing blue spectacles, while in the dark there will be no colour at all, though to touch and hearing the table will be unchanged. This colour is not something which is inherent in the table, but something depending upon the table and the spectator and the way the light falls on the table. When, in ordinary life, we speak of *the* colour of the table, we only mean the sort of colour which it will seem to have to a normal spectator from an ordinary point of view under usual conditions of light. But the other colours which appear under other conditions have just as good a right to be considered real; and therefore, to avoid favouritism, we are compelled to deny that, in itself, the table has any one particular colour.

The same thing applies to the texture. With the naked eye one can see the grain, but otherwise the table looks smooth and even. If we looked at it through a microscope, we should see roughnesses and hills and valleys, and all sorts of differences that are imperceptible to the naked eye. Which of these is the 'real' table? We are naturally tempted to say that what we see through the microscope is more real, but that in turn would be changed by a still more powerful microscope. If, then, we cannot trust what we see with the naked eye, why should we trust what we see through a microscope? Thus, again, the confidence in our senses with which we began deserts us.

The *shape* of the table is no better. We are all in the habit of judging as to the 'real' shapes of things, and we do this so unreflectingly that we come to think we actually see the real shapes. But, in fact, as we all have to learn if we try to draw, a given thing looks different in shape from every different point of view. If our table is 'really' rectangular, it will look, from almost all points of view, as if it had two acute angles and two obtuse angles. If opposite sides are parallel, they will look as if they converged to a point away from the spectator; if they are of equal length, they will look as if the nearer side were longer. All these things are not commonly noticed in looking at a table, because experience has taught us to construct the 'real' shape from the apparent shape, and the 'real' shape is what interests us as practical men. But the 'real' shape is not what we see; it is something inferred from what we see. And what we see is constantly changing in shape as we move about the room; so that here again the senses seem not to give us the truth about the table itself, but only about the appearance of the table.

Similar difficulties arise when we consider the sense of touch. It is true that the table always gives us a sensation of hardness, and we feel that it resists pressure. But the sensation we obtain depends upon how hard we press the table and also upon what part of the body we press with; thus the various sensations due to various pressures or various parts of the body cannot be supposed to reveal *directly* any definite property of the table, but at most to be *signs* of some property which perhaps *causes* all the sensations, but is not actually apparent in any of them. And the same applies still more obviously to the sounds which can be elicited by rapping the table.

Thus it becomes evident that the real table, if there is one, is not the same as what we immediately experience by sight or touch or hearing. The real table, if there is one, is not *immediately* known to us at all, but must be an inference from what is immediately known. Hence, two very difficult questions at once arise; namely, (1) Is there a real table at all? (2) If so, what sort of object can it be?

It will help us in considering these questions to have a few simple terms of which the meaning is definite and clear. Let us give the name of "sense-data" to the things that are immediately known in sensation: such things as colours, sounds, smells, hardnesses, roughnesses, and so on. We shall give the name 'sensation' to the experience of being immediately aware of these things. Thus, whenever we see a colour, we have a sensation *of* the colour, but the colour itself is a sense-datum, not a sensation. The colour is that *of* which we are immediately aware, and the awareness itself is the sensation. It is plain that if we are to know anything about the table, it must be by means of the sense-data—brown colour, oblong shape, smoothness, etc.—which we associate with the table; but, for the reasons which have been given, we cannot say that the table *is* the sense-data, or even that the sense-data are directly properties of the table. Thus a problem arises as to the relation of the sense-data to the real table, supposing there is such a thing.

The real table, if it exists, we will call a 'physical object.' Thus we have to consider the relation of sense-data to physical objects. The collection of all physical objects is called 'matter.' Thus our two questions may be re-stated as follows: (1) Is there any such thing as matter? (2) If so, what is its nature?

The philosopher who first brought prominently forward the reasons for regarding the immediate objects of our senses as not existing independently of us was Bishop Berkeley (1685–1753). His *Three Dialogues between Hylas and Philonous, in Opposition to Sceptics and Atheists*, undertake to prove that there is no such thing as matter at all, and that the world consists of nothing but minds and their ideas. Hylas has hitherto believed in matter, but he is no match for Philonous, who mercilessly drives him into contradictions and paradoxes, and makes his own denial of matter seem, in the end, as if it were almost common sense. The arguments employed are of very different value: some are important and sound, others are confused or quibbling. But Berkeley retains the merit of having shown that the existence of matter is capable of being denied without absurdity, and that if there are any things that exist independently of us they cannot be the immediate objects of our sensations.

There are two different questions involved when we ask whether matter exists, and it is important to keep them clear. We commonly mean by 'matter' something which is opposed to 'mind,' something which we think of as occupying space and as radically incapable of any sort of thought or consciousness. It is chiefly in this sense that Berkeley denies matter; that is to say, he does not deny that the sense-data which we commonly take as signs of the existence of the table are really signs of the existence of *something* independent of us, but he does deny that this something is nonmental, that it is neither mind nor ideas entertained by some mind. He admits that there must be something which continues to exist when we go out of the room or shut our eyes, and that what we call seeing the table does really give us reason for believing in something which persists even when we are not seeing it. But he thinks that this something cannot be radically different in nature from what we see, and cannot be independent of seeing altogether, though it must be independent of *our* seeing. He is thus led to regard the 'real' table as an idea in the mind of God. Such an idea has the required permanence and independence of ourselves, without being—as matter would otherwise be—something quite unknowable, in the sense that we can only infer it, and can never be directly and immediately aware of it.

Other philosophers since Berkeley have also held that, although the table does not depend for its existence upon being seen by me, it does depend upon being seen (or otherwise apprehended in sensation) by *some* mind—not necessarily the mind of God, but more often the whole collective mind of the universe. This they hold, as Berkeley does, chiefly because they think there can be nothing real—or at any rate nothing known to be real—except minds and their thoughts and feelings. We might state the argument by which they support their view in some such way as this: 'Whatever can be thought of is an idea in the mind of the person thinking of it; therefore nothing can be thought of except ideas in minds; therefore anything else is inconceivable and what is inconceivable cannot exist.'

Such an argument, in my opinion, is fallacious; and of course those who advance it do not put it so shortly or so crudely. But whether valid or not, the argument has been very widely advanced in one form or another; and very many philosophers, perhaps a majority, have held that there is nothing real except minds and their ideas. Such philosophers are called 'idealists.' When they come to explaining matter, they either say, like Berkeley, that matter is really nothing but a collection of ideas, or they say, like Leibniz (1646–1716), that what appears as matter is really a collection of more or less rudimentary minds.

But these philosophers, though they deny matter as opposed to mind, nevertheless, in another sense, admit matter. It will be remembered that we asked two questions; namely, (1) Is there a real table at all? (2) If so, what sort of object can it be? Now both Berkeley and Leibniz admit that there is a real table, but Berkeley says it is certain ideas in the mind of God, and Leibniz says it is colony of souls. Thus both of them answer our first question in the affirmative, and only diverge from the views of ordinary mortals in their answer to our second question. In fact, almost all philosophers seem to be agreed that there is a real table: They almost all agree that, however much our sense-data—colour, shape, smoothness, etc.—may depend upon us, yet their occurrence is a sign of something existing independently of us, something differing, perhaps, completely from our sense-data, and yet to be regarded as causing those sense-data whenever we are in a suitable relation to the real table.

Now obviously this point in which the philosophers are agreed—the view that there *is* a real table, whatever its nature may be—is vitally important, and it will be worth while to consider what reasons there are for accepting this view before we go on to the further question as to the nature of the real table. . . .

Before we go farther it will be well to consider for a moment what it is that we have discovered so far. It has appeared that, if we take any common object of the sort that is supposed to be known by the senses, what the senses *immediately* tell us is not the truth about the object as it is apart from us, but only the truth about certain sense-data which, so far as we can see, depend upon the relations between us and the object. Thus what we directly see and feel is merely 'appearance,' which we believe to be a sign of some 'reality' behind. But if the reality is not what appears, have we any means of knowing whether there is any reality at all? And if so, have we any means of finding out what it is like?

Such questions are bewildering, and it is difficult to know that even the strangest hypotheses may not be true. Thus our familiar table, which has roused but the slightest thoughts in us hitherto, has become a problem full of surprising possibilities. The one thing we know about it is that it is not what it seems. Beyond this modest result, so far, we have the most complete liberty of conjecture. Leibniz tells us it is a community of souls: Berkeley tells us it is an idea in the mind of God; sober science, scarcely less wonderful, tells us it is a vast collection of electric charges in violent motion.

Among these surprising possibilities, doubt suggests that perhaps there is no table at all. Philosophy, if it cannot *answer* so many questions as we could wish, has at least the power of *asking* questions which increase the interest of the world, and show the strangeness and wonder lying just below the surface even in the commonest things of daily life.

Discussion Questions

1. How do you answer Russell's opening question? What would it mean to answer it "carelessly and dogmatically, as we do in ordinary life"?
2. Knowing that others view objects differently than you (i.e., his initial account of sensing the table), what relevance does that have in your everyday life?
3. In Russell's examination of the table's texture, which of the views of the table—if any—represent the real table? Do you think that a more detailed examination yields a more correct view (i.e., that the real table is the view under the most powerful microscope)? Why/why not?
4. If we really didn't have access to the sort of reality about which Russell says we may only access as appearance, how would this matter to you? Do you agree that there is virtue in just showing the "strangeness and wonder lying just below the surface" of common things?

Is the Sex of the Knower Epistemologically Significant?

Lorraine Code

Lorraine Code teaches philosophy, social and political thought, and women's studies at York University. She has published two books and a number of journal articles focusing on feminist epistemology (theory of knowledge).

This selection is from the first chapter of her book *What Can She Know? Feminist Theory and the Construction of Knowledge.* In it, she examines the significance of the person making the knowledge claim. This is a slight divergence from other theories of knowledge that typically focus on just *how* we know things. Because the majority of academic writing is from a male point of view, the feminist approach is a relatively recent addition to the discussion.

Reading Questions

1. How does Code define "epistemological relativism"? Explain the three critiques she offers regarding epistemological relativism and then the advantages she suggests.
2. According to Code, how important is the sex of the knower when one makes a knowledge claim?
3. Why does she mention Descartes and his (Cartesian) project?
4. Why does she mention the list of "western thinkers" and their theories regarding females?

The Question

A question that focuses on the knower, as the title of this chapter does, claims that there are good reasons for asking who that knower is.[1] Uncontroversial as such a suggestion would be in ordinary conversations about knowledge, academic philosophers commonly treat 'the knower' as a featureless abstraction. Sometimes, indeed, she or he is merely a place holder in the proposition 'S knows that p.' Epistemological analyses of the proposition tend to focus on the 'knowing that,' to determine conditions under which a knowledge claim can legitimately be made. Once discerned, it is believed, such conditions will hold across all possible utterances of the proposition. Indeed, throughout the history of modern philosophy the central 'problem of knowledge' has been to determine necessary and sufficient conditions for the possibility and justification of knowledge claims. Philosophers have sought ways of establishing a relation of correspondence between knowledge and 'reality' and/or ways of establishing the coherence of particular knowledge claims within systems of already-established truths. They have

Source: Reprinted from Lorraine Code: *What Can She Know? Feminist Theory and the Construction of Knowledge.* Copyright © 1991 by Cornell University. Used by permission of the publisher, Cornell University Press.

proposed methodologies for arriving at truth, and criteria for determining the validity of claims to the effect that 'S knows that p.' Such endeavors are guided by the putatively self-evident principle that truth once discerned, knowledge once established, claim their status as truth and knowledge by virtue of a grounding in or coherence within a permanent, objective, ahistorical, and circumstantially neutral framework or set of standards.

The question 'Who is S?' is regarded neither as legitimate nor as relevant in these endeavors. As inquirers into the nature and conditions of human knowledge, epistemologists commonly work from the assumption that they need concern themselves only with knowledge claims that meet certain standards of *purity*. Questions about the circumstances of knowledge acquisition serve merely to clutter and confuse the issue with contingencies and other impurities. The question 'Who is S?' is undoubtedly such a question. If it matters who S is, then it must follow that something peculiar to S's character or nature could bear on the validity of the knowledge she or he claims: that S's *identity* might count among the conditions that make that knowledge claim possible. For many philosophers, such a suggestion would undermine the cherished assumption that knowledge can—and should—be evaluated on its own merits. More seriously still, a proposal that it matters who the knower is looks suspiciously like a move in the direction of epistemological relativism. For many philosophers, an endorsement of relativism signals the end of knowledge and of epistemology.

Broadly described, epistemological relativists hold that knowledge, truth, or even 'reality' can be understood only in relation to particular sets of cultural or social circumstances, to a theoretical framework, a specifiable range of perspectives, a conceptual scheme, or a form of life. Conditions of justification, criteria of truth and falsity, and standards of rationality are likewise relative: There is no universal, unchanging framework or scheme for rational adjudication among competing knowledge claims.

Critics of relativism often argue that relativism entails incommensurability: that a relativist cannot evaluate knowledge claims comparatively. This argument is based on the contention that epistemological relativism entails conceptual relativism: that it contextualizes language just as it contextualizes knowledge, so that there remains no 'common' or neutral linguistic framework for discussion, agreement, *or* disagreement. Other critics maintain that the very concept 'knowledge' is rendered meaningless by relativism: that the only honest—and logical—move a relativist can make is once and for all to declare her or his skepticism. Where there are no universal standards, the argument goes, there can be no knowledge worthy of the name. Opponents often contend that relativism is simply incoherent because of its inescapable self-referentiality. Relativism, they argue, is subject to the same constraints as every other claim to knowledge and truth. Any claim for the truth of relativism must itself be relative to the circumstances of the claimant; hence relativism itself has no claim to objective or universal truth. In short, relativism is often perceived as a denial of the very possibility of epistemology.[2]

Now posing the question 'Who is S?'—that is, 'Who is the knowing subject?'— does indeed count as a move in the direction of relativism, and my intention in posing it is to suggest that the answer has epistemological import. But I shall invoke certain caveats to demonstrate that such a move is not the epistemological disaster that many theorists of knowledge believe it to be.

It is true that, on its starkest construal, relativism may threaten to slide into subjectivism, into a position for which knowledge claims are indistinguishable from expressions of personal opinion, taste, or bias. But relativism need not be construed so starkly, nor do its *limitations* warrant exclusive emphasis. There are advantages to endorsing a measure of epistemological relativism that make of it an enabling rather than a constraining position. By no means the least of these advantages is the fact that relativism is one of the more obvious means of avoiding reductive explanations, in terms of drastically simplified paradigms of knowledge, monolithic explanatory modes, or privileged, decontextualized positions. For a relativist, who contends that there can be many valid ways of knowing any phenomenon, there is the possibility of taking several constructions, many perspectives into account. Hence relativism keeps open a range of interpretive possibilities. At the same time, because of the epistemic choices it affirms, it creates stringent accountability requirements of which knowers have to be cognizant. Thus it introduces a moral-political component into the heart of epistemological enquiry.[3]

There probably is no absolute authority, no practice of all practices or scheme of all schemes. Yet it does not follow that conceptual schemes, practices, and paradigms are radically idiosyncratic or purely subjective. Schemes, practices, and paradigms evolve out of communal projects of inquiry. To sustain viability and authority, they must demonstrate their adequacy in enabling people to negotiate the everyday world and to cope with the decisions, problems, and puzzles they encounter daily. From the claim that no single scheme has absolute explanatory power, it does not follow that all schemes are equally valid. Knowledge is qualitatively variable: Some knowledge is *better* than other knowledge. Relativists are in a good position to take such qualitative variations into account and to analyze their implications.

Even if these points are granted, though, it would be a mistake to believe that posing the 'Who is S?' question indicates that the circumstances of the knower are *all* that counts in knowledge evaluation. The point is, rather, that understanding the circumstances of the knower makes possible a more *discerning* evaluation. The claim that certain of those circumstances are epistemologically significant— the sex of the knower, in this instance—by no means implies that they are definitive, capable of bearing the entire burden of justification and evaluation. This point requires special emphasis. Claiming epistemological significance for the sex of the knower might seem tantamount to a dismissal, to a contention that S made such a claim only because of his or her sex. Dismissals of this sort, both of women's knowledge *and* of their claims to be knowers in any sense of the word, are only too common throughout the history of western thought. But claiming that the circumstances of the knower are not epistemologically definitive is quite different from claiming that they are of no epistemological consequence. The position I take in this book is that the sex of the knower is one of a cluster of *subjective* factors (i.e., factors that pertain to the circumstances of cognitive agents) constitutive of received conceptions of knowledge and of what it means to be a knower. I maintain that subjectivity and the specificities of cognitive agency can and must be accorded central epistemological significance, yet that so doing does not commit an inquirer to outright subjectivism. Specificities count, and they require a place in epistemological evaluation, but they cannot tell the whole story.

Knowers and the Known

The only thing that is clear about S from the standard proposition 'S knows that p' is that S is a (would-be) knower. Although the question 'Who is S?' rarely arises, certain assumptions about S as knower permeate epistemological inquiry. Of special importance for my argument is the assumption that knowers are self-sufficient and solitary individuals, at least in their knowledge-seeking activities. This belief derives from a long and venerable heritage, with its roots in Descartes's quest for a basis of perfect certainty on which to establish his knowledge. The central aim of Descartes's endeavors is captured in this claim: "I shall have the right to conceive high hopes if I am happy enough to discover one thing only which is certain and indubitable."[4] That "one thing," Descartes believed, would stand as the fixed, pivotal, Archimedean point on which all the rest of his knowledge would turn. Because of its systematic relation to that point, his knowledge would be certain and indubitable.

Most significant for this discussion is Descartes's conviction that his quest will be conducted in a private, introspective examination of the contents of his own mind. It is true, in the last section of the *Discourse on the Method*, Descartes acknowledges the benefit "others may receive from the communication of [his] reflection," and he states his belief that combining "the lives and labours of many"[5] is essential to progress in scientific knowledge. It is also true that this individualistically described act of knowing exercises the aspect of the soul that is common to and alike in all knowers: namely, the faculty of reason. Yet his claim that knowledge seeking is an introspective activity of an individual mind accords no relevance either to a knower's embodiment or to his (or her) intersubjective relations. For each knower, the Cartesian route to knowledge is through private, abstract thought, through the efforts of reason unaided either by the senses or by consultation with other knowers. It is this individualistic, self-reliant, private aspect of Descartes's philosophy that has been influential in shaping subsequent epistemological ideals.

Reason is conceived as autonomous in the Cartesian project in two ways, then. Not only is the quest for certain knowledge an independent one, undertaken separately by each rational being, but it is a journey of reason alone, unassisted by the senses. For Descartes believed that sensory experiences had the effect of distracting reason from its proper course.

The custom of formulating knowledge claims in the 'S knows that p' formula is not itself of Cartesian origin. The point of claiming Cartesian inspiration for an assumption implicit in the formulation is that the knower who is commonly presumed to be the subject of that proposition is modeled, in significant respects, on the Cartesian pure inquirer. For epistemological purposes, all knowers are believed to be alike with respect both to their cognitive capacities and to their methods of achieving knowledge. In the empiricist tradition this assumption is apparent in the belief that simple, basic observational data can provide the foundation of knowledge just because perception is invariant from observer to observer, in standard observation conditions. . . .

Just what am I asking, then, with this question about the epistemological *significance* of the sex of the knower? First, I do not expect that the question will elicit the answer that the sex of the knower is pertinent among conditions for the existence of knowledge, in the sense that taking it into account will make it possible to avoid skepticism. Again, it is unlikely that information about the sex of the knower could count among criteria of evidence or means of justifying knowledge claims. Nor is it prima facie obvious that the sex of the knower will have a legitimate bearing on the qualitative judgments that could be made about certain claims to know. Comparative judgments of the following kind are not what I expect to elicit: that if the knower is female, her knowledge is likely to be better grounded; if the knower is male, his knowledge will likely be more coherent.

In proposing that the sex of the knower is epistemologically significant, I am claiming that the scope of epistemological inquiry has been too narrowly defined. My point is not to denigrate projects of establishing the best foundations possible or of developing workable criteria of coherence. I am proposing that even if it is not possible (or not *yet* possible) to establish an unassailable foundationlist or coherentist position, there are numerous questions to be asked about knowledge whose answers matter to people who are concerned to know well. Among them are questions that bear not just on criteria of evidence, justification, and warrantability, but on the 'nature' of cognitive agents: questions about their character; their material, historical, cultural circumstances; their interests in the inquiry at issue. These are questions about how credibility is established, about connections between knowledge and power, about the place of knowledge in ethical and aesthetic judgments, and about political agendas and the responsibilities of knowers. I am claiming that all of these questions are epistemologically significant.

The Sex of the Knower

What, then, of the sex of the knower? In the rest of this chapter . . . I examine some attempts to give content to the claim that the sex of the knower *is* epistemologically significant.[6] Many of these endeavors have been less than satisfactory. Nonetheless, I argue that the claim itself is accurate.

Although it has rarely been spelled out prior to the development of feminist critiques, it has long been tacitly assumed that S is male. Nor could S be just any man, the apparently infinite substitutability of the 'S' term notwithstanding. The S who could count as a model, paradigmatic knower has most commonly—if always tacitly—been an adult (but not old), white, reasonably affluent (latterly middle-class) educated man of status, property, and publicly acceptable accomplishments. In theory of knowledge he has been allowed to stand for all men.[7] This assumption does not merely derive from habit or coincidence, but is a manifestation of engrained philosophical convictions. Not only has it been taken for granted that knowers properly so-called are male, but when male philosophers have paused to note this fact, as some indeed have done, they have argued that things are as they should be. Reason may be alike in all men, but it would be a mistake to believe that 'man,' in this respect, 'embraces woman.' Women have been judged incapable, for many reasons, of achieving knowledge worthy of the name. It is no exaggeration to say that anyone who wanted to *count* as a knower has commonly had to be male.

In the *Politics*, Aristotle observes: "The freeman rules over the slave after another manner from that in which the male rules over the female, or the man over the child; although the parts of the soul are present in all of them, they are present in different degrees. For the slave has no deliberative faculty at all; the woman has, but it is without authority, and the child has, but it is immature."[8] Aristotle's assumption that a woman will naturally be ruled by a man connects directly with his contention that a woman's deliberative faculty is "without authority." Even if a woman could, in her sequestered, domestic position, acquire deliberative skills, she would remain reliant on her husband for her sources of knowledge and information. She must be ruled by a man because, in the social structure of the *polis*, she enjoys neither the autonomy nor the freedom to put into visible practice the results of the deliberations she may engage in, in private. If she can claim no authority for her rational, deliberative endeavors, then her chances of gaining recognition as a knowledgeable citizen are seriously limited, whatever she may do.[9]

Aristotle is just one of a long line of western thinkers to declare the limitations of women's cognitive capacities.[10] Rousseau maintains that young men and women should be educated quite differently because of women's inferiority in reason and their propensity to be dragged down by their sensual natures. For Kierkegaard, women are merely aesthetic beings: Men alone can attain the (higher) ethical and religious levels of existence. And for Nietzsche, the Apollonian (intellectual) domain is the male preserve, whereas women are Dionysian (sensuous) creatures. Nineteenth-century philosopher and linguist Wilhelm von Humboldt, who writes at length about women's knowledge, sums up the central features of this line of thought as follows: "A sense of truth exists in [women] quite literally as a sense: . . . their nature also contains a lack or a failing of analytic capacity which draws a strict line of demarcation between ego and world; therefore, they will not come as close to the ultimate investigation of truth as man."[11] The implication is that women's knowledge, if ever the products of their projects deserve that label, is inherently and inevitably *subjective*—in the most idiosyncratic sense—by contrast with the best of men's knowledge.

Objectivity, quite precisely construed, is commonly regarded as a defining feature of knowledge per se.[12] So if women's knowledge is declared to be *naturally* subjective, then a clear answer emerges to my question. The answer is that if the would-be knower is female, then her sex is indeed epistemologically significant, for it disqualifies her as a knower in the fullest sense of that term. Such disqualifications will operate differently for women of different classes, races, ages, and allegiances, but in every circumstance they will operate asymmetrically for women and for men. . . .

The presuppositions I have just cited claim more than the rather simple fact that many kinds of knowledge and skill have, historically, been inaccessible to women on a purely practical level. It is true, historically speaking, that even women who were the racial and social 'equals' of standard male knowers were only rarely able to become learned. The thinkers I have cited (and others like them) claim to find a rationale for this state of affairs through appeals to dubious 'facts' about women's natural incapacity for rational thought. Yet deeper questions still need to be asked: Is there knowledge that is, quite simply, inaccessible to members of the female, or the male, sex? Are there kinds of knowledge that only men, or only women, can acquire? Is the sex of the knower crucially determining in this respect, across all other specificities? The answers to these questions should not address only the *practical* possibilities that have existed for members of either sex. Such practical possibilities are the constructs of complex social arrangements that are themselves constructed out of historically specific choices, and are, as such, open to challenge and change.

Knowledge, as it achieves credence and authoritative status at any point in the history of the male-dominated mainstream, is commonly held to be a product of the individual efforts of human knowers. References to Pythagoras's theorem, Copernicus's revolution, and Newtonian and Einsteinian physics signal an epistemic community's attribution of pathbreaking contributions to certain of its individual members. The implication is that *that* person, singlehandedly, has effected a leap of progress in a particular field of inquiry. In less publicly spectacular ways, other cognitive agents are represented as contributors to the growth and stability of public knowledge.

Now any contention that such contributions are the results of independent endeavor is highly contestable. As I argue elsewhere,[13] a complex of historical and other sociocultural factors produces the conditions that make 'individual' achievement possible, and 'individuals' themselves are socially constituted.[14] The claim that individual *men* are the creators of the authoritative (often Kuhn-paradigm-establishing) landmarks of western intellectual life is particularly interesting for the fact that the contributions—both practical and substantive—of their lovers, wives, children, servants, neighbors, friends, and colleagues rarely figure in analyses of their work.[15]

The historical attribution of such achievements to specific cognitive agents does, nonetheless, accord a significance to individual efforts which raises questions pertinent to my project. It poses the problem, in another guise, of whether aspects of human specificity could, in fact, constitute conditions for the existence of knowledge or determine the kinds of knowledge that a knower can achieve. It would seem that such incidental physical attributes as height, weight, or hair color would not count among factors that would determine a person's capacities to know (though the arguments that skin color *does* count are too familiar). It is not necessary to consider how much Archimedes weighed when he made his famous discovery, nor is there any doubt that a thinner or a fatter person could have reached the same conclusion. But in cultures in which sex differences figure prominently in virtually every mode of human interaction,[16] being female or male is far more fundamental to the construction of subjectivity than are such attributes as size or hair color. So the question is whether femaleness or maleness are the kinds of subjective factor (i.e., factors about the circumstances of a knowing subject) that are constitutive of the form and content of knowledge. Attempts to answer this question are complicated by the fact that sex/gender does not function uniformly and universally, even in western societies. Its implications vary across class, race, age, ability, and numerous other interwoven specificities. A separated analysis of sex/gender, then, always risks abstraction and is limited in its scope by the abstracting process. Further, the question seems to imply that sex and gender are themselves constants, thus obscuring the processes of *their* sociocultural construction. Hence the formulation of adequately nuanced answers is problematic and necessarily partial.

Even if it should emerge that gender-related factors play a crucial role in the construction of knowledge, then, the inquiry into the epistemological significance of the sex of the knower would not be complete. The task would remain of considering whether a distinction between 'natural' and socialized capacity can retain any validity. The equally pressing question as to how the hitherto devalued products of *women's* cognitive projects can gain acknowledgment as 'knowledge' would need to be addressed so as to uproot entrenched prejudices about knowledge, epistemology, and women. 'The epistemological project' will look quite different once its tacit underpinnings are revealed. . . .

Knowledge, Methodology, and Power

. . . Feminist philosophy simply did not exist until philosophers learned to perceive the near-total absence of women in philosophical writings from the very beginning of western philosophy, to stop assuming that 'man' could be read as a generic term. Explicit denigrations of women, which became the focus of philosophical writing in the early years of the contemporary women's movement, were more readily perceptible. The authors of derogatory views about women in classical texts clearly needed power to be able to utter their pronouncements with impunity: a power they claimed from a 'received' discourse that represented women's nature in such a way that women undoubtedly merited the negative judgments that Aristotle or Nietzsche made about them. Women are now in a position to recognize and refuse these overt manifestations of contempt.

The covert manifestations are more intransigent. Philosophers, when they have addressed the issue at all, have tended to group philosophy with science as the most gender-neutral of disciplines. But feminist critiques reveal that this alleged neutrality masks a bias in favor of institutionalizing stereotypical masculine values into the fabric of the discipline—its methods, norms, and contents. In so doing, it suppresses values, styles, problems, and concerns stereotypically associated with femininity. Thus, whether by chance or by design, it creates a hegemonic philosophical practice in which the sex of the knower is, indeed, epistemologically significant.

Discussion Questions

1. When evaluating a claim, do you take into account *who* is making it? In what ways does the knower affect what is known? Age? Sex? Culture? Time in history?
2. Many suggest that, to some extent, males and females view the world differently. Do you agree with this? In what way? Given that, how do you think areas like history, philosophy, politics, ethics, and science would be different if these endeavors were done equally by males and females versus how they have been done up to this point—a huge majority by males?
3. Is all of your knowledge *absolute* knowledge, or do you know things to a certain degree? How does this relate to a subjective approach to epistemology?

Movie Titles

1. *The Matrix* (R)—Deals with themes of reality, how active our brain is in creating our perception, and free will.
2. *Existenz* (R)—About a futuristic virtual reality game. What level of the game is reality?
3. *Rashomon*—1950s film about four witnesses' versions of a crime. Is an objective view of reality possible? What might prevent us from seeing/remembering events as they "really" happened?
4. *Twelve Angry Men*—A good example of critical thinking and talking through a topic thoroughly in order to come to a conclusion.
5. *Alice in Wonderland*—Portrays Lewis Carroll's playful use of language and logic.
6. *Pi* (R)—One disturbed man's view of a reality totally driven by mathematics. To what extent does math depict reality?

Song Lyrics

The Beatles—"Within You Without You"
311—"Reconsider Everything"
311—"Still Dreaming"
Bad Religion—"The Answer"
Queens of the Stone Age—"No One Knows"
Eyedeas and Abilities—"Birth Of A Fish . . ."
Eyedeas and Abilities—". . . Powdered Water Too"
The Mighty Mighty Bosstones—"I Know More"

Notes

1. This question is the title of my paper published in *Metaphilosophy* 12 (July–October 1981): 267–276. In this early essay I endorse an essentialism with respect to masculinity and femininity, and convey the impression that 'positive thinking' can bring an end to gender imbalances. I would no longer make these claims.

2. I consider some of these objections to relativism at greater length in "The Importance of Historicism of a Theory of Knowledge," *International Philosophical Quarterly* 22 (June 1982): 157–174.

3. I discuss some of these accountability requirements, and the normative realism from which they derive, in my *Epistemic Responsibility* (Hanover, N.H.: University Press of New England, 1987).

4. René Descartes, *Meditations*, in *The Philosophical Works of Descartes*, trans. Elizabeth S. Haldane and G.R.T Ross (Cambridge: Cambridge University Press, 1969), 1:149.

5. René Descartes, *Discourse on the Method of Rightly Conducting the Reason and Seeking* for *Truth in the Sciences* in ibid., pp. 124, 120.

6. In this chapter I discuss the sex of the knower in a way that may seem to conflate biological sex differences with their cultural elaborations and manifestations as gender differences. I retain the older term—albeit inconsistently—for two reasons. The first, personally historical, reason connects this text with my first thoughts on these matters, published in my *Metaphilosophy* paper (see note 1, above). The second, philosophically historical, reason reflects the relatively recent appearance of 'gender' as a theoretical term of art. In the history of 'the epistemological project,' which I discuss in these early chapters, 'sex' would have been the term used, had these questions been raised.

7. To cite just one example: in *The Theory of Epistemic Rationality* (Cambridge: Harvard University Press, 1987), Richard Foley appeals repeatedly to the epistemic judgments of people who are "like the rest of us" (p. 108). He contrasts their beliefs with beliefs that seem "crazy or bizarre or outlandish . . . beliefs to most of the rest of us" (p. 114), and argues that an account of rational belief is plausible only if it can be presented from "some nonweird perspective" (p. 140). Foley contends that "an individual has to be at least minimally like us in order for charges of irrationality even to make sense" (p. 240). Nowhere does he address the question of who 'we' are. (I take this point up again in Chapter 7.)

8. Aristotle, *Politics*, trans. Benjamin Jowett, in *The Basic Works of Aristotle*, ed. Richard McKenn (New York: Random House, 1941), 1260b.

9. I discuss the implications of this lack of authority more fully in Chapters 9 and 6. See Elizabeth V. Spelman, *Inessential Woman: Problems of Exclusion in Feminist Thought* (Boston: Beacon, 1988), for an interesting discussion of some more complex exclusions effected by Aristotle's analysis.

10. It would be inaccurate, however, to argue that this line is unbroken. Londa Schiebinger demonstrates that in the history of science—and, by implication, the history of the achievement of epistemic authority—there were many periods when women's intellectual achievements were not only recognized but respected. The "long line" I refer to is the dominant, historically most visible one. Schiebinger, *The Mind Has No Sex? Women in the Origins of Modern Science* (Cambridge: Harvard University Press, 1989).

11. *Humanist without Portfolio: An Anthology of the Writings of Wilhelm von Humboldt*, trans. with intro. by Marianne Cowan (Detroit: Wayne State University Press, 1963), p. 349.

12. I analyze this precise construal of objectivity in Chapter 2.

13. See chap. 7, "Epistemic Community," of my *Epistemic Responsibility*.

14. I discuss the implications of these points for analysis of subjectivity in Chapter 3.

15. I owe this point—and the list—to Polly Young-Eisendrath, "The Female Person and How We Talk about Her," in Mary M. Gergen, ed., *Feminist Thought and the Structure of Knowledge* (New York: New York University Press, 1988).

16. Marilyn Frye points out: "Sex-identification intrudes into every moment of our lives and discourse, no matter what the supposedly primary focus or topic of the moment is. Elaborate, systematic, ubiquitous and redundant marking of a distinction between two sexes of humans and most animals is customary and obligatory. One *never* can ignore it." Frye, *The Politics of Reality: Essays in Feminist Theory* (Trumansburg, N.Y.: Crossing Press 1983), p. 19.

Chapter 2

Self, Mind, and Soul

An ancient paradox given to us by Plutarch goes something like this: A ship's parts are replaced slowly over time and stored in a warehouse. Eventually, every part of the ship has been replaced so that every original part (now all somewhat dilapidated) lies in the warehouse and the ship floating in the harbor—with the same name, function, etc., as before—has entirely new parts. If we want to identify the *actual* ship, which one is it? The reassembled collection of original parts in the warehouse or the one in the harbor? It cannot be *both*—while the two could be similar, they can't be identical. So, if it's the one in the warehouse, when did the original ship cease to be that ship? And if it's the one in the harbor, how do you justify it, given that *nothing* on that ship remains from its inception?

A similar situation occurs with persons. As you may have seen in the movies or at least heard the science-fiction dilemma, your brain is taken out of your head and put into the head of another body. Where are *you* now? In another situation, just your *thoughts* and *memories* are taken from your brain and placed in the brain of another. Were *you* transferred to that other brain? When *you* go to the afterlife, what about *you* goes there? When your body completely changes over an 80-year life span, along with your thoughts and memories, where does the *self* remain?

One popular answer to this last question is often given as something non-physical or metaphysical ("beyond physics"), such as the *soul* or *mind*. This, however, introduces a myriad of new problems. How does something non-physical reside in and affect a physical body? When did humans acquire souls in history, and when do individual humans acquire their respective souls?

This section is not only of great philosophical import, but has practical consequences as well. These topics relate to many present-day issues and those on the cusp of the future: cloning, abortion, and end-of-life issues; artificial intelligence; animal rights; plastic surgery; alien life forms; and intimately connected religious issues as well. It can have great personal value as well in helping to provide a genuine answer to the question "Who am I?"

The first part of this section deals with the philosophical issue of "personal identity"—what it means to be the same person (i.e., identical to your self) over time. Both Hume and the Buddhist theory hold that this concept is a fiction—that the *self* is not a real thing but merely a concept that we build into the universe in order to help us explain things. Daniel Dennett provides an overview of the issue through a fictional story.

The second part of this section examines the notion of the mind and soul. Descartes first proposes what this soul is and how it functions. Searle helps to frame the issues surrounding the notion, and Nagel provides us with a defense of the mind, given the fact that not everything can be broken down ("reduced") into physical components, which is a theory defended by Smart. Ryle takes a different approach by arguing against a soul based on language—that we simply speak incorrectly when we speak of a body *and* a soul.

Of Personal Identity

David Hume

Many refer to Scottish philosopher David Hume as the "consummate skeptic"—casting doubt on much of what we consider true, and even common, knowledge. He has also been called the most important philosopher who has ever written in English. Hume wrote on many subjects, including politics, epistemology, and metaphysics, and even tutored Adam Smith in political economy. He became known as a religious skeptic and this kept him from holding positions at Edinburgh and Glasgow Universities in Scotland. This freed him to write a six-volume *History of England*, as well as his *Natural History of Religion*.

In this passage, from his *A Treatise of Human Nature* (published anonymously at age 27), Hume refutes the commonly held notion of the "self"—something that persists over time and maintains sameness or identity. He not only gives a positive account as to why this is the case, but also defends against others' positions, including John Locke's notion that our consistent consciousness and memories provide the basis for our maintaining sameness over time.

Reading Questions

1. In the opening paragraphs, Hume argues against the positions held by "some philosophers." How does he frame *their* positions and then what problem does he have with them?
2. What are the two ideas of identity that Hume describes? What is his purpose in making this distinction?
3. Explain Hume's mention of *purpose* as it relates to identity (and to his analogy of a ship).
4. How does he apply the following analogies?
    a. The mind-as-theater
    b. The ship
    c. A particular noise and a church as they relate to "numerical sameness"
    d. The river
    e. The soul as compared to a republic/commonwealth
5. How does Hume show that identity fails to be maintained by his three suggested criteria: contiguity, resemblance, and causation?
6. What problem does Hume suggest occurs when we assert that our identity over time is couched in memory?

There are some philosophers, who imagine we are every moment intimately conscious of what we call our *self*; that we feel its existence and its continuance in, existence; and are certain, beyond the evidence of a demonstration, both of its perfect identity and simplicity. The strongest sensation, the most violent passion, say they, instead of distracting us from this view, only fix it the more

Source: *A Treatise of Human Nature*, first published 1793. Section 6 of Part IV.

intensely, and make us consider their influence on *self* either by their pain or pleasure. To attempt a farther proof of this were to weaken its evidence; since no proof
can be derived from any fact of which we are so intimately conscious; nor is there
any thing, of which we can be certain, if we doubt of this.

Unluckily all these positive assertions are contrary to that very experience
which is pleaded for them; nor have we any idea of *self*, after the manner it is here
explained. For, from what impression could this idea be derived? This question
'tis impossible to answer without a manifest contradiction and absurdity; and yet
'tis a question which must necessarily be answered, if we would have the idea of
self pass for clear and intelligible. It must be some one impression that gives rise
to every real idea. But self or person is not any one impression, but that to which
our several impressions and ideas are supposed to have a reference. If any impression gives rise to the idea of self, that impression must continue invariably the
same, through the whole course of our lives; since self is supposed to exist after
that manner. But there is no impression constant and invariable. Pain and pleasure, grief and joy, passions and sensations succeed each other, and never all exist
at the same time. It cannot therefore be from any of these impressions, or from
any other, that the idea of self is derived; and consequently there is no such idea.

But farther, what must become of all our particular perceptions upon this
hypothesis? All these are different, and distinguishable, and separable from each
other, and may be separately considered, and may exist separately, and have no
need of any thing to support their existence. After what manner therefore do they
belong to self, and how are they connected with it? For my part, when I enter
most intimately into what I call *myself*, I always stumble on some particular perception or other, of heat or cold, light or shade, love or hatred, pain or pleasure. I
never can catch *myself* at any time without a perception, and never can observe
any thing but the perception. When my perceptions are removed for any time, as
by sound sleep, so long am I insensible of *myself*, and may truly be said not to
exist. And were all my perceptions removed by death, and could I neither think,
nor feel, nor see, nor love, nor hate, after the dissolution of my body, I should be
entirely annihilated, nor do I conceive what is farther requisite to make me a perfect nonentity. If any one, upon serious and unprejudiced reflection, thinks he has
a different notion of *himself*, I must confess I can reason no longer with him. All I
can allow him is, that he may be in the right as well as I, and that we are essentially
different in this particular. He may, perhaps, perceive something simple and
continued, which he calls *himself*; though I am certain there is no such principle
in me.

But setting aside some metaphysicians of this kind, I may venture to affirm of
the rest of mankind, that they are nothing but a bundle or collection of different
perceptions, which succeed each other with an inconceivable rapidity, and are in
a perpetual flux and movement. Our eyes cannot turn in their sockets without
varying our perceptions. Our thought is still more variable than our sight; and all
our other senses and faculties contribute to this change; nor is there any single
power of the soul, which remains unalterably the same, perhaps for one moment.
The mind is a kind of theatre, where several perceptions successively make their

appearance; pass, repass, glide away, and mingle in an infinite variety of postures and situations. There is properly no *simplicity* in it at one time, nor *identity* in different, whatever natural propension we may have to imagine that simplicity and identity. The comparison of the theatre must not mislead us. They are the successive perceptions only, that constitute the mind; nor have we the most distant notion of the place where these scenes are represented, or of the materials of which it is composed.

What then gives us so great a propension to ascribe an identity to these successive perceptions, and to suppose ourselves possessed of an invariable and uninterrupted existence through the whole course of our lives? In order to answer this question, we must distinguish betwixt personal identity, as it regards our thought or imagination, and as it regards our passions or the concern we take in ourselves. The first is our present subject; and to explain it perfectly we must take the matter pretty deep, and account for that identity, which we attribute to plants and animals; there being a great analogy betwixt it and the identity of a self or person.

We have a distinct idea of an object that remains invariable and uninterrupted through a supposed variation of time; and this idea we call that of *identity* or *sameness*. We have also a distinct idea of several different objects existing in succession, and connected together by a close relation; and this to an accurate view affords as perfect a notion of *diversity*, as if there was no manner of relation among the objects. But though these two ideas of identity, and a succession of related objects, be in themselves perfectly distinct, and even contrary, yet 'tis certain that, in our common way of thinking, they are generally confounded with each other. That action of the imagination, by which we consider the uninterrupted and invariable object, and that by which we reflect on the succession of related objects, are almost the same to the feeling; nor is there much more effort of thought required in the latter case than in the former. The relation facilitates the transition of the mind from one object to another, and renders its passage as smooth as if it contemplated one continued object. This resemblance is the cause of the confusion and mistake, and makes us substitute the notion of identity, instead of that of related objects. However at one instant we may consider the related succession as variable or interrupted, we are sure the next to ascribe to it a perfect identity, and regard it as invariable and uninterrupted. Our propensity to this mistake is so great from the resemblance above mentioned, that we fall into it before we are aware; and though we incessantly correct ourselves by reflection, and return to a more accurate method of thinking, yet we cannot long sustain our philosophy, or take off this bias from the imagination. Our last resource is to yield to it, and boldly assert that these different related objects are in effect the same, however interrupted and variable. In order to justify to ourselves this absurdity, we often feign some new and unintelligible principle, that connects the objects together, and prevents their interruption or variation. Thus, we feign the continued existence of the perceptions of our senses, to remove the interruption; and run into the notion of a *soul*, and *self*, and *substance*, to disguise the variation. But, we may farther observe, that where we do not give rise to such a fiction, our propension to confound identity with relation is so great, that we are apt to imagine something unknown and mysterious,* connecting the parts, beside their relation; and this I take to be the case with regard to the identity we ascribe to plants and vegetables. And even when this does not take place, we still feel a propensity to confound these ideas, though we are not able fully to satisfy ourselves in that particular, nor find any thing invariable and uninterrupted to justify our notion of identity.

Thus, the controversy concerning identity is not merely a dispute of words. For, when we attribute identity, in an improper sense, to variable or interrupted objects, our mistake is not confined to the expression, but is commonly attended with a fiction, either of something invariable and uninterrupted, or of something mysterious and inexplicable, or at least with a propensity to such fictions. What will suffice to prove this hypothesis to the satisfaction of every fair inquirer, is to show, from daily experience and observation, that the objects which are variable or interrupted, and yet are supposed to continue the same, are such only as consist of a succession of parts, connected together by resemblance, contiguity, or causation. For as such a succession answers evidently to our notion of diversity, it can only be by mistake we ascribe to it an identity; and as the relation of parts, which leads us into this mistake, is really nothing but a quality, which produces an association of ideas, and an easy transition of the imagination from one to another, it can only be from the resemblance, which this act of the mind bears to that by which we contemplate one continued object, that the error arises. Our chief business, then, must be to prove, that all objects, to which we ascribe identity, without observing their invariableness and uninterruptedness, are such as consist of a succession of related objects.

In order to this, suppose any mass of matter, of which the parts are contiguous and connected, to be placed before us; 'tis plain we must attribute a perfect identity to this mass, provided all the parts continue uninterruptedly and invariably the same, whatever motion or change of place we may observe either in the whole or in any of the parts. But supposing some very *small* or *inconsiderable* part to be added to the mass, or subtracted from it; though this absolutely destroys the identity of the whole, strictly speaking, yet as we seldom think so accurately, we scruple not to pronounce a mass of matter the same, where we find so trivial an alteration. The passage of the thought from the object before the change to the object after it, is so smooth and easy, that we scarce perceive the transition, and are apt to imagine, that 'tis nothing but a continued survey of the same object.

There is a very remarkable circumstance that attends this experiment; which is, that though the change of any considerable part in a mass of matter destroys the identity of the whole, yet we must measure the greatness of the part, not absolutely, but by its *proportion* to the whole. The addition or diminution of a mountain would not be sufficient to produce a diversity in a planet; though the

*If the reader is desirous to see how a great genius may be influenced by these seemingly trivial principles of the imagination, as well as the mere vulgar, let him read my Lord Shaftsbury's reasonings concerning the uniting principle of the universe, and the identity of plants and animals. See his *Moralists*, or *Philosophical Rhapsody*.

change of a very few inches would be able to destroy the identity of some bodies. 'Twill be impossible to account for this, but by reflecting that objects operate upon the mind, and break or interrupt the continuity of its actions, not according to their real greatness, but according to their proportion to each other; and therefore, since this interruption makes an object cease to appear the same, it must be the uninterrupted progress of the thought which constitutes the imperfect identity.

This may be confirmed by another phenomenon. A change in any considerable part of a body destroys its identity; but 'tis remarkable, that where the change is produced *gradually* and *insensibly,* we are less apt to ascribe to it the same effect. The reason can plainly be no other, than that the mind, in following the successive changes of the body, feels an easy passage from the surveying its condition in one moment, to the viewing of it in another, and in no particular time perceives any interruption in its actions. From which continued perception, it ascribes a continued existence and identity to the object.

But whatever precaution we may use in introducing the changes gradually, and making them proportionable to the whole, 'tis certain, that where the changes are at last observed to become considerable, we make a scruple of ascribing identity to such different objects. There is, however, another artifice, by which we may induce the imagination to advance a step farther; and that is, by producing a reference of the parts to each other, and a combination to some *common end* or purpose. A ship, of which a considerable part has been changed by frequent reparations, is still considered as the same; nor does the difference of the materials hinder us from ascribing an identity to it. The common end, in which the parts conspire, is the same under all their variations, and affords an easy transition of the imagination from one situation of the body to another.

But this is still more remarkable, when we add a *sympathy* of parts to their *common end,* and suppose that they bear to each other the reciprocal relation of cause and effect in all their actions and operations. This is the case with all animals and vegetables; where not only the several parts have a reference to some general purpose, but also a mutual dependence on, and connexion with, each other. The effect of so strong a relation is, that though every one must allow, that in a very few years both vegetables and animals endure a *total* change, yet we still attribute identity to them, while their form, size, and substance, are entirely altered. An oak that grows from a small plant to a large tree is still the same oak, though there be not one particle of matter or figure of its parts the same. An infant becomes a man, and is sometimes fat, sometimes lean, without any change in his identity.

We may also consider the two following phenomena, which are remarkable in their kind. The first is, that though we commonly be able to distinguish pretty exactly betwixt numerical and specific identity, yet it sometimes happens that we confound them, and in our thinking and reasoning employ the one for the other. Thus, a man who hears a noise that is frequently interrupted and renewed, says it is still the same noise, though 'tis evident the sounds have only a specific identity or resemblance, and there is nothing numerically the same but the cause which produced them. In like manner it may be said, without breach of the propriety of language, that such a church, which was formerly of brick, fell to ruin, and that the parish rebuilt the same church of freestone, and according to modern architecture. Here neither the form nor materials are the same, nor is there any thing common to the two objects but their relation to the inhabitants of the parish; and yet this alone is sufficient to make us denominate them the same. But we must observe, that in these cases the first object is in a manner annihilated before the second comes into existence; by which means, we are never presented, in any one point of time, with the idea of difference and multiplicity; and for that reason are less scrupulous in calling them the same.

Secondly, we may remark, that though, in a succession of related objects, it be in a manner requisite that the change of parts be not sudden nor entire, in order to preserve the identity, yet where the objects are in their nature changeable and inconstant, we admit of a more sudden transition than would otherwise be consistent with that relation. Thus, as the nature of a river consists in the motion and change of parts, though in less than four-and-twenty hours these be totally altered, this hinders not the river from continuing the same during several ages. What is natural and essential to any thing is, in a manner, expected; and what is expected makes less impression, and appears of less moment than what is unusual and extraordinary. A considerable change of the former kind seems really less to the imagination than the most trivial alteration of the latter; and by breaking less the continuity of the thought, has less influence in destroying the identity.

We now proceed to explain the nature of *personal identity*, which has become so great a question in philosophy, especially of late years, in England, where all the abstruser sciences are studied with a peculiar ardour and application. And here 'tis evident the same method of reasoning must be continued which has so successfully explained the identity of plants, and animals, and ships, and houses, and of all the compounded and changeable productions either of art or nature. The identity which we ascribe to the mind of man is only a fictitious one, and of a like kind with that which we ascribe to vegetables and animal bodies. It cannot therefore have a different origin, but must proceed from a like operation of the imagination upon like objects.

But lest this argument should not convince the reader, though in my opinion perfectly decisive, let him weigh the following reasoning, which is still closer and more immediate. 'Tis evident that the identity which we attribute to the human mind, however perfect we may imagine it to be, is not able to run the several different perceptions into one, and make them lose their characters of distinction and difference, which are essential to them. 'Tis still true that every distinct perception which enters into the composition of the mind, is a distinct existence, and is different, and distinguishable, and separable from every other perception, either contemporary or successive. But as, notwithstanding this distinction and separability, we suppose the whole train of perceptions to be united by identity, a question naturally arises concerning this relation of identity, whether it be something that really binds our several perceptions together, or only associates their ideas in the imagination; that is, in other words, whether, in pronouncing concerning the identity of a person, we observe some real bond among his perceptions, or only feel one among the ideas we form of them. This question we might easily decide, if we would recollect what has been already proved at large, that the understanding never observes any real connexion among objects, and that even the union of cause and effect, when strictly examined, resolves itself into a customary association of ideas. For from thence it evidently follows, that identity is nothing really belonging to these different perceptions, and uniting them together, but is merely a quality which we attribute to them, because of the union of their ideas in the imagination when we reflect upon them. Now, the only qualities which can give ideas an union in the imagination, are these three relations above mentioned. These are the uniting principles in the ideal world, and without them every distinct object is separable by the mind, and may be separately considered, and appears not to have any more connexion with any other object than if disjoined by the greatest difference and remoteness. 'Tis therefore on some of these three relations of resemblance, contiguity, and causation, that identity depends; and as the very essence of these relations consists in their producing an easy transition of ideas, it follows, that our notions of personal identity proceed entirely from the smooth and uninterrupted progress of the thought along a train of connected ideas, according to the principles above explained.

The only question, therefore, which remains is, by what relations this uninterrupted progress of our thought is produced, when we consider the successive existence of a mind or thinking person. And here 'tis evident we must confine ourselves to resemblance and causation, and must drop contiguity, which has little or no influence in the present case.

To begin with *resemblance*; suppose we could see clearly into the breast of another, and observe that succession of perceptions which constitutes his mind or thinking principle, and suppose that he always preserves the memory of a considerable part of past perceptions, 'tis evident that nothing could more contribute to the bestowing a relation on this succession amidst all its variations. For what is the memory but a faculty, by which we raise up the images of past perceptions? And as an image necessarily resembles its object, must not the frequent placing of these resembling perceptions in the chain of thought, convey the imagination more easily from one link to another, and make the whole seem like the continuance of one object? In this particular, then, the memory not only discovers the identity, but also contributes to its production, by producing the relation of resemblance among the perceptions. The case is the same, whether we consider ourselves or others.

As to *causation*; we may observe, that the true idea of the human mind, is to consider it as a system of different perceptions or different existences, which are linked together by the relation of cause and effect, and mutually produce, destroy, influence, and modify each other. Our impressions give rise to their correspondent idea; and these ideas, in their turn, produce other impressions. One thought chases another, and draws after it a third, by which it is expelled in its turn. In this respect, I cannot compare the soul more properly to any thing than to a republic or commonwealth, in which the several members are united by the reciprocal ties of government and subordination, and give rise to other persons who propagate the same republic in the incessant changes of its parts. And as the same individual republic may not only change its members, but also its laws and constitutions; in like manner the same person may vary his character and disposition, as well as his impressions and ideas, without losing his identity. Whatever changes he endures, his several parts are still connected by the relation of causation. And in this view our identity with regard to the passions serves to corroborate that with regard to the imagination, by the making our distant perceptions influence each other, and by giving us a present concern for our past or future pains or pleasures.

As memory alone acquaints us with the continuance and extent of this succession of perceptions, 'tis to be considered, upon that account chiefly, as the source of personal identity. Had we no memory, we never should have any notion of causation, nor consequently of that chain of causes and effects, which constitute our self or person. But having once acquired this notion of causation from the memory, we can extend the same chain of causes, and consequently the identity of our persons beyond our memory, and can comprehend times, and circumstances, and actions, which we have entirely forgot, but suppose in general to have existed. For how few of our past actions are there, of which we have any memory? Who can tell me, for instance, what were his thoughts and actions on the first of January 1715, the eleventh of March 1719, and the third of August 1733? Or will he affirm, because he has entirely forgot the incidents of these days, that the present self is not the same person with the self of that time; and by that means overturn all the most established notions of personal identity? In this view, therefore, memory does not so much *produce* as *discover* personal identity, by showing us the relation of cause and effect among our different perceptions. 'Twill be incumbent on those who affirm that memory produces entirely our personal identity, to give a reason why we can thus extend our identity beyond our memory.

The whole of this doctrine leads us to a conclusion, which is of great importance in the present affair, viz. that all the nice and subtle questions concerning personal identity can never possibly be decided, and are to be regarded rather as grammatical than as philosophical difficulties. Identity depends on the relations of ideas; and these relations produce identity, by means of that easy transition they occasion. But as the relations, and the easiness of the transition may diminish by insensible degrees, we have no just standard by which we can decide any dispute concerning the time when they acquire or lose a title to the name of identity. All the disputes concerning the identity of connected objects are merely verbal, except so far as the relation of parts gives rise to some fiction or imaginary principle of union.

Discussion Questions

1. Has Hume successfully argued against arguments for personal identity? Are you satisfied with his definition and criteria for personal identity or has he defined it too strictly? What are your criteria, if any, for maintaining sameness/identity over time?

2. Hume makes the point of *proportional change*: A few *feet* of change in a mountain affects an entire planet's identity much less than a few *inches* of change affects a person's identity. Does this make notions of change and identity relative to the object being examined? Does it force you to consider an object's *essence*?

3. What about you could *not* change in order for you to be the *same* person that you were before the change?

Where Am I?

Daniel C. Dennett

Daniel Dennett currently teaches philosophy at Tufts University and serves as the director of the Center for Cognitive Studies. He has published numerous articles, anthologies, and books on the philosophy of mind.

This essay is from a collection of his essays entitled *Brainstorms: Philosophical Essays on Mind and Psychology*. In it he explores a landscape of thought experiments regarding the self and mind in a science-fiction setting. In doing so, he carefully examines notions of the self in regards to both space (location) and time, further illuminating just what it means to locate the "I," or self.

Reading Questions

1. What problem arises for Dennett when his brain is taken from his body? What are the pros and cons he gives regarding the three scenarios with Hamlet and Yorick?

2. What happens that causes Dennett to change his point of view from his no longer being buried alive in Oklahoma to his actually *being* in Houston? How does this lead him to believing to have proved the existence of an immaterial soul?

3. Explain what happens in the end when he flips the switch for the last time.

Now that I've won my suit under the Freedom of Information Act, I am at liberty to reveal for the first time a curious episode in my life that may be of interest not only to those engaged in research in the philosophy of mind, artificial intelligence, and neuroscience but also to the general public.

Several years ago, I was approached by Pentagon officials who asked me to volunteer for a highly dangerous and secret mission. In collaboration with NASA and Howard Hughes, the Department of Defense was spending

Source: Daniel Dennett, "Where Am I?" From *Brainstorms: Philosophical Essays on Mind and Psychology,* copyright © 1978 by Bradford Books, Publishers. Reprinted by permission of the MIT Press.

billions to develop a Supersonic Tunneling Underground Device, or STUD. It was supposed to tunnel through the earth's core at great speed and deliver a specially designed atomic warhead "right up the Red's missile silos," as one of the Pentagon brass put it.

The problem was that in an early test they had succeeded in lodging a warhead about a mile deep under Tulsa, Oklahoma, and they wanted me to retrieve it for them. "Why me?" I asked. Well, the mission involved some pioneering applications of current brain research, and they had heard of my interest in brains and of course my Faustian curiosity and great courage and so forth. . . . Well, how could I refuse? The difficulty that brought the Pentagon to my door was that the device I'd been asked to recover was fiercely radioactive, in a new way. According to monitoring instruments, something about the nature of the device and its complex interactions with pockets of material deep in the earth had produced radiation that could cause severe abnormalities in certain tissues of the brain. No way had been found to shield the brain from these deadly rays, which were apparently harmless to other tissues and organs of the body. So it had been decided that the person sent to recover the device should *leave his brain behind*. It would be kept in a safe place where it could execute its normal control functions by elaborate radio links. Would I submit to a surgical procedure that would completely remove my brain, which would then be placed in a life-support system at the Manned Spacecraft Center in Houston? Each input and output pathway, as it was severed, would be restored by a pair of microminiaturized radio transceivers, one attached precisely to the brain, the other to the nerve stumps in the empty cranium. No information would be lost, all the connectivity would be preserved. At first I was a bit reluctant. Would it really work? The Houston brain surgeons encouraged me. "Think of it," they said, "as a mere *stretching* of the nerves. If your brain were just moved over an *inch* in your skull, that would not alter or impair your mind. We're simply going to make the nerves indefinitely elastic by splicing radio links into them."

I was shown around the life-support lab in Houston and saw the sparkling new vat in which my brain would be placed, were I to agree. I met the large and brilliant support team of neurologists, hematologists, biophysicists, and electrical engineers, and after several days of discussions and demonstrations, I agreed to give it a try. I was subjected to an enormous array of blood tests, brain scans, experiments, interviews, and the like. They took down my autobiography at great length, recorded tedious lists of my beliefs, hopes, fears, and tastes. They even listed my favorite stereo recordings and gave me a crash session of psychoanalysis.

The day for surgery arrived at last and of course I was anesthetized and remember nothing of the operation itself. When I came out of anesthesia, I opened my eyes, looked around, and asked the inevitable, the traditional, the lamentably hackneyed postoperative question: "Where am I?" The nurse smiled down at me. "You're in Houston," she said, and I reflected that this still had a good chance of being the truth one way or another. She handed me a mirror. Sure enough, there were the tiny antennae poling up through their titanium ports cemented into my skull.

"I gather the operation was a success," I said. "I want to go see my brain." They led me (I was a bit dizzy and unsteady) down a long corridor and into the life-support lab. A cheer went up from the assembled support team, and I responded with what I hoped was a jaunty salute. Still feeling lightheaded, I was helped over to the life-support vat. I peered through the glass. There, floating in what looked like ginger ale, was undeniably a human brain, though it was almost covered with printed circuit chips, plastic tubules, electrodes, and other paraphernalia. "Is that mine?" I asked. "Hit the output transmitter switch there on the side of the vat and see for yourself," the project director replied. I moved the switch to OFF, and immediately slumped, groggy and nauseated, into the arms of the technicians, one of whom kindly restored the switch to its ON position. While I recovered my equilibrium and composure, I thought to myself: "Well, here I am sitting on a folding chair, staring through a piece of plate glass at my own brain. . . . But wait," I said to myself, "shouldn't I have thought, 'Here I am, suspended in a bubbling fluid, being stared at by my own eyes'?" I tried to think this latter thought. I tried to project into the tank, offering it hopefully to my brain, but I failed to carry off the exercise with any conviction. I tried again. "Here am *I*, Daniel Dennett, suspended in a bubbling fluid, being stared at by my own eyes." No, it just didn't work. Most puzzling and confusing. Being a philosopher of firm physicality conviction, I believed unswervingly that the tokening of my thoughts was occurring somewhere in my brain: yet, when I thought "here I am," where the thought occurred to me was *here*, outside the vat, where I, Dennett, was standing staring at my brain.

I tried and tried to think myself into the vat, but to no avail. I tried to build up to the task by doing mental exercises. I thought to myself, "The sun is shining *over there*," five times in rapid succession, each time mentally ostending a different place: in order, the sunlit corner of the lab, the visible front lawn of the hospital, Houston, Mars, and Jupiter. I found I had little difficulty in getting my "there" 's to hop all over the celestial map with their proper references. I could loft a "there" in an instant through the farthest reaches of space, and then aim the next "there" with pinpoint accuracy at the upper left quadrant of a freckle on my arm. Why was I having such trouble with "there"? "Here in Houston" worked well enough, and so did "here in the lab," and even "here in this part of the lab," but "here in the vat" always seemed merely an unmeant mental mouthing. I tried closing my eyes while thinking it. This seemed to help, but still I couldn't manage to pull it off, except perhaps for a fleeting instant. I couldn't be sure. The discovery that I couldn't be sure was also unsettling. How did I know *where* I meant by "here" when I thought "here"? Could I *think* I meant one place when in fact I meant another? I didn't see how that could be admitted without untying the few bonds of intimacy between a person and his own mental life that had survived the onslaught of the brain scientists and philosophers, the physicalists and behaviorists. Perhaps I was incorrigible about where I *meant* when I said "here." But in my present circumstances it seemed that either I was doomed by sheer force of mental habit to thinking systematically false indexical thoughts, or where a person is (and hence where his thoughts are tokened for purposes of semantic analysis) is not necessarily where his brain, the physical seat of his soul, resides. Nagged by confusion, I attempted to orient myself by falling back on a favorite philosopher's ploy. I began naming things.

"Yorick," I said aloud to my brain, "you are my brain. The rest of my body, seated in this chair, I dub 'Hamlet.'" So here we all are: Yorick's my brain, Hamlet's my body, and I am Dennett. *Now,* where am I? And when I think "where am I?" where's that thought tokened? Is it tokened in my brain, lounging about in the vat, or right here between my ears where it *seems* to be tokened? Or nowhere? Its *temporal* coordinates give me no trouble; must it not have spatial coordinates as well? I began making a list of the alternatives.

1. *Where Hamlet goes, there goes Dennett.*   This principle was easily refuted by appeal to the familiar brain-transplant thought experiments so enjoyed by philosophers. If Tom and Dick switch brains, Tom is the fellow with Dick's former body—just ask him; he'll claim to be Tom, and tell you the most intimate details of Tom's autobiography. It was clear enough, then, that my current body and I could part company, but not likely that I could be separated from my brain. The rule of thumb that emerged so plainly from the thought experiments was that in a brain-transplant operation, one wanted to be the *donor,* not the recipient. Better to call such an operation a *body* transplant, in fact. So perhaps the truth was,

2. *Where Yorick goes, there goes Dennett.*   This was not at all appealing, however. How could I be in the vat and not about to go anywhere, when I was so obviously outside the vat looking in and beginning to make guilty plans to return to my room for a substantial lunch? This begged the question I realized, but it still seemed to be getting at something important. Casting about for some support for my intuition, I hit upon a legalistic sort of argument that might have appealed to Locke.

Suppose, I argued to myself, I were now to fly to California, rob a bank, and be apprehended. In which state would I be tried: In California, where the robbery took place, or in Texas, where the brains of the outfit were located? Would I be a California felon with an out-of-state brain, or a Texas felon remotely controlling an accomplice of sorts in California? It seemed possible that I might beat such a rap just on the undecidability of that jurisdictional question, though perhaps it would be deemed an interstate, and hence Federal, offense. In any event, suppose I were convicted. Was it likely that California would be satisfied to throw Hamlet into the brig, knowing that Yorick was living the good life and luxuriously taking the waters in Texas? Would Texas incarcerate Yorick, leaving Hamlet free to take the next boat to Rio? This alternative appealed to me.

Barring capital punishment or other cruel and unusual punishment, the state would be obliged to maintain the life-support system for Yorick though they might move him from Houston to Leavenworth, and aside from the unpleasantness of the opprobrium, I, for one, would not mind at all and would consider myself a free man under those circumstances. If the state has an interest in forcibly relocating persons in institutions, it would fail to relocate *me* in any institution by locating Yorick there. If this were true, it suggested a third alternative.

3. *Dennett is wherever he thinks he is.* Generalized, the claim was as follows: At any given time a person has a *point of view*, and the location of the point of view (which is determined internally by the content of the point of view) is also the location of the person.

Such a proposition is not without its perplexities, but to me it seemed a step in the right direction. The only trouble was that it seemed to place one in a heads-I-win/tails-you-lose situation of unlikely infallibility as regards location. Hadn't I myself often been wrong about where I was, and at least as often uncertain? Couldn't one get lost? Of course, but getting lost *geographically* is not the only way one might get lost. If one were lost in the woods one could attempt to reassure oneself with the consolation that at least one knew where one was: One was right *here* in the familiar surroundings of one's own body. Perhaps in this case one would not have drawn one's attention too much to be thankful for. Still, there were worse plights imaginable, and I wasn't sure I wasn't in such a plight right now.

Point of view clearly had something to do with personal location, but it was itself an unclear notion. It was obvious that the content of one's point of view was not the same as or determined by the content of one's beliefs or thoughts. For example, what should we say about the point of view of the Cinerama viewer who shrieks and twists in his seat as the roller-coaster footage overcomes his psychic distancing? Has he forgotten that he is safely seated in the theater? Here I was inclined to say that the person is experiencing an illusory shift in point of view. In other cases, my inclination to call such shifts illusory was less strong. The workers in laboratories and plants who handle dangerous materials by operating feedback-controlled mechanical arms and hands undergo a shift in point of view that is crisper and more pronounced than anything Cinerama can provoke. They can feel the heft and slipperiness of the containers they manipulate with their metal fingers. They know perfectly well where they are and are not fooled into false beliefs by the experience, yet it is as if they were inside the isolation chamber they are peering into. With mental effort, they can manage to shift their point of view back and forth, rather like making a transparent Necker cube or an Escher drawing change orientation before one's eyes. It does seem extravagant to suppose that in performing this bit of mental gymnastics, they are transporting *themselves* back and forth.

Still their example gave me hope. If I was in fact in the vat in spite of my intuitions, I might be able to train myself to adopt that point of view even as a matter of habit. I should dwell on images of myself comfortably floating in my vat, beaming volitions to that familiar body *out there*. I reflected that the ease or difficulty of this task was presumably independent of the truth about the location of one's brain. Had I been practicing before the operation, I might now be finding it second nature. You might now yourself try such a *trompe l'oeil*. Imagine you have written an inflammatory letter which has been published in the *Times*, the result of which is that the government has chosen to impound your brain for a probationary period of three years in its Dangerous Brain Clinic in Bethesda, Maryland. Your body of course is allowed freedom to earn a salary and thus continue its function of laying up income to be taxed. At this moment, however, your body is seated in an auditorium listening to a peculiar account by Daniel Dennett of his own similar experience. Try it. Think yourself to Bethesda, and then hark back longingly to your body, far away, and yet *seeming* so near. It is only with long-distance restraint (yours? the government's) that you can control your impulse to get those hands clapping in polite applause before navigating the old body to the rest room and a well-deserved glass of evening sherry in the lounge. The task of imagination is certainly difficult, but if you achieve your goal the results might be consoling.

Anyway, there I was in Houston, lost in thought as one might say, but not for long. My speculations were soon interrupted by the Houston doctors, who wished to test out my new prosthetic nervous system before sending me off on my hazardous mission. As I mentioned before, I was a bit dizzy at first, and not surprisingly, although I soon habituated myself to my new circumstances (which were, after all, well nigh indistinguishable from my old circumstances). My accommodation was not perfect, however, and to this day I continue to be plagued by minor coordination difficulties. The speed of light is fast, but finite, and as my brain and body move farther and farther apart, the delicate interaction of my feedback systems is thrown into disarray by the time lags. Just as one is rendered close to speechless by a delayed or echoic hearing of one's speaking voice so, for instance, I am virtually unable to track a moving object with my eyes whenever my brain and my body are more than a few miles apart. In most matters my impairment is scarcely detectable, though I can no longer hit a slow curve ball with the authority of yore. There are some compensations of course. Though liquor tastes as good as ever, and warms my gullet while corroding my liver, I can drink it in any quantity I please, without becoming the slightest bit inebriated, a curiosity some of my close friends may have noticed (though I occasionally have *feigned* inebriation, so as not to draw attention to my unusual circumstances). For similar reasons, I take aspirin orally for a sprained wrist, but if the pain persists I ask Houston to administer codeine to me *in vitro*. In times of illness the phone bill can be staggering.

But to return to my adventure. At length, both the doctors and I were satisfied that I was ready to undertake my subterranean mission. And so I left my brain in Houston and headed by helicopter for Tulsa. Well, in any case, that's the way it seemed to me. That's how I would put it, just off the top of my head as it were. On the trip I reflected further about my earlier anxieties and decided that my first postoperative speculations had been tinged with panic. The matter was not nearly as strange or metaphysical as I had been supposing. Where was I? In two places, clearly: both inside the vat and outside it. Just as one can stand with one foot in Connecticut and the other in Rhode Island, I was in two places at once. I had become one of those scattered individuals we used to hear so much about. The more I considered this answer, the more obviously true it appeared. But, strange to say, the more true it appeared, the less important the question to which it could be the true answer seemed. A sad, but not unprecedented, fate for a philosophical question to suffer. This answer did not completely satisfy me, of course. There lingered some question to which I should have liked an answer, which was neither

"Where are all my various and sundry parts?" nor "What is my current point of view?" Or at least there seemed to be such a question. For it did seem undeniable that in some sense *I* and not merely *most of me* was descending into the earth under Tulsa in search of an atomic warhead.

When I found the warhead, I was certainly glad I had left my brain behind, for the pointer on the specially built Geiger counter I had brought with me was off the dial. I called Houston on my ordinary radio and told the operation control center of my position and my progress. In return, they gave me instructions for dismantling the vehicle, based upon my on-site observations. I had set to work with my cutting torch when all of a sudden a terrible thing happened. I went stone deaf. At first I thought it was only my radio earphones that had broken, but when I tapped on my helmet, I heard nothing. Apparently the auditory transceivers had gone on the fritz. I could no longer hear Houston or my own voice, but I could speak, so I started telling them what had happened. In midsentence, I knew something else had gone wrong. My vocal apparatus had become paralyzed. Then my right hand went limp—another transceiver had gone. I was truly in deep trouble. But worse was to follow. After a few more minutes, I went blind. I cursed my luck, and then I cursed the scientists who had led me into this grave peril. There I was, deaf, dumb, and blind, in a radioactive hole more than a mile under Tulsa. Then the last of my cerebral radio links broke, and suddenly I was faced with a new and even more shocking problem: whereas an instant before I had been buried alive in Oklahoma, now I was disembodied in Houston. My recognition of my new status was not immediate. It took me several very anxious minutes before it dawned on me that my poor body lay several hundred miles away, with heart pulsing and lungs respirating, but otherwise as dead as the body of any heart-transplant donor, its skull packed with useless, broken electronic gear. The shift in perspective I had earlier found well nigh impossible now seemed quite natural. Though I could think myself back into my body in the tunnel under Tulsa, it took some effort to sustain the illusion. For surely it was an illusion to suppose I was still in Oklahoma: I had lost all contact with that body.

It occurred to me then, with one of those rushes of revelation of which we should be suspicious, that I had stumbled upon an impressive demonstration of the immateriality of the soul based upon physicalist principles and premises. For as the last radio signal between Tulsa and Houston died away, had I not changed location from Tulsa to Houston at the speed of light? And had I not accomplished this without any increase in mass? What moved from A to B at such speed was surely myself, or at any rate my soul or mind—the massless center of my being and home of my consciousness. My *point of view* had lagged somewhat behind, but I had already noted the indirect bearing of point of view on personal location. I could not see how a physicalist philosopher could quarrel with this except by taking the dire and counterintuitive route of banishing all talk of persons. Yet the notion of personhood was so well entrenched in everyone's world view, or so it seemed to me, that any denial would be as curiously unconvincing, as systematically disingenuous, as the Cartesian negation, "non sum."

The joy of philosophic discovery thus tided me over some very bad minutes or perhaps hours as the helplessness and hopelessness of my situation became more apparent to me. Waves of panic and even nausea swept over me, made all the more horrible by the absence of their normal body-dependent phenomenology. No adrenaline rush of tingles in the arms, no pounding heart, no premonitory salivation. I did feel a dread sinking feeling in my bowels at one point, and this tricked me momentarily into the false hope that I was undergoing a reversal of the process that landed me in this fix—a gradual undisembodiment. But the isolation and uniqueness of that twinge soon convinced me that it was simply the first of a plague of phantom body hallucinations that I, like any other amputee, would be all too likely to suffer.

My mood then was chaotic. On the one hand, I was fired up with elation of my philosophic discovery and was wracking my brain (one of the few familiar things I could still do), trying to figure out how to communicate my discovery to the journals; while on the other, I was bitter, lonely, and filled with dread and uncertainty. Fortunately, this did not last long, for my technical support team sedated me into a dreamless sleep from which I awoke, hearing with magnificent fidelity the familiar opening strains of my favorite Brahms piano trio. So that was why they had wanted a list of my favorite recordings! It did not take me long to realize that I was hearing the music without ears. The output from the stereo stylus was being fed through some fancy rectification circuitry directly into my auditory nerve. I was mainlining Brahms, an unforgettable experience for any stereo buff. At the end of the record it did not surprise me to hear the reassuring voice of the project director speaking into a microphone that was now my prosthetic ear. He confirmed my analysis of what had gone wrong and assured me that steps were being taken to re-embody me. He did not elaborate, and after a few more recordings, I found myself drifting off to sleep. My sleep lasted, I later learned, for the better part of a year, and when I awoke, it was to find myself fully restored to my senses. When I looked into the mirror, though, I was a bit startled to see an unfamiliar face. Bearded and a bit heavier, bearing no doubt a family resemblance to my former face, and with the same look of spritely intelligence and resolute character, but definitely a new face. Further self-explorations of an intimate nature left me no doubt that this was a new body, and the project director confirmed my conclusions. He did not volunteer any information on the past history of my new body and I decided (wisely, I think in retrospect) not to pry. As many philosophers unfamiliar with my ordeal have more recently speculated, the acquisitions of a new body leaves one's *person* intact. And after a period of adjustment to a new voice, new muscular strengths and weaknesses, and so forth, one's *personality* is by and large also preserved. More dramatic changes in personality have been routinely observed in people who have undergone extensive plastic surgery, to say nothing of sex-change operations, and I think no one contests the survival of the person in such cases. In any event I soon accommodated to my new body, to the point of being unable to recover any of its novelties to my consciousness or even memory. The view in the mirror soon became utterly familiar.

That view, by the way, still revealed antennae, and so I was not surprised to learn that my brain had not been moved from its haven in the life-support lab.

I decided that good old Yorick deserved a visit. I and my new body, whom we might as well call Fortinbras, strode into the familiar lab to another round of applause from the technicians, who were of course congratulating themselves, not me. Once more I stood before the vat and contemplated poor Yorick, and on a whim I once again cavalierly flicked off the output transmitter switch. Imagine my surprise when nothing unusual happened. No fainting spell, no nausea, no noticeable change. A technician hurried to restore the switch to ON, but still I felt nothing. I demanded an explanation, which the project director hastened to provide. It seems that before they had even operated on the first occasion, they had constructed a computer duplicate of my brain, reproducing both the complete information-processing structure and the computational speed of my brain in a giant computer program. After the operation, but before they had dared to send me off on my mission to Oklahoma, they had run this computer system and Yorick side by side. The incoming signals from Hamlet were sent simultaneously to Yorick's transceivers and to the computer's array of inputs. And the outputs from Yorick were not only beamed back to Hamlet, my body; they were recorded and checked against the simultaneous output of the computer program, which was called "Hubert" for reasons obscure to me. Over days and even weeks, the outputs were identical and synchronous, which of course did not *prove* that they had succeeded in copying the brain's functional structure, but the empirical support was greatly encouraging.

Hubert's input, and hence activity, had been kept parallel with Yorick's during my disembodied days. And now, to demonstrate this, they had actually thrown the master switch that put Hubert for the first time in on-line control of my body—not Hamlet, of course, but Fortinbras. (Hamlet, I learned, had never been recovered from its underground tomb and could be assumed by this time to have largely returned to the dust. At the head of my grave still lay the magnificent bulk of the abandoned device, with the word STUD emblazoned on its side in large letters—a circumstance which may provide archeologists of the next century with a curious insight into the burial rites of their ancestors.)

The laboratory technicians now showed me the master switch, which had two positions, labeled B, for Brain (they didn't know my brain's name was Yorick) and H, for Hubert. The switch did indeed point to H, and they explained to me that if I wished, I could switch it back to B. With my heart in my mouth (and my brain in its vat), I did this. Nothing happened. A click, that was all. To test their claim, and with the master switch now set at B, I hit Yorick's output transmitter switch on the vat and sure enough, I began to faint. Once the output switch was turned back on and I had recovered my wits, so to speak, I continued to play with the master switch, flipping it back and forth. I found that with the exception of the transitional click, I could detect no trace of a difference. I could switch in mid-utterance, and the sentence I had begun speaking under the control of Yorick was finished without a pause or hitch of any kind under the control of Hubert. I had a spare brain, a prosthetic device which might some day stand me in very good stead, were some mishap to befall Yorick. Or alternatively, I could keep Yorick as a spare and use Hubert. It didn't seem to make any difference which I chose, for the wear and tear and fatigue on my body did not have any debilitating effect on either brain, whether or not it was actually causing the motions of my body, or merely spilling its output into thin air.

The one truly unsettling aspect of this new development was the prospect, which was not long in dawning on me, of someone detaching the spare—Hubert or Yorick, as the case might be—from Fortinbras and hitching it to yet another body—some Johnny-come-lately Rosencrantz or Guildenstern. Then (if not before) there would be *two* people, that much was clear. One would be me, and the other would be a sort of super-twin brother. If there were two bodies, one under the control of Hubert and the other being controlled by Yorick, then which would the world recognize as the true Dennett? And whatever the rest of the world decided, which one would be *me*? Would I be the Yorick-brained one, in virtue of Yorick's causal priority and former intimate relationship with the original Dennett body, Hamlet? That seemed a bit legalistic, a bit too redolent of the arbitrariness of consanguinity and legal possession, to be convincing at the meta physical level. For suppose that before the arrival of the second body on the scene, I had been keeping Yorick as the spare for years, and letting Hubert's output drive my body—that is, Fortinbras—all that time. The Hubert-Fortinbras couple would seem then by squatter's rights (to combat one legal intuition with another) to be the true Dennett and the lawful inheritor of everything that was Dennett's. This was an interesting question, certainly, but not nearly so pressing as another question that bothered me. My strongest intuition was that in such an eventuality *I* would survive so long as *either* brain-body couple remained intact, but I had mixed emotions about whether I should want both to survive.

I discussed my worries with the technicians and the project director. The prospect of two Dennetts was abhorrent to me, I explained, largely for social reasons. I didn't want to be my own rival for the affections of my wife, nor did I like the prospect of the two Dennetts sharing my modest professor's salary. Still more vertiginous and distasteful, though, was the idea of knowing *that much* about another person, while he had the very same goods on me. How could we ever face each other? My colleagues in the lab argued that I was ignoring the bright side of the matter. Weren't there many things I wanted to do but, being only one person, had been unable to do? Now one Dennett could stay at home and be the professor and family man, while the other could strike out on a life of travel and adventure—missing the family of course, but happy in the knowledge that the other Dennett was keeping the home fires burning. I could be faithful and adulterous at the same time. I could even cuckold myself—to say nothing of other more lurid possibilities my colleagues were all too ready to force upon my overtaxed imagination. But my ordeal in Oklahoma (or was it Houston?) had made me less adventurous, and I shrank from this opportunity that was being offered (though of course I was never quite sure it was being offered to *me* in the first place).

There was another prospect even more disagreeable: that the spare, Hubert or Yorick as the case might be, would be detached from any input from Fortinbras and just left detached. Then, as in the other case, there would be two Dennetts, or at least two claimants to my name and possessions, one embodied in Fortinbras, and the other sadly, miserably disembodied. Both selfishness and altruism bade me take steps to prevent this from happening. So I asked that measures be taken to ensure that no one could ever tamper with the transceiver connections or the master switch without my (our? no, *my*) knowledge and consent. Since I had no desire to spend my life guarding the equipment in Houston, it was mutually decided that all the electronic connections in the lab would be carefully locked. Both those that controlled the life-support system for Yorick and those that controlled the power supply for Hubert would be guarded with fail-safe devices, and I would take the only master switch, outfitted for radio remote control, with me wherever I went. I carry it strapped around my waist and—wait a moment—*here it is.* Every few months I reconnoiter the situation by switching channels. I do this only in the presence of friends, of course, for if the other channel were, heaven forbid, either dead or otherwise occupied, there would have to be somebody who had my interests at heart to switch it back, to bring me back from the void. For while I could feel, see, hear, and otherwise sense whatever befell my body, subsequent to such a switch, I'd be unable to control it. By the way, the two positions on the switch are intentionally unmarked, so I never have the faintest idea whether I am switching from Hubert to Yorick or vice versa. (Some of you may think that in this case I really don't know *who* I am, let alone where I am. But such reflections no longer make much of a dent on my essential Dennettness, on my own sense of who I am. If it is true that in one sense I don't know who I am then that's another one of your philosophical truths of underwhelming significance.)

In any case, every time I've flipped the switch so far, nothing has happened. *So let's give it a try. . . .*

"THANK GOD! I THOUGHT YOU'D NEVER FLIP THAT SWITCH! You can't imagine how horrible it's been these last two weeks—but now you know; it's your turn in purgatory. How I've longed for this moment! You see, about two weeks ago—excuse me, ladies and gentlemen, but I've got to explain this to my . . . um, brother, I guess you could say, but he's just told you the facts, so you'll understand—about two weeks ago our two brains drifted just a bit out of synch. I don't know whether *my* brain is now Hubert or Yorick, any more than you do, but in any case, the two brains drifted apart, and of course once the process started, it snowballed, for I was in a slightly different receptive state for the input we both received, a difference that was soon magnified. In no time at all the illusion that I was in control of my body—our body—was completely dissipated. There was nothing I could do—no way to call you. YOU DIDN'T EVEN KNOW I EXISTED! It's been like being carried around in a cage, or better, like being possessed—hearing my own voice say things I didn't mean to say, watching in frustration as my own hands performed deeds I hadn't intended. You'd scratch our itches, but not the way I would have, and you kept me awake, with your tossing and turning. I've been totally exhausted, on the verge of a nervous breakdown, carried around helplessly by your frantic round of activities, sustained only by the knowledge that some day you'd throw the switch.

"Now it's your turn, but at least you'll have the comfort of knowing *I* know you're in there. Like an expectant mother, I'm eating—or at any rate tasting, smelling, seeing—for *two* now, and I'll try to make it easy for you. Don't worry. Just as soon as this colloquium is over, you and I will fly to Houston, and we'll see what can be done to get one of us another body. You can have a female body— your body could be any color you like. But let's think it over. I tell you what—to be fair, if we both want this body, I promise I'll let the project director flip a coin to settle which of us gets to keep it and which then gets to choose a new body. That should guarantee justice, shouldn't it? In any case, I'll take care of you, I promise. These people are my witnesses.

"Ladies and gentlemen, this talk we have just heard is not exactly the talk *I* would have given, but I assure you that everything he said was perfectly true. And now if you'll excuse me, I think I'd—we'd—better sit down."

Discussion Questions

1. Which of the scenarios do you side with when Dennett's brain is taken out of his head initially? Does your answer tell you anything about your view of the self?

2. Dennett "receives" a new body and questions whether his *person* is still intact. In doing so, he mentions plastic surgery and sex-change operations. In what ways do these operations change or even affect one's identity? In Kafka's *Metamorphosis,* the main character wakes up as a cockroach. How would a drastic change like this affect one's identity?

3. If you had a computer copy of your brain (like "Hubert" here), would that allow you to achieve immortality? Why/why not?

The Buddhist Theory of "No-Self"

Serge-Christophe Kolm

Serge-Christophe Kolm has published over thirty books and hundreds of journal articles. As a former director and professor of the Institute for Advanced Studies in the Social Sciences, he focuses primarily on economics, theories of justice, and the social sciences in general.

This following selection is part of a chapter taken from Kolm's book in which he examines how one can minimize suffering—*dukkha*—while maximizing utility in one's life. The article first provides a brief overview of the goal of Buddhism and its underlying moral foundation. This background helps us to understand the main focus of this article— framing the Buddhist notion of the *self* or, more appropriately, the *lack* of self. In achieving this, one can better achieve the goal of avoidance of suffering.

Source: Excerpts by Serge-Christophe Kolm from *The Multiple Self,* edited by Jon Elster, 1985, pp. 244–245, 252–260. Reprinted with the permission of Cambridge University Press.

Reading Questions

1. Why isn't the Buddhist practice considered to be "cynically egoistical"? In what way might the Buddhist seem overtly egoistical and unsympathetic? How is this an incorrect view?
2. How does the Buddhist argue that the "self" does not exist? What then is the "self" that people so often reference?
3. In what way is the Buddhist "dismantling of being" different from the Western approach of reducing/dismantling the self? How does it compare to Hume's view of the self (see the selection in this section)?
4. Define and explain the Buddhist term *dharma*.
5. What value does the Buddhist find in realizing that the self is an illusion?
6. Explain Kolm's analogy of a cart to the soul (and mind).

Buddhist Egoism, Its Limits and Its Meanings

All the above Buddhist precepts are strategies aimed at improving one's personal situation. Thus, they are entirely egoistical, as is most of ordinary Buddhist practice. In terms of most Western morality, which holds that one only becomes altruistic by ceasing to be egoistical, the ethical doctrine of Awakening and the Buddhist sage seem to be cynically egoistical. The doctrine has subtler ramifications, however.

First, the detachment to which Buddhists aspire implies a diminution in, and then a cessation of, feelings of hostility towards other human beings, of malevolence, hatred, spite, cruelty, envy, and jealousy in particular. This represents a lowering of negative attitudes towards others rather than an enhancement of positive attitudes towards them, but it is a general tendency of Buddhism to consider the negative rather than the positive aspect of things. In many respects, Buddhism takes negation to be more real than affirmation. It is no small thing, after all, to reduce these hostile sentiments. At least no Buddhist has ever killed another man in order to win salvation or happiness for himself, his victim, man in general or any idol whatsoever.

Moreover, even if we discount his attitudes, his knowledge alone prevents a Buddhist from entertaining negative feelings towards another human being, since the *self*, and therefore that of another, is merely an illusion. One cannot hate something which does not exist, nor can one detest or despise it. This in itself is something of an achievement. But one cannot love it either. At most one can 'love one's neighbour as oneself,' since 'one' does not exist either. . . .

A Buddhist cannot pity his fellow any more than he pities himself. He could, however, go through the motions of expressing sympathy with you, in order to console you and thereby to lessen your pain. But he would be rendering you a disservice, for the cure thus effected would be superficial and short-term rather than definitive. You would be no further along the road to an effective and lasting cure; in fact it would lead you to a dead end. Worse still, it might well reinforce your illusion regarding your *I*, and thus distance you from the proper solution and entrench you yet more deeply in this suffering and in that of others. Furthermore, why should a Buddhist take a genuine interest in your being when he is marshalling all his intelligence in order to logically understand that such a being does not exist, and furthermore all his sensibility in order to become aware that the being who might be interested in it does not exist either? A Buddhist does not sympathize with the misfortunes of others, not because there is no misfortune (in fact that is all there is), but because, in reality, *others* no more exist than *the self* does. He may therefore often seem to be extraordinarily insensitive to the misfortunes of others and, in this sense of the word, inhuman. But this is precisely what a Buddhist strives to be towards all things of this world. It is his wish, his only wish even, to reduce misfortune. But he wishes to reduce misfortune in general, and to do so effectively and thoroughly. . . .

The object of Buddhism is indeed to lessen suffering, and not exclusively, or even particularly, one's own. But this latter is part of the overall suffering, and Buddhist psychological and therapeutic theories hold that it is basically on this part that the individual can act effectively and deeply. Through making an effort on myself, I am able to detach myself, to humble or suppress my desires, but I cannot hope to have the same effect on you and yours; it is you and you alone who can do that and the best I could do would be to point you towards therapeutic theories or prescriptions which you could then apply yourself. Consequently, in order to reduce the suffering of the world, the Buddhist is led to concern himself essentially with acting on his own self. Hence his egoistical behaviour. . . .

The well-known Chinese story which holds that it is better to teach someone how to fish than to give him a fish is a Buddhist apologue. Only help another if you do not know how to advise him to help himself. Tangible generosity and devotion are last resorts reserved for ignorant people incapable of speaking well. Only in the last resort should good action be substituted for good speech.

Once again, it was Nietzsche who perceived this: 'In the teaching of the Buddha egoism becomes a duty: the "one thing needful," the "how can *you* get rid of suffering" regulates and circumscribes the entire spiritual diet.[1]

This interpretation of Buddhism is both in strict accordance with its expressed teachings and logically compatible with the doctrine of the no-self. All Buddhist doctrine speaks of reducing suffering, but practically only provides few indications as to how one is to lessen one's own. The writings of the 'ancient school of wisdom' state quite unambiguously that 'No one can be saved by another.' This has been taken to mean that Karmic merits cannot be transferred, and in this respect it has been to some extent breached by *mahayana* Buddhism, but the deep psychological meaning of *karma* actually lends credence to our present argument. It has also been observed that the not-self that implies the concept of suffering exists on its own. Buddhaghosa, for instance, says: 'Only suffering exists, but there is no sufferer.' . . .

In the West, we have altruism, charity and fraternity, in the East, the no-self. In the former case the opposite of the me is the *you*, in the latter it is the *not-me*. I have just observed, admittedly, that Buddhist practice contains many altruistic features. But they always seem to be a means or a consequence stemming from the basic quest, which is the effacement of oneself.

Western ethics may also involve an attenuation of the *ego,* but in general as means rather than as an end, and it never pursues this to the limit. The renunciating of one's attachments is a value in the West, but it exists as a means to help or serve others or God better (one distributes one's 'worldly goods' to 'the poor') not, as is the case in Buddhism, as a direct means to achieve the absence of suffering. The individual may also be devalued in comparison with the social class of which he is a member, but the Buddhist will retort that in fact such an individual does not exist, that he is merely an illusion. Humility, as when one says that the self is small when compared with God, is largely a way of increasing God's stature by relying upon a very resilient self for support. In fact, a Buddhist will reply, none of that exists, neither God nor self (or, more precisely, there is undoubtedly no God for the *theravada* Buddhist and there is definitely no self for all Buddhists). . . .

Badness, Unhappiness, and the Self: the Great Illusion. Buddhist Ontology

For Buddhism it is clear, therefore, that *badness is unhappiness.* The true unhappiness, however, is not poverty but attachment, which is virtually its opposite, and the bad that there is in attaching oneself consists not in the attachment but in the self that is attached. Fortunately, however, this 'self' does not really exist, it is merely an illusion. One simply has to become aware of this for one's attachments, and therefore one's miseries, to cease.

In order to prove that the 'self' does not exist, Buddhism employs a fairly impressive argument. It consists in considering the person as a set of simple elements which has no reality in itself but only in the mind of the observer. And one is advised to apply this perspective to oneself, whilst taking great care to ensure that the corresponding knowledge is itself a set of elements belonging to those that it uncovers. If one genuinely succeeds in bringing off this ploy, all discomfort would seem to disappear. One would also seem to require more than one life to understand it, and several to apply it, declares the *tathagata* Guatama (the Tibetan Milarepa, a long time after him, is the only one to have effected this in a single life). All the more reason, then, to start straightaway.

One begins by acknowledging that a person is composed of several elements. The profane person would see this as a 'decomposition' of the still perceptible person into several elements. One would then make him see that what he believed to be a person *is only* this set of elements that he stubbornly persisted in regarding as a whole: There is nothing else, the world is empty of 'self.'

The West has long been habituated to such analytic dismantling of being. From Plato, through Descartes to Freud, we find a division between appetite, reason, and mind, or we hear of the ghost in the machine, or of id, ego, and superego, or of conscious and subconscious, or of conscious, unconscious, and preconscious, or of the cognitive, the conative, and the affective, etc. But the dismantling that the Buddha (a century before Plato) proposes is infinitely more refined than the crude divisions into two or three elements imagined by Westerners. Even when Hume says, much as a Buddhist would, that 'the mind is only a bundle or collection of different perceptions' linked by causalities, he only grasps one out of the six *skandhas* (it may be that he employs the word 'perception' in a slightly wider sense, but he is hardly explicit about this).

Buddhism is concerned with elementary or simple, indecomposable elements, ontological 'atoms,' as it were, which are said by it to be the only things enjoying any reality, and which are called *dharmas* in Sanskrit (*dhammas* in Pali). This word also refers to the Buddha's doctrine, a double reference which is frequent in Buddhist language (*dharma* has many other meanings also, and although most Buddhist terms have several meanings it is probably the richest of them all). As a consequence, the first two words of the Buddhist *credo*, *ye dhamma*, mean both 'I follow the doctrine' and 'I am only [composed of] simple elements.' If these two apparently very different meanings coexist, it is because the deepest meaning of *dharma* is 'ultimate reality' (or 'ultimate truth'). These *dharma* elements occur in many different forms. The elementary manuals in the monasteries describe several dozen of them, but several hundred are said to exist. These types of *dharma* are classed in different ways, according to different criteria. Before being ordained as *bhikkhus*, the novices must learn three of these classifications: in terms of *skandhas*, in terms of *ayatanas*, and in terms of *dhatus*. The most famous is the classification in terms of *skandhas* or 'aggregates' (of *dharmas*), which are five in number. To begin with, there are the ten properties of matter, of material things, which, where a person is concerned, means his body and the things which he owns, with the body referring also to his ideas, thoughts, and mental images. Then there are the sensations of the six senses (the sixth sense involves perception and sensation of ideas, thoughts, and mental images by the mental and cerebral organ – an expression that John Locke was later to reinvent). Then there are the fifty-eight volitions, impulses or 'mental formations.' Finally, the consciousnesses of all the above crown the whole series. The classification into *ayatanas* obeys a cognitive criterion; its twelve categories are the six senses and the things that they know, the latter being the sixty-four types of mental *dharma*. The division into *dhatus* serves to describe the 'current' (*santana*) of causal relations between *dharmas* which seem to constitute an 'individual' (*pudgala*). It consists of eighteen classes, adding the consciousnesses of the corresponding properties-perceptions-sensations to the twelve of the preceding classification. But Buddhism sometimes puts itself at the level of modern scholarship by distinguishing three categories, matter, spirit, and forces, a classification which it teaches to small children and to them only. The dual division between spirit and matter is also present.

The important point to note is that, once the person is dissolved in this way, Buddhism sees no reason to reassemble these elements into so-called individuals. It dismantles the human machine conceptually, and with great finesse, but then it disdains to put it together again. Man remains in detached and scattered pieces.

A Buddhist observing you will see a pile of elements, a bag containing several hundred types of things, an aggregate of aggregates, a flux of events, a current of causal relations, but not *you*. The Buddhist gaze is a ray which disintegrates being. It is fortunate, then, that it is himself that a Buddhist will spend his time thus scrutinizing.

What thus is this thing which so interests people, which activates their passions, which they care for so intensely, about which they talk so much, their self? It is a concept, a construction of the reason and of the imagination, a way of seeing and of composing the world, but not an entity which really exists. In other words, it is an *illusion*. But does not man excel most at transforming his ideas into suffering? The idea of the 'self,' Buddhism says, is the heart of all pain. The worst possible thing to do would therefore be to reassemble the robot, and to believe that this montage on the part of the mind has a real existence.

The idea of the 'self' is not the only thing, Buddhism generously adds, to which this argument applies. The same is true of every mental construction. For instance, a cart consists of wheels, shafts, frame, etc. It *is* these elements; the entity 'cart' is a creature of the mind, an illusion. Or, to put it another way, one must not say that this fruit *has* this form, this colour, this smell, but rather that this fruit *is* this form and this colour and this smell and so on. Likewise, the mind doesn't *have* sensations, sentiments, ideas, volitions, etc., but what one calls 'mind' is these things. And the 'self' is that plus material elements. But to believe in a cart or in a pear does not have the same consequences as believing in oneself.

The main conclusion we can draw from this is that the 'self' is a mental construction, and by realizing this one may suppress pain. Precise analysis of the causes of suffering, of the perceptions which bring it, of its sensation of the consciousness of these facts, enables one either to remove this conscious sensation or to take a detached and objective view of it, and thereby to remove the pain. It is worth noting that Buddhism claims that this latter method is its own peculiar achievement, arrived at thanks to the no-self (the cutting off of sensation, reputed to have been the means employed by the Buddha's last *guru*, did not satisfy the Buddha, inducing him to search for his own answer by embarking upon a long mediation, from which he was to emerge 'awakened' to the solution.) At any rate, more or less training is required to produce these results. This is particularly the case with physical sufferings, where one has to overcome the danger and the fear that its absence would deprive us of the warning that the body is incurring some serious destruction. And things are much easier in the case of self-love, jealousy, hatred, pride, and of shame, honour, or love! When one understands the causes and mechanisms of suffering, when one becomes aware of their basic sequences, suffering ceases. In the West, Spinoza (in his *Ethics*, in particular) had certain intuitions about this phenomenon, but he provided no account of the precise mode of functioning, or even of the structure of the psyche such as would enable one to understand it, and such as Buddhism provides. One is tempted, however, to improve the latter doctrine by saying; only strive to dismantle mentally those things which do you harm; attach yourself when it is possible and painless or agreeable, disengage yourself when it ceases to be so; opt for the agreeable side of things, and only analyse the rest in a Buddhist manner! This should be all the more possible that Buddhist psychology provides all the warning and knowledge which are required in order to prevent that a voluntary attachment turns into a sadistic master.

In this diagnosis of the cause of human unhappiness, and therefore in the therapeutic practice which derives from it, Buddhism proves to be the exact opposite of the Western tradition (which includes both Marx and Freud). The latter sees unhappiness, despair, neurosis, alienation, etc., in human beings who are divided, in fragments and internally dismembered, and equilibrium, the necessary condition for happiness (and a concept reminiscent of that of *nirvana*), in the integrated personality. Buddhism, by contrast, regards the latter as the cause of all ills. In order to remedy it, it shatters man (the illusion of man in man's eyes) and is only too glad to leave him in pieces. Is there then a fundamental contradiction between these two theories, each of which is firmly anchored in a tradition? The important thing to note is that the divisions of the personality identified by these two traditions are by no means the same. In Buddhism, the elements are psychological categories which, although connected, belong to different planes, whilst for Freud, for example, the superego and id may collide head-on over particular choices.

To be more precise, however large the number of 'things' (or, more exactly, of 'facts') Buddhism sees in an 'individual,' there is one which he will not find there, namely, the 'I,' the heart of being, which would be at once the subject of volitions and the object of suffering, and therefore a link between desire and *dukkha*. Chapter 19 in Kolm (1982) analyses precisely and in detail this question of the 'I,' and it explains that Buddhist advanced philosophy considers in fact many kinds of 'I,' some of which are real by definition or by nature and some of which are illusory. It is the illusion of the 'I in itself,' both based upon and providing the basis for desires and attachments, which Buddhists hold to be the specific cause common to all sufferings. Critical examination of the 'self' enables one to show that an individual contains no entity of this sort. When, therefore, one has succeeded in realizing this and in convincing oneself of it, both desires and pains fade away.

Having thus presented a more detailed account of the Buddhist conception of the self, we are now in a better position to gauge whether it can be reconciled with the theory of choices. If the 'self' is simply an illusion, what reality can the 'order of preferences' have? If it is composed of various 'aggregates' and specified elements, can the whole of behaviour be explained in terms of this ultra-simple entity? If everything is provisional, 'impermanent,' and in a perpetual flux of change, as Buddhism declares it to be, what can the stability of these preferences be worth? If 'everything has a cause' and 'everything is determined,' which is another base of this philosophy, it applies to individual's actions, and can one then speak of a person's free choice, or even of choice at all? And if 'I' do not exist, who is it that does the choosing?

An illusion is something quite real for the person observing someone who is in a state of illusion (his theoretician, as it were), and if this illusion guides or influences its victim's acts, one can perhaps describe this effect in terms of the theory of choices.

But, for a Buddhist, the illusion of the *self* has a crucial effect on the decisions of a non-Buddhist or, more exactly, on non-Buddhist decisions. Only an *arahant,* because he has understood, is an exception to this, but he is a rare phenomenon and undoubtedly acts very little. On the other hand, the action entailed by the theory of choices is indeed caused by constraints and preferences, which are themselves caused by something else. The instability of preferences, for its part, does not obstruct the pure theory of choices which dates them; it may, however, hinder certain of its practical applications. Buddhism states that everything changes, everything disappears, without specifying the speed of this process or the delays that occur. It may take a lifetime, or an aeon. Finally, the fact that out of five 'aggregates' one may only derive one 'self' does not necessarily imply that one cannot derive an order of preferences from them. For the *perceptions* of the available alternatives produce more or less agreeable sensations, and this gives rise to an order which is a *mental and volitional formation,* all of this being liable to be more or less *conscious* (with certainly a higher degree of rationality in the sense of transitivity the more conscious it is).

Discussion Questions

1. Given your (likely) Western habits, could you cause your concept of a *self* to disappear into an illusion? Even if you could, would you value this? What possible downsides might arise?
2. In what ways does your *self* or your *ego* cause you to suffer? If you could eradicate the *self,* would you be able to then avoid feelings like jealousy, hatred, and shame? How about actual physical suffering?
3. What value is there in being able to eliminate your desires?

On the Soul

René Descartes

(For a biography of Descartes, see the earlier selection in chapter 1.)

While the notion of a mind and soul had been popularized long before Descartes—not by just Plato well before him, but by the Church as well—Descartes added a key element to the doctrine: a logical, almost scientific defense (or "proof," depending on how convinced one is) of the spiritual component of human existence.

This selection builds on his proof of knowledge (printed in the "Knowledge" chapter of this anthology). Here Descartes investigates the "I" of his famous statement, "I think, therefore I am." At the point of his proving this, the "I" was merely a thinking (doubting) thing. Through an examination of differences between the corporeal (physical) and noncorporeal components of his self, along with a further investigation of how we attain knowledge, he shows not only that the immaterial component exists, but what it is like.

Source: Excerpts from "Second Meditation" and "Sixth Meditation" by René Descartes from *Meditations on First Philosophy,* translated by John Cottingham, 1984, pp. 20–23, 54, 56–61. Reprinted with the permission of Cambridge University Press.

Reading Questions

1. What point does Descartes make in reference to the piece of wax? Why can't we truly know the wax with our senses alone? What else is needed? Why? How does this relate to how we know the "I"?
2. Why is it important for Descartes to show that he perceives his mind more clearly and distinctly than his body?
3. Explain the relevance of Descartes's disanalogy of the body being like a ship with a sailor.
4. How does Descartes show that the mind is distinct from the body when he examines the notion of its being indivisible?
5. What is the overall relation of the mind to the body according to Descartes?

Second Meditation: The nature of the human mind, and how it is better known than the body.

Let us consider the things which people commonly think they understand most distinctly of all; that is, the bodies which we touch and see. I do not mean bodies in general—for perceptions are apt to be somewhat more confused—but one particular body. Let us take, for example, this piece of wax. It has just been taken from the honeycomb; it has not yet quite lost the taste of the honey; it retains some of the scent of the flowers from which it was gathered; its colour, shape, and size are plain to see; it is hard, cold, and can be handled without difficulty; if you rap it with your knuckle it makes a sound. In short, it has everything which appears necessary to enable a body to be known as distinctly as possible. But even as I speak, I put the wax by the fire, and look: The residual taste is eliminated, the smell goes away, the colour changes, the shape is lost, the size increases; it becomes liquid and hot; you can hardly touch it, and if you strike it, it no longer makes a sound. But does the same wax remain? It must be admitted that it does; no one denies it, no one thinks otherwise. So what was it in the wax that I understood with such distinctness? Evidently none of the features which I arrived at by means of the senses; for whatever came under taste, smell, sight, touch, or hearing has now altered—yet the wax remains.

Perhaps the answer lies in the thought which now comes to my mind; namely, the wax was not after all the sweetness of the honey, or the fragrance of the flowers, or the whiteness, or the shape, or the sound, but was rather a body which presented itself to me in these various forms a little while ago, but which now exhibits different ones. But what exactly is it that I am now imagining? Let us concentrate, take away everything which does not belong to the wax, and see what is left: merely something extended, flexible, and changeable. But what is meant here by 'flexible' and 'changeable'? Is it what I picture in my imagination: that this piece of wax is capable of changing from a round shape to a square shape, or from a square shape to a triangular shape? Not at all; for I can grasp that the wax is capable of countless changes of this kind, yet I am unable to run through this immeasurable number of changes in my imagination, from which it follows that it is not the faculty of imagination that gives me my grasp of the wax as flexible and changeable. And what is meant by 'extended'? Is the extension of the wax also unknown? For it increases if the wax melts, increases again if it boils, and is greater still if the heat is increased. I would not be making a correct judgement about the nature of wax unless I believed it capable of being extended in many more different ways than in I will ever encompass in my imagination. I must therefore admit that the nature of this piece of wax is in no way revealed by my imagination, but is perceived by the mind alone. (I am speaking of this particular piece of wax; the point is even clearer with regard to wax in general.) But what is this wax which is perceived by the mind alone?[2] It is of course the same wax which I see, which I touch, which I picture in my imagination, in short the same wax which I thought it to be from the start. And yet, and here is the point, the perception I have of it[3] is a case not of vision or touch or imagination—nor has it ever been, despite previous appearances—but of purely mental scrutiny; and this can be imperfect and confused, as it was before, or clear and distinct as it is now, depending on how carefully I concentrate on what the wax consists in.

But as I reach this conclusion I am amazed at how (weak and) prone to error my mind is. For although I am thinking about these matters within myself, silently and without speaking, nonetheless the actual words bring me up short, and I am almost tricked by ordinary ways of talking. We say that we see the wax itself, if it is there before us, not that we judge it to be there from its colour or shape; and this might lead me to conclude without more ado that knowledge of the wax comes from what the eye sees, and not from the scrutiny of the mind alone. But then if I look out of the window and see men crossing the square, as I just happen to have done, I normally say that I see the men themselves, just as I say that I see the wax. Yet do I see any more than hats and coats which could conceal automations? I *judge* that they are men. And so something which I thought I was seeing with my eyes is in fact grasped solely by the faculty of judgement which is in my mind.

However, one who wants to achieve knowledge above the ordinary level should feel ashamed at having taken ordinary ways of talking as a basis for doubt. So let us proceed, and consider on which occasion my perception of the nature of the wax was more perfect and evident. Was it when I first looked at it, and believed I knew it by my external senses, or at least by what they call the 'common' sense—that is, the power of imagination? Or is my knowledge more perfect now, after a more careful investigation of the nature of the wax and of the means by which it is known? Any doubt on this issue would clearly be foolish; for what distinctness was there in my earlier perception? Was there anything in it which an animal could not possess? But when I distinguish the wax from its outward forms—take the clothes off, as it were, and consider it naked—then although my judgement may still contain errors, at least my perception now requires a human mind.

But what am I to say about this mind, or about myself? (So far, remember, I am not admitting that there is anything else in me except a mind.) What, I ask, is this 'I' which seems to perceive the wax so distinctly? Surely my awareness of my own self is not merely much truer and more certain than my awareness of the wax, but also much more distinct and evident. For if I judge that the wax exists from the fact that I see it, clearly this same fact entails much more evidently that I myself also exist. It is possible that what I see is not really the wax; it is possible that I do not even have eyes with which to see anything. But when I see, or think I see (I am not here distinguishing the two), it is simply not possible that I who am now thinking am not something. By the same token, if I judge that the wax exists from the fact that I touch it, the same result follows, namely that I exist. If I judge that it exists from the fact that I imagine it, or for any other reason, exactly the same thing follows. And the result that I have grasped in the case of the wax may be applied to everything else located outside me. Moreover, if my perception of the wax seemed more distinct[4] after it was established not just by sight or touch but by many other considerations, it must be admitted that I now know myself even more distinctly. This is because every consideration whatsoever which contributes to my perception of the wax, or of any other body, cannot but establish even more effectively the nature of my own mind. But besides this, there is so much else in the mind itself which can serve to make my knowledge of it more distinct, that it scarcely seems worth going through the contributions made by considering bodily things.

I see that without any effort I have now finally got back to where I wanted. I now know that even bodies are not strictly perceived by the senses or the faculty of imagination but by the intellect alone, and that this perception derives not from their being touched or seen but from their being understood; and in view of this I know plainly that I can achieve an easier and more evident perception of my own mind than of anything else. But since the habit of holding on to old opinions cannot be set aside so quickly, I should like to stop here and mediate for some time on this new knowledge I have gained, so as to fix it more deeply in my memory.

Sixth Meditation: The existence of material things, and the real distinction between mind and body.

. . . The fact that I can clearly and distinctly understand one thing apart from another is enough to make me certain that the two things are distinct, since they are capable of being separated, at least by God. The question of what kind of power is required to bring about such a separation does not affect the judgement that the two things are distinct. Thus, simply by knowing that I exist and seeing at the same time that absolutely nothing else belongs to my nature or essence except that I am a thinking thing, I can infer correctly that my essence consists solely in the fact that I am a thinking thing. It is true that I may have (or, to anticipate, that I certainly have) a body that is very closely joined to me. But nevertheless, on the one hand I have a clear and distinct idea of myself, in so far as I am simply a thinking, non-extended thing; and on the other hand I have a distinct idea of body,[5] in so far as this is simply an extended, non-thinking thing. And accordingly, it is certain that I[6] am really distinct from my body, and can exist without it.

Besides this, I find in myself faculties for certain special modes of thinking,[7] namely imagination and sensory perception. Now I can clearly and distinctly understand myself as a whole without these faculties; but I cannot, conversely, understand these faculties without me, that is, without an intellectual substance to inhere in. This is because there is an intellectual act included in their essential definition; and hence I perceive that the distinction between them and myself corresponds to the distinction between the modes of a thing and the thing itself.[8] Of course I also recognize that there are other faculties (like those of changing position, of taking on various shapes, and so on) which, like sensory perception and imagination, cannot be understood apart from some substance for them to inhere in, and hence cannot exist without it. But it is clear that these other faculties, if they exist, must be in a corporeal or extended substance and not an intellectual one; for the clear and distinct conception of them includes extension, but does not include any intellectual act whatsoever. . . .

There is nothing that my own nature teaches me more vividly than that I have a body, and that when I feel pain there is something wrong with the body, and that when I am hungry or thirsty the body needs food and drink, and so on. So I should not doubt that there is some truth in this.

Nature also teaches me, by these sensations of pain, hunger, thirst and so on, that I am not merely present in my body as a sailor is present in a ship,[9] but that I am very closely joined and, as it were, intermingled with it, so that I and the body form a unit. If this were not so, I, who am nothing but a thinking thing, would not feel pain when the body was hurt, but would perceive the damage purely by the intellect, just as a sailor perceives by sight if anything in his ship is broken. Similarly, when the body needed food or drink, I should have an explicit understanding of the fact, instead of having confused sensations of hunger and thirst. For these sensations of hunger, thirst, pain, and so on are nothing but confused modes of thinking which arise from the union and, as it were, intermingling of the mind with the body.

I am also taught by nature that various other bodies exist in the vicinity of my body, and that some of these are to be sought out and others avoided. And from the fact that I perceive by my senses a great variety of colours, sounds, smells, and tastes, as well as differences in heat, hardness, and the like, I am correct in inferring that the bodies which are the source of these various sensory perceptions possess differences corresponding to them, though perhaps not resembling them. Also, the fact that some of the perceptions are agreeable to me while others are disagreeable makes it quite certain that my body, or rather my whole self, in so far as I am a combination of body and mind, can be affected by the various beneficial or harmful bodies which surround it.

There are, however, many other things which I may appear to have been taught by nature, but which in reality I acquired not from nature but from a habit of making ill-considered judgements; and it is therefore quite possible that these are false. Cases in point are the belief that any space in which nothing is occurring to stimulate my senses must be empty; or that the heat in a body is something exactly resembling the idea of heat which is in me; or that when a body is white or green, the selfsame whiteness or greenness which I perceive through my senses is present in the body; or that in a body which is bitter or sweet there is the selfsame taste which I experience, and so on; or, finally, that stars and towers and other distant bodies have the same size and shape which they present to my senses, and other examples of this kind. But to make sure that my perceptions in this matter are sufficiently distinct, I must more accurately define exactly what I mean when I say that I am taught something by nature. In this context I am taking nature to be something more limited than the totality of things bestowed on me by God. For this includes many things that belong to the mind alone—for example my perception that what is done cannot be undone, and all other things that are known by the natural light;[10] but at this stage I am not speaking of these matters. It also includes much that relates to the body alone, like the tendency to move in a downward direction, and so on; but I am not speaking of these matters either. My sole concern here is with what God has bestowed on me as a combination of mind and body. My nature, then, in this limited sense, does indeed teach me to avoid what induces a feeling of pain and to seek out what induces feelings of pleasure, and so on. But it does not appear to teach us to draw any conclusions from these sensory perceptions about things located outside us without waiting until the intellect has examined[11] the matter. For knowledge of the truth about such things seems to belong to the mind alone, not to the combination of mind and body. Hence, although a star has no greater effect on my eye than the flame of a small light, that does not mean that there is any real or positive inclination in me to believe that the star is no bigger than the light; I have simply made this judgement from childhood onwards without any rational basis. Similarly, although I feel heat when I go near a fire and feel pain when I go too near, there is no convincing argument for supposing that there is something in the fire which resembles the heat, any more than for supposing that there is something which resembles the pain. There is simply reason to suppose that there is something in the fire, whatever it may eventually turn out to be, which produces in us the feelings of heat or pain. And likewise, even though there is nothing in any given space that stimulates the senses, it does not follow that there is no body there. In these cases and many others I see that I have been in the habit of misusing the order of nature. For the proper purpose of the sensory perceptions given me by nature is simply to inform the mind of what is beneficial or harmful for the composite of which the mind is a part; and to this extent they are sufficiently clear and distinct. But I misuse them by treating them as reliable touchstones for immediate judgements about the essential nature of the bodies located outside us; yet this is an area where they provide only very obscure information.

I have already looked in sufficient detail at how, notwithstanding the goodness of God, it may happen that my judgements are false. But a further problem now comes to mind regarding those very things which nature presents to me as objects which I should seek out or avoid, and also regarding the internal sensations, where I seem to have detected errors[12]—e.g., when someone is tricked by the pleasant taste of some food into eating the poison concealed inside it. Yet in this case, what the man's nature urges him to go for is simply what is responsible for the pleasant taste, and not the poison, which his nature knows nothing about. The only inference that can be drawn from this is that his nature is not omniscient. And this is not surprising, since man is a limited thing, and so it is only fitting that his perfection should be limited.

And yet it is not unusual for us to go wrong even in cases where nature does urge us towards something. Those who are ill, for example, may desire food or drink that will shortly afterwards turn out to be bad for them. Perhaps it may be said that they go wrong because their nature is disordered, but this does not remove the difficulty. A sick man is no less one of God's creatures than a healthy one, and it seems no less a contradiction to suppose that he has received from God a nature which deceives him. Yet a clock constructed with wheels and weights observes all the laws of its nature just as closely when it is badly made and tells the wrong time as when it completely fulfils the wishes of the clockmaker. In the same way, I might consider the body of a man as a kind of machine equipped with and made up of bones, nerves, muscles, veins, blood, and skin in such a way that, even if there were no mind in it, it would still perform all the same movements as it now does in those cases where movement is not under the control of the will or, consequently, of the mind.[13] I can easily see that if such a body suffers from dropsy, for example, and is affected by the dryness of the throat which normally produces in the mind the sensation of thirst, the resulting condition of the nerves and other parts will dispose the body to take a drink, with the result that the disease will be aggravated. Yet this is just as natural as the body's being stimulated by a similar dryness of the throat to take a drink when there is no such illness and the drink is beneficial. Admittedly, when I consider the purpose of the clock, I may say that it is departing from its nature when it does not tell the right time; and similarly when I consider the mechanism of the human body, I may think that, in relation to the movements which normally occur in it, it too is deviating from its nature if the throat is dry at a time when drinking is not beneficial to its continued health. But I am well aware that 'nature' as I have just used it has a very different significance from 'nature' in the other sense. As I have just used it, 'nature' is simply a label which depends on my thought; it is quite extraneous to the things to which it is applied, and depends simply on my comparison between the idea of a sick man and a badly-made clock, and the idea of a healthy man and a well-made clock. But by 'nature' in the other sense I understand something which is really to be found in the things themselves; in this sense, therefore, the term contains something of the truth.

When we say, then, with respect to the body suffering from dropsy, that it has a disordered nature because it has a dry throat and yet does not need drink, the term 'nature' is here used merely as an extraneous label. However, with respect to the composite, that is, the mind united with this body, what is involved is not a mere label, but a true error of nature, namely that it is thirsty at a time when drink is going to cause it harm. It thus remains to inquire how it is that the goodness of God does not prevent nature, in this sense, from deceiving us.

The first observation I make at this point is that there is a great difference between the mind and the body, inasmuch as the body is by its very nature always divisible, while the mind is utterly indivisible. For when I consider the mind, or myself in so far as I am merely a thinking thing, I am unable to distinguish any parts within myself; I understand myself to be something quite single and complete. Although the whole mind seems to be united to the whole body, I recognize that if a foot or arm or any other part of the body is cut off, nothing has thereby been taken away from the mind. As for the faculties of willing, of understanding, of sensory perception and so on, these cannot be termed parts of the mind, since it is one and the same mind that wills, and understands and has sensory perceptions. By contrast, there is no corporeal or extended thing that I can think of which in my thought I cannot easily divide into parts; and this very fact makes me understand that it is divisible. This one argument would be enough to show me that the mind is completely different from the body, even if I did not already know as much from other considerations.

My next observation is that the mind is not immediately affected by all parts of the body, but only by the brain, or perhaps just by one small part of the brain, namely the part which is said to contain the 'common' sense.[14] Every time this part of the brain is in a given state, it presents the same signals to the mind, even though the other parts of the body may be in a different condition at the time. This is established by countless observations, which there is no need to review here.

I observe, in addition, that the nature of the body is such that whenever any part of it is moved by another part which is some distance away, it can always be moved in the same fashion by any of the parts which lie in between, even if the more distant part does nothing. For example, in a cord ABCD, if one end D is pulled so that the other end A moves, the exact same movement could have been brought about if one of the intermediate points B or C had been pulled, and D had not moved at all. In similar fashion, when I feel a pain in my foot, physiology tells me that this happens by means of nerves distributed throughout the foot, and that these nerves are like cords which go from the foot right up to the brain. When the nerves are pulled in the foot, they in turn pull on inner parts of the brain to which they are attached, and produce a certain motion in them; and nature has laid it down that this motion should produce in the mind a sensation of pain, as occurring in the foot. But since these nerves, in passing from the foot to the brain, must pass through the calf, the thigh, the lumbar region, the back and the neck, it can happen that, even if it is not the part in the foot but one of the intermediate parts which is being pulled, the same motion will occur in the brain as occurs when the foot is hurt, and so it will necessarily come about that the mind feels the same sensation of pain. And we must suppose the same thing happens with regard to any other sensation.

My final observation is that any given movement occurring in the part of the brain that immediately affects the mind produces just one corresponding sensation; and hence the best system that could be devised is that it should produce the one sensation which, of all possible sensations, is most especially and most frequently conducive to the preservation of the healthy man. And experience shows that the sensations which nature has given us are all of this kind; and so there is absolutely nothing to be found in them that does not bear witness to the power and goodness of God. For example, when the nerves in the foot are set in motion in a violent and unusual manner, this motion, by way of the spinal cord, reaches the inner parts of the brain, and there gives the mind its signal for having a certain sensation, namely the sensation of a pain as occurring in the foot. This stimulates the mind to do its best to get rid of the cause of the pain, which it takes to be harmful to the foot. It is true that God could have made the nature of man such that this particular motion in the brain indicated something else to the mind; it might, for example, have made the mind aware of the actual motion occurring in the brain, or in the foot, or in any of the intermediate regions; or it might have indicated something else entirely. But there is nothing else which would have been so conducive to the continued well-being of the body. In the same way, when we need drink, there arises a certain dryness in the throat; this sets in motion the nerves of the throat, which in turn move the inner parts of the brain. This motion produces in the mind a sensation of thirst, because the most useful thing for us to know about the whole business is that we need drink in order to stay healthy. And so it is in the other cases.

Discussion Questions

1. When one melts, or even boils, a cube of solid wax, do you agree that the result is still the *same* wax? How does this relate to your own sameness/identity over time? If you were changed as drastically as being melted, would you still be the *same*?
2. Descartes states (and defends elsewhere) that God is not a deceiver. The popular conception of God is that He is good/loving. Why is that? Could a creator be otherwise?
3. Descartes argues that, because the mind is distinct from the body in a number of ways, it is *known* differently; it is indivisible. This is proof that the mind exists. Does this argument persuade you? Why/why not?

The Mind-Body Problem
John Searle

John Searle teaches philosophy at U. C. Berkeley and has published sixteen books, nearly all of which focus on the philosophy of mind. This selection is the first chapter of his book *Minds, Brains, and Science*. In it, he provides a brief overview of the problem. In doing so, he sets forth what he believes to be four key features of mental phenomena that many often have trouble converging with the current (scientific) world-view. Following that, he goes on to defend his own position, dissolving the problems and providing what he believes to be a consistent framework for the mind-body problem.

Source: Reprinted by permission of the publisher from *Minds, Brains, and Science* by John R. Searle, pp. 13, 14, 15–27, Cambridge, Mass.: Harvard University Press, copyright © 1984 by John R. Searle.

Reading Questions

1. What four features of mental phenomena does Searle suggest make it hard to discuss the mind-body problem in a "scientific" way?
2. What sort of cause-and-effect does Searle suggest will help us think about the mind-brain relationship more clearly? How does his analogy of liquidity and water relate to the mental phenomena and the brain?
3. How does Searle defend each of the four initially stated features of mental phenomena that seemed problematic?
4. How does Searle define "naïve physicalism" and "naïve mentalism," and why does he think they can both be true?

For thousands of years, people have been trying to understand their relationship to the rest of the universe. For a variety of reasons many philosophers today are reluctant to tackle such big problems. Nonetheless, the problems remain. . . .

At the moment, the biggest problem is this: We have a certain commonsense picture of ourselves as human beings which is very hard to square with our overall 'scientific' conception of the physical world. We think of ourselves as *conscious, free, mindful, rational* agents in a world that science tells us consists entirely of mindless, meaningless physical particles. Now, how can we square these two conceptions? How, for example, can it be the case that the world contains nothing but unconscious physical particles, and yet that it also contains consciousness? How can a mechanical universe contain intentionalistic human beings – that is, human beings that can represent the world to themselves? How, in short, can an essentially meaningless world contain meanings?. . .

I want to plunge right into what many philosophers think of as the hardest problem of all: What is the relation of our minds to the rest of the universe? This, I am sure you will recognise, is the traditional mind-body or mind-brain problem. In its contemporary version it usually takes the form: How does the mind relate to the brain?

I believe that the mind-body problem has a rather simple solution, one that is consistent both with what we know about neurophysiology and with our commonsense conception of the nature of mental states—pains, beliefs, desires, and so on. But before presenting that solution, I want to ask why the mind-body problem seems so intractable. Why do we still have in philosophy and psychology after all these centuries a 'mind-body problem' in a way that we do not have, say, a 'digestion-stomach problem'? Why does the mind seem more mysterious than other biological phenomena?

I am convinced that part of the difficulty is that we persist in talking about a twentieth-century problem in an outmoded seventeenth-century vocabulary. When I was an undergraduate, I remember being dissatisfied with the choices that were apparently available in the philosophy of mind: You could be either a monist or a dualist. If you were a monist, you could be either a materialist or an idealist. If you were a materialist, you could be either a behaviourist or a physical-ist. And so on. One of my aims in what follows is to try to break out of these tired old categories. Notice that nobody feels he has to choose between monism and dualism where the 'digestion-stomach problem' is concerned. Why should it be any different with the 'mind-body problem'?

But, vocabulary apart, there is still a problem or family of problems. Since Descartes, the mind-body problem has taken the following form: How can we account for the relationships between two apparently completely different kinds of things? On the one hand, there are mental things, such as our thoughts and feelings; we think of them as subjective, conscious, and immaterial. On the other hand, there are physical things; we think of them as having mass, as extended in space, and as causally interacting with other physical things. Most attempted solutions to the mind-body problem wind up by denying the existence of, or in some way downgrading the status of, one or the other of these types of things. Given the successes of the physical sciences, it is not surprising that in our stage of intellectual development the temptation is to downgrade the status of men-tal entities. So, most of the recently fashionable materialist conceptions of the mind—such as behaviourism, functionalism, and physicalism—end up by deny-ing, implicitly or explicitly, that there are any such things as minds as we ordinar-ily think of them. That is, they deny that we do really *intrinsically* have subjective, conscious, mental states and that they are as real and as irreducible as anything else in the universe.

Now, why do they do that? Why is it that so many theorists end up denying the intrinsically mental character of mental phenomena? If we can answer that question, I believe that we will understand why the mind-body problem has seemed so intractable for so long.

There are four features of mental phenomena which have made them seem impossible to fit into our 'scientific' conception of the world as made up of mate-rial things. And it is these four features that have made the mind-body problem really difficult. They are so embarrassing that they have led many thinkers in phi-losophy, psychology, and artificial intelligence to say strange and implausible things about the mind.

The most important of these features is consciousness. I, at the moment of writing this, and you, at the moment of reading it, are both conscious. It is just a plain fact about the world that it contains such conscious mental states and events, but it is hard to see how mere physical systems could have consciousness. How could such a thing occur? How, for example, could this grey and white gook inside my skull be conscious?

I think the existence of consciousness ought to seem amazing to us. It is easy enough to imagine a universe without it, but if you do, you will see that you have imagined a universe that is truly meaningless. Consciousness is the central fact of specifically human existence because without it all of the other specifically human aspects of our existence—language, love, humour, and so on—would be impossible. I believe it is, by the way, something of a scandal that contemporary discussions in philosophy and psychology have so little of interest to tell us about consciousness.

The second intractable feature of the mind is what philosophers and psychologists call 'intentionality,' the feature by which our mental states are directed at, or about, or refer to, or are of objects and states of affairs in the world other than themselves. 'Intentionality,' by the way, doesn't just refer to intentions, but also to beliefs, desires, hopes, fears, love, hate, lust, disgust, shame, pride, irritation, amusement, and all of those mental states (whether conscious or unconscious) that refer to, or are about, the world apart from the mind. Now the question about intentionality is much like the question about consciousness. How can this stuff inside my head be *about* anything? How can it *refer* to anything? After all, this stuff in the skull consists of 'atoms in the void,' just as all of the rest of material reality consists of atoms in the void. Now how, to put it crudely, can atoms in the void represent anything?

The third feature of the mind that seems difficult to accommodate within a scientific conception of reality is the subjectivity of mental states. This subjectivity is marked by such facts as that I can feel my pains, and you can't. I see the world from my point of view; you see it from your point of view. I am aware of myself and my internal mental states, as quite distinct from the selves and mental states of other people. Since the seventeenth century we have come to think of reality as something which must be equally accessible to all competent observers—that is, we think it must be objective. Now, how are we to accommodate the reality of *subjective* mental phenomena with the scientific conception of reality as totally *objective*?

Finally, there is a fourth problem, the problem of mental causation. We all suppose, as part of common sense, that our thoughts and feelings make a real difference to the way we behave, that they actually have some *causal* effect on the physical world. I decide, for example, to raise my arm and—lo and behold—my arm goes up. But if our thoughts and feelings are truly mental, how can they affect anything physical? How could something mental make a physical difference? Are we supposed to think that our thoughts and feelings can somehow produce chemical effects on our brains and the rest of our nervous system? How could such a thing occur? Are we supposed to think that thoughts can wrap themselves around the axons or shake the dendrites or sneak inside the cell wall and attack the cell nucleus?

But unless some such connection takes place between the mind and the brain, aren't we just left with the view that the mind doesn't matter, that it is as unimportant causally as the froth on the wave is to the movement of the wave? I suppose if the froth were conscious, it might think to itself: 'What a tough job it is pulling these waves up on the beach and then pulling them out again, all day long!' But we know the froth doesn't make any important difference. Why do we suppose our mental life is any more important than a froth on the wave of physical reality?

These four features, consciousness, intentionality, subjectivity, and mental causation are what make the mind-body problem seem so difficult. Yet, I want to say, they are all real features of our mental lives. Not every mental state has all of them. But any satisfactory account of the mind and of mind-body relations must take account of all four features. If your theory ends up by denying any one of them, you know you must have made a mistake somewhere.

The first thesis I want to advance toward 'solving the mind-body problem' is this:

> Mental phenomena, all mental phenomena whether conscious or unconscious, visual or auditory, pains, tickles, itches, thoughts, indeed, all of our mental life, are caused by processes going on in the brain.

To get a feel for how this works, let's try to describe the causal processes in some detail for at least one kind of mental state. For example, let's consider pains. Of course, anything we say now may seem wonderfully quaint in a generation, as our knowledge of how the brain works increases. Still, the *form* of the explanation can remain valid even though the *details* are altered. On current views, pain signals are transmitted from sensory nerve endings to the spinal cord by at least two types of fibres—there are Delta A fibres, which are specialised for prickling sensations, and C fibres, which are specialised for burning and aching sensations. In the spinal cord, they pass through a region called the tract of Lissauer and terminate on the neurons of the cord. As the signals go up the spine, they enter the brain by two separate pathways: the prickling pain pathway and the burning pain pathway. Both pathways go through the thalamus, but the prickling pain is more localised afterwards in the somato-sensory cortex, whereas the burning pain pathway transmits signals, not only upwards into the cortex, but also laterally into the hypothalamus and other regions at the base of the brain. Because of these differences, it is much easier for us to localise a prickling sensation—we can tell fairly accurately where someone is sticking a pin into our skin, for example—whereas burning and aching pains can be more distressing because they activate more of the nervous system. The actual sensation of pain appears to be caused both by the stimulation of the basal regions of the brain, especially the thalamus, and the stimulation of the somato-sensory cortex.

Now for the purposes of this discussion, the point we need to hammer home is this: Our sensations of pains are caused by a series of events that begin at free nerve endings and end in the thalamus and in other regions of the brain. Indeed, as far as the actual sensations are concerned, the events inside the central nervous system are quite sufficient to cause pains—we know this both from the phantom-limb pains felt by amputees and the pains caused by artificially stimulating relevant portions of the brain. I want to suggest that what is true of pain is true of mental phenomena generally. To put it crudely, and counting all of the central nervous system as part of the brain for our present discussion, everything that matters for our mental life, all of our thoughts and feelings, are caused by processes inside the brain. As far as causing mental states is concerned, the crucial step is the one that goes on inside the head, not the external or peripheral stimulus. And the argument for this is simple. If the events outside the central nervous system occurred, but nothing happened in the brain, there would be no mental events. But if the right things happened in the brain, the mental events would occur even if there was no outside stimulus. (And that, by the way, is the principle on which surgical anaesthesia works: The outside stimulus is prevented from having the relevant effects on the central nervous system.)

But if pains and other mental phenomena are caused by processes in the brain, one wants to know: What are pains? What are they really? Well, in the case of pains, the obvious answer is that they are unpleasant sorts of sensations. But that answer leaves us unsatisfied because it doesn't tell us how pains fit into our overall conception of the world.

Once again, I think the answer to the question is obvious, but it will take some spelling out. To our first claim—that pains and other mental phenomena are caused by brain processes, we need to add a second claim:

> Pains and other mental phenomena just are features of the brain (and perhaps the rest of the central nervous system).

One of the primary aims of this chapter is to show how *both* of these propositions can be true together. How can it be both the case that brains cause minds and yet minds just are features of brains? I believe it is the failure to see how both these propositions can be true together that has blocked a solution to the mind-body problem for so long. There are different levels of confusion that such a pair of ideas can generate. If mental and physical phenomena have cause and effect relationships, how can one be a feature of the other? Wouldn't that imply that the mind caused itself—the dreaded doctrine of *causa sui*? But at the bottom of our puzzlement is a misunderstanding of causation. It is tempting to think that whenever A causes B there must be two discrete events, one identified as the cause, the other identified as the effect; that all causation functions in the same way as billiard balls hitting each other. This crude model of the causal relationships between the brain and the mind inclines us to accept some kind of dualism; we are inclined to think that events in one material realm, the 'physical,' cause events in another insubstantial realm, the 'mental.' But that seems to me a mistake. And the way to remove the mistake is to get a more sophisticated concept of causation. To do this, I will turn away from the relations between mind and brain for a moment to observe some other sorts of causal relationships in nature.

A common distinction in physics is between micro- and macro-properties of systems—the small and large scales. Consider, for example, the desk at which I am now sitting, or the glass of water in front of me. Each object is composed of micro-particles. The micro-particles have features at the level of molecules and atoms as well as at the deeper level of sub-atomic particles. But each object also has certain properties such as the solidity of the table, the liquidity of the water, and the transparency of the glass, which are surface or global features of the physical systems. Many such surface or global properties can be causally explained by the behaviour of elements at the micro-level. For example, the solidity of the table in front of me is explained by the lattice structure occupied by the molecules of which the table is composed. Similarly, the liquidity of the water is explained by the nature of the interactions between the H_2O molecules. Those macro-features are causally explained by the behaviour of elements at the micro-level.

I want to suggest that this provides a perfectly ordinary model for explaining the puzzling relationships between the mind and the brain. In the case of liquidity, solidity, and transparency, we have no difficulty at all in supposing that the surface features are *caused by* the behaviour of elements at the micro-level, and at the same time we accept that the surface phenomena *just are* features of the very systems in question. I think the clearest way of stating this point is to say that the surface feature is both *caused by* the behaviour of micro-elements, and at the same time is *realised in* the system that is made up of the micro-elements. There is a cause and effect relationship, but at the same time the surface features are just higher level features of the very system whose behaviour at the micro-level causes those features.

In objecting to this someone might say that liquidity, solidity, and so on are identical with features of the micro-structure. So, for example, we might just define solidity as the lattice structure of the molecular arrangement, just as heat often is identified with the mean kinetic energy of molecule movements. This point seems to me correct but not really an objection to the analysis that I am proposing. It is a characteristic of the progress of science that an expression that is originally defined in terms of surface features, features accessible to the senses, is subsequently defined in terms of the micro-structure that causes the surface features. Thus, to take the example of solidity, the table in front of me is solid in the ordinary sense that it is rigid, it resists pressure, it supports books, it is not easily penetrable by most other objects such as other tables, and so on. Such is the commonsense notion of solidity. And in a scientific vein one can define solidity as whatever micro-structure causes these gross observable features. So one can then say either that solidity just is the lattice structure of the system of molecules and that solidity so defined causes, for example, resistance to touch and pressure. Or one can say that solidity consists of such high level features as rigidity and resistance to touch and pressure and that it is caused by the behaviour of elements at the micro-level.

If we apply these lessons to the study of the mind, it seems to me that there is no difficulty in accounting for the relations of the mind to the brain in terms of the brain's functioning to cause mental states. Just as the liquidity of the water is caused by the behaviour of elements at the micro-level, and yet at the same time it is a feature realised in the system of micro-elements, so in exactly that sense of 'caused by' and 'realised in' mental phenomena are caused by processes going on in the brain at the neuronal or modular level, and at the same time they are realised in the very system that consists of neurons. And just as we need the micro/macro distinction for any physical system, so for the same reasons we need the micro/macro distinction for the brain. And though we can say of a system of particles that it is 10°C or it is solid or it is liquid, we cannot say of any given particle that this particle is solid, this particle is liquid, this particle is 10°C. I can't for example reach into this glass of water, pull out a molecule and say: 'This one's wet.'

In exactly the same way, as far as we know anything at all about it, though we can say of a particular brain: 'This brain is conscious,' or: 'This brain is experiencing thirst or pain,' we can't say of any particular neuron in the brain: 'This neuron is in pain, this neuron is experiencing thirst.' To repeat this point, though there are enormous empirical mysteries about how the brain works in detail, there are no logical or philosophical or metaphysical obstacles to accounting for the relation between the mind and the brain in terms that are quite familiar to us from the rest of nature. Nothing is more common in nature than for surface features of a phenomenon to be both caused by and realised in a micro-structure, and those are exactly the relationships that are exhibited by the relation of mind to brain.

Let us now return to the four problems that I said faced any attempt to solve the mind-brain problem.

First, how is consciousness possible?

The best way to show how something is possible is to show how it actually exists. We have already given a sketch of how pains are actually caused by neurophysiological processes going on in the thalamus and the sensory cortex. Why is it then that many people feel dissatisfied with this sort of answer? I think that by pursuing an analogy with an earlier problem in the history of science we can dispel this sense of puzzlement. For a long time many biologists and philosophers thought it was impossible, in principle, to account for the existence of *life* on purely biological grounds. They thought that in addition to the biological processes some other element must be necessary, some *élan vital* must be postulated in order to lend life to what was otherwise dead and inert matter. It is hard today to realise how intense the dispute was between vitalism and mechanism even a generation ago, but today these issues are no longer taken seriously. Why not? I think it is not so much because mechanism won and vitalism lost, but because we have come to understand better the biological character of the processes that are characteristic of living organisms. Once we understand how the features that are characteristic of living beings have a biological explanation, it no longer seems mysterious to us that matter should be alive. I think that exactly similar considerations should apply to our discussions of consciousness. It should seem no more mysterious, in principle, that this hunk of matter, this grey and white oatmeal-textured substance of the brain, should be conscious than it seems mysterious that this other hunk of matter, this collection of nucleo-protein molecules stuck onto a calcium frame, should be alive. The way, in short, to dispel the mystery is to understand the processes. We do not yet fully understand the processes, but we understand their general *character*, we understand that there are certain specific electrochemical activities going on among neurons or neuron-modules and perhaps other features of the brain and these processes cause consciousness.

Our second problem was, how can atoms in the void have intentionality? How can they be about something?

As with our first question, the best way to show how something is possible is to show how it actually exists. So let's consider thirst. As far as we know anything about it, at least certain kinds of thirst are caused in the hypothalamus by sequences of nerve firings. These firings are in turn caused by the action of angiotensin in the hypothalamus, and angiotensin, in turn, is synthesised by renin, which is secreted by the kidneys. Thirst, at least of these kinds, is caused by a series of events in the central nervous system, principally the hypothalamus, and it is realised in the hypothalamus. To be thirsty is to have, among other things, the desire to drink. Thirst is therefore an intentional state: It has content; its content determines under what conditions it is satisfied, and it has all the rest of the features that are common to intentional states.

As with the 'mysteries' of life and consciousness, the way to master the mystery of intentionality is to describe in as much detail as we can how the phenomena are caused by biological processes while being at the same time realised in biological system. Visual and auditory experiences, tactile sensations, hunger, thirst, and sexual desire, are all caused by brain processes and they are realised in the structure of the brain, and they are all intentional phenomena.

I am not saying we should lose our sense of the mysteries of nature. On the contrary, the examples I have cited are all in a sense astounding. But I am saying that they are neither more nor less mysterious than other astounding features of the world, such as the existence of gravitational attraction, the process of photosynthesis, or the size of the Milky Way.

Our third problem: how do we accommodate the subjectivity of mental states within an objective conception of the real world?

It seems to me a mistake to suppose that the definition of reality should exclude subjectivity. If 'science' is the name of the collection of objective and systematic truths we can state about the world, then the existence of subjectivity is an objective scientific fact like any other. If a scientific account of the world attempts to describe how things are, then one of the features of the account will be the subjectivity of mental states, since it is just a plain fact about biological evolution that it has produced certain sorts of biological systems, namely human and certain animal brains, that have subjective features. My present state of consciousness is a feature of my brain, but its conscious aspects are accessible to me in a way that they are not accessible to you. And your present state of consciousness is a feature of your brain and its conscious aspects are accessible to you in a way that they are not accessible to me. Thus the existence of subjectivity is an objective fact of biology. It is a persistent mistake to try to define 'science' in terms of certain features of existing scientific theories. But once this provincialism is perceived to be the prejudice it is, then any domain of facts whatever is a subject of systematic investigation. So, for example, if God existed, then that fact would be a fact like any other. I do not know whether God exists, but I have no doubt at all that subjective mental states exist, because I am now in one and so are you. If the fact of subjectivity runs counter to a certain definition of 'science,' then it is the definition and not the fact which we will have to abandon.

Fourth, the problem of mental causation for our present purpose is to explain how mental events can cause physical events. How, for example, could anything as 'weightless' and 'ethereal' as a thought give rise to an action?

The answer is that thoughts are not weightless and ethereal. When you have a thought, brain activity is actually going on. Brain activity causes bodily movements by physiological processes. Now, because mental states are features of the brain, they have two levels of description—a higher level in mental terms, and a lower level in physiological terms. The very same causal powers of the system can be described at either level.

Once again, we can use an analogy from physics to illustrate these relationships. Consider hammering a nail with a hammer. Both hammer and nail have a certain kind of solidity. Hammers made of cottonwool or butter will be quite useless, and hammers made of water or steam are not hammers at all. Solidity is a real causal property of the hammer. But the solidity itself is caused by the behaviour of particles at the micro-level and it is realised in the system which consists of micro-elements. The existence of two causally real levels of description in the brain, one a macro-level of mental processes and the other a micro-level of neuronal processes is exactly analogous to the existence of two causally real levels of description of the hammer. Consciousness, for example, is a real property of the brain that can cause things to happen. My conscious attempt to perform an action such as raising my arm causes the movement of the arm. At the higher level of description, the intention to raise my arm causes the movement of the arm. But at the lower level of description, a series of neuron firings starts a chain of events that results in the contraction of the muscles. As with the case of hammering a nail, the same sequence of events has two levels of description. Both of them are causally real, and the higher level causal features are both caused by and realised in the structure of the lower level elements.

To summarise: On my view, the mind and the body interact, but they are not two different things, since mental phenomena just are features of the brain. One way to characterise this position is to see it as an assertion of both physicalism and mentalism. Suppose we define 'naive physicalism' to be the view that all that exists in the world are physical particles with their properties and relations. The power of the physical model of reality is so great that it is hard to see how we can seriously challenge naive physicalism. And let us define 'naive mentalism' to be the view that mental phenomena really exist. There really are mental states; some of them are conscious; many have intentionality; they all have subjectivity; and many of them function causally in determining physical events in the world. The thesis of this first chapter can now be stated quite simply. Naive mentalism and naive physicalism are perfectly consistent with each other. Indeed, as far as we know anything about how the world works, they are not only consistent, they are both true.

Discussion Questions

1. If we account for surgical anesthesia (something that should be painful but is not) and for phantom pains (an amputee can feel a pain in a limb that he or she does not have), what does this tell us about pain itself?

2. Do you find Searle's mention of water and liquidity as analogous to mental phenomena and the brain?

3. Which of Searle's four features of mental phenomena are philosophically problematic for you? Does he solve any that were?

4. Searle attempts to solve the problem of "causal interactionism" (that an immaterial mind cannot affect the material body). Has he done so in a satisfactory way? Does his account allow for an immaterial mind/soul, or has he just rephrased the problem using different words? Is "causal interactionism" a problem for you?

What Is It Like to Be a Bat?

Thomas Nagel

Professor of law and of philosophy at Princeton University and now at New York University, Thomas Nagel has published numerous books in many fields, with a focus on the philosophy of mind.

Here he presents an argument against reductionism—the notion that consciousness can be broken down and viewed objectively through the scientific process, thus supporting materialism. For example, a reductionist would claim that something like love is just certain chemicals behaving in the brain in a certain way and that the soul or mind is not needed to explain this experience.

Reading Questions

1. How does Nagel determine if an organism has "conscious mental states"?
2. What is the significance here of a "point of view"?
3. What point does Nagel make when he explores the answer to the question "What is it like to be a bat?"
4. How does Nagel explain the difference in the way that we (or even Martians) know about rainbows, lightning, etc.? How important is a human viewpoint in examining these sorts of things?
5. What results from a shift toward greater objectivity in attempting to discover the subjective character of experience?
6. Does Nagel believe he has successfully proved physicalism to be incorrect? If no, why?

Consciousness is what makes the mind-body problem really intractable. Perhaps that is why current discussions of the problem give it little attention or get it obviously wrong. The recent wave of reductionist euphoria has produced several analyses of mental phenomena and mental concepts designed to explain the possibility of some variety of materialism, psychophysical identification, or reduction. But the problems dealt with are those common to this type of reduction and other types, and what makes the mind-body problem unique, and unlike the water-H_2O problem or the Turing machine-IBM machine problem or the lightning-electrical discharge problem or the gene-DNA problem or the oak tree-hydrocarbon problem, is ignored.

Every reductionist has his favorite analogy from modern science. It is most unlikely that any of these unrelated examples of successful reduction will shed light on the relation of mind to brain. But philosophers share the general human weakness for explanations of what is incomprehensible in terms suited for what is

Source: Thomas Nagel, "What Is It Like to Be a Bat?" in The Philosophical Review, Volume 83, pp. 435–450.
Copyright © 1974, Cornell University Press. All rights reserved. Used by permission of the current publisher, Duke University Press.

incomprehensible in terms suited for what is familiar and well understood, though entirely different. This has led to the acceptance of implausible accounts of the mental largely because they would permit familiar kinds of reduction. I shall try to explain why the usual examples do not help us to understand the relation between mind and body—why, indeed, we have at present no conception of what an explanation of the physical nature of a mental phenomenon would be. Without consciousness the mind-body problem would be much less interesting. With consciousness it seems hopeless. The most important and characteristic feature of conscious mental phenomena is very poorly understood. Most reductionist theories do not even try to explain it. And careful examination will show that no currently available concept of reduction is applicable to it. Perhaps a new theoretical form can be devised for the purpose, but such a solution, if it exists, lies in the distinct intellectual future.

Conscious experience is a widespread phenomenon. It occurs at many levels of animal life, though we cannot be sure of its presence in the simpler organisms, and it is very difficult to say in general what provides evidence of it. (Some extremists have been prepared to deny it even of mammals other than man.) No doubt it occurs in countless forms totally unimaginable to us, on other planets in other solar systems throughout the universe. But no matter how the form may vary, the fact that an organism has conscious experience *at all* means, basically, that there is something it is like to *be* that organism. There may be further implications about the form of the experience; there may even (though I doubt it) be implications about the behavior of the organism. But fundamentally an organism has conscious mental states if and only if there is something that it is like to *be* that organism—something it is like *for* the organism.

We may call this the subjective character of experience. It is not captured by any of the familiar, recently devised reductive analyses of the mental, for all of them are logically compatible with its absence. It is not analyzable in terms of any explanatory system of functional states, or intentional states, since these could be ascribed to robots or automata that behaved like people though they experienced nothing. It is not analyzable in terms of the causal role of experiences in relation to typical human behavior—for similar reasons. I do not deny that conscious mental states and events cause behavior, nor that they may be given functional characterizations. I deny only that this kind of thing exhausts their analysis. Any reductionist program has to be based on an analysis of what is to be reduced. If the analysis leaves something out, the problem will be falsely posed. It is useless to base the defense of materialism on any analysis of mental phenomena that fails to deal explicitly with their subjective character. For there is no reason to suppose that a reduction which seems plausible when no attempt is made to account for consciousness can be extended to include consciousness. Without some idea, therefore, of what the subjective character of experience is, we cannot know what is required of a physicalist theory.

While an account of the physical basis of mind must explain many things, this appears to be the most difficult. It is impossible to exclude the phenomenological features of experience from a reduction in the same way that one excludes the phenomenal features of an ordinary substance from a physical or chemical reduction of it—namely, by explaining them as effects on the minds of human observers. If physicalism is to be defended, the phenomenological features must themselves be given a physical account. But when we examine their subjective character it seems that such a result is impossible. The reason is that every subjective phenomenon is essentially connected with a single point of view, and it seems inevitable that an objective, physical theory will abandon that point of view.

Let me first try to state the issue somewhat more fully than by referring to the relation between the subjective and the objective, or between the *pour-soi* and the *en-soi*. This is far from easy. Facts about what it is like to be an *X* are very peculiar, so peculiar that some may be inclined to doubt their reality, or the significance of claims about them. To illustrate the connection between subjectivity and a point of view, and to make evident the importance of subjective features, it will help to explore the matter in relation to an example that brings out clearly the divergence between the two types of conception, subjective and objective.

I assume we all believe that bats have experience. After all, they are mammals, and there is no more doubt that they have experience than that mice or pigeons or whales have experience. I have chosen bats instead of wasps or flounders because if one travels too far down the phylogenetic tree, people gradually shed their faith that there is experience there at all. Bats, although more closely related to us than those other species, nevertheless present a range of activity and a sensory apparatus so different from ours that the problem I want to pose is exceptionally vivid (though it certainly could be raised with other species). Even without the benefit of philosophical reflection, anyone who has spent some time in an enclosed space with an excited bat knows what it is to encounter a fundamentally *alien* form of life.

I have said that the essence of the belief that bats have experience is that there is something that it is like to be a bat. Now we know that most bats (the microchiroptera, to be precise) perceive the external world primarily by sonar, or echolocation, detecting the reflections, from objects within range, of their own rapid, subtly modulated, high-frequency shrieks. Their brains are designed to correlate the outgoing impulses with the subsequent echoes, and the information thus acquired enables bats to make precise discriminations of distance, size, shape, motion, and texture comparable to those we make by vision. But bat sonar, though clearly a form of perception, is not similar in its operation to any sense that we possess, and there is no reason to suppose that it is subjectively like anything we can experience or imagine. This appears to create difficulties for the notion of what it is like to be a bat. We must consider whether any method will permit us to extrapolate to the inner life of the bat from our own case, and if not, what alternative methods there may be for understanding the notion.

Our own experience provides the basic material for our imagination, whose range is therefore limited. It will not help to try to imagine that one has webbing on one's arms, which enables one to fly around at dusk and dawn catching insects in one's mouth; that one has very poor vision, and perceives the surrounding world by a system of reflected high-frequency sound signals; and that one spends the day hanging upside down by one's feet in an attic. In so far as I can imagine this (which is not very far), it tells me only what it would be like for *me* to behave as a bat behaves. But that is not the question. I want to know what it is like for a *bat* to be a bat. Yet if I try to imagine this, I am restricted to the resources of my own mind, and those resources are inadequate to the task. I cannot perform it either by imagining additions to my present experience, or by imagining segments gradually subtracted from it, or by imagining some combination of additions, subtractions, and modifications.

To the extent that I could look and behave like a wasp or a bat without changing my fundamental structure, my experiences would not be anything like the experiences of those animals. On the other hand, it is doubtful that any meaning can be attached to the supposition that I should possess the internal neurophysiological constitution of a bat. Even if I could by gradual degrees be transformed into a bat, nothing in my present constitution enables me to imagine what the experiences of such a future stage of myself thus metamorphosed would be like. The best evidence would come from the experiences of bats, if we only knew what they were like.

So if extrapolation from our own case is involved in the idea of what it is like to be a bat, the extrapolation must be incompletable. We cannot form more than a schematic conception of what it *is* like. For example, we may ascribe general *types* of experience on the basis of the animal's structure and behavior. Thus we describe bat sonar as a form of three-dimensional forward perception; we believe that bats feel some versions of pain, fear, hunger, and lust, and that they have other, more familiar types of perception besides sonar. But we believe that those experiences also have in each case a specific subjective character, which it is beyond our ability to conceive. And if there is conscious life elsewhere in the universe, it is likely that some of it will not be describable even in the most general experiential terms available to us. (The problem is not confined to exotic cases, however, for it exists between one person and another. The subjective character of the experience of a person deaf and blind from birth is not accessible to me, for example, nor presumably is mine to him. This does not prevent us each from believing that the other's experience has such a subjective character.)

If anyone is inclined to deny that we can believe in the existence of facts like this whose exact nature we cannot possibly conceive, he should reflect that in contemplating the bats we are in much the same position that intelligent bats or Martians would occupy if they tried to form a conception of what it was like to be us. The structure of their own minds might make it impossible for them to succeed, but we know they would be wrong to conclude that there is not anything precise that it is like to be us: that only certain general types of mental state could be ascribed to us (perhaps perception and appetite would be concepts common to us both; perhaps not). We know they would be wrong to draw such a skeptical conclusion because we know what it is like to be us. And we know that while it includes an enormous amount of variation and complexity, and while we do not possess the vocabulary to describe it adequately, its subjective character is highly specific, and in some respects describable in terms that can be understood only by creatures like us. The fact that we cannot expect ever to accommodate in our language a detailed description of Martian or bat phenomenology should not lead us to dismiss as meaningless the claim that bats and Martians have experiences fully comparable in richness of detail to our own. It would be fine if someone were to develop concepts and a theory that enabled us to think about those things; but such an understanding may be permanently denied to us by the limits of our nature. And to deny the reality or logical significance of what we can never describe or understand is the crudest form of cognitive dissonance.

This brings us to the edge of a topic that requires much more discussion than I can give it here: namely, the relation between facts on the one hand and conceptual schemes or systems of representation on the other. My realism about the subjective domain in all its forms implies a belief in the existence of facts beyond the reach of human concepts. Certainly it is possible for a human being to believe that there are facts which humans never *will* possess the requisite concepts to represent or comprehend. Indeed, it would be foolish to doubt this, given the finiteness of humanity's expectations. After all, there would have been transfinite numbers even if everyone had been wiped out by the Black Death before Cantor discovered them. But one might also believe that there are facts which *could* not ever be represented or comprehended by human beings, even if the species lasted forever—simply because our structure does not permit us to operate with concepts of the requisite type. This impossibility might even be observed by other beings, but it is not clear that the existence of such beings, or the possibility of their existence, is a precondition of the significance of the hypothesis that there are humanly inaccessible facts. (After all, the nature of beings with access to humanly inaccessible facts is presumably itself a humanly inaccessible fact.) Reflection on what it is like to be a bat seems to lead us, therefore, to the conclusion that there are facts that do not consist in the truth of propositions expressible in a human language. We can be compelled to recognize the existence of such facts without being able to state or comprehend them.

I shall not pursue this subject, however. Its bearing on the topic before us (namely, the mind-body problem) is that it enables us to make a general observation about the subjective character of experience. Whatever may be the status of facts about what it is like to be a human being, or a bat, or a Martian, these appear to be facts that embody a particular point of view.

I am not adverting here to the alleged privacy of experience to its possessor. The point of view in question is not one accessible only to a single individual. Rather it is a *type*. It is often possible to take up a point of view other than one's own, so the comprehension of such facts is not limited to one's own case. There is a sense in which phenomenological facts are perfectly objective: One person can know or say of another what the quality of the other's experience is. They are subjective, however, in the sense that even this objective ascription of experience is possible only for someone sufficiently similar to the object of ascription to be able to adopt his point of view—to understand the ascription in the first person as well as in the third, so to speak. The more different from oneself the other experiencer is, the less success one can expect with this enterprise. In our own case we occupy the relevant point of view, but we will have as much difficulty understanding our own experience properly if we approach it from another point of view as we would if we tried to understand the experience of another species without taking up *its* point of view.

This bears directly on the mind-body problem. For if the facts of experience—facts about what it is like *for* the experiencing organism—are accessible only from one point of view, then it is a mystery how the true character of experiences could be revealed in the physical operation of that organism. The latter is a domain of objective facts *par excellence*—the kind that can be observed and understood from many points of view and by individuals with differing perceptual systems. There are no comparable imaginative obstacles to the acquisition of knowledge about bat neurophysiology by human scientists, and intelligent bats or Martians might learn more about the human brain than we ever will.

This is not by itself an argument against reduction. A Martian scientist with no understanding of visual perception could understand the rainbow, or lightning, or clouds as physical phenomena, though he would never be able to understand the human concepts of rainbow, lightning, or cloud, or the place these things occupy in our phenomenal world. The objective nature of the things picked out by these concepts could be apprehended by him because, although the concepts themselves are connected with a particular point of view and a particular visual phenomenology, the things apprehended from that point of view are not: They are observable from the point of view but external to it; hence they can be comprehended from other points of view also, either by the same organisms or by others. Lightning has an objective character that is not exhausted by its visual appearance, and this can be investigated by a Martian without vision. To be precise, it has a *more* objective character than is revealed in its visual appearance. In speaking of the move from subjective to objective characterization, I wish to remain noncommittal about the existence of an end point, the completely objective intrinsic nature of the thing, which one might or might not be able to reach. It may be more accurate to think of objectivity as a direction in which the understanding can travel. And in understanding a phenomenon like lightning, it is legitimate to go as far away as one can from a strictly human viewpoint.

In the case of experience, on the other hand, the connection with a particular point of view seems much closer. It is difficult to understand what could be meant by the *objective* character of an experience, apart from the particular point of view from which its subject apprehends it. After all, what would be left of what it was like to be a bat if one removed the viewpoint of the bat? But if experience does not have, in addition to its subjective character, an objective nature that can be apprehended from many different points of view, then how can it be supposed that a Martian investigating my brain might be observing physical processes which were my mental processes (as he might observe physical processes which were bolts of lightning), only from a different point of view? How, for that matter, could a human physiologist observe them from another point of view.

We appear to be faced with a general difficulty about psycho-physical reduction. In other areas the process of reduction is a move in the direction of greater objectivity, toward a more accurate view of the real nature of things. This is accomplished by reducing our dependence on individual or species-specific points of view toward the object of investigation. We describe it not in terms of the impressions it makes on our senses, but in terms of its more general effects and of properties detectable by means other than the human senses. The less it depends on a specifically human viewpoint, the more objective is our description. It is possible to follow this path because although the concepts and ideas we employ in thinking about the external world are initially applied from a point of view that involves our perceptual apparatus, they are used by us to refer to things beyond themselves—toward which we *have* the phenomenal point of view. Therefore we can abandon it in favor of another, and still be thinking about the same things.

Experience itself, however, does not seem to fit the pattern. The idea of moving from appearance to reality seems to make no sense here. What is the analogue in this case to pursuing a more objective understanding of the same phenomena by abandoning the initial subjective viewpoint toward them in favor of another that is more objective but concerns the same thing? Certainly it *appears* unlikely that we will get closer to the real nature of human experience by leaving behind the particularity of our human point of view and striving for a description in terms accessible to beings that could not imagine what it was like to be us. If the subjective character of experience is fully comprehensible only from one point of view, then any shift to greater objectivity—that is, less attachment to a specific viewpoint—does not take us nearer to the real nature of the phenomenon: It takes us farther away from it.

In a sense, the seeds of this objection to the reducibility of experience are already detectable in successful cases of reduction; for in discovering sound to be, in reality, a wave phenomenon in air or other media, we leave behind one viewpoint to take up another, and the auditory, human or animal viewpoint that we leave behind remains unreduced. Members of radically different species may both understand the same physical events in objective terms, and this does not require that they understand the phenomenal forms in which those events appear to the senses of members of the other species. Thus it is a condition of their referring to a common reality that their more particular viewpoints are not part of the common reality that they both apprehend. The reduction can succeed only if the species-specific viewpoint is omitted from what is to be reduced.

But while we are right to leave this point of view aside in seeking a fuller understanding of the external world, we cannot ignore it permanently, since it is the essence of the internal world, and not merely a point of view on it. Most of the neobehaviorism of recent philosophical psychology results from the effort to substitute an objective concept of mind for the real thing, in order to have nothing left over which cannot be reduced. If we acknowledge that a physical theory of mind must account for the subjective character of experience, we must admit that no presently available conception gives us a clue how this could be done. The problem is unique. If mental processes are indeed physical processes, then there is something it is like, intrinsically, to undergo certain physical processes. What it is for such a thing to be the case remains a mystery.

What moral should be drawn from these reflections, and what should be done next? It would be a mistake to conclude that physicalism must be false. Nothing is proved by the inadequacy of physicalist hypotheses that assume a faulty objective analysis of mind. It would be truer to say that physicalism is a position we cannot understand because we do not at present have any conception of how it might be true. Perhaps it will be thought unreasonable to require such a conception as a condition of understanding. After all, it might be said, the meaning of physicalism is clear enough: Mental states are states of the body; mental events are physical events. We do not know *which* physical states and events they are, but that should not prevent us from understanding the hypothesis. What could be clearer than the words "is" and "are"?

But I believe it is precisely this apparent clarity of the word "is" that is deceptive. Usually, when we are told that X is Y we know *how* it is supposed to be true, but that depends on a conceptual or theoretical background and is not conveyed by the "is" alone. We know how both "X" and "Y" refer, and the kinds of things to which they refer, and we have a rough idea how the two referential paths might converge on a single thing, be it an object, a person, a process, an event, or whatever. But when the two terms of the identification are very disparate it may not be so clear how it could be true. We may not have even a rough idea of how the two referential paths could converge, or what kind of things they might converge on, and a theoretical framework may have to be supplied to enable us to understand this. Without the framework, an air of mysticism surrounds the identification.

This explains the magical flavor of popular presentations of fundamental scientific discoveries, given out as propositions to which one must subscribe without really understanding them. For example, people are now told at an early age that all matter is really energy. But despite the fact that they know what "is" means most of them never form a conception of what makes this claim true, because they lack the theoretical background.

At the present time the status of physicalism is similar to that which the hypothesis that matter is energy would have had if uttered by a pre-Socratic philosopher. We do not have the beginnings of a conception of how it might be true. In order to understand the hypothesis that a mental event is a physical event, we require more than an understanding of the word "is." The idea of how a mental and a physical term might refer to the same thing is lacking, and the usual analogies with theoretical identification in other fields fail to supply it. They fail because if we construe the reference of mental terms to physical events on the usual model, we either get a reappearance of separate subjective events as the effects through which mental reference to physical events is secured, or else we get a false account of how mental terms refer (for example, a causal behaviorist one).

Strangely enough, we may have evidence for the truth of something we cannot really understand. Suppose a caterpillar is locked in a sterile safe by someone unfamiliar with insect metamorphosis, and weeks later the safe is reopened, revealing a butterfly. If the person knows that the safe has been shut the whole time, he has reason to believe that the butterfly is or was once the caterpillar, without having any idea in what sense this might be so. (One possibility is that the caterpillar contained a tiny winged parasite that devoured it and grew into the butterfly.)

It is conceivable that we are in such a position with regard to physicalism. Donald Davidson has argued that if mental events have physical causes and effects, they must have physical descriptions. He holds that we have reason to believe this even though we do not—and in fact *could* not—have a general psychophysical theory. His argument applies to intentional mental events, but I think we also have some reason to believe that sensations are physical processes, without being in a position to understand how. Davidson's position is that certain physical events have irreducibly mental properties, and perhaps some view describable in this way is correct. But nothing of which we can now form a conception corresponds to it; nor have we any idea what a theory would be like that enabled us to conceive of it.

Very little work has been done on the basic question (from which mention of the brain can be entirely omitted) whether any sense can be made of experiences' having an objective character at all. Does it make sense, in other words, to ask what my experiences are *really* like, as opposed to how they appear to me? We cannot genuinely understand the hypothesis that their nature is captured in a physical description unless we understand the more fundamental idea that they *have* an objective nature (or that objective processes can have a subjective nature).

I should like to close with a speculative proposal. It may be possible to approach the gap between subjective and objective from another direction. Setting aside temporarily the relation between the mind and the brain, we can pursue a more objective understanding of the mental in its own right. At present we are completely unequipped to think about the subjective character of experience without relying on the imagination—without taking up the point of view of the experiential subject. This should be regarded as a challenge to form new concepts and devise a new method—an objective phenomenology not dependent on empathy or the imagination. Though presumably it would not capture everything, its goal would be to describe, at least in part, the subjective character of experiences in a form comprehensible to beings incapable of having those experiences.

We would have to develop such a phenomenology to describe the sonar experiences of bats; but it would also be possible to begin with humans. One might try, for example, to develop concepts that could be used to explain to a person blind from birth what it was like to see. One would reach a blank wall eventually, but it should be possible to devise a method of expressing in objective terms much more than we can at present, and with much greater precision. The loose intermodal analogies—for example, "Red is like the sound of a trumpet"—which crop up in discussions of this subject are of little use. That should be clear to anyone who has both heard a trumpet and seen red. But structural features of perception might be more accessible to objective description, event though something would be left out. And concepts alternative to those we learn in the first person may enable us to arrive at a kind of understanding even of our own experience which is denied us by the very ease of description and lack of distance that subjective concepts afford.

Apart from its own interest, a phenomenology that is in this sense objective may permit questions about the physical basis of experience to assume a more intelligible form. Aspects of subjective experience that admitted this kind of objective description might be better candidates for objective explanations of a more familiar sort. But whether or not this guess is correct, it seems unlikely that any physical theory of mind can be contemplated until more thought has been given to the general problem of subjective and objective. Otherwise we cannot even pose the mind-body problem without sidestepping it.

Discussion Questions

1. Are you happy with Nagel's attack on materialism? How would you deal with the criticism that the human experience is not reducible to physical properties only because science hasn't solved that/figured that out yet?
2. For what other beings could we ask, "What is it like to be X?" A dog? A bacterium? An alien? A robot?
3. How does this relate to our knowledge of other people? Does it shed any light on the common saying "If I were you, I would . . ."?
4. How would you answer Nagel's question, "Does it make sense . . . to ask what my experiences are *really* like, as opposed to how they appear to me?"
5. Elsewhere, Nagel wrote that *scientism*—a view that "assumes that everything there is must be understandable by the employment of scientific theories"—"puts one type of human understanding in charge of the universe and what can be said about it." He believes this to be incorrect (and "myopic"). Do you agree?

The Concept of Mind: Descartes's Myth
Gilbert Ryle

Gilbert Ryle spent a majority of his career serving as both the chair of the Oxford University philosophy department and as the editor of *Mind*—considered one of the most well-respected philosophy journals—from 1947–1971. During this time, he influenced many philosophers, including two of his students cited in this collection, Daniel Dennett and J.J.C. Smart. His argument here is consistent with his views on behaviorism—the notion that there are no mental states above and beyond observable behavior. In a sense, mental events like love can just be reduced to behavior of one in love.

Ryle's book *The Concept of Mind* is considered one of the most important philosophical works to examine the metaphysical concepts of the mind and soul. Chapter 1 of the book, reprinted here, first defines the "Cartesian Dualism" (Descartes's notion that we have an immaterial soul separate from the brain and body—see the reading in this section on

Source: The Concept of Mind. London: Routledge, and Chicago: The University of Chicago Press, 1984. Originally published by Hutchinson's University Library, 1949. Chapter 1 (edited).

Descartes). Ryle refers to the popular notion of the embodied soul in a derogatory way as "the ghost in the machine." He then sets out to illuminate this "dogma" as being based on false reasoning and, more simply, as a problem of language. Ryle sympathizes with dualism as he explains reasons for its wide acceptance: namely that it helps us avoid being just another mechanical part in a deterministic (controlled by the forces of nature) system, like all other objects.

Reading Questions

1. Why does Ryle mention that minds cannot be spatially inside another thing?
2. Explain the notion of a "category mistake" in relation to the "university" or "team spirit."
3. Explain the two main cruxes upon which Descartes's theory of mind rested: Why *would* it be important to have an immaterial mind?
4. How does Ryle explain that the "dogma of the ghost in the machine" commits a category mistake?
5. Does Ryle argue that mental processes do not occur? How?
6. What does he say about reducing (breaking down) mental states to physical processes?
7. Summarize Ryle's "Historical Note."

1. The Official Doctrine

There is a doctrine about the nature and place of minds which is so prevalent among theorists and even among laymen that it deserves to be described as the official theory. Most philosophers, psychologists, and religious teachers subscribe, with minor reservations, to its main articles and, although they admit certain theoretical difficulties in it, they tend to assume that these can be overcome without serious modifications being made to the architecture of the theory. It will be argued here that the central principles of the doctrine are unsound and conflict with the whole body of what we know about minds when we are not speculating about them.

The official doctrine, which hails chiefly from Descartes, is something like this. With the doubtful exceptions of idiots and infants in arms every human being has both a body and a mind. Some would prefer to say that every human being is both a body and a mind. His body and his mind are ordinarily harnessed together, but after the death of the body his mind may continue to exist and function.

Human bodies are in space and are subject to the mechanical laws which govern all other bodies in space. Bodily processes and states can be inspected by external observers. So a man's bodily life is as much a public affair as are the lives of animals and reptiles and even as the careers of trees, crystals, and planets.

But minds are not in space, nor are their operations subject to mechanical laws. The workings of one mind are not witnessable by other observers; its career is private. Only I can take direct cognisance of the states and processes of my own mind. A person therefore lives through two collateral histories, one consisting of what happens in and to his body, the other consisting of what happens in and to his mind. The first is public, the second private. The events in the first history are events in the physical world, those in the second are events in the mental world.

It has been disputed whether a person does or can directly monitor all or only some of the episodes of his own private history; but, according to the official doctrine, of at least some of these episodes he has direct and unchallengeable cognisance. In consciousness, self-consciousness and introspection he is directly and authentically apprised of the present states and operations of his mind. He may have great or small uncertainties about concurrent and adjacent episodes in the physical world, but he can have none about at least part of what is momentarily occupying his mind.

It is customary to express this bifurcation of his two lives and of his two worlds by saying that the things and events which belong to the physical world, including his own body, are external, while the workings of his own mind are internal. This antithesis of outer and inner is of course meant to be construed as a metaphor, since minds, not being in space, could not be described as being spatially inside anything else, or as having things going on spatially inside themselves. But relapses from this good intention are common and theorists are found speculating how stimuli, the physical sources of which are yards or miles outside a person's skin, can generate mental responses inside his skull, or how decisions framed inside his cranium can set going movements of his extremities.

Even when 'inner' and 'outer' are construed as metaphors, the problem how a person's mind and body influence one another is notoriously charged with theoretical difficulties. What the mind wills, the legs, arms, and the tongue execute; what affects the ear and the eye has something to do with what the mind perceives; grimaces and smiles betray the mind's moods and bodily castigations lead, it is hoped, to moral improvement. But the actual transactions between the episodes of the private history and those of the public history remain mysterious, since by definition they can belong to neither series. They could not be reported among the happenings described in a person's autobiography of his inner life, but nor could they be reported among those described in someone else's biography of that person's overt career. They can be inspected neither by introspection nor by laboratory experiment. They are theoretical shuttlecocks which are forever being bandied from the physiologist back to the psychologist and from the psychologist back to the physiologist.

Underlying this partly metaphorical representation of the bifurcation of a person's two lives there is a seemingly more profound and philosophical assumption. It is assumed that there are two different kinds of existence or status. What exists or happens may have the status of physical existence, or it may have the status of mental existence. Somewhat as the faces of coins are either heads or tails, or somewhat as living creatures are either male or female, so, it is supposed, some existing is physical existing, other existing is mental existing. It is a necessary feature of what has physical existence that it is in space and time; it is a necessary feature of what has mental existence that is in time but not in space. What has physical existence is composed of matter, or else is a function of matter; what has mental existence consists of consciousness, or else is a function of consciousness.

There is thus a polar opposition between mind and matter, an opposition which is often brought out as follows. Material objects are situated in a common field, known as 'space,' and what happens to one body in one part of space is mechanically connected with what happens to other bodies in other parts of space. But mental happenings occur in insulated fields, known as 'minds,' and there is, apart maybe from telepathy, no direct causal connexion between what happens in one mind and what happens in another. Only through the medium of the public physical world can the mind of one person make a difference to the mind of another. The mind is its own place and in his inner life each of us lives the life of a ghostly Robinson Crusoe. People can see, hear and jolt one another's bodies, but they are irremediably blind and deaf to the workings of one another's minds and inoperative upon them.

What sort of knowledge can be secured of the workings of a mind? On the one side, according to the official theory, a person has direct knowledge of the best imaginable kind of the workings of his own mind. Mental states and processes are (or are normally) conscious states and processes, and the consciousness which irradiates them can engender no illusions and leaves the door open for no doubts. A person's present thinkings, feelings, and willings, his perceivings, rememberings, and imaginings are intrinsically 'phosphorescent'; their existence and their nature are inevitably betrayed to their owner. The inner life is a stream of consciousness of such a sort that it would be absurd to suggest that the mind whose life is that stream might be unaware of what is passing down it.

True, the evidence adduced recently by Freud seems to show that there exist channels tributary to this stream, which run hidden from their owner. People are actuated by impulses the existence of which they vigorously disavow; some of their thoughts differ from the thoughts which they acknowledge; and some of the actions which they think they will to perform they do not really will. They are thoroughly gulled by some of their own hypocrisies and they successfully ignore facts about their mental lives which on the official theory ought to be patent to them. Holders of the official theory tend, however, to maintain that anyhow in normal circumstances a person must be directly and authentically seized of the present state and workings of his own mind.

Besides being currently supplied with these alleged immediate data of consciousness, a person is also generally supposed to be able to exercise from time to time a special kind of perception, namely inner perception, or introspection. He can take a (non-optical) 'look' at what is passing in his mind. . . .

2. The Absurdity of the Official Doctrine

Such in outline is the official theory. I shall often speak of it, with deliberate abusiveness, as 'the dogma of the Ghost in the Machine.' I hope to prove that it is entirely false, and false not in detail but in principle. It is not merely an assemblage of particular mistakes. It is one big mistake and a mistake of a special kind. It is, namely, a category-mistake. It represents the facts of mental life as if they belonged to one logical type or category (or range of types or categories), when they actually belong to another. The dogma is therefore a philosopher's myth. . . .

I must first indicate what is meant by the phrase 'Category-mistake.' This I do in a series of illustrations.

A foreigner visiting Oxford or Cambridge for the first time is shown a number of colleges, libraries, playing fields, museums, scientific departments, and administrative offices. He then asks 'But where is the University? I have seen where the members of the Colleges live, where the Registrar works, where the scientists experiment and the rest. But I have not yet seen the University in which reside and work the members of your University.' It has then to be explained to him that the University is not another collateral institution, some ulterior counterpart to the colleges, laboratories, and offices which he has seen. The University is just the way in which all that he has already seen is organized. When they are seen and when their coordination is understood, the University has been seen. His mistake lay in his innocent assumption that it was correct to speak of Christ Church, the Bodleian Library, the Ashmolean Museum, *and* the University, to speak, that is, as if 'the University' stood for an extra member of the class of which these other units are members. He was mistakenly allocating the University to the same category as that to which the other institutions belong. . . .

One more illustration. A foreigner watching his first game of cricket learns what are the functions of the bowlers, the batsmen, the fielders, the umpires, and the scorers. He then says 'But there is no one left on the field to contribute the famous element of team-spirit. I see who does the bowling, the batting and the wicket-keeping, but I do not see whose role it is to exercise *esprit de corps.*' Once more, it would have to be explained that he was looking for the wrong type of thing. Team-spirit is not another cricketing-operation supplementary to all of the other special tasks. It is, roughly, the keenness with which each of the special tasks is performed, and performing a task keenly is not performing two tasks. Certainly exhibiting team spirit is not the same thing as bowling or catching, but nor is it a third thing such that we can say that the bowler first bowls *and* then exhibits team-spirit or that a fielder is at a given moment *either* catching *or* displaying *esprit de corps.*

These illustrations of category-mistakes have a common feature which must be noticed. The mistakes were made by people who did not know how to wield the concepts *University* . . . and *team-spirit.* Their puzzles arose from inability to use certain items in the English vocabulary.

The theoretically interesting category-mistakes are those made by people who are perfectly competent to apply concepts, at least in the situations with which they are familiar, but are still liable in their abstract thinking to allocate those concepts to logical types to which they do not belong. . . .

My destructive purpose is to show that a family of radical category-mistakes is the source of the double-life theory. The representation of a person as a ghost mysteriously ensconced in a machine derives from this argument. . . .

3. The Origin of the Category-Mistake

One of the chief intellectual origins of what I have yet to prove to be the Cartesian category-mistake seems to be this. When Galileo showed that his methods of scientific discovery were competent to provide a mechanical theory which should cover every occupant of space, Descartes found in himself two conflicting motives. As a man of scientific genius he could not but endorse the claims of mechanics, yet as a religious and moral man he could not accept as Hobbes accepted, the discouraging rider to those claims, namely that human nature differs only in degree of complexity from clockwork. The mental could not be just a variety of the mechanical.

He and subsequent philosophers naturally but erroneously availed themselves of the following escape-route. Since mental-conduct words are not to be construed as signifying the occurrence of mechanical processes, they must be construed as signifying the occurrence of non-mechanical processes; since mechanical laws explain movements in space as the effects of other movements in space, other laws must explain some of the non-spatial workings of minds as the effects of other non-spatial workings of minds. The difference between the human behaviours which we describe as intelligent and those which we describe as unintelligent must be a difference in their causation; so, while some movements of human tongues and limbs are the effects of mechanical causes, others must be the effects of non-mechanical causes, i.e., some issue from movements of particles of matter, others from workings of the mind.

The differences between the physical and the mental were thus represented as differences inside the common framework of the categories of 'thing,' 'stuff,' 'attribute,' 'state,' 'process,' 'change,' 'cause,' and 'effect.' Minds are things, but different sorts of things from bodies; mental processes are causes and effects, but different sorts of causes and effects from bodily movements. And so on. Somewhat as the foreigner expected the University to be an extra edifice, rather like a college but also considerably different, so the repudiators of mechanism represented minds as extra centres of causal processes, rather like machines but also considerably different from them. Their theory was a para-mechanical hypothesis.

That this assumption was at the heart of the doctrine is shown by the fact that there was from the beginning felt to be a major theoretical difficulty in explaining how minds can influence and be influenced by bodies. How can a mental process, such as willing, cause spatial movements like the movements of the tongue? How can a physical change in the optic nerve have among its effects a mind's perception of a flash of light? This notorious crux by itself shows the logical mould into which Descartes pressed his theory of the mind. It was the self-same mould into which he and Galileo set their mechanics. Still unwittingly adhering to the grammar of mechanics, he tried to avert disaster by describing minds in what was merely an obverse vocabulary. The workings of minds had to be described by the mere negatives of the specific descriptions given to bodies; they are not in space, they are not motions, they are not modifications of matter, they are not accessible to public observation. Minds are not bits of clockwork, they are just bits of not-clockwork.

As thus represented, minds are not merely ghosts harnessed to machines, they are themselves just spectral machines. Though the human body is an engine, it is not quite an ordinary engine, since some of its workings are governed by another engine inside it—this interior governor-engine being one of a very special sort. It is invisible, inaudible, and it has no size or weight. It cannot be taken to bits and the laws it obeys are not those known to ordinary engineers. Nothing is known of how it governs the bodily engine.

A second major crux points the same moral. Since, according to the doctrine, minds belong to the same category as bodies and since bodies are rigidly governed by mechanical laws, it seemed to many theorists to follow that minds must be similarly governed by rigid non-mechanical laws. The physical world is a deterministic system, so the mental world must be a deterministic system. Bodies cannot help the modifications that they undergo, so minds cannot help pursuing the careers fixed for them. *Responsibility, choice, merit,* and *demerit* are therefore inapplicable concepts—unless the compromise solution is adopted of saying that the laws governing mental processes, unlike those governing physical processes, have the congenial attribute of being only rather rigid. The problem of the Freedom of the Will was the problem how to reconcile the hypothesis that minds are to be described in terms drawn from the categories of mechanics with the knowledge that higher-grade human conduct is not of a piece with the behaviour of machines. . . .

When two terms belong to the same category, it is proper to construct conjunctive propositions embodying them. Thus a purchaser may say that he bought a left-hand glove and a right-hand glove, but not that he bought a left-hand glove, a right-hand glove, and a pair of gloves. 'She came home in a flood of tears and a sedan-chair' is a well known joke based on the absurdity of conjoining terms of different types. It would have been equally ridiculous to construct the disjunction. 'She came home either in a flood of tears or else in a sedan-chair.' Now the dogma of the Ghost in the Machine does just this. It maintains that there exist both bodies and minds; that there occur physical processes and mental processes; that there are mechanical causes of corporeal movements and mental causes of corporeal movements. I shall argue that these and other analogous conjunctions are absurd; but, it must be noticed, the argument will not show that either of the illegitimately conjoined propositions is absurd in itself. I am not, for example, denying that there occur mental processes. Doing long division is a mental process and so is making a joke. But I am saying that the phrase 'there occur mental processes' does not mean the same sort of thing as 'there occur physical processes,' and, therefore, that it makes no sense to conjoin or disjoin the two.

If my argument is successful, there will follow some interesting consequences. First, the hallowed contrast between Mind and Matter will be dissipated, but dissipated not by either of the equally hallowed absorptions of Mind by Matter or of Matter by Mind, but in quite a different way. For the seeming contrast of the two will be shown to be as illegitimate as would be the contrast of 'she came home in a flood of tears' and 'she came home in a sedan-chair.' The belief that there is a polar opposition between Mind and Matter is the belief that they are terms of the same logical type.

It will also follow that both Idealism and Materialism are answers to an improper question. The 'reduction' of the material world to mental states and processes, as well as the 'reduction' of mental states and processes to physical states and processes, presupposes the legitimacy of the disjunction 'Either there exist minds or there exist bodies (but not both).' It would be like saying, 'Either she bought a left-hand and right-hand glove or she bought a pair of gloves (but not both).'

It is perfectly proper to say, in one logical tone of voice, that there exist minds, and to say, in another logical tone of voice, that there exist bodies. But these expressions do not indicate two different species of existence, for 'existence' is not a generic word like 'coloured' or 'sexed.' They indicate two different senses of 'exist,' somewhat as 'rising' has different senses in 'the tide is rising,' 'hopes are rising,' and 'the average age of death is rising.' A man would be thought to be making a poor joke who said that three things are now rising, namely the tide, hopes, and the average age of death. It would be just as good or bad a joke to say that there exist prime numbers and Wednesdays and public opinions and navies; or that there exist both minds and bodies. . . .

4. Historical Note

It would not be true to say that the official theory derives solely from Descartes's theories, or even from a more widespread anxiety about the implications of seventeenth-century mechanics. Scholastic and Reformation theology had schooled the intellects of the scientists as well as of the laymen, philosophers, and clerics of that age. Stoic-Augustinian theories of the will were embedded in the Calvinist doctrines of sin and grace; Platonic and Aristotelian theories of the intellect shaped the orthodox doctrines of the immortality of the soul. Descartes was reformulating already prevalent theological doctrines of the soul in the new syntax of Galileo. The theologian's privacy of conscience became the philosopher's privacy of consciousness, and what had been the bogy of Predestination reappeared as the body of Determinism.

It would also not be true to say that the two-worlds myth did no theoretical good. Myths often do a lot of theoretical good, while they are still new. One benefit bestowed by the para-mechanical myth was that it partly superannuated the then prevalent para-political myth. Minds and their Faculties had previously been described by analogies with political superiors and political subordinates. The idioms used were those of ruling, obeying, collaborating, and rebelling. They survived and still survive in many ethical and some epistemological discussions. As, in physics, the new myth of occult Forces was a scientific improvement on the old myth of Final Causes, so, in anthropological and psychological theory, the new myth of hidden operations, impulses, and agencies was an improvement on the old myth of dictations, deferences, and disobediences.

Discussion Questions

1. In the opening paragraph, Ryle notes that we claim to know things about the mind without really thinking/speculating about it. How much time have you spent thinking about what it means (or would mean) to have a mind or a soul? Is it just something you assumed you had (or didn't have) without thinking about what it was? In what sense is dualism truly a dogma?
2. Ryle holds that a mistake has been made partly due to the way we speak about the mind. Do you think that the mind is something that can correctly be summarized by language? Is it somehow outside the realm of language and logic? If so, then how could you be justified in talking about your mind if you can't express just what it is?
3. Do you agree that, in order to maintain the freedom of the will, we need a soul so that we can avoid a purely machine-like (and thus, deterministic) existence?
4. Some consider the mind and soul to be metaphors. In what ways do you agree with this?

Sensations and Brain Processes

J.J.C. Smart

Australian philosopher John Jamieson Carswell Smart (Jack) now serves as Emeritus Professor at Australia National University. A physicalist, Smart argues that the mind and brain are identical. In the following article, he sets forth his position and then defends it against many of the most common objections.

One of Smart's primary positions relies on "Occam's Razor." Also called the Principle of Parsimony ("parsimony" meaning simplicity), Occam's Razor holds that, when choosing among competing theories, it is prudent to choose the simplest theory for, with fewer "components" there is a lesser likelihood for error (and thus, a greater likelihood that the simplest theory will be correct).

Other terms and references Smart makes that may be unclear to the unindoctrinated reader are:

- The Morning Star and Evening Star—Both terms refer to the planet Venus as it appears brightly in the sky at both sunrise and sunset.
- The argument *ignoratio elenchi* (translated as "ignorance of the issue")—This is a logical fallacy that occurs when one states an argument that does not address the particular issue being addressed. If done intentionally, this falls into the class of fallacies known as a "red herring," which is thought to have gotten its name from the herring fish that would lead dogs astray when following a particular scent.
- The "beetle in a box"—This is a reference to philosopher Wittgenstein: Imagine that everyone has a box that contains a "beetle," yet no one is ever allowed to view another's

Source: J.J.C. Smart, "Sensations and Brain Processes," in *The Philosophical Review,* Volume 68, no. 2, pp. 141–156. Copyright © 1959 Cornell University Press. All rights reserved. Used by permission of the current publisher, Duke University Press.

box. Over time, the word "beetle" comes to stand for "the thing in the box." Wittgenstein argues this could be just like the mind: We all have something inside ourselves that is private and known only to us, but this doesn't mean that there must be some actual thing called a mind. "Mind" may just be what we refer to as our private experience as taught to us through language.

- Epiphenominalism—This is the theory that the mind is created by the brain but does not affect or interact with the brain. It could be much like a shadow that is created by a physical tree but does not "do" anything.

Reading Questions

1. Explain Smart's position as to how sensations (i.e., after-images, pain) relate to brain processes. How does his analogy of nations-and-citizens help to illuminate this?
2. Explain the objections given to Smart's identity thesis and how Smart replies to each of them.
3. What final objection does Smart give in his summary when he considers the objection/suggestion of epiphenomenalism? How does he relate epiphenomenalism to the thesis that the Earth was created as per the *Genesis* account in 4000 B.C.?

The suggestion I wish if possible to avoid is . . . that "I am in pain" is a genuine report, and that what it reports is an irreducibly psychical something. And similarly the suggestion I wish to resist is also that to say "I have a yellowish orange after-image" is to report something irreducibly psychical.

Why do I wish to resist this suggestion? Mainly because of Occam's razor. It seems to me that science is increasingly giving us a viewpoint whereby organisms are able to be seen as physicochemical mechanisms:[15] it seems that even the behavior of man himself will one day be explicable in mechanistic terms. There does seem to be, so far as science is concerned, nothing in the world but increasingly complex arrangements of physical constituents. All except for one place: in consciousness. That is, for a full description of what is going on in a man you would have to mention not only the physical processes in his tissue, glands, nervous system, and so forth, but also his states of consciousness: his visual, auditory, and tactual sensations, his aches and pains. That these should be *correlated* with brain processes does not help, for to say that they are *correlated* is to say that they are something "over and above [them]." You cannot correlate something with itself. You correlate footprints with burglars, but not Bill Sikes the burglar with Bill Sikes the burglar. So sensations, states of consciousness, do seem to be the one sort of thing left outside the physicalist picture, and for various reasons I just cannot believe that this can be so. That everything should be explicable in terms of physics (together of course with descriptions of the ways in which the parts are put together), . . . except the occurrence of sensations seems to me to be frankly unbelievable. . . . It is the object of this paper to show that there are no philosophical arguments which compel us to be dualists. . . .

Why should not sensations just be brain processes of a certain sort? There are, of course, well-known (as well as lesser-known) philosophical objections to the view that reports of sensations are reports of brain-processes, but I shall try to argue that these arguments are by no means as cogent as is commonly thought to be the case.

Let me first try to state more accurately the thesis that sensations are brain processes. It is not the thesis that, for example, "after-image" or "ache" means the same as "brain process of sort X (where "X" is replaced by a description of a certain sort of brain process). It is that, in so far as "after-image" or "ache" is a report of a process, it is a report of a process that *happens to be* a brain process. It follows that the thesis does not claim that sensation statements can be *translated* into statements about brain processes.[16] Nor does it claim that the logic of a sensation statement is the same as that of a brain-process statement. All it claims is that in so far as a sensation statement is a report of something, that something is in fact a brain process. Sensations are nothing over and above brain processes. Nations are nothing "over and above" citizens, but this does not prevent the logic of nation statements being very different from the logic of citizen statements, nor does it insure the translatability of nation statements into citizen statements. (I do not, however, wish to assert that the relation of sensation statements to brain-process statements is very like that of nation statements to citizen statements. Nations do not just *happen to be* nothing over and above citizens, for example. I bring in the "nations" example merely to make a negative point: that the fact that the logic of A-statements is different from that of B-statements does not insure that A's are anything over and above B's.)

Remarks on identity. When I say that a sensation is a brain process or that lightning is an electric discharge, I am using "is" in the sense of strict identity. (Just as in the—in this case necessary—proposition "7 is identical with the smallest prime number greater than 5.") When I say that a sensation is a brain process or that lightning is an electric discharge I do not mean just that the sensation is somehow spatially or temporally continuous with the brain process or that the lightning is just spatially or temporally continuous with the discharge. . . . I distinguish these two senses of "is identical with" because I wish to make it clear that the brain-process doctrine asserts identity in the *strict* sense.

I shall now discuss various possible objections to the view that the processes reported in sensation statements are in fact processes in the brain. Most of us have met some of these objections in our first year as philosophy students. All the more reason to take a good look at them. Others of the objections will be more recondite and subtle.

Objection 1. Any illiterate peasant can talk perfectly well about his after-images, or how things look or feel to him, or about his aches and pains, and yet he may know nothing whatever about neurophysiology. A man may, like Aristotle, believe that the brain is an organ for cooling the body without any impairment of his ability to make true statements about his sensations. Hence the things we are talking about when we describe our sensations cannot be processes in the brain.

Reply. You might as well say that a nation of slug-abeds, who never saw the morning star or knew of its existence, or who had never thought of the expression "the Morning Star," but who used the expression "the Evening Star" perfectly well, could not use this expression to refer to the same entity as we refer to (and describe as) "the Morning Star."[17]

You may object that the Morning Star is in a sense not the very same thing as the Evening Star, but only something spatio-temporally continuous with it. That is, you may say that the Morning Star is not the Evening Star in the strict sense of "identity" that I distinguished earlier. I can perhaps forestall this objection by considering the slug-abeds to be New Zealanders and the early risers to be Englishmen. Then the thing the New Zealanders describe as "the Morning Star" could be the very same thing (in the strict sense) as the Englishmen describe as "the Evening Star." And yet they could be ignorant of this fact.

There is, however, a more plausible example. Consider lightning.[18] Modern physical science tells us that lightning is a certain kind of electrical discharge due to ionization of clouds of water-vapor in the atmosphere. This, it is now believed, is what the true nature of lightning is. Note that there are not two things: a flash of lightning and an electrical discharge. There is one thing, a flash of lightning, which is described scientifically as an electrical discharge to the earth from a cloud of ionized water-molecules. The case is not at all like that of explaining a footprint by reference to a burglar. We say that what lightning really is, what its true nature as revealed by science is, is an electric discharge. (It is not the true nature of a footprint to be a burglar.) . . .

In short, the reply to Objection 1 is that there can be contingent statements of the form "A is identical with B," and a person may well know that something is an A without knowing that it is a B. An illiterate peasant might well be able to talk about his sensations without knowing about his brain processes, just as he can talk about lightning though he knows nothing of electricity.

Objection 2. It is only a contingent fact (if it is a fact) that when we have a certain kind of sensation there is a certain kind of process in our brain. Indeed it is possible, though perhaps in the highest degree unlikely, that our present physiological theories will be as out of date as the ancient theory connecting mental processes with goings on in the heart. It follows that when we report a sensation we are not reporting a brain-process.

Reply. The objection certainly proves that when we say "I have an after-image" we cannot *mean* something of the form "I have such and such a brain-process." But this does not show that what we report (having an after-image is not *in fact* a brain process. "I see lightning" does not *mean* "I see an electric discharge." Indeed it is logically possible (though highly unlikely) that the electrical discharge account of lightning might one day be given up. Again, "I see the Evening Star" does not *mean* the same as "I see the Morning Star," and yet "the Evening Star and Morning Star are one and the same thing" is a contingent proposition. Possibly Objection 2 derives some of its apparent strength from a "Fido"-Fido theory of meaning. If the meaning of an expression were what the expression named, then of course it *would* follow from the fact that "sensation" and "brain-process" have different meanings that they cannot name one and the same thing.

Objection 3.[19] Even if objections 1 and 2 do not prove that sensations are something over and above brain-processes, they do prove that the qualities of sensations are something over and above the qualities of brain-processes. That is, it may be possible to get out of asserting the existence of irreducibly psychic processes, but not out of asserting the existence of irreducibly psychic *properties*. For suppose we identify the Morning Star with the Evening Star. Then there must be some properties which logically imply that of being the Morning Star, and quite distinct properties which entail that of being the Evening Star. Again, there must be some properties (for example, that of being a yellow flash) which are logically distinct from those in the physicalist story.

Indeed, it might be thought that the objection succeeds at one jump. For consider the property of "being a yellow flash." It might seem that this property lies inevitably outside the physicalist framework within which I am trying to work (either by "yellow" being an objective emergent property of physical objects, or else by being a power to produce yellow sense-data, where "yellow," in this second instantiation of the word, refers to a purely phenomenal or introspectible quality). I must therefore digress for a moment and indicate how I deal with secondary qualities. I shall concentrate on color.

First of all, let me introduce the concept of a normal percipient. One person is more a normal percipient than another if he can make color discriminations that the other cannot. For example, if A can pick a lettuce leaf out of a heap of cabbage leaves, whereas B cannot though he can pick a lettuce leaf out of a heap of beetroot leaves, then A is more normal than B. (I am assuming that A and B are not given time to distinguish the leaves by their slight difference in shape, and so forth.) From the concept of "more normal than" it is easy to see how we can introduce the concept of "normal." Of course, Eskimos may make the finest discriminations at the blue end of the spectrum, Hottentots at the red end. In this case the concept of a normal percipient is a slightly idealized one, rather like that of "the mean sun" in astronomical chronology. There is no need to go into such subtleties now. I say that "This is red" means something roughly like "A normal percipient would not easily pick this out of a clump of geranium petals though he would pick it out of a clump of lettuce leaves." Of course it does not exactly mean this: A person might know the meaning of "red" without knowing anything about geraniums, or even about normal percipients. But the point is that a person can be trained to say "This is red" of objects which would not easily be picked out of geranium petals by a normal percipient, and so on. (Note that even a color-blind person can reasonably assert that something is red, though of course he needs to use another human being, not just himself, as his "color meter.") This account of secondary qualities explains their unimportance in physics. For obviously the discriminations and lack of discriminations made by a very complex neurophysiological mechanism are hardly likely to correspond to simple and nonarbitrary distinctions in nature.

I therefore elucidate colors as powers, in Locke's sense, to evoke certain sorts of discriminatory responses in human beings. They are also, of course, powers to cause sensations in human beings (an account still nearer Locke's). But these sensations, I am arguing, are identifiable with brain processes.

Now how do I get over the objection that a sensation can be identified with a brain process only if it has some phenomenal property, not possessed by brain processes, whereby one-half of the identification may be, so to speak, pinned down?

My suggestion is as follows. When a person says, "I see a yellowish-orange after-image," he is saying something like this: "*There is something going on which is like what is going on when* I have my eyes open, am awake, and there is an orange illuminated in good light in front of me, that is, when I really see an orange." (And there is no reason why a person should not say the same thing when he is having a veridical sense-datum, so long as we construe "like" in the last sentence in such a sense that something can be like itself.) Notice that the italicized words, namely "there is something going on which is like what is going on when," are all quasi-logical or topic-neutral words. This explains why the ancient Greek peasant's reports about his sensations can be neutral between dualistic metaphysics or my materialistic metaphysics. It explains how sensations can be brain-processes and yet how those who report them need know nothing about brain-processes. For he reports them only very abstractly as "something going on which is like what is going on when. . . ." Similarly, a person may say "someone is in the room," thus reporting truly that the doctor is in the room, even though he has never heard of doctors. (There are not two people in the room: "someone" *and* the doctor.) This account of sensation statements also explains the singular elusiveness of "raw feels"—why no one seems to be able to pin any properties on them.[20] Raw feels, in my view, are colorless for the very same reason that *something* is colorless. This does not mean that sensations do not have properties, for if they are brain-processes they certainly have properties. It only means that in speaking of them as being like or unlike one another we need not know or mention these properties.

This, then, is how I would reply to Objection 3. The strength of my reply depends on the possibility of our being able to report that one thing is like another without being able to state the respect in which it is like. I am not sure whether this is so or not, and that is why I regard Objection 3 as the strongest with which I have to deal.

Objection 4. The after-image is not in physical space. The brain-process is. So the after-image is not a brain-process.

Reply. This is an *ignoratio elenchi.* I am not arguing that the after-image is a brain-process, but that the experience of having an after-image is a brain-process. It is the *experience* which is reported in the introspective report. Similarly, if it is objected that the after-image is yellowy-orange but that a surgeon looking into your brain would see nothing yellowy-orange, my reply is that it is the experience of seeing yellowy-orange that is being described, and this experience is not a yellowy-orange something. So to say that a brain-process cannot be yellowy-orange is not to say that a brain-process cannot in fact be the experience of having a yellowy-orange after-image. There is, in a sense, no such thing as an after-image or a sense-datum, though there is such a thing as the experience of having an image, and this experience is described indirectly in material object language, not in phenomenal language, for there is no such thing.[21] We describe the experience by saying, in effect, that it is like the experience we have when, for example, we really see a yellowy-orange patch on the wall. Trees and wallpaper can be green, but not the experience of seeing or imagining a tree or wallpaper. (Or if they are described as green or yellow this can only be in a derived sense.)

Objection 5. It would make sense to say of a molecular movement in the brain that it is swift or slow, straight or circular, but it makes no sense to say this of the experience of seeing something yellow.

Reply. So far we have not given sense to talk of experiences as swift or slow, straight or circular. But I am not claiming that "experience" and "brain-process" mean the same or even that they have the same logic. "Somebody" and "the doctor" do not have the same logic, but this does not lead us to suppose that talking about somebody telephoning is talking about someone over and above, say, the doctor. The ordinary man when he reports an experience is reporting that something is going on, but he leaves it open as to what sort of thing is going on, whether in a material solid medium, or perhaps in some sort of gaseous medium, or even perhaps in some sort of nonspatial medium (if this makes sense). All that I am saying is that "experience" and "brain-process" may in fact refer to the same thing, and if so we may easily adopt a convention (which is not a change in our present rules for the use of experience words but an addition to them) whereby it would make sense to talk of an experience in terms appropriate to physical processes.

Objection 6. Sensations are private, brain-processes are *public*. If I sincerely say, "I see a yellowish-orange after-image" and I am not making a verbal mistake, then I cannot be wrong. But I can be wrong about a brain-process. The scientist looking into my brain might be having an illusion. Moreover, it makes sense to say that two or more people are observing the same brain-process but not that two or more people are reporting the same inner experience.

Reply. This shows that the language of introspective reports has a different logic from the language of material processes. It is obvious that until the brain-process theory is much improved and widely accepted there will be no *criteria* for saying "Smith has an experience of such-and-such a sort" *except* Smith's introspective reports. So we have adopted a rule of language that (normally) what Smith says goes.

Objection 7. I can imagine myself turned to stone and yet having images, aches, pains, and so on.

Reply. I can imagine that the electrical theory of lightning is false, that lightning is some sort of purely optical phenomenon. I can imagine that lightning is not an electrical discharge. I can imagine that the Evening Star is not the Morning Star. But it is. All the objection shows is that "experience" and "brain-process" do not have the same meaning. It does not show that an experience is not in fact a brain-process. . . .

Objection 8. The "beetle in the box" objection (see Wittgenstein, *Philosophical Investigations*, paragraph 293). How could descriptions of experiences, if these are genuine reports, get a foothold in language? For any rule of language must have public criteria for its correct application.

Reply. The change from describing how things are to describing how we feel is just a change from uninhibitedly saying "this is so" to saying "this looks so." That is, when the naive person might be tempted to say, "There is a patch of light on the wall which moves whenever I move my eyes" or "A pin is being stuck into me," we have learned how to resist this temptation and say "It *looks as though* there is a patch of light on the wallpaper" or "It *feels as though* someone were sticking a pin into me." The introspective account tells us about the individual's state of consciousness in the same way as does "I see a patch of light" or "I feel a pin being stuck into me": It differs from the corresponding perception statement in so far as (a) in the perception statement the individual "goes beyond the evidence of his senses" in describing his environment and (b) in the introspective report he withholds descriptive epithets he is inclined to ascribe to the environment, perhaps because he suspects that they may not be appropriate to the actual state of affairs. Psychologically speaking, the change from talking about the environment to talking about one's state of consciousness is simply a matter of inhibiting descriptive reactions not justified by appearances alone, and of disinhibiting descriptive reactions which are normally inhibited because the individual has learned that they are unlikely to provide a reliable guide to the state of the environment in the prevailing circumstances.[22] To say that something looks green to me is to say that my experience is like the experience I get when I see something that really is green. In my reply to Objection 3, I pointed out the extreme openness or generality of statements which report experiences. This explains why there is no language of private qualities. (Just as "someone," unlike "the doctor," is a colorless word.)

If it is asked what is the difference between those brain processes which, in my view, are experiences and those brain processes which are not, I can only reply that this is at present unknown. . . .

I have now considered a number of objections to the brain-process thesis. I wish now to conclude by some remarks on the logical status of the thesis itself. U. T. Place seems to hold that it is a straight-out scientific hypothesis.[23] If so, he is partly right and partly wrong. If the issue is between (say) a brain-process thesis and a heart thesis, or a liver thesis, or a kidney thesis, then the issue is a purely empirical one, and the verdict is overwhelmingly in favor of the brain. The right sorts of things don't go on in the heart, liver, or kidney, nor do these organs possess the right sort of complexity of structure. On the other hand, if the issue is between a brain-or-heart-or-liver-or-kidney thesis (that is, some form of materialism) on the one hand and epiphenomenalism on the other and, then the issue is not an empirical one. For there is no conceivable experiment which could decide between materialism and epiphenomenalism. This latter issue is not like the average straight-out empirical issue in science, but like the issue between the nineteenth-century English naturalist Philip Gosse[24] and the orthodox geologists and paleontologists of his day. According to Gosse, the earth was created about 4000 B.C. exactly as described in *Genesis*, with twisted rock strata, "evidence" of erosion, and so forth, and all sorts of fossils, all in their appropriate strata, just as if the usual evolutionist story had been true. Clearly this theory is in a sense irrefutable: No evidence can possibly tell against it. Let us ignore the theological setting in which Philip Gosse's hypothesis had been placed, thus ruling out objections of a theological kind, such as "what a queer God who would go to such elaborate lengths to deceive us." Let us suppose that it is held that the universe just *began* in 4004 B.C. with the initial conditions just everywhere as they were in 4004 B.C., and in particular that our own planet began with sediment in the rivers, eroded cliffs, fossils in the rocks, and so on. No scientist would ever entertain this as a serious hypothesis, consistent though it is with all possible evidence. The hypothesis offends against the principles of parsimony and simplicity. There would be far too many brute and inexplicable facts. Why are pterodactyl bones just as they are? No explanation in terms of the evolution of pterodactyls from earlier forms of life would any longer be possible. We would have millions of facts about the world as it was in 4004 B.C. that just have to be *accepted*.

The issue between the brain-process theory and epiphenomenalism seems to be of the above sort. (Assuming that a behavioristic reduction of introspective reports is not possible.) If it be agreed that there are no cogent philosophical arguments which force us into accepting dualism, and if the brain-process theory and dualism are equally consistent with the facts, then the principles of parsimony and simplicity seem to me to decide overwhelmingly in favor of the brain-process theory. As I pointed out earlier, dualism involves a large number of irreducible psychophysical laws . . . of a queer sort, that just have to be taken on trust, and are just as difficult to swallow as the irreducible facts about the paleontology of the earth with which we are faced on Philip Gosse's theory.

Discussion Questions

1. Smart writes that someday our behavior will be explainable in mechanistic, scientific terms. Do you agree? Do you think it is possible to explain something considered by most as a product of the mind/soul (love, for example) as eventually explained by science?

2. If ignorance of identity (Smart's reply to Objection 1) is not relevant in claming that mind and body are different things, how could we ever know if we had done "enough" investigating to know if two things were the same?

3. In what way do you think notions of the mind and soul are just like Wittgenstein's "beetle in a box"—mere words created to help us explain how things seem versus how things *really are*?

Movie Titles

1. Theme: Memory—How important is a person's memory to their identity?
   • *Memento* (R)
   • *Eternal Sunshine of a Spotless Mind* (R)

- *Total Recall* (R)
- *Groundhog Day*
- *Fifty First Dates*

2. Theme: Artificial Intelligence—Are these robots persons? Do they have minds? Have they achieved consciousness? Should they have rights?
   - *I Robot*
   - *Bicentennial Man*
   - *AI: Artificial Intelligence*
   - *2001: A Space Odyssey*

3. *Crash* (R)—What role does race play in identity? More importantly, how does society affect the way you view others?

4. *Being John Malkovich* (R)—Does the main character "become" John Malkovich?

5. *The Jerk* (R)—How much is the main character's identity affected by his material/monetary possessions? By his realization regarding his family history?

6. *Heaven Can Wait*—What does it mean to come back to life in another body? What is the meaning of death if our soul lives on?

7. *Gattaca*—How important is one's body and physical composition to his or her identity? What is the harm in using technology to create what we believe to be "more fit" people?

8. *The Fountainhead*—What does it mean to be an "authentic" person? Is this possible? Which architect do you admire more and why?

Song Lyrics

Tool—"Parabola"
The Dave Matthews Band—"Dancing Nancies"
Ben Folds Five—"Best Imitation of Myself"
Thrice—"To What End"
Dream Theater—"The Spirit Carries On"
The History of the Concept of the Soul—"The Mr. T Experience"

Notes

1. Nietzsche (1968).
2. '. . . which can be conceived only by the understanding or the mind' (French version).
3. '. . . or rather the act whereby it is perceived' (added in French version).
4. The French version has 'more clear and distinct' and, at the end of this sentence, 'more evidently, distinctly, and clearly.'
5. The Latin term *corpus* as used here by Descartes is ambiguous as between 'body' (i.e., corporeal matter in general) and 'the body' (i.e., this particular body of mine). The French version preserves the ambiguity.
6. '. . . that is, my soul, by which I am what I am' (added in French version).

7. '. . . certain modes of thinking which are quite special and distinct from me' (French version).
8. '. . . between the shapes, movements, and other modes or accidents of a body and the body which supports them' (French version).
9. '. . . as a pilot in his ship' (French version).
10. '. . . without any help from the body' (added in French version).
11. '. . . carefully and maturely examined' (French version).
12. '. . . and thus seem to have been directly deceived by my nature' (added in French version).
13. '. . . but occurs merely as a result of the disposition of the organs' (French version).
14. The supposed faculty which integrates the data from the five specialized senses (the notion goes back ultimately to Aristotle). 'The seat of the common sense must be very mobile, to receive all the impressions coming from the senses, but must be moveable only by the spirits which transmit these impressions. Only the *conarion* [pineal gland] fits these conditions' (letter to Mersenne, 21 April 1641).
15. On this point see Paul Oppenheim and Hilary Putnam, "Unity of Science as a Working Hypothesis," in *Minnesota Studies in the Philosophy of Science*, II, 336; also my note "Plausible Reasoning in Philosophy," *Mind*, LXVI (1957), 75–78.
16. See Place, *op. cit.*, p. 45, near top, and Feigl, *op. cit.*, p. 390, near top.
17. Cf. Feigl, *op. cit.*, p. 439.
18. See Place, *op. cit.*, p. 47; also Feigl, *op. cit.*, p. 438.
19. I think this objection was first put to me by Professor Max Black. I think it is the most subtle of any of those I have considered and the one which I am least confident of having satisfactorily met.
20. See B. A. Farrell, "Experience," *Mind*, LIX (1950), especially 174.
21. Dr. J. R. Smythies claims that a sense-datum language could be taught independently of the material object language ("A Note on the Fallacy of the 'Phenomenological Fallacy,'" *British Journal of Psychology*, XLVIII, 1957, 141–144.) I am not so sure of this: There must be some public criteria for a person having got a rule wrong before we can teach him the rule. I suppose someone might *accidentally* learn color words by Dr. Symthies' procedure. I am not, of course, denying that we can learn a sense-datum language in the sense that we can learn to report out experience. Nor would Place deny it.
22. I owe this point to Place, in correspondence.
23. See his article "Towards an Information Flow Model of Human Behaviour," *British Journal of Psychology*, XLVII (1956), 30–43.
24. See the entertaining account of Gosse's took *Omphalos* by Martin Gardner in *Fads and Fallacies in the Name of Science* (2nd ed., New York, 1957).

Chapter 3

Science

High school students spend so much time in science courses but rarely are asked to consider such questions as: What is science, non-science, and pseudo-science? To which do we ascribe more value and why? How do we distinguish these from each other? Is astrology science and, if not, why not? Is creationism (the idea that a supernatural being created the universe) science? And how does science function in the first place? What is the role of a *theory* and a *law*?

For most people, science class represents an experience comprised mainly of memorizing formulas, biochemical pathways, and chemical compounds—and then restating them on an exam as facts. But we also realize that science has been wrong in the past. Scientists before Copernicus, for example, all believed they had proved the Earth to be the center of the universe. Because science works through the method of induction (assuming that the future will be like the past), it thus never achieves *absolute* certainty. Though science has undoubtedly provided us with great truths and useful theories throughout history and in our everyday lives.

When examining the value of science, it is important to understand the institution of science from all perspectives—historical, psychological, sociological, and logical. Science does have limits. Most agree that it simply cannot examine supernatural and metaphysical entities such as God, the soul, the mind, and even some topics in psychology and in ethics (though not all agree on this). And with the continued focus on the creationism/evolution debate and how each should be taught in our public schools (if at all), this discussion becomes even more important.

In the readings here, Salmon first explores the inductive method on which science relies and, in doing so, addresses the famous "problem of induction" noted by Hume. Kuhn then provides an historical view of science, illustrating its development as well as what psychological and sociological effects this has on scientists and the public at large. Popper then defends what has been considered by most philosophers of science to be a suitable criterion for determining a specific investigation as scientific. Thagard then applies this notion to astrology as a case study in application of this and other criteria.

Science is not without its critics. In Feyerabend's piece, he first points out the numerous logical flaws of science and then warns us of following this "monster," while Longino applies a feminist review of science claiming that, because of the subjective nature of science, we must beware of portraying a one-sided view of what we see as reality. Scientist Richard Dawkins answers these concerns (and more) as he provides a scientist's view of science and the critiques aimed at science.

An Encounter with David Hume
Wesley C. Salmon

One of the preeminent experts in the philosophy of science, Wesley Salmon earned his PhD in Philosophy of Science at UCLA working under Hans Reichenbach, another main figure in the philosophy of science (and also referenced in this article). Salmon lectured in the History and Philosophy of Science primarily at Indiana University, University of Arizona, and finally at the University of Pittsburgh where he retired in 1999, and he also held visiting professorships at several universities throughout the world. He has written and edited numerous books with a strong focus in the history and philosophy of science as well as in logic.

Here, Salmon frames "Hume's Problem of Induction" in a story-like format. This problem is considered one of Hume's main contributions to philosophy. Hume argues that a reliance on induction is circular in nature and, thus, illogical. Basically, to prove induction (that the future will resemble the past), one must rely on induction (that induction will continue to provide results because it has done so in the past). After stating "Hume's problem," Salmon then provides various responses given by philosophers in attempts to solve the problem, as well as responses to those. Salmon presents Hume's position through the character "Professor Philo" (in reference to "Philo" of Hume's "Dialogues Concerning Natural Religion," in Chapter 4 of this book).

Reading Questions

1. Explain the difference between the "swinging ball" and the "maniac driver" as explained by the second student and then Professor Salvia. How do these relate to Hume's two kinds of reasoning?
2. What is the difference between the "vitamin C/cold" example and the "five swinging balls" example?
3. What is the law of conservation of momentum? How is it demonstrated? What practical applications are given?
4. How does Professor Philo attempt to show that the student's line of reasoning regarding the proof of the law of conservation of momentum is faulty?
5. How does Professor Salvia discuss the "certainty" of scientific laws? What is Hume's "more fundamental"/"more devastating" point?
6. How is Hume's point reinforced by the student's discussion of the "hidden forces" that allow Professor Silva's coffee cup to sit on the table top?
7. According to Hume, why can't we know the "connection" among objects about which we discover generalities?
8. How does Professor Philo relate Hume's view of "scientific reasoning" to the psychological conditioning of Pavlov's Dogs?
9. How does Professor Philo summarize Hume's critique of the scientific method as involving circular reasoning? Explain the relevance of her check-cashing analogy.

Source: Permission granted by estate of Wesley C. Salmon.

A Day in The Life of a Hypothetical Student

In the Physics 1A Lecture Hall, Professor Salvia[1] has had a bowling ball suspended from a high ceiling by a long rope so that it can swing back and forth like a pendulum. Standing well over to one side of the room, he holds the bowling ball at the tip of his nose. He releases it (taking great care not to give it a push). It swings through a wide arc, gaining considerable speed as it passes through the low portion of its swing beneath the point of suspension from the ceiling. It continues to the other side of the room, where it reaches the end of its path, and then returns. The professor stands motionless as the bowling ball moves faster and faster back toward his nose. As it passes through the midpoint of the return arc, it is again traveling very rapidly, but it begins to slow down, and it stops just at the tip of his nose. Some of the students think he is cool. "This demonstration," he says, "illustrates the faith that the physicist has in nature's regularity." (See Figure 1.)

Imagine that you have witnessed this demonstration just after your philosophy class, where the subject of discussion was Hume's *Enquiry Concerning Human*

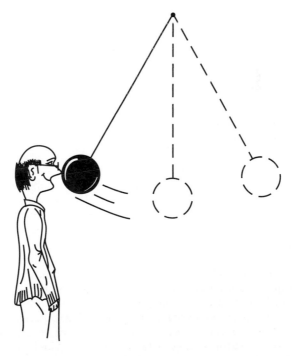

Figure 1
Professor Salvia's Pendulum. After swinging to the opposite of the lecture hall, the bowling ball swings right back to the tip of the prof's nose, which remains motionless during the entire procedure.

Understanding. You raise your hand. "How did you *know* that the bowling ball would stop where it did, just short of bashing your nose into your face?" you ask.

"This is a standard demonstration," he replies; "I do it every year in this class, and it has often been used by many other physics teachers." In an attempt to inject a little humor, he adds, "If I had had any doubt about its working, I'd have had the teaching assistant do it."

"Are you saying, then, that you trusted the experiment to work this time simply because it has been tried so many times in the past, and has never failed?" You recall Hume's discussion of the collisions of billiard balls. In the first instance, according to Hume, before you have any experience with material objects colliding with one another, you would not know what to expect when you see a moving billiard ball approaching a stationary one, but after a good deal of experience you confidently expect some motion to be transferred to the stationary ball as a result of the collision. As your experience accumulates, you learn to predict the exact manner in which the second ball will move after being struck by the first. But you cannot really accept that answer, and neither, you feel sure, will your physics professor. Without waiting for an answer, you follow up your first question with another.

"I have this friend," you continue, "who drives like a maniac. It scares me to ride with him, but he always tells me not to worry—he has never had an accident, or even a traffic ticket. Should I conclude—assuming he is telling the truth (just as I assume you are telling me the truth about this demonstration)—that it is as safe for me to ride with him as it is for you to perform the bowling ball trick?"

"It's not the same thing at all," another student chimes in; "you can prove, mathematically, that the pendulum will not swing back beyond its original starting point, but you certainly can't prove mathematically that your friend won't have a wreck. In a way it's just the opposite; you can prove that he is likely to have an accident if he keeps on driving like that."

"What you say is partly right," says Professor Salvia to the second student, "but it isn't only a matter of mathematics. We have to rely upon the laws of physics as well. With the pendulum we were depending mainly upon the law of conservation of energy, one of the most fundamental laws of nature. As the pendulum goes through its swing, potential energy is transformed into kinetic energy, which is transformed back into potential energy; and so forth. As long as the total amount of energy remains unchanged, my nose is safe."

Since you have not yet studied the concept of energy, you do not worry too much about the details of the explanation. You are satisfied that you will understand why the pendulum behaves as it does when you have learned more about the concepts and laws that were mentioned. But you do remember something Hume wrote. There are two kinds of reasoning: reasoning concerning relations of ideas, and reasoning concerning matters of fact and existence. Mathematical reasoning falls into the former category (relations of ideas) and consequently, by itself, cannot provide any information about matters of fact. The pendulum and the professor's nose are, however, matters of fact, so we need something in addition to mathematics to get the information we want concerning that situation. Professor Salvia has told us what it is—we need the laws of nature as well.

Since physics is your last class in the morning, you head for the cafeteria when it is over to get a sandwich and coffee. The philosophy class is still bugging you. What was it Hume said about bread? That we do not know the "secret power" by which it nourishes us? Now we do, of course; we understand metabolism, the mechanism by which the body converts food into energy. Hume (living in the eighteenth century) did not understand about power and energy, as he said repeatedly. He did not know why bread is suitable food for humans, but not for tigers and lions. In biology class, you recall, you studied herbivorous, carnivorous, and omnivorous species. Biologists must now understand why some species can metabolize vegetables and others cannot. Modern physics, chemistry, and biology can provide a complete explanation of the various forms of energy, the ways they can be converted from one form to another, and the ways in which they can be utilized by a living organism.

Taking a sip of the hot coffee, you recall some other things Hume said—for example, remarks about the "connection" between heat and flame. We now know that heat is really a form of energy; that temperature is a measure of the average kinetic energy of the molecules. Now, it seems, we know a great deal about the "secret powers," "energy," etc., that so perplexed Hume. Modern physics knows that ordinary objects are composed of molecules, which are in turn composed of atoms, which are themselves made up of subatomic particles. Modern science can tell us what holds atoms and molecules together, and why the things that consist of them have the properties they do. What was it that Hume said about a piece of ice and a crystal (e.g., a diamond)? That we do not know why one is caused by cold and the other by heat? I'll just bet, you think, that Salvia could answer that one without a bit of trouble. Why, you wonder, do they make us read these old philosophers who are now so out of date? Hume was, no doubt, a very profound thinker in his day, but why do we have to study him now, when we know the answers to all of those questions? If I were majoring in history that might be one thing, but that doesn't happen to be my field of interest. Oh, I suppose they'd say that getting an education means that you have to learn something about the "great minds of the past," but why doesn't the philosophy professor come right out and tell us the answers to these questions? It's silly to pretend that they are still great mysteries.

After lunch, let's imagine, you go to a class in contemporary social and political problems, a class you particularly like because of the lively discussions. A lot of time is spent talking about such topics as population growth, ecology and the environment, energy demands and uses, food production, and pollution. You discuss population trends, the extrapolation of such trends, and the predication that by the year 2000 A.D., world population will reach 7 billion. You consider the various causes and possible effects of increasing concentrations of carbon dioxide in the atmosphere. You discuss solutions to various of these problems in terms of strict governmental controls, economic sanctions and incentives, and voluntary compliance on the part of enlightened and concerned citizens.

"If people run true to form," you interject, "if they behave as they always have, you can be sure that you won't make much progress relying on the good will and good sense of the populace at large."

"What is needed is more awareness and education," another student remarks, "for people can change if they see the need. During World War II people willingly sacrificed in order to support the war effort. They will do the same again, if they see that the emergency is really serious. That's why we need to provide more education and make stronger appeals to their humanitarian concerns."

"What humanitarian concerns?" asks still another student with evident cynicism.

"People *will* change," says another. "I have been reading that we are entering a new era, the Age of Aquarius, when man's finer, gentler, more considerate nature will be manifest."

"Well, I don't know about all of this astrology," another remarks in earnest tones, "but I do not believe that God will let His world perish if we mend our ways and trust in Him. I have complete faith in His goodness."

You find this statement curiously reminiscent of Professor Salvia's earlier mention of his faith in the regularity of nature.

That night, after dinner, you read an English assignment. By the time you finish it, your throat feels a little scratchy, and you notice that you have a few sniffles. You decide to begin taking large doses of vitamin C; you have read that there is quite some controversy as to whether this helps to ward off colds, but that there is no harm in taking this vitamin in large quantities. Before going to the drug store to buy some vitamin C, you write home to request some additional funds; you mail your letter in the box by the pharmacy. You return with the vitamin C, take a few of the pills, and turn in for the night—confident that the sun will rise tomorrow morning, and hoping that you won't feel as miserable as you usually do when you catch a cold. David Hume is the farthest thing from your mind.

Hume Revisited

The next morning, you wake up feeling fine. The sun is shining brightly, and you have no sign of a cold. You are not sure whether the vitamin C cured your cold, or whether it was the good night's sleep, or whether it wasn't going to develop into a real cold regardless. Perhaps, even, it was the placebo effect; in psychology you learned that people can often be cured by totally inert drugs (e.g., sugar pills) if they believe in them. You don't really know what caused your prompt recovery, but frankly, you don't really care. If it was the placebo effect that is fine with you; you just hope it will work as well the next time.

You think about what you will do today. It is Thursday, so you have a philosophy discussion section in the morning and a physics lab in the afternoon. Thursday, you say to yourself, has got to be the lousiest day of the week. The philosophy section is a bore, and the physics lab is a drag. If only it were Saturday, when you have no classes! For a brief moment you consider taking off. Then you remember the letter you wrote last night, think about your budget and your grades, and resign yourself to the prescribed activities for the day.

The leader of the discussion section starts off with the question, "What was the main problem—I mean the really *basic* problem—bothering Hume in the *Enquiry*?" You feel like saying, "Lack of adequate scientific knowledge" (or words to that effect), but restrain yourself. No use antagonizing the guy who will decide what grade to give you. Someone says that he seemed to worry quite a lot about causes and effects, to which the discussion leader (as usual) responds. "But *why*?" Again, you stifle an impulse to say, "Because he didn't know too much about them."

After much folderol, the leader finally elicits the answer, "Because he wanted to know how we can find out about things we don't actually see (or hear, smell, touch, taste, etc.)."

"In other words," the leader paraphrases, "to examine the basis for making inferences from what we observe to what we cannot (at the moment) observe. Will someone," he continues, "give me an example of something you believe in which you are not now observing?"

You think of the letter you dropped into the box last night, of your home and parents, and of the money you hope to receive. You do not see the letter now, but you are confident it is somewhere in the mails; you do not see your parents now, but you firmly believe they are back home where you left them; you do not yet see the money you hope to get, but you expect to see it before too long. The leader is pleased when you give those examples. "And what do causes and effects have to do with all of this?" he asks, trying to draw you out a little more. Still thinking of your grade you cooperate. "I believe the letter is somewhere in the mails because I wrote it and dropped it in the box. I believe my parents are at home because they are always calling me up to tell me what to do. And I believe that the money will come as an effect of my eloquent appeal." The leader is really happy with that; you can tell you have an A for today's session.

"But," he goes on, "do you see how this leads us immediately into Hume's next question? If cause-effect relations are the whole basis for our knowledge of things and events we do not observe, how do we know whether one event causes another, or whether they just happen together as a matter of coincidence?" Your mind is really clicking now.

"I felt a cold coming on last night, and I took a massive dose of vitamin C," you report. "This morning I feel great, but I honestly don't know whether the vitamin C actually cured it."

"Well, how could we go about trying to find out," retorts the discussion leader.

"By trying it again when I have the first symptoms of a cold," you answer, "and by trying it on other people as well." At that point the bell rings, and you leave class wondering whether the vitamin C really did cure your incipient cold.

You keep busy until lunch, doing one thing and another, but sitting down and eating, you find yourself thinking again about the common cold and its cure. It seems to be a well-known fact that the cold is caused by one or more viruses, and the human organism seems to have ways of combating virus infections. Perhaps the massive doses of vitamin C trigger the body's defenses, in some way or other, or perhaps it provides some kind of antidote to the toxic effects of the virus. You don't know much about all of this, but you can't help speculating that science has had a good deal of success in finding causes and cures of various diseases. If continued research reveals the physiological and chemical processes in the cold's infection and in the body's response, then surely it would be possible to find out whether the vitamin C really has any effect upon the common cold or not. It seems that we could ascertain whether a causal relation exists in this instance if only we could discover the relevant laws of biology and chemistry.

At this point in your musings, you notice that it is time to get over to the physics lab. You remember that yesterday morning you were convinced that predicting the outcome of an experiment is possible if you know which physical laws apply. That certainly was the outcome of the discussion in the physics class. Now, it seems, the question about the curative power of vitamin C hinges on exactly the same thing—the laws of nature. As you hurry to the lab it occurs to you that predicting the outcome of an experiment, before it is performed, is a first-class example of what you were discussing in philosophy—making inferences from the observed to the unobserved. We observe the set-up for the experiment (or demonstration) before it is performed, and we predict the outcome before we observe it. Salvia certainly was confident about the prediction he made. Also, recalling one of Hume's examples, you were at least as confident, when you went to bed last night, that the sun would rise this morning. But Hume *seemed* to be saying that the basis for this confidence was the fact that the sun has been observed to rise every morning since the dawn of history. "That's wrong," you say to yourself as you reach the physics lab. "My confidence in the rising of the sun is based upon the laws of astronomy. So here we are back at the laws again."

Inside the lab you notice a familiar gadget; it consists of a frame from which five steel balls are suspended so that they hang in a straight line, each one touching its neighbors. Your little brother got a toy like this, in a somewhat smaller size, for his birthday a couple of years ago. You casually raise one of the end balls, and let it swing back. It strikes the nearest of the four balls left hanging, and the ball at the other end swings out (the three balls in the middle keeping their place). The ball at the far end swings back again, striking its neighbor, and then the ball on the near end swings out, almost to the point from which you let it swing originally. The process goes on for a while, with the two end balls alternately swinging out and back. It has a pleasant rhythm. (See Figure 2.)

While you are enjoying the familiar toy, the lab instructor, Dr. Sagro,[2] comes over to you. "Do you know why just the ball on the far end moves—instead of, say, two on the far end, or all four of the remaining ones—when the ball on this end strikes?"

"Not exactly, but I suppose it has something to do with conservation of energy," you reply, recalling what Salvia said yesterday in answer to the question about the bowling ball.

"That's right," says Dr. Sagro, "but it also depends upon conservation of momentum." Before you have a chance to say anything she continues, "Let me ask you another question. What would happen if you raised two balls at this end; and let them swing together toward the remaining three?"

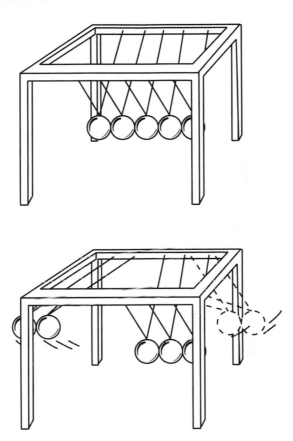

Figure 2
The Energy-Momentum Toy. When two balls at the right collide with the remaining three, two balls swing away from the left side. What happens when three on the right collide with the remaining two?

"I think two balls will swing away at the other end," you reply, remembering the way your brother's toy worked.

"Why don't you test it to find out if you are right?" says the instructor. You do, and you find that the result is as you had predicted. Without saying anything about it, you assume that this, too, can be explained by means of the laws of conservation of energy and momentum.

Dr. Sagro poses another question. "What will happen," she asks, "if you start by swinging three balls from this end?" Since there are only two remaining balls you don't know what to say, so you confess ignorance. She suggests you try it, in order to find out what will happen. When you do, you see that three balls swing to the other side, and three swing back again; the middle ball swings back and forth, acting as the third ball in each group. This was a case in which you didn't know what to expect as a result until you tried the experiment. This was like some of Hume's examples; not until you have actually had the experience do you know what result to expect. But there is also something different. Hume said that you must try the experiment many times in order to know what to expect; nevertheless, after just one trial you are sure what will happen whenever the experiment is repeated. This makes it rather different from the problem of whether vitamin C cured your cold. In that case, it seemed necessary to try the experiment over and over again, preferably with a number of different people. Reflecting upon this difference, you ask the lab instructor a crucial question, "If you knew the laws of conservation of momentum and energy, but had never seen the experiment with the three balls performed, would you have been able to predict the outcome?"

"Yes," she says simply.

"Well," you murmur inaudibly, "it seems as if the whole answer to Hume's problem regarding inferences about things we do not immediately observe, including predictions of future occurrences, rests squarely upon the laws of nature."

Knowing the Laws

Given that the laws are so fundamental, you decide to find out more about them. The laws of conservation of energy and momentum are close at hand, so to speak, so you decide to start there. "O.K.," you say to the lab instructor, "what are these laws of nature, which enable you to predict so confidently how experiments will turn out before they are performed? I'd like to learn something about them."

"Fine," she says, delighted with your desire to learn; "let's start with conservation of momentum. (See Figure 3.) . . .

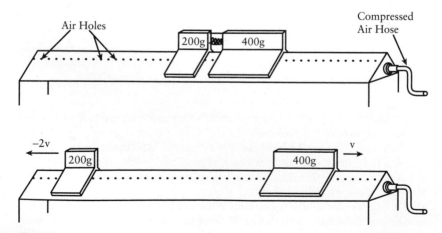

Figure 3
Cars on the Air Track. Top: Cars tied together against spring under tension. Bottom: Cars moving apart after "explosion." $400\,g \times v + 200\,g \times (-2v) = 0$. Momentum is conserved.

When two bodies (such as cars) interact with one another (as in a collision), the total momentum of the system consisting of those two bodies is the same before and after the interaction. . . .

"There are many other applications of the law of conservation of momentum," she continues. "When a rifle recoils upon being fired, when a jet engine propels an airplane, when a rocket engine lifts an artificial satellite into orbit, or when you step out of an untethered rowboat and are surprised to feel it moving out from under you—these are all cases of conservation of momentum."

"Is this law ever violated?" you ask.

"No," she answers, "there are no known exceptions to it." You leave the lab with the feeling that you know at least one fundamental law, and that you have seen it proved experimentally right before your eyes. You can't wait to tell your philosophy professor about it.

When you go to your philosophy class the next morning, the topic is still Hume's *Enquiry Concerning Human Understanding* and the problem of how we can have knowledge of things we do not observe. As the lecture begins, Professor Philo[3] is saying, "As we saw during the last lecture, Hume maintains that our knowledge of what we do not observe is based entirely upon cause and effect relations, but that raises the question of how we can gain knowledge of these relations. Hume maintained that this knowledge can result only from repeated observation of one type of event (a cause) to see whether it is always followed by an event of another kind (its effect). Hume therefore analyzed the notion of causality in terms of constant conjunction of events. Consider for a moment Hume's favorite example, the colliding billiard balls . . ."

You raise your hand. "It seems to me that Hume was wrong about this," you begin, and then you relate briefly yesterday's experiences in the physics lab. "If you know the relevant laws of nature," you conclude, "you can predict the outcomes of future experiments on the basis of a single trial, or perhaps even without benefit of any trials at all."

"But how," asks Professor Philo, "can we establish knowledge of the laws of nature?"

You had a hunch she might ask some such question, and you are ready with your reply, "We *proved* it experimentally."

"Well," says Professor Philo, "I'm not a physicist, so perhaps you had better explain in a little more detail just what the experimental proof consists of. You mentioned something about an explosion—how did that go?"

You explain carefully. . . . "In every case," you conclude, "the momentum of the two cars was equal in amount and opposite in direction, just as the law of conservation of momentum says it should be."

"Now let me see if I understand your line of reasoning," says the professor in a tone that is altogether too calm to suit you. "If the law of conservation of momentum is correct, then the two cars will part in the manner you described. The cars did move apart in just that way. Therefore, the law of conservation of momentum is correct. Is that your argument?"

"I guess so," you reply a bit hesitantly, because it looks as if she is trying to trap you.

"Do you think that kind of argument is valid?" she responds.

"What do you mean?" you ask, beginning to feel a little confused.

"Well," she says, "isn't that rather like the following argument: If this defendant is guilty, he will refuse to testify at his own trial; he does refuse to testify; therefore, he is guilty. Would any judge allow that argument in a court of law?"

"Of course not," you reply, "but it isn't the same thing at all. We tested the law of conservation of momentum many times in many different ways, and in every case we got the expected result (allowing for the usual small inaccuracies in the measurements)."

"If I remember what you said," Ms. Philo goes on, "in one of your experiments you had one car with a mass of 200 grams and another with a mass of 400 grams, and in that case the lighter car recoiled with twice the speed of the more massive one. How many times did you repeat this particular experiment?"

"Once or twice, as nearly as I can recall."

"Yet, you seem to believe that the result would be the same, no matter how many times the experiment was repeated—is that correct?"

"I suppose so," you reply somewhat uncomfortably.

"And with how many different masses and how many different recoil velocities did you try it? Do you believe it would work the same way if the masses were thousands or billions of kilograms instead of a few grams? And do you suppose that it would work the same way if the velocities were very great—somewhere near the speed of light?"

Since you have heard that strange things happen when speeds approach that of light, your hesitancy increases, but you reply tentatively, "Well, the lab instructor told me that there are no exceptions to the law."

"Did she say that," asks Philo, "or did she say no *known* exceptions?"

"I guess that was it," you reply lamely, feeling quite crushed.

Professor Philo endeavors to summarize the discussion. "What is considered experimental 'proof of a law of nature' is actually a process of testing *some* of its logical consequences. That is, you ask what would have to happen *if* your hypothesis is true, and then you perform an experiment to see if it turns out that way *in fact*. Since any law of nature is a generalization, it has an unlimited number of consequences. We can never hope to test them all. In particular, any *useful* law of nature will have consequences that pertain to the future; they enable us to make predictions. We can never test these consequences until it is too late to use them for the purpose of prediction. To suppose that testing *some* of the consequences of a law constitutes a *conclusive proof* of the law would clearly be an outright logical fallacy." The bell rings and you leave the class, convinced that she has merely been quibbling.

During your physics class you brood about the previous discussion in the philosophy class, without paying very close attention to the lecture. Similar thoughts keep nagging at you during lunch. The objections brought up by Professor Philo seem to be well-founded, you conclude, but you wonder how they can be reconciled with the apparent reliability and certainty of scientific knowledge. In desperation, you decide to talk it over with Professor Salvia during his office hour this very afternoon. When you arrive, you don't know exactly where to begin, so you decide to go back to the pendulum demonstration, which was the thing that got you started on this whole mess. "When you performed that demonstration," you ask, "were you *absolutely certain* how it would turn out? Has it ever failed?"

"Well, to be perfectly honest," he says, "it has been known to fail. Once when a friend of mine was doing it in front of a large auditorium, the suspension in the ceiling broke and the ball landed right on his foot. He was in a cast for months!"

"But that's no fault of the law of conservation of energy is it?" you ask. "The breaking of the suspension didn't mean that conservation of energy is false, did it?"

"Of course not," he answers, "we still believe firmly in conservation of energy."

"But are you *certain* of the law of conservation of energy, or any other law of nature?" you ask, and before he has a chance to answer, you tell him about the discussion in the philosophy class this morning.

"So that's what's bothering you," he says, after hearing the whole story. "Professor Philo has an important point. No matter how thoroughly we have tested a scientific law—better, let's say 'hypothesis'—there is always the possibility that new evidence will show up to prove it false. For instance, around the close of the nineteenth century, many physicists seemed virtually certain that Newtonian mechanics was absolutely correct. A wide variety of its consequences had been tested under many different circumstances, and Newton's laws stood up extremely well. But early in the twentieth century it became clear that what we now call 'classical physics' would have to undergo major revisions, and a profound scientific revolution ensued. Modern physics, which includes quantum mechanics and relativity theory, was the result. We can never be sure that any hypothesis we currently accept as correct will not have to be abandoned or modified at some time in the future as a result of new evidence."

"What about the law of conservation of momentum?" you ask, recalling yesterday's experience in the lab. "The lab instructor said it has no known exceptions."

"That is correct," says Salvia, "and it is a rather interesting case. Conservation of momentum is a consequence of Newton's laws of motion; therefore, any consequence of conservation of momentum is a consequence of Newton's laws. But we now regard Newton's laws as not strictly true—they break down, for example, with objects traveling close to the speed of light—but conservation of momentum holds even in these cases. So we have a good example of a case where we believe a lot of consequences, but we do not believe in the laws (Newton's) from which the consequences follow."

It occurs to you that this is a rather important set of supposed laws; perhaps the philosophy professor was not merely quibbling when she said that it was not valid to conclude that a hypothesis is true just because we know many of its consequences to be true.

"Since you cannot be certain of any so-called law of nature," you ask, "why do you believe in them so firmly?"

"Because," answers Salvia, "we consider them very well confirmed. We accept well-confirmed hypotheses, knowing that we may later have to change our minds in the light of new evidence. Science can no longer claim infallible truth."

"Does that mean that scientific results are highly probable, but not absolutely certain?" you ask, trying to be sure you have understood what he has said.

"Yes, you could put it that way," he agrees.

You leave with the feeling that you have a pretty good comprehension of the situation. As a result of your study of physics and philosophy you now understand why science cannot claim infallibility for its findings, but must be content with results that are well confirmed. With that, you take off for the weekend. (And what you do with your weekend is your own business.)

Hume's Bombshell

A little tired, but basically in a cheerful mood, you arrive at your philosophy class on Monday morning. You meet the professor a few minutes before class outside the room, and you tell her very briefly of your conversation with the physics professor. You explain that you now understand why it is that scientific laws can never be considered completely certain, but only as well-confirmed hypotheses. With her help, and with that of Professor Salvia, you now understand what Hume was driving at—and you see, moreover, that Hume was right. She smiles, and you both go into the classroom, where she begins her lecture.

"Last Friday, as you may recall, we had quite a lively discussion about the status of scientific laws—the law of conservation of momentum, in particular. We saw that such laws cannot be proved conclusively by any amount of experimental evidence. This is a point with which, I am happy to report, many (if not most) contemporary scientists agree. They realize that the most they can reasonably claim for their hypotheses is strong confirmation. Looking at the matter this way, one could conclude that it is wise to believe in scientific predictions, for if they are not certain to be true, they are a good bet. To believe in scientific results is to bet with the best available odds.

"However," she continues, "while this view may be correct as far as it goes, Hume was making a much more fundamental, and I should add, much more devastating point. Hume was challenging not merely our right to claim that scientific predictions will always be right, but also our right to claim that they will usually, or often, or indeed ever, be correct. Take careful note of what he says in Section IV:

> Let the course of things be allowed hitherto ever so regular; that alone, without some new argument or inference, proves not that, for the future, it will continue so. In vain do you pretend to have learned the nature of bodies from your past experience. Their secret nature, and consequently all their effects

and influence, may change, without any change in their sensible qualities. This happens sometimes, and with regard to some objects: Why may it not happen always and with regard to all objects? What logic, what process of argument secures you against this supposition?

He is saying, as I hope you understood from your reading, that no matter how reliably a law seems to have held in the past, there is no logical reason why it must do so in the future *at all*. It is therefore possible that *every* scientific prediction, based on *any* law or laws whatever, may turn out to be false from this moment on. The stationary billiard ball that is struck by a moving one may remain motionless where it is—while the moving ball may bounce straight back in the direction from whence it came, or it may go straight up in the air, or it might vanish in a puff of smoke. Any of these possibilities can be imagined; none of them involves any logical contradiction. This is the force of Hume's skeptical arguments. The conclusion seems to be that we have no *reason* to believe in scientific predictions—no more reason than to believe on the basis of astrology, crystal gazing, or sheer blind guessing."

You can hardly believe your ears; what is she saying? You raise your hand, and when you are recognized, you can hardly keep your intense irritation from showing as you assert, "But certainly we can say that scientific predictions are more probable than those based, for example, upon astrology." As you speak, you are reminded of the remark in contemporary problems last Wednesday concerning the coming of the Age of Aquarius. Science has got to be better than *that*! As these thoughts cross your mind Professor Philo is saying, ". . . but that depends upon what you mean by 'probable,' doesn't it?"

The physics lecture today is on Newton's law of gravitation, and the professor is explaining that every bit of matter in the universe is attracted to every other by a force proportional to the masses and inversely proportional to the square of the distance between them. He goes on to explain how Kepler's laws of planetary motion and Galileo's law of falling bodies are (when suitably corrected) consequences of Newton's laws. You listen carefully, but you recognize this as another law that enables scientists to make impressive predictions. Indeed, Salvia is now telling how Newton's laws were used to explain the tides on the oceans and to predict the existence of two planets, Neptune and Pluto, that had not been known before. At the same time, you are wondering whether there is anything in what Hume seemed to be saying about such laws. Is it possible that suddenly, at the very next moment, matter would cease to have gravitational attraction, so that the whole solar system would go flying apart? It's a pretty chilling thought.

At lunch you are thinking about this question, and you glance back at some of the readings that were assigned from Hume's *Enquiry*. You notice again Hume's many references to secret powers and forces. Well, gravitation is surely a force, though there has not been any great secret about it since Newton's time. It is the "power" which keeps the solar system together. You remember reading somewhere that, according to Hume, you cannot know that it is safer to leave a building by way of the halls, stairways, and doors than it would be to step out of the third-story window. Well, Newton's law makes it clear why you don't want to step out of the third-story window, but what assurance have you that the building will continue to stand, rather than crashing down around your ears before you can get out? The engineers who design and build towers and bridges have a great deal of knowledge of the "secret powers" of their materials, so they must know a great deal more than Hume did about the hidden properties of things.

At this very moment, a lucky coincidence occurs—you see Dr. Sagro, your physics lab instructor, entering the cafeteria. You wave to her, and she sits down with you, putting her coffee cup on the table. You begin to ask her some questions about structural materials, and she responds by inquiring whether you would be satisfied if she could explain how the table supports the cup of coffee. You recognize it as just the kind of question you have in mind, and urge her to proceed.

"Certain materials, such as the metal in this table," she begins, "have a rather rigid crystalline structure, and for this reason they stick together and maintain their shape unless subjected to large forces. These crystals consist of very regular (and very beautiful) arrays of atoms, and they are held together by forces, essentially electrostatic in origin, among the charged particles that make up the atoms. Have you studied Coulomb's law of electrostatic forces?"

"No," you reply, "we are just doing Newton's law of gravitation. I think Salvia said electricity and magnetism would come up next semester."

"Well," she says, "these electrostatic forces are a lot like gravitational forces (they vary inversely with the square of the distance), but there are a couple of very important differences. First, as you know, there are two types of charges, positive and negative. The proton in the nucleus of the atom carries a positive charge, and the electrons that circulate about the nuclei have a negative charge. Two particles with opposite signs (such as a proton and an electron) attract one another, while two particles with like signs (e.g., two electrons or two protons) repel each other. This is different from gravity, because all matter attracts all other matter; there is no such thing as gravitational repulsion. The second main difference is that the electrostatic force is fantastically stronger than the gravitational force—roughly a billion billion billion billion times more powerful—but we don't usually notice it because most objects we deal with in everyday life are electrically neutral, containing equal amounts of positive and negative electric charge, or very nearly so. If you could somehow strip all of the electrons away from an apple, and all of the protons away from the earth, the force of attraction between the apple and the earth would be unbelievable.

"It is these *extremely* strong attractive and repulsive forces among the electrons and protons in the metal that maintain a stable and rigid form. That's why the table doesn't collapse. And the reason the coffee cup stays on top of the table, without penetrating its surface or slipping through, is that the electrons in the surface of the cup strongly repel those in the surface of the table. Actually, there is also a quantum mechanical force that prevents the weight of the cup from noticeably compressing the table, but we needn't go into that, because the effect is mostly due to the electrostatic forces."

Pleased with this very clear explanation, you thank her, but follow it up with another question. "Is there any logical reason why it has to be that way—why opposite charges attract and like charges repel? Can you prove that it is impossible for like charges to attract and unlike charges to repel? What would happen if *that* were suddenly to become the law?"

"It would certainly result in utter catastrophe," she replies, "with all of the atomic nuclei bunching up together in one place and all of the electrons rushing away from them to congregate elsewhere. But to answer your question, no, there is no logical proof that it couldn't be that way. In our physical world we find that there are, in fact, two types of charges, and they obey the Coulomb law rather than the one you just formulated."

"Can you prove that the world will not switch from the one law to the other, say, tomorrow?" you ask.

"No, frankly, I can't," she answers, "but I, and all other physicists assume—call it an article of faith if you like—that it won't happen."

There's that word "faith" again, you muse as you leave the cafeteria.

The more you think about it, the more clearly you see that the physicists have not shown you how to get around the basic problem Hume raised; rather, they have really reinforced it. Maybe this problem is tougher than I thought, you say to yourself, and you head for Professor Philo's office to talk further about it. "I was thinking about all these 'secret powers' Hume talks about," you begin, "and so I asked my physics instructor about them. She explained, as an example, how a table supports a coffee cup, but she did it on the basis of laws of nature— Coulomb's law of electrostatics was one of them. This law is very well confirmed, I suppose, but she admitted that it is quite possible to imagine that this law would fail tomorrow, and—if you'll pardon the expression—all hell would break loose. Now, my question is, how can we find out about these secret powers that Hume keeps saying we need to know? How can we discover the real underlying causes of what happens?"

"I think you are really beginning to get the point Hume was driving at," she replies, "namely, that there is *no way*, even in principle, of finding any hidden causes or secret powers. You can, of course, find regularities in nature—such as conservation of energy, conservation of momentum, universal gravitation, and electrostatic attraction and repulsion—but these can only be known to have held up to the present. There is no further kind of hidden connection or causal relation that can be discovered by more careful observation, or examination with some kind of super-microscope. Of course, we do discover regularities, and we explain them. For instance, Kepler's laws of planetary motion are regularities that are explained by Newton's laws of motion and gravitation, but these do not reveal any secret powers. They simply provide more general regularities to cover the more restricted ones.

"In his discussion of 'the idea of necessary connection,' Hume tries to bring out precisely this point. We can observe, as you were saying in class the other day, that recoil experiments always yield a particular type of result—namely, momentum is conserved. We have observed this many times. And now we expect, on future trials, that the same thing will happen. But we do not observe, nor can we discover in any way, an *additional* factor which constitutes a necessary connection between the 'explosion' and the subsequent motion of the cars. This seems to be what Hume had in mind when he wrote:

> These ultimate springs and principles are totally shut up from human curiosity and enquiry. Elasticity, gravity, cohesion of parts, communication of motion by impulse; these are probably the ultimate causes and principles which we ever discover in nature; and we may esteem ourselves sufficiently happy, if, by accurate inquiry and reasoning, we can trace up the particular phenomena to, or near to, these general principles.

Hume is acknowledging that we can discover general regularities in nature, but he is denying that an additional 'connection' can be found. And Hume was dedicated to the maxim, as are modern scientists, that we have no business talking about things it is impossible in principle for us to know anything about.

"When he asks why we do, in fact, expect so confidently that the future experiments will have outcomes similar to those of the past trials, Hume finds that it is nothing other than a matter of psychological conditioning. When we see one type of cause repeatedly followed by a particular type of effect, we come to expect that the same type of effect will follow the next time we come across that kind of cause. But this is not a matter of logical reasoning. Have you heard of Pavlov's conditioning experiments with dogs?" You nod. "When the bell rings the dog starts to salivate. He is *not* reasoning that, since the sounding of the bell has, in the past, been associated with the bringing of food, therefore, on this occasion the food will (at least probably) appear soon after the bell rings. According to Hume's analysis, what is called 'scientific reasoning' is no more rational or logical than your watering at the mouth when you are hungry and hear the dinner bell. It is something you cannot help doing, Hume says, but that does not mean that it has any logical foundation."

"That brings up a question I've wanted to ask," you say. "Hume seems to think that people necessarily reason in that way—inductive reasoning, I think it is called—but I've noticed that lots of people don't seem to. For instance, many people (including a student in my current problems course) believe in things like astrology; they believe that the configuration of the planets has a bearing on human events, when experience shows that it often doesn't work that way." The professor nods in agreement. You continue, "So if there is no logical justification for believing in scientific predictions, why isn't it just as reasonable to believe in astrological predictions?"

"That," replies the prof, "is a very profound and difficult question. I doubt that any philosopher has a completely satisfactory answer to it."

Modern Answers[4]

The Wednesday philosophy lecture begins with a sort of rhetorical question, "What reason do we have (Hume is, at bottom, asking) for trusting the scientific method; what grounds do we have for believing that scientific predictions are reliable?" You have been pondering that very question quite a bit in the last couple of days, and—rhetorical or not—your hand shoots up. You have a thing or two to say on the subject.

"Philosophers may have trouble answering such questions," you assert, "but it seems to me there is an obvious reply. As my physics professor has often said, the scientist takes a very practical attitude. He puts forth a hypothesis; if it works he believes in it, and he continues to believe in it as long as it works. If it starts giving him bad predictions, he starts looking for another hypothesis, or for a way of revising his old one. Now the important thing about the scientific method, it seems to me, is that it works. Not only has it led to a vast amount of knowledge about the physical world, but it has been applied in all sorts of practical ways—and although these applications may not have been uniformly beneficial—for better or worse they were successful. Not always, of course, but by and large. Astrology, crystal gazing, and other such superstitious methods simply do not work very well. That's good enough for me."[5]

"That is, indeed, a very tempting answer," Professor Philo replies, "and in one form or another, it has been advanced by several modern philosophers. But Hume actually answered that one himself. You might put it this way. We can all agree that science has, up till now, a very impressive record of success in predicting the future. The question we are asking, however, is this: should we *predict* that science will continue to have the kind of success it has had in the past? It is quite natural to assume that its record will continue, but this is just a case of applying the scientific method to itself. In studying conservation of momentum, you inferred that future experiments would have results similar to those of your past experiments; in appraising the scientific method, you are assuming that its future success will match its past success. But using the scientific method to judge the scientific method is circular reasoning. It is as if a man goes to a bank to cash a check. When the teller refuses, on the grounds that he does not know this man, the man replies, 'That is no problem; permit me to introduce myself—I am John Smith, just as it says on the check.'

"Suppose that I were a believer in crystal gazing. You tell me that your method is better than mine because it has been more successful than mine. You say that this is a good reason for preferring your method to mine, I object. Since you are using your method to judge my method (as well as your method), I demand the right to use my method to evaluate yours. I gaze into my crystal ball and announce the result: From now on crystal gazing will be very successful in predicting the future, while the scientific method is due for a long run of bad luck."

You are about to protest, but she continues.

"The trouble with circular arguments is that they can be used to prove anything; if you assume what you are trying to prove, then there isn't much difficulty in proving it. You find the scientific justification of the scientific method convincing because you already trust the scientific method; if you had equal trust in crystal gazing, I should think you would find the crystal gazer's justification of his method equally convincing. Hume puts it this way:

> When a man says, *I have found, in all past instances, such sensible qualities conjoined with such secret powers:* And when he says, *Similar sensible qualities will always be conjoined with similar secret powers,* he is not guilty of a tautology, nor are these propositions in any respect the same. You can say that the one proposition is an inference from the other. But you must confess that the inference is not intuitive; neither is it demonstrative: Of what nature is it, then? To say it is experimental is begging the question. For all inferences from experience suppose, as their foundation, that the future will resemble the past, and that similar powers will be conjoined with similar sensible qualities.

If the assumption that the future is like the past is the presupposition of the scientific method, we cannot assume that principle in order to justify the scientific method. Once more, we can hardly find a clearer statement than Hume's:

> We have said that all arguments concerning existence are founded on the relation of cause and effect; that our knowledge of that relation is derived entirely from experience; and that all our experimental conclusions proceed upon the supposition that the future will be conformable to the past. To endeavour, therefore, the proof of this last supposition by probable arguments, or arguments regarding existence, must evidently be going in a circle, and taking that for granted, which is the very point in question.

"The principle that the future will be like the past, or that regularities which have held up to the present will persist in the future, has traditionally been called *the principle of uniformity of nature.* Some philosophers, most notably Immanuel Kant, have regarded it as an a priori truth.[6] It seems to me, however, that Hume had already provided a convincing refutation of that claim by arguing that irregularities, however startling to common sense, are by no means inconceivable— that is, they cannot be ruled out a priori. Recall what he said:

> . . . it implies no contradiction that the course of nature may change, and that an object, seemingly like those which we have experienced, may be attended with different or contrary effects. May I not clearly and distinctly conceive that a body, falling from the clouds, and which, in all other respects, resembles snow, has yet the taste of salt or feeling of fire? . . . Now whatever is

intelligible, and can be distinctly conceived, implies no contradiction, and can never be proved false by any demonstrative argument or abstract reasoning *a priori.*

. . . "Scientific confirmation is a subtle and complex matter to which contemporary philosophers have devoted a great deal of attention; some have tried to construct systems of inductive logic that would capture this kind of scientific reasoning. Such efforts have, at best, met with limited success; inductive logic is in a primitive state compared with deductive logic. Until we have a reasonably clear idea of what such inference consists of, however, it is unlikely that we will be able to go very far in meeting the fundamental challenge Hume issued concerning the justification of scientific reasoning. Unless we can at least say what inductive inference is, and what constitutes uniformity of nature (or natural law), we can hardly argue that inductive reasoning—and, only inductive reasoning—will prove successful in predicting the future if nature is uniform. And even if those concepts were clarified, the argument would still be intricate indeed."

"Do you think there is any chance that answers to such problems can be found?" you ask.

"I think it's just possible."

"Thanks," you say as you get up to leave.

"And my thanks to you," she replies. "You can not possibly know how satisfying it is to talk with someone like you—someone intelligent—who takes such philosophical problems seriously and thinks hard about them. If you keep it up, you might be the very person to find some of the answers. I wish you well."

Discussion Questions

1. It was once believed that a sneeze resulted from either a demon trying to enter the body or the soul trying to escape (hence, "Bless You"). These "secret powers" were then explained by science. Hume did not know about the "secret powers" of bread's nourishment for humans. What current phenomena cannot be explained scientifically (naturalistically)? Do you agree that all phenomena can be (or eventually will be) explained by science and are caused by natural (not *super*natural) forces?

2. How do you answer the student's question, "Why do they make us read these old philosophers who are now so out of date?" What virtue is there in reading the theories of antiquated thinkers who based their ideas and theories on science that is now outdated?

3. Salmon mentions "faith" in regard to both God and science: faith that God will protect us and faith in the regularity of nature. Do you think the word means the same thing in both instances?

4. Given Philo's point—that evidence could turn up that would prove a scientific law to be false—does this affect your view of scientific laws in any way? Does Hume's proposed circularity of induction affect your approach to scientific claims?

The Structure of Scientific Revolutions
Thomas Kuhn

Thomas Kuhn earned a bachelor's degree in physics at Harvard University graduating *summa cum laude* and went on to earn a master's and PhD in the same field. He stayed at Harvard to begin his teaching career (which later took him to U.C. Berkeley, Princeton, and MIT), where he focused on the history of science, teaching in both the history and philosophy departments.

This selection is taken from his work *The Structure of Scientific Revolutions*, which has sold over one million copies and has been translated into sixteen languages. It is one of the most cited books in the twentieth century, as it influences areas not just in science and philosophy, but also in history, economics, and sociology. From this work, Kuhn is often credited with popularizing the terms "paradigm" and "paradigm shift."

Kuhn often references "*ad hoc* hypotheses." These occur when an initial hypothesis is shown to be false and, instead of abandoning the hypothesis, one adds a corollary hypothesis in order to maintain the initial hypothesis. Another notion important in Kuhn's work is the "gestalt" view, exemplified by the duck/rabbit illustration. Link to duck/rabbit illustration: http://www.answers.com/topic/duck-rabbit-illusion.jpg.

Reading Questions

1. What is a paradigm and what are the two characteristics that a scientific achievement maintains in order to be considered a paradigm?
2. What is the significance of Kuhn's discussion of the discovery of oxygen?
3. What is an anomaly in scientific terms? Why does Kuhn argue that anomalies may be difficult to recognize? How does this relate to the playing-card study?
4. Why are paradigms so difficult to change?
5. What is the result of a crisis in a scientific paradigm? What causes the crisis?
6. How does devising "*ad hoc* modifications" help to "eliminate any apparent conflict" with an anomaly in science?
7. Why must we reject a scientific paradigm *only* when another is available?
8. What are the parallels between scientific and political revolutions?
9. Why is it difficult or, as Kuhn claims, illogical, to compare two paradigms?
10. What does Kuhn mean when he writes, "after a revolution scientists are responding to a different world"? How does he relate this to the duck/rabbit example?
11. What does Kuhn hope to do in his mention of art?

The Route to Normal Science

In this essay, 'normal science' means research firmly based upon one or more past scientific achievements, achievements that some particular scientific community acknowledges for a time as supplying the foundation for its further practice.

Source: Excerpts from *The Structure of Scientific Revolutions*, 3rd Edition, by Thomas Kuhn, copyright © 1996 University of Chicago Press. Reprinted by permission of the publisher.

Today such achievements are recounted, though seldom in their original form, by science textbooks, elementary and advanced. These textbooks expound the body of accepted theory, illustrate many or all of its successful applications, and compare these applications with exemplary observations and experiments. Before such books became popular early in the nineteenth century (and until even more recently in the newly matured sciences), many of the famous classics of science fulfilled a similar function. Aristotle's *Physica*, Ptolemy's *Almagest*, Newton's *Principia* and *Opticks*, Franklin's *Electricity*, Lavoisier's *Chemistry*, and Lyell's *Geology*—these and many other works served for a time implicitly to define the legitimate problems and methods of a research field for succeeding generations of practitioners. They were able to do so because they shared two essential characteristics. Their achievement was sufficiently unprecedented to attract an enduring group of adherents away from competing modes of scientific activity. Simultaneously, it was sufficiently open-ended to leave all sorts of problems for the redefined group of practitioners to resolve.

Achievements that share these two characteristics I shall henceforth refer to as 'paradigms,' a term that relates closely to 'normal science.' By choosing it, I mean to suggest that some accepted examples of actual scientific practice—examples which include law, theory, application, and instrumentation together—provide models from which spring particular coherent traditions of scientific research. These are the traditions which the historian describes under such rubrics as 'Ptolemaic astronomy' (or 'Copernican'), 'Aristotelian dynamics' (or 'Newtonian'), 'corpuscular optics' (or 'wave optics'), and so on. The study of paradigms, including many that are far more specialized than those named illustratively above, is what mainly prepares the student for membership in the particular scientific community with which he will later practice. Because he there joins men who learned the bases of their field from the same concrete models, his subsequent practice will seldom evoke overt disagreement over fundamentals. Men whose research is based on shared paradigms are committed to the same rules and standards for scientific practice. That commitment and the apparent consensus it produces are prerequisites for normal science, i.e., for the genesis and continuation of a particular research tradition. . . .

The Nature of Normal Science

What then is the nature of the more professional and esoteric research that a group's reception of a single paradigm permits? If the paradigm represents work that has been done once and for all, what further problems does it leave the united group to resolve? Those questions will seem even more urgent if we now note one respect in which the terms used so far may be misleading. In its established usage, a paradigm is an accepted model or pattern, and that aspect of its meaning has enabled me, lacking a better word, to appropriate 'paradigm' here. But it will shortly be clear that the sense of 'model' and 'pattern' that permits the appropriation is not quite the one usual in defining 'paradigm.' In grammar, for example, *'amo, amas, amat'* is a paradigm because it displays the pattern to be used in conjugating a large number of other Latin verbs, e.g., in producing *'laudo, laudas, laudat.'* In this standard application, the paradigm functions by permitting the replication of examples any one of which could in principle serve to replace it. In a science, on the other hand, a paradigm is rarely an object for replication. Instead, like an accepted judicial decision in the common law, it is an object for further articulation and specification under new or more stringent conditions.

To see how this can be so, we must recognize how very limited in both scope and precision a paradigm can be at the time of its first appearance. Paradigms gain their status because they are more successful than their competitors in solving a few problems that the group of practitioners has come to recognize as acute. To be more successful is not, however, to be either completely successful with a single problem or notably successful with any large number. The success of a paradigm—whether Aristotle's analysis of motion, Ptolemy's computations of planetary position, Lavoisier's application of the balance, or Maxwell's mathematization of the electromagnetic field—is at the start largely a promise of success discoverable in selected and still incomplete examples. Normal science consists in the actualization of that promise, an actualization achieved by extending the knowledge of those facts that the paradigm displays as particularly revealing, by increasing the extent of the match between those facts and the paradigm's predictions, and by further articulation of the paradigm itself. . . .

Anomaly and the Emergence of Scientific Discoveries

Normal science, the puzzle-solving activity we have just examined, is a highly cumulative enterprise, eminently successful in its aim, the steady extension of the scope and precision of scientific knowledge. In all these respects it fits with great precision the most usual image of scientific work. Yet one standard product of the scientific enterprise is missing. Normal science does not aim at novelties of fact or theory and, when successful, finds none. New and unsuspected phenomena are, however, repeatedly uncovered by scientific research, and radical new theories have again and again been invented by scientists. History even suggests that the scientific enterprise has developed a uniquely powerful technique for producing surprises of this sort. If this characteristic of science is to be reconciled with what has already been said, then research under a paradigm must be a particularly effective way of inducing paradigm change. That is what fundamental novelties of fact and theory do. Produced inadvertently by a game played under one set of rules, their assimilation requires the elaboration of another set. After they have become parts of science, the enterprise, at least of those specialists in whose particular field the novelties lie, is never quite the same again.

We must now ask how changes of this sort can come about, considering first discoveries, or novelties of fact, and then inventions, or novelties of theory. That distinction between discovery and invention or between fact and theory will, however, immediately prove to be exceedingly artificial. Its artificiality is an important clue to several of this essay's main theses. Examining selected discoveries in the rest of this section, we shall quickly find that they are not isolated events but extended episodes with a regularly recurrent structure. Discovery commences with the awareness of anomaly, i.e., with the recognition that nature has somehow violated the paradigm-induced expectations that govern normal science. It then continues with a more or less extended exploration of the area of anomaly. And it closes only when the paradigm theory has been adjusted so that the anomalous has become the expected. Assimilating a new sort of fact demands a more than additive adjustment of theory, and until that adjustment is completed— until the scientist has learned to see nature in a different way—the new fact is not quite a scientific fact at all.

To see how closely factual and theoretical novelty are intertwined in scientific discovery examine a particularly famous example, the discovery of oxygen. At least three different men have a legitimate claim to it and several other chemists must, in the early 1770s, have had enriched air in a laboratory vessel without knowing it. The progress of normal science, in this case of pneumatic chemistry, prepared the way to a breakthrough quite thoroughly. The earliest of the claimants to prepare a relatively pure sample of the gas was the Swedish apothecary, C. W. Scheele. We may, however, ignore his work since it was not published until oxygen's discovery had repeatedly been announced elsewhere and thus had no effect upon the historical pattern that most concerns us here. The second in time to establish a claim was the British scientist and divine, Joseph Priestley, who collected the gas released by heated red oxide of mercury as one item in a prolonged normal investigation of the "airs" evolved by a large number of solid substances. In 1774 he identified the gas thus produced as nitrous oxide and in 1775, led by further tests, as common air with less than its usual quantity of phlogiston. The third claimant, Lavoisier, started the work that led him to oxygen after Priestley's experiments of 1774 and possibly as the result of a hint from Priestley. Early in 1775 Lavoisier reported that the gas obtained by heating the red oxide of mercury was "air itself entire without alteration [except that] . . . it comes out more pure, more respirable." By 1777, probably with the assistance of a second hint from Priestley, Lavoisier had concluded that the gas was a distinct species, one of the two main constituents of the atmosphere, a conclusion that Priestley was never able to accept. . . .

To a greater or lesser extent (corresponding to the continuum from the shocking to the anticipated result), the characteristics common to the . . . example above are characteristic of all discoveries from which new sorts of phenomena emerge. Those characteristics include: the previous awareness of anomaly, the gradual and simultaneous emergence of both observational and conceptual recognition, and the consequent change of paradigm categories and procedures often accompanied by resistance. There is even evidence that these same characteristics are built into the nature of the perceptual process itself. In a psychological experiment that deserves to be far better known outside the trade, Bruner and Postman asked experimental subjects to identify on short and controlled exposure a series of playing cards. Many of the cards were normal, but some were made anomalous, e.g., a red six of spades and a black four of hearts. Each experimental run was constituted by the display of a single card to a single subject in a series of gradually increased exposures. After each exposure the subject was asked what he had seen, and the run was terminated by two successive correct identifications.

Even on the shortest exposures many subjects identified most of the cards, and after a small increase all the subjects identified them all. For the normal cards these identifications were usually correct, but the anomalous cards were almost always identified, without apparent hesitation or puzzlement, as normal. The black four of hearts might, for example, be identified as the four of either spades or hearts. Without any awareness of trouble, it was immediately fitted to one of the conceptual categories prepared by prior experience. One would not even like to say that the subjects had seen something different from what they identified. With a further increase of exposure to the anomalous cards, subjects did begin to hesitate and to display awareness of anomaly. Exposed, for example, to the red six of spades, some would say: That's the six of spades, but there's something wrong with it—the black has a red border. Further increase of exposure resulted in still more hesitation and confusion until finally, and sometimes quite suddenly, most subjects would produce the correct identification without hesitation. Moreover, after doing this with two or three of the anomalous cards, they would have little further difficulty with the others. A few subjects, however, were never able to make the requisite adjustment of their categories. Even at forty times the average exposure required to recognize normal cards for what they were, more than 10 percent of the anomalous cards were not correctly identified. And the subjects who then failed often experienced acute personal distress. One of them exclaimed: "I can't make the suit out, whatever it is. It didn't even look like a card that time. I don't know what color it is now or whether it's a spade or a heart. I'm not even sure now what a spade looks like. My God!" In the next section we shall occasionally see scientists behaving this way too.

Either as a metaphor or because it reflects the nature of the mind, that psychological experiment provides a wonderfully simple and cogent schema for the process of scientific discovery. In science, as in the playing card experiment, novelty emerges only with difficulty, manifested by resistance, against a background provided by expectation. Initially, only the anticipated and usual are experienced even under circumstances where anomaly is later to be observed. Further acquaintance, however, does result in awareness of something wrong or does relate the effect to something that has gone wrong before. That awareness of anomaly opens a period in which conceptual categories are adjusted until the initially anomalous has become the anticipated. At this point the discovery has been completed. I have already urged that that process or one very much like it is involved in the emergence of all fundamental scientific novelties. Let me now point out that, recognizing the process, we can at last begin to see why normal science, a pursuit not directed to novelties and tending at first to suppress them, should nevertheless be so effective in causing them to arise.

In the development of any science, the first received paradigm is usually felt to account quite successfully for most of the observations and experiments easily accessible to that science's practitioners. Further development, therefore, ordinarily calls for the construction of elaborate equipment, the development of an esoteric vocabulary and skills, and a refinement of concepts that increasingly lessens their resemblance to their usual common-sense prototypes. That professionalization leads, on the one hand, to an immense restriction of the scientist's vision and to a considerable resistance to paradigm change. The science has become increasingly rigid. On the other hand, within those areas to which the paradigm directs the attention of the group, normal science leads to a detail of information and to a precision of the observation-theory match that could be achieved in no other way. Furthermore, that detail and precision-of-match have a value that transcends their not always very high intrinsic interest. Without the special apparatus that is constructed mainly for anticipated functions, the results that lead ultimately to novelty could not occur. And even when the apparatus exists, novelty ordinarily emerges only for the man who, knowing *with precision* what he should expect, is able to recognize that something has gone wrong. Anomaly appears only against the background provided by the paradigm. The more precise and far-reaching that paradigm is, the more sensitive an indicator it provides of anomaly and hence of an occasion for paradigm change. In the normal mode of discovery, even resistance to change has a use. . . . By ensuring that the paradigm will not be too easily surrendered, resistance guarantees that scientists will not be lightly distracted and that the anomalies that lead to paradigm change will penetrate existing knowledge to the core. The very fact that a significant scientific novelty so often emerges simultaneously from several laboratories is an index both to the strongly traditional nature of normal science and to the completeness with which that traditional pursuit prepares the way for its own change. . . .

The Response to Crisis

. . . Once it has achieved the status of paradigm, a scientific theory is declared invalid only if an alternate candidate is available to take its place. No process yet disclosed by the historical study of scientific development at all resembles the methodological stereotype of falsification by direct comparison with nature. That remark does not mean that scientists do not reject scientific theories, or that experience and experiment are not essential to the process in which they do so. But it does mean—what will ultimately be a central point—that the act of judgment that leads scientists to reject a previously accepted theory is always based upon more than a comparison of that theory with the world. The decision to reject one paradigm is always simultaneously the decision to accept another, and the judgment leading to that decision involves the comparison of both paradigms with nature *and* with each other.

There is, in addition, a second reason for doubting that scientists reject paradigms because confronted with anomalies or counterinstances. . . . They will devise numerous articulations and *ad hoc* modifications of their theory in order to eliminate any apparent conflict. . . .

Though history is unlikely to record their names, some men have undoubtedly been driven to desert science because of their inability to tolerate crisis. Like artists, creative scientists must occasionally be able to live in a world out of joint—elsewhere I have described that necessity as "the essential tension" implicit in scientific research. But that rejection of science in favor of another occupation is, I think, the only sort of paradigm rejection to which counterinstances by themselves can lead. Once a first paradigm through which to view nature has been found, there is no such thing as research in the absence of any paradigm. To reject one paradigm without simultaneously substituting another is to reject science itself. That act reflects not on the paradigm but on the man. Inevitably he will be seen by his colleagues as "the carpenter who blames his tools." . . .

The Nature and Necessity of Scientific Revolutions

. . . What are scientific revolutions, and what is their function in scientific development? Much of the answer to these questions has been anticipated in earlier sections. In particular, the preceding discussion has indicated that scientific revolutions are here taken to be those non-cumulative developmental episodes in which an older paradigm is replaced in whole or in part by an incompatible new one. There is more to be said, however, and an essential part of it can be introduced by asking one further question. Why should a change of paradigm be called a revolution? In the face of the vast and essential differences between political and scientific development, what parallelism can justify the metaphor that finds revolutions in both? . . .

Political revolutions aim to change political institutions in ways that those institutions themselves prohibit. Their success therefore necessitates the partial relinquishment of one set of institutions in favor of another, and in the interim, society is not fully governed by institutions at all. Initially it is crisis alone that attenuates the role of political institutions as we have already seen it attenuate the role of paradigms. In increasing numbers individuals become increasingly estranged from political life and behave more and more eccentrically within it. Then, as the crisis deepens, many of these individuals commit themselves to some concrete proposal for the reconstruction of society in a new institutional framework. At that point the society is divided into competing camps or parties, one seeking to defend the old institutional constellation, the others seeking to institute some new one. And, once that polarization has occurred, *political recourse fails*. Because they differ about the institutional matrix within which political change is to be achieved and evaluated, because they acknowledge no supra-institutional framework for the adjudication of revolutionary difference, the parties to a revolutionary conflict must finally resort to the techniques of mass persuasion, often including force. Though revolutions have had a vital role in the evolution of political institutions, that role depends upon their being partially extrapolitical or extrainstitutional events.

The remainder of this essay aims to demonstrate that the historical study of paradigm change reveals very similar characteristics in the evolution of the sciences. Like the choice between competing political institutions, that between competing paradigms proves to be a choice between competing modes of community life. Because it has that character, the choice is not and cannot be determined merely by the evaluative procedures characteristic of normal science, for these depend in part upon a particular paradigm, and that paradigm is at issue. When paradigms enter, as they must, into a debate about paradigm choice, their role is necessarily circular. Each group uses its own paradigm to argue in that paradigm's defense. . . .

As in political revolutions, so in paradigm choice—there is no standard higher than the assent of the relevant community. To discover how scientific revolutions are effected, we shall therefore have to examine not only the impact of nature and of logic, but also the techniques of persuasive argumentation effective within the quite special groups that constitute the community of scientists.

To discover why this issue of paradigm choice can never be unequivocally settled by logic and experiment alone, we must shortly examine the nature of the differences that separate the proponents of a traditional paradigm from their revolutionary successors. . . .

Are there intrinsic reasons why the assimilation of either a new sort of phenomenon or a new scientific theory must demand the rejection of an older paradigm?

First notice that if there are such reasons, they do not derive from the logical structure of scientific knowledge. . . .

Previously, we had principally examined the paradigm's role as a vehicle for scientific theory. In that role it functions by telling the scientist about the entities that nature does and does not contain and about the ways in which those entities behave. That information provides a map whose details are elucidated by mature scientific research. And since nature is too complex and varied to be explored at random, that map is as essential as observation and experiment to science's continuing development. Through the theories they embody, paradigms prove to be constitutive of the research activity. They are also, however, constitutive of science in other respects, and that is now the point. In particular, our most recent examples show that paradigms provide scientists not only with a map but also with some of the directions essential for map-making. In learning a paradigm the scientist acquires theory, methods, and standards together, usually in an inextricable mixture. Therefore, when paradigms change, there are usually significant shifts in the criteria determining the legitimacy both of problems and of proposed solutions.

That observation returns us to the point from which this section began, for it provides our first explicit indication of why the choice between competing paradigms regularly raises questions that cannot be resolved by the criteria of normal science. To the extent, as significant as it is incomplete, that two scientific schools disagree about what is a problem and what a solution, they will inevitably talk through each other when debating the relative merits of their respective paradigms. In the partially circular arguments that regularly result, each paradigm will be shown to satisfy more or less the criteria that it dictates for itself and to fall short of a few of those dictated by its opponent. There are other reasons, too, for the incompleteness of logical contact that consistently characterizes paradigm debates. For example, since no paradigm ever solves all the problems it defines and since no two paradigms leave all the same problems unsolved, paradigm debates always involve the question: Which problems is it more significant to have solved? Like the issue of competing standards, that question of values can be answered only in terms of criteria that lie outside of normal science altogether, and it is that recourse to external criteria that most obviously makes paradigm debates revolutionary. Something even more fundamental than standards and values is, however, also at stake. I have so far argued only that paradigms are constitutive of science. Now I wish to display a sense in which they are constitutive of nature as well.

Revolutions as Changes of World View

Examining the record of past research from the vantage of contemporary historiography, the historian of science may be tempted to exclaim that when paradigms change, the world itself changes with them. Led by a new paradigm, scientists adopt new instruments and look in new places. Even more important, during revolutions scientists see new and different things when looking with familiar instruments in places they have looked before. It is rather as if the professional community had been suddenly transported to another planet where familiar objects are seen in a different light and are joined by unfamiliar ones as well. Of course, nothing of quite that sort does occur: There is no geographical transplantation; outside the laboratory everyday affairs usually continue as before. Nevertheless, paradigm changes do cause scientists to see the world of their research-engagement differently. In so far as their only recourse to that world is through what they see and do, we may want to say that after a revolution scientists are responding to a different world.

It is as elementary prototypes for these transformations of the scientist's world that the familiar demonstrations of a switch in visual gestalt prove so suggestive. What were ducks in the scientist's world before the revolution are rabbits afterwards. The man who first saw the exterior of the box from above later sees its interior from below. Transformations like these, though usually more gradual and almost always irreversible, are common concomitants of scientific training. Looking at a contour map, the student sees lines on paper, the cartographer a picture of a terrain. Looking at a bubble-chamber photograph, the student sees confused and broken lines, the physicist a record of familiar subnuclear events. Only after a number of such transformations of vision does the student become an inhabitant of the scientist's world, seeing what the scientist sees and responding as the scientist does. The world that the student then enters is not, however, fixed once and for all by the nature of the environment, on the one hand, and of science, on the other. Rather, it is determined jointly by the environment and the particular normal-scientific tradition that the student has been trained to pursue. Therefore, at times of revolution, when the normal-scientific tradition changes, the scientist's perception of his environment must be re-educated—in some familiar situations he must learn to see a new gestalt. After he has done so the world of his research will seem, here and there, *incommensurable* with the one he had inhabited before. That is another reason why schools guided by different paradigms are always slightly at cross-purposes.

In their most usual form, of course, gestalt experiments illustrate only the nature of perceptual transformations. They tell us nothing about the role of paradigms or of previously assimilated experience in the process of perception. But on that point there is a rich body of psychological literature, much of it stemming from the pioneering work of the Hanover Institute. An experimental subject who puts on goggles fitted with inverting lenses initially sees the entire world upside down. At the start his perceptual apparatus functions as it had been trained to function in the absence of the goggles, and the result is extreme disorientation, an acute personal crisis. But after the subject has begun to learn to deal with his new world, his entire visual field flips over, usually after an intervening period in which vision is simply confused. Thereafter, objects are again seen as they had been before the goggles were put on. The assimilation of a previously anomalous visual field has reacted upon and changed the field itself. Literally as well as metaphorically, the man accustomed to inverting lenses has undergone a revolutionary transformation of vision.

The subjects of the anomalous playing-card experiment discussed in Section VI experienced a quite similar transformation. Until taught by prolonged exposure that the universe contained anomalous cards, they saw only the types of cards for which previous experience had equipped them. Yet once experience had provided the requisite additional categories, they were able to see all anomalous cards on the first inspection long enough to permit any identification at all. Still other experiments demonstrate that the perceived size, color, and so on, of experimentally displayed objects also varies with the subject's previous training and experience. Surveying the rich experimental literature from which these examples are drawn makes one suspect that something like a paradigm is prerequisite to perception itself. What a man sees depends both upon what he looks at and also upon what his previous visual-conceptual experience has taught him to see. In the absence of such training there can only be, in William James's phrase, "a bloomin' buzzin' confusion." . . .

Progress Through Revolutions

. . . If this description has at all caught the essential structure of a science's continuing evolution, it will simultaneously have posed a special problem: Why should the enterprise sketched above move steadily ahead in ways that, say, art, political theory, or philosophy does not? Why is progress a perquisite reserved almost exclusively for the activities we call science? . . .

For many centuries, both in antiquity and again in early modern Europe, painting was regarded as *the* cumulative discipline. During those years the artist's goal was assumed to be representation. Critics and historians, like Pliny and

Vasari, then recorded with veneration the series of inventions from foreshortening through chiaroscuro that had made possible successively more perfect representations of nature. But those are also the years, particularly during the Renaissance, when little cleavage was felt between the sciences and the arts. Leonardo was only one of many men who passed freely back and forth between fields that only later became categorically distinct. Furthermore, even after that steady exchange had ceased, the term 'art' continued to apply as much to technology and the crafts, which were also seen as progressive, as to painting and sculpture. Only when the latter unequivocally renounced representation as their goal and began to learn again from primitive models did the cleavage we now take for granted assume anything like its present depth. . . .

Ask now why an enterprise like normal science should progress, and begin by recalling a few of its most salient characteristics. Normally, the members of a mature scientific community work from a single paradigm or from a closely related set. Very rarely do different scientific communities investigate the same problems. In those exceptional cases the groups hold several major paradigms in common. Viewed from within any single community, however, whether of scientists or of non-scientists, the result of successful creative work is progress. How could it possibly be anything else? We have, for example, just noted that while artists aimed at representation as their goal, both critics and historians chronicled the progress of the apparently united group. Other creative fields display progress of the same sort. The theologian who articulates dogma or the philosopher who refines the Kantian imperatives contributes to progress, if only to that of the group that shares his premises. No creative school recognizes a category of work that is, on the one hand, a creative success, but is not, on the other, an addition to the collective achievement of the group. If we doubt, as many do, that non-scientific fields make progress, that cannot be because individual schools make none. Rather, it must be because there are always competing schools, each of which constantly questions the very foundations of the others. The man who argues that philosophy, for example, has made no progress emphasizes that there are still Aristotelians, not that Aristotelianism has failed to progress. . . .

In the sciences there need not be progress of another sort. We may, to be more precise, have to relinquish the notion, explicit or implicit, that changes of paradigm carry scientists and those who learn from them closer and closer to the truth.

It is now time to notice that until the last very few pages the term 'truth' had entered this essay only in a quotation from Francis Bacon.* And even in those pages it entered only as a source for the scientist's conviction that incompatible rules for doing science cannot coexist except during revolutions when the profession's main task is to eliminate all sets but one. The developmental process described in this essay has been a process of evolution *from* primitive beginnings—a process whose successive stages are characterized by an increasingly detailed and refined understanding of nature. But nothing that has been or will

---

* "Truth emerges more readily from error than from confusion."

be said makes it a process of evolution *toward* anything. Inevitably that lacuna will have disturbed many readers. We are all deeply accustomed to seeing science as the one enterprise that draws constantly nearer to some goal set by nature in advance.

But need there be any such goal? Can we not account for both science's existence and its success in terms of evolution from the community's state of knowledge at any given time? Does it really help to imagine that there is some one full, objective, true account of nature and that the proper measure of scientific achievement is the extent to which it brings us closer to that ultimate goal? If we can learn to substitute evolution-from-what-we-do-know for evolution-toward-what-we-wish-to-know, a number of vexing problems may vanish in the process. Somewhere in this maze, for example, must lie the problem of induction. . . .

Anyone who has followed the argument this far will nevertheless feel the need to ask why the evolutionary process should work. What must nature, including man, be like in order that science be possible at all? Why should scientific communities be able to reach a firm consensus unattainable in other fields? Why should consensus endure across one paradigm change after another? And why should paradigm change invariably produce an instrument more perfect in any sense than those known before? From one point of view those questions, excepting the first, have already been answered. But from another they are as open as they were when this essay began. It is not only the scientific community that must be special. The world of which that community is a part must also possess quite special characteristics, and we are no closer than we were at the start to knowing what these must be. That problem—What must the world be like in order that man may know it?—was not, however, created by this essay. On the contrary, it is as old as science itself, and it remains unanswered. But it need not be answered in this place. Any conception of nature compatible with the growth of science by proof is compatible with the evolutionary view of science developed here. Since this view is also compatible with close observation of scientific life, there are strong arguments for employing it in attempts to solve the host of problems that still remain.

Discussion Questions

1. How might you apply the lesson of the playing-card study to your own life?
2. Is science just one map of reality? If so, what are examples of other maps? If you make a map of your room, how would you do it? Would it be an exact replica of reality? In what ways would it be lacking?
3. If a theory is useful and successful at prediction, does it matter to you if it is really true? Why/why not?
4. Kuhn mentions the notion of progress in science and in art. Do you think that art improves over time and that there is artistic progress? Is art now *better* then it was in prehistoric times, for example?
5. If rules of science are chosen as a matter of taste (as opposed to objectively chosen), what does that tell you about science?

Science: Conjectures and Refutations

Karl Popper

Born in 1902, Karl Popper wrote extensively in the philosophy of science as well as on political theories. Nobel Prize winner Peter Medawar referred to Popper as "incomparably the greatest philosopher of science who ever lived," while famous cosmologist Frank Tipler claims that Popper's book *The Logic of Scientific Discovery* is the most important book of the twentieth century. Knighted in England in 1946, Sir Karl Popper not only established a criterion for distinguishing science from other ventures, but also proposed a unique solution to Hume's "problem of induction."

This selection portrays many of his most prominent ideas and establishes him as one of the primary influences in the philosophy of science. Popper originally gave this as a lecture at Peterhouse College in Cambridge in 1953 and it is now included in his book *Conjectures and Refutations: The Growth of Scientific Knowledge.*

Reading Questions

1. In what way is Popper concerned with the *truth* of a theory?
2. Explain the significance of Popper's example with a man pushing a child in the water (or saving it) as it relates to the question of Freud and Adler's theories as being scientific. What difference does Einstein's theory exhibit?
3. What role does myth play regarding Popper's discussion of testability?
4. According to Popper, how important is induction as a demarcation for science?
5. Why does Popper write in his mention of Hume that it is not possible to infer a theory from observation, but only to refute it?
6. After having read the selection, explain the significance of the epigram that cites Trollope.
7. What is Hume's "problem of induction"? Why does it lead to an infinite regress?
8. Why does Popper claim that our interpretations of the world come *before* our observations? How does he show this in his example of telling his physics students to "observe"?
9. According to Popper, what are the "critical attitude" and the "dogmatic attitude" and how does he distinguish the two?
10. In what two ways does Popper suggest that Hume used the term "belief" when he writes that Hume concluded our "belief" in theories was irrational? How does Popper evaluate the correctness of each usage?
11. According to Popper, what creates the dogmatic (pseudoscientific) thinking in science? How should we test hypotheses in order to test them critically and non-dogmatically?

Source: Excerpts from *Conjectures and Refutations: The Growth of Scientific Knowledge.* 5th Edition, by Karl Popper, 1989, pp. 43–51, 55–71. First published 1963 by Routledge & Kegan Paul, London; 5th Edition (revised) published 1989 by Routledge, London and New York. Copyright © Karl Popper 1963.

Mr. Turnbull had predicted evil consequences, . . . and was now doing the best in his power to bring about the verification of his own prophecies.
ANTHONY TROLLOPE

I

When I received the list of participants in this course and realized that I had been asked to speak to philosophical colleagues I thought, after some hesitation and consultation, that you would probably prefer me to speak about those problems which interest me most, and about those developments with which I am most intimately acquainted. I therefore decided to do what I have never done before: to give you a report on my own work in the philosophy of science, since the autumn of 1919 when I first began to grapple with the problem, '*When should a theory be ranked as scientific?*' or '*Is there a criterion for the scientific character or status of a theory?*'

The problem which troubled me at the time was neither, 'When is a theory true?' nor, 'When is a theory acceptable?' My problem was different. I *wished to distinguish between science and pseudo science*; knowing very well that science often errs, and that pseudo-science may happen to stumble on the truth. . . .

It was during the summer of 1919 that I began to feel more and more dissatisfied with . . . three theories—the Marxist theory of history, [Freud's] psychoanalysis, and [Alfred Adler's] individual psychology; and I began to feel dubious about their claims to scientific status. My problem perhaps first took the simple form, 'What is wrong with Marxism, psycho-analysis, and individual psychology? Why are they so different from physical theories, from Newton's theory, and especially from the theory of relativity?'

To make this contrast clear I should explain that few of us at the time would have said that we believed in the *truth* of Einstein's theory of gravitation. This shows that it was not my doubting the *truth* of those other three theories which bothered me, but something else. Yet neither was it that I merely felt mathematical physics to be more *exact* than the sociological or psychological type of theory. Thus what worried me was neither the problem of truth, at that stage at least, nor the problem of exactness or measurability. It was rather that I felt that these other three theories, though posing as sciences, had in fact more in common with primitive myths than with science; that they resembled astrology rather than astronomy.

I found that those of my friends who were admirers of Marx, Freud, and Adler, were impressed by a number of points common to these theories, and especially by their apparent *explanatory power*. These theories appeared to be able to explain practically everything that happened within the fields to which they referred. The study of any of them seemed to have the effect of an intellectual conversion or revelation, opening your eyes to a new truth hidden from those not yet initiated. Once your eyes were thus opened you saw confirming instances everywhere: The world was full of *verifications* of the theory. Whatever happened always confirmed it. Thus its truth appeared manifest; and unbelievers were clearly people who did not want to see the manifest truth; who refused to see it, either because it was against their class interest, or because of their repressions which were still 'un-analysed' and crying out for treatment.

The most characteristic element in this situation seemed to me the incessant stream of confirmations, of observations which 'verified' the theories in question; and this point was constantly emphasized by their adherents. A Marxist could not open a newspaper without finding on every page confirming evidence for his interpretation of history; not only in the news, but also in its presentation—which revealed the class bias of the paper—and especially of course in what the paper did not say. The Freudian analysts emphasized that their theories were constantly verified by their 'clinical observations.' As for Adler, I was much impressed by a personal experience. Once, in 1919, I reported to him a case which to me did not seem particularly Adlerian, but which he found no difficulty in analysing in terms of his theory of inferiority feelings, although he had not even seen the child. Slightly shocked, I asked him how he could be so sure. 'Because of my thousandfold experience', he replied; whereupon I could not help saying: 'And with this new case, I suppose, your experience has become thousand-and-one-fold.'

What I had in mind was that his previous observations may not have been much sounder than this new one; that each in its turn had been interpreted in the light of 'previous experience,' and at the same time counted as additional confirmation. What, I asked myself, did it confirm? No more than that a case could be interpreted in the light of the theory. But this meant very little, I reflected, since every conceivable case could be interpreted in the light of Adler's theory, or equally of Freud's. I may illustrate this by two very different examples of human behaviour: that of a man who pushes a child into the water with the intention of drowning it; and that of a man who sacrifices his life in an attempt to save the child. Each of these two cases can be explained with equal ease in Freudian and in Adlerian terms. According to Freud the first man suffered from repression (say, of some component of his Oedipus complex), while the second man had achieved sublimation. According to Adler the first man suffered from feelings of inferiority (producing perhaps the need to prove to himself that he dared to commit some crime), and so did the second man (whose need was to prove to himself that he dared to rescue the child). I could not think of any human behaviour which could not be interpreted in terms of either theory. It was precisely this fact—that they always fitted, that they were always confirmed—which in the eyes of their admires constituted the strongest argument in favour of these theories. It began to dawn on me that this apparent strength was in fact their weakness.

With Einstein's theory the situation was strikingly different. Take one typical instance—Einstein's prediction, just then confirmed by the findings of Eddington's expedition. Einstein's gravitational theory had led to the result that light must be attracted by heavy bodies (such as the sun), precisely as material bodies were attracted. As a consequence it could be calculated that light from a distant fixed star whose apparent position was close to the sun would reach the earth from such a direction that the star would seem to be slightly shifted away from the sun; or, in other words, that stars close to the sun would look as if they had moved a little away from the sun, and from one another. This is a thing which cannot normally be observed since such stars are rendered invisible in daytime by the sun's overwhelming brightness; but during an eclipse it is possible to take photographs of them. If the same constellation is photographed at night one can measure the distances on the two photographs, and check the predicted effect.

Now the impressive thing about this case is the risk involved in a prediction of this kind. If observation shows that the predicted effect is definitely absent, then the theory is simply refuted. The theory is *incompatible with certain possible results of observation*—in fact with results which everybody before Einstein would have expected.[7] This is quite different from the situation I have previously described, when it turned out that the theories in question were compatible with the most divergent human behaviour, so that it was practically impossible to describe any human behaviour that might not be claimed to be a verification of these theories.

These considerations led me in the winter of 1919–20 to conclusions which I may now reformulate as follows.

(1) It is easy to obtain confirmations, or verifications, for nearly every theory—if we look for confirmations.

(2) Confirmations should count only if they are the result of *risky predictions*; that is to say, if, unenlightened by the theory in question, we should have expected an event which was incompatible with the theory—an event which would have refuted the theory.

(3) Every 'good' scientific theory is a prohibition: It forbids certain things to happen. The more a theory forbids, the better it is.

(4) A theory which is not refutable by any conceivable event is non-scientific. Irrefutability is not a virtue of a theory (as people often think) but a vice.

(5) Every genuine *test* of a theory is an attempt to falsify it, or to refute it. Testability is falsifiability; but there are degrees of testability: Some theories are more testable, more exposed to refutation, than others; they take, as it were, greater risks.

(6) Confirming evidence should not count *except when it is the result of a genuine test of the theory*; and this means that it can be presented as a serious but unsuccessful attempt to falsify the theory. (I now speak in such cases of 'corroborating evidence.')

(7) Some genuinely testable theories, when found to be false, are still upheld by their admirers—for example by introducing *ad hoc* some auxiliary assumption, or by re-interpreting the theory *ad hoc* in such a way that it escapes refutation. Such a procedure is always possible, but it rescues the theory from refutation only at the price of destroying, or at least lowering, its scientific status. (I later described such a rescuing operation as a '*conventionalist twist*' or a '*conventionalist stratagem*.')

One can sum up all this by saying that *the criterion of the scientific status of a theory is its falsifiability, or refutability, or testability.*

II

I may perhaps exemplify this with the help of the various theories so far mentioned. Einstein's theory of gravitation clearly satisfied the criterion of falsifiability. Even if our measuring instruments at the time did not allow us to pronounce on the results of the tests with complete assurance, there was clearly a possibility of refuting the theory.

Astrology did not pass the test. Astrologers were greatly impressed, and mis-led, by what they believed to be confirming evidence—so much so that they were quite unimpressed by any unfavourable evidence. Moreover, by making their interpretations and prophecies sufficiently vague they were able to explain away anything that might have been a refutation of the theory had the theory and the prophecies been more precise. In order to escape falsification they destroyed the testability of their theory. It is a typical soothsayer's trick to predict things so vaguely that the predictions can hardly fail: that they become irrefutable.

The Marxist theory of history, in spite of the serious efforts of some of its founders and followers, ultimately adopted this soothsaying practice. In some of its earlier formulations (for example in Marx's analysis of the character of the 'coming social revolution') their predictions were testable, and in fact falsified. Yet instead of accepting the refutations the followers of Marx re-interpreted both the theory and the evidence in order to make them agree. In this way they rescued the theory from refutation; but they did so at the price of adopting a device which made it irrefutable. They thus gave a 'conventionalist twist' to the theory; and by this stratagem they destroyed its much advertised claim to scientific status.

The two psycho-analytic theories were in a different class. They were simply non-testable, irrefutable. There was no conceivable human behaviour which could contradict them. This does not mean that Freud and Adler were not seeing certain things correctly: I personally do not doubt that much of what they say is of considerable importance, and may well play its part one day in a psychological science which is testable. But it does mean that those 'clinical observations' which analysts naïvely believe confirm their theory cannot do this any more than the daily confirmations which astrologers find in their practice.[8] And as for Freud's epic of the Ego, the Super-ego, and the Id, no substantially stronger claim to scientific status can be made for it than for Homer's collected stories from Olympus. These theories describe some facts, but in the manner of myths. They contain most interesting psychological suggestions, but not in a testable form.

At the same time I realized that such myths may be developed, and become testable; that historically speaking all—or very nearly all—scientific theories origi-nate from myths, and that a myth may contain important anticipations of scientific theories. Examples are Empedocles' theory of evolution by trial and error, or Parmenides' myth of the unchanging block universe in which nothing ever happens and which, if we add another dimension, becomes Einstein's block universe (in which, too, nothing ever happens, since everything is, four-dimensionally speaking, determined and laid down from the beginning). I thus felt that if a theory is found to be non-scientific, or "metaphysical" (as we might say), it is not thereby found to be unimportant, or insignificant, or 'meaningless', or 'nonsensical.'[9] But it cannot claim to be backed by empirical evidence in the scientific sense—although it may easily be, in some genetic sense, the 'result of observation.' . . .

Thus the problem which I tried to solve by proposing the criterion of falsifia-bility was neither a problem of meaningfulness or significance, nor a problem of truth or acceptability. It was the problem of drawing a line (as well as this can be done) between the statements, or systems of statements, of the empirical sciences, and all other statements—whether they are of a religious or of a metaphysical character, or simply pseudo-scientific. Years later—it must have been in 1928 or 1929—I called this first problem of mine the 'problem of demarcation.' The criterion of falsifiability is a solution to this problem of demarcation, for it says that statements or systems of statements, in order to be ranked as scientific, must be capable of conflicting with possible, or conceivable, observations. . . .

IV

I have discussed the problem of demarcation in some detail because I believe that its solution is the key to most of the fundamental problems of the philosophy of science. I am going to give you later a list of some of these other problems, but only one of them—the *problem of induction*—can be discussed here at any length.

I had become interested in the problem of induction in 1923. Although this problem is very closely connected with the problem of demarcation, I did not fully appreciate the connection for about five years.

I approached the problem of induction through Hume. Hume, I felt, was perfectly right in pointing out that induction cannot be logically justified. He held that there can be no valid logical[10] arguments allowing us to establish 'that those instances, of which we have had no experience, resemble those, of which we have had experience.' Consequently 'even after the observation of the frequent or constant conjunction of objects, we have no reason to draw any inference concerning any object beyond those of which we have had experience.' For 'shou'd it be said that we have experience'[11]—experience teaching us that objects constantly conjoined with certain other objects continue to be so conjoined—then, Hume says, 'I wou'd renew my question, *why from this experience we form any conclusion beyond those past instances, of which we have had experience.*' This 'renew'd question' indicates that an attempt to justify the practice of induction by an appeal to experience must lead to an *infinite regress*. As a result we can say that theories can never be inferred from observation statements, or rationally justified by them.

I found Hume's refutation of inductive inference clear and conclusive. But I felt completely dissatisfied with his psychological explanation of induction in terms of custom or habit. . . .

Hume, I felt, had never accepted the full force of his own logical analysis. Having refuted the logical idea of induction he was faced with the following problem: How do we actually obtain our knowledge, as a matter of psychological fact, if induction is a procedure which is logically invalid and rationally unjustifiable? There are two possible answers: (1) We obtain our knowledge by a non-inductive procedure. This answer would have allowed Hume to retain a form of rationalism. (2) We obtain our knowledge by repetition and induction, and therefore by a logically invalid and rationally unjustifiable procedure, so that all apparent knowledge is merely a kind of belief—belief based on habit. This answer would imply that even scientific knowledge is irrational, so that rationalism is absurd, and must be given up. . . .

It seems that Hume never seriously considered the first alternative. Having cast out the logical theory of induction by repetition he struck a bargain with common sense, meekly allowing the re-entry of induction by repetition, in the guise of a psychological fact. I proposed to turn the tables upon this theory of Hume's. Instead of explaining our propensity to expect regularities as the result of repetition, I proposed to explain repetition-for-us as the result of our propensity to expect regularities and to search for them.

Thus I was led by purely logical considerations to replace the psychological theory of induction by the following view. Without waiting, passively, for repetitions to impress or impose regularities upon us, we actively try to impose regularities upon the world. We try to discover similarities in it, and to interpret it in terms of laws invented by us. Without waiting for premises we jump to conclusions. These may have to be discarded later, should observation show that they are wrong.

This was a theory of trail and error—of *conjectures and refutations*. It made it possible to understand why our attempts to force interpretations upon the world were logically prior to the observation of similarities. Since there were logical reasons behind this procedure, I thought that it would apply in the field of science also; that scientific theories were not the digest of observations, but that they were inventions—conjectures boldly put forward for trial, to be eliminated if they clashed with observations; with observations which were rarely accidental but as a rule undertaken with the definite intention of testing a theory by obtaining, if possible, a decisive refutation.

V

The belief that science proceeds from observation to theory is still so widely and so firmly held that my denial of it is often met with incredulity. I have even been suspected of being insincere—of denying what nobody in his senses can doubt.

But in fact the belief that we can start with pure observations alone, without anything in the nature of a theory, is absurd; as may be illustrated by the story of the man who dedicated his life to natural science, wrote down everything he could observe, and bequeathed his priceless collection of observations to the Royal Society to be used as inductive evidence. This story should show us that though beetles may profitably be collected, observations may not.

Twenty-five years ago I tried to bring home the same point to a group of physics students in Vienna by beginning a lecture with the following instructions: 'Take pencil and paper; carefully observe, and write down what you have observed!' They asked, of course, *what* I wanted them to observe. Clearly the instruction, 'Observe!' is absurd.[12] (It is not even idiomatic, unless the object of the transitive verb can be taken as understood.) Observation is always selective. It needs a chosen object, a definite task, an interest, a point of view, a problem. And its description presupposes a descriptive language, with property words; it presupposes similarity and classification, which in their turn presuppose interests, points of view, and problems. 'A hungry animal,' writes Katz,[13] 'divides the environment into edible and inedible things. An animal in flight sees roads to escape and hiding places . . . Generally speaking, objects change . . . according to the needs of the animal.' We may add that objects can be classified, and can become similar or dissimilar, *only* in this way—by being related to needs and interests. This rule applies not only to animals but also to scientists. For the animal a point of view is provided by its needs, the task of the moment, and its expectations; for the scientist by his theoretical interests, the special problem under investigation, his conjectures and anticipations, and the theories which he accepts as a kind of background: his frame of reference, his 'horizon of expectations.'

The problem 'Which comes first, the hypothesis (H) or the observation (O)?' is soluble; as is the problem, 'Which comes first, the hen (H) or the egg (O)?' The reply to the latter is, 'An earlier kind of egg'; to the former, 'An earlier kind of hypothesis.' It is quite true that any particular hypothesis we choose will have been preceded by observations—the observations, for example, which it is designed to explain. But these observations, in their turn, presupposed the adoption of a frame of reference: a frame of expectations: a frame of theories. If they were significant, if they created a need for explanation and thus gave rise to the invention of a hypothesis, it was because they could not be explained within the old theoretical framework, the old horizon of expectations. There is no danger here of an infinite regress. Going back to more and more primitive theories and myths we shall in the end find unconscious, *inborn* expectations.

The theory of inborn *ideas* is absurd, I think; but every organism has inborn *reactions* or *responses*; and among them, responses adapted to impending events. These responses we may describe as 'expectations' without implying that these 'expectations' are conscious. The newborn baby 'expects,' in this sense, to be fed (and, one could even argue, to be protected and loved). In view of the close relation between expectation and knowledge we may even speak in quite a reasonable sense of 'inborn knowledge.' This 'knowledge,' however, is not *valid a priori;* an inborn expectation, no matter how strong and specific, may be mistaken. (The newborn child may be abandoned, and starve.)

Thus we are born with expectations; with 'knowledge' which, although not *valid a priori*, is *psychologically or genetically a priori*, i.e., prior to all observational experience. One of the most important of these expectations is the expectation of finding a regularity. It is connected with an inborn propensity to look out for regularities, or with a *need to find* regularities, as we may see from the pleasure of the child who satisfies this need. . . .

VI

Our propensity to look out for regularities, and to impose laws upon nature, leads to the psychological phenomenon of *dogmatic thinking* or, more generally, dogmatic behaviour: We expect regularities everywhere and attempt to find them even where there are none; events which do not yield to these attempts we are inclined to treat as a kind of 'background noise'; and we stick to our expectations even when they are inadequate and we ought to accept defeat. This dogmatism is to some extent necessary. It is demanded by a situation which can only be dealt with by forcing our conjectures upon the world. Moreover, this dogmatism allows us to approach a good theory in stages, by way of approximations: If we accept defeat too easily, we may prevent ourselves from finding that we were very nearly right.

It is clear that this *dogmatic attitude*, which makes us stick to our first impression, is indicative of a strong belief; while a *critical attitude*, which is ready to modify its tenets, which admits doubt and demands tests, is indicative of a weaker belief. Now according to Hume's theory, and to the popular theory, the strength of a belief should be a product of repetition; thus it should always grow with experience, and always be greater in less primitive persons. But dogmatic thinking, an uncontrolled wish to impose regularities, a manifest pleasure in rites and in repetition as such, are characteristic of primitives and children; and increasing experience and maturity sometimes create an attitude of caution and criticism rather than of dogmatism. . . .

VII

My logical criticism of Hume's psychological theory . . . may seem a little removed from the field of the philosophy of science. But the distinction between dogmatic and critical thinking, or the dogmatic and the critical attitude, brings us right back to our central problem. For the dogmatic attitude is clearly related to the tendency to *verify* our laws and schemata by seeking to apply them and to confirm them, even to the point of neglecting refutations, whereas the critical attitude is one of readiness to change them—to test them; to refute them; to *falsify* them, if possible. This suggests that we may identify the critical attitude with the scientific attitude, and the dogmatic attitude with the one which we have described as pseudo-scientific.

It further suggests that genetically speaking the pseudo-scientific attitude is more primitive than, and prior to, the scientific attitude: that it is a pre-scientific attitude. And this primitivity or priority also has its logical aspect. For the critical attitude is not so much opposed to the dogmatic attitude as super-imposed upon it: Criticism must be directed against existing and influential beliefs in need of critical revision—in other words, dogmatic beliefs. A critical attitude needs for its raw material, as it were, theories or beliefs which are held more or less dogmatically.

Thus science must begin with myths, and with the criticism of myths; neither with the collection of observations, nor with the invention of experiments, but with the critical discussion of myths, and of magical techniques and practices. The scientific tradition is distinguished from the pre-scientific tradition in having two layers. Like the latter, it passes on its theories; but it also passes on a critical attitude towards them. The theories are passed on, not as dogmas, but rather with the challenge to discuss them and improve upon them. This tradition is Hellenic: It may be traced back to Thales, founder of the first *school* (I do not mean 'of the first *philosophical* school,' but simply 'of the first school') which was not mainly concerned with the preservation of a dogma.[14]

The critical attitude, the tradition of free discussion of theories with the aim of discovering their weak spots so that they may be improved upon, is the attitude of reasonableness, of rationality. It makes far-reaching use of both verbal argument and observation—of observation in the interest of argument, however. The Greeks' discovery of the critical method gave rise at first to the mistaken hope that it would lead to the solution of all the great old problems; that it would establish certainty; that it would help to *prove* our theories, to *justify* them. But this hope was a residue of the dogmatic way of thinking; in fact nothing can be justified or proved (outside of mathematics and logic). The demand for rational proofs in science indicates a failure to keep distinct the broad realm of rationality and the narrow realm of rational certainty: It is an untenable, an unreasonable demand.

Nevertheless, the role of logical argument, of deductive logical reasoning, remains all-important for the critical approach; not because it allows us to prove our theories, or to infer them from observation statements, but because only by purely deductive reasoning is it possible for us to discover what our theories imply, and thus to criticize them effectively. Criticism, I said, is an attempt to find the weak spots in a theory, and these, as a rule, can be found only in the more remote logical consequences which can be derived from it. It is here that purely logical reasoning plays an important part in science.

Hume was right in stressing that our theories cannot be validly inferred from what we can know to be true—neither from observations nor from anything else. He concluded from this that our belief in them was irrational. If 'belief' means here our inability to doubt our natural laws, and the constancy of natural regularities, then Hume is again right: This kind of dogmatic belief has, one might say, a physiological rather than a rational basis. If, however, the term 'belief' is taken to cover our critical acceptance of scientific theories—a *tentative* acceptance combined with an eagerness to revise the theory if we succeed in designing a test which it cannot pass—then Hume was wrong. In such an acceptance of theories there is nothing irrational. There is not even anything irrational in relying for practical purposes upon well-tested theories, for no more rational course of action is open to us.

Assume that we have deliberately made it our task to live in this unknown world of ours; to adjust ourselves to it as well as we can; to take advantage of the opportunities we can find in it; and to explain it, if possible (we need not assume that it is), and as far as possible, with the help of laws and explanatory theories. *If we have made this our task, then there is no more rational procedure than the method of trial and error—of conjecture and refutation:* of boldly proposing theories; of trying our best to show that these are erroneous; and of accepting them tentatively if our critical efforts are unsuccessful.

From the point of view here developed all laws, all theories, remain essentially tentative, or conjectural, or hypothetical, even when we feel unable to doubt them any longer. Before a theory has been refuted we can never know in what way it may have to be modified. That the sun will always rise and set within twenty-four hours is still proverbial as a law 'established by induction beyond reasonable doubt.' . . .

The critical attitude might be described as the result of a conscious attempt to make our theories, our conjectures, suffer in our stead in the struggle for the survival of the fittest. It gives us a chance to survive the elimination of an inadequate hypothesis—when a more dogmatic attitude would eliminate it by eliminating us. (There is a touching story of an Indian community which disappeared because of its belief in the holiness of life, including that of tigers.) We thus obtain the fittest theory within our reach by the elimination of those which are less fit. (By 'fitness' I do not mean merely 'usefulness' but truth. . . .) I do not think that this procedure is irrational or in need of any further rational justification.

VIII

. . . I recently came across an interesting formulation of this belief in a remarkable philosophical book by a great physicist—Max Born's *Natural Philosophy of Cause and Chance*.[15] He writes: 'Induction allows us to generalize a number of observations into a general rule: that night follows day and day follows night . . . But while everyday life has no definite criterion for the validity of an induction, . . . science has worked out a code, or rule of craft, for its application.' Born nowhere reveals the contents of this inductive code (which, as his wording shows, contains a 'definite criterion for the validity of an induction'); but he stresses that 'there is no logical argument' for its acceptance: 'it is a question of faith'; and he is therefore 'willing to call induction a metaphysical principle.' But why does he believe that such a code of valid inductive rules must exist? This becomes clear when he speaks of the 'vast communities of people ignorant of, or rejecting, the rule of science, among them the members of anti-vaccination societies and believers in astrology. It is useless to argue with them; I cannot compel them to accept the same criteria of valid induction in which I believe: the code of scientific rules.' This makes it quite clear that *'valid induction' was here meant to serve as a criterion of demarcation between science and pseudo-science*.

But it is obvious that this rule or craft of 'valid induction' is not even metaphysical: It simply does not exist. No rule can ever guarantee that a generalization inferred from true observations, however often repeated, is true. (Born himself does not believe in the truth of Newtonian physics, in spite of its success, although he believes that it is based on induction.) And the success of science is not based upon rules of induction, but depends upon luck, ingenuity, and the purely deductive rules of critical argument.

I may summarize some of my conclusions as follows:

(1) Induction, i.e., inference based on many observations, is a myth. It is neither a psychological fact, nor a fact of ordinary life, nor one of scientific procedure.

(2) The actual procedure of science is to operate with conjectures: to jump to conclusions—often after one single observation (as noticed for example by Hume and Born).

(3) Repeated observations and experiments function in science as tests of our conjectures or hypotheses, i.e., as attempted refutations.

(4) The mistaken belief in induction is fortified by the need for a criterion of demarcation which, it is traditionally but wrongly believed, only the inductive method can provide.

(5) The conception of such an inductive method, like the criterion of verifiability, implies a faulty demarcation.

(6) None of this is altered in the least if we say that induction makes theories only probable rather than certain.

Discussion Questions

1. Imagine the following "Sugar Cereal Theory": Young children who consume sugar cereals will either consume excessive amounts of sugar as adults or will avoid eating an excess of sugary foods as adults. How strong is this theory? Do you think this theory could be confirmed in numerous (all) cases? How useful is this as a prediction tool? How would Popper evaluate it?

2. Popper mentions that, while Freud's and Adler's theories are not falsifiable (and thus, non-scientific), he has no doubt that "much of what they say is of considerable importance." How do you value theories (like Freud's) that are not scientific? How important is it for something to be considered scientific?

3. Popper mentions the lack of falsifiability of astrology. Do you agree? If astrology is unscientific, does it thus lose any meaning for you? What is your view of astrology as a source of knowledge of any sort?

4. Elsewhere, Popper cites physicist Max Born who wrote that the acceptance of induction in science is "a question of faith." How do you assess this? In what way does faith in induction and science differ from religious faith?

5. How might you apply Popper's command (to seek to *falsify*/disprove hypotheses versus to verify/support them) to your life? In what ways might ignoring this command lead to dogmatism or "blind knowledge"?

How to Defend Society Against Science

Paul Feyerabend

At the Austrian College Society, Paul Feyerabend chose Karl Popper (also featured in this section) as a supervisor of his until realizing that "I had fallen for [Popper's ideas]." Feyerabend spent most of his professional career writing and teaching at various colleges throughout England, Germany, and New Zealand and also taught at U. C. Berkeley in 1958 after becoming a United States citizen.

In what was originally given as a talk, Feyerabend promotes what has been called an "anarchistic" view of science—that science does *not* adhere to a consistent method. His main aim in his talk is to first provide a two-premise argument as to why science maintains a high status in our society. He then argues against both of these premises and provides insight on how to act on this conclusion. His view is considered controversial (and somewhat unorthodox) and summarizes many of the themes from his principal book, *Against Method*, which further advanced his attack on science.

Source: Paul Feyerabend "How to Defend Society Against Science." This article first appeared in *Radical Philosophy*, 11, 1975, and is reprinted with permission.

Reading Questions

1. Why does Feyerabend compare today's science with yesterday's "religious 'facts'"?
2. What does Feyerabend say about the defense of science that it has "found the truth"?
3. What is Feyerabend's point about the lack of "standards of judgement" for choosing among competing theories?
4. What is Feyerabend's argument "against results"? How does an examination of Copernicus' findings (along with mention of artisans, midwives, and witches) support Feyerabend's argument?
5. Does Feyerabend say that science is totally useless and should be done away with? Why/why not?
6. Why does Feyerabend suggest a "separation of state and science"?
7. Does Feyerabend think that the Biblical account of creating in *Genesis* should be included in science textbooks? How about creation stories from other religions? Why/why not?
8. What point does Feyerabend make about educating students using stories and myth?

Practitioners of a strange trade, friends, enemies, ladies, and gentlemen: Before starting with my talk, let me explain to you, how it came into existence.

About a year ago I was short of funds. So I accepted an invitation to contribute to a book dealing with the relation between science and religion. To make the book sell I thought I should make my contribution a provocative one and the most provocative statement one can make about the relation between science and religion is that science is a religion. Having made the statement the core of my article I discovered that lots of reasons, lots of excellent reasons, could be found for it. I enumerated the reasons, finished my article, and got paid. That was stage one.

Next I was invited to a Conference for the Defense of Culture. I accepted the invitation because it paid for my flight to Europe. I also must admit that I was rather curious. When I arrived in Nice I had no idea what I would say. Then while the conference was taking its course I discovered that everyone thought very highly of science and that everyone was very serious. So I decided to explain how one could defend culture from science. All the reasons collected in my article would apply here as well and there was no need to invent new things. I gave my talk, was rewarded with an outcry about my "dangerous and ill-considered ideas," collected my ticket and went on to Vienna. That was stage number two.

Now I am supposed to address you. I have a hunch that in some respect you are very different from my audience in Nice. For one, you look much younger. My audience in Nice was full of professors, businessmen, and television executives, and the average age was about $58\frac{1}{2}$. Then I am quite sure that most of you are considerably to the left of some of the people in Nice. As a matter of fact, speaking somewhat superficially I might say that you are a leftist audience while my audience in Nice was a rightist audience. Yet despite all these differences you have some things in common. Both of you, I assume, respect science and knowledge.

Science, of course, must be reformed and must be made less authoritarian. But once the reforms are carried out, it is a valuable source of knowledge that must not be contaminated by ideologies of a different kind. Secondly, both of you are serious people. Knowledge is a serious matter, for the Right as well as for the Left, and it must be pursued in a serious spirit. Frivolity is out, dedication and earnest application to the task at hand is in. These similarities are all I need for repeating my Nice talk to you with hardly any change. So, here it is.

Fairy Tales

I want to defend society and its inhabitants from all ideologies, science included. All ideologies must be seen in perspective. One must not take them too seriously. One must read them like fairytales which have lots of interesting things to say but which also contain wicked lies, or like ethical prescriptions which may be useful rules of thumb but which are deadly when followed to the letter.

Now, is this not a strange and ridiculous attitude? Science, surely, was always in the forefront of the fight against authoritarianism and superstition. It is to science that we owe our increased intellectual freedom vis-à-vis religious beliefs; it is to science that we owe the liberation of mankind from ancient and rigid forms of thought. Today these forms of thought are nothing but bad dreams—and this we learned from science. Science and enlightenment are one and the same thing—even the most radical critics of society believe this. Kropotkin wants to overthrow all traditional institutions and forms of belief, with the exception of science. Ibsen criticizes the most intimate ramifications of nineteenth-century bourgeois ideology, but he leaves science untouched. Levi-Strauss has made us realize that Western Thought is not the lonely peak of human achievement it was once believed to be, but he excludes science from his relativization of ideologies. Marx and Engels were convinced that science would aid the workers in their quest for mental and social liberation. Are all these people deceived? Are they all mistaken about the role of science? Are they all the victims of a chimera?

To these questions my answer is a firm *Yes and No*.

Now, let me explain my answer.

My explanation consists of two parts, one more general, one more specific.

The general explanation is simple. Any ideology that breaks the hold a comprehensive system of thought has on the minds of men contributes to the liberation of man. Any ideology that makes man question inherited beliefs is an aid to enlightenment. A truth that reigns without checks and balances is a tyrant who must be overthrown, and any falsehood that can aid us in the overthrow of this tyrant is to be welcomed. It follows that seventeenth- and eighteenth-century science indeed *was* an instrument of liberation and enlightenment. It does not follow that science is bound to *remain* such an instrument. There is nothing inherent in science or in any other ideology that makes it *essentially* liberating. Ideologies can deteriorate and become stupid religions. Look at Marxism. And that the science of today is very different from the science of 1650 is evident at the most superficial glance.

For example, consider the role science now plays in education. Scientific "facts" are taught at a very early age and in the very same manner in which religious "facts" were taught only a century ago. There is no attempt to waken the critical abilities of the pupil so that he may be able to see things in perspective. At the universities the situation is even worse, for indoctrination is here carried out in a much more systematic manner. Criticism is not entirely absent. Society, for example, and its institutions, are criticized most severely and often most unfairly and this already at the elementary school level. But science is excepted from the criticism. In society at large the judgement of the scientist is received with the same reverence as the judgement of bishops and cardinals was accepted not too long ago. The move towards "demythologization," for example, is largely motivated by the wish to avoid any clash between Christianity and scientific ideas. If such a clash occurs, then science is certainly right and Christianity wrong. Pursue this investigation further and you will see that science has now become as oppressive as the ideologies it had once to fight. Do not be misled by the fact that today hardly anyone gets killed for joining a scientific heresy. This has nothing to do with science. It has something to do with the general quality of our civilization. Heretics in science are still made to suffer from the *most severe* sanctions this relatively tolerant civilization has to offer.

But—is this description not utterly unfair? Have I not presented the matter in a very distorted light by using tendentious and distorting terminology? Must we not describe the situation in a very different way? I have said that science has become rigid, that it has ceased to be an instrument of *change* and *liberation*, without adding that it has found the *truth*, or a large part thereof. Considering this additional fact we realize, so the objection goes, that the rigidity of science is not due to human willfulness. It lies in the nature of things. For once we have discovered the truth—what else can we do but follow it?

This trite reply is anything but original. It is used whenever an ideology wants to reinforce the faith of its followers. "Truth" is such a nicely neutral word. Nobody would deny that it is commendable to speak the truth and wicked to tell lies. Nobody would deny that—and yet nobody knows what such an attitude amounts to. So it is easy to twist matters and to change allegiance to truth in one's everyday affairs into allegiance to the Truth of an ideology which is nothing but the dogmatic defense of that ideology. And it is of course *not* true that we *have* to follow the truth. Human life is guided by many ideas. Truth is one of them. Freedom and mental independence are others. If Truth, as conceived by some ideologists, conflicts with freedom, then we have a *choice*. We may abandon freedom. But we may also abandon Truth. (Alternatively, we may adopt a more sophisticated idea of truth that no longer contradicts freedom; that was Hegel's solution.) My criticism of modern science is that it inhabits freedom of thought. If the reason is that it has found the truth and now follows it, then I would say that there are better things than first finding, and then following such a monster.

This finishes the general part of my explanation.

There exists a more specific argument to defend the exceptional position science has in society today. Put in a nutshell the argument says (1) that science has finally found the correct *method* for achieving results and (2) that there are many *results* to prove the excellence of the method. The argument is mistaken—but most attempts to show this lead into a dead end. Methodology has by now become so crowded with empty sophistication that it is extremely difficult to perceive the simple errors at the basis. It is like fighting the hydra—cut off one ugly head, and eight formalizations take its place. In this situation the only answer is superficiality: When sophistication loses content then the only way of keeping in touch with reality is to be crude and superficial. This is what I intend to be.

Against Method

There is a method, says part (1) of the argument. What is it? How does it work?

One answer which is no longer as popular as it used to be is that science works by collecting facts and inferring theories from them. The answer is unsatisfactory as theories never *follow from* facts in the strict logical sense. To say that they may yet be *supported* from facts assumes a notion of support that (a) does not show this defect and (b) is sufficiently sophisticated to permit us to say to what extent, say, the theory of relativity is supported by the facts. No such notion exists today, nor is it likely that it will ever be found (one of the problems is that we need a notion of support in which grey ravens can be said to support "all ravens are black"). This was realized by conventionalists and transcendental idealists who pointed out that theories *shape* and *order* facts and can therefore be retained come what may. They can be retained because the human mind either consciously or unconsciously carries out its ordering function. The trouble with these views is that they assume for the mind what they want to explain for the world, viz., that it works in a regular fashion. There is only one view which overcomes all these difficulties. It was invented twice in the nineteenth century, by Mill, in his immortal essay *On Liberty*, and by some Darwinists who extended Darwinism to the battle of ideas. This view takes the bull by the horns: Theories cannot be justified and their excellence cannot be shown without reference to other theories. We may explain the *success* of a theory by reference to a more comprehensive theory (we may explain the success of Newton's theory by using the general theory of relativity); and we may explain our *preference* for it by comparing it with other theories.

Such a comparison does not establish the intrinsic excellence of the theory we have chosen. As a matter of fact, the theory we have chosen may be pretty lousy. It may contain contradictions, it may conflict with well-known facts, it may be cumbersome, unclear, ad hoc in decisive places, and so on. But it may still be better than any other theory that is available at the time. It may in fact be the best lousy theory there is. Nor are the standards of judgment chosen in an absolute manner. Our sophistication increases with every choice we make, and so do our standards. Standards compete just as theories compete and we choose the standards most appropriate to the historical situation in which the choice occurs. The rejected alternatives (theories; standards; "facts") are not eliminated. They serve as correctives (after all, we may have made the wrong choice) and they also explain the content of the preferred views (we understand relativity better when we understand the structure of its competitors; we know the full meaning of freedom only when we have an idea of life in a totalitarian state, of its advantages—and there are many advantages—as well as of its disadvantages). Knowledge so conceived is an ocean of alternatives channeled and subdivided by an ocean of standards. It forces our mind to make imaginative choices and thus makes it grow. It makes our mind capable of choosing, imagining, criticizing.

Today this view is often connected with the name of Karl Popper. But there are some very decisive differences between Popper and Mill. To start with, Popper developed his view to solve a special problem of epistemology—he wanted to solve "Hume's problem." Mill, on the other hand, is interested in conditions favorable to human growth. His epistemology is the result of a certain theory of man, and not the other way around. Also Popper, being influenced by the Vienna Circle, improves on the logical form of a theory before discussing it, while Mill uses every theory in the form in which it occurs in science. Thirdly, Popper's standards of comparison are rigid and fixed, while Mill's standards are permitted to change with the historical situation. Finally, Popper's standards eliminate competitors once and for all: Theories that are either not falsifiable or falsifiable and falsified have no place in science. Popper's criteria are clear, unambiguous, precisely formulated; Mill's criteria are not. This would be an advantage if science itself were clear, unambiguous, and precisely formulated. Fortunately it is not.

To start with, no new and revolutionary scientific theory is ever formulated in a manner that permits us to say under what circumstances we must regard it as endangered: Many revolutionary theories are unfalsifiable. Falsifiable versions do exist, but they are hardly ever in agreement with accepted basic statements: Every moderately interesting theory is falsified. Moreover, theories have formal flaws, many of them contain contradictions, ad hoc adjustments, and so on and so forth. Applied resolutely, Popperian criteria would eliminate science without replacing it by anything comparable. They are useless as an aid to science. In the past decade this has been realized by various thinkers, Kuhn and Lakatos among them. Kuhn's ideas are interesting but, alas, they are much too vague to give rise to anything but lots of hot air. If you don't believe me, look at the literature. Never before has the literature on the philosophy of science been invaded by so many creeps and incompetents. Kuhn encourages people who have no idea why a stone falls to the ground to talk with assurance about scientific method. Now I have no objection to incompetence but I do object when incompetence is accompanied by boredom and self-righteousness. And this is exactly what happens. We do not get interesting false ideas, we get boring ideas or words connected with no ideas at all. Secondly, wherever one tries to make Kuhn's ideas more definite one finds that they are *false*. Was there ever a period of normal science in the history of thought? No—and I challenge anyone to prove the contrary.

Lakatos is immeasurably more sophisticated than Kuhn. Instead of theories he considers research programs which are sequences of theories connected by methods of modification, so-called heuristics. Each theory in the sequence may be full of faults. It may be beset by anomalies, contradictions, ambiguities. What counts is not the shape of the single theories, but the tendency exhibited by the sequence. We judge historical developments and achievements over a period of time, rather than the situation at a particular time. History and methodology are combined into a single enterprise. A research program is said to progress if the sequence of theories leads to novel predictions. It is said to degenerate if it is reduced to absorbing facts that have been discovered without its help. A decisive feature of Lakatos's methodology is that such evaluations are no longer tied to methodological rules which tell the scientist either to retain or to abandon a research program. Scientists may stick to a degenerating program; they may even succeed in making the program overtake its rivals and they therefore proceed rationally whatever they are doing (provided they continue calling degenerating programs degenerating and progressive programs progressive). This means that Lakatos offers *words* which *sound* like the elements of a methodology; he does not offer a methodology. There is no method according to the most advanced and sophisticated methodology in existence today. This finishes my reply to part (1) of the specific argument.

Against Results

According to part (2), science deserves a special position because it has produced *results*. This is an argument only if it can be taken for granted that nothing else has ever produced results. Now it may be admitted that almost everyone who discusses the matter makes such an assumption. It may also be admitted that it is not easy to show that the assumption is false. Forms of life different from science either have disappeared or have degenerated to an extent that makes a fair comparison impossible. Still, the situation is not as hopeless as it was only a decade ago. We have become acquainted with methods of medical diagnosis and therapy which are effective (and perhaps even more effective than the corresponding parts of Western medicine) and which are yet based on an ideology that is radically different from the ideology of Western science. We have learned that there are phenomena such as telepathy and telekinesis which are obliterated by a scientific approach and which could be used to do research in an entirely novel way (earlier thinkers such as Agrippa of Nettesheim, John Dee, and even Bacon were aware of these phenomena). And then—is it not the case that the Church saved souls while science often does the very opposite? Of course, nobody now believes in the ontology that underlies this judgment. Why? Because of ideological pressures identical with those which today make us listen to science to the exclusion of everything else. It is also true that phenomena such as telekinesis and acupuncture may eventually be absorbed into the body of science and may therefore be called "scientific." But note that this happens only after a long period of resistance during which a science *not yet* containing the phenomena wants to get the upper hand over forms of life that contain them. And this leads to a further objection against part (2) of the specific argument. The fact that science has results counts in its favor only if these results were achieved by science alone, and without any outside help. A look at history shows that science hardly ever gets its results in this way. When Copernicus introduced a new view of the universe, he did not consult *scientific* predecessors, he consulted a crazy Pythagorean such as Philolaos. He adopted his ideas and he maintained them in the face of all sound rules of scientific method. Mechanics and optics owe a lot to artisans, medicine to midwives and witches. And in our own day we have seen how the interference of the state can advance science: When the Chinese communists refused to be intimidated by the judgment of experts and ordered traditional medicine back into universities and hospitals there was an outcry all over the world that science would now be ruined in China. The very opposite occurred: Chinese science advanced and Western science learned from it. Wherever we look we see that great scientific advances are due to outside interference which is made to prevail in the face of the most basic and most "rational" methodological rules. The lesson is plain: There does not exist a single argument that could be used to support the exceptional role which science today plays in society. Science has done many things, but so have other ideologies. Science often proceeds systematically, but so do other ideologies (just consult the records of the many doctrinal debates that took place in the Church) and, besides, there are no overriding rules which are adhered to under any circumstances; there is no "scientific methodology" that can be used to separate science from the rest. *Science is just one of the many ideologies that propel society and it should be treated as such* (this statement applies even to the most progressive and most dialectical sections of science). What consequences can we draw from this result?

The most important consequence is that there must be a *formal separation between state and science* just as there is now a formal separation between state and church. Science may influence society but only to the extent to which any political or other pressure group is permitted to influence society. Scientists may be consulted on important projects but the final judgement must be left to the democratically elected consulting bodies. These bodies will consist mainly of laymen. Will the laymen be able to come to a correct judgement? Most certainly, for the competence, the complications, and the successes of science are vastly exaggerated. One of the most exhilarating experiences is to see how a lawyer, who is a layman, can find holes in the testimony, the technical testimony, of the most advanced expert and thus prepare the jury for its verdict. Science is not a closed book that is understood only after years of training. It is an intellectual discipline that can be examined and criticized by anyone who is interested and that looks difficult and profound only because of a systematic campaign of obfuscation carried out by many scientists (though, I am happy to say, not by all). Organs of the state should never hesitate to reject the judgement of scientists when they have reason for doing so. Such rejection will educate the general public, will make it more confident, and it may even lead to improvement. Considering the sizeable chauvinism of the scientific establishment we can say: the more Lysenko affairs, the better (it is not the *interference* of the state that is objectionable in the case of Lysenko, but the *totalitarian* interference which kills the opponent rather than just neglecting his advice). Three cheers to the fundamentalists in California who succeeded in having a dogmatic formulation of the theory of evolution removed from the textbooks and an account of Genesis included. (But I know that they would become as chauvinistic and totalitarian as scientists are today when given the chance to run society all by themselves. Ideologies are marvelous when used in the companies of other ideologies. They become boring and doctrinaire as soon as their merits lead to the removal of their opponents.) The most important change, however, will have to occur in the field of *education.*

Education and Myth

The purpose of education, so one would think, is to introduce the young into life, and that means: into the *society* where they are born and into the *physical* universe that surrounds the society. The method of education often consists in the teaching of some *basic myth*. The myth is available in various versions. More advanced versions may be taught by initiation rites which firmly implant them into the mind. Knowing the myth, the grownup can explain almost everything (or else he can turn to experts for more detailed information). He is the master of Nature and of Society. He understands them both and he knows how to interact with them. However, *he is not the master of the myth that guides his understanding.*

Such further mastery was aimed at, and was partly achieved, by the Presocratics. The Presocratics not only tried to understand the *world*. They also tried to understand, and thus to become the masters of, the *means of understanding the world*. Instead of being content with a single myth they developed many and so diminished the power which a well-told story has over the minds of men. The sophists introduced still further methods for reducing the debilitating effect of interesting, coherent, "empirically adequate," et cetera, et cetera tales. The achievements of these thinkers were not appreciated and they certainly are not understood today. When teaching a myth we want to increase the chance that it will be understood (i.e., no puzzlement about any feature of the myth), believed, *and accepted*. This does not do any harm when the myth is counterbalanced by other myths: Even the most dedicated (i.e., totalitarian) instructor in a certain version of Christianity cannot prevent his pupils from getting in touch with Buddhists, Jews, and other disreputable people. It is very different in the case of science, or of rationalism where the field is almost completely dominated by the believers. In this case it is of paramount importance to strengthen the minds of the young, and "strengthening the minds of the young" means strengthening them *against* any easy acceptance of comprehensive views. What we need here is an education that makes people *contrary, countersuggestive*, without making them incapable of devoting themselves to the elaboration of any single view. How can this aim be achieved?

It can be achieved by protecting the tremendous imagination which children possess and by developing to the full the spirit of contradiction that exists in them. On the whole children are much more intelligent than their teachers. They succumb, and give up their intelligence because they are bullied, or because their teachers get the better of them by emotional means. Children can learn, understand, and keep separate two to three different languages ("children" and by this I mean three- to five-year-olds, *not* eight-year-olds who were experimented upon quite recently and did not come out too well; why? because they were already loused up by incompetent teaching at an earlier age). Of course, the languages must be introduced in a more interesting way than is usually done. There are marvelous writers in all languages who have told marvelous stories—let us begin our language teaching with *them* and not with "der Hund hat einen Schwanz" and similar inanities. Using stories we may of course also introduce "scientific" accounts, say, of the origin of the world and thus make the children acquainted with science as well. But science must not be given any special position except for pointing out that there are lots of people who believe in it. Later on the stories which have been told will be supplemented with "reasons," where by reasons I mean further accounts of the kind found in the tradition to which the story belongs. And, of course, there will also be contrary reasons. Both reasons and contrary reasons will be told by the experts in the fields and so the young generation becomes acquainted with all kinds of sermons and all types of wayfarers. It becomes acquainted with them, it becomes acquainted with their stories, and every individual can make up his mind which way to go. By now everyone knows that you can earn a lot of money and respect and perhaps even a Nobel Prize by becoming a scientist, so many will become scientists. They will *become* scientists *without having been taken in by the ideology of science*, they will *be* scientists *because they have made a free choice*. But has not much time been wasted on unscientific subjects and will this not detract from their competence once they have become scientists? Not at all! The progress of science, of good science depends on novel ideas and on intellectual freedom: Science has very often been advanced by outsiders (remember that Bohr and Einstein regarded themselves as outsiders). Will not many people make the wrong choice and end up in a dead end? Well, that depends on what you mean by a "dead end." Most scientists today are devoid of ideas, full of fear, intent on producing some paltry result so that they can add to the flood of inane papers that now constitutes "scientific progress" in many areas. And, besides, what is more important? To lead a life which one has chosen with open eyes, or to spend one's time in the nervous attempt of avoiding what some not so intelligent people call "dead ends"? Will not the number of scientists decrease so that in the end there is nobody to run our precious laboratories? I do not think so. Given a choice many people may choose science, for a science that is run by free agents looks much more attractive than the science of today which is run by slaves, slaves of institutions and slaves of "reason." And if there is a temporary shortage of scientists the situation may always be remedied by various kinds of incentives. Of course, scientists will not play any predominant role in the society I envisage. They will be more than balanced by magicians, or priests, or astrologers. Such a situation is unbearable for many people, old and young, right and left. Almost all of you have the firm belief that at least some kind of truth has been found, that it must be preserved, and that the method of teaching I advocate and the form of society I defend will dilute it and make it finally disappear. You have this firm belief; many of you may even have reasons. *But what you have to consider is that the absence of good contrary reasons is due to a historical accident*; it does *not* lie in the nature of things. Build up the kind of society I recommend and the views you now despise (without knowing them, to be sure) will return in such splendor that you will have to work hard to maintain your own position and will perhaps be entirely unable to do so. You do not believe me? Then look at history. Scientific astronomy was firmly founded on Ptolemy and Aristotle, two of the greatest minds in the history of Western Thought. Who upset their well-argued, empirically adequate, and precisely formulated system? Philolaos the mad and antediluvian Pythagorean. How was it that Philolaos could stage such a comeback? Because he found an able defender: Copernicus. Of course, you may follow your intuitions as I am following mine. But remember that your intuitions are the result of your "scientific" training where by science I also mean the science of Karl Marx. My training, or, rather, my nontraining, is that of a journalist who is interested in strange and bizarre events. Finally, is it not utterly irresponsible, in the present world situation, with millions of people starving, others enslaved, downtrodden, in abject misery of body and mind, to think luxurious thoughts such as these? Is not freedom of choice a luxury under such circumstances? Is not the flippancy and the humor I want to see combined with the freedom of choice a luxury under such circumstances? Must we not give up all self-indulgence and *act*? Join together, and *act*? This is the most important objection which today is raised against an approach such as the one recommended by me. It has tremendous appeal, it has the appeal of unselfish dedication. Unselfish dedication—to what? Let us see!

We are supposed to give up our selfish inclinations and dedicate ourselves to the liberation of the oppressed. And selfish inclinations are what? They are our wish for maximum liberty of thought in the society in which we live *now*, maximum liberty not only of an abstract kind, but expressed in appropriate institutions and methods of teaching. This wish for concrete intellectual and physical liberty in our own surroundings is to be put aside, for the time being. This assumes, first, that we do not need this liberty for our task. It assumes that we can carry out our task with a mind that is firmly closed to some alternatives. It assumes that the correct way of liberating others *has always been found* and that all that is needed is to carry it out. I am sorry, I cannot accept such doctrinaire self-assurance in such extremely important matters. Does this mean that we cannot act at all? It does not. But it means that *while acting we have to try to realize as much of the freedom I have recommended so that our actions may be corrected in the light of the ideas we get while increasing our freedom.* This will slow us down, no doubt, but are we supposed to charge ahead simply because some people tell us that they have found an explanation for all the misery and an excellent way out of it? Also we want to liberate people not to make them succumb to a new kind of slavery, *but to make them realize their own wishes,* however different these wishes may be from our own. Self-righteous and narrow-minded liberators cannot do this. As a rule they soon impose a slavery that is worse, because more systematic, than the very sloppy slavery they have removed. And as regards humor and flippancy the answer should be obvious. Why would anyone want to liberate anyone else? Surely not because of some *abstract* advantage of liberty but because liberty is the best way to free development and *thus to happiness.* We want to liberate people so that *they can smile.* Shall we be able to do this if we ourselves have forgotten how to smile and are frowning on those who still remember? Shall we then not spread another disease, comparable to the one we want to remove, the disease of puritanical self-righteousness? Do not object that dedication and humor do not go together—Socrates is an excellent example to the contrary. *The hardest task needs the lightest hand or else its completion will not lead to freedom but to a tyranny much worse than the one it replaces.*

Discussion Questions

1. In what ways does science "inhibit freedom of thought"? Have you ever been asked by teachers to question science? If not, should this occur more?
2. Feyerabend notes that other ideologies (he mentions the Church) also proceed systematically like science. Is merely having a "system" what's important regarding the doing of science, or is it a *particular* system? What do you think? How would Feyerabend respond?
3. What do you think about Feyerabend's suggestion that we separate "state and science"? Would it be a good idea to put current scientific hypotheses to a vote by "laymen" (non-scientists)? Why/why not?
4. Do you agree with Feyerabend on any level? If so, what related changes in education would you suggest in order to improve it?
5. If you were in the audience where Feyerabend gave this talk, what question would you ask of him?

Why Astrology Is a Pseudoscience

Paul R. Thagard

Paul Thagard is professor of philosophy, psychology, and computer science at the University of Waterloo and also serves as the director of the Cognitive Science Program there. He has published a great deal of articles and books focused in the areas of philosophy of science and cognitive science.

In this article, Thagard gives a brief overview of astrology and then provides past attempts to show why astrology is considered pseudoscientific. He shows that these past efforts fall short and then offers his own reasoning as to the pseudoscientific nature of astrology.

Reading Questions

1. How does astrology work? How does it make predictions?
2. What three areas do Bok et al. reference in claiming that astrology is not scientific? How does Thagard approach these claims? How do they relate to the question of astrology's being scientific or not?
3. What point does Thagard make in his first footnote (#16 here)?
4. What does it mean for a theory to be verifiable? To be falsifiable? How does Thagard connect these criteria with astrology?
5. What is Thagard's criterion to demark a theory as pseudoscientific? What four reasons does he provide that show this?
6. How does Thagard explain that a particular theory can be scientific at one point but pseudoscientific at another?
7. Why does Thagard think that defining pseudoscience is important?

Source: "Why Astrology is a Pseudoscience" by Paul Thagard from *Proceedings of Philosophy of Science Association*, 1978, Volume One, pp. 223–224, edited by P.D. Asquith and I. Hacking. Reprinted by permission of the publisher.

Most philosophers and historians of science agree that astrology is a pseudoscience, but there is little agreement on *why* it is a pseudoscience. Answers range from matters of verifiability and falsifiability, to questions of progress and Kuhnian normal science, to the different sort of objections raised by a large panel of scientists recently organized by *The Humanist* magazine. Of course there are also Feyerabendian anarchists and others who say that no demarcation of science from pseudoscience is possible. However, I shall propose a complex criterion for distinguishing disciplines as pseudoscientific; this criterion is unlike verificationist and falsificationist attempts in that it introduces social and historical features as well as logical ones.

I begin with a brief description of astrology. It would be most unfair to evaluate astrology by reference to the daily horoscopes found in newspapers and popular magazines. These horoscopes deal only with sun signs, whereas a full horoscope makes reference to the "influences" also of the moon and the planets, while also discussing the ascendant sign and other matters.

Astrology divides the sky into twelve regions, represented by the familiar signs of the Zodiac: Aquarius, Libra, and so on. The sun sign represents the part of the sky occupied by the sun at the time of birth. For example, anyone born between September 23 and October 22 is a Libran. The ascendant sign, often assumed to be at least as important as the sun sign, represents the part of the sky rising on the eastern horizon at the time of birth, and therefore changes every two hours. To determine this sign, accurate knowledge of the time and place of birth is essential. The moon and the planets (of which there are five or eight depending on whether Uranus, Neptune, and Pluto are taken into account) are also located by means of charts on one of the parts of the Zodiac. Each planet is said to exercise an influence in a special sphere of human activity; for example, Mars governs drive, courage, and daring, while Venus governs love and artistic endeavor. The immense number of combinations of sun, ascendant, moon, and planetary influences allegedly determines human personality, behavior, and fate.

Astrology is an ancient practice, and appears to have its origins in Chaldea, thousands of years B.C.E. By 700 B.C.E., the Zodiac was established, and a few centuries later the signs of the Zodiac were very similar to current ones. The conquests of Alexander the Great brought astrology to Greece, and the Romans were exposed in turn. Astrology was very popular during the fall of the Republic, with many notables such as Julius Caesar having their horoscopes cast. However, there was opposition from such men as Lucretius and Cicero.

Astrology underwent a gradual codification culminating in Ptolemy's *Tetrabiblos*, written in the second century C.E. This work describes in great detail the powers of the sun, moon, and planets, and their significance in people's lives. It is still recognized as a fundamental textbook of astrology. Ptolemy took astrology as seriously as he took his famous work in geography and astronomy; this is evident from the introduction to the *Tetrabiblos*, where he discusses two available means of making predictions based on the heavens. The first and admittedly more effective of these concerns the relative movements of the sun, moon, and planets, which Ptolemy had already treated in his celebrated *Almagest*. The secondary but still legitimate means of prediction is that in which we use the "natural character" of the aspects of movement of heavenly bodies to "investigate the changes which they bring about in that which they surround." He argues that this method of prediction is possible because of the manifest effects of the sun, moon, and planets on the earth, for example on weather and the tides.

The European Renaissance is heralded for the rise of modern science, but occult arts such as astrology and alchemy flourished as well. Arthur Koestler has described Kepler's interest in astrology: Not only did astrology provide Kepler with a livelihood, he also pursued it as a serious interest, although he was skeptical of the particular analyses of previous astrologers. Astrology was popular both among intellectuals and the general public through the seventeenth century. However, astrology lost most of this popularity in the eighteenth century, when it was attacked by such figures of the Enlightenment as Swift and Voltaire. Only since the 1930s has astrology again gained a huge audience: Most people today know at least their sun signs, and a great many believe that the stars and planets exercise an important influence on their lives.

In an attempt to reverse this trend, Bart Bok, Lawrence Jerome, and Paul Kurtz drafted in 1975 a statement attacking astrology; the statement was signed by 192 leading scientists, including 19 Nobel Prize winners. The statement raises three main issues: Astrology originated as part of a magical world view, the planets are too distant for there to be any physical foundation for astrology, and people believe it merely out of longing for comfort. None of these objections is ground for condemning astrology as pseudoscience. To show this, I shall briefly discuss articles written by Bok and Jerome in support of the statement.

According to Bok, to work on statistical tests of astrological predictions is a waste of time unless it is demonstrated that astrology has some sort of physical foundation. He uses the smallness of gravitational and radiative effects of the stars and planets to suggest that there is no such foundation. He also discusses the psychology of belief in astrology, which is the result of individuals' desperation in seeking solutions to their serious personal problems. Jerome devotes most of his article to the origins of astrology in the magical principle of correspondences. He claims that astrology is a system of magic rather than science, and that it fails "not because of any inherent inaccuracies due to precession or lack of exact knowledge concerning time of birth or conception, but rather because its interpretations and predictions are grounded in the ancients' magical world view." He does however discuss some statistical tests of astrology, which I shall return to below.

These objections do not show that astrology is a pseudoscience. First, origins are irrelevant to scientific status. The alchemical origins of chemistry and the occult beginnings of medicine are as magical as those of astrology, and historians have detected mystical influences in the work of many great scientists, including Newton and Einstein. Hence astrology cannot be condemned simply for the magical origins of its principles. Similarly, the psychology of popular belief is also in itself irrelevant to the status of astrology: People often believe even good theories for illegitimate reasons, and even if most people believe astrology for personal, irrational reasons, good reasons may be available.[16] Finally the lack of a physical foundation hardly marks a theory as unscientific. Examples: When Wegener proposed continental drift, no mechanism was known, and a link between smoking and cancer has been established statistically though the details of carcinogenesis remain to be discovered. Hence the objections of Bok, Jerome, and Kurtz fail to mark astrology as pseudoscience.

Now we must consider the application of the criteria of verifiability and falsifiability to astrology. Roughly, a theory is said to be verifiable if it is possible to deduce observation statements from it. Then in principle, observations can be used to confirm or disconfirm the theory. A theory is scientific only if it is verifiable. The vicissitudes of the verification principle are too well known to recount here. Attempts by A. J. Ayer to articulate the principle failed either by ruling out most of science as unscientific, or by ruling out nothing. Moreover, the theory/observation distinction has increasingly come into question. All that remains is a vague sense that testability somehow is a mark of scientific theories.

Well, astrology *is* vaguely testable. Because of the multitude of influences resting on tendencies rather than laws, astrology is incapable of making precise predictions. Nevertheless, attempts have been made to test the reality of these alleged tendencies, using large-scale surveys and statistical evaluation. The pioneer in this area was Michel Gauquelin, who examined the careers and times of birth of 25,000 Frenchmen. Astrology suggests that people born under certain signs or planets are likely to adopt certain occupations: For example, the influence of the warlike planet Mars tends to produce soldiers or athletes, while Venus has an artistic influence. Notably, Gauquelin found *no significant correlation* between careers and either sun sign, moon sign, or ascendant sign. However, he did find some statistically interesting correlations between certain occupations of people and the position of certain planets at the time of their birth. For example, just as astrology would suggest, there is a greater than chance association of athletes and Mars, and a greater than chance association association of scientists and Saturn, where the planet is rising or at its zenith at the moment of the individual's birth.

These findings and their interpretation are highly controversial, as are subsequent studies in a similar vein. Even if correct, they hardly verify astrology, especially considering the negative results found for the most important astrological categories. I have mentioned Gauquelin in order to suggest that through the use of statistical techniques astrology is at least *verifiable*. Hence the verification principle does not mark astrology as pseudoscience.

Because the predictions of astrologers are generally vague, a Popperian would assert that the real problem with astrology is that it is not falsifiable: Astrologers cannot make predictions which if unfulfilled would lead them to give up their theory. Hence because it is unfalsifiable, astrology is unscientific.

But the doctrine of falsifiability faces serious problems as described by Duhem, Quine, and Lakatos. Popper himself noticed early that no observation ever guarantees falsification: A theory can always be retained by introducing or modifying auxiliary hypotheses, and even observation statements are not incorrigible. Methodological decisions about what can be tampered with are required to block the escape from falsification. However, Lakatos has persuasively argued that making such decision in advance of tests is arbitrary and may often lead to overhasty rejection of a sound theory which *ought* to be saved by antifalsificationist stratagems. Falsification only occurs when a better theory comes along. Then falsifiability is only a matter of replaceability by another theory, and since astrology is in principle replaceable by another theory, falsifiability provides no criterion for rejecting astrology as pseudoscientific. We saw in the discussion of Gauquelin that astrology can be used to make predictions about statistical regularities, but the nonexistence of these regularities does not falsify astrology; but here astrology does not appear worse than the best of scientific theories which also resist falsification until alternative theories arise.

Astrology cannot be condemned as pseudoscientific on the grounds proposed by verificationists, falsificationists, or Bok and Jerome. But undoubtedly astrology today faces a great many unsolved problems. One is the negative result found by Gauquelin concerning careers and signs. Another is the problem of the precession of the equinoxes, which astrologers generally take into account when heralding the "Age of Aquarius" but totally neglect when figuring their charts. Astrologers do not always agree on the significance of the three planets, Neptune, Uranus, and Pluto, that were discovered since Ptolemy. Studies of twins do not show similarities of personality and fate that astrology would suggest. Nor does astrology make sense of mass disasters, where numerous individuals with very different horoscopes come to similar ends.

But problems such as these do not in themselves show that astrology is either false or pseudoscientific. Even the best theories face unsolved problems throughout their history. To get a criterion demarcating astrology from science, we need to consider it in a wider historical and social context.

A demarcation criterion requires a matrix of three elements: [theory, community, historical context]. Under the first heading, "theory," fall familiar matters of structure, prediction, explanation, and problem solving. We might also include the issue raised by Bok and Jerome about whether the theory has a physical foundation. Previous demarcationists have concentrated on this theoretical element, evident in the concern of the verification and falsification principles with prediction. But we have seen that this approach is not sufficient for characterizing astrology as pseudoscientific.

We must also consider the *community* of advocates of the theory, in this case the community of practitioners of astrology. Several questions are important here. First, are the practitioners in agreement on the principles of the theory and on how to go about solving problems which the theory faces? Second, do they care, that is, are they concerned about explaining anomalies and comparing the success of their theory to the record of other theories? Third, are the practitioners actively involved in attempts at confirming and disconfirming their theory?

The question about comparing the success of a theory with that of other theories introduces the third element of the matrix, historical context. The historical work of Kuhn and others has shown that in general a theory is rejected only when (1) it has faced anomalies over a long period of time and (2) it has been challenged by another theory. Hence under the heading of historical context we must consider two factors relevant to demarcation: the record of a theory over time in explaining new facts and dealing with anomalies, and the availability of alternative theories.

We can now propose the following principles of demarcation:

A theory or discipline which purports to be scientific is pseudoscientific if and only if:

1. It has been less progressive than alternative theories over a long period of time, and faces many unsolved problems; but
2. the community of practitioners makes little attempt to develop the theory towards solutions of the problems, shows no concern for attempts to evaluate the theory in relation to others, and is selective in considering confirmations and disconfirmations.

Progressiveness is a matter of the success of the theory in adding to its set of facts explained and problems solved.

This principle captures, I believe, what is most importantly unscientific about astrology. First, astrology is dramatically unprogressive, in that it has changed little and has added nothing to its explanatory power since the time of Ptolemy. Second, problems such as the precession of equinoxes are outstanding. Third, there are alternative theories of personality and behavior available: One need not be an uncritical advocate of behaviorist, Freudian, *or* Gestalt theories to see that since the nineteenth century psychological theories have been expanding to deal with many of the phenomena which astrology explains in terms of heavenly influences. The important point is not that any of these psychological theories is established or true, only that they are growing alternatives to a long-static astrology. Fourth and finally, the community of astrologers is generally unconcerned with advancing astrology to deal with outstanding problems or with evaluating the theory in relation to others. For these reasons, my criterion marks astrology as pseudoscientific.

This demarcation criterion differs from those implicit in Lakatos and Kuhn. Lakatos has said that what makes a series of theories constituting a research program scientific is that it is progressive: Each theory in the series has greater corroborated content than its predecessor. While I agree with Lakatos that progressiveness is a central notion here, it is not sufficient to distinguish science from pseudoscience. We should not brand a nonprogressive discipline as pseudoscientific unless it is being maintained against more progressive alternatives. Kuhn's discussion of astrology focuses on a different aspect of my criterion. He says that what makes astrology unscientific is the absence of the paradigm-dominated puzzle-solving activity characteristic of what he calls normal science. But as Watkins has suggested, astrologers are in some respects model normal scientists: They concern themselves with solving puzzles at the level of individual horoscopes, unconcerned with the foundations of their general theory or paradigm. Hence that feature of normal science does not distinguish science from pseudoscience. What makes astrology pseudoscientific is not that it lacks periods of Kuhnian normal science, but that its proponents adopt uncritical attitudes of "normal" scientists despite the existence of more progressive alternative theories. (Note that I am not agreeing with Popper that Kuhn's normal scientists are unscientific; they can become unscientific only when an alternative paradigm has been developed.) However, if one looks not at the puzzle solving at the level of particular astrological predictions, but at the level of theoretical problems such as the precession of the equinoxes, there is some agreement between my criterion and Kuhn's; astrologers do not have a paradigm-induced confidence about solving theoretical problems.

Of course, the criterion is intended to have applications beyond astrology. I think that discussion would show that the criterion marks as pseudoscientific such practices as witchcraft and pyramidology, while leaving contemporary physics, chemistry, and biology unthreatened. The current fad of biorhythms, implausibly based like astrology on date of birth, cannot be branded as pseudoscientific because we lack alternative theories giving more detailed accounts of cyclical variations in human beings, although much research is in progress.

One interesting consequence of the above criterion is that a theory can be scientific at one time but pseudoscientific at another. In the time of Ptolemy or even Kepler, astrology had few alternatives in the explanation of human personality and behavior. Existing alternatives were scarcely more sophisticated or corroborated than astrology. Hence astrology should be judged as not pseudoscientific in classical or Renaissance times, even though it is pseudoscientific today. Astrology was not simply a perverse sideline of Ptolemy and Kepler, but part of their scientific activity, even if a physicist involved with astrology today should be looked at askance. Only when the historical and social aspects of science are neglected does it become plausible that pseudoscience is an unchanging category. Rationality is not a property of ideas eternally: Ideas, like actions, can be rational at one time but irrational at others. Hence relativizing the science/pseudoscience distinction to historical periods is a desirable result.

But there remains a challenging historical problem. According to my criterion, astrology only became pseudoscientific with the rise of modern psychology in the nineteenth century. But astrology was already virtually excised from scientific circles by the beginning of the eighteenth. How could this be? The simple answer is that a theory can take on the appearance of an unpromising project well before it deserves the label of pseudoscience. The Copernican revolution and the mechanism of Newton, Descartes, and Hobbes undermined the plausibility of astrology. Lynn Thorndike has described how the Newtonian theory pushed aside what had been accepted as a universal natural law, that inferiors such as inhabitants of earth are ruled and governed by superiors such as the stars and the planets. William Stahlman has described how the immense growth of science in the seventeenth century contrasted with stagnation of astrology. These developments provided good reason for discarding astrology as a promising pursuit, but they were not yet enough to brand it as pseudoscientific, or even to refute it.

Because of its social aspect, my criterion might suggest a kind of cultural relativism. Suppose there is an isolated group of astrologers in the jungles of South America, practicing their art with no awareness of alternatives. Are we to say that astrology is *for them* scientific? Or, going in the other direction, should we count as alternative theories ones which are available to extraterrestrial beings, or which someday will be conceived? This wide construal of "alternative" would have the result that our best current theories are probably pseudoscientific. These two questions employ, respectively, a too narrow and too broad view of alternatives. By an alternative theory I mean one generally available in the world. This assumes first that there is some kind of communication network to which a community has, or should have, access. Second, it assumes that the onus is on individuals and communities to find out about alternatives. I would argue (perhaps against Kuhn) that this second assumption is a general feature of rationality; it is at least sufficient to preclude ostrichism as a defense against being judged pseudoscientific.

In conclusion, I would like to say why I think the question of what constitutes a pseudoscience is important. Unlike the logical positivists, I am not grinding an antimetaphysical ax, and unlike Popper, I am not grinding an anti-Freudian or anti-Marxian one. My concern is social: Society faces the twin problems of lack of public concern with the advancement of science, and lack of public concern with the important ethical issues now arising in science and technology, for example around the topic of genetic engineering. One reason for this dual lack of concern is the wide popularity of pseudoscience and the occult among the general public. Elucidation of how science differs from pseudoscience is the philosophical side of an attempt to overcome public neglect of genuine science.

Discussion Questions

1. Do you make any decisions based on astrological readings? Why/why not? Do you ever read your horoscope? Do you believe your sign (and the signs of others) tell you something about yourself (and others)? If you agree that astrology is unscientific, do you still see any value in it?

2. A decade-long religious-funded study at Harvard University recently (2006) showed that prayer has no positive effect on hospital patients. If you pray, would this finding affect your prayer?

3. In 2006, many Chinese employers made hiring choices based on their system of astrology—they avoided hiring otherwise competent employees because they were born in the Year of the Dog. Do you think this is fair? What if, instead of hiring based on astrological signs, people were hired based on religious affiliations?

4. Do you agree with Thagard that defining pseudoscience is important? Why/why not?

5. How popular would astrology and horoscopes be if they told the *whole* story, as Thagard notes in his first footnote?

What Is True?

Richard Dawkins

Richard Dawkins is considered one of today's most well-known evolutionary scientists, theorists, and ethologists (one who studies animal behavior) and has written numerous best-selling books on these topics. He currently serves as the Chair in Public Understanding

Source: "Hall of Mirrors" by Richard Dawkins from October 2, 2000 *Forbes ASAP*. Reprinted by permission of FORBES ASAP Magazine © 2007 Forbes Media LLC.

of Science at Oxford University and tours extensively, giving lectures and television appearances focusing on science and its relevance.

In this article, Dawkins addresses the concern of "truth-hecklers"—those like Kuhn, Popper, and others who criticize science from a philosophical standpoint. Originally published as a contribution to a symposium (entitled "What Is True?") in *Forbes ASAP* magazine, Dawkins chose it for an anthology of his own writings highlighting his 25-year career. In his introduction of this article he writes, "It's hard enough coaxing nature to give up her truths, without spectators and hangers-on strewing gratuitous obstacles in our way. My essay argues that we should at least be consistent. Truths about everyday life are just as much—or as little—open to philosophical doubt as scientific truths. Let us shun double standards."

Reading Questions

1. In your words, what is the "cultural relativism" that Dawkins portrays?
2. Why does Dawkins claim that scientific "truth" is preferable to other (i.e., religious) "truth"?
3. Why does Dawkins make the analogy of the Necker Cube?
4. What criticisms of Popper and Kuhn does Dawkins offer?
5. Why does Dawkins mention the limited human mind?

A little learning is a dangerous thing. This has never struck me as a particularly profound or wise remark,* but it comes into its own in the special case where the little learning is in philosophy (as it often is). A scientist who has the temerity to utter the t-word ('true') is likely to encounter a form of philosophical heckling which goes something like this:

> There is no absolute truth. You are committing an act of personal faith when you claim that the scientific method, including mathematics and logic, is the privileged road to truth. Other cultures might believe that truth is to be found in a rabbit's entrails, or the ravings of a prophet up a pole. It is only your personal faith in science that leads you to favour your brand of truth.

That strand of half-baked philosophy goes by the name of cultural relativism. It is one aspect of the *Fashionable Nonsense* detected by Alan Sokal and Jean Bricmont, or the *Higher Superstition* of Paul Gross and Norman Levitt. The feminist version is ably exposed by Daphne Patai and Noretta Koertge, authors of *Professing Feminism: Cautionary Tales from the Strange World of Women's Studies*:

> Women's Studies students are now being taught that logic is a tool of domination . . . the standard norms and methods of scientific inquiry are sexist because they are incompatible with 'women's ways of knowing' . . . These 'subjectivist' women see the methods of logic, analysis and abstraction

---

*Pope's original is wonderful, but the aphorism doesn't survive isolation from its context.

as 'alien territory belonging to men' and 'value intuition as a safer and more fruitful approach to truth.'

How should scientists respond to the allegation that our 'faith' in logic and scientific truth is just that—faith—nor 'privileged' (favourite inword) over alternative truths? A minimal response is that science gets results. As I put it in *River Out of Eden*,

> Show me a cultural relativist at 30,000 feet and I'll show you a hypocrite . . . If you are flying to an international congress of anthropologists or literary critics, the reason you will probably get there—the reason you don't plummet into a ploughed field—is that a lot of Western scientifically trained engineers have got their sums right.

Science boosts its claim to truth by its spectacular ability to make matter and energy jump through hoops on command, and to predict what will happen and when.

But is it still just our Western scientific bias to be impressed by accurate prediction; impressed by the power to slingshot rockets around Jupiter to reach Saturn, or intercept and repair the Hubble telescope; impressed by logic itself? Well, let's concede the point and think sociologically, even democratically. Suppose we agree, temporarily, to treat scientific truth as just one truth among many, and lay it alongside all the rival contenders: Trobriand truth, Kikuyu truth, Maori truth, Inuit truth, Navajo truth, Yanomamo truth, !Kung San truth, feminist truth, Islamic truth, Hindu truth. The list is endless—and thereby hangs a revealing observation.

In theory, people could switch allegiance from any one 'truth' to any other if they decide it has greater merit. On what basis might they do so? Why would one change from, say, Kikuyu truth to Navajo truth? Such merit-driven switches are rare. With one crucially important exception. Scientific truth is the only member of the list which regularly persuades converts of its superiority. People are loyal to other belief systems for one reason only: They were brought up that way, and they have never known anything better. When people are lucky enough to be offered the opportunity to vote with their feet, doctors and their kind prosper while witch doctors decline. Even those who do not, or cannot, avail themselves of a scientific education, choose to benefit from the technology that is made possible by the scientific education of others. Admittedly, religious missionaries have successfully claimed converts in great numbers all over the underdeveloped world. But they succeed not because of the merits of their religion but because of the science-based technology for which it is pardonably, but wrongly, given credit.

> Surely the Christian God must be superior to our Juju, because Christ's representatives come bearing rifles, telescopes, chainsaws, radios, almanacs that predict eclipses to the minute, and medicines that work.

So much for cultural relativism. A different type of truth-heckler prefers to drop the name of Karl Popper or (more fashionably) Thomas Kuhn:

> There is no absolute truth. Your scientific truths are merely hypotheses that have so far failed to be falsified, destined to be superseded. At worst, after the next scientific revolution, today's 'truths' will seem quaint and absurd, if not actually false. The best you scientists can hope for is a series of approximations which progressively reduce errors but never eliminate them.

The Popperian heckle partly stems from the accidental fact that philosophers of science are traditionally obsessed with one piece of scientific history: the comparison between Newton's and Einstein's theories of gravitation. It is true that Newton's inverse square law has turned out to be an approximation, a special case of Einstein's more general formula. If this is the only piece of scientific history you know, you might indeed conclude that all apparent truths are mere approximations, fated to be superseded. There is even a quite interesting sense in which all our sensory perceptions—the 'real' things that we 'see with our own eyes'—may be regarded as unfalsified 'hypotheses' about the world, vulnerable to change. This provides a good way to think about illusions such as the Necker Cube.

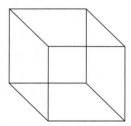

The flat pattern of ink on paper is compatible with two alternative 'hypotheses' of solidity. So we see a solid cube which, after a few seconds, 'flips' to a different cube, then flips back to the first cube, and so on. Perhaps sense data only ever confirm or reject mental 'hypotheses' about what is out there.

Well, that is an interesting theory; so is the philosopher's notion that science proceeds by conjecture and refutation; and so is the analogy between the two. This line of thought—all our percepts are hypothetical models in the brain—might lead us to fear some future blurring of the distinction between reality and illusion in our descendants, whose lives will be even more dominated by computers capable of generating vivid models of their own. Without venturing into the high-tech worlds of virtual reality, we already know that our senses are easily deceived. Conjurors—professional illusionists—can persuade us, if we lack a sceptical foothold in reality, that something supernatural is going on. Indeed, some notorious erstwhile conjurors make a fat living doing exactly that: a living much fatter than they ever enjoyed when they frankly admitted that they were conjurors.* Scientists, alas, are not best equipped to unmask telepathists, mediums, and spoon-bending charlatans. This is a job which is best handed over to the professionals, and that means other conjurors. The lesson that conjurors, the honest variety and the impostors, teach us is that an uncritical faith in our own senses is not an infallible guide to truth.

But none of this seems to undermine our ordinary concept of what it means for something to be true. If I am in the witness box, and prosecuting counsel wags his stern finger and demands, 'Is it or is it not true that you were in Chicago on the night of the murder?' I should get pretty short shrift if I said,

> What do you mean by true? The hypothesis that I was in Chicago has not so far been falsified, but it is only a matter of time before we see that it is a mere approximation.

Or, reverting to the first heckle, I would not expect a jury, even a Bongolese jury, to give a sympathetic hearing to my plea that,

> It is only in your western scientific sense of the word 'in' that I was in Chicago. The Bongolese have a completely different concept of 'in,' according to which you are only truly 'in' a place if you are an anointed elder entitled to take snuff from the dried scrotum of a goat.

It is simply true that the Sun is hotter than the Earth, true that the desk on which I am writing is made of wood. These are not hypotheses awaiting falsification; not temporary approximations to an ever-elusive truth; not local truths that might be denied in another culture. And the same can safely be said of many scientific truths, even where we can't see them 'with our own eyes.' It is forever true that DNA is a double helix, true that if you and a chimpanzee (or an octopus or a kangaroo) trace your ancestors back far enough you will eventually hit a shared ancestor. To a pedant, these are still hypotheses which might be falsified tomorrow. But they never will be. Strictly, the truth that there were no human beings in the Jurassic Period is still a conjecture, which could be refuted at any time by the discovery of a single fossil, authentically dated by a battery of radiometric methods. It could happen. Want a bet? Even if they are nominally hypotheses on probation, these statements are true in exactly the same sense as the ordinary truths of everyday life; true in the same sense as it is true that you have a head, and that my desk is wooden. If scientific truth is open to philosophic doubt, it is no more so than common sense truth. Let's at least be even-handed in our philosophical heckling.

---

*Performing psychics and mystics, who happily perform in front of scientists, will conveniently plead a headache and refuse to go on if informed that a contingent of professional conjurors is in the front row of the stalls. It is for the same reason that the then Editor of *Nature*, John Maddox, took James 'The Amazing' Randi with him when investigating a suspected case of homeopathic fraud. This caused some resentment at the time, but it was an entirely reasonable decision. Any genuine scientist has nothing to fear from a sceptical conjuror looking over his shoulder.

A more profound difficulty now arises for our scientific concept of truth. Science is very much not synonymous with common sense. Admittedly, that doughty scientific hero T. H. Huxley said:

> Science is nothing but trained and organized common sense, differing from the latter only as a veteran may differ from a raw recruit: and its methods differ from those of common sense only as far as the guardsman's cut and thrust differ from the manner in which a savage wields his club.

But Huxley was talking about the methods of science, not its conclusions. As Lewis Wolpert emphasized in *The Unnatural Nature of Science*, the conclusions can be disturbingly counter-intuitive. Quantum theory is counter-intuitive to the point where the physicist sometimes seems to be battling insanity. We are asked to believe that a single quantum behaves like a particle in going through one hole instead of another, but simultaneously behaves like a wave in interfering with a non-existent copy of itself, if another hole is opened through which that non-existent copy *could* have travelled (if it had existed). It gets worse, to the point where some physicists resort to a vast number of parallel but mutually unreachable worlds, which proliferate to accommodate every alternative quantum event; while other physicists, equally desperate, suggest that quantum events are determined retrospectively by our decision to examine their consequences. Quantum theory strikes us as so weird, so defiant of common sense, that even the great Richard Feynman was moved to remark, 'I think I can safely say that nobody understands quantum mechanics.' Yet the many predictions by which quantum theory has been tested stand up, with an accuracy so stupendous that Feynman compared it to measuring the distance between New York and Los Angeles accurately to the width of one human hair. On the basis of these stunningly successful predictions, quantum theory, or some version of it, seems to be as true as anything we know.

Modern physics teaches us that there is more to truth than meets the eye; or than meets the all too limited human mind, evolved as it was to cope with medium-sized objects moving at medium speeds through medium distances in Africa. In the face of these profound and sublime mysteries, the low-grade intellectual poodling of pseudo-philosophical poseurs seems unworthy of adult attention.

Discussion Questions

1. How do you choose which methods (i.e., science, religion, logic, astrology, etc.) you use to determine *truth*?
2. Is science better at determining truth than religion? If so, why? If not, how would you respond to Dawkins?
3. If philosophy points out problems with science (i.e., Dawkins' "truth-hecklers"), yet a scientist discounts these criticisms as irrelevant, how seriously do you take the criticisms? Could there be any sort of compromise?

Subjects, Power, and Knowledge: Description and Prescription in Feminist Philosophies of Science

Helen E. Longino

Currently a philosophy professor at Stanford University, Helen Longino has also taught philosophy and women's studies at Mills College, Rice University, and the University of Minnesota. She has published numerous articles and a number of books, including *Science as Social Knowledge: Values and Objectivity in Scientific Inquiry*, and *The Fate of Knowledge*.

In this article, Longino explores not just her own ideas on feminism in science, but also past approaches and their strengths and shortcomings. In doing so, she helps defend against the potential relativism of the feminist view of science while still highlighting the problems of an androcentric (male-centered) epistemology (method of knowledge gathering). She connects the problem in a historical context in referencing Plato's allegory of the cave (included in this anthology) in which knowledge is attained by ignoring the passions, as well as a Cartesian method (i.e., relating to Descartes's approach—attaining "epistemic autonomy" through a detachment of the (rational) mind from body).

She explores the notion of a "theory laden" epistemology: that science is not a purely objective enterprise in that humans view the world differently and subjectively, including the more general differences of men and women's view of the world. A key statement in her article summarizes much of her project: "If observation is theory laden, then observation cannot serve as an independent constraint on theories, thus permitting subjective elements to constrain theory choice."

Reading Questions

1. What examples does Longino give to illustrate that science may not be value-neutral?
2. How does Longino describe the typical ("paradigmatic") knower? How does she relate this to Plato? To Descartes?
3. What three strategies does Longino review as offered attempts to "change the subject" and also highlight the male/masculine bias in science?
4. What is "standpoint theory" and what problems does it encounter?
5. Explain the distinction between dynamic autonomy and static autonomy.
6. What is the traditional view of science according to Longino? How does the notion of "theory laden" observation challenge this view?
7. What importance does the notion of *community* have for Longino regarding scientific knowledge?
8. How does Longino define "true relativism"? How does she claim that her suggestion regarding the communal aspect of scientific knowledge avoids relativism?
9. Explain the "dilemmas of pluralism." What two solutions does Longino offer?

Source: Copyright © 1993 from *Feminist Epistemologies*, edited by Linda Alcoff and Elizabeth Potter. Reproduced by permission of Routledge, a division of Taylor & Francis Group.

10. What does Longino mean when she writes, "The structure as specified is neither true nor false; it is just a structure"? How does this relate to models and metaphors? According to Longino, what problems arise from models/ metaphors in science? How does she use the idea of a model/map to illuminate feminist issues in science?
11. Explain the two consequences Longino notes of treating science as a practice.

Prologue

Feminists, faced with traditions in philosophy and in science that are deeply hostile to women, have had practically to invest new and more appropriate ways of knowing the world. These new ways have been less invention out of whole cloth than the revival or re-evaluation of alternative or suppressed traditions. They range from the celebration of insight into nature through identification with it to specific strategies of survey research in the social sciences. Natural scientists and lay persons anxious to see the sciences change have celebrated Barbara McClintock's loving identification with various aspects of the plants she studied, whether whole organism or its chromosomal structure revealed under the microscope. Social scientists from Dorothy Smith to Karen Sacks have stressed designing research *for* rather than merely about women, a goal that requires attending to the specificities of women's lives and consulting research subjects themselves about the process of gathering information about them. Such new ways of approaching natural and social phenomena can be seen as methods of discovery, ways of getting information about the natural and social worlds not available via more traditional experimental or investigative methods.

Feminists have rightly pointed out the blinders imposed by the philosophical distinction between discovery and justification; a theory of scientific inquiry that focuses solely on the logic of justification neglects the selection processes occurring in the context of discovery that limit what we get to know about. . . .

Nevertheless, ignoring the context of justification for the context of discovery is equally problematic. I wish in this essay to explore some of the tensions between descriptivism and normativism (or prescriptivism) in the theory of knowledge, arguing that although many of the most familiar feminist accounts of science have helped us to redescribe the process of knowledge (or belief) acquisition, they stop short of an adequate normative theory. However, these accounts do require a new approach in normative epistemology because of their redescription.

Feminists have been struck by the interlocking character of several aspects of knowledge and power in the sciences. Women have been excluded from the practice of science, even as scientific inquiry gets described both as a masculine activity and as demonstrating women's unsuitability to engage in it, whether because of our allegedly deficient mathematical abilities or our insufficient independence. Some of us notice the location of women in the production of the artifacts made possible by new knowledge: swift and nimble fingers on the microelectronics assembly line. Others notice the neglect of women's distinctive health issues by the biomedical sciences, even as new techniques for preserving the fetuses they carry are introduced into hospital delivery rooms. The sciences become even more suspect as analysis of their metaphors (for example, in cell biology and in microbiology) reveals an acceptance (and hence reinforcement) of the cultural identification of the male with activity and of the female with passivity. Finally, feminists have drawn a connection between the identification of nature as female and the scientific mind as male and the persistent privileging of explanatory models constructed around relations of unidirectional control over models constructed around relations of interdependence. Reflection on this connection has prompted feminist critics to question the very idea of a scientific method capable of adjudicating the truth or probability of theories in a value-neutral way.

Although the sciences have increased human power over natural processes, they have, according to this analysis, done so in a lopsided way, systematically perpetuating women's cognitive and political disempowerment (as well as that of other groups marginalized in relation to the Euro-American drama). One obvious question, then, is whether this appropriation of power is an intrinsic feature of science or whether it is an incidental feature of the sciences as practised in the modern period, a feature deriving from the social structures within which the sciences have developed. A second question is whether it is possible to seek and possess empowering knowledge without expropriating the power of others. Is seeking knowledge inevitably an attempt at domination? And are there criteria of knowledge other than the ability to control the phenomena about which one seeks knowledge? Feminists have answered these questions in a number of ways. I will review some of these before outlining my own answer.

Feminist Epistemological Strategies 1: Changing the Subject

Most traditional philosophy of science (with the problematic exception of Descartes's) has adopted some form of empiricism. Empiricism's silent partner has been a theory of the subject, that is, of the knower.[17] The paradigmatic knower in Western epistemology is an individual—an individual who, in several classic instances, has struggled to free himself from the distortions in understanding and perception that result from attachment. Plato, for example, maintained that knowledge of the good is possible only for those whose reason is capable of controlling their appetites and passions, some of which have their source in bodily needs and pleasures and others of which have their source in our relations with others. The struggle for epistemic autonomy is even starker for Descartes, who suspends belief in all but his own existence in order to recreate a body of knowledge cleansed of faults, impurities, and uncertainties. For Descartes, only those grounds available to a single, unattached, disembodied mind are acceptable principles for the construction of a system of beliefs. Most subsequent epistemology has granted Descartes's conditions and disputed what those grounds are and whether any proposed grounds are sufficient grounds for knowledge. Descartes's creation of the radically and in principle isolated individual as the ideal epistemic agent has for the most part gone unremarked.[18] Locke, for example, adopts the Cartesian identification of the thinking subject with the disembodied soul without even remarking upon the individualism of the conception he inherits and then struggles with the problem of personal identity. Explicitly or implicitly in modern epistemology, whether rationalist or empiricist, the individual consciousness that is the subject of knowledge is transparent to itself, operates according to principles that are independent of embodied experience, and generates knowledge in a value-neutral way.

One set of feminist epistemological strategies, sometimes described as modifications or rejections of empiricism, can also, and perhaps better, be described as changing the subject. I will review three such strategies of replacement, arguing that although they enrich our understanding of how we come to have the beliefs we have and so are more descriptively adequate than the theories they challenge, they fall short of normative adequacy. The strategies identify the problems of contemporary science as resulting from male or masculinist bias. Each strategy understands both the bias and its remedy differently. One holds out the original ideal of uncontaminated or unconditioned subjectivity. A second identifies bias as a function of social location. A third identifies bias in the emotive substructure produced by the psychodynamics of individuation.

Feminist empiricism has by now taken a number of forms. That form discussed and criticized by Sandra Harding is most concerned with those fields of scientific research that have misdescribed or misanalysed women's lives and bodies. . . .

From this perspective, certain areas of science having to do with sex and gender are deformed by gender ideology, but the methods of science are not themselves masculinist and can be used to correct the errors produced by ideology. The ideal knower is still the purified mind, and epistemic or cognitive authority inheres in this purity. This strategy, as Harding has observed, is not effective against those research programmes that feminists find troublesome but that cannot be faulted by reference to the standard methodological precepts of scientific inquiry. I have argued, for example, that a critique of research on the influence of prenatal gonadal hormones on behavioural sex differences that is limited to methodological critique of the data fails to bring out the role of the explanatory model that both generates the research and gives evidential relevance to that data.[19]

Another approach is, therefore, the standpoint approach. There is no one position from which value-free knowledge can be developed, but some positions are better than others.

By valorizing the perspectives uniquely available to those who are socially disadvantaged, standpoint theorists turn the table on traditional epistemology; the ideal epistemic agent is not an unconditioned subject but the subject conditioned by the social experiences of oppression. The powerless are those with epistemic legitimacy, even if they lack the power that could turn that legitimacy into authority. One of the difficulties of the standpoint approach comes into high relief, however, when it is a women's or a feminist standpoint that is in question. Women occupy many social locations in a racially and economically stratified society. If genuine or better knowledge depends on the correct or a more correct standpoint, social theory is needed to ascertain which of these locations is the epistemologically privileged one. But in a standpoint epistemology, a standpoint is needed to justify such a theory. What is that standpoint and how do we identify *it*? If no single standpoint is privileged, then either the standpoint theorist must embrace multiple and incompatible knowledge positions or offer some means of transforming or integrating multiple perspectives into one. Both of these moves require either the abandonment or the supplementation of standpoint as an epistemic criterion.

Standpoint theory faces another problem as well. It is by now commonplace to note that standpoint theory was developed by and for social scientists. It has been difficult to see what its implications for the natural sciences might be. But another strategy has seemed more promising. Most standpoint theorists locate the epistemic advantage in the productive/reproductive experience of the oppressed whose perspective they champion. A different change of subject is proposed by those identifying the problems with science as a function of the psychodynamics of individuation. Evelyn Fox Keller has been asking, among other things, why the scientific community privileges one kind of explanation or theory over others. In particular she has asked why, when both linear reductionist and interactionist perspectives are available, the scientific community has preferred the linear or 'master molecule' theory that understands a natural process as controlled by a single dominant factor. This question was made vivid by her discussion of her own research on slime mould aggregation and the fate of Barbara McClintock's work on genetic transposition.[20]

Keller's original response, spelled out in *Reflections on Gender and Science*, involved an analysis of the traditional ideal of scientific objectivity, which she understood as the ideal of the scientist's detachment from the object of study.[21] . . .

She, therefore, proposed an alternative conceptualization of autonomy, contrasting static autonomy with what she called dynamic autonomy, an ability to move in and out of intimate connection with the world. Dynamic autonomy provides the emotional substructure for an alternative conception of objectivity: dynamic objectivity. The knower characterized by dynamic objectivity, in contrast to the knower characterized by static objectivity, does not seek power over phenomena but acknowledges instead the ways in which knower and phenomena are in relationship as well as the ways in which phenomena themselves are complexly interdependent. . . .

Both standpoint theory and the psychodynamic perspective suggest the inadequacy of an ideal of a pure transparent subjectivity that registers the world as it is in itself (or, for Kantians, as structured by universal conditions of apperception or categories of understanding). I find it most useful to read them as articulating special instances of more general descriptive claims that subjectivity is conditioned by social and historical location and that our cognitive efforts have an ineluctably affective dimension. Classical standpoint theory identifies relation to production/reproduction as the key, but there are multiple, potentially oppositional relations to production/reproduction in a complex society, and there are other kinds of social relation and location that condition subjectivity. For example, one of the structural features of a male-dominant society is asymmetry of sexual access. Men occupy a position of entitlement to women's bodies, whereas women, correspondingly, occupy the position of that to which men are entitled. Complications of the asymmetry arise in class- and race-stratified societies. There may be other structural features as well, such as those related to the institutions of heterosexuality, that condition subjectivity. Because each individual occupies a location in a multidimensional grid marked by numerous interacting structures of power asymmetry, the analytical task is not to determine which is epistemically most adequate. Rather, the task is to understand how these complexly conditioned subjectivities are expressed in action and belief. I would expect that comparable complexity can be introduced into the psychodynamic account.

Treating subjectivity as variably conditioned and cognition as affectively modulated opens both opportunities and problems. The opportunities are the possibilities of understanding phenomena in new ways; by recognizing that mainstream accounts of natural processes have been developed from particular locations and reflect particular affective orientations, we can entertain the possibility that quite different accounts might emerge from other locations with the benefit of different emotional orientations. Although either transferring or diffusing power, the strategies discussed so far have in common a focus on the individual epistemic agent, on the autonomous subject. (The subject in the second and third approaches comes to be in a social context and as a consequence of social interactions, but its knowledge is still a matter of some relation between it and the subject matter.) The standpoint and psychodynamically based theories recommend certain new positions and orientations as superior to others but fail to explain how we are to decide or to justify decisions between what seem to be conflicting claims about the character of some set of natural processes. On what grounds can one social location or affective orientation be judged epistemically superior to another?

Feminist science critics have provided analyses of the context of discovery that enable us to see how social values, including gender ideology in various guises, could be introduced into science. Some theories that have done so go on to recommend an alternate subject position as epistemically superior. But arguments are missing—and it's not clear that any particular subject position could be adequate to generate knowledge. Can a particular subject position be supported by an a priori argument? It can, but only by an argument that claims a particular structure for the world and then identifies a particular subjectivity as uniquely capable of knowing that structure. The problem with such arguments is that they beg the question. The one subject position that could be advanced as epistemically superior to others without presupposing something about the structure of the world is the unconditioned position, the position of no position that provides a view from nowhere. Attractive as this ideal might seem, arguments in the philosophy of science suggest that this is a chimera. Let me turn to them.

Feminist Epistemological Strategies 2: Multiplying Subjects

The ideal of the unconditioned (or universally conditioned) subject is the traditional proposal for escaping the particularity of subjectivity. Granting the truth of the claim that individual subjectivities are conditioned, unconditioned subjectivity is treated as an achievement rather than a natural endowment. The methods of the natural sciences constitute means to that achievement. . . . The difficulty just outlined for the feminist epistemological strategy of changing the subject, however, has a parallel in developments in the philosophy of science. Both dilemmas suggest the individual knower is an inappropriate focus for the purpose of understanding (and changing) science.

In the traditional view, the natural sciences are characterized by a methodology that purifies scientific knowledge of distortions produced by scientists' social and personal allegiances. The essential features of this methodology— explored in great detail by positivist philosophers of science—are observation and logic. Much philosophy of science in the last twenty-five years has been preoccupied with two potential challenges to this picture of scientific methodology—the claim of Kuhn, Feyerabend, and Hanson that observation is theory laden and the claim of Pierre Duhem that theories are underdetermined by data. One claim challenges the stability of observations themselves, the other the stability of evidential relations. Both accounts have seemed (at least to their critics and to some of their proponents) to permit the unrestrained expression of scientists' subjective preferences in the content of science. If observation is theory laden, then observation cannot serve as an independent constraint on theories, thus permitting subjective elements to constrain theory choice. Similarly, if observations acquire evidential relevance only in the context of a set of assumptions, a relevance that changes with a suitable change in assumptions, then it's not clear what protects theory choice from subjective elements hidden in background assumptions. Although empirical adequacy serves as a constraint on theory acceptance, it is not sufficient to pick out one theory from all contenders as the true theory about a domain of the natural world. These analyses of the relation between observation, data, and theory are often thought to constitute arguments against empiricism, but, like the feminist epistemological strategies, they are more effective as arguments against empiricism's silent partner, the theory of the unconditioned subject. The conclusion to be drawn from them is that what has been labelled scientific method does not succeed as a means to the attainment of unconditioned subjectivity on the part of individual knowers. And as long as the scientific knower is conceived of as an individual, knowing best when freed from external influences and attachment (that is, when detached or free from her/his context), the puzzles introduced by the theory-laden nature of observation and the dependence of evidential relations on background assumptions will remain unsolved.

It need not follow from these considerations, however, that scientific knowledge is impossible of attainment. Applying what I take to be a feminist insight—that we are all in relations of interdependence—I have suggested that scientific knowledge is constructed not by individuals applying a method to the material to be known but by individuals in interaction with one another in ways that modify their observations, theories and hypotheses, and patterns of reasoning. Thus scientific method includes more than just the complex of activities that constitutes hypothesis testing through comparison of hypothesis statements with (reports of) experiential data, in principle an activity of individuals. Hypothesis testing itself consists of more than the comparison of statements but involves equally centrally the subjection of putative data, of hypotheses, and of the background assumptions in light of which they seem to be supported by those data to varieties of conceptual and evidential scrutiny and criticism.[22] Conceptual criticism can include investigation into the internal and external consistency of a hypothesis and investigation of the factual, moral, and social implications of background assumptions; evidential criticism includes not only investigation of the quality of the data but of its organization, structuring, and so on. Because background assumptions can be and most frequently are invisible to the members of the scientific community for which they are background and because unreflective acceptance of such assumptions can come to define what it is to be a member of such a community (thus making criticism impossible), effective criticism of background assumptions requires the presence and expression of alternative points of view. This sort of account allows us to see how social values and interests can become enshrined in otherwise acceptable research programmes (i.e., research programmes that strive for empirical adequacy and engage in criticism). As long as representatives of alternative points of view are not included in the community, shared values will not be identified as shaping observation or reasoning.

Scientific knowledge, on this view, is an outcome of the critical dialogue in which individuals and groups holding different points of view engage with each other. It is constructed not by individuals but by an interactive dialogic community. A community's practice of inquiry is productive of knowledge to the extent that it facilitates transformative criticism. The constitution of the scientific community is crucial to this end as are the interrelations among its members. Community level criteria can, therefore, be invoked to discriminate among the products of scientific communities, even though context-independent standards of justification are not attainable. At least four criteria can be identified as necessary to achieve the transformative dimension of critical discourse:

1. There must be publicly recognized forums for the criticism of evidence, of methods, and of assumptions and reasoning.
2. The community must not merely tolerate dissent, but its beliefs and theories must change over time in response to the critical discourse taking place within it.
3. There must be publicly recognized standards by reference to which theories, hypotheses, and observational practices are evaluated and by appeal to which criticism is made relevant to the goals of the inquiring community.

With the possible exception of empirical adequacy, there needn't be (and probably isn't) a set of standards common to all communities. The general family of standards from which those locally adopted might be drawn would include such cognitive virtues as accuracy, coherence, and breadth of scope, and such social virtues as fulfilling technical or material needs or facilitating certain kinds of interactions between a society and its material environment or among the society's members.

4. Finally, communities must be characterized by equality of intellectual authority. What consensus exists must not be the result of the exercise of political or economic power or of the exclusion of dissenting perspectives; it must be the result of critical dialogue in which all relevant perspectives are represented.

Although requiring diversity in the community, this is not a relativist position. True relativism, as I understand it, holds that there are no legitimate constraints on what counts as reasonable to believe apart from the individual's own beliefs. Equality of intellectual authority does not mean that anything goes but that everyone is regarded as equally capable of providing arguments germane to the construction of scientific knowledge. The position outlined here holds that both nature and logic impose constraints. It fails, however, to narrow reasonable belief to a single one among all contenders, in part because it does not constrain belief in a wholly unmediated way. Nevertheless, communities are constrained by the standards operating within them, and individual members of communities are further constrained by the requirement of critical interaction relative to those standards. To say that there may be irreconcilable but coherent and empirically adequate systems for accounting for some portion of the world is not to endorse relativism but to acknowledge that cognitive needs can vary and that this variation generates cognitive diversity.

Dilemmas of Pluralism

This sort of account is subject to the following dilemma.[23] What gets produced as knowledge depends on the consensus reached in the scientific community. For knowledge to count as genuine, the community must be adequately diverse. But the development of a theoretical idea or hypothesis into something elaborate enough to be called knowledge requires a consensus. The questions must stop somewhere, at some point, so that a given theory can be developed sufficiently to be applied to concrete problems. How is scientific knowledge possible while pursuing socially constituted objectivity? That is, if objectivity requires pluralism in the community, then scientific knowledge becomes elusive, but if consensus is pursued, it will be at the cost of quieting critical oppositional positions.

My strategy for avoiding this dilemma is to detach scientific knowledge from consensus, if consensus means agreement of the entire scientific community regarding the truth or acceptability of a given theory. This strategy also means detaching knowledge from an ideal of absolute and unitary truth. I suggest that we look at the aims of inquiry (at least some) as satisfied by embracing multiple and, in some cases, incompatible theories that satisfy local standards. This detachment of knowledge from universal consensus and absolute truth can be made more palatable than it might first appear by two moves. One of these is implicit in treating science as a practice or set of practices; the other involves taking up some version of a semantic or model-theoretic theory of theories.

Beginning with the second of these, let me sketch what I take to be the relevant aspects of implications of the semantic view.[24] This view is proposed as an alternative to the view of theories as sets of propositions (whether axiomatized or not). If we take the semantic view, we understand a theory as a specification of a set of relations among objects or processes characterized in a fairly abstract way. Another characterization would be that on the semantic view, a theory is the specification of a structure. The structure as specified is neither true nor false; it is just a structure. The theoretical claim is that the structure is realized in some actual system. As Mary Hesse has shown, models are proposed as models of some real world system on the basis of an analogy between the model and the system, that is, the supposition that the model and the system share some significant features in common.[25] Models often have their start as metaphors. Examples of such metaphoric models are typical philosophers' examples like the billiard ball model of particle interactions or the solar system model of the atom. What many feminists have pointed out (or can be understood as having pointed out) is the use of elements of gender ideology and social relations as metaphors for natural processes and relations. Varieties of heterosexual marriage have served as the metaphoric basis for models of the relation between nucleus and cytoplasm in the cell, for example.[26] The master molecule approach to gene action, characterized by unidirectional control exerted on organismal processes by the gene, reflects relations of authority in the patriarchal household. Evelyn Fox Keller has recently been investigating the basis of models in molecular biology in androcentric metaphors of sexuality and procreation.[27] When Donna Haraway says that during and after the Second World War the organism changed from a factory to a cybernetic system, she can be understood as saying that the metaphor generating models of orgasmic structure and function shifted from a productive system organized by a hierarchical division of labour to a system for generating and processing information.[28] Alternatively put, cells, gene action, and organisms have been modelled as marriage, families, and factories and cybernetic networks, respectively. Supporting such analysis of particular theories or models requires not merely noticing the analogies of structure but also tracing the seepage of language and meaning from one domain to another as well as studying the uses to which the models are put.

The adequacy of a theory conceived as a model is determined by our being able to map some subset of the relations/structures posited in the model onto some portion of the experienced world. (Now the portions of the world stand in many relations to many other portions.) Any given model or schema will necessarily select among those relations. So its adequacy is not just a function of isomorphism of one of the interpretations of the theory with a portion of the world but of the fact that the relations it picks out are ones in which we are interested. A model guides our interactions with the interventions in the world. We want models that guide the interactions and interventions we seek. Given that different subcommunities within the larger scientific community may be interested in different relations or that they may be interested in objects under different descriptions, different models (that if taken as claims about an underlying reality would be incompatible) may well be equally adequate and provide knowledge, in the sense of an ability to direct our interactions and interventions, even in the absence of a general consensus as to what's important. Knowledge is not detached from knowers in a set of propositions but consists in our ability to understand the structural features of a model and to apply it to some particular portion of the world; it is knowledge of that portion of the world through its structuring by the model we use. The notion of theories as sets of propositions requires that we view the adequacy of a theory as a matter of correspondence of the objects, processes, and relations described in the propositions of the theory with the objects, processes, and relations in the domain of the natural world that the theory purports to explain; that is, it requires that adequacy be conceptualized as truth. The model-theoretic approach allows us to evaluate theories in relation to our aims as well as in relation to the model's isomorphism with elements of the modelled domain and permits the adequacy of different and incompatible models serving different and incompatible aims. Knowledge is not contemplative but active.

The second move to escape the dilemma develops some consequences of treating science as practice. There are two worth mentioning. If we understand science as practice, then we understand inquiry as ongoing, that is, we give up the idea that there is a terminus of inquiry that just is the set of truths about the world. . . . Scientific knowledge from this perspective is not the static end point of inquiry but a cognitive or intellectual expression of an ongoing interaction with our natural and social environments. Indeed, when we attempt to identify the goals of inquiry that organize scientific cognitive practices, it becomes clear that there are several, not all of which can be simultaneously pursued.[29] Scientific knowledge, then, is a body of diverse theories and their articulations onto the world that changes over time in response to the changing cognitive needs of those who develop and use the theories, in response to the new questions and anomalous empirical data revealed by applying theories, and in response to changes in associated theories. Both linear-reductionist and interactionist models reveal aspects of natural processes, some common to both and some uniquely describable with the terms proper to one but not both sorts of model. If we recognize the partiality of theories, as we can when we treat them as models, we can recognize pluralism in the community as one of the conditions for the continued development of scientific knowledge in this sense.

In particular, the models developed by feminists and others dissatisfied with the valuative and affective dimensions of models in use must at the very least (given that they meet the test of empirical adequacy) be recognized as both revealing the partiality of those models in use and as revealing some aspects of natural phenomena and processes that the latter conceal. These alternative models may have a variety of forms and a variety of motivations, and they need not repudiate the aim of control. We engage in scientific inquiry to direct our interactions with the interventions in the world. . . . If we aim for effective action in the natural world, something is to be controlled. The issue should be not whether but what and how. Rather than repudiate it, we can set the aim of control within the larger context of overall purposes and develop a more refined sense of the varieties of control made possible through scientific inquiry.

A second consequence for feminist and other oppositional scientists of adopting both the social knowledge thesis and a model-theoretic analysis of theories is that the constructive task does not consist in finding the one best or correct feminist model. Rather, the many models that can be generated from the different subject positions ought to be articulated and elaborated. Very few will be exclusively feminist if that means exclusively gender-based or developed only by feminists. Some will be more appropriate for some domains, others for others, and some for none. We can't know this unless models get sufficiently elaborated to be used as guides for interactions. Thus, this joint perspective implies the advocacy of subcommunities characterized by local standard. To the extent that they address a common domain and to the extent that they share some standards in common, these subcommunities must be in critical dialogue with each other as well as with those subcommunities identified with more mainstream science. The point of dialogue from this point of view is not to produce a general and universal consensus but to make possible the refinement, correction, rejection, and sharing of models. Alliances, mergers, and revisions of standards as well as of models are all possible consequences of this dialogic interaction.

Conclusions

Understanding scientific knowledge in this way supports at least two further reflections on knowledge and power. First of all, the need for models within which we can situate ourselves and the interactions we desire with the natural world will militate against the inclusiveness required for an adequate critical practice, if only because the elaboration of any model requires a substantial commitment of material and intellectual resources on the part of a community.[30] This means that, in a power-stratified society, the inclusion of the less powerful and hence of models that could serve as a resource for criticism of the received wisdom in the community of science will always be a matter of conflict. At the same time, the demand for inclusiveness should not be taken to mean that every alternative view is equally deserving of attention. Discussion must be conducted in reference to public standards, standards which, as noted above, do not provide timeless criteria, but which change in response to changes in cognitive and social needs. Nevertheless, by appeal to standards adopted and legitimated through processes of public scrutiny and criticism, it is possible to set aside as irrelevant positions such as New Age 'crystalology' or creationism. To the extent that these satisfy none of the central standards operative in the scientific communities of their cultures, they indeed qualify as crackpot. Programmes for low-tech science appropriate to settings and problems in developing nations may, by contrast, be equally irritating to or against the grain of some of the institutionalized aspects of science in the industrialized nations, but as long as they do satisfy some of the central standards of those communities, then the perspectives they embody must be included in the critical knowledge-constructive dialogue. Although there is always a danger that the politically marginal will be conflated with the crackpot, one function of public and common standards is to remind us of that distinction and to help us draw it in particular cases. I do not know of any simple or formulaic solution to this problem.

Second, . . . the structures of cognitive authority themselves must change. No segment of the community, whether powerful or powerless, can claim epistemic privilege. If we can see our way to the dissolution of those structures, then we need not understand the appropriation of power in the form of cognitive authority as intrinsic to science. Nevertheless, the creation of cognitive democracy, of democratic science, is as much a matter of conflict and hope as is the creation of political democracy.

Discussion Questions

1. Can you think of any examples in your science education in which males are identified as active and females as passive?
2. The stoic approach and a popular conception of "pure knowledge" is of one who is completely detached and void of all emotion and passions as relates to what is known. Do you agree with this? In what ways do your passions/intuitions help or hinder your ability to attain knowledge?
3. Linguist Alfred Korzybski coined the term, "The map is not the territory." Longino writes of maps and models. In what way is science a map of the territory? If it is only one map, what others could there be? In what ways might males make maps differently than females? Do you think this difference is innate or a result of social factors?
4. In Popper's book (excerpted in this anthology) he recounts asking a group of physics graduate students to take a pencil and paper and observe. They responded, "Observe what?" He uses this to allude to the theory-laden nature of science. In what ways does this embody what Longino discusses here?

Movie Titles

1. *What the Bleep Do We Know?*—How do recent findings in physics affect your view of God and spirituality? Does knowing more about your world add to or subtract from its wonder?

2. *Inherit the Wind*—A film about the 1925 "Scopes Monkey Trial" involving creationism/evolution in schools. If creationism is not a science, should it be taught in a science course? Should it be taught in another course? What does it mean for evolution to be "only a theory"? Is teaching creationism (God-created universe) in a public school a violation of church and state?

3. *Mindwalk*—Basically, a conversation between a physicist, a politician, and a poet/philosopher. They apply a lot of scientific theory to their views of reality.

4. *A Brief History of Time*—Based on the ideas of one of the most influential contemporary physicists, Steven Hawking. Mostly topical instead of a movie with a plot.

Song Lyrics

System of a Down—"Science"
The Aquabats—"The Cat With Two Heads"
Zager and Evans—"In the Year 2525"

Notes

1. Professor Salvia is a descendant of Salviati, the protagonist in Galileo's dialogues. The name was shortened when the family immigrated to America.

2. Dr. Sagro is married to a descendant of Sagredo, another character in Galileo's dialogues.

3. She is a direct descendant of Philo, the protagonist in Hume's "Dialogues Concerning Natural Religion."

4. All of the attempts to deal with Hume's problem which are treated in this section are discussed in detail in Wesley C. Salmon, *The Foundations of Scientific Inference* (Pittsburgh; University of Pittsburgh Press, 1967); this book will be cited hereafter as *Foundations*.

5. This is an inductive justification; see *Foundations,* chapter II, section I.

6. For discussion of justification by means of synthetic a priori principles, see *Foundations,* chapter II, section 4.

7. This is a slight oversimplification, for about half of the Einstein effect may be derived from the classical theory, provided we assume a ballistic theory of light.

8. 'Clinical observations,' like all other observations, are *interpretations in the light of theories* (see below, sections iv ff.); and for this reason alone they are apt to seem to support those theories in the light of which they were interpreted. But real support can be obtained only from observation undertaken as tests (by 'attempted refutations'); and for this purpose *criteria of refutation* have to be laid down beforehand: It must be agreed which observable situations, if actually observed, mean that the theory is refuted. But what kind of clinical responses would refute to the satisfaction of the analyst not merely a particular analytic diagnosis but psycho-analysis itself? And have such criteria ever been discussed or agreed upon by analysts? Is there not, on the contrary, a whole family of analytic concepts, such as 'ambivalence' (I do not suggest that there is no such thing as ambivalence), which would make it difficult, if not impossible, to agree upon such criteria? Moreover, how much headway has been made in investigating the question of the extent to which the (conscious or unconscious) expectations and theories held

by the analyst influence the 'clinical responses' of the patient? (To say nothing about the conscious attempts to influence the patient by proposing interpretations to him, etc.) Years ago I introduced the term 'Oedipus effect' to describe the influence of a theory or expectation or prediction *upon the event which it predicts* or describes: It will be remembered that the causal chain leading to Oedipus' parricide was started by the oracle's prediction of this event. This is a characteristic and recurrent theme of such myths, but one which seems to have failed to attract the interest of the analysts, perhaps not accidentally. (The problem of confirmatory dreams suggested by the analyst is discussed by Freud, for example in *Gesammelte Schriften*, III, 1925, where he says on p. 314: 'If anybody asserts that most of the dreams which can be utilized in an analysis . . . owe their origin to [the analyst's] suggestion, then no objection can be made from the point of view of analytic theory. Yet there is nothing in this fact,' he surprisingly adds, 'which would detract from the reliability of our results.')

9. The case of astrology, nowadays a typical pseudo-science, may illustrate this point. It was attacked, by Aristotelians and other rationalists, down to Newton's day, for the wrong reason—for its now accepted assertion that the planets had an 'influence' upon terrestrial ('sublunar') events. In fact Newton's theory of gravity, and especially the lunar theory of the tides, was historically speaking an offspring of astrological lore. Newton, it seems, was most reluctant to adopt a theory which came from the same stable as for example the theory that 'influenza' epidemics are due to an astral 'influence.' And Galileo, no doubt for the same reason, actually rejected the lunar theory of the tides; and his misgivings about Kepler may easily be explained by his misgivings about astrology.

10. Hume does not say 'logical' but 'demonstrative,' a terminology which, I think, is a little misleading. The following two quotations are from the *Treatise of Human Nature*, Book I, Part III, sections vi and xii. (The italics are all Hume's.)

11. This and the next quotation are from *loc. cit.*, section vi. See also Hume's *Enquiry Concerning Human Understanding*, section iv, Part II, and his *Abstract*, edited 1938 by J. M. Keynes and P. Sraffa, p. 15, and quoted in *L.Sc.D.*, new appendix *vii, text to note 6.

12. See section 30 of *L.Sc.D.*

13. Katz, *loc. cit.*

14. Further comments on these developments may be found in chs. 4 and 5, below.

15. Max Born, *Natural Philosophy of Cause and Chance*, Oxford, 1949, p. 7.

16. However, astrology would doubtlessly have many fewer supporters if horoscopes tended less toward compliments and pleasant predictions and more toward the kind of analysis included in the following satirical horoscope from the December, 1977, issue of *Mother Jones*: VIRGO (Aug. 23–Sept. 22). You are the logical type and hate disorder. This nitpicking is sickening to your friends. You are cold and unemotional and sometimes fall asleep while making love. Virgos make good bus drivers.

17. Empiricist philosophers have found themselves in great difficulty when confronting the necessity to make their theory of the knower explicit, a difficulty most eloquently expressed in David Hume's Appendix to *A Treatise of Human Nature*, ed. L. A. Selby-Bigge (Oxford: Clarendon Press, 1960).

18. The later philosophy of Wittgenstein does challenge the individualist ideal. Until recently few commentators have developed the anti-individualist implications of his work. See Naomi Scheman, 'Individualism and the Objects of Psychology,' in Sandra Harding and Merrill Hintikka (eds.), *Discovering Reality* (Boston: Reidel, 1983), 225–244.

19. Cf. Longino, 'Can There Be A Feminist Science?' in *Hypatia* 2/3 (Autumn 1987); and ch. 7 of Longino, *Science as Social Knowledge* (Princeton: Princeton University Press, 1990).

20. Cf. Evelyn F. Keller, 'The Force of the Pacemaker Concept in Theories of Slime Mold Aggregation,' in *Perspectives in Biology and Medicine*, 26 (1983), 515–521; and *A Feeling for the Organism* (San Francisco: W. H. Freeman, 1983).

21. Evelyn F. Keller, *Reflections on Gender and Science* (New Haven: Yale University Press, 1984).

22. For argument for and exposition of these points, see Longino, *Science as Social Knowledge*, esp. ch. 4.

23. Thanks to Sandra Mitchell for this formulation.

24. My understanding of the semantic view is shaped by its presentations in Bas van Fraassen, *The Scientific Image* (New York: Oxford University Press, 1980); and Ronald Giere, *Explaining Science* (Chicago: University of Chicago Press, 1988).

25. Mary Hesse, *Models and Anglogies in Science* (Notre Dame, Ind.: Notre Dame University Press, 1966).

26. The Gender and Biology Study Group, 'The Importance of Feminist Critique for Contemporary Cell Biology,' in *Hypatia*, 3/1 (1988).

27. Evelyn Fox Keller, 'Making Gender Visible in the Pursuit of Nature's Secrets,' in Teresa de Lauretis (ed.), *Feminist Studies/Critical Studies* (Bloomington: Indiana University Press, 1986), 67–77; and 'Gender and Science,' in *The Great Ideas Today* (Chicago: Encyclopedia Britannica, 1990).

28. Donna Haraway, 'The Biological Enterprise: Sex, Mind, and Profit from Human Engineering to Sociobiology,' in *Radical History Review*, 20 (1979): 206–237.

29. This point is developed further in *Science as Social Knowledge*, ch. 2.

30. For a somewhat different approach to a similar question, see Philip Kitcher, 'The Division of Cognitive Labour,' in *Journal of Philosophy*, 87/1 (Jan. 1990), 5–23.

Chapter 4

God and Creation

God—whether considered a supernatural being, a spiritual force, a metaphor, or as love—shapes much of our culture, politics, morality, and values that we may assign throughout life. Because of the vast influence that the topic of God has in so many areas, philosophers throughout history have spent a considerable amount of time focused on the philosophy of religion. A number of important issues arise, many of which will be covered in subsequent chapters:

Did God create everything? Can we demonstrate that through science?
If God is all-good and all-powerful, how can He allow for evil and suffering?
What is the role of faith in our investigation of God and other claims?
How do other cultures—namely Eastern paradigms—treat God and spirituality?

Beliefs relating to God's existence are typically categorized as follows:

Deism—God exists though does not interact with the world and thus is not a being with whom one has a relationship; He can be known through reason and not divine revelation and thus there is no need for holy books or organized religion.

Theism—God exists and is immanent (can and does affect the world) and can be known through divine revelation and holy books. Polytheism holds that many of these gods exist, while monotheism holds that only one god exists.

Atheism—God does not exist.

Agnosticism—One cannot know if God exists—either it is impossible to ever know or, while it may be possible to know at some point, it currently is not.

In this chapter, the first two selections provide two of the most well-known *a priori* proofs for God's existence. They are *a priori* (Latin for "without experience") because they do not rely on either experience or going out and testing the environment, but instead rely on reasoning. Aquinas defends five different demonstrations of God's existence, which he also believes show God's qualities. Anselm's *a priori* reasoning is based on the notion of perfection—his article contains a challenge from a monk named Gaunilo. The selection that follows examines the agnostic position and whether the existence of God can be known, and Ramakrishna's piece looks at the monotheistic position and whether this notion of one true religion is true itself.

In the second part of this chapter, we focus on a different sort of proof sometimes offered by theists: the *teleological*—goal-based—proof of God's existence. The most oft-cited analogy is given by William Paley. He imagines that, upon finding a watch (a goal-based system itself), we could imagine that it came together as a matter of chance, but it is much more likely that it was designed. This idea has been extrapolated to the universe and held that because of the order found in nature, this supports the existence of an intelligent designer. Harris and Calvert hold this position but have much to add to it since the writing of Paley's article—they provide some of the motivation for changing the theory of *creationism* to *intelligent design science* in order that it become more accepted in today's science-dominated paradigm. Hume, though, expresses philosophical concern with the design argument, and Dawkins provides both scientific and philosophical arguments to counter the intelligent design argument. In Kitcher's piece, he takes more of a philosophical approach in which it will be important to recall much of the discussion from the chapter here on science.

This topic has particular relevance given the ongoing court battles as to whether creationism can be taught in public schools. Some argue that creationism (and "intelligent design science") is religion disguised as science and thus should not be taught in a science course. Though others argue that it is science and that evolutionary theory is "just a theory" and not fully substantiated.

Five Proofs of God's Existence

Thomas Aquinas

Thomas Aquinas is one of thirty-three "Doctors of the Catholic Church" and considered by most as the greatest theologian of the Catholic Church. Educated at the University of Naples, Aquinas studied logic and natural science along with the standard Catholic doctrine. For a theologian, he wrote quite a bit in philosophy, as can be seen in the titles of a few of his other works: *On Being and Essence* and *The Principles of Nature*. When he wrote the *Summa Theologica*, from which this selection is taken, he considered it a manual of Christian doctrine. Aside from his five proofs of God's existence, this work also includes other important ideas for the Church, such as Just War Theory and ideas on ethics, as well as the afterlife.

Following his death in 1274, he was canonized by Pope John XX11 in 1323. Over fifteen colleges and universities throughout the world are named after him, as well as a number of secondary schools.

Reading Questions

1. How does the potential of wood to become hot and its relation to fire relate to Aquinas' argument of motion?
2. What is meant by the term "efficient cause"? Why can't something be the efficient cause of itself?
3. How does the gradation of hotter things in relation to fire relate to the gradation of good and God?
4. Briefly explain, in your own words, each of Aquinas's proofs.
5. Explain how the following qualities of God are ascribed by Aquinas along with each proof:
   a. eternal
   b. creator
   c. sustains the universe
   d. all-good/perfect
   e. all-knowing/directs the course of nature

. . . The existence of God can be proved in five ways.

The first and more manifest way is the argument from motion. It is certain, and evident to our senses, that in the world some things are in motion. Now whatever is moved is moved by another, for nothing can be moved except it is in potentiality to that towards which it is moved; whereas a thing moves inasmuch as it is in the act. For motion is nothing else than the reduction of something

Source: Excerpt from *The Basic Writings of St. Thomas Aquinas*, Vol. 1, edited by Anton C. Pegis, 1945, 1997 by Hackett Publishing Company, pp. 20–24. Reprinted by permission of Hackett Publishing Company, Inc.

from potentiality to actuality. But nothing can be reduced from potentiality to actuality, except by something in a state of actuality. Thus that which is actually hot, as fire, makes wood, which is potentially hot, to be actually hot, and thereby moves and changes it. Now it is not possible that the same thing should be at once in actuality and potentiality in the same respect, but only in different respects. For what is actually hot cannot simultaneously be potentially hot; but it is simultaneously potentially cold. It is therefore impossible that in the same respect and in the same way a thing should be both mover and moved, i.e., that it should move itself. Therefore, whatever is moved must be moved by another. If that by which it is moved be itself moved, then this also must be moved by another, and that by another again. But this cannot go on to infinity because then there would be no first mover, and, consequently, no other mover, seeing that subsequent movers move only inasmuch as they are moved by the first mover; as the staff moves only because it is moved by the hand. Therefore it is necessary to arrive at a first mover, moved by no other; and this everyone understands to be God.

The second way is from the nature of efficient cause. In the world of sensible things we find there is an order of efficient causes. There is no case known (neither is it, indeed, possible) in which a thing is found to be the efficient cause of itself; for so it would be prior to itself, which is impossible. Now in efficient causes it is not possible to go on to infinity, because in all efficient causes following in order, the first is the cause of the intermediate cause, and the intermediate is the cause of the ultimate cause, whether the intermediate cause be several, or one only. Now to take away the cause is to take away the effect. Therefore, if there be no first cause among efficient causes, there will be no ultimate, nor any intermediate, cause. But if in efficient causes it is possible to go on to infinity, there will be no first efficient cause, neither will there be an ultimate effect, nor any intermediate efficient causes; all of which is plainly false. Therefore it is necessary to admit a first efficient cause, to which everyone gives the name of God.

The third way is taken from possibility and necessity, and runs thus. We find in nature things that are possible to be and not to be, since they are found to be generated, and to be corrupted, and consequently, it is possible for them to be and not to be. But it is impossible for these always to exist, for that which cannot-be at some time is not. Therefore, if everything cannot-be, then at one time there was nothing in existence. Now if this were true, even now there would be nothing in existence, because that which does not exist begins to exist only through something already existing. Therefore, if at one time nothing was in existence, it would have been impossible for anything to have begun to exist; and thus even now nothing would be in existence—which is absurd. Therefore, not all beings are merely possible but there must exist something the existence of which is necessary. But every necessary thing either has its necessity caused by another, or not. Now it is impossible to go on to infinity in necessary things which have their necessity caused by another, as has been already proved in regard to efficient causes. Therefore we cannot but admit the existence of some being having of itself its own necessity, and not receiving it from another, but rather causing in others their necessity. This all men speak of as God.

The fourth way is taken from the gradation to be found in things. Among beings there are some more and some less good, true, noble, and the like. But *more* and *less* are predicated of different things according as they resemble in their different ways something which is the maximum, as a thing is said to be hotter according as it more nearly resembles that which is hottest; so that there is something which is truest, something best, something noblest, and, consequently, something which is most being, for those things that are greatest in truth are greatest in being, as it is written in [Aristotle's] *Metaphysics* ii. Now the maximum in any genus is the cause of all in that genus, as fire, which is the maximum of heat, is the cause of all hot things, as is said in the same book. Therefore there must also be something which is to all beings the cause of their being, goodness, and every other perfection; and this we call God.

The fifth way is taken from the governance of the world. We see that things which lack knowledge, such as natural bodies, act for an end, and this is evident from their acting always, or nearly always, in the same way, so as to obtain the best result. Hence it is plain that they achieve their end, not fortuitously, but designedly. Now whatever lacks knowledge cannot move towards an end, unless it be directed by some being endowed with knowledge and intelligence; as the arrow is directed by the archer. Therefore some intelligent being exists by whom all natural things are directed to their end: and this being we call God. . . .

Discussion Questions

1. Are you satisfied with Aquinas' reason why there cannot be an infinite series of movers? Do you agree with him?
2. Do you agree with Aquinas' point that if everything has the capacity to not exist (i.e., is finite), then at one time there was nothing in existence (proof number three)?
3. Regarding Aquinas' fourth "way," if there are bad things in existence, then there must be an "ultimate bad." What would he likely say about this?
4. What is an example of something that lacks knowledge (e.g., a watch) yet *acts* for an end/goal (see his fifth proof)? Is this its *true* goal/purpose, or might there be others? Do you think "acts" is the right word?
5. Aquinas concludes each of his five proofs with prose that resembles something like: *This thing whose existence I have proven is a thing we call God.* Could we call it something else? Could it *be* something else he has proven to exist in these particular arguments? Could he have proven *multiple* Gods?
6. In St. Augustine's autobiography, he cites an answer he once heard in response to the question "What was God doing before He created the Universe?": Before He created Heaven and Earth, God created hell to be used for people such as you who ask this kind of question. What do you think of this response? *Are* there any such questions that simply are not worth asking?

The Ontological Argument
Anselm of Canterbury

St. Anselm was a monk who went on to serve as the Archbishop of Canterbury—the head of the church in England—from 1093 until he died in 1109. He placed a great deal of importance on the use of reason in an attempt to shed light on God and God's existence.

   In this selection, he puts forth the "ontological argument" for God's existence—"ontological" meaning "the study of what exists." He does so in a way that relies on reason alone, and also attempts to prove God's superior nature. Included in this reading is a response from a contemporary of Anselm's—Gaunilo—and Anselm's reply.

Reading Questions

1. Anselm's argument relies heavily on his definition of God. How does he define God?
2. Why does Anselm argue that God *must* exist?
3. How does Gaunilo argue against Anselm's argument? How, then, does Anselm defend his argument against Gaunilo?
4. Different people have different conceptions of what a "greatest possible being" would be. Does this matter for Anselm's argument? Why/why not?

Chapter II. That God Truly Is

O Lord, you who give understanding to faith, so far as you know it to be beneficial, give me to understand that you are just as we believe, and that you are what we believe.

   We certainly believe that you are something than which nothing greater can be conceived.

   But is there any such nature, since "the fool has said in his heart: God is not"?

   However, when this very same fool hears what I say, when he hears of "something than which nothing greater can be conceived," he certainly understands what he hears.

   What he understands stands in relation to his understanding (*esse in intellectu*), even if he does not understand that it exists. For it is one thing for a thing to stand in relation to our understanding; it is another thing for us to understand that it really exists. For instance, when a painter imagines what he is about to paint, he has it in relation to his understanding. However, he does not yet understand that it exists, because he has not yet made it. After he paints it, then he both has it in relation to his understanding and understands that it exists. Therefore, even the fool is convinced that "something than which nothing greater

Source: Reprinted with the permission of Scribner, an imprint of Simon & Schuster Adult Publishing Group, from *The Many-Faced Argument* edited by John H. Hick and Arthur C. McGill. Copyright © 1967 by John H. Hick and Arthur C. McGill; copyright renewed 1997 by John H. Hick and Arthur C. McGill. All rights reserved.

can be conceived" at least stands in relation to his understanding, because when he hears of it he understands it, and whatever he understands stands in relation to his understanding.

And certainly that than which a greater cannot be conceived cannot stand only in relation to the understanding. For if it stands at least in relation to the understanding, it can be conceived to be also in reality, and this is something greater. Therefore, if "that than which a greater cannot be conceived" only stood in relation to the understanding, then "that than which a greater cannot be conceived" would be something than which a greater can be conceived. But this is certainly impossible.

Therefore, something than which a greater cannot be conceived undoubtedly both stands in relation to the understanding and exists in reality.

Chapter III. That It Is Impossible to Conceive That God Is Not

This so truly is that it is impossible to think of it as not existing.

It can be conceived to be something such that we cannot conceive of it as not existing.

This is greater than something which we can conceive of as not existing.

Therefore, if that than which a greater cannot be conceived could be conceived not to be, we would have an impossible contradiction: That than which a greater cannot be conceived would not be that than which a greater cannot be conceived.

Therefore, something than which a greater cannot be conceived so truly is, that it is impossible even to conceive of it as not existing.

This is you, O Lord our God. You so truly are that you cannot be thought not to be. And rightly so.

For if some mind could conceive of something better than you, the creature would rise above its Creator and would judge its Creator, which would be completely absurd.

Also, whatever else there is, except for you alone, can be conceived not to be.

Therefore, you alone, of all things exist in the truest and greatest way (*verissime et maxime esse*), for nothing else so truly exists and therefore everything else has less being.

Why, then, did the fool say in his heart: "God is not," since it is so obvious to the rational mind that you exist supremely above all things? Why, because he is stupid and foolish.

Chapter IV. How the Fool Said in His Heart What Cannot Be Conceived

How was the fool able to "say in his heart" what he was unable to conceive? Or how was it that he could not conceive what he said in his heart? For to "say in one's heart" and to "conceive" are the same thing.

However, if—or rather because—he really did conceive of it (since he said it in his heart) and yet did not really say it in his heart (since he was unable to conceive of it), then there must be more than one way for something to be said in one's heart, or to be conceived.

Indeed, a thing is conceived of in one way when the word signifying it is thought; in another way when the very thing itself is understood.

Accordingly, God can be conceived not to be in the first way, but not at all in the second. Certainly no one who understands what God is can conceive that God is not. It is possible, however, for him to say this word in his heart, while giving it either no meaning at all or some alien meaning.

God is that than which a greater cannot be conceived. Whoever understands this correctly at least understands that he exists in such a way that even for thought he cannot not exist. Therefore, whoever understands that God is so cannot even conceive that he is not.

My thanksgiving to you, good Lord, my thanksgiving to you. For what I first believed through your giving I now so understand through your illumination that even if I did not want to believe that you are, I would be unable not to understand it.

Gaunilo

Consider this example: Certain people say that somewhere in the ocean there is an island, which they call the "Lost Island" because of the difficulty or, rather, the impossibility of finding what does not exist. They say that it is more abundantly filled with inestimable riches and delights than the Isles of the Blessed, and that although it has no owner or inhabitant, it excels all the lands that men inhabit taken together in the unceasing abundance of its fertility.

When someone tells me that there is such an island, I easily understand what is being said, for there is nothing difficult here. Suppose, however, as a consequence of this, that he then goes on to say: You cannot doubt that this island, more excellent than all lands, actually exists somewhere in reality, because it undoubtedly stands in relation to your understanding. Since it is more excellent, not simply to stand in relation to the understanding, but to be in reality as well, therefore this island must necessarily be in reality. Otherwise, any other land that exists in reality would be more excellent than this island, and this island, which you understand to be the most excellent of all lands would than not be the most excellent.

If, I repeat, someone should wish by this argument to demonstrate to me that this island truly exists and is no longer to be doubted, I would think he were joking; or, if I accepted the argument, I do not know whom I would regard as the greater fool, me for accepting it or him for supposing that he had proved the existence of this island with any kind of certainty. He should first show that this excellent island exists as a genuine and undeniable real thing, and not leave it standing in relation to my understanding as a false or uncertain something.

Anselm

My reasoning, you claim, is as if something should say that there is an island in the ocean, which surpasses the whole earth in its fertility, but which is called a "Lost Island" because of the difficulty, or even impossibility, of finding something that does not exist; and as if he should then argue that no one can doubt that it actually does exist because the words describing it are easily understood.

I can confidently say that if anyone discovers for me something existing either in fact or at least in thought, other than "that than which a greater cannot be conceived," and is able to apply the logic of my argument to it, I shall find that "Lost Island" for him and shall give it to him as something which he will never lose again.

Gaunilo

When it is asserted to the fool [in *Proslogion III*] that this "greater than all things" is such that even to thought it cannot not be, and yet when this is proved to him on no other ground than that otherwise this "greater than all things" would not be greater than all things, he can give the same answer and reply: When did *I* ever say that such a being, one that is "greater than all things," exists in reality, so that from this you could prove to me that it exists so fully in reality that it cannot be conceived not to be? First of all, it should be proved by some most certain argument that some superior reality, that is, a nature which is greater and better than everything that is, actually exists. From this we can then prove all the other qualities which must not be lacking from that which is greater and better than all things.

Anselm

That which cannot possibly not be is obviously something that can be conceived and understood. He who conceives of this conceives of something greater than he who conceives of that which has the possibility of not being. Therefore, while he is conceiving of "that than which a greater cannot be conceived," if he conceives that it has the possibility of not being, he is obviously not conceiving of "that than which a greater cannot be conceived." However, the same thing cannot be both conceived and not conceived at the same time. Therefore, he who conceives of "that than which a greater cannot be conceived" is not conceiving of what can, but of what cannot possibly, not be. For that reason, what he is conceiving must necessarily exist, because whatever is able not to exist is not that of which he is conceiving.

Discussion Questions

1. Do you accept Anselm's definition of God? Even if you are an atheist (a "fool" in Anselm's terms) can you still agree with a definition of God? Must you define God in order to believe/disbelieve in Him?

2. Anselm believes he has given a deductively valid proof of God's existence. Do you agree? If not, where has he gone awry?
3. Do you think God's existence can be proved in any way? If so, how? If not, why not? And if not, how could one think that He exists?

Theology and Falsification
Antony Flew, R. M. Hare, Basil Mitchell

This selection is taken from a symposium in the 1950s from talks given by three prominent professors at British universities. Flew has written over thirty books—most on the philosophy of religion—and is considered by many to be the world's foremost philosophical atheist—a position he held nearly all of his life (born in 1923) until 2004 when he renounced his atheism (though he also refrained from embracing many of the tenets held by popular religions). The other two take the theist position: Hare was the White's Professor of Moral Philosophy at the University of Oxford from 1966 to 1983, and Mitchell taught primarily at Kelbe College in Oxford (1947–1967) while giving lectures at numerous other universities, including Cambridge (1959–1962) and Princeton (1959–1962).

In this selection, the philosophers examine not so much whether God exists, but whether the statement "God exists" has any meaning.

Reading Questions
1. What is the lesson of Wisdom's parable, *Gods*? How does this relate to Flew's point about God's love for us?
2. What point does Hare make in his parable of the *bliks*?
3. What point does Mitchell make in his parable of the Stranger? What position must the Christian take according to Mitchell regarding this type of issue as it relates to God?
4. What relevant *dis*analogies does Flew note regarding Mitchell's Stranger?
5. What two problems does Flew note regarding Hare's *bliks*?
6. What is *doublethink*? Why does Flew mention it in his conclusion?

Antony Flew

Let us begin with a parable. It is a parable developed from a tale told by John Wisdom in his haunting and revelatory article 'Gods.' Once upon a time two explorers came upon a clearing in the jungle. In the clearing were growing many

Source: Reprinted with the permission of Scribner, an imprint of Simon & Schuster Adult Publishing Group, from *New Essays in Philosophical Theology* edited by Antony Flew and Alasdair MacIntyre. Copyright © 1955 by Antony Flew and Alasdair MacIntyre; copyright renewed © 1983. All rights reserved.

flowers and many weeds. One explorer says, 'Some gardener must tend this plot.' The other disagrees, 'There is no gardener.' So they pitch their tents and set a watch. No gardener is ever seen.'But perhaps he is an invisible gardener.' So they set up a barbed-wire fence. They electrify it. They patrol with bloodhounds. (For they remember how H. G. Wells's *The Invisible Man* could be both smelt and touched though he could not be seen.) But no shrieks ever suggest that some intruder has received a shock. No movements of the wire ever betray an invisible climber. The bloodhounds never give cry. Yet still the Believer is not convinced. 'But there is a gardener, invisible, intangible, insensible to electric shocks, a gardener who has no scent and makes no sound, a gardener who comes secretly to look after the garden which he loves.' At last the Sceptic despairs, 'But what remains of your original assertion? Just how does what you call an invisible, intangible, eternally elusive gardener differ from an imaginary gardener or even from no gardener at all?'

In this parable we can see how what starts as an assertion, that something exists or that there is some analogy between certain complexes of phenomena, may be reduced step by step to an altogether different status, to an expression perhaps of a 'picture preference.'[1] The Sceptic says there is no gardener. The Believer says there is a gardener (but invisible, etc.). One man talks about sexual behaviour. Another man prefers to talk of Aphrodite (but knows that there is not really a superhuman person additional to, and somehow responsible for, all sexual phenomena). The process of qualification may be checked at any point before the original assertion is completely withdrawn and something of that first assertion will remain (Tautology). Mr. Wells's invisible man could not, admittedly, be seen, but in all other respects he was a man like the rest of us. But though the process of qualification may be, and of course usually is, checked in time, it is not always judiciously so halted. Someone may dissipate his assertion completely without noticing that he has done so. A fine brash hypothesis may thus be killed by inches, the death by a thousand qualifications.

And in this, it seems to me, lies the peculiar danger, the endemic evil, of theological utterance. Take such utterances as 'God has a plan,' 'God created the world', 'God loves us as a father loves his children.' They look at first sight very much like assertions, vast cosmological assertions. Of course, this is no sure sign that they either are, or are intended to be, assertions. But let us confine ourselves to the cases where those who utter such sentences intend them to express assertions. . . .

Now it often seems to people who are not religious as if there was no conceivable event or series of events the occurrence of which would be admitted by sophisticated religious people to be a sufficient reason for conceding 'There wasn't a God after all' or 'God does not really love us then.' Someone tells us that God loves us as a father loves his children. We are reassured. But then we see a child dying of inoperable cancer of the throat. His earthly father is driven frantic in his efforts to help, but his Heavenly Father reveals no obvious sign of concern. Some qualification is made—God's love is 'not a merely human love' or it is 'an inscrutable love,' perhaps—and we realize that such sufferings are quite compatible with the truth of the assertion that 'God loves us as a father (but, of course, . . .).' We are reassured again. But then perhaps we ask: What is this assurance of God's (appropriately qualified) love worth, what is this apparent guarantee really a guarantee against? Just what would have to happen not merely (morally and wrongly) to tempt but also (logically and rightly) to entitle us to say 'God does not love us' or even 'God does not exist'? I therefore put to the succeeding symposiasts the simple central questions, 'What would have to occur or to have occurred to constitute for you a disproof of the love of, or of the existence of, God?'

R. M. Hare

I wish to make it clear that I shall not try to defend Christianity in particular, but religion in general—not because I do not believe in Christianity, but because you cannot understand what Christianity is until you have understood what religion is.

I must begin by confessing that, on the ground marked out by Flew, he seems to me to be completely victorious. I therefore shift my ground by relating another parable. A certain lunatic is convinced that all dons want to murder him. His friends introduce him to all the mildest and most respectable dons that they can find, and after each of them has retired, they say, 'You see, he doesn't really want to murder you; he spoke to you in a most cordial manner; surely you are convinced now?' But the lunatic replies 'Yes, but that was only his diabolical cunning; he's really plotting against me the whole time, like the rest of them; I know it I tell you.' However many kindly dons are produced, the reaction is still the same.

Now we say that such a person is deluded. But what is he deluded about? About the truth or falsity of an assertion? Let us apply Flew's test to him. There is no behaviour of dons that can be enacted which he will accept as counting against his theory; and therefore his theory, on this test, asserts nothing. But it does not follow that there is no difference between what he thinks about dons and what most of us think about them—otherwise we should not call him a lunatic and ourselves sane, and dons would have no reason to feel uneasy about his presence in Oxford.

Let us call that in which we differ from this lunatic, our respective *bliks*. He has an insane *blik* about dons; we have a sane one. It is important to realize that we have a sane one, not no *blik* at all; for there must be two sides to any argument—if he has a wrong *blik* then those who are right about dons must have a right one. Flew has shown that a *blik* does not consist in an assertion or system of them; but nevertheless it is very important to have the right *blik*.

Let us try to imagine what it would be like to have different *bliks* about other things than dons. When I am driving my car, it sometimes occurs to me to wonder whether my movements of the steering wheel will always continue to be followed by corresponding alterations in the direction of the car. I have never had a steering failure, though I have had skids, which must be similar. Moreover, I know enough about how the steering of my car is made, to know the sort of things that would have to go wrong for the steering to fail—steel joints would have to part, or steel rods break, or something—but how do I know that this won't happen? The truth is, I don't know; I just have a *blik* about steel and its properties, so that normally I trust the steering of my car; but I find it not at all difficult to imagine what it would be like to lose this *blik* and acquire the opposite one. People would say I was silly about steel; but there would be no mistaking the reality of the difference between our respective *bliks*—for example, I should never go in a motor-car. Yet I should hesitate to say that the difference between us was the difference between contradictory assertions. No amount of safe arrivals or bench-tests will remove my *blik* and restore the normal one; for my *blik* is compatible with any finite number of such tests. . . .

Basil Mitchell

Flew's article is searching and perceptive, but there is, I think, something odd about his conduct of the theologian's case. The theologian surely would not deny that the fact of pain counts against the assertion that God loves men. This very incompatibility generates the most intractable of theological problems—the problem of evil. So the theologian *does* recognize the fact of pain as counting against Christian doctrine. But it is true that he will not allow it—or anything—to count decisively against it; for he is committed by his faith to trust in God. His attitude is not that of the detached observer, but of the believer.

Perhaps this can be brought out by yet another parable. In time of war in an occupied country, a member of the resistance meets one night a stranger who deeply impresses him. They spend that night together in conversation. The Stranger tells the partisan that he himself is on the side of the resistance—indeed that he is in command of it, and urges the partisan to have faith in him no matter what happens. The partisan is utterly convinced at that meeting of the Stranger's sincerity and constancy and undertakes to trust him.

They never meet in conditions of intimacy again. But sometimes the Stranger is seen helping members of the resistance, and the partisan is grateful and says to his friends, 'He is on our side.'

Sometimes he is seen in the uniform of the police handing over patriots to the occupying power. On these occasions his friends murmur against him: but the partisan still says, 'He is on our side.' He still believes that, in spite of appearances, the Stranger did not deceive him. Sometimes he asks the Stranger for help and receives it. He is then thankful. Sometimes he asks and does not receive it. Then he says, 'The Stranger knows best.' Sometimes his friends, in exasperation, say 'Well, what *would* he have to do for you to admit that you were wrong and that he is not on our side?' But the partisan refuses to answer. He will not consent to put the Stranger to the test. And sometimes his friends complain, 'Well, if *that's* what you mean by his being on our side, the sooner he goes over to the other side the better.'

The partisan of the parable does not allow anything to count decisively against the proposition 'The Stranger is on our side.' This is because he has committed himself to trust the Stranger. But he of course recognizes that the Stranger's ambiguous behaviour *does* count against what he believes about him. It is precisely this situation which constitutes the trial of his faith.

When the partisan asks for help and doesn't get it, what can he do? He can (a) conclude that the stranger is not on our side or; (b) maintain that he is on our side, but that he has reasons for withholding help.

The first he will refuse to do. How long can he uphold the second position without it becoming just silly?

I don't think one can say in advance. It will depend on the nature of the impression created by the Stranger in the first place. It will depend, too, on the manner in which he takes the Stranger's behaviour. If he blandly dismisses it as of no consequence, as having no bearing upon his belief, it will be assumed that he is thoughtless or insane. And it quite obviously won't do for him to say easily, 'Oh, when used of the Stranger the phrase "is on our side" *means* ambiguous behaviour of this sort.' In that case he would be like the religious man who says blandly of a terrible disaster 'It is God's will.' No, he will only be regarded as sane and reasonable in his belief, if he experiences in himself the full force of the conflict.

It is here that my parable differs from Hare's. The partisan admits that many things may and do count against his belief: whereas Hare's lunatic who has a *blik* about dons doesn't admit that anything counts against his *blik*. Nothing *can* count against *bliks*. Also the partisan has a reason for having in the first instance committed himself, viz. the character of the Stranger; whereas the lunatic has no reason for his *blik* about dons—because, of course, you can't have reasons for *bliks*.

This means that I agree with Flew that theological utterances must be assertions. The partisan is making an assertion when he says, 'The stranger is on our side.'

Do I want to say that the partisan's belief about the Stranger is, in any sense, an explanation? I think I do. It explains and makes sense of the Stranger's behaviour: It helps to explain also the resistance movement in the context of which he appears. In each case it differs from the interpretation which the others put upon the same facts.

'God loves men' resembles 'the Stranger is on our side' (and many other significant statements, e.g., historical ones) in not being conclusively falsifiable. They can both be treated in at least three different ways: (1) As provisional hypotheses to be discarded if experience tells against them; (2) As significant articles of faith; (3) As vacuous formulae (expressing, perhaps, a desire for reassurance) to which experience makes no difference and which make no difference to life.

The Christian, once he has committed himself, is precluded by his faith from taking up the first attitude: 'Thou shalt not tempt the Lord thy God.' He is in constant danger, as Flew has observed, of slipping into the third. But he need not; and, if he does, it is a failure in faith as well as in logic.

Antony Flew

It has been a good discussion: and I am glad to have helped to provoke it. But now—at least in *University*—it must come to an end: And the Editors of *University* have asked me to make some concluding remarks. Since it is impossible to deal with all the issues raised or to comment separately upon each contribution, I will concentrate on Mitchell and Hare, as representative of two very different kinds of response to the challenge made in 'Theology and Falsification.'

The challenge, it will be remembered, ran like this. Some theological utterances seem to, and are intended to, provide explanations or express assertions. Now an assertion, to be an assertion at all, must claim that things stand thus and thus; *and not otherwise*. Similarly an explanation, to be an explanation at all, must explain why this particular thing occurs; *and not something else*. Those last clauses are crucial. And yet sophisticated religious people—or so it seemed to me—are apt to overlook this, and tend to refuse to allow, not merely that anything actually does occur, but that anything conceivably could occur, which would count against their theological assertions and explanations. But in so far as they do this their supposed explanations are actually bogus, and their seeming assertions are really vacuous.

Mitchell's response to this challenge is admirably direct, straightforward, and understanding. He agrees 'that theological utterances must be assertions.' He agrees that if they are to be assertions, there must be something that would count against their truth. He agrees, too, that believers are in constant danger of transforming their would-be assertions into 'vacuous formulae.' But he takes me to task for an oddity in my 'conduct of the theologian's case. The theologian surely would not deny that the fact of pain counts against the assertion that God loves men. This very incompatibility generates the most intractable of theological problems, the problem of evil.' I think he is right. I should have made a distinction between two very different ways of dealing with what looks like evidence against the love of God: The way I stressed was the expedient of qualifying the original assertion; the way the theologian usually takes, at first, is to admit that it looks bad but to insist that there is—there must be—some explanation which will show that, in spite of appearances, there really is a God who loves us. His difficulty, it seems to me, is that he has given God attributes which rule out all possible saving explanations. In Mitchell's parable of the

Stranger it is easy for the believer to find plausible excuses for ambiguous behaviour: for the Stranger is a man. But suppose the Stranger is God. We cannot say that he would like to help but cannot: God is omnipotent. We cannot say that he would help if he only knew: God is omniscient. We cannot say that he is not responsible for the wickedness of others: God creates those others. Indeed an omnipotent, omniscient God must be an accessory before (and during) the fact to every human misdeed; as well as being responsible for every non-moral defect in the universe. So, though I entirely concede that Mitchell was absolutely right to insist against me that the theologian's first move is to look for an *explanation*, I still think that in the end, if relentlessly pursued, he will have to resort to the avoiding action of *qualification*. And there lies the danger of that death by a thousand qualifications, which would, I agree, constitute 'a failure in faith as well as in logic.'

Hare's approach is fresh and bold. He confesses that 'on the ground marked out by Flew, he seems to me to be completely victorious.' He therefore introduces the concept of *blik*. But while I think that there is room for some such concept in philosophy, and that philosophers should be grateful to Hare for his invention, I nevertheless want to insist that any attempt to analyse Christian religious utterances as expressions or affirmations of a *blik* rather than as (at least would-be) assertions about the cosmos is fundamentally misguided. *First,* because thus interpreted they would be entirely unorthodox. If Hare's religion really is a *blik*, involving no cosmological assertions about the nature and activities of a supposed personal creator, then surely he is not a Christian at all? *Second,* because thus interpreted, they could scarcely do the job they do. If they were not even intended as assertions then many religious activities would become fraudulent, or merely silly. If 'You ought *because* it is God's will' asserts no more than 'You ought,' then the person who prefers the former phraseology is not really giving a reason, but a fraudulent substitute for one, a dialectical dud cheque. If 'My soul must be immortal *because* God loves his children, etc.' asserts no more than 'My soul must be immortal,' then the man who reassures himself with theological arguments for immortality is being as silly as the man who tries to clear his overdraft by writing his bank a cheque on the same account. (Of course neither of these utterances would be distinctively Christian: But this discussion never pretended to be so confined.) Religious utterances may indeed express false or even bogus assertions: But I simply do not believe that they are not both intended and interpreted to be or at any rate to presuppose assertions, at least in the context of religious practice; whatever shifts may be demanded, in another context, by the exigencies of theological apologetic.

One final suggestion. The philosophers of religion might well draw upon George Orwell's last appalling nightmare *1984* for the concept of *doublethink*. '*Doublethink* means the power of holding two contradictory beliefs simultaneously, and accepting both of them. The party intellectual knows that he is playing tricks with reality, but by the exercise of *doublethink* he also satisfies himself that reality is not violated' (*1984*, p. 220). Perhaps religious intellectuals too are sometimes driven to doublethink in order to retain their faith in a loving God in face of the reality of a heartless and indifferent world. But of this more another time, perhaps.

Discussion Questions

1. How is belief in God similar to or different from the portrayal of the belief of the invisible gardener in Wisdom's parable?
2. If you believe in God, how do you answer the question that Flew finishes with in his first talk?
3. Is it consistent to try to blend religious faith with logic? Why/why not?
4. How relevant do you find the numerous parables in this selection to the topic of God's existence? Which do you find most convincing/relevant and why?

Against Religious Dogmatism

Ramakrishna

After losing his father at age seven, Ramakrishna (originally named Gadadhar—"Bearer of the Mace"—a nickname for the Hindu god Vishnu) became very spiritual, and by age nine he was conferred with sacred responsibilities in his community. He was disinterested in education and instead pursued a spiritual life as he believed it would "illuminate my heart and give me satisfaction forever." He came to acquire hundreds of disciples and is believed by many Hindus to be a messenger of God.

This selection is taken from the 1000-page recording of Ramakrishna's teachings by one of his most devoted disciples, Mahendranath "M." Gupta. Ramakrishna addressed numerous topics, often highlighting the problems caused by lust and greed (what he referenced as "gold and women") and focusing on the oneness of the universe and quest to know God. Here, he not only dispels numerous apparent paradoxes, but embraces them and explains them away as a mere problem of human language. More importantly, he justifies and embraces the different and unique paths to knowing God, showing through numerous parables and analogies that this is not only acceptable, but may be required given each person's unique composition.

Reading Questions

1. What point does Ramakrishna make in his analogy of the bee?
2. How does Ramakrishna deal with the criticism that religion may contain errors?
3. How and why does he employ his analogy of a chameleon?

Source: From *The Gospel of Sri Ramakrishna,* as translated into English by Swami Nikhilananda and published by the Ramakrishna-Vivekananda Center of New York. Copyright © 1942 by Swami Nikhilananda. Reprinted by permission of the publisher.

4. How does Ramakrishna address dogmatism with regard to organized religions and their belief systems?
5. Explain the significance of the parable of the blind men and the elephant.
6. How does Ramakrishna explain the apparently contradictory view that God is both formless and with form?
7. According to Ramakrishna, what is the relevance of the actual name one gives to God?
8. Explain Ramakrishna's analogy of the bel-fruit.

God exists in all beings. Who, then, is a devotee? He whose mind dwells on God. But this is not possible as long as one has egotism and vanity. The water of God's grace cannot collect on the high mound of egotism. It runs down. I am a mere machine.

(*To Kedar and the other devotees*) "God can be realized through all paths. All religions are true. The important thing is to reach the roof. You can reach it by stone stairs or by wooden stairs or by bamboo steps or by a rope. You can also climb up by a bamboo pole.

"You may say that there are many errors and superstitions in another religion. I should reply: Suppose there are. Every religion has errors. Everyone thinks that his watch alone gives the correct time. It is enough to have yearning for God. It is enough to love Him and feel attracted to Him. Don't you know that God is the Inner Guide? He sees the longing of our heart and the yearning of our soul. Suppose a man has several sons. The older boys address him distinctly as 'Bābā' or 'Pāpā,' but the babies can at best call him 'Bā' or 'Pā.' Now, will the father be angry with those who address him in this indistinct way? The father knows that they too are calling him, only they cannot pronounce his name well. All children are the same to the father. Likewise, the devotees call on God alone, though by different names. They call on one Person only. God is one, but His names are many." . . .

BRĀHMO DEVOTEE: "Sir, why are there so many different opinions about the nature of God? Some say that God has form, while others say that He is formless. Again, those who speak of God with form tell us about His different forms. Why all this controversy?"

MASTER: "A devotee thinks of God as he sees Him. In reality there is no confusion about God. God explains all this to the devotee if the devotee only realizes Him somehow. You haven't set your foot in that direction. How can you expect to know all about God?

"Listen to a story. Once a man entered a wood and saw a small animal on a tree. He came back and told another man that he had seen a creature of a beautiful red colour on a certain tree. The second man replied: 'When I went into the wood, I also saw that animal. But why do you call it red? It is green.' Another man who was present contradicted them both and insisted that it was yellow. Presently others arrived and contended that it was grey, violet, blue, and so forth and so on. At last they started quarrelling among themselves. To settle the dispute they all went to the tree. They saw a man sitting under it. On being asked, he replied: 'Yes, I live under this tree and I know the animal very well. All your descriptions are true. Sometimes it appears red, sometimes yellow, and at other times blue, violet, grey, and so forth. It is a chameleon. And sometimes it has no colour at all. Now it has a colour, and now it has none.'

"In like manner, one who constantly thinks of God can know His real nature; he alone knows that God reveals Himself to seekers in various forms and aspects. God has attributes; then again He has none. Only the man who lives under the tree knows that the chameleon can appear in various colours, and he knows, further, that the animal at times has no colour at all. It is the others who suffer from the agony of futile argument. . . .

(To the goswāmi) "With sincerity and earnestness one can realize God through all religions. The Vaishnavas will realize God, and so will the Sāktas, the Vedāntists, and the Brāhmos. The Mussalmāns and Christians will realize Him too. All will certainly realize God if they are earnest and sincere.

"Some people indulge in quarrels, saying, 'One cannot attain anything unless one worships our Krishna,' or, 'Nothing can be gained without the worship of Kāli, our Divine Mother,' or, 'One cannot be saved without accepting the Christian religion.' This is pure dogmatism. The dogmatist says, 'My religion alone is true, and the religions of others are false.' This is a bad attitude. God can be reached by different paths.

"Further, some say that God has form and is not formless. Thus they start quarrelling. A Vaishnava quarrels with a Vedāntist.

"One can rightly speak of God only after one has seen Him. He who has seen God knows really and truly that God has form and that He is formless as well. He has many other aspects that cannot be described.

"Once some blind men chanced to come near an animal that someone told them was an elephant. They were asked what the elephant was like. The blind men began to feel its body. One of them said the elephant was like a pillar; he had touched only its leg. Another said it was like a winnowing-fan; he had touched only its ear. In this way the others, having touched its tail or belly, gave their different versions of the elephant. Just so, a man who has seen only one aspect of God limits God to that alone. It is his conviction that God cannot be anything else.

(To the goswāmi) "How can you say that the only truth about God is that He has form? It is undoubtedly true that God comes down to earth in a human form, as in the case of Krishna. And it is true as well that God reveals Himself to His devotees in various forms. But it is also true that God is formless; He is the Indivisible Existence Knowledge Bliss Absolute. He has been described in the Vedas both as formless and as endowed with form. He is also described there both as attributeless and as endowed with attributes.

"Do you know what I mean? Satchidānanda is like an infinite ocean. Intense cold freezes the water into ice, which floats on the ocean in blocks of various forms. Likewise, through the cooling influence of bhakti, one sees forms of God in the Ocean of the Absolute. These forms are meant for the bhaktas, the lovers of God. But when the Sun of Knowledge rises, the ice melts; it becomes the same water it was before. Water above and water below, everywhere nothing but water. Therefore a prayer in the *Bhāgavata* says: 'O Lord, Thou hast form, and Thou art also formless. Thou walkest before, us, O Lord, in the shape of a man; again, Thou hast been described in the Vedas as beyond words and thought.'

"But you may say that for certain devotees God assumes eternal forms. There are places in the ocean where the ice doesn't melt at all. It assumes the form of quartz."

". . . Suppose you have separated the shell, flesh, and seeds of a bel-fruit and someone asks you the weight of the fruit. Will you leave aside the shell and the seeds, and weigh only the flesh? Not at all. To know the real weight of the fruit, you must weigh the whole of it—the shell, the flesh, and the seeds. Only then can you tell its real weight. The shell may be likened to the universe, and the seeds to living beings. While one is engaged in discrimination one says to oneself that the universe and the living beings are non-Self and unsubstantial. At that time one thinks of the flesh alone as the substance, and the shell and seeds as unsubstantial. But after discrimination is over, one feels that all three parts of the fruit together form a unity. Then one further realizes that the stuff that has produced the flesh of the fruit has also produced the shell and seeds. To know the real nature of the bel-fruit one must know all three.

"It is the process of evolution and involution. The world, after its dissolution, remains involved in God; and God, at the time of creation, evolves as the world. Butter goes with buttermilk, and buttermilk goes with butter. If there is a thing called buttermilk, then butter also exists; and if there is a thing called butter, then buttermilk also exists. If the Self exists, then the non-Self must also exist. . . .

"I see people who talk about religion constantly quarrelling with one another. Hindus, Mussalmāns, Brāhmos, Śākras, Vaishnavas, Śaivas, all quarrel with one another. They haven't the intelligence to understand that He who is called Krishna is also Śiva and the Primal Śakti, and that it is He, again, who is called Jesus and Allāh. 'There is only one Rāma and He has a thousand names.'

"Truth is one; only It is called by different names. All people are seeking the same Truth; the variance is due to climate, temperament, and name. A lake has many ghāts. From one ghāt the Hindus, take water in jars and call it 'jal.' From another ghāt the Mussalmāns take water in leather bags and call it 'pāni.' From a third the Christians take the same thing and call it 'water.' Suppose someone says that the thing is not 'jal' but 'pāni,' or that it is not 'pāni' but 'water,' or that it is not 'water' but 'jal,' It would indeed be ridiculous. But this very thing is at the root of the friction among sects, their misunderstandings and quarrels. This is why people injure and kill one another, and shed blood, in the name of religion. But this is not good. Everyone is going toward God. They will all realize Him if they have sincerity and longing of heart.

. . . Hanumanpuri[2] in Calcutta. It is with them that you will have to wrestle, (*Pointing to the people assembled there*) These are mere sheep!

"Innumerable are the ways that lead to God. . . ."

Discussion Questions

1. How do you assess Ramakrishna's claim that God is different to different people? If God is an actual entity, isn't God a specific thing? Or is it more important to have a belief in the idea or concept of God, regardless of what God actually is?

2. In what ways might Ramakrishna's approach to dissolving religious dogmatism help alleviate certain problems in today's culture?

3. Given that certain religions literally hold antithetical beliefs (i.e., diet restrictions, consent or prohibition of certain drug use, creation beliefs, views on medicine, etc.) how could you apply Ramakrishna's thesis to addressing this? How is it possible for such different beliefs to apply to a single god?

4. What problems might arise from people employing belief in a god that they define for themselves in any way they choose?

5. How agreeable is Ramakrishna's statement "My religion is right, but I do not know whether other religions are right or wrong"?

6. How do you juxtapose Ramakrishna's view on worship and religion with that of the "Ten Commandments" command to "worship no false idols"?

Dialogues Concerning Natural Religion

David Hume

(For a biographical sketch of Hume, please see his selection earlier in this text.)

Presented here in dialogue form, David Hume was thought to have hidden his arguments against the theistic defense of God's existence due to the social climate at the time. With his *Dialogues Concerning Natural Religion* being published in 1779, this was within a hundred years of the time when atheists were having their tongues pulled out and burned to death and the climate was still somewhat reminiscent of that. While many scholars hold that Hume represents his skeptical views of theism through the character Philo, the dialogue here leaves the question open for readers to draw their own conclusions.

The dialogue involves three characters: Cleanthes, who defends the argument from design and holds that God's attributes can be known; Demea, who defends the argument from design and holds that God's true nature is unknowable; and Philo, the skeptic who argues against the argument from design (though he agrees with Demea that God's nature cannot be known).

There are two types of arguments being addressed here:

- *a priori* (prior to experience); the cosmological (first cause) argument—Through simply reasoning, one can deduce that there must be a first cause.
- *a posteriori* (on the basis of experience); the argument from design—By looking around (i.e., through experience), one sees design and infers the existence of a designer.

Source: First published in 1779. This is a reprint of that edition.

Other distinctions to be made:

- Theism—One believes in a personal god who is involved with the universe (i.e., answers prayers, oversees the function of the universe, etc.).
- Deism—God's existence can be proven, but this god does not "meddle" in human affairs (i.e., does not answer prayers, does not participate in divine revelation, etc.); nor can he be known.
- Anthropomorphism—God can be understood in human terms.
- Fideism—Religious knowledge cannot be based on reason but only on faith.
- Empirical theism—Religious knowledge can be attained through discovery of evidence.

Reading Questions

1. What is the summary of Father Malebranche's comment as quoted by Demea in Part II? How does Philo react to Demea's main point?
2. What is the conclusion of Philo's syllogism in Part II: "Our ideas reach no further than our experience. We have no experience of divine attributes"?
3. Explain Cleanthes' position with regard to his analogy of a machine. What is Demea's response? How does Philo respond by way of analyzing Cleanthes' analogy and making his own analogy of a house?
4. Explain Philo's counter-argument regarding comparing the parts to the whole: "From observing the growth of a hair, can we learn any thing concerning the generation of a man?"
5. Why does Philo reference the "other earths" such as Venus, the moon, etc., in response to Cleanthes?
6. Explain Cleanthes' defense in his analogy (in Part III) of books and animals.
7. In Cleanthes' response to Demea in Part IV, why does he say that those like Demea are atheists "without knowing it"?

Part II

. . . Demea: The question is not concerning the *being* but the *nature* of God. This I affirm, from the infirmities of human understanding, to be altogether incomprehensible and unknown to us. The essence of that supreme Mind, his attributes, the manner of his existence, the very nature of his duration—these and every particular which regards so divine a Being are mysterious to men. Finite, weak, and blind creatures, we ought to humble ourselves in his august presence, and, conscious of our frailties, adore in silence his infinite perfections which eye hath not seen, ear hath not heard, neither hath it entered into the heart of man to conceive. They are covered in a deep cloud from human curiosity; it is profaneness to attempt penetrating through these sacred obscurities, and, next to the impiety of denying his existence, is the temerity of prying into his nature and essence, decrees and attributes.

But lest you should think that my *piety* has here got the better of my *philosophy*, I shall support my opinion, if it needs any support, by a very great authority. I might cite all the divines, almost from the foundation of Christianity, who have ever treated of this or any other theological subject; but I shall confine myself, at present, to one equally celebrated for piety and philosophy. It is Father Malebranche who, I remember, thus expresses himself. "One ought not so much," says he, "to call God a spirit in order to express positively what he is, as in order to signify that he is not matter. He is a Being infinitely perfect—of this we cannot doubt. But in the same manner as we ought not to imagine, even supposing him corporeal, that he is clothed with a human body, as the anthropomorphites asserted, under colour that that figure was the most perfect of any, so neither ought we to imagine that the spirit of God has human ideas or bears any resemblance to our spirit, under colour that we know nothing more perfect than a human mind. We ought rather to believe that as he comprehends the perfections of matter without being material . . . he comprehends also the perfections of spirits without being spirit, in the manner we conceive spirit: that his true name is *He that is*, or, in other words, Being without restriction, All Being, the Being infinite and universal."

After so great an authority, Demea, replied Philo, as that which you have produced, and a thousand more which you might produce, it would appear ridiculous in me to add my sentiment or express my approbation of your doctrine. But surely, where reasonable men treat these subjects, the question can never be concerning the *being* but only the *nature* of the Deity. The former truth, as you well observe, is unquestionable and self-evident. Nothing exists without a cause; and the original cause of this universe (whatever it be) we call God, and piously ascribe to him every species of perfection. Whoever scruples this fundamental truth deserves every punishment which can be inflicted among philosophers, to wit, the greatest ridicule, contempt, and disapprobation. But as all perfection is entirely relative, we ought never to imagine that we comprehend the attributes of this divine Being, or to suppose that his perfections have any analogy or likeness to the perfections of a human creature. Wisdom, thought, design, knowledge— these we justly ascribe to him because these words are honourable among men, and we have no other language or other conceptions by which we can express our adoration of him. But let us beware lest we think that our ideas anywise correspond to his perfections, or that his attributes have any resemblance to these qualities among men. He is infinitely superior to our limited view and comprehension, and is more the object of worship in the temple than of disputation in the schools.

In reality, Cleanthes, continued he, there is no need of having recourse to that affected scepticism so displeasing to you in order to come at this determination. Our ideas reach no further than our experience. We have no experience of divine attributes and operations. I need not conclude my syllogism, you can draw the inference yourself. And it is a pleasure to me (and I hope to you, too) that just reasoning and sound piety here concur in the same conclusion, and both of them establish the adorably mysterious and incomprehensible nature of the Supreme Being.

Not to lose any time in circumlocutions, said Cleanthes, addressing himself to Demea, much less in replying to the pious declamations of Philo, I shall briefly explain how I conceive this matter. Look round the world, contemplate the whole and every part of it: You will find it to be nothing but one great machine, subdivided into an infinite number of lesser machines, which again admit of subdivisions to a degree beyond what human senses and faculties can trace and explain. All these various machines, and even their most minute parts, are adjusted to each other with an accuracy which ravishes into admiration all men who have ever contemplated them. The curious adapting of means to ends, throughout all nature, resembles exactly, though it much exceeds, the productions of human contrivance—of human design, thought, wisdom, and intelligence. Since therefore the effects resemble each other, we are led to infer, by all the rules of analogy, that the causes also resemble, and that the Author of nature is somewhat similar to the mind of man, though possessed of much larger faculties, proportioned to the grandeur of the work which he has executed. By this argument *a posteriori,* and by this argument alone, do we prove at once the existence of a Deity and his similarity to human mind and intelligence.

I shall be so free, Cleanthes, said Demea, as to tell you that from the beginning I could not approve of your conclusion concerning the similarity of the Deity to men, still less can I approve of the mediums by which you endeavour to establish it. What! No demonstration of the Being of God! No abstract arguments! No proofs *a priori*! Are these which have hitherto been so much insisted on by philosophers all fallacy, all sophism? Can we reach no farther in this subject than experience and probability? I will not say that this is betraying the cause of a Deity; but surely, by this affected candour, you give advantages to atheists which they never could obtain by the mere dint of argument and reasoning.

What I chiefly scruple in this subject, said Philo, is not so much that all religious arguments are by Cleanthes reduced to experience, as that they appear not to be even the most certain and irrefragable of that inferior kind. That a stone will fall, that fire will burn, that the earth has solidity, we have observed a thousand and a thousand times; and when any new instance of this nature is presented, we draw without hesitation the accustomed inference. The exact similarity of the cases gives us a perfect assurance of a similar event, and a stronger evidence is never desired nor sought after. But wherever you depart, in the least, from the similarity of the cases, you diminish proportionably the evidence, and may at last bring it to a very weak *analogy*, which is confessedly liable to error and uncertainty. After having experienced the circulation of the blood in human creatures, we make no doubt that it takes place in Titius and Maevius; but from its circulation in frogs and fishes it is only a presumption, though a strong one, from analogy that it takes place in men and other animals. The analogical reasoning is much weaker when we infer the circulation of the sap in vegetables from our experience that the blood circulates in animals; and those who hastily followed that imperfect analogy are found, by more accurate experiments, to have been mistaken.

If we see a house, Cleanthes, we conclude, with the greatest certainty, that it had an architect or builder because this is precisely that species of effect which we have experienced to proceed from that species of cause. But surely you will not affirm that the universe bears such a resemblance to a house that we can with the same certainty infer a similar cause, or that the analogy is here entire and perfect. The dissimilitude is so striking that the utmost you can here pretend to is a guess, conjecture, a presumption concerning a similar cause; and how that pretension will be received in the world, I leave you to consider.

It would surely be very ill received, replied Cleanthes; and I should be deservedly blamed and detested did I allow that the proofs of Deity amounted to no more than a guess or conjecture. But is the whole adjustment of means to ends in a house and in the universe so slight a resemblance? the economy of final causes? the order, proportion, and arrangement of every part? Steps of a stair are plainly contrived that human legs may use them in mounting; and this inference is certain and infallible. Human legs are also contrived for walking and mounting; and this inference, I allow, is not altogether so certain because of the dissimilarity which you remark; but does it, therefore, deserve the name only of presumption or conjecture?

Good God! cried Demea, interrupting him, where are we? Zealous defenders of religion allow that the proofs of a Deity fall short of perfect evidence! And you, Philo, on whose assistance I depended in proving the adorable mysteriousness of the Divine Nature, do you assent to all these extravagant opinions of Cleanthes? For what other name can I give them? or, why spare my censure when such principles are advanced, supported by such an authority, before so young a man as Pamphilus?

You seem not to apprehend, replied Philo, that I argue with Cleanthes in his own way, and, by showing him the dangerous consequences of his tenets, hope at last to reduce him to our opinion. But what sticks most with you, I observe, is the representation which Cleanthes has made of the argument *a posteriori*; and, finding that the argument is likely to escape your hold and vanish into air, you think it so disguised that you can scarcely believe it to be set in its true light. Now, however much I may dissent, in other respects, from the dangerous principle of Cleanthes, I must allow that he has fairly represented that argument, and I shall endeavour so to state the matter to you that you will entertain no further scruples with regard to it.

Were a man to abstract from everything which he knows or has seen, he would be altogether incapable, merely from his own ideas, to determine what kind of scene the universe must be, or to give the preference to one state or situation of things above another. For as nothing which he clearly conceives could be esteemed impossible or implying a contradiction, every chimera of his fancy would be upon an equal footing; nor could he assign any just reason why he adheres to one idea or system, and rejects the others which are equally possible.

Again, after he opens his eyes and contemplates the world as it really is, it would be impossible for him at first to assign the cause of any one event, much less of the whole of things, or of the universe. He might set his fancy a rambling, and she might bring him in an infinite variety of reports and representations. These would all be possible, but, being all equally possible, he would never of himself give a satisfactory account for his preferring one of them to the rest. Experience alone can point out to him the true cause of any phenomenon.

Now, according to this method of reasoning, Demea, it follows (and is, indeed, tacitly allowed by Cleanthes himself) that order, arrangement, or the adjustment of final causes, is not of itself any proof of design, but only so far as it has been experienced to proceed from that principle. For aught we can know *a priori*, matter may contain the source or spring of order originally within itself, as well as mind does; and there is no more difficulty in conceiving that the several elements, from an internal unknown cause, may fall into the most exquisite arrangement, than to conceive that their ideas, in the great universal mind, from a like internal unknown cause, fall into that arrangement. The equal possibility of both these suppositions is allowed. But, by experience, we find (according to Cleanthes) that there is a difference between them. Throw several pieces of steel together, without shape or form, they will never arrange themselves so as to compose a watch. Stone and mortar and wood, without an architect, never erect a house. But the ideas in a human mind, we see, by an unknown, inexplicable economy, arrange themselves so as to form the plan of a watch or house. Experience, therefore, proves that there is an original principle of order in mind, not in matter. From similar effects we infer similar causes. The adjustment of means to ends is alike in the universe, as in a machine of human contrivance. The causes, therefore, must be resembling.

I was from the beginning scandalized, I must own, with this resemblance which is asserted between the Deity and human creatures, and must conceive it to imply such a degradation of the Supreme Being as no sound theist could endure. With your assistance, therefore, Demea, I shall endeavour to defend what you justly call the adorable mysteriousness of the Divine Nature, and shall refute this reasoning of Cleanthes, provided he allows that I have made a fair representation of it.

When Cleanthes had assented, Philo, after a short pause, proceeded in the following manner.

That all inferences, Cleanthes, concerning fact are founded on experience, and that all experimental reasonings are founded on the supposition that similar causes prove similar effects, and similar effects similar causes, I shall not at present much dispute with you. But observe, I entreat you, with what extreme caution all just reasoners proceed in the transferring of experiments to similar cases. Unless the cases be exactly similar, they repose no perfect confidence in applying their past observation to any particular phenomenon. Every alteration of circumstances occasions a doubt concerning the event; and it requires new experiments to prove certainly that the new circumstances are of no moment or importance. A change in bulk, situation, arrangement, age, disposition of the air, or surrounding bodies—any of these particulars may be attended with the most unexpected consequences. And unless the objects be quite familiar to us, it is the highest temerity to expect with assurance, after any of these changes, an event similar to that which before fell under our observation. The slow and deliberate steps of philosophers here, if anywhere, are distinguished from the precipitate march of the vulgar, who, hurried on by the smallest similitude, are incapable of all discernment or consideration.

But can you think, Cleanthes, that your usual phlegm and philosophy have been preserved in so wide a step as you have taken when you compared to the universe houses, ships, furniture, machines, and, from their similarity in some circumstances, inferred a similarity in their causes? Thought, design, intelligence, such as we discover in men and other animals, is no more than one of the springs and principles of the universe, as well as heat or cold, attraction or repulsion, and a hundred others which fall under daily observation. It is an active cause by which some particular parts of nature, we find, produce alterations on other parts. But can a conclusion, with any propriety, be transferred from parts to the whole? Does not the great disproportion bar all comparison and inference? From observing the growth of a hair, can we learn anything concerning the generation of a man? Would the manner of a leaf's blowing, even though perfectly known, afford us any instruction concerning the vegetation of a tree?

But allowing that we were to take the *operations* of one part of nature upon another for the foundation of our judgment concerning the *origin* of the whole (which never can be admitted), yet why select so minute, so weak, so bounded a principle as the reason and design of animals is found to be upon this planet? What peculiar privilege has this little agitation of the brain which we call *thought,* that we must thus make it the model of the whole universe? Our partiality in our own favour does indeed present it on all occasions, but sound philosophy ought carefully to guard against so natural an illusion.

So far from admitting, continued Philo, that the operations of a part can afford us any just conclusion concerning the origin of the whole, I will not allow any one part to form a rule for another part if the latter be very remote from the former. Is there any reasonable ground to conclude that the inhabitants of other planets possess thought, intelligence, reason, or anything similar to these faculties in men? When nature has so extremely diversified her manner of operation in this small globe, can we imagine that she incessantly copies herself throughout so immense a universe? And if thought, as we may well suppose, be confined merely to this narrow corner and has even there so limited a sphere of action, with what propriety can we assign it for the original cause of all things? The narrow views of a peasant who makes his domestic economy the rule for the government of kingdoms is in comparison a pardonable sophism.

But were we ever so much assured that a thought and reason resembling the human were to be found throughout the whole universe, and were its activity elsewhere vastly greater and more commanding than it appears in this globe, yet I cannot see why the operations of a world constituted, arranged, adjusted, can with any propriety be extended to a world which is in its embryo state, and is advancing towards that constitution and arrangement. By observation we know somewhat of the economy, action, and nourishment of a finished animal, but we must transfer with great caution that observation to the growth of a fetus in the womb, and still more to the formation of an animalcule in the loins of its male parent. Nature, we find, even from our limited experience, possesses an infinite number of springs and principles which incessantly discover themselves on every change of her position and situation. And what new and unknown principles would actuate her in so new and unknown a situation as that of the formation of a universe, we cannot, without the utmost temerity, pretend to determine.

A very small part of this great system, during a very short time, is very imperfectly discovered to us; and do we thence pronounce decisively concerning the origin of the whole?

Admirable conclusion! Stone, wood, brick, iron, brass, have not, at this time, in this minute globe of earth, an order or arrangement without human art and contrivance; therefore, the universe could not originally attain its order and arrangement without something similar to human art. But is a part of nature a rule for another part very wide of the former? Is it a rule for the whole? Is a very small part a rule for the universe? Is nature in one situation a certain rule for nature in another situation vastly different from the former?

And can you blame me, Cleanthes, if I here imitate the prudent reserve of Simonides, who, according to the noted story, being asked by Hiero, *What God was?* desired a day to think of it, and then two days more; and after that manner continually prolonged the term, without ever bringing in his definition or description? Could you even blame me if I had answered, at first, *that I did not know,* and was sensible that this subject lay vastly beyond the reach of my faculties? You might cry out sceptic and raillier, as much as you pleased; but, having found in so many other subjects much more familiar the imperfections and even contradictions of human reason, I never should expect any success from its feeble conjectures in a subject so sublime and so remote from the sphere of our observation. When two *species* of objects have always been observed to be conjoined together, I can *infer,* by custom, the existence of one wherever I *see* the existence of the other; and this I call an argument from experience. But how this argument can have place where the objects, as in the present case, are single, individual, without parallel or specific resemblance, may be difficult to explain. And will any man tell me with a serious countenance that an orderly universe must arise from some thought and art like the human because we have experience of it? To ascertain this reasoning it were requisite that we had experience of the origin of worlds; and it is not sufficient, surely, that we have seen ships and cities arise from human art and contrivance.

Philo was proceeding in this vehement manner, somewhat between jest and earnest, as it appeared to me, when he observed some signs of impatience in Cleanthes, and then immediately stopped short. What I had to suggest, said Cleanthes, is only that you would not abuse terms, or make use of popular expressions to subvert philosophical reasonings. You know that the vulgar often distinguish reason from experience, even where the question relates only to matter of fact and existence, though it is found, where that *reason* is properly analyzed, that it is nothing but a species of experience. To prove by experience the origin of the universe from mind is not more contrary to common speech than to prove the motion of the earth from the same principle. And a caviller might raise all the same objections to the Copernican system which you have urged against my reasonings. Have you other earths, might he say, which you have seen to move? Have . . .

Yes! cried Philo, interrupting him, we have other earths. Is not the moon another earth, which we see to turn around its centre? Is not Venus another earth, where we observe the same phenomenon? Are not the revolutions of the sun also a confirmation, from analogy, of the same theory? All the planets, are they not earths which revolve about the sun? Are not the satellites moons which move round Jupiter and Saturn, and along with these primary planets round the sun? These analogies and resemblances, with others which I have not mentioned, are the sole proofs of the Copernican system; and to you it belongs to consider whether you have any analogies of the same kind to support your theory.

In reality, Cleanthes, continued he, the modern system of astronomy is now so much received by all inquirers, and has become so essential a part even of our earliest education, that we are not commonly very scrupulous in examining the reasons upon which it is founded. It is now become a matter of mere curiosity to study the first writers of that subject who had the full force of prejudice to encounter, and were obliged to turn their arguments on every side in order to render them popular and convincing. But if we peruse Galileo's famous *Dialogues* concerning the system of the world, we shall find that that great genius, one of the sublimest that ever existed, first bent all his endeavours to prove that there was no foundation for the distinction commonly made between elementary and celestial substances. The schools, proceeding from the illusions of sense, had carried this distinction very far; and had established the latter substances to be ingenerable, incorruptible, unalterable, impassible; and had assigned all the opposite qualities to the former. But Galileo, beginning with the moon, proved its similarity in every particular to the earth: its convex figure, its natural darkness when not illuminated, its density, its distinction into solid and liquid, the variations of its phases, the mutual illuminations of the earth and moon, their mutual eclipses, the inequalities of the lunar surface, etc. After many instances of this kind, with regard to all the planets, men plainly saw that these bodies became proper objects of experience, and that the similarity of their nature enabled us to extend the same arguments and phenomena from one to the other.

In this cautious proceeding of the astronomers you may read your own condemnation, Cleanthes, or rather may see that the subject in which you are engaged exceeds all human reason and inquiry. Can you pretend to show any such similarity between the fabric of a house and the generation of a universe? Have you ever seen nature in any such situation as resembles the first arrangement of the elements? Have worlds ever been formed under your eye, and have you had leisure to observe the whole progress of the phenomenon, from the first appearance of order to its final consummation? If you have, then cite your experience and deliver your theory.

Part III

How the most absurd argument, replied Cleanthes, in the hands of a man of ingenuity and invention, may acquire an air of probability! Are you not aware, Philo,
that it became necessary for Copernicus and his first disciples to prove the similarity of the terrestrial and celestial matter because several philosophers, blinded
by old systems and supported by some sensible appearances, had denied this similarity? But that it is by no means necessary that theists should prove the similarity of the works of *nature* to those of *art* because this similarity is self-evident and
undeniable? The same matter, a like form; what more is requisite to show an analogy between their causes, and to ascertain the origin of all things from a divine
purpose and intention? Your objections, I must freely tell you, are no better than
the abstruse cavils of those philosophers who denied motion, and ought to be
refuted in the same manner—by illustrations, examples, and instances rather
than by serious argument and philosophy.

Suppose, therefore, that an articulate voice were heard in the clouds, much
louder and more melodious than any which human art could ever reach; suppose
that this voice were extended in the same instant over all nations and spoke to
each nation in its own language and dialect; suppose that the words delivered not
only contain a just sense and meaning, but convey some instruction altogether
worthy of a benevolent Being superior to mankind—could you possibly hesitate a
moment concerning the cause of this voice, and must you not instantly ascribe it
to some design or purpose? Yet I cannot see but all the same objections (if they
merit that appellation) which lie against the system of theism may also be produced against this inference.

Might you not say that all conclusions concerning fact were founded on
experience; that, when we hear an articulate voice in the dark and thence infer a
man, it is only the resemblance of the effects which leads us to conclude that
there is a like resemblance in the cause; but that this extraordinary voice, by its
loudness, extent, and flexibility to all languages, bears so little analogy to any
human voice that we have no reason to suppose any analogy in their causes; and,
consequently, that a rational, wise, coherent speech proceeded, you know not
whence, from some accidental whistling of the winds, not from any divine
reason or intelligence? You see clearly your own objections in these cavils, and
I hope too you see clearly that they cannot possibly have more force in the one
case than in the other.

But to bring the case still nearer the present one of the universe, I shall make
two suppositions which imply not any absurdity or impossibility. Suppose that
there is a natural, universal, invariable language, common to every individual of
human race, and that books are natural productions which perpetuate themselves in the same manner with animals and vegetables, by descent and propagation. Several expressions of our passions contain a universal language: All brute
animals have a natural speech, which, however limited, is very intelligible to
their own species. And as there are infinitely fewer parts and less contrivance in
the finest composition of eloquence than in the coarsest organized body, the

propagation of an *Iliad* or *Aeneid* is an easier supposition than that of any plant or animal.

Suppose, therefore, that you enter into your library thus peopled by natural volumes containing the most refined reason and most exquisite beauty; could you possibly open one of them and doubt that its original cause bore the strongest analogy to mind and intelligence? When it reasons and discourses; when it expostulates, argues, and enforces its views and topics; when it applies sometimes to the pure intellect, sometimes to the affections; when it collects, disposes, and adorns every consideration suited to the subject; could you persist in asserting that all this, at the bottom, had really no meaning, and that the first formation of this volume in the loins of its original parent proceeded not from thought and design? Your obstinacy, I know, reaches not that degree of firmness; even your sceptical play and wantonness would be abashed at so glaring an absurdity.

But if there be any difference, Philo, between this supposed case and the real one of the universe, it is all to the advantage of the latter. The anatomy of an animal affords many stronger instances of design than the perusal of Livy or Tacitus; and any objection which you start in the former case, by carrying me back to so unusual and extraordinary a scene as the first formation of worlds, the same objection has place on the supposition of our vegetating library. Choose, then, your party, Philo, without ambiguity or evasion; assert either that a rational volume is no proof of a rational cause or admit of a similar cause to all the works of nature. . . .

Your instance, Cleanthes, said he, drawn from books and language, being familiar, has, I confess, so much more force on that account; but is there not some danger, too, in this very circumstance, and may it not render us presumptuous, by making us imagine we comprehend the Deity and have some adequate idea of his nature and attributes? When I read a volume, I enter into the mind and intention of the author; I become him, in a manner, for the instant, and have an immediate feeling and conception of those ideas which revolved in his imagination while employed in that composition. But so near an approach we never surely can make to the Deity. His ways are not our ways, his attributes are perfect but incomprehensible. And this volume of nature contains a great and inexplicable riddle, more than any intelligible discourse or reasoning.

The ancient Platonists, you know, were the most religious and devout of all the pagan philosophers, yet many of them, particularly Plotinus, expressly declare that intellect or understanding is not to be ascribed to the Deity, and that our most perfect worship of him consists, not in acts of veneration, reverence, gratitude, or love, but in a certain mysterious self-annihilation or total extinction of all our faculties. These ideas are, perhaps, too far stretched, but still it must be acknowledged that, by representing the Deity as so intelligible and comprehensible, and so similar to a human mind, we are guilty of the grossest and most narrow partiality, and make ourselves the model of the whole universe. . . .

Part IV

. . . In reality, Cleanthes, consider what it is you assert when you represent the Deity as similar to the human mind and understanding. What is the soul of man? A composition of various faculties, passions, sentiments, ideas—united, indeed, into one self or person, but still distinct from each other. When it reasons, the ideas which are the parts of its discourse arrange themselves in a certain form or order which is not preserved entire for a moment, immediately gives place to another arrangement. New opinions, new passions, new affections, new feelings arise which continually diversify the mental scene and produce in it the greatest variety and most rapid succession imaginable. How is this compatible with that perfect immutability and simplicity which all true theists ascribe to the Deity? By the same act, say they, he sees past, present, and future; his love and hatred, his mercy and justice, are one individual operation; he is entire in every point of space, and complete in every instant of duration. No succession, no change, no acquisition, no diminution. What he is implies not in it any shadow of distinction or diversity. And what he is this moment he ever has been and ever will be, without any new judgment, sentiment, or operation. He stands fixed in one simple, perfect state; nor can you ever say, with any propriety, that this act of his is different from that other, or that this judgment or idea has been lately formed and will give place, by succession, to any different judgment or idea.

I can readily allow, said Cleanthes, that those who maintain the perfect simplicity of the Supreme Being, to the extent in which you have explained it, are complete mystics, and chargeable with all the consequences which I have drawn from their opinion. They are, in a word, atheists, without knowing it. For though it be allowed that the Deity possesses attributes of which we have no comprehension, yet ought we never to ascribe to him any attributes which are absolutely incompatible with that intelligent nature essential to him. A mind whose acts and sentiments and ideas are not distinct and successive, one that is wholly simple and totally immutable, is a mind which has no thought, no reason, no will, no sentiment, no love, no hatred; or, in a word, is no mind at all. It is an abuse of terms to give it that appellation, and we may as well speak of limited extension without figure, or of number without composition.

Discussion Questions

1. Demea says that one shouldn't even attempt to understand the infinite nature of God given our finite minds. Do you agree? If so, how can one believe in something that one can't understand? If not, how is it possible to understand something so other-worldly?

2. How do you view Cleanthes' analogy of a machine (similar to Paley's analogy of the watch)? Does it support/prove a designer? An *intelligent* designer?

3. As Philo argues, we tend to assign order to a universe from our own perspective ("There is an original principle of order in mind, not in matter."). Do you agree? Can you think of any examples where this might be exhibited?

4. Philo asks us to imagine inhabitants of other planets: We often portray them (in film, art, etc.) as relatively human-like. Why would we do this? Do you think it's a fair inference to make?

The Watchmaker and Design
William Paley

Intelligent design theory holds that, due to the orderliness of nature and (as many intelligent design theorists hold) because the competing theory—evolutionary theory—has flaws, there must have been a designer responsible for creation. The idea dates back to the ancient Greeks, including both Aristotle and Plato. And in another section in this anthology from St. Thomas Aquinas, he too defends the notion of a "prime mover." One version of this argument is referenced in much of the intelligent design literature repeatedly, even today. The selection here is by Christian apologist and philosopher William Paley, from his 1802 book *Natural Theology*.

Reading Questions

1. What is Paley's purpose for discussing the creation of a watch?
2. Why does Paley mention all of the intricacies and complexities that are involved in the making and function of a watch?
3. Paley lists three potential shortcomings of his watch analogy in Part I. What are they and how does he address them?
4. How does Paley address the notion of imperfections and irregularities in relation to design?
5. What point does he make in his discussion of the eye and a telescope?

Chapter One: State of the Argument

In crossing a heath, suppose I pitched my foot against a *stone* and were asked how the stone came to be there, I might possibly answer that for anything I knew to the contrary it had lain there forever; nor would it, perhaps, be very easy to show the absurdity of this answer. But suppose I had found a *watch* upon the ground, and it should be inquired how the watch happened to be in that place, I should hardly think of the answer which I had before given, that for anything I knew the watch might have always been there. Yet why should not this answer serve for the watch as well as for the stone; why is it not as admissible in the second case as in the first? For this reason, and for no other, namely, that when we come to inspect the watch, we perceive—what we could not discover in the stone—that its several parts are framed and put together for a purpose, e.g., that

Source: From William Paley's *Natural Theology* (1802). Chapters 1 and 3 (edited).

they are so formed and adjusted as to produce motion, and that motion so regulated as to point out the hour of the day; that if the different parts had been differently shaped from what they are, or placed after any other manner or in any other order than that in which they are placed, either no motion at all would have been carried on in the machine, or none which would have answered the use that is now served by it. To reckon up a few of the plainest of these parts and of their offices, all tending to one result: We see a cylindrical box containing a coiled elastic spring, which, by its endeavor to relax itself, turns round the box. We next observe a flexible chain—artificially wrought for the sake of flexure—communicating the action of the spring from the box to the fusee. We then find a series of wheels, the teeth of which catch in and apply to each other, conducting the motion from the fusee to the balance and from the balance to the pointer, and at the same time, by the size and shape of those wheels, so regulating that motion as to terminate in causing an index, by an equable and measured progression, to pass over a given space in a given time. We take notice that the wheels are made of brass, in order to keep them from rust; the springs of steel, no other metal being so elastic; that over the face of the watch there is placed a glass, a material employed in no other part of the work, but in the room of which, if there had been any other than a transparent substance, the hour could not be seen without opening the case. This mechanism being observed—it requires indeed an examination of the instrument, and perhaps some previous knowledge of the subject, to perceive and understand it; but being once, as we have said, observed and understood—the inference we think is inevitable, that the watch must have had a maker—that there must have existed, at some time and at some place or other, an artificer or artificers who formed it for the purpose which we find it actually to answer, who completely comprehended its construction and designed its use.

I. Nor would it, I apprehend, weaken the conclusion, that we had never seen a watch made—that we had never known an artist capable of making one—that we were altogether incapable of executing such a piece of workmanship ourselves, or of understanding in what manner it was performed; all this being no more than what is true of some exquisite remains of ancient art, of some lost arts, and, to the generality of mankind, of the more curious productions of modern manufacture. Does one man in a million know how oval frames are turned? Ignorance of this kind exalts our opinion of the unseen and unknown artist's skill, if he be unseen and unknown, but raises no doubt in our minds of the existence and agency of such an artist, at some former time and in some place or other. Nor can I perceive that it varies at all the inference, whether the question arise concerning a human agent or concerning an agent of a different species, or an agent possessing in some respects a different nature.

II. Neither, secondly, would it invalidate our conclusion, that the watch sometimes went wrong or that it seldom went exactly right. The purpose of the machinery, the design, and the designer might be evident, and in the case supposed, would be evident, in whatever way we accounted for the irregularity of the movement, or whether we could account for it or not. It is not necessary that a machine be perfect in order to show with what design it was made: still less necessary, where the only question is whether it were made with any design at all. . . .

Chapter Three: Application of the Argument

. . . Every indication of contrivance, every manifestation of design which existed in the watch, exists in the works of nature, with the difference on the side of nature of being greater and more, and that in a degree which exceeds all computation. I mean that the contrivances of nature surpass the contrivances of art in the complexity, subtlety, and curiosity of the mechanism; and still more, if possible, do they go beyond them in number and variety; yet, in a multitude of cases, are not less evidently mechanical, not less evidently contrivances, not less evidently accommodated to their end or suited to their office than are the most perfect productions of human ingenuity.

I know no better method of introducing so large a subject than that of comparing a single thing with a single thing: an eye, for example, with a telescope. As far as the examination of the instrument goes, there is precisely the same proof that the eye was made for vision as there is that the telescope was made for assisting it. They are made upon the same principles, both being adjusted to the laws by which the transmission and refraction of rays of light are regulated. I speak not of the origin of the laws themselves; but such laws being fixed, the construction in both cases is adapted to them. For instance, these laws require, in order to produce the same effect, that rays of light in passing from water into the eye should be refracted by a more convex surface than when it passes out of air into the eye. Accordingly, we find that the eye of a fish, in that part of it called the crystalline lens, is much rounder than the eye of terrestrial animals. What plainer manifestation of design can there be than this difference? What could a mathematical instrument maker have done more to show his knowledge of his principle, his application of that knowledge, his suiting of his means to his end—I will not say to display the compass or excellence of his skill and art, for in these all comparison is indecorous, but to testify counsel, choice, consideration, purpose?

To some it may appear a difference sufficient to destroy all similitude between the eye and the telescope, that the one is a perceiving organ, the other an unperceiving instrument. The fact is that they are both instruments. And as to the mechanism, at least as to the mechanism being employed, and even as to the kind of it, this circumstance varies not the analogy at all.

Discussion Questions

1. What important differences are there between a watch and a rock? Do you like Paley's analogy of the watch to a living organism? Why/why not?
2. Paley addresses the near impossibility of a watch coming together *randomly*. If evolution progresses by natural *selection* (i.e., the "parts" are "selected"

depending on how they help the organism survive) is Paley's analogy apt? Why/why not? If not, how would you change it?

3. While a watch does appear to have a clear purpose, do humans have a clear purpose? Does the universe? Is it possible to use a watch incorrectly? What would that mean?

4. Some argue that the eye seems very inefficient and, *if* designed, is designed poorly (i.e., the light has to go all the way through the eye before being detected, the image is inverted and seems to take a somewhat circuitous route, etc.). What does this say about design? What about *intelligent* design?

Intelligent Design: The Scientific Alternative to Evolution

William S. Harris and John H. Calvert

William Harris and John Calvert currently serve as the managing directors of the Intelligent Design Network. Harris earned a PhD in nutritional biochemistry from the University of Minnesota and has published over seventy scientific papers. He is a professor of medicine at the University of Missouri, where he has an endowed chair in metabolism and vascular biology. Calvert earned a degree in geology before going on to practice law, where he has done so for thirty-two years in Kansas City. For the past four years he has been primarily focused on the legal side of the creationism–evolution debate and getting origins science taught in the school system.

This article is listed as the primary source on the Intelligent Design Network website in response to the question "Where can I find a good overview of the controversy?" Harris and Calvert not only provide some background, but also cover the philosophy and science behind the debate, as well as social and ethical ramifications.

Reading Questions

1. The authors mention that there are two possible answers to the question "Are we here for a purpose?" What are they? Do you agree there are only two?

2. What are the two unique characteristics of "origin science"? Why is the historical component of such importance to the authors' position?

3. How do the authors define "naturalism"? How do they define "scientific materialism"?

4. How do the authors address the "rules" of science (naturalism, scientific materialism, etc.) and their effect on the institution of science and creationism?

5. What is intelligent design? Creation science? How do they differ?

6. How do they define a "deist"? How does a deist differ from a theist?

Source: Reprinted with permission from *The National Catholic Bioethics Quarterly* 3.4 (Autumn 2005): 531–561. Copyright © 2003 The National Catholic Bioethics Center. All rights reserved.

7. Explain the relevance of "nonoverlapping magisteria." How would this solve the science-vs.-creationism dilemma? Why do the authors claim that it doesn't solve it?

8. What is Dembski's "design-detection filter"? How does it apply to the word "DESIGN"? What is the relevance of the requirements of *complexity* and *specification*?

9. Explain "irreducible complexity." How is a bacterial flagellum irreducibly complex? How does this seem to discredit evolutionary theory?

10. How do they address the notion of *similarity* among species as it relates to the two theories?

A little science estranges a man from God; a little more brings him back.
FRANCIS BACON (1561–1626)

Sooner or later everyone asks the question, "Where do we come from?" The answer carries profound, life-molding implications. Until this question is answered we cannot solve another fundamental question that is key to ethics, religion, and the meaning of life (if any): "Are we here for a purpose?"

There are two possible answers: the universe and life and its diversity—natural phenomena—are the product of (1) a combination of only natural laws and chance (the "naturalistic hypothesis"); or (2) a combination of law, chance, and design—the activity of a mind or some form of intelligence that has the power to manipulate matter and energy (the "design hypothesis"). The latter produces purpose, the former does not.

The naturalistic hypothesis is supported by theories of chemical evolution (with respect to the origin of the universe and of life) and by Darwinian evolution (with respect to the origin of the diversity of life). The design hypothesis is supported by the purposeful characteristics of exceedingly complex natural systems that are frequently described as "fine tuned." Each hypothesis is densely laden with philosophical and religious baggage, and clear thinking is required in order to separate the science from the philosophy, the evidence from the implications, and reality from imagination.

The authors are trained in scientific research and law. In this article, we hope to convince the reader that a substantial scientific controversy exists about our origins, that the controversy cannot be resolved without objective consideration of intelligent design (ID) and its challenge to evolution, and that a resolution of the controversy is enormously important to our worldviews about science, religion, ethics, and morals. In discussing the issues, we make several propositions: (1) that the most important, defining characteristic of Darwinian evolution is that it is an unguided, unplanned, and purposeless process; (2) that ID is science and not religion; and (3) that there are profound religious, ethical, and moral implications associated with each origins theory.

This article begins with a comprehensive discussion of key terms and concepts. It then proceeds to a consideration of the detection of design, the evidence supporting both origins hypotheses, and finally it reflects on how ID impacts bioethics.

Terms of the Debate

Much confusion about evolution and ID stems from imprecise and elusive definitions of terms.

Origins Science

As used in this essay, origins science is the science that seeks to explain the origin (or causes) of the universe, of the earth, and of life and its diversity. Origins science is historical rather than strictly empirical in nature. Thus, it differs from experimental disciplines like chemistry and physics because experiments cannot be used to directly test its hypotheses. The historical nature of origins science is explained by Harvard Professor Ernst Mayr.

> For example, Darwin introduced historicity into science. Evolutionary biology, in contrast with physics and chemistry, is a historical science—the evolutionist attempts to explain events and processes that have already taken place. *Laws and experiments are inappropriate techniques for the explication of such events and processes.* Instead *one constructs a historical narrative*, consisting of a tentative reconstruction of the particular scenario that led to the events one is trying to explain.

The historical-empirical distinction is critically important. Contrary to purely empirical sciences whose conclusions are held to rigorous objectivity by "laws and experiments," the explanations of a historian are held to no such standard or discipline. This allows the historian's explanations to be subjective, influenced not only by supportive data but also by imagination, philosophy, and religious (or nonreligious) views.

The second unique characteristic of origins science is that it addresses the same questions as do all religions, and thus unavoidably impacts religious belief. Any answer to the question, "Where do we come from?" is certain to offend someone.

Accordingly, the historical, subjective, and religious nature of origins science demands that it be conducted objectively and without philosophic or religious bias, and that all relevant evidence be properly evaluated regardless of its implications.

Evolution

In common parlance, evolution refers to things changing over time. Many things "evolve" in this sense: car designs, political systems, computer software, interpersonal relationships, etc. This definition is noncontroversial. Everyone agrees that things change. Even when applied to living systems, we note that "things change." A fertilized egg becomes a baby, a child, a teenager, and an adult.

Dandelions change from a golden flower to a dusty ball of seeds, and caterpillars become butterflies. Even closer to home, we know that different breeds of dogs, cats, and livestock have been "created" by artificial selection via planned, selective breeding. Thus, evolution as change is accepted by all scientists. The question is not, has there been change, but what has *caused* the change?

Darwinian Evolution

It was "artificial" (i.e., intelligence-driven) selection that Charles Darwin had in mind when he coined his term "natural" selection[3] in his 1859 book *The Origin of Species*. Darwin argued that if intelligent agents could engender such radical changes in animal forms in a few years by planned breeding, then mindless processes could probably do the same thing if they had enough time, with environmental factors allowing the "most fit" members of a population to survive (and reproduce) better than the "less fit." Darwin knew well that life forms, body plans, and structures have changed over long periods of time. Fossils alone attest to the stunning variety of increasingly complex plants and animals no longer living. No doubt life has changed. But what *caused* the change? Darwin and his successors contend that an unguided, mindless natural process caused the changes, that law and chance alone (natural selection acting on random variation) are sufficient to explain all of life's diversity and life's origin.

The National Association of Biology Teachers in 1995 provided the following definition of evolution:

> The diversity of life on earth *is* the outcome of evolution: an unsupervised, impersonal, unpredictable, and natural process of temporal descent with genetic modification that is affected by natural selection, chance, historical contingencies, and changing environments.

Thus, evolution is, by definition, a completely unguided and undirected process in which a mind plays no part. It is purposeless because only minds generate purpose.

The purposelessness of the process is made clear by those who advance the Darwinian theory:

> Darwin did two things: he showed that evolution was a fact contradicting scriptural legends of creation, and that its cause, natural selection, was automatic with no room for divine guidance or design.

> Man is the result of a purposeless and natural process that did not have him in mind.

> Darwin's immeasurably important contribution to science was to show how mechanistic causes could also explain all biological phenomena, despite their apparent evidence of design and purpose. By coupling undirected, purposeless

variation to the blind, uncaring process of natural selection, Darwin made theological or spiritual explanations of the life processes superfluous.

Man has to understand that he is a mere accident.

When biologists speak of "evolution," this is what they mean. Not just *change* but unguided, unintended, purposeless change uninfluenced by a higher intelligence. These statements make it clear that evolution excludes the intervention of any natural or supernatural mind. According to Darwinists, we are "occurrences" and not "designs." . . .

Naturalism/Scientific Materialism

Evolution is undergirded by a philosophy called naturalism. Naturalism is the doctrine that the laws of cause and effect (as in chemistry and physics) are adequate to account for all phenomena, and that design or teleological conceptions of nature are invalid.[4] The last phrase means that the design hypothesis is invalid a priori, as a matter of principle—not as a deduction from evidence. It requires a belief that we just "occur" as natural phenomena and that we are not designed or created for any purpose. By eliminating design, the philosophy of naturalism effectively eliminates supernatural explanations for any event occurring in nature. Indeed, the very function of naturalism is to eliminate the possibility of supernatural intervention from all scientific explanations. It is because of the "philosophies which inspire them" that Pope John Paul II has stated that "theories of evolution . . . are incompatible with the truth about man."[5]

This irrefutable assumption against design is also called "scientific materialism." It holds that all phenomena, even consciousness, can be reduced to matter and energy and that only physical causes operate. Design, which reflects the activity of a nonphysical mind, is not permitted. Although philosophers catalog numerous varieties of naturalism and materialism, they all reject design as an operative cause.

The commitment to a naturalistic worldview is clearly set forth by Professor Richard Lewontin, a Harvard geneticist:

> We take the side of science in spite of the patent absurdity of some of its constructs, in spite of its failure to fulfill many of its extravagant promises of health and life, in spite of the tolerance of the scientific community for just-so stories, because we have a prior commitment, a commitment to materialism. It is not that the methods and institutions of science somehow compel us to accept a material explanation of the phenomenal world, but, on the contrary, that we are forced by our a priori adherence to material causes to create an apparatus of investigation and a set of concepts that produce material explanations, no matter how counterintuitive, no matter how mystifying to the uninitiated. Moreover, that materialism is absolute, for we cannot allow a Divine Foot in the door.

This statement illustrates how ID's opponents avoid engaging the two central problems associated with placing philosophical restrictions on origins science. First, we are not discussing all of science, we are discussing how life and its diversity originated. How something works and how it came to be are vastly different questions. Lewontin is correct that in the workaday world where scientists try to discover how life works, supernatural explanations are not invoked. But to assert that intelligence forces *never* played any role in the origin of life or its diversity is clearly a presupposition, a problematic assertion that cannot be tested by experiment or direct observation. Secondly, Lewontin completely ignores the obvious impact of the "commitment to materialism" on theistic belief.

Perhaps the clearest expression of how naturalism blinds science to evidence was made by Kansas State University biologist Scott Todd who said that "even if all the data point to an intelligent designer, such an hypothesis is excluded from science because it is not naturalistic." Obviously, then, naturalism is not a deduction from experimental observations but a defining philosophy, a worldview. It presupposes only certain causes and eliminates all others by *definition*, not by *data*. . . .

Intelligent Design

ID is a scientific theory that intelligent causes may have played a crucial role in the origin of the universe and of life and its diversity. It holds that design is empirically detectable in nature, and particularly in living systems. ID is an intellectual movement that includes a scientific research program for investigating intelligent causes and that challenges naturalistic explanations of origins that currently drive science education and research.

The theory of intelligent design has been described by ID theorist Professor William Dembski of Baylor University as follows:

> Intelligent design begins with the observation that intelligent causes can do things that undirected natural causes cannot. Undirected natural causes can place scrabble pieces on a board, but cannot arrange the pieces as meaningful words and sentences. To obtain a meaningful arrangement requires an intelligent cause. This intuition, that there is a fundamental distinction between undirected natural causes on the one hand and intelligent causes on the other, has underlain the design arguments of past centuries.

To the unbiased eye, the design hypothesis veritably leaps from the study of nature. It is an instinctive mental reaction to the observed data. Even the most ardent evolutionary biologist acknowledges that living systems look designed for a purpose.[6] Currently ID scientists are developing ways to empirically and objectively test and confirm the hypothesis that life and certain aspects of its diversity may be the product of an intelligent cause. They do this not only by showing positive evidence of design that "rules in" the hypothesis (e.g., the existence of cellular message-bearing systems), but also by seeking evidence that "rules out" the competing naturalistic hypotheses of chemical evolution, Darwinian evolution, and a variety of new "self organization" theories.

Creation Science

Creation science seeks to validate a literal interpretation of creation as contained in the book of Genesis in the Bible. Creation science was defined in a statute that was litigated in a 1982 Arkansas case. In that case, the district court found that, as defined, the teaching of "creation science" was unconstitutional because it was, in effect, a restatement of the Genesis account of origins, and that teaching this material would have the effect of promoting that particular religious view. A similar "creation science" statute was held to be unconstitutional by the Supreme Court in the case of *Edwards v. Aguillard* where the holding was based on the same reason—that the statute had the effect of promoting a particular religious view.

Relationship Between Intelligent Design and Creation Science

Intelligent Design is not creation science. ID is simply an hypothesis about the direct cause of certain past events based on an observation and analysis of data. ID does not arise from any religious text, nor does it seek to validate any scriptural account of origins. An ID proponent recognizes that ID theory may be disproved by new evidence.

ID is like a large tent under which many religious and nonreligious origins theories may find a home. ID proposes nothing more than that life and its diversity were the product of an intelligence with power to manipulate matter and energy. Period. This is not inconsistent with "literal Biblical creationism," nor Islamic, American Indian, or any religious heritage that invokes a Creator. ID simply does not address the specifics of creation—the why and who—not because ID theorists are protecting a hidden agenda but because the data do not compel firm answers to those questions. ID addresses one question only: Is life the product of a guided or an unguided process? Did it arise from a mind or from the meaningless meandering of molecules in mindless motion?

Theistic Evolution

According to Gallup Polls taken over the last two decades (Table 1), over eighty percent of Americans believe in some form of God-guided process, although they may not know it by the term intelligent design. About half of these hold to a "young earth, literal Genesis" perspective, and the other half to what has been termed "theistic" or "God-guided" evolution.

If evolution is defined as "change over time," then clearly one can believe in God *and* evolution because God could have directed the change. But it is precisely here where definitions are so critical, because if one defines evolution as do the

TABLE 1   Gallup Polls[a]

Year	Creation Science[b]	Theistic Evolution[c]	God-Guided Process[d]	Atheistic (or Deistic) Evolution[e]	No Opinion
1982	44%	38%	82%	9%	9%
1991	47%	40%	87%	9%	4%
1993	47%	35%	82%	11%	7%
1997	44%	39%	83%	10%	7%
1999	47%	40%	87%	9%	4%
2001	45%	37%	82%	12%	6%

[a]Column headings are the authors', not the Gallup Organization's.
[b]Agreed with the statement, "God created human beings pretty much in their present form at one time within the last 10,000 years or so."
[c]Agreed with the statement, "Human beings have developed over millions of years from less advanced forms of life, but God guided this process."
[d]Sum of Creation and Theistic Evolution
[e]Agreed with the statement, "Human beings have developed over millions of years from less advanced forms of life. God had no part in this process."

scientists quoted above (i.e., unguided and unplanned accidents), then it is logically difficult to believe in a God other than one who has simply thrown the dice without intending any particular outcome. Thus if God used a random evolutionary process, by definition only purposeless and unintended outcomes will result. It is self-contradictory to believe in a "guided, unguided" process. Professor Kenneth Miller discusses this dilemma:

> As [Kurt] Wise makes clear, he believes that the real danger of evolutionary biology to Christianity is not at all what most scientists might suspect. It is not that evolution's version of natural history threatens to unseat the central Biblical myths of unitary creation and the Flood. Rather, it is the chilling prospect that evolution might succeed in convincing humanity of the fundamental purposelessness of life. Without purpose to the universe, there is no meaning, there are no absolutes, and there is no reason for existence.

Those who believe in a "dice-throwing" god are closer to deists than to theists. A deist is one who is happy to allow the existence of a god that perhaps created matter and the laws of nature, but then took a walk and has not been seen since. This god "let the chips fall where they may." Such a god does not intervene in the natural world; he started the ball rolling and then vanished, leaving evolution to do the real "creating." This is not the view of God that most theistic religions (Christian, Jewish, Muslim) embrace.

Some attempt to reconcile science with religion by defining each as "nonoverlapping magisteria," two completely separate and distinct "ways of knowing."[7]

According to this concept the function of science is to provide "objective" knowledge of reality while religion deals only with "subjective" spiritual impressions. This attempted demarcation only exacerbates the problem rather than solving it because the magisteria actually do overlap when both offer an answer to the same question: Where do we come from? Theism holds that humanity was designed for a purpose, while science claims that design and the purposes it serves are an illusion.[8] A recent example of the depth of the confusion is a resolution adopted by the Presbyterian Church USA (PCUSA) in which "evolution" is held to be consistent with a "God as Creator." The problem is that evolution is not defined in the resolution. If by evolution, the PCUSA means "change over time," then the statement may be accurate, but if evolution means "unguided, blind, unintended change," then the statement is logically inconsistent.

The deistic evolutionist also holds that because there is no evidence of design in nature, belief in a God cannot be based on "natural revelation," that is, on evidence for God in nature. According to Christian scriptures, the design apparent in nature is real. As a consequence, the deistic evolutionist is left only with subjective personal spiritual experience as a basis for belief. Logically the deistic evolutionist would be virtually indistinguishable from a strict Darwinist. The theistic evolutionist, who believes that life was somehow planned, would find support in ID theory.

Richard Dawkins has said that the attempt to meld naturalism with theism is just "an attempt to woo the sophisticated theological lobby and to get them into our camp and put the creationists into another camp. It's good politics. But it's intellectually disreputable."

The Detection of Design

The central claim of ID theory is that design is empirically detectable. For most people, design detection is an intuitive process that occurs without any thoughtful deliberation. This was most famously described over two hundred years ago by William Paley in his book *Natural Theology*. While walking in the countryside, he would frequently encounter stones on the ground. If he thought about it at all, he would conclude that they were simply natural objects formed by materialistic forces. On the other hand, if he happened upon a pocket watch lying in the grass, his conclusion would be that it was formed by an intelligent source. Why? Because upon inspection he would discover that the watch, unlike the stone, was made up of multiple finely shaped and interacting parts all working together to accomplish one purpose: to tell time. While such a scenario is easily imagined, and his conclusion would not be challenged by any reasonable person, he did not reach it by a direct, step-by-step scientific process. He just "knew" it to be designed. If Paley found a cell phone on the ground, he would still conclude that it had been designed even though he would have no idea of its purpose. Recall the stir that a Coke bottle falling from the sky engendered among the African tribe in the movie, *The Gods Must Be Crazy*. One mind can "sense" the creative activity of another mind.

Although this intuition works well for human-made objects, can it be applied to living objects that we absolutely know were not "handcrafted?" In other words, can it apply to biology? Gene Myers, one of the lead scientists on the Human Genome project, stated in an interview in 2000: "'What really astounds me is the architecture of life,' he said. 'The system is extremely complex. It's like it was designed. . . . There's a huge intelligence there.'" How can we know if Myers's intuition is correct? What if his (and our) minds are fooling us? What if our intuition is wrong and the design we see in living systems is just an illusion, as evolutionary biologists claim? Is there any way to check or confirm our intuition?

Methods of Design Detection

If we are to scientifically determine whether an object or event was designed, we have to have more than intuition at our disposal. We need a formalized, objective, and systematic approach to the question. That is precisely what William Dembski has begun to explore. In his book *The Design Inference*, Dembski outlines a methodology for detection of design using a "design-detection filter." This logical construct recognizes that there are only three explanatory causes for any event, pattern, or object (past or present): chance, necessity (natural law), and design. The naturalistic hypothesis assumes that only chance and necessity have operated to generate life and its diversity, whereas the design hypothesis postulates that all three causes may have played a role. Design detection essentially seeks evidence that rules in design and that also rules out chance and necessity.

A way to apply Dembski's filter is to first ask whether a pattern in question exhibits function, structure, or purpose that is independent of the meaning or significance of each of the elements that make up the pattern. For example, the pattern "DESIGN" conveys a recognizable meaning that is independent of the significance or meaning of each of the letters which comprise the pattern. Professor Dembski call this a "specification." The sequence "NDISGN," lacks a specification and therefore cannot support a design inference.

The next step is to determine whether this apparently meaningful pattern could be explained by some law or regularity. Is the pattern required to be so? Do the elements that make up the pattern *have* to take that specific form? If so, then design may not be inferred.

If the pattern is not required, then we proceed to the final step, which is to determine whether the pattern could have occurred by chance. If the pattern is relatively simple, so that chance could reasonably explain it, then design may not be inferred. However, if it is too complex to be explained by chance, then the design inference is warranted. A pattern which is deemed by the filter to have been designed is one that exhibits what Dembski calls "specified complexity." A design inference requires not only complexity, but specification. It must match an independently given pattern.

"TDIPH,B;5H;Nn;E/" is a complex pattern, but it lacks specification, it has no meaning. A wave pattern on a beach is regular but lacks complexity. Similarly, the pattern "DESIGN" is specified, but being only six characters long lacks sufficient complexity to confidently lead to the conclusion that it appeared on purpose instead of accidentally. The Gettysburg Address, on the other hand, is both complex and specified. The following discussion of the three causes should help the reader understand this important concept.

The Three Explanatory Causes

Chance. Events can occur by chance. A chance event is one that (a) cannot be predicted, and (b) is not controlled by intent or law. Anyone who has patronized a casino, played cards, or flipped a coin knows the meaning of chance. With the use of statistical calculations we can predict the likelihood that a given event will occur although we cannot know for certain when or where it will occur. For example, how likely would it be that we could spell the word "DESIGN" by blindly pulling Scrabble tiles out of a bag of twenty-six tiles (one for each letter of the English alphabet that is replaced after each drawing)? This can be calculated. The chance of pulling the D is 1 in 26; the chance of pulling D *and* E in sequence is $1/26^2$ which is 1 in 676. Thus, the chance of spelling D-E-S-I-G-N out of the bag is $1/26^6$ or one chance in 308,915,776 (or $10^{8.5}$). Stated more simply (but less precisely), it would take us nearly 309 million cycles of pulling six tiles out of the bag to be sure we would assemble the word DESIGN at least once. This is only a six-letter pattern; if we wanted to spell "HAMBURGERS," it would take 141 *million million* cycles (i.e., the chances are 1 in 10^{14} that you could obtain this pattern on the first try). Clearly, as the complexity of the pattern increases, the probability that it was "caused" by chance decreases exponentially. Most scientists would acknowledge that any event having a probability of occurring that is less than 1 in 10^{150} is virtually impossible.

Necessity (or Natural Law). Events, patterns, or objects can also arise by "necessity." A necessary event is one that is required to occur by the laws of chemistry and physics. A salt crystal is an example of a pattern arranged only by chance and necessity without any direct input from a mind. When a solution of sodium and chlorine ions becomes supersaturated, the positively charged sodium ions will be attracted to the negatively charged chlorine ions to form a cube. The path a river takes as it crosses the continent is dictated by the law of gravity and the presence of matter (water, rocks, etc.). The rainbow that appears when white light is passed through a prism is the result of the interaction of electromagnetic radiation with a certain shape of glass. In each of these cases the pattern is "caused" by the natural and forever reproducible behavior of matter driven by natural law.

Design. The third possible cause for an event, object, or pattern is design. A designed event, object, or pattern is one that was originally conceived by a mind or intelligence, and then brought into being "on purpose" by manipulation of matter and energy. Every human-made object in history was the result of design; each was intended. This very document consists of a pattern of many events (letters, numbers, characters, and punctuation marks in a unique sequence) arranged by a mind and using the material elements of ink and paper. Both design (choosing the language and the words) and necessity (ink has to stick to paper) "caused" this document. Nature is filled with both human and nonhuman "minds," and some scientists are searching for alien minds. Hence, it is not absurd to postulate the existence of other unseen minds that may have operated in the past.

An example of all three "causes" at work in a series of three events is the flipping of a coin. The decision and action of flipping are designed or intended; the falling of the coin in topsy-turvy flight up and down is dictated by the law of gravity; and the outcome—heads or tails—is the result of chance.

Many well-accepted, uncontroversial scientific disciplines are utterly dependent on detecting design, on inferring the past actions of an intelligent agent by examining present evidence:

- Forensic Sciences, where a death is investigated to determine whether the person died by accident (i.e., chance/necessity) or by intent (i.e., murder).
- Cryptanalysis, where code breakers examine patterns of characters to determine whether they convey a message or are simply random and meaningless noise.
- Archaeology, where artifacts are examined to determine whether they were fashioned by man or by nature. Is the rock just a stone, or a tool?
- Arson investigation, where one attempts to discern from charred remains whether the fire was set intentionally (by design) or resulted from a frayed wire (chance/necessity).
- Copyright infringement and plagiarism, where scientists examine writings to determine whether they were accidentally or intentionally similar to the work of others. . . .

Evidence Supporting Intelligent Design

The evidence for design theory is composed of both evidence *for* design as well as evidence *against* the naturalistic theory. As noted above, when there are only two possible explanations, evidence against one is evidence for the other.

Apparent Design

Perhaps the most direct and compelling evidence for design is simply the *appearance* of design in living systems. It is the evidence that we detect with our intuition when we find an arrowhead or study the human eye. It is the evidence that convinced Aristotle, Socrates, Plato, Copernicus, Galileo, Newton, Bacon, Boyle, and even Einstein of design in the universe. Apparent design formed the foundation for science until very recently, and it is this intuition that led Richard Dawkins and Gene Myers (quoted above) to see design in biology.

In science, the most obvious and simplest explanation is usually accepted first but may be challenged by new data. Until such data (not hints, suggestions, or wishful thinking) actually disprove the original hypothesis, it should not be abandoned. For the first four thousand years of recorded human history, the design hypothesis was virtually universally accepted, and the job of the scientist was not to discover how the world came to be (that was a given), but how the created world worked. In the mid-eighteenth century Hume challenged the logic of the design inference but offered no alternative. Darwin provided that alternative— a viable competing naturalistic hypothesis. Much of his world (which like him was completely ignorant of the true complexity of life) was easily convinced. But modern science (especially in the last half of the twentieth century) has discovered the mind-boggling intricacy of cellular (and cosmic) structure and function. It is these discoveries that have begun to drive scientists to reconsider the merits of the design hypothesis.

Irreducible Complexity

"Law and luck" explanations of life's origins are rendered less likely in light of observations relating to the nature of cellular complexity. Biochemist Michael Behe has argued that many biological mechanisms in living organisms are "irreducibly complex." An irreducibly complex system is a "single system [which is] necessarily composed of several well-matched interacting parts that contribute to the basic function, wherein the removal of any one of the parts causes the system to effectively cease functioning." The adjective "irreducible" means the system cannot be "reduced" to a simpler, *functioning* system that could develop into a more complex system.

Behe points to the bacterial flagellum as an example of an irreducibly complex biological system. This biological machine is a high-speed rotary motor that turns a propeller to move a bacterium towards food or away from danger. It requires at least forty, highly complex, interlocking, moving protein components for assembly and operation and is believed to have been a fully functioning component of the most primitive cells. It will not work unless all the parts are present together at the same time. Dr. Behe contends that natural selection cannot build such a machine because, in isolation, the individual parts have no Darwinian selective value (i.e., they have no survival function that natural selection can "choose" because it works better than the original). In Behe's words,

> An irreducibly complex system cannot be produced directly (that is, by continuously improving the initial function, which continues to work by the same mechanism) by slight, successive modifications of a precursor system, because any precursor to an irreducibly complex biological system, if there is such a thing, would be a powerful challenge to Darwinian evolution. Since natural selection can only choose systems that are already working, then if a biological system cannot be produced gradually it would have to arise as an integrated unit, in one fell swoop, for natural selection to have anything to act on.

Natural law and chance alone have never been shown to assemble even one of the protein subunits of the hundreds of highly complex, integrated, multicomponent, macromolecular machines present in single-celled organisms. Absent the faculty of a mind to perceive, decide, plan, and direct the arrangement and coordination of events, mechanisms of chance and necessity appear to be creatively impotent in concept alone.

Biological Information

Living systems are characterized by the presence of vast amounts of *information* (e.g., DNA). There is no known physical or chemical law or process that can produce information that has a semantic characteristic; complexity, yes, but not information. The semantic or meaningful quality does not flow from matter or energy alone. The only force in our experience known to produce meaning is a mind. For example, the letter sequence "SGIDNE" conveys no meaning. However the same letters rearranged into "DESIGN" have something new—meaning, information derived from a mind—but no more matter. This is explained by astronomer Paul Davies:

> Snowflakes contain syntactic information in the specific arrangement of their hexagonal shapes, but these patterns have no semantic content, no meaning for anything beyond the structure itself. By contrast, the distinctive feature of biological information is that it is replete with meaning. DNA stores the instructions needed to build a functioning organism; it is a blueprint or an algorithm for a specified, predetermined product. Snowflakes don't code for or symbolize anything, whereas genes most definitely do. To explain life fully, it is not enough simply to identify a source of free energy, or negative entropy, to provide biological information. We also have to understand how *semantic* information comes into being. It is the quality, not the mere existence, of information that is the real mystery here.

Similarities in Biological and Human-Made Systems

Those favoring Darwinism and the power of evolution to "create" depend heavily on arguments from similarities: Molecules across life forms are *similar*, body plans of different animals are *similar*, etc. Of course, similarity can just as easily point to a common designer, and the evolutionists' failure to exclude that possibility (based on evidence and not philosophy) keeps design as a live possibility. Scientists are discovering that many biological systems have the same characteristics as human-made systems. One example is the Morse Code's conceptual similarity to the genetic code. In fact the latter was discovered using human-made coding systems as an analogy. A falcon is far more complex than the F-16 Fighting Falcon that bears its name, and the nano-scale motor that drives the bacterial flagellum outperforms any human-made electric motor. The similarity between complex human-made and biomolecular machines and information processing systems supports the design hypothesis. If "similarities" are admissible evidence for the Darwinian position, then they are admissible for the design hypothesis.

Abrupt Appearance of Fossil Phyla

Darwin's theory of natural selection is based on the assumption that differences in life forms develop gradually over long periods of time through an accumulation of very small changes. However, the fossil record contradicts this prediction. To begin with, current evidence suggests that the first living cells appeared on earth almost immediately (within a few million years) after the temperature on earth became habitable to life. Although scientists initially predicted that it would take billions of years for life to arise, the appearance of bacterial life so close to the time that the earth's temperature fell below boiling suggests a sudden rather than gradual appearance of life. The rapid advent of over forty new and distinct life forms is also chronicled in the "Cambrian explosion" which took place about 550 million years ago. The essentially simultaneous appearance of virtually all the major body plans is directly contrary to Darwinian theory. Stephen J. Gould and Niles Elderidge proposed the theory of "punctuated equilibrium" in an attempt to "explain" the sudden appearance of life forms. Unfortunately it does not actually *explain* anything; it simply posits that evolution happened in fits and starts when no one was looking, and animals changed so quickly that there was either not enough time for fossilization or there were too few "intermediates" to fossilize. This is not evidence—it is wishful thinking, and there are no known biochemical mechanisms that can support sudden, large scale changes in the genome. In either case, both a gradual or an abrupt appearance of life over time can be accommodated by the intelligent design theory since ID is not about the *rate* of change but about the *control* of life's development.

ID does not claim that no evolutionary process is involved in the origin of various species. It merely claims that evolution is inadequate to explain all of the diversity of life.

The Fine Tuning of the Universe

Many astrophysicists and cosmologists have recognized for years that the universe appears to be "fine tuned." "Fine tuned" (synonym for "designed") refers to the existence of very precise and intricately balanced mathematical constants underlying physical laws. The force of gravity, the mass of the electron, the charge of the proton, etc. are specific, real values. Were they even slightly different from what they are, not only would life not exist, *nothing* (of any significance) would exist. Martin Rees admits that the only two satisfying solutions to the observed fine tuning are either design or the very speculative possibility that our universe might just be one of an infinite number of independent, parallel universes, thereby rendering the existence of our "fine tuned" universe more probable. As a committed naturalist, he must invoke the evidenceless existence of multiple unseen and undetectable universes in order to avoid a design conclusion. Consider the Earth. Far from being just a minor planet in a minor solar system revolving around a minor star in the backyard of one very average galaxy among billions, evidence has been presented that the location of the Earth in the universe is remarkably unique. Thus, the evidence of the "fine tuning" of the universe and the placement of the Earth are evidence favoring design.

In addition to these signs and evidences *for* ID, there are findings that fail to support the counterargument. These further strengthen the design position.

Discussion Questions

1. The authors spend a lot of time on the "purposelessness" inherent in evolution theory. How important is this to the truth of a theory? Would you prefer a theory to another simply because the one provided purpose and meaning in your life?

2. How relevant are the Gallup Polls data to their argument? What purpose does this data serve in a study like this one?

3. The authors cite the movie *The Gods Must Be Crazy* as support for the design argument. Does the fact that the Coke bottle *was* designed, but by *humans* (not God), affect this analogy in any way?

4. In what ways might the Search for Extraterrestrial Intelligence (SETI) be a good analogy for a "search for ID"?

5. Much of this controversy is in how we define science. Look at the definitions/criteria for science here (and in other selections). Is there any agreement? How do *you* define it? Who should be the deciding voice in this discussion?

6. Later in their article, the authors suggest that a strong focus on science and materialism would result in "no absolute guiding principles" and also a total lack of moral laws. How do you address this? Some scientists suggest that our conscience guides morality and this is a product of evolution. Is morality possible in light of evolutionary theory? And if not, how important is this regarding the *truth* of a theory?

7. The authors later ask the following rhetorical questions—how do you answer them: "If life is an accident, why not alter it to suit our needs? If we can, why not make human clones? Why not abort unwanted children? Why not euthanize the 'useless' aged? Why not end a challenging marriage?"

The Blind Watchmaker

Richard Dawkins

(For a biographical sketch of Dawkins, please see his selection earlier in this text.)

This selection is extracted from Dawkins' national bestseller, *The Blind Watchmaker*. As you can discern from the title, Dawkins here references William Paley's argument (also included in this section of readings) in which the watchmaker, according to Paley, is God. Dawkins illustrates the weakness of Paley's analogy as it relates to arguments of supernatural design, as suggested by the subtitle of the book, *Why the Evidence of Evolution Reveals a Universe Without Design*. Dawkins instead promotes the "blind" forces of nature—in doing so, he explains the process of natural selection and the role of chance and randomness. He also addresses the more current procreationist notion of Irreducible Complexity (IC). IC holds that certain organs (i.e., the eye) and biological processes could not have evolved because they need all parts intact in order to function. As an evolutionary biologist, Dawkins holds that many of the design arguments rest on the fact that a majority of people do not have a basic understanding of the natural forces and the process by which evolution proceeds.

Reading Questions

1. Briefly describe William Paley's analogy of the watch. How does he relate it to the human eye? How does Dawkins argue that this analogy is false?
2. What does it mean for a structure to be "heterogeneous"? How does it relate to complexity?
3. Regarding probability, how does Mont Blanc differ from an airplane?
4. Explain the significance of Dawkins' quote, "However many ways there may be of being alive, it is certain that there are vastly more ways of being dead."
5. Explain the difference between single-step and cumulative selection. How does Dawkins illustrate the differences between the two with his example of the typing monkey? How, then, does this example relate to life on this planet?
6. What role do randomness and chance play in evolution? How do some people misunderstand this?
7. In what way does Dawkins suggest that the monkey/Shakespeare model is misleading as it relates to natural selection?
8. Summarize the argument given by Francis Hitching. In what ways does Dawkins argue against it?
9. How does Dawkins explain the circular nature of the argument, "Because life has arisen here, it can't be too terribly improbable"?
10. Explain the SGP. How does Dawkins connect it with the hypothesized number of planets? What does he hope to demonstrate in doing so?

Source: "Hall of Mirrors" by Richard Dawkins from October 2, 2000 *Forbes ASAP.* Reprinted by permission of FORBES ASAP Magazine © 2007 Forbes Media LLC.

Explaining the Very Improbable

. . . Each one of us is a machine, like an airliner only much more complicated. Were we designed on a drawing board too, and were our parts assembled by a skilled engineer? The answer is no. It is a surprising answer, and we have known and understood it for only a century or so. When Charles Darwin first explained the matter, many people either wouldn't or couldn't grasp it. I myself flatly refused to believe Darwin's theory when I first heard about it as a child. Almost everybody throughout history, up to the second half of the nineteenth century, has firmly believed in the opposite—the Conscious Designer theory. Many people still do, perhaps because the true, Darwinian explanation of our own existence is still, remarkably, not a routine part of the curriculum of a general education. It is certainly very widely misunderstood.

The watchmaker of my title is borrowed from a famous treatise by the eighteenth-century theologian William Paley. His *Natural Theology—or Evidences of the Existence and Attributes of the Deity Collected from the Appearances of Nature,* published in 1802, is the best-known exposition of the 'Argument from Design,' always the most influential of the arguments for the existence of a God. It is a book that I greatly admire, for in his own time its author succeeded in doing what I am struggling to do now. He had a point to make, he passionately believed in it, and he spared no effort to ram it home clearly. He had a proper reverence for the complexity of the living world, and he saw that it demands a very special kind of explanation. The only thing he got wrong—admittedly quite a big thing!—was the explanation itself. He gave the traditional religious answer to the riddle, but he articulated it more clearly and convincingly than anybody had before. The true explanation is utterly different, and it had to wait for one of the most revolutionary thinkers of all time, Charles Darwin.

Paley begins *Natural Theology* with a famous passage:

> In crossing a heath, suppose I pitched my foot against a *stone*, and were asked how the stone came to be there; I might possibly answer, that, for anything I knew to the contrary, it had lain there for ever: nor would it perhaps be very easy to show the absurdity of this answer. But suppose I had found a *watch* upon the ground, and it should be inquired how the watch happened to be in that place; I should hardly think of the answer which I had before given, that for anything I knew, the watch might have always been there.

Paley here appreciates the difference between natural physical objects like stones, and designed and manufactured objects like watches. He goes on to expound the precision with which the cogs and springs of a watch are fashioned, and the intricacy with which they are put together. If we found an object such as a watch upon a heath, even if we didn't know how it had come into existence, its own precision and intricacy of design would force us to conclude that the watch must have had a maker: that there must have existed, at some time, and at some place or other, an artificer or artificers, who formed it for the purpose which we find it actually to answer, who comprehended its construction, and designed its use.

Nobody could reasonably dissent from this conclusion, Paley insists, yet that is just what the atheist, in effect, does when he contemplates the works of nature for:

every indication of contrivance, every manifestation of design, which existed in the watch, exists in the works of nature; with the difference, on the side of nature, of being greater or more, and that in a degree which exceeds all computation.

Paley drives his point home with beautiful and reverent descriptions of the dissected machinery of life, beginning with the human eye, a favourite example which Darwin was later to use and which will reappear throughout this book. Paley compares the eye with a designed instrument such as a telescope, and concludes that 'there is precisely the same proof that the eye was made for vision, as there is that the telescope was made for assisting it.' The eye must have had a designer, just as the telescope had.

Paley's argument is made with passionate sincerity and is informed by the best biological scholarship of his day, but it is wrong, gloriously and utterly wrong. The analogy between telescope and eye, between watch and living organism, is false. All appearances to the contrary, the only watchmaker in nature is the blind forces of physics, albeit deployed in a very special way. A true watchmaker has foresight: He designs his cogs and springs, and plans their interconnections, with a future purpose in his mind's eye. Natural selection, the blind, unconscious, automatic process which Darwin discovered, and which we now know is the explanation for the existence and apparently purposeful form of all life, has no purpose in mind. It has no mind and no mind's eye. It does not plan for the future. It has no vision, no foresight, no sight at all. If it can be said to play the role of watchmaker in nature, it is the *blind* watchmaker.

I shall explain all this, and much else besides. But one thing I shall not do is belittle the wonder of the living 'watches' that so inspired Paley. On the contrary, I shall try to illustrate my feeling that here Paley could have gone even further. When it comes to feeling awe over living 'watches' I yield to nobody. I feel more in common with the Reverend William Paley than I do with the distinguished modern philosopher, a well-known atheist, with whom I once discussed the matter at dinner. I said that I could not imagine being an atheist at any time before 1859, when Darwin's *Origin of Species* was published. 'What about Hume?', replied the philosopher. 'How did Hume explain the organized complexity of the living world?', I asked. 'He didn't,' said the philosopher. 'Why does it need any special explanation?'

Paley knew that it needed a special explanation, Darwin knew it, and I suspect that in his heart of hearts my philosopher companion knew it too. In any case it will be my business to show it here. As for David Hume himself, it is sometimes said that that great Scottish philosopher disposed of the Argument from Design a century before Darwin. But what Hume did was criticize the logic of using apparent design in nature as *positive* evidence for the existence of a God. He did not offer any *alternative* explanation for apparent design, but left the question open. An atheist before Darwin could have said, following Hume: 'I have no explanation for complex biological design. All I know is that God isn't a good explanation, so we must wait and hope that somebody comes up with a better one.' I can't help feeling that such a position, though logically sound, would have left one feeling pretty unsatisfied, and that although atheism might have been *logically* tenable before Darwin, Darwin made it possible to be an intellectually fulfilled atheist. I like to think that Hume would agree, but some of his writings suggest that he underestimated the complexity and beauty of biological design. The boy naturalist Charles Darwin could have shown him a thing or two about that, but Hume had been dead 40 years when Darwin enrolled in Hume's university of Edinburgh.

I have talked glibly of complexity, and of apparent design, as though it were obvious what these words mean. In a sense it is obvious—most people have an intuitive idea of what complexity means. But these notions, complexity and design, are so pivotal to this book that I must try to capture a little more precisely, in words, our feeling that there is something special about complex, and apparently designed things.

So, what is a complex thing? How should we recognize it? In what sense is it true to say that a watch or an airliner or an earwig or a person is complex, but the moon is simple? The first point that might occur to us, as a necessary attribute of a complex thing, is that it has a heterogeneous structure. A pink milk pudding or blancmange is simple in the sense that, if we slice it in two, the two portions will have the same internal constitution: A blancmange is homogeneous. A car is heterogeneous: Unlike a blancmange, almost any portion of the car is different from other portions. Two times half a car does not make a car. This will often amount to saying that a complex object, as opposed to a simple one, has many parts, these parts being of more than one kind.

Such heterogeneity, or 'many-partedness,' may be a necessary condition, but it is not sufficient. Plenty of objects are many-parted and heterogeneous in internal structure, without being complex in the sense in which I want to use the term. Mont Blanc, for instance, consists of many different kinds of rock, all jumbled together in such a way that, if you sliced the mountain anywhere, the two portions would differ from each other in their internal constitution. Mont Blanc has a heterogeneity of structure not possessed by a blancmange, but it is still not complex in the sense in which a biologist uses the term.

Let us try another tack in our quest for a definition of complexity, and make use of the mathematical idea of probability. Suppose we try out the following definition: A complex thing is something whose constituent parts are arranged in a way that is unlikely to have arisen by chance alone. To borrow an analogy from an eminent astronomer, if you take the parts of an airliner and jumble them up at random, the likelihood that you would happen to assemble a working Boeing is vanishingly small. There are billions of possible ways of putting together the bits of an airliner, and only one, or very few, of them would actually be an airliner. There are even more ways of putting together the scrambled parts of a human.

This approach to a definition of complexity is promising, but something more is still needed. There are billions of ways of throwing together the bits of Mont Blanc, it might be said, and only one of them is Mont Blanc. So what is it that makes the airliner and the human complicated, if Mont Blanc is simple? Any old jumbled collection of parts is unique and, *with hindsight*, is as improbable as any other. The scrap-heap at an aircraft breaker's yard is unique. No two scrap-heaps are the same. If you start throwing fragments of aeroplanes into heaps, the odds of your happening to hit upon exactly the same arrangement of junk twice are just about as low as the odds of your throwing together a working airliner. So, why don't we say that a rubbish dump, or Mont Blanc, or the moon, is just as complex as an aeroplane or a dog, because in all these cases the arrangement of atoms is 'improbable'?

The combination lock on my bicycle has 4,096 different positions. Every one of these is equally 'improbable' in the sense that, if you spin the wheels at random, every one of the 4,096 positions is equally unlikely to turn up. I can spin the wheels at random, look at whatever number is displayed and exclaim with hindsight: 'How amazing. The odds against that number appearing are 4,096: 1. A minor miracle!' That is equivalent to regarding the particular arrangement of rocks in a mountain, or of bits of metal in a scrap-heap, as 'complex.' But one of those 4,096 wheel positions really is interestingly unique: The combination 1207 is the only one that opens the lock. The uniqueness of 1207 has nothing to do with hindsight: It is specified in advance by the manufacturer. If you spun the wheels at random and happened to hit 1207 first time, you would be able to steal the bike, and it would seem a minor miracle. If you struck lucky on one of those multi-dialled combination locks on bank safes, it would seem a very major miracle, for the odds against it are many millions to one, and you would be able to steal a fortune.

Now, hitting upon the lucky number that opens the bank's safe is the equivalent, in our analogy, of hurling scrap metal around at random and happening to assemble a Boeing 747. Of all the millions of unique and, with hindsight equally improbable, positions of the combination lock, only one opens the lock. Similarly, of all the millions of unique and, with hindsight equally improbable, arrangements of a heap of junk, only one (or very few) will fly. The uniqueness of the arrangement that flies, or that opens the safe, is nothing to do with hindsight. It is specified in advance. The lock-manufacturer fixed the combination, and he has told the bank manager. The ability to fly is a property of an airliner that we specify in advance. If we see a plane in the air we can be sure that it was not assembled by randomly throwing scrap metal together, because we know that the odds against a random conglomeration's being able to fly are too great.

Now, if you consider all possible ways in which the rocks of Mont Blanc could have been thrown together, it is true that only one of them would make Mont Blanc as we know it. But Mont Blanc as we know it is defined with hindsight. Any one of a very large number of ways of throwing rocks together would be labelled a mountain, and might have been named Mont Blanc. There is nothing special about the particular Mont Blanc that we know, nothing specified in advance, nothing equivalent to the plane taking off, or equivalent to the safe door swinging open and the money tumbling out. . . .

Accumulating Small Change

. . . The essential difference between single-step selection and cumulative selection is this. In single-step selection the entities selected or sorted, pebbles or whatever they are, are sorted once and for all. In cumulative selection, on the other hand, they 'reproduce,' or in some other way the results of one sieving process are fed into a subsequent sieving, which is fed into . . . , and so on. The entities are subjected to selection or sorting over many 'generations' in succession. The end-product of one generation of selection is the starting point for the next generation of selection, and so on for many generations. It is natural to borrow such words as 'reproduce' and 'generation,' which have associations with living things, because living things are the main examples we know of things that participate in cumulative selection. They may in practice be the only things that do. But for the moment I don't want to beg that question by saying so outright.

Sometimes clouds, through the random kneading and carving of the winds, come to look like familiar objects. There is a much published photograph, taken by the pilot of a small aeroplane, of what looks a bit like the face of Jesus, staring out of the sky. We have all seen clouds that reminded us of something—a sea horse, say, or a smiling face. These resemblances come about by single-step selection, that is to say by a single coincidence. They are, consequently, not very impressive. The resemblance of the signs of the zodiac to the animals after which they are named, Scorpio, Leo, and so on, is as unimpressive as the predictions of astrologers. We don't feel overwhelmed by the resemblance, as we are by biological adaptations—the products of cumulative selection. We describe as weird, uncanny or spectacular, the resemblance of, say, a leaf insect to a leaf or a praying mantis to a cluster of pink flowers. The resemblance of a cloud to a weasel is only mildly diverting, barely worth calling to the attention of our companion. Moreover, we are quite likely to change our mind about exactly what the cloud most resembles.

HAMLET: Do you see yonder cloud that's almost in shape of a camel?
POLONIUS: By the mass, and 'tis like a camel, indeed.
HAMLET: Methinks it is like a weasel.
POLONIUS: It is backed like a weasel.
HAMLET: Or like a whale?
POLONIUS: Very like a whale.

I don't know who it was first pointed out that, given enough time, a monkey bashing away at random on a typewriter could produce all the works of Shakespeare. The operative phrase is, of course, given enough time. Let us limit the task facing our monkey somewhat. Suppose that he has to produce, not the complete works of Shakespeare but just the short sentence 'Methinks it is like a weasel,' and we shall make it relatively easy by giving him a typewriter with a restricted keyboard, one with just the 26 (capital) letters, and a space bar. How long will he take to write this one little sentence?

The sentence has 28 characters in it, so let us assume that the monkey has a series of discrete 'tries,' each consisting of 28 bashes at the keyboard. If he types the phrase correctly, that is the end of the experiment. If not, we allow him another 'try' of 28 characters. I don't know any monkeys, but fortunately my 11-month old daughter is an experienced randomizing device, and she proved only too eager to step into the role of monkey typist. Here is what she typed on the computer:

UMMK JK CDZZ F ZD DSDSKSM
S SS FMCV PU I DDRGLKDXRRDO
RDTE QDWFDVIOY UDSKZWDCCVYT
H CHVY NMGNBAYTDFCCVD D
RCDFYYYRM N DFSKD LD K WDWK
JJKAUIZMZI UXDKIDISFUMDKUDXI

She has other important calls on her time, so I was obliged to program the computer to simulate a randomly typing baby or monkey:

WDLDMNLT DTJBKWJR7REZLMQCO P
Y YVMQKZPGJXWVHGLAWFVCHQYOPY
MWR SWTNUXMLCDLEUBXTQHNZVJQF
FU OVAODVYKDGXDEKYVMOGGS VT
HZQZDSFZIHIVPHZPETPWVOVPMZGF
GEWRGZRPBCTPGQMCKHFDBGW ZCCF

And so on and on. It isn't difficult to calculate how long we should reasonably expect to wait for the random computer (or baby or monkey) to type METHINKS IT IS LIKE A WEASEL. Think about the total number of *possible* phrases of the right length that the monkey or baby or random computer *could* type. It is the same kind of calculation as we did for haemoglobin, and it produces a similarly large result. There are 27 possible letters (counting 'space' as one letter) in the first position. The chance of the monkey happening to get the first letter—M—right is therefore 1 in 27. The chance of it getting the first two letters—ME—right is the chance of it getting the second letter—E—right (1 in 27) *given that* it has also got the first letter—M—right, therefore $1/27 \times 1/27$, which equals 1/729. The chance of it getting the first word—METHINKS—right is 1/27 for each of the 8 letters, therefore $(1/27) \times (1/27) \times (1/27) \times (1/27) \ldots$, etc. 8 times, or (1/27) to the power 8. The chance of it getting the entire phrase of 28 characters right is (1/27) to the power 28, i.e., (1/27) multiplied by itself 28 times. These are very small odds, about

1 in 10,000 million million million million million million. To put it mildly, the phrase we seek would be a long time coming, to say nothing of the complete works of Shakespeare.

So much for single-step selection of random variation. What about cumulative selection, how much more effective should this be? Very very much more effective, perhaps more so than we at first realize, although it is almost obvious when we reflect further. We again use our computer monkey, but with a crucial difference in its program. It again begins by choosing a random sequence of 28 letters, just as before:

WDLMNLT DTJBKWIRZREZLMQCO P

It now 'breeds from' this random phrase. It duplicates it repeatedly, but with a certain chance of random error—'mutation'—in the copying. The computer examines the mutant nonsense phrases, the 'progeny' of the original phrase, and chooses the one which, *however slightly*, most resembles the target phrase, METHINKS IT IS LIKE A WEASEL. In this instance the winning phrase of the next 'generation' happened to be:

WDLTMNLT DTJBSWIRZREZLMQCO P

Not an obvious improvement! But the procedure is repeated, again mutant 'progeny' are 'bred from' the phrase, and a new 'winner' is chosen. This goes on, generation after generation. After 10 generations, the phrase chosen for 'breeding' was:

MDLDMNLS ITJISWHRZREZ MECS P

After 20 generations it was:

MELDINLS IT ISWPRKE Z WECSEL

By now, the eye of faith fancies that it can see a resemblance to the target phrase. By 30 generations there can be no doubt:

METHINGS IT ISWLIKE B WECSEL

Generation 40 takes us to within one letter of the target:

METHINKS IT IS LIKE I WEASEL

And the target was finally reached in generation 43. A second run of the computer began with the phrase:

Y YVMQKZPFJXWVHGLAWFVCHQXYOPY,

passed through (again reporting only every tenth generation):

Y YVMQKSPFTXWSHLIKEFV HQYSPY
YETHINKSPITXISHLIKEFA WQYSEY
METHINKS IT ISSLIKE A WEFSEY
METHINKS IT ISBLIKE A WEASES
METHINKS IT ISJLIKE A WEASEO
METHINKS IT IS LIKE A WEASEP

and reached the target phrase in generation 64. In a third run the computer started with:

GEWRGZRPBCTPGQMCKHFDBGW ZCCF

and reached METHINKS IT IS LIKE A WEASEL in 41 generations of selective 'breeding.'

The exact time taken by the computer to reach the target doesn't matter. If you want to know, it completed the whole exercise for me, the first time, while I was out to lunch. It took about half an hour. (Computer enthusiasts may think this unduly slow. The reason is that the program was written in BASIC, a sort of computer baby-talk. When I rewrote it in Pascal, it took 11 seconds.) Computers are a bit faster at this kind of thing than monkeys, but the difference really isn't significant. What matters is the difference between the time taken by *cumulative* selection, and the time which the same computer, working flat out at the same rate, would take to reach the target phrase if it were forced to use the other procedure of *single-step selection*: about a million million million million million years. This is more than a million million million times as long as the universe has so far existed. Actually it would be fairer just to say that, in comparison with the time it would take either a monkey or a randomly programmed computer to type our target phrase, the total age of the universe so far is a negligibly small quantity, so small as to be well within the margin of error for this sort of back-of-an-envelope calculation. Whereas the time taken for a computer working randomly but with the constraint of *cumulative selection* to perform the same task is of the same order as humans ordinarily can understand, between 11 seconds and the time it takes to have lunch.

There is a big difference, then, between cumulative selection (in which each improvement, however slight, is used as a basis for future building), and single-step selection (in which each new 'try' is a fresh one). If evolutionary progress had had to rely on single-step selection, it would never have got anywhere. If, however, there was any way in which the necessary conditions for *cumulative* selection could have been set up by the blind forces of nature, strange and wonderful might have been the consequences. As a matter of fact that is exactly what happened on this planet, and we ourselves are among the most recent, if not the strangest and most wonderful, of those consequences.

It is amazing that you can still read calculations like my haemoglobin calculation, used as though they constituted arguments *against* Darwin's theory. The people who do this, often expert in their own field, astronomy or whatever it may be, seem sincerely to believe that Darwinism explains living organization in terms of chance—'single-step selection'—alone. This belief, that Darwinian evolution is 'random,' is not merely false. It is the exact opposite of the truth. Chance is a minor ingredient in the Darwinian recipe, but the most important ingredient is cumulative selection which is quintessentially *non*random.

Clouds are not capable of entering into cumulative selection. There is no mechanism whereby clouds of particular shapes can spawn daughter clouds resembling themselves. If there were such a mechanism, if a cloud resembling a weasel or a camel could give rise to a lineage of other clouds of roughly the same shape, cumulative selection would have the opportunity to get going. Of course, clouds do break up and form 'daughter' clouds sometimes, but this isn't enough for cumulative selection. It is also necessary that the 'progeny' of any given cloud should resemble its 'parent' *more* than it resembles any old 'parent' in the 'population.' This vitally important point is apparently misunderstood by some of the philosophers who have, in recent years, taken an interest in the theory of natural selection. It is further necessary that the chances of a given cloud's surviving and spawning copies should depend upon its shape. Maybe in some distant galaxy these conditions did arise, and the result, if enough millions of years have gone by, is an ethereal, wispy form of life. This might make a good science fiction story—*The White Cloud*, it could be called—but for our purposes a computer model like the monkey/Shakespeare model is easier to grasp.

Although the monkey/Shakespeare model is useful for explaining the distinction between single-step selection and cumulative selection, it is misleading in important ways. One of these is that, in each generation of selective 'breeding,' the mutant 'progeny' phrases were judged according to the criterion of resemblance to a *distant ideal* target, the phrase METHINKS IT IS LIKE A WEASEL. Life isn't like that. Evolution has no long-term goal. There is no long-distance target, no final perfection to serve as a criterion for selection, although human vanity cherishes the absurd notion that our species is the final goal of evolution. In real life, the criterion for selection is always short-term, either simple survival or, more generally, reproductive success. If, after the aeons, what looks like progress towards some distant goal seems, with hindsight, to have been achieved, this is always an incidental consequence of many generations of short-term selection. The 'watchmaker' that is cumulative natural selection is blind to the future and has no long-term goal. . . .

I quote from Francis Hitching's book of 1982 called *The Neck of the Giraffe* or *Where Darwin Went Wrong*. I could have quoted basically the same words from almost any Jehovah's Witness tract, but I choose this book because a reputable publisher (Pan Books Ltd) saw fit to publish it, despite a very large number of errors which would quickly have been spotted if an unemployed biology graduate, or indeed undergraduate, had been asked to glance through the manuscript. (My favourites, if you'll indulge me just two in-jokes, are the conferring of a knighthood on Professor John Maynard Smith, and the description of Professor Ernst Mayr, that eloquent and most unmathematical arch-critic of mathematical genetics, as 'the high priest' of mathematical genetics.)

For the eye to work the following minimum perfectly coordinated steps have to take place (there are many others happening simultaneously, but even a grossly simplified description is enough to point up the problems for

Darwinian theory). The eye must be clean and moist, maintained in this state by the interaction of the tear gland and movable eyelids, whose eyelashes also act as a crude filter against the sun. The light then passes through a small transparent section of the protective outer coating (the *cornea*), and continues via a *lens* which focuses it on the back of the *retina*. Here 130 million light-sensitive rods and cones cause photochemical reactions which transform the light into electrical impulses. Some 1,000 million of these are transmitted every second, by means that are not properly understood, in a brain which then takes appropriate action.

Now it is quite evident that if the slightest thing goes wrong *en route*—if the cornea is fuzzy, or the pupil fails to dilate, or the lens becomes opaque, or the focusing goes wrong—then a recognizable image is not formed. The eye either functions as a whole, or not at all. So how did it come to evolve by slow, steady, infinitesimally small Darwinian improvements? Is it really plausible that thousands upon thousands of lucky chance mutations happened coincidentally so that the lens and the retina, which cannot work without each other, evolved in synchrony? What survival value can there be in an eye that doesn't see?

This remarkable argument is very frequently made, presumably because people *want* to believe its conclusion. Consider the statement that 'if the slightest thing goes wrong . . . if the focusing goes wrong . . . a recognizable image is not formed.' The odds cannot be far from 50/50 that you are reading these words through glass lenses. Take them off and look around. Would you agree that 'a recognizable image is not formed'? If you are male, the odds are about 1 in 12 that you are colourblind. You may well be astigmatic. It is not unlikely that, without glasses, your vision is a misty blur. One of today's most distinguished (though not yet knighted) evolutionary theorists so seldom cleans his glasses that his vision is probably a misty blur anyway, but he seems to get along pretty well and, by his own account, he used to play a mean game of monocular squash. If you have lost your glasses, it may be that you upset your friends by failing to recognize them in the street. But you yourself would be even more upset if somebody said to you: 'Since your vision is now not absolutely perfect, you might as well go around with your eyes tight shut until you find your glasses again.' Yet that is essentially what the author of the passage I have quoted is suggesting.

He also states, as though it were obvious, that the lens and the retina cannot work without each other. On what authority? Someone close to me has had a cataract operation in both eyes. She has no lenses in her eyes at all. Without glasses she couldn't even begin to play lawn tennis or aim a rifle. But she assures me that you are far better off with a lensless eye than with no eye at all. You can tell if you are about to walk into a wall or another person. If you were a wild creature, you could certainly use your lensless eye to detect the looming shape of a predator, and the direction from which it was approaching. In a primitive world where some creatures had no eyes at all and others had lensless eyes, the ones with lensless eyes would have all sorts of advantages. And there is a continuous series of Xs, such that each tiny improvement in sharpness of image, from swimming blur to perfect human vision, plausibly increases the organism's chances of surviving.

The book goes on to quote Stephen Jay Gould, the noted Harvard palaeontologist, as saying:

> We avoid the excellent question, What good is 5 percent of an eye? by arguing that the possessor of such an incipient structure did not use it for sight.

An ancient animal with 5 percent of an eye might indeed have used it for something other than sight, but it seems to me at least as likely that it used it for 5 percent vision. And actually I don't think it is an excellent question. Vision that is 5 percent as good as yours or mine is very much worth having in comparison with no vision at all. So is 1 percent vision better than total blindness. And 6 percent is better than 5, 7 percent better than 6, and so on up the gradual, continuous series. . . .

Origins are Miracles
. . . There are some levels of sheer luck, not only too great for puny human imaginations, but too great to be allowed in our hard-headed calculations about the origin of life. But, to repeat the question, how great a level of luck, how much of a miracle, *are* we allowed to postulate? Don't let's run away from this question just because large numbers are involved. It is a perfectly valid question, and we can at least write down what we would need to know in order to calculate the answer.

Now here is a fascinating thought. The answer to our question—of how much luck we are allowed to postulate—depends upon whether our planet is the only one that has life, or whether life abounds all around the universe. The one thing we know for certain is that life has arisen once, here on this very planet. But we have no idea at all whether there is life anywhere else in the universe. It is entirely possible that there isn't. Some people have calculated that there must be life elsewhere, on the following grounds (I won't point out the fallacy until afterwards). There are probably at least 10^{20} (i.e., 100 billion billion) roughly suitable planets in the universe. We know that life has arisen here, so it can't be *all* that improbable. Therefore it is almost inescapable that at least some among all those billions of billions of other planets have life.

The flaw in the argument lies in the inference that, *because life has arisen here*, it can't be too terribly improbable. You will notice that this inference contains the built-in assumption that whatever went on Earth is likely to have gone on elsewhere in the universe, and this begs the whole question. In other words, that kind of statistical argument, that there must be life elsewhere in the universe because there is life here, builds in, as an assumption, what it is setting out to prove. This doesn't mean that the conclusion that life exists all around the universe is necessarily wrong. My guess is that it is probably right. It simply means that that particular argument that led up to it is no argument at all. It is just an assumption.

Let us, for the sake of discussion, entertain the alternative assumption that life has arisen only once, ever, and that was here on Earth. It is tempting to object to this assumption on the following emotional grounds. Isn't there something terribly medieval about it? Doesn't it recall the time when the church taught that our Earth was the centre of the universe, and the stars just little pinpricks of light set in the sky for our delight (or, even more absurdly presumptuous, that the stars go out of their way to exert astrological influences on our little lives)? How very conceited to assume that, out of all the billions of billions of planets in the universe, our own little backwater of a world, in our own local backwater of a solar system, in our own local backwater of a galaxy, should have been singled out for life? Why, for goodness sake, should it have been *our* planet?

I am genuinely sorry, for I am heartily thankful that we have escaped from the small-mindedness of the medieval church and I despise modern astrologers, but I am afraid that the rhetoric about backwaters in the previous paragraph is just empty rhetoric. It is *entirely* possible that our backwater of a planet is literally the only one that has ever borne life. The point is that if there *were* only one planet that had ever borne life, then it would *have* to be our planet, for the very good reason that 'we' are here discussing the question! If the origin of life *is* such an improbable event that it happened on only one planet in the universe, then our planet has to be that planet. So, we can't use the fact that Earth has life to conclude that life must be probable enough to have arisen on another planet. Such an argument would be circular. We have to have some independent arguments about how easy or difficult it is for life to originate on a planet, before we can even begin to answer the question of how many other planets in the universe have life.

But that isn't the question we set out with. Our question was, how much luck are we allowed to assume in a theory of the origin of life on Earth? I said that the answer depends upon whether life has arisen only once, or many times. Begin by giving a name to the probability, however low it is, that life will originate on any randomly designated planet of some particular type. Call this number the spontaneous generation probability or SGP. It is the SGP that we shall arrive at if we sit down with our chemistry textbooks, or strike sparks through plausible mixtures of atmospheric gases in our laboratory, and calculate the odds of replicating molecules springing spontaneously into existence in a typical planetary atmosphere. Suppose that our best guess of the SGP is some very very small number, say one in a billion. This is obviously such a small probability that we haven't the faintest hope of duplicating such a fantastically lucky, miraculous event as the origin of life in our laboratory experiments. Yet if we assume, as we are perfectly entitled to do for the sake of argument, that life has originated only once in the universe, it follows that we are *allowed* to postulate a very large amount of luck in a theory, because there are so many planets in the universe where life *could* have originated. If, as one estimate has it, there are 100 billion billion planets, this is 100 billion times greater than even the very low SGP that we postulated. To conclude this argument, the maximum amount of luck that we are allowed to assume, before we reject a particular theory of the origin of life, has odds of one in N, where N is the number of suitable planets in the universe. There is a lot hidden in that word 'suitable,' but let us put an upper limit of 1 in 100 billion billion for the maximum amount of luck that this argument entitles us to assume.

Think about what this means. We go to a chemist and say: Get out your textbooks and your calculating machine; sharpen your pencil and your wits; fill your head with formulae, and your flasks with methane and ammonia and hydrogen and carbon dioxide and all the other gases that a primeval nonliving planet can be expected to have; cook them all up together; pass strokes of lightning through your simulated atmospheres, and strokes of inspiration through your brain; bring all your clever chemist's methods to bear, and give us your best chemist's estimate of the probability that a typical planet will spontaneously generate a self-replicating molecule. Or, to put it another way, how long would we have to wait before random chemical events on the planet, random thermal jostling of atoms and molecules, resulted in a self-replicating molecule?

Chemists don't know the answer to this question. Most modern chemists would probably say that we'd have to wait a long time by the standards of a human lifetime, but perhaps not all that long by the standards of cosmological time. The fossil history of earth suggests that we have about a billion years—one 'aeon,' to use a convenient modern definition—to play with, for this is roughly the time that elapsed between the origin of the Earth about 4.5 billion years ago and the era of the first fossil organisms. But the point of our 'numbers of planets' argument is that, even if the chemist said that we'd have to wait for a 'miracle,' have to wait a billion billion years—far longer than the universe has existed, we can still accept this verdict with equanimity. There are probably more than a billion billion available planets in the universe. If each of them lasts as long as Earth, that gives us about a billion billion billion planet-years to play with. That will do nicely! A miracle is translated into practical politics by a multiplication sum.

Discussion Questions

1. Early in the article Dawkins writes, "Each one of us in a machine." Some people believe that this view of humanity diminishes the value that we place on human beings. How does this affect your view of humans?

2. Elsewhere in Dawkins' book he writes, "Words are our servants, not our masters." What does this mean to you? In what ways can words be "masters" of us and what problems might result from this?

3. Imagine holding the opposite view that you currently hold regarding creationism (God created everything as it is) and evolution. How does this affect your view of other issues such as morality, science, the soul, humanity, etc.?

Believing Where We Cannot Prove

Philip Kitcher

A philosophy professor at Columbia University, Philip Kitcher has taught at numerous other universities, including Vassar College, University of Vermont, University of Minnesota, and University of California at San Diego. He focuses primarily on philosophy of science. He has published over one hundred articles in academic journals, as well as eight books.

In this selection, taken from Chapter 2 of his book *Abusing Science: The Case Against Creationism*, Kitcher gives a philosophical analysis of the creationism–evolution debate. In first defining science and then portraying creationism as non-scientific, he argues that creationism should not be given "equal time" in science classes (a current goal of the creationist "movement").

Reading Questions

1. What criticisms of evolution by creationists does Kitcher cite in the opening pages?
2. What does Kitcher say about the fallibility of science? How does he compare it to the fallibility of our senses and of math?
3. How does this statement of Kitcher's defend evolutionary theory: "Scientific theories . . . rest on indirect arguments from the observational evidence"? What does Kitcher say about scientific *theories*?
4. Explain "deductive interference" and "deductive validity."
5. Explain the critique of evolutionary theory cited in (a) and (b) of the first paragraph under "Predictive Failure." Then, explain why Kitcher says they are "mutually contradictory."
6. What problem does Kitcher suggest regarding Popper's criterion of falsifiablity in science?
7. What is Pierre Duhem's insight and how does it apply to the example of Newton's theory and the discovery of Venus? What other two "morals of the story" (characteristics of science) does Kitcher draw from the "Venus example"?
8. How does Kitcher respond to the creationist claim that evolutionary theory is not science?
9. At the end, why does Kitcher mention unsolved problems in evolutionary theory?

Opening Moves

Simple distinctions come all too easily. Frequently we open the way for later puzzlement by restricting the options we take to be available. So, for example, in contrasting science and religion, we often operate with a simple pair of categories.

Source: Philip Kitcher, "Believing Where We Cannot Prove" from *Abusing Science,* pp. 30–34, 34–36, 37–39, 44–54. Copyright © 1982 The Massachusetts Institute of Technology. Reprinted by permission of The MIT Press.

On one side there is science, proof, and certainty; on the other, religion, conjecture, and faith.

The opening lines of Tennyson's *In Memoriam* offer an eloquent statement of the contrast:

Strong Son of God, immortal love,
Whom we, that have not seen Thy face,
By faith, and faith alone, embrace,
Believing where we cannot prove.

A principal theme of Tennyson's great poem is his struggle to maintain faith in the face of what seems to be powerful scientific evidence. Tennyson had read a popular work by Robert Chambers, *Vestiges of the Natural History of Creation*, and he was greatly troubled by the account of the course of life on earth that the book contains. *In Memoriam* reveals a man trying to believe where he cannot prove, a man haunted by the thought that the proofs may be against him.

Like Tennyson, contemporary Creationists accept the traditional contrast between science and religion. But where Tennyson agonized, they attack. While they are less eloquent, they are supremely confident of their own solution. They open their onslaught on evolutionary theory by denying that it is a science. In *The Troubled Waters of Evolution*, Henry Morris characterizes evolutionary theory as maintaining that large amounts of time are required for evolution to produce "new kinds." As a result, we should not expect to see such "new kinds" emerging. Morris comments, "Creationists in turn insist that this belief is not scientific evidence but only a statement of faith. The evolutionist seems to be saying, Of course, we cannot really *prove* evolution, since this requires ages of time, and so, therefore, you should accept it as a proved fact of science! Creationists regard this as an odd type of logic, which would be entirely unacceptable in any other field of science." David Watson makes a similar point in comparing Darwin with Galileo: "So here is the difference between Darwin and Galileo: Galileo set a demonstrable *fact* against a few words of Bible poetry which the Church at that time had understood in an obviously naive way; Darwin set an unprovable *theory* against eleven chapters of straightforward history which cannot be reinterpreted in any satisfactory way."

The idea that evolution is conjecture, faith, or "philosophy" pervades Creationist writings. It is absolutely crucial to their case for equal time for "scientific" Creationism. This ploy has succeeded in winning important adherents to the Creationist cause. As he prepared to defend Arkansas law 590, Attorney General Steven Clark echoed the Creationist judgment. "Evolution," he said, "is just a theory." Similar words have been heard in Congress. William Dannemeyer, a congressman from California, introduced a bill to limit funding to the Smithsonian with the following words: "If the theory of evolution is just that—a theory—and if that theory can be regarded as a religion . . . then it occurs to this

Member that other Members might prefer it not to be given exclusive or top billing in our Nation's most famous museum but equal billing or perhaps no billing at all."

In their attempt to show that evolution is not science, Creationists receive help from the least likely sources. Great Scientists sometimes claim that certain facts about the past evolution of organisms are "demonstrated" or "indubitable." But Creationists also can (and do) quote scientists who characterize evolution as "dogma" and contend that there is no conclusive proof of evolutionary theory. Evolution is not part of science because, as evolutionary biologists themselves concede, science demands proof, and, as other biologists point out, proof of evolution is not forthcoming.

The rest of the Creationist argument flows easily. We educate our children in evolutionary theory as if it were a proven fact. We subscribe officially, in our school system, to one faith—an atheistic, materialistic faith—ignoring rival beliefs. Antireligious educators deform the minds of children, warping them to accept as gospel a doctrine that has no more scientific support than the true Gospel. The very least that should be done is to allow for both alternatives to be presented.

We should reject the Creationists' gambit. Eminent scientists notwithstanding, science is not a body of demonstrated truths. Virtually all of science is an exercise in believing where we cannot prove. Yet, scientific conclusions are not embraced by faith alone. Tennyson's dichotomy was too simple.

Inconclusive Evidence

Sometimes we seem to have conclusive reasons for accepting a statement as true. It is hard to doubt that 2 + 2 = 4. If, unlike Lord Kelvin's ideal mathematician, we do not find it obvious that

$$\int_{-\infty}^{+\infty} e^{-x^2}\, dx = \sqrt{\pi},$$

at least the elementary parts of mathematics appear to command our agreement. The direct evidence of our senses seems equally compelling. If I see the pen with which I am writing, holding it firmly in my unclouded view, how can I doubt that it exists? The talented mathematician who has proved a theorem and the keen-eyed witness of an episode furnish our ideals of certainty in knowledge. What they tell us can be engraved in stone, for there is no cause for worry that it will need to be modified.

Yet, in another mood, one that seems "deeper" or more "philosophical," skeptical doubts begin to creep in. Is there really anything of which we are so certain that later evidence could not give us reason to change our minds? Even when we think about mathematical proof, can we not imagine that new discoveries may cast doubt on the cogency of our reasoning? (The history of mathematics reveals that sometimes what seems for all the world like a proof may have a false conclusion.) Is it not possible that the most careful observer may have missed something? Or that the witness brought preconceptions to the observation that subtly biased what was reported? Are we not *always* fallible?

I am mildly sympathetic to the skeptic's worries. Complete certainty is best seen as an ideal toward which we strive and that is rarely, if ever, attained. Conclusive evidence always eludes us. Yet even if we ignore skeptical complaints and imagine that we are sometimes lucky enough to have conclusive reasons for accepting a claim as true, we should not include scientific reasoning among our paradigms of proof. Fallibility is the hallmark of science.

This point should not be so surprising. The trouble is that we frequently forget it in discussing contemporary science. When we turn to the history of science, however, our fallibility stares us in the face. The history of the natural sciences is strewn with the corpses of intricately organized theories, each of which had, in its day, considerable evidence in its favor. When we look at the confident defenders of those theories we should see anticipations of ourselves. The eighteenth-century scientists who believed that heat is a "subtle fluid," the atomic theorists who maintained that water molecules are compounded out of one atom of hydrogen and one of oxygen, the biochemists who identified protein as the genetic material, and the geologists who thought that continents cannot move were neither unintelligent nor ill informed. Given the evidence available to them, they were eminently reasonable in drawing their conclusions. History proved them wrong. It did not show that they were unjustified.

Why is science fallible? Scientific investigation aims to disclose the general principles that govern the workings of the universe. These principles are not intended merely to summarize what some select groups of humans have witnessed. Natural science is not just natural history. It is vastly more ambitious. Science offers us laws that are supposed to hold universally, and it advances claims about things that are beyond our power to observe. The nuclear physicist who sets down the law governing a particular type of radioactive decay is attempting to state a truth that holds throughout the entire cosmos and also to describe the behavior of things that we cannot even see. Yet, of necessity, the physicist's ultimate evidence is highly restricted. Like the rest of us, scientists are confined to a relatively small region of space and time and equipped with limited and imperfect senses.

How is science possible at all? How are we able to have any confidence about the distant regions of the cosmos and the invisible realm that lies behind the surfaces of ordinary things? The answer is complicated. Natural science follows intricate and ingenious procedures for fathoming the secrets of the universe. Scientists devise ways of obtaining especially revealing evidence. They single out some of the things we are able to see as crucial clues to the way that nature works. These clues are used to answer questions that cannot be addressed by direct observation. Scientific theories, even those that are most respected and most successful, rest on indirect arguments from the observational evidence. New discoveries can always call those arguments into question, showing scientists that the observed data should be understood in a different way, that they have misread their evidence. . . .

Once we have appreciated the fallibility of natural science and recognized its sources, we can move beyond the simple opposition of proof and faith. Between these extremes lies the vast field of cases in which we believe something on the basis of good—even excellent—but inconclusive evidence.

If we want to emphasize the fact that what scientists believe today may have to be revised in the light of observations made tomorrow, then we can describe all our science as "theory." But the description should not confuse us. To concede that evolutionary biology is a theory is not to suppose that there are alternatives to it that are equally worthy of a place in our curriculum. All theories are revisable, but not all theories are equal. Even though our present evidence does not *prove* that evolutionary biology—or quantum physics, or plate tectonics, or any other theory—is true, evolutionary biologists will maintain that the present evidence is overwhelmingly in favor of their theory and overwhelmingly against its supposed rivals. Their enthusiastic assertions that evolution is a proven fact can be charitably understood as claims that the (admittedly inconclusive) evidence we have for evolutionary theory is as good as we ever obtain for any theory in any field of science.

Hence the Creationist try for a quick Fools' Mate can easily be avoided. Creationists attempt to draw a line between evolutionary biology and the rest of science by remarking that large-scale evolution cannot be observed. This tactic fails. Large-scale evolution is no more inaccessible to observation than nuclear reactions or the molecular composition of water. For the Creationists to succeed in divorcing evolutionary biology from the rest of science, they need to argue that evolutionary theory is less well supported by the evidence than are theories in, for example, physics and chemistry. It will come as no surprise to learn that they try to do this. To assess the merits of their arguments we need a deeper understanding of the logic of inconclusive justification. We shall begin with a simple and popular idea: Scientific theories earn our acceptance by making successful predictions.

Predictive Success

Imagine that somebody puts forward a new theory about the origins of hay fever. The theory makes a number of startling predictions concerning connections that we would not have thought worth investigating. For example, it tells us that people who develop hay fever invariably secrete a particular substance in certain fatty tissues and that anyone who eats rhubarb as a child never develops hay fever. The theory predicts things that initially appear fantastic. Suppose that we check up on these predictions and find that they are borne out by clinical tests. Would we not begin to believe—and believe reasonably—that the theory was *at least* on the right track?

This example illustrates a pattern of reasoning that is familiar in the history of science. Theories win support by producing claims about what can be observed, claims that would not have seemed plausible prior to the advancement of the theory, but that are in fact found to be true when we make the appropriate observations. A classic (real) example is Pascal's confirmation of Torricelli's hypothesis that we live at the bottom of an ocean of air that presses down upon us. Pascal reasoned that if Torricelli's hypothesis were true, then air pressure should decrease at higher altitudes (because at higher altitudes we are closer to the "surface" of the atmosphere, so that the length of the column of air that presses down is shorter). Accordingly, he sent his brother-in-law to the top of a mountain to make some barometric measurements. Pascal's clever working out of the observational predictions of Torricelli's theory led to a dramatic predictive success for the theory.

The idea of predictive success has encouraged a popular picture of science. (We shall see later that this picture, while popular, is not terribly accurate.) Philosophers sometimes regard a theory as a collection of claims or statements. Some of these statements offer generalizations about the features of particular, recondite things (genes, atoms, gravitational force, quasars, and the like). These statements are used to infer statements whose truth or falsity can be decided by observation. (This appears to be just what Pascal did.) Statements belonging to this second group are called the *observational consequences* of the theory. Theories are supported when we find that their observational consequences (those that we have checked) are true. The credentials of a theory are damaged if we discover that some of its observational consequences are false. . . .

We can now make the second point much more precise. Any theory that has a false observational consequence must contain some false statement (or statements). For if all the statements in the theory were true, then, according to the standard definitions of *deductive validity* and *observational consequence*, any observational consequence would also has to be true. Hence, if a theory is found to have a false observational consequence, we must conclude that one or more statements of the theory is false.

This means that theories can be conclusively falsified, through the discovery that they have false observational consequences. Some philosophers, most notably Sir Karl Popper, have taken this point to have enormous significance for our understanding of science. According to Popper, the essence of a scientific theory is that it should be *falsifiable*. That is, if the theory is false, then it must be possible to show that it is false. Now, if a theory has utterly no observational consequences, it would be extraordinarily difficult to unmask that theory as false. So, to be a genuine scientific theory, a group of statements must have observational consequences. It is important to realize that Popper is not suggesting that every good theory must be false. The difference between being falsifiable and being false is like the difference between being vulnerable and actually being hurt. A good scientific theory should not be false. Rather, it must have observational consequences that could reveal the theory as mistaken if the experiments give the wrong results.

While these ideas about theory testing may seem strange in their formal attire, they emerge quite frequently in discussions of science. They also find their way into the creation-evolution debate.

Predictive Failure

From the beginning, evolutionary theory has been charged with just about every possible type of predictive failure. Critics of the theory have argued that (a) the theory makes no predictions (it is unfalsifiable and so fails Popper's criterion for science), (b) the theory makes false predictions (it is falsified), (c) the theory does not make the kinds of predictions it ought to make (the observations and experiments that evolutionary theorists undertake have no bearing on the theory). Many critics, including several Creationists, manage to advance all these objections in the same work. This is somewhat surprising, since points (a) and (b) are, of course, mutually contradictory.

The first objection is vitally important to the Creationist cause. Their opponents frequently insist that Creationism fails the crucial test for a scientific theory. The hypothesis that all kinds of organisms were separately fashioned by some "originator" is unfalsifiable. Creationists retort that they can play the same game equally well. *Any* hypothesis about the origins of life, including that advanced by evolutionary theory, is not subject to falsification. Hence we cannot justify a decision to teach evolutionary theory and not to teach Creationism by appealing to the Popperian criterion for genuine science.

The allegation that evolutionary theory fails to make any predictions is a completely predictable episode in any Creationist discussion of evolution. Often the point is made by appeal to the authority of Popper. Here are two sample passages:

> The outstanding philosopher of science, Karl Popper, though himself an evolutionist, pointed out cogently that evolution, no less than creation, is untestable and thus unprovable.
>
> Thus, for a theory to qualify as a scientific theory, it must be supported by events, processes or properties which can be observed, and the theory must be useful in predicting the outcome of future natural phenomena or laboratory experiments. An additional limitation usually imposed is that the theory must be capable of falsification. That is, it must be possible to conceive some experiment, the failure of which would disprove the theory.
>
> It is on the basis of such criteria that most evolutionists insist that creation be refused consideration as a possible explanation for origins. Creation has not been witnessed by human observers, it cannot be tested experimentally, and as a theory it is nonfalsifiable.

The general theory of evolution also fails to meet all three of these criteria, however.

These passages, and many others, draw on the picture of science sketched above. It is not clear that the Creationists really understand the philosophical views that they attempt to apply. Gish presents the most articulate discussion of the falsifiability criterion. Yet he muddles the issue by describing falsifiability as an "additional limitation" beyond predictive power. (The previous section shows that theories that make predictions are automatically falsifiable.) Nevertheless, the Creationist challenge is a serious one, and, if it could not be met, evolutionary theory would be in trouble.

Creationists buttress their charge of unfalsifiability with further objections. They are aware that biologists frequently look as though they are engaged in observations and experiments. Creationists would allow that researchers in biology sometimes make discoveries. What they deny is that the discoveries support evolutionary theory. They claim that laboratory manipulations fail to teach us about evolution in nature: "Even if modern scientists should ever actually achieve the artificial creation of life from non-life, or of higher kinds from lower kinds, in the laboratory, this would not *prove* in any way that such changes did, or even could, take place in the past by random natural processes". The standards of evidence to be applied to evolutionary biology have suddenly been raised. In this area of inquiry, it is not sufficient that a theory yield observational consequences whose truth or falsity can be decided in the laboratory. Creationists demand special kinds of predictions, and will dismiss as irrelevant any laboratory evidence that evolutionary theorists produce. [In this way, they try to defend point (c).] . . .

Naive Falsificationism

. . . The falsifiability criterion adopted from Popper—which I shall call the *naive falsificationist* criterion—is hopelessly flawed. It runs aground on a fundamental fact about the relation between theory and prediction: On their own, individual scientific laws, or the small groups of laws that are often identified as theories, do not have observational consequences. This crucial point about theories was first understood by the great historian and philosopher of science Pierre Duhem. Duhem saw clearly that individual scientific claims do not, and cannot, confront the evidence one by one. Rather, in his picturesque phrase, "Hypotheses are tested in bundles." Besides ruling out the possibility of testing an individual scientific theory (read, small group of laws), Duhem's insight has another startling consequence. We can only test relatively large bundles of claims. What this means is that when our experiments go awry we are not logically compelled to select any particular claim as the culprit. We can always save a cherished hypothesis from refutation by rejecting (however implausibly) one of the other members of the bundle. Of course, this is exactly what I did in the illustration of Newton and the apple above. Faced with disappointing results, I suggested that we could abandon the (tacit) additional claim that no large forces besides gravity were operating on the apple.

Creationists wheel out the ancient warhorse of naive falsificationism so that they can bolster their charge that evolutionary theory is not a science. The (very) brief course in deductive logic plus the whirlwind tour through naive falsificationism and its pitfalls enable us to see what is at the bottom of this seemingly important criticism. Creationists can appeal to naive falsificationism to show that evolution is not a science. But, given the traditional picture of theory and evidence I have sketched, one can appeal to naive falsificationism to show that *any* science is not a science. So, as with the charge that evolutionary change is unobservable, Creationists have again failed to find some "fault" of evolution not shared with every other science. (And, as we shall see, Creationists like some sciences, especially thermodynamics.) Consistent application of naive falsificationism can show that anybody's favorite science (whether it be quantum physics, molecular biology, or whatever) is not science. Of course, what this shows is that the naive falsificationist criterion is a very poor test of genuine science. To be fair, this point can cut both ways. Scientists who charge that "scientific" Creationism is unfalsifiable are not insulting the theory as much as they think.

Successful Science

Despite the inadequacies of naive falsificationism, there is surely something right in the idea that a science can succeed only if it can fail. An invulnerable "science" would not be science at all. To achieve a more adequate understanding of how a science can succeed and how it runs the risk of failure, let us look at one of the most successful sciences and at a famous episode in its development.

Newtonian celestial mechanics is one of the star turns in the history of science. Among its numerous achievements were convincing explanations of the orbits of most of the known planets. Newton and his successors viewed the solar system as a collection of bodies subject only to gravitational interactions; they used the law of gravitation and the laws of motion to compute the orbits. (Bodies whose effects were negligible in any particular case would be disregarded. For example, the gravitational attraction due to Mercury would not be considered in working out the orbit of Saturn.) The results usually tallied beautifully with astronomical observations. But one case proved difficult. The outermost known planet, Uranus, stubbornly followed an orbit that diverged from the best computations. By the early nineteenth century it was clear that something was wrong. Either astronomers erred in treating the solar system as a Newtonian gravitational system or there was some particular difficulty in applying the general method to Uranus.

Perhaps the most naive of falsificationists would have recommended that the central claim of Newtonian mechanics—the claim that the solar system is a Newtonian gravitational system—be abandoned. But there was obviously a more sensible strategy. Astronomers faced one problematical planet, and they asked themselves what made Uranus so difficult. Two of them, John Adams and Urbain Leverrier, came up with an answer. They proposed (independently) that there was a hitherto unobserved planet beyond Uranus. They computed the orbit of the postulated planet and demonstrated that the anomalies of the motion of Uranus could be explained if a planet followed this path. There was a straightforward way to test their proposal. Astronomers began to look for the new planet. Within a few years, the planet—Neptune—was found.

I will extract several morals from this success story. The first: . . . What is the proper use of auxiliary hypotheses? Adams and Leverrier saved the central claim of Newtonian celestial mechanics by offering an auxiliary hypothesis. They maintained that there were more things in the heavens than had been dreamed of in previous natural philosophy. The anomalies in the orbit of Uranus could be explained on the assumption of an extra planet. Adams and Leverrier worked out the exact orbit of that planet so that they could provide a detailed account of the perturbations—and so that they could tell their fellow astronomers where to look for Neptune. Thus, their auxiliary hypothesis was *independently testable*. The evidence for Neptune's existence was not just the anomalous motion of Uranus. The hypothesis could be checked independently of any assumptions about Uranus or about the correctness of Newtonian celestial mechanics—by making telescopic observations.

Since hypotheses are always tested in bundles, this method of checking presupposed other assumptions, in particular, the optical principles that justify the use of telescopes. The crucial point is that, while hypotheses are always tested in bundles, they can be tested in *different* bundles. An auxiliary hypothesis ought to be testable independently of the particular problem it is introduced to solve, independently of the theory it is designed to save. . . .

We can draw a second moral. A science should be *unified*. A thriving science is not a gerrymandered patchwork but a coherent whole. Good theories consist of just one problem-solving strategy, or a small family of problem-solving strategies, that can be applied to a wide range of problems. The theory succeeds as it is able to encompass more and more problem areas. Failure looms when the basic problem-solving strategy (or strategies) can resolve almost none of the problems in its intended domain without the "aid" of untestable auxiliary hypotheses. . . .

The final moral I want to draw from this brief look at Newtonian physics concerns *fecundity*. A great scientific theory, like Newton's, opens up new areas of research. Celestial mechanics led to the discovery of a previously unknown planet. Newtonian physics as a whole led to the development of previously unknown sciences. Because a theory presents a new way of looking at the world, it can lead us to ask new questions, and so to embark on new and fruitful lines of inquiry. Of the many flaws with the earlier picture of theories as sets of statements, none is more important than the misleading presentation of sciences as static and insular. Typically, a flourishing science is incomplete. At any time, it raises more questions than it can currently answer. But incompleteness is no vice. On the contrary, incompleteness is the mother of fecundity. Unresolved problems present challenges that enable a theory to flower in unanticipated ways. They also make the theory hostage to future developments. A good theory should be productive; it should raise new questions and presume that those questions can be answered without giving up its problem-solving strategies.

I have highlighted three characteristics of successful science. *Independent testability* is achieved when it is possible to test auxiliary hypotheses independently of the particular cases for which they are introduced. *Unification* is the result of applying a small family of problem-solving strategies to a broad class of cases. *Fecundity* grows out of incompleteness when a theory opens up new and profitable lines of investigation. . . .

The most global Creationist attack on evolutionary theory is the claim that evolution is not a science. If this claim were correct, then the dispute about what to teach in high school science classes would be over. In earlier parts of this chapter, we saw how Creationists were able to launch their broad criticisms. If one accepts the idea that science requires proof, or if one adopts the naive falsificationist criterion, then the theory of evolution—and every other scientific theory—will turn out not to be a part of science. So Creationist standards for science imply that there is no science to be taught. ·

However, we have seen that Creationist standards rest on a very poor understanding of science. In light of a clearer picture of the scientific enterprise, I have provided a more realistic group of tests for good science, bad science, and pseudoscience. Using this more sophisticated approach, I now want to address seriously the global Creationist questions about the theory of evolution. Is it a pseudoscience? Is it a poor science? On is it a great science? These are very important questions, for the appropriateness of granting equal time to Creation "science" depends, in part, on whether it can be regarded as the equal of the theory of evolution.

Darwin's Daring

The heart of Darwinian evolutionary theory is a family of problem-solving strategies, related by their common employment of a particular style of historical narrative. A *Darwinian history* is a piece of reasoning of the following general form. The first step consists in a description of an ancestral population of organisms. The reasoning proceeds by tracing the modification of the population through subsequent generations, showing how characteristics were selected, inherited, and became prevalent. . . .

Since Darwin's day, biologists have contributed parts of evolutionary theory that help to answer . . . important questions. Geneticists have advanced our understanding of the transmission of characteristics between generations and have enabled us to see how new characteristics can arise. Population geneticists have analyzed the variation present in populations of organisms; they have suggested how that variation is maintained and have specified ways in which characteristics can be fixed or eliminated. Workers in morphology and physiology have helped us to see how variations of particular kinds might yield advantages in particular environments. Ecologists have studied the ways in which interactions among populations can affect survival and fecundity.

The moral is obvious. Darwin gambled. He trusted that the questions he left open would be answered by independent biological sciences and that the deliverances of these sciences and that the deliverances of these sciences would be consistent with the presuppositions of Darwinian histories. Because of the breadth of his vision, Darwin made his theory vulnerable from a number of different directions. To take just one example, it could have turned out the mechanisms of heredity would have made it impossible for advantageous variations to be preserved and to spread. Indeed, earlier in this century, many biologists felt that the emerging views about inheritance did not fit into Darwin's picture, and the fortunes of Darwinian evolutionary theory were on the wane.

When we look at the last 120 years of the history of biology, it is impossible to ignore the fecundity of Darwin's ideas. Not only have inquiries into the presuppositions of Darwinian histories yielded new theoretical disciplines (like population genetics), but the problem-solving strategies have been extended to cover phenomena that initially appeared troublesome. One recent triumph has been the development of explanations for social interactions among animals. Behavior involving one animal's promotion of the good of others seems initially to pose a problem for evolutionary theory. How can we construct Darwinian histories for the emergence of such behavior? W. D. Hamilton's concept of inclusive fitness, and the deployment of game-theoretic ideas by R. L. Trivers and John Maynard Smith, revealed how the difficulty could be resolved by a clear extension of traditional Darwinian concepts.

Yet puzzles remain. One problem is the existence of sex. When an organism forms gametes (sperm cells or egg cells) there is a meiotic division, so that in sexual reproduction only half of an organism's genes are transmitted to each of its progeny. Because of this "cost of meiosis," it is hard to see how genotypes for sexual reproduction might have become prevalent. (Apparently, they will spread only half as fast as their asexual rivals.) So why is there sex? We do not have a compelling answer to the question. Despite some ingenious suggestions by orthodox Darwinians, there is no convincing Darwinian history for the emergence of sexual reproduction. However, evolutionary theorists believe that the problem will be solved without abandoning the main Darwinian insights—just as early nineteenth-century astronomers believed that the problem of the motion of Uranus could be overcome without major modification of Newton's celestial mechanics.

The comparison is apt. Like Newton's physics in 1800, evolutionary theory today rests on a huge record of successes. In both cases, we find a unified theory whose problem-solving strategies are applied to illuminate a host of diverse phenomena. Both theories offer problem solutions that can be subjected to rigorous independent checks. Both open up new lines of inquiry and have a history of surmounting apparent obstacles. The virtues of successful science are clearly displayed in both.

There is a simple way to put the point. Darwin is the Newton of biology. Evolutionary theory is not simply an area of science that has had some success at solving problems. It has unified biology and it has inspired important biological disciplines. Darwin himself appreciated the unification achieved by his theory and its promise of further development. Over a century later, at the beginning of his authoritative account of current views of species and their origins, Ernst Mayr explained how that promise had been fulfilled: "The theory of evolution is quite rightly called the greatest unifying theory in biology. The diversity of organisms, similarities and differences between kinds of organisms, patterns of distribution and behavior, adaptation and interaction, all this was merely a bewildering chaos of facts until given meaning by the evolutionary theory." Dobzhansky put the point even more concisely: "Nothing in biology makes sense except in the light of evolution."

Discussion Questions

1. What things do you believe "where we cannot prove"?
2. Examine your belief regarding God (either for or against). Do you think that your belief has been proven? If not, could it? And what, if anything, would have to be shown in order to change your belief?
3. In what way do you think that science also requires *faith* in a theory or in the method of science?
4. Do you like Kitcher's three criteria for science? Can you think of any more?
5. What do you think of Kitcher's reference to issues that evolutionary theory has failed to explain? How would a creationist answer these unsolved issues?

Movie Titles

1. *Bruce Almighty*—A personification of God. What would you do if you were all-powerful?
2. *Dogma* (R)—Brings up many issues surrounding God including omniscience, omnipotence, salvation, and evil.
3. *The Gods Must Be Crazy*—How does the Coke bottle shed any light on creationism? Do they use the bottle "incorrectly"? What other issues arise from the outside influence of the Coke bottle?

4. *Oh, God!*—God attempting to spread the word about Himself. Touches on God's omnipotence, miracles, His being perfect, and a bit on the problems of pain and evil as well.

Song Lyrics

Monty Python—"The Galaxy Song"
Jars of Clay—"Flood"
DC Talk—"So Help Me God"
Rakim—"Mystery (Who is God)"
Billy Preston—"That's The Way God Planned It"
Dan Hart—"Intelligent Design"

Notes

1. Cf. J. Wisdom, 'Other minds,' *Mind*, 1940; reprinted in his *Other Minds* (Blackwell, 1952).
2. A noted wrestler of the time.
3. Selection is a term that implies the making of a choice, a decision. Synonyms include picking out, choosing, and preferring. A mindless process cannot "select" in this sense. A river does not choose to follow the path of least resistance; sodium and chloride ions do not choose to form a salt crystal; gasoline, oxygen, and a spark do not choose to explode; and a colander does not choose to retain noodles. The term "natural selection" is an oxymoron and its widespread use contributes to the pervasive confusion so characteristic of this topic.
4. Teleology is the study of the evidences of design or purpose in nature.
5. "Consequently, theories of evolution which, in accordance with the philosophies inspiring them, consider the mind as emerging from the forces of living matter, or as a mere epiphenomenon of this matter, are incompatible with the truth about man. Nor are they able to ground the dignity of the human person." Pope John Paul II, message to the Pontifical Academy of Sciences (October 22, 1996), "Magisterium Is Concerned with Question of Evolution, for It Involves Conception of Man," *L'Osservatore Romano* (English), October 30, 1996, n. 5.
6. "Biology is the study of complicated things that give the appearance of having been designed for a purpose." Richard Dawkins, *The Blind Watchmaker: Why the Evidence of Evolution Reveals a Universe without Design* (New York: W.W. Norton & Company, 1996), 1. According to Francis Crick (codiscoverer of the structure of DNA, Nobel laureate, 1962), "biologists must constantly keep in mind that what they see was not designed, but rather evolved." Francis Crick, *What Mad Pursuit: A Personal View of Scientific Discovery* (London: Penguin Books, 1990), 138.
7. "Magisteria" is derived from the Latin word for "teacher." Stephen J. Gould asserts that science and religion are separate and distinct teaching authorities. Unfortunately, no true intellectual weight is given to the pronouncements of the latter. See idem., *Rocks of Ages: Science and Religion in the Fullness of Life* (London: Jonathan Cape, 2001).
8. Mano Singham describes the inherent problem with the overlapping magisteria in "The Science and Religion Wars," *Phi Delta Kappan* 81 (February 2000): 426. Although recognizing the problem as very real and significant, he has no solution. The solution we suggest is

for science to simply stick to what we expect it to do—investigate and explain origins objectively using the scientific method without bias and confine its explanations to those permitted by the data and logical analysis. The emerging speculative issues such as the inherent purpose of life, if any, then naturally fall into the domain of religion. So long as science conducts the investigation objectively like an umpire at a ball game, neither side should have cause to complain (other than the normal litany of epithets that are hurled at any umpire!).

Chapter 5

The Religious Problem of Evil

Loving parents let their children experience some challenges, some difficulties, and even some suffering, all with the hope that the child learn and grow from the experiences. Could it be that an all-good, all-powerful being created the universe in a similar manner— to allow for some suffering such that one can experience even greater virtues? Or does the existence of evil and suffering preclude the existence of such a being?

Could it be possible that we just don't understand evil, or that evil is merely a human-made concept that is not part of the world? Or maybe it is just the result of the divine gift of free will, or that it serves as a testing-ground for admission into the realm of the afterlife.

This has been a problem for many who posit the existence of the typically Western conception of God as all-good, all-powerful, and all-knowing. This section provides an overview of the problem. George Smith argues against the existence of God by addressing the position of the defender of God. Hick then provides a more contemporary defense of God (literally translated as "theodicy").

Atheism: The Case Against God

George Smith

George Smith served as the Senior Research Fellow at George Mason University for sixteen years, lecturing primarily in political philosophy and history. He has been the Director for the Forum for Philosophical Studies in Los Angeles and has published over one hundred articles in popular newspapers and magazines, as well as three books, all of which focus primarily on atheism and the problems and inconsistencies of religion. This selection is extracted from his first book *Atheism: The Case Against God*.

   Smith first states the "problem of evil"—considered a "problem" for religions such as Christianity that posit the existence of an all-powerful, all-knowing, all-good God. He then examines the most popular approaches to "theodicy"—attempts to defend/justify God in the face of evil—that have been suggested throughout the history of this problem.

Reading Questions

1. State the problem of evil in your own words while referencing God's attributes of omniscience, omnipotence, and omnibenevolence.
2. According to Smith, why is it inconsistent for the Christian to attempt to resolve the problem of evil by claiming that one cannot distinguish good from evil?
3. Why doesn't the portrayal of evil as a privation (a lack of good) solve the problem?
4. How does Smith first paraphrase the solution to the problem with regard to human free will? For what reasons does he then suggest it falls short?
5. What problem does Smith have with the attempted solution involving the reward of an afterlife? Why does he write, "The Christian God appears an immoral fiend of cosmic dimensions"?
6. How do *physical evils* differ from *moral evils*? How do physical evils factor into Smith's argument?
7. Why does Smith claim that the response to the suggestion of physical evils pushes us into agnosticism?
8. Explain Smith's critique of Hick's position. Why does Smith claim it to be *dogma*?

Briefly, the problem of evil is this: If God does not know there is evil, he is not omniscient. If God knows there is evil but cannot prevent it, he is not omnipotent. If God knows there is evil and can prevent it but desires not to, he is not omnibenevolent. If, as the Christian claims, God is all-knowing and all-powerful, we must conclude that God is not all-good. The existence of evil in the universe excludes this possibility.

Source: From *Atheism: The Case Against God* by George H. Smith (1989), pp. 81–87, Amherst, NY: Prometheus Books. Copyright © 1979 by George H. Smith. Reprinted with permission of the publisher.

There have been various attempts to escape from the problem of evil, and we shall briefly consider the more popular of these. But one point requires emphasis. The Christian, by proclaiming that God is good, commits himself to the position that man is capable of distinguishing good from evil—for, if he is not, how did the Christian arrive at his judgment of "good" as applied to God? Therefore, any attempt to resolve the problem of evil by arguing that man cannot correctly distinguish good from evil, destroys the original premise that it purports to defend and thus collapses from the weight of an internal inconsistency. If the human standards of good and evil are somehow invalid, the Christian's claim that God is good is equally invalid.

One general theological approach to the problem of evil consists of the claim that evil is in some way unreal or purely negative in character. This argument, however, is so implausible that few Christians care to defend it. The first problem with it, as Antony Flew notes, is: "If evil is really nothing then what is all the fuss about sin about: nothing?"

In *Some Dogmas of Religion*, John McTaggart quickly disposes of the claim that evil is in some way unreal:

> Supposing that it could be proved that all that we think evil was in reality good, the fact would still remain that we think it evil. This may be called a delusion or mistake. But a delusion or mistake is as *real* as anything else. A savage's erroneous belief that the earth is stationary is just as real a fact as an astronomer's correct belief that it moves. The delusion that evil exists, then, is real. But then . . . it seems certain that a delusion or an error which hid from us the goodness of the universe would itself be evil. And so there would be real evil after all. . . . However many times we pronounce evil unreal, we always leave a reality behind, which in its turn is to be pronounced evil.

As for the argument that evil is purely negative, a privation of the good (as disease may be said to be the absence of health), Wallace Matson provides this illuminating example in *The Existence of God*.

> It may console the paralytic to be told that paralysis is mere lack of mobility, nothing positive, and that insofar as he *is*, he is perfect. It is not clear, however, that this kind of comfort is available to the sufferer from malaria. He will reply that his trouble is not that he lacks anything, but rather that he has too much of something, namely protozoans of the genus *Plasmodium*.

Any attempt to absolve God of the responsibility for evil by claiming that, in the final analysis, there is no such thing as evil is, as Matson puts it, "an unfunny joke." This approach merely ends up by negating our human standards of good and evil, which, as previously indicated, undercuts the argument at its root.

Another common effort to reconcile God and evil is to argue that evil is the consequence of man's freely chosen actions. God, through his gift of free will, gave man the ability to distinguish and choose between good and evil, right and wrong. As a free agent, man has the potential to reach a higher degree of perfection and goodness than if he were a mere robot programmed to behave in a given manner. Thus it is good that man has free will. But this entails the opportunity for man to select evil instead of good, which has been the case in the instances of torture, murder, and cruelty which some men inflict upon others. The responsibility for these actions, however, rests with man, not with God. Therefore, concludes the Christian, evil does not conflict with the infinite goodness of God.

While this approach has some initial plausibility, it falls far short of solving the problem of evil. We are asked to believe that God created man with the power of choice in the hope that man would voluntarily pursue the good, but that man thwarts this desire of God through sin and thus brings evil upon himself. But, to begin with, to speak of frustrating or acting contrary to the wishes of an omnipotent being makes no sense whatsoever. There can be no barriers to divine omnipotence, no obstacles to thwart his desires, so we must assume that the present state of the world is precisely as God desires it to be. If God wished things to be other than they are, nothing could possibly prevent them from being other than they are, man's free will notwithstanding. In addition, we have seen that free will is incompatible with the foreknowledge possessed by an omniscient being, so the appeal to free will fails in this respect as well. In any case, God created man with full knowledge of the widespread suffering that would ensue, and, given his ability to prevent this situation, we must presume that God desired and willed these immoral atrocities to occur.

It is unfair to place the responsibility for immoral actions on man's free will in general. Individual men commit atrocities, not the bloodless abstraction "man." Some men commit blatant injustices, but others do not. Some men murder, rob, and cheat, but others do not. Some men choose a policy of wanton destructiveness, but others do not. And we must remember that crimes are committed by men against other men, innocent victims, who cannot be held responsible. The minimum requirement for a civilized society is a legal system whereby the individual liberties of men are protected from the aggressive activities of other men. We regard the recognition and protection of individual rights as a moral necessity, and we condemn governments that fail to provide a fair system of justice. How, then, are we to evaluate a God who permits widespread instances of injustice when it is easily within his power to prevent them? The Christian believes in a God who displays little, if any, interest in the protection of the innocent, and we must wonder how such a being can be called "good."

The standard reply to this objection is that God rewards the virtuous and punishes the wicked in an afterlife, so there is an overall balance of justice. An extreme variation of this tactic was reported in the *New York Times* of September 11, 1950. Referring to the Korean War, this article states: "Sorrowing parents whose sons have been drafted or recalled for combat duty were told yesterday in St. Patrick's Cathedral [by Monsignor William T. Greene] that death in battle was part of God's plan for populating 'the kingdom of heaven.'"

This approach is so obviously an exercise in theological rationalization that it deserves little comment. If every instance of evil is to be rectified by an appeal to an afterlife, the claim that God is all-good has no relevance whatsoever to our present life. Virtually any immoral action, no matter how hideous or atrocious, can be explained away in this fashion—which severs any attempt to discuss the alleged goodness of a creator from reference to empirical evidence. More importantly, no appeal to an afterlife can actually eradicate the problem of evil. An injustice always remains an injustice, regardless of any subsequent efforts to comfort the victim. If a father, after beating his child unmercifully, later gives him a lollipop as compensation, this does not erase the original act or its evil nature. Nor would we praise the father as just and loving. The same applies to God, but even more so. The Christian may believe that God will punish the perpetrators of evil and compensate the victims of injustice, but this does not explain why a supposedly benevolent and omnipotent being created a world with evildoers and innocent victims in the first place. Again, we must assume that there are innocent victims because God desires innocent victims; from the standpoint of Christian theism, there is simply no other explanation. If an omnipotent God did not want innocent victims, they could not exist—and, by human standards, the Christian God appears an immoral fiend of cosmic dimensions.

Even if we overlook the preceding difficulties, the appeal to free will is still unsuccessful, because it encompasses only so-called *moral* evils (i.e., the actions of men). There remains the considerable problem of *physical* evils, such as natural disasters, over which man has no control. Why are there floods, earthquakes, and diseases that kill and maim millions of persons? The responsibility for these occurrences obviously cannot be placed on the shoulders of man. From an atheistic standpoint, such phenomena are inimical to man's life and may be termed evil, but since they are the result of inanimate, natural forces and do not involve conscious intent, they do not fall within the province of moral judgment. But from a Christian perspective, God—the omnipotent creator of the natural universe—must bear ultimate responsibility for these occurrences, and God's deliberate choice of these evil phenomena qualifies him as immoral.

There is an interesting assortment of arguments designed to explain the existence of natural evils. Some theologians argue that evil exists for the sake of a greater good: Others maintain that apparent evils disappear into a universal harmony of good. Although something may appear evil to man, we are assured by the Christian that God is able to view the overall perspective, and any apparent evil always turns out for the best. These approaches share the premise that man cannot understand the ways of God, but this simply pushes us into agnosticism. It will not do for the Christian to posit an attribute of God and, when asked to defend that attribute, contend that man cannot understand it.

If we are incorrect in calling natural disasters, diseases, and other phenomena evil, then man is incapable of distinguishing good from evil. But if this is the case, by what standard does the Christian claim that God is good? What criterion is the Christian using?

If man cannot pass correct moral judgments, he cannot validly praise *or* condemn anything—including the Christian God. To exclude God from the judgment of evil is to exclude him from the judgment of good as well; but if man can distinguish good from evil, a supernatural being who willfully causes or permits the continuation of evil on his creatures merits unequivocal moral condemnation.

Some Christians resort to incredible measures to absolve their God from the responsibility for evil. Consider this passage from *Evil and the God of Love* in which John Hick attempts to reconcile the existence of an omnibenevolent deity with the senseless disasters that befall man:

> . . . men and women often act in true compassion and massive generosity and self-giving in the face of unmerited suffering, especially when it comes in such dramatic forms as an earthquake or a mining disaster. It seems, then, that in a world that is to be the scene of compassionate love and self-giving for others, suffering must fall upon mankind with something of the haphazardness and inequity that we now experience. It must be apparently unmerited, pointless, and incapable of being morally rationalized. For it is precisely this feature of our common human lot that creates sympathy between man and man and evokes the unselfish kindness and goodwill which are among the highest values of personal life.

Aside from displaying a low regard for man's "highest values" and their origins, Hick illustrates an important point: *There is virtually nothing which the Christian will accept as evidence of God's evil.* If disasters that are admittedly "unmerited, pointless, and incapable of being morally rationalized" are compatible with the "goodness" of God, what could possibly qualify as contrary evidence? The "goodness" of God, it seems, is compatible with any conceivable state of affairs. While we evaluate a man with reference to his actions, we are not similarly permitted to judge God. God is immune from the judgment of evil as a matter of principle.

Here we have a concrete illustration of theological "reasoning." Unlike the philosopher, the theologian adopts a position, a dogma, and then commits himself to a defense of that position come what may. While he may display a willingness to defend this dogma, closer examination reveals this to be a farce. His defense consists of distorting and rationalizing all contrary evidence to meet his desired specifications. In the case of divine benevolence, the theologian will grasp onto any explanation, no matter how implausible, before he will abandon his dogma. And when finally pushed into a corner, he will argue that man cannot understand the true meaning of this dogma.

This brings us to our familiar resting place. The "goodness" of God is different in kind from goodness as we comprehend it. To say that God's "goodness" is compatible with the worst disasters imaginable, is to empty this concept of its meaning. By human standards, the Christian God cannot be good. By divine standards, God may be "good" in some unspecified, unknowable way—but this term no longer makes any sense. And so, for the last time, we fail to comprehend the Christian God.

Discussion Questions

1. Do you think evil exists? If not, why? If so, what is it?
2. If you could create a universe, would you decrease the amount of evil and suffering? How?

3. The "Greater Goods Theory" (that evil and suffering allow/result in greater goods) is critiqued by saying that it results in a meaningless use of "good": An all-powerful God should be able to create/allow for goodness without having events like the 2004 tsunami that killed over 200,000 people. How do you address this issue?

4. If suffering really does create greater goods, then would you hope for more suffering for you and your loved ones? Why/why not?

5. Looking back on your life, what goods were likely greater due to any pain or suffering you endured?

6. Think back to your experience of the September 11 terrorist action. In what way did this change your perspective on life? In what ways did the behavior and concerns of others around you change? Could the good that resulted be valid support of the Greater Goods Theory?

7. If it is true that no conceivable event could disprove God's omnipotence and love, does that result in a weakness of the Christian's position? Does it matter if the Christian's position is unfalsifiable and irrefutable?

8. Does Smith overlook any good solutions to the problem of evil? If so, which ones? If not, has he successfully refuted all attempted solutions?

9. Taking the analogy of the parent child relationship, in what ways does the parent allow or cause pain and suffering of their children in a *justifiable* way? Is this ever the case? Is this a good analogy in examining the God-creation relationship?

10. Leibniz argued that "this is the best of all possible worlds." Do you agree? In what ways could you make it better? Is it even possible for a mortal to know the answer to this question?

The Problem of Evil

John Hick

John Hick has published eighteen books and hundreds of articles, all with a focus on religion and the philosophy of religion. He has taught philosophy of religion as well as theology at numerous universities throughout the world and serves as a Fellow of the Institute for Advanced Research in Arts & Social Sciences and is the Vice-President for both the British Society for the Philosophy of Religion and the World Congress of Faiths.

In this selection, taken from his book *Philosophy of Religion*, he attempts to give a justification of God's existence in a universe that has evil—known as theodicy from the Greek words for God (*theos*) and righteous (*dike*).

Source: Philosophy of Religion, 1st Edition, pp. 105–111. Copyright © 1963. Reprinted by permission of Pearson Education, Inc., Upper Saddle River, NJ.

Reading Questions

1. How does Hick describe the "problem of evil"?
2. Why isn't claiming evil as an illusion an acceptable solution?
3. What two types of evil does Hick mention? What is the difference between them?
4. What solution does Hick provide with regard to human freedom (free will)? How does Mackie argue against it?
5. What is the significance of Hick's mention of "a person who is not a person"?
6. Explain what Hick means when he writes, "We can never provide a complete causal explanation of a free act; if we could, it would not be a free act." Why wouldn't it?
7. How does Hick explain that the skeptic has gone wrong in framing God's creation as a paradise?
8. How does the notion of "soul making" address the suffering/natural evils component of the problem of evil?
9. Why does Hick have us imagine an ultimate paradise with no pain or suffering of any kind? What problems would arise? Why might this paradise be the "worst of all possible worlds"?
10. How can the death of Christ be seen as a metaphor for explaining the ultimate good that arises from evil?

To many, the most powerful positive objection to belief in God is the fact of evil. Probably for most agnostics it is the appalling depth and extent of human suffering, more than anything else, that makes the idea of a loving Creator seem so implausible and disposes them toward one or another of the various naturalistic theories of religion.

As a challenge to theism, the problem of evil has traditionally been posed in the form of a dilemma; if God is perfectly loving, he must wish to abolish evil; and if he is all-powerful, he must be able to abolish evil. But evil exists; therefore God cannot be both omnipotent and perfectly loving.

Certain solutions, which at once suggest themselves, have to be ruled out so far as the Judaic-Christian faith is concerned.

To say, for example (with contemporary Christian Science), that evil is an illusion of the human mind, is impossible within a religion based upon the stark realism of the Bible. Its pages faithfully reflect the characteristic mixture of good and evil in human experience. They record every kind of sorrow and suffering, every mode of man's inhumanity to man and of his painfully insecure existence in the world. There is no attempt to regard evil as anything but dark, menacingly ugly, heart-rending, and crushing. In the Christian scriptures, the climax of this history of evil is the crucifixion of Jesus, which is presented not only as a case of utterly unjust suffering, but as the violent and murderous rejection of God's Messiah. There can be no doubt, then, that for biblical faith, evil is unambiguously evil, and stands in direct opposition to God's will.

Again, to solve the problem of evil by means of the theory . . . of a finite deity who does the best he can with a material, intractable and coeternal with himself, is to have abandoned the basic premise of Hebrew-Christian monotheism; for the theory amounts to rejecting belief in the infinity and sovereignty of God.

Indeed, any theory which would avoid the problem of the origin of evil by depicting it as an ultimate constituent of the universe, coordinate with good, has been repudiated in advance by the classic Christian teaching, first developed by Augustine, that evil represents the going wrong of something which in itself is good. Augustine holds firmly to the Hebrew-Christian conviction that the universe is *good*—that is to say, it is the creation of a good God for a good purpose. He completely rejects the ancient prejudice, widespread in his day, that matter is evil. There are, according to Augustine, higher and lower, greater and lesser goods in immense abundance and variety; but everything which has being is good in its own way and degree, except in so far as it may have become spoiled or corrupted. Evil—whether it be an evil will, an instance of pain, or some disorder or decay in nature—has not been set there by God, but represents the distortion of something that is inherently valuable. Whatever exists is, as such, and in its proper place, good; evil is essentially parasitic upon good, being disorder and perversion in a fundamentally good creation. This understanding of evil as something negative means that it is not willed and created by God; but it does not mean (as some have supposed) that evil is unreal and can be disregarded. Clearly, the first effect of this doctrine is to accentuate even more the question of the origin of evil.

Theodicy, as many modern Christian thinkers see it, is a modest enterprise, negative rather than positive in its conclusions. It does not claim to explain, nor to explain away, every instance of evil in human experience, but only to point to certain considerations which prevent the fact of evil (largely incomprehensible though it remains) from constituting a final and insuperable bar to rational belief in God.

In indicating these considerations it will be useful to follow the traditional division of the subject. There is the problem of *moral evil* or wickedness; why does an all-good and all-powerful God permit this? And there is the problem of the *nonmoral evil* of suffering or pain, both physical and mental: Why has an all-good and all-powerful God created a world in which this occurs?

Christian thought has always considered moral evil in its relation to human freedom and responsibility. To be a person is to be a finite center of freedom, a (relatively) free and self-directing agent responsible for one's own decisions. This involves being free to act wrongly as well as to act rightly. The idea of a person who can be infallibly guaranteed always to act rightly is self-contradictory. There can be no guarantee in advance that a genuinely free moral agent will never choose amiss. Consequently, the possibility of wrongdoing or sin is logically inseparable from the creation of finite persons, and to say that God should not have created beings who might sin amounts to saying that he should not have created people.

This thesis has been challenged in some recent philosophical discussions of the problem of evil, in which it is claimed that no contradiction is involved in saying that God might have made people who would be genuinely free and who could yet be guaranteed always to act rightly. A quotation from one of these discussions follows:

> If there is no logical impossibility in a man's freely choosing the good on one, or on several occasions, there cannot be a logical impossibility in his freely choosing the good on every occasion. God was not, then, faced with a choice between making innocent automata and making beings, who, in acting freely, would sometimes go wrong: there was open to him the obviously better possibility of making beings who would act freely but always go right. Clearly, his failure to avail himself of this possibility is inconsistent with his being both omnipotent and wholly good.

A reply to this argument is suggested in another recent contribution to the discussion. If by a free action we mean an action which is not externally compelled but which flows from the nature of the agent as he reacts to the circumstances in which he finds himself, there is, indeed, no contradiction between our being free and our actions being "caused" (by our own nature), and therefore, being in principle predictable. There is a contradiction, however, in saying that God is the cause of our acting as we do but that we are free beings in relation to God. There is, in other words, a contradiction in saying that God has made us so that we shall of necessity act in a certain way, and that we are genuinely independent persons in relation to him. If all our thoughts and actions are divinely predestined, however free and morally responsible we may seem to be ourselves, we cannot be free and morally responsible in the sight of God, but must instead be his helpless puppets. Such "freedom" is like that of a patient acting out a series of posthypnotic suggestions: He appears, even to himself, to be free, but his volitions have actually been predetermined by another will, that of the hypnotist, in relation to whom the patient is not a free agent.

A different objector might raise the question of whether or not we deny God's omnipotence if we admit that he is unable to create persons who are free from the risks inherent in personal freedom. The answer that has always been given is that to create such beings is logically impossible. It is no limitation upon God's power that he cannot accomplish the logically impossible, since there is nothing here to accomplish, but only a meaningless conjunction of words[1]—in this case "person who is not a person." God is able to create beings of any and every conceivable kind; but creatures who lack moral freedom, however superior they might be to human beings in other respects, would not be what we mean by persons. They would constitute a different form of life which God might have brought into existence instead of persons. When we ask why God did not create such beings in place of persons, the traditional answer is that only persons could, in any meaningful sense, become "children of God," capable of entering into a personal relationship with their Creator by a free and uncompelled response to his love.

When we turn from the possibility of moral evil as a correlate of man's personal freedom to its actuality, we face something which must remain inexplicable even when it can be seen to be possible. For we can never provide a complete causal explanation of a free act; if we could, it would not be a free act. The origin of moral evil lies forever concealed within the mystery of human freedom.

The necessary connection between moral freedom and the possibility, now actualized, of sin throws light upon a great deal of the suffering which afflicts mankind. For an enormous amount of human pain arises either from the inhumanity or the culpable incompetence of mankind. This includes such major scourges as poverty, oppression and persecution, war, and all the injustice, indignity, and inequity which occur even in the most advanced societies. These evils are manifestations of human sin. Even disease is fostered to an extent, the limits of which have not yet been determined by psychosomatic medicine, by moral and emotional factors seated both in the individual and in his social environment. To the extent that all of these evils stem from human failures and wrong decisions, their possibility is inherent in the creation of free persons inhabiting a world which presents them with real choices which are followed by real consequences.

We may now turn more directly to the problem of suffering. Even though the major bulk of actual human pain is traceable to man's misused freedom as a sole or part cause, there remain other sources of pain which are entirely independent of the human will, for example, earthquake, hurricane, storm, flood, drought, and blight. In practice, it is often impossible to trace a boundary between the suffering which results from human wickedness and folly and that which falls upon mankind from without. Both kinds of suffering are inextricably mingled together in human experience. For our present purpose, however, it is important to note that the latter category does exist and that it seems to be built into the very structure of our world. In response to it, theodicy, if it is wisely conducted, follows a negative path. It is not possible to show positively that each item of human pain serves the divine purpose of good; but, on the other hand, it does seem possible to show that the divine purpose as it is understood in Judaism and Christianity could not be forwarded in a world which was designed as a permanent hedonistic paradise.

An essential premise of this argument concerns the nature of the divine purpose in creating the world. The skeptic's assumption is that man is to be viewed as a completed creation and that God's purpose in making the world was to provide a suitable dwelling place for this fully formed creature. Since God is good and loving, the environment which he has created for human life to inhabit is naturally as pleasant and comfortable as possible. The problem is essentially similar to that of a man who builds a cage for some pet animal. Since our world, in fact, contains sources of hardship, inconvenience, and danger of innumerable kinds, the conclusion follows that this world cannot have been created by a perfectly benevolent and all-powerful deity.[2]

Christianity, however, has never supposed that God's purpose in the creation of the world was to construct a paradise whose inhabitants would experience a maximum of pleasure and a minimum of pain. The world is seen, instead, as a place of "soul-making" in which free beings grappling with the tasks and challenges of their existence in a common environment, may become "children of God" and "heirs of eternal life." A way of thinking theologically of God's continuing creative purpose for man was suggested by some of the early Hellenistic Fathers of the Christian Church, especially Irenaeus. Following hints from St. Paul, Irenaeus taught that a man has been made as a person in the image of God but has not yet been brought as a free and responsible agent into the finite likeness of God, which is revealed in Christ. Our world, with all its rough edges, is the sphere in which this second and harder stage of the creative process is taking place.

This conception of the world (whether or not set in Irenaeus's theological framework) can be supported by the method of negative theodicy. Suppose, contrary to fact, that this world were a paradise from which all possibility of pain and suffering were excluded. The consequences would be very far-reaching. For example, no one could ever injure anyone else: The murderer's knife would turn to paper or his bullets to thin air; the bank safe, robbed of a million of dollars, would miraculously become filled with another million dollars (without this device, on however large a scale, proving inflationary); fraud, deceit, conspiracy, and treason would somehow always leave the fabric of society undamaged. Again, no one would ever be injured by accident: The mountain-climber, steeplejack, or playing child falling from a height would float unharmed to the ground; the reckless driver would never meet with disaster. There would be no need to work; since no harm could result from avoiding work; there would be no call to be concerned for others in time of need or danger, for in such a world there could be no real needs or dangers.

To make possible this continual series of individual adjustments, nature would have to work by "special providences" instead of running according to general laws which men must learn to respect on penalty of pain or death. The laws of nature would have to be extremely flexible: Sometimes gravity would operate, sometimes not; sometimes an object would be hard and solid, sometimes soft. There could be no sciences, for there would be no enduring world structure to investigate. In eliminating the problems and hardships of an objective environment, with its own laws, life would become like a dream in which, delightfully but aimlessly, we would float and drift at ease.

One can at least begin to imagine such a world. It is evident that our present ethical concepts would have no meaning in it. If, for example, the notion of harming someone is an essential element in the concept of a wrong action, in our hedonistic paradise there could be no wrong actions—nor any right actions in distinction from wrong. Courage and fortitude would have no point in an environment in which there is, by definition, no danger or difficulty. Generosity, kindness, the *agape* aspect of love, prudence, unselfishness, and all other ethical notions which presuppose life in a stable environment, could not even be formed. Consequently, such a world, however well it might promote pleasure, would be very ill adapted for the development of the moral qualities of human personality. In relation to this purpose it would be the worst of all possible worlds.

It would seem, then, that an environment intended to make possible the growth in free beings of the finest characteristics of personal life, must have a good deal in common with our present world. It must operate according to general and dependable laws; and it must involve real dangers, difficulties, problems, obstacles, and possibilities of pain, failure, sorrow, frustration, and defeat. If it did not contain the particular trials and perils which—subtracting man's own very considerable contribution—our world contains, it would have to contain others instead.

To realize this is not, by any means, to be in possession of a detailed theodicy. It is to understand that this world, with all its "heartaches and the thousand natural shocks that flesh is heir to," an environment so manifestly not designed for the maximization of human pleasure and the minimization of human pain, may be rather well adapted to the quite different purpose of "soul-making."

These considerations are related to theism as such. Specifically, Christian theism goes further in the light of the death of Christ, which is seen paradoxically both (as the murder of the divine Son) as the worst thing that has ever happened and (as the occasion of Man's salvation) as the best thing that has ever happened. As the supreme evil turned to supreme good, it provides the paradigm for the distinctively Christian reaction to evil. Viewed from the standpoint of Christian faith, evils do not cease to evils; and certainly, in view of Christ's healing work, they cannot be said to have been sent by God. Yet, it has been the persistent claim of those seriously and wholeheartedly committed to Christian discipleship that tragedy, though truly tragic, may nevertheless be turned, through a man's reaction to it, from a cause of despair and alienation from God to a stage in the fulfillment of God's loving purpose for that individual. As the greatest of all evils, the crucifixion of Christ, was made the occasion of man's redemption, so good can be won from other evils. As Jesus saw his execution by the Romans as an experience which God desired him to accept, an experience which was to be brought within the sphere of the divine purpose and made to serve the divine ends, so the Christian response to calamity is to accept the adversities, pains, and afflictions which life brings, in order that they can be turned to a positive spiritual use.

At this point, theodicy points forward in two ways to the subject of life after death.

First, although there are many striking instances of good being triumphantly brought out of evil through a man's or a woman's reaction to it, there are many other cases in which the opposite has happened. Sometimes obstacles breed strength of character, dangers evoke courage and unselfishness, and calamities produce patience and moral steadfastness. But sometimes they lead, instead, to resentment, fear, grasping selfishness, and disintegration of character. Therefore, it would seem that any divine purpose of soul-making which is at work in earthly history must continue beyond this life if it is ever to achieve more than a very partial and fragmentary success.

Second, if we ask whether the business of soul-making is worth all the toil and sorrow of human life, the Christian answer must be in terms of a future good which is great enough to justify all that has happened on the way to it.

Discussion Questions

1. Often, the analogy of loving parents and their children is given when looking at the religious problem of evil. Parenting styles that completely shelter and protect children from any harm are not considered to be in the children's best interests. Does this analogy relate to the problem of evil? Why/why not?

2. A proposed argument that supports the problem of evil is that an all-powerful god *could* have created *free* humans who can only choose the good (versus choosing any evil). Would this constitute *freedom*? Hick gives the example of people under hypnosis who think they're acting freely, but they're not. Is this a good analogy for this?

3. Regarding the notion of "soul making," does all pain and natural disaster build souls for the afterlife? How would an anonymous death (an example that has been provided in the past is that of a deer burning to death unknown in the forest) build a soul?

4. Can you think of any middle ground between how things are now and Hick's imaginary paradise? Under an all-powerful god, could we still have the virtue of soul making with less pain and suffering?

5. Does a normal life full of suffering, yet justified by eternal happiness, conflict with a god who is *all* good?

Movie Titles

1. *The Devil's Advocate* (R)—A Hollywood version of the devil and antichrist at work. Explores notions of free will, fate, and the "force" of evil.

2. *The Seventh Seal*—A 1958 film that addresses issues of death and God.

3. *Left Behind*—Based on the novel (which is based on Biblical references), this movie looks at the times just before and after the rapture (end time). Is Earth a testing ground of some sort?

Song Lyrics

XTC—"Dear God"
Tracy Chapman—"Heaven's Here on Earth"
Amboy Kelso—"Perfectly Imperfect"
Blues Traveler—"Sweet Pain"

Notes

1. As Aquinas said, ". . . nothing that implies a contradiction falls under the scope of God's omnipotence." *Summa Theologica*, Part 1. Question 25, article 4.

2. This is the nature of David Hume's argument in his discussion of the problem of evil in his *Dialogues*, Part XI.

Chapter 6

Faith and Reason

The phrase "a leap of faith" has become entrenched in our culture as having more than just a religious connotation. One can act with faith in one's personal relationships, in obstacles they attempt to overcome, and many other secular ventures. Though many argue that the only way to truly know God is through a similar "leap"—a leap beyond pure reason, logic, and science.

This section explores the notion of faith as a means of knowing. William James holds the position that we not only can, but must, at certain times, rely on non-rational methods (which he calls one's *passional nature*) and that we all do this to some extent, even though we may not be aware of it. Likewise, Kierkegaard explores the limits of rational knowledge (namely, its subjective nature) and also defends the necessity of faith with regard to religion. Mathematician Blaise Pascal suggests a rational means in support of a belief in an eternal god—he even defends this belief as the only prudent "wager" one could make from a rational standpoint.

Many consider Clifford's position as the antithesis of James's—he suggests that to rely on non-rational means when making decisions (especially monumental decisions) is not only irresponsible, but unethical. And neuroscientist Steven Pinker provides a psycho-biological explanation for people's belief in supernatural entities.

Thoughts

Blaise Pascal

Initially known for his mathematical prowess, French-born Blaise Pascal wrote a treatise on projective geometry at age sixteen in which he posited "Pascal's Theorem." By nineteen he had invented one of the earliest calculators. He also influenced ideas in economics, social science, and the scientific method. Following a near-death experience in a carriage, he changed his focus to philosophy and theology, penning two important works, the second—*Thoughts*—from which this selection is extracted. It wasn't published until after his death at age thirty-nine. In his series *The Story of Civilization*, Will Durant refers to it as "the most eloquent book in French prose." In honor of Pascal, the term "Pascal" is given to an important principle in hydrostatics (Pascal's Law), as well as a computer programming language and a unit of pressure.

The influence of mathematics is obvious in this selection. As the reader will notice, this is not a proof of God's existence, but instead a defense of belief in God (as opposed to non-belief). He also explores the relation of the heart/faith to reason, and how this relationship plays out in more than our religious lives.

Reading Questions

1. What point does Pascal make about the even/odd nature of the "infinity in number" in the opening paragraph here? How does he relate our knowledge of infinity to knowledge of God?
2. According to Pascal, why *must* you wager?
3. What is Pascal's point when he first imagines that you have two or three lives to gain and then suggests that you have *infinite* lives to gain?
4. What does Pascal suggest for the person who agrees with him intellectually but simply does not have faith?
5. What does Pascal say in response to the critique that we should act based only on *certainty*? How does Pascal argue that religion is more certain than our seeing tomorrow?
6. Why does Pascal ask, "Is it by reason that you love yourself?"
7. Explain the significance of Pascal's final remarks here regarding *thought*.

233

. . . We know that there is an infinite, and are ignorant of its nature. As we know it to be false that numbers are finite, it is therefore true that there is an infinity in number. But we do not know what it is. It is false that it is even, it is false that it is odd; for the addition of a unit can make no change in its nature. Yet it is a number, and every number is odd or even (this is certainly true of every finite number). So we may well know that there is a God without knowing what He is. Is there not one substantial truth, seeing there are so many things which are not the truth itself?

We know then the existence and nature of the finite, because we also are finite and have extension. We know the existence of the infinite, and are ignorant of its nature, because it has extension like us, but not limits like us. But we know neither the existence nor the nature of God, because He has neither extension nor limits.

But by faith we know His existence; in glory we shall know His nature. Now, I have already shown that we may well know the existence of a thing, without knowing its nature.

Let us now speak according to natural lights.

If there is a God, He is infinitely incomprehensible, since, having neither parts nor limits, He has no affinity to us. We are then incapable of knowing either what He is or if He is. This being so, who will dare to undertake the decision of the question? Not we, who have no affinity to Him.

Who then will blame Christians for not being able to give a reason for their belief, since they profess a religion for which they cannot give a reason? They declare, in expounding it to the world, that it is a foolishness, stultitiam; and then you complain that they do not prove it! If they proved it, they would not keep their word; it is in lacking proofs, that they are not lacking in sense. "Yes, but although this excuses those who offer it as such, and take away from them the blame of putting it forward without reason, it does not excuse those who receive it." Let us then examine this point, and say, "God is, or He is not." But to which side shall we incline? Reason can decide nothing here. There is an infinite chaos which separates us. A game is being played at the extremity of this infinite distance where heads or tails will turn up. What will you wager? According to reason, you can do neither the one thing nor the other; according to reason, you can defend neither of the propositions.

Do not then reprove for error those who have made a choice; for you know nothing about it. "No, but I blame them for having made, not this choice, but a choice; for again both he who chooses heads and he who chooses tails are equally at fault, they are both in the wrong. The true course is not to wager at all."

Yes; but you must wager. It is not optional. You are embarked. Which will you choose then? Let us see. Since you must choose, let us see which interests you least. You have two things to lose, the true and the good; and two things to stake, your reason and your will, your knowledge and your happiness; and your nature has two things to shun, error and misery. Your reason is no more shocked in choosing one rather than the other, since you must of necessity choose. This is one point settled. But your happiness? Let us weigh the gain and the loss in wagering that God is. Let us estimate these two chances. If you gain, you gain all; if you lose, you lose nothing. Wager then without hesitation that He is. "That is very fine. Yes, I must wager; but I may perhaps wager too much." Let us see. Since there is an equal risk of gain and of loss, if you had only to gain two lives, instead of one, you might still wager. But if there were three lives to gain, you would have to play (since you are under the necessity of playing), and you would be imprudent, when you are forced to play, not to chance your life to gain three at a game where there is an equal risk of loss and gain. But there is an eternity of life and happiness. And this being so, if there were an infinity of chances, of which one only would be for you, you would still be right in wagering one to win two, and you would act stupidly, being obliged to play, by refusing to stake one life against three at a game in which out of an infinity of chances there is one for you, if there were an infinity of an infinitely happy life to gain. But there is here an infinity of an infinitely happy life to gain, a chance of gain against a finite number of chances of loss, and what you stake is finite. It is all divided; wherever the infinite is and there is not an infinity of chances of loss against that of gain, there is no time to hesitate, you must give all. And thus, when one is forced to play, he must renounce reason to preserve his life, rather than risk it for infinite gain, as likely to happen as the loss of nothingness.

For it is no use to say it is uncertain if we will gain, and it is certain that we risk, and that the infinite distance between the certainty of what is staked and the uncertainty of what will be gained, equals the finite good which is certainly staked against the uncertain infinite. It is not so, as every player stakes a certainty to gain an uncertainty, and yet he stakes a finite certainty to gain a finite uncertainty, without transgressing against reason. There is not an infinite distance between the certainty staked and the uncertainty of the gain; that is untrue. In truth, there is an infinity between the certainty of gain and the certainty of loss. But the uncertainty of the gain is proportioned to the certainty of the stake according to the proportion of the chances of gain and loss. Hence it comes that, if there are as many risks on one side as on the other, the course is to play even; and then the certainty of the stake is equal to the uncertainty of the gain, so far is it from fact that there is an infinite distance between them. And so our proposition is of infinite force, when there is the finite to stake in a game where there are equal risks of gain and of loss, and the infinite to gain. This is demonstrable; and if men are capable of any truths, this is one.

"I confess it, I admit it. But still is there no means of seeing the faces of the cards?" Yes, Scripture and the rest, etc. "Yes, but I have my hands tied and my mouth closed; I am forced to wager, and am not free. I am not released, and am so made that I cannot believe. What then would you have me do?"

True. But at least learn your inability to believe, since reason brings you to this, and yet you cannot believe. Endeavour then to convince yourself, not by increase of proofs of God, but by the abatement of your passions. You would like to attain faith, and do not know the way; you would like to cure yourself of unbelief, and ask the remedy for it. Learn of those who have been bound like you, and who now stake all their possessions. These are people who know the way which you would follow, and who are cured of an ill of which you would be cured. Follow the way by which they began; by acting as if they believe, taking the holy water, having masses said, etc. Even this will naturally make you believe, and deaden your acuteness. "But this is what I am afraid of." And why? What have you to lose?

But to show you that this leads you there, it is this which will lessen the passions, which are your stumbling-blocks . . .

234

If we must not act save on a certainty, we ought not to act on religion, for it is not certain. But how many things we do on an uncertainty, sea voyages, battles! I say then we must do nothing at all, for nothing is certain, and that there is more certainty in religion than there is as to whether we may see to-morrow; for it is not certain that we may see to-morrow, and it is certainly possible that we may not see it. We cannot say as much about religion. It is not certain that it is; but who will venture to say that it is certainly possible that it is not; Now when we work for to-morrow, and so on an uncertainty, we act reasonably; for we ought to work for an uncertainty according to the doctrine of chance which was demonstrated above. . . .

239

Objection. Those who hope for salvation are so far happy; but they have as a counterpoise the fear of hell.

Reply. Who has most reason to fear hell: he who is in ignorance whether there is a hell, and who is certain of damnation if there is; or he who certainly believes there is a hell, and hopes to be saved if there is?

240

"I would soon have renounced pleasure," say they, "had I faith." For my part I tell you, "You would soon have faith, if you renounced pleasure." Now, it is for you to begin. If I could, I would give you faith. I cannot do so, nor therefore test the truth of what you say. But you can well renounce pleasure, and test whether what I say is true.

241

Order. I would have far more fear of being mistaken, and of finding that the Christian religion was true, than of not being mistaken in believing it true. . . .

277

The heart has its reasons, which reason does not know. We feel it in a thousand things. I say that the heart naturally loves the Universal Being, and also itself naturally, according as it gives itself to them; and it hardens itself against one or the other at its will. You have rejected the one, and kept the other. Is it by reason that you love yourself?

278

It is the heart which experiences God, and not the reason. This, then, is faith: God felt by the heart, not by the reason.

279

Faith is a gift of God; do not believe that we said it was a gift of reasoning. Other religions do not say this of their faith. They only gave reasoning in order to arrive at it, and yet it does not bring them to it. . . .

365

Thought. All the dignity of man consists in thought. Thought is therefore by its nature a wonderful and incomparable thing. It must have strange defects to be contemptible. But it has such, so that nothing is more ridiculous. How great it is in its nature! How vile it is in its defects!

Discussion Questions

1. How do you approach the apparent paradox suggested by Pascal in the opening paragraph? If it is false that a particular number is even and false that it is odd, then what are our options? How do you treat the concept of infinity? Does it relate to your knowledge-claims in any other areas (i.e., God)?
2. Do you agree that by "wagering" on a belief in God that you "lose nothing"? What *might* you lose?
3. Pascal gives a caricature of the religious position by stating that "it is in lacking proofs that they are not lacking in sense." What do you think of this position? What problems might arise from a belief system like this? What virtue might there be in this?
4. Do you find Pascal's defense of the rationality of belief in God convincing? Why/why not?
5. Even if you agree that it is in your best interest to believe in God, what control do you have over your beliefs? When someone professes their belief or disbelief in God, how often is an intellectual, *rational* answer given? If never, is a *rational* defense of religious belief sensible?
6. Can you change your belief in God? How? Do you agree with Pascal's suggested method for changing one's belief in God?
7. Some argue that Pascal's argument falls short: How can we know *which* God to believe in? If the true God is a jealous, vengeful God and you believe in another God, would that pose a problem? Explain.
8. In what ways can you apply Pascal's famous quote to your life: "The heart has its reasons, which reason does not know"? Explain.

Concluding Unscientific Postscript

Søren Kierkegaard

Danish philosopher and theologian Søren Kierkegaard is considered by many to be one of the earliest existential philosophers, often referred to as the "father of existentialism." Considered by Ludwig Wittgenstein as, "by far, the most profound thinker of the nineteenth century," Kierkegaard focused primarily on the relationship of faith and rationality, though his scope was very broad.

Source: Concluding Unscientific Postscript to Philosophical Fragments (2 vols.). Copyright © 1992 Princeton University Press. Reprinted by permission of Princeton University Press.

Known by many today for his term "leap of faith," Kierkegaard held that there are moments in our lives that require us to transcend ("leap over") pure rationality, science, logic, and reason and instead rely on our non-rational (faith, passion) inclinations. In a deeper sense, faith and love actually *require* that we have doubts and recognize our objective shortcomings. He notes the importance of subjectivity and passion in that it is this that guides our decision-making. For a skeptic to instead claim that pure objectivity allows one to come to decisions is, according to Kierkegaard, "chimerical"—a mere illusion (a "chimera" is the term from Greek mythology for creatures made from parts of other creatures that, as we now know, do not exist).

Reading Questions

1. What is the relation of faith to scientific inquiry according to Kierkegaard? How does proof of *or* against Christianity relate to the beliefs held prior to that proof? Why does he write that faith "must even regard proof as its enemy"?
2. What does Kierkegaard mean when he writes repeatedly of an *approximation*?
3. Why does the elimination of subjectivity and passion result in the elimination of decisiveness and the ability to make decisions?
4. In what way does Socrates' "bit of uncertainty" actually help in his examination of immortality? How does Kierkegaard relate this to the "young girl" and her enjoying the "sweetness of love"?
5. Explain the significance of Kierkegaard's comment, "subjectivity is the truth."
6. Why does an objective grasp of God result in Kierkegaard's *in*ability to believe?

Let us assume that the critics have succeeded in proving about the Bible everything that any learned theologian in his happiest moments has ever wished to prove about the Bible. These books, and no others belong to the canon; they are authentic; they are integral; their authors are trustworthy—one could say that it is as if every word were inspired. Well, everything being assumed to be in order with respect to the Scriptures, what follows? Has anyone who previously did not have faith been brought a step nearer to its acquisition? No, not a single step. Faith does not result simply from scientific inquiry; it does not come directly at all. On the contrary, in this objectivity one tends to lose the infinite personal interestedness in passion which is the condition of faith—the "everywhere and nowhere" in which faith can come into being. Would anyone who previously had faith gain anything with respect to its strength and power, from this new certainty? No, not in the least. Rather it is the case that in this voluminous knowledge, this certainty that lurks at the door of faith and threatens to devour it, he is in so dangerous a situation that much effort will be needed, in great fear and trembling, lest he fall victim to the temptation to confuse knowledge with faith. While faith has hitherto had a valuable schoolmaster in the existing uncertainty, it would have its most dangerous enemy in the new certainty. For if passion is eliminated, faith no longer exists, and certainty and passion do not go together. Whoever believes that there is a God, and an over-ruling providence, finds it easier to preserve his faith, easier to acquire something that definitely is faith and not an illusion, in an imperfect world where passion is kept alive, than in an absolutely perfect world. In such a world faith is unthinkable. And hence the teaching that faith is abolished in eternity.

How fortunate, then, that this wishful hypothesis, this beautiful dream of critical theology, is an impossibility, because even the most perfect realization would still remain an approximation. And again how fortunate for the critics that the fault is by no means in them! If all the angels in heaven were to put their heads together, they could still bring to pass only an approximation, because an approximation is the only certainty attainable for historical knowledge—but also an inadequate basis for eternal happiness.

I assume now the opposite, that the opponents have succeeded in proving what they desire about the Scriptures, with a certainty transcending the most ardent wish of the most passionate hostility—what then? Have the opponents thereby abolished Christianity? By no means. Has the believer been harmed? By no means, not in the least. Has the opponent made good a right to be relieved of responsibility for not being a believer? By no means. Because these books are not written by these authors, are not authentic, are not in an integral condition, are not inspired (though this cannot be disproved, since it is an object of faith), it does not follow that these authors have not existed; and above all it does not follow that Christ has not existed. As far as all this goes, the believer is equally free to assume it—equally free (let us note this well) since if he had assumed it by virtue of any proof he would have been on the verge of giving up his faith. If matters ever come to this pass, the believer will have some share of the guilt, in so far as he has himself invited this procedure, and begun to play into the hands of unbelief by proposing to provide a proof.

Here is the crux of the matter, and I come back to the case of learned theology. For whose sake is it that the proof is sought? Faith does not need it. Indeed it must even regard the proof as its enemy. But when faith begins to feel embarrassed and ashamed like a young woman for whom her love is no longer sufficient, but secretly feels ashamed of her lover and must therefore have it established that there is something remarkable about him—when faith thus begins to lose its passion, when faith ceases to be faith, then a proof becomes necessary so as to command respect from the side of unbelief . . .

When the question is treated in an objective manner it becomes impossible for the subject to face the decision with passion, least of all with an infinitely interested passion. It is a self-contradiction, and therefore comical, to be infinitely interested in that which at its maximum still always remains an approximation. If, in spite of this, passion is nevertheless imported, we get fanaticism. For an infinitely interested passion every iota will be of infinite value. The fault is not in the infinitely interested passion, but in the fact that its object has become an approximation-object.

The objective mode of approach to the problem persists from generation to generation precisely because the individuals, the contemplative individuals, become more and more objective, less and less possessed by an infinite passionate interest. Supposing that we continue in this manner to prove and seek the proof of Christianity, the remarkable phenomenon would finally emerge that just when the proof of its truth became completely realized, Christianity would cease to exist as a present fact. It would then have become so completely a historical phenomenon as to be something entirely past, whose truth, i.e., whose historical truth, had finally been brought to a satisfactory determination.

The more objective the contemplative enquirer, the less he bases an eternal happiness, i.e., his eternal happiness, upon his relationship to the enquiry; for there can be no question of an eternal happiness except for the passionately and infinitely interested subject. Objectively, the contemplative enquirer, whether learned scholar or dilettante member of the laity, understands himself in the following farewell words as he faces the final end: "When I was a young man, such and such books were in doubt; now their genuineness has been demonstrated, but then again a doubt has recently been raised about certain books which have never before been under suspicion. But there will doubtless soon arise a scholar who will . . ." And so forth.

The accommodating and objective subject holds himself aloof, displaying an applauded heroism. He is completely at your service, and ready to accept the truth as soon as it is brought to light. But the goal towards which he strives is far distant—undeniably so, since an approximation can continue indefinitely; and while the grass grows under his feet the enquirer dies, his mind at rest, for he was objective. It is not without reason that you have been praised, O Wonderful Objectivity, for you can do all things; not even the firmest believer was ever so certain of his eternal happiness and above all of not losing it, as the objective subject! Unless this objective and accommodating temper should perhaps be in the wrong place, so that it is possibly unchristian; in that case, it would naturally be a little dubious to have arrived at the truth of Christianity in this manner. Christianity is spirit, spirit is inwardness, inwardness is subjectivity, subjectivity is essential passion, and at its maximum an infinite, personal, passionate interest in one's eternal happiness.

As soon as subjectivity is eliminated, and passion eliminated from subjectivity, and the infinite interest eliminated from passion, there is in general no decision at all, either in this problem or in any other. All decisiveness, all essential decisiveness, is rooted in subjectivity. A contemplative spirit, and this is what the objective subject is, feels nowhere any infinite need of a decision, and sees no decision anywhere. This is the falsity that is inherent in all objectivity; and this is the significance of mediation as the mode of transition in the continuous process where nothing is fixed and nothing is infinitely decided. For the moment turns back upon itself and again turns back, so that the movement is chimerical, and the philosopher is wise only after the event. But there is no decisive result anywhere. This is quite as it should be, since decisiveness adheres in subjectivity alone, and essentially in its passion. . . .

When the question of truth is raised in an objective manner, reflection is directed objectively to the truth, as an object to which the knower is related. Reflection is not focused upon the relationship, however, but upon the question of whether it is the truth to which the knower is related. If only the object to which he is related is the truth, the subject is accounted to be in the truth. When the question truth is raised subjectively, reflection is directed subjectively to the nature of the individual's relationship: If only the mode of this relationship is in the truth, the individual is in the truth, *even if he should happen to be thus related to what is not true.*

Let us take as an example the knowledge of God. Objectively, reflection is directed to the problem of whether this object is the true God; subjectively, reflection is directed to the question whether the individual is related to a something *in such a manner* that his relation is in truth a God-relationship. On which side is the truth now to be found? May we not here resort to a mediation, and say "it is on neither side, but in the mediation of both"? Excellently well said, provided we could have it explained how an existing individual manages to be in a state of mediation. For to be in that state is to be finished, while to exist is to become. Nor can an existing individual be in two places at the same time—he cannot be an identity of subject and object. When he is nearest to being in two places at the same time, he is in passion; but passion is momentary, and passion is also the highest expression of subjectivity.

The existing individual who chooses to pursue the objective way enters upon the entire approximation-process by which it is proposed to bring God to light objectively. But this is in all eternity impossible, because God is a subject, and therefore exists only for subjectivity in inwardness. The existing individual who chooses the subjective way apprehends instantly the entire dialectical difficulty involved in having to use some time, perhaps a long time, in to finding God objectively; and he feels this dialectical difficulty, in all its painfulness, because every moment is wasted in which he does not have God. That very instant he has God, not by virtue of any objective deliberation, but by virtue of the infinite passion of inwardness.

It is at this point, so difficult dialectically, that the way swings off for everyone who knows what it means to think and to think existentially. This is something very different from sitting at a desk and writing about what one has never done, something very different from writing *de omnibus dubitandum* [one ought to doubt everything], and at the same time being as credulous existentially as the most sensuous of men. Here is where the way swings off, and the change is marked by the fact that while the objective knowledge rambles comfortably on by way of the long road of approximation without being impelled by the urge of passion, subjective knowledge counts every deadly peril, and the decision so infinitely important and so instantly pressing that it is as if the opportunity had already passed.

Now when the problem is to reckon up on which side there is most truth, whether on the side of one who seeks the true God objectively, and who pursues the approximate truth of the God-idea, or on the side of one who, driven by the infinite passion of his need of God, feels an infinite concern for his own relationship with God in truth . . . the answer cannot be in doubt for anyone who has not been demoralized with the aid of science. If one who lives in the midst of Christendom goes up to the house of God, the house of the true God, with the true conception of God in his knowledge, and prays, but prays in a false spirit; if he who lives in an idolatrous community prays with the passion of the [...]e, although his eyes rest upon the image of an idol: Where is the most [...]he one prays in truth to God though he worships an idol; the other prays [...]he true God, and hence worships in fact an idol.

When one man investigates objectively the problem of immortality, and another embraces an uncertainty with the passion of the infinite, where is there most truth and who has the greater certainty? The one who has entered upon a never-ending approximation, for the certainty of immortality lies precisely in the subjectivity of the individual; the other is immortal, and fights for this immortality by struggling with the uncertainty. Let us consider Socrates. Nowadays everyone dabbles in a few proofs; some have several such proofs, others fewer. But Socrates! He puts the question objectively in a problematic manner: *if* there is immortality. Must he therefore be accounted a doubter in comparison with one of our modern thinkers with their "three proofs"? By no means. On this "if" he risks his entire life; he has the courage to meet death; and he has with the passion of the infinite so determined the pattern of his life that it must be found acceptable—*if* there is immortality. Is any better proof capable of being given for the immortality of the soul? But those who have the three proofs do not at all determine their lives in conformity with them; if there is immortality it must feel disgust over the manner of their lives. Can any better refutation be given of the three proofs? The fact that Socrates had a bit of uncertainty helped him because he himself contributed the passion of the infinite; the three proofs that the others had did not profit them at all, because they are dead to spirit and to enthusiasm. And their three proofs—instead of proving something else—prove precisely that. A young girl may enjoy all the sweetness of love on the basis of what is merely a weak hope that she is beloved, because she rests everything on this weak hope. But many a wedded matron, more than once subjected to the strongest expressions of love, has to this extent indeed had proofs, but strangely enough has not enjoyed *quod erat demonstrandum* [that which was to be proved]. The Socratic ignorance, which Socrates held fast with the entire passion of his inwardness, was thus an expression of the principle that eternal truth *is* related to the existing individual, and that this truth must therefore be a paradox for the individual as long as he exists. And yet it is possible that there was more truth in the Socratic ignorance, as it was in him, than in the entire objective truth of the System which flirts with what the times demand, and accommodates itself to the university lecturers.

The objective accent falls on WHAT is said, the subjective accent on HOW it is said. . . . Objectively the interest is focused merely on the thought-content, subjectively on the inwardness. At its maximum this inward "how" is the passion of the infinite, and the passion of the infinite is the truth. But the passion of the infinite is precisely subjectivity, and thus subjectivity becomes truth. Objectively there is no infinite decisiveness, and hence it is objectively appropriate to annul the difference between good and evil, together with the principle of contradiction and therewith also the infinite difference between the true and the false. Only in subjectivity is there decisiveness; to seek objectivity is to be in error. It is the passion of the infinite that is the decisive factor, and not its content, for its content is precisely itself. In this manner subjectivity and the subjective "how" constitute truth.

When subjectivity is the truth, the conceptual determination of the truth must include an expression for the antithesis to objectivity—a memento of the fork in the road where the way swings off. And at the same time this expression will serve as an indication of the subjective inwardness. Here is such a definition of truth: *The truth is an objective uncertainty held fast in an appropriation-process of the most passionate inwardness.* This is the highest truth attainable for an *existing* individual. At the point where the way swings off (and where this is cannot be specified objectively, since it is a matter of subjectivity) there objective knowledge is placed in abeyance. Thus the subject merely has, objectively, the uncertainty; but it is this which precisely increases the tension of that infinite passion which constitutes his inwardness. The truth is precisely the venture which chooses an objective uncertainty with the passion of the infinite. I contemplate the order of nature in the hope of finding God, and I see omnipotence and wisdom; but I also see much else which disturbs my mind and excites anxiety. The sum of all this is an objective uncertainty. But it is for this very reason that the inwardness becomes as intense as it is, for it embraces this objective uncertainty with the entire passion of the infinite. In the case of a mathematical proposition, the objectivity is given, but for this reason the truth of such a proposition is also an indifferent truth.

But the above definition of truth is an equivalent expression of faith. Without risk there is no faith. Faith is precisely the contradiction between the infinite passion of the individual's inwardness and the objective uncertainty. If I am capable of grasping God objectively, I do not believe; but precisely because I cannot do this, I must believe. If I wish to preserve myself in faith, I must constantly be intent on holding fast the objective uncertainty, so as to remain out upon the deep, over seventy thousand fathoms of water, still preserving my faith.

Discussion Questions

1. Do you agree that if everything in the Bible were proven to be true that atheists would *still* not have faith? What if everything in the Bible were proven to be *incorrect*? Would Christians lose their faith? Why/why not?

2. Philosopher Alastair MacIntyre writes that if Christianity could be proven beyond any doubt (for example, any who deny Christian doctrine are struck down by God) then the Christian faith would actually be *destroyed*: "For all the possibility of free choice would have been done away." Do you agree? Why/why not? How does this relate to Kierkegaard's position? Is this position counterintuitive? Ironic?

3. How do you distinguish *faithfulness* from *fanaticism*?

4. Kierkegaard writes, "While the grass grows under his feet the enquirer dies, his mind at rest, for he was objective." How does Kierkegaard's approach differ from Clifford's (see selection in this section)?

5. Kierkegaard claims that subjectivity—not objectivity—provides for decisiveness. In what way do you agree or disagree with Kierkegaard?

6. In what other areas of life are you required to make a similar "leap" of faith and thus act, despite a complete attainment of objective knowledge? If there are other areas, then how do you treat a similar "leap" regarding religious belief?

The Ethics of Belief
William K. Clifford

Educated at King's College London (where he was admitted at age 15) and then at Trinity College, William Clifford wrote primarily in mathematics, though he also contributed much to philosophy. He co-invented "geometric algebra," which was later more fully developed by Einstein.

In this article, he sets up an argument for assigning ethical status to the beliefs that one holds. This essay precedes William James's (in this section of the anthology) by twenty years and is almost antithetical to it. Clifford argues that one is morally responsible when acting in the absence of sufficient evidence. Thus, one cannot act based merely on one's hunches and one's *passional* nature, but, instead, must more scientifically gather knowledge in order to properly inform one's actions. He gives not just a defense of investigating one's beliefs, but explains the psychology behind why we avoid doing so and provides an ethical account of our doing so as well.

Reading Questions

1. What point does Clifford hope to make with his parable of the ship owner? If the ship did not sink, does Clifford exonerate the ship owner? Why/why not?
2. What, for Clifford, is more important: drawing the correct conclusion or drawing the conclusion in a diligent manner? Why?
3. Why does Clifford argue that we all have a duty to question what we believe? How do our beliefs relate to the rest of society?
4. What difficulty does the practice of doubt present?
5. How does Clifford compare stealing money from an unknowing victim to claiming knowledge unjustifiably?

I. The Duty of Inquiry

A shipowner was about to send to sea an emigrant-ship. He knew that she was old, and not overwell built at the first; that she had seen many seas and climes, and often had needed repairs. Doubts had been suggested to him that possibly she was not seaworthy. These doubts preyed upon his mind, and made him unhappy; he thought that perhaps he ought to have her thoroughly overhauled and refitted,

Source: Originally published in *Contemporary Review*, 1877. Reprinted in *Lectures and Essays* (1879).

even though this should put him at great expense. Before the ship sailed, however, he succeeded in overcoming these melancholy reflections. He said to himself that she had gone safely through so many voyages and weathered so many storms that it was idle to suppose she would not come safely home from this trip also. He would put his trust in Providence, which could hardly fail to protect all these unhappy families that were leaving their fatherland to seek for better times elsewhere. He would dismiss from his mind all ungenerous suspicions about the honesty of builders and contractors. In such ways he acquired a sincere and comfortable conviction that his vessel was thoroughly safe and seaworthy; he watched her departure with a light heart, and benevolent wishes for the success of the exiles in their strange new home that was to be; and he got his insurance-money when she went down in mid-ocean and told no tales.

What shall we say of him? Surely this that he was verily guilty of the death of those men. It is admitted that he did sincerely believe in the soundness of his ship; but the sincerity of his conviction can in no wise help him, because *he had no right to believe on such evidence as was before him*. He had acquired his belief not by honestly earning it in patient investigation, but by stifling his doubts. And although in the end he may have felt so sure about it that he could not think otherwise, yet inasmuch as he had knowingly and willingly worked himself into that frame of mind, he must be held responsible for it.

Let us alter the case a little, and suppose that the ship was not unsound after all; that she made her voyage safely, and many others after it. Will that diminish the guilt of her owner? Not one jot. When an action is once done, it is right or wrong for ever; no accidental failure of its good or evil fruits can possibly alter that. The man would not have been innocent, he would only have been not found out. The question of right or wrong has to do with the origin of his belief, not the matter of it; not what it was, but how he got it; not whether it turned out to be true or false, but whether he had a right to believe on such evidence as was before him.

There was once an island in which some of the inhabitants professed a religion teaching neither the doctrine of original sin nor that of eternal punishment. A suspicion got abroad that the professors of this religion had made use of unfair means to get their doctrines taught to children. They were accused of wresting the laws of their country in such a way as to remove children from the care of their natural and legal guardians; and even of stealing them away and keeping them concealed from their friends and relations. A certain number of men formed themselves into a society for the purpose of agitating the public about this matter. They published grave accusations against individual citizens of the highest position and character, and did all in their power to injure these citizens in their exercise of their professions. So great was the noise they made, that a Commission was appointed to investigate the facts; but after the Commission had carefully inquired into all the evidence that could be got, it appeared that the accused were innocent. Not only had they been accused of insufficient evidence, but the evidence of their innocence was such as the agitators might easily have obtained, if they had attempted a fair inquiry. After these disclosures the inhabitants of that country looked upon the members of the agitating society, not only as persons whose judgment was to be distrusted, but also as no longer to be counted honourable men. For although they had sincerely and conscientiously believed in the charges they had made, *yet they had no right to believe on such evidence as was before them.* Their sincere convictions, instead of being honestly earned by patient inquiring, were stolen by listening to the voice of prejudice and passion.

Let us vary this case also, and suppose, other things remaining as before, that a still more accurate investigation proved the accused to have been really guilty. Would this make any difference in the guilt of the accusers? Clearly not; the question is not whether their belief was true or false, but whether they entertained it on wrong grounds. They would no doubt say, "Now you see that we were right after all; next time perhaps you will believe us." And they might be believed, but they would not thereby become honourable men. They would not be innocent, they would only be not found out. Every one of them, if he chose to examine himself *in foro conscientiae* would know that he had acquired and nourished a belief, when he had no right to believe on such evidence as was before him; and therein he would know that he had done a wrong thing.

It may be said, however, that in both these supposed cases it is not the belief which is judged to be wrong, but the action following upon it. The shipowner might say, "I am perfectly certain that my ship is sound, but still I feel it my duty to have her examined, before trusting the lives of so many people to her." And it might be said to the agitator, "However convinced you were of the justice of your cause and the truth of your convictions, you ought not to have made a public attack upon any man's character until you had examined the evidence on both sides with the utmost patience and care."

In the first place, let us admit that, so far as it goes, this view of the case is right and necessary; right, because even when a man's belief is so fixed that he cannot think otherwise, he still has a choice in the action suggested by it, and so cannot escape the duty of investigating on the ground of the strength of his convictions; and necessary, because those who are not yet capable of controlling their feelings and thoughts must have a plain rule dealing with overt acts."

But this being premised as necessary, it becomes clear that it is not sufficient, and that our previous judgment is required to supplement it. For it is not possible so to sever the belief from the action it suggests as to condemn the one without condemning the other. No man holding a strong belief on one side of a question, or even wishing to hold a belief on one side, can investigate it with such fairness and completeness as if he were really in doubt and unbiased; so that the existence of a belief not founded on fair inquiry unfits a man for the performance of this necessary duty.

Nor is it that truly a belief at all which has not some influence upon the actions of him who holds it. He who truly believes that which prompts him to an action has looked upon the action to lust after it, he has committed it already in his heart. If a belief is not realized immediately in open deeds, it is stored up for the guidance of the future. It goes to make a part of that aggregate of beliefs which is the link between sensation and action at every moment of all our lives, and which is so organized and compacted together that no part of it can be isolated from the rest, but every new addition modifies the structure of the whole. No real belief, however trifling and fragmentary it may seem, is ever truly insignificant; it prepares us to receive more of its like, confirms those which resembled it before, and weakens others; and so gradually it lays a stealthy train in our inmost thoughts, which may someday explode into overt action, and leave its stamp upon our character for ever.

And no one man's belief is in any case a private matter which concerns himself alone. Our lives are guided by that general conception of the course of things which has been created by society for social purposes. Our words, our phrases, our forms and processes and modes of thought, are common property, fashioned and perfected from age to age; an heirloom which every succeeding generation inherits as a precious deposit and a sacred trust to be handled on to the next one, not unchanged but enlarged and purified, with some clear marks of its proper handiwork. Into this, for good or ill, is woven every belief of every man who has speech of his fellows. A awful privilege, and an awful responsibility, that we should help to create the world in which posterity will live.

In the two supposed cases which have been considered, it has been judged wrong to believe on insufficient evidence, or to nourish belief by suppressing doubts and avoiding investigation. The reason of this judgment is not far to seek: it is that in both these cases the belief held by one man was of great importance to other men. But forasmuch as no belief held by one man, however seemingly trivial the belief, and however obscure the believer, is ever actually insignificant or without its effect on the fate of mankind, we have no choice but to extend our judgment to all cases of belief whatever. Belief, that sacred faculty which prompts the decisions of our will, and knits into harmonious working all the compacted energies of our being, is ours not for ourselves but for humanity. It is rightly used on truths which have been established by long experience and waiting toil, and which have stood in the fierce light of free and fearless questioning. Then it helps to bind men together, and to strengthen and direct their common action. It is desecrated when given to unproved and unquestioned statements, for the solace and private pleasure of the believer; to add a tinsel splendour to the plain straight road of our life and display a bright mirage beyond it; or even to drown the common sorrows of our kind by a self-deception which allows them not only to cast down, but also to degrade us. Whoso would deserve well of his fellows in this matter will guard the purity of his beliefs with a very fanaticism of jealous care, lest at any time it should rest on an unworthy object, and catch a stain which can never be wiped away.

It is not only the leader of men, statesmen, philosopher, or poet, that owes this bounden duty to mankind. Every rustic who delivers in the village alehouse his slow, infrequent sentences, may help to kill or keep alive the fatal superstitions which clog his race. Every hard-worked wife of an artisan may transmit to her children beliefs which shall knit society together, or rend it in pieces. No simplicity of mind, no obscurity of station, can escape the universal duty of questioning all that we believe.

It is true that this duty is a hard one, and the doubt which comes out of it is often a very bitter thing. It leaves us bare and powerless where we thought that we were safe and strong. To know all about anything is to know how to deal with it under all circumstances. We feel much happier and more secure when we think we know precisely what to do, no matter what happens, then when we have lost our way and do not know where to turn. And if we have supposed ourselves to know all about anything, and to be capable of doing what is fit in regard to it, we naturally do not like to find that we are really ignorant and powerless, that we have to begin again at the beginning, and try to learn what the thing is and how it is to be dealt with—if indeed anything can be learnt about it. It is the sense of power attached to a sense of knowledge that makes men desirous of believing, and afraid of doubting.

This sense of power is the highest and best of pleasures when the belief on which it is founded is a true belief, and has been fairly earned by investigation. For then we may justly feel that it is common property, and hold good for others as well as for ourselves. Then we may be glad, not that *I* have learned secrets by which I am safer and stronger, but that *we men* have got mastery over more of the world; and we shall be strong, not for ourselves but in the name of Man and his strength. But if the belief has been accepted on insufficient evidence, the pleasure is a stolen one. Not only does it deceive ourselves by giving us a sense of power which we do not really possess, but it is sinful, because it is stolen in defiance of our duty to mankind. That duty is to guard ourselves from such beliefs as from pestilence, which may shortly master our own body and then spread to the rest of the town. What would be thought of one who, for the sake of a sweet fruit, should deliberately run the risk of delivering a plague upon his family and his neighbours?

And, as in other such cases, it is not the risk only which has to be considered; for a bad action is always bad at the time when it is done, no matter what happens afterwards. Every time we let ourselves believe for unworthy reasons, we weaken our powers of self-control, of doubting, of judicially and fairly weighing evidence. We all suffer severely enough from the maintenance and support of false beliefs and the fatally wrong actions which they lead to, and the evil born when one such belief is entertained is great and wide. But a greater and wider evil arises when the credulous character is maintained and supported, when a habit of believing for unworthy reasons is fostered and made permanent. If I steal money from any person, there may be no harm done from the mere transfer of possession; he may not feel the loss, or it may prevent him from using the money badly. But I cannot help doing this great wrong towards Man, that I make myself dishonest. What hurts society is not that it should lose its property, but that it should become a den of thieves, for then it must cease to be society. This is why we ought not to do evil, that good may come; for at any rate this great evil has come, that we have done evil and are made wicked thereby. In like manner, if I let myself believe anything on insufficient evidence, there may be no great harm done by the mere belief; it may be true after all, or I may never have occasion to exhibit it in outward acts. But I cannot help doing this great wrong towards Man, that I make myself credulous. The danger to society is not merely that it should believe wrong things, though that is great enough; but that it should become credulous, and lose the habit of testing things and inquiring into them; for then it must sink back into savagery.

The harm which is done by credulity in a man is not confined to the fostering of a credulous character in others, and consequent support of false beliefs. Habitual want of care about what I believe leads to habitual want of care in others about the truth of what is told to me. Men speak the truth of one another when each reveres the truth in his own mind and in the other's mind; but how shall my friend revere the truth in my mind when I myself am careless about it, when I believe things because I want to believe them, and because they are comforting and pleasant? Will he not learn to cry, "Peace," to me, when there is no peace? By such a course I shall surround myself with a thick atmosphere of falsehood and fraud, and in that I must live. It may matter little to me, in my cloud-castle of sweet illusions and darling lies; but it matters much to Man that I have made my neighbours ready to deceive. The credulous man is father to the liar and the cheat; he lives in the bosom of this his family, and it is no marvel if he should become even as they are. So closely are our duties knit together, that whoso shall keep the whole law, and yet offend in one point, he is guilty of all.

To sum up: it is wrong always, everywhere, and for anyone, to believe anything upon insufficient evidence.

If a man, holding a belief which he was taught in childhood or persuaded of afterwards, keeps down and pushes away any doubts which arise about it in his mind, purposely avoids the reading of books and the company of men that call into question or discuss it, and regards as impious those questions which cannot easily be asked without disturbing it—the life of that man is one long sin against mankind.

If this judgment seems harsh when applied to those simple souls who have never known better, who have been brought up from the cradle with a horror of doubt, and taught that their eternal welfare depends on *what* they believe, then it leads to the very serious question, *Who hath made Israel to sin?*

It may be permitted me to fortify this judgment with the sentence of Milton:

A man may be a heretic in the truth; and if he believe things only because his pastor says so, or the assembly so determine, without knowing other reason, though his belief be true, yet the very truth he holds becomes his heresy.

And with this famous aphorism of Coleridge:

He who begins by loving Christianity better than Truth, will proceed by loving his own sect or Church better than Christianity, and end loving himself better than all.

Inquiry into the evidence of a doctrine is not to be made once for all, and then taken as finally settled. It is never lawful to stifle a doubt; for either it can be honestly answered by means of the inquiry already made, or else it proves that the inquiry was not complete.

"But," says one, "I am a busy man; I have no time for the long course of study which would be necessary to make me in any degree a competent judge of certain questions, or even able to understand the nature of the arguments."

Then he should have no time to believe.

II. The Weight of Authority

Are we then to become universal sceptics, doubting everything, afraid always to put one foot before the other until we have personally tested the firmness of the road? Are we to deprive ourselves of the help and guidance of that vast body of knowledge which is daily growing upon the world, because neither we nor any other one person can possibly test a hundredth part of it by immediate experiment or observation, and because it would not be completely proved if we did? Shall we steal and tell lies because we have had no personal experience wide enough to justify the belief that it is wrong to do so?

There is no practical danger that such consequences will ever follow from scrupulous care and self-control in the matter of belief. Those men who have most nearly done their duty in this respect have found that certain great principles, and these most fitted for the guidance of life, have stood out more and more clearly in proportion to the care and honesty with which they were tested, and have acquired in this way a practical certainty. The beliefs about right and wrong which guide our actions in dealing with men in society, and the beliefs about physical nature which guide our actions in dealing with animate and inanimate bodies, these never suffer from investigation; they can take care of themselves, without being propped up by "acts of faith," the clamour of paid advocates, or the suppression of contrary evidence. Moreover there are many cases in which it is our duty to act upon probabilities, although the evidence is not such as to justify present belief; because it is precisely by such action, and by observation of its fruits, that evidence is got which may justify future belief. So that we have no reason to fear lest a habit of conscientious inquiry should paralyse the actions of our daily life.

But because it is not enough to say, "It is wrong to believe on unworthy evidence," without saying also what evidence is worthy, we shall now go on to inquire under what circumstances it is lawful to believe on the testimony of others; and then, further, we shall inquire more generally when and why we may believe that which goes beyond our own experience, or even beyond the experience of mankind.

Discussion Questions

1. Does the ship owner act immorally in this case? What should he have done differently? If the ship did *not* sink, would it have been wrong to let it go to sea?
2. Can you think of any instances in which it would be immoral to act before gathering enough evidence? What about acting out toward another based on religious beliefs that many argue cannot be "purely rational"? What about acting based on what one is told by an astrologer or his or her horoscope?

3. What is the difference between *holding* a belief and *acting* on that belief? Can it be immoral to hold a belief, even if it is horrendous (i.e., to be extremely racist without acting on it)?

4. If we accept Clifford's position, how would we ever know that we had "enough" evidence to act? Does it seem like you could always find ways to gather more evidence in every account?

5. How would Clifford approach Pascal's Wager (see article in this anthology)? How could one attain "sufficient evidence" when determining that God does or does not exist?

6. Which do you favor more when making decisions: rational/evidence gathering or passion/faith/intuition?

7. Which of Plato's criteria for knowledge (from *Theatetus* in this anthology) does Clifford focus on here: justification, truth, belief? Explain.

8. Eighty-five percent of religious people adhere to the religious beliefs of the families in which they were raised. To what extent should they, along the lines of Clifford's argument, investigate the numerous other religions (estimated at over 1000) and atheism before they secure their particular belief?

The Will to Believe

William James

Considered a psychologist as much as a philosopher, James was one of the original pragmatists, focusing on the usefulness of certain statements in relation to their truth. He was educated at Harvard Medical School and went on to teach physiology and psychology at Harvard. He published many well-known works, primarily in psychology and pragmatism, solidifying him as one of the first popular American philosophers. This selection here, his most cited piece, is from an address he gave to the philosophical clubs of Yale and Brown Universities.

One key component in his foundation of knowledge was belief. Here, James attempts to give a rational defense of belief and faith, in contrast with some who think that we should only act on pure reason and logic (see the essay by Clifford). He also addresses the "pyrrhonistic skeptics" who hold that it is best to withhold judgment and remain agnostic. As James says of them, they "do not decide, but leave the question open."

Key to his essay is the role that he assigns to the passions of not just the "faith affirmer" but also to the typically non-faith-affirming skeptic. James discusses the risks assumed by both—one the risk of being in error, one the risk of missing out on truth—and argues that both types of risk are passional (or non-intellectual, sympathetic) in nature.

Reading Questions

1. What is the difference between a living and dead hypothesis? Why is being live or dead not an intrinsic property of a hypothesis?

2. What is a genuine option? Explain.

3. What does James say about Pascal's Wager with regard to it being a live or dead option? Later, why does he refer to the *wager* as a "clincher"?
4. Why does James mention belief in molecules and democracy, etc.?
5. What, for James, is behind the supposed rule that we disbelieve all theories for which we have no use?
6. What "great commandments" of knowing does James suggest?
7. According to James, when *is* it permissible to withhold judgment and refrain from making up our minds?
8. What does James say about "moral questions" and their relation to science and to our hearts? How does this relate to his overall position?
9. What point is James making with his example of the train of passengers? How does he use this to defend his position regarding faith and facts?
10. How does James argue that religion is a genuine option?
11. Why does James argue that skepticism doesn't involve just the intellect, but is "Intellect with one passion laying down its law"?
12. What point does James make through his analogy of the man who believes no one else's word without proof?
13. What is James's position on agnosticism (that knowledge of God is not possible; one cannot know whether He exists or not)?

I have long defended to my own students the lawfulness of voluntarily adopted faith; but as soon as they have got well imbued with the logical spirit, they have as a rule refused to admit my contention to be lawful philosophically, even though in point of fact they were personally all the time chock-full of some faith or other themselves. I am all the while, however, so profoundly convinced that my own position is correct, that your invitation has seemed to me a good occasion to make my statements more clear. Perhaps your minds will be more open than those with which I have hitherto had to deal. I will be as little technical as I can, though I must begin by setting up some technical distinctions that will help us in the end.

I

Let us give the name of hypothesis to anything that may be proposed to our belief; and just as the electricians speak of live and dead wires, let us speak of any hypothesis as either live or dead. A live hypothesis is one which appeals as a real possibility to him to whom it is proposed. If I ask you to believe in the Mahdi, the notion makes no electric connection with your nature—it refuses to scintillate with any credibility at all. As an hypothesis it is completely dead. To an Arab, however (even if he be not one of the Mahdi's followers), the hypothesis is among the mind's possibilities: It is alive. This shows that deadness and liveness in an hypothesis are not intrinsic properties, but relations to the individual thinker. They are measured by his willingness to act. The maximum of liveness in hypothesis means willingness to act irrevocably. Practically, that means belief; but there is some believing tendency wherever there is willingness to act at all.

Next, let us call the decision between two hypotheses an option. Options may be several kinds. They may be:

1. living or dead;
2. forced or avoidable;
3. momentous or trivial;

and for our purpose we may call an option a genuine option when it of the forced, living, and momentous kind.

1. A living option is one in which both hypotheses are live ones. If I say to you: "Be a theosophist or be a Mohammedan," it is probably a dead option, because for you neither hypothesis is likely to be alive. But if I say: "Be an agnostic or be Christian," it is otherwise: trained as you are, each hypothesis makes some appeal, however small, to your belief.

2. Next, if I say to you: "Choose between going out with your umbrella or without it," I do not offer you a genuine option, for it is not forced. You can easily avoid it by not going out at all. Similarly, if I say, "Either love me or hate me," "Either call my theory true or call it false," your option is avoidable. You may remain indifferent to me, neither loving nor hating, and you may decline to offer any judgment as to my theory. But if I say, "Either accept this truth or go without it," I put on you a forced option, for there is no standing place outside of the alternative. Every dilemma based on a complete logical disjunction, with no possibility of not choosing, is an option of this forced kind.

3. Finally, if I were Dr. Nansen and proposed to you to join my North Pole expedition, your option would be momentous; for this would probably be your only similar opportunity, and your choice now would either exclude you from the North Pole sort of immortality altogether or put at least the chance of it into your hands. He who refuses to embrace a unique opportunity loses the prize as surely as if he tried and failed. Per contra [on the other hand], the option is trivial when the opportunity is not unique, when the stake in insignificant, or when the decision is reversible if it later prove unwise. Such trivial options abound in the scientific life. A chemist finds an hypothesis live enough to spend a year in its verification: He believes in it to that extent. But if his experiments prove inconclusive either way, he is quit for his loss of time, no vital harm being done.

It will facilitate our discussion if we keep all these distinctions well in mind.

II

The next matter to consider is the actual psychology of human opinion. When we look at certain facts, it seems as if our passional and volitional nature lay at the root of all our convictions. When we look at others, it seems as if they could do nothing when the intellect had once said its say. Let us take the latter facts up first.

Does it not seem preposterous on the very face of it to talk of our opinions being modifiable at will? Can our will either help or hinder our intellect in its perceptions of truth? Can we, by just willing it, believe that Abraham Lincoln's existence is a myth, and that the portraits of him in *McClure's Magazine* are all of some one else? Can we, by any effort of our will, or by any strength of wish that it were true, believe ourselves well and about when we are roaring with rheumatism in bed, or feel certain that the sum of the two one-dollar bills in our pocket must be a hundred dollars? We can say any of these things, but we are absolutely impotent to believe them; and of just such things is the whole fabric of the truths that we do believe in made up—matters of fact, immediate or remote, as Hume said, and relations between ideas, which are either there or not there for us if we see them so, and which if not there cannot be put there by any action of our own.

In Pascal's *Thoughts* there is a celebrated passage known in literature as Pascal's wager. In it he tries to force us into Christianity by reasoning as if our concern with truth resembled our concern with the stakes in a game of chance. Translated freely his words are these: You must either believe or not believe that God is—which will you do? Your human reason cannot say. A game is going on between you and the nature of things which at the day of judgment will bring out either heads or tails. Weigh what your gains and your losses would be if you should stake all you have on heads, or God's existence: If you win in such case, you gain eternal beatitude; if you lose, you lose nothing at all. If there were an infinity of changes, and only one for God in this wager, still you ought to stake your all on God; for though you surely risk a finite loss by this procedure, any finite loss is reasonable, even a certain one is reasonable, if there is but the possibility of infinite gain. Go, then, and take holy water, and have masses said; belief will come and stupefy your *scruples—Cela vous fera croire et vous abetira* [that will make you believe and stupefy you.] Why should you not? At bottom, what have you to lose?

You probably feel that when religious faith expresses itself thus, in the language of the gaming-table, it is put to its last trumps. Surely Pascal's own personal belief in masses and holy water had far other springs; and this celebrated page of his is but an argument for others, a last desperate snatch at a weapon against the hardness of the unbelieving heart. We feel that a faith in masses and holy water adopted willfully after such a mechanical calculation lack the inner soul of faith's reality; and if we were of the Deity, we should probably take pleasure in cutting off believers from their infinite reward. It is evident that unless there be some preexisting tendency to believe in masses and holy water, the option offered to the will by Pascal is not a living option. Certainly no Turk ever took to masses and holy water on its account; and even to us Protestants these seem such foregone impossibilities that Pascal's logic, invoked for them specifically, leaves us unmoved. As well might the Mahdi write to us, saying, "I am the Expected One whom God has created in his effulgence. You shall be infinitely happy if you confess me; otherwise you shall be cut off from the light of the sun. Weigh, then, your infinite gain if I am genuine against your finite sacrifice if I am not!" His logic would be that of Pascal; but he would vainly use it on us, for the hypothesis he offers us is dead. No tendency to act on it exists in us to any degree. . . .

III

All this strikes one as healthy, even when expressed, as by Clifford, with somewhat too much of robustious pathos in the voice. Free-will and simple wishing do seem, in the matter of our credences, to be only fifth wheels to the coach. Yet if any one should thereupon assume that intellectual insight is what remains after wish and will and sentimental preference have taken wing, or that pure reason is what then settles our opinions, he would fly quite as directly in the teeth of the facts.

It is only our already dead hypotheses that our willing nature is unable to bring to life again. But what has made them dead for us is for the most part a previous action of our willing nature of an antagonistic kind. When I say 'willing nature,' I do not mean only such deliberate volitions as may have set up habits of belief that we cannot now escape from—I mean all such factors of belief as fear and hope, prejudice and passion, imitation and partisanship, the circumpressure of our caste and set. As a matter of fact we find ourselves believing, we hardly know how or why. Mr. Balfour gives the name of 'authority' to all those influences, born of the intellectual climate, that make hypotheses possible or impossible for us, alive or dead. Here in this room, we all of us believe in molecules and the conservation of energy, in democracy and necessary progress, in Protestant Christianity and the duty of fighting for 'the doctrine of the immortal Monroe,' all for no reasons worthy of the name. We see into these matters with no more inner clearness, and probably with much less, than any disbeliever in them might possess. His unconventionality would probably have some grounds to show for its conclusions; but for us, not insight, but the prestige of the opinions, is what makes the spark shoot from them and light up our sleeping magazines of faith. Our reason is quite satisfied, in nine hundred and ninety-nine cases out of every thousand of us, if it can find a few arguments that will do to recite in case our credulity is criticised by some one else. Our faith is faith in some one else's faith, and in the greatest matters this is most the case. Our belief in truth itself, for instance, that there is a truth, and that our minds and it are made for each other—what is it but a passionate affirmation of desire, in which our social system backs us up? We want to have a truth; we want to believe that our experiments and studies and discussions must put us in a continually better and better position towards it; and on this line we agree to fight out our thinking lives. But if a pyrrhonistic sceptic asks us how we know all this, can our logic find a reply? No! certainly it cannot. It is just one volition against another—we willing to go in for life upon a trust or assumption which he, for his part, does not care to make.

As a rule we disbelieve all facts and theories for which we have no use. Clifford's cosmic emotions find no use for Christian feelings. Huxley belabors the bishops because there is no use for sacerdotalism in his scheme of life. Newman, on the contrary, goes over to Romanism, and finds all sorts of reasons good for staying there, because a priestly system is for him an organic need and delight. Why do so few 'scientists' even look at the evidence for telepathy, so called?

Because they think, as a leading biologist, now dead, once said to me, that even if such a thing were true, scientists ought to band together to keep it suppressed and concealed. It would undo the uniformity of Nature and all sorts of other things without which scientists cannot carry on their pursuits. But if this very man had been shown something which as a scientist he might do with telepathy, he might not only have examined the evidence, but even have found it good enough. This very law which the logicians would impose upon us—if I may give the name of logicians to those who would rule out our willing nature here—is based on nothing but their own natural wish to exclude all elements for which they, in their professional quality of logicians, can find no use.

Evidently, then, our non-intellectual nature does influence our convictions. There are passional tendencies and volitions which run before and others which come after belief, and it is only the latter that are too late for the fair; and they are not too late when the previous passional work has been already in their own direction. Pascal's argument, instead of being powerless, then seems a regular clincher, and is the last stroke needed to make our faith in masses and holy water complete. The state of things is evidently far from simple; and pure insight and logic, whatever they might do ideally, are not the only things that really do produce our creeds.

IV

. . . The thesis I defend is, briefly stated, this: Our passional nature not only lawfully may, but must, decide an option between propositions, whenever it is a genuine option that cannot by its nature be decided on intellectual grounds; for to say, under such circumstances, "Do not decide, but leave the question open," is itself a passional decision—just like deciding yes or no—and is attended with the same risk of losing the truth. . . .

VII

. . . There are two ways of looking at our duty in the matter of opinion—ways entirely different, and yet ways about whose difference the theory of knowledge seems hitherto to have shown very little concern. *We must know the truth; and we must avoid error*—these are our first and great commandments as would-be knowers; but they are not two ways of stating an identical commandment, they are two separable laws. . . .

Believe truth! Shun error!—these, we see, are two materially different laws; and by choosing between them we may end by coloring differently our whole intellectual life. We may regard the chase for truth as paramount, and the avoidance of error as secondary; or we may, on the other hand, treat the avoidance of error as more imperative, and let truth take its chance. Clifford . . . exhorts us to the latter course. Believe nothing, he tells us, keep your mind in suspense forever, rather than by closing it on insufficient evidence incur the awful risk of believing lies. You, on the other hand, may think that the risk of being in error is a very small matter when compared with the blessings of real knowledge, and be ready to be duped many times in your investigation rather than postpone indefinitely the chance of guessing true. I myself find it impossible to go with Clifford. We must remember that these feelings of our duty about either truth or error are in any case only expressions of our passional life. Biologically considered, our minds are as ready to grind out falsehood as veracity, and he who says, "Better go without belief forever than believe a lie!" merely shows his own preponderant private horror of becoming a dupe. He may be critical of many of his desires and fears, but this fear he slavishly obeys. He cannot imagine any one questioning its binding force. For my own part, I have also a horror of being duped; but I can believe that worse things than being duped may happen to a man in this world: So Clifford's exhortation has to my ears a thoroughly fantastic sound. It is like a general informing his soldiers that it is better to keep out of battle forever than to risk a single wound. Not so are victories either over enemies or over nature gained. Our errors are surely not such awfully solemn things. In a world where we are so certain to incur them in spite of all our caution, a certain lightness of heart seems healthier than this excessive nervousness on their behalf.

VIII

. . . Wherever the option between losing truth and gaining it is not momentous, we can throw the chance of guining truth away, and at any rate save ourselves from any chance of believing falsehood, by not making up our minds at all till objective evidence has come. In scientific questions, this is almost always the case; and even in human affairs in general, the need of acting is seldom so urgent that a false belief to act on is better than no belief at all. Law courts, indeed, have to decide on the best evidence attainable for the moment, because a judge's duty is to make law as well as to ascertain it, and (as a learned judge once said to me) few cases are worth spending much time over: The great thing is to have them decided on any acceptable principle, and got out of the way. But in our dealings with objective nature we obviously are recorders, not makers, of the truth; and decisions for the mere sake of deciding promptly and getting on to the next business would be wholly out of place. Throughout the breadth of physical nature facts are what they are quite independently of us, and seldom is there any such hurry about them that the risks of being duped by believing a premature theory need be faced. The questions here are always trivial options, the hypotheses are hardly living (at any rate not living for us spectators), the choice between believing truth or falsehood is seldom forced. The attitude of sceptical balance is therefore the absolutely wise one if we would escape mistakes. What difference, indeed, does it make to most of us whether we have or have not a theory of the Röntgen rays [x-rays], whether we believe or not in mind-stuff, or have a conviction about the causality of conscious states? It makes no difference. Such options are not forced on us. On every account it is better not to make them, but still keep weighing reasons pro et contra with an indifferent hand. . . .

IX

Moral questions immediately present themselves as questions whose solution cannot wait for sensible proof. A moral question is a question not of what sensibly exists, but of what is good, or would be good if it did exist. Science can tell us what exists; but to compare the worths, both of what exists and of what does not exist, we must consult not science, but what Pascal calls our heart. Science herself consults her heart when she lays it down that the infinite ascertainment of fact and correction of false belief are the supreme goods for man. Challenge the statement, and science can only repeat it oracularly, or else prove it by showing that such ascertainment and correction bring man all sorts of other goods which man's heart in turn declares. The question of having moral beliefs at all or not having them is decided by our will. Are our moral preferences true or false, or are they only odd biological phenomena, making things good or bad for us, but in themselves indifferent? How can your pure intellect decide? If your heart does not want a world of moral reality, your head will assuredly never make you believe in one. . . .

The desire for a certain kind of truth here brings about that special truth's existence; and so it is in innumerable cases of other sorts. . . .

Wherever a desired result is achieved by the co-operation of many independent persons, its existence as a fact is a pure consequence of the precursive faith in one another of those immediately concerned. A government, an army, a commercial system, a ship, a college, an athletic team, all exist on this condition, without which not only is nothing achieved, but nothing is even attempted. A whole train of passengers (individually brave enough) will be looted by a few highwaymen, simply because the latter can count on one another, while each passenger fears that if he makes a movement of resistance, he will be shot before any one else backs him up. If we believed that the whole car-full would rise at once with us, we should each severally rise, and train-robbing would never even be attempted. There are, then, cases where a fact cannot come at all unless a preliminary faith exists in its coming. And where faith in a fact can help create the fact, that would be an insane logic which should say that faith running ahead of scientific evidence is the 'lowest kind of immorality' into which a thinking being can fall. Yet such is the logic by which our scientific absolutists pretend to regulate our lives!

X

In truths dependent on our personal action, then, faith based on desire is certainly a lawful and possibly an indispensable thing. . . .

What then do we now mean by the religious hypothesis? Science says things are; morality says some things are better than other things; and religion says essentially two things.

First, she says that the best things are the more eternal things, the overlapping things, the things in the universe that throw the last stone, so to speak, and say the final word. "Perfection is eternal"—this phrase of Charles Secretan seems a good way of putting this first affirmation of religion, an affirmation which obviously cannot yet be verified scientifically at all.

The second affirmation of religion is that we are better off even now if we believe her first affirmation to be true.

Now, let us consider what the logical elements of this situation are in case the religious hypothesis in both its branches be really true. (Of course, we must admit that possibility at the outset. If we are to discuss the question at all, it must involve a living option. If for any of you religion be a hypothesis that cannot, by any living possibility be true, then you need go no farther. I speak to the 'saving remnant' alone.) So proceeding, we see, first that religion offers itself as a momentous option. We are supposed to gain, even now, by our belief, and to lose by our nonbelief, a certain vital good. Secondly, religion is a forced option, so far as that good goes. We cannot escape the issue by remaining sceptical and waiting for more light, because, although we do avoid error in that way if religion be untrue, we lose the good, if it be true, just as certainly as if we positively chose to disbelieve. It is as if a man should hesitate indefinitely to ask a certain woman to marry him because he was not perfectly sure that she would prove an angel after he brought her home. Would he not cut himself off from that particular angel-possibility as decisively as if he went and married some one else? Scepticism, then, is not avoidance of option; it is option of a certain particular kind of risk. Better risk loss of truth than chance of error—that is your faith—vetoer's exact position. He is actively playing his stake as much as the believer is; he is backing the field against the religious hypothesis, just as the believer is backing the religious hypothesis against the field. To preach scepticism to us as a duty until 'sufficient evidence' for religion be found, is tantamount therefore to telling us, when in presence of the religious hypothesis, that to yield to our fear of its being error is wiser and better than to yield to our hope that it may be true. It is not intellect against all passions, then; it is only intellect with one passion laying down its law. And by what, forsooth, is the supreme wisdom of this passion warranted? Dupery for dupery, what proof is there that dupery through hope is so much worse than dupery through fear? I, for one, can see no proof; and I simply refuse obedience to the scientist's command to imitate his kind of option, in a case where my own stake is important enough to give me the right to choose my own form of risk. If religion be true and the evidence for it be still insufficient, I do not wish, by putting your extinguisher upon my nature (which feels to me as if it had after all some business in this matter), to forfeit my sole chance in life of getting upon the winning side—that chance depending, of course, on my willingness to run the risk of acting as if my passional need of taking the world religiously might be prophetic and right.

All this is on the supposition that it really may be prophetic and right, and that, even to us who are discussing the matter, religion is a live hypothesis which may be true. Now, to most of us religion comes in a still further way that makes a veto on our active faith even more illogical. The more perfect and more eternal aspect of the universe is represented in our religions as having personal form. The universe is no longer a mere It to us, but a Thou, if we are religious; and any relation that may be possible from person to person might be possible here. For instance, although in one sense we are passive portions of the universe, in another we show a curious autonomy, as if we were small active centres on our own account. We feel, too, as if the appeal of religion to us were made to our own active good-will, as if evidence might be forever withheld from us unless we met the hypothesis half-way. To take a trivial illustration: Just as a man who in a company of gentlemen made no advances, asked a warrant for every concession, and believed no one's word without proof, would cut himself off by such churlishness from all the social rewards that a more trusting spirit would earn—so here, one who should shut himself up in snarling logicality and try to make the gods extort his recognition willy-nilly, or not get it at all, might cut himself off forever from his only opportunity of making the gods' acquaintance. This feeling, forced on us we know not whence, that by obstinately believing that there are gods (although not to do so would be so easy both for our logic and our life) we are doing the universe the deepest service we can, seems part of the living essence of the religious hypothesis. If the hypothesis were true in all its parts, including this one, then pure intellectualism, with its veto on our making willing advances, would be an absurdity; and some participation of our sympathetic nature would be logically required. I, therefore, for one, cannot see my way to accepting the agnostic rules for truth-seeking, or wilfully agree to keep my willing nature out of the game. I cannot do so for this plain reason, that *a rule of thinking which would absolutely prevent me from acknowledging certain kinds of truth if those kinds of truth were really there, would be an irrational rule.* That for me is the long and short of the formal logic of the situation, no matter what the kinds of truth might materially be.

I confess I do not see how this logic can be escaped. But sad experience makes me fear that some of you may still shrink from radically saying with me, *in abstracto*, that we have the right to believe at our own risk any hypothesis that is live enough to tempt our will. I suspect, however, that if this is so, it is because you have got away from the abstract logical point of view altogether, and are thinking (perhaps without realizing it) of some particular religious hypothesis which for you is dead. The freedom to 'believe what we will' you apply to the case of some patent superstition; and the faith you think of is the faith defined by the schoolboy when he said, "Faith is when you believe something that you know ain't true." I can only repeat that this is misapprehension. *In concreto*, the freedom to believe can only cover living options which the intellect of the individual cannot by itself resolve; and living options never seem absurdities to him who has them to consider. When I look at the religious question as it really puts itself to concrete men, and when I think of all the possibilities which both practically and theoretically it involves, then this command that we shall put a stopper on our heart, instincts, and courage, and wait-acting of course meanwhile more or less as if religion were not true [Since belief is measured by action, he who forbids us to believe religion to be true, necessarily also forbids us to act as we should if we did believe it to be true. The whole defence of religious faith hinges upon action. If the action required or inspired by the religious hypothesis is in no way different from that dictated by the naturalistic hypothesis, then religious faith is a pure superfluity, better pruned away, and controversy about its legitimacy is a piece of idle trifling, unworthy of serious minds. I myself believe, of course, that the religious hypothesis gives to the world an expression which specifically determines our reactions, and makes them in a large part unlike what they might be on a purely naturalistic scheme of belief.] till doomsday, or till such time as our intellect and senses working together may have raked in evidence enough—this command, I say, seems to me the queerest idol ever manufactured in the philosophic cave. Were we scholastic absolutists, there might be more excuse. If we had an infallible intellect with its objective certitudes, we might feel ourselves disloyal to such a perfect organ of knowledge in not trusting to it exclusively, in not waiting for its releasing word. But if we are empiricists [pragmatists], if we believe that no bell in us tolls to let us know for certain when truth is in our grasp, then it seems a piece of idle fantasticality to preach so solemnly our duty of waiting for the bell. Indeed we may wait if we will—I hope you do not think that I am denying that—but if we do so, we do so at our peril as much as if we believed. In either case we act, taking our life in our hands. No one of us ought to issue vetoes to the other, nor should we bandy words of abuse. We ought, on the contrary, delicately and profoundly to respect one another's mental freedom: then only shall we bring about the intellectual republic; then only shall we have that spirit of inner tolerance without which all our outer tolerance is soulless, and which is empiricism's glory; then only shall we live and let live, in speculative as well as in practical things.

I began by a reference to Fitz James Stephen; let me end by a quotation from him. "What do you think of yourself? What do you think of the world? . . . These are questions with which all must deal as it seems good to them. They are riddles of the Sphinx, and in some way or other we must deal with them. . . . In all important transactions of life we have to take a leap in the dark. . . . If we decide to leave the riddles unanswered, that is a choice; if we waver in our answer, that, too, is a choice: but whatever choice we make, we make it at our peril. If a man chooses to turn his back altogether on God and the future, no one can prevent him; no one can show beyond reasonable doubt that he is mistaken. If a man thinks otherwise and acts as he thinks, I do not see that any one can prove that he is mistaken. Each must act as he thinks best; and if he is wrong, so much the worse for him. We stand on a mountain pass in the midst of whirling snow and blinding mist through which we get glimpses now and then of paths which may be deceptive. If we stand still we shall be frozen to death. If we take the wrong road we shall be dashed to pieces. We do not certainly know whether there is any right one. What must we do? 'Be strong and of a good courage.' Act for the best, hope for the best, and take what comes. . . . If death ends all, we cannot meet death better." [*Liberty, Equality, Fraternity*, p. 353, second edition. London, 1874.]

Discussion Questions

1. Do you have control over your beliefs? Over all of them? None of them? Could you change your belief in God simply by willing it?
2. Which motivates you more: attaining the truth/knowledge or avoiding error?
3. Do you think it is possible to *know* about God's existence? It is true that God either exists or does not? So mustn't every person believe one way or the other?
4. In what situations, if any, is it okay (or even necessary) to make a decision based on something other than purely objective evidence? Can you ever have *all* the information about a specific decision before deciding? How does this relate to "momentous" decisions in your own life (i.e., belief in God, decision to go to college, decision to marry, etc.)?
5. If we do need faith to attain some knowledge—especially religious knowledge—do you agree with James that this is logical? St. Augustine wrote, "Unless I believe, I cannot understand." Does faith help in your knowing certain things, or does your knowledge of things help establish your faith?

The Evolution of Religious Belief

Steven Pinker

(For a biographical sketch of Pinker, please see his selection earlier in this text.)

In this excerpt, taken from Pinker's book *How The Mind Works*, he explores the mind's involvement in religious beliefs. He provides a biological, psychological, and sociological explanation for the prominence of belief in such religious issues as supernatural entities and miracles.

Reading Questions

1. Why does Pinker claim that we cannot equate religion with our human, spiritual journeys?
2. What is the practicality of the following according to Pinker?
   a. Ancestor worship
   b. An immortal soul
   c. Food taboos
   d. Rites of passage
   e. Painful initiations
   What relevance do these have to Pinker's overall position?

Source: From *How the Mind Works* by Steven Pinker. Copyright © 1997 by Steven Pinker. Used by permission of W. W. Norton & Company, Inc.

3. What is the common thread of religions according to Ruth Benedict? What function does prayer serve?
4. What reasons do Boyer and Sperber give to explain how "inventing ghosts and bribing them for good weather" fits with the view that human reasoning is designed to determine how the world works?
5. Explain Pinker's analogy of his experience at the dentist as it relates to one's belief in miracles.
6. How does Edward Taylor suggest that our beliefs in spirits stem from our everyday lives?

"The most common of all follies," wrote H.L. Mencken, "is to believe passionately in the palpably not true. It is the chief occupation of mankind." In culture after culture, people believe that the soul lives on after death, that rituals can change the physical world and divine the truth, and that illness and misfortune are caused and alleviated by spirits, ghosts, saints, fairies, angels, demons, cherubim, djinns, devils, and gods. According to polls, more than a quarter of today's Americans believe in witches, almost half believe in ghosts, half believe in the devil, half believe that the book of Genesis is literally true, 69 percent believe in angels, 87 percent believe that Jesus was raised from the dead, and more than 90 percent believe in a God or universal spirit.

How does religion fit into a mind that one might have thought was designed to reject the palpably not true? The common answer—that people take comfort in the thought of a benevolent shepherd, a universal plan, or an afterlife—is unsatisfying, because it only raises the question of why a mind would evolve to find comfort in beliefs it can plainly see are false. A freezing person finds no comfort in believing he is warm; a person face-to-face with a lion is not put at ease by the conviction that it is a rabbit.

What is religion? The psychology of religion has been muddied by scholars' attempts to exalt it while understanding it. Religion cannot be equated with our higher, spiritual, humane, ethical yearnings (though it sometimes overlaps with them). The Bible contains instructions for genocide, rape, and the destruction of families, and even the Ten Commandments, read in context, prohibit murder, lying, and theft only within the tribe, not against outsiders. Religions have given us stonings, witch-burnings, crusades, inquisitions, jihads, fatwas, suicide bombers, abortion-clinic gunmen, and mothers who drown their sons so they can be happily reunited in heaven. As Blaise Pascal wrote, "Men never do evil so completely and cheerfully as when they do it from religious conviction."

Religion is not a single topic. What we call religion in the modern West is an alternative culture of laws and customs that survived alongside those of the nation-state because of accidents of European history. Religions, like other cultures, have produced great art, philosophy, and law, but their customs, like those of other cultures, often serve the interests of the people who promulgate them. Ancestor worship must be an appealing idea to people who are about to become ancestors. As one's days dwindle, life begins to shift from an iterative prisoner's dilemma, in which defection can be punished and cooperation rewarded, to a one-shot prisoner's dilemma, in which enforcement is impossible. If you can convince your children that your soul will live on and watch over their affairs, they are less emboldened to defect while you are alive. Food taboos keep members of the tribe from becoming intimate with outsiders. Rites of passage demarcate the people who are entitled to the privileges of social categories (fetus or family member, child or adult, single or married) so as to preempt endless haggling over gray areas. Painful initiations weed our anyone who wants the benefits of membership without being committed to paying the costs. Witches are often mothers-in-law and other inconvenient people. Shamans and priests are Wizards of Oz who use special effects, from sleight-of-hand and ventriloquism to sumptuous temples and cathedrals, to convince others that they are privy to forces of power and wonder.

Let's focus on the truly distinctive part of the psychology of religion. The anthropologist Ruth Benedict first pointed out the common thread of religious practice in all cultures: Religion is a technique for success. Ambrose Bierce defined *to pray* as "to ask that the laws of the universe be annulled on behalf of a single petitioner confessedly unworthy." People everywhere beseech gods and spirits for recovery from illness, for success in love or on the battlefield, and for good weather. Religion is a desperate measure that people resort to when the stakes are high and they have exhausted the usual techniques for the causation of success—medicines, strategies, courtship, and, in the case of the weather, nothing.

What kind of mind would do something as useless as inventing ghosts and bribing them for good weather? How does that fit into the idea that reasoning comes from a system of modules designed to figure our how the world works? The anthropologists Pascal Boyer and Dan Sperber have shown that it fits rather well. First, nonliterate peoples are not psychotic hallucinators who are unable to distinguish fantasy from reality. They know there is a humdrum world of people and objects driven by the usual laws, and find the ghosts and spirits of their belief system to be terrifying and fascinating precisely *because* they violate their own ordinary intuitions about the world.

Second, the spirits, talismans, seers, and other sacred entities are never invented out of whole cloth. People take a construct from one of the cognitive modules—an object, person, animal, natural substance, or artifact—and cross out a property or write in a new one, letting the construct keep the rest of its standard-issue traits. A tool or weapon or substance will be granted some extra causal power but otherwise is expected to behave as it did before. It lives at one place at one time, is unable to pass through solid objects, and so on. A spirit is stipulated to be exempt from one or more of the laws of biology (growing, aging, dying), physics (solidity, visibility, causation by contact), or psychology (thoughts and desires are known only through behavior). But otherwise the spirit is recognizable as a kind of person or animal. Spirits see and hear, have a memory, have beliefs and desires, act on conditions that they believe will bring about a desired effect, make decisions, and issue threats and bargains. When the elders spread religious beliefs, they never bother to spell out these defaults. No one ever says, "If the spirits promise us good weather in exchange for a sacrifice, and they know we want good weather, they predict that we will make the sacrifice." They don't have to, because they know that the minds of the pupils will automatically supply these beliefs from their tacit knowledge of psychology. Believers also avoid working out the strange logical consequences of these piecemeal revisions of ordinary things.

They don't pause to wonder why a God who knows our intentions has to listen to our prayers, or how a God can both see into the future and care about how we choose to act. Compared to the mind-bending ideas of modern science, religious beliefs are notable for their lack of imagination (God is a jealous man; heaven and hell are places; souls are people who have sprouted wings). That is because religious concepts are human concepts with a few emendations that make them wondrous and a longer list of standard traits that make them sensible to our ordinary ways of knowing.

But where do people get the emendations? Even when all else has failed, why would they waste time spinning ideas and practices that are useless, even harmful? Why don't they accept that human knowledge and power have limits and conserve their thoughts for domains in which they can do some good? I have alluded to one possibility: The demand for miracles creates a market that would-be priests compete in, and they can succeed by exploiting people's dependence on experts. I let the dentist drill my teeth and the surgeon cut into my body even though I cannot possibly verify for myself the assumptions they use to justify those mutilations. That same trust would have made me submit to medical quackery a century ago and to a witch doctor's charms millennia ago. Of course, witch doctors must have *some* track record or they would lose all credibility, and they do blend their hocus-pocus with genuine practical knowledge such as herbal remedies and predictions of events (for instance, the weather) that are more accurate than chance.

And beliefs about a world of spirits do not come from nowhere. They are hypotheses intended to explain certain data that stymie our everyday theories. Edward Tylor, an early anthropologist, noted that animistic beliefs are grounded in universal experiences. When people dream, their body stays in bed but some other part of them is up and about in the world. The soul and the body also part company in the trance brought on by an illness or a hallucinogen. Even when we are awake, we see shadows and reflections in still water that seem to carry the essence of a person without having mass, volume, or continuity in time and space. And in death the body has lost some invisible force that animates it in life. One theory that brings these facts together is that the soul wanders off when we sleep, lurks in the shadows, looks back at us from the surface of a pond, and leaves the body when we die.

Discussion Questions

1. Which of the things in the first paragraph do you believe? Why do you believe/disbelieve them? Why does Pinker mention these statistics?
2. People who act violently in the name of religion, such as abortion clinic gunmen and suicide bombers, are typically written off as religious extremists

just like Christians do not believe that Hitler was "acting in accordance with the will of the Almighty Creator." How do you respond to this? Does *religion* lead to these atrocities or is it just people's misuse of religion?

3. Why would it cause reason for wonder "Why a God who knows our intentions has to listen to our prayers"?

4. If there is a biological and psychological explanation for religious beliefs as Pinker suggests, how does this affect your own views of religious belief?

5. Explain the relevance of the finding that 85 percent of religious peoples adopt the religious beliefs of their parents.

Movie Titles

1. *Contact*—Involves issues of faith in both science and God. Also addresses the relevance of the rational in creating belief systems. What would it take for you to believe in extraterrestrial life? Is there any sort of proof for God?

2. THEME: Feelings and Knowledge—What is the role of emotion and intuition in framing your worldview? In what ways do emotion and passion get in the way of your ability to see the world clearly? In what ways do they help and add to your life and allow you to see even more clearly?
   - *Pleasantville*
   - *The Passion of Ayn Rand* (Not Rated)
   - *Equilibrium* (R)

Song Lyrics

Stevie Wonder—"Superstition"
Carter Peace Mission—"I Would Never Write"
DC Talk—"Mrs. Morgan"
Thrice—"The Melting Point of Wax"

Chapter 7

Eastern Thought

In many philosophy courses, the Eastern paradigm is often ignored or taught as a separate course (i.e., "Eastern Philosophy"). Given that this book attempts to provide the "landscape" of philosophical thought, it would be a disservice to ignore the foundation of thought for such a large part of the population's world view. Likewise, you may find that this approach solves (or at least sheds light on) some of the conundrums throughout Western thought.

Many of the problems of Western philosophy result from inconsistencies, contradictions, and paradoxes in language. Eastern religions and approaches tend to eschew these problems by recognizing language as lacking to begin with. As an Eastern proverb suggests, "If one asks about the Tao and the other answers, neither knows it." To the Western mind, this likely seems problematic (and it can make teaching about the Tao difficult). But as you will see, avoiding the numerous contradictions of language and logic can also be liberating.

Likewise, the Eastern approach addresses issues of pain and suffering by attempting to eliminate its root cause: desire. In doing so, one not only avoids worldly suffering (or at least can embrace it for what it is), but also transcends the numerous obstacles obstructing the *oneness* of the universe. This has real-life consequences when we examine notions of political philosophy, as well as morality and religious suffering.

In this chapter, the selection from the Buddha not only explores more deeply the issue of suffering, but also provides a guide for dealing with the suffering and allowing oneself to flourish in spite of (or because of) it. Gandhi also provides insights as to how to approach worldly suffering and how to apply this approach to a method of revolt that is peaceful and consistent with Hindu ethic. The selection from the *Dao De Jing*—the primary source for Taoism—illuminates some of its main tenets in the form of poetry. (Other selections in this text also highlight areas in Eastern thought such as those by Kolm and Ramakrishna.)

The Four Noble Truths
The Buddha

"Buddha" means "Enlightened (or Awakened) One" and is the name originally given to Siddhartha Gautama. Siddhartha grew up in a royal family in Nepal around the time of 560 B.C. and lived a luxurious life. One day he ventured outside of his palace and realized the great suffering (*dukkha*) going on throughout the world. This resulted in his leaving the palace and living a simple, ascetic life in search of the solution to suffering. He nearly starved to death in his ascetic quest for enlightenment and purportedly devised the *Four Noble Truths* and *Eightfold Path* (included here, in this section) while meditating under a "Bo-tree" known as the "Tree of Enlightenment." He went on to teach and developed a sect of monks and, after his death (thirteen years before Socrates was born), the religion of Buddhism grew and is now very popular worldwide.

The *Four Noble Truths* is considered by most as the cornerstone of Buddhist teaching. The four "truths" basically illuminate the problem of suffering (also referred to as imperfection or stress) and how to alleviate it. The Buddha held that there are three types of suffering: ordinary suffering (i.e., sickness, loss of loved ones), impermanence, and suffering of the mind. It is the latter that the Buddha hopes to alleviate and, in doing so, aid in the attainment of wisdom and, eventually, nirvana.

In the first Noble Truth, he explains the "five aggregates" of suffering. Here, he refers to the components of the human being: *form*—the physical component; *feelings*—sensations; *perception*—awareness of particular sensations; *mental formations*—emotions tied to the sensations that lead to action; and *consciousness*—awareness of the other four aggregates working together.

In the fourth Noble Truth, known also as the "Middle Path," the Buddha puts forth his approach for eradicating suffering known as the Eightfold Path. This prescription for the avoidance of suffering has eight interconnected principles and aims to provide a middle-ground between the extremes of pursuit of happiness through sensual pleasure and its opposite, asceticism—avoidance of any sensual pleasure. The Eightfold Path can be broken down into three basic categories: wisdom (numbers 1 and 2), ethical conduct (numbers 3–5), and mental discipline (numbers 6–8).

Reading Questions

1. What are the "Four Noble Truths"?
2. What are the five aggregates of stress/suffering, and how do they relate to the Four Noble Truths?
3. What is the origin of suffering? What does the Buddha mean when he writes that one origin is "Craving for existence, and craving for non-existence"?
4. In your own words, explain each point of the Eightfold Path.

Source: Copyright © Maurice Walshe 1987, 1995. Reprinted from *The Long Discourses of Buddha: A Translation of The Digha Nikaya* with permission of Wisdom Publications, 199 Elm Street, Somerville, MA 02144 U.S.A., www.wishdompubs.org.

17. "Again, monks, a monk abides contemplating mind-objects as mind-objects in respect of the Four Noble Truths. How does he do so? Here, a monk knows as it really is: 'This is suffering' he knows as it really is: 'This is the origin of suffering' he knows as it really is: 'This is the cessation of suffering' he knows as it really is: 'This is the way of practice leading to the cessation of suffering.'

18. "And what, monks, is the Noble Truth of suffering? Birth is suffering, aging is suffering, death is suffering, sorrow, lamentation, pain, sadness, and distress are suffering. Being attached to the unloved is suffering, being separated from the loved is suffering, not getting what one wants is suffering. In short, the five aggregates of grasping are suffering. . . .

"And how, monks, in short, are the five aggregates of grasping suffering? They are as follows: the aggregate of grasping that is form, the aggregate of grasping that is feeling, the aggregate of grasping that is perception, the aggregate of grasping that is the mental formations, the aggregate of grasping that is consciousness. These are, in short, the five aggregates of grasping that are suffering. And that, monks, is called the Noble Truth of Suffering.

19. "And what, monks, is the Noble Truth of the Origin of Suffering? It is that craving which gives rise to rebirth, bound up with pleasure and lust, finding fresh delight now here, now there: that is to say sensual craving, craving for existence, and craving for non-existence.

"And where does this craving arise and establish itself? Wherever in the world there is anything agreeable and pleasurable, there this craving arises and establishes itself.

"And what is there in the world that is agreeable and pleasurable? The eye in the world is agreeable and pleasurable, the ear . . . , the nose . . . , the tongue . . . , the body . . . , the mind in the world is agreeable and pleasurable, and there this craving arises and establishes itself. Sights, sounds, smells, tastes, tangibles, mind-objects in the world are agreeable and pleasurable, and there this craving arises and establishes itself.

"The craving for sights, sounds, smells, tastes, tangibles, mind-objects in the world is agreeable and pleasurable, and there this craving arises and establishes itself.

"Thinking of sights, sounds, smells, tastes, tangibles, mind-objects in the world is agreeable and pleasurable, and there this craving arises and establishes itself.

"Pondering on sights, sounds, smells, tastes, tangibles, and mind-objects in the world is agreeable and pleasurable, and there this craving arises and establishes itself. And that, monks, is called the Noble Truth of the Origin of Suffering.

20. "And what, monks, is the Noble Truth of the Cessation of Suffering? It is the complete fading-away and extinction of this craving, its forsaking and abandonment, liberation from it, detachment from it. And how does this craving come to be abandoned, how does its cessation come about? . . .

21. "And what, monks, is the Noble Truth of the Way of Practice Leading to the Cessation of Suffering? It is just this Noble Eightfold Path, namely:—Right

View, Right Thought; Right Speech, Right Action, Right Livelihood; Right Effort, Right Mindfulness, Right Concentration.

"And what, monks, is Right View? It is, monks, the knowledge of suffering, the knowledge of the origin of suffering, the knowledge of the cessation of suffering, and the knowledge of the way of practice leading to the cessation of suffering. This is called Right View.

"And what, monks, is Right Thought? The thought of renunciation, the thought of non-ill-will, the thought of harmlessness. This, monks, is called Right Thought.

"And what, monks, is Right Speech? Refraining from lying, refraining from slander, refraining from harsh speech, refraining from frivolous speech. This is called Right Speech.

"And what, monks, is Right Action? Refraining from taking life, refraining from taking what is not given, refraining from sexual misconduct. This is called Right Action.

"And what, monks, is Right Livelihood? Here, monks, the Ariyan disciple, having given up wrong livelihood, keeps himself by right livelihood.

"And what, monks, is Right Effort? Here, monks, a monk rouses his will, makes an effort, stirs up energy, exerts his mind, and strives to prevent the arising of unarisen evil unwholesome mental states. He rouses his will . . . and strives to overcome evil unwholesome mental states that have arisen. He rouses his will . . . and strives to produce unarisen wholesome mental states. He rouses his will makes an effort, stirs up energy, exerts his mind, and strives to maintain wholesome mental states that have arisen, not to let them fade away, to bring them to greater growth, to the full perfection of development. This is called Right Effort.

"And what, monks, is Right Mindfulness? Here, monks, a monk abides contemplating body as body, ardent, clearly aware, and mindful, having put aside hankering and fretting for the world; he abides contemplating feelings as feelings . . . ; he abides contemplating mind as mind . . . ; he abides contemplating mind-objects as mind-objects, ardent, clearly aware and mindful, having put aside hankering and fretting for the world. This is called Right Mindfulness.

"And what, monks, is Right Concentration? Here, a monk, detached from sense-desires, detached from unwholesome mental states, enters and remains in the first jhāna, which is with thinking and pondering, born of detachment, filled with delight and joy. And with the subsiding of thinking and pondering, by gaining inner tranquility and oneness of mind, he enters and remains in the second jhāna, which is without thinking and pondering, born of concentration, filled with delight and joy. And with the fading away of delight, remaining imperturbable, mindful and clearly aware, he experiences in himself the joy of which the Noble Ones say: 'Happy is he who dwells with equanimity and mindfulness,' he enters the third jhāna. And, having given up pleasure and pain, and with the disappearance of former gladness and sadness, he enters and remains in the fourth jhāna, which is beyond pleasure and pain, and purified by equanimity and mindfulness. This is called Right Concentration. And that, monks, is called the way of practice leading to the cessation of suffering."

Discussion Questions

1. What are the immediate causes of stress/suffering in your own life? Does the Buddha's approach here give you insight as to how to alleviate these? Why/why not?

2. How do your desires and cravings cause suffering? Do *all* cravings cause suffering? What about a craving to help others? To eat? To raise a family?

3. In what way is suffering caused by not getting what one wants? Would you prefer that you got everything you ever wanted?

4. In the second noble truth, he writes, "Wherever in the world there is anything agreeable and pleasurable, there this craving arises." What role does pleasure play in your pursuit of happiness? If cravings are caused by agreeable and pleasurable things, and cravings cause suffering, then in what ways do pleasurable things cause suffering in your life? Pursuing them? Attaining them?

5. Does the realization of universal impermanence help alleviate stress or does it in some way increase your stress? Think about times you have experienced sorrow, or when you have lost or broken a treasured object. Think in reference to yourself and loved ones. Think in reference to our planet and the universe.

6. How does the avoidance of suffering in this passage differ from the Western approaches taken in the "Religious Problem of Evil" section of this book?

Selected Writings
Gandhi

While the philosophy of Mohandas Gandhi (also called "Mahatma," meaning "great soul") combined many different approaches—such as the teachings of Christ, Buddha, Mahavira, and the *Bhagavad Gita*—he considered himself a Hindu. Gandhi was a major contributor to India's earning independence from Britain in 1947. His approach to gaining India's independence is referenced in this selection from his writings: Instead of returning the often violent nature of Britain's rule, Gandhi promoted tactics like nonviolent protest, fasting, and boycotting British goods. He is well known for saying, "An eye for an eye makes the whole world blind," as well as, "You must be the change you wish to see in the world."

Source: Excerpts from *Young India* and *Yeravda Mandir* by Mahatma Gandhi (as published in *Great Political Thinkers*, 6e, pp. 742–752). Reprinted by permission of Navajivan Trust.

See the citations at the bottom of each page. The first are taken from his newsletter, *Young India*, on the dates included on the photocopied sheets. The sections on and following "Truth" are from Gandhi's, *Yeavda Mandir:* Rupees Three © Navajivan Trust, 1932. First edition, 1932, ISBN 81-7229-135-3. Printed and published by Jitendra T. Desai.

Reading Questions

1. What is *Satyagraha*? Why does Gandhi believe that humans are not competent to punish others?
2. What role does self-purification have in *Satyagraha*?
3. How do Truth and God interrelate? How does this relationship affect suffering?
4. How does Gandhi suggest that we find this Truth?
5. How does Gandhi suggest that we deal with those who create great difficulty for us? Why does he make this particular suggestion?
6. How does Gandhi explain the "path of *ahimsa*" with his example of the thieves? How does *ahimsa* relate to Truth?
7. Why does Gandhi write that in obeying the law of *ahimsa* alone, this would prevent one from marrying and having a family?
8. Explain *brahmacharya* in your own words. What role do the mind and body play with regard to this?
9. Explain Gandhi's philosophy regarding our worldly possessions. In what way is the body a possession? What about thoughts?

*Satyagraha, Civil Disobedience, Passive Resistance, Non-Cooperation**

Satyagraha is literally holding on to Truth and it means, therefore, Truth-force. Truth is soul or spirit. It is, therefore, known as soul-force. It excludes the use of violence because man is not capable of knowing the absolute truth and, therefore, not competent to punish. The word was coined in South Africa to distinguish the non-violent resistance of the Indians of South Africa from the contemporary 'passive resistance' of the suffragetters and others. It is not conceived as a weapon of the weak. . . .

*Some Rules of Satyagraha**

Satyagraha literally means insistence on truth. This insistence arms the votary with matchless power. This power or force is connoted by the word *Satyagraha*. *Satyagraha*, to be genuine, may be offered against one's wife or one's children, against rulers, against fellow citizens, even against the whole world.

Such a universal force necessarily makes no distinction between kinsmen and strangers, young and old, man and woman, friend and foe. The force to be so applied can never be physical. There is in it no room for violence. The only force of universal application can, therefore, be that of *ahimsa* or love. In other words it is soul-force.

Young India, 23–2–'21.
Young India, 27–2–'30.

Love does not burn others, it burns itself. Therefore, a *Satyagrahi*, i.e., a civil resister, will joyfully suffer even unto death.

It follows, therefore, that a civil resister, whilst he will strain every nerve to compass the end of the existing rule, will do no intentional injury in thought, word or deed. . . .

*Qualifications for Satyagraha**

Satyagraha presupposes self-discipline, self-control, self-purification, and a recognized social status in the person offering it. A *Satyagrahi* must never forget the distinction between evil and the evil-doer. He must not harbor ill-will or bitterness against the latter. He may not even employ needlessly offensive language against the evil person, however unrelieved his evil might be. For it should be an article of faith with every *Satyagrahi* that there is none so fallen in this world but can be converted by love. A *Satyagrahi* will always try to overcome evil by good, anger by love, untruth by truth, *himsa* by *ahimsa*. There is no other way of purging the world of evil. Therefore a person who claims to be a *Satyagrahi* always tries by close and prayerful self-introspection and self-analysis to find out whether he is himself completely free from the taint of anger, ill-will, and such other human infirmities, whether he is not himself capable of those very evils against which he is out to lead a crusade. In self-purification and penance lies half the victory of a *Satyagrahi*. A *Satyagrahi* has faith that the silent and undemonstrative action of truth and love produces far more permanent and abiding results than speeches or such other showy performances. . . .

The word *Satya* (Truth) is derived from *Sat*, which means 'being.' Nothing is or exists in reality except Truth. That is why *Sat* or Truth is perhaps the most important name of God. In fact it is more correct to say that Truth is God, than to say that God is Truth. But as we cannot do without a ruler or a general, names of God such as 'King of Kings' or 'the Almighty' are and will remain generally current. On deeper thinking, however, it will be realized, that *Sat* or *Satya* is the only correct and fully significant name for God.

And where there is Truth, there also is knowledge which is true. Where there is no Truth, there can be no true knowledge. That is why the word *Chit* or knowledge is associated with the name of God. And where there is true knowledge, there is always bliss (*Ananda*). Sorrow has no place there. And even as Truth is eternal, so is the bliss derived from it. Hence we know God as *Satchit-ananda*, One who combines in Himself Truth, Knowledge, and Bliss.

Devotion to this Truth is the sole justification for our existence. . . .

But how is one to realize this Truth, which may be likened to the philosopher's stone or the cow of plenty? By single-minded devotion (*abhyasa*) and indifference to all other interests in life (*vairagya*)—replies the *Bhagavadgita*. In

---

Young India, 8–8–'29.

spite, however, of such devotion, what may appear as truth to one person will often appear as untruth to another person. But that need not worry the seeker. Where there is honest effort, it will be realized that what appear to be different truths are like the countless and apparently different leaves of the same tree. Does not God Himself appear to different individuals in different aspects? Yet we know that He is one. But Truth is the right designation of God. Hence there is nothing wrong in every man following Truth according to his lights. Indeed it is his duty to do so. Then if there is a mistake on the part of any one so following Truth, it will be automatically set right. For the quest of Truth involves *tapas*—self-suffering, sometimes even unto death. There can be no place in it for even a trace of self-interest. In such selfless search for Truth nobody can lose his bearings for long. Directly he takes to the wrong path he stumbles, and is thus redirected to the right path. Therefore the pursuit of Truth is truth *bhakti* (devotion). It is the path that leads to God. There is no place in it for cowardice, no place for defeat. It is the talisman by which death itself becomes the portal to life eternal. . . .

Ahimsa or Love

. . . One can realize Truth and *ahimsa* only by ceaseless striving.

But it is impossible for us to realize perfect Truth so long as we are imprisoned in this mortal frame. We can only visualize it in our imagination. We cannot, through the instrumentality of this ephemeral body, see face to face Truth which is eternal. That is why in the last resort one must depend on faith.

It appears that the impossibility of full realization of Truth in this mortal body led some ancient seeker after Truth to the appreciation of *ahimsa*. The question which confronted him was: "Shall I bear with those who create difficulties for me, or shall I destroy them?" The seeker realized that he who went on destroying others did not make headway but simply stayed where he was, while the man who suffered those who created difficulties marched ahead, and at times even took the others with him. The first act of destruction taught him that the Truth which was the object of his quest was not outside himself but within. Hence the more he took to violence, the more he receded from Truth. For in fighting the imagined enemy without, he neglected the enemy within.

We punish thieves, because we think they harass us. They may leave us alone; but they will only transfer their attentions to another victim. This other victim however is also a human being, ourselves in a different form, and so we are caught in a vicious circle. The trouble from thieves continues to increase, as they think it is their business to steal. In the end we see that it is better to endure the thieves than to punish them. The forbearance may even bring them to their senses. By enduring them we realize that thieves are not different from ourselves, they are our brethren, our friends, and may not be punished. But whilst we may bear with the thieves, we may not endure the infliction. That would only induce cowardice. So we realize a further duty. Since we regard the thieves as our kith and kin, they must be made to realize the kinship. And so we must take pains to devise ways and means of winning them over. This is the path of *ahimsa*. It may entail continuous suffering and the cultivating of endless patience. Given these two conditions, the thief is bound in the end to turn away from his evil ways. Thus step by step we learn how to make friends with all the world; we realize the greatness of God—of Truth. Our peace of mind increases in spite of suffering; we become braver and more enterprising; we understand more clearly the difference between what is everlasting and what is not; we learn how to distinguish between what is our duty and what is not. Our pride melts away, and we become humble. Our worldly attachments diminish, and the evil within us diminishes from day to day.

Ahimsa is not the crude thing it has been made to appear. Not to hurt any living thing is not doubt a part of *ahimsa*. But it is its least expression. The principle of *ahimsa* is hurt by every evil thought, by undue haste, by lying, by hatred, by wishing ill to anybody. It is also violated by our holding on to what the world needs. But the world needs even what we eat day by day. In the place where we stand there are millions of microorganisms to whom the place belongs, and who are hurt by our presence there. What should we do then? Should we commit suicide? Even that is no solution, if we believe, as we do, that so long as the spirit is attached to the flesh, on every destruction of the body it weaves for itself another. The body will cease to be only when we give up all attachment to it. This freedom from all attachment is the realization of God as Truth. Such realization cannot be attained in a hurry. The body does not belong to us. While it lasts, we must use it as a trust handed over to our charge. Treating in this way, the things of the flesh, we may one day expect to become free from the burden of the body. Realizing the limitations of the flesh, we must strive day by day towards the ideal with what strength we have in us.

It is perhaps clear from the foregoing, that without *ahimsa* it is not possible to seek and find Truth. *Ahimsa* and Truth are so intertwined that it is practically impossible to disentangle and separate them. They are like the two sides of a coin, or rather of a smooth unstamped metallic disc. Who can say, which is the obverse, and which is the reverse? Nevertheless *ahimsa* is the means; Truth is the end. Means to be means must always be within our reach, and so *ahimsa* is our supreme duty. If we take care of the means, we are bound to reach the end sooner or later. When once we have grasped this point, final victory is beyond question. Whatever difficulties we encounter, whatever apparent reverses we sustain, we may not give up the quest for Truth which alone is, being God Himself.

Brahmacharya or Chastity

The third among our observances is *brahmacharya*. As a matter of fact all observances are deducible from Truth, and are meant to subserve it. The man, who is wedded to Truth and worships Truth alone, proves unfaithful to her, if he applies his talents to anything else. How then can he minister to the senses? A man, whose activities are wholly consecrated to the realization of Truth, which requires utter selflessness, can have no time for the selfish purpose of begetting children and running a household. Realization of Truth through self-gratification should, after what has been said before, appear a contradiction in terms.

If we look at it from the standpoint of *ahimsa* (nonviolence), we find that the fulfilment of *ahimsa* is impossible without utter selflessness. *Ahimsa* means Universal Love. If a man gives his love to one woman, or a woman to one man, what is there left for all the world besides? It simply means, "We two first, and the devil take all the rest of them." As a faithful wife must be prepared to sacrifice her all for the sake of her husband, and a faithful husband for the sake of his wife, it is clear that such persons cannot rise to the height of Universal Love, or look upon all mankind as kith and kin. For they have created a boundary wall round their love. The larger their family, the farther are they from Universal Love. Hence one who would obey the law of *ahimsa* cannot marry, not to speak of gratification outside the marital bond.

Then what about people who are already married? Will they never be able to realize Truth? Can they never offer up their all at the altar of humanity? There is a way out for them. They can behave as if they were not married. Those who have enjoyed this happy condition will be able to bear me out. Many have to my knowledge successfully tried the experiment. If the married couple can think of each other as brother and sister, they are freed for universal service. The very thought that all the women in the world are his sisters, mothers, or daughters will at once ennoble a man and snap his chains. The husband and wife do not lose any thing here, but only add to their resources and even to their family. Their love becomes free from the impurity of lust and so grows stronger. With the disappearance of this impurity, they can serve each other better, and the occasions for quarrelling become fewer. There are more occasions for quarrelling where the love is selfish and bounded. . . .

Brahmacharya, like all other observances, must be observed in thought, word and deed. We are told in the *Gita*, and experience will corroborate the statement, that the foolish man, who appears to control his body, but is nursing evil thoughts in his mind, makes a vain effort. It may be harmful to suppress the body, if the mind is at the same time allowed to go astray. Where the mind wanders, the body must follow sooner or later.

It is necessary here to appreciate a distinction. It is one thing to allow the mind to harbor impure thoughts; it is a different thing altogether if it strays among them in spite of ourselves. Victory will be ours in the end, if we non-cooperate with the mind in its evil wanderings.

We experience every moment of our lives, that often while the body is subject to our control, the mind is not. This physical control should never be relaxed, and in addition we must put forth a constant endeavour to bring the mind under control. We can do nothing more, nothing less. If we give way to the mind, the body and the mind will put different ways, and we shall be false to ourselves. Body and mind may be said to go together, so long as we continue to resist the approach of every evil thought.

The observance of *brahmacharya* has been believed to be very difficult, almost impossible. In trying to find a reason for this belief, we see that the term *brahmacharya* has been taken in a narrow sense. Mere control of animal passion has been thought to be tantamount to observing *brahmacharya*. I feel, that this conception is incomplete and wrong. *Brahmacharya* means control of all the organs of sense. He, who attempts to control only one organ, and allows all the others free play, is bound to find his effort futile. To hear suggestive stories with the ears, to see suggestive sights with the eyes, to taste stimulating food with the tongue, to touch exciting things with the hands, and then at the same time expect to control the only remaining organ is like putting one's hands in the fire, and expecting to escape being burnt. He therefore who is resolved to control the one must be likewise determined to control the rest. I have always felt, that much harms has been done by the narrow definition of *brahmacharya*. If we practice simultaneous self-control in all directions, the attempt will be scientific and possible of success. Perhaps the palate is the chief sinner. That is why in the *Ashram* we have assigned to control of the palate a separate place among our observances.

Let us remember the root meaning of *brahmacharya*. *Charya* means course of conduct; *brahmacharya* conduct adapted to the search of *Brahma*, i.e., Truth. From this etymological meaning arises the special meaning, viz., control of all the senses. We must entirely forget the incomplete definition which restricts itself to the sexual aspect only.

Non-Possession

Possession implies provision for the future. A seeker after Truth, a follower of the law of Love cannot hold anything against tomorrow. God never stores for the morrow; He never creates more than what is strictly needed for the moment. If therefore we repose faith in His providence, we should rest assured that He will give us every day our daily bread, meaning everything that we require. . . . The rich have a superfluous store of things which they do not need, and which are therefore neglected and wasted; while millions are starved to death for want of sustenance. If each retained possession only of what he needed, no one would be in want, and all would live in contentment. As it is, the rich are discontented no less than the poor. The poor man would fain become a millionaire, and the millionaire a multimillionaire. The rich should take the initiative in dispossession with a view to a universal diffusion of the spirit of contentment. If only they keep their own property within moderate limits, the starving will be easily fed, and will learn the lesson of contentment along with the rich. . . .

Civilization, in the real sense of the term, consists not in the multiplication, but in the deliberate and voluntary reduction of wants. This alone promotes real happiness and contentment, and increases the capacity for service. Judging by this criterion, we find that in the Ashram we possess many things, the necessity for which cannot be proved, and we thus tempt our neighbors to thieve.

From the standpoint of pure Truth, the body too is a possession. It has been truly said that desire for enjoyment creates bodies for the soul. When this desire vanishes, there remains no further need for the body, and man is free from the vicious cycle of births and deaths. The soul is omnipresent; why should she care to be confined within the cagelike body, or do evil and even kill for the sake of that cage? We thus arrive at the ideal of total renunciation, and learn to use the body for the purposes of service so long as it exists, so much so that service, and not bread, becomes with us the staff of life. We eat and drink, sleep and wake, for service alone. Such an attitude of mind brings us real happiness, and the beatific vision in the fulness of time. Let us all examine ourselves from this standpoint.

We should remember, that Non-possession is a principle applicable to thoughts, as well as to things. A man who fills his brain with useless knowledge violates that inestimable principle. Thoughts, which turn us away from God, or do not turn us towards Him, constitute impediments in our way. . . .

Discussion Questions

1. Arguments against the death penalty are often rooted in the idea that any human judicial system is imperfect and, thus, we should abolish the death penalty. What do you think about this argument? What do you think about this argument as it relates to other forms of punishment as well?
2. Much of what Gandhi writes goes against much of what we consider to be human nature, such as avoiding feelings of jealousy, desire for revenge, lust, etc. Do you think his philosophy is realistic? If not, is it still worth striving for? In what ways is it truly possible to "joyfully suffer until death," as Gandhi writes?
3. In what ways do your worldly possessions cause you stress and suffering? Would you be better off by having more or fewer possessions?
4. Which phrase encapsulates your view: "An eye for an eye," or "An eye for an eye makes the whole world blind"? What are the positive and negative ramifications of each?

The *Dao De Jing*

Laozi

Written by Laozi (also spelled Lao Tzu, translated as "Old Master") around the time of 600–400 B.C., the *Dao De Jing* (also spelled *Tao Te Ching*) is the second most translated book in history (second to the Christian Bible) and is central to the philosophy of Taoism (pronounced "dow-ism"; Tao pronounced "dow"), as well as Buddhism. The book contains two sections: the first, the *Tao* (Chapters 1–37) is often translated as "the way." Though the *Tao* is considered as unable to be defined, as it is not an actual *thing* but rather the ultimate reality and beyond distinction, thus beyond the scope of mere language. The second section, the *Te* (Chapters 38–81) is translated as "virtue" or "power." Thus, the title of the book has been translated as "The Great Book of the Way and Its Power."

Source: Chan, Wing-tsit; *A Source Book In Chinese Philosophy.* Copyright © 1963 Princeton University Press, 1991 renewed PUP. Reprinted by permission of Princeton University Press.

Written in poetic form, the *Dao De Jing* primarily sets forth ethical considerations and a guide for how one ought to live, as well as to govern, but it also explains the underlying metaphysical philosophy of Taoism and its basic principles of reality. The selections here focus more on the later project. Commentary by a scholar follows each chapter for further clarification. Try distilling meaning from each poem on your own before reading the comments that follow each poem.

Reading Questions

1. What role does naming something play in Taoism? What problem occurs when the Tao is named?
2. In much of Western society, something cannot both *be* and *not be*. How is this approached in the *Dao De Jing*?
3. What relation does beauty have to ugliness? Good to evil? What role do opposites play in Chinese philosophy?
4. Why is there virtue in teaching through actions?
5. What does it mean for the *Tao* to be empty, like a bowl? What does Laozi mean when he writes that the *Tao* "becomes one with the dusty world"?
6. Explain the significance of non-being. What three examples does Laozi provide to show the importance of non-being. What is the non-being of a door?
7. What is the relation of the "manifest" to the "hidden"?
8. What relation does the *Tao* have to left/right, small/great? How is the *Tao* like the Christian God?

1

The Tao that can be told of is not the eternal Tao;
The name that can be named is not the eternal name.
The Nameless is the origin of Heaven and Earth;
The Named is the mother of all things.

Therefore let there always be non-being, so we may see their subtlety,
And let there always be being, so we may see their outcome.
The two are the same,
But after they are produced, they have different names.
They both may be called deep and profound.
Deeper and more profound,
The door of all subtleties!

Comment

This is the most important of all chapters, for in one stroke the basic characteristics of Tao as the eternal, the nameless, the source, and the substance of all things are explicitly or implicitly affirmed. It is no wonder the opening sentences are among the most often quoted or even chanted sayings in Chinese.

The key Taoist concepts of the named and the nameless are also introduced here. The concept of name is common to all ancient Chinese philosophical schools, but Taoism is unique in this respect. Most schools insist on the correspondence of names and actualities and accept names as necessary and good; Taoism, on the contrary, rejects names in favor of the nameless. This, among other things, shows its radical and unique character. To Lao Tzu, Tao is nameless and is the simplicity without names; when names arise, that is, when the simple oneness of Tao is split up into individual things with names, it is time to stop.

The cardinal ideas of being and non-being are also important here, for in Taoism the nameless (*wu-ming*) is equivalent to non-being and the named (*yu-ming*) is equivalent to being. For this reason, when he comments on the saying about the named and the nameless, Wang Pi says, "All being originated in non-being." As students of Chinese thought well know, the ideas of being and non-being have been dominant throughout the history of Chinese philosophy. They are central concepts in Neo-Taoism, Chinese Buddhism, and also Neo-Confucianism. It was the importance of these concepts, no doubt, that led the Neo-Confucianist Wang An-shih to deviate from tradition and punctuate the phrases "always be no desires" and "always be desires" to read "Let there always be non-being, so we may . . . ," and "Let there always be being, so we may. . . ."

Wang's punctuation not only underlines the importance of these ideas; it also shows the new metaphysical interest in Neo-Confucianism. Confucianism had been fundamentally ethical in tradition, but under the impact of Buddhist and Taoist metaphysics, the Neo-Confucianists developed Confucianism along metaphysical lines. In this case, in substituting the ideas of being and non-being for the ideas of having desires and having no desires, Wang shows a greater recognition of the philosophical content of the *Lao Tzu*, as it deserves.

2

When the people of the world all know beauty as beauty,
There arises the recognition of ugliness.
When they all know the good as good,
There arises the recognition of evil.
Therefore:
 Being and non-being produce each other;
 Difficult and easy complete each other;
 Long and short contrast each other;
 High and low distinguish each other;
 Sound and voice harmonize each other;
 Front and behind accompany each other.
Therefore the sage manages affairs without action
And spreads doctrines without words.
All things arise, and he does not turn away from them.
He produces them but does not take possession of them.

He acts but does not rely on his own ability.
He accomplishes his task but does not claim credit for it.
It is precisely because he does not claim credit that his
    accomplishment remains with him.

Comment

That everything has its opposite, and that these opposites are the mutual causations of each other, form a basic part of Chuang Tzu's philosophy and later Chinese philosophy. It is important to note that opposites are here presented not as irreconcilable conflicts but as complements. The traditional Chinese ideal that opposites are to be synthesized and harmonized can be said to have originated with Lao Tzu.

The idea of teaching without words anticipated the Buddhist tradition of silent transmission of the mystic doctrine, especially in the Zen (Ch'an) school. This is diametrically opposed to the Confucian ideal, according to which a superior man acts and thus "becomes the model of the world," and speaks and thus "becomes the pattern for the world." It is true that Confucianists say that a superior man "is truthful without any words," but they would never regard silence itself as a virtue. . . .

4

Tao is empty (like a bowl).
    It may be used but its capacity is never exhausted.
It is bottomless, perhaps the ancestor of all things.
It blunts its sharpness,
It unties its tangles.
It softens its light.
It becomes one with the dusty world.
Deep and still, it appears to exist forever.
I do not know whose son it is.
It seems to have existed before the Lord.

Comment

This chapter, on the substance and function of Tao, shows clearly that in Taoism function is no less important than substance. Substance is further described in chapters 14 and 21, but here, as in chapters 11 and 45, function (*yung*, also meaning "use") is regarded with equal respect. There is no deprecation of phenomena, as is the case with certain Buddhist schools. To describe the world as dusty may suggest a lack of enthusiasm for it; indeed both Buddhism and later Taoism employ the word "dust" to symbolize the dirty world from which we should escape. It is significant to note, however, that Taoism in its true sense calls for identification with, not escape from, such a world. . . .

11

Thirty spokes are united around the hub to make a wheel,
   But it is on its non-being that the utility of the carriage depends.
Clay is molded to form a utensil,
   But it is on its non-being that the utility of the utensil depends.
Doors and windows are cut out to make a room,
   But it is on its non-being that the utility of the room depends.
Therefore turn being into advantage, and turn non-being into utility.

Comment

Nowhere else in Chinese philosophy is the concept of non-being more strongly emphasized. This chapter alone should dispel any idea that Taoism is negativistic, for non-being—the hole in the hub, the hollowness of a utensil, the empty space in the room—is here conceived not as nothingness but as something useful and advantageous.

The Taoist interest in non-being has counteracted the positivistic tendency in certain Chinese philosophical schools, especially the Legalist and Confucian, which often overlook what seems to be nonexistent. It has prepared the Chinese mind for the acceptance of the Buddhist doctrine of Emptiness, although neither the Taoist concept of non-being nor that of vacuity is identical with that of the Buddhist Void. In addition, it was because of the Taoist insistence on the positive value of non-being that empty space has been utilized as a constructive factor in Chinese landscape painting. In this greatest art of China, space is used to combine the various elements into an organic whole and to provide a setting in which the onlooker's imagination may work. By the same token, much is left unsaid in Chinese poetry, for the reader must play a creative role to bring the poetic idea into full realization. The Zen Buddhists have developed to the fullest the themes that real existence is found in the nonexistent and that true words are spoken in silence, but the origin of these themes must be traced to early Taoism. . . .

14

We look at it and do not see it;
   Its name is The Invisible.
We listen to it and do not hear it;
   Its name is The Inaudible.
We touch it and do not find it;
   Its name is The Subtle (formless).
These three cannot be further inquired into,
And hence merge into one.
Going up high, it is not bright, and coming down low, it is not dark.
Infinite and boundless, it cannot be given any name;

It reverts to nothingness.
This is called shape without shape,
Form without objects.
It is The Vague and Elusive.
Meet it and you will not see its head.
Follow it and you will not see its back.
Hold on to the Tao of old in order to master the things of the present.
From this one may know the primeval beginning (of the universe).
This is called the bond[1] of Tao.

Comment

Subtlety is an important characteristic of Tao and is more important than its manifestations. The Confucianists, on the other hand, emphasize manifestation. There is nothing more manifest than the hidden (subtle), they say, and "a man who knows that the subtle will be manifested can enter into virtue." The Buddhists and Neo-Confucianists eventually achieved a synthesis, saying that "there is no distinction between the manifest and the hidden."

To describe reality in terms of the invisible, the inaudible, and the subtle is an attempt to describe it in terms of non-being. Because the three Chinese words are pronounced *i, hsi*, and *wei*, respectively, they have been likened to *Jod, Heh, Vav*, indicating the name Jehovah, and to the Hindu god Ishvara, but any similarity is purely accidental. The threefold description does not suggest any idea of trinity either. Basically, Taoist philosophy is naturalistic, if not atheistic, and any idea of a god is alien to it. . . .

34

The Great Tao flows everywhere.
It may go left or right.
All things depend on it for life, and it does not turn away from them.
It accomplishes its task, but does not claim credit for it.
It clothes and feeds all things but does not claim to be master over them.
Always without desires, it may be called The Small.
All things come to it and it does not master them; it may be called The Great.
Therefore (the sage) never strives himself for the great, and thereby the great
    is achieved.

Comment

In commenting on this chapter, Yen Fu says that the left and the right, the small and the great, are relative terms, and that Tao in its original substance transcends all these relative qualities. Of greater significance, however, is the paradoxical character of Tao. This character is affirmed more than once in the *Lao Tzu*. In Neo-Confucianism, principle is both immanent and transcendent, as is the Christian God. Ultimate being or reality is by nature paradoxical. . . .

42

Tao produced the One.
The One produced the two.
The two produced the three.
And the three produced the ten thousand things.
The ten thousand things carry the yin and embrace the yang, and through
    the blending of the material force they achieve harmony.
People hate to be children without parents, lonely people without spouses,
    or men without food to eat,
And yet kings and lords call themselves by these names.
Therefore it is often the case that things gain by losing and lose by gaining.

What others have taught, I teach also:
"Violent and fierce people do not die a natural death."
I shall make this the father of my teaching.

Comment

It is often understood that the One is the original material force of the Great Ultimate, the two are yin and yang, the three are their blending with the original material force, and the ten thousand things are things carrying yin and embracing yang. The similarity of this process to that of the *Book of Changes,* in which the Great Ultimate produces the Two Forces (yin and yang) and then the myriad things, is amazing. The important point, however, is not the specific similarities, but the evolution from the simple to the complex. This theory is common to nearly all Chinese philosophical schools.

It should be noted that the evolution here, as in the *Book of Changes,* is natural. Production (*sheng*) is not personal creation or purposeful origination, but natural causation.

Discussion Questions

1. What virtue is there in stripping language of its importance? For example, when he writes, "The *Tao* that can be told of is not the eternal *Tao*"? If we cannot tell of the *Tao,* then how do we ever know it? Then again, how might language prevent us from ever truly knowing something?

2. In what way do a person's "accomplishments remain with him" just because "he does not claim credit" for tasks accomplished? How does seeking credit for accomplishments diminish the rewards? In what ways does it heighten them?

3. Similar to Question 2 above, in what ways is it true that, in avoiding striving to be great, one thereby achieves greatness (see Poem 34)? In what ways does the pursuit of greatness serve as an obstacle for greatness? In what ways does it help one to achieve greatness? In the following two cases, what types of greatness will each artist likely achieve:
   a. The artist who strives to be a "best seller" and creates work for that purpose;
   b. The artist who ignores the pursuit of public accolades and pursues art for its own sake.

4. What importance, if any, do you place in "non-being"—in the empty space on a landscape or building; silence in a song (i.e., what's played between the notes); "reading between the lines" of a poem or work of fiction? How might you use non-being in your own life to create more value?

5. In what ways does Taoism help to alleviate apparent problems or contradictions in Western logic? How would the Taoist approach problems such as "God's not all powerful because He can't create a rock that He can't lift," or Zeno's Paradox: Motion is impossible because there are infinite halfway points that we must traverse in order to move?

━━━━━━━━

Movie Titles

1. *Gandhi*—Depicts Gandhi's application of non-violence. How much more successful is this method than other more aggressive methods? Could you use non-violence in your life, even at a less severe level than does Gandhi?

2. *The Tao of Steve* (R)—A comedy in which the main character applies his knowledge of Eastern philosophy to attract women.

Song Lyrics

John Lennon—"Imagine"
The Police—"Synchronicity"
Jack Johnson—"Gone"
Cloud Cult—"Transistor Radio"

Notes

1. *Chi*, literally, "a thread," denotes tradition, discipline, principle, order, essence, etc. Generally it means the system, principle, or continuity that binds things together.

Chapter 8

Free Will

The topic of free will has great relevance in much of today's society. It directly relates to how we justify punishing people and holding them morally accountable—how could we do so if what they did was not a free action? If you act based on forces out of your control, in what way can you be held accountable? It also relies heavily on the notion of the soul as being the source for our freely willed actions. And as we see in this section, free will is important when we investigate mind control (as in the case of advertising, cults, etc.) and artificial intelligence (i.e., can a computer exhibit free will?).

Free will is of special importance to us as individuals as well. We tend to value (maybe more than anything else) making free, authentic choices for ourselves—authoring our characters, in a sense. And we certainly disparage the idea of ourselves as mere puppets being forced to act at the whims of some other force. Even if we hold that we are not wholly free, recognizing where we lack this freedom is illuminating and important. As the saying goes, "Determine your actions, don't let your actions determine you."

The theory of determinism holds that we do not maintain free will—that we are like any other machine that acts based on factors out of its immediate control, even though some of these factors may be unrecognized.

Taylor provides a broad overview of the problem and offers numerous alternative viewpoints. d'Holbach's excerpt then frames the determinist position and holds that we are material entities in a mechanistic universe, and thus subject to the same laws and forces of other material entities. The next three philosophers focus on a specific portion of the debate. Hospers examines the role that unconscious forces play in our examination of seemingly free actions; Kane provides an analogy en route to defending the libertarian position (that we do have free will); and Stace argues for a compromise known as *compatiblism*: He holds that free will and determinism are not mutually exclusive theories and can instead be consistently held simultaneously.

The next three selections address two important topics in relation to free will. The first regards advertising's affect on consumers: If we are not free in all respects and can be controlled, then it is important to see how advertisers gain this control over us, as well as what deleterious affects advertising may have over our own world view and within society at large.

The final two selections examine the topic of artificial intelligence and help address questions such as: What would it mean for a computer to think or be conscious? How could a computer be said to act freely? And in what ways do computers differ from our own "computer-like" brains? Both employing analogies to help frame the issue, Searle argues against artificial intelligence, while Lycan argues that a computer can, in fact, achieve consciousness.

Freedom and Determinism
Richard Taylor

Richard Taylor taught philosophy at Brown, Columbia, and Rochester universities. Considered an expert on metaphysics, he has also authored a number of books, and is also an expert beekeeper. This selection is taken from his oft-cited book, *Metaphysics*, in which he first provides an overview of the freewill–determinism debate and then suggests his solution to the problem.

Reading Questions

1. How does Taylor define "free actions"?
2. What are the three criteria of soft determinism?
3. What is Taylor's critique of soft determinism?
4. Explain the significance of the "ingenious psychologist" example.
5. How does indeterminism attempt to solve the problem of determinism? What is the main flaw of this theory?
6. How does Taylor frame what he believes to be the correct view in this debate? Explain the two "metaphysical notions" that relate to his view.
7. What is the difference between fatalism and determinism?

Determinism

Reflections such as this suggest that, in the case of everything that exists, there are antecedent conditions, known or unknown, which, because they are given, mean that things could not be other than they are. That is an exact statement of the metaphysical thesis of determinism. More loosely, it says that everything, including every cause, is the effect of some cause or causes; or that everything is not only determinate but causally determined. The statement, moreover, makes no allowance for time, for past, or for future. Hence, if true, it holds not only for all things that have existed but for all things that do or ever will exist.

Of course people rarely think of such a principle, and hardly one in a thousand will ever formulate it to himself in words. Yet all do seem to assume it in their daily affairs, so much so that some philosophers have declared it an *a priori* principle of the understanding, that is, something that is known independently of experience, while others have deemed it to be at least a part of the common sense of mankind. Thus, when I hear a noise I look up to see where it came from. I never suppose that it was just a noise that came from nowhere and had no cause. Everyone does the same—even animals, though they have never once thought about metaphysics or the principle of universal determinism. People believe, or at least act as though they believed, that things have causes, without exception.

Source: Metaphysics, 4th Edition, pp. 36–38, 43–49, 51–53, 55–56, © 1992. Reprinted by permission of Pearson Education, Inc., Upper Saddle River, NJ. One Lake Street.

When a child or animal touches a hot stove for the first time, it unhesitatingly believes that the pain then felt was caused by that stove, and so firm and immediate is that belief that hot stoves are avoided ever after. We all use our metaphysical principles, whether we think of them or not, or are even capable of thinking of them. If I have a bodily or other disorder—a rash, for instance, or a fever or a phobia—I consult a physician for a diagnosis and explanation in the hope that the cause of it might be found and removed or moderated. I am never tempted to suppose that such things just have no causes, arising from nowhere, else I would take no steps to remove the causes. The principle of determinism is here, as in everything else, simply assumed, without being thought about.

Determinism and Human Behavior

I am a part of the world. So is each of the cells and minute parts of which I am composed. The principle of determinism, then, in case it is true, applies to me and to each of those minute parts, no less than to the sand, wheat, winds, and waters of which we have spoken. There is no particular difficulty in thinking so, as long as I consider only what are sometimes called the "purely physiological" changes of my body, like growth, the pulse, glandular secretions, and the like. But what of my thoughts and ideas? And what of my behavior that is supposed to be deliberate, purposeful, and perhaps morally significant? These are all changes of my own being, changes that I undergo, and if these are all but the consequences of the conditions under which they occur, and these conditions are the only ones that could have obtained, given the state of the world just before and when they arose, what now becomes of my responsibility for my behavior and of the control over my conduct that I fancy myself to possess? What am I but a helpless product of nature, destined by her to do whatever I do and to become whatever I become?

There is no moral blame nor merit in anyone who cannot help what he does. It matters not whether the explanation for his behavior is found within him or without, whether it is expressed in terms of ordinary physical causes or allegedly "mental" ones, or whether the causes be proximate or remote. I am not responsible for being a man rather than a woman, nor for having the temperament and desires characteristic of that sex. I was never asked whether these should be given to me. The kleptomaniac, similarly, steals from compulsion, the alcoholic drinks from compulsion, and sometimes even the hero dies from compulsive courage. Though these causes are within them, they compel no less for that, and their victims never chose to have them inflicted upon themselves. To say they are compulsions is to say only that they compel. But to say that they compel is only to say that they cause; for the cause of a thing being given, the effect cannot fail to follow. By the thesis of determinism, however, everything whatever is caused, and not one single thing could ever be other than exactly what it is. Perhaps one thinks that the kleptomaniac and the drunkard did not have to become what they are, that they could have done better at another time and thereby ended up better than they are now, or that the hero could have done worse and then ended up a coward. But this shows only an unwillingness to understand what made them become as they are. Having found that their behavior is caused from within them, we can hardly avoid asking what caused these inner springs of action, and then asking what were the causes of these causes, and so on through the infinite past. We shall not, certainly, with our small understanding and our fragmentary knowledge of the past ever know why the world should at just this time and place have produced just this thief, this drunkard, and this hero, but the vagueness and smattered nature of our knowledge should not tempt us to imagine a similar vagueness in nature herself. Everything in nature is and always has been determinate, with no loose edges at all, and she was forever destined to bring forth just what she has produced, however slight may be our understanding of the origins of these works. Ultimate responsibility for anything that exists, and hence for any person and his deeds, can thus rest only with the first cause of all things, if there is such a cause, or nowhere at all, in case there is not. Such, at least, seems to be the unavoidable implication of determinism. . . .

Freedom

To say that it is, in a given instance, up to me what I do is to say that I am in that instance *free* with respect to what I then do. Thus, I am sometimes free to move my finger this way and that, but not, certainly, to bend it backward or into a knot. But what does this mean?

It means, first that there is no *obstacle* or *impediment* to my activity. Thus, there is sometimes no obstacle to my moving my finger this way and that, though there are obvious obstacles to my moving it backward or into a knot. Those things, accordingly, that pose obstacles to my motions limit my freedom. If my hand were strapped in such a way as to permit only a leftward motion of my finger, I would not then be free to move it to the right. If it were encased in a tight cast that permitted no motion, I would not be free to move it at all. Freedom of motion, then, is limited by obstacles.

Further, to say that it is, in a given instance, up to me what I do, means that nothing *constrains* or *forces* me to do one thing rather than another. Constraints are like obstacles, except that while the latter prevent, the former enforce. Thus, if my finger is being forcibly bent to the left—by a machine, for instance, or by another person, or by any force that I cannot overcome—then I am not free to move it this way and that. I cannot, in fact, move it at all; I can only watch to see how it is moved, and perhaps vainly resist: Its motions are not up to me, or within my control, but in the control of some other thing or person.

Obstacles and constraints, then, both obviously limit my freedom. To say that I am free to perform some action thus means at least that there is no obstacle to my doing it, and that nothing constrains me to do otherwise.

Now if we rest content with this observation, as many have, and construe free activity simply as activity that is unimpeded and unconstrained, there is evidently no inconsistency between affirming both the thesis of determinism and the claim that I am sometimes free. For to say that some action of mine is neither impeded nor constrained does not by itself imply that it is not causally determined. The absence of obstacles and constraints is a mere negative condition, and does not by itself rule out the presence of positive causes. It might seem, then, that we can say of some of my actions that there are conditions antecedent to their performance so that no other actions were possible, and also that these actions were unobstructed and unconstrained. And to say that would logically entail that such actions were both causally determined, and free.

Soft Determinism

It is this kind of consideration that has led many philosophers to embrace what is sometimes called "soft determinism." All versions of this theory have in common three claims, by means of which, it is naïvely supposed, a reconciliation is achieved between determinism and freedom. Freedom being, furthermore, a condition of moral responsibility and the only condition that metaphysics seriously questions, it is supposed by the partisans of this view that determinism is perfectly compatible with such responsibility. This, no doubt, accounts for its great appeal and wide acceptance, even by some people of considerable learning.

The three claims of soft determinism are (1) that the thesis of determinism is true, and that accordingly all human behavior, voluntary or other, like the behavior of all other things, arises from antecedent conditions, given which no other behavior is possible—in short, that all human behavior is caused and determined; (2) that voluntary behavior is nonetheless free to the extent that it is not externally constrained or impeded; and (3) that, in the absence of such obstacles and constraints, the causes of voluntary behavior are certain states, events, or conditions within the agent himself; namely, his own acts of will or volitions, choices, decisions, desires, and so on.

Thus, on this view, I am free, and therefore sometimes responsible for what I do, provided nothing prevents me from acting according to my own choice, desire, or volition, or constrains me to act otherwise. There may, to be sure, be other conditions for my responsibility—such as, for example, an understanding of the probable consequences of my behavior, and that sort of thing—but absence of constraint or impediment is, at least, one such condition. And, it is claimed, it is a condition that is compatible with the supposition that my behavior is caused—for it is, by hypothesis, caused by my own inner choices, desires, and volitions.

The Refutation of This

The theory of soft determinism looks good at first—so good that it has for generations been solemnly taught from innumerable philosophical chairs and implanted in the minds of students as sound philosophy—but no great acumen is needed to discover that far from solving any problem, it only camouflages it.

My free actions are those unimpeded and unconstrained motions that arise from my own inner desires, choices, and volitions; let us grant this provisionally. But now, whence arise those inner states that determine what my body shall do? Are they within my control or not? Having made my choice or decision and acted upon it, could I have chosen otherwise or not?

Here the determinist, hoping to surrender nothing and yet to avoid the problem implied in that question, bids us not to ask it; the question itself, he announces, is without meaning. For to say that I could have done otherwise, he says, means only that I *would* have done otherwise, *if* those inner states that determined my action had been different; if, that is, I had decided or chosen differently. To ask, accordingly, whether I could have chosen or decided differently is only to ask whether, had I decided to decide differently or chosen to choose differently, or willed to will differently, I *would* have decided or chosen or willed differently. And this, of course, is unintelligible nonsense.

But it is not nonsense to ask whether the causes of my actions—my own inner choices, decisions, and desires—are themselves caused. And of course they are, if determinism is true, for on that thesis everything is caused and determined. And if they are, then we cannot avoid concluding that, given the causal conditions of those inner states, I could not have decided, willed, chosen, or desired other than I, in fact, did, for this is a logical consequence of the very definition of determinism. Of course we can still say that, *if* the causes of those inner states, whatever they were, had been different, then their effects, those inner states themselves, would have been different, and that in this hypothetical sense I could have decided, chosen, willed, or desired differently—but that only pushes our problem back still another step. For we will then want to know whether the causes of those inner states were within my control, and so on *ad infinitum*. We are, at each step, permitted to say "could have been otherwise" only in a provisional sense—provided, that is, that something else had been different—but must then retract it and replace it with "could not have been otherwise" as soon as we discover, as we must at each step, that whatever would have to have been different could not have been different.

Examples

Such is the dialectic of the problem. The easiest way to see the shadowy quality of soft determinism, however, is by means of examples.

Let us suppose that my body is moving in various ways, that these motions are not externally constrained or impeded, and that they are all exactly in accordance with my own desires, choices, or acts of will and whatnot. When I will that my arm should move in a certain way, I find it moving in that way, unobstructed and unconstrained. When I will to speak, my lips and tongue move, unobstructed and unconstrained, in a manner suitable to the formation of the words I choose to utter. Now, given that this is a correct description of my behavior, namely, that it consists of the unconstrained and unimpeded motions of my body in response to my own volitions, then it follows that my behavior is free, on the soft determinist's definition of "free." It follows further that I am responsible for that behavior; or at least, that if I am not, it is not from any lack of freedom on my part.

But if the fulfillment of these conditions renders my behavior free—that is to say, if my behavior satisfies the conditions of free action set forth in the theory of soft determinism—then my behavior will be no less free if we assume further conditions that are perfectly consistent with those already satisfied.

We suppose further, accordingly, that while my behavior is entirely in accordance with my own volitions, and thus "free" in terms of the conception of freedom we are examining, my volitions themselves are caused. To make this graphic, we can suppose that an ingenious physiologist can induce in me any volition he pleases, simply by pushing various buttons on an instrument to which, let us suppose, I am attached by numerous wires. All the volitions I have in that situation are, accordingly, precisely the ones he gives me. By pushing one button, he evokes in me the volition to raise my hand; and my hand, being unimpeded, rises in response to that volition. By pushing another, he induces the volition in me to kick, and my foot, being unimpeded, kicks in response to that volition. We can even suppose that the physiologist puts a rifle in my hands, aims it at some passerby, and then, by pushing the proper button, evokes in me the volition to squeeze my finger against the trigger, whereupon the passerby falls dead of a bullet wound.

This is the description of a man who is acting in accordance with his inner volitions, a man whose body is unimpeded and unconstrained in its motions, these motions being the effects of those inner states. It is hardly the description of a free and responsible agent. It is the perfect description of a puppet. To render someone your puppet, it is not necessary forcibly to constrain the motions of his limbs, after the fashion that real puppets are moved. A subtler but no less effective means of making a person your puppet would be to gain complete control of his inner states, and ensuring, as the theory of soft determinism does ensure, that his body will move in accordance with them.

The example is somewhat unusual, but it is no worse for that. It is perfectly intelligible, and it does appear to refute the soft determinist's conception of freedom. One might think that, in such a case, the agent should not have allowed himself to be so rigged in the first place, but this is irrelevant; we can suppose that he was not aware that he was and was hence unaware of the source of those inner states that prompted his bodily motions. The example can, moreover, be modified in perfectly realistic ways, so as to coincide with actual and familiar cases. One can, for instance, be given a compulsive desire for certain drugs, simply by having them administered over a course of time. Suppose, then, that I do, with neither my knowledge nor consent, thus become a victim of such a desire and act upon it. Do I act freely, merely by virtue of the fact that I am unimpeded in my quest for drugs? In a sense I do, surely, but I am hardly free with respect to whether or not I shall use drugs. I never chose to have the desire for them inflicted upon me.

Nor does it, of course, matter whether the inner states that allegedly prompt all my "free" activity are evoked in me by another agent or by perfectly impersonal forces. Whether a desire that causes my body to behave in a certain way is inflicted upon me by another person, for instance, or derived from hereditary factors, or indeed from anything at all, matters not the least. In any case, if it is in fact the cause of my bodily behavior, I cannot help but act in accordance with it. Wherever it came from, whether from personal or impersonal origins, it was entirely caused or determined, and not within my control. Indeed, if determinism is true, as the theory of soft determinism holds it to be, all those inner states that cause my body to behave in whatever ways it behaves must arise from circumstances that existed before I was born; for the chain of causes and effects is infinite, and none could have been the least different, given those that preceded.

Simple Indeterminism

We might at first now seem warranted in simply denying determinism, and saying that, insofar as they are free, my actions are not caused; or that, if they are caused by my own inner states—my own desires, impulses, choices, volitions, and whatnot—then these, in any case, are not caused. This is a perfectly clear sense in which a person's action, assuming that it was free, could have been otherwise. If it was uncaused, then, even given the conditions under which it occurred and all that preceded, some other act was nonetheless possible, and he did not have to do what he did. Or if his action was the inevitable consequence of his own inner states, and could not have been otherwise, given these, we can nevertheless say that these inner states, being uncaused, could have been otherwise, and could thereby have produced different actions.

Only the slightest consideration will show, however, that this simple denial of determinism has not the slightest plausibility. For let us suppose it is true, and that some of my bodily motions—namely, those that I regard as my free acts—are not caused at all or, if caused by my own inner states, that these are not caused. We shall thereby avoid picturing a puppet, to be sure—but only by substituting something even less like a human being; for the conception that now emerges is not that of a free person, but of an erratic and jerking phantom, without any rhyme or reason at all.

Suppose that my right arm is free, according to this conception; that is, that its motions are uncaused. It moves this way and that from time to time, but nothing causes these motions. Sometimes it moves forth vigorously, sometimes up, sometimes down, sometimes it just drifts vaguely about—these motions all being wholly free and uncaused. Manifestly I have nothing to do with them at all; they just happen, and neither I nor anyone can ever tell what this arm will be doing next. It might seize a club and lay it on the head of the nearest bystander, no less to my astonishment than his. There will never be any point in asking why these motions occur, or in seeking any explanation of them, for under the conditions assumed there is no explanation. They just happen, from no causes at all.

This is no description of free, voluntary, or responsible behavior. Indeed, so far as the motions of my body or its parts are entirely uncaused, such motions cannot even be ascribed to me as my behavior in the first place, since I have nothing to do with them. The behavior of my arm is just the random motion of a foreign object. Behavior that is mine must be behavior that is within my control, but motions that occur from no causes are beyond the control of anyone. I can have no more to do with, and no more control over, the uncaused motions of my limbs than a gambler has over the motions of an honest roulette wheel. I can only, like him, idly wait to see what happens.

Nor does it improve things to suppose that my bodily motions are caused by my own inner states, so long as we suppose these to be wholly uncaused. The result will be the same as before. My arm, for example, will move this way and that, sometimes up and sometimes down, sometimes vigorously and sometimes just drifting about, always in response to certain inner states, to be sure. But since these are supposed to be wholly uncaused, it follows that I have no control over them and hence none over their effects. If my hand lays a club forcefully on the nearest bystander, we can indeed say that this motion resulted from an inner club-wielding desire of mine; but we must add that I had nothing to do with that desire, and that it arose, to be followed by its inevitable effect, no less to my astonishment than to his. Things like this do, alas, sometimes happen. We are all sometimes seized by compulsive impulses that arise we know not whence, and we do sometimes act upon these. But because they are far from being examples of free, voluntary, and responsible behavior, we need only to learn that the behavior was of this sort to conclude that it was not free, voluntary, or responsible. It was erratic, impulsive, and irresponsible. . . .

The Theory of Agency

The only conception of action that accords with our data is one according to which people—and perhaps some other things too—are sometimes, but of course not always, self-determining beings; that is, beings that are sometimes the causes of their own behavior. In the case of an action that is free, it must not only be such that it is caused by the agent who performs it, but also such that no antecedent conditions were sufficient for his performing just that action. In the case of an action that is both free and rational, it must be such that the agent who performed it did so for some reason, but this reason cannot have been the cause of it.

Now, this conception fits what people take themselves to be; namely, beings who act, or who are agents, rather than beings that are merely acted upon, and whose behavior is simply the causal consequence of conditions that they have not wrought. When I believe that I have done something, I do believe that it was I who caused it to be done, I who made something happen, and not merely something within me, such as one of my own subjective states, which is not identical with myself. If I believe that something not identical with myself was the cause of my behavior—some event wholly external to myself, for instance, or even one internal to myself, such as a nerve impulse, volition, or whatnot—then I cannot regard that behavior as being an act of mine, unless I further believe that I was the cause of that external or internal event. My pulse, for example, is caused and regulated by certain conditions existing within me, and not by myself. I do not, accordingly, regard this activity of my body as my action, and would be no more tempted to do so if I became suddenly conscious within myself of those conditions or impulses that produce it. This is behavior with which I have nothing to do, behavior that is not within my immediate control, behavior that is not only not free activity, but not even the activity of an agent to begin with; it is nothing but a mechanical reflex. Had I never learned that my very life depends on this pulse beat, I would regard it with complete indifference, as something foreign to me, like the oscillations of a clock pendulum that I idly contemplate.

Now this conception of activity, and of an agent who is the cause of it, involves two rather strange metaphysical notions that are never applied elsewhere in nature. The first is that of a *self* or *person*—for example, a man—who is not merely a collection of things or events, but a self-moving being. For on this view it is a person, and not merely some part of him or something within him, that is the cause of his own activity. Now, we certainly do not know that a human being is anything more than an assemblage of physical things and processes that act in accordance with those laws that describe the behavior of all other physical things and processes. Even though he is a living being, of enormous complexity, there is nothing, apart from the requirements of this theory, to suggest that his behavior is so radically different in its origin from that of other physical objects, or that an understanding of it must be sought in some metaphysical realm wholly different from that appropriate to the understanding of nonliving things.

Second, this conception of activity involves an extraordinary conception of causation according to which an agent, which is a substance and not an event, can nevertheless be the cause of an event. Indeed, if he is a free agent then he can, on this conception, cause an event to occur—namely, some act of his own—without anything else causing him to do so. This means that an agent is sometimes a cause, without being an antecedent sufficient condition; for if I affirm that I am the cause of some act of mine, then I am plainly not saying that my very existence is sufficient for its occurrence, which would be absurd. If I say that my hand causes my pencil to move, then I am saying that the motion of my hand is, under the other conditions then prevailing, sufficient for the motion of the pencil. But if I then say that I cause my hand to move, I am not saying anything remotely like this, and surely not that the motion of my self is sufficient for the motion of my arm and hand, since these are the only things about me that are moving.

This conception of the causation of events by things that are not events is, in fact, so different from the usual philosophical conception of a cause that it should not even bear the same name, for "being a cause" ordinarily just means "being an antecedent sufficient condition or set of conditions." Instead, then, of speaking of agents as *causing* their own acts, it would perhaps be better to use another word entirely, and say, for instance, that they *originate* them, *initiate* them, or simply that they *perform* them.

Now this is, on the face of it, a dubious conception of what a person is. Yet it is consistent with our data, reflecting the presuppositions of deliberation, and appears to be the only conception that is consistent with them, as determinism and simple indeterminism are not. The theory of agency avoids the absurdities of simple indeterminism by conceding that human behavior is caused, while at the same time avoiding the difficulties of determinism by denying that every chain of causes and effects is infinite. Some such causal chains, on this view, have beginnings, and they begin with agents themselves. Moreover, if we are to suppose that it is sometimes up to me what I do, and understand this in a sense that is not consistent with determinism, we must suppose that I am an agent or a being who initiates his own actions, sometimes under conditions that do not determine what action I shall perform. Deliberation becomes, on this view, something that is not only possible but quite rational, for it does make sense to deliberate about activity that is truly my own and that depends in its outcome upon me as its author, and not merely upon something more or less esoteric that is supposed to be intimately associated with me, such as my thoughts, volitions, choices or whatnot.

One can hardly affirm such a theory of agency with complete comfort, however, and not wholly without embarrassment, for the conception of agents and their powers which is involved in it is strange indeed, if not positively mysterious. In fact, one can hardly be blamed here for simply denying our data outright, rather than embracing this theory to which they do most certainly point. Our data—to the effect that we do sometimes deliberate before acting, and that, when we do, we presuppose among other things that it is up to us what we are going to do—rest upon nothing more than fairly common consent. These data might simply be illusions. It might, in fact, be that no one ever deliberates but only imagines that he does, that from pure conceit he supposes himself to be the master of his behavior and the author of his acts. Spinoza has suggested that if a stone, having been thrown into the air, were suddenly to become conscious, it would suppose itself to be the source of its own motion, being then conscious of what it was doing but not aware of the real cause of its behavior. Certainly we are *sometimes* mistaken in believing that we are behaving as a result of choice deliberately arrived at. A man might, for example, easily imagine that his embarking upon matrimony is the result of the most careful and rational deliberation, when in fact the causes, perfectly sufficient for that behavior, might be of an entirely physiological, unconscious origin. If it is sometimes false that we deliberate and then act as the result of a decision deliberately arrived at, even when we suppose it to be true, it might always be false. No one seems able, as we have noted, to describe deliberation without metaphors, and the conception of a thing's being "within one's power" or "up to him" seems to defy analysis or definition altogether, if taken in a sense that the theory of agency appears to require.

These are, then, dubitable conceptions, despite their being so well implanted in common sense. Indeed, when we turn to the theory of fatalism, we shall find formidable metaphysical considerations that appear to rule them out altogether. Perhaps here, as elsewhere in metaphysics, we should be content with discovering difficulties, with seeing what is and what is not consistent with such convictions as we happen to have, and then drawing such satisfaction as we can from the realization that, no matter where we begin, the world is mysterious and that we who try to understand it are even more so. This realization can, with some justification, make one feel wise, even in the full realization of his ignorance. . . .

Fatalism and Determinism

Determinism, it will be recalled, is the theory that all events are rendered unavoidable by their causes. The attempt is sometimes made to distinguish this from fatalism by saying that, according to the fatalist, certain events are going to happen *no matter what*, or in other words, regardless of causes. But this is enormously contrived. It would be hard to find in the whole history of thought a single fatalist, on that conception of it.

Fatalism is the belief that whatever happens is unavoidable. That is the clearest expression of the doctrine, and it provides the basis of the attitude of calm acceptance that the fatalist is thought, quite correctly, to embody. One who endorses the claim of universal causation, then, and the theory of the causal determination of all human behavior, is a kind of fatalist—or at least he should be, if he is consistent. For that theory, as we have seen, once it is clearly spelled out and not hedged about with unresolved "ifs," does entail that whatever happens is rendered inevitable by the causal conditions preceding it, and is therefore unavoidable. One can indeed think of verbal formulas for distinguishing the two theories, but if we think of a fatalist as one who has a certain attitude, we find it to be the attitude that a thoroughgoing determinist should, in consistency, assume. That some philosophical determinists are not fatalists does not so much illustrate a great difference between fatalism and determinism but rather the humiliation to one's pride that a fatalist position can deliver, and the comfort that can sometimes be found in evasion.

Fatalism with Respect to the Future and the Past

A fatalist, then, is someone who believes that whatever happens is and always was unavoidable. He thinks it is not up to him what will happen a thousand years hence, next year, tomorrow, or the very next moment. Of course he does not pretend always to *know* what is going to happen. Hence, he might try sometimes to read signs and portents, as meteorologists and astrologers do, or to contemplate the effects upon him of the various things that might, for all he knows, be fated to occur. But he does not suppose that whatever happens could ever have really been avoidable.

A fatalist thus thinks of the future in the way we all think of the past, for everyone is a fatalist as he looks *back* on things. To a large extent we know what has happened—some of it we can even remember—whereas the future is still obscure to us, and we are therefore tempted to imbue it, in our imagination, with all sorts of "possibilities." The fatalist resists this temptation, knowing that mere ignorance can hardly give rise to any genuine possibility in things. He thinks of both past and future "under the aspect of eternity," the way God is supposed to view them. We all think of the past this way, as something settled and fixed, to be taken for what it is. We are never in the least tempted to try to modify it. It is not in the least up to us what happened last year, yesterday, or even a moment ago, any more than are the motions of the heavens or the political developments in Tibet. If we are not fatalists, then we might think that past things once *were* up to us, to bring about or prevent, as long as they were still future—but this expresses our attitude toward the future, not the past.

Such is surely our conception of the whole past, whether near or remote. But the consistent fatalist thinks of the future in the same way. We say of past things that they are no longer within our power. The fatalist says they never were.

Discussion Questions

1. In what ways might we be like Spinoza's rock example in which the rock, falling through the air, would think (if it could) that it was choosing to do so without knowing otherwise?

2. How would your view of life change given the different paradigms of determinism, fatalism, and free will?

3. If determinism were true, would we be justified in punishing people? If so, how? If not, why not?

The Illusion of Free Will
Paul d'Holbach

French philosopher Paul d'Holbach was one of the first to publicly defend atheism and, because of this, published much of his work anonymously to avoid persecution by the Church. He argued that organized religion detracted from happiness and resulted in immorality in comparison with his atheistic view. d'Holbach was a major contributor to the 17-volume *Encyclopédie*—an encyclopedia published in France with many contributors, including Rousseau and Voltaire—penning 414 articles on chemistry, politics, and religion. The selection is extracted from his most well-known work, *System of Nature*, which presented a mechanistic view of nature and was considered by Goethe as the most repulsive book ever written. Considered by many as a generous man of great integrity, d'Holbach was generous with the great deal of inheritance acquired from his wealthy uncle.

In d'Holbach's defense of "hard determinism" here, his materialistic and mechanistic view of reality is obvious. He argues that even though we may seem to be free agents—beings who make free, uncoerced choices—this is a mere chimera (false belief). Instead, when we make one of these apparently free choices, there is some "anterior impulse" that takes priority—some other (likely unknown) force that acts first (*ante* is Latin for "before").

Source: System of Nature by Baron Paul d'Holbach, published 1770. Translated by H. D. Robinson. Chapter XI: Of the System of Man's Free Agency (edited).

Reading Questions

1. By what "shackles" (i.e., handcuffs) are humans bound according to d'Holbach? How does he reference these shackles to argue that we only *pretend* to be free?
2. How does the assumption of freedom relate to religion? To punishment? To "human vanity"?
3. How does d'Holbach suggest that our brain affects/*causes* our will? How does he relate thirst—and the subsequent poisoning of water —to this?
4. What role does desire play in the discussion of free will? What *causes* these desires according to d'Holbach?
5. How does d'Holbach respond to one who claims that the simple calculated choice to move or not move one's hand proves free agency? What about one's decision to throw oneself out of a window?
6. How does d'Holbach define "free agency"?
7. How does d'Holbach defend Socrates' submission to execution (even though he could have avoided it) as an un-free act? What does d'Holbach say about those who apparently choose *freely* to act against their inclination?
8. How are humans like the swimmer in a stream?

Motives and the Determination of the Will

In whatever manner man is considered, he is connected to universal nature, and submitted to the necessary and immutable laws that she imposes on all the beings she contains, according to their peculiar essences or to the respective properties with which, without consulting them, she endows each particular species. Man's life is a line that nature commands him to describe upon the surface of the earth, without his ever being able to swerve from it, even for an instant. He is born without his own consent; his organization does in nowise depend upon himself; his ideas come to him involuntarily; his habits are in the power of those who cause him to contract them; he is unceasingly modified by causes, whether visible or concealed, over which he has no control, which necessarily regulate his mode of existence, give the hue to his way of thinking, and determine his manner of acting. He is good or bad, happy or miserable, wise or foolish, reasonable or irrational, without his will being for anything in these various states. Nevertheless, in spite of the shackles by which he is bound, it is pretended he is a free agent, or that independent of the causes by which he is moved, he determines his own will and regulates his own condition.

However slender the foundation of his opinion, of which everything ought to point out to him the error, it is current at this day and passes for an incontestable truth with a great number of people, otherwise extremely enlightened; it is the basis of religion, which supposing relations between man and the unknown being she has placed above nature, has been incapable of imagining how man could merit reward or deserve punishment from this being, if he was not a free agent. Society has been believed interested in his system; because an idea has gone abroad, that if all the actions of man were to be contemplated as necessary, the right of punishing those who injure their associates would no longer exist. At length human vanity accommodated itself to a hypothesis which, unquestionably, appears to distinguish man from all other physical beings, by assigning to him the special privilege of a total independence of all other causes, but of which a very little reflection would have shown him the impossibility.

The will . . . is a modification of the brain, by which it is disposed to action, or prepared to give play to the organs. This will is necessarily determined by the qualities, good or bad, agreeable or painful, of the object or the motive that acts upon his senses, or of which the idea remains with him, and is resuscitated by his memory. In consequence, he acts necessarily, his action is the result of the impulse he receives either from the motive, from the object, or from the idea which has modified his brain, or disposed his will. When he does not act according to this impulse, it is because there comes some new cause, some new motive, some new idea, which modifies his brain in a different manner, gives him a new impulse, determines his will in another way, by which the action of the former impulse is suspended: Thus, the sight of an agreeable object, or its idea, determines his will to set him in action to procure it; but if a new object or a new idea more powerfully attracts him, it gives a new direction to his will, annihilates the effect of the former, and prevents the action by which it was to be procured. This is the mode in which reflection, experience, reason, necessarily arrests or suspends the action of man's will: Without this he would of necessity have followed the anterior impulse which carried him towards a then desirable object. In all this he always acts according to necessary laws from which he has no means of emancipating himself.

If when tormented with violent thirst, he figures to himself an idea, or really perceives a fountain, whose limpid streams might cool his feverish want, is he sufficient master of himself to desire or not to desire the object competent to satisfy so lively a want? It will no doubt be conceded, that it is impossible he should not be desirous to satisfy it; but it will be said—if at this moment it is announced to him that the water he so ardently desires is poisoned, he will, notwithstanding his vehement thirst, abstain from drinking it: And it has, therefore, been falsely concluded that he is a free agent. The fact, however, is, that the motive in either case is exactly the same: his own conservation. The same necessity that determined him to drink before he knew the water was deleterious upon this new discovery equally determined him not to drink; the desire of conserving himself either annihilates or suspends the former impulse; the second motive becomes stronger than the preceding, that is, the fear of death, or the desire of preserving himself, necessarily prevails over the painful sensation caused by his eagerness to drink: but, it will be said, if the thirst is very parching, an inconsiderate man without regarding the danger will risk swallowing the water. Nothing is gained by this remark: In this case, the anterior impulse only regains the ascendancy; he is persuaded that life may possibly be longer preserved, or that he shall derive a greater good by drinking the poisoned water than by enduring the torment, which, to his mind, threatens instant dissolution: Thus the first becomes the strongest and necessarily urges him on to action. Nevertheless, in either case, whether he partakes of the water, or whether he does not, the two actions will be equally necessary; they will be the effect of that motive which finds itself most puissant; which consequently acts in the most coercive manner upon his will.

This example will serve to explain the whole phenomena of the human will. This will, or rather the brain, finds itself in the same situation as a bowl, which, although it has received an impulse that drives it forward in a straight line, is deranged in its course whenever a force superior to the first obliges it to change its direction. The man who drinks the poisoned water appears a madman; but the actions of fools are as necessary as those of the most prudent individuals. The motives that determine the voluptuary and the debauchee to risk their health, are as powerful, and their actions are as necessary, as those which decide the wise man to manage his. But, it will be insisted, the debauchee may be prevailed on to change his conduct: this does not imply that he is a free agent; but that motives may be found sufficiently powerful to annihilate the effect of those that previously acted upon him; then these new motives determine his will to the new mode of conduct he may adopt as necessarily as the former did to the old mode. . . .

The errors of philosophers on the free agency of man, have arisen from their regarding his will as . . . the original motive of his actions; for want of recurring back, they have not perceived the multiplied, the complicated causes which, independently of him, give motion to the will itself; or which dispose and modify his brain, whilst he himself is purely passive in the motion he receives. Is he the master of desiring or not desiring an object that appears desirable to him? Without doubt it will be answered, no: But he is the master of resisting his desire, if he reflects on the consequences. But, I ask, is he capable of reflecting on these consequences, when his soul is hurried along by a very lively passion, which entirely depends upon his natural organization, and the causes by which he is modified? Is it in his power to add to these consequences all the weight necessary to counterbalance his desire? Is he the master of preventing the qualities which render an object desirable from residing in it? I shall be told: He ought to have learned to resist his passions; to contract a habit of putting a curb on his desires. I agree to it without any difficulty. But in reply, I again ask, is his nature susceptible of this modification? Does his boiling blood, his unruly imagination, the igneous fluid that circulates in his veins, permit him to make, enable him to apply true experience in the moment when it is wanted? And even when his temperament has capacitated him, has his education, the examples set before him, the ideas with which he has been inspired in early life, been suitable to make him contract this habit of repressing his desires? Have not all these things rather contributed to induce him to seek with avidity, to make him actually desire those objects which you say he ought to resist? . . .

In short, the actions of man are never free; they are always the necessary consequence of his temperament, of the received ideas, and of the notions, either true or false, which he has formed to himself of happiness; of his opinions, strengthened by example, by education, and by daily experience. So many crimes are witnessed on the earth only because every thing conspires to render man vicious and criminal; the religion he has adopted, his government, his education, the examples set before him, irresistibly drive him on to evil: Under these circumstances, morality preaches virtue to him in vain. In those societies where vice is esteemed, where crime is crowned, where venality is constantly recompensed, where the most dreadful disorders are punished only in those who are too weak to enjoy the privilege of committing them with impunity, the practice of virtue is considered nothing more than a painful sacrifice of happiness. Such societies chastise, in the lower orders, those excesses, which they respect in the higher ranks; and frequently have the injustice to condemn those in the penalty of death, whom public prejudices, maintained by constant example, have rendered criminal.

Man, then, is not a free agent in any one instant of his life; he is necessarily guided in each step by those advantages, whether real of fictitious, that he attaches to the objects by which his passions are roused: These passions themselves are necessary in a being who unceasingly tends towards his own happiness; their energy is necessary, since that depends on his temperament; his temperament is necessary, because it depends on the physical elements which enter into his composition; the modification of this temperament is necessary, as it is the infallible and inevitable consequence of the impulse he receives from the incessant action of moral and physical beings.

Choice Does Not Prove Freedom

In spite of these proofs of the want of free agency in man, so clear to unprejudiced minds, it will, perhaps, be insisted upon with no small feeling of triumph, that if it be proposed to any one, to move or not to move his hand, an action in the number of those called indifferent, he evidently appears to be the master of choosing; from which it is concluded that evidence has been offered of free agency. The reply is, this example is perfectly simple; man in performing some action which he is resolved on doing, does not by any means prove his free agency: The very desire of displaying this quality, excited by the dispute, becomes a necessary motive, which decides his will either for the one or the other of these actions: What deludes him in this instance, or that which persuades him he is a free agent at this moment, is, that he does not discern the true motive which sets him in action, namely, the desire of convincing his opponent: If in the heat of the dispute he insists and asks, "Am I not the master of throwing myself out of the window?" I shall answer him, no; that whilst he preserves his reason there is no probability that the desire of proving his free agency, will become a motive sufficiently powerful to make him sacrifice his life to the attempt: If, notwithstanding this, to prove he is a free agent, he should actually precipitate himself from the window, it would not be a sufficient warranty to conclude he acted freely, but rather that it was the violence of his temperament which spurred him on to this folly. Madness is a state, that depends upon the heat of the blood, not upon the will. A fanatic or a hero, braves death as necessarily as a more phlegmatic man or coward flies from it.

There is, in point of fact, no difference between the man that is cast out of the window by another, and the man who throws himself out of it, except that the impulse in the first instance comes immediately from without whilst that which determines the fall in the second case, springs from within his own peculiar machine, having its more remote cause also exterior. When Mutius Scaevola held his hand in the fire, he was as much acting under the influence of necessity (caused by interior motives) that urged him to this strange action, as if his arm had been held by strong men: Pride, despair, the desire of braving his enemy, a wish to astonish him, and anxiety to intimidate him, etc., were the visible chains that held his hand bound to the fire. The love of glory, enthusiasm for their country, in like manner caused Codrus and Decius to devote themselves for their fellow-citizens. The Indian Colanus and the philosopher Peregrinus were equally obliged to burn themselves, by desire of exciting the astonishment of the Grecian assembly.

It is said that free agency is the absence of those obstacles competent to oppose themselves to the actions of man, or to the exercise of his faculties: It is pretended that he is a free agent whenever, making use of these faculties, he produces the effect he has proposed to himself. In reply to this reasoning, it is sufficient to consider that it in nowise depends upon himself to place or remove the obstacles that either determine or resist him; the motive that causes his action is no more in his own power than the obstacle that impedes him, whether this obstacle or motive be within his own machine or exterior of his person: He is not master of the thought presented to his mind, which determines his will; this thought is excited by some cause independent of himself.

To be undeceived on the system of his free agency, man has simply to recur to the motive by which his will is determined; he will always find this motive is out of his own control. It is said: That in consequence of an idea to which the mind gives birth, man acts freely if he encounters no obstacle. But the question is, what gives birth to this idea in his brain? Was he the master either to prevent it from presenting itself, or from renewing itself in his brain? Does not this idea depend either upon objects that strike him exteriorly and in despite of himself, or upon causes, that without his knowledge, act within himself and modify his brain? Can he prevent his eyes, cast without design upon any object whatever, from giving him an idea of this object, and from moving his brain? He is not more master of the obstacles; they are the necessary effects of either interior or exterior causes, which always act according to their given properties. A man insults a coward; this necessarily irritates him against his insulter; but his will cannot vanquish the obstacle that cowardice places to the object of his desire, because his natural conformation, which does not depend upon himself, prevents his having courage. In this case, the coward is insulted in spite of himself; and against his will is obliged patiently to brook the insult he has received.

Absence of Restraint Is Not Absence of Necessity

The partisans of the system of free agency appear ever to have confounded constraint with necessity. Man believes he acts as a free agent, every time he does not see any thing that places obstacles to his actions; he does not perceive that the motive which causes him to will, is always necessary and independent of himself. A prisoner loaded with chains is compelled to remain in prison; but he is not a free agent in the desire to emancipate himself; his chains prevent him from acting, but they do not prevent him from willing; he would save himself if they would loose his fetters; but he would not save himself as a free agent; fear or the idea of punishment would be sufficient motives for his action.

Man may, therefore, cease to be restrained, without, for that reason, becoming a free agent: In whatever manner he acts, he will act necessarily, according to motives by which he shall be determined. He may be compared to a heavy body that finds itself arrested in its descent by any obstacle whatever: Take away this obstacle, it will gravitate or continue to fall; but who shall say this dense body is free to fall or not? Is not its descent the necessary effect of its own specific gravity? The virtuous Socrates submitted to the laws of his country, although they were unjust; and though the doors of his jail were left open to him, he would not save himself; but in this he did not act as a free agent: The invisible chains of opinion, the secret love of decorum, the inward respect of the laws, even when they were iniquitous, the fear of tarnishing his glory, kept him in his prison; they were motives sufficiently powerful with this enthusiast for virtue, to induce him to await death with tranquility; it was not in his power to save himself, because he could find no potential motive to bring him to depart, even for an instant, from those principles to which his mind was accustomed.

Man, it is said, frequently acts against his inclination, from whence it is falsely concluded he is a free agent; but when he appears to act contrary to his inclination, he is always determined to it by some motive sufficiently efficacious to vanquish this inclination. A sick man, with a view to his cure, arrives at conquering his repugnance to the most disgusting remedies: The fear of pain, or the dread of death, then become necessary motives; consequently this sick man cannot be said to act freely.

When it is said, that man is not a free agent, it is not pretended to compare him to a body moved by a single impulsive cause: He contains within himself causes inherent to his existence; he is moved by an interior organ, which has its own peculiar laws, and is itself necessarily determined in consequence of ideas formed from perception resulting from sensation which it receives from exterior objects. As the mechanism of these sensations, of these perception, and the manner they engrave ideas on the brain of man, are not known to him; because he is unable to unravel all these motions; because he cannot perceive the chain of operations in his soul, or the motive principle that acts within him, he supposes himself a free agent; which literally translated, signifies, that he moves himself by himself; that he determines himself without cause: when he rather ought to say, that he is ignorant how or why he acts in the manner he does. It is true the soul enjoys an activity peculiar to itself: But it is equally certain that this activity would never be displayed, if some motive or some cause did not put it in a condition to exercise itself: At least it will not be pretended that the soul is able either to love or to hate without being moved, without knowing the objects, without having some idea of their qualities. Gunpowder has unquestionably a particular activity, but this activity will never display itself, unless fire be applied to it; this, however, immediately sets it in motion.

The Complexity of Human Conduct and the Illusion of Free Agency

... If, for a short time, each man was willing to examine his own peculiar actions, search out their true motives to discover their concatenation, he would remain convinced that the sentiment he has of his natural free agency, is a chimera that must speedily be destroyed by experience.

Nevertheless it must be acknowledged that the multiplicity and diversity of the causes which continually act upon man, frequently without even his knowledge, render it impossible, or at least extremely difficult for him to recur to the true principles of his own peculiar actions, much less the actions of others: They frequently depend upon causes so fugitive, so remote from their effects, and which, superficially examined, appear to have so little analogy, so slender a relation with them, that it requires singular sagacity to bring them into light. This is what renders the study of the moral man a task of such difficulty; this is the reason why his heart is an abyss, of which it is frequently impossible for him to fathom the depth. . . .

If he understood the play of his organs, if he were able to recall to himself all the impulsions they have received, all the effects they have produced, he would perceive that all his actions are submitted to that fatality, which regulates his own particular system, as it does the entire system of the universe: No one effect in him, any more than in nature, produces itself by chance; this, as has been before proved, is word void of sense. All that passes in him; all that is done by him; as well as all that happens in nature, or that is attributed to her, is derived from necessary causes, which act according to necessary laws, and which produce necessary effects from whence necessarily flow others.

Fatality, is the eternal, the immutable, the necessary order, established in nature; or the indispensable connexion of causes that act, with the effects they operate. Conforming to this order, heavy bodies fall; light bodies rise; that which is analogous in matter reciprocally attracts; that which is heterogeneous mutually repels; man congregates himself in society, modifies each his fellow; becomes either virtuous or wicked; either contributes to his mutual happiness, or reciprocates his misery; either loves his neighbour, or hates his companion necessarily, according to the manner in which the one acts upon the other. From whence it may be seen, that the same necessity which regulates the physical, also regulates the moral world, in which everything is in consequence submitted to fatality. Man, in running over, frequently without his own knowledge, often in spite of himself, the route which nature has marked out for him, resembles a swimmer who is obliged to follow the current that carries him along: He believes himself a free agent, because he sometimes consents, sometimes does not consent, to glide with the stream, which, notwithstanding, always hurries him forward; he believes himself the master of his condition, because he is obliged to use his arms under the fear of sinking.

Discussion Questions

1. If you had a chance to speak with d'Holbach, do you think you could suggest any *conceivable* action that he would agree *could* be considered free? If so, what? If not, does this pose a problem for his theory (think back to Popper's criterion of *falsifiability*)?

2. Do you agree with d'Holbach's definition of free agency? How important is the definition in this discussion?

3. How do you answer d'Holbach's question: Are you "the master of desiring or not desiring an object that appears desirable" to you? What control do you have over your own desires? Do they arise *freely*?

4. How do your adopted religion, government, education, and examples set for you contribute to your decisions? What about the time in history that you were born? Would you have the same interests and desires if all these factors were different? How does that relate to your view of free will?

5. Many claim that certain acts/decisions can be coerced (and thus not free). For example, having a gun put to one's head and being told to act in a particular manner, or having a *mandatory* class meeting. What does it mean to respond to a critic by saying you "had to" do something? Are you ever truly *forced* to act?

6. Does a deterministic view (such as the one d'Holbach portrays here) add to or take away from your view of your own existence? In what way does it affect your world view?

7. If you were to argue against d'Holbach, how would you do so?

Meaning and Free Will

John Hospers

John Hospers is Professor Emeritus of Philosophy at the University of Southern California. His area of focus includes aesthetics, ethics, and political philosophy, all of which he has written on extensively, publishing nearly 150 scholarly articles, as well as numerous books. He served as the editor of *The Personalist, The Monist,* and *Liberty* magazine, and in 1972 he was the first U.S. presidential candidate to run under the Libertarian Party.

In this article, Hospers focuses on the relevance of the unconscious forces in relation to the topic of free will. The power of the unconscious is nearly universally accepted, though it has been explained in many different ways. Hospers here uses the Freudian paradigm to explain how the unconscious affects (causes) our behavior. Austrian neurologist Sigmund Freud (1856–1939) is considered the "father of psychoanalysis" by many and brought to light many issues relevant to our unconscious, such as defense mechanisms, dream analysis, and the "Freudian slip of the tongue."

Source: "Meaning and Free Will" [*Philosophy and Phenomenological Research* 10 (March 1950): 307–330]. Reprinted by permission of the publisher.

Reading Questions

1. How does Hospers suggest that moralists define a *free* act? What problem with this definition arises regarding one's character?
2. What are the "Big Three" components of the unconscious, and what do they do?
3. How does Hospers relate the topic of human unconscious to the discussion of free will?
4. Explain the role of the unconscious in Hospers' following examples:
   a. Man deciding to kill
   b. Divorced woman
   c. Gambling man
   d. Hand-washing compulsion
   e. *Faux pas* student
   f. Woman on train
5. What is the significance of one's conscious rationalization to explain away the actions of one's unconscious?
6. How does Hospers relate the unconscious drive as it relates to punishment? To being held *responsible*?

In practice most of us would not call free many persons who behave voluntarily and even with calculation aforethought, and under no compulsion either of any obvious sort. A metropolitan newspaper headlines an article with the words "Boy Killer Is Doomed Long before He is Born," and then goes on to describe how a twelve-year-old boy has just been sentenced to thirty years in Sing Sing for the murder of a girl; his family background includes records of drunkenness, divorce, social maladjustment, epilepsy, and paresis. He early displays a tendency to sadistic activity to hide an underlying masochism and "prove that he's a man"; being coddled by his mother only worsens this tendency, until, spurned by a girl in his attempt on her, he kills her—not simply in a fit of anger, but calculatingly, deliberately. Is he free in respect of his criminal act, or for that matter in most of the acts of his life? Surely to ask this question is to answer it in the negative. . . . Though not everyone has criminotic tendencies, everyone has been moulded by influences which in large measure at least determine his present behavior; he is literally the product of these influences, stemming from periods prior to his "years of discretion," giving him a host of character traits that he cannot change now even if he would. So obviously does what a man is depend upon how a man comes to be, that it is small wonder that philosophers and sages have considered man far indeed from being the master of his fate. It is not as if man's will were standing high and serene above the flux of events that have moulded him; it is itself caught up in this flux, itself carried along on the current. An act is when it is determined by the man's character, when there was nothing the man could do to shape his character, and even the degree of will power available to him in shaping his habits and disciplining himself to overcome the influence of his early environment is a factor over which he has no control, what are we to say of this kind of "freedom?" Is it not rather like the freedom of the machine to stamp labels on cans when it has been devised for just that purpose? Some machines can do so more efficiently than others, but only because they have been better constructed.

It is not my purpose here to establish this thesis in general, but only in one specific respect which has received comparatively little attention, namely, the field referred to by psychiatrists as that of unconscious motivation. In what follows I shall restrict my attention to it because it illustrates as clearly as anything the points I wish to make.

Let me try to summarize very briefly the psychoanalytic doctrine on this point. The conscious life of the human being, including the conscious decisions and volitions, is merely a mouthpiece for the unconscious—not directly for the enactment of unconscious drivers, but of the compromise between unconscious drives and unconscious reproaches. There is a Big Three behind the scenes which the automaton called the conscious personality carries out: The id, an "eternal gimme," presents its wish and demands its immediate satisfaction; the super-ego says no to the wish immediately upon presentation, and The unconscious ego, the mediator between the two, tries to keep peace by means of compromise.

To go into examples of the functioning of these three "bosses" would be endless; psychoanalytic case books supply hundreds of them. The important point for us to see in the present context is that it is the unconscious that determines what the conscious impulse and the conscious action shall be. . . .

We have always been conscious of the fact that we are not masters of our fate in every respect—that there are many things which we cannot do, that nature is more powerful than we are, that we cannot disobey laws without danger of reprisals, etc. Lately we have become more conscious, too, though novelists, and dramatists have always been fairly conscious of it, that we are not free with respect to the emotions that we feel—whom we love or hate, what types we admire, and the like. More lately still we have been reminded that there are unconscious motivations for our basic attractions and repulsions, our compulsive actions or inabilities to act. But what is not welcome news is that our very acts of volition, and the entire train of deliberations leading up to them, are but facades for the expression of unconscious wishes, or rather, unconscious compromises and defenses.

A man is faced by a choice: Shall he kill another person or not? Moralists would say, here is a free choice—the result of deliberation, an action consciously entered into. And yet, though the agent himself does not know it, and has no awareness of the forces that are at work within him, his choice is already determined for him: His conscious will is only an instrument, a slave, in the hands of a deep unconscious motivation which determines his action. If he has a great deal of what the analyst calls "free-floating guilt," he will not; but if the guilt is such as to demand immediate absorption in the form of self-damaging behavior, this accumulated guilt will have to be discharged in some criminal action. The man himself does not know what the inner clockwork is; he is like the hands on the clock, thinking they move freely over the face of the clock.

A woman has married and divorced several husbands. Now she is faced with a choice for the next marriage: Shall she marry Mr. A, or Mr. B, or nobody at all? She may take considerable time to "decide" this question, and her decision may appear as a final triumph of her free will. Let us assume that A is a normal, well-adjusted, kind, and generous man, while B is a leech, an impostor, one who will become entangled constantly in quarrels with her. If she belongs to a certain classifiable psychological type, she will inevitably choose B, and she will do so even if her previous husbands have resembled B, so that one would think that she "had learned from experience." Consciously, she will of course "give the matter due consideration," etc., etc. To the psychoanalyst all this is irrelevant chaff in the wind—only a camouflage for the inner workings about which she knows nothing consciously. If she is of a certain kind of masochistic strain, as exhibited in her previous set of symptoms, she *must* choose B: Her superego, always out to maximize the torment in the situation, seeing what dazzling possibilities for self-damaging behavior are promised by the choice of B, compels her to make the choice she does, and even to conceal the real basis of the choice behind an elaborate facade of rationalizations.

A man is addicted to gambling. In the service of his addiction he loses all his money, spends what belongs to his wife, even sells his property and neglects his children. For a time perhaps he stops: Then, inevitably, he takes it up again, although he himself may think he chose to. The man does not know that he is a victim rather than an agent; or, if he sometimes senses that he is in the throes of something-he-knows-not-what, he will have no inkling of its character and will soon relapse into the illusion that he (his conscious self) is freely deciding the course of his own actions. What he does not know, of course, is that he is still taking out on his mother the original lesion to his infantile narcissism, getting back at her for her fancied refusal of his infantile wishes—and this by rejecting everything identified with her, namely education, discipline, logic, common sense, training. At the roulette wheel, almost alone among adult activities, chance—the opposite of all these things—rules supreme; and his addiction represents his continued and emphatic reiteration of his rejection of Mother and all she represents to his unconscious.

This pseudo-aggression of his is of course masochistic in its effects. In the long run he always loses; he can never quit while he is winning. And far from playing in order to win, rather one can say that his losing is a *sine qua non* of his psychic equilibrium (as it was for example with Dostoyevsky): Guilt demands punishment, and in the ego's "deal" with the super-ego the super-ego has granted satisfaction of infantile wishes in return for the self-damaging conditions obtaining. Winning would upset the neurotic equilibrium.

A man has wash-compulsion. He must be constantly washing his hands—he uses up perhaps 400 towels a day. Asked why he does this, he says, "I need to, my hands are dirty"; and if it is pointed out to him that they are not really dirty, he says "They feel dirty anyway, I feel better when I wash them." So once again he washes them. He "freely decides" every time; he feels that he must wash them, he deliberates for a moment perhaps, but always ends by washing them. What he does not see, of course, is the invisible wires inside him pulling him inevitably to do the thing he does: The infantile id-wish concerns preoccupation with dirt, the super-ego charges him with this, and the terrified ego must respond, "No, I don't like dirt, see how clean I like to be, look how I wash my hands!" . . .

Let us take, finally, a less colorful, more everyday example. A student at a university, possessing wealth, charm, and all that is usually considered essential to popularity, begins to develop the following personality-pattern: Although well taught in the graces of social conversation, he always makes a *faux pas* somewhere, and always in the worst possible situation; to his friends be makes cutting remarks which hurt deeply—and always apparently aimed in such a way as to hurt the most: A remark that would not hurt A but would hurt B he invariably makes to B rather than to A, and so on. None of this is conscious. Ordinarily he is considerate of people, but he contrives always (unconsciously) to impose on just those friends who would resent it most, and at just the times when he should know that he should not impose: at 3 o'clock in the morning, without forewarning, he phones a friend in a near-by city demanding to stay at his apartment for the weekend; naturally the friend is offended, but the person himself is not aware that he has provoked the grievance ("common sense" suffers a temporary eclipse when the neurotic pattern sets in, and one's intelligence, far from being of help in such a situation, is used in the interest of the neurosis), and when the friend is cool to him the next time they meet, he wonders why and feels unjustly treated. Aggressive behavior on his part invites resentment and aggression in turn, but all that he consciously sees is other's behavior toward him—and he considers himself the innocent victim of an unjustified "persecution."

Each of these choices is, from the moralist's point of view, free: He chose to phone his friend at 3 a.m.; he chose to make the cutting remark that he did, etc. What he does not know is that an ineradicable masochistic pattern has set in. His unconscious is far more shrewd and clever than is his conscious intellect; it sees with uncanny accuracy just what kind of behavior will damage him most, and unerringly forces him into that behavior. Consciously, the student "doesn't know why he did it"—he gives different "reasons" at different times, but they are all, once again, rationalizations cloaking the unconscious mechanism which propels him willy-nilly into actions that his "common sense" eschews.

The more of this sort of thing you see, the more you can see what the psychoanalyst means when he talks about "the illusion of free-will." And the more of a psychiatrist you become, the more you are overcome with a sense of what an illusion this precious free-will really is. In some kinds of cases most of us can see it already: It takes no psychiatrist to look at the epileptic and sigh with sadness at the thought that soon this person before you will be as one possessed, not the same thoughtful intelligent person you knew. But people are not aware of this in other contexts, for example when they express surprise at how a person whom they have been so good to could treat them so badly. Let us suppose that you help a person financially or morally or in some other way, so that he is in your debt; suppose further that he is one of the many neurotics who unconsciously identify kindness with weakness and aggression with strength, then he will unconsciously take your kindness to him as weakness and use it as the occasion for enacting some aggression against you. He can't help it, he may regret it himself later; still, he will be driven to do it. If we gain a little knowledge of psychiatry, we can look at him with pity, that a person otherwise so worthy should be so unreliable—but we will exercise realism too and be aware that there are some types of people that you cannot be good to in "free" acts of their conscious volition, they will use your own goodness against you.

Sometimes the persons themselves will become dimly aware that "something behind the scenes" is determining their behavior. The divorcee will sometimes view herself with detachment, as if she were some machine (and indeed the psychoanalyst does call her a "repeating-machine"): "I know I'm caught in a net, that I'll fall in love with this guy and marry him and the whole ridiculous merry-go-round will start all over again."

We talk about free will, and we say, yes, the person is free to do so-and-so if he can do so *if* he wants to—and we forget that his wanting to is itself caught up in the stream of determinism, that unconscious forces drive him into the wanting or not wanting to do the thing in question. The idea of the puppet whose motions are manipulated from behind by invisible wires, or better still, by springs inside, is no mere figure of speech. The analogy is a telling one at almost every point . . .

Now, what of the notion of responsibility? What happens to it on our analysis?

Let us begin with an example, not a fictitious one. A woman and her two-year-old baby are riding on a train to Montreal in mid-winter. The child is ill. The woman wants badly to get to her destination. She is, unknown to herself, the victim of a neurotic conflict whose nature is irrelevant here except for the fact that it forces her to behave aggressively toward the child, partly to spite her husband whom she despises and who loves the child, but chiefly to ward off super-ego charges of masochistic attachment. Consciously she loves the child, and when she says this she says it sincerely, but she must behave aggressively toward it neverthe-less, just as many children love their mothers but are nasty to them most of the time in neurotic pseudo-aggression. The child becomes more ill as the train approaches Montreal; the heating system of the train is not working, and the con-ductor advises the woman to get off the train at the next town and get the child to a hospital at once. The woman says no, she must get to Montreal. Shortly after-ward, as the child's condition worsens, and the mother does all she can to keep it alive, without, however, leaving the train, for she declares that it is absolutely nec-essary that she reach her destination. But before she gets there the child is dead. After that, of course, the mother grieves, blames herself, weeps hysterically, and joins the church to gain surcease from the guilt that constantly overwhelms her when she thinks of how her aggressive behavior has killed her child.

Was she responsible for her deed? In ordinary life, after making a mistake, we say, "Chalk it up to experience." Here we say, "Chalk it up to the neurosis." No, she is not responsible. She could not help it if her neurosis forced her to act this way—she didn't even know what was going on behind the scenes, she merely acted out the part assigned to her. This is far more true than is generally realized: Criminal actions in general are not actions for which their agents are responsible; the agents are passive, not active—they are victims of a neurotic conflict. Their very hyper-activity is unconsciously determined.

To say this is, of course, not to say that we should not punish criminals. Clearly, for our own protection, we must remove them from our midst so that they can no longer molest and endanger organized society. And, of course, if we use the world "responsible" in such a way that justly to hold someone responsible for a deed is by definition identical with being justified in punishing him, then we can and do hold people responsible. But this is like the sense of "free" in which free acts are voluntary ones. It does not go deep enough. In a deeper sense we cannot hold the person responsible: we may hold his neurosis responsible, but he is not responsible for his neurosis, particularly since the age at which its onset was inevitable was an age before he could even speak.

The neurosis is responsible—but isn't the neurosis a part of *him*? We have been speaking all the time as if the person and his unconscious were two separate beings; but isn't he one personality, including conscious and unconscious departments together?

I do not wish to deny this. But it hardly helps us here; for what people want when they talk about freedom, and what they hold to when they champion it, is the idea that the *conscious* will is the master of their destiny. "I am the master of my fate, I am the captain of my soul"—and they surely mean their conscious selves, the self that they can recognize and search and introspect. Between an unconscious that willy-nilly determines your actions, and an external force which pushes you, there is little if anything to choose. The unconscious is just as *if* it were an outside force; and indeed psychiatrists will assert that the inner Hitler can torment you far more than any external Hitler can. Thus the kind of freedom that people want, the only kind they will settle for, is precisely the kind that psychiatry says that they cannot have . . . .

Let us . . . put the situation schematically in the form of a deductive argument.

1. An occurrence over which we had no control is something we cannot be held responsible for.
2. Events E, occurring during our babyhood, were events over which we had no control.
3. Therefore events E were events which we cannot be held responsible for.
4. But if there is something we cannot be held responsible for, neither can we be held responsible for something that inevitably results from it.
5. Events E have as inevitable consequence Neurosis N, which in turn has as inevitable consequence Behavior B.
6. Since N is the inevitable consequence of E and B is the inevitable consequence of N, B is the inevitable consequence of E.
7. Hence, not being responsible for E, we cannot be responsible for B.

Discussion Questions

1. In what sense are you *not* free with respect to your emotions? In what way *are* you free?
2. Given the force of your own unconscious on you, in what ways might you counteract this?

3. Do you see any value in psychoanalysis? Why/why not?
4. Are you ever aware of your own ability to rationalize actions of yours that you realize are unpleasing to you? How do you explain this?
5. Freud held that we occasionally make seemingly harmless "slips of the tongue" caused by our unconscious and reveal truths outside of our conscious awareness (now called "Freudian slips"). Have you ever done this? In what ways do you notice your unconscious manifesting itself? What about body language?

Free Will: Ancient Dispute, New Themes
Robert Kane

Robert Kane earned his PhD in 1964 from Yale where he wrote his dissertation on intentionality and the mind. Following a number of short teaching assignments, he has taught at the University of Texas at Austin, where he now serves as Distinguished Teaching Professor. He has written and edited numerous books, primarily focusing on the topic of free will.

In this article he frames the issue of free will, comparing it with allegories from works of fiction and showing its relevance in terms of punishment. He then puts forth his views through a reframing of the issue and concluding with an analogy to help illuminate his libertarian (proponent of free will) position.

Reading Questions

1. Explain the problem regarding freedom expressed by the angels in Milton's *Paradise Lost*.
2. How does Kane answer his question, "Why do we want freedom?"
3. What distinction does Kane make between *surface* and *deeper* freedom? How are the types of freedom portrayed in *Walden Two*? What role does conditioning play with regard to free will?
4. How do these types of freedom relate to punishment?
5. Why isn't deeper freedom compatible with determinism? With indeterminism?
6. What relevance do self-forming choices/actions (SFA) have in Kane's discussion? How does his example of the businesswoman's dilemma illustrate his notion of SFA's?
7. How does Kane overcome the objection that one's possibilities of choices are arbitrary to begin with?
8. Explain Kane's writer/character analogy.

Source: Reprinted by permission of the author. Robert Kane is also the author of *A Contemporary Introduction to Free Will* (Oxford: Oxford University Press, 2005).

I

"There is a disputation that will continue till mankind are raised from the dead, between the necessitarians and the partisans of free will." These are the words of twelfth-century Persian poet, Jalalu'ddin Rumi. The problem of free will and necessity (or determinism), of which Rumi speaks, has puzzled the greatest minds for centuries—including famous philosophers, literary figures, theologians, scientists, legal theorists, and psychologists—as well as many ordinary people. It has affected and been affected by both religion and science.

In his classic poem, *Paradise Lost*, John Milton describes the angels debating how some of them could have sinned of their own free wills given that God had made them intelligent and happy. Why would they have done it? And why were they responsible for it rather than God, since God had made them the way they were and had complete foreknowledge of what they would do? While puzzling over such questions, even the angels, Milton tells us, were "in Endless Mazes lost" (not a comforting thought for us humans). On the scientific front, issues about free will lead us to ask about the nature of the physical universe and our place in it (are we determined by physical laws and movements of the atoms?), about human psychology and the springs of action (can our actions be predicted by those who know our psychology?), about social conditioning, moral responsibility, crime and punishment, right and wrong, good and evil, and much more.

To dive into these questions, the best way to begin is with the idea of *freedom* itself. Nothing could be more important than freedom to the modern world. All over the globe, the trend (often against resistance) is toward societies that are more free. But why do we want freedom? The simple, and not totally adequate, answer is that to be more free is to have the capacity and opportunity to satisfy more of our desires. In a free society we can walk into a store and buy almost anything we want. We can choose what movies to see, what music to listen to, whom to vote for.

But these are what you might call *surface* freedoms. What is meant by *free will* runs deeper than these everyday freedoms. To see how, suppose we had maximal freedom to make such choices to satisfy our desires and yet the choices we actually made were manipulated by others, by the powers-that-be. In such a world we would have a great deal of everyday freedom to do whatever we wanted, yet our free *will* would be severely limited. We would be free to *act* or choose *as* we will, but would not have the ultimate say about what it is that we will. Someone else would be pulling the strings, not by coercing us against our wishes, but by manipulating us into having the wishes they wanted us to have.

You may be thinking that, to some extent, we do live in such a world, where we are free to make numerous choices, but are manipulated into making many of our choices by advertising, television, public relations, spin doctors, salespersons, marketers, and sometimes even by friends, parents, relatives, rivals, or enemies. One indication of how important free will is to us is that people generally feel revulsion at such manipulation. When people find out that what they thought were their own wishes were actually manipulated by others who wanted them to choose in just the way they did, they feel demeaned. Such situations are demeaning because we realize we were not our own persons; and having free will is about being your own person.

The problem is brought out in a striking way by twentieth-century utopian novels, such as Aldous Huxley's *Brave New World* and B. F. Skinner's *Walden Two*. In the fictional societies described in these famous works, people can have and do what they will or choose, but only to the extent that they have been conditioned by behavioral engineers or neuro-chemists to will or choose what they can have and do. In *Brave New World*, the lower-echelon workers are under the influence of powerful drugs so that they do not dream of things they cannot have. They are quite content to play miniature golf all weekend. They can do what they want, though their wants are meager and controlled by drugs.

The citizens of Skinner's *Walden Two* have a richer existence than the workers of *Brave New World*. Yet their desires and purposes are also covertly controlled, in this case by behavioral engineers. Walden Two-ers live collectively in a kind of rural commune; and because they share duties of farming and raising children, they have plenty of leisure. They pursue arts, sciences, crafts, engage in musical performances, and enjoy what appears to be a pleasant existence. The fictional founder of Walden Two, a fellow named Frazier, forthrightly says that their pleasant existence is brought about by the fact that, in his community, persons can do whatever they want or choose because they have been behaviorally conditioned since childhood to want and choose only what they can have and do. In other words, they have maximal *surface freedom* of action and choice (they can choose or do anything they want), but they lack a *deeper freedom* of the will because their desires and purposes are created by their behavioral conditioners or controllers. Their wills are not of "their own" making. Indeed, what happens in Walden Two is that their surface freedom to act and choose as they will is maximized by minimizing the deeper freedom to have the ultimate say about what they will.

Thus Frazier can say that Walden Two "is the freest place on earth," because he has surface freedom in mind. For there is no *coercion* in Walden Two and no *punishment* because no one has to be forced to do anything against his or her will. The citizens can have anything they want because they have been conditioned not to want anything they cannot have. As for the deeper freedom, or free will, it does not exist in Walden Two, as Frazier himself admits. But this is no loss, according to Frazier. Echoing *Walden Two's* author, B. F. Skinner (a foremost defender of behaviorism in psychology), Frazier thinks the deeper freedom of the will is an illusion in the first place. We do not have it anyway, inside or outside Walden Two. In our ordinary lives, he argues, we are just as much the products of upbringing and social conditioning as the citizens of Walden Two, though we may delude ourselves into thinking otherwise. The difference is that, unlike Walden Two, our everyday conditioning is often haphazard, incompetent, and harmful.

Why then, Skinner asks, reject the maximal surface freedom and happiness of Walden Two for a deeper freedom of the will that is something we do not and cannot have anyway? Along with many other scientists, he thinks the idea that we could be *ultimate* determiners of our own ends or purposes (which is what the deeper freedom of the will would require) is an impossible ideal that cannot fit into the modern scientific picture of the world. To have such freedom, we would have to have been the original creators of our own wills—causes of ourselves. But if we trace the psychological springs of action back further and further to childhood, we find that we were less free back then, not more, and more subject to conditioning. We thus delude ourselves into thinking that we have sacrificed some real (deeper) freedom for the happiness of Walden Two. Rather we have gained a maximum amount of the only kind of freedom we really can have (surface freedom), while giving up an illusion (free will).

Seductive as these arguments may be, there are many people (myself included) who continue to believe that something important is missing in Walden Two and that the deeper freedom is not a mere illusion. Such persons want to be the ultimate designers of their own lives as Frazier was for the lives of Walden Two. They want to be the creators, as he was, not the pawns—at least for their own lives. What they long for is what was traditionally meant by "free will."

Here is yet another way of looking at it. Free will in this deeper sense is also intimately related to notions of moral responsibility, blameworthiness, and praiseworthiness. Suppose a young man is on trial for an assault and robbery in which his victim was beaten to death. Let us say we attend his trial on a daily basis. At first, our thoughts of the young man are filled with anger and resentment. But as we listen daily to how he came to have such a mean character and perverse motives—a sordid story of parental neglect, child abuse, sexual abuse, bad role models—some of our resentment against the young man is shifted over to the parents and others who abused and influenced him. We begin to feel angry with them as well as him. Yet we aren't quite ready to shift all of the blame away from the young man himself. We wonder whether some residual responsibility may not belong to him. Our questions become: To what extent is *he* responsible for becoming the sort of person he now is? Was it *all* a question of bad parenting, societal neglect, social conditioning, and the like, or did he have any role to play in it?

These are crucial questions about free will, and about what may be called *ultimate responsibility*. We know that parenting and society, genetic makeup and upbringing, have an influence on what we become and what we are. But were these influences entirely *determining* or did they "leave anything over" for us to be responsible for? That's what we wanted to know about the young man. The question of whether he is merely a victim of his bad circumstances or has some residual responsibility for being what he is depends on whether these other factors were or were not *entirely* determining.[1]

Turning this around, if there were factors or circumstances that entirely determined what he did, then to be ultimately responsible, he would have had to be responsible to some degree for some of those factors by virtue of earlier acts through which he formed his present character. As the philosopher Aristotle put it centuries ago, if a man is responsible for the wicked acts that flow from his character, then he must at one time in the past have been responsible for forming the character from which these acts flow. But, of course, if *all* of our choices and actions were entirely determined by prior circumstances, we would have had to be responsible to some degree for some of these earlier circumstances by still earlier acts of ours, and so on indefinitely backward in time—an impossibility for finite creatures like ourselves. At some point, if we are to be ultimately responsible for being what we are, there must be acts in our life histories in which parenting and society, genetic make-up, and other factors did not completely determine how we acted, but left something over for us to be responsible for then and there. This is why many people have thought that the deeper freedom of the will is not compatible with being completely determined by the past. Surface freedoms (to do or choose what we will) may be compatible with determinism, but free will does not seem to be (as Skinner himself realized).

II

Yet such thoughts only lead to a further problem that has haunted free will debates for centuries: If this deeper freedom of the will is not compatible with determinism, it does not seem to be compatible with *indeterminism* either. An event that is undetermined might occur or might not occur, given the entire past. (A determined event *must* occur, given the entire past.) Thus, whether or not an undetermined event actually occurs, given its past, is a matter of chance. But chance events occur spontaneously and are not under the control of anything, hence not under the control of agents. How then could they be free and responsible actions? If, for example, a choice occurred by virtue of a quantum jump or other undetermined event in your brain, it would seem a fluke or accident rather than a responsible choice. Undetermined events in the brain or body, it seems, would inhibit or interfere with freedom, occurring spontaneously and not under our control. They would turn out to be a nuisance—or perhaps a curse, like epilepsy—rather than an enhancement of our freedom.

Or look at the problem in another way that goes a little deeper. If my choice is really undetermined, that means I could have made a different choice *given exactly the same past* right up to the moment when I did choose. This is what indeterminism and the denial of determinism mean: exactly the same past, different outcomes. Imagine, for example, that I had been deliberating about where to spend my vacation, in Hawaii or Colorado, and after much thought and deliberation had decided I preferred Hawaii, and chose it. If the choice was undetermined, then exactly the same deliberation, the same thought processes, the same beliefs, desires, and other motives—not a sliver of difference—that led to my favoring and choosing Hawaii over Colorado, might by chance have resulted in my choosing Colorado instead. That is very strange. If such a thing happened it would seem a fluke or accident, like that quantum jump in the brain just mentioned, not a rational choice. Because I had come to favor Hawaii and was about to choose it, when by chance I chose Colorado, I would wonder what went wrong in my brain and perhaps consult a neurologist.

For reasons such as these, people have argued that undetermined free choices would be "arbitrary," "capricious," "random," "irrational," "uncontrolled," "inexplicable," or merely "matters of luck or chance," not really free and responsible choices at all. If free will is not compatible with determinism, it does not seem to be compatible with indeterminism either.

. . . Libertarian stratagems, to their critics, are reminiscent of the old debates about vital forces in the biology of the nineteenth century, where obscure forces were postulated to explain what otherwise could not be explained about living things. They remind of the Arkansas farmer when he first saw an automobile. He listened intently to the explanation of how the internal combustion engine worked, and nodded in agreement, but insisted on looking under the hood anyway because, as he said, "there must be a horse in there somewhere."

Thus, defenders of a nondeterminist free will are faced with a dilemma that was expressed by philosopher Thomas Hobbes at the beginning of the modern era. When trying to explain free will, these incompatibilist or libertarian defenders tend to fall either into "confusion" or "emptiness"—the confusion of identifying free will with indeterminism or the emptiness of mysterious accounts of agency in terms of noumenal selves, transempirical power centers, non-occurrent or agent-causes, or other stratagems whose operations remain obscure and unexplained. What is needed to escape this dilemma is some new thinking about how free will can be reconciled with indeterminism and how it might fit into the modern scientific picture of the world, without appealing to extra factors that have made it seem so mysterious. In the remainder of this essay, I want to suggest some new ways of thinking about this problem and about free will generally, which may stir you to do likewise.

III

The first thing to note is that indeterminism does not have to be a factor in all acts done "of our own free wills." Not all of them have to be undetermined. Frequently in everyday life we act from existing motives without having to think or deliberate about what to do. At such times, we may very well be determined by our existing characters and motives. Yet we may also at such times be acting "of our own free wills" to the extent that we formed our present characters and motives (our own wills) by earlier choices or actions that were not themselves determined. Recall again Aristotle's claim that if a man is responsible for the wicked acts that flow from his character, he must at one time in the past have been responsible for forming the character from which these acts flow. Not all choices or acts done "of our own free wills" have to be undetermined, but only those choices or acts in our lifetimes by which we made ourselves into the kinds of persons we are. Let us call these "self-forming choices or actions" or SFAs.

I believe that such undetermined self-forming choices and actions (SFAs) occur at those difficult times of life when we are torn between competing visions of what we should do or become, and that they are more frequent than we think. Perhaps we are torn between doing the moral thing or acting from ambition, or between powerful present desires and long-term goals, or we are faced with difficult tasks for which we have aversions. In all such cases, we are faced with competing motivations and have to make an effort to overcome temptation to do something else we also strongly want. At such times, there is tension and uncertainty in our minds about what to do. I suggest this is reflected in appropriate regions of our brains by movement away from thermodynamic equilibrium—in short, a kind of stirring up of chaos in the brain that makes it sensitive to micro-indeterminacies at the neuronal level. The uncertainty and inner tension we feel at such soul-searching moments of self-formation would thus be reflected in the indeterminacy of our neural processes themselves. What is experienced personally as uncertainty corresponds physically to the opening of a window of opportunity that temporarily screens off complete determination by influences of the past. (By contrast, when we act from predominant motives or settled dispositions, the uncertainty or indeterminacy is muted. If it did play a role in such cases, it would be a mere nuisance or fluke, as critics suggest, like the choice of Colorado when we favored Hawaii.)

When we do decide under such conditions of uncertainty, the outcome is not determined because of the preceding indeterminacy—and yet it can be willed (and hence rational and voluntary) either way owing to the fact that, in such self-formation, the agents' prior wills are divided by conflicting motives. Consider a businesswoman who faces a conflict of this kind. She is on the way to a business meeting important to her career when she observes an assault taking place in an alley. An inner struggle ensues between her moral conscience telling her to stop and call for help, and her career ambitions telling her she cannot miss this meeting. She has to make an effort of will to overcome the temptation to go on to her meeting. If she overcomes this temptation, it will be the result of her effort, but if she fails, it will be because she did not *allow* her effort to succeed. And this is because, while she wanted to overcome temptation, she also wanted to fail, for quite different and incommensurable reasons. When we, like the businesswoman, decide in such circumstances, and the indeterminate efforts we are making become determinate choices, we *make* one set of competing reasons or motives prevail over the others then and there *by deciding*. . . .

Let me conclude with one final objection that is perhaps the most telling and has not yet been discussed. Even if one granted that persons, such as the businesswoman, could make genuine self-forming choices that were undetermined, isn't there something to the charge that such choices would be "arbitrary"? A residual arbitrariness seems to remain in all self-forming choices because the agents cannot in principle have sufficient or overriding *prior* reasons for making one option and one set of reasons prevail over the other. The agents *make* one set of reasons prevail *by* choosing, to be sure, but they could as well have made the other set of reasons prevail by choosing differently.

I agree that there is some truth to this charge as well. But I would argue that such arbitrariness relative to prior reasons also tells us something important about free will. It tells us that every undetermined self-forming free choice is the initiation of what might be called a "value experiment" whose justification lies in the future and is not fully explained by past reasons. In making such a choice we say, in effect, "Let's try this. It is not required by my past, but is consistent with my past and is one branching pathway my life can now meaningfully take. Whether it is the right choice, only time will tell. Meanwhile, I am willing to take responsibility for it one way or the other."

It is worth noting that the term "arbitrary" comes from the Latin *arbitrium*, which means "judgment"—as in *liberum arbitrium voluntatis,* "free judgment of the will" (the medieval philosophers' designation for free will). Imagine a writer in the middle of a novel. The novel's heroine faces a crisis and the writer has not yet developed her character in sufficient detail to say exactly how she will act. The author makes a "judgment" about this that is not determined by the heroine's already formed past, which does not give unique direction. In this sense, the judgment (*arbitrium*) of how she will react is "arbitrary," but not entirely so. It had input from the heroine's fictional past and in turn gave input to her projected future. In a similar way, agents who exercise free will are both authors of and characters in their own stories all at once. By virtue of "self-forming" judgments of the will (*arbitria voluntatis*), they are "arbiters" of their own lives, "making themselves" out of a past that, if they are truly free, does not limit their future pathways to one.

Suppose we were to say to them, "But look, you didn't have sufficient or *conclusive* prior reasons for choosing as you did since you also had viable reasons for choosing the other way." They might reply, "True enough. But I did have *good* reasons for choosing as I did, which I'm willing to stand by and take responsibility for. If they were not sufficient or conclusive reasons, that's because, like the heroine of the novel, I was not a fully formed person before I chose (and still am not, for that matter). Like the author of the novel described above, I am in the process of writing an unfinished story and forming an unfinished character who, in my case, is myself."

Discussion Questions

1. In what ways might our current society resemble that of Skinner's *Walden Two*? What effect do the following have on your choices: "advertising, television, publics relations, spin doctors, salespersons, marketers, . . . friends, parents, relatives, rivals, enemies"? How is our everyday conditioning "haphazard, incompetent, and harmful"?

2. What role does education play in your making free choices? Does it provide you with more or less freedom?

3. What is the role of self-forming actions (SFA) in your life? What was the last SFA you made?

4. Aristotle writes, "You are what you do." One could then argue that the more self-forming actions you have, the *more* (not less) determined you become, making you less free to make choices in the future. How do you respond to this?

Free Will and Morality

W. T. Stace

Born in London in 1886 and educated in philosophy at Trinity College in Dublin, Walter Stace went on to earn his D. Litt. from Trinity College after spending twenty-two years in the British Civil Service. During that time, he not only served as mayor of Colombo (where "Stace Street" still stands), but wrote three philosophy books on varying subjects. From that point, he went to Princeton University, where he was appointed Stuart Professor of Philosophy in 1935 and taught there until his retirement, penning numerous award-winning books in philosophy.

In this article, Stace puts forth a view known as *compatiblism*, holding that free will and determinism can (and do) consistently coexist, as opposed to it being an either-or situation.

Reading Questions

1. Why does Stace claim that without free will there can be no morality?
2. How does Stace argue that the dispute surrounding free will is just a semantic problem?
3. How does Stace rule out the criterion of indeterminism (being uncaused) from the definition of free will?
4. State Stace's definition of free will in your own words.
5. How does Stace address the issue of predictability as it relates to free will?
6. What "puzzling case" arises from Stace's definition of free will? How does he overcome it?
7. What two justifications does Stace provide for punishing someone? How does punishment relate to Stace's overall discussion?

[A] great problem which the rise of scientific naturalism has created for the modern mind concerns the foundations of morality. The old religious foundations have largely crumbled away, and it may well be thought that the edifice built upon them by generations of men is in danger of collapse. A total collapse of moral behavior is . . . very unlikely. For a society in which this occurred could not survive. Nevertheless the danger to moral standards inherent in the virtual disappearance of their old religious foundations is not illusory.

I shall first discuss the problem of free will, for is certain that if there is no free will there can be no morality. Morality is concerned with what men ought and ought not to do. But if a man has no freedom to choose what he will do, if whatever he does is done under compulsion, then it does not make sense to tell him that he ought not to have done what he did and that he ought to do something different. All moral precepts would in such case be meaningless. Also if he acts

Source: Pages 248–258 (with one minor edit) from *Religion and the Modern Mind* by W. T. Stace. Copyright © 1952 by W. T. Stace, renewed © 1980 by Blanche Stace. Reprinted by permission of HarperCollins Publishers.

always under compulsion, how can he be held morally responsible for his actions? How can he, for example, be punished for what he could not help doing?

It is to be observed that those learned professors of philosophy or psychology who deny the existence of free will do so only in their professional moments and in their studies and lecture rooms. For when it comes to doing anything practical, even of the most trivial kind, they invariably behave as if they and others were free. They inquire from you at dinner whether you will choose this dish or that dish. They will ask a child why he told a lie, and will punish him for not having chosen the way of truthfulness. All of which is inconsistent with a disbelief in free will. This should cause us to suspect that the problem is not a real one; and this, I believe, is the case. The dispute is merely verbal, and is due to nothing but a confusion about the meanings of words. It is what is now fashionably called a semantic problem.

How does a verbal dispute arise? Let us consider a case which, although it is absurd in the sense that no one would ever make the mistake which is involved in it, yet illustrates the principle which we shall have to use in the solution of the problem. Suppose that someone believed that the word "man" means a certain sort of five-legged animal; in short that "five-legged animal" is the correct *definition* of man. He might then look around the world, and rightly observing that there are no five-legged animals in it, he might proceed to deny the existence of men. This preposterous conclusion would have been reached because he was using an incorrect definition of "man." All you would have to do to show him his mistake would be to give him the correct definition; or at least to show him that his definition was wrong. Both the problem and its solution would, of course, be entirely verbal. The problem of free will, and its solution, I shall maintain, is verbal in exactly the same way. The problem has been created by the fact that learned men, especially philosophers, have assumed an incorrect definition of free will, and then finding that there is nothing in the world which answers to their definition, have denied its existence. As far as logic is concerned, their conclusion is just as absurd as that of the man who denies the existence of men. The only difference is that the mistake in the latter case is obvious and crude, while the mistake which the deniers of free will have made is rather subtle and difficult to detect.

Throughout the modern period, until quite recently, it was assumed, both by the philosophers who denied free will and by those who defended it, that *determinism is inconsistent with free will*. If a man's actions were wholly determined by chains of causes stretching back into the remote past, so that they could be predicted beforehand by a mind which knew all the causes, it was assumed that they could not in that case be free. This implies that a certain definition of actions done from free will was assumed, namely that they are actions *not* wholly determined by causes or predictable beforehand. Let us shorten this by saying that free will was defined as meaning indeterminism. This is the incorrect definition which has led to the denial of free will. As soon as we see what the true definition is we shall find that the question whether the world is deterministic, as Newtonian science implied, or in a measure indeterministic, as current physics teaches, is wholly irrelevant to the problem.

Of course there is a sense in which one can define a word arbitrarily in any way one pleases. But a definition may nevertheless be called correct or incorrect. It is correct if it accords with a *common usage* of the word defined. It is incorrect if it does not. And if you give an incorrect definition, absurd and untrue results are likely to follow. For instance, there is nothing to prevent you from arbitrarily defining a man as a five-legged animal, but this is incorrect in the sense that it does not accord with the ordinary meaning of the word. Also it has the absurd result of leading to a denial of the existence of men. This shows that *common usage is the criterion for deciding whether a definition is correct or not.* And this is the principle which I shall apply to free will. I shall show that indeterminism is not what is meant by the phrase "free will" *as it is commonly used.* And I shall attempt to discover the correct definition by inquiring how the phrase is used in ordinary conversation.

Here are a few samples of how the phrase might be used in ordinary conversation. It will be noticed that they include cases in which the question whether a man acted with free will is asked in order to determine whether he was morally and legally responsible for his acts.

JONES: I once went without food for a week.
SMITH: Did you do that of your own free will?
JONES: No. I did it because I was lost in a desert and could find no food.

But suppose that the man who had fasted was Mahatma Gandhi. The conversation might then have gone:

GANDHI: I once fasted for a week.
SMITH: Did you do that of your own free will?
GANDHI: Yes. I did it because I wanted to compel the British Government to give India its independence.

Take another case. Suppose that I had stolen some bread, but that I was as truthful as George Washington. Then, if I were charged with the crime in court, some exchange of the following sort might take place:

JUDGE: Did you steal the bread of your own free will?
STACE: Yes. I stole it because I was hungry.

Or in different circumstances the conversation might run:

JUDGE: Did you steal of your own free will?
STACE: No. I stole because my employer threatened to beat me if I did not.

At a recent murder trial in Trenton some of the accused had signed confessions, but afterwards asserted that they had done so under police duress. The following exchange might have occurred:

JUDGE: Did you sign this confession of your own free will?
PRISONER: No. I signed it because the police beat me up.

Now suppose that a philosopher had been a member of the jury. We could imagine this conversation taking place in the jury room.

FOREMAN OF THE JURY: The prisoner says he signed the confession because he was beaten, and not of his own free will.
PHILOSOPHER: This is quite irrelevant to the case. There is no such thing as free will.
FOREMAN: Do you mean to say that it makes no difference whether he signed because his conscience made him want to tell the truth or because he was beaten?
PHILOSOPHER: None at all. Whether he was caused to sign by a beating or by some desire of his own—the desire to tell the truth, for example—in either case his signing was causally determined, and therefore in neither case did he act of his own free will. Since there is no such thing as free will, the question whether he signed of his own free will ought not to be discussed by us.

The foreman and the rest of the jury would rightly conclude that the philosopher must be making some mistake. What sort of a mistake could it be? There is only one possible answer. The philosopher must be using the phrase "free will" in some peculiar way of his own which is not the way in which men usually use it when they wish to determine a question of moral responsibility. That is, he must be using an incorrect definition of it as implying action not determined by causes.

Suppose a man left his office at noon, and were questioned about it. Then we might hear this:

JONES: Did you go out of your own free will?
SMITH: Yes. I went out to get my lunch.

But we might hear:

JONES: Did you leave your office of your own free will?
SMITH: No. I was forcibly removed by the police.

We have now collected a number of cases of actions which, in the ordinary usage of the English language, would be called cases in which people have acted of their own free will. We should also say in all these cases that they *chose* to act as they did. We should also say that they could have acted otherwise, if they had chosen. For instance, Mahatma Gandhi was not compelled to fast; he chose to do so. He could have eaten if he had wanted to. When Smith went out to get his lunch, he chose to do so. He could have stayed and done some more work, if he had wanted to. We have also collected a number of cases of the opposite kind. They are cases in which men were not able to exercise their free will. They had no choice. They were compelled to do as they did. The man in the desert did not fast of his own free will. He had no choice in the matter. He was compelled to fast because there was nothing for him to eat. And so with the other cases. It ought to be quite easy, by an inspection of these cases, to tell what we ordinarily mean when we say that a man did or did not exercise free will. We ought therefore to be able to extract from them the proper definition of the term. Let us put the cases in a table:

Free Acts	Unfree Acts
Gandhi fasting because he wanted to free India.	The man fasting in the desert because there was no food.
Stealing bread because one is hungry.	Stealing because one's employer threatened to beat one.
Signing a confession because one wanted to tell the truth.	Signing because the police beat one.
Leaving the office because one wanted one's lunch.	Leaving because forcibly removed.

It is obvious that to find the correct definition of free acts we must discover what characteristic is common to all the acts in the left-hand column, and is, at the same time, absent from all the acts in the right-hand column. This characteristic which all free acts have, and which no unfree acts have, will be the defining characteristic of free will.

Is being uncaused, or not being determined by causes, the characteristic of which we are in search? It cannot be, because although it is true that all the acts in the right-hand column have causes, such as the beating by the police or the absence of food in the desert, so also do the acts in the left-hand column. Mr. Gandhi's fasting was caused by his desire to free India, the man leaving his office by his hunger, and so on. Moreover there is no reason to doubt that these causes of the free acts were in turn caused by prior conditions, and that these were again the results of causes, and so on back indefinitely into the past. Any physiologist can tell us the causes of hunger. What caused Mr. Gandhi's tremendously powerful desire to free India is no doubt more difficult to discover. But it must have had causes. Some of them may have lain in peculiarities of his glands or brain, others in his past experiences, others in his heredity, others in his education. Defenders of free will have usually tended to deny such facts. But to do so is plainly a case of special pleading, which is unsupported by any scrap of evidence. The only reasonable view is that all human actions, both those which are freely done and those which are not, are either wholly determined by causes, or at least as much determined as other events in nature. It may be true, as the physicists tell us, that nature is not as deterministic as was once thought. But whatever degree of determinism prevails in the world, human actions appear to be as much determined as anything else. And if this is so, it cannot be the case that what distinguishes actions freely chosen from those which are not free is that the latter are determined by causes while the former are not. Therefore, being uncaused or being undetermined by causes, must be an incorrect definition of free will.

What, then, is the difference between acts which are freely done and those which are not? What is the characteristic which is present to all the acts in the left-hand column and absent from all those in the right-hand column? Is it not obvious that, although both sets of actions have causes, the causes of those in the left-hand column are *of a different kind* from the causes of those in the right-hand column? The free acts are all caused by desires, or motives, or by some sort of internal psychological states of the agent's mind. The unfree acts, on the other hand, are all caused by physical forces or physical conditions, outside the agent. Police arrest means physical force exerted from the outside; the absence of food in the desert in a physical condition of the outside world. We may therefore frame the following rough definitions. *Acts freely done are those whose immediate causes are psychological states in the agent. Acts not freely done are those whose immediate causes are states of affairs external to the agent.*

It is plain that if we define free will in this way, then free will certainly exists, and the philosopher's denial of its existence is seen to be what it is—nonsense. For it is obvious that all those actions of men which we should ordinarily attribute to the exercise of their free will, or of which we should say that they freely chose to do them, are in fact actions which have been caused by their own desires, wishes, thoughts, emotions, impulses, or other psychological states.

In applying our definition we shall find that it usually works well, but that there are some puzzling cases which it does not seem exactly to fit. These puzzles can always be solved by paying careful attention to the ways in which words are used, and remembering that they are not always used consistently. I have space for only one example. Suppose that a thug threatens to shoot you unless you give him your wallet, and suppose that you do so. Do you, in giving him your wallet, do so of your own free will or not? If we apply our definition, we find that you acted freely, since the immediate cause of the action was not an actual outside force but the fear of death, which is a psychological cause. Most people, however, would say that you did not act of your own free will but under compulsion. Does this show that our definition is wrong? I do not think so. Aristotle, who gave a solution of the problem of free will substantially the same as ours (though he did not use the term "free will") admitted that there are what he called "mixed" or borderline cases in which it is difficult to know whether we ought to call the acts free or compelled. In the case under discussion, though no actual force was used, the gun at your forehead so nearly approximated to actual force that we tend to say the case was one of compulsion. It is a borderline case.

Here is what may seem like another kind of puzzle. According to our view an action may be free though it could have been predicted beforehand with certainty. But suppose you told a lie, and it was certain beforehand that you would tell it. How could one then say, "You could have told the truth"? The answer is that it is perfectly true that you could have told the truth *if* you had wanted to. In fact you would have done so, for in that case the causes producing your action, namely your desires, would have been different, and would therefore have produced different effects. It is a delusion that predictability and free will are incompatible. This agrees with common sense. For if, knowing your character, I predict that you will act honorably, no one would say when you do act honorably, that this shows you did not do so of your own free will.

Since free will is a condition of moral responsibility, we must be sure that our theory of free will gives a sufficient basis for it. To be held morally responsible for one's actions means that one may be justly punished or rewarded, blamed or praised, for them. But it is not just to punish a man for what he cannot help doing. How can it be just to punish him for an action which it was certain beforehand that he would do? We have not attempted to decide whether, as a matter of fact, all events, including human actions, are completely determined. For that question is irrelevant to the problem of free will. But if we assume for the purposes of argument that complete determinism is true, but that we are nevertheless free, it may then be asked whether such a deterministic free will is compatible with moral responsibility. For it may seem unjust to punish a man for an action which it could have been predicted with certainty beforehand that he would do.

But that determinism is incompatible with moral responsibility is as much a delusion as that it is incompatible with free will. You do not excuse a man for doing a wrong act because, knowing his character, you felt certain beforehand that he would do it. Nor do you deprive a man of a reward prize because, knowing his goodness or his capabilities, you felt certain beforehand that he would win it.

Volumes have been written on the justification of punishment. But so far as it affects the question of free will, the essential principles involved are quite simple. The punishment of a man for doing a wrong act is justified, either on the ground that it will correct his own character, or that it will deter other people from doing similar acts. The instrument of punishment has been in the past, and no doubt still is, often unwisely used; so that it may often have done more harm than good. But that is not relevant to our present problem. Punishment, if and when it is justified, is justified only on one or both of the grounds just mentioned. The question then is how, if we assume determinism, punishment can correct character or deter people from evil actions.

Suppose that your child develops a habit of telling lies. You give him a mild beating. Why? Because you believe that his personality is such that the usual motives for telling the truth do not cause him to do so. You therefore supply the missing cause, or motive, in the shape of pain and the fear of future pain if he repeats his untruthful behavior. And you hope that a few treatments of this kind will condition him to the habit of truth-telling, so that he will come to tell the truth without the infliction of pain. You assume that his actions are determined by causes, but that the usual causes of truth-telling do not in him produce their usual effects. You therefore supply him with an artificially injected motive, pain and fear, which you think will in the future cause him to speak truthfully.

The principle is exactly the same where you hope, by punishing one man, to deter others from wrong actions. You believe that the fear of punishment will cause those who might otherwise do evil to do well.

We act on the same principle with non-human, and even with inanimate, things, if they do not behave in the way we think they ought to behave. The rose bushes in the garden produce only small and poor blooms, whereas we want large and rich ones. We supply a cause which will produce large blooms, namely fertilizer. Our automobile does not go properly. We supply a cause which will make it go better, namely oil in the works. The punishment for the man, the fertilizer for the plant, and the oil for the car, are all justified by the same principle and in the same way. The only difference is that different kinds of things require different kinds of causes to make them do what they should. Pain may be the appropriate remedy to apply, in certain cases, to human beings, and oil to the machine. It is, of course, of no use to inject motor oil into the boy or to beat the machine.

Thus we see that moral responsibility is not only consistent with determinism, but requires it. The assumption on which punishment is based is that human behavior is causally determined. If pain could not be a cause of truth-telling there would be no justification at all for punishing lies. If human actions and volitions were uncaused, it would be useless either to punish or reward, or indeed to do anything else to correct people's bad behavior. For nothing that you could do would in any way influence them. Thus moral responsibility would entirely disappear. If there were no determinism of human beings at all, their actions would be completely unpredictable and capricious, and therefore irresponsible. And this is in itself a strong argument against the common view of philosophers that free will means being undetermined by causes.

Discussion Questions

1. Do you agree with Stace's statement, "If there is no free will there can be no morality"? *Can* we hold someone morally accountable for what they could not help doing? What would that mean?

2. Do you agree that Stace's examples of the prisoner who signed the confession because of threat and the thief who stole because of his employer's threat are examples of non-free acts? *Couldn't* they still have refrained from signing/stealing?

3. Do you accept Stace's definition of free will? Does it solve cases like the "thug" that he gives? What if the thug threatened just to punch you once versus shoot you? What level of compulsion is necessary to deem an act as unfree? Are you free to leave the classroom whenever you want to? Are you free to break any laws that you choose?

4. Do you agree with the statement, "It may seem unjust to punish a man for an action which it could have been predicted with certainty beforehand that he would do"? In the movie *Minority Report,* they do just this—if you could know ahead of time that someone would commit a crime, would you be justified in punishing them?

5. There are typically three justifications for the government punishing its citizens: for utilitarian reasons (to deter others from committing crimes and to prevent the particular criminal from committing more); for retributive reasons (because the person *deserves* it/has *earned* it); to rehabilitate (to *teach* or change the person). How would your justification for punishment change with regard to your view of human free will?

How Advertising Changes the Way We Think and Feel

Jean Kilbourne

Jean Kilbourne earned her PhD in education from Boston University and has worked as a Visiting Research Scholar at the Wellesley College Center for Women since 1984. She is considered a pioneer in advertising research. Along with the book cited here, she has also produced six documentary films, each of which focuses on the negative effects of advertising. She has lectured at nearly half of the college campuses throughout the United States and Canada and has twice been chosen as "Lecturer of the Year" by the National Association for Campus Activities.

This selection is taken from her book *Can't Buy My Love: How Advertising Changes the Way We Think and Feel*. She first sets forth a defense of advertising's power over people—noting the fact that much of this is not consciously recognized. Then, she not only highlights the resulting effects of consumer purchasing behavior, but also the effects this has on even more important issues, such as body image, addiction, attitudes toward food, and the negative light in which women (and sometimes men) are depicted. This discussion relies on themes relevant to the topic of free will (i.e., how *freely* do we choose the products we purchase? how authentic are our choices in regards to our relationships? etc.) and also morality (i.e., what moral responsibility, if any, do advertisers have, given the impact they have on individuals and society?).

Reading Questions

1. What evidence does Kilbourne provide to dispel the notion that advertising does not strongly affect us?
2. What effect does Kilbourne suggest advertising has on our view of the poor?
3. What role do neuroscientists, psychologists, and anthropologists have in creating commercials?
4. What is the average time one spends viewing television commercials? What percentage of the ad's message is absorbed by the conscious mind?
5. What point does Kilbourne make regarding the Sprite commercials?
6. Explain the significance of the mind-as-combination-lock analogy.
7. What negative attitudes does Kilbourne suggest arise from the portrayal of food in commercials?
8. According to researchers, what effect do magazines have on a woman's view of her body? How do they affect men's view of women?
9. What is *weightism*, and how is it relevant?
10. Explain the significance of the study done in Fiji.
11. How does Kilbourne show that alcohol advertisers do seem to target children?
12. Explain some of the advertising statistics of cigarette commercials.

Source: Excerpted with the permission of the Free Press, a Division of Simon & Schuster, Inc., from *Can't Buy My Love: How Advertising Changes the Way We Think and Feel* (previously published in hardcover as *Deadly Persuasion*) by Jean Kilbourne. Copyright © 1999 by Jean Kilbourne. All rights reserved.

Although much more attention has been paid to the cultural impact of advertising in recent years than ever before, just about everyone in America still feels personally exempt from advertising's influence. Almost everyone holds the misguided belief that advertisements don't affect *them*, don't shape their attitudes, don't help define their dreams. What I hear more than anything else, as I lecture throughout the country, is "I don't pay attention to ads . . . I just tune them out . . . they have no effect on me." Of course, I hear this most often from young men wearing Budweiser caps. In truth, we are all influenced by advertising. There is no way to tune out this much information, especially when it is carefully designed to break through the "tuning out" process.

The fact is that much of advertising's power comes from this belief that advertising does not affect us. The most effective kind of propaganda is that which is not recognized as propaganda. Because we think advertising is silly and trivial, we are less on guard, less critical, than we might otherwise be. It's all in fun, it's ridiculous. While we're laughing, sometimes sneering, the commercial does its work.

Some of the most talented and creative people in the world are dedicated to this work. Indeed, the most skillful propagandists of our time are not working for dictators, they are certainly not working exclusively for the Democratic party or the Republicans either. They are working for Foote, Cone & Belding, Ogilvy & Mather, and DDB Needham Worldwide. Their job is very specific: They are to use all of their powers of persuasion, explicit and implicit, to sell a particular product. That's all! No moral, no obligation to any other set of values. They just have to use their wits to put together a hip, funny, seductive, *persuasive* ad campaign. If they don't, another agency will take away the account. These folks are just doing their job—and maybe they're even doing us a service by giving us information about products and entertaining us while they're at it. What's the harm in that? . . .

Like a very potent drug, advertising is designed to do one particular job, but along the way it often has other, much broader results. Although some of this is intentional on the part of advertisers, much of it is not. Advertising often sells more than products, but advertisers generally don't care about that. If the cumulative effect of some advertising, for example, is to degrade women or to sexualize children or to increase eating disorders, surely that is not the *intent* of the advertisers. It is simply an unfortunate side effect.

Even in the case of addictive products, the aim of advertisers is to make money, not to create addicts. Unfortunately, they can't do the former without doing the latter. Indeed, the addict is the ideal consumer. Ten percent of drinkers consume over 60 percent of all the alcohol sold. These aren't the folks who are having an occasional Cabernet Sauvignon with dinner or one beer with their pizza. Advertisers spend enormous amounts of money on psychological research and understand addiction at least as well as, if not better than, any other group in the country. They use this knowledge to target children (because if you hook them early, they are yours for life), to encourage all people to consume more, in spite of often dangerous consequences for all of us, and to create a climate of denial in which all kinds of addictions flourish. This they do with full intent, as we see so clearly in the "secret" documents of the tobacco industry that have been made available to the public in recent years. . . .

One certainly doesn't have to be an alcoholic or any kind of addict to have suffered from a sense of emptiness. Our materialistic culture encourages this because people who feel empty make great consumers. The emptier we feel, the more likely we are to turn to products, especially potentially addictive products, to fill us up, to make us feel whole. Not everyone has to give up these things (although some of us do), but we all can profit from becoming more conscious of their role in our lives. They all serve to distance us from our feelings and to deflect attention from that which might really make a difference in our lives. . . .

We Are the Product

If you're like most people, you think that advertising has no influence on you. This is what advertisers want you to believe. But, if that were true, why would companies spend over $200 billion a year on advertising? Why would they be willing to spend over $250,000 to produce an average television commercial and another $250,000 to air it? If they want to broadcast their commercial during the Super Bowl, they will gladly spend over a million dollars to produce it and over one and a half million to air it. After all, they might have the kind of success that Victoria's Secret did during the 1999 Super Bowl. When they paraded bra-and-panty-clad models across TV screens for a mere thirty seconds, one million people turned away from the game to log on to the Website promoted in the ad. No influence?

Ad agency Arnold Communications of Boston kicked off an ad campaign for a financial services group during the 1999 Super Bowl that represented eleven months of planning and twelve thousand "man-hours" of work. Thirty hours of footage were edited into a thirty-second spot. An employee flew to Los Angeles with the ad in a lead-lined bag, like a diplomat carrying state secrets or a courier with crown jewels. Why? Because the Super Bowl is one of the few sure sources of big audiences—especially male audiences, the most precious commodity for advertisers. Indeed, the Super Bowl is more about advertising than football: The four hours it takes include only about twelve minutes of actually moving the ball. . . .

Although we like to think of advertising as unimportant, it is in fact the most important aspect of the mass media. It is the point. Advertising supports more than 60 percent of magazine and newspaper production and almost 100 percent of the electronic media. Over $40 billion a year in ad revenue is generated for television and radio and over $30 billion for magazines and newspapers. As one ABC executive said, "The network is paying affiliates to carry network commercials, not programs. What we are is a distribution system for Procter & Gamble." And the CEO of Westinghouse Electric, owner of CBS, said, "We're here to serve advertisers. That's our raison d'être." . . .

Not surprisingly, there are no magazines or Internet sites or television programs for the poor or for people on welfare. They might not be able to afford the magazines or computers but more important, they are of no use to advertisers.

This emphasis on the affluent surely has something to do with the invisibility of the poor in our society. Since advertisers have no interest in them, they are not reflected in the media. We know so much about the rich and famous that it becomes a problem for many who seek to emulate them, but we know very little about the lifestyles of the poor and desperate. It is difficult to feel compassion for people we don't know. . . .

The media . . . spend a fortune on research to learn a lot about us, using techniques like polls, trends analysis, focus groups, and PRIZM, a marketing program that garners information about consumers from their ZIP codes—and that is advertised in *Advertising Age* as "the targeting tool that turns birds of a feather into sitting ducks."

Many companies these days are hiring anthropologists and psychologists to examine consumers' product choices, verbal responses, even body language for deeper meanings. They spend time in consumers' homes, listening to their conversations and exploring their closets and bathroom cabinets. Ad agency Leo Burnett's director of planning calls these techniques "getting in under the radar." Robert Deutsch, a neuroscientist and anthropologist who works for ad agency DDB Needham, likens himself to a vampire—"I suck information out of people, and they love it."

One new market research technique involves monitoring brain-wave signals to measure how "engaged" viewers are in what they are watching. According to the president of the company doing this research, "We are the only company in the industry reading people's thoughts and emotions. Someone's going to be a billionaire doing this. I think it will be us."

Through focus groups and depth interviews, psychological researchers can zero in on very specific target audiences—and their leaders. "Buy this 24-year-old and get all his friends absolutely free," proclaims an ad for MTV directed to advertisers. MTV presents itself publicly as a place for rebels and nonconformists. Behind the scenes, however, it tells potential advertisers that its viewers are lemmings who will buy whatever they are told to buy. . . .

Advertising Is Our Environment

. . . The average American is exposed to at least three thousand ads every day and will spend three years of his or her life watching television commercials. Advertising makes up about 70 percent of our newspapers and 40 percent of our mail. Of course, we don't pay direct attention to very many of these ads, but we are powerfully influenced, mostly on an unconscious level, by the experience of being immersed in an advertising culture, a market-driven culture, in which all our institutions, from political to religious to educational, are increasingly for sale to the highest bidder. According to Rance Crain, editor-in-chief of *Advertising Age*, the major publication of the advertising industry, "Only eight percent of an ad's message is received by the conscious mind; the rest is worked and reworked deep within the recesses of the brain, where a product's positioning and repositioning takes shape." It is in this sense that advertising is subliminal: not in the sense of hidden messages embedded in ice cubes, but in the sense that we aren't consciously aware of what advertising is doing. . . .

A Sprite . . . commercial features teenagers partying on a beach while drinking a soft drink called Jooky. As the camera pulls back, we see that this is a fictional television commercial being watched by two teens, who open their own cans of Jooky and experience absolutely nothing. "Image is nothing. Thirst is everything," says the slogan. However, there is nothing in the ad about thirst—or taste, for that matter—or anything intrinsic to Sprite. The campaign is about nothing but image. Of course, what other way is there to sell sweetened, flavored carbonated water? If thirst is really everything, our best bet is water, and not high-priced bottled water either, such as Evian, which costs more than some champagne (no wonder that Evian backward spells "naive"). . . .

Some advertisers use what they chillingly call "viral communications" as a way to reach teenagers alienated from traditional forms of advertising. They use posters on construction sites and lampposts, sidewalk markings, and e-mail to infiltrate youth culture and cultivate the perception that their product is hot. One marketing consultant suggests picturing the mind as a combination lock and says, "One has to know what the particular stimuli are that are the 'clicks' heard by the inner mind of the target market and then allow the target market to open the lock so it is their own 'Aha!'—their own discovery, and so their own commitment."

Some ads make fun of high-pressure tactics. "Perhaps you'd consider buying one," says an ad for Saturn, and then in brackets below, "Sorry, we didn't mean to pressure you like that." Another car ad declares, "We're not trying to sell you this car. We're just letting you know it exists." An ad for sneakers tells us that "marketing is just hype." This is a bit like a man unbuttoning a woman's blouse, all the while telling her that she is far too smart to be seduced by the likes of him. . . .

Many teens fantasize that objects will somehow transform their lives, give them social standing and respect. When they wear a certain brand of sneaker or jacket, they feel, "This is important, therefore I am important." The brand gives instant status. No wonder they are willing, even eager, to spend money for clothes that advertise the brands. A *USA Today*–CNN–Gallup Poll found that 61 percent of boys and 44 percent of girls considered brand names on clothes "very important" or "somewhat important." . . .

In the beginning these labels were somewhat discreet. Today we see sweatshirts with fifteen-inch "Polo" logos stamped across the chest, jeans with four-inch "Calvin Klein" labels stitched on them, and a jacket with "Tommy Hilfiger" in five-inch letters across the back. Some of these outfits are so close to sandwich boards that I'm surprised people aren't paid to wear them. Before too long, the logo-free product probably will be the expensive rarity.

What people who wear these clothes are really buying isn't a garment, of course, but an *image*. And increasingly, an image is all that advertising has to sell. . . .

Industrialization gave rise to the burgeoning ability of businesses to mass-produce goods. Since it was no longer certain there would be a market for the goods, it became necessary not just to mass-produce the goods but to mass-produce markets hungry for the goods. The problem became not too little candy produced but not enough candy consumed, so it became the job of the advertisers to _produce consumers_. This led to an increased use of psychological research and emotional ploys to sell products. Consumer behavior became recognized as a science in the late 1940s.

As luxury goods, prepared foods, and nonessential items have proliferated, it has become crucial to create artificial needs in order to sell unnecessary products. Was there such a thing as static cling before there were fabric softeners and sprays? An ad for a "lip renewal cream" says, "I never thought of my lips as a problem area until Andrea came up with the solution."

Most brands in a given category are essentially the same. Most shampoos are made by two or three manufacturers. Blindfolded smokers or beer-drinkers can rarely identify what brand they are smoking or drinking, including their own. Whether we know it or not, we select products primarily because of the image reflected in their advertising. Very few ads give us any real information at all. Sometimes it is impossible to tell what is being advertised. "This is an ad for the hair dryer," says one ad, featuring a woman lounging on a sofa. If we weren't told, we would never know. A joke made the rounds a while ago about a little boy who wanted a box of tampons so that he could effortlessly ride bicycles and horses, ski, and swim.

Almost all tobacco and alcohol ads are entirely image-based. Of course, when you're selling a product that kills people, it's difficult to give honest information about it. Think of all the cigarette ads that never show cigarettes or even a wisp of smoke. One of the most striking examples of image advertising is the very successful and long-running campaign for Absolut vodka. This campaign focuses on the shape of the bottle and the word "Absolut," as in "Absolut Perfection," which features the bottle with a halo. This campaign has been so successful that a coffee-table book collection of the ads published just in time for Christmas . . . sold over 150,000 copies. Collecting Absolut ads is now a common pastime for elementary-school children, who swap them like baseball cards.

Adbusters magazine often parodies the Absolut ads. One such parody, headlined "Absolut Nonsense," pictures a bottle with the following copy on the label: "This superb marketing scheme has been carefully distilled for smoothness. . . . Although no one pays attention to advertising, after one year of this campaign, sales soared from 54,000 cases to 2.4 million cases." Since all vodka is essentially the same, all the campaign can sell us is image. . . .

The Corruption of Relationships

. . . Taken individually, . . . ads are silly, sometimes funny, certainly nothing to worry about. But cumulatively they create a climate of cynicism and alienation that is poisonous to relationships. Many people end up feeling romantic about material objects

yet deeply cynical about other human beings. In a society in which one of two marriages ends in divorce, we are offered constancy through our products. As one ad
says, "Some people need only one man. Or one woman. Or one watch." Okay, so we
can't be monogamous—at least we can be faithful to our watches. Because of the
pervasiveness of this kind of advertising message, we learn from childhood that it is
far safer to make a commitment to a product than to a person, far easier to be loyal
to a brand. Ad after ad portrays our real lives and relationships as dull and ordinary,
and commitment to human beings as something to be avoided.

"Who says guys are afraid of commitment? He's had the same backpack for
years," states an ad that features photographs of a young man with several different women, but always the same backpack. The young women are the accessories,
the backpack is the intimate partner. The copy assures the reader that the backpack "comes with a lifetime guarantee not to rip, tear, break, or ask for a ring." You
know, people are so annoying—they want promises, permanence. Such a drag. So
much easier to snuggle up with your undemanding backpack. . . .

If a guy does get roped into marriage, he can always drown his sorrows in booze.
"Hang on to your spirit," says an ad for Southern Comfort, which features an anxious
groom with a hangman's rope around his neck. The bride is smiling, completely
oblivious to the true feelings of this moron she is so, so lucky to marry. Another ad in
this campaign pictures a man accompanying a woman on a shopping expedition. In
addition to being laden with packages, he has a ball and chain around his ankle. . . .

Crazy for Cars

. . . Until recently the car was always symbolized as a woman. A Toyota Celica is
described as having "vivacious curves, a shimmering body and . . . striking good
looks." And Mercedes-Benz ran an ad featuring a photo of Marilyn Monroe's face,
with the Mercedes-Benz symbol replacing her famous mole. No words were necessary. It was clear from the image that the car and the sex goddess were somehow
one and the same. Sales increased by 35 percent. Vespa, the Italian motorcycle,
also exploited Monroe in an ad entitled "Marilyn Vespoe," which features the
motorcycle on pink satin sheets.

This is taken a step further in a newspaper ad for Autique stores in which the
car is a nude woman "accessorized" with automobile parts, such as tires and head-
lights. The objectification of the woman is particularly chilling in this ad, as she is
barely human. There is also implicit violence in the metal chain around her neck,
her extreme passivity, the blood-red background. Once again, lovers are things
and things are lovers.

Of course, this has been going on a long time. Ever since Vance Packard wrote
The Hidden Persuaders, we've known that cars are often men's symbolic mistresses.
Sometimes the copy for car ads reads like pornography. A Subaru ad from the 1970s,
headlined "Like a Spirited Woman Who Yearns to Be Tamed," says, "Sleek. Agile. The
sculptured lines of the one-piece body invite you in . . . Go to her. . . . Surround yourself with the lushness of her interior appointments. . . . Now. Turn her on." . . .

Falling in Love with Food

. . . Advertisers spend a lot of money on psychological research. They know that many people, especially women, use food to help us deal with loneliness and disappointment and also as a way to connect. The ads play on this. . . .

One of the most erotic commercials I have ever seen is a British one (no doubt too racy for America) that features a man and a woman making love while feeding each other something. Because the commercial is shot with infrared film, we see only their shapes and intense patterns of red and yellow and blue. "Make Yourself Comfortable" is playing on the record player. They lick some substance off each other's bodies, while an elderly man below bangs on the ceiling with a broomstick, shouting "Mr. Rogers" (thus playing on the British slang "to roger," meaning to have intercourse, and also implying that the man is single and that this is a tryst, not a marriage). At the very end of the commercial we see that the couple's erotic toy is a pint of Häagen-Dazs ice cream. "Dedicated to pleasure" is the slogan.

This campaign ran in print too, with erotic black and white photographs by French photographer Jeanloup Sieff. In just a few months after the campaign broke in upscale magazines such as *Tatler* and *Vogue*, sales of Häagen-Dazs in Great Britain rose 400 percent. This spectacular success indicates that advertisers do indeed sometimes know what they are doing.

Of course, we are not stupid. We don't for a minute believe that we're actually going to improve our relationships with ice cream or pasta sauce. But these ads do contribute to a cultural climate in which relationships are constantly trivialized and we are encouraged to connect via consumption. An obsession with food interferes with real relationships just as any other obsession does, yet food advertising often normalizes and glamorizes such an obsession. . . .

Another problematic aspect of the cumulative impact of food advertising is that many ads normalize and glamorize harmful and often dangerous attitudes toward food and eating. And we suffer drastically as a culture from the negative consequences of these attitudes. About eighty million Americans are clinically obese, and nearly three out of four are overweight. Indeed, in a culture seemingly obsessed with thinness and fitness. Americans are fatter than ever and fatter than people in most other cultures. Eight million Americans suffer from an eating disorder and as many as 10 percent of all college-age women are bulimic. Eating disorders are the third most common chronic illness among females. In fact, they are so common it really is misleading to refer to them as "disorders" More accurately, they are a common way that women cope with the difficulties in their lives and with the cultural contradictions involving food and eating. Few of us aren't touched by some kind of problem with food (not to mention the thirty million at risk for hunger and malnutrition).

There are many reasons for these problems, ranging from the decrease in physical education in our schools to our use of the automobile to the development of the TV remote control to fear of crime, which keeps people indoors, often in front of the television set with its blaring litany of commercials for junk food and diet products. American children see over ten thousand commercials for food on television each year. Ninety-five percent are for four food groups: soft drinks, candy, fast food, and sugar-coated cereal. There's a lot of money at stake: Americans spend an estimated $14 billion a year on snack foods, $15 billion on chocolate, and $86 billion on fast food restaurants.

The commercials are only one part of the problem, but they are a significant part. Just as alcohol ads teach us that drinking leads inevitably to good times, great sex, athletic prowess, and success, without any risks or negative consequences whatsoever, so do the food ads associate eating and overeating with only good things. The negative consequences are obliterated. Indeed, in order to maximize their profits, the junk food and the diet industries need to normalize and glamorize disordered and destructive attitudes toward food and eating. . . .

The success of the diet industry primarily depends on women being dissatisfied with their bodies. Many people say that advertising simply reflects the society. But certainly the body images of women that advertising reflects today are as distorted as the reflections in a funhouse mirror. Since advertising cashes in on women's body-hatred and distorted self-images, it sometimes deliberately promotes such distortion. A yogurt ad says, "How to go from seeing yourself like this . . . to seeing yourself like this," and portrays the "before" image with a pear. In fact, it is perfectly normal for a woman to be pear-shaped. Many more women have pear-shaped bodies than have the V-shaped bodies of the models, but we don't see them in the media. Instead, we get the message that this shape is unacceptable.

The use of body doubles in films and commercials makes it even less likely that we'll see real women's bodies. A photograph of Julia Roberts and Richard Gere that was widely used to advertise the hit film *Pretty Woman* featured Julia Roberts's head but not her body. Apparently, even *her* body wasn't good enough or thin enough to be in the ad. A body double was also used for Roberts when she was nude or partially nude in the film. This is common practice in the industry. Not surprisingly, at least 85 percent of body doubles have breast implants.

Unfortunately, the obsession with thinness is becoming a problem throughout the developed world. "Le diete S.O.S.," the title of an article featured on the cover of an Italian magazine, is understood in many languages. Italy used to be a country where voluptuous women could still feel desirable, but the model on the cover shown measuring her waist is extremely thin by any standards.

The dieter, even more than the addict, is the ideal consumer. She (most dieters are women) will spend a lot on food and then spend even more to lose weight—and the cycle never stops. Sales of low-fat frozen yogurt soar, but so do sales of high-fat premium ice cream. The diet industry, which includes diet drugs and other products, diet workshops and books, health spas, and more, has tripled in recent years, increasing from a $10 billion to a $36 billion-a-year industry. No one loses, especially the dieter (although she doesn't win either). . . .

Cutting Girls Down to Size

. . . Although troubled young women are especially vulnerable, these messages affect all girls. A researcher at Brigham and Women's Hospital in Boston found that the more frequently girls read magazines, the more likely they were to diet and to feel that magazines influence their ideal body shape. Nearly half reported wanting to lose weight because of a magazine picture (but only 29 percent were actually overweight). Studies at Stanford University and the University of Massachusetts found that about 70 percent of college women say they feel worse about their own looks after reading women's magazines. Another study, this one of 350 young men and women, found that a preoccupation with one's appearance takes a toll on mental health. Women scored much higher than men on what the researchers called "self-objectification." This tendency to view one's body from the outside in—regarding physical attractiveness, sex appeal, measurements, and weight as more central to one's physical identity than health, strength, energy level, coordination, or fitness—has many harmful effects, including diminished mental performance, increased feelings of shame and anxiety, depression, sexual dysfunction, and the development of eating disorders.

These images of women seem to affect men most strikingly by influencing how they judge the real women in their lives. Male college students who viewed just one episode of *Charlie's Angels*, the hit television show of the 1970s that featured three beautiful women, were harsher in their evaluations of the attractiveness of potential dates than were males who had not seen the episode. In another study, male college students shown centerfolds from *Playboy* and *Penthouse* were more likely to find their own girlfriends less sexually attractive. . . .

Some studies have found that from 40 to 80 percent of fourth-grade girls are dieting. Today at least one-third of twelve- to thirteen-year-old girls are actively trying to lose weight by dieting, vomiting, using laxatives, or taking diet pills. One survey found that 63 percent of high-school girls were on diets, compared with only 16 percent of men. And a survey in Massachusetts found that the single largest group of high-school students considering or attempting suicide are girls who feel they are overweight. Imagine. Girls made to feel so terrible about themselves that they would rather be dead than fat. This wouldn't be happening, of course, if it weren't for our last "socially acceptable" prejudice—weightism. Fat children are ostracized and reduced from the moment they enter school, and fat adults, women in particular, are subjected to public contempt and scorn. This strikes terror into the hearts of all women, many of whom, unfortunately, identify with the oppressor and become vicious to themselves and each other.

No wonder it is hard to find a woman, especially a young woman, in America today who has a truly healthy attitude toward her body and toward food. . . .

The influence of the media is strikingly illustrated in a recent study that found a sharp rise in eating disorders among young women in Fiji soon after the introduction of television to the culture. Before television was available, there was little talk of dieting in Fiji. "You've gained weight" was a traditional compliment and "going thin" the sign of a problem. In 1995 television came to the island. Within three years, the number of teenagers at risk for eating disorders more than doubled, 74 percent of the teens in the study said they felt "too big or too fat," and 62 percent said they had dieted in the past month. Of course, this doesn't prove a direct causal link between television and eating disorders. Fiji is a culture in transition in many ways. However, it seems more than coincidental that the Fiji girls who were heavy viewers of television were 50 percent more likely to describe themselves as fat and 30 percent more likely to diet than those girls who watched television less frequently. As Ellen Goodman says. "The big success story of our entertainment industry is our ability to export insecurity. We can make any woman anywhere feel perfectly rotten about her shape." . . .

"Make a statement without saying a word," says an ad for perfume. And indeed this is one of the primary messages of the culture to adolescent girls. "The silence of a look can reveal more than words," says another perfume ad, this one featuring a woman lying on her back. "More than words can say," says yet another perfume ad, and a clothing ad says, "Classic is speaking your mind (without saying a word)." An ad for lipstick says, "Watch your mouth, young lady," while one for nail polish says, "Let your fingers do the talking," and one for hairspray promises "hair that speaks volumes." In another ad, a young woman's turtleneck is pulled over her mouth. And an ad for a movie soundtrack features a chilling image of a young woman with her lips sewn together.

It is not only the girls themselves who see these images, of course. Their parents and teachers and doctors see them and they influence their sense of how girls should be. A 1999 study done at the University of Michigan found that, beginning in preschool, girls are told to be quiet much more often than boys. Although boys were much noisier than girls, the girls were told to speak softly or to use a "nicer" voice about three times more often. Girls were encouraged to be quiet, small, and physically constrained. The researcher concluded that one of the consequences of this socialization is that girls grow into women afraid to speak up for themselves or to use their voices to protect themselves from a variety of dangers. . . .

Alcohol and Rebellion

The number-one illegal drug in America is . . . beer. Because beer is the drug of choice for young people. Although we hear a lot about marijuana, cocaine, and heroin, the truth is our children are at much greater risk from alcohol than from these other drugs. A 1999 study found that almost 8 percent of nine-year-olds are already drinking beer. Fifteen percent of eighth-graders and 30 percent of twelfth-graders are binge drinkers, which means they've had five or more drinks at one sitting within the past two weeks. In college, the percentage of binge drinkers rises to 45 percent. . . .

Anheuser-Busch, the largest brewer in the world and the maker of Budweiser, supplies almost one-fourth of all the alcohol that Americans consume and spends over a quarter of a billion dollars a year on advertising and promotion. Of course, they deny that this advertising attracts young people. According to one vice-president, "We do not target our advertising toward young people. Period." A look at some of their ads reveals a different story. . . .

Do these [beer] ads affect children? Children certainly notice them: the Budweiser frog campaign is the most popular of all among children over the age of six—more popular than commercials for McDonald's, Pepsi, or Nike. According to a 1996 survey by the Center on Alcohol Advertising, almost as many children between the ages of nine and eleven know that frogs say "Budweiser" (73 percent) as know that Bugs Bunny says "What's up, Doc?" (80 percent). Laurie Leiber, the center's director, said, "After a single year of advertising, the Budweiser frogs have assumed a friendly place in our children's psyches between Bugs Bunny and Smokey the Bear."

A survey of eight- to twelve-year-olds in Washington, D.C., found that students could name more brands of beer than they could U.S. presidents. . . .

The brewers broadcast their ads on cable television during youth viewing hours, and on shows such as *Beavis and Butthead*, whose audiences are predominantly underage. Despite their denials, leading brewers have run commercials on MTV during time periods when half or more of the audience was below the legal drinking age. Both Budweiser and Miller, along with makers of distilled spirits, sponsor the "extreme" sports that especially appeal to young people, such as snowboarding, mountain biking, and in-line skating, and sell sports paraphernalia with the brand logo through marketing campaigns like Budweiser's "Buy the Beer, Get the Gear." According to a Jose Cuervo tequila spokesperson, "It's essential to our brand image to sponsor the boldest, most surprising stuff because our audience is young and rebellious and that's how they know us."

The alcohol industry also reaches young people via magazines such as *Spin* and *Allure*, with almost half of their readers under twenty-one, and via flashy Websites on the Internet. In 1998 the Center for Media Education found that 82 percent of beer Websites and 72 percent of distilled spirits sites used techniques that are particularly attractive to underage audiences (compared with only 10 percent of wine sites). . . .

Rage and Rebellion in Cigarette Advertising

. . . Highly addictive, the damage they do to health has been documented by over sixty thousand research studies. Cigarettes kill more Americans each year than alcohol, cocaine, heroin, fires, car crashes, homicide, suicide, and AIDS *combined*. Indeed, smoking is the single largest preventable cause of death in America (and, according to former surgeon general C. Everett Koop, the most important public health issue of our time). Yet we sell cigarettes in pharmacies, we sell them in candy stores to children. Over one thousand people die every day due to cigarette-related diseases, in the United States alone. In the twentieth century, tobacco has killed more people than war. Based on current trends, by the year 2030, the worldwide death toll will rise to ten million per year, with 70 percent occurring in developing countries. . . .

In spite of these appalling statistics, smoking has been promoted for decades by the most massive marketing campaign ever dedicated to a single product. While spending over five billion dollars a year in the United States alone on advertising and promotion, the tobacco industry ironically denies that this advertising has any effect. It insists that it does not target nonsmokers or young people and that the whole point of all that advertising is simply to get smokers to switch brands. Only 10 percent of the nation's fifty-five million smokers switch brands every year. It is obvious that the tobacco industry needs to aggressively recruit new smokers to replace those who die or quit. When you're selling a product that kills people, you've got a problem. Your best customers die.

Nowhere is the distorted perspective of advertising, a perspective that manages to screen out almost all unpleasant reality except the strictly personal (such as bad breath, facial hair, and fat), more obvious than in the cigarette ads. The contradictions abound. Macho men apparently owe their freedom and independence, indeed their very masculinity, to their Marlboros, although the evidence is clear that cigarettes are linked with impotence, lower testosterone count, and sterility.

In fact, Marlboros began as a cigarette designed for women. It came with a red tip so the smoker's lipstick wouldn't show, and the slogan was "Cherry tips to match your ruby lips." It didn't take long for Philip Morris, makers of Marlboro, to realize that this wasn't a good idea. A woman will most often freely use a product designed for men, but God forbid that a man would ever use a product designed for women. How many men smoke Virginia Slims? The group with higher status rarely wants to use a product designed for a lower-status group. So in 1956 Marlboro was repositioned as the ultimate man's cigarette, with the image of the cowboy. This campaign has been phenomenally successful. Almost one-third of American smokers smoke Marlboros, the most heavily advertised cigarette in the world, and the Marlboro Man was recently named by *Advertising Age* as the top advertising icon of the century. At least one writer for the magazine mentioned the irony of a "supposed symbol of rugged independence" really being a "symbol of enslavement to an addictive drug." . . .

A 1999 study found that more than two-thirds of the fifty G-rated animated films released by major studios during the past sixty years portray alcohol or tobacco use without any clear messages of negative health effects. Current research suggests that tobacco advertising has two major effects: It creates the perception that more people smoke than actually do and it makes smoking look cool. It seems that the rest of the media help further these perceptions.

One of the most successful campaigns in the history of advertising was the one for Camel cigarettes that ran from 1988 until 1997. Just about everyone remembers this campaign, which featured a cartoon camel doing lots of "cool" things, like playing in a rock band, shooting pool, and riding a motorcycle. This camel, known as Old Joe, is now as recognizable to six-year-olds as is Mickey Mouse. One-third of all three-year-olds can link him with cigarettes.

Before the advent of this campaign, Camels did not especially appeal to young people. Of smokers under the age of eighteen, less than 1 percent smoked who Camels. Soon after the introduction of Joe Camel, the percentage of teen smokers who smoked Camels sky-rocketed to 33 percent. This certainly says something about the power of advertising. . . .

Addiction as a Relationship

. . . No wonder advertising often normalizes disordered attitudes and even symptoms of addiction. The most obvious example is obsession. Alcohol, cigarettes, food, sex are at the center of the ads just as they are at the center of the addict's life. The ads imply, for example, that alcohol is an appropriate adjunct to almost every activity, from making love to white-water canoeing. They also rationalize drinking at any time and for any reason, just as the alcoholic does. "A full day of shopping?" asks an ad for scotch, "Now that calls for a drink." Another features a bottle of champagne on ice with the tagline "The meter maid actually bought your story." I recently passed two billboards within a block of each other. The first offered beer as a reward and celebration because "Life is good." The second offered tequila as a consolation because "Life is harsh." Whatever one's state of mind, whatever one's circumstances, ads tell us that the appropriate response is to drink. Alcoholics are all too eager to believe this.

The wine industry has recently begun a campaign designed to deflate its special-occasion-only image. One commercial says, "You're actually home watching TV? This is a special occasion." A print ad says, "It is well to remember that there are five reasons for drinking: the arrival of a friend; one's present or future thirst; the excellence of the wine; or any other reason." And an ad aimed at the woman at home, alone except for her children says, "This is the wine you sip between the evening news, spilled milk, & 'How was your day?'" Another in the same campaign says, "The while-you-set-the-table wine that usually gets invited to dinner," and describes the product as "a wine you drink just about every day." Of course, drinking alone just about every day is both a sign of and a route to trouble with alcohol—but in this campaign it is presented as just another innocuous part of one's daily routine. The beer commercials that are indistinguishable from soft-drink commercials have a similar effect. This isn't a drug, they seem to say, this is a harmless beverage that you can indulge in any time without consequences.

Progression is also one of the hallmarks of addiction. Most people begin the addictive process gradually—one or two drinks, a few cigarettes a day, a dish of ice cream, a joint, one hit of cocaine. Gradually they need more of the substance in order to achieve the same effect. Eventually they feel they cannot live without it and it becomes the center of their lives.

A classic example of normalizing progression occurred in a national beer campaign several years ago. In the late 1970s the slogan for Michelob was "Holidays were made for Michelob." A year or so later it became "Weekends were made for Michelob." It must have been apparent to the makers of Michelob that they would not make nearly enough money if people only drank their product on weekends, so the next slogan was "Put a little weekend in your week." Eventually the slogan became "The night belongs to Michelob." . . .

Of course, alcohol has long been advertised to men as a way to seduce women. An ad for Cherry Kijafa from the 1970s features a virginal young woman dressed entirely in white and the headline "Put a little cherry in your life." Such double entendres abound, ranging from a cocktail called "Sex on the Beach" to an ad featuring a young man dressed as a fencer declaring, "I'm as sure of myself on each thrust as I am when choosing my scotch." In a series of suggestive print and television ads in the 1980s, Billy Dee Williams promised that Colt 45 malt liquor "works every time." Years later a radio ad, also for malt liquor and also targeting young African-American men, said, "Grab a six-pack and get your girl in the mood quicker. Get your jimmy thicker with St. Ides malt liquor." Imagine—our kids are growing up in this kind of environment and some people think it's enough to tell them to "just say no" to sex. "Get your jimmy thicker" but keep it in your pants? . . .

One of the most chilling commercials I've ever seen is a 1999 one for Michelob. It opens with an African-American man and woman in bed, clearly just after making love. A fire is blazing and romantic music is playing. "Baby, do you love me?" the woman asks. "Of course I do," the man replies. "What do you love about me most?" she asks. The man looks thoughtful, "Well, Michelob, I love you more than life itself." "What did you call me?" the woman asks indignantly. "I called you Theresa," he replies. "No, you did not," she says, leaping from the bed, "You just called me Michelob. I'm outta here." "Wait, wait," the man says. "What?" she asks. "While you're up," the man says, "could you get me a Michelob?" On the surface, this commercial is intended to be funny, of course. But on a deeper level, and I believe intentionally on the part of the advertisers, it is meant to normalize and trivialize a symptom of alcoholism. The terrible truth is that alcoholics do love alcohol more than the people in their lives and indeed more than life itself. . . .

Advertising and Violence

. . . "Wear it out and make it scream," says a jeans ad portraying a man sliding his hands under a woman's transparent blouse. This could be a seduction, but it could as easily be an attack. Although the ad that ran in the Czech version of *Elle* portraying three men attacking a woman seems unambiguous, the terrifying image is being used to sell jeans *to women*. So someone must think that women would find this image compelling or attractive. Why would we? Perhaps it is simply designed to get our attention, by shocking us and by arousing unconscious anxiety. Or perhaps the intent is more subtle and it is designed to play into the fantasies of domination and even rape that some women use in order to maintain an illusion of being in control (we are the ones having the fantasies, after all, we are the directors).

A camera ad features a woman's torso wrapped in plastic, her hands tied behind her back. A smiling woman in a lipstick ad has a padlocked chain around her neck. An ad for MTV shows a vulnerable young woman, her breasts exposed, and the simple copy "Bitch." A perfume ad features a man shadowboxing with what seems to be a woman.

Sometimes women are shown dead or in the process of being killed. "Great hair never dies," says an ad featuring a female corpse lying on a bed, her breasts exposed. An ad in the Italian version of *Vogue* shows a man aiming a gun at a nude woman wrapped in plastic, a leather briefcase covering her face. And an ad for Bitch skateboards, for God's sake, shows a cartoon version of a similar scene, this time clearly targeting young people. We believe we are not affected by these images, but most of us experience visceral shock when we pay conscious attention to them. Could they be any less shocking to us on an unconscious level?

Discussion Questions

1. Kilbourne writes, "People who feel empty make great consumers." In what sense do products—food, clothing, alcohol—fill needs of "empty consumers"? How do you notice commercials aimed at creating this feeling of emptiness?

2. Do you feel slighted in any way once you realize how much research (biological, psychological, sociological) is involved in creating commercials aimed to get you to purchase something?

3. Knowledge is often considered neutral, but what one does with it is not. In what ways are advertisers morally responsible for attempting to create desires in consumers? More specifically:

   a. desires for harmful products such as alcohol and cigarettes

   b. attitudes and desires relating to body image, the opposite sex, food, etc.

   Are they morally responsible for their portrayal of women (and men)? Or is this still the responsibility of the consumer? What about child consumers?

4. Think of how advertising has affected you. Were you aware of this before reading this piece and more closely examining the issue?

5. Do you wear any clothes that prominently display a brand name or logo? If so, why? What role does the brand have when you purchase an item? What do particular brands represent? Would you pay more for a brand name item when an equally suitable item is available for less? Why/why not?

6. Kilbourne writes that advertisers "create artificial needs in order to sell unnecessary products." What artificial needs do you have (or are you aware of)? How were they created? What does she mean here?

7. How seriously do you take Kilbourne's argument? Do you agree with her analysis of the ads she mentions specifically? Pay attention to the advertisements you see and hear after reading this piece. Do you notice any trends? Notice how many ads you are exposed to daily—billboards, sponsors of sporting events, radio, etc. Are you surprised at what you realized once you became conscious of this?

Minds, Brains, and Programs

John Searle

(For a biographical sketch of John Searle, see earlier selection.)

In this article published in *Behavioral and Brain Sciences*, John Searle presents an argument against "Strong Artificial Intelligence." In doing so, he explores the meaning of a "machine," what types of machines exist, and the role of *programs* in a computer. This article highlights one of the most well-known "thought experiments" (referred to by Searle here as *Gedankenexperiment* in reference to Hans Ørsted, who first used the term meaning "experiment conducted in the thoughts"): "The Chinese Room." Along with defending his own position, he also addresses numerous responses from the academic community and responds to them as well.

Reading Questions

1. Explain the difference between what Searle calls "'strong' AI" and "'weak' AI."
2. Why do some argue that Schank's machine supports strong AI?
3. Explain the Chinese Room example. What conclusions does Searle draw? How does he use this to address the two claims made by strong AI supporters with regard to Schank's machine? What important factor is there in the English case as opposed to the Chinese case?
4. What explanation does Searle provide as to why we tend to assign mental states to our cars, computers, etc.? What is "intentionality," and how is it relevant here?
5. Briefly summarize each of the responses to Searle as well as Searle's rejoinder.
6. How does Searle answer the question, "Could a machine think?" What is the relevance of simulations? How does he compare the brain with a digital computer?
7. Explain the difference between syntax and semantics and their relevance in Searle's discussion.
8. How does dualism factor into Searle's discussion?

What psychological and philosophical significance should we attach to recent efforts at computer simulations of human cognitive capacities? In answering this question, I find it useful to distinguish what I will call "strong" AI from "weak" or "cautious" AI (artificial intelligence). According to weak AI, the principal value of the computer in the study of the mind is that it gives us a very powerful tool. For example, it enables us to formulate and test hypotheses in a more rigorous and precise fashion. But according to strong AI, the computer is not merely a tool in

Source: Excerpts from "Minds, Brains, and Programs" in *Behavioral and Brain Sciences*, Vol. 3, 1980, pp. 417–424. Reprinted with the permission of Cambridge University Press and the author.

the study of the mind; rather, the appropriately programmed computer really is a mind, in the sense that computers given the right programs can be literally said to *understand* and have other cognitive states. In strong AI, because the programmed computer has cognitive states, the programs are not mere tools that enable us to test psychological explanations; rather, the programs are themselves the explanations.

I have no objection to the claims of weak AI, at least as far as this article is concerned. My discussion here will be directed at the claims I have defined as those of strong AI, specifically the claim that the appropriately programmed computer literally has cognitive states and that the programs thereby explain human cognition. When I hereafter refer to AI, I have in mind the strong version, as expressed by these two claims. . . .

Very briefly, and leaving out the various details, one can describe [Roger] Schank's program as follows: The aim of the program is to simulate the human ability to understand stories. It is characteristic of human beings' story-understanding capacity that they can answer questions about the story even though the information that they give was never explicitly stated in the story. Thus, for example, suppose you are given the following story: "A man went into a restaurant and ordered a hamburger. When the hamburger arrived it was burned to a crisp, and the man stormed out of the restaurant angrily, without paying for the hamburger or leaving a tip." Now, if you are asked "Did the man eat the hamburger?" you will presumably answer, "No, he did not." Similarly, if you are given the following story: "A man went into a restaurant and ordered a hamburger; when the hamburger came he was very pleased with it; and as he left the restaurant he gave the waitress a large tip before paying his bill," and you are asked the question, "Did the man eat the hamburger?" you will presumably answer, "Yes, he ate the hamburger." Now Schank's machines can similarly answer, questions about restaurants in this fashion. To do this, they have a "representation" of the sort of information that human beings have about restaurants, which enables them to answer such questions as those above, given these sorts of stories. When the machine is given the story and then asked the question, the machine will print out answers of the sort that we would expect human beings to give if told similar stories. Partisans of strong AI claim that in this question and answer sequence the machine is not only simulating a human ability but also (1) that the machine can literally be said to *understand* the story and provide the answers to questions, and (2) that what the machine and its program do *explains* the human ability to understand the story and answer questions about it.

Both claims seem to me to be totally unsupported by Schank's work, as I will attempt to show in what follows.

One way to test any theory of the mind is to ask oneself what it would be like if my mind actually worked on the principles that the theory says all minds work on. Let us apply this test to the Schank program with the following *Gedankenexperiment*. Suppose that I'm locked in a room and given a large batch of Chinese writing. Suppose furthermore (as is indeed the case) that I know no

Chinese, either written or spoken, and that I'm not even confident that I could recognize Chinese writing as Chinese writing distinct from, say, Japanese writing or meaningless squiggles. To me, Chinese writing is just so many meaningless squiggles. Now suppose further that after this first batch of Chinese writing I am given a second batch of Chinese script together with a set of rules for correlating the second batch with the first batch. The rules are in English, and I understand these rules as well as any other native speaker of English. They enable me to correlate one set of formal symbols with another set of formal symbols, and all that "formal" means here is that I can identify the symbols entirely by their shapes. Now suppose also that I am given a third batch of Chinese symbols together with some instructions, again in English, that enable me to correlate elements of this third batch with the first two batches, and these rules instruct me how to give back certain Chinese symbols with certain sorts of shapes in response to certain sorts of shapes given me in the third batch. Unknown to me, the people who are giving me all of these symbols call the first batch a "script," they call the second batch a "story," and they call the third batch "questions." Furthermore, they call the symbols I give them back in response to the third batch "answers to the questions," and the set of rules in English that they gave me, they call the "program." Now just to complicate the story a little, imagine that these people also give me stories in English, which I understand, and they then ask me questions in English about these stories, and I give them back answers in English. Suppose also that after a while I get so good at following the instructions for manipulating the Chinese symbols and the programmers get so good at writing the programs that from the external point of view—that is, from the point of view of somebody outside the room in which I am locked—my answers to the questions are absolutely indistinguishable from those of native Chinese speakers. Nobody just looking at my answers can tell that I don't speak a word of Chinese. Let us also suppose that my answers to the English questions are, as they no doubt would be, indistinguishable from those of other native English speakers, for the simple reason that I am a native English speaker. From the external point of view—from the point of view of someone reading my "answers"—the answers to the Chinese questions and the English questions are equally good. But in the Chinese case, unlike the English case, I produce the answers by manipulating uninterpreted formal symbols. As far as the Chinese is concerned, I simply behave like a computer; I perform computational operations on formally specified elements. For the purposes of the Chinese, I am simply an instantiation of the computer program.

Now the claims made by strong AI are that the programmed computer understands the stories and that the program in some sense explains human understanding. But we are now in a position to examine these claims in light of our thought experiment.

(1) As regards the first claim, it seems to me quite obvious in the example that I do not understand a word of the Chinese stories. I have inputs and outputs that are indistinguishable from those of the native Chinese speaker, and I can have any formal program you like, but I still understand nothing. For the same reasons,

Schank's computer understands nothing of any stories, whether in Chinese, English, or whatever, since in the Chinese case the computer is me, and in cases where the computer is not me, the computer has nothing more than I have in the case where I understand nothing.

(2) As regards the second claim, that the program explains human understanding, we can see that the computer and its program do not provide sufficient conditions of understanding since the computer and the program are functioning, and there is no understanding. But does it even provide a necessary condition or a significant contribution to understanding? One of the claims made by the supporters of strong AI is that when I understand a story in English, what I am doing is exactly the same—or perhaps more of the same—as what I was doing in manipulating the Chinese symbols. It is simply more formal symbol manipulation that distinguishes the case in English, where I do understand, from the case in Chinese, where I don't. I have not demonstrated that this claim is false, but it would certainly appear an incredible claim in the example. Such plausibility as the claim has derives from the supposition that we can construct a program that will have the same inputs and outputs as native speakers, and in addition we assume that speakers have some level of description where they are also instantiations of a program. On the basis of these two assumptions we assume that even if Schank's program isn't the whole story about understanding, it may be part of the story. Well, I suppose that is an empirical possibility, but not the slightest reason has so far been given to believe that it is true, since what is suggested—though certainly not demonstrated—by the example is that the computer program is simply irrelevant to my understanding of the story. In the Chinese case I have everything that artificial intelligence can put into me by way of a program, and I understand nothing; in the English case I understand everything, and there is so far no reason at all to suppose that my understanding has anything to do with computer programs, that is, with computational operations on purely formally specified elements. As long as the program is defined in terms of computational operations on purely formally defined elements, what the example suggests is that these by themselves have no interesting connection with understanding. They are certainly not sufficient conditions, and not the slightest reason has been given to suppose that they are necessary conditions or even that they make a significant contribution to understanding. Notice that the force of the argument is not simply that different machines can have the same input and output while operating on different formal principles—that is not the point at all. Rather, whatever purely formal principles you put into the computer, they will not be sufficient for understanding, since a human will be able to follow the formal principles without understanding anything. No reason whatever has been offered to suppose that such principles are necessary or even contributory, since no reason has been given to suppose that when I understand English I am operating with any formal program at all.

Well, then, what is it that I have in the case of the English sentences that I do not have in the case of the Chinese sentences? The obvious answer is that I know what the former mean, while I haven't the faintest idea what the latter mean. But in what does this consist and why couldn't we give it to a machine, whatever it is? I will return to this question later, but first I want to continue with the example.

I have had the occasions to present this example to several workers in artificial intelligence, and, interestingly, they do not seem to agree on what the proper reply to it is. I get a surprising variety of replies, and in what follows I will consider the most common of these (specified along with their geographic origins).

But first I want to block some common misunderstandings about "understanding": In many of these discussions one finds a lot of fancy footwork about the word "understanding." My critics point out that there are many different degrees of understanding; that "understanding" is not a simple two-place predicate; that there are even different kinds and levels of understanding, and often the law of excluded middle doesn't even apply in a straightforward way to statements of the form "x understands y"; that in many cases it is a matter for decision and not a simple matter of fact whether x understands y; and so on. To all of these points I want to say: of course, of course. But they have nothing to do with the points at issue. There are clear cases in which "understanding" literally applies and clear cases in which it does not apply; and these two sorts of cases are all I need for this argument.[2] I understand stories in English; to a lesser degree I can understand stories in French; to a still lesser degree, stories in German; and in Chinese, not at all. My car and my adding machine, on the other hand, understand nothing: They are not in that line of business. We often attribute "understanding" and other cognitive predicates by metaphor and analogy to cars, adding machines, and other artifacts, but nothing is proved by such attributions. We say, "The door *knows* when to open because of its photoelectric cell," "The adding machine *knows how* (*understands how*, is *able*) to do addition and subtraction but not division," and "The thermostat *perceives* changes in the temperature." The reason we make these attributions is quite interesting, and it has to do with the fact that in artifacts we extend our own intentionality;[3] our tools are extensions of our purposes, and so we find it natural to make metaphorical attributions of intentionality to them; but I take it no philosophical ice is cut by such examples. The sense in which an automatic door "understands instructions" from its photoelectric cell is not at all the sense in which I understand English. If the sense in which Schank's programmed computers understand stories is supposed to be the metaphorical sense in which the door understands, and not the sense in which I understand English, the issue would not be worth discussing. But Newell and Simon (1963) write that the kind of cognition they claim for computers is exactly the same as for human beings. I like the straightforwardness of this claim, and it is the sort of claim I will be considering. I will argue that in the literal sense the programmed computer understands what the car and the adding machine understand, namely, exactly nothing. The computer understanding is not just (like my understanding of German) partial or incomplete; it is zero.

Now to the replies:

(1) The Systems Reply (Berkeley). "While it is true that the individual person who is locked in the room does not understand the story, the fact is that he is merely part of a whole system, and the system does understand the story. The person has a large ledger in front of him in which are written the rules, he has a lot of

scratch paper and pencils for doing calculations, he has 'data banks' of sets of Chinese symbols. Now, understanding is not being ascribed to the mere individual; rather it is being ascribed to this whole system of which he is a part."

My response to the systems theory is quite simple: Let the individual internalize all of these elements of the system. He memorizes the rules in the ledger and the data banks of Chinese symbols, and he does all the calculations in his head. The individual then incorporates the entire system. There isn't anything at all to the system that he does not encompass. We can even get rid of the room and suppose he works outdoors. All the same, he understands nothing of the Chinese, and a fortiori neither does the system, because there isn't anything in the system that isn't in him. If he doesn't understand, then there is no way the system could understand because the system is just a part of him.

Actually I feel somewhat embarrassed to give even this answer to the systems theory because the theory seems to me so implausible to start with. The idea is that while a person doesn't understand Chinese, somehow the *conjunction* of that person and bits of paper might understand Chinese. It is not easy for me to imagine how someone who was not in the grip of an ideology would find the idea at all plausible. Still, I think many people who are committed to the ideology of strong AI will in the end be inclined to say something very much like this. . . .

The systems reply would appear to lead to consequences that are independently absurd. If we are to conclude that there must be cognition in me on the grounds that I have a certain sort of input and output and a program in between, then it looks like all sorts of noncognitive subsystems are going to turn out to be cognitive. For example, there is a level of description at which my stomach does information processing, and it instantiates any number of computer programs, but I take it we do not want to say that it has any understanding. But if we accept the systems reply, then it is hard to see how we avoid saying that stomach, heart, liver, and so on are all understanding subsystems, since there is no principle way to distinguish the motivation for saying the Chinese subsystem understands from saying that the stomach understands. It is, by the way, not an answer to this point to say that the Chinese system has information as input and output and the stomach has food and food products as input and output, since from the point of view of the agent, from my point of view, there is no information in either the food or the Chinese—the Chinese is just so many meaningless squiggles. The information in the Chinese case is solely in the eyes of the programmers and the interpreters, and there is nothing to prevent them from treating the input and output of my digestive organs as information if they so desire. . . .

(2) The Robot Reply (Yale). "Suppose we wrote a different kind of program from Schank's program. Suppose we put a computer inside a robot, and this computer would not just take in formal symbols as input and give out formal symbols as output, but rather would actually operate the robot in such a way that the robot does something very much like perceiving, walking, moving about, hammering nails, eating, drinking—anything you like. The robot would, for example, have a television camera attached to it that enabled it to see, it would have arms

and legs that enabled it to 'act,' and all of this would be controlled by its computer 'brain.' Such a robot would, unlike Schank's computer, have genuine understanding and other mental states."

The first thing to notice about the robot reply is that it tacitly concedes that cognition is not solely a matter of formal symbol manipulation, since this reply adds a set of causal relations with the outside world. But the answer to the robot reply is that the addition of such "perceptual" and "motor" capacities adds nothing by way of understanding, in particular, or intentionality, in general, to Schank's original program. To see this, notice that the same thought experiment applies to the robot case. Suppose that instead of the computer inside the robot, you put me inside the room and, as in the original Chinese case, you give me more Chinese symbols with more instructions in English for matching Chinese symbols to Chinese symbols and feeding back Chinese symbols to the outside. Suppose, unknown to me, some of the Chinese symbols that come to me come from a television camera attached to the robot and other Chinese symbols that I am giving out serve to make the motors inside the robot move the robot's legs or arms. It is important to emphasize that all I am doing is manipulating formal symbols: I know none of these other facts. I am receiving "Information" from the robot's perceptual apparatus and I am giving out "instructions" to its motor apparatus without knowing either of these facts. I am the robot's homunculus, but unlike the traditional homunculus, I don't know what's going on. I don't understand anything except the rules for symbol manipulation. Now in this case I want to say that the robot has no intentional states at all; it is simply moving about as a result of its electrical wiring and its program. And furthermore, by instantiating the program I have no intentional states of the relevant type. All I do is follow formal instructions about manipulating formal symbols.

(3) The Brain Simulator Reply (Berkeley and M.I.T.). "Suppose we design a program that doesn't represent information that we have about the world, such as the information in Schank's scripts, but simulates the actual sequence of neuron firings at the synapses of the brain of a native Chinese speaker when he understands stories in Chinese and gives answers to them. The machine takes in Chinese stories and questions about them as input, it simulates the formal structure of actual Chinese brains in processing these stories, and it gives out Chinese answers as outputs. We can even imagine that the machine operates, not with a single serial program, but with a whole set of programs operating in parallel, in the manner that actual human brains presumably operate when they process natural language. Now surely in such a case we would have to say that the machine understood the stories; and if we refuse to say that, wouldn't we also have to deny that native Chinese speakers understood the stories? At the level of the synapses, what would or could be different about the program of the computer and the program of the Chinese brain?"

Before countering this reply I want to digress to note that it is an odd reply for any partisan of artificial intelligence (or functionalism, etc.) to make: I thought the whole idea of strong AI is that we don't need to know how the brain works to know how the mind works. The basic hypothesis, or so I had supposed, was that there is a level of mental operations consisting of computational processes over formal elements that constitute the essence of the mental and can be realized in all sorts of different brain processes, in the same way that any computer program can be realized in different computer hardwares: On the assumptions of strong AI, the mind is to the brain as the program is to the hardware, and thus we can understand the mind without doing neurophysiology. If we had to know how the brain worked to do AI, we wouldn't bother with AI. However, even getting this close to the operation of the brain is still not sufficient to produce understanding. To see this, imagine that instead of a monolingual man in a room shuffling symbols we have the man operate an elaborate set of water pipes with valves connecting them. When the man receives the Chinese symbols, he looks up in the program, written in English, which valves he has to turn on and off. Each water connection corresponds to a synapse in the Chinese brain, and the whole system is rigged up so that after doing all the right firings, that is after turning on all the right faucets, the Chinese answers pop out at the output end of the series of pipes.

Now where is the understanding in this system? It takes Chinese as input, it simulates the formal structure of the synapses of the Chinese brain, and it gives Chinese as output. But the man certainly doesn't understand Chinese, and neither do the water pipes, and if we are tempted to adopt what I think is the absurd view that somehow the *conjunction* of man *and* water pipes understands, remember that in principle the man can internalize the formal structure of the water pipes and do all the "neuron firings" in his imagination. The problem with the brain simulator is that it is simulating the wrong things about the brain. As long as it simulates only the formal structure of the sequence of neuron firings at the synapses, it won't have simulated what matters about the brain, namely its causal properties, its ability to produce intentional states. And that the formal properties are not sufficient for the causal properties is shown by the water pipe example: We can have all the formal properties carved off from the relevant neurobiological causal properties.

(4) The Combination Reply (Berkeley and Stanford). "While each of the previous three replies might not be completely convincing by itself as a refutation of the Chinese room counterexample, if you take all three together they are collectively much more convincing and even decisive. Imagine a robot with a brain-shaped computer lodged in its cranial cavity, imagine the computer programmed with all the synapses of a human brain, imagine the whole behavior of the robot is indistinguishable from human behavior, and now think of the whole thing as a unified system and not just as a computer with inputs and outputs. Surely in such a case we would have to ascribe intentionality to the system."

I entirely agree that in such a case we would find it rational and indeed irresistible to accept the hypothesis that the robot had intentionality, as long as we knew nothing more about it. Indeed, besides appearance and behavior, the other elements of the combination are really irrelevant. If we could build a robot whose behavior was indistinguishable over a large range from human behavior, we would attribute intentionality to it, pending some reason not to. We wouldn't need to know in advance that its computer brain was a formal analogue of the human brain.

But I really don't see that this is any help to the claims of strong AI, and here's why: According to strong AI, instatitiating a formal program with the right input and output is a sufficient condition of, indeed is constitutive of, intentionality. As Newell (1979) puts it, the essence of the mental is the operation of a physical symbol system. But the attributions of intentionality that we make to the robot in this example have nothing to do with formal programs. They are simply based on the assumption that if the robot looks and behaves sufficiently like us, then we would suppose, until proven otherwise, that it must have mental states like ours that cause and are expressed by its behavior and it must have an inner mechanism capable of producing such mental states. If we knew independently how to account for its behavior without such assumptions we would not attribute intentionality to it, especially if we knew it had a formal program. And this is precisely the point of my earlier reply to objection II. . . .

(5) The Other Minds Reply (Yale). "How do you know that other people understand Chinese or anything else? Only by their behavior. Now the computer can pass the behavioral tests as well as they can (in principle), so if you are going to attribute cognition to other people you must in principle also attribute it to computers."

This objection really is only worth a short reply. The problem in this discussion is not about how I know that other people have cognitive states, but rather what it is that I am attributing to them when I attribute cognitive states to them. The thrust of the argument is that it couldn't be just computational processes and their output because the computational processes and their output can exist without the cognitive state. It is no answer to this argument to feign anesthesia. In "cognitive sciences" one presupposes the reality and knowability of the mental in the same way that in physical sciences one has to presuppose the reality and knowability of physical objects. . . .

By way of concluding I want to try to state some of the general philosophical points implicit in the argument. For clarity I will try to do it in a question-and-answer fashion, and I begin with that old chestnut of a question:

"Could a machine think?" The answer is, obviously, yes. We are precisely such machines.

"Yes, but could an artifact, a man-made machine, think?"

Assuming it is possible to produce artificially a machine with a nervous system, neurons with axons and dendrites, and all the rest of it, sufficiently like ours, again the answer to the question seems to be obviously, yes. If you can exactly duplicate the causes, you could duplicate the effects. And indeed it might be possible to produce consciousness, intentionality, and all the rest of it using some other sorts of chemical principles than those that human beings use. It is, as I said, an empirical question.

"OK, but could a digital computer think?"

If by "digital computer" we mean anything at all that has a level of description where it can correctly be described as the instantiation of a computer program, then again the answer is, of course, yes, since we are the instantiations of any number of computer programs, and we can think.

"But could something think, understand, and so on *solely* in virtue of being a computer with the right sort of program? Could instantiating a program, the right program of course, by itself be a sufficient condition of understanding?"

This I think is the right question to ask, though it is usually confused with one or more of the earlier questions, and the answer to it is no.

"Why not?"

Because the formal symbol manipulations by themselves don't have any intentionality; they are quite meaningless; they aren't even *symbol* manipulations, since the symbols don't symbolize anything. In the linguistic jargon, they have only a syntax but no semantics. Such intentionality as computers appear to have is solely in the minds of those who program them and those who use them, those who send in the input and those who interpret the output.

The aim of the Chinese room example was to try to show this by showing that as soon as we put something into the system that really does have intentionality (a man), and we program him with the formal program, you can see that the formal program carries no additional intentionality. It adds nothing, for example, to a man's ability to understand Chinese. . . .

"Well if programs are in no way constitutive of mental processes, why have so many people believed the converse? That at least needs some explanation."

I don't really know the answer to that one. The idea that computer simulations could be the real thing ought to have seemed suspicious in the first place because the computer isn't confined to simulating mental operations, by any means. No one supposes that computer simulations of a five-alarm fire will burn the neighborhood down or that a computer simulation of a rainstorm will leave us all drenched. Why on earth would anyone suppose that a computer simulation of understanding actually understood anything? It is sometimes said that it would be frightfully hard to get computers to feel pain or fall in love, but love and pain are neither harder nor easier than cognition or anything else. For simulation, all you need is the right input and output and a program in the middle that transforms the former into the latter. That is all the computer has for anything it does. To confuse simulation with duplication is the same mistake, whether it is pain, love, cognition, fires, or rainstorms.

Still, there are several reasons why AI must have seemed—and to many people perhaps still does seem—in some way to reproduce and thereby explain mental phenomena, and I believe we will not succeed in removing these illusions until we have fully exposed the reasons that give rise to them.

First, and perhaps most important, is a confusion about the notion of "information processing": Many people in cognitive science believe that the human brain, with its mind, does something called "information processing," and analogously the computer with its program does information processing; but fires and rainstorms, on the other hand, don't do information processing at all. Thus, though the computer can simulate the formal features of any process whatever, it stands in a special relation to the mind and brain because when the computer is properly programmed, ideally with the same program as the brain, the information processing is identical in the two cases, and this information processing is really the essence of the mental. But the trouble with this argument is that it rests on an ambiguity in the notion of "information." In the sense in which people "process information" when they reflect, say, on problems in arithmetic or when they read and answer questions about stories, the programmed computer does not do "information processing." Rather, what it does is manipulate formal symbols. The fact that the programmer and the interpreter of the computer output use the symbols to stand for objects in the world is totally beyond the scope of the computer. The computer, to repeat, has a syntax but no semantics. Thus, if you type into the computer "2 plus 2 equals?" it will type out "4." But it has no idea that "4" means 4 or that it means anything at all. And the point is not that it lacks some second-order information about the interpretation of its first-order symbols, but rather that its first-order symbols don't have any interpretations as far as the computer is concerned. All the computer has is more symbols. The introduction of the notion of "information processing" therefore produces a dilemma: either we construe the notion of "information processing" in such a way that it implies intentionality as part of the process or we don't. If the former, then the programmed computer does not do information processing, it only manipulates formal symbols. If the latter, then, though the computer does information processing, it is only doing so in the sense in which adding machines, typewriters, stomachs, thermostats, rainstorms, and hurricanes do information processing; namely, they have a level of description at which we can describe them as taking information in at one end, transforming it, and producing information as output. But in this case it is up to outside observers to interpret the input and output as information in the ordinary sense. And no similarity is established between the computer and the brain in terms of any similarity of information processing.

Second, in much of AI there is a residual behaviorism or operationalism. Since appropriately programmed computers can have input-output patterns similar to those of human beings, we are tempted to postulate mental states in the computer similar to human mental states. But once we see that it is both conceptually and empirically possible for a system to have human capacities in some realm without having any intentionality at all, we should be able to overcome this impulse. My desk adding machine has calculating capacities, but no intentionality, and in this paper I have tried to show that a system could have input and output capabilities that duplicated those of a native Chinese speaker and still not understand Chinese, regardless of how it was programmed. The Turing test is typical of the tradition in being unashamedly behavioristic and operationalistic, and I believe that if AI workers totally repudiated behaviorism and operationalism much of the confusion between simulation and duplication would be eliminated.

Third, this residual operationalism is joined to a residual form of dualism; indeed strong AI only makes sense given the dualistic assumption that, where the mind is concerned, the brain doesn't matter. In strong AI (and in functionalism, as well) what matters are programs, and programs are independent of their realization in machines; indeed, as far as AI is concerned, the same program could be realized by an electronic machine, a Cartesian mental substance, or a Hegelian world spirit. The single most surprising discovery that I have made in discussing these issues is that many AI workers are quite shocked by my idea that actual human mental phenomena might be dependent on actual physical-chemical properties of actual human brains. But if you think about it a minute you can see that I should not have been surprised; for unless you accept some form of dualism, the strong AI project hasn't got a chance. The project is to reproduce and explain the mental by designing programs, but unless the mind is not only conceptually but empirically independent of the brain you couldn't carry out the project, for the program is completely independent of any realization. Unless you believe that the mind is separable from the brain both conceptually and empirically—dualism in a strong form—you cannot hope to reproduce the mental by writing and running programs since programs must be independent of brains or any other particular forms of instantiation. If mental operations consist in computational operations on formal symbols, then it follows that they have no interesting connection with the brain; the only connection would be that the brain just happens to be one of the indefinitely many types of machines capable of instantiating the program. This form of dualism is not the traditional Cartesian variety that claims there are two sorts of *substances*, but it is Cartesian in the sense that it insists that what is specifically mental about the mind has no intrinsic connection with the actual properties of the brain. This underlying dualism is masked from us by the fact that AI literature contains frequent fulminations against "dualism"; what the authors seem to be unaware of is that their position presupposes a strong version of dualism. "Could a machine think?" My own view is that *only* a machine could think, and indeed only very special kinds of machines, namely brains and machines that had the same causal powers as brains. And that is the main reason strong AI has had little to tell us about thinking, since it has nothing to tell us about machines. By its own definition, it is about programs, and programs are not machines. Whatever else intentionality is, it is a biological phenomenon, and it is as likely to be as causally dependent on the specific biochemistry of its origins as lactation, photosynthesis, or any other biological phenomena. No one would suppose that we could produce milk and sugar by running a computer simulation of the formal sequences in lactation and photosynthesis, but where the mind is concerned many people are willing to believe in such a miracle because of a deep and abiding dualism: The mind they suppose is a matter of formal processes and is independent of quite specific material causes in the way that milk and sugar are not. In defense of this dualism the hope is often expressed that the brain is a digital computer (early computers, by the way, were often called "electronic brains"). But that is no help. Of course the brain is a digital computer. Since everything is a digital computer, brains are too. The point is that the brain's causal capacity to produce intentionality cannot consist in its instantiating a computer program, since for any program you like it is possible for something to instantiate that program and still not have any mental states. Whatever it is that the brain does to produce intentionality, it cannot consist in instantiating a program since no program, by itself, is sufficient for intentionality.[4]

Discussion Questions

1. What do you think about Schank's machine? Has it achieved artificial intelligence? Does it *understand*?
2. How do *you* determine whether a computer could think and could understand? What criteria, if any, are required?
3. Do you find Searle's example of the Chinese Room convincing? Does the Chinese Room achieve thought? Intelligence? A mind? Why/why not? If you think the Chinese Room fails to exhibit understanding/intentionality, then how do you assert that any other beings (i.e., humans) do?
4. Could a computer/robot be programmed to be sarcastic? To be happy? Depressed? Dishonest?
5. If you played against a computer in tic-tac-toe and the computer moved twice without you making a move and then flashed "I Win" on the screen, would you think the computer had cheated? Why/why not? How does free will factor into this discussion? Intentionality?

Machine Consciousness

William Lycan

A professor of philosophy at the University of North Carolina since 1982, William Lycan has authored over 150 academic articles in academic journals, as well as seven books, with a focus on the philosophy of mind language.

In this selection, excerpted from his book *Consciousness*, Lycan explores what is essential to *personhood*—the moral sense in which we distinguish certain beings as having rights. In conjunction with this, he explores what it means to maintain consciousness. Many claim that machines (i.e., computers/robots) cannot achieve personhood or consciousness because they cannot react to "contingencies"—occurrences that require the ability to react or adapt to unique events in one's environment. Lycan, though, provides two thought experiments that he believes support our being justified in certain types of robots being conscious, *prima facie* (Latin for "on its first appearance"—a term often used in legal cases to "present one's case" and proceed based on initial evidence). Through his two cases—"Harry" and "Henrietta"—he concludes that machines can, in fact, achieve consciousness.

Reading Questions

1. How does Lycan use the word "intelligence"? In what ways do we differ from machines?
2. How is a digital computer similar to "higher animals"? Explain the two *limitations* of a computer that Lycan suggests.
3. Explain in your own words the three types of questions that AI researchers ask. In what ways are types one and two "empirical"?

Source: "Robots and Minds" from *Consciousness*, pp. 123–130. Copyright © 1987 Massachusetts Institute of Technology. Reprinted by permission of The MIT Press, 55 Hayward Street.

4. How does Lycan suggest that we determine if Harry—or any other creature—is conscious?
5. What differences between Harry and ourselves does the "human chauvinist" proclaim? What does Lycan say about these claims?
6. Explain the experiment involving "Henrietta." What point does Lycan make here?
7. In what ways is this issue parallel with animal rights, as Lycan suggests?
8. How does the McCullough-Pitts model of the neuron paint the human being as a computing machine? How has this model been overcome, and what further conclusions have been drawn in this area?
9. How does Lycan define Soft Determinism, and what is the relevance to his argument?
10. For what two reasons does Lycan consider it "slander" to claim that Harry and Henrietta are *un*-free and "only do what they are programmed to do"?
11. What "matters to mentality" for Lycan? How does this relate to his overall position?

Artificial intelligence is, very crudely, the science of getting machines to perform jobs that normally require intelligence and judgment. Researchers at any number of AI labs have designed machines that prove mathematical theorems, play chess, sort mail, guide missiles, assemble auto engines, diagnose illnesses, read stories and other written texts, and converse with people in a rudimentary way. This is, we might say, intelligent behavior.

But what is this "intelligence"? As a first pass, I suggest that intelligence of the sort I am talking about is a kind of flexibility, a responsiveness to contingencies. A dull or stupid machine must have just the right kind of raw materials presented to it in just the right way, or it is useless: The electric can opener must have an appropriately sized can fixed under its drive wheel *just so*, in order to operate at all. Humans (most of us, anyway) are not like that. We deal with the unforeseen. We take what comes and make the best of it, even though we may have had no idea what it would be. We play the ball from whatever lie we are given, and at whatever angle to the green; we read and understand texts we have never seen before; we find our way back to Chapel Hill after getting totally lost in downtown Durham (or downtown Washington, D.C., or downtown Lima, Peru).

Our pursuit of our goals is guided while in progress by our ongoing perception and handling of interim developments. Moreover, we can pursue any number of different goals at the same time, and balance them against each other. We are sensitive to contingencies, both external and internal, that have a very complex and unsystematic structure.

It is almost irresistible to speak of *information* here, even if the term were not as trendy as it is. An intelligent creature, I want to say, is an *information-sensitive* creature, one that not only *registers* information through receptors such as sense-organs but somehow stores and manages and finally uses that information. Higher animals are intelligent beings in this sense, and so are we, even though virtually nothing is known about how we organize or manage the vast, seething profusion of information that comes our way. And there is one sort of machine that is information-sensitive also: the digital computer. A computer *is* a machine specifically designed to be fed complexes of information, to store them, manage them, and produce appropriate theoretical or practical conclusions on demand. Thus, if artificial intelligence is what one is looking for, it is no accident that one looks to the computer.

Yet a computer has two limitations in common with machines of less elite and grandiose sorts, both of them already signaled in the characterization I have just given. First, a (present-day) computer must be *fed* information, and the choice of what information to feed and in what form is up to a human programmer or operator. (For that matter, a present-day computer must be plugged into an electrical outlet and have its switch turned to ON, but this is a very minor contingency given the availability of nuclear power packs.) Second, the *appropriateness* and effectiveness of a computer's output depends entirely on what the programmer or operator had in mind and goes on to make of it. A computer has intelligence in the sense I have defined, but has no judgment, since it has no goals and purposes of its own and no internal sense of appropriateness, relevance, or proportion.

For essentially these reasons—that computers are intelligent in my minimal sense, and that they are nevertheless limited in the two ways I have mentioned—AI theorists, philosophers, and intelligent laymen have inevitably compared computers to human minds, but at the same time debated both technical and philosophical questions raised by this comparison. The questions break down into three main groups or types: (A) Questions of the form "Will a computer ever be able to do X?" where X is something that intelligent humans can do. (B) Questions of the form "Given that a computer can or could do X, have we any reason to think that it does X in the same way that humans do X?" (C) Questions of the form "Given that some futuristic supercomputer were able to do $X, Y, Z, \ldots$, for some arbitrarily large range and variety of human activities, would that show that the computer had property P?" where P is some feature held to be centrally, vitally characteristic of human minds, such as thought, consciousness, feeling, sensation, emotion, creativity, or freedom of the will.

Questions of type A are empirical questions and cannot be settled without decades, perhaps centuries, of further research—compare ancient and medieval speculations on the question of whether a machine could ever fly. Questions of type B are brutely empirical too, and their answers are unavailable to AI researchers *per se*, lying squarely in the domain of cognitive psychology, a science or alleged science barely into its infancy. Questions of type C are philosophical and conceptual, and so I shall essay to answer them all at one stroke.

Let us begin by supposing that all questions of types A and B have been settled affirmatively—that one day we might be confronted by a much-improved version of Hal, the soft-spoken computer in Kubrick's 2001 (younger readers may substitute Star Wars' C3PO or whatever subsequent cinematic robot is the most lovable). Let us call this more versatile machine "Harry." Harry (let us say) is humanoid in form—he is a miracle of miniaturization and has lifelike plastic skin—and he can converse intelligently on all sorts of subjects, play golf *and* the viola, write passable poetry, control his occasional nervousness pretty well, make love, prove mathematical theorems (of course), show envy when outdone, throw gin bottles at annoying children, etc., etc. We may suppose he fools people into thinking he is human. Now the question is, is Harry really a *person?* Does he have thoughts, feelings, and so on? Is he actually conscious, or is he just a mindless walking hardware store whose movements are astoundingly *like* those of a person?[5]

Plainly his acquaintances would tend from the first to see him as a person, even if they were aware of his dubious antecedents. I think it is a plain psychological fact, if nothing more, that we could not help treating him as a person, unless we resolutely made up our minds, on principle, not to give him the time of day. But how could we really tell that he is conscious?

Well, how do we really tell that any humanoid creature is conscious? How do you tell that I am conscious, and how do I tell that you are? Surely we tell, and decisively, on the basis of our standard behavioral tests for mental states, to revert to [an earlier theme of this book]: We know that a human being has such-and-such mental states when it behaves, to speak very generally, in the ways we take to be appropriate to organisms that are in those states. (The point is of course an epistemological one only, no metaphysical implications intended or tolerated.) We know for practical purposes that a creature has a mind when it fulfills all the right criteria. And by hypothesis, Harry fulfills all our behavioral criteria with a vengeance; moreover, he does so *in the right way* (cf. questions of type B): the processing that stands causally behind his behavior is just like ours. It follows that we are at least *prima facie* justified in believing him to be conscious.

We have not *proved* that he is conscious, of course—any more than you have proved that I am conscious. An organism's merely behaving in a certain way is no logical guarantee of sentience; from my point of view it is at least imaginable, a bare logical possibility, that my wife, my daughter, and my chairman are not conscious, even though I have excellent, overwhelming behavioral reason to think that they are. But for that matter, our "standard behavioral tests" for mental states yield practical or moral certainty only so long as the situation is not palpably extraordinary or bizarre. A human chauvinist—in this case, someone who denies that Harry has thoughts and feelings, joys and sorrows—thinks precisely that Harry is as bizarre as they come. But *what is bizarre about him?* There are quite a few chauvinist answers to this, but what they boil down to, and given our hypothesized facts all they could boil down to, are two differences between Harry and ourselves: his *origin* (a laboratory is not a proper mother), and the *chemical composition of his anatomy*, if his creator has used silicon instead of carbon, for example. To exclude him from our community for either or both of *those* reasons seems to me to be a clear case of racial or ethnic prejudice (literally) and nothing more. I see no obvious way in which either a creature's origin or its subneuroanatomical chemical composition should matter to its psychological processes or any aspect of its mentality.

My argument can be reinforced by a thought-experiment . . . : Imagine that we take a normal human being, Henrietta, and begin gradually replacing parts of her with synthetic materials—first a few prosthetic limbs, then a few synthetic arteries, then some neural fibers, and so forth. Suppose that the surgeons who perform the successive operations (particularly the neurosurgeons) are so clever and skillful that Henrietta survives in fine style: Her intelligence, personality, perceptual acuity, poetic abilities, etc., remain just as they were before. But after the replacement process has eventually gone on to completion, Henrietta will have become an artifact—at least, her body will then be nothing but a collection of artifacts. Did she lose consciousness at some point during the sequence of operations, despite her continuing to behave and respond normally? When? It is hard to imagine that there is some privileged portion of the human nervous system that is for some reason indispensable, even though kidneys, lungs, heart, and any given bit of brain could in principle be replaced by a prosthesis (for *what* reason?); and it is also hard to imagine that there is some *pro*portion of the nervous system such that removal of more than that proportion causes loss of consciousness or sentience despite perfect maintenance of all intelligent capacities.

If this quick but totally compelling defense of Harry and Henrietta's personhood is correct, then the two, and their ilk, will have not only mental lives like ours, but *moral* lives like ours, and moral rights and privileges accordingly. Just as origin and physical constitution fail to affect psychological personhood, if a creature's internal organization is sufficiently like ours, so do they fail to affect moral personhood. We do not discriminate against a person who has a wooden leg, or a mechanical kidney, or a nuclear heart regulator; no more should we deny any human or civil right to Harry or Henrietta on grounds of their origin or physical makeup, which they cannot help.

But this happy egalitarianism raises a more immediate question: *In real life*, we shall soon be faced with medium-grade machines, which have some intelligence and are not "mere" machines like refrigerators or typewriters but which fall far short of flawless human stimulators like Harry. For AI researchers may well build machines that will appear to have some familiar mental capacities but not others. The most obvious example is that of a sensor or perceptron, which picks up information from its immediate environment, records it, and stores it in memory for future printout. (We already have at least crude machines of this kind. When they become versatile and sophisticated enough, it will be quite natural to say that they see or hear and that they remember.) But the possibility of "specialist" machines of this kind raises an unforeseen contingency: There is an enormous and many-dimensional range of possible beings in between our current "mere" machines and our fully developed, flawless human simulators; we have not even begun to think of all the infinitely possible variations on this theme. And once we do begin to think of these hard cases, we will be at a loss as to where to draw the "personhood" line between them. How complex, eclectic, and impressive must a machine be, and in what respects, before we award it the accolade of personhood and/or of consciousness? There is, to say the least, no clear answer to be had *a priori*, Descartes's notorious view of animals to the contrary notwithstanding.*

---

*Descartes claimed in his *Discourse on Method* that animals are mere machines.

This typical philosophical question would be no more than an amusing bon-bon, were it not for the attending moral conundrum: What moral rights would an intermediate or marginally intelligent machine have? Adolescent machines of this sort will confront us much sooner than will any good human simulators, for they are easier to design and construct; more to the moral point, they will be designed mainly as *labor-saving devices*, as servants who will work for free, and servants of this kind are (literally) made to be exploited. If they are intelligent to any degree, we should have qualms in proportion.

I suggest that this moral problem, which may become a real and pressing one, is parallel to the current debate over animal rights. Luckily I have never wanted to cook and eat my Compaq Portable.

Suppose I am right about the irrelevance of biochemical constitution to psychology; and suppose I was also right about the coalescing of the notions *computation, information, intelligence*. Then our mentalized theory of computation suggests in turn a computational theory of mentality, and a computational picture of the place of human beings in the world. In fact, philosophy aside, that picture has already begun to get a grip on people's thinking—as witness the filtering down of computer jargon into contemporary casual speech—and that grip is not going to loosen. Computer science is the defining technology of our time, and in this sense the computer is the natural cultural successor to the steam engine, the clock, the spindle, and the potter's wheel. Predictably, an articulate computational theory of the mind has also gained credence among professional psychologists and philosophers.[6] I have been trying to support it here and elsewhere; I shall say no more about it for now, save to note again its near-indispensability in accounting for intentionality (noted), and to address the ubiquitous question of computer creativity and freedom:

Soft Determinism or **Libertarianism** may be true of humans. But many people have far more rigidly deterministic intuitions about computers. Computers, after all, (let us all say it together:) "only do what they are told/programmed to do"; they have no spontaneity and no freedom of choice. But human beings choose all the time, and the ensuing states of the world often depend entirely on these choices.[7] Thus the "computer analogy" supposedly fails.

The alleged failure of course depends on what we think freedom really is. As a Soft Determinist, I think that to have freedom of choice in acting is (roughly) for one's action to proceed out of one's own desires, deliberation, will, and intention, rather than being compelled or coerced by external forces regardless of my desires or will. As before, free actions are not *uncaused* actions. My free actions are those that *I* cause, i.e., that are caused by my own mental processes rather than by something pressing on me from the outside. I have argued . . . that I am free in that my beliefs, desires, deliberations, and intentions are all functional or computational states and processes within me that do interact in characteristic ways to produce my behavior. Note now that the same response vindicates our skilled human-simulating machines from the charge of puppethood. The word "robot" is often used as a veritable synonym for "puppet," so it may seem that Harry and

Henrietta are paradigm cases of *unfree* mechanisms that "only do what they are programmed to do." This is a slander—for two reasons:

First, even an ordinary computer, let alone a fabulously sophisticated machine like Harry, is in a way unpredictable. You are at its mercy. You *think* you know what it is going to do; you know what it should do, what it is supposed to do, but there is no guarantee—and it may do something *awful* or at any rate something that you could not have predicted and could not figure out if you tried with both hands. This practical sort of unpredictability would be multiplied a thousandfold in the case of a machine as complex as the human brain, and it is notably characteristic of *people*.

The unpredictability has several sources. (i) Plain old physical defects, as when Harry's circuits have been damaged by trauma, stress, heat, or the like. (ii) Bugs in one or more of his programs. (I have heard that once upon a time, somewhere, a program was written that had not a single bug in it, but this is probably an urban folk tale.) (iii) Randomizers, quantum-driven or otherwise; elements of Harry's behavior may be *genuinely,* physically random. (iv) Learning and analogy mechanisms; if Harry is equipped with these, as he inevitably would be, then his behavior-patterns will be modified in response to his experiential input from the world, which would be neither controlled nor even observed by us. *We don't know where he's been.* (v) The relativity of reliability to goal-description. This last needs a bit of explanation.

People often say things like, "A computer just crunches binary numbers; provided it isn't broken, it just chugs on mindlessly through whatever flipflop settings are predetermined by its electronic makeup." But such remarks ignore the multileveled character of real computer programming. At any given time, as we have noted [earlier], a computer is running *each of any number of* programs, depending on how it is described and on the level of functional organization that interests us. True, it is always crunching binary numbers, but in crunching them it is also doing any number of more esoteric things. And (more to the point) what counts as a mindless, algorithmic procedure at a very low level of organization may constitute, at a higher level, a hazardous do-or-die heuristic that might either succeed brilliantly or (more likely) fail and leave its objective unfulfilled.

As a second defense, remember that Harry too has beliefs, desires, and intentions (provided my original argument is sound). If this is so, then his behavior normally proceeds out of his own mental processes rather than being externally compelled; and so he satisfies the definition of freedom-of-action formulated above. In most cases it will be appropriate to say that Harry could have done other than what he did do (but in fact chose after some ratiocination to do what he did, instead). Harry acts in the same sense as that in which we act, though one might continue to quarrel over what sense that is.

Probably the most popular remaining reason for doubt about machine consciousness has to do with the raw qualitative character of experience. Could a mere bloodless runner-of-programs have states that *feel to it* in any of the various dramatic ways in which our mental states feel to us?

The latter question is usually asked rhetorically, expecting a resounding answer "NO!!" But I do not hear it rhetorically, for I do not see why the negative answer is supposed to be at all obvious, even for machines as opposed to biologic humans. Of course there is an incongruity *from our human point of view* between human feeling and printed circuitry or silicon pathways; that is to be expected, since we are considering those high-tech items from an external, third-person perspective and at the same time comparing them to our own first-person feels. But argumentatively, that *Gestalt* phenomenon counts for no more in the present case than it did in that of human consciousness, viz., for nothing, especially if my original argument about Harry was successful in showing that biochemical constitution is irrelevant to psychology. What matters to mentality is not the stuff of which one is made, but the complex way in which that stuff is organized. If after years of close friendship we were to open Harry up and find that he is stuffed with microelectronic gadgets instead of protoplasm, we would be taken aback—no question. But our *Gestalt* clash on the occasion would do nothing *at all* to show that Harry does not have his own rich inner qualitative life. If an objector wants to insist that computation alone cannot provide consciousness with its qualitative character, the objector will have to take the initiative and come up with a further, substantive argument to show why not.[8] We have already seen that such arguments have failed wretchedly for the case of humans; I see no reason to suspect that they would work any better for the case of robots. We must await further developments. But at the present stage of inquiry I see no compelling feel-based objection to the hypothesis of machine consciousness.

Discussion Questions

1. Do you think the description of Harry the machine is a *person* in the moral sense (not to be confused with a *human being*, as it obviously doesn't have human DNA)? Does Harry have thoughts and feelings?
2. How do you answer the above questions regarding Henrietta? And "How complex, eclectic, and impressive must a machine be . . . before we award it the accolade of personhood and/or of consciousness"?
3. How *do* you determine if any other creature is conscious?
4. Do you accept Lycan's criticism of the "human chauvinist" claim that robots aren't conscious due to their *origin* and *chemical composition*? *Is* this similar to ethnic or racial prejudice? How might this relate to animal rights?
5. How do you evaluate Lycan's claim (and the five sources/causes) that computers are unpredictable? If they are, does this affect your view of free will with regard to computers? How important is *unpredictability* to your assigning free will to beings?
6. How would your view of your best friend or close family member change if you discovered that they were composed of "microelectronic gadgets instead of protoplasm"? Would this change their moral status and the way in which you treated them? How would you answer these questions with regard to discovering they instead had alien DNA?
7. What importance does the discussion of AI have in general?

Movie Titles

1. *Sliding Doors* (R)—How much do the "little things" matter? Is it true that everything happens for a reason? Do you believe in fate?
2. Theme: How can we be held morally responsible if our actions are out of our control?
   - *A Clockwork Orange* (R)
   - *Dead Man Walking* (R)
   - *Liar Liar*
3. *Minority Report*—Are our actions determined ahead of time? What is the purpose of punishment—to keep people from doing bad things or because they deserve it?
4. *I Heart Huckabees*—How does the "consultants'" view of life differ from yours?

Song Lyrics

Rush—"Freewill"
Natalie Evans—"Que Sera Sera"
They Might Be Giants—"Where Your Eyes Don't Go"
Fugazi—"Suggestion"
John Hartford—"(If I Had Not Been There) I Would Not Be Here"
Crimpshrine—"Free Will"
Incubus—"Privilege"

Notes

1. This is why we are naturally inclined to ask in cases like this whether someone else in exactly these circumstances might have acted differently.
2. Also, "understanding" implies both the possession of mental (intentional) states and the truth (validity, success) of these states. For the purposes of this discussion we are concerned only with the possession of the states.
3. Intentionality is by definition that feature of certain mental states by which they are directed at or about objects and states of affairs in the world. Thus, beliefs, desires, and intentions are intentional states; undirected forms of anxiety and depression are not.
4. I am indebted to a rather large number of people for discussion of these matters and for their patient attempts to overcome my ignorance of artificial intelligence. I would especially like to thank Ned Block, Hubert Dreyfus, John Haugeland, Roger Schank, Robert Wilensky, and Terry Winograd.
5. It is interesting that children seem instinctively to reject the hypothesis of machine consciousness, usually on the grounds that computers are not alive. (One day when my daughter Jane was three years old, we were fooling with some piece of software or other, and I

quite unreflectively remarked "It thinks you want it to [do such-and-such]." She did an enormous take, and then replied, "Computers can't think!—Is that 'just an expression'??")

6. The computational picture of mentality is by no means new. For one thing, the idea of mechanical intelligence goes back to the seventeenth century at least, long before Charles Babbage's celebrated Analytical Engine. And the computer model of the mind received a decisive boost from the McCullough-Pitts model of the neuron (1947), according to which a neuron is nothing but a little on-off device, that either *fires* or does not. If a brain is just an organized collection of neurons, and a neuron is just an on-off switch, it follows *straightway* that a brain is a digital computer and anything interesting that it does is a computation over binary formulas. Thus a human being is not only a featherless biped, a rational animal, and the only creature on earth that laughs, but the only computing machine on earth that is made by unskilled labor.

The McCullough-Pitts model is no longer current (no pun intended): Neurons are now known to be very complicated little agents, not mere on-off switches. But the computational picture of mentality still receives strong encouragement from other quarters. It has two separate philosophical motivations, in particular, the first of which I have already noted: It exploits and explains the coalescence of the notions of computation, information, and intelligence. The computer is the only thing in the world that displays potential intelligence *and* whose workings are well understood. It is the only answer we currently know to the question: By what means *could* Mother Nature have crafted an intelligent being (in our sense of responsiveness to contingencies) out of nothing but a large bunch of individually insensate biological cells? To deny that there may be other answers would be presumptuous at best, and there are plenty of human capacities that do not seem to admit of computational simulation in any way at all—but anyone who manages to think up a genuinely distinct alternative to the digital-computer paradigm will have achieved a major conceptual breakthrough. For the foreseeable future, computation is our only model for intelligence.

Computationalism as a form of Homunctionalism also affords us a way of acknowledging our place as physical organisms amid the closed causal order we call Nature, without benefit of intervention by ghosts. (Actually I hear there are some physicists who speculate that quantum indeterminacies afford gaps in nature that are in principle permeable to Cartesian minds, and that immaterial egos do insert themselves into quantum gaps, thus taking over the role of hidden variables. But (i) it would have to be shown how such quantum phenomena could be combined and multiplied into macroscopic effects characteristic of intelligence, i.e., how the brain could act as a "quantum magnifier," and (ii) to avoid *ad-hoc*ness of the crassest sort, one would have to find *physical reason* to think that Cartesian intervention does occur, which task I take to be almost definitionally impossible.)

7. Of course, this re-emphasizes the question of human freedom: if humans are just wetware or liveware, are they not then essentially soft puppets? This in turn suggests—however speciously in light of the arguments made [earlier]—that the computational view of people must therefore be drastically wrong.

8. That mental acts do not *feel* digital is not an objection either. To infer from that fact that mental acts are not digital would be a clear case of what Armstrong (1968a) calls the "headless woman" fallacy.

Chapter 9

Politics and Society

How we ought to govern ourselves is one of the most current and relevant philosophical questions we can ask. Inherent to that question are issues of rights, equality, freedom, and justice. Social and political philosophy forces us to ask what it means to have an "inalienable *right*" to something like liberty (and to ask just what "liberty" means). Where does this right come from and to what does it entitle the holder? How is it that we can justify establishing a government, thereby taking certain liberties away from citizens (i.e., through a legal system), and likewise, how can we assume that the citizens rightly consent to being governed in the first place?

Within this system, we must also examine how the goods within the community ought to be distributed. How should the people be taxed—if at all—and what purpose does tax money serve? One might like to simply say that it should be done fairly, but the mere notion of fairness comes into question as well: Do we mean that the goods should be equally available to each citizen, or that the goods should be made available based on one's merit—on their earning the specific goods? And what truth do we discover in phrases like "Might makes right" and "Life isn't fair"?

The first selection is taken from Plato, who wrote much on political philosophy and how we ought to establish a republic. In this selection, he aims to home in on a suitable definition of justice and also provides an analogy to help examine the questions "Why be moral?" and "Does might make right?" Hobbes and Locke both explore the "State of Nature"—what life would be like without a government—and from here provide a justification of an established government. In doing so, they examine notions of rights, punishment, property ownership, and justifying government rule.

Young examines issues relating to the distribution of goods within a society. In doing so she highlights the unjust system of distribution based on merit.

Justice and Morality
Plato

(For a biographical sketch of Plato, see the earlier selection in this text.)

The first part of this reading showcases a good illustration of the "Socratic Method"—the asking of relevant questions in order to first expose the inconsistency of another's position and then to establish your own. Socrates discusses the notion of justice as opposed to injustice, first examining if justice lies solely in the phrase "Might makes right," and then attempts to show the virtue and profitability inherent in being just. Through a later discussion, the speakers attempt to more precisely define justice, as well as examine individuals' motivations for being just.

Reading Questions

1. How does Thrasymachus define justice initially?
2. How does Socrates attempt to show that Thrasymachus' definition of justice leads to the following contradiction: "Justice, according to your argument, is not only obedience to the interest of the stronger but [also] the reverse"?
3. Explain the relevance of Socrates' analogy of the ship's captain and the doctor.
4. What is the relevance of wage-earning in Socrates' discussion?
5. What contradiction arises when Socrates asks Thrasymachus to determine if justice is a virtue or a vice? How does Socrates demonstrate that justice is actually a virtue?
6. How does Socrates employ the notion of *function* (of the eyes, ears, soul) to show that injustice is less profitable than justice?
7. What three types of goods does Glaucon suggest exist? Give an example of each.
8. In what way is justice initially defined as the mean between the extremes of "the best and the worst"?
9. Why does Glaucon claim that those who practice justice do so only because they don't have the power to do injustice?
10. What is the story of the ring of Gyges? How does Gyges use it to support his position?
11. Why does Glaucon claim that one should not simply want to be just, but that one should want to be believed to be just? How does he use the examples of two different men to support this?
12. What two defenses of justice does Adeimantus provide?
13. How does Adeimantus address the concern that doing injustice will lead to a difficult afterlife?

Source: Plato, *Republic.* Written in 380 B.C. This translation by Benjamin Jowett, Encyclopedia Britannica, Inc.

Book I

. . . I proclaim that justice is nothing else than the interest of the stronger. And now why do you not praise me? But of course you won't.

Let me first understand you, I replied. Justice, as you say, is the interest of the stronger. What, Thrasymachus, is the meaning of this? You cannot mean to say that because Polydamas, the pancratiast, is stronger than we are, and finds the eating of beef conducive to his bodily strength, that to eat beef is therefore equally for our good who are weaker than he is, and right and just for us?

That's abominable of you, Socrates; you take the words in the sense which is most damaging to the argument.

Not at all, my good sir, I said; I am trying to understand them; and I wish that you would be a little clearer.

Well, he said, have you never heard that forms of government differ; there are tyrannies, and there are democracies, and there are aristocracies?

Yes, I know.

And the government is the ruling power in each state?

Certainly.

And the different forms of government make laws democratical, aristocratical, tyrannical, with a view to their several interests; and these laws, which are made by them for their own interests, are the justice which they deliver to their subjects, and him who transgresses them they punish as a breaker of the law, and unjust. And that is what I mean when I say that in all states there is the same principle of justice, which is the interest of the government; and as the government must be supposed to have power, the only reasonable conclusion is, that everywhere there is one principle of justice, which is the interest of the stronger.

Now I understand you, I said; and whether you are right or not I will try to discover. But let me remark, that in defining justice you have yourself used the word "interest" which you forbade me to use. It is true, however, that in your definition the words "of the stronger" are added.

A small addition, you must allow, he said.

Great or small, never mind about that: we must first enquire whether what you are saying is the truth. Now we are both agreed that justice is interest of some sort, but you go on to say "of the stronger"; about this addition I am not so sure, and must therefore consider further.

Proceed.

I will; and first tell me, Do you admit that it is just for subjects to obey their rulers?

I do.

But are the rulers of states absolutely infallible, or are they sometimes liable to err?

To be sure, he replied, they are liable to err.

Then in making their laws they may sometimes make them rightly, and sometimes not?

True.

When they make them rightly, they make them agreeably to their interest; when they are mistaken, contrary to their interest; you admit that?

Yes.

And the laws which they make must be obeyed by their subjects—and that is what you call justice?

Doubtless.

Then justice, according to your argument, is not only obedience to the interest of the stronger but the reverse?

What is that you are saying? he asked.

I am only repeating what you are saying, I believe. But let us consider: Have we not admitted that the rulers may be mistaken about their own interest in what they command, and also that to obey them is justice? Has not that been admitted?

Yes.

Then you must also have acknowledged justice not to be for the interest of the stronger, when the rulers unintentionally command things to be done which are to their own injury. For if, as you say, justice is the obedience which the subject renders to their commands, in that case, O wisest of men, is there any escape from the conclusion that the weaker are commanded to do, not what is for the interest, but what is for the injury of the stronger?

Nothing can be clearer, Socrates, said Polemarchus.

Yes, said Cleitophon, interposing, if you are allowed to be his witness.

But there is no need of any witness, said Polemarchus, for Thrasymachus himself acknowledges that rulers may sometimes command what is not for their own interest, and that for subjects to obey them is justice.

Yes, Polemarchus—Thrasymachus said that for subjects to do what was commanded by their rulers is just.

Yes, Cleitophon, but he also said that justice is the interest of the stronger, and, while admitting both these propositions, he further acknowledged that the stronger may command the weaker who are his subjects to do what is not for his own interest; whence follows that justice is the injury quite as much as the interest of the stronger.

But, said Cleitophon, he meant by the interest of the stronger what the stronger thought to be his interest—this was what the weaker had to do; and this was affirmed by him to be justice.

Those were not his words, rejoined Polemarchus.

Never mind, I replied, if he now says that they are, let us accept his statement. Tell me, Thrasymachus, I said, did you mean by justice what the stronger thought to be his interest, whether really so or not?

Certainly not, he said. Do you suppose that I call him who is mistaken the stronger at the time when he is mistaken?

Yes, I said, my impression was that you did so, when you admitted that the ruler was not infallible but might be sometimes mistaken.

You argue like an informer, Socrates. Do you mean, for example, that he who is mistaken about the sick is a physician in that he is mistaken? or that he who errs in arithmetic or grammar is an arithmetician or grammarian at the time when he is making the mistake, in respect of the mistake? True, we say that the physician or arithmetician or grammarian has made a mistake, but this is only a way of speaking; for the fact is that neither the grammarian nor any other person of skill ever makes a mistake in so far as he is what his name implies; they none of them err unless their skill fails them, and then they cease to be skilled artists. No artist or sage or ruler errs at the time when he is what his name implies; though he is commonly said to err, and I adopt the common mode of speaking. But to be perfectly accurate, since you are such a lover of accuracy, we should say that the ruler, in so far as he is a ruler, is unerring and, being unerring, always commands that which is for his own interest; and the subject is required to execute his commands; and therefore, as I said at first and now repeat, justice is the interest of the stronger.

Indeed, Thrasymachus, and do I really appear to you to argue like an informer?

Certainly, he replied.

And do you suppose that I ask these questions with any design of injuring you in the argument?

Nay, he replied, "suppose" is not the word—I know it; but you will be found out, and by sheer force of argument you will never prevail.

I shall not make the attempt, my dear man; but to avoid any misunderstanding occurring between us in future, let me ask, in what sense do you speak of a ruler or stronger whose interest, as you were saying, he being the superior, it is just that the inferior should execute—is he a ruler in the popular or in the strict sense of the term?

In the strictest of all senses, he said. And now cheat and play the informer if you can; I ask no quarter at your hands. But you never will be able, never.

And do you imagine, I said, that I am such a madman as to try and cheat Thrasymachus? I might as well shave a lion.

Why, he said, you made the attempt a minute ago, and you failed.

Enough, I said, of these civilities. It will be better that I should ask you a question: Is the physician, taken in that strict sense of which you are speaking, a healer of the sick or a maker of money? And remember that I am now speaking of the true physician.

A healer of the sick, he replied.

And the pilot—that is to say, the true pilot—is he a captain of sailors or a mere sailor?

A captain of sailors.

The circumstance that he sails in the ship is not to be taken into account; neither is he to be called a sailor; the name pilot by which he is distinguished has nothing to do with sailing, but is significant of his skill and of his authority over the sailors.

Very true, he said.

Now, I said, every art has an interest?

Certainly.

For which the art has to consider and provide?

Yes, that is the aim of art.

And the interest of any art is the perfection of it—this and nothing else?

What do you mean?

I mean what I may illustrate negatively by the example of the body. Suppose you were to ask me whether the body is self-suffering or has wants, I should reply: Certainly the body has wants; for the body may be ill and require to be cured, and has therefore interests to which the art of medicine ministers; and this is the origin and intention of medicine, as you will acknowledge. Am I not right?

Quite right, he replied.

But is the art of medicine or any other art faulty or deficient in any quality in the same way that the eye may be deficient in sight or the ear fail of hearing, and therefore requires another art to provide for the interests of seeing and hearing—has art in itself, I say, any similar liability to fault or defect, and does every art require another supplementary art to provide for its interests, and that another and another without end? Or have the arts to look only after their own interests? Or have they no need either of themselves or of another?—having no faults or defects, they have no need to correct them, either by the exercise of their own art or of any other; they have only to consider the interest of their subject-matter. For every art remains pure and faultless while remaining true—that is to say, while perfect and unimpaired. Take the words in your precise sense, and tell me whether I am not right.

Yes, clearly.

Then medicine does not consider the interest of medicine, but the interest of the body?

True, he said.

Nor does the art of horsemanship consider the interests of the art of horsemanship, but the interests of the horse; neither do any other arts care for themselves, for they have no needs; they care only for that which is the subject of their art?

True, he said.

But surely, Thrasymachus, the arts are the superiors and rulers of their own subjects?

To this he assented with a good deal of reluctance.

Then, I said, no science or art considers or enjoins the interest of the stronger or superior, but only the interest of the subject and weaker?

He made an attempt to contest this proposition also, but finally acquiesced.

Then, I continued, no physician, in so far as he is a physician, considers his own good in what he prescribes, but the good of his patient; for the true physician is also a ruler having the human body as a subject, and is not a mere money-maker; that has been admitted?

Yes.

And the pilot likewise, in the strict sense of the term, is a ruler of sailors and not a mere sailor?

That has been admitted.

And such a pilot and ruler will provide and prescribe for the interest of the sailor who is under him, and not for his own or the ruler's interest?

He gave a reluctant "Yes."

Then, I said, Thrasymachus, there is no one in any rule who, in so far as he is a ruler, considers or enjoins what is for his own interest, but always what is for the interest of his subject or suitable to his art; to that he looks, and that alone he considers in everything which he says and does.

When we had got to this point in the argument, and everyone saw that the definition of justice had been completely upset, Thrasymachus, instead of replying to me, said: Tell me, Socrates, have you got a nurse?

Why do you ask such a question, I said, when you ought rather to be answering?

Because she leaves you to snivel, and never wipes your nose: She has not even taught you to know the shepherd from the sheep.

What makes you say that? I replied.

Because you fancy that the shepherd or neatherd fattens or tends the sheep or oxen with a view to their own good and not to the good of himself or his master; and you further imagine that the rulers of states, if they are true rulers, never think of their subjects as sheep, and that they are not studying their own advantage day and night. Oh, no; and so entirely astray are you in your ideas about the just and unjust as not even to know that justice and the just are in reality another's good; that is to say, the interest of the ruler and stronger, and the loss of the subject and servant; and injustice the opposite; for the unjust is lord over the truly simple and just: he is the stronger, and his subjects do what is for his interest, and minister to his happiness, which is very far from being their own. Consider further, most foolish Socrates, that the just is always a loser in comparison with the unjust. First of all, in private contracts: Wherever the unjust is the partner of the just you will find that, when the partnership is dissolved, the unjust man has always more and the just less. Secondly, in their dealings with the State: When there is an income-tax, the just man will pay more and the unjust less on the same amount of income; and when there is anything to be received the one gains nothing and the other much. Observe also what happens when they take an office; there is the just man neglecting his affairs and perhaps suffering other losses, and getting nothing out of the public, because he is just; moreover he is hated by his friends and acquaintance for refusing to serve them in unlawful ways. But all this is reversed in the case of the unjust man. I am speaking, as before, of injustice on a large scale in which the advantage of the unjust is more apparent; and my meaning will be most clearly seen if we turn to that highest form of injustice in which the criminal is the happiest of men, and the sufferers or those who refuse to do injustice are the most miserable—that is to say tyranny, which by fraud and force takes away the property of others, not little by little but wholesale; comprehending in one, things sacred as well as profane, private and public; for which acts of wrong, if he were detected perpetrating any one of them singly, he would be punished and incur great disgrace—they who do such wrong in particular cases are called robbers of temples, and man-stealers and burglars and swindlers and thieves. But when a man besides taking away the money of the citizens has made slaves of them, then, instead of these names of reproach, he is termed happy and blessed, not only by the citizens but by all who hear of his having achieved the consummation of injustice. For mankind censure injustice, fearing that they may be the victims of it and not because they shrink from committing it. And thus, as I have shown, Socrates, injustice, when on a sufficient scale, has more strength and freedom and mastery than justice; and, as I said at first, justice is the interest of the stronger, whereas injustice is a man's own profit and interest.

Thrasymachus, when he had thus spoken, having, like a bathman, deluged our ears with his words, had a mind to go away. But the company would not let him; they insisted that he should remain and defend his position; and I myself added my own humble request that he would not leave us. Thrasymachus, I said to him, excellent man, how suggestive are your remarks! And are you going to run away before you have fairly taught or learned whether they are true or not? Is the attempt to determine the way of man's life so small a matter in your eyes—to determine how life may be passed by each one of us to the greatest advantage?

And do I differ from you, he said, as to the importance of the enquiry?

You appear rather, I replied, to have no care or thought about us, Thrasymachus—whether we live better or worse from not knowing what you say know, is to you a matter of indifference. Prithee, friend, do not keep your knowledge to yourself; we are a large party; and any benefit which you confer upon us will be amply rewarded. For my own part I openly declare that I am not convinced, and that I do not believe injustice to be more gainful than justice, even if uncontrolled and allowed to have free play. For, granting that there may be an unjust man who is able to commit injustice either by fraud or force, still this does not convince me of the superior advantage of injustice, and there may be others who are in the same predicament with myself. Perhaps we may be wrong; if so, you in your wisdom should convince us that we are mistaken in preferring justice to injustice.

And how am I to convince you, he said, if you are not already convinced by what I have just said; what more can I do for you? Would you have me put the proof bodily into your souls?

Heaven forbid! I said; I would only ask you to be consistent; or, if you change, change openly and let there be no deception. For I must remark, Thrasymachus, if you will recall what was previously said, that although you began by defining the true physician in an exact sense, you did not observe a like exactness when speaking of the shepherd; you thought that the shepherd as a shepherd tends the sheep not with a view to their own good, but like a mere diner or banquetter with a view to the pleasures of the table; or, again, as a trader for sale in the market, and not as a shepherd. Yet surely the art of the shepherd is concerned only with the good of his subjects; he has only to provide the best for them, since the perfection of the art is already ensured whenever all the requirements of it are satisfied. And that was what I was saying just now about the ruler. I conceived that the art of the ruler, considered as ruler, whether in a state or in private life, could only regard the good of his flock or subjects; whereas you seem to think that the rulers in states, that is to say, the true rulers, like being in authority.

Think! Nay, I am sure of it.

Then why in the case of lesser offices do men never take them willingly without payment, unless under the idea that they govern for the advantage not of themselves but of others? Let me ask you a question: Are not the several arts different, by reason of their each having a separate function? And, my dear illustrious friend, do say what you think, that we may make a little progress.

Yes, that is the difference, he replied.

And each art gives us a particular good and not merely a general one—medicine, for example, gives us health; navigation, safety at sea, and so on?

Yes, he said.

And the art of payment has the special function of giving pay: But we do not confuse this with other arts, any more than the art of the pilot is to be confused with the art of medicine, because the health of the pilot may be improved by a sea voyage. You would not be inclined to say, would you, that navigation is the art of medicine, at least if we are to adopt your exact use of language?

Certainly not.

Or because a man is in good health when he receives pay you would not say that the art of payment is medicine?

I should say not.

Nor would you say that medicine is the art of receiving pay because a man takes fees when he is engaged in healing?

Certainly not.

And we have admitted, I said, that the good of each art is specially confined to the art?

Yes.

Then, if there be any good which all artists have in common, that is to be attributed to something of which they all have the common use?

True, he replied.

And when the artist is benefited by receiving pay the advantage is gained by an additional use of the art of pay, which is not the art professed by him?

He gave a reluctant assent to this.

Then the pay is not derived by the several artists from their respective arts. But the truth is, that while the art of medicine gives health, and the art of the builder builds a house, another art attends them which is the art of pay. The various arts may be doing their own business and benefiting that over which they preside, but would the artist receive any benefit from his art unless he were paid as well?

I suppose not.

But does he therefore confer no benefit when he works for nothing?

Certainly, he confers a benefit.

Then now, Thrasymachus, there is no longer any doubt that neither arts nor governments provide for their own interests; but, as we were before saying, they rule and provide for the interests of their subjects who are the weaker and not the stronger—to their good they attend and not to the good of the superior. And this is the reason, my dear Thrasymachus, why, as I was just now saying, no one is willing to govern; because no one likes to take in hand the reformation of evils which are not his concern without remuneration. For, in the execution of his work, and in giving his orders to another, the true artist does not regard his own interest, but always that of his subjects; and therefore in order that rulers may be willing to rule, they must be paid in one of three modes of payment, money, or honour, or a penalty for refusing.

What do you mean, Socrates? said Glaucon. The first two modes of payment are intelligible enough, but what the penalty is I do not understand, or how a penalty can be a payment.

You mean that you do not understand the nature of this payment which to the best men is the great inducement to rule? Of course you know that ambition and avarice are held to be, as indeed they are, a disgrace?

Very true.

And for this reason, I said, money and honour have no attraction for them; good men do not wish to be openly demanding payment for governing and so to get the name of hirelings, nor by secretly helping themselves out of the public revenues to get the name of thieves. And not being ambitious they do not care about honour. Wherefore necessity must be laid upon them, and they must be induced to serve from the fear of punishment. And this, as I imagine, is the reason why the forwardness to take office, instead of waiting to be compelled, has been deemed dishonourable. Now the worst part of the punishment is that he who refuses to rule is liable to be ruled by one who is worse than himself. And the fear of this, as I conceive, induces the good to take office, not because they would, but because they cannot help—not under the idea that they are going to have any benefit or enjoyment themselves, but as a necessity, and because they are not able to commit the task of ruling to any one who is better than themselves, or indeed as good. For there is reason to think that if a city were composed entirely of good men, then to avoid office would be as much an object of contention as to obtain office is at present; then we should have plain proof that the true ruler is not meant by nature to regard his own interest, but that of his subjects; and every one who knew this would choose rather to receive a benefit from another than to have the trouble of conferring one. So far am I from agreeing with Thrasymachus that justice is the interest of the stronger. This latter question need not be further discussed at present; but when Thrasymachus says that the life of the unjust is more advantageous than that of the just, his new statement appears to me to be of a far more serious character. Which of us has spoken truly? And which sort of life, Glaucon, do you prefer?

I for my part deem the life of the just to be the more advantageous, he answered.

Did you hear all the advantages of the unjust which Thrasymachus was rehearsing?

Yes, I heard him, he replied, but he has not convinced me.

Then shall we try to find some way of convincing him, if we can, that he is saying what is not true?

Most certainly, he replied.

If, I said, he makes a set speech and we make another recounting all the advantages of being just, and he answers and we rejoin, there must be a numbering and measuring of the goods which are claimed on either side, and in the end we shall want judges to decide; but if we proceed in our enquiry as we lately did, by making admissions to one another, we shall unite the offices of judge and advocate in our own persons.

Very good, he said.

And which method do I understand you to prefer? I said.

That which you propose.

Well, then, Thrasymachus, I said, suppose you begin at the beginning and answer me. You say that perfect injustice is more gainful than perfect justice?

Yes, that is what I say, and I have given you my reasons.

And what is your view about them? Would you call one of them virtue and the other vice?

Certainly.

I suppose that you would call justice virtue and injustice vice?

What a charming notion! So likely too, seeing that I affirm injustice to be profitable and justice not.

What else then would you say?

The opposite, he replied.

And would you call justice vice?

No, I would rather say sublime simplicity.

Then would you call injustice malignity?

No; I would rather say discretion.

And do the unjust appear to you to be wise and good?

Yes, he said; at any rate those of them who are able to be perfectly unjust, and who have the power of subduing states and nations; but perhaps you imagine me to be talking of cutpurses. Even this profession if undetected has advantages, though they are not to be compared with those of which I was just now speaking.

I do not think that I misapprehend your meaning, Thrasymachus, I replied; but still I cannot hear without amazement that you class injustice with wisdom and virtue, and justice with the opposite.

Certainly I do so class them.

Now, I said, you are on more substantial and almost unanswerable ground; for if the injustice which you were maintaining to be profitable had been admitted by you as by others to be vice and deformity, an answer might have been given to you on received principles; but now I perceive that you will call injustice honourable and strong, and to the unjust you will attribute all the qualities which were attributed by us before to the just, seeing that you do not hesitate to rank injustice with wisdom and virtue.

You have guessed most infallibly, he replied. . . .

Very good, Thrasymachus, I said; and now to take the case of the arts: You would admit that one man is a musician and another not a musician?

Yes.

And which is wise and which is foolish?

Clearly the musician is wise, and he who is not a musician is foolish.

And he is good in as far as he is wise, and bad in as far as he is foolish?

Yes.

And you would say the same sort of thing of the physician?

Yes.

And do you think, my excellent friend, that a musician when he adjusts the lyre would desire or claim to exceed or go beyond a musician in the tightening and loosening the strings?

I do not think that he would.

But he would claim to exceed the non-musician?

Of course.

And what would you say of the physician? In prescribing meats and drinks would he wish to go beyond another physician or beyond the practice of medicine?

He would not.

But he would wish to go beyond the non-physician?

Yes.

And about knowledge and ignorance in general; see whether you think that any man who has knowledge ever would wish to have the choice of saying or doing more than another man who has knowledge. Would he not rather say or do the same as his like in the same case?

That, I suppose, can hardly be denied.

And what of the ignorant? Would he not desire to have more than either the knowing or the ignorant?

I dare say.

And the knowing is wise?

Yes.

And the wise is good?

True.

Then the wise and good will not desire to gain more than his like, but more than his unlike and opposite?

I suppose so.

Whereas the bad and ignorant will desire to gain more than both?

Yes.

But did we not say, Thrasymachus, that the unjust goes beyond both his like and unlike? Were not these your words?

They were.

And you also said that the just will not go beyond his like but his unlike?

Yes.

Then the just is like the wise and good, and the unjust like the evil and ignorant?

That is the inference.

And each of them is such as his like is?

That was admitted.

Then the just has turned out to be wise and good and the unjust evil and ignorant.

Thrasymachus made all these admissions, not fluently, as I repeat them, but with extreme reluctance; it was a hot summer's day, and the perspiration poured from him in torrents; and then I saw what I had never seen before, Thrasymachus blushing. As we were now agreed that justice was virtue and wisdom, and injustice vice and ignorance, I proceeded to another point:

Well, I said, Thrasymachus, that matter is now settled; but were we not also saying that injustice had strength; do you remember?

Yes, I remember, he said, but do not suppose that I approve of what you are saying or have no answer; if however I were to answer, you would be quite certain to accuse me of haranguing; therefore either permit me to have my say out, or if you would rather ask, do so, and I will answer "Very good," as they say to storytelling old women, and will nod "Yes" and "No."

Certainly not, I said, if contrary to your real opinion.

Yes, he said, I will, to please you, since you will not let me speak. What else would you have?

Nothing in the world, I said; and if you are so disposed I will ask and you shall answer.

Proceed.

Then I will repeat the question which I asked before, in order that our examination of the relative nature of justice and injustice may be carried on regularly. A statement was made that injustice is stronger and more powerful than justice, but now justice, having been identified with wisdom and virtue, is easily shown to be stronger than injustice, if injustice is ignorance; this can no longer be questioned by any one. But I want to view the matter, Thrasymachus, in a different way: You would not deny that a state may be unjust and may be unjustly attempting to enslave other states, or may have already enslaved them, and may be holding many of them in subjection?

True, he replied; and I will add that the best and most perfectly unjust state will be most likely to do so.

I know, I said, that such was your position; but what I would further consider is, whether this power which is possessed by the superior state can exist or be exercised without justice or only with justice.

If you are right in your view, and justice is wisdom, then only with justice; but if I am right, then without justice.

I am delighted, Thrasymachus, to see you not only nodding assent and dissent, but making answers which are quite excellent.

That is out of civility to you, he replied.

You are very kind, I said; and would you have the goodness also to inform me, whether you think that a state, or an army, or a band of robbers and thieves, or any other gang of evildoers could act at all if they injured one another?

No indeed, he said, they could not.

But if they abstained from injuring one another, then they might act together better?

Yes.

And this is because injustice creates divisions and hatreds and fighting, and justice imparts harmony and friendship; is not that true, Thrasymachus?

I agree, he said, because I do not wish to quarrel with you.

How good of you, I said; but I should like to know also whether injustice, having this tendency to arouse hatred, wherever existing, among slaves or among freemen, will not make them hate one another and set them at variance and render them incapable of common action?

Certainly.

And even if injustice be found in two only, will they not quarrel and fight, and become enemies to one another and to the just?

They will.

And suppose injustice abiding in a single person, would your wisdom say that she loses or that she retains her natural power?

Let us assume that she retains her power.

Yet is not the power which injustice exercises of such a nature that wherever she takes up her abode, whether in a city, in an army, in a family, or in any other body, that body is, to begin with, rendered incapable of united action by reason of sedition and distraction; and does it not become its own enemy and at variance with all that opposes it, and with the just? Is not this the case?

Yes, certainly.

And is not injustice equally fatal when existing in a single person; in the first place rendering him incapable of action because he is not at unity with himself, and in the second place making him an enemy to himself and the just? Is not that true, Thrasymachus?

Yes.

And O my friend, I said, surely the gods are just?

Granted that they are.

But if so, the unjust will be the enemy of the gods, and the just will be their friend?

Feast away in triumph, and take your fill of the argument; I will not oppose you, lest I should displease the company.

Well then, proceed with your answers, and let me have the remainder of my repast. For we have already shown that the just are clearly wiser and better and abler than the unjust, and that the unjust are incapable of common action; nay more, that to speak as we did of men who are evil acting at any time vigorously together, is not strictly true, for if they had been perfectly evil, they would have laid hands upon one another; but it is evident that there must have been some remnant of justice in them, which enabled them to combine; if there had not been they would have injured one another as well as their victims; they were but half-villains in their enterprises; for had they been whole villains, and utterly unjust, they would have been utterly incapable of action. That, as I believe, is the truth of the matter, and not what you said at first. But whether the just have a better and happier life than the unjust is a further question which we also proposed to consider. I think that they have; and for the reasons which I have given; but still I should like to examine further, for no light matter is at stake, nothing less than the rule of human life.

Proceed.

I will proceed by asking a question: Would you not say that a horse has some end?

I should.

And the end or use of a horse or of anything would be that which could not be accomplished, or not so well accomplished, by any other thing?

I do not understand, he said.

Let me explain: Can you see, except with the eye?

Certainly not.

Or hear, except with the ear?

No.

These then may be truly said to be the ends of these organs?

They may.

But you can cut off a vine-branch with a dagger or with a chisel, and in many other ways?

Of course.

And yet not so well as with a pruning-hook made for the purpose?

True.

May we not say that this is the end of a pruning-hook?

We may.

Then now I think you will have no difficulty in understanding my meaning when I asked the question whether the end of anything would be that which could not be accomplished, or not so well accomplished, by any other thing?

I understand your meaning, he said, and assent.

And that to which an end is appointed has also an excellence? Need I ask again whether the eye has an end?

It has.

And has not the eye an excellence?

Yes.

And the ear has an end and an excellence also?

True.

And the same is true of all other things; they have each of them an end and a special excellence?

That is so.

Well, and can the eyes fulfil their end if they are wanting in their own proper excellence and have a defect instead?

How can they, he said, if they are blind and cannot see?

You mean to say, if they have lost their proper excellence, which is sight; but I have not arrived at that point yet. I would rather ask the question more generally, and only enquire whether the things which fulfil their ends fulfil them by their own proper excellence, and fail of fulfilling them by their own defect?

Certainly, he replied.

I might say the same of the ears; when deprived of their own proper excellence they cannot fulfil their end?

True.

And the same observation will apply to all other things?

I agree.

Well; and has not the soul an end which nothing else can fulfil? For example, to superintend and command and deliberate and the like. Are not these functions proper to the soul, and can they rightly be assigned to any other?

To no other.

And is not life to be reckoned among the ends of the soul?

Assuredly, he said.

And has not the soul an excellence also?

Yes.

And can she or can she not fulfil her own ends when deprived of that excellence?

She cannot.

Then an evil soul must necessarily be an evil ruler and superintendent, and the good soul a good ruler?

Yes, necessarily.

And we have admitted that justice is the excellence of the soul, and injustice the defect of the soul?

That has been admitted.

Then the just soul and the just man will live well, and the unjust man will live ill?

That is what your argument proves.

And he who lives well is blessed and happy, and he who lives ill the reverse of happy?

Certainly.

Then the just is happy, and the unjust miserable?

So be it.

But happiness and not misery is profitable.

Of course.

Then, my blessed Thrasymachus, injustice can never be more profitable than justice.

Let this, Socrates, he said, be your entertainment at the Bendidea.

For which I am indebted to you, I said, now that you have grown gentle towards me and have left off scolding. Nevertheless, I have not been well entertained; but that was my own fault and not yours. As an epicure snatches a taste of every dish which is successively brought to table, he not having allowed himself time to enjoy the one before, so have I gone from one subject to another without having discovered what I sought at first, the nature of justice. I left that enquiry and turned away to consider whether justice is virtue and wisdom or evil and folly; and when there arose a further question about the comparative advantages of justice and injustice, I could not refrain from passing on to that. And the result of the whole discussion has been that I know nothing at all. For I know not what justice is, and therefore I am not likely to know whether it is or is not a virtue, nor can I say whether the just man is happy or unhappy.

Book II

With these words I was thinking that I had made an end of the discussion; but the end, in truth, proved to be only a beginning. For Glaucon, who is always the most pugnacious of men, was dissatisfied at Thrasymachus' retirement; he wanted to have the battle out. So he said to me: Socrates, do you wish really to persuade us, or only to seem to have persuaded us, that to be just is always better than to be unjust?

I should wish really to persuade you, I replied, if I could.

Then you certainly have not succeeded. Let me ask you now:—How would you arrange goods—are there not some which we welcome for their own sakes, and independently of their consequences, as, for example, harmless pleasures and enjoyments, which delight us at the time, although nothing follows from them?

I agree in thinking that there is such a class, I replied.

Is there not also a second class of goods, such as knowledge, sight, health, which are desirable not only in themselves, but also for their results?

Certainly, I said.

And would you not recognize a third class, such as gymnastic, and the care of the sick, and the physician's art; also the various ways of money-making—these do us good but we regard them as disagreeable; and no one would choose them for their own sakes, but only for the sake of some reward or result which flows from them?

There is, I said, this third class also. But why do you ask?

Because I want to know in which of the three classes you would place justice?

In the highest class, I replied—among those goods which he who would be happy desires both for their own sake and for the sake of their results.

Then the many are of another mind; they think that justice is to be reckoned in the troublesome class, among goods which are to be pursued for the sake of rewards and of reputation, but in themselves are disagreeable and rather to be avoided.

I know, I said, that this is their manner of thinking, and that this was the thesis which Thrasymachus was maintaining just now, when he censured justice and praised injustice. But I am too stupid to be convinced by him.

I wish, he said, that you would hear me as well as him, and then I shall see whether you and I agree. For Thrasymachus seems to me, like a snake, to have been charmed by your voice sooner than he ought to have been; but to my mind the nature of justice and injustice have not yet been made clear. Setting aside their rewards and results, I want to know what they are in themselves, and how they inwardly work in the soul. If you please, then, I will revive the argument of Thrasymachus. And first I will speak of the nature and origin of justice according to the common view of them. Secondly, I will show that all men who practise justice do so against their will, of necessity, but not as a good. And thirdly, I will argue that there is reason in this view, for the life of the unjust is after all better far than the life of the just—if what they say is true, Socrates, since I myself am not of their opinion. But still I acknowledge that I am perplexed when I hear the voices of Thrasymachus and myriads of others dinning in my ears; and, on the other hand, I have never yet heard the superiority of justice to injustice maintained by any one in a satisfactory way. I want to hear justice praised in respect of itself; then I shall be satisfied, and you are the person from whom I think that I am most likely to hear this; and therefore I will praise the unjust life to the utmost of my power, and my manner of speaking will indicate the manner in which I desire to hear you too praising justice and censuring injustice. Will you say whether you approve of my proposal?

Indeed I do; nor can I imagine any theme about which a man of sense would oftener wish to converse.

I am delighted, he replied, to hear you say so, and shall begin by speaking, as I proposed, of the nature and origin of justice.

They say that to do injustice is, by nature, good; to suffer injustice, evil; but that the evil is greater than the good. And so when men have both done and suffered injustice and have had experience of both, not being able to avoid the one and obtain the other, they think that they had better agree among themselves to have neither; hence there arise laws and mutual covenants; and that which is ordained by law is termed by them lawful and just. This they affirm to be the origin and nature of justice—it is a mean or compromise, between the best of all, which is to do injustice and not be punished, and the worst of all, which is to suffer injustice without the power of retaliation; and justice, being at a middle point between the two, is tolerated not as a good, but as the lesser evil, and honoured by reason of the inability of men to do injustice. For no man who is worthy to be called a man would ever submit to such an agreement if he were able to resist; he would be mad if he did. Such is the received account, Socrates, of the nature and origin of justice.

Now that those who practise justice do so involuntarily and because they have not the power to be unjust will best appear if we imagine something of this kind: Having given both to the just and the unjust power to do what they will, let us watch and see whither desire will lead them; then we shall discover in the very act the just and unjust man to be proceeding along the same road, following their interest, which all natures deem to be their good, and are only diverted into the path of justice by the force of law. The liberty which we are supposing may be most completely given to them in the form of such a power as is said to have been possessed by Gyges the ancestor of Croesus the Lydian. According to the tradition, Gyges was a shepherd in the service of the king of Lydia; there was a great storm, and an earthquake made an opening in the earth at the place where he was feeding his flock. Amazed at the sight, he descended into the opening, where, among other marvels, he beheld a hollow brazen horse, having doors, at which he stooping and looking in saw a dead body of stature, as appeared to him, more than human, and having nothing on but a gold ring; this he took from the finger of the dead and reascended. Now the shepherds met together, according to custom, that they might send their monthly report about the flocks to the king; into their assembly he came having the ring on his finger, and as he was sitting among them he chanced to turn the collet of the ring inside his hand, when instantly he became invisible to the rest of the company and they began to speak of him as if he were no longer present. He was astonished at this, and again touching the ring he turned the collet outwards and reappeared; he made several trials of the ring, and always with the same result—when he turned the collet inwards he became invisible, when outwards he reappeared. Whereupon he contrived to be chosen one of the messengers who were sent to the court; where as soon as he arrived he seduced the queen, and with her help conspired against the king and slew him, and took the kingdom. Suppose now that there were two such magic rings, and the just put on one of them and the unjust the other; no man can be imagined to be of such an iron nature that he would stand fast in justice. No man would keep his hands off what was not his own when he could safely take what he liked out of the market, or go into houses and lie with any one at his pleasure, or kill or release from prison whom he would, and in all respects be like a God among men. Then the actions of the just would be as the actions of the unjust; they would both come at last to the same point. And this we may truly affirm to be a great proof that a man is just, not willingly or because he thinks that justice is any good to him individually, but of necessity, for wherever any one thinks that he can safely be unjust, there he is unjust. For all men believe in their hearts that injustice is far more profitable to the individual than justice, and he who argues as I have been supposing, will say that they are right. If you could imagine any one obtaining this power of becoming invisible, and never doing any wrong or touching what was another's, he would be thought by the lookers-on to be a most wretched idiot, although they would praise him to one another's faces, and keep up appearances with one another from a fear that they too might suffer injustice. Enough of this.

Now, if we are to form a real judgment of the life of the just and unjust, we must isolate them; there is no other way; and how is the isolation to be effected? I answer: Let the unjust man be entirely unjust, and the just man entirely just; nothing is to be taken away from either of them, and both are to be perfectly furnished for the work of their respective lives. First, let the unjust be like other distinguished masters of craft; like the skilful pilot or physician, who knows intuitively his own powers and keeps within their limits, and who, if he fails at any point, is able to recover himself. So let the unjust make his unjust attempts in the right way, and lie hidden if he means to be great in his injustice (he who is found out is nobody): For the highest reach of injustice is, to be deemed just when you are not. Therefore I say that in the perfectly unjust man we must assume the most perfect injustice; there is to be no deduction, but we must allow him, while doing the most unjust acts, to have acquired the greatest reputation for justice. If he have taken a false step he must be able to recover himself; he must be one who can speak with effect, if any of his deeds come to light, and who can force his way where force is required by his courage and strength, and command of money and friends. And at his side let us place the just man in his nobleness and simplicity, wishing, as Aeschylus says, to be and not to seem good. There must be no seeming, for if he seem to be just he will be honoured and rewarded, and then we shall not know whether he is just for the sake of justice or for the sake of honours and rewards; therefore, let him be clothed in justice only, and have no other covering; and he must be imagined in a state of life the opposite of the former. Let him be the best of men, and let him be thought the worst; then he will have been put to the proof; and we shall see whether he will be affected by the fear of infamy and its consequences. And let him continue thus to the hour of death; being just and seeming to be unjust. When both have reached the uttermost extreme, the one of justice and the other of injustice, let judgment be given which of them is the happier of the two.

Heavens! my dear Glaucon, I said, how energetically you polish them up for the decision, first one and then the other, as if they were two statues.

I do my best, he said. And now that we know what they are like there is no difficulty in tracing out the sort of life which awaits either of them. This I will proceed to describe; but as you may think the description a little too coarse, I ask you to suppose, Socrates, that the words which follow are not mine. Let me put them into the mouths of the eulogists of injustice: They will tell you that the just man who is thought unjust will be scourged, racked, bound—will have his eyes burnt out; and, at last, after suffering every kind of evil, he will be impaled: Then he will understand that he ought to seem only, and not to be, just; the words of Aeschylus may be more truly spoken of the unjust than of the just. For the unjust is pursuing a reality; he does not live with a view to appearances—he wants to be really unjust and not to seem only:

> His mind has a soil deep and fertile,
> Out of which spring his prudent counsels.

In the first place, he is thought just, and therefore bears rule in the city; he can marry whom he will, and give in marriage to whom he will; also he can trade and deal where he likes, and always to his own advantage, because he has no misgivings about injustice; and at every contest, whether in public or private, he gets the better of his antagonists, and gains at their expense, and is rich, and out of his gains he can benefit his friends, and harm his enemies; moreover, he can offer sacrifices, and dedicate gifts to the gods abundantly and magnificently, and can honour the gods or any man whom he wants to honour in a far better style than the just, and therefore he is likely to be dearer than they are to the gods. And thus, Socrates, gods and men are said to unite in making the life of the unjust better than the life of the just.

I was going to say something in answer to Glaucon, when Adeimantus, his brother, interposed: Socrates, he said, you do not suppose that there is nothing more to be urged?

Why, what else is there? I answered.

The strongest point of all has not been even mentioned, he replied.

Well, then, according to the proverb, "Let brother help brother"—if he fails in any part do you assist him; although I must confess that Glaucon has already said quite enough to lay me in the dust, and take from me the power of helping justice.

Nonsense, he replied. But let me add something more: There is another side to Glaucon's argument about the praise and censure of justice and injustice, which is equally required in order to bring out what I believe to be his meaning. Parents and tutors are always telling their sons and their wards that they are to be just; but why? not for the sake of justice, but for the sake of character and reputation; in the hope of obtaining for him who is reputed just some of those offices, marriages, and the like which Glaucon has enumerated among the advantages accruing to the unjust from the reputation of justice. More, however, is made of appearances by this class of persons than by the others; for they throw in the good opinion of the gods, and will tell you of a shower of benefits which the heavens, as they say, rain upon the pious; and this accords with the testimony of the noble Hesiod and Homer, the first of whom says, that the gods make the oaks of the just—

> To bear acorns at their summit, and bees in the middle;
> And the sheep are bowed down with the weight of their fleeces,

and many other blessings of a like kind are provided for them. And Homer has a very similar strain; for he speaks of one whose fame is—

> As the fame of some blameless king who, like a god,
> Maintains justice; to whom the black earth brings forth
> Wheat and barley, whose trees are bowed with fruit,
> And his sheep never fail to bear, and the sea gives him fish.

Still grander are the gifts of heaven which Musaeus and his son[*] vouchsafe to the just; they take them down into the world below, where they have the saints lying on couches at a feast, everlastingly drunk, crowned with garlands; their idea seems to be that an immortality of drunkenness is the highest meed of virtue. Some extend their rewards yet further; the posterity, as they say, of the faithful and just shall survive to the third and fourth generation. This is the style in which they praise justice. But about the wicked there is another strain; they bury them in a slough in Hades, and make them carry water in a sieve; also while they are yet living they bring them to infamy, and inflict upon them the punishments which Glaucon described as the portion of the just who are reputed to be unjust; nothing else does their invention supply. Such is their manner of praising the one and censuring the other.

Once more, Socrates, I will ask you to consider another way of speaking about justice and injustice, which is not confined to the poets, but is found in prose writers. The universal voice of mankind is always declaring that justice and virtue are honourable, but grievous and toilsome; and that the pleasures of vice and injustice are easy of attainment, and are only censured by law and opinion. They say also that honesty is for the most part less profitable than dishonesty; and they are quite ready to call wicked men happy, and to honour them both in public and private when they are rich or in any other way influential, while they despise and overlook those who may be weak and poor, even though acknowledging

___
[*] Eumolpus

them to be better than the others. But most extraordinary of all is their mode of speaking about virtue and the gods: They say that the gods apportion calamity and misery to many good men, and good and happiness to the wicked. And mendicant prophets go to rich men's doors and persuade them that they have a power committed to them by the gods of making an atonement for a man's own or his ancestor's sins by sacrifices or charms, with rejoicings and feasts; and they promise to harm an enemy, whether just or unjust, at a small cost; with magic arts and incantations binding heaven, as they say, to execute their will. And the poets are the authorities to whom they appeal, now smoothing the path of vice with the words of Hesiod:

> Vice may be had in abundance without trouble; the way is smooth and her dwelling-place is near. But before virtue the gods have set toil,

and a tedious and uphill road: then citing Homer as a witness that the gods may be influenced by men; for he also says:—

> The gods, too, may be turned from their purpose; and men pray to them and avert their wrath by sacrifices and soothing entreaties, and by libations and the odour of fat, when they have sinned and transgressed.

And they produce a host of books written by Musaeus and Orpheus, who were children of the Moon and the Muses—that is what they say—according to which they perform their ritual, and persuade not only individuals, but whole cities, that expiations and atonements for sin may be made by sacrifices and amusements which fill a vacant hour, and are equally at the service of the living and the dead; the latter sort they call mysteries, and they redeem us from the pains of hell, but if we neglect them no one knows what awaits us.

He proceeded: And now when the young hear all this said about virtue and vice, and the way in which gods and men regard them, how are their minds likely to be affected, my dear Socrates—those of them, I mean, who are quick-witted, and, like bees on the wing, light on every flower, and from all that they hear are prone to draw conclusions as to what manner of persons they should be and in what way they should walk if they would make the best of life? Probably the youth will say to himself in the words of Pindar—

> Can I by justice or by crooked ways of deceit ascend a loftier tower which may be a fortress to me all my days?

For what men say is that, if I am really just and am not also thought just, profit there is none, but the pain and loss on the other hand are unmistakable. But if, though unjust, I acquire the reputation of justice, a heavenly life is promised to me. Since then, as philosophers prove, appearance tyrannizes over truth and is lord of happiness, to appearance I must devote myself. I will describe around me a picture and shadow of virtue to be the vestibule and exterior of my house; behind I will trail the subtle and crafty fox, as Archilochus, greatest of sages, recommends. But I hear some one exclaiming that the concealment of wickedness is often difficult; to which I answer, Nothing great is easy. Nevertheless, the argument indicates this, if we would be happy, to be the path along which we should proceed. With a view to concealment we will establish secret brotherhoods and political clubs. And there are professors of rhetoric who teach the art of persuading courts and assemblies; and so, partly by persuasion and partly by force, I shall make unlawful gains and not be punished. Still I hear a voice saying that the gods cannot be deceived, neither can they be compelled. But what if there are no gods? or, suppose them to have no care of human things—why in either case should we mind about concealment? And even if there are gods, and they do care about us, yet we know of them only from tradition and the genealogies of the poets; and these are the very persons who say that they may be influenced and turned by "sacrifices and soothing entreaties and by offerings." Let us be consistent then, and believe both or neither. If the poets speak truly, why then we had better be unjust, and offer of the fruits of injustice; for if we are just, although we may escape the vengeance of heaven, we shall lose the gains of injustice; but, if we are unjust, we shall keep the gains, and by our sinning and praying, and praying and sinning, the gods will be propitiated, and we shall not be punished. "But there is a world below in which either we or our posterity will suffer for our unjust deeds." Yes, my friend, will be the reflection, but there are mysteries and atoning deities, and these have great power. That is what mighty cities declare and the children of the gods, who were their poets and prophets, bear a like testimony.

On what principle, then, shall we any longer choose justice rather than the worst injustice? when, if we only unite the latter with a deceitful regard to appearances, we shall fare to our mind both with gods and men, in life and after death, as the most numerous and the highest authorities tell us. Knowing all this, Socrates, how can a man who has any superiority of mind or person or rank or wealth, be willing to honour justice; or indeed to refrain from laughing when he hears justice praised? And even if there should be some one who is able to disprove the truth of my words, and who is satisfied that justice is best, still he is not angry with the unjust, but is very ready to forgive them, because he also knows that men are not just of their own free will; unless, peradventure, there be some one whom the divinity within him may have inspired with a hatred of injustice, or who has attained knowledge of the truth—but no other man. He only blames injustice who, owing to cowardice or age or some weakness, has not the power of being unjust. And this is proved by the fact that when he obtains the power, he immediately becomes unjust as far as he can be.

The cause of all this, Socrates, was indicated by us at the beginning of the argument, when my brother and I told you how astonished we were to find that of all the professing panegyrists of justice—beginning with the ancient heroes of whom any memorial has been preserved to us, and ending with the men of our own time—no one has ever blamed injustice or praised justice except with a view to the glories, honours, and benefits which flow from them. No one has ever adequately described either in verse or prose the true essential nature of either of them abiding in the soul, and invisible to any human or divine eye; or shown that of all the things of a man's soul which he has within him, justice is the greatest good, and injustice the greatest evil. Had this been the universal strain, had you sought to persuade us of this from our youth upwards, we should not have been on the watch to keep one another from doing wrong, but every one would have been his own watchman, because afraid, if he did wrong, of harbouring in himself the greatest of evils. I dare say that Thrasymachus and others would seriously hold the language which I have been merely repeating, and words even stronger than these about justice and injustice, grossly, as I conceive, perverting their true nature. But I speak in this vehement manner, as I must frankly confess to you, because I want to hear from you the opposite side; and I would ask you to show not only the superiority which justice has over injustice, but what effect they have on the possessor of them which makes the one to be a good and the other an evil to him. And please, as Glaucon requested of you, to exclude reputations; for unless you take away from each of them his true reputation and add on the false, we shall say that you do not praise justice, but the appearance of it; we shall think that you are only exhorting us to keep injustice dark, and that you really agree with Thrasymachus in thinking that justice is another's good and the interest of the stronger, and that injustice is a man's own profit and interest, though injurious to the weaker. Now as you have admitted that justice is one of that highest class of goods which are desired indeed for their results, but in a far greater degree for their own sakes—like sight or hearing or knowledge or health, or any other real and natural and not merely conventional good—I would ask you in your praise of justice to regard one point only: I mean the essential good and evil which justice and injustice work in the possessors of them. Let others praise justice and censure injustice, magnifying the rewards and honours of the one and abusing the other; that is a manner of arguing which, coming from them, I am ready to tolerate, but from you who have spent your whole life in the consideration of this question, unless I hear the contrary from your own lips, I expect something better. And therefore, I say, not only prove to us that justice is better than injustice, but show what they either of them do to the possessor of them, which makes the one to be a good and the other an evil, whether seen or unseen by gods and men.

Discussion Questions

1. Historically, there have been many laws that we now consider immoral and not for the best of the citizens (slavery, for example). Can you think of any others now? How do you treat these laws from a moral standpoint? Is it better to follow an immoral law or to break the law?

2. What truth do you see, if any, in the phrase "Might makes right"? How is it true that "A just man always gets less than an unjust one"? Is this true in sports and games? In which ways do people or governments seem to follow this? What downside results?

3. How do you assess Socrates' comment "The greatest punishment . . . is to be ruled by someone worse than oneself"? Have you ever had a ruler—or a leader, team captain, coach, boss—who you believed to be "worse" than yourself? How did you react to this? Did it make you (a seemingly "decent person") desire to rule as Socrates suggests it would?

4. How would you act any differently if you had a ring that made you invisible (such as the ring of Gyges)? What immoral acts could you imagine yourself committing, if any? What do you think others would do? What does this thought experiment tell you about the human condition and morality and justice?

5. How do you answer the question "Why be moral?" What motivation do you have to act morally?

6. How do you asses Glaucon's following comments?
   a. "No one believes justice to be a good when it is kept private."
   b. "One shouldn't want to be just but to be believed to be just."

7. How important is your reputation—regardless of its accuracy—to you? Why?

Leviathan

Thomas Hobbes

Following his education at Oxford, Thomas Hobbes spent many years tutoring younger children of nobility and traveling throughout Europe. Much of his earlier writings focused on science and metaphysics, including a treatise attacking Descartes's view of dualism in favor of a materialistic, mechanistic universe. As civil unrest and rebellion arose in England, though, Hobbes focused primarily on political philosophy, inquiring about the status of governance and the source of political authority. His primary work, *Leviathan* (from which this selection is extracted), became widely circulated and also became a great source of trouble for Hobbes, as it disrupted much of the current paradigm—denying that kings rule by divine providence, attacking organized religion, and defending materialism along with a less romantic view of the human condition. Despite this turmoil, he continued to defend his thesis in *Leviathan*. The title, which he also uses to name the governed state that he describes, is a reference to the Old Testament in which "Leviathan" is a fire-breathing sea-monster with many heads that, as written in the book of Revelations, stands as the final battle for God before the world's end.

Hobbes first provides his overview of the Natural State—the condition in which humanity would exist without the affects of government or, what he calls, *common rule*. He then goes

Source: Thomas Hobbes, *Leviathan*. First published in London in 1651. Chapters 13–15, 17–18 (edited). Numerous sources exist, including M. Oakshott (Oxford: Blackwell, 1946) and C. B. Macpherson (Harmondsworth: Penguin, 1968).

on to show that it is manifest (obvious) that this common rule is necessary and explores laws that can be put in place through reason to help establish this governed state and justify the power of the ruler (or rulers), as well as exploring rational reasons for individuals to renounce certain privileges for the good of the state and, eventually, the individual.

Reading Questions

1. How and why does Hobbes argue that all people are basically equal? What issues does he suggest arise from this?
2. What three principles of human nature does Hobbes suggest as "causes of quarrel"? Briefly explain their significance.
3. How does Hobbes defend his position that, without governance, humans are in a state of *war*?
4. What results from an ungoverned society?
5. What anthropological reference does Hobbes use to defend his position? How does he do this?
6. In a warring state, why can no action be unjust? Why is there no concept of property?
7. Explain the difference between a *right* of nature and a *law* of nature.
8. What is the first law of nature? How does Hobbes arrive at it?
9. What is the second law of nature? How does Hobbes arrive at it? How does he relate it to the "Golden Rule" of the gospel?
10. Explain the relation of a *right* to a duty. How does one *renounce* and *transfer* a right?
11. What justification does Hobbes provide for a person's failing to abandon a right? What three cases does he provide as examples?
12. What is a *contract*? How does it differ from a *covenant, keeping of promise,* and a *gift*?
13. In what ways can one enter into a contract?
14. How does the existence of a common power make covenants valid that would otherwise be void?
15. What does Hobbes say about covenants with animals? With God? To not defend oneself from force by force?
16. What is the third law of nature? How does it provide a definition of *justice*? What *is* justice?
17. Explain the difference between commutative and distributive justice.
18. Briefly summarize laws five and six.
19. How does law seven deal with revenge? How does the end (purpose) of the revenge factor into this law?
20. What does Hobbes say about the distribution of goods?
21. From where, and how, does Hobbes derive moral truths?
22. Briefly explain the six reasons Hobbes provides as to why humans cannot live sociably together in the way other political/social animals do.
23. Why should a person submit their will to a sovereign leader/leaders? How does one attain sovereign power?

Of the Natural Condition of Mankind as Concerning Their Felicity and Misery

Nature has made men so equal in the faculties of the body and mind as that, though there be found one man sometimes manifestly stronger in body or of quicker mind than another, yet, when all is reckoned together, the difference between man and man is not so considerable as that one man can thereupon claim to himself any benefit to which another may not pretend as well as he. For as to the strength of body, the weakest has strength enough to kill the stronger, either by secret machination or by confederacy with others that are in the same danger with himself.

And as to the faculties of the mind, setting aside the arts grounded upon words, and especially that skill of proceeding upon general and infallible rules called science—which very few have and but in few things, as being not a native faculty born with us, nor attained, as prudence, while we look after somewhat else—I find yet a greater equality among men than that of strength. For prudence is but experience, which equal time equally bestows on all men in those things they equally apply themselves unto. That which may perhaps make such equality incredible is but a vain conceit of one's own wisdom, which almost all men think they have in a greater degree than the vulgar—that is, than all men but themselves and a few others whom, by fame or for concurring with themselves, they approve. For such is the nature of men that howsoever they may acknowledge many others to be more witty or more eloquent or more learned, yet they will hardly believe there be many so wise as themselves; for they see their own wit at hand and other men's at a distance. But this proves rather than men are in that point equal than unequal. For there is not ordinarily a greater sign of the equal distribution of anything than that every man is contented with his share.

From this equality of ability arises equality of hope in the attaining of our ends. And therefore if any two men desire the same thing, which nevertheless they cannot both enjoy, they become enemies; and in the way to their end, which is principally their own conservation, and sometimes their delectation only, endeavor to destroy or subdue one another. And from hence it comes to pass that where an invader has no more to fear than another man's single power, if one plant, sow, build, or possess a convenient seat, others may probably be expected to come prepared with forces united to dispossess and deprive him, not only of the fruit of his labor, but also of his life or liberty. And the invader again is in the like danger of another.

And from this diffidence of one another there is no way for any man to secure himself so reasonable as anticipation—that is, by force or wiles to master the persons of all men he can, so long till he see no other power great enough to endanger him; and this is no more than his own conservation requires, and is generally allowed. Also, because there be some that take pleasure in contemplating their own power in the acts of conquest, which they pursue farther than their security requires, if others that otherwise would be glad to be at ease within modest bounds should not by invasion increase their power, they would not be able, long time, by standing only on their defense, to subsist. And by consequence, such augmentation of dominion over men being necessary to a man's conservation, it ought to be allowed him.

Again, men have no pleasure, but on the contrary a great deal of grief, in keeping company where there is no power able to overawe them all. For every man looks that his companion should value him at the same rate he sets upon himself; and upon all signs of contempt or undervaluing naturally endeavors, as far as he dares (which among them that have no common power to keep them in quiet is far enough to make them destroy each other), to extort a greater value from his contemners by damage and from others by the example.

So that in the nature of man we find three principal causes of quarrel: first, competition; secondly, diffidence; thirdly, glory.

The first makes men invade for gain, the second for safety, and the third for reputation. The first use violence to make themselves masters of other men's persons, wives, children, and cattle; the second, to defend them; the third, for trifles, as a word, a smile, a different opinion, and any other sign of undervalue, either direct in their persons or by reflection in their kindred, their friends, their nation, their profession, or their name.

Hereby it is manifest that, during the time men live without a common power to keep them all in awe, they are in that condition which is called war, and such a war as is of every man against every man. For WAR consists not in battle only, or the act of fighting, but in a tract of time wherein the will to contend by battle is sufficiently known; and therefore the notion of *time* is to be considered in the nature of war as it is in the nature of weather. For as the nature of foul weather lies not in a shower or two of rain but in an inclination thereto of many days together, so the nature of war consists not in actual fighting but in the known disposition thereto during all the time there is no assurance to the contrary. All other time is PEACE.

Whatsoever, therefore, is consequent to a time of war where every man is enemy to every man, the same is consequent to the time wherein men live without other security than what their own strength and their own invention shall furnish them withal. In such condition there is no place for industry, because the fruit thereof is uncertain: and consequently no culture of the earth; no navigation nor use of the commodities that may be imported by sea; no commodious building; no instruments of moving and removing such things as require much force; no knowledge of the face of the earth; no account of time; no arts; no letters; no society; and, which is worst of all, continual fear and danger of violent death; and the life of man solitary, poor, nasty, brutish, and short.

It may seem strange to some man that has not well weighed these things that nature should thus dissociate and render men apt to invade and destroy one another; and he may therefore, not trusting to this inference made from the passions, desire perhaps to have the same confirmed by experience. Let him therefore consider with himself—when taking a journey he arms himself and seeks to go well accompanied, when going to sleep he locks his doors, when even in his house he locks his chests, and this when he knows there be laws and public officers, armed, to revenge all injuries shall be done him—what opinion he has of his fellow subjects when he rides armed, of his fellow citizens when he locks his doors, and of his children and servants when he locks his chests. Does he not there as much accuse mankind by his actions as I do by my words? But neither of us accuse man's nature in it. The desires and other passions of man are in themselves no sin. No more are the actions that proceed from those passions till they know a law that forbids them, which, till laws be made, they cannot know, nor can any law be made till they have agreed upon the person that shall make it.

It may peradventure be thought there was never such a time nor condition of war as this, and I believe it was never generally so over all the world; but there are many places where they live so now. For the savage people in many places of America, except the government of small families, the concord whereof depends on natural lust, have no government at all and live at this day in that brutish manner as I said before. Howsoever, it may be perceived what manner of life there would be where there were no common power to fear by the manner of life which men that have formerly lived under a peaceful government use to degenerate into in a civil war. . . .

To this war of every man against every man, this also is consequent: that nothing can be unjust. The notions of right and wrong, justice and injustice, have there no place. Where there is no common power, there is no law; where no law, no injustice. Force and fraud are in war the two cardinal virtues. Justice and injustice are none of the faculties neither of the body nor mind. If they were, they might be in a man that were alone in the world, as well as his senses and passions. They are qualities that relate to men in society, not in solitude. It is consequent also to the same condition that there be no propriety, no dominion, no *mine* and *thine* distinct; but only that to be every man's that he can get, and for so long as he can keep it. And thus much for the ill condition which man by mere nature is actually placed in, though with a possibility to come out of it consisting partly in the passions, partly in his reason.

The passions that incline men to peace are fear of death, desire of such things as are necessary to commodious living, and a hope by their industry to obtain them. And reason suggests convenient articles of peace, upon which men may be drawn to agreement. These articles are they which otherwise are called the Laws of Nature, whereof I shall speak more particularly in the two following chapters.

Of the First and Second Natural Laws, and of Contracts

The right of nature, which writers commonly call *jus naturale*, is the liberty each man has to use his own power, as he will himself for the preservation of his own nature—that is to say, of his own life—and consequently of doing anything which, in his own judgment and reason, he shall conceive to be the aptest means thereunto.

By LIBERTY is understood, according to the proper signification of the word, the absence of external impediments; which impediments may oft take away part of a man's power to do what he would, but cannot hinder him from using the power left him according as his judgment and reason shall dictate to him.

A LAW OF NATURE, *lex naturalis*, is a precept or general rule, found out by reason, by which a man is forbidden to do that which is destructive of his life or takes away the means of preserving the same and to omit that by which he thinks it may be best preserved. For though they that speak of this subject use to confound *jus* and *lex*, *right* and *law*, yet they ought to be distinguished; because RIGHT consists in liberty to do or to forbear, whereas LAW determines and binds to one of them; so that law and right differ as much as obligation and liberty, which in one and the same matter are inconsistent.

And because the condition of man, as has been declared in the precedent chapter, is a condition of war of every one against every one, . . . it follows that in such a condition every man has a right to everything, even to one another's body. And therefore, as long as this natural right of every man to everything endures, there can be no security to any man, how strong or wise soever he be, of living out the time which nature ordinarily allows men to live. And consequently it is a precept or general rule of reason *that every man ought to endeavor peace, as far as he has hope of obtaining it; and when he cannot obtain it, that he may seek and use all helps and advantages of war.* The first branch of which rule contains the first and fundamental law of nature, which is *to seek peace and follow it.* The second, the sum of the right of nature, which is, *by all means we can to defend ourselves.*

From this fundamental law of nature, by which men are commanded to endeavor peace, is derived this second law: *that a man be willing, when others are so too, as far forth as for peace and defense of himself he shall think it necessary, to lay down this right to all things, and be contented with so much liberty against other men as he would allow other men against himself.* For as long as every man holds this right of doing anything he likes, so long are all men in the condition of war. But if other men will not lay down their right as well as he, then there is no reason for anyone to divest himself of his, for that were to expose himself to prey, which no man is bound to rather than to dispose himself to peace. This is that law of the gospel: *whatsoever you require that others should do to you, that do ye to them.* And that law of all men, *quod tibi fieri non vis, alteri ne feceris.*

To *lay down* a man's *right* to anything is to *divest* himself of the *liberty* of hindering another of the benefit of his own right to the same. For he that renounces or passes away his right gives not to any other man a right which he had not before—because there is nothing to which every man had not right by nature—but only stands out of his way, that he may enjoy his own original right without hindrance from him, not without hindrance from another. So that the effect which redounds to one man by another man's defect of right is but so much diminution of impediments to the use of his own right original. Right is laid aside either by simply renouncing it or by transferring it to another. By *simply* RENOUNCING, when he cares not to whom the benefit thereof redounds. By TRANSFERRING, when he intends the benefit thereof to some certain person or persons. And when a man has in either manner abandoned or granted away his right, then he is said to be OBLIGED or BOUND not to hinder those to whom such right is granted or abandoned from the benefit of it; and that he *ought*, and it is his DUTY, not to make void that voluntary act of his own; and that such hindrance is INJUSTICE and INJURY as being *sine jure*, the right being before renounced or transferred. So that *injury* or *injustice* in the controversies of the world is somewhat like to that which in the disputations of scholars is called *absurdity*. For as it is there called an absurdity to contradict what one maintained in the beginning, so in the world it is called injustice and injury voluntarily to undo that which from the beginning he had voluntarily done. The way by which a man either simply renounces or transfers his right is a declaration or signification by some voluntary and sufficient sign or signs that he does so renounce or transfer, or has so renounced or transferred, the same to him that accepts it. And these signs are either words only or actions only; or as it happens most often, both words and actions. And the same are the BONDS by which men are bound and obliged—bonds that have their strength, not from their own nature, for nothing is more easily broken than a man's word, but from fear of some evil consequence upon the rupture.

Whensoever a man transfers his right or renounces it, it is either in consideration of some right reciprocally transferred to himself or for some other good he hopes for thereby. For it is a voluntary act; and of the voluntary acts of every man, the object is some *good to himself*. And therefore there be *some rights* which no man can be understood by any words or other signs to have abandoned or transferred. As, first, a man cannot lay down the right of resisting them that assault him by force to take away his life, because he cannot be understood to aim thereby at any good to himself. The same may be said of wounds and chains and imprisonment, both because there is no benefit consequent to such patience as there is to the patience of suffering another to be wounded or imprisoned, as also because a man cannot tell, when he sees men proceed against him by violence, whether they intend his death or not. And, lastly, the motive and end for which this renouncing and transferring of right is introduced is nothing else but the security of a man's person in his life and in the means of so preserving life as not to be weary of it. And therefore if a man by words or other signs seem to despoil himself of the end for which those signs were intended, he is not to be understood as if he meant it or that it was his will, but that he was ignorant of how such words and actions were to be interpreted.

The mutual transferring of right is that which men call CONTRACT.

There is difference between transferring of right to the thing and transferring, or tradition—that is, delivery—of the thing itself. For the thing may be delivered together with the translation of the right, as in buying and selling with ready money or exchange of goods or lands, and it may be delivered some time after.

Again, one of the contractors may deliver the thing contracted for on his part and leave the other to perform his part at some determinate time after and in the meantime be trusted, and then the contract on his part is called PACT or COVENANT; or both parts may contract now to perform hereafter, in which cases he that is to perform in time to come, being trusted, his performance is called *keeping of promise* or faith, and the failing of performance, if it be voluntary, *violation of faith*.

When the transferring of right is not mutual, but one of the parties transfers in hope to gain thereby friendship or service from another or from his friends, or in hope to gain the reputation of charity or magnanimity, or to deliver his mind from the pain of compassion, or in hope of reward in heaven—this is not contract but GIFT, FREE GIFT, GRACE, which words signify one and the same thing.

Signs of contract are either *express* or *by inference*. Express are words spoken with understanding of what they signify, and such words are either of the time *present* or *past*—as *I give, I grant, I have given, I have granted, I will that this be yours*—or of the future—as *I will give, I will grant*—which words of the future are called PROMISE.

Signs by inference are sometimes the consequence of words, sometimes the consequence of silence, sometimes the consequence of actions, sometimes the consequence of forbearing an action; and generally a sign by inference of any contract is whatsoever sufficiently argues the will of the contractor. . . .

If a covenant be made wherein neither of the parties perform presently but trust one another, in the condition of mere nature, which is a condition of war of every man against every man, upon any reasonable suspicion, it is void; but if there be a common power set over them both, with right and force sufficient to compel performance, it is not void. For he that performs first has no assurance the other will perform after, because the bonds of words are too weak to bridle men's ambition, avarice, anger, and other passions without the fear of some coercive power which in the condition of mere nature, where all men are equal and judges of the justness of their own fears, cannot possibly be supposed. And therefore he which performs first does but betray himself to his enemy, contrary to the right he can never abandon of defending his life and means of living.

But in a civil estate, where there is a power set up to constrain those that would otherwise violate their faith, that fear is no more reasonable; and for that cause, he which by the covenant is to perform first is obliged so to do.

The cause of fear which makes such a covenant invalid must be always something arising after the covenant made, as some new fact or other sign of the will not to perform; else it cannot make the covenant void. For that which could not hinder a man from promising ought not to be admitted as a hindrance of performing. . . .

To make covenants with brute beasts is impossible because, not understanding our speech, they understand not nor accept of any translation of right, nor can translate any right to another; and without mutual acceptation there is no covenant.

To make covenant with God is impossible but by mediation of such as God speaks to, either by revelation supernatural or by his lieutenants that govern under him and in his name; for otherwise we know not whether our covenants be accepted or not. And therefore they that vow anything contrary to any law of nature vow in vain, as being a thing unjust to pay such vow. And if it be a thing commanded by the law of nature, it is not the vow but the law that binds them. . . .

A covenant not to defend myself from force by force is always void. For, as I have showed before, no man can transfer or lay down his right to save himself from death, wounds, and imprisonment, the avoiding whereof is the only end of laying down any right; and therefore the promise of not resisting force in no covenant transfers any right, nor is obliging. For though a man may covenant thus: *Unless I do so or so, kill me*, he cannot covenant thus: *Unless I do so or so, I will not resist you when you come to kill me*. For man by nature chooses the lesser evil, which is danger of death in resisting, rather than the greater, which is certain and present death in not resisting. And this is granted to be true by all men, in that they lead criminals to execution and prison with armed men, notwithstanding that such criminals have consented to the law by which they are condemned. . . .

Of Other Laws of Nature

From that law of nature by which we are obliged to transfer to another such rights as, being retained, hinder the peace of mankind, there follows a third, which is this: *that men perform their covenants made;* without which covenants are in vain and but empty words, and, the right of all men to all things remaining, we are still in the condition of war.

And in this law of nature consists the fountain and original of JUSTICE. For where no covenant has preceded there has no right been transferred, and every man has right to every thing; and consequently to action can be unjust. But when a covenant is made, then to break it is *unjust*; and the definition of INJUSTICE is no other than *the not performance of covenant*. And whatsoever is not unjust is *just*.

But because covenants of mutual trust, where there is a fear of not performance on either part, as has been said in the former chapter, are invalid, though the original of justice be the making of covenants, yet injustice actually there can be none till the cause of such fear be taken away, which, while men are in the natural condition of war, cannot be done. Therefore, before the names of just and unjust can have place, there must be some coercive power to compel men equally to the performance of their covenants by the terror of some punishment greater than the benefit they expect by the breach of their covenant, and to make good that propriety which by mutual contract men acquire in recompense of the universal right they abandon; and such power there is none before the erection of a commonwealth. And this is also to be gathered out of the ordinary definition of justice in the Schools, for they say that *justice is the constant will of giving to every man his own*. And therefore where there is no *own*—that is, no propriety—there is no injustice; and where there is no coercive power erected—that is, where there is no commonwealth—there is no propriety, all men having right to all things; therefore, where there is no commonwealth, there nothing is unjust. So that the nature of justice consists in keeping of valid covenants; but the validity of covenants begins not but with the constitution of civil power sufficient to compel men to keep them; and then it is also that propriety begins. . . .

Justice, therefore—that is to say, keeping of covenant—is a rule of reason by which we are forbidden to do anything destructive to our life, and consequently a law of nature. . . .

Justice of actions is by writers divided into *commutative* and *distributive*; and the former they say consists in proportion arithmetical, the latter in proportion geometrical. Commutative, therefore, they place in the equality of value of the things contracted for, and distributive in the distribution of equal benefit to men of equal merit. As if it were injustice to sell dearer than we buy, or to give more to a man than he merits. The value of all things contracted for is measured by the appetite of the contractors, and therefore the just value is that which they be contented to give. And merit (besides that which is by covenant, where the performance on one part merits the performance of the other part, and falls under justice commutative, not distributive) is not due by justice, but is rewarded of grace only. And therefore this distinction, in the sense wherein it uses to be expounded, is not right. To speak properly, commutative justice is the justice of a contractor—that is, a performance of covenant in buying and selling, hiring and letting to hire, lending and borrowing, exchanging, bartering, and other acts of contract.

And distributive justice, the justice of an arbitrator—that is to say, the act of defining what is just. Wherein, being trusted by them that make him arbitrator, if he perform his trust, he is said to distribute to every man his own; and this is indeed just distribution, and may be called, though improperly, distributive justice, but more properly equity, which also is a law of nature, as shall be shown in due place.

As justice depends on antecedent covenant, so does GRATITUDE depend on antecedent grace—that is to say, antecedent free gift—and is the fourth law of nature, which may be conceived in this form: *that a man which receives benefit from another of mere grace endeavor that he which gives it have no reasonable cause to repent him of his good will.* For, no man gives but with intention of good to himself, because gift is voluntary, and of all voluntary acts the object is to every man his own good; of which if men see they shall be frustrated, there will be no beginning of benevolence or trust nor consequently of mutual help nor of reconciliation of one man to another; and therefore they are to remain still in the condition of *war*, which is contrary to the first and fundamental law of nature, which commands men to *seek peace.* The breach of this law is called *ingratitude,* and has the same relation to grace that injustice has to obligation by covenant.

A fifth law of nature is COMPLAISANCE—that is to say, *that every man strive to accommodate himself to the rest.* . . . For seeing every man, not only by right but also by necessity of nature, is supposed to endeavor all he can to obtain that which is necessary for his conservation, he that shall oppose himself against it for things superfluous is guilty of the war that thereupon is to follow, and therefore does that which is contrary to the fundamental law of nature, which commands *to seek peace.* The observers of this law may be called SOCIABLE (the Latins call them *commodi*), the contrary *stubborn, insociable, forward, intractable.*

A sixth law of nature is this: *that upon caution of the future time, a man ought to pardon the offenses past of them that, repenting, desire it.* For PARDON is nothing but granting of peace, which, though granted to them that persevere in their hostility, be not peace but fear, yet, not granted to them that give caution of the future time, is sign of an aversion to peace, and therefore contrary to the law of nature.

A seventh is *that in revenges*—that is, retribution of evil for evil—*men look not at the greatness of the evil past, but the greatness of the good to follow.* Whereby we are forbidden to inflict punishment with any other design than for correction of the offender or direction of others. For this law is consequent to the next before it that commands pardon upon security of the future time. Besides, revenge without respect to the example and profit to come is a triumph or glorying in the hurt of another, tending to no end; for the end is always somewhat to come, and glorying to no end is vainglory and contrary to reason; and to hurt without reason tends to the introduction of war, which is against the law of nature and is commonly styled by the name of *cruelty.* . . .

Another law: *that such things as cannot be divided be enjoyed in common, if it can be; and if the quantity of the thing permit, without stint; otherwise proportionably to the number of them that have right.* For otherwise the distribution is unequal and contrary to equity.

But some things there be that can neither be divided nor enjoyed in common. Then the law of nature, which prescribes equity, requires *that the entire right, or else—making the use alternate—the first possession, be determined by lot.* For equal distribution is of the law of nature; and other means of equal distribution cannot be imagined.

Of *lots* there be two sorts: *arbitrary* and *natural.* Arbitrary is that which is agreed on by the competitors; natural is either *primogeniture* (which the Greek calls κληρονομία which signifies *given by lot*) or *first seizure.*

And therefore those things which cannot be enjoyed in common, nor divided, ought to be adjudged to the first possessor; and in some cases to the first-born, as acquired by lot. . . .

The laws of nature are immutable and eternal, for injustice, ingratitude, arrogance, pride, iniquity, acception of persons, and the rest can never be made lawful. For it can never be that war shall preserve life and peace destroy it.

The same laws, because they oblige only to a desire and endeavor—I mean an unfeigned and constant endeavor—are easy to be observed. For in that they require nothing but endeavor, he that endeavors their performance fulfills them; and he that fulfills the law is just.

And the science of them is the true and only moral philosophy. For moral philosophy is nothing else but the science of what is *good* and *evil* in the conversation and society of mankind. *Good* and *evil* are names that signify our appetites and aversions, which in different tempers, customs, and doctrines of men are different; and divers men differ not only in their judgment on the senses of what is pleasant and unpleasant to the taste, smell, hearing, touch, and sight but also of what is conformable or disagreeable to reason in the actions of common life. Nay, the same man in divers times differs from himself, and one time praises—that is, calls good—what another time he dispraises and calls evil; from whence arise disputes, controversies, and at last war. And therefore so long as a man is in the condition of mere nature, which is a condition of war, private appetite is the measure of good and evil; and consequently all men agree on this: that peace is good, and therefore also the way or means of peace, which, as I have showed before, are *justice, gratitude, modesty, equity, mercy,* and the rest of the laws of nature, are good—that is to say, *moral virtues*—and their contrary *vices* evil. Now the science of virtue and vice is moral philosophy; and therefore the true doctrine of the laws of nature is the true moral philosophy. But the writers of moral philosophy, though they acknowledge the same virtues and vices, yet, not seeing wherein consisted their goodness nor that they come to be praised as the means of peaceable, sociable, and comfortable living, place them in a mediocrity of passions; as if not the cause but the degree of daring made fortitude, or not the cause but the quantity of a gift made liberality.

These dictates of reason men used to call by the name of laws, but improperly, for they are but conclusions or theorems concerning what conduces to the conservation and defense of themselves, whereas law, properly, is the word of him that by right has command over others. But yet if we consider the same theorems as delivered in the word of God, that by right commands all things, then are they properly called laws.

Part II: Of Commonwealth

Chapter XVII: Of the Causes, Generation, and Definition of a Commonwealth

. . . It is true that certain living creatures, as bees and ants, live sociably one with another (which are therefore by *Aristotle* numbered amongst political creatures), and yet have no other direction than their particular judgments and appetites; nor speech, whereby one of them can signify to another what he thinks expedient for the common benefit: And therefore some man may perhaps desire to know why mankind cannot do the same. To which I answer,

First, that men are continually in competition for honour and dignity, which these creatures are not; and consequently amongst men there ariseth on that ground, envy, and hatred, and finally war; but amongst these not so.

Secondly, that amongst these creatures the common good differeth not from the private; and being by nature inclined to their private, they procure thereby the common benefit. But man, whose joy consisteth in comparing himself with other men, can relish nothing but what is eminent.

Thirdly, that these creatures, having not, as man, the use of reason, do not see, nor think they see, any fault in the administration of their common business: Whereas amongst men there are very many that think themselves wiser and abler to govern the public better than the rest, and these strive to reform and innovate, one this way, another that way; and thereby bring it into distraction and civil war.

Fourthly, that these creatures, though they have some use of voice in making known to one another their desires and other affections, yet they want that art of words by which some men can represent to others that which is good in the likeness of evil; and evil, in the likeness of good; and augment or diminish the apparent greatness of good and evil, discontenting men and troubling their peace at their pleasure.

Fifthly, irrational creatures cannot distinguish between *injury* and *damage*; and therefore as long as they be at ease, they are not offended with their fellows: Whereas man is then most troublesome when he is most at ease; for then it is that he loves to show his wisdom, and control the actions of them that govern the commonwealth.

Lastly, the agreement of these creatures is natural; that of men is by covenant only, which is artificial: And therefore it is no wonder if there be somewhat else required, besides covenant, to make their agreement constant and lasting; which is a common power to keep them in awe and to direct their actions to the common benefit.

The only way to erect such a common power, as may be able to defend them from the invasion of foreigners, and the injuries of one another, and thereby to secure them in such sort as that by their own industry and by the fruits of the earth they may nourish themselves and live contentedly, is to confer all their power and strength upon one man, or upon one assembly of men, that may reduce all their wills, by plurality of voices, unto one will: which is as much as to say, to appoint one man, or assembly of men, to bear their person; and every one to own and acknowledge himself to be author of whatsoever he that so beareth their person shall act, or cause to be acted, in those things which concern the common peace and safety; and therein to submit their wills, every one to his will, and their judgments to his judgment. This is more than consent, or concord; it is a real unity of them all in one and the same person, made by covenant of every man with every man, in such manner as if every man should say to every man: *I authorise and give up my right of governing myself to this man, or to this assembly of men, on this condition; that thou give up, thy right to him, and authorise all his actions in like manner.* This done, the multitude so united in one person is called a *commonwealth*; in Latin, *civitas*. This is the generation of that great *Leviathan*, or rather, to speak more reverently, of that *Mortal God* to which we owe, under the *Immortal God*, our peace and defence. For by this authority, given him by every particular man in the commonwealth, he hath the use of so much power and strength conferred on him that, by terror thereof, he is enabled to form the wills of them all, to peace at home, and mutual aid against their enemies abroad. And in him consisteth the essence of the commonwealth; which, to define it, is: *one person, of whose acts a great multitude, by mutual covenants one with another, have made themselves every one the author, to the end he may use the strength and means of them all as he shall think expedient for their peace and common defence.*

And he that carryeth this person is called sovereign, and said to have *sovereign power*, and every one besides, his subject.

The attaining to this sovereign power is by two ways. One, by natural force: As when a man maketh his children to submit themselves, and their children, to his government, as being able to destroy them if they refuse; or by war subdueth his enemies to his will, giving them their lives on that condition. The other, is when men agree amongst themselves to submit to some man, or assembly of men, voluntarily, on confidence to be protected by him against all others. This latter may be called a political commonwealth, or commonwealth by *institution*; and the former, a commonwealth by *acquisition*. And first, I shall speak of a commonwealth by institution.

Chapter XVIII: Of the Rights of Sovereigns by Institution

A *commonwealth* is said to be *instituted* when a *multitude* of men do agree, and *covenant, every one with every one*, that to whatsoever *man*, or *assembly of men*, shall be given by the major part the *right* to *present* the person of them all, that is to say, to be their *representative*; every one, as well he that *voted for it* as he that *voted against it*, shall *authorize* all the actions and judgements of that man, or assembly of men, in the same manner as if they were his own, to the end to live peaceably amongst themselves, and be protected against other men.

From this institution of a commonwealth are derived all the *rights* and *faculties* of him, or them, on whom the sovereign power is conferred by the consent of the people assembled. . . .

Discussion Questions

1. Do you agree that humans would be in a constant state of war without any common governance ruling over them? How would you support your position?
2. What does it mean to you to have a right to life? To liberty? To the pursuit of happiness?
3. Have you ever made a promise to someone and followed through with it, even when it was an inconvenience? What motivated you to keep this promise? Was it somehow in your best interest, as Hobbes claims? He writes, "no man gives but with intention of good to himself." Do you agree? If not, why? What *could* he mean here?
4. Look at Hobbes' six reasons as to why humans cannot live together in the way other social animals do. Humans are often considered *better* than other species. Do you agree that we are? How do you apply your ideas to Hobbes' six reasons here? Do you agree with Hobbes here?
5. The defense of anarchy—living without a sovereign power governing the people—rests on the notion that to surrender one's autonomy and deep sense of freedom is worse than the goods provided by this government. How do you evaluate this claim?

Two Treatises of Government
John Locke

It is purported that John Locke initially wrote *Two Treatises of Government* in order to justify the revolution against Charles II in 1681 by the Whigs. Though he later revised it and hoped, as he cited in the Preface, it would be "sufficient to establish the throne of our great restorer, our present King William."

Like Hobbes, Locke discusses the *state of nature*—what life would be like without any established government (state). Locke, though, held that a *law of nature* would exist that could govern people, but that it still left things wanting (lacking)—this is where the government becomes necessary. Locke discusses justifications of punishment, property ownership, and his famous notion of *tacit consent*—that, simply by participating in the state, one agrees to the rules therein.

Reading Questions

1. According to Locke, what liberties do people have and not have in the "state of liberty"? From where does the law originate?
2. In what circumstances does Locke justify punishment?
3. How does Locke justify war? What signifies the difference between a state of nature and of war?
4. How does Locke explain someone's rightly acquiring property? What about rightly acquiring resources?
5. What is required to form a political/civil society? How does Locke suggest that someone consents to being governed and thus authorizes the state to make laws over him or her?
6. What is the primary end (goal) in people establishing a commonwealth? In your own words, summarize the three things wanting (lacking) in the state of nature that are not lacking under a government.
7. What are the limits of the government?

Of the State of Nature

To understand political power aright, and derive it from its original, we must consider, what state all men are naturally in, and that is, a state of perfect freedom to order their actions, and dispose of their possessions and persons, as they think fit, within the bounds of the law of nature, without asking leave, or depending upon the will of any other man.

A state also of equality, wherein all the power and jurisdiction is reciprocal, no one having more than another; there being nothing more evident, than that creatures of the same species and rank, promiscuously born to all the same

Source: John Locke, *The Second Treatise of Civil Government.* 1690.

advantages of nature, and the use of the same faculties, should also be equal one amongst another without subordination or subjection, unless the lord and master of them all should, by any manifest declaration of his will, set one above another, and confer on him, by an evident and clear appointment, an undoubted right to dominion and sovereignty. . . .

But though this be a state of liberty, yet it is not a state of licence: Though man in that state have an uncontrollable liberty to dispose of his person or possessions, yet he has not liberty to destroy himself, or so much as any creature in his possession, but where some nobler use than its bare preservation calls for it. The state of nature has a law of nature to govern it, which obliges every one, and reason, which is that law, teaches all mankind, who will but consult it, that being all equal and independent, no one ought to harm another in his life, health, liberty, or possessions: for men being all the workmanship of one omnipotent, and infinitely wise maker; all the servants of one sovereign master, sent into the world by his order, and about his business; they are his property, whose workmanship they are, made to last during his, not one another's pleasure: And being furnished with like faculties, sharing all in one community of nature, there cannot be supposed any such subordination among us, that may authorize us to destroy one another, as if we were made for one another's uses, as the inferior ranks of creatures are for ours. Every one, as he is bound to preserve himself, and not to quit his station wilfully, so by the like reason, when his own preservation comes not in competition, ought he as much as he can to preserve the rest of mankind, and not unless it be to do justice on an offender, take away, or impair the life, or what tends to the preservation of the life, the liberty, health, limb or goods of another.

And that all men may be restrained from invading others' rights, and from doing hurt to one another, and the law of nature be observed, which willeth the peace and preservation of all mankind, the execution of the law of nature is, in that state, put into every man's hands, whereby every one has a right to punish the transgressors of that law to such a degree, as may hinder its violation. For the law of nature would, as all other laws that concern men in this world, be in vain, if there were nobody that in the state of nature had a power to execute that law, and thereby preserve the innocent and restrain offenders. And if any one in the state of nature may punish another for any evil he has done, every one may do so: For in that state of perfect equality where naturally there is no superiority or jurisdiction of one over another, what any may do in prosecution of that law, every one must needs have a right to do.

And thus, in the state of nature, one man comes by a power over another; but yet no absolute or arbitrary power, to use a criminal, when he has got him in his hands, according to the passionate heats, or boundless extravagancy of his own will; but only to retribute to him, so far as calm reason and conscience dictates, what is proportionate to his transgression, which is so much as may serve for reparation and restraint: For these two are the only reasons why one man may lawfully do harm to another, which is that we call punishment. In transgressing the law of nature, the offender declares himself to live by another rule than that of reason and common equity, which is that measure God has set to the actions of men for their mutual security, and so he becomes dangerous to mankind, the tie, which is to secure them from injury and violence, being slighted and broken by him, which being a trespass against the whole species, and the peace and safety of it, provided for by the law of nature, every man upon this score, by the right he hath to preserve mankind in general, may restrain, or where it is necessary, destroy things noxious to them, and so may bring such evil on any one, who hath transgressed that law, as may make him repent the doing of it, and thereby deter him, and, by his example others, from doing the like mischief. And in this case, and upon this ground, every man hath a right to punish the offender, and be executioner of the law of nature. . . .

Besides the crime which consists in violating the law, and varying from the right rule of reason, whereby a man so far becomes degenerate, and declares himself to quit the principles of human nature and to be a noxious creature, there is commonly injury done, and some person or other, some other man receives damage by his transgression; in which case he who hath received any damage, has, besides the right of punishment common to him with other men, a particular right to seek reparation from him that has done it: And any other person, who finds it just, may also join with him that is injured, and assist him in recovering from the offender so much as may make satisfaction for the harm he has suffered.

From these two distinct rights, the one of punishing the crime for restraint, and preventing the like offence, which right of punishing is in everybody; the other of taking reparation, which belongs only to the injured party, comes it to pass that the magistrate, who by being magistrate hath the common right of punishing put into his hands, can often, where the public good demands not the execution of the law, remit the punishment of criminal offences by his own authority, but yet cannot remit the satisfaction due to any private man for the damage he has received. That, he who has suffered the damage has a right to demand in his own name, and he alone can remit: The damnified person has this power of appropriating to himself the goods or service of the offender, by right of self-preservation, as every man has a power to punish the crime, to prevent its being committed again, by the right he has of preserving all mankind, and doing all reasonable things he can in order to that end: And thus it is, that every man, in the state of nature, has a power to kill a murderer, both to deter others from doing the like injury, which no reparation can compensate, by the example of the punishment that attends it from every body, and also to secure men from the attempts of a criminal, who having renounced reason, the common rule and measure God hath given to mankind, hath, by the unjust violence and slaughter he hath committed upon one, declared war against all mankind, and therefore may be destroyed as a lion or a tiger, one of those wild savage beasts, with whom men can have no society nor security: and upon this is grounded that great law of nature, *Whoso sheddeth man's blood, by man shall his blood be shed.* And Cain was so fully convinced, that every one had a right to destroy such a criminal, that after the murder of his brother, he cries out, *Every one that findeth me shall slay me*; so plain was it writ in the hearts of all mankind.

By the same reason may a man in the state of nature punish the lesser breaches of that law. It will perhaps be demanded, with death? I answer, each transgression may be punished to that degree, and with so much severity, as will suffice to make it an ill bargain to the offender, give him cause to repent, and terrify others from doing the like. Every offence, that can be committed in the state of nature, may in the state of nature be also punished equally, and as far forth as it may, in a commonwealth: for though it would be besides my present purpose, to enter here into the particulars of the law of nature, or its measures of punishment; yet, it is certain there is such a law, and that too as intelligible and plain to a rational creature, and a studier of that law, as the positive laws of commonwealths: nay, possibly plainer; as much as reason is easier to be understood, than the fancies and intricate contrivances of men, following contrary and hidden interests put into words; for so truly are a great part of the municipal laws of countries, which are only so far right, as they are founded on the law of nature, by which they are to be regulated and interpreted.

To this strange doctrine, viz., that in the state of nature every one has the executive power of the law of nature, I doubt not but it will be objected, that it is unreasonable for men to be judges in their own cases, that self-love will make men partial to themselves and their friends: And on the other side, ill-nature, passion, and revenge will carry them too far in punishing others; and hence nothing but confusion and disorder will follow; and that therefore God hath certainly appointed government to restrain the partiality and violence of men. I easily grant that civil government is the proper remedy for the inconveniences of the state of nature, which must certainly be great where men may be judges in their own case, since 'tis easy to be imagined, that he who was so unjust as to do his brother an injury, will scarce be so just as to condemn himself for it; but I shall desire those who make this objection, to remember, that absolute monarchs are but men; and if government is to be the remedy of those evils, which necessarily follow from men's being judges in their own cases, and the state of nature is therefore not to be endured, I desire to know what kind of government that is, and how much better it is than the state of nature, where one man commanding a multitude, has the liberty to be judge in his own case, and may do to all his subjects whatever he pleases, without the least question or control of those who execute his pleasure? and in whatsoever he doth, whether led by reason, mistake or passion, must be submitted to? which men in the state of nature are not bound to do one to another. And if he that judges, judges amiss in his own, or any other case, he is answerable for it to the rest of mankind. . . .

Of the State of War

The state of war is a state of enmity and destruction; and therefore declaring by word or action, not a passionate and hasty, but sedate, settled design upon another man's life, puts him in a state of war with him against whom he has declared such an intention, and so has exposed his life to the other's power to be taken away by him, or any one that joins with him in his defence, and espouses his quarrel, it being reasonable and just I should have a right to destroy that which threatens me with destruction; for by the fundamental law of nature, man being to be preserved, as much as possible, when all cannot be preserved, the safety of the innocent is to be preferred; and one may destroy a man who makes war upon him, or has discovered an enmity to his being, for the same reason that he may kill a wolf or a lion, because such men are not under the ties of the common law of reason, have no other rule but that of force and violence, and so may be treated as beasts of prey, those dangerous and noxious creatures that will be sure to destroy him whenever he falls into their power.

And hence it is that he who attempts to get another man into his absolute power does thereby put himself into a state of war with him; it being to be understood as a declaration of a design upon his life. For I have reason to conclude that he who would get me into his power without my consent would use me as he pleased when he had got me there, and destroy me too when he had a fancy to it, for nobody can desire to have me in his absolute power unless it be to compel me by force to that which is against the right of my freedom—i.e., make me a slave. To be free from such force is the only security of my preservation, and reason bids me look on him as an enemy to my preservation who would take away that freedom which is the fence to it; so that he who makes an attempt to enslave me thereby puts himself into a state of war with me. He that in the state of nature would take away the freedom that belongs to any one in that state must necessarily be supposed to have a design to take away everything else, that freedom being the foundation of all the rest; as he that in the state of society would take away the freedom belonging to those of that society or commonwealth must be supposed to design to take away from them everything else, and so be looked on as in a state of war.

This makes it lawful for a man to kill a thief who has not in the least hurt him, nor declared any design upon his life, any farther than by the use of force, so to get him in his power as to take away his money, or what he pleases, from him; because using force, where he has no right to get me into his power, let his pretence be what it will, I have no reason to suppose that he who would take away my liberty would not, when he had me in his power, take away everything else. And therefore it is lawful for me to treat him as one who has put himself into a state of war with me—i.e., kill him if I can; for to that hazard does he justly expose himself whoever introduces a state of war, and is aggressor in it.

And here we have the plain difference between the state of nature and the state of war, which however some men have confounded, are as far distant as a state of peace, goodwill, mutual assistance, and preservation; and a state of enmity, malice, violence, and mutual destruction are one from another. Men living together according to reason without a common superior on earth, with authority to judge between them, are properly in the state of nature. But force, or a declared design of force upon the person of another, where there is no common superior on earth to appeal to for relief, is the state of war; and 'tis the want of such an appeal gives a man the right of war even against an aggressor, though he be in society and a fellow-subject. Thus, a thief whom I cannot harm, but by appeal to the law, for having stolen all that I am worth, I may kill when he sets on me to rob me but of my horse or coat, because the law, which was made for my preservation, where it cannot interpose to secure my life from present force, which if lost is capable of no reparation, permits me my own defence and the right of war, a liberty to kill the aggressor, because the aggressor allows not time to appeal to our common judge, nor the decision of the law, for remedy in a case where the mischief may be irreparable. Want of a common judge with authority puts all men in a state of nature; force without right upon a man's person makes a state of war both where there is, and is not, a common judge. . . .

Of Property

. . . Though the earth and all inferior creatures be common to all men, yet every man has a *property* in his own *person*. This nobody has any right to but himself. The *labour* of his body and the *work* of his hands, we may say, are properly his. Whatsoever, then, he removes out of the state that nature hath provided and left it in, he hath mixed his labour with it, and joined to it something that is his own, and thereby makes it his property. It being by him removed from the common state nature placed it in, it hath by this labour something annexed to it that excludes the common right of other men. For this labour being the unquestionable property of the labourer, no man but he can have a right to what that is once joined to, at least where there is enough, and as good left in common for others.

He that is nourished by the acorns he picked up under an oak, or the apples he gathered from the trees in the wood, has certainly appropriated them to himself. Nobody can deny but the nourishment is his. I ask, then, when did they begin to be his? when he digested? or when he ate? or when he boiled? or when he brought them home? or when he picked them up? And 'tis plain, if the first gathering made them not his, nothing else could. That labour put a distinction between them and common. That added something to them more than Nature, the common mother of all, had done, and so they became his private right. And will any one say he had no right to those acorns or apples he thus appropriated because he had not the consent of all mankind to make them his? Was it a robbery thus to assume to himself what belonged to all in common? If such a consent as that was necessary, man had starved, notwithstanding the plenty God had given him. We see in commons, which remain so by compact, that 'tis the taking any part of what is common, and removing it out of the state Nature leaves it in, which begins the property, without which the common is of no use. And the taking of this or that part does not depend on the express consent of all the commoners. Thus, the grass my horse has bit, the turfs my servant has cut, and the ore I have digged in any place, where I have a right to them in common with others, become my property without the assignation or consent of any body. The labour that was mine, removing them out of that common state they were in, hath fixed my property in them. . . .

It will perhaps be objected to this, that if gathering the acorns or other fruits of the earth, etc., makes a right to them, then any one may engross as much as he will. To which I answer, Not so. The same law of nature that does by this means give us property, does also bound that property too. *God has given us all things richly*, I *Tim.* vi. 12. Is the voice of reason confirmed by inspiration? But how far has he given it us, *to enjoy*? As much as any one can make use of to any advantage of life before it spoils, so much he may by his labour fix a property in. Whatever is beyond this is more than his share, and belongs to others. Nothing was made by God for man to spoil or destroy. And thus considering the plenty of natural provisions there was a long time in the world, and the few spenders, and to how small a part of that provision the industry of one man could extend itself and engross it to the prejudice of others, especially keeping within the bonds set by reason of what might serve for his use, there could be then little room for quarrels or contentions about property so established. . . .

Of Political or Civil Society

Man being born, as has been proved, with a title to perfect freedom and an uncontrolled enjoyment of all the rights and privileges of the law of nature, equally with any other man, or number of men in the world, hath by nature a power not only to preserve his property, that is, his life, liberty, and estate, against the injuries and attempts of other men, but to judge of and punish the breaches of that law in others, as he is persuaded the offence deserves, even with death itself, in crimes where the heinousness of the fact, in his opinion, requires it. But because no political society can be, nor subsist, without having in itself the power to preserve the property, and in order thereunto punish the offences of all those of that society: There, and there only, is political society, where every one of the members hath quitted this natural power, resigned it up into the hands of the community in all cases that exclude him not from appealing for protection to the law established by it. And thus all private judgement of every particular member being excluded, the community comes to be umpire, by settled standing rules; indifferent, and the same to all parties: And by men having authority from the community for the execution of those rules, decides all the differences that may happen between any members of that society concerning any matter of right, and punishes those offences which any member hath committed against the society with such penalties as the law has established; whereby it is easy to discern who are, and who are not, in political society together. Those who are united into one body, and have a common established law and judicature to appeal to, with authority to decide controversies between them and punish offenders, are in civil society one with, another; but those who have no such common appeal, I mean on earth, are still in the state of nature, each being, where there is no other, judge for himself and executioner; which is, as I have before showed it, the perfect state of nature.

And thus the commonwealth comes by a power to set down what punishment shall belong to the several transgressions they think worthy of it, committed amongst the members of that society (which is the power of making laws) as well as it has the power to punish any injury done unto any of its members by anyone that is not of it (which is the power of war and peace); and all this for the preservation of the property of all the members of that society, as far as is possible. But though every man entered into society has quitted his power to punish offences against the law of nature in prosecution of his own private judgement, yet with the judgement of offences which he has given up to the legislative in all cases where he can appeal to the magistrate, he has given up a right to the commonwealth to employ his force for the execution of the judgements of the commonwealth whenever he shall be called to it, which, indeed, are his own judgement, they being made by himself or his representative. And herein we have the original of the legislative and executive power of civil society, which is to judge by standing laws how far offences are to be punished when committed within the commonwealth; and also by occasional judgements founded on the present circumstances of the fact, how far injuries from without are to be vindicated, and in both these to employ all the force of all the members when there shall be need.

Wherever therefore any number of men are so united into one society as to quit every one his executive power of the law of nature, and to resign it to the public, there and there only is a political or civil society. And this is done wherever any number of men, in the state of nature, enter into society to make one people, one body politic under one supreme government: or else when anyone joins himself to and incorporates with any government already made. For hereby he authorizes the society, or which is all one, the legislative thereof, to make laws for him as the public good of he society shall require, to the execution whereof his own assistance (as to his own decrees) is due. And this puts men out of a state of nature into that of a commonwealth, by setting up a judge on earth with authority to determine all the controversies and redress the injuries that may happen to any member of the commonwealth; which judge is the legislative or magistrates appointed by it. And wherever there are any number of men, however associated, that have no such decisive power to appeal to, there they are still in the state of nature.

And hence it is evident that absolute monarchy, which by some men is counted for the only government in the world, is indeed inconsistent with civil society, and so can be no form of civil government at all. For the end of civil society being to avoid and remedy those inconveniences of the state of nature which necessarily follow from every man's being judge in his own case, by setting up a known authority, to which everyone of that society may appeal upon any injury received, or controversy that may arise, and which everyone of the society ought to obey, wherever any persons are who have not such an authority to appeal to, for the decision of any difference between them there, those persons are still in the state of nature. And so is every absolute prince in respect of those who are under his *dominion*. . . .

Men being, as has been said, by nature all free, equal, and independent, no one can be put out of this estate and subjected to the political power of another without his own consent, which is done by agreeing with other men, to join and unite into a community for their comfortable, safe, and peaceable living, one amongst another, in a secure enjoyment of their properties, and a greater security against any that are not of it. This any number of men may do, because it injures not the freedom of the rest; they are left, as they were, in the liberty of the state of Nature. When any number of men have so consented to make one community or government, they are thereby presently incorporated, and make one body politic, wherein the majority have a right to act and conclude the rest.

For, when any number of men have, by the consent of every individual, made a community, they have thereby made that community one body, with a power to act as one body, which is only by the will and determination of the majority. For that which acts any community, being only the consent of the individuals of it, and it being one body, must move one way, it is necessary the body should move that way whither the greater force carries it, which is the consent of the majority, or else it is impossible it should act or continue one body, one community, which the consent of every individual that united into it agreed that is should; and so every one is bound by that consent to be concluded by the majority. And therefore we see that in assemblies empowered to act by positive laws where no number is set by that positive law which empowers them, the act of the majority passes for the act of the whole, and of course determines as having, by the law of Nature and reason, the power of the whole.

And thus every man, by consenting with others to make one body politic under one government, puts himself under an obligation to every one of that society to submit to the determination of the majority, and to be concluded by it; or else this original compact, whereby he with others incorporates into one society, would signify nothing, and be no compact if he be left free and under no other ties than he was in before in the state of Nature. For what appearance would there be of any compact? What new engagement if he were no farther tied by any decrees of the society than he himself thought fit and did actually consent to? This would be still as great a liberty as he himself had before his compact, or any one else in the state of Nature, who may submit himself and consent to any acts of it if he thinks fit.

For if the consent of the majority shall not in reason be received as the act of the whole, and conclude every individual, nothing but the consent of every individual can make anything to be the act of the whole, which, considering the infirmities of health and avocations of business, which in a number though much less than that of a commonwealth, will necessarily keep many away from the public assembly; and the variety of opinions and contrariety of interests which unavoidably happen in all collections of men, it is next impossible ever to be had. And, therefore, if coming into society be upon such terms, it will be only like Cato's coming into the theatre, *tantum ut exirt*. Such a constitution as this would make the mighty leviathan of a shorter duration than the feeblest creatures, and not let it outlast the day it was born in, which cannot be supposed till we can think that rational creatures should desire and constitute societies only to be dissolved. For where the majority cannot conclude the rest, there they cannot act as one body, and consequently will be immediately dissolved again.

Whosoever, therefore, out of a state of Nature unite into a community, must be understood to give up all the power necessary to the ends for which they unite into society to the majority of the community, unless they expressly agreed in any number greater than the majority. And this is done by barely agreeing to unite into one political society, which is all the compact that is, or needs be, between the individuals that enter into or make up a commonwealth. And thus, that which begins and actually constitutes any political society is nothing but the consent of any number of freemen capable of majority, to unite and incorporate into such a society. And this is that, and that only, which did or could give beginning to any lawful government in the world. . . .

Of the Ends of Political Society and Government Of the Extent of Legislative Power

If man in the state of nature be so free as has been said; if he be absolute lord of his own person and possessions; equal to the greatest and subject to no body, why will he part with his freedom? Why will he give up this empire, and subject himself to the dominion and control of any other power? To which 'tis obvious to answer, that though in the state of nature he hath such a right, yet the enjoyment of it is very uncertain and constantly exposed to the invasion of others; for all being kings as much as he, every man his equal, and the greater part no strict observers of equity and justice, the enjoyment of the property he has in this state is very unsafe, very unsecure. This makes him willing to quit this condition which, however free, is full of fears and continual dangers; and 'tis not without reason that he seeks out and is willing to join in society with others who are already united, or have a mind to unite for the mutual preservation of their lives, liberties, and estates, which I call by the general name, property.

The great and chief end therefore, of men's uniting into commonwealths, and putting themselves under government, is the preservation of their property; to which in the state of nature there are many things wanting.

First, There wants an established, settled, known law, received and allowed by common consent to be the standard of right and wrong, and the common measure to decide all controversies between them. For though the law of nature be plain and intelligible to all rational creatures, yet men, being biased by their interest, as well as ignorant for want of study of it, are not apt to allow of it as a law binding to them in the application of it to their particular cases.

Secondly, In the state of nature there wants a known and indifferent judge, with authority to determine all differences according to the established law. For everyone in that state being both judge and executioner of the law of nature, men being partial to themselves, passion and revenge is very apt to carry them too far, and with too much heat in their own cases, as well as negligence and unconcernedness, make them too remiss in other men's.

Thirdly, In the state of nature there often wants power to back and support the sentence when right, and to give it due execution. They who by any injustice offended, will seldom fail where they are able by force to make good their injustice. Such resistance many times makes the punishment dangerous, and frequently destructive to those who attempt it.

Thus mankind, notwithstanding all the privileges of the state of nature, being but in an ill condition while they remain in it, are quickly driven into society. Hence it comes to pass, that we seldom find any number of men live any time together in this state. The inconveniences that they are therein exposed to by the irregular and uncertain exercise of the power every man has of punishing the transgressions of others, make them take sanctuary under the established laws of government, and therein seek the preservation of their property. 'Tis this makes them so willingly give up every one his single power of punishing to be exercised by such alone as shall be appointed to it amongst them, and by such rules as the community, or those authorized by them to that purpose, shall agree on. And in this we have the original right and rise of both the legislative and executive power as well as of the governments and societies themselves. . . .

The Limits of Government

The great end of men's entering into society being the enjoyment of their properties in peace and safety, and the great instrument and means of that being the laws established in that society, the first and fundamental positive law of all commonwealths is the establishing of the legislative power; as the first and fundamental natural law, which is to govern even the legislative itself, is the preservation of the society, and (as far as will consist with the public good) of every person in it. This legislative is not only the supreme power of the commonwealth, but sacred and unalterable in the hands where the community have once placed it; nor can any edict of anybody else, in what form soever conceived, or by what power soever backed, have the force and obligation of a law which has not its sanction from that legislative which the public has chosen and appointed; for without this the law could not have that which is absolutely necessary to its being a law, the consent of the society, over whom nobody can have a power to make laws but by their own consent and by authority received from them; and therefore all the obedience, which by the most solemnities anyone can be obliged to pay, ultimately terminates in this supreme power, and is directed by those laws which it enacts. Nor can any oaths to any foreign power whatsoever, or any domestic subordinate power, discharge any member of the society from his obedience to the legislative, acting pursuant to their trust, nor oblige him to any obedience contrary to the laws so enacted or father than they do allow, it being ridiculous to imagine one can be tied ultimately to obey any power in the society which is not the supreme. . . .

These are the bounds which the trust that is put in them by the society and the law of God and nature have set to the legislative power of every commonwealth, in all forms of government.

First, They are to govern by promulgated established laws, not to be varied in particular cases, but to have one rule for rich and poor, for the favourite at Court, and the countryman at plough.

Secondly, These laws also ought to be designed for no other end ultimately but the good of the people.

Thirdly, They must not raise taxes on the property of the people without the consent of the people given by themselves or their deputies. And this properly concerns only such governments where the legislative is always in being, or at least where the people have not reserved any part of the legislative to deputies, to be from time to time chosen by themselves.

Fourthly, The legislative neither must nor can transfer the power of making laws to anybody else, or place it anywhere but where the people have.

Discussion Questions

1. There are currently three popular paradigms of punishment—ways to justify the state punishing its citizens. They are:
   a. Utilitarianism—for the greater good of society (to deter others, etc.)
   b. Retributivism—because the citizen deserves/earned the punishment
   c. Rehabilitationism—to help improve the criminal's actions
   Which of these do you support and why? How does this shape your views on the death penalty?

2. Have you ever considered why you and others willingly give up certain liberties? Why/how the government is justified in taking away certain liberties from its citizens? Why/why not? How important is your right to the pursuit of happiness? To liberty? (How do you define *liberty*?)

3. *Just War Theory* (dating back to St. Thomas Aquinas) puts forth the following criteria to suggest when going to war is justified. Going to war is *just* if:
   a. It serves a just cause.
   b. It is declared by proper authority.
   c. It is carried out for the right intention.
   d. It has a reasonable chance for success.
   e. The objective of the war is proportional to the methods used.
   Are the criteria sufficient? What problems might arise from them? Do you think going to war is ever justified?

4. Locke's notion of tacit consent—by voluntarily participating in society, one agrees to "play by the rules"—has been used in defense of a moral mandate

for rule-following in sports. In what way are you morally required to follow the rules of a game in which you voluntarily participate? How does this frame your analysis of slogans such as "It's only cheating if you get caught" and "If you're not cheating, you're not trying"?

The Myth of Merit

Iris Young

Iris Marion Young graduated with honors in philosophy from Queens College before going on to earn her PhD in philosophy at Pennsylvania State University. She held two major teaching posts—nine years at the Graduate School of Public and International Affairs at the University of Pittsburgh and then a professorship in political science at the University of Chicago—and also many visiting professorships at universities throughout the world. She published five books that have been translated into over twenty languages with a focus on social justice, democracy, and feminist theory.

This selection is from a chapter in her first and most well-known book, *Justice and the Politics of Difference.* In it, she questions popular assumptions held by social philosophers. In doing so, she questions whether a just form of merit-based awards is attainable, suggesting that "subordinate groups" (i.e., racial minorities and, in many cases, females) cannot reap the same benefits from merit awards due to the subjectivity and hierarchy inherent in the system. In the remainder of the chapter (not included here), she applies this to examine the issue of affirmative action.

Reading Questions

1. Explain the two assumptions Young mentions that are usually held by philosophers and policymakers, yet which she questions.
2. How does Young define the principle of merit? What purpose does it serve?
3. What four conditions does Young suggest must be met in order to consider the principle of merit as just?
4. How does Fishkin address the fourth criterion of Young's regarding the neutrality of cultural norms in ranking the performance of individuals? Briefly explain Young's four impediments for objective job assessment.
5. How does Young relate the principle of equality, of contribution and effort, and the priority of basic needs to her conclusion?
6. What practical problems arise in merit evaluation? What two sources disadvantage the subordinated groups? Explain the relevance of the examples and studies mentioned by Young.

Source: Justice and the Politics of Difference. Copyright © 1990 Princeton University Press. Reprinted by permission of Princeton University Press.

The Myth of Merit

> We have no words to speak about our oppression, our distress, our bitterness, and our revolt against the exhaustion, the stupidity, the monotony, the lack of meaning of our work and of our life, against the contempt in which our work is held; against the despotic hierarchy of the factory; against a society in which we remain the underdogs and in which goods and enjoyments that are considered normal by other classes are denied to us and are parceled out to us only reluctantly, as though we were asking for a privilege. We have no words to say what it is and how it feels to be workers, to be held in suspicion, to be ordered around by people who have more and who pretend to know more and who compel us to work according to rules *they* set and for purposes that are *theirs*, not ours. And we have no words to say all this because the ruling class has monopolized not only the power of decision-making and of material wealth; they have also monopolized culture and language.

> —ANDRÉ GORZ

. . . Philosophers and policymakers usually assume as given, and thus as not unjust, a hierarchical division of labor with scarce positions of high income, power, and prestige at the top, and less privileged positions at the bottom. They also assume that these positions should be distributed according to merit, by measuring the individual technical competence of persons and awarding the most competitive positions to those judged most qualified according to impartial measures of such competence. I question both these assumptions. . . .

This chapter examines in detail two assumptions about institutional structure that usually underlie affirmative action debate: the assumption that positions should be distributed to the most qualified, and the assumption that a hierarchical division of labor is just. . . .

The merit principle holds that positions should be awarded to the most qualified individuals, that is, to those who have the greatest aptitude and skill for performing the tasks those positions require. This principle is central to legitimating a hierarchical division of labor in a liberal democratic society which assumes the equal moral and political worth of all persons. Assuming as given a structural division between scarce highly rewarded positions and more plentiful less rewarded positions, the merit principle asserts that this division of labor is just when no group receives privileged positions by birth or right, or by virtue of arbitrary characteristics such as race, ethnicity, or sex. The unjust hierarchy of caste is to be replaced by a "natural" hierarchy of intellect and skill.

Just how this principle or merit should be interpreted, and whether it should function as the principle of the distribution of positions and rewards, is the subject of some controversy. Rawls, for example, argues that using natural talents as a criterion for awarding positions can be considered just as arbitrary as awarding them according to race or sex, because a person is just as little responsible for his or her talents as for his or her race. Thus many argue that effort and achievement should be a large part of merit criteria. Many argue, further, that a principle of merit distribution should apply only after basic needs are met for everyone. Others question whether a principle of merit has any moral force, arguing that claims about efficiency or productivity cannot support claims of right or desert.

In his thorough and thoughtful study of the conflict of values he perceives in the goals of equal opportunity, James Fishkin defines the merit principle as entailing "widespread procedural fairness in the evaluation of qualifications for positions." Procedural fairness requires that the processes of evaluation "approach the model of an impartial competition." Qualifications are "criteria that are job related in that they fairly can be interpreted as indicators of competence or motivation for an individual's performance in a given position." Education, job history, fairly administered test results, or other tokens of ability or effort, says Fishkin, can all be used to assess qualifications. A fair assessment of an individual's qualifications must rest on that person's own past or present actual performance of relevant tasks; determination of qualifications cannot rest on statistical inferences.

Use of a principle of merit to allocate scarce and desirable positions in a job hierarchy, and in the educational institutions that train people for those jobs, is just only if several conditions are met. First, qualifications must be defined in terms of technical skills and competence, independently of and neutral with respect to values and culture. By technical competence I mean competence at producing specified results. If merit criteria do not distinguish between technical skills and normative or cultural attributes, there is no way to separate being a "good" worker of a certain sort from being the sort kind of person—with the right background, way of life, and so on. Second, to justify differential job privilege the purely technical skills and competences must be "job related," in that they operate as predictors for excellent performance in the position. Third, for merit criteria to be applied justly, performance and competence must be judged individually. In order to say that one individual is more qualified than another, finally, the performances and predicted performances of individuals must be compared and ranked according to measures which are independent of and neutral with respect to values and culture.

Proponents of a merit principle rarely doubt that these conditions can be met. Fishkin, for example, finds it obvious that the technical competence of individuals can be measured and predicted apart from values, purposes, and cultural norms. "It is hard to believe," he says, "in a modern industrial society, with a complex differentiation of tasks that qualifications that are performance related could not be defined so as to predict better performances." It may be hard to believe, but in fact such normatively and culturally neutral measures of individual performance do not exist for most jobs. The idea of merit criteria that are objective and unbiased with respect to personal attributes is a version of the ideal of impartiality, and is just as impossible.

First, most jobs are too complex and multifaceted to allow for a precise identification of their tasks and thus measurement of levels of performance of those tasks. Precise, value-neutral, task-specific measures of job performance are possible only for jobs with a limited number of definable functions each of which is a fairly straightforward identifiable task, requiring little verbal skill, imagination, or judgment. Data entry work or quality control sorting may satisfy these requirements, but a great many jobs do not. A travel agent, for example, must keep records, communicate effectively on the telephone and through ever-changing computer networks of information, and study and keep at hand options in tour packages for many places. Service sector work, a vastly expanding portion of jobs, in general can rarely be evaluated in terms of the criteria of productivity and efficiency applied to industrial production, because it makes much less sense to count services rendered than items that come off the assembly line.

Second, in complex industrial and office organizations, it is often not possible to identify the contribution that each individual makes, precisely because the workers cooperate in producing an outcome or product. The performance of a team, department, or firm may be measurable, but this is of little use in justifying the position or level of reward of any particular team members.

Third, a great many jobs require wide discretion in what the worker does and how best to do it. In many jobs the worker's role is more negative than positive; he or she oversees a process and intervenes to prevent something from going wrong. In automated processes, from individual machines to entire factories, for example, workers routinely contribute little to the actual making of things, but they must be vigilant in tending the machines to make sure the process goes as it should. The negative role increases worker discretion about whether, when, and how often to intervene. Perhaps there is one easily identifiable and measurable way to perform many positive actions. But there are many ways of preventing a process from going wrong, and it is not usually possible to measure a worker's productivity level in terms of the costs that would have been incurred if she or he had not intervened, or the costs that would have been saved if she or he had intervened differently.

Finally, the division of labor in most large organizations means that those evaluating a worker's performance often are not familiar with the actual work process. Modern organizational hierarchies are what Claus Offe calls task discontinuous hierarchies. In a task continuous hierarchy, like that exemplified by medieval guild production, superiors do the same kind of work as their subordinates, but with a greater degree of skill and competence. In the task discontinuous hierarchies of contemporary organizations, job ladders are highly segregated. Superiors do not do the same kind of work as subordinates, and may never have done that sort of work. Thus the superior is often not competent to evaluate the technical work performance itself, and must rely on evaluating workers' attitudes, their compliance with the rules, their self-presentation, their cooperativeness—that is, their social comportment.

While these four impediments to a normatively and culturally neutral definition and assessment of job performance occur in many types of work, they are most apparent in professional and managerial work. These types of work usually involve a wide diversity of skills and tasks. Most or all of these tasks rely on the use of judgment, discretion, imagination, and verbal acuity, and none of these qualities is precisely measurable according to some objective, value-neutral scale. The achievement of professional and managerial objectives usually involves a complex series of social relationships and dependencies, to the extent that it is often unreasonable to hold professionals responsible for not meeting objectives. Professional and managerial jobs, finally, often are evaluated not only by superiors in a task discontinuous hierarchy, but by clients who are even less aware of the nature of the jobs and the skills required, and who are thus not in a position to apply criteria of technical performance that are normatively and culturally neutral. . . .

Criteria of evaluation necessarily carry normative and cultural implications and so often will not be group-neutral. These criteria often carry assumptions about ways of life, styles of behavior, and values that derive from and reflect the experience of the privileged groups who design and implement them. Since the ideology of impartiality leads evaluators to deny the particularity of these standards, groups with different experiences, values, and ways of life are evaluated as falling short. For example, . . . many supposedly neutral and unquestioned norms of the corporate workplace implicitly assume male socialization and a male life style. To take another example, an employee who does not look a white male employer in the eye may be perceived as shifty or dishonest; but the employee may have been raised in a culture where averting the eyes is a sign of deference.

Second, . . . everyday judgment of and interaction with women, people of color, gay men and lesbians, disabled people, and old people is often influenced by unconscious aversions and devaluations. Thus evaluators, especially those belonging to groups defined as neutral, often carry unconscious biases and prejudices against specially marked groups. A number of studies have shown, for example, that many whites rate black job candidates more negatively than whites with identical credentials. Similar studies have shown that the same résumé receives a significantly lower rating when it has a woman's name than when it has a man's.

Discussion Questions

1. How do you react to Gorz's quote in the epigram?
2. Look at the two assumptions noted by Young in the beginning of her piece that she holds questionable. Do you also question them, or do you agree with the assumptions as stated? Why?
3. Have you been awarded (or denied) anything due to a merit-based system (e.g., a school award, job offer, job promotion)? In what ways was the process fair? In what ways was it unfair? How does this apply to other merit-based systems that have not directly affected you?
4. The title of the chapter from which this piece was extracted is "Affirmative Action and the Myth of Merit." How do you apply Young's argument to the issue of affirmative action?
5. In reference to what sorts of things do you typically hear the phrase, "Life isn't fair"? In what ways is this phrase true and/or not true? If you agree that

life is not *fair*, do you think efforts should be made to change that, or does this "truth of life" justify the seemingly inherent unfairness?

Movie Titles

1. Theme: Individual in Society—How can one be a true individual while part of society? Do you have to give up part of yourself to participate in a community? What is your view of a utopia?
   * *Antz*
   * *1984 (R)*
   * *Modern Times*
2. *Fahrenheit 9/11* (R)—What is the duty of the media and government to share/portray the news objectively and truthfully?
3. *Fahrenheit 451*—If you can control what people know, then is knowledge relative?
4. *The People vs. Larry Flint* (R)—Even if you disagree with what Flint does, would you want to prevent him from doing so? Would that infringe upon the right to free speech? How might you be justified in censoring him?
5. *The Fog of War*—When, if ever, is war justified?
6. *Lord of the Flies*—How would you set up a government if there was none? Do you think it is fair to restrict people's rights for the good of the whole?
7. *The Corporation*—What virtues and vices do you see in a capitalistic society? What alternatives would be better?
8. *Sicko*—What role should the government play in regard to health care?

Song Lyrics

Rush—"The Trees"
Bad Religion—"You Are (The Government)"
The Police—"Spirits in a Material World"
Fugazi—"Lockdown"
Fugazi—"And The Same"

Chapter 10

Aesthetics

I remember walking into the Boston Museum of Art with my mother when I was thirteen and finding it very problematic that they had on display a big red canvas. Granted, it was by Andy Warhol, but this didn't mean anything to me at the time. And they wouldn't let me take a photo of it! Obviously, this particular work of art had some impact on me, as I'm writing about it years later as an introductory piece in a philosophy book, but I remember thinking to myself, "Could this really be art?"

The title of Leo Tolstoy's book referenced in this section captures the major question explored in this branch of philosophy: What is art? We can take this further and ask, "What is *good* art?" One may be inclined to say *everything* is art—but this just makes the term meaningless: There would be no point in asking the question, "Is this particular object art?"

These questions have pragmatic value as well. Many countries fund art in some way or another. In the United States, the National Endowment for the Arts (NEA) spends public money on art, art education, and other related endeavors. As you can imagine, the question "Is this art?" has great relevance when discerning whether a government agency ought to spend tax dollars on a particular work. Likewise, the definition of "good" as in "Is this good art?" arises, or at the least, what is it that we value in terms of art?

Some philosophers have attempted to find universal qualities that relate to all art and even to all good art. Some draw on the intent of the artist, others on the materials and methods used to create the art, and still others on the aesthetic feeling created by the viewers. David Hume focuses on the feelings associated with art, asking that we not address this question as a matter of *a priori* (before experience) knowledge, but only *through* experience. In this section Tolstoy suggests criteria for art and for good art, as well as touching on the importance of art in society. The second reading frames the issue of government funding of art through the NEA. Helms addresses concerns with funding specific types of art—namely art that is obscene or degrading.

What Is Art?

Leo Tolstoy

Russian author and philosopher Leo Tolstoy is best known for his novels *War and Peace* and *Anna Karenina*. Throughout his life, he became very interested in reforming society. Tolstoy believed that a strong education system was of paramount importance, and he started a school for peasant children, as well as editing a number of educational journals. He and his wife had thirteen children, and in his later life, he shifted his focus from writing novels to exploring his Christian conversion and writing more on moral, religious, and philosophical issues.

In this piece from his later writings, Tolstoy first examines the moral issues of art and sheds some light on the discussion of government funding of art. He then puts forth criteria for determining not just what we can consider art (as opposed to counterfeit art), but what can be considered *good* art as well. He writes that the experience of art is so important that, without it, we would be like Kaspar Houser—a teenage boy imprisoned most of his life who, when found on the streets of Nuremberg, Germany, could say only his name.

Reading Questions

1. For Tolstoy, how is art a moral issue as it regards both the time/energy of the artists and government funding?
2. Explain the relevance of transmission of feelings with regard to art.
3. According to Tolstoy, why is the activity of art important?
4. What indication does Tolstoy claim distinguishes real art from counterfeit art?
5. Explain Tolstoy's explanation of the connection between perceiver ("receiver") and artist in a "true artistic impression." How does the receiver's "infection" relate to the quality of the art?
6. What does Tolstoy say about an artist creating art for the sake of the receiver? What is the importance of *sincerity* according to Tolstoy?

Chapter One

Take up any one of our ordinary newspapers and you will find a part devoted to the theatre and music. In almost every number you will find a description of some art exhibition, or of some particular picture, and you will always find reviews of new works of art that have appeared, of volumes of poems, of short stories, or of novels. . . .

For the support of art in Russia (where for the education of the people only a hundredth part is spent of what would be required to give everyone the opportunity of instruction), the government grants millions of roubles in subsidies to academics, conservatories, and theatres. In France twenty million francs are assigned for art, and similar grants are made in Germany and England.

Source: What is Art? Chapters 1, 2, 5, 15 (edited). Translation: Aylmer Maude (London: Brotherhood Publishing Company, 1891).

In every large town enormous buildings are erected for museums, academies, conservatories, dramatic schools, and for performances and concerts. Hundreds of thousands of workmen—carpenters, masons, painters, joiners, paperhangers, tailors, hairdressers, jewellers, moulders, typesetters—spend their whole lives in hard labour to satisfy the demands of art, so that hardly any other department of human activity, except the military, consumes so much energy as this.

Not only is enormous labour spent on this activity, but in it, as in war, the very lives of men are sacrificed. Hundreds of thousands of people devote their lives from childhood to learning to twirl their legs rapidly (dancers), or to touch notes and strings very rapidly (musicians), or to draw with paint and represent what they see (artists), or to turn every phrase inside out and find a rhyme to every word. And these people, often very kind and clever, and capable of all sorts of useful labour, grow savage over their specialized and stupefying occupations, and become one-sided and self-complacent specialists, dull to all the serious phenomena of life and skilful only at rapidly twisting their legs, their tongues, or their fingers.

But even this stunting of human life is not the worst. I remember being once at the rehearsal of one of the most ordinary of the new operas which are produced at all the opera houses of Europe and America.

I arrived when the first act had already begun. To reach the auditorium I had to pass through the stage entrance. By dark entrances and passages I was led through the vaults of an enormous building, past immense machines for changing the scenery and for lighting, and there in the gloom and dust I saw workmen busily engaged. One of these men, pale, haggard, in a dirty blouse, with dirty, work-worn hands and cramped fingers, evidently tired and out of humour, went past me, angrily scolding another man. Ascending by a dark stair, I came out on the boards behind the scenes. Amid various poles and rings and scattered scenery, decorations and curtains, stood and moved dozens, if not hundreds, of painted and dressed-up men, in costumes fitting tight to their thighs and calves, and also women, as usual, as nearly nude as might be. These were all singers, or members of the chorus, or ballet dancers, waiting their turns. My guide led me across the stage and, by means of a bridge of boards across the orchestra (in which perhaps a hundred musicians of all kinds, from kettledrum to flute and harp, were seated), to the dark pitstalls.

On an elevation, between two lamps with reflectors, and in an armchair placed before a music stand, sat the director of the musical part, baton in hand, managing the orchestra and singers, and, in general, the production of the whole opera.

The performance had already begun, and on the stage a procession of Indians who had brought home a bride was being presented. Besides men and women in costume, two other men in ordinary clothes bustled and ran about on the stage; one was the director of the dramatic part, and the other, who stepped about in soft shoes and ran from place to place with unusual agility, was the dancing master, whose salary per month exceeded what ten labourers earn in a year. . . .

Instinctively the question presents itself: For whom is this being done? Whom can it please? If there are, occasionally, good melodies in the opera to which it is pleasant to listen, they could have been sung simply, without these stupid costumes and all the processions and recitatives and handwavings.

The ballet, in which half-naked women make voluptuous movements, twisting themselves into various sensual writhings, is simply a lewd performance.

So one is quite at a loss as to whom these things are done for. The man of culture is heartily sick of them, while to a real working man they are utterly incomprehensible. If anyone can be pleased by these things (which is doubtful), it can only be some young footman or depraved artisan who has contracted the spirit of the upper classes but is not yet satiated with their amusements and wishes to show his breeding.

And all this nasty folly is prepared, not simply, nor with kindly merriment, but with anger and brutal cruelty.

It is said that it is all done for the sake of art, and that art is a very important thing. But is it true that art is so important that such sacrifices should be made for its sake? This question is especially urgent because art, for the sake of which the labour of millions, the lives of men, and, above all, love between man and man, are being sacrificed—this very art is becoming something more and more vague and uncertain to human perception. . . .

So art, which demands such tremendous labour sacrifices from the people, which stunts human lives and transgresses against human love, is not only *not* a thing clearly and firmly defined, but is understood in such contradictory ways by its own devotees that it is difficult to say what is meant by art, and especially what is good, useful art—art for the sake of which we might condone such sacrifices as are being offered at its shrine.

Chapter Two

For the production of every ballet, circus, opera, operetta, exhibition, picture, concert, or printed book, the intense and unwilling labour of thousands of people is needed at what is often harmful and humiliating work. It were well if artists made all they require for themselves, but, as it is, they all need the help of workmen, not only to produce art, but also for their own usually luxurious maintenance. And, one way or other, they get it, either through payments from rich people or through subsidies given by government (in Russia, for instance, in grants of millions of roubles to theatres, conservatories, and academies). This money is collected from the people, some of whom have to sell their only cow to pay the tax and who never get those aesthetic pleasures which art gives.

It was all very well for a Greek or Roman artist, or even for a Russian artist of the first half of our century (when there were still slaves and it was considered right that there should be), with a quiet mind to make people serve him and his art; but in our day, when in all men there is at least some dim perception of the equal rights of all, it is impossible to constrain people to labour unwillingly for art without first deciding the question whether it is true that art is so good and so important an affair as to redeem this evil.

If not, we have the terrible probability to consider that while fearful sacrifices of the labour and lives of men, and of morality itself, are being made to art, that same art may be not only useless but even harmful.

And therefore it is necessary for a society in which works of art arise and are supported, to find out whether all that professes to be art is really art, whether (as is presupposed in our society) all that which is art is good, and whether it is important and worth those sacrifices which it necessitates. It is still more necessary for every conscientious artist to know this that he may be sure that all he does has a valid meaning; that it is not merely an infatuation of the small circle of people among whom he lives which excites in him the false assurance that he is doing a good work; and that what he takes from others for the support of his often very luxurious life will be compensated for by those productions at which he works. And that is why answers to the above questions are especially important in our time.

What is this art which is considered so important and necessary for humanity that for its sake these sacrifices of labour, of human life, and even of goodness may be made? . . .

Chapter Five

In order correctly to define art, it is necessary, first of all, to cease to consider it as a means to pleasure and to consider it as one of the conditions of human life. Viewing it in this way we cannot fail to observe that art is one of the means of intercourse between man and man.

Every work of art causes the receiver to enter into a certain kind of relationship both with him who produced, or is producing, the art, and with all those who, simultaneously, previously, or subsequently, receive the same artistic impression.

Speech, transmitting the thoughts and experiences of men, serves as a means of union among them, and art acts in a similar manner. The peculiarity of this latter means of intercourse, distinguishing it from intercourse by means of words, consists in this, that whereas by words a man transmits his thoughts to another, by means of art he transmits his feelings.

The activity of art is based on the fact that a man, receiving through his sense of hearing or sight another man's expression of feeling, is capable of experiencing the emotion which moved the man who expressed it. To take the simplest example; one man laughs, and another who hears becomes merry; or a man weeps, and another who hears feels sorrow. A man is excited or irritated, and another man seeing him comes to a similar state of mind. By his movements or by the sounds of his voice, a man expresses courage and determination or sadness and calmness, and this state of mind passes on to others. A man suffers, expressing his sufferings by groans and spasms, and this suffering transmits itself to other people; a man expresses his feeling of admiration, devotion, fear, respect, or love to certain objects, persons, or phenomena, and others are infected by the same feelings of admiration, devotion, fear, respect, or love to the same objects, persons, and phenomena.

And it is upon this capacity of man to receive another man's expression of feeling and experience those feelings himself, that the activity of art is based.

If a man infects another or others directly, immediately, by his appearance or by the sounds he gives vent to at the very time he experiences the feeling; if he causes another man to yawn when he himself cannot help yawning, or to laugh or cry when he himself is obliged to laugh or cry, or to suffer when he himself is suffering—that does not amount to art.

Art begins when one person, with the object of joining another or others to himself in one and the same feeling, expresses that feeling by certain external indications. To take the simplest example: A boy, having experienced, let us say, fear on encountering a wolf, relates that encounter; and, in order to evoke in others the feeling he has experienced, describes himself, his condition before the encounter, the surroundings, the woods, his own lightheartedness, and then the wolf's appearance, its movements, the distance between himself and the wolf, etc. All this, if only the boy, when telling the story, again experiences the feelings he had lived through and infects the hearers and compels them to feel what the narrator had experienced is art. If even the boy had not seen a wolf but had frequently been afraid of one, and if, wishing to evoke in others the fear he had felt, he invented an encounter with a wolf and recounted it so as to make his hearers share the feelings he experienced when he feared the world, that also would be art. And just in the same way it is art if a man, having experienced either the fear of suffering or the attraction of enjoyment (whether in reality or in imagination) expresses these feelings on canvas or in marble so that others are infected by them. And it is also art if a man feels or imagines to himself feelings of delight, gladness, sorrow, despair, courage, or despondency and the transition from one to another of these feelings, and expresses these feelings by sounds so that the hearers are infected by them and experience them as they were experienced by the composer.

The feelings with which the artist infects others may be most various—very strong or very weak, very important or very insignificant, very bad or very good: feelings of love for one's own country, self-devotion and submission to fate or to God expressed in a drama, raptures of lovers described in a novel, feelings of voluptuousness expressed in a picture, courage expressed in a triumphal march, merriment evoked by a dance, humor evoked by a funny story, the feeling of quietness transmitted by an evening landscape or by a lullaby, or the feeling of admiration evoked by a beautiful arabesque—it is all art.

If only the spectators or auditors are infected by the feelings which the author has felt, it is art.

To evoke in oneself a feeling one has once experienced, and having evoked it in oneself, then, by means of movements, lines, colors, sounds, or forms expressed in words, so to transmit that feeling that others may experience the same feeling—his is the activity of art.

Art is a human activity consisting in this, that one man consciously, by means of certain external signs, hands on to others feelings he has lived through, and that other people are infected by these feelings and also experience them.

Art is not, as the metaphysicians say, the manifestation of some mysterious idea of beauty or God; it is not, as the aesthetical physiologists say, a game in which man lets off his excess of stored-up energy; it is not the expression of man's emotions by external signs; it is not the production of pleasing objects; and, above all, it is not pleasure; but it is a means of union among men, joining them together in the same feelings, and indispensable for the life and progress toward well-being of individuals and of humanity.

As, thanks to man's capacity to express thoughts by words, every man may know all that has been done for him in the realms of thought by all humanity before his day, and can in the present, thanks to this capacity to understand the thoughts of others, become a sharer in their activity and can himself hand on to his contemporaries and descendants the thoughts he has assimilated from others, as well as those which have arisen within himself; so, thanks to man's capacity to be infected with the feelings of others by means of art, all that is being lived through by his contemporaries is accessible to him, as well as the feelings experienced by men thousands of years ago, and he has also the possibility of transmitting his own feelings to others.

If people lacked this capacity to receive the thoughts conceived by the men who preceded them and to pass on to others their own thoughts, men would be like wild beasts, or like Kaspar Houser.

And if men lacked this other capacity of being infected by art, people might be almost more savage still, and, above all, more separated from, and more hostile to, one another.

And therefore the activity of art is a most important one, as important as the activity of speech itself and as generally diffused. . . .

Chapter Fifteen

Art, in our society, has been so perverted that not only has bad art come to be considered good, but even the very perception of what art really is has been lost. In order to be able to speak about the art of our society, it is, therefore, first of all necessary to distinguish art from counterfeit art.

There is one indubitable indication distinguishing real art from its counterfeit, namely, the infectiousness of art. If a man, without exercising effort and without altering his standpoint on reading, hearing, or seeing another man's work, experiences a mental condition which unites him with that man and with other people who also partake of that work of art, then the object evoking that condition is a work of art. And however poetical, realistic, effectful, or interesting a work may be, it is not a work of art if it does not evoke that feeling (quite distinct from all other feelings) of joy and of spiritual union with another (the author) and with others (those who are also infected by it).

It is true that this indication is an internal one, and that there are people who have forgotten what the action of real art is, who expect something else from art (in our society the great majority are in this state), and that therefore such people may mistake for this aesthetic feeling the feeling of diversion and a certain excitement which they receive from counterfeits of art. But though it is impossible to undeceive these people, just as it is impossible to convince a man suffering from "Daltonism" [a type of color blindness] that green is not red, yet, for all that, this indication remains perfectly definite to those whose feeling for art is neither perverted nor atrophied, and it clearly distinguishes the feeling produced by art from all other feelings.

The chief peculiarity of this feeling is that the receiver of a true artistic impression is so united to the artist that he feels as if the work were his own and not someone else's—as if what it expresses were just what he had long been wishing to express. A real work of art destroys, in the consciousness of the receiver, the separation between himself and the artist—not that alone, but also between himself and all whose minds receive this work of art. In this freeing of our personality from its separation and isolation, in this uniting of it with others, lies the chief characteristic and the great attractive force of art.

If a man is infected by the author's condition of soul, if he feels this emotion and this union with others, then the object which has effected this is art; but if there be no such infection, if there be no this union with the author and with others who are moved by the same work—then it is not art. And not only is infection a sure sign of art, but the degree of infectiousness is also the sole measure of excellence in art.

The stronger the infection, the better is the art as art, speaking now apart from its subject matter, i.e., not considering the quality of the feelings it transmits.

And the degree of the infectiousness of art depends on three conditions:

1. On the greater or lesser individuality of the feeling transmitted;
2. On the greater or lesser clearness with which the feeling is transmitted;
3. On the sincerity of the artist, i.e., on the greater or lesser force with which the artist himself feels the emotion he transmits.

The more individual the feeling transmitted the more strongly does it act on the receiver; the more individual the state of soul into which he is transferred, the more pleasure does the receiver obtain, and therefore the more readily and strongly does he join in it.

The clearness of expression assists infection because the receiver, who mingles in consciousness with the author, is the better satisfied the more clearly the feeling is transmitted, which, as it seems to him, he has long known and felt, and for which he has only now found expression.

But most of all is the degree of infectiousness of art increased by the degree of sincerity in the artist. As soon as the spectator, hearer, or reader feels that the artist is infected by his own production, and writes, sings, or plays for himself, and not merely to act on others, this mental condition of the artist infects the receiver; and contrariwise, as soon as the spectator, reader, or hearer feels that the author is not writing, singing, or playing for his own satisfaction—does not himself feel what he wishes to express—but is doing it for him, the receiver, a resistance immediately springs up, and the most individual and the newest feelings and the cleverest technique not only fail to produce any infection but actually repel.

I have mentioned three conditions of contagiousness in art, but they may be all summed up into one, the last, sincerity, i.e., that the artist should be impelled by an inner need to express his feeling. That condition includes the first; for if the artist is sincere he will express the feeling as he experienced it. And as each man is different from everyone else, his feeling will be individual for everyone else; and the more individual it is—the more the artist has drawn it from the depths of his nature—he more sympathetic and sincere will it be. And this same sincerity will impel the artist to find a clear expression of the feeling which he wishes to transmit.

Therefore this third condition—sincerity—is the most important of the three. It is always complied with in peasant art, and this explains why such art always acts so powerfully; but it is a condition almost entirely absent from our upper-class art, which is continually produced by artists actuated by personal aims of covetousness or vanity.

Such are the three conditions which divide art from its counterfeits, and which also decide the quality of every work of art apart from its subject matter.

The absence of any one of these conditions excludes a work form the category of art and relegates it to that of art's counterfeits. If the work does not transmit the artist's peculiarity of feeling and is therefore not individual, if it is unintelligibly expressed, or if it has not proceeded from the author's inner need for expression—it is not a work of art. If all these conditions are present, even in the smallest degree, then the work, even if a weak one, is yet a work of art.

The presence in various degrees of these three conditions—individuality, clearness, and sincerity—decides the merit of a work of art as art, apart from subject matter. All works of art take rank of merit according to the degree in which they fulfill the first, the second, and the third of these conditions. In one the individuality of the feeling transmitted may predominate; in another, clearness of expression; in a third, sincerity; while a fourth may have sincerity and individuality but be deficient in clearness; a fifth, individuality and clearness but less sincerity; and so forth, in all possible degrees and combinations.

Thus is art divided from that which is not art, and thus is the quality of art as art decided, independently of its subject matter, i.e., apart from whether the feelings it transmits are good or bad.

Discussion Questions

1. How do you assess Tolstoy's moral concerns with regard to art? How could we determine if people were wasting time and energy creating/practicing art? How should we determine if the government should tax its citizens to help fund art? And how much should the government spend on the arts?
2. What does Tolstoy mean in the opening sentence of Chapter Five? Do you agree?
3. Tolstoy suggests that the basis of art is being able to share in the emotion of the artist, and he later writes that insincere art causes a resistance amongst perceivers. How would you feel if you found out an artist whose work you enjoyed was not sharing genuine emotion (i.e., imagine a songwriter singing about love when she did not believe in love herself)? Would you feel betrayed? Does this devalue the art for you?

4. When you have an intense aesthetic feeling, does that affect how you feel toward the artist (even if you've never met him/her)?
5. Can species other than humans be affected by art? What role does empathy play in aesthetic appreciation?
6. Do you agree with Tolstoy's opening line in Chapter Fifteen? Why/why not?
7. Do you agree with the following criterion for art suggested by Tolstoy: "If only the spectators or auditors are infected by the feelings which the author has felt, it is art"? How do you react to his suggestion that the quality of the work is also determined by the reaction ("infection") of the viewer? What problems arise when we define art—and assign values such as good or bad to it—by the reaction of viewers? What benefits are there?
8. Given the vast differences in people's aesthetic tastes, what role does an art/music/etc. critic serve?
9. In learning more about a specific work of art—i.e., the specific notes and progressions of a song, or the chromatic structure of a painting—does your enjoyment and appreciation of the piece increase or decrease? Why? How much does your knowledge of an artist's life add to/subtract from your enjoyment/appreciation of the art?

The NEA Should Not Fund Obscenity

Jesse Helms

Jesse Helms served as a U.S. Senator (Republican, representing North Carolina) from 1973–2003, elected for five consecutive terms. In 2005, he published a memoir entitled *Where I Stand.*

In this piece, an amendment proposed by Helms, he argues that the government ought not provide funding for art that is obscene or denigrating. He references a number of specific pieces of art, of which he provides a brief description. Established in 1965, the National Endowment for the Arts' (NEA) mission statement states that it is "a public agency dedicated to supporting excellence in the arts, both new and established; bringing the arts to all Americans; and providing leadership in arts education." (For more on the purpose and function of the NEA, visit the website: *www.nea.gov*) The NEA supports not just individual artists, but also literature fellowships, opera houses and museums, public television and radio programs, and much more.

Reading Questions

1. Explain Helms's point about the people's support of specific artists in the marketplace (which he also references later by a quote from Ronald Reagan).

Source: Jesse Helms, *Amendment 420: The NEA Should Not Fund Obscenity*. U.S. Senate, July 26, 1989. Reprinted in Bolton, Richard, ed. *Culture Wars*, New Press, 1992, pp. 73–77.

2. What does Helms say regarding critics who claim his proposal would result in censorship?
3. What problem does Helms illuminate with regard to the process by which artists (i.e., Mapplethorpe) obtain NEA grants?
4. How does Helms use the funding of churches to support his position?

Amendment No. 420

(Purpose: To prohibit the use of appropriated funds for the dissemination, promotion, or production of obscene or indecent materials or materials denigrating a particular religion)

MR. HELMS. Mr. President, I send an amendment to the desk and ask for its immediate consideration.

The PRESIDING OFFICER. The clerk will report.

The legislative clerk read as follows:

The Senator from North Carolina [Mr. Helms] proposes an amendment numbered 420.

Mr. HELMS. Mr. President, I ask unanimous consent that reading of the amendment be dispensed with.

The PRESIDING OFFICER. Without objection, it is so ordered.

The amendment is as follows:

On page 94, line 16, strike the period and insert the following: "provided that this section will become effective one day after the date of enactment.

Sec. limitations.

None of the funds authorized to be appropriated pursuant to this Act may be used to promote, disseminate, or produce—

1. obscene or indecent materials, including but not limited to depictions of sadomasochism, homoeroticism, the exploitation of children, or individuals engaged in sex acts; or
2. material which denigrates the objects or beliefs of the adherents of a particular religion or nonreligion; or
3. material which denigrates, debases, or reviles a person, group or class of citizens on the basis of race, creed, sex, handicap, age, or national origin.

Mr. HELMS. Mr. President, this amendment has been agreed to on both sides, I believe. I very much appreciate it.

Mr. President, I believe we are all aware of the controversy surrounding the use of Federal funds, via the National Endowment for the Arts [NEA], to support so-called works of art by Andres Serrano and Robert Mapplethorpe. My amendment would prevent the NEA from funding such immoral trash in the future. Specifically, my amendment prohibits the use of the NEA's funds to support obscene or indecent materials, or materials which denigrate the objects or beliefs of a particular religion.

I applaud the efforts of my distinguished colleagues from West Virginia, Mr. BYRD, and from Idaho, Mr. McCLURE, to address this issue in both the Appropriations Subcommittee on the Interior, and the full Appropriations Committee. Cutting off funding to the Southeastern Center for Contemporary Art [SECCA] in Winston-Salem and the Institute for Contemporary Art in Philadelphia will certainly prevent them from misusing Federal funds for the next five years. However, as much as I agree with the measures, the committee's efforts do not go far enough because they will not prevent such blasphemous or immoral behavior by other institutions or artists with Government funds. That is why I have offered my amendment.

Frankly, Mr. President, I have fundamental questions about why the Federal Government is involved in supporting artists the taxpayers have refused to support in the marketplace. My concern in this regard is heightened when I hear the arts community and the media saying that any restriction at all on Federal funding would amount to censorship. What they seem to be saying is that we in Congress must choose between: First, absolutely no Federal presence in the arts; or second, granting artists the absolute freedom to use tax dollars as they wish, regardless of how vulgar, blasphemous, or despicable their works may be.

If we indeed must make this choice, then the Federal Government should get out of the arts. However, I do not believe we are limited to those two choices and my amendment attempts to make a compromise between them. It simply provides for some common sense restrictions on what is and is not an appropriate use of Federal funding for the arts. It does not prevent the production or creation of vulgar works, it merely prevents the use of Federal funds to support them.

Mr. President, I remind my colleagues that the distinguished Senator from New York and I called attention to Mr. Serrano's so-called work of art, which portrays Jesus Christ submerged in a bottle of the artist's urine, on May 18. We pointed out that the National Endowment for the Arts had not only supported a $15,000 award honoring Mr. Serrano for it, but they also helped promote and exhibit the work as well.

Over 25 Senators—Democrats and Republicans—expressed their outrage that day by cosigning a letter to Hugh Southern, the Endowment's acting chairman, asking him to review their procedures and to determine what steps are needed to prevent such abuses from recurring in the future. Mr. Southern replied on June 6 that he too was personally offended by Mr. Serrano's so-called art, but that—as I have heard time after time on this issue—the Endowment is prevented by its authorizing language from promoting or suppressing particular points of view.

Mr. Southern's letter goes on to endorse the Endowment's panel review system as a means of ensuring competence and integrity in grant decisions, and he states that the Endowment will review their processes to be sure they are effective and maintain the highest artistic integrity and quality.

However, Mr. President, shortly after receiving Mr. Southern's response, I became aware of yet another example of the competence, integrity, and quality of the Endowment's panel review system. It is a federally supported exhibit entitled: "Robert Mapplethorpe: The Perfect Moment." The Corcoran Gallery of Art had planned to open the show here in Washington on July 1, but abruptly canceled it citing the danger the exhibit poses to future Federal funding for the arts. The Washington Project for the Arts subsequently agreed to make their facilities available and opened the show last Friday, July 21.

Mr. President, the National Endowment, the Corcoran, and others in the arts community felt the Mapplethorpe exhibit endangered Federal funding for the arts because the patently offensive collection of homoerotic pornography and sexually explicit nudes of children was put together with the help of a $30,000 grant from the Endowment. The exhibit was assembled by the University of Pennsylvania's Institute for Contemporary Art as a retrospective look at Mr. Mapplethorpe's work after his recent death from AIDS. It has already appeared in Philadelphia and Chicago with the Endowment's official endorsement.

I have a catalog of the show and Senators need to see it to believe it. However, the catalog is only a survey, not a complete inventory, of what was in the Endowment's show. If Senators are interested, I have a list and description of the photographs appearing in the show but not the catalog because even the catalog's publishers knew they were too vulgar to be included—as sick as that book is.

Vanity Fair magazine ran an article on another collection of Mapplethorpe's works which appears at the Whitney Museum of Modern Art in New York. This collection included many of the photographs currently in the NEA funded exhibit. There are unspeakable portrayals which I cannot describe on the floor of the Senate.

Mr. President, this pornography is sick. But Mapplethorpe's sick art does not seem to be an isolated incident. Yet another artist exhibited some of this sickening obscenity in my own State. The Duke Museum of Art at Duke University had a show deceptively titled "Morality Tales: History Painting in the 1980's." One painting, entitle "First Sex," depicts a nude woman on her back, legs open, knees up, and a little boy leaning against her leg looking into her face while two sexually aroused older boys wait in the background. Another work shows a man urinating on a boy lying in a gutter. Other, more despicable, works were included as well.

I could go on and on, Mr. President, about the sick art that has been displayed around the country. These shows are outrageous. And, like Serrano's blasphemy, the most outrageous thing is that some of the shows like Mapplethorpe's are financed with our tax dollars. Again, I invite Senators to see what taxpayers got for $30,000 dollars.

Mr. President, how did the Endowment's vaunted panel review system approve a grant for this pornography? It was approved because the panel only received a description, provided by the Endowment's staff, which read as follows:

"To support a mid-career summary of the work of photographer Robert Mapplethorpe. Although all aspects of the artist's work—the still-lifes, nudes, and portraits—will be included, the exhibition will focus on Mapplethorpe's unique pieces where photographic images interact with richly textured fabrics within carefully design frames."

Mr. President, what a useless and misleading description. No legitimate panel of experts would know from this description that the collection included explicit homoerotic pornography and child obscenity. Yet none of the descriptions for other projects funded by the Endowment at the time were any better. Indeed, Mr. Jack Neusner—who sat on the panel approving the Mapplethorpe exhibit—was mystified as to how he had approved a show of this character. He knows now that he was misled.

Mr. President, I was hopeful Washington would be spared this exhibit when the Corcoran canceled it. I only wish the Corcoran had canceled the show out of a sense of public decency and not as part of a calculated attempt to shield themselves and the Endowment from criticism in Congress.

Some accuse us of censorship because we threaten to cut off Federal funding, yet they are the ones who refuse to share the contents of their exhibits with the taxpayers' elected representatives. For example, the Southeastern Center for Contemporary Art in Winston-Salem refused to send me copies of requested works despite their earlier promises to the contrary. If what such institutions promote and exhibit is legitimate art, then why are they afraid for the taxpayers and Congress to see what they do?

Mr. President, there is a fundamental difference between Government censorship—the preemption of publication or production—and governmental refusal to pay for such publication and production. Artists have a right, it is said, to express their feelings as they wish: Only a philistine would suggest otherwise. Fair enough, but no artist has a preemptive claim on the tax dollars of the American people: time for them, as President Reagan used to say, "to go out and test the magic of the marketplace."

Congress attaches strings to Federal funds all the time. Churches must follow strict Federal guidelines in order to participate in Federal programs for the poor and needy—even when those guidelines violate their religious tenets. For example, a U.S. District Court in Alabama recently held that a practicing witch employed by the Salvation Army in a women's shelter could not be fired because the shelter was federally funded.

Mr. President, there have been instances where public outrage has forced artists to remove works from public display. For instance, shortly after Mayor Harold Washington's death, a work portraying him as a transvestite was forcibly removed from a show in Chicago. Another work on display at Richmond's airport was voluntarily removed after the night crew complained about a racial epithet which had been inscribed on it. There was little real protest from the arts community in these instances.

Mr. President, at a minimum, we need to prohibit the Endowment from using Federal dollars to fund filth like Mr. Serrano's and Mr. Mapplethorpe's. If it does not violate criminal statutes and the private sector is willing to pay for it, fine! However, if Federal funds are used, then Congress needs to ensure the sensitivities of all groups—regardless of race, creed, sex, national origin, handicap, or age—are respected.

Federal funding for sadomasochism, homoeroticism, and child pornography is an insult to taxpayers. Americans for the most part are moral, decent people and they have a right not to be denigrated, offended, or mocked with their own tax dollars. My amendment would protect that right.

Mr. President, if Senators want the Federal Government funding pornography, sadomasochism, or art for pedophiles, they should vote against my amendment. However, if they think most voters and taxpayers are offended by Federal support for such art, they should vote for my amendment.

Discussion Questions

1. What do you think about Helms' proposal and three suggested classes of art that should not receive government funding? What potential problems do you find with any of the language in the proposal?
2. What are your views on censorship? Should the government censor anything (i.e., attempt to prevent its production/distribution) and, if so, what? If the NEA is in place, in what ways is the government's refusing to fund certain works a form of censorship?
3. Some argue that the First Amendment's "freedom of speech" clause can be overruled when the speech causes harm. For example, one is not "free" to yell "Fire!" in a crowded theater when they believe there to be no fire. Does this relate to censorship? Why/why not?
4. What value, if any, do you find in the work mentioned of Serrano's and the "Duke museum"? Are you offended by it? Do you wish the government had not funded it? Why/why not?
5. How do you evaluate the claim that, instead of artists receiving government grants, they make their money by "testing the marketplace"? What strengths and/or weaknesses do you see in this?
6. In 1964, Supreme Court Justice Potter Stewart said, in his attempt to define hardcore pornography, "I'll know it when I see it." How do you distinguish between pornography and art? What role do definitions—i.e., art, *good* art, pornography, offensiveness—play in the discussion about the NEA?

Movie Titles

1. Theme: The Life of the Artist—How much does knowledge of the artist influence your appreciation of an artwork?
   Can you appreciate an artwork just because it challenged the boundaries of the artistic paradigm of its time? How do you determine good art from others? Art from non-art? How do you assess the art of the artists depicted in these films?
   - *Pollock*
   - *My Kid Could Paint That*
   - *Surviving Picasso* (R)
   - *Frida* (R)
   - *Basquiat* (R)

Song Lyrics

311—"Plain"

Chapter 11

Morality

One of the most challenging yet important issues in philosophy regards morality—determining not only what *you* ought to do, but what *everyone* ought to do. Even that comes into question, in the subjectivist's response "What's right for you isn't necessarily right for me." But as soon as we accept this form of relativism (that morality is just a matter of personal taste), it leads to potentially drastic results. Hitler, for example, could attempt to justify his actions as being right for him and something that he was even morally required to do (to "purify" the human race, he might suggest, in a morally abhorrent manner).

Though once we decide to assert universal moral rules, we encounter new problems. If it is *always* wrong to lie, what should you do when a lie could prevent wrongful death (imagine that you are housing innocent castaways and criminals ask you of their whereabouts). And if it is always wrong to kill innocent people (or allow for innocent deaths), what if killing one innocent person could save the lives of many others (this dilemma is often portrayed as a "life boat scenario" in which a life boat has one too many people on it and, if one is not done away with, all will die).

Determining a universal moral law that all agree on and that covers all situations proves to be extremely difficult for philosophers and non-philosophers alike. Yet most agree that we do have moral obligations to ourselves and to others. Many different foundations for morality have been provided throughout history. Such efforts include:

Divine Command Theory: A particular God or gods determine morality.

Utilitarianism: Morality is determined in relation to what results in the greatest good.

Deontology: Doing one's duty, regardless of the consequences, is the foundation for morality.

Virtue Ethics: Development of proper character determines moral actions.

Ethical Egoism: One ought to do what is best for oneself.

Care Ethics: One ought to act out of care for others, not just in accord with some impersonal set of rules.

Naturalized Ethics: Ethics is an evolved phenomenon, and like any other natural phenomenon, it can be explained and discovered through science.

In this chapter, Rachels first examines the allure of cultural relativism (that morality is determined by a particular culture's practices) and then illustrates the pitfalls of holding such a position. Aristotle discusses virtue ethics and derives his ideas from an examination of human purpose and what it means to flourish. In doing so, he avoids the constructs of a set of rules and allows one to focus more on developing a character that resonates with human flourishing. Kant employs reason to determine a set of rules (duties) that we ought to follow, despite how we may be inclined to act, while Mill focuses more on the consequences of our actions in defense of utilitarianism. Rand explores the virtue of selfishness and frames the ethical egoist position. And Gilligan first assesses previous attempts to determine moral theory, pointing out flaws of such systems—namely, that they represent a very androcentric (male-oriented) viewpoint and fail to account for *all* situations *all* the time—and then provides the basis for care ethics and how we might view morality in a different "voice."

The Challenge of Cultural Relativism

James Rachels

James Rachels taught philosophy at the University of Alabama from 1977 until his death in 2003. During this time, he authored four books—each focused on moral theory—edited seven others, and published over sixty academic articles.

This excerpt—Chapter 2 of his book *The Elements of Moral Philosophy* (now in its fourth edition)—first illustrates the moral theory known as cultural relativism along with showing the initial allure. He then discusses the problems that result from holding this theory, highlights reasons behind the theory's appeal and suggests insights we can still take from it.

Reading Questions

1. What point does Rachels make in his opening account of the Greeks and Callations? What examples does he then use from Eskimo culture to make the same point?
2. Provide a definition of the moral theory of *cultural relativism*. Why does cultural relativism challenge the notion of objective moral truths?
3. Why does Rachels believe the Cultural Differences Argument to be unsound? How does he use the reference of some people's *belief* that the Earth is flat to demonstrate this?
4. Explain each of Rachels' three consequences of taking cultural relativism seriously.
5. How does Rachels contrast *belief systems* with *values* in his example of the "Cow Culture"? How does he extrapolate this to the Eskimo practice of infanticide?
6. What values does Rachels suggest that cultures have in common? With what reasoning does he believe each of these to be the case?
7. According to Rachels, what two lessons can we learn from cultural relativism?

How Different Cultures Have Different Moral Codes

Darius, a king of ancient Persia, was intrigued by the variety of cultures he encountered in his travels. He had found, for example, that the Callatians (a tribe of Indians) customarily ate the bodies of their dead fathers. The Greeks, of course, did not do that—the Greeks practiced cremation and regarded the funeral pyre as the natural and fitting way to dispose of the dead. Darius thought that a sophisticated understanding of the world must include an

Source: Excerpt from *The Elements of Moral Philosophy* by James Rachels. Copyright © 1986 by Random House, Inc. Reprinted by permission of McGraw-Hill Companies.

appreciation of such differences between cultures. One day, to teach this lesson, he summoned some Greeks who happened to be present at his court and asked them what they would take to eat the bodies of their dead fathers. They were shocked, as Darius knew they would be, and replied that no amount of money could persuade them to do such a thing. Then Darius called in some Callatians, and while the Greeks listened asked them what they would take to burn their dead fathers' bodies. The Callatians were horrified and told Darius not even to mention such a dreadful thing.

This story, recounted by Herodotus in his *History*, illustrates a recurring theme in the literature of social science: Different cultures have different moral codes.[1] What is thought right within one group may be utterly abhorrent to the members of another group, and vice versa. Should we eat the bodies of the dead or burn them? If you were a Greek, one answer would seem obviously correct; but if you were a Callatian, the opposite would seem equally certain.

It is easy to give additional examples of the same kind. Consider the Eskimos. They are a remote and inaccessible people. Numbering only about 25,000, they live in small, isolated settlements scattered mostly along the northern fringes of North America and Greenland. Until the beginning of this century, the outside world knew little about them. Then explorers began to bring back strange tales.

Eskimo customs turned out to be very different from our own. The men often had more than one wife, and they would share their wives with guests, lending them for the night as a sign of hospitality. Moreover, within a community, a dominant male might demand—and get—regular sexual access to other men's wives. The women, however, were free to break these arrangements simply by leaving their husbands and taking up with new partners—free, that is, so long as their former husbands chose not to make trouble. All in all, the Eskimo practice was a volatile scheme that bore little resemblance to what we call marriage.

But it was not only their marriage and sexual practices that were different. The Eskimos also seemed to have less regard for human life. Infanticide, for example, was common. Knud Rasmussen, one of the most famous early explorers, reported that he met one woman who had borne twenty children but had killed ten of them at birth. Female babies, he found, were especially liable to be destroyed, and this was permitted simply at the parents' discretion, with no social stigma attached to it. Old people also, when they became too feeble to contribute to the family, were left out in the snow to die. So there seemed to be, in this society, remarkably little respect for life.[2]

To the general public, these were disturbing revelations. Our own way of living seems so natural and right that for many of us it is hard to conceive of others living so differently. And when we do here of such things, we tend immediately to categorize those other peoples as "backward" or "primitive." But to anthropologists and sociologists, there was nothing particularly surprising about the Eskimos. Since the time of Herodotus, enlightened observers have been accustomed to the idea that conceptions of right and wrong differ from culture to culture. If we assume that *our* ideas of right and wrong will be shared by all peoples at all times, we are merely naive.

Cultural Relativism

To many thinkers, this observation—"Different cultures have different moral codes"—has seemed to be the key to understanding morality. The idea of universal truth in ethics, they say, is a myth. The customs of different societies are all that exist. These customs cannot be said to be "correct" or "incorrect," for that implies we have an independent standard of right and wrong by which they may be judged. But there is no such independent standard; every standard is culture-bound. The great pioneering sociologist William Graham Sumner, writing in 1906, put the point like this:

> The "right" way is the way which the ancestors used and which has been handed down. The tradition is its own warrant. It is not held subject to verification by experience. The notion of right is in the folkways. It is not outside of them, of independent origin, and brought to test them. In the folkways, whatever is, is right. This is because they are traditional, and therefore contain in themselves the authority of the ancestral ghosts. When we come to the folkways we are at the end of our analysis.[3]

This line of thought has probably persuaded more people to be skeptical about ethics than any other single thing. *Cultural Relativism*, as it has been called, challenges our ordinary belief in the objectivity and universality of moral truth. It says, in effect, that there is no such thing as universal truth in ethics; there are only the various cultural codes, and nothing more. Moreover, our own code has no special status; it is merely one among many.

As we shall see, this basic idea is really a compound of several different thoughts. It is important to separate the various elements of the theory because, on analysis, some parts of the theory turn out to be correct, whereas others seem to be mistaken. As a beginning, we may distinguish the following claims, all of which have been made by cultural relativists:

1. Different societies have different moral codes.
2. There is no objective standard that can be used to judge one societal code better than another.
3. The moral code of our own society has no special status; it is merely one among many.
4. There is no "universal truth" in ethics—that is, there are no moral truths that hold for all peoples at all times.
5. The moral code of a society determines what is right within that society; that is, if the moral code of a society says that a certain action is right, then that action *is* right, at least within that society.
6. It is mere arrogance for us to try to judge the conduct of other peoples. We should adopt an attitude of tolerance toward the practices of other cultures.

Although it may seem that these six propositions go naturally together, they are independent of one another, in the sense that some of them might be true even if others are false. In what follows, we will try to identify what is correct in Cultural Relativism, but we will also be concerned to expose what is mistaken about it.

The Cultural Differences Argument

Cultural Relativism is a theory about the nature of morality. At first blush it seems quite plausible. However, like all such theories, it may be evaluated by subjecting it to rational analysis; and when we analyze Cultural Relativism we find that it is not so plausible as it first appears to be.

The first thing we need to notice is that at the heart of Cultural Relativism there is a certain *form of argument*. The strategy used by cultural relativists is to argue from facts about the differences between cultural outlooks to a conclusion about the status of morality. Thus we are invited to accept this reasoning:

1. The Greeks believed it was wrong to eat the dead, whereas the Callatians believed it was right to eat the dead.
2. Therefore, eating the dead is neither objectively right nor objectively wrong. It is merely a matter of opinion, which varies from culture to culture.

Or, alternatively:

1. The Eskimos see nothing wrong with infanticide, whereas Americans believe infanticide is immoral.
2. Therefore, infanticide is neither objectively right nor objectively wrong. It is merely a matter of opinion, which varies from culture to culture.

Clearly, these arguments are variations of one fundamental idea. They are both special cases of a more general argument, which says:

1. Different cultures have different moral codes.
2. Therefore, there is no objective "truth" in morality. Right and wrong are only matters of opinion, and opinions vary from culture to culture.

We may call this the *Cultural Differences Argument*. To many people, it is very persuasive. But from a logical point of view, is it a *sound* argument?

It is not sound. The trouble is that the conclusion does not really follow from the premise—that is, even if the premise is true, the conclusion still might be false. The premise concerns what people *believe*: In some societies, people believe one thing; in other societies, people believe differently. The conclusion, however, concerns *what really is the case*. The trouble is that this sort of conclusion does not follow logically from this sort of premise.

Consider again the example of the Greeks and Callatians. The Greeks believed it was wrong to eat the dead; the Callatians believed it was right. Does it follow, *from the mere fact that they disagreed*, that there is no objective truth in the matter? No, it does not follow; for it *could* be that the practice was objectively right (or wrong) and that one or the other of them was simply mistaken.

To make the point clearer, consider a very different matter. In some societies, people believe the earth is flat. In other societies, such as our own, people believe the earth is (roughly) spherical. Does it follow, *from the mere fact that they disagree*, that there is no "objective truth" in geography? Of course not; we would never draw such a conclusion because we realize that, in their beliefs about the world, the members of some societies might simply be wrong. There is no reason to think that if the world is round everyone must know it. Similarly, there is no reason to think that if there is moral truth everyone must know it. The fundamental mistake in the Cultural Differences Argument is that it attempts to derive a substantive conclusion about a subject (morality) from the mere fact that people disagree about it.

It is important to understand the nature of the point that is being made here. We are *not* saying (not yet, anyway) that the conclusion of the argument is false. Insofar as anything being said here is concerned, it is still an open question whether the conclusion is true. We *are* making a purely logical point and saying that the conclusion does not *follow from* the premise. This is important, because in order to determine whether the conclusion is true, we need arguments in its support. Cultural Relativism proposes this argument, but unfortunately the argument turns out to be fallacious. So it proves nothing.

The Consequences of Taking Cultural Relativism Seriously

Even if the Cultural Differences Argument is invalid, Cultural Relativism might still be true. What would it be like if it were true?

In the passage quoted above, William Graham Summer summarizes the essence of Cultural Relativism. He says that there is no measure of right and wrong other than the standards of one's society: "The notion of right is in the folkways. It is not outside of them, of independent origin, and brought to test them. In the folkways, whatever is, is right."

Suppose we took this seriously. What would be some of the consequences?

(1) *We could no longer say that the customs of other societies are morally inferior to our own.* This, of course, is one of the main points stressed by Cultural Relativism. We would have to stop condemning other societies merely because they are "different." So long as we concentrate on certain examples, such as the funerary practices of the Greeks and Callatians, this may seem to be a sophisticated, enlightened attitude.

However, we would also be stopped from criticizing other, less benign practices. Suppose a society waged war on its neighbors for the purpose of taking slaves. Or suppose a society was violently anti-Semitic, and its leaders set out to destroy the Jews. Cultural Relativism would preclude us from saying that either of these practices was wrong. We would not even be able to say that a society tolerant of Jews is *better* than the anti-Semitic society, for that would imply some sort of transcultural standard of comparison. The failure to condemn *these* practices does not seem "enlightened"; on the contrary, slavery and anti-Semitism seem wrong *wherever* they occur. Nevertheless, if we took Cultural Relativism seriously, we would have to admit that these social practices also are immune from criticism.

(2) *We could decide whether actions are right or wrong just by consulting the standards of our society.* Cultural Relativism suggests a simple test for determining what is right and what is wrong: All one has to do is ask whether the action is in accordance with the code of one's society. Suppose a resident of South Africa is wondering whether his country's policy of *apartheid*—rigid racial segregation—is morally correct. All he has to do is ask whether this policy conforms to his society's moral code. If it does, there is nothing to worry about, at least from a moral point of view.

This implication of Cultural Relativism is disturbing because few of us think that our society's code is perfect—we can think of ways it might be improved. Yet Cultural Relativism would not only forbid us from criticizing the codes of *other* societies; it would stop us from criticizing our *own*. After all, if right and wrong are relative to culture, this must be true for our own culture just as much as for others.

(3) *The idea of moral progress is called into doubt.* Usually, we think that at least some changes in our society have been for the better. (Some, of course, may have been changes for the worse.) Consider this example: Throughout most of Western history the place of women in society was very narrowly circumscribed. They could not own property; they could not vote or hold political office; with a few exceptions, they were not permitted to have paying jobs; and generally they were under the almost absolute control of their husbands. Recently much of this has changed, and most people think of it as progress.

If Cultural Relativism is correct, can we legitimately think of this as progress? Progress means replacing a way of doing things with a *better* way. But by what standard do we judge the new ways as better? If the old ways were in accordance with the social standards of their time, then Cultural Relativism would say it is a mistake to judge them by the standards of a different time. Eighteenth-century society was, in effect, a different society from the one we have now. To say that we have made progress implies a judgment that present-day society is better, and that is just the sort of transcultural judgment that, according to Cultural Relativism, is impermissible.

Our idea of social *reform* will also have to be reconsidered. A reformer such as Martin Luther King, Jr., seeks to change his society for the better. Within the constraints imposed by Cultural Relativism, there is one way this might be done. If a society is not living up to its own ideals, the reformer may be regarded as acting for the best: The ideals of the society are the standard by which we judge his or her proposals as worthwhile. But the "reformer" may not challenge the ideals themselves, for those ideals are by definition correct. According to Cultural Relativism, then, the idea of social reform makes sense only in this very limited way.

These three consequences of Cultural Relativism have led many thinkers to reject it as implausible on its face. It does make sense, they say, to condemn some practices, such as slavery and anti-Semitism, wherever they occur. It makes sense to think that our own society has made some moral progress, while admitting that it is still imperfect and in need of reform. Because Cultural Relativism says that these judgments make no sense, the argument goes, it cannot be right.

Why There Is Less Disagreement Than It Seems

The original impetus for Cultural Relativism comes from the observation that cultures differ dramatically in their views of right and wrong. But just how much do they differ? It is true that there are differences. However, it is easy to overestimate the extent of those differences. Often, when we examine what *seems* to be a dramatic difference, we find that the cultures do not differ nearly as much as it appears.

Consider a culture in which people believe it is wrong to eat cows. This may even be a poor culture, in which there is not enough food; still, the cows are not to be touched. Such a society would *appear* to have values very different from our own. But does it? We have not yet asked why these people will not eat cows. Suppose it is because they believe that after death the souls of humans inhabit the bodies of animals, especially cows, so that a cow may be someone's grandmother. Now do we want to say that their values are different from ours? No, the difference lies elsewhere. The difference is in our belief systems, not in our values. We agree that we shouldn't eat Grandma; we simply disagree about whether the cow *is* (or could be) Grandma.

The general point is this. Many factors work together to produce the customs of a society. The society's values are only one of them. Other matters such as the religious and factual beliefs held by its members and the physical circumstances in which they must live, are also important. We cannot conclude, then, merely because customs differ, that there is a disagreement about *values*. The difference in customs may be attributable to some other aspect of social life. Thus there may be less disagreement about values than there appears to be.

Consider the Eskimos again. They often kill perfectly normal infants, especially girls. We do not approve of this at all; a parent who did this in our society would be locked up. Thus there appears to be a great difference in the values of our two cultures. But suppose we ask *why* the Eskimos do this. The explanation is not that they have less affection for their children or less respect for human life. An Eskimo family will always protect its babies if conditions permit. But they live in a harsh environment, where food is often in short supply. A fundamental postulate of Eskimo thought is: "Life is hard, and the margin of safety small." A family may want to nourish its babies but be unable to do so.

As in many "primitive" societies, Eskimo mothers will nurse their infants over a much longer period of time than mothers in our culture. The child will take nourishment from its mother's breast for four years, perhaps even longer. So even in the best of times there are limits to the number of infants that one mother can sustain. Moreover, the Eskimos are a nomadic people—unable to farm, they must move about in search of food. Infants must be carried, and a mother can carry only one baby in her parka as she travels and goes about her outdoor work. Other family members can help, but this is not always possible.

Infant girls are more readily disposed of because, first, in this society the males are the primary food providers—they are the hunters, according to the traditional division of labor—and it is obviously important to maintain a sufficient number of food gatherers. But there is an important second reason as well. Because the hunters suffer a high casualty rate, the adult men who die prematurely far outnumber the women who die early. Thus if male and female infants survived in equal numbers, the female adult population would greatly outnumber the male adult population. Examining the available statistics, one writer concluded that "were it not for female infanticide. . . there would be approximately one-and-a-half times as many females in the average Eskimo local group as there are food-producing males."[4]

So among the Eskimos, infanticide does not signal a fundamentally different attitude toward children. Instead, it is a recognition that drastic measures are sometimes needed to ensure the family's survival. Even then, however, killing the baby is not the first option considered. Adoption is common; childless couples are especially happy to take a more fertile couple's "surplus." Killing is only the last resort. I emphasize this in order to show that the raw data of the anthropologists can be misleading; it can make the differences in values between cultures appear greater than they are. The Eskimos' values are not all that different from our values. It is only that life forces upon them choices that we do not have to make.

How All Cultures Have Some Values in Common

It should not be surprising that, despite appearances, the Eskimos are protective of their children. How could it be otherwise? How could a group survive that did *not* value its young? This suggests a certain argument, one which shows that all cultural groups must be protective of their infants:

1. Human infants are helpless and cannot survive if they are not given extensive care for a period of years.
2. Therefore, if a group did not care for its young, the young would not survive, and the older members of the group would not be replaced. After a while the group would die out.
3. Therefore, any cultural group that continues to exist must care for its young. Infants that are *not* cared for must be the exception rather than the rule.

Similar reasoning shows that other values must be more or less universal. Imagine what it would be like for a society to place no value at all on truth telling. When one person spoke to another, there would be no presumption at all that he was telling the truth—for he could just as easily be speaking falsely. Within that society, there would be no reason to pay attention to what anyone says. (I ask you what time it is, and you say "four o'clock." But there is no presumption that you are speaking truly; you could just as easily have said the first thing that came into your head. So I have no reason to pay attention to your answer—in fact, there was no point in my asking you in the first place!) Communication would then be extremely difficult, if not impossible. And because complex societies cannot exist without regular communication among their members, society would become impossible. It follows that in any complex society there *must* be a presumption in favor of truthfulness. There may of course be exceptions to this rule: There may be situations in which it is thought to be permissible to lie. Nevertheless, these will be exceptions to a rule that *is* in force in the society.

Let me give one further example of the same type. Could a society exist in which there was no prohibition on murder? What would this be like? Suppose people were free to kill other people at will, and no one thought there was anything wrong with it. In such a "society," no one could feel secure. Everyone would have to be constantly on guard. People who wanted to survive would have to avoid other people as much as possible. This would inevitably result in individuals trying to become as self-sufficient as possible—after all, associating with others would be dangerous. Society on any large scale would collapse. Of course, people might band together in smaller groups with others that they *could* trust not to harm them. But notice what this means: They would be forming smaller societies that *did* acknowledge a rule against murder. The prohibition of murder, then, is a necessary feature of all societies.

There is a general theoretical point here, namely, that *there are some moral rules that all societies will have in common, because those rules are necessary for society to exist.* The rules against lying and murder are two examples. And in fact, we do find these rules in force in all viable cultures. Cultures may differ in what they regard as legitimate exceptions to the rules, but this disagreement exists against a background of agreement on the larger issues. Therefore, it is a mistake to overestimate the amount of difference between cultures. Not *every* moral rule can vary from society to society.

What Can Be Learned From Cultural Relativism

At the outset, I said that we were going to identify both what is right and what is wrong in Cultural Relativism. Thus far I have mentioned only its mistakes: I have said that it rests on an invalid argument, that it has consequences that make it implausible on its face, and that the extent of cultural disagreement is far less than it implies. This all adds up to a pretty thorough repudiation of the theory. Nevertheless, it is still a very appealing idea, and the reader may have the feeling that all this is a little unfair. The theory *must* have something going for it, or else why has it been so influential? In fact, I think there *is* something right about Cultural Relativism, and now I want to say what that is. There are two lessons we should learn from the theory, even if we ultimately reject it.

(1) Cultural Relativism warns us, quite rightly, about the danger of assuming that all our preferences are based on some absolute rational standard. They are not. Many (but not all) of our practices are merely peculiar to our society, and it is easy to lose sight of that fact. In reminding us of it, the theory does a service.

Funerary practices are one example. The Callatians, according to Herodotus, were "men who eat their fathers"—a shocking idea, to us at least. But eating the flesh of the dead could be understood as a sign of respect. It could be taken as a symbolic act that says: We wish this person's spirit to dwell within us. Perhaps this was the understanding of the Callatians. On such a way of thinking, burying the dead could be seen as an act of rejection, and burning the corpse as positively scornful. If this is hard to imagine, then we may need to have our imaginations stretched. Of course we may feel a visceral repugnance at the idea of eating human flesh in any circumstances. But what of it? This repugnance may be, as the relativists say, only a matter of what is customary in our particular society.

There are many other matters that we tend to think of in terms of objective right and wrong, but that are really nothing more than social conventions. Should women cover their breasts? A publicly exposed breast is scandalous in our society, whereas in other cultures it is unremarkable. Objectively speaking, it is neither right nor wrong —there is no objective reason why either custom is better. Cultural Relativism begins with the valuable insight that many of our practices are like this—they are only cultural products. Then it goes wrong by concluding that, because *some* practices are like this, *all* must be.

(2) The second lesson has to do with keeping an open mind. In the course of growing up, each of us has acquired some strong feelings: We have learned to think of some types of conduct as acceptable, and others we have learned to regard as simply unacceptable. Occasionally, we may find those feelings challenged. We may encounter someone who claims that our feelings are mistaken. For example, we may have been taught that homosexuality is immoral, and we may feel quite uncomfortable around gay people and see them as alien and "different." Now someone suggests that this may be a mere prejudice; that there is nothing evil about homosexuality; that gay people are just people, like anyone else, who happen, through no choice of their own, to be attracted to others of the same sex. But because we feel so strongly about the matter, we may find it hard to take this seriously. Even after we listen to the arguments, we may still have the unshakable feeling that homosexuals *must*, somehow, be an unsavory lot.

Cultural Relativism, by stressing that our moral views can reflect the prejudices of our society, provides an antidote for this kind of dogmatism. When he tells the story of the Greeks and Callatians, Herodotus adds:

> For if anyone, no matter who, were given the opportunity of choosing from amongst all the nations of the world the set of beliefs which he thought best, he would inevitably, after careful consideration of their relative merits, choose that of his own country. Everyone without exception believes his own native customs, and the religion he was brought up in, to be the best.[5]

Realizing this can result in our having more open minds. We can come to understand that our feelings are not necessarily perceptions of the truth—they may be nothing more than the result of cultural conditioning. Thus when we hear it suggested that some element of our social code is *not* really the best, and we find ourselves instinctively resisting the suggestion, we might stop and remember this. Then we may be more open to discovering the truth, whatever that might be.

We can understand the appeal of Cultural Relativism, then, even though the theory has serious shortcomings. It is an attractive theory because it is based on a genuine insight—that many of the practices and attitudes we think so natural are really only cultural products. Moreover, keeping this insight firmly in view is important if we want to avoid arrogance and have open minds. These are important points, not to be taken lightly. But we can accept these points without going on to accept the whole theory.

Discussion Questions

1. How do *you* morally assess the "burial process" of the Callations and the sexual conduct and infanticide practice of Eskimos (as he describes in the opening section)? If you judge them to be immoral, how do you defend your position?
2. Does learning more about the Eskimos (later in Rachels' piece) change your view of the moral status of infanticide in their culture? Why/why not?
3. If you believe that cultural relativism is true, how do you respond to each of Rachels' consequences of this theory? If you believe it to be false, why?
4. In Africa and the Middle East, approximately 6000 girls per day undergo female genital mutilation (FGM), in which all or part of the genitalia is removed. This is culturally accepted, as late Kenyan president Jomo Kenyatta noted: "Abolition [of FGM] . . . will destroy the tribal system." It can result not just in pain, but serious infections, kidney damage, decreased sexual pleasure, psychological trauma, and death. How do you view the moral status of this practice?

Nicomachean Ethics

Aristotle

At age seventeen, Aristotle went to study under Plato at Plato's university, the Academy. (He later established his own university—the Lyceum—which lasted for over 500 years.) Aristotle wrote extensively, completing nearly 150 works on a huge variety of subjects, including rhetoric, metaphysics, mathematics, logic, botany, political science, meteorology, the philosophy and history of science, love, friendship, and the natural sciences. Darwin highly praised Aristotle's work in biology and zoology. Aristotle even wrote poetry.

Aristotle's system of ethics, which he describes here, is *teleological*—*telos* meaning goal or purpose. Aristotle often mentions the *end*, or goal, of objects and activities; in doing so, he discusses (and he believes that he determines) the end (goal) of humans, in order that he may more correctly determine just *how* to achieve that end—namely, how *ought* one to act? Through this system of *politics* (used by Aristotle to refer to the study of living in a society) he helps to determine the ultimate virtues. Virtue—in Greek, *arête*—is meant more as "excellence," and in conjunction with the *ends* of humans, Aristotle aims to determine just what it is that makes an *excellent person*. In admitting that ethics is not an exact science, he

Source: Aristotle, *Nicomachean Ethics*. Translated by H. Rackham, M.A. London: William Heinemann, 1926.

then suggests a method—the Doctrine of the Mean—by which we can approach virtue in our own lives. Aristotle's ethics (the investigation of human happiness) focuses not on a set of rules (as many moral codes do), but on one's character and way of life.

Reading Questions

1. How does Aristotle relate the ends (goals) of crafts to the corresponding actions? Why does he argue the ends of activities cannot go on infinitely?
2. How does Aristotle argue that young people are not properly suited for deliberating about ethics and politics?
3. What is the general consensus of the good at which every action aims? What causes people to differ on how this good is achieved?
4. What is the role of one's upbringing according to Aristotle?
5. What are the three types of life Aristotle mentions, and what does he say about the way they reflect the good? Why does Aristotle dismiss considering money-making as a way of life?
6. How does Aristotle defend *happiness* as that which is desirable in and of itself?
7. What is the role of *function* in Aristotle's discussion? What is the function of humans? How does he defend this?
8. How does Aristotle defend the claim (in Book I, Chapter 8) that a virtuous action must be pleasant in itself?
9. How does Aristotle's discussion of the parts of the soul relate to virtues?
10. Explain the two sorts of character.
11. Explain how he uses the following examples to defend the importance of *habit:*
    a. A stone moving upward
    b. Builders
    c. Citizens of states/cities
12. Why is Aristotle's inquiry more than just theoretical? What is the role of *action?*
13. Explain how Aristotle posits bravery and temperance as virtues by examining their respective excesses and deficiencies.
14. What is the role of pleasure and pain in relation to virtue?
15. In what two ways does Aristotle address the criticism "How can we be good without being good already?"
16. Explain the three things found in the soul. Why are virtues (and vices) neither *passions* nor *faculties*, and why *does* Aristotle consider them to be *states* of character?
17. How does Aristotle more exactly define *virtue?* What five components does he include in his definition?
18. What situations arise in which there is no mean? How should one respond to these situations?
19. What are the extremes—the excesses and deficiencies—relating to each virtue (mean)?
    a. Courage/bravery
    b. Temperance

      c. Liberality/generosity
      d. Magnificence
      e. Greatness of Soul/proper pride
      f. Gentleness/good temper
      g. Truthfulness
      h. Wittiness
      i. Friendliness
      j. Righteous indignation

20. Since we are not immediately drawn to the mean, how does Aristotle suggest we approach it?
21. What eight reasons does Aristotle provide in support of his claim that understanding/reason is the best thing and that it can be achieved through study and contemplation?

Book I

IV

2   . . . Let us discuss what it is that we pronounce to be . . . the highest of all the goods that action can achieve. As far as the name goes, we may almost say that the great majority of mankind are agreed about this; for both the multitude and persons of refinement speak of it as Happiness, and conceive 'the good life' or 'doing well'

3   to be the same thing as 'being happy.' But what constitutes happiness is a matter of dispute; and the popular account of it is not the same as that given by the philosophers. Ordinary people identify it with some obvious and visible good, such as pleasure or wealth or honour—some say one thing and some another, indeed very often the same man says different things at different times: When he falls sick he thinks health is happiness, when he is poor, wealth. At other times, feeling conscious of their own ignorance, men admire those who propound something grand and above their heads; and it has been held by some thinkers that beside the many good things we have mentioned, there exists another Good, that is good in itself, and stands to all those goods as the cause of their being good.

4   Now perhaps it would be a somewhat fruitless task to review all the different opinions that are held. It will suffice to examine those which are most widely accepted, or which seem to be supported by some measure of reason.

5   And we must not overlook the distinction between arguments that start from first principles and those that lead to first principles. This is a matter that was rightly raised by Plato, who used to enquire whether the true procedure is to start from or to lead up to one's first principles, as in a race-course one may run from the judges to the far end of the track or the reverse. Now no doubt it is proper to start from the known. But 'the known' has two meanings—'what is familiar to us,' which is one thing, and 'what is intelligible in itself,' which is another. Perhaps

6   then for us at all events it is proper to start from what is known to us. This is why in order to be a competent student of the Right and Just, and in short of the top-

7   ics of Politics in general, the pupil is bound to have had a right moral upbringing.

For the starting-point or first principle is the fact that a thing is so; if this be satisfactorily ascertained, there will be no need also to know the reason why it is so. And the man of good moral training knows first principles already, or can easily acquire them. . . .

V

But let us continue from the point where we digressed. To judge from the recognized types of Lives, the more or less reasoned conceptions of the Good or Happiness that prevail are the following. On the one hand the generality of men and the most vulgar identify the Good with pleasure, and accordingly look no   *2* higher than the Life of Enjoyment—for there are three specially prominent Lives, the one just mentioned, the Life of Politics, and thirdly, the Life of   *3* Contemplation. The generality of mankind then show themselves to be utterly slavish, by preferring what is only a life for cattle; but they get a hearing for their view as reasonable because many persons of high position share the feelings of Sardanapallus.

Men of refinement, on the other hand, and men of action think that the   *4* Good is honour—for this may be said to be the end of the Life of Politics. But honour after all seems too superficial to be the Good for which we are seeking; since it appears to depend on those who confer it more than on him upon whom it is conferred, whereas we instinctively feel that the Good must be something proper to its possessor and not easy to be taken away from him. Moreover   *5* men's motive in pursuing honour seems to be to assure themselves of their own merit; at least they seek to be honoured by men of judgement and by people who know them, that is, they desire to be honoured on the ground of virtue. It is clear therefore that in the opinion at all events of men of action, virtue is a greater good than honour; and one might perhaps accordingly suppose that virtue rather than honour is the end of the Political Life. But even virtue proves   *6* on examination to be too incomplete to be the End; since it appears possible to possess it while you are asleep, or without putting it into practice throughout the whole of your life; and also for the virtuous man to suffer the greatest misery and misfortune—though no one would pronounce a man living a life of misery to be happy, unless for the sake of maintaining a paradox. But we need not pursue this subject, since it has been sufficiently treated in the ordinary discussions.

The third type of life is the Life of Contemplation, which we shall consider in   *7* the sequel.

The Life of Money-making is a hard kind of life; and clearly wealth is not the   *8* Good we are in search of, for it is only good as being useful, a means to something else. On this score indeed one might conceive the ends before mentioned to have a better claim, for they are approved for their own sakes. But even they do not really seem to be the Supreme Good; however, many arguments against them have been disseminated, so we may dismiss them. . . .

VII

We may now return to the Good which is the object of our search, and try to find out what exactly it can be. For good appears to be one thing in one pursuit or art and another in another: It is different in medicine from what it is in strategy, and so on with the rest of the arts. What definition of the Good then will hold true in all the arts? Perhaps we may define it as that for the sake of which everything else is done. This applies to something different in each different art—to health in the case of medicine, to victory in that of strategy, to a house in architecture, and to something else in each of the other arts; but in every pursuit or undertaking it describes the end of that pursuit or under- taking, since in all of them it is for the sake of the end that everything else is done. Hence if there be something which is the end of all the things done by human action, this will be the practicable Good—or if there be several such

2 ends, the sum of these will be the Good. Thus by changing its ground the argument has reached the same result as before. We must attempt however to render this still more precise.

3 Now there do appear to be several ends at which our actions aim; but as we choose some of them—for instance wealth, or flutes, and instruments generally—as a means to something else, it is clear that not all of them are final ends; whereas the Supreme Good seems to be something final or perfect. Consequently if there be some one thing which alone is a final end, this thing—or

4 if there be several final ends, the one among them which is the most final—will be the Good which we are seeking. In speaking of degrees of finality, we mean that a thing pursued as an end in itself is more final than one pursued as a means to something else, and that a thing never chosen as a means to anything else is more final than things chosen both as ends in themselves and as means to that thing;

5 and accordingly a thing chosen always as an end and never as a means we call absolutely final. Now happiness above all else appears to be absolutely final in this sense, since we always choose it for its own sake and never as a means to some- thing else; whereas honour, pleasure, intelligence, and excellence in its various forms, we choose indeed for their own sakes (since we should be glad to have each of them although no extraneous advantage resulted from it), but we also choose them for the sake of happiness, in the belief that they will be a means to our securing it. But no one chooses happiness for the sake of honour, pleasure, etc., nor as a means to anything whatever other than itself.

6 The same conclusion also appears to follow from a consideration of the self- sufficiency of happiness—for it is felt that the final good must be a thing suffi- cient in itself. The term self-sufficient, however, we employ with reference not to oneself alone, living a life of isolation, but also to one's parents and children and wife, and one's friends and fellow citizens in general, since man is by nature a

7 social being. On the other hand a limit has to be assumed in these relationships; for if the list be extended to one's ancestors and descendants and to the friends of one's friends, it will go on *ad infinitum*. But this is a point that must be considered later on; we take a self-sufficient thing to mean a thing which merely standing by

itself alone renders life desirable and lacking in nothing, and such a thing we deem happiness to be. Moreover, we think happiness the most desirable of all good things without being itself reckoned as one among the rest; for if it were so reckoned, it is clear that we should consider it more desirable when even the smallest of other good things were combined with it, since this addition would result in a larger total of good, and of two goods the greater is always the more desirable.

Happiness, therefore, being found to be something final and self-sufficient, is the End at which all actions aim.

To say however that the Supreme Good is happiness will probably appear a truism; we still require a more explicit account of what constitutes happiness. Perhaps then we may arrive at this by ascertaining what is man's function. For the goodness or efficiency of a flute-player or sculptor or craftsman of any sort, and in general of anybody who has some function or business to perform, is thought to reside in that function; and similarly it may be held that the good of man resides in the function of man, if he has a function.

Are we then to suppose that, while the carpenter and the shoemaker have definite functions or businesses belonging to them, man as such has none, and is not designed by nature to fulfil any function? Must we not rather assume that just as the eye, the hand, the foot, and each of the various members of the body manifestly has a certain function of its own, so a human being also has a certain function over and above all the functions of his particular members? What then precisely can this function be? The mere act of living appears to be shared even by plants, whereas we are looking for the function peculiar to man; we must therefore set aside the vital activity of nutrition and growth. Next in the scale will come some form of sentient life; but this too appears to be shared by horses, oxen, and animals generally. There remains therefore what may be called the practical life of the rational part of man. (This part has two divisions, one rational as obedient to principle, the other as possessing principle and exercising intelligence). Rational life again has two meanings; let us assume that we are here concerned with the active exercise of the rational faculty, since this seems to be the more proper sense of the term. If then the function of man is the active exercise of the soul's faculties in conformity with rational principle, or at all events not in dissociation from rational principle, and if we acknowledge the function of an individual and of a good individual of the same class (for instance, a harper and a good harper, and so generally with all classes) to be generically the same, the qualification of the latter's superiority in excellence being added to the function in his case (I mean that if the function of a harper is to play the harp, that of a good harper is to play the harp well): If this is so, and if we declare that the function of man is a certain form of life, and define that form of life as the exercise of the soul's faculties and activities in association with rational principle, and say that the function of a good man is to perform these activities well and rightly, and if a function is well performed when it is performed in accordance with its own proper excellence—if then all this be so, the Good of man proves to be the active exercise of his soul's faculties in conformity with excellence or virtue, or if there be several

8

9

10

11

12

13

14

15

human excellences or virtues, in conformity with the best and most perfect among them.

16   Moreover, to be happy takes a complete lifetime. For one swallow does not make summer, nor does one fine day; and similarly one day or a brief period of happiness does not make a man supremely blessed and happy. . . .

VIII

Accordingly we must examine our first principle not only as a logical conclusion deduced from certain premises but also in the light of the current opinions on the subject. For if a proposition be true, all the facts harmonize with it, but if it is false, it is quickly seen to be discordant with them.

Now things good have been divided into three classes, external goods on the
2   one hand, and goods of the soul and of the body on the other; and of these three kinds of goods, those of the soul are commonly said to be the highest, and good in the fullest degree. But our actions, that is, the soul's active exercise of its functions, must be placed in the class of things of the soul; hence so far as this opinion goes—and it is of long standing, and generally accepted by students of philosophy—it supports the correctness of our definition of Happiness.

3   It also shows it to be right in declaring the End to consist in certain actions or activities, for thus the End is included among goods of the soul, and not among external goods.

4   Again, our definition accords with the description of the happy man as one who 'lives well' or 'does well'; for it has virtually identified happiness with a form of good life or doing well.

5   And moreover all the various characteristics that are looked for in happiness
6   are found to belong to the Good as we define it. Some people think happiness is goodness or virtue, others prudence, others a form of wisdom; others again say it is all of these things, or one of them, in combination with pleasure, or accompanied by pleasure as an indispensable adjunct; another school include external
7   prosperity as a concomitant factor. Some of these views have been held by many people and from ancient times, others by a few distinguished men, and neither class is likely to be altogether mistaken; the probability is that their beliefs are at least partly, or indeed mainly, correct.

8   Now with those who pronounce happiness to be virtue, or some particular virtue, our definition is in agreement; for 'activity in conformity with virtue'
9   involves virtue. But no doubt it makes a great difference whether we conceive the Supreme Good to depend on possessing virtue or on displaying it—on disposition, or on the manifestation of a disposition in action. For a man may possess the disposition without its producing any good result, as for instance when he is asleep, or has ceased to function from some other cause; but virtue in active exercise cannot be inoperative—it will of necessity act, and act well. And just as at the Olympic games the wreaths of victory are not bestowed upon the handsomest and strongest persons present, but on men who enter for the competitions—since

it is among these that the winners are found,—so it is those who *act* rightly who carry off the prizes and good things of life.

And further, the life of active virtue is essentially pleasant. For on the one   *10*
hand, the feeling of pleasure is an experience of the soul. Also, when a man is described as "fond of" so-and-so, the thing in question gives him pleasure: For instance a horse gives pleasure to one fond of horses, a play to one fond of the theatre, and similarly just actions are pleasant to the lover of justice, and acts conforming with virtue generally to the lover of virtue. But whereas the mass of   *11*
mankind take pleasure in things that conflict with one another, because they are not pleasant of their own nature, the lovers of what is noble take pleasure in things pleasant by nature. But lovers of the noble take pleasure in actions conforming with virtue. Therefore actions in conformity with virtue are pleasant essentially as well as pleasant to lovers of the right. Thus their life has no need of pleasure as a   *12*
sort of additional appendage, but contains its pleasure in itself. For there is the further consideration that the man who does not enjoy doing noble actions is not a good man at all: No one would call a man just if he did not like acting justly, nor liberal if he did not like doing liberal things, and similarly with the other virtues.   *13*
But if so, actions in conformity with virtue must be essentially pleasant.

But they are also of course both good and noble, and each in the highest degree, if the good man judges them rightly; and his judgement is as we have said. It follows   *14*
therefore that happiness is at once the best, the noblest, and the pleasantest of things: these qualities are not separated as the inscription at Delos makes out—

Justice is noblest, and health is best,
But the heart's desire is the pleasantest—,

for the best activities possess them all; and it is the best activities, or one activity which is the best of all, in which according to our definition happiness consists.

Nevertheless it is manifest that happiness also requires external goods in   *15*
addition, as we said; for it is impossible, or at least not easy, to play a noble part unless furnished with the necessary equipment. For many noble actions require instruments for their performance, in the shape of friends or wealth or political power; also   *16*
there are certain external advantages, the lack of which sullies supreme felicity, such as good birth, satisfactory children, and personal beauty: A man of very ugly appearance or low birth, or childless and alone in the world, is not our idea of a happy man, and still less so perhaps is one who has children or friends that are worthless, or who has had good ones but lost them by death. As we said therefore, happiness does seem   *17*
to require the addition of external prosperity, and this is why some people identify it with good fortune (though others identify it with virtue).

IX

It is this that gives rise to the question whether happiness is a thing that can be learnt, or acquired by training, or cultivated in some other manner, or whether it is bestowed by some divine dispensation or even by fortune. . . .   *2*

3   Light is also thrown on the question by our definition of happiness, which said that it is a certain kind of activity of the soul; whereas the remaining good things are either merely indispensable conditions of happiness, or are of the

4   nature of auxiliary means, and useful instrumentally. This conclusion moreover agrees with what we laid down at the outset; for we stated that the Supreme Good was the end of the political science, but the principal care of this science is to produce a certain character in the citizens, namely to make them virtuous, and capable of performing noble actions.

5   We have good reasons therefore for not speaking of an ox or horse or any other animal as being happy, because none of these is able to participate in noble

6   activities. For this cause also children cannot be happy, for they are not old enough to be capable of noble acts; when children are spoken of as happy, it is in compliment to their promise for the future. Happiness, as we said, requires both

7   complete goodness and a complete lifetime. For many reverses and vicissitudes of all sorts occur in the course of life, and it is possible that the most prosperous man may encounter great disasters in his declining years, as the story is told of Priam in the epics; but no one calls a man happy who meets with misfortunes like Priam's, and comes to a miserable end. . . .

XIII

But inasmuch as happiness is a certain activity of soul in conformity with perfect virtue, it is necessary to examine the nature of virtue. For this will probably assist

2   us in our investigation of the nature of happiness. . . .

3   Now the virtue that we have to consider is clearly human virtue, since the

4   good or happiness which we set out to seek is human good and human happiness. But human virtue means in our view excellence of soul, not excellence of body;

5   indeed our definition of happiness is an activity of the soul. Now if this is so, clearly it behooves the statesman to have some acquaintance with psychology, just as the physician who is to heal the eye or the other parts of the body must know their anatomy. . . .

6   Now on the subject of psychology some of the teaching current in extraneous discourses is satisfactory, and may be adopted here: namely that the soul consists

7   of two parts, one irrational and the other capable of reason. (Whether these two parts are really distinct in the sense that the parts of the body or of any other divisible whole are distinct, or whether though distinguishable in thought as two they are inseparable in reality, like the convex and concave sides of a curve, is a

8   question of no importance for the matter in hand.) Of the irrational part of the soul again one division appears to be common to all living things, and of a vegetative nature: I refer to the part that causes nutrition and growth; for we must assume that a vital faculty of this nature exists in all things that assimilate nourishment, including embryos—the same faculty being present also in the fully-developed organism (this is more reasonable than to assume a different nutritive

9   faculty in the latter). The excellence of this faculty therefore appears to be

common to all animate things and not peculiar to man; for it is believed that this faculty or part of the soul is most active during sleep, but when they are asleep you cannot tell a good man from a bad one (whence the saying that for half their lives there is no difference between the happy and the miserable). This is a natural result of the fact that sleep is a cessation of the soul from the functions on which its goodness or badness depend—except that in some small degree certain of the bodily processes may emerge into consciousness during sleep, and consequently the dreams of the good are better than those of ordinary men. We need not however pursue this subject further, but may omit from consideration the nutritive part of the soul, since it exhibits no specifically human excellence.

But there also appears to be another element in the soul, which, though irra- 10 tional, yet in a manner participates in rational principle. In self-restrained and unrestrained people we approve their principle, or the rational part of their souls, because it urges them in the right way and exhorts them for their good; but their nature seems also to contain another element beside that of rational princi- ple, which combats and resists that principle. Exactly the same thing may take 11 place in the soul as occurs with the body in a case of paralysis: when the patient wills to move his limbs to the right they swerve to the left; and similarly in unre- strained persons their impulses run counter to their principle. But whereas in the body we see the erratic member, in the case of the soul we do not see it; neverthe- less it cannot be doubted that in the soul also there is an element beside that of principle, which opposes and runs counter to principle (though in what sense the two are distinct does not concern us here). But this second element also seems, as 12 we said, to participate in rational principle; at least in the self-restrained man it obeys the behest of principle—and no doubt in the temperate and brave man it is still more amenable, for all parts of his nature are in harmony with principle.

Thus we see that the irrational part, as well as the soul as a whole, is double. 13 One division of it, the vegetative, does not share in rational principle at all; the other, the seat of the appetites and of desire in general, does in a sense participate in principle, as being amenable and obedient to it (in the sense in fact in which we speak of 'paying heed' to one's father and friends, not in the sense of the term 'rational' in mathematics). And that principle can in a manner appeal to the irra- tional part, is indicated by our practice of admonishing delinquents, and by our employment of rebuke and exhortation generally.

If on the other hand it be more correct to speak of the appetitive part of 14 the soul also as rational, in that case it is the rational part which, as well as the whole soul, is divided into two, the one division having rational principle in the proper sense and in itself, the other in the sense in which a child listens to its father.

Now virtue also is differentiated in correspondence with this division of the 15 soul. Some forms of virtue are called intellectual virtues, others moral virtues: Wisdom, Understanding, and Prudence are intellectual, Liberality and Temperance are moral virtues. When describing a man's moral character we do not say that he is wise or intelligent, but gentle or temperate; but a wise man also is praised for his disposition, and praiseworthy dispositions we term virtues.

Book II

i   Virtue being, as we have seen, of two kinds, intellectual and moral, intellectual virtue is for the most part both produced and increased by instruction, and therefore requires experience and time; whereas moral or ethical virtue is the product

2   of habit (*ethos*), and has indeed derived its name, with a slight variation of form, from that word. And therefore it is clear that none of the moral virtues is engendered in us by nature, for no natural property can be altered by habit. For instance, it is the nature of a stone to move downwards, and it cannot be trained to move upwards, even though you should try to train it to do so by throwing it up into the air ten thousand times; nor can fire be trained to move downwards, nor can anything else that naturally behaves in one way be trained into a habit of

3   behaving in another way. The virtues therefore are engendered in us neither by nature nor yet in violation of nature; nature gives us the capacity to receive them, and this capacity is brought to maturity by habit.

4   Moreover, the faculties given us by nature are bestowed on us first in a potential form; we develop their actual exercise afterwards. This is clearly so with our senses: We did not acquire the faculty of sight or hearing by repeatedly seeing or repeatedly listening, but the other way about—because we had the senses we began to use them, we did not get them by using them. The virtues on the other hand we acquire by first having actually practised them, just as we do the arts. We learn an art or craft by doing the things that we shall have to do when we have learnt it: for instance, men become builders by building houses, harpers by playing on the harp. Similarly

5   we become just by doing just acts, temperate by doing temperate acts, brave by doing brave acts. This truth is attested by the experience of states: Lawgivers make the citizens good by training them in habits of right action—this is the aim of all legislation, and if it fails to do this it is a failure; this is what distinguishes a good

6   form of constitution from a bad one. Again, the actions from or through which any virtue is produced are the same as those through which it also is destroyed—just as is the case with skill in the arts, for both the good harpers and the bad ones are produced by harping, and similarly with builders and all the other craftsmen: As you

7   will become a good builder from building well, so you will become a bad one from building badly. Were this not so, there would be no need for teachers of the arts, but everybody would be born a good or bad craftsman as the case might be. The same then is true of the virtues. It is by taking part in transactions with our fellow-men that some of us become just and others unjust; by acting in dangerous situations and forming a habit of fear or of confidence we become courageous or cowardly. And the same holds good of our dispositions with regard to the appetites, and anger; some men become temperate and gentle, other profligate and irascible, by actually comporting themselves in one way or the other in relation to those pas-

8   sions. In a word, our moral dispositions are formed as a result of the corresponding activities. Hence it is incumbent on us to control the character of our activities, since on the quality of these depends the quality of our dispositions. It is therefore not of small moment whether we are trained from childhood in one set of habits or another; on the contrary it is of very great, or rather of supreme, importance.

As then our present study, unlike the other branches of philosophy, has a *ii* practical aim (for we are not investigating the nature of virtue for the sake of knowing what it is, but in order that we may become good, without which result our investigation would be of no use), we have consequently to carry our enquiry into the region of conduct, and to ask how we are to act rightly; since our actions, as we have said, determine the quality of our dispositions.

Now the formula 'to act in conformity with right principle' is common *2* ground, and may be assumed as the basis of our discussion. . . .

But let it be granted to begin with that the whole theory of conduct is bound *3* to be an outline only and not an exact system, in accordance with the rule we laid down at the beginning, that philosophical theories must only be required to correspond to their subject matter; and matters of conduct and expediency have nothing fixed or invariable about them, any more than have matters of health. And if this is true of the general theory of ethics, still less is exact precision possi- *4* ble in dealing with particular cases of conduct; for these come under no science or professional tradition, but the agents themselves have to consider what is suited to the circumstances on each occasion, just as is the case with the art of *5* medicine or of navigation. But although the theory we are now investigating is thus necessarily inexact, we must do our best to help it out.

First of all then we have to observe, that moral qualities are so constituted as *6* to be destroyed by excess and by deficiency—as we see is the case with bodily strength and health (for one is forced to explain what is invisible by means of vis- ible illustrations). Strength is destroyed both by excessive and by deficient exer- cise; and similarly health is destroyed both by too much and by too little food and drink, while it is produced, increased, and preserved by a suitable quantity. The *7* same therefore is true of Temperance, Courage, and the other virtues. The man who runs away from everything in fear and never endures anything becomes a coward; the man who fears nothing whatsoever but encounters everything becomes foolhardy. Similarly he that indulges in every pleasure and refrains from none turns out a profligate, and he that shuns all pleasure, as boorish persons do, becomes what may be called insensible. Thus Temperance and Courage are destroyed by excess and deficiency, and preserved by the observance of the mean.

But not only are the virtues both generated and fostered on the one hand, *8* and destroyed on the other, from and by the same actions, but they will also find their full exercise in the same actions. This is clearly the case with the other more visible qualities, such as bodily strength: For strength is produced by taking much food and undergoing much exertion, while also it is the strong man who will be able to eat most food and endure most exertion. The same holds good with the *9* virtues. We become temperate by abstaining from pleasures, and at the same time we are best able to abstain from pleasures when we have become temperate. And so with Courage: We become brave by training ourselves to despise and endure terrors, and we shall be best able to endure terrors when we have become brave.

An index of our dispositions is afforded by the pleasure or pain that accom- *iii* panies our actions. A man is temperate if he abstains from bodily pleasures and finds this abstinence itself enjoyable, profligate if he feels it irksome; he is brave if he faces danger with pleasure or at all events without pain, cowardly if he does so with pain.

In fact pleasures and pains are the things with which moral virtue is concerned.

2   For (1) pleasure causes us to do base actions and pain causes us to abstain from doing noble actions. Hence the importance, as Plato points out, of having been definitely trained from childhood to like and dislike the proper things; this is what good education means.

3   (2) Again, if the virtues have to do with actions and feelings, and every feeling and every action is attended with pleasure or pain, this too shows that virtue has to do with pleasure and pain.

4   (3) Another indication is the fact that pain is the medium of punishment; for punishment is a sort of medicine, and it is the nature of medicine to work by means of opposites.

5   (4) Again . . . every formed disposition of the soul realizes its full nature in relation to and in dealing with that class of objects by which it is its nature to be corrupted or improved. But men are corrupted through pleasures and pains, that is, either by pursuing and avoiding the wrong pleasures and pains, or by pursuing and avoiding them at the wrong time, or in the wrong manner, or in one of the other wrong ways under which errors of conduct can be logically classified. This is why some thinkers define the virtues as states of impassivity or tranquillity, though they make a mistake in using these terms absolutely, without adding 'in the right (or wrong) manner' and 'at the right (or wrong) time' and the other qualifications.

6   Therefore it is established that moral virtue is the quality of acting in the best way in relation to pleasures and pains, and that vice is the opposite.

7   But the following considerations also will give us further light on the same point.

(5) There are three things that are the motives of choice and three that are the motives of avoidance; namely, the noble, the expedient, and the pleasant, and their opposites, the base, the harmful, and the painful. Now in respect of all these the good man is likely to go right and the bad to go wrong, but especially in respect of pleasure; for pleasure is common to man with the lower animals, and also it is a concomitant of all the objects of choice, since both the noble and the expedient appear to us pleasant.

8   (6) Again, the susceptibility to pleasure has grown up with all of us from the cradle. Hence this feeling is hard to eradicate, being engrained in the fabric of our lives.

9   (7) Again, pleasure and pain are also the standards by which we all, in a greater or less degree, regulate our actions. On this account therefore pleasure and pain are necessarily our main concern, since to feel pleasure and pain rightly or wrongly has a great effect on conduct.

10   (8) And again, it is harder to fight against pleasure than against anger (hard as that is, as Heracleitus says); but virtue, like art, is constantly dealing with what is harder, since the harder the task the better is success. For this reason also therefore

pleasure and pain are necessarily the main concern both of virtue and of political science, since he who comports himself towards them rightly will be good, and he who does so wrongly, bad.

We may then take it as established that virtue has to do with pleasures and   11
pains, that the actions which produce it are those which increase it, and also, if differently performed, destroy it, and that the actions from which it was produced are also those in which it is exercised.

A difficulty may however be raised as to what we mean by saying that in order   iv
to become just men must do just actions, and in order to become temperate they must do temperate actions. For if they do just and temperate actions, they are just and temperate already, just as, if they spell or play music correctly, they are scholars or musicians.

But perhaps this is not the case even with the arts. It is possible to spell a word   2
correctly by chance, or because some one else prompts you; hence you will be a scholar only if you spell correctly in the scholar's way, that is, in virtue of the scholarly knowledge which you yourself possess.

Moreover the case of the arts is not really analogous to that of the virtues.   3
Works of art have their merit in themselves, so that it is enough if they are produced having a certain quality of their own; but acts done in conformity with the virtues are not done justly or temperately if they themselves are of a certain sort, but only if the agent also is in a certain state of mind when he does them: First he must act with knowledge; secondly he must deliberately choose the act, and choose it for its own sake; and thirdly the act must spring from a fixed and permanent disposition of character. For the possession of an art, none of these conditions is included, except the mere qualification of knowledge; but for the possession of the virtues, knowledge is of little or no avail, whereas the other conditions, so far from being of little moment, are all-important, inasmuch as virtue results from the repeated performance of just and temperate actions. Thus   4
although actions are entitled just and temperate when they are such acts as just and temperate men would do, the agent is just and temperate not when he does these acts merely, but when he does them in the way in which just and temperate men do them. It is correct therefore to say that a man becomes just by doing just   5
actions and temperate by doing temperate actions; and no one can have the remotest chance of becoming good without doing them. But the mass of   6
mankind, instead of doing virtuous acts, have recourse to discussing virtue, and think that they are pursuing philosophy and that this will make them good men. In so doing they act like invalids who listen carefully to what the doctor says, but entirely neglect to carry out his prescriptions. That sort of philosophy will no more lead to a healthy state of soul than will that mode of treatment produce health of body.

We have next to consider the formal definition of virtue.

A state of the soul is either (1) a feeling, (2) a capacity, or (3) a disposition;   v
virtue therefore must be one of these three things. By the feelings, I mean desire,   2
anger, fear, confidence, envy, joy, friendship, hatred, longing, jealousy, pity; and generally those states of consciousness which are accompanied by pleasure or pain.

The capacities are the faculties in virtue of which we can be said to be liable to the feelings, for example, capable of feeling anger or pain or pity. The dispositions are the formed states of character in virtue of which we are well or ill disposed in respect of the feelings; for instance, we have a bad disposition in regard to anger if we are disposed to get angry too violently or not violently enough, a good disposition if we habitually feel a moderate amount of anger; and similarly in respect of the other feelings.

3   Now the virtues and vices are not feelings, because we are not pronounced good or bad according to our feelings, but we are according to our virtues and vices; nor are we either praised or blamed for our feelings—a man is not praised for being frightened or angry, nor is he blamed for being angry merely, but for being angry in a certain way—but we are praised or blamed for our virtues and

4   vices. Again, we are not angry or afraid from choice, but the virtues are certain modes of choice, or at all events involve choice. Moreover, we are said to be 'moved' by the feelings, whereas in respect of the virtues and vices we are not said to be 'moved' but to be 'disposed' in a certain way.

5   And the same considerations also prove that the virtues and vices are not capacities; since we are not pronounced good or bad, praised or blamed, merely by reason of our capacity for feelings. Again, we possess certain capacities by nature, but we are not born good or bad by nature: of this however we spoke before.

6   If then the virtues are neither feelings nor capacities, it remains that they are dispositions.

Thus we have stated what virtue is generically.

vi   But it is not enough merely to define virtue generically as a disposition; we
2   must also say what species of disposition it is. It must then be premised that all excellence has a twofold effect on the thing to which it belongs: It not only renders the thing itself good, but it also causes it to perform its function well. For example, the effect of excellence in the eye is that the eye is good *and* functions well; since having good eyes means having good sight. Similarly excellence in a horse
3   makes it *a* good horse, and also good at galloping, at carrying its rider, and at facing the enemy. If therefore this is true of all things, excellence or virtue in a man will be the disposition which renders him a good man and also which will cause
4   him to perform his function well. We have already indicated what this means; but it will throw more light on the subject if we consider what constitutes the specific nature of virtue.

Now of everything that is continuous and divisible, it is possible to take the larger part, or the smaller part, or an equal part, and these parts may be larger, smaller, and equal either with respect to the thing itself or relatively to us; the
5   equal part being a mean between excess and deficiency. By the mean of the thing I denote a point equally distant from either extreme, which is one and the same for everybody; by the mean relative to us, that amount which is neither too much
6   nor too little, and this is not one and the same for everybody. For example, let 10 be many and 2 few; then one takes the mean with respect to the thing if one
7   takes 6, since $6 - 2 = 10 - 6$; this is the mean given by arithmetical proportion.

But we cannot arrive by this method at the mean relative to us. Suppose that 10 lb. of food is a large ration for anybody and 2 lb. a small one: it does not follow that a trainer will prescribe 6 lb., for perhaps even this will be a large ration, or a small one, for the particular athlete who is to receive it; it is a small ration for a Milo, but a large one for a man just beginning to go in for athletics. And similarly with the amount of running or wrestling exercise to be taken. In the same way then an expert in any art avoids excess and deficiency, and seeks and adopts the mean— the mean, that is, not of the thing but relative to us. If therefore the way in which every art or science performs its work well is by looking to the mean and applying that as a standard to its productions (hence the common remark about a perfect work of art, that you could not take from it nor add to it—meaning that excess and deficiency destroy perfection, while adherence to the mean preserves it)—if then, as we say, good craftsmen look to the mean as they work, and if virtue, like nature, is more accurate and better than any form of art, it will follow that virtue aims at hitting the mean. I refer to moral virtue, for this is concerned with feelings and actions, in which one can have excess or deficiency or a due mean. For example, one can be frightened or bold, feel desire or anger or pity, and experience pleasure and pain in general, either too much or too little, and in both cases wrongly; whereas to feel these feelings at the right time, on the right occasion, towards the right people, for the right purpose and in the right manner, is to feel the best amount of them, which is the mean amount—and the best amount is of course the mark of virtue. And similarly there can be excess, deficiency, and the due mean in actions. Now feelings and actions are the objects with which virtue is concerned; and in feelings and actions excess and deficiency are errors, while the mean amount is praised, and constitutes success; and to be praised and to be successful are both marks of virtue. Virtue, therefore, is a mean state in the sense that it aims at hitting the mean. Again, error is multiform (for evil is a form of the unlimited, as in the old Pythagorean imagery, and good of the limited), whereas success is possible in one way only (which is why it is easy to fail and difficult to succeed—easy to miss the target and difficult to hit it); so this is another reason why excess and deficiency are a mark of vice, and observance of the mean a mark of virtue:

Goodness is simple, badness manifold.

Virtue then is a settled disposition of the mind as regards the choice of actions and feelings, consisting essentially in the observance of the mean relative to use, this being determined by principle, that is, as the prudent man would determine it.

And it is a mean state between two vices, one of excess and one of defect. Furthermore, it is a mean state in that whereas the vices either fall short of or exceed what is right in feelings and in actions, virtue ascertains and adopts the mean. Hence while in respect of its essence and the definition that states its original being virtue is the observance of the mean, in point of excellence and rightness it is an extreme.

18   Not every action or feeling however admits of the observance of a due mean. Indeed the very names of some essentially denote evil, for instance malice, shamelessness, envy, and, of actions, adultery, theft, murder. All these and similar actions and feelings are blamed as being bad in themselves; it is not the excess or deficiency of them that we blame. It is impossible therefore ever to go right in regard to them—one must always be wrong; nor does right or wrong in their case depend on the circumstances, for instance, whether one commits adultery with

19   the right woman, at the right time, and in the right manner; the mere commission of any of them is wrong. One might as well suppose there could be a due mean and excess and deficiency in acts of injustice or cowardice or profligacy, which would imply that one could have a medium amount of excess and of deficiency, an excessive amount of excess and a deficient amount of deficiency.

20   But just as there can be no excess or deficiency in temperance and justice, because the mean is in a sense an extreme, so there can be no observance of the mean nor excess nor deficiency in the corresponding vicious acts mentioned above, but however they are committed, they are wrong; since, to put it in general terms, there is no such thing as observing a mean in excess or deficiency, nor as exceeding or falling short in the observance of a mean.

vii   We must not however rest content with stating this general definition, but must show that it applies to the particular virtues. In practical philosophy, although universal principles have a wider application, those covering a particular part of the field possess a higher degree of truth; because conduct deals with particular facts, and our theories are bound to accord with these.

Let us then take the particular virtues from the diagram.

2   The observance of the mean in fear and confidence is Courage. The man that exceeds in fearlessness is not designated by any special name (and this is the case with many of the virtues and vices); he that exceeds in confidence is Rash; he that

3   exceeds in fear and is deficient in confidence is Cowardly. In respect of pleasures and pains—not all of them, and to a less degree in respect of pains—the observance of the mean is Temperance, the excess Profligacy. Men deficient in the enjoyment of pleasures scarcely occur, and hence this character also has not been

4   assigned a name, but we may call it Insensible. In regard to giving and getting money, the observance of the mean is Liberality; the excess and deficiency are Prodigality and Meanness, and these exceed and fall short in opposite ways: the

5   prodigal exceeds in giving and is deficient in getting, whereas the mean man exceeds in getting and is deficient in giving. For the present then we describe these qualities in outline and summarily, which is enough for the purpose in hand. . . .

6   There are also other dispositions in relation to money, namely, the mode of observing the mean called Magnificence (the magnificent man being different from the liberal, as the former deals with large amounts and the latter with small ones), the excess called Tastelessness or Vulgarity, and the defect called Shabbiness. . . .

7   In respect of honour and dishonour, the observance of the mean is Greatness of Soul, the excess a sort of Vanity, as it may be called, and the deficiency,

8   Smallness of Soul. And just as we said that Liberality is related to Magnificence, differing from it in being concerned with small amounts of money, so there is a certain quality related to Greatness of Soul, which is concerned with great honours, while this quality itself is concerned with small honours; for it is possible to aspire to minor honours in the right way, or more than is right, or less. He who exceeds in these aspirations is called ambitious, he who is deficient, unambitious; but the middle character has no name. . . .

In respect of anger also we have excess, deficiency, and the observance of the   9
mean. These states are virtually without names, but as we call a person of the middle character gentle, let us name the observance of the mean Gentleness, while of the extremes, he that exceeds may be styled irascible and his vice Irascibility, and he that is deficient, spiritless, and the deficiency Spiritlessness.

There are also three other modes of observing a mean which bear some resem-   10
blance to each other, and yet are different; all have to do with intercourse in conversation and action, but they differ in that one is concerned with truthfulness of speech and behaviour, and the other with pleasantness, in its two divisions of pleasantness in social amusement and pleasantness in the general affairs of life. We must then discuss these qualities also, in order the better to discern that in all things the observance of the mean is to be praised, while the extremes are neither right nor praiseworthy, but reprehensible. Most of these qualities also are unnamed, but in these as in the other cases we must attempt to coin names for them ourselves, for the sake of clearness and so that our meaning may be easily followed.

In respect of truth then, the middle character may be called truthful, and the   11
observance of the mean Truthfulness; pretence in the form of exaggeration is Boastfulness, and its possessor a boaster; in the form of understatement, Self-depreciation, and its possessor the self-depreciator.

In respect of pleasantness in social amusement, the middle character is witty   12
and the middle disposition Wittiness; the excess is Buffoonery and its possessor a buffoon; the deficient man may be called boorish, and his disposition Boorishness. In respect of general pleasantness in life, the man who is pleasant in   13
the proper manner is friendly, and the observance of the mean is Friendliness: he that exceeds, if from no interested motive, is complaisant, if for his own advantage, a flatterer; he that is deficient, and unpleasant in all the affairs of life, may be called peevish and surly.

There are also modes of observing a mean in the sphere of and in relation to   14
the feelings. For in these also one man is spoken of as moderate and another as excessive—for example the grovelling man who is ashamed of everything; while he that is deficient in shame, or ashamed of nothing, whatsoever, is shameless, and the man of middle character modest. For though Modesty is not a virtue, it is praised, and so is the modest man.

Again, Righteous Indignation is the observance of a mean between Envy and   15
Malice, and these qualities are concerned with pain and pleasure felt at the fortunes of one's neighbours. The righteously indignant man is pained by undeserved good fortune; the jealous man exceeds him and is pained by all the good fortune of others; while the malicious man so far falls short of being pained that he actually feels pleasure. . . .

viii There are then three dispositions—two vices, one of excess and one of defect, and one virtue which is the observance of the mean; and each of them is in a certain way opposed to both the others. For the extreme states are the opposite both
2 of the middle state and of each other, and the middle state is the opposite of both extremes; since just as the equal is greater in comparison with the less and less in comparison with the greater, so the middle states of character are in excess as compared with the defective states and defective as compared with the excessive states, whether in the case of feelings or of actions. For instance, a brave man appears rash in contrast with a coward and cowardly in contrast with a rash man; similarly a temperate man appears profligate in contrast with a man insensible to pleasure and pain, but insensible in contrast with a profligate; and a liberal man
3 seems prodigal in contrast with a mean man, mean in contrast with one who is prodigal. Hence either extreme character tries to push the middle character towards the other extreme; a coward calls a brave man rash and a rash man calls him a coward, and correspondingly in other cases.
4 But while all three dispositions are thus opposed to one another, the greatest degree of opposition exists between the two extremes. For the extremes are farther apart from each other than from the mean, just as great is farther from small
5 and small from great than either from equal. Again some extremes show a certain likeness to the mean—for instance, Rashness resembles Courage, Prodigality Liberality, whereas the extremes display the greatest unlikeness to one another. But it is things most remote from each other that are defined as opposites, so that the more remote things are the more opposed they are.
6 And in some cases the defect, in others the excess, is more opposed to the mean; for example, Cowardice, which is a vice of deficiency, is more opposed to Courage than is Rashness, which is a vice of excess; but Profligacy, or excess of
7 feeling, is more opposed to Temperance than is Insensibility, or lack of feeling. This results from either of two causes. One of these arises from the thing itself: owing to one extreme being nearer to the mean and resembling it more, we count not this but rather the contrary extreme as the opposite of the mean; for example, because Rashness seems to resemble Courage more than Cowardice does, and to be nearer to it, we reckon Cowardice rather than Rashness as the opposite of
8 Courage; for those extremes which are more remote from the mean seem to be the more opposed to it. This then is one cause, arising out of the thing itself. The other cause has its origin in us: those things appear more opposed to the mean to which we are ourselves more inclined by our nature. For example, we are of ourselves more inclined to pleasure, which is why we are liable to Profligacy [more than to Sobriety]. We therefore rather call those things the opposite of the mean, into which we are more inclined to lapse; and hence Profligacy, the excess, is more particularly the opposite of Temperance.
ix Enough has now been said to show that moral virtue is a mean, and in what sense this is so, namely that it is a mean between two vices, one of excess and the other of defect; and that it is such a mean because it aims at hitting the middle
2 point in feelings and in actions. This is why it is a hard task to be good, for it is

hard to find the middle point in anything: For instance, not everybody can find the centre of a circle, but only someone who knows geometry. So also anybody can become angry—that is easy, and so it is to give and spend money; but to be angry with or give money to the right person, and to the right amount, and at the right time, and for the right purpose, and in the right way—this is not within everybody's power and is not easy; so that to do these things properly is rare, praiseworthy, and noble.

Hence the first rule in aiming at the mean is to avoid that extreme which is 3
the more opposed to the mean, as Calypso advises—

Steer the ship clear of yonder spray and surge.

For of the two extremes one is a more serious error than the other. Hence, 4
inasmuch as to hit the mean extremely well is difficult, the second best way to sail, as the saying goes, is to take the least of the evils; and the best way to do this is the way we enjoin.

The second rule is to notice what are the errors to which we are ourselves most prone (as different men are inclined by nature to different faults)—and we shall discover what these are by observing the pleasure or pain that we experi- 5
ence—; then we must drag ourselves away in the opposite direction, for by steering wide of our besetting error we shall make a middle course. This is the method adopted by carpenters to straighten warped timber.

Thirdly, we must in everything be most of all on our guard against what is 6
pleasant and against pleasure; for when pleasure is on her trial we are not impartial judges. The right course is therefore to feel towards pleasure as the elders of the people felt towards Helen, and to apply their words to her on every occasion; for if we roundly bid her be gone, we shall be less likely to err.

These then, to sum up the matter, are the precautions that will best enable 7
us to hit the mean. But no doubt it is a difficult thing to do, and especially in particular cases: For instance, it is not easy to define in what manner and with what people and on what sort of grounds and how long one ought to be angry; and in fact we sometimes praise men who err on the side of defect in this matter and call them gentle, sometimes those who are quick to anger and style them manly. However, though we do not blame one who diverges only a little 8
from the right course, whether on the side of the too much or of the too little, we do blame one who diverges more widely, and to a noticeable extent. Yet to what degree and how seriously a man must err to be blamed is not easy to define on principle. For in fact no object of perception is easy to define; and such questions of degree depend on particular circumstances, and the decision lies with perception.

Thus much then is clear, that it is the middle disposition in each department 9
of conduct that is to be praised, but that one should lean sometimes to the side of excess and sometimes to that of deficiency, since this is the easiest way of hitting the mean and the right course.

Book X

VII

But if happiness consists in activity in accordance with virtue, it is reasonable that it should be activity in accordance with the highest virtue; and this will be the virtue of the best part of us. Whether then this be the intellect, or whatever else it be that is thought to rule and lead us by nature, and to have cognizance of what is noble and divine, either as being itself also actually divine, or as being relatively the divinest part of us, it is the activity of this part of us in accordance with the virtue proper to it that will constitute perfect happiness; and it has been stated already that this activity is the activity of contemplation.

2   And that happiness consists in contemplation may be accepted as agreeing both with the results already reached and with the truth. For contemplation is at once the highest form of activity, since the intellect is the highest thing in us, and the objects with which the intellect deals are the highest things that can be known; and also it is the most continuous, for we can reflect more continuously than we can carry on any

3   form of action. And again we suppose that happiness must contain an element of pleasure; now activity in accordance with wisdom is admittedly the most pleasant of the activities in accordance with virtue: At all events it is held that philosophy or the pursuit of wisdom contains pleasures of marvelous purity and permanence, and it is reasonable to suppose that the enjoyment of knowledge is a still pleasanter occupa-

4   tion than the pursuit of it. Also the activity of contemplation will be found to possess in the highest degree the quality that is termed self-sufficiency; for while it is true that the wise man equally with the just man and the rest requires the necessaries of life, yet, these being adequately supplied, whereas the just man needs other persons towards whom or with whose aid he may act justly, and so likewise do the temperate man and the brave man and the others, the wise man on the contrary can also contemplate by himself, and the more so the wiser he is; no doubt he will study better

5   with the aid of fellow-workers, but still he is the most self-sufficient of men. Also the activity of contemplation may be held to be the only activity that is loved for its own sake: It produces no result beyond the actual act of contemplation, whereas from practical pursuits we look to secure some advantage, greater or smaller, beyond the

6   action itself. Also happiness is thought to involve leisure; for we do business in order that we may have leisure, and carry on war in order that we may have peace. . . .

7   The activity of the intellect is felt to excel in serious worth, consisting as it does in contemplation, and to aim at no end beyond itself, and also to contain a pleasure peculiar to itself, and therefore augmenting its activity: and if accordingly the attributes of this activity are found to be self-sufficiency, leisuredness, such freedom from fatigue as is possible for man, and all the other attributes of blessedness: It follows that it is the activity of the intellect that constitutes complete human happiness—provided it be granted a complete span of life, for nothing that belongs to happiness can be incomplete.

8   Such a life as this however will be higher than the human level: not in virtue of his humanity will a man achieve it, but in virtue of something within him that is divine; and by as much as this something is superior to his composite nature, by

so much is its activity superior to the exercise of the other forms of virtue. If then the intellect is something divine in comparison with man, so is the life of the intellect divine in comparison with human life. Nor ought we to obey those who enjoin that a man should have man's thoughts and a mortal the thoughts of mortality, but we ought so far as possible to achieve immortality, and do all that man may to live in accordance with the highest thing in him; for though this be small in bulk, in power and value it far surpasses all the rest.

It may even be held that this is the true self of each, inasmuch as it is the ruling and better part; and therefore it would be a strange thing if a man should choose to live not his own life but the life of some other than himself.   9

Moreover what was said before will apply here also: That which is best and most pleasant for each creature is that which is proper to the nature of each; accordingly the life of the intellect is the best and the pleasantest life for man, inasmuch as the intellect especially is man; therefore this life will be the happiest.

The life of moral virtue, on the other hand, is happy only in a secondary degree. For   *vii* the moral activities are purely human: Justice, I mean, Courage and the other virtues we display in our intercourse with our fellows, when we observe what is due to each in contracts and services and in our various actions, and in our emotions also; and all of these things seem to be purely human affairs. And some moral qualities are thought to be the outcome of the physical constitution, and moral virtue is thought   2 to have a close affinity in many respects with the passions. Moreover, Prudence   3 is intimately connected with Moral Virtue, and this with Prudence, inasmuch as the first principles which Prudence employs are determined by the Moral Virtues, and the right standard for the Moral Virtues is determined by Prudence. But these being also connected with the passions are related to our composite nature; now the virtues of our composite nature are purely human; so therefore also is the life that manifests these virtues, and the happiness that belongs to it. Whereas the happiness that belongs to the intellect is separate: So much may be said about it here, for a full discussion of the matter is beyond the scope of our present purpose.

And such happiness would appear to need but little external equipment, or   4 less than the happiness based on moral virtue. Both, it may be granted, require the mere necessaries of life, and that in an equal degree (though the politician does as a matter of fact take more trouble about bodily requirements and so forth than the philosopher); for in this respect there may be little difference between them. But for the purpose of their special activities their requirements will differ widely. The liberal man will need wealth in order to do liberal actions, and so indeed will the just man in order to discharge his obligations (since mere intentions are invisible, and even the unjust pretend to wish to act justly); and the brave man will need strength if he is to perform any action displaying his virtue; and the temperate man opportunity for indulgence: Otherwise how can he, or the possessor of any other virtue, show that he is virtuous? It is disputed also whether purpose or per-   5 formance is the more important factor in virtue, as it is alleged to depend on both; now the perfection of virtue will clearly consist in both; but the performance of virtuous actions requires much outward equipment, and the more so the greater and more noble the actions are. But the student, so far as the pursuit of his activity   6 is concerned, needs no external apparatus: On the contrary, worldly goods may almost be said to be a hindrance to contemplation; though it is true that, being a man and living in the society of others, he chooses to engage in virtuous action, and so will need external goods to carry on his life as a human being.

7   The following considerations also will show that perfect happiness is some form of contemplative activity. The gods, as we conceive them, enjoy supreme felicity and happiness. But what sort of actions can we attribute to them? Just actions? But will it not seem ridiculous to think of them as making contracts, restoring deposits and the like? Then brave actions—enduring terrors and running risks for the nobility of so doing? Or liberal actions? But to whom will they give? Besides, it would be absurd to suppose that they actually have a coinage or currency of some sort! And temperate actions—what will these mean in their case? Surely it would be derogatory to praise them for not having evil desires! If we go through the list we shall find that all forms of virtuous conduct seem trifling and unworthy of the gods. Yet nevertheless they have always been conceived as, at all events, living, and therefore living actively, for we cannot suppose they are always asleep like Endymion. But for a living being, if we eliminate action, and *a fortiori* creative action, what remains save contemplation? It follows that the activity of God, which is transcendent in blessedness, is the activity of contemplation; and therefore among human activities that which is most akin to the divine activity of contemplation will be the greatest source of happiness.

8   A further confirmation is that the lower animals cannot partake of happiness, because they are completely devoid of the contemplative activity. The whole of the life of the gods is blessed, and that of man is so in so far as it contains some likeness to the divine activity; but none of the other animals possess happiness, because they are entirely incapable of contemplation. Happiness therefore is co-extensive in its range with contemplation: The more a class of beings possesses the faculty of contemplation, the more it enjoys happiness, not as an accidental concomitant of contemplation but as inherent in it, since contemplation is valuable in itself. It follows that happiness is some form of contemplation.

9   But the philosopher being a man will also need external well-being, since man's nature is not self-sufficient for the activity of contemplation, but he must also have bodily health and a supply of food and other requirements. Yet if supreme blessedness is not possible without external goods, it must not be supposed that happiness will demand many or great possessions; for self-sufficiency

10   does not depend on excessive abundance, nor does moral conduct, and it is possible to perform noble deeds even without being ruler of land or sea: One can do virtuous acts with quite moderate resources. This may be clearly observed in experience: private citizens do not seem to be less but more given to doing virtuous actions than princes and potentates. It is sufficient then if moderate resources are forthcoming; for a life of virtuous activity will be essentially a happy life.

11   Solon also doubtless gave a good description of happiness, when he said that in his opinion those men were happy who, being moderately equipped with external goods, had performed noble exploits and had lived temperately; for it is possible for a man of but moderate possessions to do what is right. Anaxagoras again does not seem to have conceived the happy man as rich or powerful, since he says

that he would not be surprised if his notion of happiness were to appear strange in the eyes of the many; for most men judge by externals, which are all that they can   *12* perceive. So our theories seem to be in agreement with the opinions of the wise.

Such arguments then carry some degree of conviction; but it is by the practical experience of life and conduct that the truth is really tested, since it is there that the final decision lies. We must therefore examine the conclusions we have advanced by bringing them to the test of the facts of life. If they are in harmony with the facts, we may accept them; if found to disagree, we must deem them mere theories.

And it seems likely that the man who pursues intellectual activity, and who   *13* cherishes his intellect and keeps that in the best condition, is also the man most beloved of the gods. For if, as is generally believed, the gods exercise some superintendence over human affairs, then it will be reasonable to suppose that they take pleasure in that part of man which is best and most akin to themselves, namely the intellect, and that they recompense with their favours those men who esteem and honour this most, because these care for the things dear to themselves, and act rightly and nobly. Now it is clear that all these attributes belong most of all to the wise man. He therefore is most beloved by the gods; and if so, he is naturally most happy. Here is another proof that the wise man is the happiest.

Discussion Questions

1. Aristotle argues that some activities and objects are desired for their own sake, as opposed to some things we desire for the sake of something else. What do you desire for its own sake, i.e., as an end in itself? Are these things somehow better than those that you desire only for the sake of something else?

2. Aristotle writes that the young people will be misguided in their study of ethics because they rely on their passions and feelings. Do you agree? How do your feelings either help or hinder your ability to deliberate?

3. Think about what makes you happy and then examine this notion of *happiness*. Is your happiness a good in and of itself, or do you desire happiness for some other reason? What does this tell you about your quest for happiness? How does that quest differ from other quests?

4. How important was your training as regards your moral character? What are examples of your own moral training? If you *are* (likely) a good/just person through proper training/upbringing, do you think you could be so without this sort of training?

5. In what sense is Aristotle right when he writes, "You are what you do"? How does this apply to your own life?

6. Can you apply Aristotle's Doctrine of the Mean to your own life? In what ways do you already adhere to it? Do you find it to be a worthy guide to being a virtuous person? Does it permit any acts that you consider "*non-virtuous*"?

7. How do you evaluate the common phrase, "The right thing to do isn't always the easy one"? Do you agree? What is an example of a right/ethical decision you made that wasn't the easy one?

8. How might you employ Aristotle's Doctrine of the Mean regarding truth-telling? Is it *always* morally necessary to tell the truth? Should you *ever* tell it? What examples help you find the mean of truthfulness, or do you believe it is *always* wrong to lie?

9. Do you agree with the respective extremes of the virtues suggested by Aristotle in Book II, Chapter 7? Which do you believe to be the "least of the evils" among the two extremes for each virtue?

Foundations of the Metaphysics of Morals
Immanuel Kant

Considered one of the most important philosophers throughout history, German philosopher Immanuel Kant put forth many original yet philosophically rigorous ideas on numerous subjects while working as a professor of logic and metaphysics at the University of Königsberg for twenty-six years. In his monumental *A Critique of Pure Reason*, he introduced a new way of viewing certain knowledge claims, noting specifically that metaphysical claims (about God, the soul, etc.) were of a different sort than others (he termed them *synthetic a priori* propositions because they are known without experience yet also without logically relating the ideas). In this piece, you can see Kant's focus on *a priori* truths—those that are attainable *prior to experience* in the way one attains mathematical truths (as opposed to *a posteriori* claims, which must be determined through experience, such as "The grass is green").

In this selection, from his *Foundations of the Metaphysics of Morals*, Kant first argues that moral laws do exist, and then he demonstrates that, through *reason*, we discover the "supreme principle of morality," what he calls the Categorical Imperative. He shows how we can apply our own subjective guidelines—*maxims*—and attempt to make them applicable to everyone (*universalize* them).

Kant's system of morals is *deontological* in that it is based on determining one's *duty* and then adhering to that duty, regardless of one's inclinations and whims. He does not account for the consequences of the action either, as this would not necessarily accord with duty. Throughout his writing, he establishes not only how to properly determine duty, but why we should follow it. He also determines the categorical imperative of treating people as ends in themselves (versus as means to an end, i.e., as *using* them for some other purpose). This is all done through pure reason, such as not to be led astray by other, less accurate methods.

Reading Questions

1. Why does Kant argue that *good will* is the only route to true goodness and happiness?

2. Which of the two ways that one can act consistently with virtue/duty (listed below) does Kant find to be morally superior? Explain.

Source: Beck, Lewis White, Immanuel Kant: *Foundations of the Metaphysics of Morals,* 2nd Edition, pp. 642–648, 653–654. Copyright © 1990. Reprinted by permission of Pearson Education, Inc., Upper Saddle River, NJ.

    a. actions done *in accord* with duty (i.e., when an agent's natural inclination happens to agree with her duty)

    b. actions done *from* duty alone (i.e., when an agent acts strictly out of duty)

How does he show this with the following examples?

    a. the dealer (shopkeeper)

    b. the preservation of one's life

    c. being kind to others

    d. being happy

    e. loving one's enemies

3. What role do one's personal *maxims* have in Kant's system of morals? How does Kant use the notion of promise-keeping to illustrate his position?

4. What is an *imperative*? What is its role in morality? What two types of imperatives are there, and how do they differ?

5. Examine the four duties that Kant enumerates. What are the duties? *How* does he conclude that they are duties? In what ways do the tests of the respective maxims fail to be rationally universalized? He specifically mentions two general ways that maxims cannot be rationally universalized—what are they?

6. How does Kant argue that humans are ends in themselves and ought to be treated as such? How does he employ this imperative in addressing the following issues?

    a. suicide

    b. deceitful promises

    c. duty to oneself and one's talents

    d. duty to others

First Section: Transition from Common Sense Knowledge of Morals to the Philosophical

Nothing in the world—indeed nothing even beyond the world—can possibly be conceived which could be called good without qualification except a *good will*. Intelligence, wit, judgment, and other talents of the mind however they may be named, or courage, resoluteness, and perseverance as qualities of temperament, are doubtless in many respects good and desirable; but they can become extremely bad and harmful if the will, which is to make use of these gifts of nature and which in its special constitution is called character, is not good. It is the same with gifts of fortune. Power, riches, honor, even health, general well-being and the contentment with one's condition which is called happiness make for pride and even arrogance if there is not a good will to correct their influence on the mind and on its principle of action, so as to make it generally fitting to its entire end. It need hardly be mentioned that the sight of a being adorned with no feature of a pure and good will yet enjoying lasting good fortune can never give pleasure to an impartial rational observer. Thus the good will seems to constitute the indispensable condition even of worthiness to be happy.

Some qualities seem to be conductive to this good will and can facilitate its action, but in spite of that they have no intrinsic unconditional worth. They rather presuppose a good will, which limits the high esteem which one otherwise rightly has for them and prevents their being held to be absolutely good. Moderation in emotions and passions, self-control, and calm deliberation not only are good in many respects but seem even to constitute part of the inner worth of the person. But however unconditionally they were esteemed by the ancients, they are far from being good without qualification, for without the principles of a good will they can become extremely bad, and the coolness of a villain makes him not only far more dangerous but also more directly abominable in our eyes than he would have seemed without it.

The good will is not good because of what it effects or accomplishes or because of its competence to achieve some intended end; it is good only because of its willing (i.e., it is good in itself). And, regarded for itself, it is to be esteemed as incomparably higher than anything which could be brought about by it in favor of any inclination or even of the sum total of all inclinations. Even if it should happen that, by a particularly unfortunate fate or by the niggardly provision of a step-motherly nature, this will should be wholly lacking in power to accomplish its purpose, and if even the greatest effort should not avail it to achieve anything of its end, and if there remained only the good will—not as a mere wish, but as the summoning of all the means in our power—it would sparkle like a jewel all by itself, as something that had its full worth in itself. Usefulness or fruitlessness can neither diminish nor augment this worth. Its usefulness would be only its setting, as it were, so as to enable us to handle it more conveniently in commerce or to attract the attention of those who are not yet connoisseurs, but not to recommend it to those who are experts or to determine its worth. . . .

As nature has elsewhere distributed capacities suitable to the functions they are to perform, reason's proper function must be to produce a will good in itself and not one good merely as a means, since for the former, reason is absolutely essential. This will need not be the sole and complete good, yet it must be the condition of all others, even of the desire for happiness. In this case it is entirely compatible with the wisdom of nature that the cultivation of reason, which is required for the former unconditional purpose, at least in this life restricts in many ways—indeed, can reduce to nothing—the achievement of the latter unconditional purpose, happiness. For one perceives that nature here does not proceed unsuitably to its purpose, because reason, which recognizes its highest practical vocation in the establishment of a good will, is capable of a contentment of its own kind (i.e., one that springs from the attainment of a purpose determined by reason), even though this injures the ends of inclination.

We have, then, to develop the concept of a will which is to be esteemed as good in itself without regard to anything else. It dwells already in the natural and sound understanding and does not need so much to be taught as only to be brought to light. In the estimation of the total worth of our actions it always takes first place and is the condition of everything else. In order to show this, we shall take the concept of duty. It contains the concept of a good will, though with certain subjective restrictions and hindrances, but these are far from concealing it and making it unrecognizable, for they rather bring it out by contrast and make it shine forth all the more brightly.

I here omit all actions which are recognized as opposed to duty, even though they may be useful in one respect or another, for with these the question does not arise as to whether they may be done *from* duty, since they conflict with it. I also pass over actions which are really in accord with duty and to which one has no direct inclination, rather doing them because impelled to do so by another inclination. For it is easily decided whether an action in accord with duty is done from duty or for some selfish purpose. It is far more difficult to note this difference when the action is in accord with duty and, in addition, the subject has a direct inclination to do it. For example, it is in accord with duty that a dealer should not overcharge an inexperienced customer, and wherever there is much trade the prudent merchant does not do so, but has a fixed price for everyone so that a child may buy from him as cheaply as any other. Thus the customer is honestly served, but this is far from sufficient to warrant the belief that the merchant has behaved in this way from duty and principles of honesty. His own advantage required this behavior, but it cannot be assumed that over and above that he had a direct inclination to his customers and that, out of love, as it were, he gave none an advantage in price over another. The action was done neither from duty nor from direct inclination but only for a selfish purpose.

On the other hand, it is a duty to preserve one's life, and moreover everyone has a direct inclination to do so. But for that reason, the often anxious care which most men take of it has no intrinsic worth, and the maxim of doing so has no moral import. They preserve their lives according to duty, but not from duty. But if adversities and hopeless sorrow completely take away the relish for life; if an unfortunate man, strong in soul, is indignant rather than despondent or dejected over his fate and wishes for death, and yet preserves his life without loving it and from neither inclination nor fear but from duty—then his maxim has moral merit.

To be kind where one can is a duty, and there are, moreover, many persons so sympathetically constituted that without any motive of vanity or selfishness they find an inner satisfaction in spreading joy and rejoice in the contentment of others which they have made possible. But I say that, however dutiful and however amiable it may be, that kind of action has no true moral worth. It is on a level with [actions done from] other inclinations, such as the inclination to honor, which, if fortunately directed to what in fact accords with duty and is generally useful and thus honorable, deserve praise and encouragement, but no esteem. For the maxim lacks the moral import of an action done not from inclination but from duty. But assume that the mind of that friend to mankind was clouded by a sorrow of his own which extinguished all sympathy with the lot of others, and though he still had the power to benefit others in distress their need left him untouched because he was preoccupied with his own. Now suppose him to tear himself, unsolicited by inclination, out of his dead insensibility and to do this action only from duty and without any inclination—then for the first time his action has genuine moral worth. Furthermore, if nature has put little sympathy into the heart of a man, and if he, though an honest man, is by temperament cold and indifferent to the sufferings of others perhaps because he is provided with special gifts of patience and fortitude and expects and even requires that others should have them too—and such a man would certainly not be the meanest product of nature—would not he find in himself a source from which to give himself a far higher worth than he could have got by having a good-natured temperament? This is unquestionably true even though nature did not make him philanthropic, for it is just here that the worth of character is brought out, which is morally the incomparably highest of all: He is beneficent not from inclination, but from duty.

To secure one's own happiness is at least indirectly a duty, for discontent with one's condition under pressure from many cares and amid unsatisfied wants could easily become a great temptation to transgress against duties. But, without any view to duty, all men have the strongest and deepest inclination to happiness, because in this Idea all inclinations are summed up. But the precept of happiness is often so formulated that it definitely thwarts some inclinations, and men can make no definite and certain concept of the sum of satisfaction of all inclinations, which goes under the name of happiness. It is not to be wondered at, therefore, that a single inclination, definite as to what it promises and as to the time at which it can be satisfied, can outweigh a fluctuating idea and that, for example, a man with the gout can choose to enjoy what he likes and to suffer what he may, because according to his calculations at least on this occasion he has not sacrificed the enjoyment of the present moment to a perhaps groundless expectation of a happiness supposed to lie in health. But even in this case if the universal inclination to happiness did not determine his will, and if health were not at least for him a necessary factor in these calculations, there would still remain, as in all other cases, a law that he ought to promote his happiness not from inclination but from duty. Only from this law could his conduct have true moral worth.

It is in this way, undoubtedly, that we should understand those passages of Scripture which command us to love our neighbor and even our enemy, for love as an inclination cannot be commanded, But beneficence from duty, even when no inclination impels it and even when it is opposed by a natural and unconquerable aversion, is practical love, not pathological love; it resides in the will and not in the propensities of feeling, in principles of action and not in tender sympathy; and it alone can be commanded. . . .

Thus the moral worth of an action does not lie in the effect which is expected from it or in any principle of action which has to borrow its motive from this expected effect. For all these effects (agreeableness of my own condition, indeed even the promotion of the happiness of others) could be brought about through other causes and would not require the will of a rational being, while the highest and unconditional good can be found only in such a will. Therefore the preeminent good can consist only in the conception of law in itself (which can be present only in a rational being) so far as this conception and not the hoped-for effect is the determining ground of the will. This preeminent good, which we call moral, is already present in the person who acts according to this conception, and we do not have to look for it first in the result.

But what kind of law can that be, the conception of which must determine the will without reference to the expected result? Under this condition alone can the will be called absolutely good without qualification. Since I have robbed the will of all impulses which could come to it from obedience to any law, nothing remains to serve as a principle of the will except universal conformity to law as such. That is, I ought never to act in such a way that I could not also will that my maxim should be a universal law. Strict conformity to law as such (without assuming any particular law applicable to certain actions) serves as the principle of the will, and it must serve as such a principle if duty is not to be a vain delusion and chimerical concept. The common sense of mankind in its practical judgments is in perfect agreement with this and has this principle constantly in view.

Let the question, for example, be: May I, when in distress, make a promise with the intention not to keep it? I easily distinguish the two meanings which the question can have, viz., whether it is prudent to make a false promise, or whether it conforms to duty. The former can undoubtedly be often the case, though I do see clearly that it is not sufficient merely to escape from the present difficulty by this expedient, but that I must consider whether inconveniences much greater than the present one may not later spring from this lie. Even with all my supposed cunning, the consequences cannot be so easily foreseen. Loss of credit might be far more disadvantageous than the misfortune I am now seeking to avoid, and it is hard to tell whether it might not be more prudent to act according to a universal maxim and to make it a habit not to promise anything without intending to fulfill it. But it is soon clear to me that such a maxim is based only on an apprehensive concern with consequences.

To be truthful from duty, however, is an entirely different thing from being truthful out of fear of untoward consequences, for in the former case the concept of the action itself contains a law for me, while in the latter I must first look about to see what results for me may be connected with it. To deviate from the principle of duty is certainly bad, but to be unfaithful to my maxim of prudence can sometimes be very advantageous to me, though it is certainly safer to abide by it. The shortest but most infallible way to find the answer to the question as to whether a deceitful promise is consistent with duty is to ask myself: Would I be content that my maxim of extricating myself from difficulty by a false promise should hold as a universal law for myself as well as for others? And could I say to myself that everyone may make a false promise when he is in a difficulty from which he otherwise cannot escape? Immediately I see that I could will the lie but not a universal law to lie. For with such a law there would be no promises at all, inasmuch as it would be futile to make a pretense of my intention in regard to future actions to those who would not believe this pretense or—if they overhastily did so—would pay me back in my own coin. Thus my maxim would necessarily destroy itself as soon as it was made a universal law.

I do not, therefore, need any penetrating acuteness to discern what I have to do in order that my volition may be morally good. Inexperienced in the course of the world, incapable of being prepared for all its contingencies, I only ask myself: Can I will that my maxim become a universal law? If not, it must be rejected, not because of any disadvantage accruing to myself or even to others, but because it cannot enter as a principle into a possible enactment of universal law, and reason extorts from me an immediate respect for such legislation. I do not as yet discern on what it is grounded (this is a question the philosopher may investigate), but I at least understand that it is an estimation of a worth which far outweighs all the worth of whatever is recommended by the inclinations, and that the necessity that I act from pure respect for the practical law constitutes my duty. To duty every other motive must give place, because duty is the condition of a will good in itself, whose worth transcends everything. . . .

Second Section: Transition from Popular Moral Philosophy to the Metaphysics of Morals

. . . Everything in nature works according to laws. Only a rational being has the capacity of acting according to the *conception* of laws (i.e., according to principles). This capacity is the will. Since reason is required for the derivation of actions from laws, will is nothing less than practical reason. If reason infallibly determines the will, the actions which such a being recognizes as objectively necessary are also subjectively necessary. That is, the will is a faculty of choosing only that which reason, independently of inclination, recognizes as practically necessary (i.e., as good). But if reason of itself does not sufficiently determine the will, and if the will is subjugated to subjective conditions (certain incentives) which do not always agree with the objective conditions—in a word, if the will is not of itself in complete accord with reason (which is the actual case with men), then the actions which are recognized as objectively necessary are subjectively contingent, and the determination of such a will according to objective laws is a constraint. That is, the relation of objective laws to a will which is not completely good is conceived as the determination of the will of a rational being by principles of reason to which this will is not by its nature necessarily obedient.

The conception of an objective principle, so far as it constrains a will, is a command (of reason), and the formula of this command is called an *imperative*.

All imperatives are expressed by an "ought" and thereby indicate the relation of an objective law of reason to a will which is not in its subjective constitution necessarily determined by this law. This relation is that of constraint. Imperatives say that it would be good to do or to refrain from doing something, but they say it to a will which does not always do something simply because the thing is presented to it as good to do. Practical good is what determines the will by means of the conception of reason and hence not by subjective causes but objectively, on grounds which are valid for every rational being as such. It is distinguished from the pleasant, as that which has an influence on the will only by means of a sensation from purely subjective causes, which hold for the senses only of this or that person and not as a principle of reason which holds for everyone.

A perfectly good will, therefore, would be equally subject to objective laws of the good, but it could not be conceived as constrained by them to accord with them, because it can be determined to act by its own subjective constitution only through the conception of the good. Thus no imperatives hold for the divine will or, more generally, for a holy will. The "ought" here is out of place, for the volition of itself is necessarily in unison with the law. Therefore imperatives are only formulas expressing the relation of objective laws of volition in general to the subjective imperfection of the will of this or that rational being, for example, the human will.

All imperatives command either *hypothetically* or *categorically*. The former present the practical necessity of a possible action as a means to achieving something else which one desires (or which one may possibly desire). The categorical imperative would be one which presented an action as of itself objectively necessary, without regard to any other end.

Since every practical law presents a possible action as good and thus as necessary for a subject practically determinable by reason, all imperatives are formulas of the determination of action which is necessary by the principle of a will which is in any way good. If the action is good only as a means to something else, the imperative is hypothetical; but if it is thought of as good in itself, and hence as necessary in a will which of itself conforms to reason as the principle of this will, the imperative is categorical.

The imperative thus says what action possible for me would be good, and it presents the practical rule in relation to a will which does not forthwith perform an action simply because it is good, in part because the subject does not always know that the action is good, and in part (when he does know it) because his maxims can still be opposed to the objective principles of a practical reason.

The hypothetical imperative, therefore, says only that the action is good to some purpose, possible or actual. In the former case, it is a problematical, in the latter an assertorical, practical principle. The categorical imperative, which declares the action to be of itself objectively necessary without making any reference to any end in view (i.e., without having any other purpose), holds as an apodictical practical principle. . . .

If I think of a hypothetical imperative as such, I do not know what it will contain until the condition is stated [under which it is an imperative]. But if I think of a categorical imperative, I know immediately what it will contain. For since the imperative contains besides the law, only the necessity of the maxim[6] of acting in accordance with the law, while the law contains no condition to which it is restricted, nothing remains except the universality of law as such to which the maxim of the action should conform; and this conformity alone is what is represented as necessary by the imperative.

There is, therefore, only one categorical imperative. It is: Act only according to that maxim by which you can at the same time will that it should become a universal law.

Now if all imperatives of duty can be derived from this one imperative as a principle, we can at least show what we understand by the concept of duty and what it means, even though it remains undecided whether that which is called duty is an empty concept or not.

The universality of law according to which effects are produced constitutes what is properly called nature in the most general sense (as to form) (i.e., the existence of things so far as it is determined by universal laws). [By analogy], then, the universal imperative of duty can be expressed as follows: Act as though the maxim of your action were by your will to become a universal law of nature.

We shall now enumerate some duties, adopting the usual division of them into duties to ourselves and to others and into perfect and imperfect duties.[7]

(1) A man who is reduced to despair by a series of evils feels a weariness with life but is still in possession of his reason sufficiently to ask whether it would not be contrary to his duty to himself to take his own life. Now he asks whether the maxim of his action could become a universal law of nature. His maxim, however is: For love of myself, I make it my principle to shorten my life when by a longer duration it threatens more evil than satisfaction. But it is questionable whether this principle of self-love could become a universal law of nature. One immediately sees a contradiction in a system of nature whose law would be to destroy life by the feeling whose special office is to impel the improvement of life. In this case it would not exist as nature; hence that maxim cannot obtain as a law of nature, and thus it wholly contradicts the supreme principle of all duty.

(2) Another man finds himself forced by need to borrow money. He well knows that he will not be able to repay it, but he also sees that nothing will be lent him if he does not firmly promise to repay it at a certain time. He desires to make such a promise, but he has enough conscience to ask himself whether it is not improper and opposed to duty to relieve his distress in such a way. Now, assuming he does decide to do so, the maxim of his action would be as follows: When I believe myself to be in need of money, I will borrow money and promise to repay it, although I know I shall never be able to do so. Now this principle of self-love or of his own benefit may very well be compatible with his whole future welfare, but the question is whether it is right. He changes the pretension of self-love into a universal law and then puts the question: How would it be if my maxim became a universal law? He immediately sees that it could never hold as a universal law of nature and be consistent with itself; rather it must necessarily contradict itself. For the universality of a law which says that anyone who believes himself to be in need could promise what he pleased with the intention of not fulfilling it would make the promise itself and the end to be accomplished by it impossible; no one would believe what was promised to him but would only laugh at any such assertion as vain pretense.

(3) A third finds in himself a talent which could, by means of some cultivation, make him in many respects a useful man. But he finds himself in comfortable circumstances and prefers indulgence in pleasure to troubling himself with broadening and improving his fortunate natural gifts. Now, however, let him ask whether his maxim of neglecting his gifts, besides agreeing with his propensity to

idle amusement, agrees also with what is called duty. He sees that a system of nature could indeed exist in accordance with such a law, even though man (like the inhabitants of the South Sea Islands) should let his talents rust and resolve to devote his life merely to idleness, indulgence, and propagation—in a word, to pleasure. But he cannot possibly will that this should become a universal law of nature or that it should be implanted in us by a natural instinct. For, as a rational being, he necessarily wills that all his faculties should be developed, inasmuch as they are given him and serve him for all sorts of purposes.

(4) A fourth man, for whom things are going well, sees that others (whom he could help) have to struggle with great hardships, and he asks, "What concern of mine is it? Let each one be as happy as heaven wills, or as he can make himself; I will not take anything from him or even envy him; but to his welfare or to his assistance in time of need I have no desire to contribute." If such a way of thinking were a universal law of nature, certainly the human race could exist, and without doubt even better than in a state where everyone talks of sympathy and good will or even exerts himself occasionally to practice them while, on the other hand, he cheats when he can and betrays or otherwise violates the right of man. Now although it is possible that a universal law of nature according to that maxim could exist, it is nevertheless impossible to will that such a principle should hold everywhere as a law of nature. For a will which resolved this would conflict with itself, since instances can often arise in which he would need the love and sympathy of others, and in which he would have robbed himself, by such a law of nature springing from his own will, of all hope of the aid he desires.

The foregoing are a few of the many actual duties, or at least of duties we hold to be actual, whose derivation from the one stated principle is clear. We must be able to will that a maxim of our action become a universal law; this is the canon of the moral estimation of our action generally. Some actions are of such a nature that their maxim cannot even be *thought* as a universal law of nature without contradiction, far from it being possible that one could will that it should be such. In others this internal impossibility is not found, though it is still impossible to *will* that that maxim should be raised to the universality of a law of nature, because such a will would contradict itself. We easily see that a maxim of the first kind conflicts with stricter or narrower (imprescriptible) duty, that of the latter with broader (meritorious) duty. Thus all duties, so far as the kind of obligation (not the object of their action) is concerned, have been completely exhibited by these examples in their dependence upon the same principle. . . .

We have thus at least established that if duty is a concept which is to have significance and actual law-giving authority for our actions, it can be expressed only in categorical imperatives and not at all in hypothetical ones. For every application of it we have also clearly exhibited the content of the categorical imperative which must contain the principle of all duty (if there is such). This is itself very much. But we are not yet advanced far enough to prove a priori that that kind of imperative really exists, that there is a practical law which of itself commands absolutely and without any incentives, and that obedience to this law is duty. . . .

The will is thought of as a faculty of determining itself to action in accordance with the conception of certain laws. Such a faculty can be found only in rational beings. That which serves the will as the objective ground of its self-determination is a purpose, and if it is given by reason alone it must hold alike for all rational beings. On the other hand, that which contains the ground of the possibility of the action, whose result is an end, is called the means. The subjective ground of desire is the incentive while the objective ground of volition is the motive. Thus arises the distinction between subjective purposes, which rest on incentives, and objective purposes, which depend on motives valid for every rational being. Practical principles are formal when they disregard all subjective purposes; they are material when they have subjective purposes and thus certain incentives as their basis. The purposes that a rational being holds before himself by choice as consequences of his action are material purposes and are without exception only relative, for only their relation to a particularly constituted faculty of desire in the subject gives them their worth. And this worth cannot afford any universal principles for all rational beings or any principles valid and necessary for every volition. That is, they cannot give rise to any practical laws. All these relative purposes, therefore, are grounds for hypothetical imperatives only.

But suppose that there were something the existence of which in itself had absolute worth, something which, as an end in itself, could be a ground of definite laws. In it and only in it could lie the ground of a possible categorical imperative (i.e., of a practical law).

Now, I say, man and, in general, every rational being exists as an end in himself and not merely as a means to be arbitrarily used by this or that will. In all his actions, whether they are directed toward himself or toward other rational beings, he must always be regarded at the same time as an end. All objects of inclination have only conditional worth, for if the inclinations and needs founded on them did not exist, their object would be worthless. The inclinations themselves as the sources of needs, however, are so lacking in absolute worth that the universal wish of every rational being must be indeed to free himself completely from them. Therefore, the worth of any objects to be obtained by our actions is at times conditional. Beings whose existence does not depend on our will but on nature, if they are not rational beings, have only relative worth as means, and are therefore called "things"; rational beings, on the other hand, are designated "persons" because their nature indicates that they are ends in themselves (i.e., things which may not be used merely as means). Such a being is thus an object of respect, and as such restricts all [arbitrary] choice. Such beings are not merely subjective ends whose existence as a result of our action has a worth for us, but are objective ends (i.e., beings whose existence is an end in itself). Such an end is one in the place of which no other end, to which these beings should serve merely as means, can be put. Without them, nothing of absolute worth could be found, and if all worth is conditional and thus contingent, no supreme practical principle for reason could be found anywhere.

Thus if there is to be a supreme practical principle and a categorical imperative for the human will, it must be one that forms an objective principle of the will from the conception of that which is necessarily an end for everyone because it is an end in itself. Hence this objective principle can serve as a universal law. The ground of this principle is: Rational nature exists as an end in itself. Man necessarily thinks of his own existence in this way, and thus far it is a subjective principle of human actions. Also every other rational being thinks of his existence on the same rational ground which holds also for myself;[8] thus it is at the same time an objective principle from which, as a supreme practical ground, it must be possible to derive all laws of the will. The practical imperative, therefore, is the following: Act so that you treat humanity, whether in your own person or in that of another, always as an end and never as a means only. Let us now see whether this can be achieved. To return to our previous examples:

First, according to the concept of necessary duty to oneself, he who contemplates suicide will ask himself whether his action can be consistent with the idea of humanity as an end in itself. If in order to escape from burdensome circumstances he destroys himself, he uses a person merely as a means to maintain a tolerable condition up to the end of life. Man, however, is not a thing, and thus not something to be used merely as a means; he must always be regarded in all his actions as an end in himself. Therefore I cannot dispose of man in my own person so as to mutilate, corrupt, or kill him. (It belongs to ethics proper to define more accurately this basic principle so as to avoid all misunderstanding, e.g., as to amputating limbs in order to preserve myself, or to exposing my life to danger in order to save it; I must therefore omit them here.)

Second, as concerns necessary or obligatory duties to others, he who intends a deceitful promise to others sees immediately that he intends to use another man merely as a means, without the latter at the same time containing the end in himself. For he whom I want to use for my own purposes by means of such a promise cannot possibly assent to my mode of acting against him and thus share in the purpose of this action. This conflict with the principle of other men is even clearer if we cite examples of attacks on their freedom and property, for then it is clear that he who violates the rights of men intends to make use of the person of others merely as means, without considering that, as rational beings, they must always be esteemed at the same time as ends (i.e., only as beings who must be able to embody in themselves the purpose of the very same action).[9]

Thirdly, with regard to contingent (meritorious) duty to oneself, it is not sufficient that the action not conflict with humanity in our person as an end in itself; it must also harmonize with it. In humanity there are capacities for greater perfection which belong to the purpose of nature with respect to humanity in our own person, and to neglect these might perhaps be consistent with the preservation of humanity as an end in itself, but not with the furtherance of that end.

Fourthly, with regard to meritorious duty to others, the natural purpose that all men have is their own happiness. Humanity might indeed exist if no one contributed to the happiness of others, provided he did not intentionally detract from it, but this harmony with humanity as an end in itself is only negative, not positive, if everyone does not also endeavor, as far as he can, to further the purposes of others. For the ends of any person, who is an end in himself, must as far as possible be also my ends, if that conception of an end in itself is to have its full effect on me.

This principle of humanity, and in general of every rational creature an end in itself, is the supreme limiting condition on the freedom of action of each man. It is not borrowed from experience, first, because of its universality, since it applies to all rational beings generally, and experience does not suffice to determine anything about them; and secondly, because in experience humanity is not thought of (subjectively) as the purpose of men (i.e., as an object which we of ourselves really make our purpose). Rather it is thought of as the objective end which ought to constitute the supreme limiting condition of all subjective ends whatever they may be. Thus this principle must arise from pure reason. Objectively the ground of all practical legislation lies (according to the first principle) in the rule and form of universality, which makes it capable of being a law (at least a natural law); subjectively it lies in the end. But the subject of all ends is every rational being as an end in itself (by the second principle); from this there follows the third practical principle of the will as the supreme condition of its harmony with universal practical reason, viz, the Idea of the will of every rational being as making universal law. . . .

The concept of any rational being as a being that must regard itself as giving universal law through all the maxims of its will, so that it may judge itself and its actions from this standpoint, leads to a very fruitful concept, namely that of a *realm of ends.*

By *realm* I understand the systematic union of different rational beings through common laws. Because laws determine which ends have universal validity, if we abstract from personal differences of rational beings, and thus from all content of their private purposes, we can think of a whole of all ends in systematic connection, a whole of rational beings as ends in themselves as well as a whole of particular purposes which each may set for himself. This is a realm of ends, which is possible on the principles stated above. For all rational beings stated under the law that each of them should treat himself and all others never merely as means, but in every case at the same time as an end in himself. Thus there arises a systematic union of rational beings through common objective laws. This is a realm which may be called a realm of ends (certainly only an ideal) because what these laws have in view is just the relation of these beings to each other as ends and means.

A rational being belongs to the realm of ends as a member when he gives universal laws in it while also himself subject to these laws. He belongs to it as sovereign when, as legislating, he is subject to the will of no other. The rational being must regard himself always as legislative in a realm of ends possible through the freedom of the will whether he belongs to it as member or as sovereign. He cannot maintain his position as sovereign merely through the maxims of his will, but only when he is a completely independent being without need and with unlimited power adequate to his will.

Morality, therefore, consists in the relation of every action to the legislation through which alone a realm of ends is possible. This legislation must be found in every rational being. It must be able to arise from his will, whose principle then is to do no action according to any maxim which would be inconsistent with its being a universal law, and thus to act only so that the will through its maxims could regard itself at the same time as giving universal law. If the maxims do not by their nature already necessarily conform to this objective principle of rational beings as giving universal law, the necessity of acting according to that principle is called practical constraint, which is to say: duty. Duty pertains not to the sovereign of the realm of ends, but rather to each member and to each in the same degree.

The practical necessity of acting according to this principle (duty) does not rest at all on feelings, impulses, and inclinations; it rests solely on the relation of rational beings to one another, in which the will of a rational being must always be regarded as legislative, for otherwise it could not be thought of as an end in itself. Reason, therefore, relates every maxim of the will as giving universal laws to every other will and also to every action towards itself; it does not do so for the sake of any other practical motive or future advantage but rather from the Idea of the dignity of a rational being who obeys no law except one which he himself also gives.

Discussion Questions

1. How do you answer Reading Question 2 (p. 594) for *yourself*? Imagine two people who walk by the same wallet sitting on a towel at the beach. Both need money, yet neither steals it. Person A does so out of pure duty (i.e., he desperately wants the money but decides, in the end, that he has a duty not to steal). Person B looks at the wallet and thinks nothing of stealing it to begin with (i.e., his inclination happens to agree with his duty). What pitfalls could arise from following duty alone? What pitfalls could arise from following inclination alone?

2. In what ways can one treat a person as a means to an end? Have you ever done this? Do you agree with Kant that one ought always to treat people as ends in themselves? Why/why not?

3. Kant mentions that you have a *duty* to preserve your own life (i.e., not to commit suicide). Do you agree? Why/why not? If not, how do you justify the moral permissibility of people treating *themselves* as a means to an end, contrary to Kant's practical imperative?

4. Think of some of the things that you consider unethical yet have not reasoned through completely (if at all)—incest, the death penalty, etc. When you begin the process of determining its moral status, do you determine it to be moral/immoral and then reason through it? Or do you reason through it and then determine its status? Which would Kant do? What does your method tell you about how you determine the moral status of actions?

5. Look at Rand's view of ethics (in this section) and how it differs from Kant's. How does each of them employ reason to derive different conclusions? Which doctrine are you more drawn to?

Utilitarianism

John Stuart Mill

John Stuart Mill was raised in London by a father with a fervent belief that a rigorous education from a very young age could produce superior intellect. In a sense, this was true for Mill, whose isolated home schooling had him learning Latin and studying logic, Greek literature (including Plato's dialogues), political economy, and philosophy, all by the age of 13. He is now considered to be the most prominent British philosopher of the nineteenth century. While he never held an academic position (Cambridge University admitted him, but his father prevented his attending, claiming that it had nothing more to offer him), he was very active in the political and intellectual community. He founded and edited the periodical *London and Westminster Review* and also served for four years as the liberal representative of the Parliament for Westminster. His writings were extensive, including the six-volume *System of Logic*, his well-known *Principles of Political Economy*, and one of the earliest feminist works, *The Subjection of Women*. He is most well known today for his work in ethics and social morality: for demonstrating the appeal of utilitarianism and how it can be applied to civilized states. He does the former in his work *Utilitarianism* (from which this selection is taken) and then later in *On Liberty*.

Here, Mill first provides an overview of the shortcomings of other moral systems and then gives a working definition of utilitarianism, followed by a defense of the theory against potential and actual criticisms. Utilitarianism is a *consequentialist* theory in that it focuses on the consequences of certain actions, regardless of motive or duty. While Mill was not the first to posit utilitarianism, his formulation, explanation, and defense of it have been the most highly regarded and accepted. In Chapter 1, Mill references English philosopher Jeremy Bentham, considered the first to formally discuss utilitarianism.

Two types of utilitarianism are often referenced, though not here in this piece. Mill primarily discusses *act* utilitarianism, which aims to increase the total utility or happiness of each particular action (i.e., I should not steal *this* object), while *rule* utilitarianism examines general rules (i.e., one should not steal objects) in order to determine if the particular rule would increase total utility or happiness.

Reading Questions

1. According to Mill, how do moral claims compare to scientific claims? How does he explain the methods of both the *intuitive* and *inductive* schools of ethics? What criticisms does Mill offer of these approaches?
2. What critique of Kant's system of ethics does Mill offer?
3. What is the *greatest happiness principle*? How is "happiness" defined? How is this principle criticized by comparing it with the life of a pig (swine)? What response does Mill provide?
4. How does he discuss the relation of quality and quantity with regard to pleasure? How should one choose between two pleasures?

Source: *Utilitarianism* by John Stuart Mill, copyright © 1979 by Hackett Publishing Company, Inc. Reprinted by permission of Hackett Publishing Company, Inc. All rights reserved.

5. What reasons does Mill give in support of the idea that "A being of higher faculties requires more to make him happy"?
6. What two initial objections does Mill site regarding the doctrine? How does he respond to them?
7. How can a utilitarian justify sacrificing one's own good for the sake of the good of others?
8. What does Mill say about the *motive* of an action as it relates to the act's moral status? How does he use the example of rescuing a drowning person to defend his position? How does Mill's opponent (Davies) respond?
9. Explain the following additional "misapprehensions" or critiques of utilitarianism that Mill cites along with his responses to each of them:
   a. It is a *godless* doctrine
   b. Its "expediency"
   c. It can be molded to fit one's tastes/temptations.

Chapter I

General Remarks

There are few circumstances among those which make up the present condition of human knowledge more unlike what might have been expected, or more significant of the backward state in which speculation on the most important subjects still lingers, than the little progress which has been made in the decision of the controversy respecting the criterion of right and wrong. From the dawn of philosophy, the question concerning the *summum bonum*, or, what is the same thing, concerning the foundation of morality, has been accounted the main problem in speculative thought, has occupied the most gifted intellects and divided them into sects and schools carrying on a vigorous warfare against one another. And after more than two thousand years the same discussions continue, philosophers are still ranged under the same contending banners, and neither thinkers nor mankind at large seem nearer to being unanimous on the subject than when the youth Socrates listened to the old Protagoras and asserted (if Plato's dialogue be grounded on a real conversation) the theory of utilitarianism against the popular morality of the so-called sophist. . . .

In science the particular truths precede the general theory, the contrary might be expected to be the case with a practical art, such as morals or legislation. All action is for the sake of some end, and rules of action, it seems natural to suppose, must take their whole character and color from the end to which they are subservient. When we engage in pursuit, a clear and precise conception of what we are pursuing would seem to be the first thing we need, instead of the last we are to look forward to. A test of right and wrong must be the means, one would think, of ascertaining what is right or wrong, and not a consequence of having already ascertained it.

The difficulty is not avoided by having recourse to the popular theory of a natural faculty, a sense of instinct, informing us of right and wrong. For—besides that the existence of such a moral instinct is itself one of the matters in dispute—those believers in it who have any pretensions to philosophy have been obliged to abandon the idea that it discerns what is right or wrong in the particular case in hand, as our other senses discern the sight or sound actually present. Our moral faculty, according to all those of its interpreters who are entitled to the name of thinkers, supplies us only with the general principles of moral judgments; it is a branch of our reason, not of our sensitive faculty, and must be looked to for the abstract doctrines of morality, not for perception of it in the concrete. The intuitive, no less than what may be termed the inductive, school of ethics insists on the necessity of general laws. They both agree that the morality of an individual action is not a question of direct perception, but of the application of a law to an individual case. They recognize also to a great extent, the same moral laws, but differ as to their evidence and the source from which they derive their authority. According to the one opinion, the principles of morals are evident *a priori*, requiring nothing to command assent except that the meaning of the terms be understood. According to the other doctrine, right and wrong, as well as truth and falsehood, are questions of observation and experience. But both hold equally that morality must be deduced from principles; and the intuitive school affirm as strongly as the inductive that there is a science of morals. Yet they seldom attempt to make out a list of the *a priori* principles which are to serve as the premises of the science; still more rarely do they make any effort to reduce those various principles to one first principle or common ground of obligation. They either assume the ordinary precepts of morals as of *a priori* authority, or they lay down as the common groundwork of those maxims some generality much less obviously authoritative than the maxims themselves, and which has never succeeded in gaining popular acceptance. Yet to support their pretensions there ought either to be some one fundamental principle or law at the root of all morality, or, if there be several, there should be a determinate order of precedence among them; and the one principle, or the rule for deciding between the various principles when they conflict, ought to be self-evident.

To inquire how far the bad effects of this deficiency have been mitigated in practice, or to what extent the moral beliefs of mankind have been vitiated or made uncertain by the absence of any distinct recognition of an ultimate standard, would imply a complete survey and criticism of past and present ethical doctrine. It would, however, be easy to show that whatever steadiness or consistency these moral beliefs have attained has been mainly due to the tacit influence of a standard not recognized. Although the nonexistence of an acknowledged first principle has made ethics not so much a guide as a consecration of men's actual sentiments, still, as men's sentiments, both of favor and of aversion, are greatly influenced by what they suppose to be the effects of things upon their happiness, the principle of utility, or, as Bentham latterly called it, the greatest happiness principle, has had a large share in forming the moral doctrines even of those who most scornfully reject its authority. Nor is there any school of thought which refuses to admit that the influence of actions on happiness is a most material and even predominant consideration in many of the details of morals, however unwilling to acknowledge it as the fundamental principle of morality and the source of moral obligation. I might go much further and say that to all those *a priori* moralists who deem it necessary to argue at all, utilitarian arguments are indispensable. It is not my present purpose to criticize these thinkers; but I cannot help referring, for illustration, to a systematic treatise by one of the most illustrious of them, the *Metaphysics of Ethics* by Kant. This remarkable man, whose system of thought will long remain one of the landmarks in the history of philosophical speculation, does, in the treatise in question, lay down a universal first principle as the origin and ground of moral obligation; it is this: "So act that the rule on which thou actest would admit of being adopted as a law by all rational beings." But when he begins to deduce from this precept any of the actual duties of morality, he fails, almost grotesquely, to show that there would be any contradiction, any logical (not to say physical) impossibility, in the adoption by all rational beings of the most outrageously immoral rules of conduct. All he shows is that the *consequences* of their universal adoption would be such as no one would choose to incur.

On the present occasion, I shall, without further discussion of the other theories, attempt to contribute something toward the understanding and appreciation of the "utilitarian" or "happiness" theory, and toward such proof as it is susceptible of. It is evident that this cannot be proof in the ordinary and popular meaning of the term. Questions of ultimate ends are not amenable to direct proof. Whatever can be proved to be good must be so by being shown to be a means to something admitted to be good without proof. . . .

Before, . . . I attempt to enter into the philosophical grounds which can be given for assenting to the utilitarian standard, I shall offer some illustrations of the doctrine itself, with the view of showing more clearly what it is, distinguishing it from what it is not, and disposing of such of the practical objections to it as either originate in, or are closely connected with, mistaken interpretations of its meaning. Having thus prepared the ground, I shall afterwards endeavor to throw such light as I can call upon the question considered as one of philosophical theory.

Chapter II

What Utilitarianism Is

. . . The creed which accepts as the foundation of morals "utility" or the "greatest happiness principle" holds that actions are right in proportion as they tend to promote happiness; wrong as they tend to produce the reverse of happiness. By happiness is intended pleasure and the absence of pain; by unhappiness, pain and the privation of pleasure. To give a clear view of the moral standard set up by the theory, much more requires to be said; in particular, what things it includes in the ideas of pain and pleasure, and to what extent this is left an open question. But these supplementary explanations do not affect the theory of life on which this theory of morality is grounded—namely, that pleasure and freedom from pain are the only things desirable as ends; and that all desirable things (which are as numerous in the utilitarian as in any other scheme) are desirable either for pleasure inherent in themselves or as means to the promotion of pleasure and the prevention of pain.

Now such a theory of life excites in many minds . . . inveterate dislike. To suppose that life has (as they express it) no higher end than pleasure—no better and nobler object of desire and pursuit—they designate as utterly mean and groveling, as a doctrine worthy only of swine, to whom the followers of Epicurus were, at a very early period, contemptuously likened; and modern holders of the doctrine are occasionally made the subject of equally polite comparisons by its German, French, and English assailants.

When thus attacked, the Epicureans have always answered that it is not they, but their accusers, who represent human nature in a degrading light, since the accusation supposes human beings to be capable of no pleasures except those of which swine are capable. If this supposition were true, the charge could not be gainsaid, but would men be no longer an imputation; for if the sources of pleasure were precisely the same to human beings and to swine, the rule of life which is good enough for the one would be good enough for the other. The comparison of the Epicurean life to that of beasts is felt as degrading, precisely because a beast's pleasures do not satisfy a human being's conceptions of happiness. Human beings have faculties more elevated than the animal appetites and, when once made conscious of them, do not regard anything as happiness which does not include their gratification. I do not indeed, consider the Epicureans to have been by any means faultless in drawing out their scheme of consequences from the utilitarian principle. To do this in any sufficient manner, many Stoic, as well as Christian, elements require to be included. But there is no known Epicurean theory of life which does not assign to the pleasures of the intellect, of the feelings and imagination, and of the moral sentiments a much higher value as pleasures than to those of mere sensation. It must be admitted, however, that utilitarian writers in general have placed the superiority of mental over bodily pleasures chiefly in the greater permanency, safety, uncostliness, etc., of the former—that is, in their circumstantial advantages rather than in their intrinsic nature. And on all these points utilitarians have fully proved their case; but they might have taken the other and, as it may be called, higher ground with entire consistency. It is quite compatible with the principle of utility to recognize the fact that some kinds of pleasure are more desirable and more valuable than others. It would be absurd that, while in estimating all other things quality is considered as well as quantity, the estimation of pleasure should be supposed to depend on quantity alone.

If I am asked what I mean by difference of quality in pleasures, or what makes one pleasure more valuable than another merely as a pleasure, except its being greater in amount, there is but one possible answer. Of two pleasures, if there be one to which all or almost all who have experience of both give a decided preference, irrespective of any feeling of moral obligation to prefer it, that is the more desirable pleasure. If one of the two is, by those who are competently acquainted with both, placed so far above the other that they prefer it, even though knowing it to be attended with a greater amount of discontent, and would not resign it for any quantity of the other pleasure which their nature is capable of, we are justified in ascribing to the preferred enjoyment a superiority in quality so far outweighing quantity as to render it, in comparison, of small account.

Now it is an unquestionable fact that those who are equally acquainted with and equally capable of appreciating and enjoying both do give a most marked preference to the manner of existence which employs their higher faculties. Few human creatures would consent to be changed into any of the lower animals for a promise of the fullest allowance of a beast's pleasures; no intelligent human being would consent to be a fool, no instructed person would be an ignoramus, no person of feeling and conscience would be selfish and base, even though they should be persuaded that the fool, the dunce, or the rascal is better satisfied with his lot than they are with theirs. They would not resign what they possess more than he for the most complete satisfaction of all the desires which they have in common with him. If they ever fancy they would, it is only in cases of unhappiness so extreme that to escape from it they would exchange their lot for almost any other, however undesirable in their own eyes. A being of higher faculties requires more to make him happy, is capable probably of more acute suffering, and certainly accessible to it at more points, than one of an inferior type; but in spite of these liabilities, he can never really wish to sink into what he feels to be a lower grade of existence. We may give what explanation we please of this unwillingness; we may attribute it to pride, a name which is given indiscriminately to some of the most and to some of the least estimable feelings of which mankind are capable; we may refer it to the love of liberty and personal independence, an appeal to which was with the Stoics one of the most effective means for the inculcation of it; to the love of power or to the love of excitement, both of which do really enter into and contribute to it; but its most appropriate appellation is a sense of dignity, which all human beings possess in one form or other, and in some, though by no means in exact, proportion to their higher faculties, and which is so essential a part of the happiness of those in whom it is strong that nothing which conflicts with it could be otherwise than momentarily an object of desire to them. Whoever supposes that this preference takes place at a sacrifice of happiness—that the superior being, in anything like equal circumstances, is not happier than the inferior—confounds the two very different ideas of happiness and content. It is indisputable that the being whose capacities of enjoyment are low has the greatest chance of having them fully satisfied; and a highly endowed being will always feel that any happiness which he can look for, as the world is constituted, is imperfect. But he can learn to bear its imperfections, if they are at all bearable; and they will not make him envy the being who is indeed unconscious of the imperfections, but only because he feels not at all the good which those imperfections qualify. It is better to be a human being dissatisfied than a pig satisfied; better to be Socrates dissatisfied than a fool satisfied. And if the fool, or the pig, are of a different opinion, it is because they only know their own side of the question. The other party to the comparison knows both sides.

It may be objected that many who are capable of the higher pleasures occasionally, under the influence of temptation, postpone them to the lower. But this is quite compatible with a full appreciation of the intrinsic superiority of the higher. Men often, from infirmity of character, make their election for the nearer good, though they know it to be the less valuable; and this no less when the choice is between two bodily pleasures than when it is between bodily and mental. They pursue sensual indulgences to the injury of health, though perfectly aware that health is the greater good. It may be further objected that many who begin with youthful enthusiasm for everything noble, as they advance in years, sink into indolence and selfishness. But I do not believe that those who undergo this very common change voluntarily choose the lower description of pleasures in preference to the higher. I believe that, before they devote themselves exclusively to the one, they have already become incapable of the other. Capacity for the nobler feelings is in most natures a very tender plant, easily killed, not only by hostile influences, but by mere want of sustenance; and in the majority of young persons it speedily dies away if the occupations to which their position in life has devoted them, and the society into which it has thrown them, are not favorable to keeping that higher capacity in exercise. Men lose their high aspirations as they lose their intellectual tastes, because they have not time or opportunity for indulging them; and they addict themselves to inferior pleasures, not because they deliberately prefer them, but because they are either the only ones to which they have access or the only ones which they are any longer capable of enjoying. It may be questioned whether anyone who has remained equally susceptible to both classes of pleasures ever knowingly and calmly preferred the lower, though many, in all ages, have broken down in an ineffectual attempt to combine both.

From this verdict of the only competent judges, I apprehend there can be no appeal. On a question which is the best worth having of two pleasures, or which of two modes of existence is the most grateful to the feelings, apart from its moral attributes and from its consequences, the judgment of these who are qualified by knowledge of both, or, if they differ, that of the majority among them, must be admitted as final. And there needs be the less hesitation to accept this judgment respecting the quality of pleasures, since there is no other tribunal to be referred to even on the question of quantity. What means are there of determining which is the acutest of two pains, or the intensest of two pleasurable sensations, except the general suffrage of those who are familiar with both? Neither pains nor pleasures are homogeneous, and pain is always heterogeneous with pleasure. What is there to decide whether a particular pleasure is worth purchasing at the cost of a particular pain, except the feelings and judgment of the experienced? When, therefore, those feelings and judgment declare the pleasures derived from the higher faculties to be preferable *in kind*, apart from the question of intensity, to those of which the animal nature, disjoined from the higher faculties, is susceptible, they are entitled on this subject to the same regard.

I have dwelt on this point as being part of a perfectly just conception of utility or happiness considered as the directive rule of human conduct. But it is by no means an indispensable condition to the acceptance of the utilitarian standard; for that standard is not the agent's own greatest happiness, but the greatest amount of happiness altogether; and if it may possibly be doubted whether a noble character is always the happier for its nobleness, there can be no doubt that it makes other people happier, and that the world in general is immensely a gainer by it. Utilitarianism, therefore, could only attain its end by the general cultivation of nobleness of character, even if each individual were only benefited by the nobleness of others, and his own, so far as happiness is concerned, were a sheer deduction from the benefit. But the bare enunciation of such an absurdity as this last renders refutation superfluous.

According to the greatest happiness principle, as above explained, the ultimate end, with reference to and for the sake of which all other things are desirable—whether we are considering our own good or that of other people—is an existence exempt as far as possible from pain, and as rich as possible in enjoyments, both in point of quantity and quality; the test of quality and the rule for measuring it against quantity being the preference felt by those who, in their opportunities of experience, to which must be added their habits of self-consciousness and self-observation, are best furnished with the means of comparison. This, being according to the utilitarian opinion the end of human action, is necessarily also the standard of morality, which may accordingly be defined "the rules and precepts for human conduct," by the observance of which an existence such as has been described might be, to the greatest extent possible, secured to all mankind; and not to them only, but, so far as the nature of things admits, to the whole sentient creation.

Against this doctrine, however, arises another class of objectors who say that happiness, in any form, cannot be the rational purpose of human life and action; because, in the first place, it is unattainable; and they contemptuously ask, What right hast thou to be happy?—a question which Mr. Carlyle clinches by the addition, What right, a short time ago, hadst thou even *to be*? Next they say that men can do *without* happiness; that all noble human beings have felt this, and could not have become noble but by learning the lesson of *Entsagen*, or renunciation; which lesson, thoroughly learned and submitted to, they affirm to be the beginning and necessary condition of all virtue.

The first of these objections would go to the root of the matter were it well founded; for if no happiness is to be had at all by human beings, the attainment of it cannot be the end of morality or of any rational conduct. Though, even in that case, something might still be said for the utilitarian theory, since utility includes not solely the pursuit of happiness, but the prevention or mitigation of unhappiness; and if the former aim be chimerical, there will be all the greater scope and more imperative need for the latter, so long at least as mankind think fit to live and do not take refuge in the simultaneous act of suicide recommended under certain conditions by Novalis. When, however, it is thus positively asserted to be impossible that human life should be happy, the assertion, if not something like a verbal quibble, is at least an exaggeration. If by happiness be meant a continuity of highly pleasurable excitement, it is evident enough that this is impossible. A state of exalted pleasure lasts only moments or in some cases, and with some intermissions, hours or days, and is the occasional brilliant flash of enjoyment, not its permanent and steady flame. Of this the philosophers who have taught that happiness is the end of life were as fully aware as those who taunt them. The happiness which they meant was not a life of rapture, but moments of such, in an existence made up of few and transitory pains, many and various pleasures, with a decided predominance of the active over the passive, and having as the foundation of the whole not to expect more from life than it is capable of bestowing. A life thus composed, to those who have been fortunate enough to obtain it, has always appeared worthy of the name of happiness. And such an existence is even now the lot of many during some considerable portion of their lives. The present wretched education and wretched social arrangements are the only real hindrance to its being attainable by almost all.

The objectors perhaps may doubt whether human beings, if taught to consider happiness as the end of life, would be satisfied with such a moderate share of it. But great numbers of mankind have been satisfied with much less. The main constituents of a satisfied life appear to be two, either of which by itself is often found sufficient for the purpose: tranquillity and excitement. With much tranquillity, many find that they can be content with very little pleasure; with much excitement, many can reconcile themselves to a considerable quantity of pain. . . .

The utilitarian morality does recognize in human beings the power of sacrificing their own greatest good for the good of others. It only refuses to admit that the sacrifice is itself a good. A sacrifice which does not increase or tend to increase the sum total of happiness, it considers as wasted. The only self-renunciation which it applauds is devotion to the happiness, or to some of the means of happiness, of others, either of mankind collectively or of individuals within the limits imposed by the collective interests of mankind.

I must again repeat what the assailants of utilitarianism seldom have the justice to acknowledge, that the happiness which forms the utilitarian standard of what is right in conduct is not the agent's own happiness but that of all concerned. As between his own happiness and that of others, utilitarianism requires him to be as strictly impartial as a disinterested and benevolent spectator. In the golden rule of Jesus of Nazareth, we read the complete spirit of the ethics of utility. "To do as you would be done by," and "to love your neighbor as yourself," constitute the ideal perfection of utilitarian morality. As the means of making the nearest approach to this ideal, utility would enjoin, first, that laws and social arrangements should place the happiness or (as, speaking practically, it may be called) the interest of every individual as nearly as possible in harmony with the interest of the whole; and, secondly, that education and opinion, which have so vast a power over human character, should so use that power as to establish in the mind of every individual an indissoluble association between his own happiness and the good of the whole, especially between his own happiness and the practice of such modes of conduct, negative and positive, as regard for the universal happiness prescribes; so that not only he may be unable to conceive the possibility of happiness to himself, consistently with conduct opposed to the general good, but also that a direct impulse to promote the general good may be in every individual one of the habitual motives of action, and the sentiments connected therewith may fill a large and prominent place in every human being's sentient existence. If the impugners of the utilitarian morality represented it to their own minds in this its true character, I know not what recommendation possessed by any other morality they could possibly affirm to be wanting to it; what more beautiful or more exalted developments of human nature any other ethical system can be supposed to foster, or what springs of action, not accessible to the utilitarian, such systems rely on for giving effect to their mandates.

The objectors to utilitarianism cannot always be charged with representing it in a discreditable light. On the contrary, those among them who entertain anything like a just idea of its disinterested character sometimes find fault with its standard as being too high for humanity. They say it is exacting too much to require that people shall always act from the inducement of promoting the general interest of society. But this is to mistake the very meaning of a standard of morals and confound the rule of action with the motive of it. It is the business of ethics to tell us what are our duties, or by what test we may know them; but no system of ethics requires that the sole motive of all we do shall be a feeling of duty; on the contrary, ninety-nine hundredths of all our actions are done from other motives, and rightly so done if the rule of duty does not condemn them. It is the more unjust to utilitarianism that this particular misapprehension should be made a ground of objection to it, inasmuch as utilitarian moralists have gone beyond almost all others in affirming that the motive has nothing to do with the morality of the action, though much with the worth of the agent. He who saves a fellow creature from drowning does what is morally right, whether his motive be duty or the hope of being paid for his trouble; he who betrays the friend that trusts him is guilty of a crime, even if his object be to serve another friend to whom he is under greater obligations.[10] But to speak only of actions done from the motive of duty, and in direct obedience to principle: It is a misapprehension of the utilitarian mode of thought to conceive it as implying that people should fix their minds upon so wide a generality as the world, or society at large. The great majority of good actions are intended not for the benefit of the world, but for that of individuals, of which the good of the world is made up; and the thoughts of the most virtuous man need not on these occasions travel beyond the particular persons concerned, except so far as is necessary to assure himself that in benefiting them he is not violating the rights, that is, the legitimate and authorized expectations, of anyone else. The multiplication of happiness is, according to the utilitarian ethics, the object of virtue: The occasions on which any person (except one in a thousand) has it in his power to do this on an extended scale—in other words, to be a public benefactor—are but exceptional; and on these occasions alone is he called on to consider public utility; in every other case, private utility, the interest or happiness of some few persons, is all he has to attend to. Those alone the influence of whose actions extends to society in general need concern themselves habitually about so large an object. In the case of abstinences indeed—of things which people forbear to do from moral considerations, though the consequences in the particular case might be beneficial—it would be unworthy of an intelligent agent not to be consciously aware that the action is of a class which, if practiced generally, would be generally injurious, and that this is the ground of the obligation to abstain from it. The amount of regard for the public interest implied in this recognition is no greater than is demanded by every system of morals, for they all enjoin to abstain from whatever is manifestly pernicious to society. . . .

It may not be superfluous to notice a few more of the common misapprehensions of utilitarian ethics. . . . We not uncommonly hear the doctrine of utility inveighed against a *godless* doctrine. If it be necessary to say anything at all against so mere an assumption, we may say that the question depends upon what idea we have formed of the moral character of the Deity. If it be a true belief that God desires, above all things, the happiness of his creatures, and that this was his purpose in their creation, utility is not only not a godless doctrine, but more profoundly religious than any other. If it be meant that utilitarianism does not recognize the revealed will of God as the supreme law of morals, I answer that a utilitarian who believes in the perfect goodness and wisdom of *God* necessarily believes that whatever God has thought fit to reveal on the subject of morals must fulfill the requirements of utility in a supreme degree. But others besides utilitarians have been of opinion that the Christian revelation was intended, and is fitted, to inform the hearts and minds of mankind with a spirit which should enable them to find for themselves what is right, and incline them to do it when found, rather than to tell them, except in a very general way, what it is; and that we need a doctrine of ethics, carefully followed out, to *interpret* to us the will of God. Whether this opinion is correct or not, it is superfluous here to discuss; since whatever aid religion, either natural or revealed, can afford to ethical investigation is as open to the utilitarian moralist as to any other. He can use it as the testimony of God to the usefulness or hurtfulness of any given course of action by as good a right as others can use it for the indication of a transcendental law having no connection with usefulness or with happiness.

Again, utility is often summarily stigmatized as an immoral doctrine by giving it the name of "*expediency*," and taking advantage of the popular use of that term to contrast it with principle. But the expedient, in the sense in which it is opposed to the right, generally means that which is expedient for the particular interest of the agent himself; as when a minister sacrifices the interests of his country to keep himself in place. When it means anything better than this, it means that which is expedient for some immediate object, some temporary purpose, but which violates a rule whose observance is expedient in a much higher degree. The expedient, in this sense, instead of being the same thing with the useful, is a branch of the hurtful. Thus it would often be expedient, for the purpose of getting over some momentary embarrassment, or attaining some object immediately useful to ourselves or others, to tell a lie. But inasmuch as the cultivation in ourselves of a sensitive feeling on the subject of veracity is one of the most useful, and the enfeeblement of that feeling one of the most hurtful, things to which our conduct can be instrumental; and inasmuch as any, even unintentional, deviation from truth does that much toward weakening the trustworthiness of human assertion, which is not only the principal support of all present social well-being, but the insufficiency of which does more than any one thing that can be named to keep back civilization, virtue, everything on which human happiness on the largest scale depends—we feel that the violation, for a present advantage, of a rule of such transcendent expediency is not expedient, and that he who, for the sake of convenience to himself or to some other individual, does what depends on him to deprive mankind of the good, and inflict upon them the evil, involved in the greater or less reliance which they can place in each other's words, acts the part of one of their worst enemies. Yet that even this rule, sacred as it is, admits of possible exceptions is acknowledged by all moralists; the chief of which is when the withholding of some fact (as of information from a malefactor, or of bad news from a person dangerously ill) would save an individual (especially an individual other than oneself) from great and unmerited evil, and when the withholding can only be effected by denial. But in order that the exception may not extend itself beyond the need, and may have the least possible effect in weakening reliance on veracity, it ought to be recognized and, if possible, its limits defined; and, if the principle of utility is good for anything, it must be good for weighing these conflicting utilities against one another and marking out the region within which one or the other preponderates.

Again, defenders of utility often find themselves called upon to reply to such objections as this—that there is not time, previous to action, for calculating and weighing the effects of any line of conduct on the general happiness. This is exactly as if anyone were to say that it is impossible to guide our conduct by Christianity because there is not time, on every occasion on which anything has to be done, to read through the Old and New Testaments. The answer to the objection is that there has been ample time, namely, the whole past duration of the human species. During all that time mankind have been learning by experience the tendencies of actions; on which experience all the prudence as well as all the morality of life are dependent. . . . That the received code of ethics is by no means of divine right; and that mankind have still much to learn as to the effects of actions on the general happiness, I admit or rather earnestly maintain. The corollaries from the principle of utility, like the precepts of every practical art, admit of indefinite improvement, and, in a progressive state of the human mind, their improvement is perpetually going on. But to consider the rules of morality as improvable is one thing; to pass over the intermediate generalization entirely and endeavor to test each individual action directly by the first principle is another. It is a strange notion that the acknowledgment of a first principle is inconsistent with the admission of secondary ones. To inform a traveler respecting the place of his ultimate destination is not to forbid the use of landmarks and direction-posts on the way. The proposition that happiness is the end and aim of morality does not mean that no road ought to be laid down to that goal, or that persons going thither should not be advised to take one direction rather than another. Men really ought to leave off talking a kind of nonsense on this subject, which they would neither talk nor listen to on other matters of practical concernment. Nobody argues that the art of navigation is not founded on astronomy because sailors cannot wait to calculate the National Almanac. Being rational creatures, they go to sea with it ready calculated; and all rational creatures go out upon the sea of life with their minds made up on the common questions of right and wrong, as well as on many of the far more difficult questions of wise and foolish. And this, as long as foresight is a human quality, it is to be presumed they will continue to do. . . .

The remainder of the stock arguments against utilitarianism mostly consist in laying to its charge the common infirmities of human nature, and the general difficulties which embarrass conscientious persons in shaping their course through life. We are told that a utilitarian will be apt to make his own particular case an exception to moral rules, and, when under temptation, will see a utility in the breach of a rule, greater than he will see in its observance. But is utility the only creed which is able to furnish us with excuses for evil-doing and means of cheating our own conscience? They are afforded in abundance by all doctrines which recognize as a fact in morals the existence of conflicting considerations, which all doctrines do that have been believed by sane persons. It is not the fault of any creed, but of the complicated nature of human affairs, that rules of conduct cannot be so framed as to require no exceptions, and that hardly any kind of action can safely be laid down as either always obligatory or always condemnable. There is no ethical creed which does not temper the rigidity of its laws by giving a certain latitude, under the moral responsibility of the agent, for accommodation to peculiarities of circumstances; and under every creed, at the opening thus made, self-deception and dishonest casuistry get in. There exists no moral system under which there do not arise unequivocal cases of conflicting obligation. These are the real difficulties, the knotty points both in the theory of ethics and in the conscientious guidance of personal conduct. They are overcome practically, with greater or with less success, according to the intellect and virtue of the individual; but it can hardly be pretended that anyone will be the less qualified for dealing with them, from possessing an ultimate standard to which conflicting rights and duties can be referred. If utility is the ultimate source of moral obligations, utility may be invoked to decide between them when their demands are incompatible. Though the application of the standard may be difficult, it is better than none at all; while in other systems, the moral laws all claiming independent authority, there is no common umpire entitled to interfere between them; their claims to precedence one over another rest on little better than sophistry, and, unless determined, as they generally are, by the unacknowledged influence of consideration of utility, afford a free scope for the action of personal desires and partialities. We must remember that only in these cases of conflict between secondary principles is it requisite that first principles should be appealed to. There is no case of moral obligation in which some secondary principle is not involved; and if only one, there can seldom be any real doubt which one it is, in the mind of any person by whom the principle itself is recognized.

Discussion Questions

1. Look at Mill's discussion of *motive* versus *consequence* regarding the moral status of an action (Chapter II). How important is motive to you when addressing a moral situation? What truth do you find in the phrase, "The road to hell is paved with good intentions"?

2. Do you agree with Mill when he writes, "Pleasure and freedom from pain are the only things desirable as [goals]"? If so, how does this affect your view of ethics. If not, why not?

3. Do you agree that someone with "higher faculties" requires more to make them happy? Are they also capable of more severe suffering as Mill suggests? If so, why would one desire to have "higher faculties"? What value do you see in being a "pig satisfied" (i.e., living a "dog's life" as opposed to being "Socrates dissatisfied")?

4. Mill addresses numerous "misapprehensions" or critiques of utilitarianism. Are you happy with his responses to these? Did he leave any out that you have?

5. Both Mill and Aristotle (see reading, this section) frequently mention happiness as a major factor in their respective ethical systems. How do they treat it differently? Is it easy for you to recognize when you are happy and what exactly it takes for you to achieve happiness?

6. Does utilitarianism seem like a suitable moral doctrine to you? Why/why not? What kinds of actions would it allow (or prevent) which you believe to be immoral (or moral)?

Care-Based Ethics

Carol Gilligan

Following her completion of a PhD in social psychology at Harvard University, Carol Gilligan remained there to teach for over thirty years and has since taught at New York and Cambridge Universities, both in the law school and with a focus on gender studies. Considered a pioneer in the moral development of girls, *Time* magazine named her one of the twenty-five most influential Americans. She has received numerous awards, including the Grawenmeyer Award for her work in education and the Heinz Award for contributions to the understanding of the human condition.

This selection is taken from her best-known book, *In a Different Voice: Psychological Theory and Women's Development*, described by the Harvard University Press as "the little book that started a revolution." In it, she highlights the predominance of androcentric (male-centered) moral frameworks and how these tend to ignore (and even devalue) the "voice" of females. Gilligan is the founder of "difference feminism"—the notion that females *do* have different tendencies than males and that this ought to be taken into account when devising a moral framework.

Also in this selection, Gilligan discusses another well-known moral researcher, Lawrence Kohlberg, for whom she worked as a research assistant in 1970. Kohlberg is best known for his six moral stages that he devised following interviews of subjects as to how they justify their decisions in a moral situation known as the "Heinz Dilemma." In this dilemma, a man's wife is dying, but he cannot afford the overly-priced drug, even after asking all of his friends for a loan. So he breaks into the drugstore and steals the drug. Kohlberg interviewed predominantly upper-class male subjects, though, and thus developed sta° that Gilligan believed to be androcentric. He classified typically male views—i.e.

involving contracts and rule-based systems—as higher/more advanced than that of the typically female-oriented approach—i.e., based on caring and relationships—and he thus (wrongly) gave the appearance of female morality as "deviant" or "deficient."

Reading Questions

1. In what way are the first student's responses contradictory?
2. According to Gilligan, what is the "essence of moral choice," and how might this affect the decisions of women (and children)?
3. How does Gilligan relate sexuality to making moral judgments?
4. According to the research mentioned (by Hann and Holstein), how do moral judgments of women differ from those of men?
5. Explain the dilemma that women face as a result of the conflict between the self and other.
6. What are Kohlberg's stages of moral development, and how do they differ?
7. What is the "distinct moral language" of women that Gilligan discusses? In what way is the female approach *psychological* and the male approach *logical*?
8. Why does "Ruth" refrain from passing moral judgment regarding the Heinz Dilemma? How does she describe the moral issue? How does Gilligan explain that Ruth avoids relativism?
9. Explain the point that Gilligan makes in her reference of Gandhi, Abraham, and the "woman who comes before Solomon."

A college student, responding to the question "If you had to say what morality meant to you, how would you sum it up?" replies:

> When I think of the word *morality*, I think of obligations. I usually think of it as conflicts between personal desires and social things, social considerations, or personal desires of yourself versus personal desires of another person or people or whatever. Morality is that whole realm of how you decide these conflicts. A moral person is one who would decide by placing themselves more often than not as equals. A truly moral person would always consider another person as their equal . . . In a situation of social interaction, something is morally wrong where the individual ends up screwing a lot of people. And it is morally right when everyone comes out better off.

Yet when asked if she can think of someone whom she considers a genuinely moral person, she replies, "Well, immediately I think of Albert Schweitzer, bec~~~~ obviously given his life to help others." Obligation and sacrifice ~~l of equality, setting up a basic contradiction in her thought.

rmission of the publisher from *In a Different Voice: Psychological Theory and Women's* iilligan, pp. 64–73, 100–105, Cambridge, Mass.: Harvard University Press, Copyright © igan.

Another undergraduate responds to the question "What does it mean to say something is morally right or wrong?" by also speaking first of responsibilities and obligations:

> It has to do with responsibilities and obligations and values, mainly values . . . In my life situation I relate morality with interpersonal relationships that have to do with respect for the other person and myself. (*Why respect other people?*) Because they have a consciousness or feelings that can be hurt, an awareness that can be hurt.

The concern about hurting others persists as a major theme in the responses of two other women students to the question "Why be moral?"

> Millions of people have to live together peacefully. I personally don't want to hurt other people. That's real criterion, a main criterion for me. It underlies my sense of justice. It isn't nice to inflict pain. I empathize with anyone in pain. Not hurting others is important in my own private morals. Years ago I would have jumped out of a window not to hurt my boyfriend. That was pathological. Even today, though, I want approval and love, and I don't want enemies. Maybe that's why there is morality—so people can win approval, love, and friendship.

> My main principle is not hurting other people as long as you aren't going against your own conscience and as long as you remain true to yourself . . . There are many moral issues, such as abortion, the draft, killing, stealing, monogamy. If something is a controversial issue like these, then I always say it is up to the individual. The individual has to decide and then follow his own conscience. There are no moral absolutes. Laws are pragmatic instruments, but they are not absolutes. A viable society can't make exceptions all the time, but I would personally . . . I'm afraid I'm heading for some big crisis with my boyfriend someday, and someone will get hurt, and he'll get more hurt than I will. I feel an obligation not to hurt him, but also an obligation not to lie. I don't know if it is possible not to lie and not to hurt.

The common thread that runs through these statements is the wish not to hurt others and the hope that in morality lies a way of solving conflicts so that no one will be hurt. This theme is independently introduced by each of the four women as the most specific item in their response to a most general question. The moral person is one who helps others; goodness is service, meeting one's obligations and responsibilities to others, if possible without sacrificing oneself. While the first of the four women ends by denying the conflict she initially introduced, the last woman anticipates a conflict between remaining true to herself and adhering to her principle of not hurting others. The dilemma that would test the limits of this judgment would be one where helping others is seen to be at the price of hurting the self.

The reticence about taking stands on "controversial issues," a willingness to "make exceptions all the time," is echoed repeatedly by other college women:

> I never feel that I can condemn anyone else. I have a very relativistic position. The basic idea that I cling to is the sanctity of human life. I am inhibited about impressing my beliefs on others.

> I could never argue that my belief on a moral question is anything that another person should accept. I don't believe in absolutes. If there is an absolute for moral decisions, it is human life.

Or as a thirty-one-year-old graduate student says when explaining why she would find it difficult to steal a drug to save her own life, despite her belief that it would be right to steal for another: "It's just very hard to defend yourself against the rules. I mean, we live by consensus, and if you take an action simply for yourself, by yourself, there's no consensus there, and that is relatively indefensible in this society now."

What emerges in these voices is a sense of vulnerability that impedes these women from taking a stand, what George Eliot regards as the girl's "susceptibility" to adverse judgments by others, which stems from her lack of power and consequent inability "to do something in the world." The unwillingness to make moral judgments that Kohlberg and Kramer and Kohlberg and Gilligan associate with the adolescent crisis of identity and belief takes the form in men of calling into question the concept of morality itself. But these women's reluctance to judge stems rather from their uncertainty about their right to make moral statements, or perhaps from the price for them that such judgment seems to entail.

When women feel excluded from direct participation in society, they see themselves as subject to a consensus or judgment made and enforced by the men on whose protection and support they depend and by whose names they are known. A divorced middle-aged woman, mother of adolescent daughters, resident of a sophisticated university community, tells the story:

> As a woman, I feel I never understood that I was a person, that I could make decisions and I had a right to make decisions. I always felt that that belonged to my father or my husband in some way, or church, which was always represented by a male clergyman. They were the three men in my life: father, husband, and clergyman, and they had much more to say about what I should or shouldn't do. They were really authority figures which I accepted. It only lately has occurred to me that I never even rebelled against it, and my girls are much more conscious of this, not in the militant sense, but just in the recognizing sense . . . I still let things happen to me rather than make them happen, than make choices, although I know all about choices. I know the procedures and the steps and all. (*Do you have any clues about why this might be true?*) Well, I think in one sense there is less responsibility involved. Because if you make a dumb decision, you have to take the rap. If it happens

to you, well, you can complain about it. I think that if you don't grow up feeling that you ever have any choices, you don't have the sense that you have emotional responsibility. With this sense of choice comes this sense of responsibility.

The essence of moral decision is the exercise of choice and the willingness to accept responsibility for that choice. To the extent that women perceive themselves as having no choice, they correspondingly excuse themselves from the responsibility that decision entails. Childlike in the vulnerability of their dependence and consequent fear of abandonment, they claim to wish only to please, but in return for their goodness they expect to be loved and cared for. This, then, is an "altruism" always at risk, for it presupposes an innocence constantly in danger of being compromised by an awareness of the trade-off that has been made. Asked to describe herself, a college senior responds:

> I have heard of the onion-skin theory. I see myself as an onion, as a block of different layers. The external layers are for people that I don't know that well, the agreeable, the social, and as you go inward, there are more sides for people I know that I show. I am not sure about the innermost, whether there is a core, or whether I have just picked up everything as I was growing up, these different influences. I think I have a neutral attitude toward myself, but I do think in terms of good and bad. Good—I try to be considerate and thoughtful of other people, and I try to be fair in situations and be tolerant. I use the words, but I try and work them out practically. Bad things—I am not sure if they are bad, if they are altruistic or I am doing them basically for approval of other people. (*Which things are these?*) The values that I try to act out. They deal mostly with interpersonal relations . . . If I were doing things for approval, it would be a very tenuous thing. If I didn't get the right feedback, there might go all my values.

Ibsen's play *A Doll's House* depicts the explosion of just such a world through the eruption of a moral dilemma that calls into question the notion of goodness which lies at its center. Nora, the "squirrel wife," living with her husband as she lived with her father, puts into action this conception of goodness as sacrifice and, with the best of intentions, takes the law into her own hands. The crisis that ensues, most painfully for her in the repudiation of that goodness by the very person who was its recipient and beneficiary, causes her to reject the suicide that she initially saw as its ultimate expression and to choose instead to seek new and firmer answers to questions of identity and moral belief.

The availability of choice, and with it the onus of responsibility, has now invaded the most private sector of the woman's domain and threatens a similar explosion. For centuries, women's sexuality anchored them in passivity, in a receptive rather than an active stance, where the events of conception and childbirth could be controlled only by a withholding in which their own sexual needs were either denied or sacrificed. That such a sacrifice entailed a cost to their intelligence as well was seen by Freud when he tied the "undoubted intellectual inferiority of so many women" to "the inhibition of thought necessitated by sexual suppression." The strategies of withholding and denial that women have employed in the politics of sexual relations appear similar to their evasion or withholding of judgment in the moral realm. The hesitance of college students to assert a belief even in the value of human life, like the reluctance to claim one's sexuality, bespeaks a self uncertain of its strength, unwilling to deal with choice, and avoiding confrontation.

Thus women have traditionally deferred to the judgment of men, although often while intimating a sensibility of their own which is at variance with that judgment. Maggie Tulliver in *The Mill on the Floss* responds to the accusations that ensue from the discovery of her secretly continued relationship with Phillip Wakeham by acceding to her brother's moral judgment, while at the same time asserting a different set of standards by which she attests to her own superiority:

> I don't want to defend myself . . . I know I've been wrong—often continually. But yet, sometimes when I have done wrong, it has been because I have feelings that you would be the better for if you had them. If *you* were in fault ever, if you had done anything very wrong, I should be sorry for the pain it brought you; I should not want punishment to be heaped on you.

Maggie's protest is an eloquent assertion of the age-old split between thinking and feeling, justice and mercy, that underlies many of the clichés and stereotypes concerning the difference between the sexes. But considered from another point of view, her protest signifies a moment of confrontation, replacing a former evasion. This confrontation reveals two modes of judging, two different constructions of the moral domain—one traditionally associated with masculinity and the public world of social power, the other with femininity and the privacy of domestic interchange. The developmental ordering of these two points of view has been to consider the masculine as more adequate than the feminine and thus as replacing the feminine when the individual moves toward maturity. The reconciliation of these two modes, however, is not clear.

Norma Haan's research on college students and Constance Holstein's three-year study of adolescents and their parents indicate that the moral judgments of women differ from those of men in the greater extent to which women's judgments are tied to feelings of empathy and compassion and are concerned with the resolution of real as opposed to hypothetical dilemmas. However, as long as the categories by which development is assessed are derived from research on men, divergence from the masculine standard can be seen only as a failure of development. As a result, the thinking of women is often classified with that of children. The absence of alternative criteria that might better encompass the development of women, however, points not only to the limitations of theories framed by men and validated by research samples disproportionately male and adolescent, but also to the diffidence prevalent among women, their reluctance to speak publicly in their own voice, given the constraints imposed on them by their lack of power and the politics of relations between the sexes.

In order to go beyond the question, "How much like men do women think, how capable are they of engaging in the abstract and hypothetical construction of reality?" it is necessary to identify and define developmental criteria that encompass the categories of women's thought. Haan points out the necessity to derive such criteria from the resolution of the "more frequently occurring, real-life moral dilemmas of interpersonal, empathic, fellow-feeling concerns" which have long been the center of women's moral concern. But to derive developmental criteria from the language of women's moral discourse, it is necessary first to see whether women's construction of the moral domain relies on a language different from that of men and one that deserves equal credence in the definition of development. This in turn requires finding places where women have the power to choose and thus are willing to speak in their own voice.

When birth control and abortion provide women with effective means for controlling their fertility, the dilemma of choice enters a central arena of women's lives. Then the relationships that have traditionally defined women's identities and framed their moral judgments no longer flow inevitably from their reproductive capacity but become matters of decision over which they have control. Released from the passivity and reticence of a sexuality that binds them in dependence, women can question with Freud what it is that they want and can assert their own answers to that question. However, while society may affirm publicly the woman's right to choose for herself, the exercise of such choice brings her privately into conflict with the conventions of femininity, particularly the moral equation of goodness with self-sacrifice. Although independent assertion in judgment and action is considered to be the hallmark of adulthood, it is rather in their care and concern for others that women have both judged themselves and been judged.

The conflict between self and other thus constitutes the central moral problem for women, posing a dilemma whose resolution requires a reconciliation between femininity and adulthood. In the absence of such a reconciliation, the moral problem cannot be resolved. The "good woman" masks assertion in evasion, denying responsibility by claiming only to meet the needs of others, while the "bad woman" forgoes or renounces the commitments that bind her in self-deception and betrayal. It is precisely this dilemma—the conflict between compassion and autonomy, between virtue and power—which the feminine voice struggles to resolve in its effort to reclaim the self and to solve the moral problem in such a way that no one is hurt. . . .

In extending Piaget's description of children's moral judgment to the moral judgment of adolescents and adults, Kohlberg distinguishes three perspectives on moral conflict and choice. Tying moral development in adolescence to the growth of reflective thought at that time, Kohlberg terms these three views of morality preconventional, conventional, and postconventional, to reflect the expansion in moral understanding from an individual to a societal to a universal point of view. In this scheme, conventional morality, or the equation of the right or good with the maintenance of existing social norms and values, is always the point of departure. Whereas preconventional moral judgment denotes an inability to construct a shared or societal viewpoint, postconventional judgment transcends that vision. Preconventional judgment is egocentric and derives moral constructs from individual needs; conventional judgment is based on the shared norms and values that sustain relationships, groups, communities, and societies; and postconventional judgment adopts a reflective perspective on societal values and constructs moral principles that are universal in application.

This shift in perspective toward increasingly differentiated, comprehensive, and reflective forms of thought appears in women's responses to both actual and hypothetical dilemmas. But just as the conventions that shape women's moral judgment differ from those that apply to men, so also women's definition of the moral domain diverges from that derived from studies of men. Women's construction of the moral problem as a problem of care and responsibility in relationships rather than as one of rights and rules ties the development of their moral thinking to changes in their understanding of responsibility and relationships, just as the conception of morality as justice ties development to the logic of equality and reciprocity. Thus the logic underlying an ethic of care is a psychological logic of relationships, which contrasts with the formal logic of fairness that informs the justice approach.

Women's constructions of the abortion dilemma in particular reveal the existence of a distinct moral language whose evolution traces a sequence of development. This is the language of selfishness and responsibility, which defines the moral problem as one of obligation to exercise care and avoid hurt. The inflicting of hurt is considered selfish and immoral in its reflection of unconcern, while the expression of care is seen as the fulfillment of moral responsibility. The reiterative use by the women of the words *selfish* and *responsible* in talking about moral conflict and choice, given the underlying moral orientation that this language reflects sets the women apart from the men whom Kohlberg studied and points toward a different understanding of moral development. . . .

The moral imperative that emerges repeatedly in interviews with women is an injunction to care, a responsibility to discern and alleviate the "real and recognizable trouble" of this world. For men, the moral imperative appears rather as an injunction to respect the rights of others and thus to protect from interference the rights to life and self-fulfillment. Women's insistence on care is at first self-critical rather than self-protective, while men initially conceive obligation to others negatively in terms of noninterference. Development for both sexes would therefore seem to entail an integration of rights and responsibilities through the discovery of the complementarity of these disparate views. For women, the integration of rights and responsibilities takes place through an understanding of the psychological logic of relationships. This understanding tempers the self-destructive potential of a self-critical morality by asserting the need of all persons for care. For men, recognition through experience of the need for more active responsibility in taking care corrects the potential indifference of a morality of noninterference and turns attention from the logic to the consequences of choice. In the development of a postconventional ethical understanding, women come to see the violence inherent in inequality, while men come to see the limitations of a conception of justice blinded to the differences in human life. . . .

Ruth, the woman who spoke of her conflicting wishes to become a college president or to have another child, sees Heinz's dilemma as a choice between selfishness and sacrifice. For Heinz to steal the drug, given the circumstances of his life, which she infers from his inability to pay two thousand dollars, he would have "to do something which is not in his best interest, in that he is going to get sent away, and that is a supreme sacrifice, a sacrifice which I would say a person truly in love might be willing to make." However, not to steal the drug "would be selfish on his part. He would have to feel guilty about not allowing her a chance to live longer." Heinz's decision to steal is considered not in terms of the logical priority of life over property, which justifies its rightness, but rather in terms of the actual consequences that stealing would have for a man of limited means and little social power.

Considered in the light of its probable outcomes—his wife dead, or Heinz in jail, brutalized by the violence of that experience and his life compromised by a record of felony—the dilemma itself changes. Its resolution has less to do with the relative weights of life and property in an abstract moral conception than with the collision between two lives, formerly conjoined but now in opposition, where the continuation of one life can occur only at the expense of the other. This construction makes clear why judgment revolves around the issue of sacrifice and why guilt becomes the inevitable concomitant of either resolution.

Demonstrating the reticence noted in women's moral judgments, Ruth explains her reluctance to judge in terms of her belief:

> I think that everybody's existence is so different that I kind of say to myself, "That might be something that I wouldn't do," but I can't say that it is right or wrong for that person. I can only deal with what is appropriate for me to do when I am faced with specific problems.

Asked if she would apply to others her own injunction against hurting, she replies:

> I can't say that it is wrong. I can't say that it is right or that it's wrong, because I don't know what the person did that the other person did something to hurt him. So it is not right that the person got hurt, but it is right that the person who just lost the job has got the anger up and out. It doesn't put any bread on

his table, but it is released. I don't mean to be copping out. I really am trying to see how to answer these questions for you.

Her difficulty in arriving at definitive answers to moral questions, her sense of strain with the construction of Heinz's problem, stems from the divergence between these questions and her own frame of reference:

> I don't even think I use the words *right* and *wrong* anymore, and I know I don't use the word *moral*, because I am not sure I know what it means. We are talking about an unjust society, we are talking about a whole lot of things that are not right, that are truly wrong—to use the word that I don't use very often—and I have no control to change that. If I could change it, I certainly would, but I can only make my small contribution from day to day, and if I don't intentionally hurt somebody, that is my contribution to a better society. And so a chunk of that contribution is also not to pass judgment on other people, particularly when I don't know the circumstances of why they are doing certain things.

The reluctance to judge remains a reluctance to hurt, but one that stems not from a sense of personal vulnerability but rather from a recognition of the limitation of judgment itself. The deference of the conventional feminine perspective thus continues at the postconventional level, not as moral relativism but rather as part of a reconstructed moral understanding. Moral judgment is renounced in an awareness of the psychological and social determination of human behavior, at the same time that moral concern is reaffirmed in recognition of the reality of human pain and suffering:

> I have a real thing about hurting people and always have, and that gets a little complicated at times, because, for example, you don't want to hurt your child. I don't want to hurt my child, but if I don't hurt her sometimes, then that's hurting her more, you see, so that was a terrible dilemma for me.

Moral dilemmas are terrible in that they entail hurt. Ruth sees Heinz's decision as "the result of anguish: Who am I hurting? Why do I have to hurt them?" The morality of Heinz's theft is not in question, given the circumstances that necessitated it. What is at issue is his willingness to substitute himself for his wife and become, in her stead, the victim of exploitation by a society which breeds and legitimizes the druggist's irresponsibility and whose injustice in thus manifest in the very occurrence of the dilemma. . . .

The blind willingness to sacrifice people to truth, however, has always been the danger of an ethics abstracted from life. This willingness links Gandhi to the biblical Abraham, who prepared to sacrifice the life of his son in order to demonstrate the integrity and supremacy of his faith. Both men, in the limitations of their fatherhood, stand in implicit contrast to the woman who comes before Solomon and verifies her motherhood by relinquishing truth in order to save the life of her child. It is the ethics of an adulthood that has become principled at the expense of care that Erikson comes to criticize in his assessment of Gandhi's life.

This same criticism is dramatized explicitly as a contrast between the sexes in *The Merchant of Venice*, where Shakespeare goes through an extraordinary complication of sexual identity, dressing a male actor as a female character who in turn poses as a male judge, in order to bring into the masculine citadel of justice the feminine plea for mercy. The limitation of the contractual conception of justice is illustrated through the absurdity of its literal execution, while the need to "make exceptions all the time" is demonstrated contrapuntally in the matter of the rings. Portia, in calling for mercy, argues for that resolution in which no one is hurt, and as the men are forgiven for their failure to keep both their rings and their word, Antonio in turn forgoes his "right" to ruin Shylock. . . .

The sequence of women's moral judgment proceeds from an initial concern with survival to a focus on goodness and finally to a reflective understanding of care as the most adequate guide to the resolution of conflicts in human relationships. The abortion study demonstrates the centrality of the concepts of responsibility and care in women's thinking constructions of the moral domain, the close tie in women's thinking between conceptions of the self and of morality, and ultimately the need for an expanded developmental theory that includes, rather than rules out from consideration, the differences in the feminine voice. Such an inclusion seems essential, not only for explaining the development of women but also for understanding in both sexes the characteristics and precursors of an adult moral conception.

Discussion Questions

1. How do you answer Gilligan's questions: What does morality mean to you? Who is a genuinely moral person (and why)?

2. Do you find it difficult/unfair to hold others accountable to your moral standards? Why/why not?

3. Do you think that men and women view moral situations differently? If so, how? Do you think this difference results more from nature (i.e., brain structure) or nurture (i.e., the influence of society/culture)?

4. What value do you see in employing more of a "care-based" morality, as described here? What shortcomings do you notice? Do you think you can employ care-based ethics and still avoid moral relativism?

5. Given that a majority of textbooks and published articles are written by Caucasian males, what other issues (aside from the one mentioned by Gilligan) might arise from this?

6. How do you answer the Heinz Dilemma (described briefly in the introduction to this reading)? Determine not just what the man should do, but justify the action (or non-action): *Why* should he do so?

Ethical Egoism and the Virtue of Selfishness
Ayn Ranð

Russian-born Ayn (rhymes with "wine") Rand is most well known for her novels, primarily *The Fountainhead* (which has sold over 5 million copies since its release in 1943) and *Atlas Shrugged*, a thousand-plus page book that Library of Congress Book of the Month Club readers chose as second to the Bible as "the most influential book for Americans today."

In her novels Rand put forth her primary philosophy, "objectivism," which held that there is an objective reality to be discovered through reason alone; and that humans should exist as "ends in themselves"—politically and economically, each person is responsible for their own well-being, and through a "hands off" system of capitalism, each person can fulfill their potential by way of "rational self-interest."

In this selection—the Introduction and another essay from her book *The Virtue of Selfishness*—Rand provides a defense of *ethical egoism*, a moral theory that states that one ought to act in accord with one's own interests. This is in contrast to the theories of duty and of *altruism* (one *can* be morally obligated to sacrifice one's own interests for the good of others). Instead of adhering to duties and ethical prescriptions demanding that an agent ignore his or her own interests, Rand asserts that the *rational* thing to do is just the opposite. Elsewhere in her book, she asserts that the main problem with other ethical theories is their reliance on foundations outside of reason (and thus *irrational*), such as "Faith—instinct—revelation—feeling—taste—urge—wish—*whim*." She thus writes that deviating from *rationality* is the reason that the world is "collapsing to a lower and ever lower rung of hell." Through reason, she hopes to establish an objective ethics (thus, her philosophy is termed *Objectivism*).

It should be noted that, while she does not mention it here, ethical egoism (EE) is often based on the more descriptive theory of psychological egoism (PE). While EE *pre*scribes what one ought to do—i.e., you should do that which serves your own interests—PE *de*scribes how we naturally act—i.e., people are naturally inclined to act in order to serve their own interests. Thus, some hold that PE proves the truth of EE: If one cannot act otherwise (i.e., against one's best interests), then one cannot be morally required to do so. Rand, though, explicitly rejects PE on the grounds that it is wholly deterministic and thus not consistent with her position that we are free agents.

Reading Questions

1. How does Rand distinguish the exact meaning of *selfishness* from the "popular usage" of the word?
2. How does Rand define altruism? How does she show it to be an immoral and unjust system of ethics in her examination of the "beneficiary-criterion" as it relates to her examples of the "industrialist and bank robber," the young man who supports his parents, and the dictator?

Source: "Introduction, pp. vii–xii," "The Ethics of Emergencies," from *The Virtue of Selfishness* by Ayn Rand. Copyright © 1961, 1964 by Ayn Rand. Used by permission of Dutton Signet, a division of Penguin Group (USA) Inc.

3. What does Rand suggest results from adhering to the beneficiary-criterion?
4. How does Rand argue that her system of ethics does not justify simply doing as one pleases, acting on whims, and defining an action as moral simply because he chose it?
5. According to Rand, what four consequences result when one accepts the ethics of altruism?
6. What is the other side of altruism's "viciously false dichotomy"?
7. What role does *sacrifice* play in the ethics of altruism? How does Rand contrast this with the "rational principle of conduct"?
8. How does Rand incorporate love into her views of selfishness and sacrifice? Explain this in terms of her example of the husband whose wife is seriously ill. Why isn't he making a sacrifice by spending a fortune in attempting to cure her? Why would it be a sacrifice to let her die?
9. How does Rand apply her moral ethic to the case of a drowning person (both a stranger and a loved one)?
10. What is *integrity*, and how does it factor into Rand's moral system? In what ways does this relate to the moral nature of loving another and to the moral status of friendship?
11. How does Rand treat strangers from a moral standpoint? When ought one aid a stranger and why?
12. Explain Rand's use of the term "malevolent universe" as it relates to her criticism of altruist ethics.
13. What is the relevance of Rand's discussion of "'lifeboat' situations"?

Introduction

. . . The meaning ascribed in popular usage to the word "selfishness" is not merely wrong: It represents a devastating intellectual "package-deal," which is responsible, more than any other single factor, for the arrested moral development of mankind.

In popular usage, the word "selfishness" is a synonym of evil; the image it conjures is of a murderous brute who tramples over piles of corpses to achieve his own ends, who cares for no living being and pursues nothing but the gratification of the mindless whims of any immediate moment.

Yet the exact meaning and dictionary definition of the word "selfishness" is: *concern with one's own interests.*

This concept does *not* include a moral evaluation; it does not tell us whether concern with one's own interests is good or evil; nor does it tell us what constitutes man's actual interests. It is the task of ethics to answer such questions.

The ethics of altruism has created the image of the brute, as its answer, in order to make men accept two inhuman tenets: (a) that any concern with one's own interests is evil, regardless of what these interests might be, and (b) that the brute's activities are *in fact* to one's own interest (which altruism enjoins man to renounce for the sake of his neighbors). . . .

There are two moral questions which altruism lumps together into one "package-deal": (1) What are values? (2) Who should be the beneficiary of values? Altruism substitutes the second for the first; it evades the task of defining a code of moral values, thus leaving man, infact, without moral guidance.

Altruism declares that any action taken for the benefit of others is good, and any action taken for one's own benefit is evil. Thus the *beneficiary* of an action is the only criterion of moral value—and so long as that beneficiary is anybody other than oneself, anything goes.

Hence the appalling immorality, the chronic injustice, the grotesque double standards, the insoluble conflicts and contradictions that have characterized human relationships and human societies throughout history, under all the variants of the altruist ethics.

Observe the indecency of what passes for moral judgments today. An industrialist who produces a fortune, and a gangster who robs a bank are regarded as equally immoral, since they both sought wealth for their own "selfish" benefit. A young man who gives up his career in order to support his parents and never rises beyond the rank of grocery clerk is regarded as morally superior to the young man who endures an excruciating struggle and achieves his personal ambition. A dictator is regarded as moral, since the unspeakable atrocities he committed were intended to benefit "the people," not himself.

Observe what this beneficiary-criterion of morality does to a man's life. The first thing he learns is that morality is his enemy; he has nothing to gain from it, he can only lose; self-inflicted loss, self-inflicted pain, and the gray, debilitating pall of an incomprehensible duty is all that he can expect. He may hope that others might occasionally sacrifice themselves for his benefit, as he grudgingly sacrifices himself for theirs, but he knows that the relationship will bring mutual resentment, not pleasure—and that, morally, their pursuit of values will be like an exchange of unwanted, unchosen Christmas presents, which neither is morally permitted to buy for himself. Apart from such times as he manages to perform some act of self-sacrifice, he possesses no moral significance: Morality takes no cognizance of him and has nothing to say to him for guidance in the crucial issues of his life; it is only his own personal, private, "selfish" life and, as such, it is regarded either as evil or, at best, *amoral*.

Since nature does not provide man with an automatic form of survival, since he has to support his life by his own effort, the doctrine that concern with one's own interests is evil means that man's desire to live is evil—that man's life, as such, is evil. No doctrine could be more evil than that.

Yet that is the meaning of altruism, implicit in such examples as the equation of an industrialist with a robber. There is a fundamental moral difference between a man who sees his self-interest in production and a man who sees it in robbery. The evil of a robber does *not* lie in the fact that he pursues his own interests, but in *what* he regards as to his own interest; *not* in the fact that he pursues his values, but in *what* he chose to value; *not* in the fact that he wants to live, but in the fact that he wants to live on a subhuman level. . . .

If it is true that what I mean by "selfishness" is not what is meant convention-ally, then *this* is one of the worst indictments of altruism: It means that altruism *permits no concept* of a self-respecting, self-supporting man—a man who sup-ports his life by his own effect and neither sacrifices himself nor others. It means that altruism permits no view of men except as sacrificial animals and profiteers-on-sacrifice, as victims and parasites—that it permits no concept of a benevolent co-existence among men—that it permits no concept of *justice.*

If you wonder about the reasons behind the ugly mixture of cynicism and guilt in which most men spend their lives, these are the reasons: cynicism, because they neither practice nor accept the altruist morality—guilt, because they dare not reject it.

To rebel against so devastating an evil, one has to rebel against its basic premise. To redeem both man and morality, it is the concept of "*selfishness*" that one has to redeem.

The first step is to assert *man's right to a moral existence*—that is: to recognize his need of a moral code to guide the course and the fulfillment of his own life. . . .

The reasons why man needs a moral code will tell you that the purpose of morality is to define man's proper values and interests, that *concern with his own interests* is the essence of a moral existence, and that *man must be the beneficiary of his own moral actions.*

Since all values have to be gained and/or kept by men's actions, any breach between actor and beneficiary necessitates an injustice: the sacrifice of some men to others, of the actors to the nonactors, of the moral to the immoral. Nothing could ever justify such a breach, and no one ever has. . . .

The actor must always be the beneficiary of his action and man must act for his own *rational* self-interest. But his right to do so is derived from his nature as man and from the function of moral values in human life—and, therefore, is applicable *only* in the context of a rational, objectively demonstrated, and vali-dated code of moral principles which define and determine his actual self-interest. It is not a license "to do as he pleases" and it is not applicable to the altruists' image of a "selfish" brute nor to any man motivated by irrational emotions, feel-ings, urges, wishes or whims.

This is said as a warning against . . . the other side of the altruist coin: the men who believe that any action, regardless of its nature, is good if it is intended for one's own benefit. Just as the satisfaction of the irrational desires of others is *not* a criterion of moral value, neither is the satisfaction of one's own irrational desires. Morality is not a contest of whims. . . .

A similar type of error is committed by the man who declares that since man must be guided by his own independent judgment, any action he chooses to take is moral if *he* chooses it. One's own independent judgment is the *means* by which one must choose one's actions, but it is not a moral criterion nor a moral valida-tion: Only reference to a demonstrable principle can validate one's choices.

Just as man cannot survive by any random means, but must discover and practice the principles which his survival requires, so man's self-interest cannot be determined by blind desires or random whims, but must be discovered and achieved by the guidance of rational principles. This is why ... ethics is a morality of *rational self-interest* or of *rational selfishness.* ...

The attack on "selfishness" is an attack on man's self-esteem; to surrender one, is to surrender the other. ...

The Ethics of Emergencies

The psychological results of altruism may be observed in the fact that a great many people approach the subject of ethics by asking such questions as: "Should one risk one's life to help a man who is: (a) drowning, (b) trapped in a fire, (c) stepping in front of a speeding truck, (d) hanging by his fingernails over an abyss?"

Consider the implications of that approach. If a man accepts the ethics of altruism, he suffers the following consequences (in proportion to the degree of his acceptance):

1. Lack of self-esteem—since his first concern in the realm of values is not how to live his life, but how to sacrifice it.
2. Lack of respect for others—since he regards mankind as a herd of doomed beggars crying for someone's help.
3. A nightmare view of existence—since he believes that men are trapped in a "malevolent universe" where disasters are the constant and primary concern of their lives.
4. And, in fact, a lethargic indifference to ethics, a hopelessly cynical amorality— since his questions involve situations which he is not likely ever to encounter, which bear no relation to the actual problems of his own life and thus leave him to live without any moral principles whatever.

By elevating the issue of helping others into the central and primary issue of ethics, altruism has destroyed the concept of any authentic benevolence or good will among men. It has indoctrinated men with the idea that to value another human being is an act of selflessness, thus implying that a man can have no personal interest in others—that *to value* another means *to sacrifice* oneself—that any love, respect, or admiration a man may feel for others is not and cannot be a source of his own enjoyment, but is a threat to his existence, a sacrificial blank check signed over to his loved ones.

The men who accept that dichotomy but choose its other side, the ultimate products of altruism's dehumanizing influence, are those psychopaths who do not challenge altruism's basic premise, but proclaim their rebellion against self-sacrifice by announcing that they are totally indifferent to anything living and would not lift a finger to help a man or a dog left mangled by a hit-and-run driver (who is usually one of their own kind).

Most men do not accept or practice either side of altruism's viciously false dichotomy, but its result is a total intellectual chaos on the issue of proper human relationships and on such questions as the nature, purpose, or extent of the help one may give to others. Today, a great many well-meaning, reasonable men do not know how to identify or conceptualize the moral principles that motivate their love, affection or good will, and can find no guidance in the field of ethics, which is dominated by the stale platitudes of altruism. . . .

Man is not a sacrificial animal and help to others is not his moral duty. . . . This present discussion is concerned with the principles by which one identifies and evaluates the instances involving a man's *nonsacrificial* help to others.

"Sacrifice" is the surrender of a greater value for the sake of a lesser one or of a nonvalue. Thus, altruism gauges a man's virtue by the degree to which he surrenders, renounces, or betrays his values (since help to a stranger or an enemy is regarded as more virtuous, less "selfish," than help to those one loves). The rational principle of conduct is the exact opposite: Always act in accordance with the hierarchy of your values, and never sacrifice a greater value to a lesser one.

This applies to all choices, including one's actions toward other men. It requires that one possess a defined hierarchy of *rational* values (values chosen and validated by a rational standard). Without such a hierarchy, neither rational conduct nor considered value judgments nor moral choices are possible.

Love and friendship are profoundly personal, selfish values: Love is an expression and assertion of self-esteem, a response to one's own values in the person of another. One gains a profoundly personal, selfish joy from the mere existence of the person one loves. It is one's own personal, selfish happiness that one seeks, earns, and derives from love.

A "selfless," "disinterested" love is a contradiction in terms: It means that one is indifferent to that which one values.

Concern for the welfare of those one loves is a rational part of one's selfish interests. If a man who is passionately in love with his wife spends a fortune to cure her of a dangerous illness, it would be absurd to claim that he does it as a "sacrifice" for *her* sake, not his own, and that it makes no difference to *him*, personally and selfishly, whether she lives or dies.

Any action that a man undertakes for the benefit of those he loves is *not a sacrifice* if, in the hierarchy of his values, in the total context of the choices open to him, it achieves that which is of greatest *personal* (and rational) importance to *him*. In the above example, his wife's survival is of greater value to the husband than anything else that his money could buy, it is of greatest importance to his own happiness and, therefore, his action is *not* a sacrifice.

But suppose he let her die in order to spend his money on saving the lives of ten other women, none of whom meant anything to him—as the ethics of altruism would require. *That* would be a sacrifice. . . . If sacrifice is the moral principle of action, then that husband *should* sacrifice his wife for the sake of ten other women. What distinguishes the wife from the ten others? Nothing but her value to the husband who has to make the choice—nothing but the fact that *his* happiness requires her survival. . . .

Your highest moral purpose is the achievement of your own happiness, your money is yours, use it to save your wife, *that* is your moral right and your rational, moral choice.

Consider the soul of the altruistic moralist who would be prepared to tell that husband the opposite. (And then ask yourself whether altruism is motivated by benevolence.)

The proper method of judging when or whether one should help another person is by reference to one's own rational self-interest and one's own hierarchy of values: The time, money or effort one gives or the risk one takes should be proportionate to the value of the person in relation to one's own happiness.

To illustrate this on the altruists' favorite example: the issue of saving a drowning person. If the person to be saved is a stranger, it is morally proper to save him only when the danger to one's own life is minimal; when the danger is great, it would be immoral to attempt it: Only a lack of selfesteem could permit one to value one's life no higher than that of any random stranger. (And, conversely, if one is drowning, one cannot expect a stranger to risk his life for one's sake, remembering that one's life cannot be as valuable to him as his own.)

If the person to be saved is not a stranger, then the risk one should be willing to take is greater in proportion to the greatness of that person's value to oneself. If it is the man or woman one loves, then one can be willing to give one's own life to save him or her—for the selfish reason that life without the loved person could be unbearable.

Conversely, if a man is able to swim and to save his drowning wife, but becomes panicky, gives in to an unjustified, irrational fear and lets her drown, then spends his life in loneliness and misery—one would not call him "selfish"; one would condemn him morally for his treason to himself and to his own values, that is: his failure to fight for the preservation of a value crucial to his own happiness. Remember that values are that which one acts to gain and/or keep, and that one's own happiness is the moral purpose of one's life, the man who fails to achieve it because of his own default, because of his failure to fight for it, is morally guilty.

The virtue involved in helping those one loves is not "selflessness" or "sacrifice," but *integrity*. Integrity is loyalty to one's convictions and values; it is the policy of acting in accordance with one's values, of expressing, upholding, and translating them into practical reality. If a man professes to love a woman, yet his actions are indifferent, inimical, or damaging to her, it is his lack of integrity that makes him immoral.

The same principle applies to relationships among friends. If one's friend is in trouble, one should act to help him by whatever nonsacrificial means are appropriate. For instance, if one's friend is starving, it is not a sacrifice, but an act of integrity to give him money for food rather than buy some insignificant gadget for oneself, because his welfare is important in the scale of one's personal values. If the gadget means more than the friend's suffering, one had no business pretending to be his friend.

The practical implementation of friendship, affection, and love consists of incorporating the welfare (the *rational* welfare) of the person involved into one's own hierarchy of values, then acting accordingly.

But this is a reward which men have to earn by means of their virtues and which one cannot grant to mere acquaintances or strangers.

What, then, should one properly grant to strangers? The generalized respect and good will which one should grant to a human being in the name of the potential value he represents—until and unless he forfeits it.

A rational man does not forget that *life* is the source of all values and, as such, a common bond among living beings (as against inanimate matter), that other men are potentially able to achieve the same virtues as his own and thus be of enormous value to him. This does not mean that he regards human lives as interchangeable with his own. He recognizes the fact that his own life is the *source*, not only of all his values, but of *his capacity to value*. Therefore, the value he grants to others is only a consequence, an extension, a secondary projection of the primary value which is himself. . . .

Since men are born *tabula rasa*, both cognitively and morally, a rational man regards strangers as innocent until proved guilty, and grants them that initial good will in the name of their human potential. After that, he judges them according to the moral character they have actualized. If he finds them guilty of major evils, his good will is replaced by contempt and moral condemnation. (If one values human life, one cannot value its destroyers.) If he finds them to be virtuous, he grants them personal, individual value and appreciation, in proportion to their virtues.

It is on the ground of that generalized good will and respect for the value of human life that one helps strangers in an emergency—*and only in an emergency*.

It is important to differentiate between the rules of conduct in an emergency situation and the rules of conduct in the normal conditions of human existence. This does not mean a double standard of morality: The standard and the basic principles remain the same, but their application to either case requires precise definitions.

An emergency is an unchosen, unexpected event, limited in time, that creates conditions under which human survival is impossible—such as a flood, an earthquake, a fire, a shipwreck. In an emergency situation, men's primary goal is to combat the disaster, escape the danger and restore normal conditions (to reach dry land, to put out the fire, etc.).

By "normal" conditions I mean *metaphysically* normal, normal in the nature of things, and appropriate to human existence. Men can live on land, but not in water or in a raging fire. Since men are not omnipotent, it is metaphysically possible for unforeseeable disasters to strike them, in which case their only task is to return to those conditions under which their lives can continue. By its nature, an emergency situation is temporary; if it were to last, men would perish.

It is only in emergency situations that one should volunteer to help strangers, if it is in one's power. For instance, a man who values human life and is caught in a shipwreck, should help to save his fellow passengers (though not at the expense of his own life). But this does not mean that after they all reach shore, he should devote his efforts to saving his fellow passengers from poverty, ignorance, neurosis, or whatever other troubles they might have. Nor does it mean that he should spend his life sailing the seven seas in search of shipwreck victims to save.

Or to take an example that can occur in everyday life: Suppose one hears that the man next door is ill and penniless. Illness and poverty are not metaphysical emergencies, they are part of the normal risks of existence; but since the man is temporarily helpless, one may bring him food and medicine, *if* one can afford it (as an act of good will, not of duty) or one may raise a fund among the neighbors to help him out. But this does not mean that one must support him from then on, nor that one must spend one's life looking for starving men to help.

In the normal conditions of existence, man has to choose his goals, project them in time, pursue them, and achieve them by his own effort. He cannot do it if his goals are at the mercy of and must be sacrificed to any misfortune happening to others. He cannot live his life by the guidance of rules applicable only to conditions under which human survival is impossible.

The principle that one should help men in an emergency cannot be extended to regard all human suffering as an emergency and to turn the misfortune of some into a first mortgage on the lives of others.

Poverty, ignorance, illness, and other problems of that kind are not metaphysical emergencies. By the *metaphysical* nature of man and of existence, man has to maintain his life by his own effort; the values he needs—such as wealth or knowledge—are not given to him automatically, as a gift of nature, but have to be discovered and achieved by his own thinking and work. One's sole obligation toward others, in this respect, is to maintain a social system that leaves men free to achieve, to gain and to keep their values.

Every code of ethics is based on and derived from a metaphysics, that is: from a theory about the fundamental nature of the universe in which man lives and acts. The altruist ethics is based on a "malevolent universe" metaphysics, on the theory that man, by his very nature, is helpless and doomed—that success, happiness, achievement are impossible to him—that emergencies, disasters, catastrophes are the norm of his life and that his primary goal is to combat them.

As the simplest empirical refutation of that metaphysics—as evidence of the fact that the material universe is not inimical to man and that catastrophes are the exception, not the rule of his existence—observe the fortunes made by insurance companies.

Observe also that the advocates of altruism are unable to base their ethics on any facts of men's normal existence and that they always offer "lifeboat" situations as examples from which to derive the rules of moral conduct. ("What should you do if you and another man are in a lifeboat that can carry only one?" etc.)

The fact is that men do not live in lifeboats—and that a lifeboat is not the place on which to base one's metaphysics.

The moral purpose of a man's life is the achievement of his own happiness. This does not mean that he is indifferent to all men, that human life is of no value to him and that he has no reason to help others in an emergency. But it *does* mean that he does not subordinate his life to the welfare of others, that he does not sacrifice himself to their needs, that the relief of their suffering is not his primary concern, that any help he gives is an *exception*, not a rule, an act of generosity, not of moral duty, that it is *marginal* and *incidental*—as disasters are marginal and incidental in the course of human existence—and that *values*, not disasters, are the goal, the first concern and the motive power of his life.

(February 1963)

Discussion Questions

1. Altruism is typically considered to be a virtue and even as the "ultimate act." How do you evaluate the four consequences of this as suggested by Rand at the beginning of her essay? What truth is there in her comment, "Altruism has destroyed the concept of any authentic benevolence"?
2. How does Rand's view of love compare to yours? In what sense is love selfish? In what sense is it self*less*?
3. Culture typically views selfishness in a negative light. How do you view selfishness? Does Rand's view of selfishness change its moral status in your mind? In what ways docs acting altruistically have greater moral worth than acting selfishly? In what ways does it demean the self and, thus, have lesser moral worth?
4. Rand mentions "lifeboat situations"—hypothetical thought experiments in which you are on a lifeboat that will sink unless one or more people sacrifice themselves for the good of the whole. Are there situations when you would sacrifice yourself for the good of those on the lifeboat? Who would have to be on the boat in order for you to take your own life? Would you *ever* forfeit your life for the sakc of others? What is the *moral* status of this decision?
5. How does Rand's theory apply to distributive justice? When *ought* you help those in need? What moral duty do you have to strangers who are starving?
6. It is argued by some that psychological egoism—we can *only* act out of self-intcrest—drives the moral doctrine of ethical egoism—that we *ought* to act out of self-interest. How do you evaluate this claim? *Can* you act in a way that is not in your own interest? What would that mean?
7. Distinguish *selfish* behavior from *self-interested* behavior. In what ways is smoking cigarettes one but not the other? Is this distinction important in determining the value of ethical egoism?

Issues in Applied Ethics

This section includes articles under the heading of what is commonly called *applied ethics*—it examines moral issues that require action and application. It differs from the preceding section that focused primarily on moral *theory* and how we can determine a system of morals to begin with.

Ethicists currently work in many areas of society. Most hospitals have medical ethicists on staff and you will find a number of articles in this section extracted from medical journals. Likewise, government agencies up through the White House often rely on ethicists to inform policy. The "President's Council on Bioethics" recently weighed in on such current issues as cloning and stem cell research, among many others.

In reading these articles, you will likely recognize the importance of many of the topics covered in previous chapters of this book: The soul and personal identity, personhood, theories of knowledge and methods of science, religion, suffering, justice, fairness, rights, morality—these are all integral in the cross-disciplinary demands of today's most challenging ethical issues.

The articles that follow are grouped together to provide a look at both sides of each topic. Your challenge as a reader is to decipher the following:

- Determine the respective author's position.
- Determine how he or she defends that position. Have they adequately defended their position? If not, why not?
- What counter-arguments have the authors considered and defended? What counter-arguments have they failed to consider?
- Have the authors provided any analogies? Do you find the analogies applicable? Do you agree with the conclusion provided by the analogies?
- Have the authors addressed any of the concerns or theories suggested by the author of the other article in that section?
- How would you apply any of the moral theories from the previous section to the issues in this section?
- What is *your* position on each issue? How do you defend that position?

Abortion

On the Moral and Legal Status of Abortion

Mary Anne Warren

The question which we must answer in order to produce a satisfactory solution to the problem of the moral status of abortion is this: How are we to define the moral community, the set of beings with full and equal moral rights, such that we can decide whether a human fetus is a member of this community or not? What sort of entity, exactly, has the inalienable rights to life, liberty, and the pursuit of happiness? Jefferson attributed these rights to all *men*, and it may or may not be fair to suggest that he intended to attribute them *only* to men. Perhaps he ought to have attributed them to all human beings. If so, then we arrive, first, at [John] Noonan's problem of defining what makes a being human, and, second, at the equally vital question which Noonan does not consider, namely, What reason is there for identifying the moral community with the set of all human beings, in whatever way we have chosen to define that term?

1. On the Definition of "Human"

One reason why this vital second question is so frequently overlooked in the debate over the moral status of abortion is that the term "human" has two distinct, but not often distinguished, senses. This fact results in a slide of meaning,

Source: Copyright © 1973 *The Monist:* An International Quarterly Journal of General Philosophical Inquiry, Peru, Illinois, USA 61354. Reprinted by permission.
Postscript on Infanticide: Wasserstrom, Richard A., *Today's Moral Problems,* 3rd Edition. Copyright © 1985, pp. 447–448. Reprinted by permission of Pearson Education, Inc., Upper Saddle River, NJ.

which serves to conceal the fallaciousness of the traditional argument that since (1) it is wrong to kill innocent human beings, and (2) fetuses are innocent human beings, then (3) it is wrong to kill fetuses. For if "human" is used in the same sense in both (1) and (2) then, whichever of the two senses is meant, one of these premises is question-begging. And if it is used in two different senses then of course the conclusion doesn't follow.

Thus, (1) is a self-evident moral truth,[11] and avoids begging the question about abortion, only if "human being" is used to mean something like "a full-fledged member of the moral community." (It may or may not also be meant to refer exclusively to members of the species *Homo sapiens*.) We may call this the *moral* sense of "human." It is not to be confused with what we will call the *genetic* sense, i.e., the sense in which *any* member of the species is a human being, and no member of any other species could be. If (1) is acceptable only if the moral sense is intended, (2) is nonquestion-begging only if what is intended is the genetic sense.

In "Deciding Who Is Human," Noonan argues for the classification of fetuses with human beings by pointing to the presence of the full genetic code, and the potential capacity for rational thought.[12] It is clear that what he needs to show, for his version of the traditional argument to be valid, is that fetuses are human in the moral sense, the sense in which it is analytically true that all human beings have full moral rights. But, in the absence of any argument showing that whatever is genetically human is also morally human, and he gives none, nothing more than genetic humanity can be demonstrated by the presence of the human genetic code. And, as we will see, the *potential* capacity for rational thought can at most show that an entity has the potential for *becoming* human in the moral sense.

2. Defining the Moral Community

Can it be established that genetic humanity is sufficient for moral humanity? I think that there are very good reasons for not defining the moral community in this way. I would like to suggest an alternative way of defining the moral community, which I will argue for only to the extent of explaining why it is, or should be, self-evident. The suggestion is simply that the moral community consists of all and only *people*, rather than all and only human beings,[13] and probably the best way of demonstrating its self-evidence is by considering the concept of personhood, to see what sorts of entity are and are not persons, and what the decision that a being is or is not a person implies about its moral rights.

What characteristics entitle an entity to be considered a person? This is obviously not the place to attempt a complete analysis of the concept of personhood, but we do not need such a fully adequate analysis just to determine whether and why a fetus is or isn't a person. All we need is a rough and approximate list of the most basic criteria of personhood, and some idea of which, or how many, of these an entity must satisfy in order to properly be considered a person.

In searching for such criteria, it is useful to look beyond the set of people with whom we are acquainted, and ask how we would decide whether a totally alien being was a person or not. (For we have no right to assume that genetic humanity is necessary for personhood.) Imagine a space traveler who lands on an unknown planet and encounters a race of beings utterly unlike any he has ever seen or heard of. If he wants to be sure of behaving morally toward these beings, he has to somehow decide whether they are people, and hence have full moral rights, or whether they are the sort of thing which he need not feel guilty about treating as, for example, a source of food.

How should he go about making this decision? If he has some anthropological background, he might look for such things as religion, art, and the manufacturing of tools, weapons, or shelters, since these factors have been used to distinguish our human from our prehuman ancestors, in what seems to be closer to the moral than the genetic sense of "human." And no doubt he would be right to consider the presence of such factors as good evidence that the alien beings were people, and morally human. It would, however, be overly anthropocentric of him to take the absence of these things as adequate evidence that they were not, since we can imagine people who have progressed beyond, or evolved without ever developing, these cultural characteristics.

I suggest that the traits which are most central to the concept of personhood, or humanity in the moral sense, are, very roughly, the following:

1. consciousness (of objects and events external and/or internal to the being), and in particular the capacity to feel pain;
2. reasoning (the *developed* capacity to solve new and relatively complex problems);
3. self-motivated activity (activity which is relatively independent of either genetic or direct external control);
4. the capacity to communicate, by whatever means, messages of an indefinite variety of types, that is, not just with an indefinite number of possible contents, but on indefinitely many possible topics;
5. the presence of self-concepts, and self-awareness, either individual or racial, or both.

Admittedly, there are apt to be a great many problems involved in formulating precise definitions of these criteria, let alone in developing universally valid behavioral criteria for deciding when they apply. But I will assume that both we and our explorer know approximately what (1)–(5) mean, and that he is also able to determine whether or not they apply. How, then, should he use his findings to decide whether or not the alien beings are people? We needn't suppose that an entity must have *all* of these attributes to be properly considered a person; (1) and (2) alone may well be sufficient for personhood, and quite probably (1)–(3) are sufficient. Neither do we need to insist that any one of these criteria is *necessary* for personhood, although once again (1) and (2) look like fairly good candidates for necessary conditions, as does (3), if "activity" is construed so as to include the activity of reasoning.

All we need to claim, to demonstrate that a fetus is not a person, is that any being which satisfies *none* of (1)–(5) is certainly not a person. I consider this claim to be so obvious that I think anyone who denied it, and claimed that a being which satisfied none of (1)–(5) was a person all the same, would thereby demonstrate that he had no notion at all of what a person is—perhaps because he had confused the concept of a person with that of genetic humanity. If the opponents of abortion were to deny the appropriateness of these five criteria, I do not know what further arguments would convince them. We would probably have to admit that our conceptual schemes were indeed irreconcilably different, and that our dispute could not be settled objectively.

I do not expect this to happen, however, since I think that the concept of a person is one which is very nearly universal (to people), and that it is common to both proabortionists and antiabortionists, even though neither group has fully realized the relevance of this concept to the resolution of their dispute. Furthermore, I think that on reflection even the antiabortionists ought to agree not only that (1)–(5) are central to the concept of personhood, but also that it is a part of this concept that all and only people have full moral rights. The concept of a person is in part a moral concept; once we have admitted that x is a person we have recognized, even if we have not agreed to respect, x's right to be treated as a member of the moral community. It is true that the claim that x *is a human being* is more commonly voiced as part of an appeal to treat x decently than is the claim that x is a person, but this is either because "human being" is here used in the sense which implies personhood, or because the genetic and moral senses of "human" have been confused.

Now if (1)–(5) are indeed the primary criteria of personhood, then it is clear that genetic humanity is neither necessary nor sufficient for establishing that an entity is a person. Some human beings are not people, and there may well be people who are not human beings. A man or woman whose consciousness has been permanently obliterated but who remains alive is a human being which is no longer a person; defective human beings, with no appreciable mental capacity, are not and presumably never will be people; and a fetus is a human being which is not yet a person, and which therefore cannot coherently be said to have full moral rights. Citizens of the next century should be prepared to recognize highly advanced, self-aware robots or computers, should such be developed, and intelligent inhabitants of other worlds, should such be found, as people in the fullest sense, and to respect their moral rights. But to ascribe full moral rights to an entity which is not a person is as absurd as to ascribe moral obligations and responsibilities to such an entity.

3. Fetal Development and the Right to Life

Two problems arise in the application of these suggestions for the definition of the moral community to the determination of the precise moral status of a human fetus. Given that the paradigm example of a person is a normal adult human being, then (1) How like this paradigm, in particular how far advanced since conception, does a human being need to be before it begins to have a right to life by virtue, not of being fully a person as of yet, but of being *like* a person? and (2) To what extent, if any, does the fact that a fetus has the *potential* for becoming a person endow it with some of the same rights? Each of these questions requires some comment.

In answering the first question, we need not attempt a detailed consideration of the moral rights of organisms which are not developed enough, aware enough, intelligent enough, etc., to be considered people, but which resemble people in some respects. It does seem reasonable to suggest that the more like a person, in the relevant respects, a being is, the stronger is the case for regarding it as having a right to life, and indeed the stronger its right to life is. Thus we ought to take seriously the suggestion that, insofar as "the human individual develops biologically in a continuous fashion . . . the rights of a human person might develop in the same way."[14] But we must keep in mind that the attributes which are relevant in determining whether or not an entity is enough like a person to be regarded as having some of the same moral rights are no different from those which are relevant to determining whether or not it is fully a person—i.e., are no different from (1)–(5)—and that being genetically human, or having recognizably human facial and other physical features, or detectable brain activity, or the capacity to survive outside the uterus, are simply not among these relevant attributes.

Thus it is clear that even though a seven- or eight-month fetus has features which make it apt to arouse in us almost the same powerful protective instinct as is commonly aroused by a small infant, nevertheless it is not significantly more personlike than is a very small embryo. It is *somewhat* more personlike; it can apparently feel and respond to pain, and it may even have a rudimentary form of consciousness, insofar as its brain is quite active. Nevertheless, it seems safe to say that it is not fully conscious, in the way that an infant of a few months is, and that it cannot reason, or communicate messages of indefinitely many sorts, does not engage in self-motivated activity, and has no self-awareness. Thus, in the *relevant* respects, a fetus, even a fully developed one, is considerably less personlike than is the average mature mammal, indeed the average fish. And I think that a rational person must conclude that if the right to life of a fetus is to be based upon its resemblance to a person, then it cannot be said to have any more right to life than, let us say, a newborn guppy (which also seems to be capable of feeling pain), and that a right of that magnitude could never override a woman's right to obtain an abortion, at any stage of her pregnancy.

There may, of course, be other arguments in favor of placing legal limits upon the stage of pregnancy in which an abortion may be performed. Given the relative safety of the new techniques of artificially inducing labor during the third trimester, the danger to the woman's life or health is no longer such an argument. Neither is the fact that people tend to respond to the thought of abortion in the later stages of pregnancy with emotional repulsion, since mere emotional responses cannot take the place of moral reasoning in determining what ought to be permitted. Nor, finally, is the frequently heard argument that legalizing abortion, especially late in the pregnancy, may erode the level of respect for human life, leading, perhaps, to an increase in unjustified euthanasia and other crimes.

For this threat, if it is a threat, can be better met by educating people to the kinds of moral distinctions which we are making here than by limiting access to abortion (which limitation may, in its disregard for the rights of women, be just as damaging to the level of respect for human rights).

Thus, since the fact that even a fully developed fetus is not personlike enough to have any significant right to life on the basis of its personlikeness shows that no legal restrictions upon the stage of pregnancy in which an abortion may be performed can be justified on the grounds that we should protect the rights of the older fetus, and since there is no other apparent justification for such restrictions, we may conclude that they are entirely unjustified. Whether or not it would be *indecent* (whatever that means) for a woman in her seventh month to obtain an abortion just to avoid having to postpone a trip to Europe, it would not, in itself, be *immoral*, and therefore it ought to be permitted.

4. Potential Personhood and the Right to Life

We have seen that a fetus does not resemble a person in any way which can support the claim that it has even some of the same rights. But what about its *potential*, the fact that if nurtured and allowed to develop naturally it will very probably become a person? Doesn't that alone give it at least some right to life? It is hard to deny that the fact that an entity is a potential person is a strong prima facie reason for not destroying it; but we need not conclude from this that a potential person has a right to life, by virtue of that potential. It may be that our feeling that it is better, other things being equal, not to destroy a potential person is better explained by the fact that potential people are still (felt to be) an invaluable resource, not to be lightly squandered. Surely, if every speck of dust were a potential person, we would be much less apt to conclude that every potential person has a right to become actual.

Still, we do not need to insist that a potential person has no right to life whatever. There may well be something immoral, and not just imprudent, about wantonly destroying potential people, when doing so isn't necessary to protect anyone's rights. But even if a potential person does have some prima facie right to life, such a right could not possibly outweigh the right of a woman to obtain an abortion, since the rights of any actual person invariably outweigh those of any potential person, whenever the two conflict. Since this may not be immediately obvious in the case of a human fetus, let us look at another case.

Suppose that our space explorer falls into the hands of an alien culture, whose scientists decide to create a few hundred thousand or more human beings, by breaking his body into its component cells, and using these to create fully developed human beings, with, of course, his genetic code. We may imagine that each of these newly created men will have all of the original man's abilities, skills, knowledge, and so on, and also have an individual self-concept, in short that each of them will be a bona fide (though hardly unique) person. Imagine that the whole project will take only seconds, and that its chances of success are extremely high, and that our explorer knows all of this, and also knows that these people will be treated fairly. I maintain that in such a situation he would have every right to escape if he could, and thus to deprive all of these potential people of their potential lives; for his right to life outweighs all of theirs together, in spite of the fact that they are all genetically human, all innocent, and all have a very high probability of becoming people very soon, if only he refrains from acting.

Indeed, I think he would have a right to escape even if it were not his life which the alien scientists planned to take, but only a year of his freedom, or, indeed, only a day. Nor would he be obligated to stay if he had gotten captured (thus bringing all these people-potentials into existence) because of his own carelessness, or even if he had done so deliberately, knowing the consequences. Regardless of how he got captured, he is not morally obligated to remain in captivity for *any* period of time for the sake of permitting any number of potential people to come into actuality, so great is the margin by which one actual person's right to liberty outweighs whatever right to life even a hundred thousand potential people have. And it seems reasonable to conclude that the rights of a woman will outweigh by a similar margin whatever right to life a fetus may have by virtue of its potential personhood.

Thus, neither a fetus's resemblance to a person, nor its potential for becoming a person provides any basis whatever for the claim that it has any significant right to life. Consequently, a woman's right to protect her health, happiness, freedom, and even her life,[15] by terminating an unwanted pregnancy, will always override whatever right to life it may be appropriate to ascribe to a fetus, even a fully developed one. And thus, in the absence of any overwhelming social need for every possible child, the laws which restrict the right to obtain an abortion, or limit the period of pregnancy during which an abortion may be performed, are a wholly unjustified violation of a woman's most basic moral and constitutional rights.[16]

Postscript on Infanticide

Since the publication of this article, many people have written to point out that my argument appears to justify not only abortion, but infanticide as well. For a newborn infant is not significantly more personlike than an advanced fetus, and consequently it would seem that if the destruction of the latter is permissible so too must be that of the former. Inasmuch as most people, regardless of how they feel about the morality of abortion, consider infanticide a form of murder, this might appear to represent a serious flaw in my argument.

Now, if I am right in holding that it is only people who have a full-fledged right to life, and who can be murdered, and if the criteria of personhood are as I have described them, then it obviously follows that killing a newborn infant isn't murder. It does *not* follow, however, that infanticide is permissible, for two reasons. In the first place, it would be wrong, at least in this country and in this period of history, and other things being equal, to kill a newborn infant, because even if its parents do not want it and would not suffer from its destruction, there are other people who would like to have it, and would, in all probability, be deprived of a great deal of pleasure by its destruction. Thus, infanticide is wrong for reasons analogous to those which make it wrong to wantonly destroy natural resources, or great works of art.

Secondly, most people, at least in this country, value infants and would much prefer that they be preserved, even if foster parents are not immediately available. Most of us would rather be taxed to support orphanages than allow unwanted infants to be destroyed. So long as there are people who want an infant preserved, and who are willing and able to provide the means of caring for it, under reasonably humane conditions, it is *ceteris paribus*, wrong to destroy it.

But, it might be replied, if this argument shows that infanticide is wrong, at least at this time and in this country, doesn't it also show that abortion is wrong? After all, many people value fetuses, are disturbed by their destruction, and would much prefer that they be preserved, even at some cost to themselves. Furthermore, as a potential source of pleasure to some foster family, a fetus is just as valuable as an infant. There is, however, a crucial difference between the two cases: So long as the fetus is unborn, its preservation, contrary to the wishes of the pregnant woman, violates her rights to freedom, happiness, and self-determination. Her rights override the rights of those who would like the fetus preserved, just as if someone's life or limb is threatened by a wild animal, his right to protect himself by destroying the animal overrides the rights of those who would prefer that the animal not be harmed.

The minute the infant is born, however, its preservation no longer violates any of its mother's rights, even if she wants it destroyed, because she is free to put it up for adoption. Consequently, while the moment of birth does not mark any sharp discontinuity in the degree to which an infant possesses the right to life, it does mark the end of its mother's right to determine its fate. Indeed, if abortion could be performed without killing the fetus, she would never possess the right to have the fetus destroyed, for the same reasons that she has no right to have an infant destroyed.

On the other hand, it follows from my argument that when an unwanted or defective infant is born into a society which cannot afford and/or is not willing to care for it, then its destruction is permissible. This conclusion will, no doubt, strike many people as heartless and immoral; but remember that the very existence of people who feel this way, and who are willing and able to provide care for unwanted infants, is reason enough to conclude that they should be preserved.

Abortion and the "Feminine Voice"

Celia Wolf-Devine

A growing number of feminists now seek to articulate the "feminine voice," to draw attention to women's special strengths, and to correct the systematic devaluation of these by our male-dominated society. Carol Gilligan's book, *In a Different Voice*, was especially important to the emergence of this strain of feminist

Source: Reprinted by permission of the author and Public Affairs Quarterly.

thought. It was her intention to help women identify more positively with their own distinctive style of reasoning about ethics, instead of feeling that there is something wrong with them because they do not think like men (as Kohlberg's and Freud's theories would imply). Inspired by her work, feminists such as Nel Noddings, Annette Baier, and the contributors to *Women and Moral Theory*,[17] have tried to articulate further the feminine voice in moral reasoning. Others such as Carol McMillan, Adrienne Rich, Sara Ruddick, and Nancy Harstock agree that women have distinct virtues, and argue that these need not be self-victimizing.[18] When properly transformed by a feminist consciousness, women's different characteristics can, they suggest, be productive of new social visions.

Similar work is also being done by feminists who try to correct for masculine bias in other areas such as our conception of human nature, the way we view the relationship between people and nature, and the kinds of paradigms we employ in thinking about society.[19]

Some of those engaged in this enterprise hold that women by *nature* possess certain valuable traits that men do not, but more frequently, they espouse the weaker position that, on the whole, the traits they label "feminine" are more common among women (for reasons which are at least partly cultural), but that they also can be found in men, and that they should be encouraged as good traits for a human being to have, regardless of sex.[20]

Virtually all of those feminists who are trying to reassert the value of the feminine voice, also express the sort of unqualified support for free access to abortion which has come to be regarded as a central tenet of feminist "orthodoxy." What I wish to argue in this paper is that: (1) abortion is, by their own accounts, clearly a masculine response to the problems posed by an unwanted pregnancy, and is thus highly problematic for those who seek to articulate and defend the "feminine voice" as the proper mode of moral response, and that (2) on the contrary the "feminine voice" as it has been articulated generates a strong presumption against abortion as a way of responding to an unwanted pregnancy.[21]

These conclusions, I believe, can be argued without relying on a precise determination of the moral status of the fetus. A case at least can be made that the fetus is a person since it is biologically a member of the human species and will, in time, develop normal human abilities. Whether the burden of proof rests on those who defend the personhood of the fetus, or on those who deny it, is a matter of moral methodology, and for that reason will depend in part on whether one adopts a masculine or feminine approach to moral issues.

I. *Masculine Voice/Feminine Voice*

A. Moral Reasoning

According to Gilligan, girls, being brought up by mothers, identify with them, while males must define themselves through separation from their mothers. As a result, girls have "a basis for empathy built into their primary definition of self in a way that boys do not."[22] Thus while masculinity is defined by separation and threatened by intimacy, femininity is defined through attachment and threatened by separation; girls come to understand themselves as imbedded within a network of personal relationships.

A second difference concerns attitudes toward general rules and principles. Boys tend to play in larger groups than girls, and become "increasingly fascinated with the legal elaboration of rules, and the development of fair procedures for adjudicating conflicts."[23] We thus find men conceiving of morality largely in terms of adjudicating fairly between the conflicting rights of self-assertive individuals.

Girls play in smaller groups, and accord a greater importance to relationships than to following rules. They are especially sensitive to the needs of the particular other, instead of emphasizing impartiality, which is more characteristic of the masculine perspective. They think of morality more in terms of having responsibilities for taking care of others, and place a high priority upon preserving the network of relationships which makes this possible. While the masculine justice perspective requires detachment, the feminine care perspective sees detachment and separation as themselves the moral problem.[24]

Inspired by Gilligan, many feminist philosophers have discovered a masculine bias in traditional ethical theories. Nel Noddings has written a book called *Caring: A Feminine Approach to Ethics,* Annette Baier has praised Hume for his emphasis on the role of the affections in ethics[25] and proposed that trust be taken as the central notion for ethical theory.[26] Christina Hoff Sommers has argued for giving a central role to special relationships in ethics.[27] And Virginia Held has suggested that the mother-child relationship be seen as paradigmatic of human relationships, instead of the economic relationship of buyer/seller (which she sees to be the ruling paradigm now).[28]

The feminine voice in ethics attends to the particular other, thinks in terms of responsibilities to care for others, is sensitive to our interconnectedness, and strives to preserve relationships. It contrasts with the masculine voice, which speaks in terms of justice and rights, stresses consistency and principles, and emphasizes the autonomy of the individual and impartiality in one's dealings with others.

B. Human Nature: Mind and Body

Feminist writers have also discovered a masculine bias in the way we think of mind and body and the relationship between them. A large number of feminists, for example, regard radical mind/body dualism as a masculine way of understanding human nature. Alison Jaggar, for example, criticizes what she calls "normative dualism" for being "male biased,"[29] and defines "normative dualism" as "the belief that what is especially valuable about human beings is a particular 'mental' capacity, the capacity for rationality."[30]

Another critic of dualism is Rosemary Radford Reuther, a theologian. Her book *New Woman, New Earth* is an extended attack upon what she calls transcendent hierarchical dualism, which she regards as a "male ideology."[31] By "transcendent dualism" she means the view that consciousness is "transcendent to visible nature"[32] and that there is a sharp split between spirit and nature. In the attempt to deny our own mortality, our essential humanity is then identified with a "transcendent divine sphere beyond the matrix of coming to be and passing away."[33] In using the term "hierarchical," she means that the mental or spiritual component is taken to be superior to the physical. Thus "the relation of spirit and body is one of repression, subjugation and mastery."[34]

Dodson Gray, whose views resemble Reuther's, poetically contrasts the feminine attitude with the masculine one as follows:

> I see that life is not a line but a circle. Why do men imagine for themselves the illusory freedom of a soaring mind, so that the body of nature becomes a cage? 'Tis not true. To be human is to be circled in the cycles of nature, rooted in the processes that nature us in life, breathing in and breathing out human life just as plants breathe in and out their photosynthesis.[35]

Feminists critical of traditional masculine ways of thinking about human nature also examine critically the conception of "reason" which has become engrained in our Western cultural heritage from the Greeks on. Genevieve Lloyd, for example, in *The Man of Reason: Male and Female in Western Philosophy*,[36] suggests that the very notion of reason itself has been defined in part by the exclusion of the feminine. And if the thing which makes us distinctively human—namely our reason—is thought of as male, women and the things usually associated with them such as the body, emotion and nature, will be placed in an inferior position.

C. Our Relationship with Nature

Many feminists hold that mind-body dualism which sees mind as transcendent to and superior to the body, leads to the devaluation of both women and nature. For the transcendent mind is conceived as masculine, and women, the body and nature assigned an inferior and subservient status.[37] As Rosemary Radford Reuther puts it:

> The woman, the body and the world are the lower half of a dualism that must be declared posterior to, created by, subject to, and ultimately alien to the nature of (male) consciousness in whose image man made his God.[38]

Women are to be subject to men, and nature may be used by man in any way he chooses. Thus the male ideology of transcendent dualism sanctions unlimited technological manipulation of nature; nature is an alien object to be conquered.

Carolyn Merchant, in her book *The Death of Nature: Women, Ecology and the Scientific Revolution*,[39] focuses on the Cartesian version of dualism as particularly disastrous to our relationship with nature, and finds the roots of our present ecological crisis to lie in the Seventeenth Century scientific revolution—

itself based on Cartesian dualism and the mechanization of nature. According to Merchant, both feminism and the ecology movement are egalitarian movements which have a vision of our interconnectedness with each other and with nature.

Feminists who stress the deep affinities between feminism and the ecology movement are often called "ecofeminists." Stephanie Leland, radical feminist and co-editor of a recent collection of ecofeminist writings, has explained that:

> Ecology is universally defined as the study of the balance and interrelationship of all life on earth. The motivating force behind feminism is the expression of the feminine principle. As the essential impulse of the feminine principle is the striving towards balance and interrelationship, it follows that feminism and ecology are inextricably connected.[40]

The masculine urge is, she says, to "separate, discriminate and control," while the feminine impulse is "towards belonging, relationship and letting be."[41] The urge to discriminate leads, she thinks, to the need to dominate "in order to feel secure in the choice of a particular set of differences."[42] The feminine attitude springs from a more holistic view of the human person and sees us as imbedded in nature rather than standing over and above it. It entails a more egalitarian attitude, regarding the needs of other creatures as important and deserving of consideration. It seeks to "let be" rather than to control, and maintains a pervasive awareness of the interconnectedness of all things and the need to preserve this if all are to flourish.

Interconnectendness, which we found to be an important theme in feminist ethics, thus reappears in the writings of the ecofeminists as one of the central aspects of the feminine attitude toward nature.

D. Paradigms of Social Life

Feminists' descriptions of characteristically masculine and feminine paradigms of social life center around two different focuses. Those influenced by Gilligan tend to stress the contrast between individualism (which they take to be characteristic of the masculine "justice tradition") and the view of society as "a web of relationships sustained by a process of communication"[43] (which they take to characterize the feminine "care perspective"). According to them, the masculine paradigm sees society as a collection of self-assertive individuals seeking rules which will allow them to pursue their own goals without interfering with each other. The whole contractarian tradition from Locke and Hobbes through Rawls is thus seen as a masculine paradigm of social life; we are only connected to others and responsible to them through our own choice to relinquish part of our autonomy in favor of the state. The feminine care perspective guides us to think about societal problems in a different way. We are already imbedded in a network of relationships, and must never exploit or hurt the other. We must strive to preserve those relationships as much as possible without sacrificing the integrity of the self.

The ecofeminists, pacifist feminists, and those whose starting point is a rejection of dualism, tend to focus more on the contrast between viewing social relationships in terms of hierarchy, power, and domination (the masculine paradigm) and viewing them in a more egalitarian and nonviolent manner (the feminine one). Feminists taking this position range from the moderate ones who believe that masculine social thought tends to be more hierarchical than feminine thought, to the extreme radicals who believe males are irredeemably aggressive and dominating, and prone to violence in order to preserve their domination.

The more moderate characterization of masculine social thought would claim that men tend to prefer a clear structure of authority; they want to know who is in control and thave a clear set of procedures or rules for resolving difficult cases. The more extreme view, common among ecofeminists and a large number of radical feminists, is that males seek to establish and maintain patriarchy (systematic domination by males) and use violence to maintain their control. These feminists thus see an affinity between feminism (which combats male violence against women) and the pacifist movement (which does so on a more global scale). Mary Daly, for example, holds that "the rulers of patriarchy—males with power—wage an unceasing war against life itself . . . female energy is essentially biophilic."[44] Another radical feminist, Sally Miller Gearhart, says that men possess the qualities of objectification, violence, and competitiveness, while women possess empathy, nurturance, and cooperation.[45] Thus the feminine virtues must prevail if we are to survive at all, and the entire hierarchical power structure must be replaced by "horizontal patterns of relationship."[46]

Women are thus viewed by the pacifist feminists as attuned in some special way to the values and attitudes underlying a pacifist commitment. Sara Ruddick, for example, believes that maternal practice, because it involves "preservative love" and nurtures growth, involves the kinds of virtues which, when put to work in the public domain, lead us in the direction of pacifism.[47]

II. Abortion

A person who had characteristically masculine traits, attitudes and values as defined above would very naturally choose abortion, and justify it ethically in the same way in which most feminists do. Conversely, a person manifesting feminine traits, attitudes and values would not make such a choice, or justify it in that way.

According to the ecofeminists, the masculine principle is insensitive to the interconnectedness of all life; it strives to discriminate, separate, and control. It does not respect the natural cycles of nature, but objectifies it, and imposes its will upon it through unrestrained technological manipulation. Such a way of thinking would naturally lead to abortion. If the woman does not *want* to be pregnant, she has recourse to an operation involving highly sophisticated technology in order to defend her control of her body. This fits the characterization of the masculine principle perfectly.

Abortion is a separation—a severing of a life-preserving connection between the woman and the fetus. It thus fails to respect the interconnectedness of all life. Nor does it respect the natural cycles of nature. The mother and the developing child together form a delicately balanced ecosystem with the woman's entire hormonal system geared towards sustaining the pregnancy.[48] The abortionist forces the cervical muscles (which have become thick and hard in order to hold in the developing fetus) open and disrupts her hormonal system by removing it.

Abortion has something further in common with the behavior ecofeminists and pacifist feminists take to be characteristically masculine; it shows a willingness to use violence in order to maintain control. The fetus is destroyed by being pulled apart by suction, cut in pieces, or poisoned. It is not merely killed inadvertently as fish might be by toxic wastes, but it is deliberately targeted for destruction. Clearly this is not the expression of a "biophilic" attitude. This point was recently brought home to me by a Quaker woman who had reached the conclusion that the abortion she had had was contrary to her pacifist principles. She said, "we must seek peaceableness both within and without."

In terms of social thought, again, it is the masculine models which are most frequently employed in thinking about abortion. If masculine thought is naturally hierarchical and oriented toward power and control, then the interests of the fetus (who has no power) would naturally be suppressed in favor of the interests of the mother. But to the extent that feminist social thought is egalitarian, the question must be raised of why the mother's interests should prevail over the child's.

Feminist thought about abortion has, in addition, been deeply pervaded by the individualism which they so ardently criticize. The woman is supposed to have the sole authority to decide the outcome of the pregnancy. But what of her interconnectedness with the child and with others? Both she and the unborn child already exist within a network of relationships ranging from the closest ones—the father, grandparents, siblings, uncles and aunts, and so on—to ones with the broader society—including the mother's friends, employer, employees, potential adoptive parents, taxpayers who may be asked to fund the abortion or subsidize the child, and all the numerous other people affected by her choice. To dismiss this already existing network of relationships as irrelevant to the mother's decision is to manifest the sort of social atomism which feminist thinkers condemn as characteristically masculine.

Those feminists who are seeking to articulate the feminine voice in ethics also face a *prima facie* inconsistency between an ethics of care and abortion. Quite simply, abortion is a failure to care for one living being who exists in a particularly intimate relationship to oneself. If empathy, nurturance, and taking responsibility for caring for others are characteristic of the feminine voice, then abortion does not appear to be a feminine response to an unwanted pregnancy. If, as Gilligan says, "an ethic of care rests on the premise of non-violence—that no one should be hurt,"[49] then surely the feminine response to an unwanted pregnancy would be to try to find a solution which does not involve injury to anyone, including the unborn.

"Rights" have been invoked in the abortion controversy in a bewildering variety of ways, ranging from the "right to life" to the "right to control one's body." But clearly those who defend unrestricted access to abortion in terms of such things as the woman's right to privacy or her right to control her body are speaking the language of an ethics of justice rather than an ethics of care. For example, Judith Jarvis Thompson's widely read article "A Defense of Abortion"[50] treats the moral issue involved in abortion as a conflict between the rights of the fetus and the mother's rights over her own body. Mary Anne Warren also sees the issue in terms of a conflict of rights, but since the fetus does not meet her criteria for being a person, she weighs the woman's rights to "freedom, happiness and self-determination" against the rights of other people in the society who would like to see the fetus preserved for whatever reason.[51] And, insofar as she appeals to consciousness, reasoning, self-motivated activity, the capacity to communicate, and the presence of self-concepts and self-awareness as criteria of personhood, she relies on the kind of opposition between mind and nature criticized by many feminists as masculine. In particular, she is committed to what Jaggar calls "normative dualism"—the view that what is especially valuable about humans is their mental capacity for rational thought.

It is rather striking that feminists defending abortion lapse so quickly into speaking in the masculine voice. Is it because they feel they must do so in order to be heard in our male-dominated society, or is it because no persuasive defense of abortion can be constructed from within the ethics of care tradition? We now consider several possible "feminine voice" defenses of abortion.

III. Possible Responses and Replies

Among the feminists seeking to articulate and defend the value of the feminine voice, very few have made any serious attempt to grapple with abortion. The writings of the ecofeminists and the pacifist feminists abound with impassioned defenses of such values as non-violence, a democratic attitude towards the needs of all living things, letting others be and nurturing them, and so on, existing side by side with impassioned defenses of "reproductive rights." They see denying women access to abortion as just another aspect of male domination and violence against women.

This will not do for several reasons. First, it is not true that males are the chief opponents of abortion. Many women are strongly opposed to it. The pro-life movement at every level is largely composed of women. For example, as of May 1988, 38 of the state delegates to the National Right to Life Board of Directors were women, and only 13 were men. Indeed as Jean Bethke Elshtain has observed,[52] the pro-life movement has mobilized into political action an enormous number of women who were never politically active before. And a Gallup poll in 1981 found that 51% of women surveyed believed a person is present at conception, compared with only 33% of the men. The pro-life movement, thus, can not be dismissed as representing male concerns and desires only. Granted, a pro-choice feminist could argue that women involved in the pro-life movement suffer from "colonized minds," but this sort of argument clearly can be made to cut both directions. After all, many of the strongest supporters of "reproductive rights" have been men—ranging from the Supreme Court in *Roe v. Wade* to the Playboy Philosopher.

Secondly, terms like violence and domination are used far too loosely by those who condemn anti-abortion laws. If there are laws against wife abuse, does this mean that abusive husbands are being subjected to domination and violence? One does not exercise violence against someone merely by crossing his or her will, or even by crossing his or her will and backing this up by threats of legal retribution.

Finally, those who see violence and domination in laws against abortion, but not in abortion itself, generally fail to look at the nature of the act itself, and thus fail to judge that act in light of their professed values and principles. This is not surprising; abortion is a bloody and distressing thing to contemplate. But one cannot talk about it intelligently without being willing to look concretely at the act itself.

One line of thought is suggested by Gilligan, who holds that at the highest level of moral development, we must balance our responsibility to care for others against our need to care for ourselves. Perhaps we could, then, see the woman who has an abortion as still being caring and nurturing in that she is acting out of a legitimate care for herself. This is an implausible view of the actual feelings of women who undergo abortions. They may believe they are "doing something for themselves" in the sense of doing what they must do to safeguard their legitimate interests. But the operation is more naturally regarded as a violation of oneself than as a nurturing of oneself. This has been noted, even by feminists who support permissive abortion laws. For example, Carolyn Whitbeck speaks of "the unappealing prospect of having someone scraping away at one's core,"[53] and Adrienne Rich says that "Abortion is violence: A deep, desperate violence inflicted by a woman upon, first of all, herself."[54]

We here come up against the problem that a directive to care, to nurture, to take responsibility for others, and so on, provides a moral orientation, but leaves unanswered many important questions and hence provides little guidance in problem situations. What do we do when caring for one person involves being uncaring toward another? How widely we must extend our circle of care? Are some kinds of not caring worse than others? Is it caring to give someone what they want even though it may be bad for them?

Thinking in terms of preserving relationships suggests another possible "feminine" defense of abortion—namely that the woman is striving to preserve her interconnectedness with her family, husband, or boyfriend. Or perhaps she is concerned to strengthen her relationship with her other children by having enough time and resources to devote to their care. To simply tell a woman to preserve *all* her existing relationships is not the answer. Besides the fact that it may not be possible (women *do* sometimes have to sever relationships), it is not clear that it would be desirable even if it were possible. Attempting to preserve our existing relationships has conservative tendencies in several unfortunate ways. It fails to invite us to reflect critically on whether those relationships are good, healthy, or worthy or preservation.[55] It also puts the unborn at a particular disadvantage, since the mother's relationship with him or her is just beginning, while her relationships with others have had time to develop. And not only the unborn, but any needy stranger who shows up at our door can be excluded on the grounds that caring for them would disrupt our existing pattern of relationships. Thus the care perspective could degenerate into a rationalization for a purely tribal morality; I take care of myself and my friends.

But how are decisions about severing relationships to be made? One possibility is suggested by Gilligan in a recent article. She looks at the network of connections within which the woman who is considering abortion finds herself entangled, and says "to ask what actions constitute care or are more caring directs attention to the parameters of connection and the *Costs of detachment* . . . (emphasis added)."[56] Thus, the woman considering abortion, should reflect upon the comparative costs of severing various relationships. This method of decision, however, makes her vulnerable to emotional and psychological pressure from others, by encouraging her to sever whichever connection is easiest to break (the squeaky wheel principle).[57]

But perhaps we can lay out some guidelines (or, at least, rules of thumb) for making these difficult decisions. One way we might reason, from the point of view of the feminine voice, is that since preserving interconnectedness is good, we should prefer a short-term estrangement to an irremediable severing of relationship. And we should choose an action which *may* cause an irremediable break in relationship over one which is certain to cause such a break. By either of these criteria, abortion is clearly to be avoided.[58]

Another consideration suggested by Gilligan's work is that since avoiding hurt to others (or non-violence) is integral to an ethics of care, severing a relationship where the other person will be only slightly hurt would be preferable to severing one where deep or lasting injury will be inflicted by our action. But on this criterion, again, it would seem she should avoid abortion, since loss of life is clearly a graver harm than emotional distress.

Two other possible criteria which would also tell against abortion are: (1) that it is permissible to cut ties with someone who behaves unjustly and oppressively toward one, but not with someone who is innocent of any wrong against one, or (2) we have special obligations to our own offspring, and thus should not sever relationship with them.

Criteria can, perhaps, be found which would dictate severing relationship with the fetus rather than others, but it is hard to specify one which clearly reflects the feminine voice. Certainly the right to control one's body will not do. The claim that the unborn is not a person and therefore does not deserve moral consideration can be faulted on several grounds. First, if the feminine voice is one which accepts the interconnectedness of all life and strives to avoid harm to nature and to other species, then the non-personhood of the fetus (supposing it could be proved) would not imply that its needs can be discounted. And secondly, the entire debate over personhood has standardly been carried on very much in the masculine voice.[59] One feminist, Janice Raymond,[60] has suggested that the question of when life begins is a masculine one, and if this is a masculine question, it would seem that personhood, with its juridical connotations, would be also. It is not clear that the care perspective has the resources to resolve this issue. If it cannot, then, one cannot rely on the non-personhood of the fetus in constructing a "feminine voice" defense of abortion. A care perspective would at least seem to place the burden of proof on those who would restrict the scope of care, in this case to those that have been born.

It seems that the only way open to the person who seeks to defend abortion from the point of view of the feminine voice is to deny that a relationship (or at least any morally significant relationship) exists between the embryo/fetus and the mother. The question of how to tell when a relationship (or a morally significant relationship) exists is a deep and important one, which has, as yet, received insufficient attention from those who are trying to articulate the feminine voice in moral reasoning. The whole ecofeminist position relies on the assumption that our relationship with nature and with other species is a real and morally significant one. They, thus, have no basis at all for excluding the unborn from moral consideration.

There are those, however, who wish to define morally significant relationships more narrowly—thus effectively limiting our obligation to extend care. While many philosophers within the "justice tradition" (for example, Kant) have seen moral significance only where there is some impact upon rational beings, Nel Noddings, coming from the "care perspective" tries to limit our obligation to extend care in terms of the possibility of "completion" or "reciprocity" in a caring relationship.[61] Since she takes the mother-child relationship to be paradigmatic of caring, it comes as something of a surprise that she regards abortion as a permissible response to an unwanted pregnancy.[62]

There are, on Noddings' view, two different ways in which we may be bound, as caring persons, to extend our care to one for whom we do not already have the sort of feelings of love and affection which would lead us to do the caring action naturally. One is by virtue of being connected with our "inner circle" of caring (which is formed by natural relations of love and friendship) through "chains" of "personal or formal relations."[63] As an example of a person appropriately linked to the inner circle, she cites her daughter's fiancé. It would certainly *seem* that the embryo in one's womb would belong to one's "inner circle" (via natural caring), or at least be connected to it by a "formal relation" (that is, that of parenthood). But Noddings does not concede this. Who is part of my inner circle, and who is connected to it in such a way that I am obligated to extend care to him or her seems to be, for Noddings, largely a matter of my feelings toward the person and/or my choice to include him or her. Thus the mother *may* "confer sacredness" upon the "information speck"[64] in her womb, but need not if, for example, her relationship with the father is not a stable and loving one. During pregnancy "many women recognize the relation as established when the fetus begins to move about. It is not a question of when life begins, but of when relation begins."

But making the existence of a relation between the unborn and the mother a matter of her choice or feelings, seems to run contrary to one of the most central insights of the feminine perspective in moral reasoning—namely that we already *are* interconnected with others, and thus have responsibilities to them. The view that we are connected with others only when we choose to be or when we *feel* we are, presupposes the kind of individualism and social atomism which Noddings and other feminists criticize as masculine.

Noddings also claims that we sometimes are obligated to care for "the proximate stranger." She says:

> We cannot refuse obligation in human affairs by merely refusing to enter relation; we are, by virtue of our mutual humanity, already and perpetually in potential relation.[65]

Why, then, are we not obligated to extend care to the unborn? She gives two criteria for when we have an obligation to extend care: there must be "the existence of or potential for present relation" and the "dynamic potential for growth in relation, including the potential for increased reciprocity. . . ." Animals are, she believes, excluded by this second criterion since their response is nearly static (unlike a human infant).

She regards the embryo/fetus as not having the potential for present relationships of caring and reciprocity, and thus as having no claim upon our care. As the fetus matures, he or she develops increasing potential for caring relationships, and thus our obligation increases also. There are problems with her position, however.

First of all, the only relationships which can be relevant to *my* obligation to extend care, for Noddings, must be relationships with *me*. Whatever the criteria for having a relationship are, it must be that at a given time, an entity either has a relationship with me or it does not. If it does not, it may either have no potential for a morally significant relationship with me (for example, my word processor), or it may have such potential in several ways: (1) The relationship may become actual at the will of one or both parties (for example, the stranger sitting next to me on the bus). (2) The relationship may become actual only after a change in relative spatial locations which will take time, and thus can occur only in the future (for example, walking several blocks to meet a new neighbor, or traveling to Tibet to meet a specific Tibetan). Or (3) The relationship may become actual only after some internal change occurs within the other (for example by waiting for a sleeping drug to wear off, for a deep but reversible coma to pass, or for the embryo to mature more fully) and thus can also happen only in the future.

In all three of these cases there is present now in the other the potential for relations of a caring and reciprocal sort. In cases (1) and (2) this is uncontroversial, but (3) requires some defense in the case of the unborn. The human embryo differs now from a rabbit embryo in that it possesses potential for these kinds of relationships although neither of them is presently able to enter into relationships of any sort.[66] That potential becomes actualized only over time, but it can become actualized only because it is there to be actualized (as it is not in the rabbit embryo).[67] Noddings fails to give any reason why the necessity for some internal change to occur in the other before relation can become actual has such moral importance that we are entitled to kill the other in case (3), but not in the others, especially since my refraining from killing it is a sufficient condition for the actualization of the embryo's potential for caring relationships. Her criterion as it stands would also seem to imply that we may kill persons in deep but predictably reversible comas.

Whichever strand of Noddings thought we choose, then, it is hard to see how the unborn can be excluded from being ones for whom we ought to care. If we focus on the narrow, tribal morality of "inner circles" and "chains," then an objective connection exists tying the unborn to the mother and other relatives. If we are to be open to the needy stranger because of the real potential for relationship and reciprocity, then we should be open to the unborn because he or she also has the real and present potential for a relationship of reciprocity and mutuality which comes with species membership.

Many feminists will object to my argument so far on the grounds that they do not, after all, consider abortion to be a *good* thing. They aren't pro-abortion in the sense that they encourage women to have abortions. They merely regard it as something which must be available as a kind of "grim option"—something a woman would choose only when the other alternatives are all immeasurably worse.[68]

First of all, the grim options view sounds very much like the "masculine voice"—we must grit our teeth, and do the distasteful but necessary deed (the more so where the deed involves killing).[69] Furthermore, it is in danger of collapsing into total subjectivism unless one is willing to specify some criteria for when an option is a genuinely grim one, beyond the agent's feeling that it is. What if she chooses to abort in order not to have to postpone her trip to Europe, or because she prefers sons to daughters? Surely these are not grim options no matter what she may say. Granted, the complicated circumstances surrounding her decision are best known to the woman herself. But this does not imply that no one is *ever* in a position to make judgments about whether her option is sufficiently grim to justify abortion. We do not generally concede that only the agent is in a position to judge the morality of his or her action.

Feminists standardly hold that absolutely no restrictions may be placed on a woman's right to choose abortion.[70] This position cannot be supported by the grim options argument. One who believes something is a grim option will be inclined to try to avoid or prevent it, and thus be willing, at least in principle, to place some restrictions on what counts as a grim option. Granted, practical problems exist about how such decisions are to be made and by whom. But someone who refuses in principle to allow any restrictions on women's right to abort, cannot in good faith claim that they regard abortion only as a grim option.

Some feminists will say: Yes, feminine virtues are a good thing for any person to have, and yes, abortion is a characteristically masculine way of dealing with an unwanted pregnancy, but in the current state of things we live in a male-dominated society, and we must be willing to use now weapons which, ideally, in a good, matriarchal society, we would not use.[71] But there are no indications that an ideal utopian society is just around the corner; thus we are condemned to a constant violation of our own deepest commitments. If the traits, values and attitudes characteristic of the "feminine voice" are asserted to be good ones, we ought to act according to them. And such values and attitudes simply do not lend support to either the choice of abortion as a way of dealing with an unwanted pregnancy in individual cases, or to the political demand for unrestricted[72] access to abortion which has become so entrenched in the feminist movement. Quite the contrary.[73]

Stonehill College, North Easton, Massachusetts

Received February 13, 1989

Death Penalty

Capital Punishment

Anthony G. Amsterdam

My discussion of capital punishment will proceed in three stages.

First, I would like to set forth certain basic factual realities about capital punishment, like the fact that capital punishment is a fancy phrase for legally killing people. Please forgive me for beginning with such obvious and ugly facts. Much of our political and philosophical debate about the death penalty is carried on in language calculated to conceal these realities and their implications. The implications, I will suggest, are that capital punishment is a great evil—surely the greatest evil except for war that our society can intentionally choose to commit.

This does not mean that we should do away with capital punishment. Some evils, like war, are occasionally necessary, and perhaps capital punishment is one of them. But the fact that it is a great evil means that we should not choose to do it without some very good and solid reason of which we are satisfactorily convinced upon sufficient evidence. The conclusion of my first point simply is that the burden of proof upon the question of capital punishment rightly rests on those who are asking us to use our laws to kill people with, and that this is a very heavy burden.

Source: "Capital Punishment" by Anthony G. Amsterdam from *Stanford* magazine, Fall/Winter 1977.
Reprinted with permission from *Stanford* magazine, published by Stanford Alumni Association, Stanford University.

Second, I want to review the justifications that have been advanced to support capital punishment. I want to explore with you concepts such as retribution and deterrence, and some of the assumptions and evidence about them. The conclusion of my second point will be that none of these reasons which we like to give ourselves for executing criminals can begin to sustain the burden of proof that rightfully rests upon them.

Third, I would like to say a word about history—about the slow but absolutely certain progress of maturing civilization that will bring an inevitable end to punishment by death. That history does not give us the choice between perpetrating and abolishing capital punishment, because we could not perpetuate it if we wanted to. A generation or two within a single nation can retard but not reverse a long-term, worldwide evolution of this magnitude. Our choice is narrower although it is not unimportant: whether we shall be numbered among the last generations to put legal killing aside. I will end by asking you to cast your choice for life instead of death. But, first, let me begin with some basic facts about the death penalty.

I.

The most basic fact, of course, is that capital punishment means taking living, breathing men and women, stuffing them into a chair, strapping them down, pulling a lever, and exterminating them. We have almost forgotten this fact because there have been no executions in this country for more than ten years, except for Gary Gilmore whose combined suicide and circus were so wildly extravagant as to seem unreal. For many people, capital punishment has become a sanitized and symbolic issue: Do you or do you not support your local police? Do you or do you not care enough about crime to get tough with criminals? These abstractions were never what capital punishment was about, although it was possible to think so during the ten-year moratorium on executions caused by constitutional challenges to the death penalty in the courts. That is no longer possible. The courts have now said that we can start up executions again, if we want to. Today, a vote for capital punishment is a vote to kill real, live people.

What this means is, first, that we bring men or women into court and put them through a trial for their lives. They are expected to sit back quietly and observe decent courtroom decorum throughout a proceeding whose purpose is systematically and deliberately to decide whether they should be killed. The jury hears evidence and votes; and you can always tell when a jury has voted for death because they come back into court and they will not look the defendant or defense counsel in the eyes. The judge pronounces sentence and the defendant is taken away to be held in a cell for two to six years, hoping that his appeals will succeed, not really knowing what they are all about, but knowing that if they fail, he will be taken out and cinched down and put to death. Most of the people in prison are reasonably nice to him, and even a little apologetic; but he realizes every day for that 700 or 2,100 days that they are holding him there helpless for the approaching slaughter; and that, once the final order is given, they will truss him up and kill him, and that nobody in that vast surrounding machinery of public officials and servants of the law will raise a finger to save him. This is why Camus once wrote that an execution

> . . . is not simply death. It is a just as different . . .from the privation of life as a concentration camp is from prison. . . . It adds to death a rule, a public premeditation known to the future victim, an organization . . . which is itself a source of moral sufferings more terrible than death . . . *[Capital punishment] is . . . the most premeditated of murders, to which no criminal's deed, however calculated . . . can be compared. . . . For there to be an equivalency, the death penalty would have to punish a criminal who had warned his victim of the date at which he would inflict a horrible death on him and who, from that moment onward, had confined him at his mercy for months. Such a monster is not encountered in private life.*

I will spare you descriptions of the execution itself. Apologists for capital punishment commonly excite their readers with descriptions of extremely gruesome, gory murders. All murders are horrible things, and executions are usually a lot cleaner physically—although, like Camus, I have never heard of a murderer who held his victim captive for two or more years waiting as the minutes and hours ticked away toward his preannounced death. The clinical details of an execution are as unimaginable to me as they are to most of you. We have not permitted public executions in this country for over 40 years. The law in every state forbids more than a few people to watch the deed done behind prison walls. In January of 1977, a federal judge in Texas ruled that executions could be photographed for television, but the attorneys general of 25 states asked the federal Court of Appeals to set aside that ruling, and it did. I can only leave to your imagination what they are trying so very hard to hide from us. Oh, of course, executions are too hideous to put on television; we all know that. But let us not forget that it is the same hideous thing, done in secret, which we are discussing under abstract labels like "capital punishment" that permit us to talk about the subject in after-dinner conversation instead of spitting up.

In any event, the advocates of capital punishment can and do accentuate their arguments with descriptions of the awful physical details of such hideous murders as that of poor Sharon Tate. All of us naturally and rightly respond to these atrocities with shock and horror. You can read descriptions of executions that would also horrify you (for example, in Byron Eshelman's 1962 book, *Death Row Chaplain*, particularly pages 160–161), but I prefer not to insult your intelligence by playing "can you top this" with issues of life and death. I ask you only to remember two things, if and when you are exposed to descriptions of terrifying murders.

First, the murders being described are not murders that are being done by us, or in our name, or with our approval; and our power to stop them is exceedingly limited even under the most exaggerated suppositions of deterrence, which I shall shortly return to question. Every execution, on the other hand, is done by our paid servants, in our collective name, and we can stop them all. Please do not be bamboozled into thinking that people who are against executions are in favor of murders. If we had the individual or the collective power to stop murders, we would stop them all—and for the same basic reason that we want to stop executions. Murders and executions are both ugly, vicious things, because they destroy the same sacred and mysterious gift of life which we do not understand and can never restore.

Second, please remember therefore that descriptions of murders are relevant to the subject of capital punishment only on the theory that two wrongs make a right, or that killing murderers can assuage their victims' sufferings or bring them back to life, or that capital punishment is the best deterrent to murder. The first two propositions are absurd, and the third is debatable—although as I shall later show, the evidence is overwhelmingly against it. My present point is only that deterrence is debatable, whereas we *know* that persons whom we execute are dead beyond recall, no matter how the debate about deterrence comes out. That is a sufficient reason, I believe, why the burden of proof on the issue of deterrence should be placed squarely upon the executioners.

There are other reasons too. Let me try to state them briefly.

Capital punishment not merely kills people, it also kills some of them in error, and these are errors which we can never correct. When I speak about legal error, I do not mean only the question whether "they got the right man" or killed somebody who "didn't do it." Errors of that sort do occur: Timothy Evans, for example, an innocent man whose execution was among the reasons for the abolition of the death penalty in Great Britain. If you read Anthony Scaduto's recent book, *Scapegoat*, you will come away with unanswerable doubts whether Bruno Ricahard Hauptmann was really guilty of the kidnapping of the Lindbergh infant for which he was executed, or whether we killed Hauptmann, too, for a crime he did not commit.

In 1975, the Florida Cabinet pardoned two black men, Freddie Lee Pitts and Wilbert Lee, who were twice tried and sentenced to death and spent 12 years apiece on death row for a murder committed by somebody else. This one, I am usually glibly told, "does not count," because Pitts and Lee were never actually put to death. Take comfort if you will but I cannot, for I know that only the general constitutional attack which we were then mounting upon the death penalty in Florida kept Pitts and Lee alive long enough to permit discovery of the evidence of their innocence. Our constitutional attack is now dead, and so would Pitts and Lee be if they were tried tomorrow. Sure, we catch some errors. But we often catch them by extremely lucky breaks that could as easily not have happened. I represented a young man in North Carolina who came within a hair's breadth of being the Gary Gilmore of his day. Like Gilmore, he became so depressed under a death sentence that he tried to dismiss his appeal. He was barely talked out of it, his conviction was reversed, and on retrial a jury acquitted him in 11 minutes.

We do not know how many "wrong men" have been executed. We think and pray that they are rare—although we can't be sure because, after a man is dead, people seldom continue to investigate the possibility that he was innocent. But that is not the biggest source of error anyway.

What about *legal* error? In 1968, the Supreme Court of the United States held that it was unconstitutional to exclude citizens from capital trial juries simply because they had general conscientious or religious objections to the death penalty. That decision was held retroactive; and I represented 60 or 70 men whose death sentences were subsequently set aside for constitutional errors in jury selection. While researching their cases, I found the cases of at least as many more men who had already been executed on the basis of trials infected with identical errors. On June 29, 1977, we finally won a decision from the Supreme Court of the United States that the death penalty is excessively harsh and therefore unconstitutional for the crime of rape. Fine, but it comes too late for the 455 men executed for rape in this country since 1930—405 of them black.

In 1975, the Supreme Court held that the constitutional presumption of innocence forbids a trial judge to tell the jury that the burden of proof is on a homicide defendant to show provocation which reduces murder to manslaughter. On June 17, 1977, the Court held that this decision was also retroactive. Jury charges of precisely that kind were standard forms for more than a century in many American states that punished murder with death. Can we even begin to guess how many people were unconstitutionally executed under this so-called retroactive decision?

Now what about errors of fact that go to the degree of culpability of a crime? In almost every state, the difference between first and second-degree murder—or between capital and noncapital murder—depends on whether the defendant acted with something called "premeditation" as distinguished from intent to kill. Premeditation means intent formed beforehand, but no particular amount of time is required. Courts tell juries that premeditation "may be as instantaneous as successive thoughts in the mind." Mr. Justice Cardozo wrote that *he* did not understand the concept of premeditation after several decades of studying and trying to apply it as a judge. Yet this is the kind of question to which a jury's answer spells out life or death in a capital trial—this, and the questions of whether the defendant had "malice aforethought," or "provocation and passion," or "insanity," or the "reasonableness" necessary for killing in self-defense.

I think of another black client, Johnny Coleman, whose conviction and death sentence for killing a white truck driver named "Screwdriver" Johnson we twice got reversed by the Supreme Court of the United States. On retrial a jury acquitted him on the grounds of self-defense upon exactly the same evidence that an earlier jury had had when it sentenced him to die. When ungraspable legal standards are thus applied to intangible mental states, there is not merely the possibility but the actuarial certainty that juries deciding substantial volumes of cases are going to be wrong in an absolutely large number of them. If you accept capital punishment, you must accept the reality—not the risk, but the reality—that we shall kill people whom the law says that it is not proper to kill.

No other outcome is possible when we presume to administer an infallible punishment through a fallible system.

You will notice that I have taken examples of black defendants as some of my
cases of legal error. There is every reason to believe that discrimination on
grounds of race and poverty fatally infect the administration of capital justice in
this country. Since 1930, an almost equal number of white and black defendants
has been executed for the crime of murder, although blacks constituted only
about a tenth of the nation's population during this period. No sufficiently careful studies have been done of these cases, controlling variables other than race, so
as to determine exactly what part race played in the outcome. But when that kind
of systemic study *was* done in rape cases, it showed beyond the statistical possibility of a doubt that black men who raped white women were disproportionately
sentenced to die on the basis of race alone. Are you prepared to believe that juries
which succumbed to conscious or unconscious racial prejudices in rape cases
were or are able to put those prejudices wholly aside where the crime charged is
murder? Is it not much more plausible to believe that even the most conscientious
juror—or judge, or prosecuting attorney—will be slower to want to inflict the
death penalty on a defendant with whom he can identify as a human being; and
that the process of identification in our society is going to be very seriously
affected by racial identity?

I should mention that there have been a couple of studies—one by the
Stanford Law Review and the other by the Texas Judicial Council—which found
no racial discrimination in capital sentencing in certain murder cases. But both of
these studies had methodological problems and limitations; and both of them
also found death-sentencing discrimination against the economically poor, who
come disproportionately from racial minorities. The sum of the evidence still
stands where the National Crime Commission found it ten years ago, when it
described the following discriminatory patterns. "The death sentence," said the
Commission, "is disproportionately imposed and carried out on the poor, the
Negro, and members of unpopular groups."

Apart from discrimination, there is a haphazard, crazy-quilt character about
the administration of capital punishment that every knowledgeable lawyer or
observer can describe but none can rationally explain. Some juries are hanging
juries, some counties are hanging counties, some years are hanging years; and
men live or die depending on these flukes.

However atrocious the crime may have been for which a particular defendant
is sentenced to die, "[e]xperienced wardens know many prisoners serving life or
less whose crimes were equally, or more atrocious." This is a quotation, by the
way, from former Attorney General Ramsey Clark's statement to a congressional
subcommittee; and wardens Lewis Lawes, Clinton Duffy, and others have said the
same thing.

With it I come to the end of my first point. I submit that the deliberate judicial extinction of human life is intrinsically so final and so terrible an act as to cast
the burden of proof for its justification upon those who want us to do it. But certainly when the act is executed through a fallible system which assures that we kill

some people wrongly, others because they are black or poor or personally unattractive or socially unacceptable, and all of them quite freakishly in the sense that whether a man lives or dies for any particular crime is a matter of luck and happenstance, *then*, at the least, the burden of justifying capital punishment lies fully and heavily on its proponents.

II.

Let us consider those justifications. The first and the oldest is the concept of *retribution*: an eye for an eye, a life for a life. You may or may not believe in this kind of retribution, but I will not waste your time debating it because it cannot honestly be used to justify the only form of capital punishment that this country has accepted for the past half-century. Even before the judicial moratorium, executions in the United States had dwindled to an average of about 30 a year. Only a rare, sparse handful of convicted murderers are being sentenced to die or executed for the selfsame crimes for which many, many times as many murderers were sent away to prison. Obviously, as Professor Herbert Wechsler said a generation ago, the issue of capital punishment is no longer "whether it is fair or just that one who takes another person's life should lose his own. . . . [W]e do not and cannot act upon . . . [that proposition] generally in the administration of the penal law. The problem rather is whether a small and highly random sample of people who commit murder . . . ought to be dispatched, while most of those convicted of . . . [identical] crimes are dealt with by imprisonment."

Sometimes the concept of retribution is modernized a little with a notion called *moral reinforcement*—the ideal that we should punish very serious crimes very severely in order to demonstrate how much we abhor them. The trouble with *this* justification for capital punishment, of course, is that it completely begs the question, which is *how severely* we ought to punish any particular crime to show appropriate abhorrence for it. The answer can hardly be found in a literal application of the eye-for-an-eye formula. We do not burn down arsonists' houses or cheat back at bunco artists. But if we ought not punish all crimes exactly according to their kind, then what is the fit moral reinforcement for murder? You might as well say burning at the stake or boiling in oil is as simple as gassing or electrocution.

Or is it not more plausible—if what we really want to say is that the killing of a human being is wrong and ought to be condemned as clearly as we can—that we should choose the punishment of prison as the fitting means to make this point? So far as moral reinforcement goes, the difference between life imprisonment and capital punishment is precisely that imprisonment continues to respect the value of human life. The plain message of capital punishment, on the other hand, is that life ceases to be sacred whenever someone with the power to take it away decides that there is a sufficiently compelling pragmatic reason to do so.

But there is still another theory of a retributive sort which is often advanced to support the death penalty, particularly in recent years. This is the argument that *we*—that is, the person making the argument—no longer believe in the outworn concept of retribution, but the *public*—they believe in retribution, and so we must let them have their prey or they will lose respect for law. Watch for this argument because it is the surest sign of democratic depravity. It is disgusting in its patronizing attribution to "the public" of a primitive, uneducable bloodthirstiness which the speaker is unprepared to defend but is prepared to exploit as a means of side-stepping the rational and moral limitations of a *just* theory of retribution. It out-judases Judas in its abnegation of governmental responsibility to respond to popular misinformation with enlightenment, instead of seizing on it as a pretext for atrocity. This argument asserts that the proper way to deal with a lynch mob is to string its victim up before the mob does.

I don't think "the public" is a lynch mob or should be treated as one. People today are troubled and frightened by crime, and legitimately so. Much of the apparent increase of violent crime in our times is the product of intensified statistics keeping, massive and instantaneous and graphic news reporting, and manipulation of figures by law enforcement agencies which must compete with other sectors of the public economy for budget allocations. But part of the increase is also real, and very disturbing. Murders ought to disturb us all, whether or not they are increasing. Each and every murder is a terrible human tragedy. Nevertheless, it is irresponsible for public officials—particularly law enforcement officials whom the public views as experts—first to exacerbate and channel legitimate public concern about crime into public support for capital punishment by advertising unsupportable claims that capital punishment is an answer to the crime problem, and then to turn around and cite public support for capital punishment as justification when all other justifications are shown to be unsupportable. Politicians do this all the time, for excellent political reasons. It is much easier to advocate simplistic and illusory solutions to the crime problem than to find real and effective solutions. Most politicians are understandably afraid to admit that our society knows frighteningly little about the causes or cure of crime, and will have to spend large amounts of taxpayers' money even to begin to find out. The facile politics of crime do much to explain our national acceptance of capital punishment, but nothing to justify it.

Another supposed justification for capital punishment that deserves equally brief treatment is the notion of *isolation or specific deterrence*—the idea that we must kill a murderer to prevent him from murdering ever again. The usual forms that this argument takes are that a life sentence does not mean a life sentence—it means parole after 7, or 12, or 25 years; and that, within prisons themselves, guards and other prisoners are in constant jeopardy of death at the hands of convicted but unexecuted murderers.

It amazes me that these arguments can be made or taken seriously. Are we really going to kill a human being because we do not trust other people—the people whom we have chosen to serve on our own parole boards—to make a proper judgment in his case at some future time? We trust this same parole board to make far more numerous, difficult, and dangerous decisions: Hardly a week passes when they do not consider the cases of armed robbers, for example, although armed robbers are much, much more likely statistically to commit future murders than any murderer is to repeat his crime. But if we really do distrust the public agencies of law—if we fear that they may make mistakes—then surely that is a powerful argument *against* capital punishment. Courts which hand out death sentences because they predict that a man will still be criminally dangerous 7 or 25 years in the future cannot conceivably make fewer mistakes than parole boards who release a prisoner after 7 or 25 years of close observation in prison have convinced them that he is reformed and no longer dangerous.

But pass this point. If we refuse to trust the parole system, then let us provide by law that the murderers whose release we fear shall be given sentences of life imprisonment without parole which *do* mean life imprisonment without parole. I myself would be against that, but it is far more humane than capital punishment, and equally safe.

As for killings inside prisons, if you examine them you will find that they are very rarely done by convicted murderers, but are almost always done by people imprisoned for crimes that no one would think of making punishable by death. Warden Lawes of Sing Sing and Governor Wallace of Alabama, among others, regularly employed murder convicts as house servants because they were among the very safest prisoners. There are exceptions, of course; but these can be handled by adequate prison security. You cannot tell me or believe that a society which is capable of putting a man on the moon is incapable of putting a man in prison, keeping him there, and keeping him from killing while he is there. And if anyone says that this is costly, and that we should kill people in order to reduce government expenditures, I can only reply that the cost of housing a man for life in prison is considerably less than the cost of putting the same man through all of the extraordinary legal proceedings necessary to kill him.

That brings me to the last supposed justification for the death penalty: *deterrence.* This is the subject that you most frequently hear debated, and many people who talk about capital punishment talk about nothing else. I have done otherwise here, partly for completeness, partly because it is vital to approach the subject of deterrence knowing precisely what question you want to ask and have answered. I have suggested that the proper question is *whether there is sufficiently convincing evidence that the death penalty deters murder better than does life imprisonment so that you are willing to accept responsibility for doing the known evil act of killing human beings—with all of the attending ugliness that I have described—on the faith of your conviction in the superior deterrent efficacy of capital punishment.*

If this is the question, then I submit that there is only one fair and reasonable answer. When the Supreme Court of the United States reviewed the evidence in 1976, it described that evidence as "inconclusive." Do not let anybody tell you—as death-penalty advocates are fond of doing—that the Supreme Court held the death penalty justifiable as a deterrent. What the Court's plurality opinion said, exactly, was that "there is no convincing evidence *either supporting or refuting . . .* [the] view" that "the death penalty may not function as a significantly greater deterrent than lesser penalties." *Because* the evidence was inconclusive, the Court held that the Constitution did not forbid judgment either way. But if the evidence is inconclusive, is it *your* judgment that we should conclusively kill people on a factual theory that the evidence does not conclusively sustain?

I hope not. But let us examine the evidence more carefully because—even though it is not conclusive—it is very, very substantial; and the overwhelming weight of it refutes the claims of those who say that capital punishment is a better deterrent than life imprisonment for murder.

For more than 40 years, criminologists have studied this question by a variety of means. They have compared homicide rates in countries and states that did and did not have capital punishment, or that actually executed people more and less frequently. Some of these studies compared large aggregates of abolitionist and retentionist states; others compared geographically adjacent pairs or triads of states, or states that were chosen because they were comparable in other socio-economic factors that might affect homicide. Other studies compared homicide rates in the same country or state before and after the abolition or reinstatement of capital punishment, or they compared homicide rates for the same geographic area during periods preceding and following well publicized executions. Special comparative studies were done relating to police killings and prison killings. All in all, there were dozens of studies. Without a single exception, *none* of them found that the death penalty had any statistically significant effect upon the rate of homicide or murder. Often I have heard advocates of capital punishment explain away its failures by likening it to a great lighthouse: "We count the ships that crash," they say, "but we never know how many saw the light and were saved." What these studies show, however, is that coastlines of the same shape and depth and tidal structure, with and without lighthouses, invariably have the same number of shipwrecks per year. On that evidence, would you invest your money in a lighthouse, or would you buy a sonar if you really wanted to save lives?

In 1975, the first purportedly scientific study ever to find that capital punishment *did* deter homicides was published. This was done by Isaac Ehrlich of Chicago, who is not a criminologist but an economist. Using regression analysis involving an elaborate mathematical model, Ehrlich reported that every execution deterred something like eight murders. Naturally supporters of capital punishment hurriedly clambered on the Ehrlich bandwagon.

Unhappily, for them, the wagon was a factory reject. Several distinguished econometricians—including a team headed by Lawrence Klein, president of the American Economy Association—reviewed Ehrlich's work and found it fatally flawed with numerous methodological errors. Some of these were technical: It appeared, for example, that Ehrlich had produced his results by the unjustified and unexplained use of a logarithmic form of regression equation instead of the more conventional linear form—which made his findings of deterrence vanish. Equally important, it was shown that Ehrlich's findings depended entirely on data from the post-1962 period, when executions declined and the homicide rate rose *as a part of a general rise in the overall crime rate that Ehrlich incredibly failed to consider.*

Incidentally, the nonscientific proponents of capital punishment are also fond of suggesting that the rise in homicide rates in the 1960s and 1970s, when executions were halted, proves that executions used to deter homicides. This is ridiculous when you consider that crime as a whole has increased during this period; that homicide rates have increased about *half* as much as the rates for all other FBI Index crimes; and that whatever factors are affecting the rise of most noncapital crimes (which *cannot* include cessation of executions) almost certainly affect the homicide-rate rise also.

In the event, Ehrlich's study was discredited and a second, methodologically inferior study by a fellow named Yunker is not even worth criticizing here. These are the only two scientific studies in 40 years, I repeat, which have ever purported to find deterrence. On the other hand, several recent studies have been completed by researchers who adopted Ehrlich's basic regression-analysis approach but corrected its defects. Peter Passell did such a study finding no deterrence. Kenneth Avio did such a study finding no deterrence. If you want to review all of these studies yourselves, you may find them discussed and cited in an excellent article in the 1976 *Supreme Court Review* by Hans Zeisel, on page 317. The conclusion you will have to draw is that—during 40 years and today—the scientific community has looked and looked and looked for any reliable evidence that capital punishment deters homicide better than does life imprisonment, and it has found no such evidence at all.

Proponents of capital punishment frequently cite a different kind of study, one that was done by the Los Angeles Police Department. Police officers asked arrested robbers who did not carry guns, or did not use them, *why* they did not; and the answers, supposedly, were frequently that the robber "did not want to get the death penalty." It is noteworthy that the Los Angeles Police Department has consistently refused to furnish copies of this study and its underlying data to professional scholars, apparently for fear of criticism. I finally obtained a copy of the study from a legislative source, and I can tell you that it shows two things. First, an arrested person will tell a police officer anything that he thinks the police officer wants to hear. Second, police officers, like all other human beings, hear what they want to hear. When a robber tries to say that he did not carry or use a gun because he did not wish to risk the penalties for homicide, he will describe those penalties in terms of whatever the law happens to be at the time and place. In Minnesota, which has no death penalty, he will say, "I didn't want to get life imprisonment." In Los Angeles, he will say, "I didn't want to get the death penalty." Both responses mean the same thing; neither tells you that death is a superior deterrent to life imprisonment.

The real mainstay of deterrence thesis, however, is not evidence but intuition. You and I ask ourselves: Are we not afraid to die? Of course! Would the threat of death, then, not intimidate us to forbear from a criminal act? Certainly! *Therefore,* capital punishment must be a deterrent. The trouble with this intuition is that the people who are doing the reasoning and the people who are doing the murdering are not the same people. You and I do not commit murder for a lot of reasons other than the death penalty. The death penalty might perhaps also deter us from murdering—but altogether needlessly, since we would not murder with it or without it. Those who are sufficiently dissocialized to murder are not responding to the world in the same way that we are, and we simply cannot "intuit" their thinking processes from ours.

Consider, for example, the well-documented cases of persons who kill *because* there is a death penalty. One of these was Pamela Watkins, a babysitter in San Jose who had made several unsuccessful suicide attempts and was frightened to try again. She finally strangled two children so that the state of California would execute her. In various bizarre forms, this "suicide-murder" syndrome is reported by psychiatrists again and again. (Parenthetically, Gary Gilmore was probably such a case.) If you intuit that somewhere, sometime, the death penalty *does* deter some potential murders, are you also prepared to intuit that their numbers mathematically exceed the numbers of these wretched people who are actually induced to murder by the existence of capital punishment?

Here, I suggest, our intuition does—or should—fail, just as the evidence certainly does fail, to establish a deterrent justification for the death penalty. There is simply no credible evidence, and there is no rational way of reasoning about the real facts once you know them, which can sustain this or any other justification with the degree of confidence that should be demanded before a civilized society deliberately extinguishes human life.

III.

I have only a little space for my final point, but it is sufficient because the point is perfectly plain. Capital punishment is a dying institution in this last quarter of the twentieth century. It has already been abandoned in law or in fact throughout most of the civilized world. England, Canada, the Scandinavian countries, virtually all of Western Europe except for France and Spain have abolished the death penalty. The vast majority of countries in the Western Hemisphere have abolished it. Its last strongholds in the world—apart from the United States—are in Asia and Africa, particularly South Africa. Even the countries which maintain capital punishment on the books have almost totally ceased to use it in fact. In the United States, considering only the last half century, executions have plummeted from 199 in 1935 to approximately 29 a year during the decade before 1967, when the ten-year judicial moratorium began.

Do you doubt that this development will continue? Do you doubt that it will continue because it is the path of civilization—the path up out of fear and terror and the barbarism that terror breeds, into self-confidence and decency in the administration of justice? The road, like any other built by men, has its detours, but over many generations it has run true, and will run true. And there will therefore come a time—perhaps in 20 years, perhaps in 50 or 100, but very surely and very shortly as the lifetime of nations is measured—when our children will look back at us in horror and unbelief because of what we did in their names and for their supposed safety, just as we look back in horror and unbelief at the thousands of crucifixions and beheadings and live disembowelments that our ancestors practiced for the supposed purpose of making our world safe from murderers and robbers, thieves, shoplifters, and pickpockets.

All of these kinds of criminals are still with us, and will be with our children—although we can certainly decrease their numbers and their damage, and protect ourselves from them a lot better, if we insist that our politicians stop pounding on the whipping boy of capital punishment and start coming up with some real solutions to the real problems of crime. Our children will cease to execute murderers for the same reason that we have ceased to string up pickpockets and shoplifters at the public crossroads, although there are still plenty of them around. Our children will cease to execute murderers because executions are a self-deluding, self-defeating, self-degrading, futile, and entirely stupid means of dealing with the crime of murder, and because our children will prefer to be something better than murderers themselves. Should we not—can we not—make the same choice now?

The Ultimate Punishment: A Defense of Capital Punishment

Ernest van den Haag

In an average year about 20,000 homicides occur in the United States. Fewer than 300 convicted murderers are sentenced to death. But because no more than thirty murderers have been executed in any recent year, most convicts sentenced to death are likely to die of old age. Nonetheless, the death penalty looms large in discussions: It raises important moral questions independent of the number of executions.

The death penalty is our harshest punishment. It is irrevocable; it ends the existence of those punished, instead of temporarily imprisoning them. Further, although not intended to cause physical pain, execution is the only corporal punishment still applied to adults. These singular characteristics contribute to the perennial, impassioned controversy about capital punishment.

I. *Distribution*

Consideration of the justice, morality, or usefulness, of capital punishment is often conflated with objections to its alleged discriminatory or capricious distribution among the guilty. Wrongly so. If capital punishment is immoral *in se*, no distribution among the guilty could make it moral. If capital punishment is moral, no distribution would make it immoral. Improper distribution cannot affect the quality of what is distributed, be it punishments or rewards. Discriminatory or capricious distribution thus could not justify abolition of the

Source: Harvard Law Review, "The Ultimate Punishment: A Defense of Capital Punishment" by Ernest van den Haag. Copyright © 1986 by Harvard Law Review Association. Reproduced with permission of Harvard Law Review Association in the format Textbook via Copyright Clearance Center.

death penalty. Further, maldistribution inheres no more in capital punishment than in any other punishment.

Maldistribution between the guilty and the innocent is, by definition, unjust. But the injustice does not lie in the nature of the punishment. Because of the finality of the death penalty, the most grievous maldistribution occurs when it is imposed upon the innocent. However, the frequent allegations of discrimination and capriciousness refer to maldistribution among the guilty and not to the punishment of the innocent.

Maldistribution of any punishment among those who deserve it is irrelevant to its justice or morality. Even if poor or black convicts guilty of capital offenses suffer capital punishment, and other convicts equally guilty of the same crimes do not, a more equal distribution, however desirable, would merely be more equal. It would not be more just to the convicts under sentence of death.

Punishments are imposed on persons, not on racial or economic groups. Guilt is personal. The only relevant question is: Does the person to be executed deserve the punishment? Whether or not others who deserve the same punishment, whatever their economic or racial group, have avoided execution is irrelevant. If they have, the guilt of the executed convicts would not be diminished, nor would their punishment be less deserved. To put the issue starkly, if the death penalty were imposed on guilty blacks, but not on guilty whites, or, if it were imposed by a lottery among the guilty, this irrationally discriminatory or capricious distribution would neither make the penalty unjust, nor cause anyone to be unjustly punished, despite the undue impunity bestowed on others.

Equality, in short, seems morally less important than justice. And justice is independent of distributional inequalities. The ideal of equal justice demands that justice be equally distributed, not that it be replaced by equality. Justice requires that as many of the guilty as possible be punished, regardless of whether others have avoided punishment. To let these others escape the deserved punishment does not do justice to them, or to society. But it is unjust to those who could not escape. . . .

Recent data reveal little direct racial discrimination in the sentencing of those arrested and convicted of murder. The abrogation of the death penalty for rape has eliminated a major source of racial discrimination. Concededly, some discrimination based on the race of murder victims may exist; yet, this discrimination affects criminal victimizers in an unexpected way. Murderers of whites are thought more likely to be executed than murderers of blacks. Black victims, then, are less fully vindicated than white ones. However, because most black murderers kill blacks, black murderers are spared the death penalty more often than are white murderers. They fare better than most white murderers. The motivation behind unequal distribution of the death penalty may well have been to discriminate against blacks, but the result has favored them. Maldistribution is thus a straw man for empirical as well as analytical reasons.

II. Miscarriages of Justice

In a recent survey Professors Hugo Adam Bedau and Michael Radalet found that 7000 persons were executed in the United States between 1900 and 1985 and that 25 were innocent of capital crimes. Among the innocents they list Sacco and Vanzetti as well as Ethel and Julius Rosenberg. Although their data may be questionable, I do not doubt that over a long enough period, miscarriages of justice will occur even in capital cases.

Despite precautions, nearly all human activities, such as trucking, lighting, or construction, cost the lives of some innocent bystanders. We do not give up these activities, because the advantages, moral or material, outweigh the unintended losses. Analogously, for those who think the death penalty just, miscarriages of justice are offset by the moral benefits and the usefulness of doing justice. For those who think the death penalty unjust even when it does not miscarry, miscarriages can hardly be decisive.

III. Deterrence

Despite much recent work, there has been no conclusive statistical demonstration that the death penalty is a better deterrent than are alternative punishments. However, deterrence is less than decisive for either side. Most abolitionists acknowledge that they would continue to favor abolition even if the death penalty were shown to deter more murders than alternatives could deter. Abolitionists appear to value the life of a convicted murderer or at least, his non-execution, more highly than they value the lives of innocent victims who might be spared by deterring prospective murderers.

Deterrence is not altogether decisive for me either. I would favor retention of the death penalty as retribution even if it were shown that the threat of execution could not deter prospective murderers not already deterred by the threat of imprisonment. Still, I believe the death penalty, because of its finality, is more feared than imprisonment, and deters some prospective murderers not deterred by the threat of imprisonment. Sparing the lives of even a few prospective victims by deterring their murderers is more important than preserving the lives of convicted murderers because of the possibility, or even the probability, that executing them would not deter others. Whereas the lives of the victims who might be saved are valuable, that of the murderer has only negative value, because of his crime. Surely the criminal law is meant to protect the lives of potential victims in preference to those of actual murderers.

Murder rates are determined by many factors; neither the severity nor the probability of the threatened sanction is always decisive. However, for the long run, I share the view of Sir James Fitzjames Stephen: "Some men, probably, abstain from murder because they fear that if they committed murder they would be hanged. Hundreds of thousands abstain from it because they regard it with horror. One great reason they regard it with horror is that murderers are hanged." Penal sanctions are useful in the long run for the formation of the internal restraints so necessary to control crime. The severity and finality of the death penalty is appropriate to the seriousness and finality of murder.

IV. Incidental Issues: Cost, Relative Suffering, Brutalization

Many nondecisive issues are associated with capital punishment. Some believe that the monetary cost of appealing a capital sentence is excessive. Yet most comparisons of the cost of life imprisonment with the cost of execution, apart from their dubious relevance, are flawed at least by the implied assumption that life prisoners will generate no judicial costs during their imprisonment. At any rate, the actual monetary costs are trumped by the importance of doing justice.

Others insist that a person sentenced to death suffers more than his victims suffered, and that this (excess) suffering is undue according to the *lex talionis* (rule of retaliation). We cannot know whether the murderer on death row suffers more than his victim suffered; however, unlike the murderer, the victim deserved none of the suffering inflicted. Further, the limitations of the *lex talionis* were meant to restrain private vengeance, not the social retribution that has taken its place. Punishment—regardless of the motivation—is not intended to revenge, offset, or compensate for the victim's suffering, or to be measured by it. Punishment is to vindicate the law and the social order undermined by the crime. This is why a kidnapper's penal confinement is not limited to the period for which he imprisoned his victim; nor the harm he caused his victim; nor is it meant only to offset the advantage he gained.

Another argument heard at least since Beccaria is that, by killing a murderer, we encourage, endorse, or legitimize unlawful killing. Yet, although all punishments are meant to be unpleasant, it is seldom argued that they legitimize the unlawful imposition of identical unpleasantness. Imprisonment is not thought to legitimize kidnapping; neither are fines thought to legitimize robbery. The difference between murder and execution, or between kidnapping and imprisonment, is that the first is unlawful and undeserved, the second a lawful and deserved punishment for an unlawful act. The physical similarities of the punishment to the crime are irrelevant. The relevant difference is not physical, but social.

V. Justice, Excess, Degradation

We threaten punishments in order to deter crime. We impose them not only to make the threats credible but also as retribution (justice) for the crimes that were not deterred. Threats and punishments are necessary to deter and deterrence is a sufficient practical justification for them. Retribution is an independent moral justification. Although penalties can be unwise, repulsive, or inappropriate, and those punished can be pitiable, in a sense the infliction of legal punishment on a guilty person cannot be unjust. By committing the crime, the criminal volunteered to assume the risk of receiving a legal punishment that he could have avoided by not committing the crime. The punishment he suffers is the punishment he voluntarily risked suffering and, therefore, it is no more unjust to him than any other event for which one knowingly volunteers to assume the risk. Thus, the death penalty cannot be unjust to the guilty criminal.

There remain, however, two moral objections. The penalty may be regarded as always excessive as retribution and always morally degrading. To regard the death penalty as always excessive, one must believe that no crime—no matter how heinous—could possibly justify capital punishment. Such a belief can neither be corroborated nor refuted; it is an article of faith.

Alternatively, or concurrently, one may believe that everybody, the murderer no less than the victim, has an imprescriptible (natural?) right to life. The law therefore should not deprive anyone of life. I share Jeremy Bentham's view that any such "natural and imprescriptible rights" are "nonsense upon stilts."

Justice Brennan has insisted that the death penalty is "uncivilized," "inhuman," inconsistent with "human dignity" and with "the sanctity of life," that it "treats members of the human race as nonhumans, as objects to be toyed with and discarded," that it is "uniquely degrading to human dignity" and "by its very nature, [involves] a denial of the executed person's humanity." Justice Brennan does not say why he thinks execution "uncivilized." Hitherto most civilizations have had the death penalty, although it has been discarded in Western Europe, where it is currently unfashionable probably because of its abuse by totalitarian regimes.

By "degrading," Justice Brennan seems to mean that execution degrades the executed convicts. Yet philosophers, such as Immanuel Kant and G. F. W. Hegel, have insisted that, when deserved, execution, far from degrading the executed convict, affirms his humanity by affirming his rationality and his responsibility for his actions. They thought that execution, when deserved, is required for the sake of the convict's dignity. (Does not life imprisonment violate human dignity more than execution, by keeping alive a prisoner deprived of all autonomy?)

Common sense indicates that it cannot be death—our common fate—that is inhuman. Therefore, Justice Brennan must mean that death degrades when it comes not as a natural or accidental event, but as a deliberate social imposition. The murderer learns through his punishment that his fellow men have found him unworthy of living; that because he has murdered, he is being expelled from the community of the living. This degradation is self-inflicted. By murdering, the murderer has so dehumanized himself that he cannot remain among the living. The social recognition of his self-degradation is the punitive essence of execution. To believe, as Justice Brennan appears to, that the degradation is inflicted by the execution reverses the direction of causality.

Execution of those who have committed heinous murders may deter only one murder per year. If it does, it seems quite warranted. It is also the only fitting retribution for murder I can think of.

Cloning

"Goodbye Dolly?" The Ethics of Human Cloning

John Harris

The recent announcement of a birth in the press heralds an event probably unparalleled for two millennia and has highlighted the impact of the genetic revolution on our lives and personal choices. More importantly perhaps, it raises questions about the legitimacy of the sorts of control individuals and society purport to exercise over something, which while it must sound portentous, is nothing less than human destiny. This birth, that of "Dolly," the cloned sheep, is also illustrative of the responsibilities of science and scientists to the communities in which they live and which they serve, and the public anxiety that sensational scientific achievements sometimes provokes.

The ethical implications of human clones have been much alluded to, but have seldom been examined with any rigor. Here I will examine the possible uses and abuses of human cloning and draw out the principle ethical dimensions, both of what might be done and its meaning, and of public and official responses.

There are two rather different techniques available for cloning individuals. One is by nuclear substitution, the technique used to create Dolly, and the other is by cell mass division or "embryo splitting." We'll start with cell mass division because this is the only technique for cloning that has, as yet, been used in humans.

Cell Mass Division

Although the technique of cloning embryos by cell mass division has, for some time been used extensively in animal models, it was used as a way of multiplying human embryos for the first time in October 1993 when Jerry Hall and Robert Stillman at George Washington Medical Center cloned human embryos by splitting early two- to eight-cell embryos into single embryo cells. Among other uses, cloning by cell mass division or embryo splitting could be used to provide a "twin" embryo for biopsy, permitting an embryo undamaged by invasive procedures to be available for implantation following the result of the biopsy on its twin, or to increase the number of embryos available for implantation in the treatment of infertility. To what extent is such a practice unethical?

Source: "Goodbye Dolly?" The Ethics of Human Cloning," *Journal of Medical Ethics*, 23, (1997): 353–360. Some notes have been omitted.

Individuals, Multiples, and Genetic Variation

Cloning does not produce identical copies of the same individual person. It can only produce identical copies of the same genotype. Our experience of identical twins demonstrates that each is a separate individual with his or her own character, preferences, and so on. Although there is some evidence of striking similarities with respect to these factors in twins, there is no question but that each twin is a distinct individual, as independent and as free as is anyone else. To clone Bill Clinton is not to create multiple Presidents of the United States. Artificial clones do not raise any difficulties not raised by the phenomenon of "natural" twins. We do not feel apprehensive when natural twins are born, why should we when twins are deliberately created?

If the objection to cloning is to the creation of identical individuals separated by time (because the twin embryos might be implanted in different cycles, perhaps even years apart), it is a weak one at best. We should remember that such twins will be "identical" in the sense that they will each have the same genotype, but they will even (unlike some but by no means all natural monozygotic twins) be identical in the more familiar sense of looking identical at the same moment in time. If we think of expected similarities in character, tastes, and so on, then the same is true. The further separated in time, the less likely they are to have similarities in *character* (the more different the environment, the more different environmental influence on individuality).

The significant ethical issue here is whether it would be morally defensible, by outlawing the creation of clones by cell mass division, to deny a woman the chance to have the child she desperately seeks. If this procedure would enable a woman to create a sufficient number of embryos to give her a reasonable chance of successfully implanting one or two of them, then the objections to it would have to be weightly indeed. . . .

Nuclear Substitution: The Birth of Dolly

This technique involves (crudely described) deleting the nucleus of an egg cell and substituting the nucleus taken from the cell of another individual. This can be done using cells from an adult. The first viable offspring produced from fetal and adult mammalian cells was reported from an Edinburgh-based group in *Nature* on February 27, 1997. The event caused an international sensation and was widely reported in the world press. President Clinton of the United States called for an investigation into the ethics of such procedures and announced a moratorium on public spending on human cloning; the British Nobel Prize winner, Joseph Rotblat, described it as science out of control, creating "a means of mass destruction," and the German newspaper *Die Welt,* evoked the Third Reich, commenting: "The cloning of human beings would fit precisely into Adolph Hitler's world view."

More sober commentators were similarly panicked into instant reaction. Dr. Hiroshi Nakajima, Director General of the World Health Organization said: "WHO considers the use of cloning for the replication of human individuals to be ethically unacceptable as it would violate some of the basic principles which govern medically assisted procreation. These include respect for the dignity of the human being and protection of the security of human genetic material."[74] The World Health Organization followed up the line taken by Nakajima with a resolution of the Fiftieth World Health Assembly which saw fit to affirm "that the use of cloning for the replication of human individuals is ethically unacceptable and contrary to human integrity and morality."[75] Federico Mayor of UNESCO, equally quick off the mark, commented: "Human beings must not be cloned under any circumstances. Moreover, UNESCO's International Bioethics Committee (IBC), which has been reflecting on the ethics of scientific progress, has maintained that the human genome must be preserved as common heritage of humanity."[76]

The European parliament rushed through a resolution on cloning, the preamble of which asserted (paragraph B):

> "[T]he cloning of human beings . . . cannot under any circumstances be justified or tolerated by any society, because it is a serious violation of fundamental human rights and is contrary to the principle of equality of human beings as it permits a eugenic and racist selection of the human race, it offends against human dignity and it requires experimentation on humans," And which went on to claim that, (clause 1) "each individual has a right to his or her own genetic identity and that human cloning is, and must continue to be, prohibited."[77]

These statements are, perhaps un-surprisingly, thin on argument and rationale; they appear to have been plucked from the air to justify an instant reaction. There are vague references to "human rights" or "basic principles" with little or no attempt to explain what these principles are, or to indicate how they might apply to cloning. The WHO statement, for example, refers to the basic principles which govern human reproduction and singles out "respect for the dignity of the human being" and "protection of the security of genetic material." How, we are entitled to ask, is the security of genetic material compromised? Is it less secure when inserted with precision by scientists, or when spread around with the characteristic negligence of the average human male?

Human Dignity

Appeals to human dignity, on the other hand, while universally attractive, are comprehensively vague and deserve separate attention. A first question to ask when the idea of human dignity is invoked is: Whose dignity is attacked and how? Is it the duplication of a large part of the genome that is supposed to constitute the attack on human dignity? If so we might legitimately ask whether and how the dignity of a natural twin is threatened by the existence of her sister? The notion of human dignity is often also linked to Kantian ethics. A typical example, and one that attempts to provide some basis for objections to cloning based on human dignity, was Axel Kahn's invocation of this principle in his commentary on cloning in *Nature*.[78]

> The creation of human clones solely for spare cell lines would, from a philosophical point of view, be in obvious contradiction to the principle expressed by Emmanuel Kant: that of human dignity. This principle demands that an individual—and I would extend this to read human life—should never be thought of as a means, but always also as an end. Creating human life for the sole purpose of preparing therapeutic material would clearly not be for the dignity of the life created.

The Kantian principle, crudely invoked as it usually is without any qualification or gloss, is seldom helpful in medical or bio-science contexts. As formulated by Kahn, for example, it would outlaw blood transfusions. The beneficiary of blood donation, neither knowing of, nor usually caring about, the anonymous donor uses the blood (and its donor) simply as a means to her own ends. It would also outlaw abortions to protect the life or health of the mother.

Instrumentalization

This idea of using individuals as a means to the purposes of others is sometimes termed "instrumentalization." Applying this idea coherently or consistently is not easy! If someone wants to have children in order to continue their genetic line do they act instrumentally? Where, as is standard practice in *in vitro fertilisation* (IVF), spare embryos are created, are these embryos created instrumentally? If not how do they differ from embryos created by embryo splitting for use of assisted reproduction?

Kahn responded in the journal *Nature* to these objections.[79] He reminds us, rightly, that Kant's famous principle states: "respect for human dignity requires that an individual is *never* used . . . *exclusively* as a means" and suggests that I have ignored the crucial use of the term "exclusively." I did not of course, and I'm happy with Kant's reformulation of the principle. It is not that Kant's principle does not have powerful intuitive force, but that it is so vague and so open to selective interpretation and its scope for application is consequently so limited, that its utility as one of the "fundamental principles of modern bioethical thought," as Kahn describes it, is virtually zero.

Kahn himself rightly points out that debates concerning the moral status of the human embryo are debates about whether embryos fall within the *scope* of Kant's or indeed any other moral principles concerning persons; so the principle itself is not illuminating in this context. Applied to the creation of individuals which are, or will become autonomous, it has limited application. True the Kantian principle rules out slavery, but so do a range of other principles based on autonomy and rights. If you are interested in the ethics of creating people then, so long as existence is in the created individual's best interests, and the individual will have the capacity of autonomy like any other, then the motives for which the individual was created are either morally irrelevant or subordinate to other moral considerations. So that even where, for example, a child is engendered exclusively to provide "a son and heir" (as so often in so many cultures) it is unclear how or whether Kant's principle applies. Either other motives are also attributed to the parent to square parental purposes with Kant, or the child's eventual autonomy, and its clear and substantial interest in or benefit from existence, take precedence over the comparatively trivial issue of parental motives. Either way the "fundamental principle of modern bioethical thought" is unhelpful and debates about whether or not an individual has been used *exclusively* as a means are sterile and usually unresolveable.

We noted earlier the possibility of using embryo splitting to allow genetic and other screening by embryo biopsy. One embryo could be tested and then destroyed to ascertain the health and genetic status of the remaining clones. Again, an objection often voiced to this is that it would violate the Kantian principle, and that "one twin would be destroyed for the sake of another."

This is a bizarre and misleading objection both to using cell mass division to create clones for screening purposes, and to creating clones by nuclear substitution to generate spare cell lines. It is surely ethically dubious to object to one embryo being sacrificed for the sake of another, but not to object to it being sacrificed for nothing. In *in vitro* fertilisation, for example, it is, in the United Kingdom, currently regarded as good practice to store spare embryos for future use by the mother or for disposal at her discretion, either to other women who require donor embryos, or for research, or simply to be destroyed. It cannot be morally worse to use an embryo to provide information about its sibling, than to use it for more abstract research or simply to destroy it. If it is permissible to use early embryos for research or to destroy them, their use in genetic and other health testing is surely also permissible. The same would surely go for their use in creating cell lines for therapeutic purposes. . . .

Genetic Variability

So many of the fears expressed about cloning, and indeed about genetic engineering more generally, invoke the idea of the effect on the gene pool or upon genetic variability or assert the sanctity of the human genome as a common resource or heritage. It is very difficult to understand what is allegedly at stake here. The issue of genetic variation need not detain us long. The numbers of twins produced by cloning will always be so small compared to the human gene pool in totality, that the effect on the variation of the human gene pool will be vanishingly small. We can say with confidence that the human genome and the human population were not threatened at the start of the present millennium in the year A.D. one, and yet the world population was then perhaps one percent of what it is today. Natural species are usually said to be endangered when the population falls to about one thousand breeding individuals; by these standards fears for humankind and its genome may be said to have been somewhat exaggerated.

The resolution of the European parliament goes into slightly more detail; having repeated the, now mandatory, waft in the direction of fundamental human rights and human dignity, it actually produces an argument. It suggests that cloning violates the principle of equality, "as it permits a eugenic and racist selection of the human race." Well, so does prenatal, and pre-implantation screening, not to mention egg donation, sperm donation, surrogacy, abortion, and human preference in choice of sexual partner. The fact that a technique could be abused does not constitute an argument against the technique, unless there is no prospect of preventing the abuse or wrongful use. To ban cloning on the grounds that it might be used for racist purposes is tantamount to saying that sexual intercourse should be prohibited because it permits the possibility of rape.

Genetic Identity

The second principle appealed to by the European parliament states, that "each individual has a right to his or her own genetic identity." Leaving aside the inevitable contribution of mitochondrial DNA,[80] we have seen that, as in the case of natural identical twins, genetic identity is not an essential component of personal identity nor is it necessary for "individuality." Moreover, unless genetic identity is required either for personal identity, or for individuality, it is not clear why there should be a right to such a thing. But if there is, what are we to do about the rights of identical twins?

Suppose there came into being a life-threatening (or even disabling) condition that affected pregnant women and that there was an effective treatment, the only side effect of which was that it cause the embryo to divide, resulting in twins. Would the existence of the supposed right conjured up by the European parliament mean that the therapy should be outlawed? Suppose that an effective vaccine for HIV was developed which had the effect of doubling the natural twinning rate; would this be a violation of fundamental human rights? Are we to foreclose the possible benefits to be derived from human cloning on so flimsy a basis? We should recall that the natural occurrence of monozygotic (identical) twins is one in 270 pregnancies. This means that in the United Kingdom, with a population of about 58 million, over 200 thousand such pregnancies have occurred. How are we to regard human rights violations on such a grand scale?

A Right to Parents

The apparently overwhelming imperative to identify some right that is violated by human cloning sometimes expresses itself in the assertion of "a right to have two parents" or as "the right to be the product of the mixture of the genes of two individuals." These are on the face of it highly artificial and problematic rights— where have they sprung from, save from a desperate attempt to conjure some rights that have been violated by cloning? However, let's take them seriously for a moment and grant that they have some force. Are they necessarily violated by the nuclear transfer technique?

If the right to have two parents is understood to be the right to have two social parents, then it is of course only violated by cloning if the family identified as the one to rear the resulting child is a one-parent family. This is not of course necessarily any more likely a result of cloning, than of the use of any of the other new reproductive technologies (or indeed of sexual reproduction). Moreover if there is such a right, it is widely violated, creating countless "victims," and there is no significant evidence of any enduring harm from the violation of this supposed right. Indeed war widows throughout the world would find its assertion highly offensive.

If, on the other hand we interpret a right to two parents as the right to be the product of the mixture of the genes of two individuals, then the supposition that this right is violated when the nucleus of the cell of one individual is inserted into the denucleated egg of another, is false in the way this claim is usually understood. There is at least one sense in which a right expressed in this form might be violated by cloning, but not in any way which has force as an objection. Firstly it is false to think that the clone is the genetic child of the nucleus donor. It is not. The clone is the twin brother or sister of the nucleus donor and the genetic offspring of the nucleus donor's own parents. Thus this type of cloned individual is, and always must be, the genetic child of two separate genotypes, of two genetically different individuals, however often it is cloned or re-cloned. . . .

What Good is Cloning?

One major reason for developing cloning in animals is said to be to permit the study of genetic diseases and indeed genetic development more generally. Whether or not there would be major advantages in human cloning by nuclear substitution is not yet clear. Certainly it would enable some infertile people to have children genetically related to them, it offers the prospect, as we have noted, of preventing some diseases caused by mitochondrial DNA, and could help "carriers" of X-linked and autosomal recessive disorders to have their own genetic children without risk of passing on the disease. It is also possible that cloning could be used for the creation of "spare parts" by for example, growing stem cells for particular cell types from non-diseased parts of an adult.

Any attempt to use this technique in the United Kingdom, is widely thought to be illegal. Whether it would in fact be illegal might turn on whether it is plausible to regard such cloning as the product of "fertilisation." Apparently only fertilized embryos are covered by the *Human Fertilisation and Embryology Act 1990*. The technique used in Edinburgh which involves deleting the nucleus of an unfertilized egg and then substituting a cell nucleus from an existing individual, by-passes what is normally considered to be fertilisation completely and may therefore turn out not to be covered by existing legislation. On the other hand, if as seems logical, we consider "fertilisation" as the moment when all forty-six chromosomes are present and the zygote is formed the problem does not arise.

The unease caused by Dolly's birth may be due to the fact that it was just such a technique that informed the plot of the film "The Boys from Brazil" in which Hitler's genotype was cloned to produce a fuehrer for the future. The prospect of limitless numbers of clones of Hitler is rightly disturbing. However, the number of clones that could be produced of any one genotype will, for the foreseeable future, be limited not by the number of copies that could be made of one genotype (using serial nuclear transfer techniques 470 copies of a single nuclear gene in cattle have been reported), but by the availability of *human* host mothers. Mass production in any democracy could therefore scarcely be envisaged. Moreover, the futility of any such attempt is obvious. Hitler's genotype might conceivably produce a "gonadically challenged" individual of limited stature, but reliability in producing an evil and vicious megalomaniac is far more problematic, for reasons already noted in our consideration of cloning by cell mass division. . . .

Immortality?

Of course some vainglorious individuals might wish to have offspring not simply with their genes but with a matching genotype. However, there is no way that they could make such an individual a duplicate of themselves. So many years later the environmental influences would be radically different, and since every choice, however insignificant, causes a life-path to branch with unpredictable consequences, the holy grail of duplication would be doomed to remain a fruitless quest. We can conclude that people who would clone themselves would probably be foolish and ill-advised, but would they be immoral and would their attempts harm society or their children significantly?

Whether we should legislate to prevent people reproducing, not 23 but all 46 chromosomes, seems more problematic for reasons we have already examined, but we might have reason to be uncomfortable about the likely standards and effects of child-rearing by those who would clone themselves. Their attempts to mould their child in their own image would be likely to be more pronounced than the average. Whether they would likely be worse than so many people's attempts to duplicate race, religion, and culture, which are widely accepted as respectable in the contemporary world, might well depend on the character and constitution of the genotype donor. Where identical twins occur naturally we might think of it as "horizontal twinning," where twins are created by nuclear substitution we have a sort of "vertical twinning." Although horizontal twins would be closer to one another in every way, we do not seem much disturbed by their natural occurrence. Why we should be disturbed either by artificial horizontal twinning or by vertical twinning (where differences between the twins would be greater) is entirely unclear.

Suppose a woman's only chance of having "her own" genetic child was by cloning herself; what are the strong arguments that should compel her to accept that it would be wrong to use nuclear substitution? We must assume that this cloning technique is safe, and that initial fears that individuals produced using nuclear substitution might age more rapidly have proven groundless. We usually grant the so-called genetic imperative as an important part of the right to found a family, of procreative autonomy. The desire of people to have "their own" genetic children is widely accepted, and if we grant the legitimacy of genetic aspirations in so many cases, and the use of so many technologies to meet these aspirations, we need appropriately serious and weighty reasons to deny them here.

It is perhaps salutary to remember that there is no necessary connection between phenomena, attitudes, or actions that make us uneasy, or even those that disgust us, and those phenomena, attitudes, and actions that there are good reasons for judging unethical. Nor does it follow that those things we are confident *are* unethical must be prohibited by legislation or regulation.

We have looked at some of the objections of human cloning and found them to be less than plausible; we should now turn to one powerful argument that has recently been advanced in favor of a tolerant attitude to varieties of human reproduction.

Procreative Autonomy

We have examined the arguments for and against permitting the cloning of human individuals. At the heart of these questions is the issue of whether or not people have rights to control their reproductive destiny and, so far as they can do so without violating the rights of others or threatening society, to choose their own procreative path. We have seen that it has been claimed that cloning violates principles of human dignity. We will conclude by briefly examining an approach which suggests rather that failing to permit cloning might violate principles of dignity.

The American philosopher and legal theorist Ronald Dworkin has outlined the arguments for a right to what he calls "procreative autonomy" and has defined this right as a "a right to control their own role in procreation unless the state has a compelling reason for denying them that control."[81] Arguably, freedom to clone one's own genes might also be defended as a dimension of procreative autonomy because so many people and agencies have been attracted by the idea of the special nature of genes and have linked the procreative imperative to the genetic imperative.

> The right of procreative autonomy follows from any competent interpretation of the due process clause and of the Supreme Court's past decisions applying it.... The First Amendment prohibits government from establishing any religion, and it guarantees all citizens free exercise of their own religion. The Fourteenth Amendment, which incorporates the First Amendment, imposes the same prohibition and same responsibility on states. These provisions also guarantee the right of procreative autonomy.[82]

The point is that the sorts of freedoms which freedom of religion guarantees, freedom to choose one's own way of life and live according to one's most deeply held beliefs are also at the heart of procreative choices. And Dworkin concludes:

> the no one may be prevented from influencing the shared moral environment, through his own private choices, tastes, opinions, and example, just because these tastes or opinions disgust those who have the power to shut him up or lock him up.[83]

Thus it may be that we should be prepared to accept some degree of offense and some social disadvantages as a price we should be willing to pay in order to protect freedom of choice in matters of procreation and perhaps this applies to cloning as much as to more straightforward or usual procreative preferences.

The nub of this argument is complex and abstract but it is worth stating at some length. I cannot improve on Dworkin's formulation of it.

> The right of procreative autonomy has an important place . . . in Western political culture more generally. The most important feature of that culture is a belief in individual human dignity: that people have the moral right—and the moral responsibility—to confront the most fundamental questions about the meaning and value of their own lives for themselves, answering to their own consciences and convictions. . . . The principle of procreative autonomy, in a broad sense, is embedded in any genuinely democratic culture.[84]

In so far as decisions to reproduce in particular ways or even using particular technologies constitute decisions concerning central issues of value, then arguably the freedom to make them is guaranteed by the constitution (written or not) of any democratic society, unless the state has a compelling reason for denying its citizens that control. To establish such a compelling reason the state (or indeed a federation or union of states, such as the European Union for example) would have to show that more was at stake than the fact that a majority found the ideas disturbing or even disgusting.

As yet, in the case of human cloning, such compelling reasons have not been produced. Suggestions have been made, but have not been sustained, that human dignity may be compromised by the techniques of cloning. Dworkin's arguments suggest that human dignity and indeed democratic constitutions may be compromised by attempts to limit procreative autonomy, at least where greater values cannot be shown to be thereby threatened.

In the absence of compelling arguments against human cloning, we can bid Dolly a cautious "hello." We surely have sufficient reasons to permit experiments on human embryos to proceed, provided, as with any such experiments, the embryos are destroyed at an early stage. While we wait to see whether the technique will ever be established as safe, we should consider the best ways to regulate its uptake until we are in a position to know what will emerge both by way of benefits and in terms of burdens.

The Wisdom of Repugnance

Leon Kass

Our habit of delighting in news of scientific and technological breakthroughs has been sorely challenged by the birth announcement of a sheep named Dolly. Though Dolly shares with previous sheep the "softest clothing, woolly, bright," William Blake's question, "Little Lamb, who made thee?" has for her a radically different answer: Dolly was, quite literally, made. She is the work not of nature or nature's God but of man, an Englishman, Ian Wilmut, and his fellow scientists. What is more, Dolly came into being not only asexually—ironically, just like "He [who] calls Himself a Lamb"—but also as the genetically identical copy (and the perfect incarnation of the form or blueprint) of a mature ewe, of whom she is a clone. This long-awaited yet not quite expected success in cloning a mammal raised immediately the prospect—and the specter—of cloning human beings: "I a child and Thou a lamb," despite our differences, have always been equal candidates for creative making, only now, by means of cloning, we may both spring from the hand of man playing at being God.

After an initial flurry of expert comment and public consternation, with opinion polls showing overwhelming opposition to cloning human beings, President Clinton ordered a ban on all federal support for human cloning research (even though none was being supported) and charged the National Bioethics Advisory Commission to report in ninety days on the ethics of human cloning research. The commission (an eighteen-member panel, evenly balanced between scientists and nonscientists, appointed by the president and reporting to the National Science and Technology Council) invited testimony from scientists, religious thinkers, and bioethicists, as well as from the general public. In its report, issued in June 1997, the commission concluded that attempting to clone a human being was "at this time . . . morally unacceptable," recommended continuing the president's moratorium on the use of federal funds to support cloning of humans, and called for federal legislation to prohibit anyone from attempting (during the next three to five years) to create a child through cloning.

Even before the commission reported, Congress was poised to act. Bills to prohibit the use of federal funds for human cloning research have been introduced in the House of Representatives and the Senate; and another bill, in the House, would make it illegal "for any person to use a human somatic cell for the process of producing a human clone." A fateful decision is at hand. To clone or not to clone a human being is no longer an academic question.

Source: Excerpted and reprinted with the author's permission from "The Wisdom of Repugnance: Why We Should Ban the Cloning of Humans" by Leon Kass from *The New Republic* 216, No. 22, 1997, pp. 17–26.
Dr. Kass is a Professor in the Committee on Social Thought at the University of Chicago and Hertog Fellow at the American Enterprise Institute.

Taking Cloning Seriously, Then and Now

Cloning first came to public attention roughly thirty years ago, following the successful asexual production, in England, of a clutch of tadpole clones by the technique of nuclear transplantation. The individual largely responsible for bringing the prospect and promise of human cloning to public notice was Joshua Lederberg, a Nobel laureate geneticist and a man of large vision. In 1996 Lederberg wrote a remarkable article in the *American Naturalist* detailing the eugenic advantages of human cloning and other forms of genetic engineering, and the following year he devoted a column in the *Washington Post,* where he wrote regularly on science and society, to the prospect of human cloning. He suggested that cloning could help us overcome the unpredictable variety that still rules human reproduction and would allow us to benefit from perpetuating superior genetic endowments. Those writings sparked a small public debate in which I became a participant. At the time a young researcher in molecular biology at the National Institutes of Health, I wrote a reply to the *Post,* arguing against Lederberg's amoral treatment of that morally weighty subject and insisting on the urgency of confronting a series of questions and objections, culminating in the suggestion that "the programmed reproduction of man will, in fact, dehumanize him."

Much has happened in the intervening years. It has become harder, not easier, to discern the true meaning of human cloning. We have in some sense been softened up to the idea—through movies, cartoons, jokes, and intermittent commentary in the mass media, some serious, most lighthearted. We have become accustomed to new practices in human reproduction: not just in vitro fertilization, but also embryo manipulation, embryo donation, and surrogate pregnancy. Animal biotechnology has yielded transgenic animals and a burgeoning science of genetic engineering, easily and soon to be transferable to humans.

Even more important, changes in the broader culture make it now vastly more difficult to express a common and respectful understanding of sexuality, procreation, nascent life, family, and the meaning of motherhood, fatherhood, and the links between the generations. Twenty-five years ago, abortion was still largely illegal and thought to be immoral, the sexual revolution (made possible by the extramarital use of the pill) was still in its infancy, and few had yet heard about the reproductive rights of single women, homosexual men, and lesbians. (Never mind shameless memoirs about one's own incest!) Then one could argue, without embarrassment, that the new technologies of human reproduction—babies without sex—and their confounding of normal kin relations—who is the mother: the egg donor, the surrogate who carries and delivers, or the one who rears?—would "undermine the justification and support that biological parenthood gives to the monogamous marriage." Today, defenders of stable, monogamous marriage risk charges of giving offense to those adults who are living in "new family forms" or to those children who, even without the benefit of assisted reproduction, have acquired either three or four parents or one or none at all. Today, one must even apologize for voicing opinions that twenty-five years ago were nearly universally regarded as the core of our culture's wisdom on those matters. In a world whose once-given natural boundaries are blurred by technological change and whose moral boundaries are seemingly up for grabs, it is much more difficult to make persuasive the still compelling case against cloning human beings. As Raskolnikov put it, "Man gets used to everything—the beast!"

Indeed, perhaps the most depressing feature of the discussions that immediately followed the news about Dolly was their ironical tone, their genial cynicism, their moral fatigue: "An Udder Way of Making Lambs" (*Nature*), "Who Will Cash in on Breakthrough in Cloning?" (*Wall Street Journal*), "Is Cloning Baaaaaaad?" (*Chicago Tribune*). Gone from the scene are the wise and courageous voices of Theodosius Dobzhansky (genetics), Hans Jonas (philosophy), and Paul Ramsey (theology), who, only twenty-five years ago, all made powerful moral arguments against ever cloning a human being. We are now too sophisticated for such argumentation; we would not be caught in public with a strong moral stance, never mind an absolutist one. We are all, or almost all, postmodernists now.

Cloning turns out to be the perfect embodiment of the ruling opinions of our new age. Thanks to the sexual revolution, we are able to deny in practice, and increasingly in thought, the inherent procreative teleology of sexuality itself. But, if sex has no intrinsic connection to generating babies, babies need have no necessary connection to sex. Thanks to feminism and the gay rights movement, we are increasingly encouraged to treat the natural heterosexual difference and its preeminence as a matter of "cultural construction." But if male and female are not normatively complementary and generatively significant, babies need not come from male and female complementarity. Thanks to the prominence and the acceptability of divorce and out-of-wedlock births, stable, monogamous marriage as the ideal home for procreation is no longer the agreed-upon cultural norm. For that new dispensation, the clone is the ideal emblem: the ultimate "single-parent child."

Thanks to our belief that all children should be *wanted* children (the more high-minded principle we use to justify contraception and abortion), sooner or later only those children who fulfill our wants will be fully acceptable. Through cloning, we can work our wants and wills on the very identity of our children, exercising control as never before. Thanks to modern notions of individualism and the rate of cultural change, we see ourselves not as linked to ancestors and defined by traditions, but as projects for our own self-creation, not only as self-made men but also man-made selves; and self-cloning is simply an extension of such rootless and narcissistic self-re-creation.

Unwilling to acknowledge our debt to the past and unwilling to embrace the uncertainties and the limitations of the future, we have a false relation to both: Cloning personifies our desire fully to control the future, while being subject to no controls ourselves. Enchanted and enslaved by the glamour of technology, we have lost our awe and wonder before the deep mysteries of nature and of life. We cheerfully take our own beginnings in our hands and, like the last man, we blink.

Part of the blame for our complacency lies, sadly, with the field of bioethics itself, and its claim to expertise in these moral matters. Bioethics was founded by people who understood that the new biology touched and threatened the deepest matters of our humanity: bodily integrity, identity and individuality, lineage and kinship, freedom and self-command, eros and aspiration, and the relations and strivings of body and soul. With its capture by analytic philosophy, however, and its inevitable routinization and professionalization, the field has by and large come to content itself with analyzing moral arguments, reacting to new technological developments, and taking on emerging issues of public policy, all performed with a naïve faith that the evils we fear can all be avoided by compassion, regulation, and a respect for autonomy. Bioethics has made some major contributions in the protection of human subjects and in other areas where personal freedom is threatened; but its practitioners, with few exceptions, have turned the big human questions into pretty thin gruel. . . .

Human cloning, though it is in some respects continuous with previous reproductive technologies, also represents something radically new, in itself and in its easily foreseeable consequences. The stakes are very high indeed. I exaggerate, but in the direction of the truth, when I insist that we are faced with having to decide nothing less than whether human procreation is going to remain human, whether children are going to be made rather than begotten, whether it is a good thing, humanly speaking, to say yes in principle to the road that leads (at best) to the dehumanized rationality of *Brave New World*. This is not business as usual, to be fretted about for a while but finally to be given our seal of approval. We must rise to the occasion and make our judgments as if the future of our humanity hangs in the balance. For so it does.

The State of the Art

If we should not underestimate the significance of human cloning, neither should we exaggerate its imminence or misunderstand just what is involved. The procedure is conceptually simple. The nucleus of a mature but unfertilized egg is removed and replaced with a nucleus obtained from a specialized cell of an adult (or fetal) organism (in Dolly's case, the donor nucleus came from mammary gland epithelium). Since almost all the hereditary material of a cell is contained within its nucleus, the renucleated egg and the individual into which that egg develops are genetically identical to the organism that was the source of the transferred nucleus. An unlimited number of genetically identical individuals—clones—could be produced by nuclear transfer. In principle, any person, male or female, newborn or adult, could be cloned, and in any quantity. With laboratory cultivation and storage of tissues, cells outliving their sources make it possible even to clone the dead.

The technical stumbling block, overcome by Wilmut and his colleagues, was to find a means of reprogramming the state of the DNA in the donor cells, reversing its differentiated expression and restoring its full totipotency, so that it could again direct the entire process of producing a mature organism. Now that the problem has been solved, we should expect a rush to develop cloning for other animals, especially livestock, to propagate in perpetuity the champion meat or milk producers. Though exactly how soon someone will succeed in cloning a human being is anybody's guess, Wilmut's technique, almost certainly applicable to humans, makes *attempting* the feat an imminent possibility.

Yet some cautions are in order and some possible misconceptions need correcting. For a start, cloning is not Xeroxing. As has been reassuringly reiterated, the clone of Mel Gibson, though his genetic double, would enter the world hairless, toothless, and peeing in his diapers, just like any other human infant. Moreover, the success rate, at least at first, will probably not be very high: The British transferred 277 adult nuclei into enucleated sheep eggs and implanted twenty-nine clonal embryos, but they achieved the birth of only one live lamb clone. For that reason, among others, it is unlikely that, at least for now, the practice would be very popular, and there is no immediate worry of mass-scale production of multicopies. The need of repeated surgery to obtain eggs and, more crucially, of numerous borrowed wombs for implantation will surely limit use, as will the expense; besides, almost everyone who is able will doubtless prefer nature's sexier way of conceiving.

Still, for the tens of thousands of people already sustaining over 200 assisted-reproduction clinics in the United States and already availing themselves of in vitro fertilization, intracytoplasmic sperm injection, and other techniques of assisted reproduction, cloning would be an option with virtually no added fuss (especially when the success rate improves). Should commercial interests develop in "nucleus-banking," as they have in sperm-banking; should famous athletes or other celebrities decide to market their DNA the way they now market their autographs and just about everything else; should techniques of embryo and germline genetic testing and manipulation arrive as anticipated, increasing the use of laboratory assistance to obtain "better" babies—should all this come to pass, then cloning, if it is permitted, could become more than a marginal practice simply on the basis of free reproductive choice, even without any social encouragement to upgrade the gene pool or to replicate superior types. Moreover, if laboratory research on human cloning proceeds, even without any intention to produce cloned humans, the existence of cloned human embryos in the laboratory, created to begin with only for research purposes, would surely pave the way for later baby-making implantations.

In anticipation of human cloning, apologists and proponents have already made clear possible uses of the perfected technology, ranging from the sentimental and compassionate to the grandiose. They include: providing a child for an infertile couple; "replacing" a beloved spouse or child who is dying or has died; avoiding the risk of genetic disease; permitting reproduction for homosexual men and lesbians who want nothing sexual to do with the opposite sex; securing a genetically identical source of organs or tissues perfectly suitable for transplantation; getting a child with a genotype of one's own choosing, not excluding oneself; replicating individuals of great genius, talent, or beauty—having a child who really could "be like Mike"; and creating large sets of genetically identical humans suitable for research on, for instance, the question of nature versus nurture, or for special missions in peace and war (not excluding espionage), in which using identical humans would be an advantage. Most people who envision the cloning of human beings, of course, want none of those scenarios. That they cannot say why is not surprising. What is surprising, and welcome, is that, in our cynical age, they are saying anything at all.

The Wisdom of Repugnance

Offensive, grotesque, revolting, repugnant, and *repulsive*—those are the words most commonly heard regarding the prospect of human cloning. Such reactions come both from the man or woman in the street and from the intellectuals, from believers and atheists, from humanists and scientists. Even Dolly's creator has said he "would find it offensive" to clone a human being.

People are repelled by many aspects of human cloning. They recoil from the prospect of mass production of human beings, with large clones of look-alikes, compromised in their individuality; the idea of father-son or mother-daughter twins; the bizarre prospects of a woman's giving birth to and rearing a genetic copy of herself, her spouse, or even her deceased father or mother; the grotesqueness of conceiving a child as an exact replacement for another who has died; the utilitarian creation of embryonic genetic duplicates of oneself, to be frozen away or created when necessary, in case of need for homologous tissues or organs for transplantation; the narcissism of those who would clone themselves and the arrogance of others who think they know who deserves to be cloned or which genotype any child-to-be should be thrilled to receive; the Frankensteinian hubris to create human life and increasingly to control its destiny; man playing God. Almost no one finds any of the suggested reasons for human cloning compelling; almost everyone anticipates its possible misuses and abuses. Moreover, many people feel oppressed by the sense that there is probably nothing we can do to prevent it from happening. That makes the prospect all the more revolting.

Revulsion is not an argument; and some of yesterday's repugnances are today calmly accepted—though, one must add, not always for the better. In crucial cases, however, repugnance is the emotional expression of deep wisdom, beyond reason's power fully to articulate it. Can anyone really give an argument fully adequate to the horror which is father-daughter incest (even with consent), or having sex with animals, or mutilating a corpse, or eating human flesh, or raping or murdering another human being? Would anybody's failure to give full rational justification for his revulsion at those practices make that revulsion ethically suspect? Not at all. On the contrary, we are suspicious of those who think that they can rationalize away our horror, say, by trying to explain the enormity of incest with arguments only about the genetic risks of inbreeding.

The repugnance at human cloning belongs in that category. We are repelled by the prospect of cloning human beings not because of the strangeness or novelty of the undertaking, but because we intuit and feel, immediately and without argument, the violation of things that we rightfully hold dear. Repugnance, here as elsewhere, revolts against the excesses of human willfulness, warning us not to transgress what is unspeakably profound. Indeed, in this age in which everything is held to be permissible so long as it is freely done, in which our given human nature no longer commands respect, in which our bodies are regarded as mere instruments of our autonomous rational wills, repugnance may be the only voice left that speaks up to defend the central core of our humanity. Shallow are the souls that have forgotten how to shudder.

The Profundity of Sex

. . . Asexual reproduction, which produces "single-parent" offspring, is a radical departure from the natural human way, confounding all normal understandings of father, mother, sibling, and grandparent and all moral relations tied thereto. It becomes even more of a radical departure when the resulting offspring is a clone derived not from an embryo, but from a mature adult to whom the clone would be an identical twin; and when the process occurs not by natural accident (as in natural twinning), but by deliberate human design and manipulation; and when the child's (or children's) genetic constitution is preselected by the parent(s) (or scientists). Accordingly, as we shall see, cloning is vulnerable to three kinds of concerns and objections, related to these three points: Cloning threatens confusion of identity and individuality, even in small-scale cloning; cloning represents a giant step (though not the first one) toward transforming procreation into manufacture, that is, toward the increasing depersonalization of the process of generation and, increasingly, toward the "production" of human children as artifacts, products of human will and design (what others have called the problem of "commodification" of new life); and cloning—like other forms of eugenic engineering of the next generation—represents a form of despotism of the cloners over the cloned, and thus (even in benevolent cases) represents a blatant violation of the inner meaning of parent child relations, of what it means to have a child, of what it means to say yes to our own demise and "replacement."

Before turning to those specific ethical objections, let me test my claim of the profundity of the natural way by taking up a challenge recently posed by a friend. What if the given natural human way of reproduction were asexual, and we now had to deal with a new technological innovation—artificially induced sexual dimorphism and the fusing of complementary gametes—whose inventors argued that sexual reproduction promised all sorts of advantages, including hybrid vigor and the creation of greatly increased individuality? Would one then be forced to defend natural asexuality because it was natural? Could one claim that it carried deep human meaning?

The response to that challenge broaches the ontological meaning of sexual reproduction. For it is impossible, I submit, for there to have been human life—or even higher forms of animal life—in the absence of sexuality and sexual reproduction. We find asexual reproduction only in the lowest forms of life: bacteria, algae, fungi, some lower invertebrates. Sexuality brings with it a new and enriched relationship to the world. Only sexual animals can seek and find complementary others with whom to pursue a goal that transcends their own existence. For a sexual being, the world is no longer an indifferent and largely homogeneous *otherness*, in part edible, in part dangerous. It also contains some very special and related and complementary beings, of the same kind but of opposite sex, toward whom one reaches out with special interest and intensity. In higher birds and mammals, the outward gaze keeps a lookout not only for food and predators, but also for prospective mates; the beholding of the many-splendored world is suffused with desire for union— the animal antecedent of human eros and the germ of sociality. Not by accident is the human animal both the sexiest animal—whose females do not go into heat but are receptive throughout the estrous cycle and whose males must therefore have greater sexual appetite and energy to reproduce successfully—and also the most aspiring, the most social, the most open, and the most intelligent animal.

The soul-elevating power of sexuality is, at bottom, rooted in its strange connection to mortality, which it simultaneously accepts and tries to overcome. Asexual reproduction may be seen as a continuation of the activity of self-preservation. When one organism buds or divides to become two, the original being is (doubly) preserved, and nothing dies. Sexuality, by contrast, means perishability and serves replacement; the two that come together to generate one soon will die. Sexual desire, in human beings as in animals, thus serves an end that is partly hidden from, and finally at odds with, the self-serving individual. Whether we know it or not, when we are sexually active we are voting with our genitalia for our own demise. The salmon swimming upstream to spawn and die tell the universal story: Sex is bound up with death, to which it holds a partial answer in procreation. . . .

The Perversities of Cloning

First, an important if formal objection: Any attempt to clone a human being would constitute an unethical experiment upon the resulting child-to-be. As the animal experiments (frog and sheep) indicate, there are grave risks of mishaps and deformities. Moreover, because of what cloning means, one cannot presume a future cloned child's consent to be a clone, even a healthy one. Thus, ethically speaking, we cannot even get to know whether or not human cloning is feasible.

I understand, of course, the philosophical difficulty of trying to compare a life with defects against nonexistence. Several bioethicists, proud of their philosophical cleverness, use that conundrum to embarrass claims that one can injure a child in its conception, precisely because it is only thanks to that complained-of conception that the child is alive to complain. But common sense tells us that we have no reason to fear such philosophisms. For we surely know that people can harm and even maim children in the very act of conceiving them, say, by paternal transmission of the AIDS virus, maternal transmission of heroin dependence, or, arguably, even by bringing them into being as bastards or with no capacity or willingness to look after them properly. And we believe that to do that intentionally, or even negligently, is inexcusable and clearly unethical.

The objection about the impossibility of presuming consent may even go beyond the obvious and sufficient point that a clonant, were he subsequently to be asked, could rightly resent having been made a clone. At issue are not just benefits and harms, but doubts about the very independence needed to give proper (even retroactive) consent, that is, not just the capacity to choose but the disposition and ability to choose freely and well. It is not at all clear to what extent a clone will fully be a moral agent. For, as we shall see, in the very fact of cloning, and especially of rearing him *as a clone*, his makers subvert the cloned child's independence, beginning with that aspect that comes from knowing that one was an unbidden surprise, a gift, to the world, rather than the designed result of someone's artful project.

Cloning creates serious issues of identity and individuality. The cloned person may experience concerns about his distinctive identity not only because he will be in genotype and appearance identical to another human being, but, in this case, because he may also be twin to the person who is his "father" or "mother"—if one can still call them that. What would be the psychic burdens of being the "child" or "parent" of your twin? The cloned individual, moreover, will be saddled with a genotype that has already lived. He will not be fully a surprise to the world. People are likely always to compare his performances in life with that of his alter ego. True, his nurture and his circumstance in life will be different; genotype is not exactly destiny. Still, one must also expect parental and other efforts to shape that new life after the original—or at least to view the child with the original version always firmly in mind. Why else did they clone from the star basketball player, mathematician, and beauty queen—or even dear old dad—in the first place? . . .

Human cloning would also represent a giant step toward turning begetting into making, procreation into manufacture (literally, something "handmade"), a process already begun with in vitro fertilization and genetic testing of embryos. With cloning, not only is the process in hand, but the total genetic blueprint of the cloned individual is selected and determined by the human artisans. To be sure, subsequent development will take place according to natural processes; and the resulting children will still be recognizably human. But we here would be taking a major step into making man himself simply another one of the man-made things. Human nature becomes merely the last part of nature to succumb to the technological project, which turns all of nature into raw material at human disposal, to be homogenized by our rationalized technique according to the subjective prejudices of the day.

How does begetting differ from making? In natural procreation, human beings come together, complementarily male and female, to give existence to another being who is formed, exactly as we were, *by what we are*: living, hence perishable, hence aspiringly erotic, human beings. In clonal reproduction, by contrast, and in the more advanced forms of manufacture to which it leads, we give existence to a being not by what we are but by what we intend and design. As with any product of our making, no matter how excellent, the artificer stands above it, not as an equal but as a superior, transcending it by his will and creative prowess. Scientists who clone animals make it perfectly clear that they are engaged in instrumental making; the animals are, from the start, designed as means to serve rational human purposes. In human cloning scientists and prospective "parents" would be adopting the same technocratic mentality to human children: Human children would be their artifacts.

Such an arrangement is profoundly dehumanizing, no matter how good the product. . . .

Finally, and perhaps most important, the practice of human cloning by nuclear transfer—like other anticipated forms of genetic engineering of the next generation—would enshrine and aggravate a profound and mischievous misunderstanding of the meaning of having children and of the parent-child relationship. . . .

Much harm is already done by parents who try to live vicariously through their children. Children are sometimes compelled to fulfill the broken dreams of unhappy parents; John Doe, Jr., or John Doe III is under the burden of having to live up to his forebear's name. Still, if most parents have hopes for their children, cloning parents will have expectations. In cloning, such overbearing parents take at the start a decisive step that contradicts the entire meaning of the open and forward-looking nature of parent-child relations. The child is given a genotype that has already lived, with full expectation that the blueprint of a past life ought to be controlling of the life that is to come. Cloning is inherently despotic, for it seeks to make one's children (or someone else's children) after one's own image (or an image of one's choosing) and their future according to one's will. In some cases the despotism may be mild and benevolent. In other cases it will be mischievous and downright tyrannical. But despotism—the control of another through one's will—it inevitably will be.

Meeting Some Objections

The defenders of cloning, of course, are not wittingly friends of despotism. Indeed, they regard themselves mainly as friends of freedom: the freedom of individuals to reproduce, the freedom of scientists and inventors to discover and devise and to foster "progress" in genetic knowledge and technique. They want large-scale cloning only for animals, but they wish to preserve cloning as a human option for exercising our "right to reproduce"—our right to have children, and children with "desirable genes." As law professor John Robertson points out, under our "right to reproduce" we already practice early forms of unnatural, artificial, and extramarital reproduction, and we already practice early forms of eugenic choice. For that reason, he argues, cloning is no big deal.

We have here a perfect example of the logic of the slippery slope, and the slippery way in which it already works in that area. Only a few years ago, slippery-slope arguments were advanced to oppose artificial insemination and in vitro fertilization using unrelated sperm donors. Principles used to justify those practices, it was said, will be used to justify more artificial and more eugenic practices, including cloning. Not so, the defenders retorted, since we can make the necessary distinctions. And now, without even a gesture at making the necessary distinctions, the continuity of practice is held by itself to be justificatory. . . .

Ban the Cloning of Humans

What, then, should we do? We should declare that human cloning is unethical in itself and dangerous in its likely consequences. In so doing, we shall have the backing of the overwhelming majority of our fellow Americans, of the human race, and (I believe) of most practicing scientists. Next, we should do all that we can to prevent the cloning of human beings. We should do that by means of an international legal ban if possible and by a unilateral national ban at a minimum.

Policy on Stem Cell Research and Veto of Stem Cell Research Enhancement Act

George W. Bush

Message to the House of Representatives

To the House of Representatives:

I am returning herewith without my approval H.R. 810, the "Stem Cell Research Enhancement Act of 2005."

Like all Americans, I believe our Nation must vigorously pursue the tremendous possibilities that science offers to cure disease and improve the lives of millions. Yet, as science brings us ever closer to unlocking the secrets of human biology, it also offers temptations to manipulate human life and violate human dignity. Our conscience and history as a Nation demand that we resist this temptation. With the right scientific techniques and the right policies, we can achieve scientific progress while living up to our ethical responsibilities.

In 2001, I set forth a new policy on stem cell research that struck a balance between the needs of science and the demands of conscience. When I took office, there was no Federal funding for human embryonic stem cell research. Under the policy I announced five years ago, my Administration became the first to make Federal funds available for this research, but only on embryonic stem cell lines derived from embryos that had already been destroyed. My Administration has made available more than $90 million for research of these lines. This policy has allowed important research to go forward and has allowed America to continue to lead the world in embryonic stem cell research without encouraging the further destruction of living human embryos.

H.R. 810 would overturn my Administration's balanced policy on embryonic stem cell research. If this bill were to become law, American taxpayers for the first time in our history would be compelled to fund the deliberate destruction of human embryos. Crossing this line would be a grave mistake and would needlessly encourage a conflict between science and ethics that can only do damage to both and harm our Nation as a whole.

Advances in research show that stem cell science can progress in an ethical way. Since I announced my policy in 2001, my Administration has expanded funding of research into stem cells that can be drawn from children, adults, and the blood in umbilical cords with no harm to the donor, and these stem cells are currently being used in medical treatments. Science also offers the hope that we may one day enjoy the potential benefits of embryonic stem cells without destroying human life. Researchers are investigating new techniques that might allow doctors and scientists to produce stem cells just as versatile as those derived from human embryos without harming life. We must continue to explore these hopeful alternatives, so we can advance the cause of scientific research while staying true to the ideals of a decent and humane society.

I hold to the principle that we can harness the promise of technology without becoming slaves to technology and ensure that science serves the cause of humanity. If we are to find the right ways to advance ethical medical research, we must also be willing when necessary to reject the wrong ways. For that reason, I must veto this bill.

George W. Bush
The White House,
July 19, 2006

President Discusses Stem Cell Research Policy

The East Room

2:08 P.M. EDT

The President: Good afternoon. Congress has just passed and sent to my desk two bills concerning the use of stem cells in biomedical research. These bills illustrate both the promise and perils we face in the age of biotechnology. In this new era, our challenge is to harness the power of science to ease human suffering without sanctioning the practices that violate the dignity of human life. (Applause.)

In 2001, I spoke to the American people and set forth a new policy on stem cell research that struck a balance between the needs of science and the demands of conscience. When I took office, there was no federal funding for human embryonic stem cell research. Under the policy I announced five years ago, my administration became the first to make federal funds available for this research, yet only on embryonic stem cell lines derived from embryos that had already been destroyed.

My administration has made available more than $90 million for research on these lines. This policy has allowed important research to go forward without using taxpayer funds to encourage the further deliberate destruction of human embryos.

One of the bills Congress has passed builds on the progress we have made over the last five years. So I signed it into law. (Applause.) Congress has also passed a second bill that attempts to overturn the balanced policy I set. This bill would support the taking of innocent human life in the hope of finding medical benefits for others. It crosses a moral boundary that our decent society needs to respect, so I vetoed it. (Applause.)

Like all Americans, I believe our nation must vigorously pursue the tremendous possibility that science offers to cure disease and improve the lives of millions. We have opportunities to discover cures and treatments that were unthinkable generations ago. Some scientists believe that one source of these cures might be embryonic stem cell research. Embryonic stem cells have the ability to grow into specialized adult tissues, and this may give them the potential to replace damaged or defective cells or body parts and treat a variety of diseases.

Yet we must also remember that embryonic stem cells come from human embryos that are destroyed for their cells. Each of these human embryos is a unique human life with inherent dignity and matchless value. We see that value in the children who are with us today. Each of these children began his or her life as a frozen embryo that was created for in vitro fertilization, but remained unused after the fertility treatments were complete. Each of these children was adopted while still an embryo, and has been blessed with the chance to grow up in a loving family.

These boys and girls are not spare parts. (Applause.) They remind us of what is lost when embryos are destroyed in the name of research. They remind us that we all begin our lives as a small collection of cells. And they remind us that in our zeal for new treatments and cures, America must never abandon our fundamental morals.

Some people argue that finding new cures for disease requires the destruction of human embryos like the ones that these families adopted. I disagree. I believe that with the right techniques and the right policies, we can achieve scientific progress while living up to our ethical responsibilities. That's what I sought in 2001, when I set forth my administration's policy allowing federal funding for research on embryonic stem cell lines where the life and death decision had already been made.

This balanced approach has worked. Under this policy, 21 human embryonic stem cell lines are currently in use in research that is eligible for federal funding. Each of these lines can be replicated many times. And as a result, the National Institutes of Health have helped make more than 700 shipments to researchers since 2001. There is no ban on embryonic stem cell research. To the contrary, even critics of my policy concede that these federally funded lines are being used in research every day by scientists around the world. My policy has allowed us to explore the potential of embryonic stem cells, and it has allowed America to continue to lead the world in this area.

Since I announced my policy in 2001, advances in scientific research have also shown the great potential of stem cells that are derived without harming human embryos. My administration has expanded the funding of research into stem cells that can be drawn from children, adults, and the blood in umbilical cords, with no harm to the donor. And these stem cells are already being used in medical treatments.

With us today are patients who have benefited from treatments with adult and umbilical-cord-blood stem cells. And I want to thank you all for coming. (Applause.)

They are living proof that effective medical science can also be ethical. Researchers are now also investigating new techniques that could allow doctors and scientists to produce stem cells just as versatile as those derived from human embryos. One technique scientists are exploring would involve reprogramming an adult cell. For example, a skin cell to function like an embryonic stem cell. Science offers the hope that we may one day enjoy the potential benefits of embryonic stem cells without destroying human life.

We must continue to explore these hopeful alternatives and advance the cause of scientific research while staying true to the ideals of a decent and humane society. The bill I sign today upholds these humane ideals and draws an important ethical line to guide our research. The Fetus Farming Prohibition Act was sponsored by Senators Santorum and Brownback—both who are here. (Applause.) And by Congressman Dave Weldon, along with Nathan Deal. Thank you, Congressmen. (Applause.) This good law prohibits one of the most egregious abuses in biomedical research, the trafficking in human fetuses that are created with the sole intent of aborting them to harvest their parts. Human beings are not a raw material to be exploited, or a commodity to be bought or sold, and this bill will help ensure that we respect the fundamental ethical line.

I'm disappointed that Congress failed to pass another bill that would have promoted good research. This bill was sponsored by Senator Santorum and Senator Arlen Specter and Congressman Roscoe Bartlett. Thanks for coming, Roscoe. (Applause.) It would have authorized additional federal funding for promising new research that could produce cells with the abilities of embryonic cells, but without the destruction of human embryos. This is an important piece of legislation. This bill was unanimously approved by the Senate; it received 273 votes in the House of Representatives, but was blocked by a minority in the House using procedural maneuvers. I'm disappointed that the House failed to authorize funding for this vital and ethical research.

It makes no sense to say that you're in favor of finding cures for terrible diseases as quickly as possible, and then block a bill that would authorize funding for promising and ethical stem cell research. At a moment when ethical alternatives are becoming available, we cannot lose the opportunity to conduct research that would give hope to those suffering from terrible diseases, and help move our nation beyond the current controversies over embryonic stem cell research.

We must pursue this research. And so I direct the Secretary of Health and Human Services, Secretary Leavitt, and the Director of the National Institutes of Health to use all the tools at their disposal to aid the search for stem cell techniques that advance promising medical science in an ethical and morally responsible way. (Applause.)

Unfortunately, Congress has sent me a bill that fails to meet this ethical test. This legislation would overturn the balanced policy on embryonic stem cell research that my administration has followed for the past five years. This bill would also undermine the principle that Congress, itself, has followed for more than a decade, when it has prohibited federal funding for research that destroys human embryos.

If this bill would have become law, American taxpayers would, for the first time in our history, be compelled to fund the deliberate destruction of human embryos. And I'm not going to allow it. (Applause.)

I made it clear to the Congress that I will not allow our nation to cross this moral line. I felt like crossing this line would be a mistake, and once crossed, we would find it almost impossible to turn back. Crossing the line would needlessly encourage a conflict between science and ethics that can only do damage to both, and to our nation as a whole. If we're to find the right ways to advance ethical medical research, we must also be willing, when necessary, to reject the wrong ways. So today, I'm keeping the promise I made to the American people by returning this bill to Congress with my veto.

As science brings us ever closer to unlocking the secrets of human biology, it also offers temptations to manipulate human life and violate human dignity. Our conscience and history as a nation demand that we resist this temptation. America was founded on the principle that we are all created equal, and endowed by our Creator with the right to life. We can advance the cause of science while upholding this founding promise. We can harness the promise of technology without becoming slaves to technology. And we can ensure that science serves the cause of humanity instead of the other way around.

America pursues medical advances in the name of life, and we will achieve the great breakthroughs we all seek with reverence for the gift of life. I believe America's scientists have the ingenuity and skill to meet this challenge. And I look forward to working with Congress and the scientific community to achieve these great and noble goals in the years ahead.

Thank you all for coming and may God bless. (Applause.)

END 2:23 P.M. EDT

Animal Rights

All Animals Are Equal

Peter Singer

. . . There are obviously important differences between humans and other animals, and these differences must give rise to some differences in the rights that each have. Recognizing this evident fact, however, is no barrier to the case for extending the basic principle of equality to nonhuman animals. The differences that exist between men and women are equally undeniable, and the supporters of women's liberation are aware that these differences may give rise to different rights. Many feminists hold that women have the right to an abortion on request. It does not follow that since these same feminists are campaigning for equality between men and women, they must support the right of men to have abortions too. Since a man cannot have an abortion, it is meaningless to talk of his right to have one. Since dogs can't vote, it is meaningless to talk of their right to vote. There is no reason why either women's liberation or animal liberation should get involved in such nonsense. The extension of the basic principle of equality from one group to another does not imply that we must treat both groups in exactly the same way or grant exactly the same rights to both groups. Whether we should do so will depend on the nature of the members of the two groups. The basic principle of equality does not require equal or identical *treatment*; it requires equal consideration. Equal consideration for different beings may lead to different treatment and different rights. . . .

Source: Reprinted by permission of the author from *Animal Liberation,* 2nd Edition, ECCO 2001. Copyright © Peter Singer 1990.

If we examine more deeply the basis on which our opposition to discrimination on grounds of race or sex ultimately rests, we will see that we would be on shaky ground if we were to demand equality for blacks, women, and other groups of oppressed humans while denying equal consideration to nonhumans. To make this clear we need to see, first, exactly why racism and sexism are wrong. When we say that all human beings, whatever their race, creed, or sex, are equal, what is it that we are asserting? Those who wish to defend hierarchical, inegalitarian societies have often pointed out that by whatever test we choose it simply is not true that all humans are equal. Like it or not we must face the fact that humans come in different shapes and sizes; they come with different moral capacities, different intellectual abilities, different amounts of benevolent feeling and sensitivity to the needs of others, different abilities to communicate effectively, and different capacities to experience pleasure and pain. In short, if the demand for equality were based on the actual equality of all human beings, we would have to stop demanding equality.

Still, one might cling to the view that the demand for equality among human beings is based on the actual equality of the different races and sexes. Although, it may be said, humans differ as individuals, there are no differences between the races and sexes as such. From the mere fact that a person is black or a woman we cannot infer anything about that person's intellectual or moral capacities. This, it may be said, is why racism and sexism are wrong. The white racist claims that whites are superior to blacks, but this is false; although there are differences among individuals, some blacks are superior to some whites in all of the capacities and abilities that could conceivably be relevant. The opponent of sexism would say the same: A person's sex is no guide to his or her abilities, and this is why it is unjustifiable to discriminate on the basis of sex.

The existence of individual variations that cut across the lines of race or sex, however, provides us with no defense at all against a more sophisticated opponent of equality, one who proposes that, say, the interests of all those with IQ scores below 100 be given less consideration than the interests of those with ratings over 100. Perhaps those scoring below the mark would, in this society, be made the slaves of those scoring higher. Would a hierarchical society of this sort really be so much better than one based on race or sex? I think not. But if we tie the moral principle of equality to the factual equality of the different races or sexes, taken as a whole, our opposition to racism and sexism does not provide us with any basis for objecting to this kind of inegalitarianism.

There is a second important reason why we ought not to base our opposition to racism and sexism on any kind of factual equality, even the limited kind that asserts that variations in capacities and abilities are spread evenly among the different races and between the sexes: We can have no absolute guarantee that these capacities and abilities really are distributed evenly, without regard to race or sex, among human beings. So far as actual abilities are concerned there do seem to be certain measurable differences both among races and between sexes. These differences do not, of course, appear in every case; they appear only when averages are taken. More important still, we do not yet know how many of these differences are really due to the different genetic endowments of the different races and sexes, and how many are due to poor schools, poor housing, and other factors that are the result of past and continuing discrimination. Perhaps all of the important differences will eventually prove to be environmental rather than genetic. Anyone opposed to racism and sexism will certainly hope that this will be so, for it will make the task of ending discrimination a lot easier; nevertheless, it would be dangerous to rest the case against racism and sexism on the belief that all significant differences are environmental in origin. The opponent of, say, racism who takes this line will be unable to avoid conceding that if differences in ability did after all prove to have some genetic connection with race, racism would in some way be defensible.

Fortunately there is no need to pin the case for equality on one particular outcome of a scientific investigation. The appropriate response to those who claim to have found evidence of genetically based differences in ability among the races or between the sexes is not to stick to the belief that the genetic explanation must be wrong, whatever evidence to the contrary may turn up; instead we should make it quite clear that the claim to equality does not depend on intelligence, moral capacity, physical strength, or similar matters of fact. Equality is a moral idea, not an assertion of fact. There is no logically compelling reason for assuming that a factual difference in ability between two people justifies any difference in the amount of consideration we give to their needs and interests. *The principle of the equality of human beings is not a description of an alleged actual equality among humans: It is a prescription of how we should treat human beings.*

Jeremy Bentham, the founder of the reforming utilitarian school of moral philosophy, incorporated the essential basis of moral equality into his system of ethics by means of the formula: "Each to count for one and none for more than one." In other words, the interests of every being affected by an action are to be taken into account and given the same weight as the like interests of any other being. A later utilitarian, Henry Sidgwick, put the point in this way: "The good of any one individual is of no more importance, from the point of view (if I may say so) of the Universe, than the good of any other." More recently the leading figures in contemporary moral philosophy have shown a great deal of agreement in specifying as a fundamental presupposition of their moral theories some similar requirement that works to give everyone's interests equal consideration—although these writers generally cannot agree on how this requirement is best formulated.

It is an implication of this principle of equality that our concern for others and our readiness to consider their interests ought not to depend on what they are like or on what abilities they may possess. Precisely what our concern or consideration requires us to do may vary according to the characteristics of those affected by what we do: Concern for the well-being of children growing up in America would require that we teach them to read; concern for the well-being of pigs may require no more than that we leave them with other pigs in a place where there is adequate food and room to run freely. But the basic element—the taking into account of the interests of the being, whatever those interests may be—must, according to the principle of equality, be extended to all beings, black or white, masculine or feminine, human or nonhuman.

Thomas Jefferson, who was responsible for writing the principle of the equality of men into the American Declaration of Independence, saw this point. It led him to oppose slavery even though he was unable to free himself fully from his slaveholding background. He wrote in a letter to the author of a book that emphasized the notable intellectual achievements of Negroes in order to refute the then common view that they had limited intellectual capacities:

> Be assured that no person living wishes more sincerely than I do, to see a complete refutation of the doubts I myself have entertained and expressed on the grade of understanding allotted to them by nature, and to find that they are on a par with ourselves . . . but whatever be their degree of talent it is no measure of their rights. Because Sir Isaac Newton was superior to others in understanding, he was not therefore lord of the property or persons of others.

Similarly, when in the 1850s the call for women's rights was raised in the United States, a remarkable black feminist named Sojourner Truth made the same point in more robust terms at a feminist convention:

> They talk about this thing in the head; what do they call it? ["Intellect," whispered someone nearby.] That's it. What's that got to do with women's rights or Negroes' rights? If my cup won't hold but a pint and yours holds a quart, wouldn't you be mean not to let me have my little half-measure full?

It is on this basis that the case against racism and the case against sexism must both ultimately rest; and it is in accordance with this principle that the attitude that we may call "speciesism," by analogy with racism, must also be condemned. Speciesism—the word is not an attractive one, but I can think of no better term—is a prejudice or attitude of bias in favor of the interests of members of one's own species and against those of members of other species. It should be obvious that the fundamental objections to racism and sexism made by Thomas Jefferson and Sojourner Truth apply equally to speciesism. If possessing a higher degree of intelligence does not entitle one human to use another for his or her own ends, how can it entitle humans to exploit nonhumans for the same purpose?

Many philosophers and other writers have proposed the principle of equal consideration of interests, in some form or other, as a basic moral principle; but not many of them have recognized that this principle applies to members of other species as well as to our own. Jeremy Bentham was one of the few who did realize this. In a forward-looking passage written at a time when black slaves had been freed by the French but in the British dominions were still being treated in the way we now treat animals, Bentham wrote:

> The day *may* come when the rest of the animal creation may acquire those rights which never could have been witholden from them but by the hand of tyranny. The French have already discovered that the blackness of the skin is no reason why a human being should be abandoned without redress to the

caprice of a tormentor. It may one day come to be recognized that the number of the legs, the villosity of the skin, or the termination of the *os sacrum* are reasons equally insufficient for abandoning a sensitive being to the same fate. What else is it that should trace the insuperable line? Is it the faculty of reason, or perhaps the faculty of discourse? But a full-grown horse or dog is beyond comparison a more rational, as well as a more conversable animal, than an infant of a day or a week or even a month, old. But suppose they were otherwise, what would it avail? The question is not, Can they *reason*? nor Can they *talk*? but, Can they *suffer*?

In this passage Bentham points to the capacity for suffering as the vital characteristic that gives a being the right to equal consideration. The capacity for suffering—or more strictly, for suffering and/or enjoyment or happiness—is not just another characteristic like the capacity for language or higher mathematics. Bentham is not saying that those who try to mark "the insuperable line" that determines whether the interests of a being should be considered happen to have chosen the wrong characteristic. By saying that we must consider the interests of all beings with the capacity for suffering or enjoyment Bentham does not arbitrarily exclude from consideration any interests at all—as those who draw the line with reference to the possession of reason or language do. The capacity for suffering and enjoyment is *a prerequisite for having interests at all*, a condition that must be satisfied before we can speak of interests in a meaningful way. It would be nonsense to say that it was not in the interests of a stone to be kicked along the road by a schoolboy. A stone does not have interests because it cannot suffer. Nothing that we can do to it could possibly make any difference to its welfare. The capacity for suffering and enjoyment is, however, not only necessary, but also sufficient for us to say that a being has interests—at an absolute minimum, an interest in not suffering. A mouse, for example, does have an interest in not being kicked along the road, because it will suffer if it is.

Although Bentham speaks of "rights" in the passage I have quoted, the argument is really about equality rather than about rights. Indeed, in a different passage, Bentham famously described "natural rights" as "nonsense" and "natural and imprescriptible rights" as "nonsense upon stilts." He talked of moral rights as a shorthand way of referring to protections that people and animals morally ought to have; but the real weight of the moral argument does not rest on the assertion of the existence of the right, for this in turn has to be justified on the basis of the possibilities for suffering and happiness. In this way we can argue for equality for animals without getting embroiled in philosophical controversies about the ultimate nature of rights.

In misguided attempts to refute the arguments of this book, some philosophers have gone to much trouble developing arguments to show that animals do not have rights. They have claimed that to have rights a being must be autonomous, or must be a member of a community, or must have the ability to respect the rights of others, or must possess a sense of justice. These claims are irrelevant to the case for animal liberation. The language of rights is a convenient political shorthand. It is even more valuable in the era of thirty-second TV news clips than it was in Bentham's day; but in the argument for a radical change in our attitude to animals, it is in no way necessary.

If a being suffers there can be no moral justification for refusing to take that suffering into consideration. No matter what the nature of the being, the principle of equality requires that its suffering be counted equally with the like suffering—insofar as rough comparisons can be made—of any other being. If a being is not capable of suffering, or of experiencing enjoyment or happiness, there is nothing to be taken into account. So the limit of sentience (using the term as a convenient if not strictly accurate shorthand for the capacity to suffer and/or experience enjoyment) is the only defensible boundary of concern for the interests of others. To mark this boundary by some other characteristic like intelligence or rationality would be to mark it in an arbitrary manner. Why not choose some other characteristic, like skin color?

Racists violate the principle of equality by giving greater weight to the interests of members of their own race when there is a clash between their interests and the interests of those of another race. Sexists violate the principle of equality by favoring the interests of their own sex. Similarly, speciesists allow the interests of their own species to override the greater interests of members of other species. The pattern is identical in each case.

Most human beings are speciesists. The following chapters show that ordinary human beings—not a few exceptionally cruel or heartless humans, but the overwhelming majority of humans—take an active part in, acquiesce in, and allow their taxes to pay for practices that require the sacrifice of the most important interests of members of other species in order to promote the most trivial interests of our own species. . . .

There are no good reasons, scientific or philosophical, for denying that animals feel pain. If we do not doubt that other humans feel pain, we should not doubt that other animals do so too.

Animals can feel pain. As we saw earlier, there can be no moral justification for regarding the pain (or pleasure) that animals feel as less important than the same amount of pain (or pleasure) felt by humans. But what practical consequences follow from this conclusion? To prevent misunderstanding I shall spell out what I mean a little more fully.

If I give a horse a hard slap across its rump with my open hand, the horse may start, but it presumably feels little pain. Its skin is thick enough to protect it against a mere slap. If I slap a baby in the same way, however, the baby will cry and presumably feel pain, for its skin is more sensitive. So it is worse to slap a baby than a horse, if both slaps are administered with equal force. But there must be some kind of blow—I don't know exactly what it would be, but perhaps a blow with a heavy stick—that would cause the horse as much pain as we cause a baby by slapping it with our hand. That is what I mean by "the same amount of pain," and if we consider it wrong to inflict that much pain on a baby for no good reason, then we must, unless we are speciesists, consider it equally wrong to inflict the same amount of pain on a horse for no good reason.

Other differences between humans and animals cause other complications. Normal adult human beings have mental capacities that will, in certain circumstances, lead them to suffer more than animals would in the same circumstances. If, for instance, we decided to perform extremely painful or lethal scientific experiments on normal adult humans, kidnapped at random from public parks for this purpose, adults who enjoy strolling in parks would become fearful that they would be kidnapped. The resultant terror would be a form of suffering additional to the pain of the experiment. The same experiments performed on nonhuman animals would cause less suffering, since the animals would not have the anticipatory dread of being kidnapped and experimented upon. This does not mean, of course, that it would be *right* to perform the experiment on animals, but only that there is a reason, which is *not* speciesist, for preferring to use animals rather than normal adult human beings, if the experiment is to be done at all. It should be noted, however, that this same argument gives us a reason for preferring to use human infants—orphans perhaps—or severely retarded human beings for experiments, rather than adults, since infants and retarded humans would also have no idea of what was going to happen to them. So far as this argument is concerned nonhuman animals and infants and retarded humans are in the same category; and if we use this argument to justify experiments on nonhuman animals, we have to ask ourselves whether we are also prepared to allow experiments on human infants and retarded adults; and if we make a distinction between animals and these humans, on what basis can we do it, other than a barefaced—and morally indefensible—preference for members of our own species? . . .

It may be objected that comparisons of the sufferings of different species are impossible to make and that for this reason when the interests of animals and humans clash the principle of equality gives no guidance. It is probably true that comparisons of suffering between members of different species cannot be made precisely, but precision is not essential. Even if we were to prevent the infliction of suffering on animals only when it is quite certain that the interests of humans will not be affected to anything like the extent that animals are affected, we would be forced to make radical changes in our treatment of animals that would involve our diet; the farming methods we use; experimental procedures in many fields of science; our approach to wildlife and to hunting, trapping, and the wearing of furs; and areas of entertainment like circuses, rodeos, and zoos. As a result, a vast amount of suffering would be avoided. . . .

Just as most human beings are speciesists in their readiness to cause pain to animals when they would not cause a similar pain to humans for the same reason, so most human beings are speciesists in their readiness to kill other animals when they would not kill human beings. . . .

Adult chimpanzees, dogs, pigs, and members of many other species far surpass the brain-damaged infant in their ability to relate to others, act independently, be self-aware, and any other capacity that could reasonably be said to give value to life. With the most intensive care possible, some severely retarded infants can never achieve the intelligence level of a dog. . . . The only thing that distinguishes the infant from the animal, in the eyes of those who claim it has a "right to life," is that it is, biologically, a member of the species *Homo sapiens*, whereas chimpanzees, dogs, and pigs are not. But to use *this* difference as the basis for granting a right to life to the infant and not to the other animals is, of course, pure speciesism. It is exactly the kind of arbitrary difference that the most crude and overt kind of racist uses in attempting to justify racial discrimination.

This does not mean that to avoid speciesism we must hold that it is as wrong to kill a dog as it is to kill a human being in full possession of his or her faculties. The only position that is irredeemably speciesist is the one that tries to make the boundary of the right to life run exactly parallel to the boundary of our own species. Those who hold the sanctity of life view do this, because while distinguishing sharply between human beings and other animals they allow no distinctions to be made within our own species, objecting to the killing of the severely retarded and the hopelessly senile as strongly as they object to the killing of normal adults.

To avoid speciesism we must allow that beings who are similar in all relevant respects have a similar right to life—and mere membership in our own biological species cannot be a morally relevant criterion for this right. Within these limits we could still hold, for instance, that it is worse to kill a normal adult human, with a capacity for self-awareness and the ability to plan for the future and have meaningful relations with others, than it is to kill a mouse, which presumably does not share all of these characteristics; or we might appeal to the close family and other personal ties that humans have but mice do not have to the same degree; or we might think that it is the consequences for other humans, who will be put in fear for their own lives, that makes the crucial difference; or we might think it is some combination of these factors, or other factors altogether.

Whatever criteria we choose, however, we will have to admit that they do not follow precisely the boundary of our own species. We may legitimately hold that there are some features of certain beings that make their lives more valuable than those of other beings; but there will surely be some nonhuman animals whose lives, by any standards, are more valuable than the lives of some humans. A chimpanzee, dog, or pig, for instance, will have a higher degree of self-awareness and a greater capacity for meaningful relations with others than a severely retarded infant or someone in a state of advanced senility. So if we base the right to life on these characteristics, we must grant these animals a right to life as good as, or better than, such retarded or senile humans.

This argument cuts both ways. It could be taken as showing that chimpanzees, dogs, and pigs, along with some other species, have a right to life and we commit a grave moral offense whenever we kill them, even when they are old and suffering and our intention is to put them out of their misery. Alternatively one could take the argument as showing that the severely retarded and hopelessly senile have no right to life and may be killed for quite trivial reasons, as we now kill animals. . . .

What we need is some middle position that would avoid speciesism but would not make the lives of the retarded and senile as cheap as the lives of pigs and dogs now are, or make the lives of pigs and dogs so sacrosanct that we think it wrong to put them out of hopeless misery. What we must do is bring nonhuman animals within our sphere of moral concern and cease to treat their lives as expendable for whatever trivial purposes we may have. At the same time, once we realize that the fact that a being is a member of our own species is not in itself enough to make it always wrong to kill that being, we may come to reconsider our policy of preserving human lives at all costs, even when there is no prospect of a meaningful life or of existence without terrible pain.

I conclude, then, that a rejection of speciesism does not imply that all lives are of equal worth. While self-awareness, the capacity to think ahead and have hopes and aspirations for the future, the capacity for meaningful relations with others, and so on are not relevant to the question of inflicting pain—since pain is pain, whatever other capacities, beyond the capacity to feel pain, the being may have—these capacities are relevant to the question of taking life. It is not arbitrary to hold that the life of a self-aware being, capable of abstract thought, of planning for the future, of complex acts of communication, and so on, is more valuable than the life of a being without these capacities. To see the difference between the issues of inflicting pain and taking life, consider how we would choose within our own species. If we had to choose to save the life of a normal human being or an intellectually disabled human being, we would probably choose to save the life of a normal human being; but if we had to choose between preventing pain in the normal human being or the intellectually disabled one—imagine that both have received painful but superficial injuries, and we have only enough painkiller for one of them—it is not nearly so clear how we ought to choose. The same is true when we consider other species. The evil of pain is, in itself, unaffected by the other characteristics of the being who feels the pain; the value of life is affected by these other characteristics. To give just one reason for this difference, to take the life of a being who has been hoping, planning, and working for some future goal is to deprive that being of the fulfillment of all those efforts; to take the life of a being with a future—much less make plans for the future—cannot involve this particular kind of loss.

Normally this will mean that if we have to choose between the life of a human being and the life of another animal, we should choose to save the life of the human; but there may be special cases in which the reverse holds true, because the human being in question does not have the capacities of a normal human being. So this view is not speciesist, although it may appear to be at first glance. The preference, in normal cases, for saving a human life over the life of an animal when a choice *has* to be made is a preference based on the characteristics that normal humans have, and not on the mere fact that they are members of our own species. This is why when we consider members of our own species who lack the characteristics of normal humans, we can no longer say that their lives are always to be preferred to those of other animals. This issue comes up in a practical way in the following chapter. In general, though, the question of when it is wrong to kill (painlessly) an animal is one to which we need give no precise answer. As long as we remember that we should give the same respect to the lives of animals as we give to the lives of those humans at a similar mental level, we shall not go far wrong.

In any case, the conclusions that are argued for here flow from the principle of minimizing suffering alone. The idea that it is also wrong to kill animals painlessly gives some of these conclusions additional support that is welcome but strictly unnecessary. Interestingly enough, this is true even of the conclusion that we ought to become vegetarians, a conclusion that in the popular mind is generally based on some kind of absolute prohibition on killing.

Tools for Research

Among the tens of millions of experiments performed, only a few can possibly be regarded as contributing to important medical research. Huge numbers of animals are used in university departments such as forestry and psychology; many more are used for commercial purposes, to test new cosmetics, shampoos, food coloring agents, and other inessential items. All this can happen only because of our prejudice against taking seriously the suffering of a being who is not a member of our own species. Typically, defenders of experiments on animals do not deny that animals suffer. They cannot deny the animals' suffering, because they need to stress the similarities between humans and other animals in order to claim that their experiments may have some relevance for human purposes. The experimenter who forces rats to choose between starvation and electric shock to see if they develop ulcers (which they do) does so because the rat has a nervous system very similar to a human being's, and presumably feels an electric shock in a similar way.

There has been opposition to experimenting on animals for a long time. This opposition has made little headway because experimenters, backed by commercial firms that profit by supplying laboratory animals and equipment, have been able to convince legislators and the public that opposition comes from uninformed fanatics who consider the interests of animals more important than the interests of human beings. But to be opposed to what is going on now it is not necessary to insist that all animal experiments stop immediately. All we need to say is that experiments serving no direct and urgent purpose should stop immediately, and in the remaining fields of research, we should, whenever possible, seek to replace experiments that involve animals with alternative methods that do not. . . .

When are experiments on animals justifiable? Upon learning of the nature of many of the experiments carried out, some people react by saying that all experiments on animals should be prohibited immediately. But if we make our demands as absolute as this, the experimenters have a ready reply: Would we be prepared to let thousands of humans die if they could be saved by a single experiment on a single animal?

This question is, of course, purely hypothetical. There has never been and never could be a single experiment that saved thousands of lives. The way to reply to this hypothetical question is to pose another: Would the experimenters be prepared to carry out their experiment on a human orphan under six months old if that were the only way to save thousands of lives?

If the experimenters would not be prepared to use a human infant, then their readiness to use nonhuman animals reveals an unjustifiable form of discrimination on the basis of species, since adult apes, monkeys, dogs, cats, rats, and other animals are more aware of what is happening to them, more self-directing, and, so far as we can tell, at least as sensitive to pain as a human infant. (I have specified that the human infant be an orphan, to avoid the complications of the feelings of parents. Specifying the case in this way is, if anything, overgenerous to those defending the use of nonhuman animals in experiments, since mammals intended for experimental use are usually separated from their mothers at an early age, when the separation causes distress for both mother and young.)

So far as we know, human infants possess no morally relevant characteristic to a higher degree than adult nonhuman animals, unless we are to count the infants' potential as a characteristic that makes it wrong to experiment on them. Whether this characteristic should count is controversial—if we count it, we shall have to condemn abortion along with experiments on infants, since the potential of the infant and the fetus is the same. To avoid the complexities of this issue, however, we can alter our original question a little and assume that the infant is one with irreversible brain damage so severe as to rule out any mental development beyond the level of a six-month-old infant. There are, unfortunately, many such human beings, locked away in special wards throughout the country, some of them long since abandoned by their parents and other relatives, and, sadly, sometimes unloved by anyone else. Despite their mental deficiencies, the anatomy and physiology of these infants are in nearly all respects identical to those of normal humans. If, therefore, we were to force-feed them with large quantities of floor polish or drip concentrated solutions of cosmetics into their eyes, we would have a much more reliable indication of the safety of these products for humans than we now get by attempting to extrapolate the results of tests on a variety of other species. The LD50 tests, the Draize eye tests, the radiation experiments, the heatstroke experiments, and many others that cause suffering to nonhuman animals could have told us more about human reactions to the experimental situation if they had been carried out on severely brain-damaged humans instead of dogs or rabbits.

So whenever experimenters claim that their experiments are important enough to justify the use of animals, we should ask them whether they would be prepared to use a brain-damaged human being at a mental level similar to that of the animals they are planning to use. I cannot imagine that anyone would seriously propose carrying out the experiments described in this chapter on brain-damaged human beings. Occasionally it has become known that medical experiments have been performed on human beings without their consent; one case did concern institutionalized intellectually disabled children, who were given hepatitis. When such harmful experiments on human beings become known, they usually lead to an outcry against the experimenters, and rightly so. They are, very often, a further example of the arrogance of the research worker who justifies everything on the grounds of increasing knowledge. But if the experimenter claims that the experiment is important enough to justify inflicting suffering on animals, why is it not important enough to justify inflicting suffering on humans at the same mental level? What difference is there between the two? Only that one is a member of our species and the other is not? But to appeal to that difference is to reveal a bias no more defensible than racism or any other form of arbitrary discrimination.

We have still not answered the question of when an experiment might be justifiable. It will not do to say "Never!" Putting morality in such black-and-white terms is appealing, because it eliminates the need to think about particular cases; but in extreme circumstances, such absolutist answers always break down. Torturing a human being is almost always wrong, but it is not absolutely wrong. If torture were the only way in which we could discover the location of a nuclear bomb hidden in a New York City basement and timed to go off within the hour, then torture would be justifiable. Similarly, if a single experiment could cure a disease like leukemia, that experiment would be justifiable. But in actual life the benefits are always more remote, and more often than not they are nonexistent. So how do we decide when an experiment is justifiable?

We have seen that experimenters reveal a bias in favor of their own species whenever they carry out experiments on nonhumans for purposes that they would not think justified using human beings, even brain-damaged ones. This principle gives us a guide toward an answer to our question. Since a speciesist bias, like a racist bias, is unjustifiable, an experiment cannot be justifiable unless the experiment is so important that the use of a brain-damaged human would also be justifiable.

This is not an absolutist principle. I do not believe that it could never be justifiable to experiment on a brain-damaged human. If it really were possible to save several lives by an experiment that would take just one life, and there were no other way those lives could be saved, it would be right to do the experiment. But this would be an extremely rare case. Certainly none of the experiments described in this chapter could pass this test. Admittedly, as with any dividing line, there would be a gray area where it was difficult to decide if an experiment could be justified. But we need not get distracted by such considerations now. As this chapter has shown, we are in the midst of an emergency in which appalling suffering is being inflicted on millions of animals for purposes that on any impartial view are obviously inadequate to justify the suffering. When we have ceased to carry out all those experiments, then there will be time enough to discuss what to do about the remaining ones which are claimed to be essential to save lives or prevent greater suffering. . . .

The Case for the Use of Animals in Biomedical Research

Carl Cohen

Using animals as research subjects in medical investigations is widely condemned on two grounds: first, because it wrongly violates the *rights* of animals,[85] and second, because it wrongly imposes on sentient creatures much

Source: Carl Cohen, "The Case for the Use of Animals in Biomedical Research" from *The New England Journal of Medicine,* Vol. 315, October 2, 1986, pp. 865–870. Copyright © 1986 Massachusetts Medical Society. All rights reserved.

avoidable *suffering*.[86] Neither of these arguments is sound. The first relies on a mistaken understanding of rights; the second relies on a mistaken calculation of consequences. Both deserve definitive dismissal.

Why Animals Have No Rights

A right, properly understood, is a claim, or potential claim, that one party may exercise against another. The target against whom such a claim may be registered can be a single person, a group, a community, or (perhaps) all humankind. The content of rights claims also varies greatly: repayment of loans, nondiscrimination by employers, noninterference by the state, and so on. To comprehend any genuine right fully, therefore, we must know *who* holds the right, *against whom* it is held, and *to what* it is a right.

Alternative sources of rights add complexity. Some rights are grounded in constitution and law (e.g., the right of an accused to trial by jury); some right are moral but give no legal claims (e.g., my right to your keeping the promise you gave me); and some rights (e.g., against theft or assault) are rooted both in morals and in law.

The differing targets, contents, and sources of rights, and their inevitable conflict, together weave a tangled web. Notwithstanding all such complications, this much is clear about rights in general: They are in every case claims, or potential claims, within a community of moral agents. Rights arise, and can be intelligibly defended, only among beings who actually do, or can, make moral claims against one another. Whatever else rights may be, therefore, they are necessarily human; their possessors are persons, human beings.

The attributes of human beings from which this moral capability arises have been described variously by philosophers, both ancient and modern: the inner consciousness of a free will (Saint Augustine[87]); the grasp, by human reason, of the binding character of moral law (Saint Thomas[88]); the self-conscious participation of human beings in an objective ethical order (Hegel[89]); human membership in an organic moral community (Bradley[90]); the development of the human self through the consciousness of other moral selves (Mead[91]); and the underivative, intuitive cognition of the rightness of an action (Prichard[92]). Most influential has been Immanuel Kant's emphasis on the universal human possession of a uniquely moral will and the autonomy its use entails.[93] Humans confront choices that are purely moral; humans—but certainly not dogs or mice—lay down moral laws, for others and for themselves. Human beings are self-legislative, morally *auto-nomous*.

Animals (that is, nonhuman animals, the ordinary sense of that word) lack this capacity for free moral judgment. They are not beings of a kind capable of exercising or responding to moral claims. Animals therefore have no rights, and they can have none. This is the core of the argument about the alleged rights of animals. The holders of rights must have the capacity to comprehend rules of duty, governing all including themselves. In applying such rules, the holders of rights must recognize possible conflicts between what is in their own interest and what is just. Only in a community of beings capable of self-restricting moral judgments can the concept of a right be correctly invoked.

Humans have such moral capacities. They are in this sense self-legislative, are members of communities governed by moral rules, and do possess rights. Animals do not have such moral capacities. They are not morally self-legislative, cannot possibly be members of a truly moral community, and therefore cannot possess rights. In conducting research on animal subjects, therefore, we do not violate their rights, because they have none to violate.

To animate life, even in its simplest forms, we give a certain natural reverence. But the possession of rights presupposes a moral status not attained by the vast majority of living things. We must not infer, therefore, that a live being has, simply in being alive, a "right" to its life. The assertion that all animals, only because they are alive and have interests, also possess the "right to life"[94] is an abuse of that phrase, and wholly without warrant.

It does not follow from this, however, that we are morally free to do anything we please to animals. Certainly not. In our dealings with animals, as in our dealings with other human beings, we have obligations that do not arise from claims against us based on rights. Rights entail obligations, but many of the things one ought to do are in no way tied to another's entitlement. Rights and obligations are not reciprocals of one another, and it is a serious mistake to suppose that they are.

Illustrations are helpful. Obligations may arise from internal commitments made: Physicians have obligations to their patients not grounded merely in their patients' rights. Teachers have such obligations to their students, shepherds to their dogs, and cowboys to their horses. Obligations may arise from differences of status: Adults owe special care when playing with young children, and children owe special care when playing with young pets. Obligations may arise from special relationships: The payment of my son's college tuition is something to which he may have no right, although it may be my obligation to bear the burden if I reasonably can; my dog has no right to daily exercise and veterinary care, but I do have the obligation to provide these things for her. Obligations may arise from particular acts or circumstances: One may be obliged to another for a special kindness done, or obliged to put an animal out of its misery in view of its condition—although neither the human benefactor nor the dying animal may have had a claim of right.

Plainly, the grounds of our obligation to humans and to animals are manifold and cannot be formulated simply. Some hold that there is a general obligation to do no gratuitous harm to sentient creatures (the principle of nonmaleficence); some hold that there is a general obligation to do good to sentient creatures when that is reasonably within one's power (the principle of beneficence). In our dealings with animals, few will deny that we are at least obliged to act humanely—that is, to treat them with the decency and concern that we owe, as sensitive human beings, to other sentient creatures. To treat animals humanely, however, is not to treat them as humans or as the holders of rights.

A common objection, which deserves a response, may be paraphrased as follows:

> If having rights requires being able to make moral claims, to grasp and apply moral laws, then many humans—the brain-damaged, the comatose, the senile—who plainly lack those capacities must be without rights. But that is

absurd. This proves [the critic concludes] that rights do not depend on the presence of moral capacities.

This objection fails; it mistakenly treats an essential feature of humanity as though it were a screen for sorting humans. The capacity for moral judgment that distinguishes humans from animals is not a test to be administered to human beings one by one. Persons who are unable, because of some disability, to perform the full moral functions natural to human beings are certainly not for that reason ejected from the moral community. The issue is one of kind. Humans are of such a kind that they may be the subject of experiments only with their voluntary consent. The choices they make freely must be respected. Animals are of such a kind that it is impossible for them, in principle, to give or withhold voluntary consent or to make a moral choice. What humans retain when disabled, animals have never had.

A second objection, also often made, may be paraphrased as follows:

Capacities will not succeed in distinguishing humans from the other animals. Animals also reason; animals also communicate with one another; animals also care passionately for their young; animals also exhibit desires and preferences.[95, 96] Features of moral relevance—rationality, interdependence, and love—are not exhibited uniquely by human beings. Therefore [this critic concludes], there can be no solid moral distinction between humans and other animals.

This criticism misses the central point. It is not the ability to communicate or to reason, or dependence on one another, or care for the young, or the exhibition of preference, or any such behavior that marks the critical divide. Analogies between human families and those of monkeys, or between human communities and those of wolves, and the like, are entirely beside the point. Patterns of conduct are not at issue. Animals do indeed exhibit remarkable behavior at times. Conditioning, fear, instinct, and intelligence all contribute to species survival. Membership in a community of moral agents nevertheless remains impossible for them. Actors subject to moral judgment must be capable of grasping the generality of an ethical premise in a practical syllogism. Humans act immorally often enough, but only they—never wolves or monkeys—can discern, by applying some moral rule to the facts of a case, that a given act ought or ought not to be performed. The moral restraints imposed by humans on themselves are thus highly abstract and are often in conflict with the self-interest of the agent. Communal behavior among animals, even when most intelligent and most endearing, does not approach autonomous morality in this fundamental sense.

Genuinely moral acts have an internal as well as an external dimension. Thus, in law, an act can be criminal only when the guilty deed, the actus reus, is done with a guilty mind, mens rea. No animal can ever commit a crime; bringing animals to criminal trial is the mark of primitive ignorance. The claims of moral right are similarly inapplicable to them. Does a lion have a right to eat a baby zebra? Does a baby zebra have a right not to be eaten? Such questions, mistakenly invoking the concept of right where it does not belong, do not make good sense. Those who condemn biomedical research because it violates "animal rights" commit the same blunder.

In Defense of "Speciesism"

Abandoning reliance on animal rights, some critics resort instead to animal sentience—their feelings of pain and distress. We ought to desist from the imposition of pain insofar as we can. Since all or nearly all experimentation on animals does impose pain and could be readily forgone, say these critics, it should be stopped. The ends sought may be worthy, but those ends do not justify imposing agonies on humans, and by animals the agonies are felt no less. The laboratory use of animals (these critics conclude) must therefore be ended—or at least very sharply curtailed.

Argument of this variety is essentially utilitarian, often expressly so[97]; it is based on the calculation of the net product, in pains and pleasures, resulting from experiments on animals. Jeremy Bentham, comparing horses and dogs with other sentient creatures, is thus commonly quoted: "The question is not, Can they reason? nor Can they talk? but, Can they suffer?"[98]

Animals certainly can suffer and surely ought not to be made to suffer needlessly. But in inferring, from these uncontroversial premises, that biomedical research causing animal distress is largely (or wholly) wrong, the critic commits two serious errors.

The first error is the assumption, often explicitly defended, that all sentient animals have equal moral standing. Between a dog and a human being, according to this view, there is no moral difference; hence the pains suffered by dogs must be weighed no differently from the pains suffered by humans. To deny such equality, according to this critic, is to give unjust preference to one species over another; it is "speciesism." The most influential statement of this moral equality of species was made by Peter Singer:

> The racist violates the principle of equality by giving greater weight to the interests of members of his own race when there is a clash between their interests and the interests of those of another race. The sexist violates the principle of equality by favoring the interests of his own sex. Similarly the speciesist allows the interests of his own species to override the greater interests of members of other species. The pattern is identical in each case.

This argument is worse than unsound; it is atrocious. It draws an offensive moral conclusion from a deliberately devised verbal parallelism that is utterly specious. Racism has no rational ground whatever. Differing degrees of respect or concern for humans for no other reason than that they are members of different races is an injustice totally without foundation in the nature of the races themselves.

Racists, even if acting on the basis of mistaken factual beliefs, do grave moral wrong precisely because there is no morally relevant distinction among the races. The supposition of such differences has led to outright horror. The same is true of the sexes, neither sex being entitled by right to greater respect or concern than the other. No dispute here.

Between species of animate life, however—between (for example) humans on the one hand and cats or rats on the other—the morally relevant differences are enormous, and almost universally appreciated. Humans engage in moral reflection; humans are morally autonomous; humans are members of moral communities, recognizing just claims against their own interest. Human beings do have rights; theirs is a moral status very different from that of cats or rats.

I am a speciesist. Speciesism is not merely plausible; it is essential for right conduct, because those who will not make the morally relevant distinctions among species are almost certain, in consequence, to misapprehend their true obligations. The analogy between speciesism and racism is insidious. Every sensitive moral judgment requires that the differing natures of the beings to whom obligations are owed be considered. If all forms of animate life—or vertebrate animal life?—must be treated equally, and if therefore in evaluating a research program the pains of a rodent count equally with the pains of a human, we are forced to conclude (1) that neither humans nor rodents possess rights, or (2) that rodents possess all the rights that humans possess. Both alternatives are absurd. Yet one or the other must be swallowed if the moral equality of all species is to be defended.

Humans owe to other humans a degree of moral regard that cannot be owed to animals. Some humans take on the obligation to support and heal others, both humans and animals, as a principal duty in their lives; the fulfillment of that duty may require the sacrifice of many animals. If biomedical investigators abandon the effective pursuit of their professional objectives because they are convinced that they may not do to animals what the service of humans requires, they will fail, objectively, to do their duty. Refusing to recognize the moral differences among species is a sure path to calamity. (The largest animal rights group in the country is People for the Ethical Treatment of Animals; its codirector, Ingrid Newkirk, calls research using animal subjects "fascism" and "supremacism." "Animal liberationists do not separate out the *human* animal," she says, "so there is no rational basis for saying that a human being has special rights. A rat is a pig is a dog is a boy. They're all mammals."[99])

Those who claim to base their objection to the use of animals in biomedical research on their reckoning of the net pleasures and pains produced make a second error, equally grave. Even if it were true—as it is surely not—that the pains of all animate beings must be counted equally, a cogent utilitarian calculation requires that we weigh all the consequences of the use, and of the nonuse, of animals in laboratory research. Critics relying (however mistakenly) on animal rights may claim to ignore the beneficial results of such research, rights being trump cards to which interest and advantage must give way. But an argument that is explicitly framed in terms of interest and benefit for all over the long run must attend also to the disadvantageous consequences of not using animals in research, and to all the achievements attained and attainable only through their use. The sum of the benefits of their use is utterly beyond quantification. The elimination of horrible disease, the increase of longevity, the avoidance of great pain, the saving of lives, and the improvement of the quality of lives (for humans and for animals) achieved through research using animals is so incalculably great that the argument of these critics, systematically pursued, establishes not their conclusion but its reverse: To refrain from using animals in biomedical research is, on utilitarian grounds, morally wrong.

When balancing the pleasures and pains resulting from the use of animals in research, we must not fail to place on the scales the terrible pains that would have resulted, would be suffered now, and would long continue had animals not been used. Every disease eliminated, every vaccine developed, every method of pain relief devised, every surgical procedure invented, every prosthetic device implanted—indeed, virtually every modern medical therapy is due, in part or in whole, to experimentation using animals. Nor may we ignore, in the balancing process, the predictable gains in human (and animal) well-being that are probably achievable in the future but that will not be achieved if the decision is made now to desist from such research or to curtail it.

Medical investigators are seldom insensitive to the distress their work may cause animal subjects. Opponents of research using animals are frequently insensitive to the cruelty of the results of the restrictions they would impose.[2] Untold numbers of human beings—real persons, although not now identifiable—would suffer grievously as the consequence of this well-meaning but shortsighted tenderness. If the morally relevant differences between humans and animals are borne in mind, and if all relevant considerations are weighed, the calculation of long-term consequences must give overwhelming support for biomedical research using animals.

Concluding Remarks

Substitution

The humane treatment of animals requires that we desist from experimenting on them if we can accomplish the same result using alternative methods—in vitro experimentation, computer simulation, or others. Critics of some experiments using animals rightly make this point.

It would be a serious error to suppose, however, that alternative techniques could soon be used in most research now using live animal subjects. No other methods now on the horizon—or perhaps ever to be available—can fully replace the testing of a drug, a procedure, or a vaccine, in live organisms. The flood of new medical possibilities being opened by the successes of recombinant DNA technology will turn to a trickle if testing on live animals is forbidden. When initial trials entail great risks, there may be no forward movement whatever without the use of live animal subjects. In seeking knowledge that may prove critical in later clinical applications, the unavailability of animals for inquiry may spell complete stymie. In the United States, federal regulations require the testing of new drugs and other products on animals, for efficacy and safety, before human beings are exposed to them.[100, 101] We would not want it otherwise.

Every advance in medicine—every new drug, new operation, new therapy of any kind—must sooner or later be tried on a living being for the first time. That trial, controlled or uncontrolled, will be an experiment. The subject of that experiment, if it is not an animal, will be a human being. Prohibiting the use of live animals in biomedical research, therefore, or sharply restricting it, must result either in the blockage of much valuable research or in the replacement of animal subjects with human subjects. These are the consequences—unacceptable to most reasonable persons—of not using animals in research.

Reduction

Should we not at least reduce the use of animals in biomedical research? No, we should increase it, to avoid when feasible the use of humans as experimental subjects. Medical investigations putting human subjects at some risk are numerous and greatly varied. The risks run in such experiments are usually unavoidable, and (thanks to earlier experiments on animals) most such risks are minimal or moderate. But some experimental risks are substantial.

When an experimental protocol that entails substantial risk to humans comes before an institutional review board, what response is appropriate? The investigation, we may suppose, is promising and deserves support, so long as its human subjects are protected against unnecessary dangers. May not the investigators be fairly asked, Have you done all that you can to eliminate risk to humans by the extensive testing of that drug, that procedure, or that device on animals? To achieve maximal safety for humans we are right to require thorough experimentation on animal subjects before humans are involved.

Opportunities to increase human safety in this way are commonly missed; trials in which risks may be shifted from humans to animals are often not devised, sometimes not even considered. Why? For the investigator, the use of animals as subjects is often more expensive, in money and time, than the use of human subjects. Access to suitable human subjects is often quick and convenient, whereas access to appropriate animal subjects may be awkward, costly, and burdened with red tape. Physician-investigators have often had more experience working with human beings and know precisely where the needed pool of subjects is to be found and how they may be enlisted. Animals, and the procedures for their use, are often less familiar to these investigators. Moreover, the use of animals in place of humans is now more likely to be the target of zealous protests from without. The upshot is that humans are sometimes subjected to risks that animals could have borne, and should have borne, in their place. To maximize the protection of human subjects, I conclude, the wide and imaginative use of live animal subjects should be encouraged rather than discouraged. This enlargement in the use of animals is our animals is our obligation.

Consistency

Finally, inconsistency between the profession and the practice of many who oppose research using animals deserves comment. This frankly ad hominem observation aims chiefly to show that a coherent position rejecting the use of animals in medical research imposes costs so high as to be intolerable even to the critics themselves.

One cannot coherently object to the killing of animals in biomedical investigations while continuing to eat them. Anesthetics and thoughtful animal husbandry render the level of actual animal distress in the laboratory generally lower than that in the abattoir. So long as death and discomfort do not substantially differ in the two contexts, the consistent objector must not only refrain from all eating of animals but also protest as vehemently against others eating them as against others experimenting on them. No less vigorously must the critic object to the wearing of animal hides in coats and shoes, to employment in any industrial enterprise that uses animal parts, and to any commercial development that will cause death or distress to animals.

Killing animals to meet human needs for food, clothing, and shelter is judged entirely reasonable by most persons. The ubiquity of these uses and the virtual universality of moral support for them confront the opponent of research using animals with an inescapable difficulty. How can the many common uses of animals be judged morally worthy, while their use in scientific investigation is judged unworthy?

The number of animals used in research is but the tiniest fraction of the total used to satisfy assorted human appetites. That these appetites, often base and satisfiable in other ways, morally justify the far larger consumption of animals, whereas the quest for improved human health and understanding cannot justify the far smaller, is wholly implausible. Aside from the numbers of animals involved, the distinction in terms of worthiness of use, drawn with regard to any single animal, is not defensible. A given sheep is surely not more justifiably used to put lamb chops on the supermarket counter than to serve in testing a new contraceptive or a new prosthetic device. The needless killing of animals is wrong; if the common killing of them for our food or convenience is right, the less common but more humane uses of animals in the service of medical science are certainly not less right.

Scrupulous vegetarianism, in matters of food, clothing, shelter, commerce, and recreation, and in all other spheres, is the only fully coherent position the critic may adopt. At great human cost, the lives of fish and crustaceans must also be protected, with equal vigor, if speciesism has been forsworn. A very few consistent critics adopt this position. It is the reductio ad absurdum of the rejection of moral distinctions between animals and human beings.

Opposition to the use of animals in research is based on arguments of two different kinds—those relying on the alleged rights of animals and those relying on the consequences for animals. I have argued that arguments of both kinds must fail. We surely do have obligations to animals, but they have, and can have, no rights against us on which research can infringe. In calculating the consequences of animal research, we must weigh all the long-term benefits of the results achieved—to animals and to humans—and in that calculation we must not assume the moral equality of all animate species.

Sports Ethics

Why the Good Foul Is Not Good

Warren Fraleigh

Understanding how rules function helps sports participants act appropriately and assists rulesmakers state and revise rules. Rules function in relation to a sports contest—an agreed-upon event in which two or more humans oppose one another in attempting to better the other's performance on the same test of moving mass in space and time by means of bodily moves which exhibit developed motor skills, physiological endurance, and socially approved tactics and strategy.[102,103]

How do rules operate to guarantee not only that the contest *exists* but that it may be the *good* contest? In general, rules function in three ways. First, rules contain positive prescriptions for what participants *must do* and what they are *allowed to do*. In basketball, for example, all participants *must* perform actions such as throwing, dribbling and batting the ball and *are allowed to* screen and to choose when they will dribble, pass, or shoot. These prescriptions describe what all other participants must do or can do; thus they define the agreed-upon test which all participants face. Such prescriptive rules may be labeled the *positively prescribed skills and tactics of the contest*.

Second, rules function to identify the within-the-contest goal toward which the performance of the positively prescribed skills and tactics is aimed. The within-the-contest goal in basketball is to throw the ball through your opponent's basket and to prevent the opponent from throwing it through yours. This is what Suits calls the pre-lusory goal of the game; that is, it is a goal which ". . . can be described before, or independently of, any game of which it may be, or come to be, a part."[104] When such a goal can be described and pursued independently from basketball, and is stated in the rules of basketball, *pre-lusory* takes on another meaning. Specifically, the goal of throwing the ball through your opponent's basket and preventing the opponent from doing it to you means that all participants *know* that all opposing participants will be trying to throw the ball through their basket and prevent them from doing the same *before* the contest begins. Thus rules prescribe both a pre-lusory goal and the lusory means by

Source: "Why the Good Foul Is Not Good" by Warren Fraleigh from *The Journal of Physical Education, Recreation & Dance,* January 1982, pp. 41–42. Reprinted by permission of JOPERD.

which that goal may be pursued.[105] These lusory means are described earlier in this article as the positively prescribed skills and tactics of the contest. Together, the pre-lusory goal of basketball and the positively prescribed skills and tactics, as stated in the rules, are agreed upon by all participants when they agree to "play basketball." Further, when people agree to play basketball they *know* that everyone else entering the agreement *knows* what the pre-lusory goal is and what the positively prescribed skills and tactics are. That is why basketball players do not ask "Shall we try to throw the ball through the basket?" or "Shall we dribble, pass, and screen?"

Third, rules function to proscribe certain illegal actions. This function is performed by rules statements which identify prohibited actions. Basketball rules, for example, prohibit double dribbles, holding, pushing, tripping, blocking, running with and kicking the ball. Negative proscriptions help to define sport. The inventor of the sport may eliminate certain skills and tactics from the sport, or rulesmakers may add new proscriptions based on the judgment that new skills are inconsistent with the nature of the sport. Basketball rules against goaltending and violations of the free throw lane by an offensive player are proscriptions added by rulesmakers after such actions occurred.

With respect to the contest, rules specify the goal-within-the-contest which all participants must necessarily pursue, the means all participants must use and are allowed to use in pursuing that goal, and the means all participants may not legally use to pursue the goal. These three kinds of rules function together, specifying what all participants in principle agree to when they enter a sport contest and what all participants know all other participants in principle agree to. The three functions of rules operate together to ensure that all participants face the same test mutually—that is, that they are *contesting*. Conversely, if *one* opponent fails to pursue the pre-lusory goal of the sport by not performing the required and permitted skills and tactics and/or does perform the prohibited skills and tactics then all participants cannot be facing the same test and, thus, the participants cannot be contesting. Obviously participants who cannot be contesting cannot have a good contest.

If we understand that the sport rules function in three ways to ensure the basis for the good sports contest, then we can comprehend why it is crucial that all participants adhere to the *letter* and the *spirit* of the rules. Because the rules of sport are violated, however, it is necessary to analyze the effects of rules violations on the good sports contest. Essentially three types of rules violations affect the good sports contest. Most commonly, rules may be violated inadvertently and unintentionally. A basketball defensive player, attempting to attain or maintain a good defensive position against an opponent who feints and then dribbles toward the basket to score, trips the offensive player unintentionally. Inadvertent rules violation temporarily disrupts the good sports contest and does not destroy the agreed-upon mutual test of entering participants. Diligent practice of the positively prescribed skills and tactics of the sport can reduce the incidence of such inadvertent rules violation and enable sports contests to become good or better.

In the second type of rules violation, a participant knowingly and intentionally violates a rule to gain an advantage, but skillfully attempts to do so while avoiding a penalty. For example, a defensive basketball player can skillfully hold without detection an offensive pivot man so offensive pivot man so that he is unable to move to receive passes thrown to him. Or a golfer can improve his lie secretly, so that his next shot becomes easier to execute well. Such intentional rules violations constitute cheating and result in deliberate disruption of the agreed-upon mutual test. Cheating destroys the good sports contest because

> competing, winning and losing in athletics are intelligible only within the framework of rules which define a specific competitive sport; a person may cheat at a game or compete at it, but it is logically impossible for him to do both. To cheat is to cease to compete.[106]

A person who wins a contest as a consequence of cheating may *say* that he has won but, because cheating is not competing, he speaks incorrectly. In short, one may *correctly* say that a person wins only when he or she has been competing in the contest. The one who has been cheating may not claim victory.

The third type of rules violation occurs when a participant knowingly violates a rule to achieve what would otherwise be difficult to achieve, but violates the rules so as to expect and willingly accept the penalty. A "good" foul in basketball occurs where a defensive player, moving behind an offensive player with the ball who is dribbling for an easy lay up shot, intentionally holds the player, forcing him to shoot two free throws to make the same number of points. Such acts are called *good* because it is in the prudent self-interest of the fouling player to force the opponent to shoot twice from a greater distance to make the same number of points as would have been made by shooting once for a lay up. Violating the rules intelligently occurs if we consider *only* the self-interest of the offending player and team.

How does the "good foul" relate to the rules functions described earlier? The "good" foul is intentionally performing skills proscribed by the rules. Holding is proscribed in basketball rules; also among the proscriptions in basketball rules are intentional fouls which carry a penalty of two shots rather than one shot or one-and-one. But, it is argued, the appearance in the rules of statements about special penalties for intentional fouls makes such acts "part of the game" or "within the rules." It should be clear that the *spirit* of such rules as they were codified by rulesmakers was to eliminate or diminish such actions so that they would *not* be part of the positively prescribed skills and tactics of the game. In short, intentional holding, tripping, and so on are not part of the game or within the rules of basketball although, as stated above, it is at times rational and prudent to do such things when one's own self-interest is all that is considered.

How does the "good" foul relate, then, to the good sports contest? The good foul necessarily detracts from the good sports contest precisely because it changes the nature of the test being faced by all participants without clear agreement, in principle, that the test change is being agreed upon. For it cannot be established unequivocally that agreeing to play basketball means for *all* basketball partici-pants that *everyone* will be performing the "good" foul. The "good" foul is a viola-tion of the agreement which *all* participants know that all participants make when they agree to play basketball namely, that all will pursue the pre-lusory goal of basketball by the necessary and allowable skills and tactics and will avoid use of proscribed skills and tactics.

Even the dominant pattern of socialization of basketball participants cannot avoid the detraction of the "good" foul from the good sports contest. Until such acts are established as agreement in principle by the positively prescribed rules and tactics, it cannot be stated unequivocally that all participants agree to per-forming the "good" foul by agreeing to play basketball. Agreeing to play basketball does not necessarily mean also agreeing to perform the "good" foul, but it neces-sarily entails the meaning of performing acts of dribbling, shooting, passing, and so on. In summary, then, intentional violation of the rules done for the purpose of achieving an end otherwise difficult to achieve, but performed in such a way that the violator expects to receive and willingly accepts the penalty, detracts from the good sports contest. Although such intentional violations, of which the "good" foul in basketball is used as *one* illustration, are "good" in terms of the rational self-interest of the violator, they are not good in terms of the good sports contest.

Criminal Punishment of Violence in Sport
Jack Bowen

On February 21, 2000, National Hockey League (NHL) player Marty McSorley skated towards Donald Brashear from behind and, with two hands on his stick, struck Brashear in the right temple. Brashear fell back, his head hitting the ice, and proceeded to go into convulsions with blood gushing from his nose.

Great discord exists amongst sport enthusiasts, journalists, and philosophers alike regarding whether any violence in a sporting event is punishable by law. I argue not only that it is, but that it ought to be. We can demand a need for pun-ishment of participants within sport through the two dominant paradigms of punishment: utilitarianism and retributivism. As athletes participate in a subset of society, it is still of society and, like any other institution, they are subject to the corresponding laws and regulations.

We can begin by imagining the extreme case of sport violence, suggested by Black, of one sport participant shooting another. Even the most vehement propo-nent of legal laissez-faire in sport would allow criminal punishment in this instance.

Source: Jack Bowen, "Criminal Punishment of Violence in Sports," from *Sensibilities,* Fall 2003, vol. 6, Issue 1. Reprinted by permission of the publisher.

The retributivist punishes such a crime because the unjust taking of another's life violates the victim's right to life; thus the perpetrator annuls his corresponding rights. I argue that an unethical act done in sport—an act which is not a test of the game, treats the competitor as a means to an end, and does not allow a competitor her fair due—which is done with the intent to harm, and results in serious bodily injury is an infringement on that individual's rights.

The utilitarian, too, justifies punishing such an act because unjustly shooting individuals is something that we hope to deter. Because we value life, and because we do not want our lives taken, we harshly punish those who perform such actions.

Likewise in sport. As Steenbergen and Tamboer write, "An ethics of sport. . . is not confined to sport's own system; its responsibilities reach beyond its own boundaries." They then relate sport to Cachay's "revitalizing reflection" in claiming that actions within sport not only reflect upon its own character but are considered within the greater good of other systems and, most importantly, the morality of the encompassing society.

The arguments against this position, though, are plentiful. On numerous accounts, athletes and officials argue that punishment for wrongful actions in a game ought to be handled by the league within which the incident occurred. This claim is based partly on the ethos of the game—that an "outsider" cannot possibly know what actions within specific leagues are wrong. NHL player Paul Mara remarks, "I think whatever happens on the ice should stay on the ice. I don't think the legal system should become involved." Why, though, should sport alone maintain the privilege (if it is such) to govern itself when it has such a great impact on society? Allowing the leagues to make such decisions would be incongruent with "the rest of" society. And, while it would be best if the on-ice occurrences stayed on the ice, this is not possible for victims of these attacks: Their injustice leaves the playing field in the form of smashed faces, broken noses, concussions, etc. Likewise, the perpetrators ought to be forced to confront those who punish society's individuals outside the confines of sport: the criminal courts.

One columnist writes, "To suggest what the league did to McSorley is punishment enough is a lot like arguing that an embezzler who is fired by a bank shouldn't have to stand trial for the money he or she stole." While relevant, this comment fails to capture the richness and importance of the sporting institution for two reasons. First, in the case of the embezzler, the bank owner is harmed and rightly desires that the perpetrator receive punishment. Though, in the case of the NHL, the owners and league officials are not harmed, on the contrary, some might argue that fans enjoy the violence of hockey, and thus the NHL may even profit from such an event. League owners would only incur a harm if McSorley were punished by law: They would lose one of their players whom the fans come to see (which translates into dollars lost) and the league would be tarnished because of the criminal charges. Margolis writes of the volatile NBA showboat Dennis Rodman: "If Rodman were a danger to the game, the NBA could suspend him indefinitely. However, Rodman sells tickets, and his brand of basketball seems to be what many fans are paying to see." Because the league officials maintain such a vested interest in their employees staying "in house," granting them the responsibility to punish presents an obvious conflict of interest.

Secondly, the case of the professional athlete maintains a more severe social consequence than that of the embezzler: While the unpunished embezzler remains relatively anonymous, the athlete's actions are displayed on newspapers nationwide and shown repeatedly on television replays. So, if we do not employ a retributivist theory of punishment for such acts then a utilitarian argument seems pertinent here. Criminally punishing such perpetrators would likely deter them and others from committing such acts in the future.

Thus arises yet another possible objection to punishing athletes criminally: that a hockey player who acts violently on the ice is only a threat on the ice and thereby only needs to be removed from that arena. Again, though, we must examine just why our society punishes. If via a retributivist account, then certainly McSorley has committed wrongs against another member of society and, thus, deserves to be punished. If by a utilitarian account, then punishing him would only condemn his actions more vehemently both on the ice and as a reflection of society, and it truly would incapacitate him from threatening any further individuals. The 23-game suspension handed down by the NHL to McSorley was his seventh suspension and the longest in league history. It seems then that (a) suspensions do not deter some individuals, and (b) leagues are not willing to remove athletes from the playing field for long periods of time, much less indefinitely.

A final objection to criminally punishing athletes regards the actual "flow" of the game which many anticipate would be hindered if the criminal courts entered the sporting arena. One law journalist writes that criminally punishing certain behavior in sport "may result in an undesirably interfering role for the criminal law in sport, paradoxically threatening the spontaneity, the athleticism and genuine competitiveness that it seeks to protect." First, while the spontaneity of a game provides great beauty, it does not seem to override the importance of respect for other persons. That said, it should first be apparent that the theoretical deficit in spontaneity and "flow" of a game are of less value than the health of its participants. Secondly, the qualities so valued and realized only in the athletic realm need not be squelched because premeditated, overtly violent acts intended to injure become outlawed. On the contrary, athletes may feel more liberated to act and play creatively knowing that a paralyzing blow from behind is less likely to occur.

Albert Camus once commented that all he knows of ethics he learned through sport. If others learn all (or even some) of ethics through sport, what should we hope they realize in regards to such acts and their moral consequences? The just punishment of overtly violent actors in sport will likely lead only to more of the unique goods which sport imparts—both on and off the field. If not for utilitarian reasons, we ought to respect athletes enough to give them their just desserts.

Movie Titles

1. Theme: Death Penalty—What are the important factors regarding the death penalty? If it kills innocent people, is that outweighed by the potential good it does? Would good does the death penalty provide?
   - *The Life of David Gale*
   - *Dead Man Walking* (R)
2. Theme: Environmental Ethics—What duty do we have to the environment and to future generations?
   - *An Inconvenient Truth*
   - *The 11th Hour*
3. *Kinsey* (R)—How much of our sexual behavior is based on our nature versus our nurture? Does it matter? Should this behavior have a moral status—i.e., in what ways, if any, are sexual acts considered immoral?
4. *Return to Paradise*—What duty do you have to a friend? What would you do in this situation and why? What if the sentence were half as short? Twice as long?
5. *Enter the Void*—Could it be right, in certain instances, to kill one or a few people in order to save others?
6. *Million Dollar Baby*—How do we determine if what he did in the end is morally permissible? Should it be up to the patient? Should it be up to the lawmakers?
7. *The Fisher King* (R)—What is the role of redemption in relation to sin? Can you truly forgive someone for serious wrongs if they repent?
8. *Boys from Brazil*—How does this movie affect your views on cloning? Is cloning immoral in itself, or is it just immoral if used for immoral purposes?
9. *The Boondock Saints* (R)—How do you relate illegal acts with immoral ones? Is breaking a law ever morally justified?
   How do you evaluate the actions of the characters in this movie? Does it change the moral status because they acted "in the name of God"?

Song Lyrics

Bob Dylan—"With God on Our Side"
Joni Mitchell—"Three Great Stimulants"
Fugazi—"Reclamation"
Peter Gabriel—"We Do What We're Told (Milgram's 37)"
Dream Theater—"The Great Debate"
Tool—"Right in Two"
Fugazi—"Burning Too"

Notes

1. Herodotus, *The Histories*, translated by Aubrey de Selincourt, revised by A. R. Burn (Harmondsworth, Middlesex: Penguin Books, 1972), pp. 219–220.
2. Information about the Eskimos was taken from Peter Freuchen, *Book of the Eskimos* (New York: Fawcett, 1961); and E. Adamson Hoebel, *The Law of Primitive Man* (Cambridge: Harvard University Press, 1954), Chapter 5.

3. William Graham Sumner, *Folkways* (Boston: Ginn and Company, 1906), p. 28.

4. Hoebel, *The Law of Primitive Man.*

5. Herodotus, *The Histories.*

6. A maxim is the subjective principle of acting and must be distinguished from the objective principle (i.e., the practical law). The former contains the practical rule which reason determines according to the conditions of the subject (often his ignorance or inclinations) and is thus the principle according to which the subject acts. The law, on the other hand, is the objective principle valid for every rational being, and the principle by which it ought to act, i.e., an imperative.

7. It must be noted here that I reserve the division of duties for a future *Metaphysics of Morals* and that the division here stands as only an arbitrary one (chosen in order to arrange my examples). For the rest, by a perfect duty I here understand a duty which permits no exception in the interest of inclination; thus I have not merely outer but also inner perfect duties. This runs contrary to the usage adopted in the schools, but I am not disposed to defend it here because it is all one to my purpose whether this is conceded or not.

8. Here I present this proposition as a postulate, but in the last Section grounds for it will be found.

9. Let it not be thought that the banal "what you do not wish to be done to you . . ." could here serve as guide or principle, for it is only derived from the principle and is restricted by various limitations. It cannot be a universal law, because it contains the ground neither of duties to one's self nor of the benevolent duties to others (for many a man would gladly consent that others should not benefit him, provided only that he might be excused from showing benevolence to them). Nor does it contain the ground of obligatory duties to another, for the criminal would argue on this ground against the judge who sentences him. And so on.

10. An opponent, whose intellectual and moral fairness it is a pleasure to acknowledge (the Rev. J. Llewellyn Davies), has objected to this passage, saying, "Surely the rightness or wrongness of saving a man from drowning does depend very much upon the motive with which it is done. Suppose that a tyrant, when his enemy jumped into the sea to escape from him, saved him from drowning simply in order that he might inflict upon him more exquisite tortures, would it tend to clearness to speak of that rescue as 'a morally right action'? Or suppose again, according to one of the stock illustrations of ethical inquiries, that a man betrayed a trust received from a friend, because the discharge of it would fatally injure that friend himself or someone belonging to him, would utilitarianism compel one to call the betrayal 'a crime' as much as if it had been done from the meanest motive?"

    I submit that he who saves another from drowning in order to kill him by torture afterwards does not differ only in motive from him who does the same thing from duty or benevolence; the act itself is different. The rescue of the man is, in the case supposed, only the necessary first step of an act far more atrocious than leaving him to drown would have been. Had Mr. Davies said, "The rightness or wrongness of saving a man from drowning does depend very much"–not upon the motive, but–"upon the *intention*," no utilitarian would have differed from him. Mr. Davies, by an oversight too common not to be quite venial, has in this case confounded the very different ideas of Motive and Intention. There is no point which utilitarian thinkers (and Bentham pre-eminently) have taken more pains to illustrate than this. The morality of the action depends entirely upon the intention— that is, upon what the agent *wills to do*. But the motive, that is, the feeling which makes him will so to do, if it makes no difference in the act, makes none in the morality: though it makes a great difference in our moral estimation of the agent, especially if it indicates a good or a bad habitual *disposition*—a bent of character from which useful, or from which hurtful actions are likely to arise.

11. Of course, the principle that it is (always) wrong to kill innocent human beings is in need of many other modifications, e.g., that it may be permissible to do so to save a greater number of other innocent human beings, but we may safely ignore these complications here.

12. John Noonan, "Deciding Who Is Human," *Natural Law Forum*, 13 (1968), 135.

13. From here on, we will use "human" to mean genetically human, since the moral sense seems closely connected to, and perhaps derived from, the assumption that genetic humanity is sufficient for membership in the moral community.

14. Thomas L. Hayes, "A Biological View," *Commonweal*, 85 (March 17, 1967), 677–78; quoted by Daniel Callahan, in *Abortion: Law, Choice and Morality* (London: Macmillan & Co., 1970).

15. That is, insofar as the death rate, for the woman, is higher for childbirth than for early abortion.

16. My thanks to the following people, who were kind enough to read and criticize an earlier version of this paper: Herbert Gold, Gene Glass, Anne Lauterbach, Judith Thomson, Mary Mothersill, and Timothy Binkley.

17. See Nel Noddings, *Caring: A Feminine Approach to Ethics* (Berkeley: University of California Press, 1984), Annette Baier, "What do Women Want in a Moral Theory?", *Nous*, vol. 9 (March, 1985), and "Hume, the Women's Moral Theorist?", in *Women and Moral Theory*, (eds.) Kittay and Meyers, (Minneapolis: University of Minnesota Press, 1987).

18. Carol McMillan, *Women, Reason and Nature*, (Princeton: Princeton University Press, 1982), Adrienne Rich, *Of Woman Born*, (N.Y.: Norton, 1976), Sara Ruddick, "Remarks on the Sexual Politics of Reason" in *Women and Moral Theory*, "Maternal Thinking" and "Preservative Love and Military Destruction: Some Reflections on Mothering and Peace" in Joyce Treblicot (ed.) *Mothering: Essays in Feminist Theory* (Totowa, N.J.: Rowman & Allanheld 1983), and Nancy Harstock "The Feminist Standpoint" in *Discovering Reality*, Harding (ed.), (Boston: D. Reidel, 1983).

19. Among them are such writers as Rosemary Radford Reuther, Susan Griffin, Elizabeth Dodson Gray, Brian Easla, Sally Miller Gearhart, Carolyn Merchant, Genevieve Lloyd, the pacifist feminists, and a number of feminists involved in the ecology movement.

20. In this paper I shall use the terms "masculine" and "feminine" only in this weaker sense, which is agnostic about the existence of biologically based differences.

21. A strong presumption against abortion is not, of course, the same thing as an absolute ban on all abortions. I do not attempt here to resolve the really hard cases: It is not clear that the feminine voice (at least as it has been articulated so far) is sufficiently fine-grained to tell us exactly where to draw the line in such cases.

22. See Carol Gilligan, *In a Different Voice*, (Cambridge, MA: Harvard University Press, 1982), p. 8.

23. *Ibid.*, p. 10.

24. See Gilligan, "Moral Orientation and Moral Development" in *Women and Moral Theory*, p. 31.

25. Annette Baier, "Hume, the Woman's Moral Theorist?" in *Women and Moral Theory* pp. 37–35.

26. "What Do Women Want in a Moral Theory," *Nous*, vol. 19 (March, 1985), p. 53.

27. Christina Hoff Sommers, "Filial Morality" in *Women and Moral Theory*, pp. 69–84.

28. Virginia Held, "Feminism and Moral Theory," in *Women and Moral Theory*, pp. 111–128.

29. Alison Jaggar, *Feminist Politics and Human Nature*, (Totowa, N.J.: Rowman & Alanheld, 1983), p. 46.

30. *Ibid.*, p. 28.
31. Rosemary Radford Reuther, *New Woman, New Earth*, (New York: The Seabury Press, 1975), p. 195.
32. *Ibid.*, p. 188.
33. *Ibid.*, p. 195.
34. *Ibid.*, p. 189.
35. Elizabeth Dodson Gray, *Why the Green Nigger* (Wellesley, MA: Roundtable Press, 1979), p. 54.
36. Genevieve Lloyd, *The Man of Reason: Male and Female in Western Philosophy* (Minneapolis: University of Minnesota Press, 1984).
37. See, e.g., Rosemary Radford Reuther, *New Woman, New Earth*, Elizabeth Dodson Gray, *Why the Green Nigger*; and Brian Easla, *Science and Sexual Oppression* (London: Weidenfeld & Nicolson, 1981).
38. Reuther, *op. cit.*, p. 195.
39. Carolyn Merchant, *The Death of Nature: Women, Ecology and the Scientific Revolution* (San Francisco: Harper & Row, 1980).
40. Stephanie Leland and Leonie Caldecott, (eds.) *Reclaim the Earth: Women Speak Out for Life on Earth* (London: The Women's Press, 1983), p. 72. For an overview of ecofeminist thought which focuses on the role of mind/body dualism, see Val Plumwood, "Ecofeminism: An Overview," *Australasian Journal of Philosophy*, Supplement to Vol. 64, (June, 1986), pp. 120–138.
41. Leland and Caldecott, *op. cit.*, p. 71.
42. *Ibid.*, p. 69.
43. Introduction to *Women and Moral Theory*, by Kittay and Meyers, p. 7.
44. Cited by Barbara Zanotti, "Patriarchy: A State of War," in *Reweaving the Web of Life*, Pam McAllister, (ed.), (Philadelphia: New Society Publishers, 1982), p. 17.
45. See, e.g., Sally Miller Gearhart, "The Future—if there is one—is Female" in *Reweaving the Web of Life*, p. 266.
46. *Ibid.*, p. 272.
47. See Sara Ruddick, "Remarks on the Sexual Politics of Reason."
48. I owe the idea of regarding mother and child as an ecosystem to a conversation with Leonie Caldecott, co-editor of *Reclaim the Earth*.
49. Gilligan, *op. cit.*, p. 174.
50. Judith Jarvis Thompson, "A Defense of Abortion," *Philosophy and Public Affairs*, vol. 1, (1971), pp. 47–66.
51. Mary Anne Warren, "On the Moral and Legal Status of Abortion," *The Monist*, vol. 57 (January, 1973), reprinted in Wasserstrom, *Today's Moral Problems* (New York: Macmillan, 1985), p. 448.
52. Jean Bethke Elshtain, *Public Man, Private Woman* (Princeton, NJ: Princeton University Press, 1981), p. 312.
53. Carolyn Whitbeck, "Women as People: Pregnancy and Personhood," in *Abortion and the Status of the Fetus*, W.B. Bondeson, et al. (ed.), (Boston: D. Reidel Publishing Co., 1983), p. 252.
54. Rich, *op. cit.*, p. 269.
55. Joan Tronto makes this point in "Beyond Gender Differences to a Theory of Care," *Signs*, vol. 22 (Summer, 1987), p. 666.
56. Carol Gilligan "Moral Orientation and Moral Development" in *Women and Moral Theory*, p. 24.
57. This was evident in the reasoning of the women in Gilligan's case studies, many of whom had abortions in order to please or placate other significant persons in their lives.

58. Some post-abortion counselors find the sense of irremediable break in relationship to be one of the most painful aspects of the post-abortion experience, and try to urge the woman to imaginatively re-create a relationship with the baby in order to be better able to complete the necessary grieving process. Conversation with Teresa Patterson, post-abortion counselor at Crisis Pregnancy Center in Walnut Creek, California.

59. For an excellent "masculine voice" discussion of the personhood issues, see, e.g., Philip E. Devine, *The Ethics of Homicide* (Ithaca, NY: Cornell University Press, 1978).

60. Janice Raymond, *The Transsexual Empire* (Boston: Beacon Press, 1979), p. 114.

61. It would seem that in using the term "obligation," Noddings is blurring the distinction between the masculine and feminine voice, since obligations imply rights. When she speaks of obligations to extend care, however, these are not absolute, but relative to the individual's choice of being a caring person as an ethical ideal. They are binding on us only as a result of our own prior choice, and our care is not something the other can claim as a matter of justice.

62. Nodding's discussion of abortion occurs on pp. 87–90 of *Caring: A Feminine Approach to Ethics, op. cit.*, and all quotes are from these pages unless otherwise noted.

63. *Ibid.*, p. 47.

64. It is inaccurate to call even the newly implanted zygote an "information speck." Unlike a blueprint or pattern of information, it is alive and growing.

65. I realize that Noddings would not be happy with the extent to which I lean on her use of the term "criteria," since she prefers to argue by autobiographical example. However, since moral intuitions about abortion vary so widely, this sort of argument is not effective here.

66. I omit here consideration of such difficult cases as severe genetic retardation.

67. The notion of potentiality I am relying on here is roughly an Aristotelean one.

68. Carolyn Whitbeck articulates a view of this sort in "Women as People: Pregnancy and Personhood," *op. cit.*

69. Granted, this sort of judgment is, at least in part, an impressionistic one. It is supported, however, by Gilligan's findings about the difference between boys and girls in their response to the "Heinz dilemma" (where the man is faced with a choice between allowing his wife to die or stealing an expensive drug from the druggist to save her.) Although the females she studies do not all respond to the dilemma in the same way (e.g., Betty at first sounds more like Hobbes than like what has been characterized as the feminine voice—pp. 75–76), some recurring patterns which she singles out as representative of the feminine voice are: resisting being forced to accept either horn of the dilemma, seeing all those involved as in relationship with each other, viewing the dilemma in terms of conflicting responsibilities rather than rights, and seeking to avoid or minimize harm to anyone (see, e.g., Sarah p. 95). Since the abortion decision involves killing and not merely letting die, it would seem that the impetus to find a way through the horns of the dilemma would be, if anything, greater than in the Heinz dilemma.

70. For example, one feminist, Roberta Steinbach, argues that we must not restrict a woman's right to abort for reasons of sex selection *against females* because it might endanger our hard won "reproductive rights"! (See "Sex Selection: From Here to Fraternity" in Carol Gould (ed.) *Beyond Domination* (Totowa, NJ: Rowman & Allanheld, 1984), p. 280.)

71. For example, Annette Baier regards trust as the central concept in a feminine ethics, but speaks of "the principled betrayal of the exploiter's trust" (Baier, "What do Women Want in a Moral Theory," p. 62.)

72. Restrictions can take many forms, including laws against abortion, mandatory counseling which includes information about the facts of fetal development and encourages the woman to choose other options, obligatory waiting periods, legal requirements to notify (and/or obtain the consent of) the father, or in the case of a minor the girls's parents, etc.

To defend the appropriateness of any particular sort of restrictions goes beyond the scope of this paper.

73. I wish to thank the following for reading and commenting on an earlier draft of this paper: Edith Black, Tony Celano, Phil Devine, James Nelson, Alan Soble, and Michael Wreen.

74. WHO press release (WHO/20 1997 Mar 11).

75. WHO document (WHA50.37 1997 May 14). Despite the findings of a meeting of the Scientific and Ethical Review Group (see Acknowledgements) which recommended that "the next step should be a thorough exploration and fuller discussion of the [issues]."

76. UNESCO press release No 97–29 1997 Feb 28.

77. The European parliament. Resolution on Cloning. Motion dated March 11 1997. Passed March 13 1997.

78. Kahn A. Clone mammals . . . clone man. *Nature* 1997; 386: 119.

79. Kahn A. Cloning, dignity and ethical revisionism. *Nature* 1997: 388: 320. Harris J. Is cloning an attack on human dignity? *Nature* 1997: 387: 754.

80. Mitochondrial DNA individualizes the genotype even of clones to some extent.

81. Dworkin R. *Life's dominion*. London: Harper-Collins, 1993: 148.

82. See reference 28: 160.

83. Dworkin R. *Freedom's law*. Oxford: Oxford University Press, 1996: 237–238.

84. See reference 27: 166–167.

85. Regan T. *The case for animal rights*. Berkeley, Calif.: University of California Press, 1983.

86. Singer P. *Animal liberation*. New York: Avon Books, 1977.

87. St. Augustine. Confessions. *Book Seven*. 397 A.D. New York: Pocketbooks, 1957:104–126.

88. St. Thomas Aquinas. *Summa theologica*. 1273 A.D. Philosophic texts. New York: Oxford University Press, 1960:353–366.

89. Hegel GWF. *Philosophy of right*. 1821. London: Oxford University Press, 1952:105–110.

90. Bradley FH. Why should I be moral? 1876. In: Melden AI, ed. *Ethical theories*. New York: Prentice-Hall, 1950:345–359.

91. Mead GH. The genesis of the self and social control. 1925. In: Reck AJ, ed. *Selected writings*. Indianapolis: Bobbs-Merrill, 1964:264–293.

92. Prichard HA. Does moral philosophy rest on a mistake? 1912. In: Cellars W, Hospers J, eds. *Readings in ethical theory*. New York: Appleton-Century-Crofts, 1952:149–163.

93. Kant I. *Fundamental principles of the metaphysic of morals*. 1785. New York: Liberal Arts Press, 1949.

94. Rollin BE. *Animal rights and human morality*. New York: Prometheus Books, 1981.

95. Hoff C. Immoral and moral uses of animals. *N Engl J Med* 1980; 302:115–118.

96. Jamieson D. Killing persons and other beings. In: Miller HB, Williams WH, eds. *Ethics and animals*. Clifton, N.J.: Humana Press, 1983:135–146.

97. Singer P. Ten years of animal liberation. *New York Review of Books* 1985; 31:46–52.

98. Bentham J. *Introduction to the principles of morals and legislation*. London: Athlone Press, 1970.

99. McCabe K. Who will live, who will die? *Washingtonian Magazine*. August 1986:115.

100. U.S. Code of Federal Regulations, Title 21, Sect. 505(i). Food, drug, and cosmetic regulations.

101. U.S. Code of Federal Regulations, Title 16, Sect. 1500.40–2. Consumer product regulations.

102. This is a revised definition from Warren P. Fraleigh, "Sport-Purpose," *Journal of the Philosophy of Sport 2* (1975), p. 78.

103. For a clear exposition on the nature of the sports contest see R. Scott Kretchmar, "From Test to Contest: An Analysis of Two Kinds of Counterpoint in Sport," *Journal of the Philosophy of Sport 2* (1975), pp. 23–30.

104. Bernard Suits, "The Elements of Sport," in *The Philosophy of Sport,* ed. Robert G. Osterhoudt (Springfield, III.: Charles C Thomas Publisher, 1973), p. 50.
105. *Ibid.,* p. 51.
106. Edwin J. Delattre, "Some Reflections on Success and Failure in Competitive Athletics," *Journal of the Philosophy of Sport 2* (1975), p. 136.

For a treatment of intentional rules violations see, also, Kathleen M. Pearson, "Deception, Sportsmanship, and Ethics," *Quest,* 19 (January 1973), pp. 115–118; reprinted in this anthology, pp. 183–184.

Major concepts in this paper have been abstracted from Warren P. Fraleigh's book *Right Actions in Sport* (Champaign, IL.: Human Kinetics, 1984).